THE
ENCYCLOPEDIA
OF
EXTRATERRESTRIAL
ENCOUNTERS

To Sheila Keller,
with Best Wishes,

Ronald D. Story
Oct. 2001

ALSO BY RONALD D. STORY

The Space-Gods Revealed

Guardians of the Universe?

The Encyclopedia of UFOs

UFOs and the Limits of Science

THE
ENCYCLOPEDIA
OF
EXTRATERRESTIAL
ENCOUNTERS

A DEFINITIVE, ILLUSTRATED A-Z GUIDE TO ALL THINGS ALIEN

COMPILED AND EDITED BY

Ronald D. Story

NEW AMERICAN LIBRARY

New American Library
Published by New American Library, a division of Penguin Putnam Inc.,
375 Hudson Street, New York, New York 10014, U.S.A.
Penguin Books Ltd, 27 Wrights Lane, London W8 5TZ, England
Penguin Books Australia Ltd, Ringwood, Victoria, Australia
Penguin Books Canada Ltd, 10 Alcorn Avenue, Toronto, Ontario, Canada M4V 3B2
Penguin Books (N.Z.) Ltd, 182–190 Wairau Road, Auckland 10, New Zealand

Penguin Books Ltd, Registered Offices: Harmondsworth, Middlesex, England

First published by New American Library, a division of Penguin Putnam Inc.

First Printing, September 2001
10 9 8 7 6 5 4 3 2 1

 REGISTERED TRADEMARK—MARCA REGISTRADA

LIBRARY OF CONGRESS CATALOGING-IN-PUBLICATION DATA:

Story, Ronald.
The encyclopedia of extraterrestrial encounters : illustrated A-Z guide to all
things alien / compiled and edited by Ronald D. Story.
p.cm.
Includes bibliographical references.
ISBN 0-451-20424-7 (alk. paper)
1. Unidentified flying objects—Encyclopedias. 2. Human-alien encounters—Encyclopedias. I. Title.

TL789.16.S762001

001.942'03—dc21   2001030809

Printed in the United States of America

BOOKS ARE AVAILABLE AT QUANTITY DISCOUNTS WHEN USED TO PROMOTE PRODUCTS OR SERVICES.
FOR INFORMATION PLEASE WRITE TO PREMIUM MARKETING DIVISION,
PENGUIN PUTNAM INC., 375 HUDSON STREET, NEW YORK, NEW YORK 10014.

IN MEMORIAM

This book is dedicated to one of the great pioneers in the search of intelligent life elsewhere—my early mentor and advisor—who inspired millions of us earthlings to continue the search for truth wherever it might lead. His inspiration will live on.

CORNELL UNIVERSITY

"We make our would significant by the courage of our questions and by the depth of our answers."
Carl Sagan (1934–1996)

THE
ENCYCLOPEDIA
OF
EXTRATERRESTRIAL
ENCOUNTERS

CONTENTS

EDITOR'S PREFACE

If our wisdom fails to match our science, we will have no second chance.

ARTHUR C. CLARKE
Science Digest (1982)

This may sound a bit wild—especially for a skeptic—but during the compilation of this encyclopedia I experienced a revelation. If this sounds alarmist, it is meant to be.

I have tried to explain my view in two entries: PROJECTION/WARNING THEORY OF UFOs AND ETs and STORY'S UFO "OBSERVATIONS." To my mind there is no question but that we have come to a crossroads in our evolution that will determine whether we enter heaven or hell for real. And real or not, this is what the ETs are saying; their messages coinciding exactly with the teachings of our greatest philosophers and religious teachers for at least the past two millennia.

As the reader will become quickly aware, *The Encyclopedia of Extraterrestrial Encounters* is not a mere collection of information about alleged UFOs and ETs. It contains the revelation that whether or not we have visitors from elsewhere, the significance of the UFO-ET phenomenon is that the human species is in big trouble, and if we do not implement the teachings of the Space People—which, again, match the perennial wisdom of the wisest Earthlings—we really will be doomed. We will be an extinct species whose tenure on Earth won't even come close to many others that have since perished.

It is easy to poke fun at the "contactees" and "abductees" as I used to do, but I now believe it is wiser to examine the *meaning* behind it all. I think that most things happen for a reason, and that includes the UFO phenomenon and the experiences that are part of it. Of course it is easy to debunk so many of the stories as complete nonsense. But I think it behooves us to *interpret* the phenomenon—as one would interpret a dream—to understand the sense within the nonsense.

Of course there are strong tendencies toward denial, and we have some powerful, built-in defense mechanisms to help us evade the truth. That is because, as Bertrand Russell once said, "Men fear truth more than anything else in the world." We literally "can't take the truth," as someone in a movie once said. But if we don't face the facts soon, it really will be too late.

If we are being mentally or physically invaded by aliens, we need to know. But we also need to know the psychology involved, if we are to keep our wits about us. How do we judge if we do not know how our instrument for obtaining knowledge—the human mind/brain—functions and malfunctions? As Jung admonished: ". . . we need more psychology. We need more understanding of human nature, because the only real danger that exists is man himself. He is the great danger, and we are pitifully unaware of it. We know nothing of man, far too little. His psyche should be studied, because we are the origin of all coming evil."

Thus, it is my intention to present *The Encyclopedia of Extraterrestrial Encounters* as an honest and reasonably complete look at the new mythology of the gods from outer space. Are they real or imaginary? Are we being invaded? Are the aliens coming for us? And if they are, are their intentions good or evil?

It is up to all of us to figure out the truth—and then what to do about it . . . while there is still time.

—Ronald D. Story
February 12, 2001

A

Abducted: Confrontations with Beings from Outer Space (Berkley, 1977). Coral and Jim Lorenzen examine eight alien abduction cases and find a pattern of aliens seeking cultural knowledge about humans. They seem particularly interested in learning more about human emotions. The Lorenzens warn that every human on the planet is a potential kidnap victim.

—RANDALL FITZGERALD

abduction The phenomenon of forcible, involuntary capture of a human being by an apparently self-serving alien, generally of the "Gray" morphology, but also including "Nordic" and reptilian types. Those who have experienced this may be termed "abductees" or "experiencers," and often report strong feelings of violation, trauma, and terror. Abduction scenarios commonly include missing time, transfer to a new locale, physical examination and implantation, and human-alien hybridization. It is a global phenomenon, but appears more commonly in American ET contact cases.

—SCOTT MANDELKER

Abduction: Human Encounters with Aliens (Charles Scribner's Sons, 1994). With this book Harvard University professor of psychiatry John E. Mack became the most reputable figure in science or medicine to profess a belief in the reality of the alien abduction phenomenon. He put seventy-six abductees through hypnosis, including thirteen persons whose cases are used in this book, and found consistent patterns in their accounts down to tiny details. The purpose of these abductions and the collection of eggs and sperm from abductees seems to be "genetic engineering for the purpose of creating human-alien hybrid offspring." Another goal of this alien program is the alteration of human consciousness to change our perceptions of ourselves as a species.

—RANDALL FITZGERALD

Abduction Transcription Project In 1992, Dan Wright (Deputy Director for the Mutual UFO Network) devised the Abduction Transcription Project on MUFON's behalf. Project participants over the next six years included twenty psychiatrists, psychologists, and others who recorded regressive hypnosis sessions to elicit memories of alien abduction. A corps of MUFON volunteers ultimately transcribed 930 audiocassettes, involving 265 separate cases, to promote advanced research.

Wright created a 300-page index of key words and phrases from those sessions—some 2000-plus separate elements. The entries described entity appearances, actions, and communications; details of the interior and exterior of alien ships viewed during abduction experiences; medical equipment, instruments, and procedures employed; resulting physical effects on the subjects' anatomies; and particular psychic abilities and other paranormal events seemingly related to the abduction episodes.

At the 1997 MUFON International UFO Symposium, Wright offered an overview of his findings to that point regarding 254 abduction cases. His conclusions addressed five themes present in human-alien interactions:

SEX AND REPRODUCTION

1. Various entity types have a keen interest in human sexuality and reproduction. This is evidenced by a preponderance of instances involving the harvesting of human male sperm;

removal of ova and/or uterine tissue from human females as well as the implantation of embryos and later removal of partially gestated fetuses; forced intercourse between the subjects and entities or other human captives; maintenance of "nurseries" on board with gestation receptacles and/or newborns; and forced breast-feeding of "hybrid" and other newborns.

DUAL IDENTITY

2. A substantial share of abductees sense an "alien connection" from a realm ostensibly outside this conscious life. Attendant to this conviction is a certainty of protection against untimely death, an entity's conveyance that the subject is "special" or "chosen," or an episode in which the individual seemingly realizes she or he is in a nonhuman form in the company of entities with similar appearance.

SENSE OF MISSION

3. Many abductees relate being told by aliens of a "mission" to perform at some unspecified future time and/or having received technical instruction. They relate episodes of memorizing ambiguous computer graphics, learning specifics of an alien ship's technical operations, and/or being told that they will intuitively know where to be at a point in time to begin an unexplained assignment.

WORLD CATASTROPHES

4. A substantial share of the abduction subjects describe an impending geophysical disaster to befall the Earth, as shown or told to them aboard a ship. Predominant among that cataclysmic imagery are a tilting of Earth's axis and/or earthquakes and volcanoes unprecedented in scope within recorded history, vast regions of the landscape on fire, and massive tidal waves inundating coastlines.

MILITARY INVOLVEMENT

5. A disturbing number of subjects in the project claim the U.S. military-intelligence apparatus is directly involved in, or has acquiesced in, an alien program of human abductions. They report (a) underground alien or shared government-alien facilities; (b) military personnel acting in concert with alien beings; and/or (c) military personnel abducting them, or aerial harassment by unmarked helicopters of their homes, in the aftermath of alien abductions.

Based on the repetition of unpublicized details arising in the transcripts he has reviewed, Wright concludes that human abductions by alien life forms are a reality. He is confident that the various entity types described arise from multiple places and are not necessarily all working in concert. Short of a startling admission by one or more governments on our planet, he doubts that the full truth of alien intrusion can ever be known.

—ETEP STAFF

POSTSCRIPT: While "abductionists" such as Budd Hopkins, David Jacobs, and Harvard University's Dr. John Mack have achieved fame (and fortune) as experts on the UFO-abduction phenomenon, the efforts of little-known researcher Dan Wright have provided more scientifically useful insights into the true nature of the phenomenon than all other abductionists combined. Wright heads a MUFON (Mutual UFO Network) committee which painstakingly transcribes the tales told by abductees—typically under hypnosis—which Wright then analyzes in a search for patterns. The results of Wright's latest analysis were reported at MUFON's recent conference in Grand Rapids, Michigan.

Wright's latest analysis is based on 906 taped transcripts of 254 alleged abductions obtained from 20 abduction researchers. These included David Jacobs, but Budd Hopkins and John Mack did not participate. Wright's recent report reveals a significant gender pattern. Of the 254 subjects, 64 percent were female, 30 percent were male, and 6 percent involved couples.

During the supposed abductions, 54 percent of the female subjects reported being subjected to some gynecological procedure. Of these, 19 percent reported having a fetus aborted, while 7 percent reported having an embryo implanted in their womb. Nearly a third reported having ova or tissue removed. (But 46 percent reported no ET interest in such matters.)

The transcripts also revealed that 32 percent of the male subjects reported having sperm extracted, or implied that such had occurred. (Seemingly, more than two-thirds of the male abductees failed to meet ET standards to "father" a hybrid.)

Four percent of the female subjects reported being forced to engage in sexual intercourse with ETs, one by a "short greenish-brown reptilian" who was trying to arouse her with its "metal claws." One male subject reported being forced to engage in sex with another male abductee.

Eleven percent of the female subjects reported they had breast-fed a hybrid baby, even though none of them had been pregnant or lactating at the time.

Seventeen percent reported one or more of the following: underground government, alien, or shared government-alien facilities; government personnel acting in concert with alien beings; government intrusion or harassment during an alien abduction.

WRIGHT'S CONCLUSIONS

Although Wright acknowledges his belief in the reality of UFO abductions, he offers a wise caveat. "Regressive hypnosis, the cornerstone of the Abduction Transcription Project, offers only evidence—not proof—of alien abductions. Some of the people in the study might have a penchant for fantasies or a need to be part of an exclusive 'club.' Moreover, many were less than carte blanche subjects, having read one or more abduction-related books prior to undergoing hypnosis sessions."

What convinces Wright of the reality of UFO abductions are the "details, sequences, cause and effect. These to the author are the proofs of an alien abduction reality."

He cites the following as an example: "Dozens of subjects said they were shown one or more infants or a room full of incubating fetuses. But, if these were only copycat images, how is it that each person placed the 'baby' presentation sequentially after—never before—procedures on an examining table. No book or TV documentary has emphasized that." However, this author suggests the contrary: that overall, most contemporary books and TV shows essentially do follow the traditional scenario with the examination first.

Possibly Wright's most significant commentary appears early in his MUFON paper: "Regressive hypnosis cannot irrefutably uncover truth stemming from significant events in one's life. Whether such episodes entail emotional or sexual abuse, a fanciful personality, or some other prosaic explanation, the subjects in this project nonetheless have concluded that unearthly beings are responsible for their recovered memories. Further, in that there are no conclusive means to discern fact from fiction in their recorded accounts, no greater weight is given to a particular case over any other."

Thus, it is impossible to determine from the content of the tales whether all 254 abduction accounts are literally true, or if some are true and some are fantasy—or if all are fantasy. No "abductee" claim is so wild as to prompt Wright to label it as fantasy.

—PHILIP J. KLASS

abductions   Also known as *Close Encounters of the Fourth Kind (CE-IV events)*, these experiences typically include: (1) capture by alien beings, (2) time spent aboard a spaceship, and (3) bizarre, sometimes gruesome medical examinations.

Abduction reports are relative newcomers to UFO lore. John G. Fuller introduced the story of Barney and Betty Hill in his book, *The Interrupted Journey*, in 1966, making the

Hill case the prototypical and most familiar abduction—though not the first on record.

Brazilian farmer, Antonio Villas Boas, described an abduction to UFOlogists in early 1958, but they suppressed his report because of the sensationalistic claim that an alien woman seduced him. The Villas Boas and Hill cases share significant points in common even though neither case could have influenced the other. Subsequent witnesses have claimed abduction dates in the 1950s and earlier, but the Villas Boas and Hill reports were the first documented accounts.

Despite the popularity of Fuller's book, abduction accounts remained scarce for many years. Herbert Schirmer received some media attention in 1967; and in 1973, a report from Pascagoula, Mississippi, made the national news when two shipyard workers, Charles Hickson and Calvin Parker, reported they had been captured by three mummy-like beings.

Then in November of 1975, Travis Walton of Snowflake, Arizona, disappeared for five days and returned with an abduction story destined for national notoriety.

After the mid-1970s a growing trickle of people stepped forward to describe fragmentary, half-hidden memories of troubling UFO encounters. Coral and Jim Lorenzen, Dr. Leo Sprinkle, Dr. James Harder, Raymond Fowler, Walter Webb, Ann Druffel, Jenny Randles, D. Scott Rogo, and other investigators began to specialize in these reports. With the help of hypnotists they sometimes recovered abduction accounts from an hour or two when the witness's memory failed.

A breakthrough came late in the decade when Budd Hopkins teamed with professional hypnotists to explore periods of memory lapse connected not just with sightings of mysterious lights but with less specific experiences, such as a stretch of roadway or a childhood recollection that provoked unaccountable anxieties. Where he found a memory gap, he often discovered an abduction, and this new realization that the phenomenon spread further than anyone suspected became the central message of his first book, *Missing Time* (1981).

Throughout the 1980s, the abduction phenomenon continued to rise to the forefront of UFOlogy. Investigation of Betty Andreasson uncovered not just one event but a lifelong series of alien encounters extending back into her childhood.

Another account, from the Tujunga Canyon area of California, led to the discovery of a series of abductions among five female acquaintances. In his second book, *Intruders* (1987), Hopkins told of a young Indianapolis woman being impregnated by aliens who removed the fetus, then later during another abduction introduced her to the child—a human-alien hybrid.

Author Whitley Strieber proved the famous were vulnerable as well and spread awareness of abductions further than ever before with his bestselling book, *Communion* (1987).

Trademark: WALKER & COLLIER

Strieber's "visitor" became an icon
after its appearance in 1987
on the cover of *Communion*

Some 300 cases had entered the literature by 1985, followed by another 500 over the next six years. An *OMNI* magazine survey in December 1987 drew some 1,200 responses from people describing abductions or abduction-like symptoms, while a Roper Poll carried out in 1992 found abduction-related experiences so common that a conservative extrapolation implicated some 2 percent of the U.S. population as likely abductees.

The subject attracted an increasingly distinguished scholarly following—both for and against—during the 1990s. Historian Dr. David M. Jacobs turned investigator and described the recurrent order he found among abductee accounts in *Secret Life* (1992); he then proposed hybridization and eventual alien domination of the earth to be the purpose behind these encounters in *The Threat* (1998).

Harvard psychiatrist, Dr. John E. Mack, also became an investigator convinced that the phenomenon is literally true, but found it benign: an interaction working to change human consciousness from materialism to a more spiritual orientation. He published his findings in *Abduction* (1994) and underwent a university-sponsored investigation by colleagues who suspected him of unscientific procedures.

Abductees, investigators, and researchers gathered for the Abduction Study Conference Held at MIT in 1992: an attempt to synthesize accumulated knowledge and plot future research summarized in the proceedings, *Alien Discussions* (1994). Noted writer, C. D. B. Bryan, observed the conference and presented his sympathetic impressions in *Close Encounters of the Fourth Kind* (1995).

Another trend of the decade has been a willingness of abductees to follow in the footsteps of Whitley Strieber and tell their own stories in print. The list includes Karla Turner, Katharina Wilson, Debbie Jordan, Travis Walton, Beth Collings, and Anna Jamerson. Abduction research has become an organized subdiscipline of UFOlogy, with Budd Hopkins's Intruders Foundation, John Mack's Program for Extraordinary Experience Research (PEER), and the Fund for UFO Research sponsoring programs to explore physical and psychological clues to the nature of the phenomenon.

Most abduction reports originate in North America, but the phenomenon is worldwide with South America, Britain, and Australia producing numerous reports. A growing number of cases have emerged from continental Europe and the former Soviet Union, while Africa and Asia have begun to contribute reports as well.

Though most abductions involve a single witness, perhaps one-fourth are multiple-witness cases, with three or more individuals sometimes taken at once. Abductees come from all walks of life, all levels of education, and all lines of work. Males and females seem about equally prone to the experience. Psychological tests of abductees have failed to uncover any overt mental illness—though their profiles indicate some of the insecurities characteristic of crime victims. Perhaps the most remarkable characteristic of abductees is their age distribution. Anyone from children to the elderly may be abducted, but by far the most abductees are less than 35 years of age when first taken.

Hypnosis became standard operating procedure to probe a period of missing time with Barney and Betty Hill, and this technique remains the most successful way to lift amnesia or remove an apparent mental block and release memories of an abduction experience. Some two-thirds to three-fourths of the known cases have included this controversial procedure, though some witnesses, such as Charles Hickson, recall everything clearly from the start.

In other instances lost memories return spontaneously within days, weeks, or months; or emerge in dreams or nightmares. Many witnesses retain some memories with hypnosis serving only to fill in minor details.

However the story emerges, the accounts seem remarkably alike. Reports contain a maximum of eight episodes:

1. **Capture**. Alien beings capture a human to take aboard a spaceship.

2. **Examination**. The beings subject their captive to a medical examination.
3. **Conference**. A meeting, lecture, or schooling session follows.
4. **Tour**. The witness is treated to a sightseeing tour of the ship.
5. **Otherworldly Journey**. The beings fly the witness to an otherworldly environment.
6. **Theophany**. The witness meets a divine being or has a religious experience.
7. **Return**. The witness returns to Earth and resumes normal activities.
8. **Aftermath**. Aftereffects of the abduction influence the witness for weeks or years to come.

Complex order extends to the capture and examination episodes as well. The capture scenario begins with some abductees taken while driving, usually in a remote area; others while at home or in bed; still others while outdoors in the open.

Aliens or their UFO first appear, then silence and stillness settle over the physical world while abductees lose the will to resist and paralysis creeps over their bodies. The beings float their captives to the ship or a beam of light draws them up and they enter suddenly, with a momentary lapse of memory.

Once the examination begins, it also follows a set course as the witness undresses and lies on a table, then the beings perform a manual examination and an eye-like device scans the witness's body. Instrumental procedures follow, then the beings take samples of bodily materials and procedures concerned with the reproductive organs, neurological system, and emotions or behavior follow in sequence.

The neurological examination may include placing an implant within the body, often the head region of the witness. One being stares into the eyes of the witness at close range and for a prolonged period during the examination.

The beings usually communicate by telepathy and limit the conversation to instructions until the examination is completed. A conference allowing for some degree of talk may follow. This conference may simply extend the

behavioral examination and explore human reactions to projected images or dramatic scenes.

In other cases a formal and distinct conference episode brings the witness face-to-face with an alien for questions and answers or to a lecture hall to hear some sort of lesson. The beings often warn of a time of tribulation ahead and prophesy disasters to come, and may school the witness for an obscure mission to be performed "when the time is right."

In recent years some abductees have reported visits to a room filled with fetuses floating in tanks, or being presented with a hybrid infant or child and encouraged to hold, play with, or "nurture" it. If the witness travels with the beings, the destination is otherworldly—but not necessarily another planet. A short trip brings the ship to an underground or undersea location: a subterranean world of great beauty but no sunlight, only a uniformly lighted sky. If the otherworld is another planet, it is often dark and desolate, showing signs of ruin and destruction.

Three stages of aftereffects make up the aftermath episode: (1) Immediate aftereffects last a week or so and include physical conditions such as reddened eyes, sunburned skin, puncture wounds, dehydration, and nausea. (2) Intermediate aftereffects follow in a week or so and are mostly psychological, with nightmares and anxiety attacks being the most common. (3) Long-term consequences may span years and include a major restructuring of the abductee's personality, for better or worse. Abductees may develop psychic powers and experience paranormal events; in time they develop new interests and habits leading to a change of careers and lifestyles. Further abductions are common sequels.

Few reports contain every possible episode or every possible event within an episode. Out of 300 reports, capture and examination were by far the most common, while theophanies occurred in only six cases. A remarkable consistency characterizes one report after another. Whenever an episode or event occurs, it follows the prescribed order in most cases, despite the absence of any logical obligation for a conference to always follow an examination or a scan to precede sample-taking. The reasonable expectation that a fantasized story would reflect the creative imagination and personal needs of the storyteller is not realized in abduction accounts. Their fidelity to a fixed order seems an integral part of the phenomenon.

The descriptive content also persists from report to report. The craft is usually a thick disk with an examination room inside. This room has rounded walls and a domed roof, a uniform fluorescence, and misty or heavy air accompanied by a chilly temperature.

Doors often open out of nowhere and disappear when they close, leaving no seam. Humanoids, humans, and monsters occupy the craft. Monsters are quite rare and human-like entities appear in no more than a fourth of the crews. Most occupants are humanoids, some tall and some short, but by far the majority represents a single type: the "standard" humanoid.

This being is three to five feet tall and has a fetal appearance, with a large rounded cranium tapering to a pointed chin and a face dominated by enormous eyes that extend around the side of the head in a "wraparound" effect. The other facial features are vestigial— the mouth is a mere hole or slit, the nose only air holes, the ears nonexistent or holes at most. The skin is usually gray and fungus-like, as if never exposed to sunlight, and completely hairless.

Sexual distinctions are seldom reported and most of these beings seem neuter. Some humanoids are robust but most appear frail, sometimes with unusually thin necks and long arms. They walk with stiff or clumsy steps but more often glide or float, and use telepathy to communicate with captives. One being is usually a little taller than the rest and serves as a leader or liaison, and may become familiar to the abductee.

Though polite, the outward courtesy of the beings hides an innate coldness. They show little concern or understanding for human feelings and care only for accomplishing their mission.

A surrealistic atmosphere surrounds abduction, from the vacuum-like cessation of sound and traffic at the beginning to the apparitions and Men in Black that sometimes haunt abductees long after the encounter. The most celebrated effect is time lapse, a loss of memory covering the period from the early stages of capture until the abductee returns to a normal environment.

Another striking effect is the flotation many abductees report. They also experience some sort of mental impairment while in captivity, an inappropriate docility or peacefulness alternating with a sense of terror. The beings usually exert something like a hypnotic influence to restore this unnatural tranquility when it weakens, or accomplish an instant relief of pain with a touch on the forehead.

Proponents of a physical phenomenon sometimes explain abduction as the result of alien visitors satisfying their scientific curiosity. Another solution that accepts alien visitors also takes into account the apparent large number of abductions, the focus on reproduction, and the deceitfulness of the aliens to conclude that they come from a planet in trouble. They face extinction and need us or our planet to forestall their fate. By collecting eggs and sperm the aliens gather the genetic materials necessary to reinvigorate their stock or hybridize with earthlings, while any altruistic pose of preparing the earth for a future catastrophe simply hides the true selfish purpose of abductions.

A more favorable viewpoint, expressed in various ways by Sprinkle, Strieber, Mack, Kenneth Ring, John Keel, and Jacques Vallée, takes into account the baffling, surreal, seemingly paraphysical aspects of the phenomenon and interprets abduction as an effort of aliens or a cosmic mind to alter human consciousness. The effort may proceed with benign intent or with blind indifference, but the end result is a fundamental reordering of human thought, perhaps an acceptance of cosmic citizenship, perhaps a new sense of unity for humans with earth and cosmos, or perhaps merely a change with no clear direction.

Skeptics note that abductions resemble fairy legends and near-death experiences. These similarities suggest a psychological source underlying the story content. Dr. Alvin Lawson experimented with non-abductees who told abduction-like stories when questioned under hypnosis and proposed that abduction content originates in memory of the birth experience. Other doubters blame hypnosis, pointing out that a hypnotized subject is highly suggestible and responds to cues from investigators eager to find an abduction.

Leading UFO debunker, Philip J. Klass, argues that subjects familiar with media portrayals of abduction either fabricate the story or fantasize the narrative in response to leading questions. The possibility that false memory syndrome provokes accusations of child abuse and satanic ritual abuse, as well as abduction claims, has generated an extensive literature of psychological and skeptical commentary during the 1990s.

Comparative study leaves no explanation entirely satisfactory. The skeptics who blame hypnosis must explain the cases retrieved without its help, while the order and details in the reports seem to recur too often for passing familiarity to explain. The tenaciousness of a single order and similar descriptions in report after report defies the usual process of variation characteristic of folk narratives or personal fantasies.

Abduction reports also demonstrate a deep coherency, since the aliens manifest an interest in reproduction at the same time as they explain outright that their planet has lost its fertility. Anyone with a casual knowledge of the abduction story might pick up these clues. Yet the reports also include a preference for youthful captives, rejection of the old or infertile as unsuitable, the devastation of the otherworld, and the unhealthy appearance of the beings themselves.

Pieces of the puzzle interlock into a meaningful picture, although this is not immediately evident. Rather, a meaningful whole appears only after comparing many more cases than most people ever examine. The same themes appear in various guises to reinforce the verisimilitude of the abduction story, and a coherent picture is undeniable.

On the other hand, aliens advanced enough to create hybrids but obliged to steal the raw materials to do so seem implausible. With all the implants, missing fetuses, and aliens on patrol that abduction claims require, lack of creditable physical evidence that can be unequivocally connected to alien beings raises doubts as well.

The mysteries of human memory and suggestibility open other paths to explore before the reality of abduction claims become acceptable. In any balanced evaluation the issue of abductions remains far from resolution.

—THOMAS EDDIE BULLARD

References

Bryan, C. D. B. *Close Encounters of the Fourth Kind: Alien Abduction, UFOs, and the Conference at M.I.T.* (Alfred A. Knopf, 1995).

Druffel, Ann, and D. Scott Rogo. *The Tujunga Canyon Contacts* (Prentice-Hall, 1980).

Fuller, John. *The Interrupted Journey* (Dial Press, 1966).

Hopkins, Budd. *Missing Time* (Richard Marek, 1981).

———. *Intruders* (Random House, 1987).

Jacobs, David M. *Secret Life* (Simon & Schuster, 1992).

———. *The Threat* (Simon & Schuster, 1998).

Jordan, Debbie, and Kathy Mitchell. *Abducted! The Story of the Intruders Continues . . .* (Carroll & Graf, 1994).

Klass, Philip J. *UFO Abductions: A Dangerous Game* (Prometheus Books, 1988).

Mack, John E. *Abducted* (Charles Scribner's Sons, 1994).

Ring, Kenneth. *The Omega Project* (William Morrow, 1992).

Story, Ronald D., ed. *The Encyclopedia of UFOs* (Doubleday/New English Library, 1980).

Walton, Travis. *Fire in the Sky* (Marlowe, 1996).

Wilson, Katharina. *The Alien Jigsaw* (Puzzle Publishing, 1993-1995).

Above Top Secret (Sidgwick and Jackson/ William Morrow, 1987). British researcher Timothy Good summarizes or reprints UFO reports and government documents from ten nations in an attempt to prove a massive worldwide cover-up of the truth about UFOs. Good also spends a chapter trying to rehabilitate the reputation and credibility of Frank Scully, whose book in 1950 claimed that a spacecraft with alien bodies crashed in New Mexico.

—RANDALL FITZGERALD

Adamski, George (1891-1965). A Polish immigrant, without formal education, who was the first to widely publicize his alleged contacts with people from outer space. His bestselling book, *Flying Saucers Have Landed* (co-authored with Desmond Leslie), and its sequels, made him the best-known of all the "contactees," several dozen of which followed his lead.

He is described by his disciples (the present-day George Adamski Foundation, based in Vista, California) as a (former) "author-lecturer on Unidentified Flying Objects, space travel, Cosmic Philosophy and Universal Laws of Life." As a child, Adamski is said to have had a deep feeling of reverence for nature and to have often pondered great philosophical questions about the interrelationship between the rest of nature and man. He was often referred to in written accounts as "Professor" Adamski, which he said was an honorary title bestowed upon him by his students. However, a significant portion of the general public was misled into believing that he was an accredited scientist.

According to Frank Edwards, writing in *Flying Saucers—Here and Now!* (1967): "Prior to becoming associated with a hamburger stand on the road to Mount Palomar, George had worked in a hamburger stand as a grill cook. With this scientific background he wrote, in his spare time, a document which he called *An Imaginary Trip to the Moon, Venus and Mars*. He voluntarily listed it with the Li-

UFO INTERNATIONAL

George Adamski

brary of Congress for copyright purposes as *a work of fiction*." Edwards claims to have read the manuscript, which he said was later offered, in revised form, as a factual account of Adamski's contact experiences.

Jerome Clark reports a similar story in his book *The Unidentified* (co-authored with Loren Coleman): "Ray Palmer has maintained for years that back in 1946, when he edited *Amazing Stories*, he rejected a manuscript Adamski had submitted. The story, which did not pretend to be anything but fantasy, concerned Jesus Christ's landing on earth in a spaceship. In 1953, when Palmer read *Flying Saucers Have Landed*, he was amazed to discover that the new story was really the old one updated, with Jesus now a Venusian and the spaceship a flying saucer." (Clark and Coleman, 1975)

Adamski claimed to have seen his first "spaceship" on October 9, 1946, over his California home in Palomar Gardens. It was a dirigible-shaped "Mother Ship," he said, which carried the smaller "flying saucers," or

"Scout craft," inside. Then in August of 1947, 184 saucers allegedly passed over the slopes of Palomar again, as Adamski watched.

It was not until November 20, 1952, that the first face-to-face meeting reportedly occurred between Adamski and his "space friends," as he sometimes called them. The location of this historic event was said to be near Desert Center, in the California desert. Also present were six witnesses who later signed a sworn affidavit. A detailed account of the incident, in which Adamski meets Orthon, a man from Venus, appears in *Flying Saucers Have Landed* (1953).

Briefly, the supposed event can be described as follows: Orthon's saucer descends from a huge "Mother Ship," hovering high above. After landing on a nearby hill, the Venusian walks over to Adamski, who remains calm and cool throughout the entire episode. Orthon was described as smooth-skinned, beardless, and well dressed. He had shoulder-length blond hair, was about five feet six inches tall, and wore what looked like a ski suit with a broad belt around the waist.

The Venusian began communicating by telepathy, informing Adamski of the Space Peoples' friendly intentions and concern over "radiations from our nuclear tests." It was made clear to George that we earthlings had better start living according to the laws of the "Creator of All," which, of course, had been taught all along by "Professor" Adamski. After about one hour had elapsed, Orthon returned to his ship and buzzed away.

Many more contacts were to follow, including rides into space and lengthy dialogues with other spacemen (such as Firkon, a Martian, and Ramu, a Saturnian), which were recounted *verbatim*—without a tape recorder—in Adamski's second book *Inside the Space Ships* (1955).

Back on Earth, Adamski was in great demand for lectures, radio and TV appearances, as well as countless interviews for newspapers and magazines. He toured the world, speaking to millions of people, and was reportedly granted private audiences with

UFO INTERNATIONAL

Cover art from Adamski's first book, *Flying Saucers Have Landed* (1953)

Queen Juliana of the Netherlands and Pope John XXIII.

In October 1957, UFO researcher James W. Moseley (now editor of *Saucer Smear*, formerly *Saucer News*) published a damaging exposé of Adamski's claims, based on personal interviews with Adamski and most of his close friends and co-workers. Among other interesting tidbits, Moseley made the following points:

1. Adamski's first book misquoted a number of people regarding statements they supposedly made in support of his claims.

2. The six "witnesses" at the November 20, 1952, "Desert Contact" all had backgrounds as UFO believers, had no special expertise, and did not see enough detail to vouch for the reality of the incident. Some of them later admitted this.

3. The "Desert Contact" was not accidental as claimed, but was *pre-planned* from detailed information and instructions that Adamski tape recorded and played for several co-workers, about a week before the incident took place.

4. In a letter to a close friend, which Moseley obtained, Adamski wrote: "Sometimes you have to use the back door to get the Truth across."

On Adamski's behalf, it can be said that he was trying to get across certain truths—regardless of whether they were coming from the "space brothers" or ancient philosophers on Earth. As one reads *Inside the Space Ships*, especially, what is strikingly evident are the obvious *metaphors* on every page. This may be the point that Desmond Leslie intended in the foreword to the book when he said: "We are in no position to sit and split hairs when the very foundations of this planet are teetering on disaster. Read, then, the following with an open mind and see whether the light of its teaching rings true." (Adamski, 1955)

To a Jungian, Adamski's tour of the space ship becomes a treasure trove of technological metaphors coinciding with virtually every principle of mystical truth found in the *philosophica perennis*—or Perennial Philosophy—and in the Holy Bible: the all-seeing "Eye of God," warnings about idolatry, the importance of self-knowledge, warnings about egotism and self-seeking, respect for natural law and the need for harmony with nature, respect for the planet and other life-forms, unity and altruism, the reconciliation of opposites, microcosm and macrocosm, oneness with the universe, death and rebirth, the law of balance, karma and the Golden Rule, and cosmic understanding, in general.

Examples of technological metaphors include: light as enlightenment; a giant lens as the "Eye of God"; the power of the space ship as the power of the mind; space travel as ascension; the secrets of space travel as the secrets of life; interplanetary travel as connecting the "gods" (for which the planets were named), which can be interpreted as integrating the potentialities within us; the speed of light as the speed of truth (or thought); and telepathy as a symbol for total honesty.

As sociologist David Stupple cleverly pointed out, Adamski and most of the other leading contactees of the 1950s were *utopians*. "George Adamski had a vision of a better world, and that vision apparently became reality for him." (Stupple, 1980)

After a successful twelve years as a famous celebrity, Adamski died of a heart attack on April 23, 1965, in Washington, D.C.

—RONALD D. STORY

References

Adamski, George, and Desmond Leslie. *Flying Saucers Have Landed* (The British Book Centre/Werner Laurie, 1953).

———. *Inside the Space Ships* (Abelard-Schuman, 1955).

Clark, Jerome, and Loren Coleman. *The Unidentified* (Warner Paperback Library, 1975).

Edwards, Frank. *Flying Saucers—Here and Now!* (Lyle Stuart, 1967).

Huxley, Aldous. *The Perennial Philosophy* (Harper & Brothers, 1945).

Moseley, James W. Personal communication, February 14, 2000.

Stupple, David. "The Man Who Talked with Venusians" in *Proceedings of the First International UFO Congress*, edited by Curtis G. Fuller (Warner Books, 1980).

Aerial Phenomena Research Organization (APRO)

APRO was founded in January 1952 by a Wisconsin couple, Jim (Leslie James) and Coral E. Lorenzen who later moved to Alamogordo, New Mexico, and finally to Tucson, Arizona, where the organization was based until it was dissolved in 1988.

The organization was based on the premise that the UFO phenomenon is important enough to warrant an objective, scientific investigation. Toward this end APRO became a pacesetter in many ways.

APRO was the first organization of its kind in the world in that it always maintained representatives in most foreign countries who kept headquarters in Tucson informed concerning UFO activity around the globe. About 10 percent of its membership were outside the United States.

In 1956, APRO began to recruit scientific personnel to investigate and evaluate cases, rather than depend on newspaper clippings as source material. A Field Investigators Network, composed of selected APRO members was spread across North America and extending overseas. These members investigated UFO cases and forwarded the results to headquarters. The advice of APRO's consultants in their various fields of specialization was relied upon to indicate appropriate areas and direction of research.

The general membership would furnish leads to be referred to Field Investigators for follow-up. Current UFO reports, results of various projects, editorial commentaries, and other features were carried in the monthly *APRO Bulletin*. The first issue of the *APRO Bulletin* was published in June 1952 and ran through most of 1987.

In 1957, APRO began building its international staff as well as its scientific consulting staff. At one time, the organization had forty-two scientists on its consulting panels—listed under four general categories: biological, medical, physical, and social sciences—and foreign representatives in forty-seven different countries.

APRO proved to be a pacesetter in other areas as well. The concept of specially selected Field Investigators originated with APRO, and in 1971 it was the first private UFO research organization to sponsor a scientific symposium on UFOs.

In 1968, APRO initiated the Field Investigator Network system, which was later adopted by both MUFON (the Mutual UFO Network) and CUFOS (the Center for UFO Studies).

In 1970, APRO published the first Field Investigator's manual. The first UFO Conference was held in Peoria, Illinois, in 1970, sponsored by APRO and the local Peoria Research Group. MUFON surfaced the same year when its leader, Walt Andrus, decided that he wanted his own group.

APRO enjoyed considerable success during the late 1960s while UFOs were leading law enforcement officers and the general public in a merry chase that resulted in the appointment of the Condon Committee, under contract to the U.S. Air Force.

When the Condon Committee closed its doors and issued its final report in 1968, the Air Force followed suit and announced its disengagement with the UFO problem in December 1969.

The last large UFO research group came upon the scene in 1973, when Dr. J. Allen Hynek founded the Center for UFO Studies.

Between 1963 and 1973, Dr. Hynek contacted the top men in the UFO field around the world and to establish the nucleus of CUFOS. Both MUFON and CUFOS are similar to APRO in their organizational structure and methodology.

Perhaps most significantly, APRO was a pacesetter in the overall modern trend in UFOlogy relating to close encounters of the third and fourth kinds (CE-3s and CE-4s): entities and abductions. From the time the first cases were publicized in the 1960s, APRO supported the idea of UFO "occupants" or "entities," as the Lorenzens called them, while rejecting most "contactee" claims.

—ETEP STAFF

Aetherius Society An international metaphysical, scientific, and religious organization, the Aetherius Society was founded in London, England, in 1956 by Dr. George King, Ph.D. (1919-1997). The American headquarters (in California) was established in 1960, and there are other branches in Detroit, Australia, West Africa, and throughout the British Isles.

The society bases its beliefs upon the contact Dr. King is said to have had with highly evolved "Masters" on other planets—mostly within this solar system—and the more than six hundred communications, or "Transmissions," he has allegedly received from them. King claims that he was first contacted, one morning in May 1954, by a "voice from space" that said, "Prepare yourself! You are to become the Voice of Interplanetary Parliament." Thus, the thirty-five-year-old Englishman became the "Primary Terrestrial Mental Channel" by authority of the voice which (he later discovered) belonged to a thirty-five-hundred-year-old Venusian Master called Aetherius (a pseudonym meaning "One Who comes from Outer Space"). Aetherius and other members of the "Hierarchy of the Solar System" had an urgent message to give to Earth through the unique Yogic mediumship of George King, and in 1955 a series of "Cosmic Transmissions" began, which continued throughout his life.

To receive them, King would go into a samadhic trance in which the consciousness is supposedly raised to a high "Psychic Center." A telepathic beam of thought was placed on him by the communicator, and the message was received and transmitted through King's brain and voice box, emerging in the form of slow-spoken, resonant English. All messages are preserved on audiotape.

The messages include warnings against the use of nuclear energy in any form and exhortations to put the world in order by returning to the "Cosmic Laws" as taught by great Masters such as Jesus, Buddha, and Krishna—all of whom are said to have come from other planets.

Life on the other planets is described as free from war, hatred, disease, want, and ignorance. The inhabitants have perfected spacecraft that can traverse the galaxy and beyond. Some of these craft, engaged in metaphysical operations around the Earth, have been termed "flying saucers."

Among their supposed missions were the following: to protect us from outside interference from hostile races, to monitor all changes in the environment and geophysical structure of the planet, and to help clear up harmful radiation in the atmosphere.

King stated that without flying saucers the world would be lifeless. Messages from the commanders of some of the craft indicate that mankind is the "problem child" of the solar system and an area of vulnerability in an otherwise well-protected sector of the galaxy. This is of special importance to the Aetherius Society in view of its belief that an intergalactic conflict is now in progress.

The society also believes in reincarnation and teaches that mankind itself originally came from another planet in this solar system, which is now the asteroid belt between Mars and Jupiter. Our original home planet is said to have been destroyed by a total atomic chain reaction, and mankind was reincarnated on Earth some 18 million years ago.

According to the society's beliefs, two previous civilizations on Earth, Lemuria and Atlantis, also perished due to an atomic war, and the Cosmic Masters are now actively concerned with preventing a third such catastrophe. It is further maintained that specially trained interplanetary Adepts are on Earth engaged in a cleansing operation to eliminate the centers of evil, which have dominated the world for eons and seek to eventually enslave all of mankind.

The plan will culminate with the arrival of an extraterrestrial Master from a flying saucer some time in the not-too-distant future. When this happens, all people on Earth will be offered the choice of following the laws of God and entering a New Age of peace and enlightenment, or rejecting the laws and passing through death to a younger planet where they will relearn the lessons of life.

The Aetherius Society has published many texts of the Transmissions and also produces a full range of cassette tapes explaining the theory and practice of Cosmic metaphysics. The society organizes lectures, seminars, and other events to publicize the Teachings of the Cosmic Masters.

Address: 6202 Afton Place
            Hollywood, CA 90028
            U.S.A

            757 Fulham Road
            London SW6 6UU
            England
Web site: www.aetherius.org

AFR (Air Force Regulation) 190-1 Issued on August 30, 1991, by the Secretary of the United States Air Force to update the official

USAF policy on Unidentified Flying Objects (UFOs):

a. The following statement may be used in response to queries: Project Blue Book, the Air Force study of UFOs, ended in 1969, after 22 years of scientific investigation. More than 12,500 reported sightings were investigated; the vast majority—about 95 percent—were explainable. They were caused by such natural phenomena as meteors, satellites, aircraft, lightning, balloons, weather conditions, reflections of other planets, or just plain hoaxes. Of the very few that remained unexplained, there was no indication of a technology beyond our own scientific knowledge, or that any sighting could be considered an extraterrestrial vehicle. Most important, throughout Project Blue Book, there was never a shred of evidence to indicate a threat to our national security. Project Blue Book was ended based on these findings, as verified by a scientific study prepared by the University of Colorado, and further verified by the National Academy of Sciences. All of the Project Blue Book materials were turned over to the Modern Military Branch, National Archives and Records Administration, 8th Street and Pennsylvania, Washington, DC 20408, and are available for public review and analysis.

b. Individuals alleging current sighting[s] should be referred, without comment, to local law enforcement officials.

—U.S. AIR FORCE

airship wave of 1896 The first major UFO wave in recorded history took place in 1896 (several years prior to any officially documented flights of airplanes or powered airships of any kind in the United States), beginning in November, with reports mostly confined to the state of California but involving also Washington State and Canada to a lesser degree.

A mystery light was first reported in the night sky over the capitol city of Sacramento on the evening of November 17, 1896. Local newspapers ran such headlines as: A Wandering Apparition, A Queer Phenomenon, and What Was It? It was said that due to a heavy overcast on the evening of the first sighting,

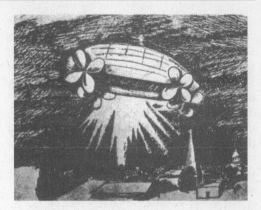

This woodcut appeared in an 1896 newspaper to illustrate the phantom "airship" that was seen before its time.

very little detail could be observed. The majority of alleged witnesses reported only a light source, but a few were said to have seen, in addition, a dark body of some sort above the luminous point (according to newspaper accounts).

The strange flying light appeared a second time, so the story goes, on the evening of November 21st, at which time the public and press are said to have taken the phenomenon much more seriously. Reportedly, witnesses to the second passage included a sizable number of the citizens of Sacramento, but, as before, a dark, cloudy sky masked any detail that would explain how the light was being carried through the atmosphere.

Soon after the light passed out of sight, it was reportedly seen over the city of Folsom, some twenty miles to the west. Later that night, reports of lights in the heavens came in from the San Francisco Bay area.

Unexplained flying lights and the story of the sighting of an airship by one R. L. Lowry prompted a San Francisco attorney to "disclose" that a man had supposedly contacted him some months earlier for legal advice concerning the "world's first practical airship," a craft that the supposed inventor asserted he had nearly completed. Flashing impressive blueprints and boasting of strong financial backing, the inventor convinced the attorney that the airship would soon be operational. The attorney, a George D. Collins, told the press that, in his opinion, the phenomenon in the skies over Sacramento must have been his client conducting nocturnal test flights before making an official announcement of his secret invention. This suggestion, a reasonable one in the minds of many, was given extensive publicity by San Francisco newspapers, stirring up imaginations all over California. Rumors and wild stories soon began to spread. For a while, the "phantom airship" was the biggest news story in northern California.

As more reports of strange lights in the sky were tallied, enhancing the mystery, attorney Collins became so tormented by reporters and curious busybodies that he regretted his earlier bragging and fled into hiding.

Cities reporting airship sightings after November 23 included Stockton, Lathrop, Sebastopol, Santa Rosa, Red Bluff, Chico, Auburn, San Jose, Modesto, Woodland, Fresno, Visalia, Hanford, Bakersfield, Tulare, Delano, Los Angeles, Redlands, and Anderson.

As to the exact nature of the mystery light, many reports were vague, mentioning only a bright light in the western sky early in the evening, indicating possible confusion with the planet Venus. Reported velocities of the light as it passed overhead were slow by modern standards, and if one considers the testimony of a number of witnesses that the light moved in an undulating fashion, this might indicate that some sightings were due to wind-blown balloons with a lantern attached. Again, some witnesses said they saw something large supporting the light but very few details were given. The most common terms used to describe the "supporting structure" were: "dark body," "misty mass," "cigar-shaped," "egg-shaped," and "barrel-shaped."

In spite of the difficulties involved, about a half-dozen reports can be explained satisfactorily. These were the sightings of three strange sights in the heavens a month before the passage of the mystery light (or lights) over Sacramento. There is a good possibility that people were confusing the "phantom airship"

with the passage of a triple-headed bolide that had crossed the night sky with majestic slowness several weeks previously.

However, all things considered, there were still some puzzling episodes that took place in November 1896:

(1) A fiery object displaying three points of light was spotted resting on the ground near Knight's Ferry, California. Two witnesses, both Methodist ministers, said the thing suddenly took off as they approached, flying away in a shallow climb.

(2) A fast-moving cigar-shaped object surrounded by a shifting luminosity and making small explosions was reported by the captain of a steamboat.

(3) According to hundreds of citizens of Tulare, California, of which fifteen are named in news accounts, something in the night sky came down quite a distance, and then went up and took a straight, quick move westward. Red, white, and blue lights were seen in succession.

(4) A resident of Tacoma, Washington, said he watched something strange in the sky over Mount Rainier one night. For over an hour, he said, an object emitted various colored rays, which shot out from the thing's center in every direction like spokes of a wheel. The "object" reportedly moved about with a waving motion, swayed back and forth, and darted from one position to another.

The Canadian press, which reported on the puzzling events taking place in California, seemed to take the airship possibility very seriously, even though one of the most intriguing reports of the year came from Rossland, British Columbia, on August 12, 1896. It told of a strange aerial body that approached the town, paused momentarily above a nearby mountain peak, made several wide circles in the sky, and then sped away on a straight course. The thing was described as a "luminous ball of fire that glowed amidst a halo of variegated colors." The object took a quarter of an hour to complete its maneuvers and was watched by many citizens of Rossland.

It is interesting to note that even back in

1896 the extraterrestrial hypothesis was suggested by some to account for the appearance of the nineteenth-century UFOs. In a letter to the editor of the *Sacramento Bee*, published in the November 24th issue, one citizen who gave his initials as ''W.A.'' stated his conviction that the observed phenomenon could only be due to the visit of a spacecraft from the planet Mars on a mission of exploration. He expressed his belief that the alien ship was made of very light metal and powered by some sort of electrical force, giving the Martian vessel the appearance of a ball of fire in flight. The speed of such an interplanetary craft he imagined to be a ''thousand miles a second.''

Perhaps even more intriguing is this early report of a ''close encounter of the third kind'': Two men told the Stockton *Evening Mail* that they had met three ''strange people'' on a road near Lodi, California. According to the story, the strange beings were very tall, with small delicate hands, and large, narrow feet. Each creature's head was bald with small ears and a small mouth, yet the eyes were big and lustrous. Instead of clothing, the creatures seemed to be covered with a natural silky growth. Conversation was impossible because the ''strange people'' could utter only a monotonous, guttural warbling. Occasionally, one of the unusual beings would breathe deeply from a nozzle attached to a bag slung under an arm and in each hand the creatures carried something the size of an egg that gave off an intense light. The weird encounter ended with an attempted kidnap of the two Californians, but failing to overpower the two men, the creatures fled to a cigar-shaped craft hovering nearby, jumped through a hatch, and zoomed away.

The California UFO wave of 1896 was over by December, but in February of 1897 reports of mysterious star-like bodies moving about the skies over western Nebraska marked the beginning of an even bigger UFO wave that would involve the greater part of the American Midwest.

—LOREN E. GROSS

airship wave of 1897   The California airship reports of November and December 1896, while recounted in some newspapers around the country, attracted relatively little attention in the Midwest and East. The arrival of 1897 saw the end of the California flap, with only isolated sightings at Lodi and Acampo in mid-January. Curiously enough, Delaware farmers, three thousand miles away, also reported airships during January.

By mid-February, unknown craft and mysterious lights in the night skies were reported in many areas of Nebraska. Sightings continued throughout March, with reports now coming from neighboring Kansas as well. To the north, in Michigan, late March brought stories of ''balls of fire'' moving through the darkness.

On the night of March 29th, hundreds of people in Omaha watched a large bright light fly over the city, hover briefly, then disappear to the northwest. An even larger audience, numbering in the thousands, witnessed the performance of an aerial mystery over Kansas City three nights later. In Everest, Kansas, the object was described as resembling an Indian canoe, some twenty-five to thirty feet in length, carrying a searchlight of varying colors.

The airships were generally described as cigar-shaped, apparently metallic, with wings, propellers, fins, and other appendages. At night, they appeared to be brilliant lights, with dark superstructures sometimes visible behind the lights.

Skeptics searched in vain for a conventional explanation, blaming the reports on the planet Venus (then brilliant in the evening sky) or the star Alpha Orionis. The reports also inspired practical jokers, who began sending aloft balloons of every description. The situation was further confused by ''enterprising'' reporters who delighted in seeing who could concoct the tallest airship tale for publication.

As the wave of reports continued throughout April, numerous stories of landed airships were published in newspapers around the country. In many such accounts, the operators of the craft were seen and communications were established by the witnesses. The airship occupants were usually described as normal-looking human beings who engaged their wondering admirers in conversation. They generally claimed to be experimenting with aerial travel, saying their craft had been constructed in secret in Iowa, New York, Tennessee, or some other locality.

There were exceptions to this contact pattern, such as a report by Judge Lawrence A. Byrne of Texarkana, Arkansas, who claimed to have met Oriental-looking occupants of a landed airship. These beings, three in number, spoke among themselves in a foreign language. They beckoned to Byrne, who went aboard the craft and later described some of the machinery inside.

In one Texas case, the airship crewmen claimed to be from an unknown region at the North Pole. A West Virginia report, only discovered in the late 1970s, tells of "Martians" aboard a grounded craft.

The people of 1897 did consider extraterrestrial explanations for the airships. Loren Gross, in his entry on the California events of 1896, has referred to a letter, published in the *Sacramento* (Calif.) *Bee* of November 24, 1896. This was the first "Martian" speculation, but others followed. The Colony (Kans.) *Free Press,* editorializing on the mystery, thought the airship was "probably operated by a party of scientists from the planet Mars." Similar theories of visitors from the Red Planet were mentioned in the St. Louis (Mo.) *Post-Dispatch,* the Memphis (Tenn.) *Commercial-Appeal,* and other newspapers of the period. The concept of life on Mars had already been brought to public consciousness by the research and theories of such astronomers as Percival Lowell and Camille Flammarion. Lowell's ideas of the Martian canals were well known, and Flammarion had speculated on possible communication with the inhabitants of Mars.

Reports of airship sightings continued throughout May of 1897, with an isolated sighting coming from Texas during June. This particular event was noteworthy, as it told of two airships seen at the same time. Sightings of more than one object were very rare, although the airships were seen in widely separated areas on the same day. For instance, on April 15th, at the height of the wave, reports came from ten different towns in Michigan, seven towns in Illinois, and one location each in Iowa and South Dakota. It would be simple enough to quote similar instances for virtually any day in April. Nor were such sightings confined to only four states in one twenty-four-hour period, as in the above example. It should be noted also that any such statistics are based on incomplete research, as the newspaper files of several states remain virtually untouched by investigators.

Hints of worldwide airship activity during 1897 are contained in reports from Sweden on July 17th, off the coast of Norway on August 13th, and from Ontario, Canada, on August 16th. In late September, an engineer in the town of Ustyug, Russia, observed a "balloon" with an "electric," or phosphorescent, sheen. As a matter of historical fact, the British and the French were known to have motor-powered balloons by this time, but the American airship reports have never been satisfactorily explained. Aviation historians state that craft such as were reported were not operational in the United States during the late 1890s. Were they, then, extraterrestrial vehicles? The descriptions hardly fit the image of sleek, streamlined spaceships, designed for interplanetary voyages. To say that the airships were from a "parallel universe," or some equally esoteric realm, is really no answer, but mere speculation. One is forced to admit that the strangers in the skies of 1897 remain as much of a mystery to us as they were to our ancestors.

—LUCIUS FARISH

alien autopsy film The Roswell crashed-saucer myth has been given renewed impetus by a controversial television program called "Alien Autopsy: Fact or Fiction?" that purports to depict the autopsy of a flying saucer occupant. The ''documentary,'' promoted by a British marketing agency that formerly handled Walt Disney products, was aired August 28 and September 4, 1995, on the Fox television network. Skeptics, as well as many UFOlogists, quickly branded the film used in the program a hoax.

''The Roswell Incident,'' as it is known, is described in several controversial books, including one of that title by Charles Berlitz and William L. Moore. Reportedly, in early July 1947, a flying saucer crashed on the ranch property of William Brazel near Roswell, New Mexico, and was subsequently retrieved by the United States government (Berlitz and Moore, 1980). Over the years, numerous rumors, urban legends, and outright hoaxes have claimed that saucer wreckage and the remains of its humanoid occupants were stored at a secret facility— e.g., a (nonexistent) ''Hangar 18'' at Wright Patterson Air Force Base—and that the small corpses were autopsied at that or another site (Berlitz and Moore, 1980; Stringfield, 1977).

UFO hoaxes, both directly and indirectly related to Roswell, have since proliferated. For example, a 1949 science fiction movie, *The Flying Saucer*, produced by Mikel Conrad, purported to contain scenes of a captured spacecraft; an actor hired by Conrad actually posed as an FBI agent and swore the claim was true. In 1950, writer Frank Scully reported in his book *Behind the Flying Saucers* that the United States government had in its possession no fewer than three Venusian spaceships, together with the bodies of their humanoid occupants. Scully, who was also a *Variety* magazine columnist, was fed the story by two confidence men who had hoped to sell a petroleum-locating device allegedly based on alien technology. Other crash-retrieval stories followed, as did various photographs of space aliens living and dead: One gruesome photo portrayed the pilot of a small plane, his aviator's glasses still visible in the picture (Clark, 1993).

Among recent Roswell hoaxes was the MJ-12 fiasco, in which supposed top secret govern-ment documents—including an alleged briefing paper for President Eisenhower and an executive order from President Truman—corroborated the Roswell crash. Unfortunately, document experts readily exposed the papers as inept forgeries (Nickell and Fischer, 1990).

Sooner or later, a Roswell ''alien autopsy'' film was bound to turn up. That predictability, together with a lack of established historical record for the bizarre film, is indicative of a hoax. So is the anonymity of the cameraman. But the strongest argument against authenticity stems from what really crashed at Roswell in 1947. According to recently released air force files, the wreckage actually came from a balloon-borne array of radar reflectors and monitoring equipment launched as part of the secret Project Mogul and intended to monitor acoustic emissions from anticipated Soviet nuclear tests. In fact, materials from the device match contemporary descriptions of the debris (foiled paper, sticks, and tape) given by rancher Brazel's children and others (Berlitz and Moore, 1980; Thomas, 1995).

Interestingly, the film failed to agree with earlier purported eyewitness testimony about the alleged autopsy. For example, multiple medical informants described the Roswell creatures as lacking ears and having only four fingers with no thumb (Berlitz and Moore, 1980), whereas the autopsy film depicts a creature with small ears and five fingers in addition to a thumb. Ergo, either the previous informants are hoaxers, or the film is a hoax, or both.

Although the film was supposedly authenticated by Kodak, only the leader tape and a single frame were submitted for examination, not the entire footage. In fact, a Kodak spokesman told the *Sunday Times* of London: ''There is no way I could authenticate this. I saw an image on the print. Sure it could be old film, but it doesn't mean it is what the aliens were filmed on.''

Various objections to the film's authenticity came from journalists, UFO researchers, and scientists who viewed the film. They noted that it bore a bogus, nonmilitary codemark

("Restricted access, AOI classification") that disappeared after it was criticized; that the anonymous photographer's alleged military status had not been verified; and that the injuries sustained by the extraterrestrial were inconsistent with an air crash. On the basis of such objections, an article in the *Sunday Times* of London advised: "RELAX. The little green men have not landed. A much-hyped film purporting to prove that aliens had arrived on earth is a hoax." (Chittenden, 1995)

Similar opinions on the film came even from prominent Roswell-crash partisans: Kent Jeffrey, an associate of the Center for UFO Studies and author of the "Roswell Declaration" (a call for an executive order to declassify any United States government information on UFOs and alien intelligence) stated "up front and unequivocally there is no (zero!!!) doubt in my mind that this film is a fraud." (1995) Even arch Roswell promoter Stanton T. Friedman said: "I saw nothing to indicate the footage came from the Roswell incident, or any other UFO incident for that matter" ("Alien or Fake?" 1995).

Still other critics found many inconsistencies and suspicious elements in the alleged autopsy. For example, in one scene the "doctors" wore white, hooded anticontamination suits that could have been neither for protection from radiation (elsewhere the personnel are examining an alien body without such suits), nor for protection from the odor of decay or from unknown bacteria or viruses (either would have required some type of breathing apparatus). Thus it appears that the outfits served no purpose except to conceal the doctors' identities.

American pathologists offered still more negative observations. Cyril Wecht, former president of the National Association of Forensic Pathologists, seemed credulous but described the viscera in terms that might apply to supermarket meat scraps and sponges: "I cannot relate these structures to abdominal contexts." Again, he said about contents of the cranial area being removed: "This is a structure that must be the brain, if it is a human

being. It looks like no brain that I have ever seen, whether it is a brain filled with a tumor, a brain that has been radiated, a brain that has been traumatized and is hemorrhagic . . . ." (Wecht, 1995) Much more critical was the assessment of nationally known pathologist Dominick Demaio who described the autopsy on television's "American Journal" (1995): "I would say it's a lot of bull."

Houston pathologist Ed Uthman (1995) was also bothered by the unrealistic viscera, stating: "The most implausible thing of all is that the 'alien' just had amorphous lumps of tissue in 'her' body cavities. I cannot fathom that an alien who had external organs so much like ours could not have some sort of definitive structural organs internally." As well, "the prosectors did not make an attempt to arrange the organs for demonstration for the camera." Uthman also observed that there was no body block, a basic piece of equipment used to prop up the trunk for examination and the head for brain removal. He also pointed out that "the prosector used scissors like a tailor, not like a pathologist or surgeon" (pathologists and surgeons place the middle or ring finger in the bottom scissors hole and use the forefinger to steady the scissors near the blades). Uthman further noted that "the initial cuts in the skin were made a little too Hollywood-like, too gingerly, like operating on a living patient" whereas autopsy incisions are made faster and deeper. Uthman faulted the film for lacking what he aptly termed "technical verisimilitude."

The degree of realism in the film has been debated, even by those who believe the film is a hoax. Some, like Kent Jeffrey (1995), thought the autopsy was done on a specially altered human corpse. On the other hand, many, including movie special effects experts, believed a dummy had been used. One suspicious point in that regard was that significant close-up views of the creature's internal organs were consistently out of focus ("Alien or Fake?" 1995).

"American Journal" (1995) also featured a special effects expert who doubted the film's authenticity and demonstrated how the autopsy "incisions"—which left a line of "blood" as the scalpel was drawn across the alien's skin—could easily have been faked. (The secret went unexplained but probably consisted of a tube fastened to the far side of the blade.)

In contrast to the somewhat credulous response of a Hollywood special effects filmmaker on the Fox program, British expert Cliff Wallace of Creature Effects provided the following assessment:

> None of us were of the opinion that we were watching a real alien autopsy, or an autopsy on a mutated human which has also been suggested. We all agreed that what we were seeing was a very good fake body, a large proportion of which had been based on a lifecast. Although the nature of the film obscured many of the things we had hoped to see, we felt that the general posture and weighting of the corpse was incorrect for a body in a prone position and had more in common with a cast that had been taken in an upright position.
>
> We did notice evidence of a possible molding seam line down an arm in one segment of the film but were generally surprised that there was little other evidence of seaming which suggests a high degree of workmanship.
>
> We felt that the filming was done in such a way as to obscure details rather than highlight them and that many of the parts of the autopsy that would have been difficult to fake, for example the folding back of the chest flaps, were avoided, as was anything but the most cursory of limb movement. We were also pretty unconvinced by the lone removal sequence. In our opinion the insides of the creature did not bear much relation to the exterior where muscle and bone shapes can be easily discerned. We all agreed that the filming of the sequence would require either the use of two separate bodies, one with chest open, one with chest closed, or significant redressing of one mortal. Either way the processes involved are fairly com-

plicated and require a high level of specialized knowledge.

Another expert, Trey Stokes—a Hollywood special effects "motion designer" whose film credits include *The Abyss, The Blob, Robocop Two, Batman Returns, Gremlins II, Tales from the Crypt,* and many others—provided an independent analysis at CSICOP's request. Interestingly, Stokes's critique also indicated that the alien figure was a dummy cast in an upright position. He further noted that it seemed lightweight and "rubbery," that it therefore moved unnaturally when handled, especially in one shot in which "the shoulder and upper arm actually are floating rigidly above the table surface, rather than sagging back against it" as would be expected. (Stokes, 1995)

CSICOP staffers (Executive Director Barry Karr, *Skeptical Inquirer* Assistant Editor Tom Genoni, Jr., and the writer) monitored developments in the case. Before the film aired, CSICOP issued a press release, briefly summarizing the evidence against authenticity and quoting CSICOP Chairman Paul Kurtz as stating: "The Roswell myth should be permitted to die a deserved death. Whether or not we are alone in the universe will have to be decided on the basis of better evidence than that provided by the latest bit of Roswell fakery. Television executives have a responsibility not to confuse programs designed for entertainment with news documentaries."

—Joe Nickell

References

"Alien or Fake?" *Sheffield Star* (August 18, 1995).

"American Journal" (September 6, 1995).

Berlitz, Charles, and William L. Moore. *The Roswell Incident* (Grosset and Dunlap, 1980; Berkley Books, 1988).

Chittenden, Maurice. "Film that 'Proves' Aliens Visited Earth Is a Hoax," (London) *Sunday Times* (July 30, 1995).

Clark, Jerome. "UFO Hoaxes" in *Encyclopedia of Hoaxes,* Stein, Gordon, ed. (Gale Research, 1993).

Kent, Jeffrey. "Bulletin 2: The Purported 1947 Roswell Film," Internet (May 26, 1995).

Kurtz, Paul. Quoted in CSICOP press release: "Alien Autopsy: Fact or Fiction? Film a Hoax Concludes Scientific Organization" (April 25, 1995).

Nickell, Joe, and John F. Fischer. "The Crashed-Saucer Forgeries," *The International UFO Reporter* (March/April 1990).

Stokes, Trey. Personal communication (August 29-31, 1995).

Stringfield, Leonard H. *Situation Red: The UFO Siege* (Doubleday, 1977).

Thomas, Dave. "The Roswell Incident and Project Mogul," *Skeptical Inquirer* (July-August, 1995).

Uthman, Ed. "Fox's 'Alien Autopsy': A Pathologist's View," Usenet, sci.med.pathology (September 15, 1995).

Wallace, Cliff. Letter to Union Pictures (August 3, 1995), quoted in Wallace's letter to Graham Birdsall, *UFO Magazine* (August 16, 1995), quoted on ParaNet (August 22, 1995).

Wecht, Cyril. Quoted on "Alien Autopsy: Fact or Fiction?" Fox Network (August 28 and September 4, 1995).

alien gallery   The illustrations that appear on the following four pages represent classic examples of alien beings that have been reported from 1947 to the present. I have researched each case in order to depict these beings as accurately as possible.

The Humanoids (Charles Bowen, et al., 1969) was a useful reference for some of the earlier cases. I have used artistic license only where insufficient information was available to determine exactly what was seen.

Whenever possible in occupant cases it is important that the investigators work with illustrators, or with the witnesses themselves, to produce drawings of the alien beings as well as getting detailed verbal descriptions. Only the combination of words and images can give a reasonably complete idea of the physical appearance of the reported beings.

For all we know, subtle differences in the pattern of scales on a reptilian being, or the shape of the eyes on a Gray being, may ultimately turn out to be very important in solving the UFO mystery.

It is hoped that this pioneering effort to document reported alien features will prove useful to serious researchers in the future.
—DAVID W. CHACE

References

Bowen, Charles, ed. *The Humanoids* (Henry Regnery, 1969).

Chace, David W. *A Visual Guide to Alien Beings* (Privately published, 1995, 1996, 1997).

alien iconography   The familiar image of the little, big-headed humanoid with large, wraparound eyes is the result of an evolutionary process. Like Jesus' portrait in art (Nickell, 1998) or the typical likeness of Santa Claus (Flynn, 1993), today's ubiquitous alien is the product of a selection process involving interaction between alleged encounterees and the popular media.

Putting aside science fiction examples, and beginning with the origin of the modern UFO era in 1947, a great variety of aliens characterized the early period (see for example Huyghe, 1996). There were the "little green men" reported in 1947 (Cohen, 1982), the beautiful, human-like beings who appeared to "contactees" in the 1950s, the hairy dwarfs common in 1954, and many other varieties of alleged extraterrestrials reported in close encounters to the present (Story, 1980).

The accompanying "Alien Time Line" (Nickell, 1997) depicts a selection of such alien beings. It has appeared in various magazines and on several television programs, including ABC's *20/20* in a documentary on the "Alien Autopsy" hoax. There it was used to show that the extraterrestrials that were supposedly retrieved from the 1947 "flying disk" crash near Roswell, New Mexico, were of a type not popularly imagined until many years later.

This type—appearing with the first widely reported alien abduction, the Betty and Barney Hill case of 1961—is now seen everywhere (in slight variations) on T-shirts, caps, ties, and other clothing items; featured on posters, wall

Villa Santina, Italy
August 14, 1947

Caracas, Venezuela
November 28, 1954

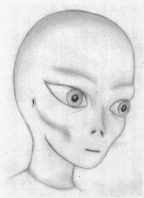

Kelly-Hopkinsville, Ky.
August 21-22, 1955

Minas Gerais, Brazil
October 15, 1957

Minas Gerais, Brazil
October 15, 1957

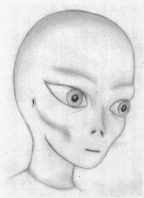

Whitfield, N.H.
September 19, 1961

South Ashburnham, Mass.
January 25, 1967

Ashland, Neb.
December 3, 1967

Houston, Tex.
May 1973

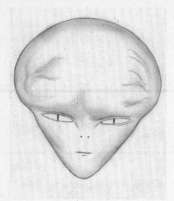

Houston, Tex.
May 1973

Baltimore, Md.
Summer 1973

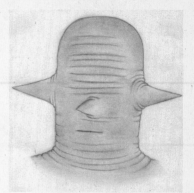

Pascagoula, Miss.
October 11, 1973

Rawlins, Wyo.
October 25, 1974

Aveley, Essex, England
October 27, 1974

Aveley, Essex, England
October 27, 1974

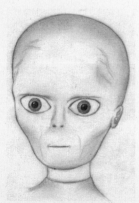

Alamogordo, N.M.
August 13, 1975

Heber-Snowflake, Ariz.
November 5, 1975

Heber-Snowflake, Ariz.
November 5, 1975

Allagash Wilderness, Me.
August 26, 1976

Allagash Wilderness, Me.
August 26, 1976

Charleston, S.C.
March 18, 1978

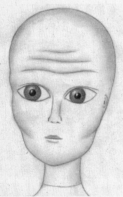

Lynnwood, Wash.
July 1981

Indianapolis, Ind.
June 30, 1983

Indianapolis, Ind.
June 30, 1983

Upstate N.Y.
December 26-27, 1985

Upstate N.Y.
December 26-27, 1985

Gulf Breeze, Fla.
December 2, 1987

Gulf Breeze, Fla.
December 2, 1987

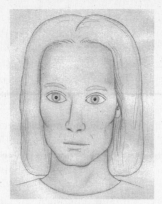

Hayes, Va.
1989

Dutch Harbor, Alaska
November 1991

Rural, Ark.
September 29, 1992

Victoria, Australia
August 8, 1993

Bothell, Wash.
February 9, 1995

Woodinville, Wash.
January 1, 1996

Varginha, Brazil
January 20, 1996

The alien archetype
in the year 2000

hangings, book jackets, etc.; and fashioned into candles, toys, keychains, and countless other items.

As part of an elaborate extraterrestrial mythology that has developed, the implication seems to be that the aliens are "time travelers"—in effect *us* as it is assumed we *will* be in our distant evolutionary future (Nickell, 1984). (This is in contrast to another mythical entity, Bigfoot, who is seen as our beastly relative from the remote past.) As futuristic beings, therefore, the aliens have dwindling bodies (due to presumed physical inactivity) and large brains (the imagined product of increased intelligence). Some critics, however, are skeptical of all human/humanoid models. As one commentator states, "While it seems incredible that life does not exist elsewhere in the universe, it is equally incredible that it should resemble man." (Palmer, 1951)

Nevertheless, although they are sometimes cute and sometimes sinister (no doubt as expressions of our collective hopes and fears), they represent a relatively standardized type that is a creation in mankind's own image.

—JOE NICKELL

References

Cohen, D. *The Encyclopedia of Monsters* (Dorsett Press, 1982).

Flynn, T. *The Trouble with Christmas.* (Prometheus Books, 1993).

Huyghe, P. *The Field Guide to Extraterrestrials* (Avon Books, 1996). (I relied heavily on this source, and Vallée 1969.)

Nickell, J. "The 'Hangar 18' tales: A folkloristic approach," *Common Ground* (June, 1984).

———. "Extraterrestrial Iconography," *Skeptical Inquirer* (September/October,1997).

Palmer, R. "New Report on the Flying Saucers." *Fate* (January, 1951).

Story, R. D. *The Encyclopedia of UFOs.* (Doubleday/New English Library, 1980).

POSTSCRIPT: Joe Nickell's "Alien Time Line" and entry on "alien iconography" could lead to misunderstandings for students of UFO culture interested in the evolution of ideas about aliens. Nickell, by his account, relied heavily on Patrick Huyghe's *Field Guide to Extraterrestrials* for the creation of the Time Line, but the book was not a comprehensive catalog of UFO entity encounters. It was a sampler of cases intended only to demonstrate the diversity of imagery. It includes only a small fraction of the total number of alien images appearing in UFO culture. Within any given type of alien, the book tends to use a representative example of the image with no preference given to it being either the first of the type or its most popular or influential manifestation. This leads to significant omissions if the interest is to display ordering in a chronology.

The most glaring omission has to be the absence of the face that appears on the cover of Whitley Strieber's bestselling book *Communion*. Since it is blatantly the template of most images of the Grays since 1987—and easily the most significant image in the history of alien images—this omission is astonishing. The omission of representations of Grays from the works of Budd Hopkins, the most visible of alien abduction authors, is also troubling if one seeks to understand the present standardization of the form of the Grays.

The aliens rendered by Steven Kilburn in *Missing Time* (Hopkins, 1981) are, for example, the first known examples of large-headed degenerate humanoids to display completely black eyes. The thin arms, disproportionately short legs, and slight paunch to the abdomen are distinctive and demonstrate an unambiguous relationship to the main alien in Steven Spielberg's 1977 blockbuster *Close Encounters of the Third Kind*.

Hopkins's next book *Intruders* (1987) introduced the thin, high necks into Gray iconography. This trait is clearly related to the Art Deco style of the main alien in Spielberg's film. Prior to that film none of the Grays drawn by alien abductees had such necks. Reinforcing the assumption is the presence of all-black eyes and a number of facial features in both the film alien and drawings in the *Intruders* book.

Whether or not Hopkins recognized the

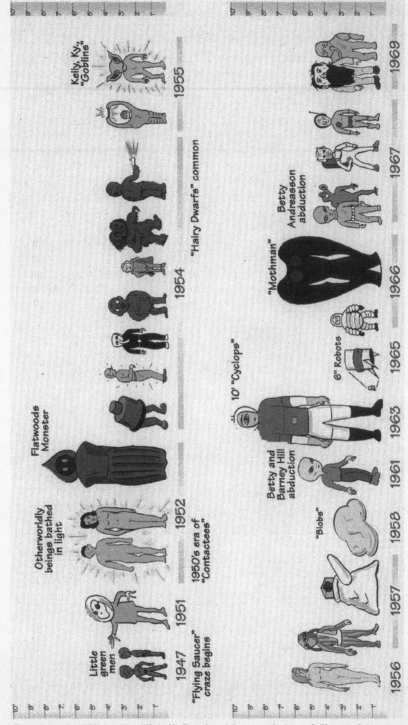

ALIEN TIME LINE

Little green men

Otherworldly beings bathed in light

Flatwoods Monster

Kelly, Ky., "Goblins"

1947 "Flying Saucer" craze begins

1951

1950's era of "Contactees"

1952

1954

"Hairy Dwarfs" common

1955

"Blobs"

Betty and Barney Hill abduction

10' "Cyclops"

6" Robots

"Mothman"

Betty Andreasson abduction

1956 1957 1958 1961 1963 1965 1966 1967 1969

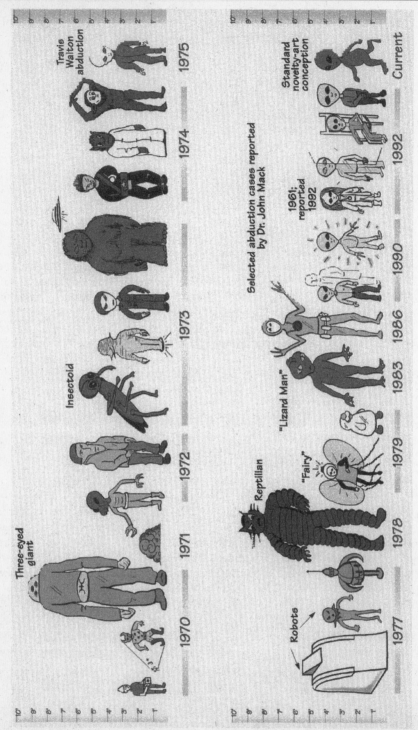

similarities, he failed to understand the influence of the film for a simple reason. He thought the aliens in the film were designed to look like aliens that had already been reported in the UFO literature. He knew that J. Allen Hynek served as a consultant, and he thought that guaranteed a basis in prior cases. He stated this in a radio interview published in the Spring 1988 *Skeptical Inquirer:* ''Allen Hynek had many drawings that he gave to Steven Spielberg for use when he made *Close Encounters of the Third Kind*, which of course was one of the biggest box office successes of all time. There was a serious attempt to follow the data that Allen Hynek and other people had gathered. So I think you can say Steven Spielberg popularized the essential physical type that the UFO reports had engendered before that time.''

This misimpression is easy to understand since *Newsweek* (November 21, 1977) reported that the chief alien was ''designed by Carlo Rimbaldi out of a consensus of reports.'' An essay by Hynek for the novelization of the film also creates such an impression with the line, ''In particular, the appearance of the 'extraterrestrials' were based on the most frequently reported features of such beings.''

Neither *Newsweek* nor Hynek offer direct quotes by the builders of the film alien. A comprehensive article on the effects work for the film in a special double issue of *Cinefantastique* in 1978 has the builders denying this. Carlo Rimbaldi specifically states, ''When we met, he told me he wanted something about 4 feet tall with a very large head and a slender body, but he gave me no actual designs.'' Rimbaldi then goes on to explain his reasoning for why the alien appears as it does:

I felt that, though humanoid in form, the extraterrestrials would be at least ten to twenty thousand years more advanced than humans, so I designed the head proportionally larger. But with their increased reliance on pure intellect, they would have a decreased need for such senses as hearing and smelling, and so the

ears and nose and other facial features would become less prominent. And because of their extreme technological orientation, I felt they would no longer smile as broadly as we do on earth; but since they would still retain certain emotions, I gave them a slight smile. Also, as the brain expanded, other parts of the body would take an opposite course. The need for muscular movements would diminish, and so their limbs would become thinner and longer. (Shay, 1978)

This is recognizably the same argument that H.G. Wells introduced many decades earlier about the future evolution of the human form. It was repeatedly used in the early science fiction pulps and even found its way into science journalism. Anyone who thinks Rimbaldi is just hyping himself in these quotes should dig up the *Cinefantastique* article and observe the paper trail of discarded concepts and drawings made by the alien builders in the course of their work. Add to this the readily confirmed observation that none of the drawings of Grays in the abduction accounts before that time had the combined traits of all-black large eyes and thin, high necks, and the role of the film in influencing subsequent UFO iconography is solidly established.

Nickell's Time Line presents a grasshopper alien over the year 1973 and labels it insectoid, implying either its origin or dominance at that time. Mike Shea said nothing about it until 1988, and he is fuzzy about whether it was 1973 or 1974. Ted Owens claimed contact with a pair of grasshopper aliens named Twitter and Tweeter as early as 1965 and was a bit more vocal about it at the time. Insectoids do not present a major presence until the 1990s after the introduction of ancient Lovecraftian godlike mantis beings by Whitley Strieber and John Lear. (Kottmeyer, 1999)

The significance of the Owens case and the intersection of UFO culture with Big Bug culture are discussed elsewhere. (Kottmeyer, 1996, 1997) The use of the Shea case on the Time Line introduces a systemic problem of method. Should the historian put a given drawing on the year a claimant alleges or believes he made contact, or on the year we can document the image was first presented?

If the interest is in the evolution of iconography, historians should favor the latter. The backdating could be fictitious for various reasons and the image subject to cultural influences between the claimed date of the experience and the putting of pen to paper. Nickell places Betty Andreasson's drawing in 1967, but no drawing was made before 1977. This is important because in 1975 the television movie *The UFO Incident* aired, presenting the true-life story of the Hill abduction. The film followed the hypnotic regression narratives of Betty and Barney Hill more faithfully than we normally expect Hollywood productions to be, but the aliens are not exact replicas of what either of the Hills described and drew.

Note the complaints by Betty Hill in a 1978 interview:

"My only serious criticism concerns the movie's depiction of the aliens' physical appearance. They did not look like that. The real ones looked more human than their humanoid counterparts. Also the movie shows them as being very short, but they weren't. I'd say the leader was my size and I'm 5 feet tall. And they weren't of such slender build." (Clark, 1978)

Similarly a comparison of the TV movie's depiction and the drawings by David Baker (done in collaboration with Barney Hill and published in the April 1972 issue of NICAP's *UFO Investigator*) uncovers a number of important differences. There is a sharp angle to the inner corners of the eye sockets in the telefilm where the original shows a rounded curve. The pupils of the eyes are larger in the film. A crease above the eye is more pronounced in the film than in the drawing. The film alien has a slit mouth and a line in the film says it has no mouth at all. Baker is told a membrane hides the mouth. The eyes in the film also display a probably unintended effect that makes one eye appear blank when seen from a glancing camera angle.

Betty Andreasson proved Raymond Fowler's statement that "her powers of visual recall seemed unusually acute" by incorporating all the film's modifications into her drawings of Quazgaa and his companions. (Fowler, 1979) The 1967 date claim makes no sense in the appearance of these details.

The drawing labeled "little green men" and set on 1947 was first published in 1964 (by Johannis Luigi). By Johannis's own account, the drawing probably was not faithful to drawings allegedly made in 1947 and subsequently lost by others. (Creighton, 1969) Of greater concern is the fact that the expression "little green men" does not seem to have been used in flying saucer journalism in 1947. (Bloecher, 1967) There is also no evidence it appeared in any newspaper clippings from the 1952 saucer wave, or for that matter in any saucer journalism between 1947 and August 1955. It seems to first appear in conjunction with the Kelly-Hopkinsville shoot-'em-up (in August of 1955). The press described the case as involving "an army of little green men" though in fact the witnesses denied the presence of any green color.

A wire service story on August 25, 1955, by Air Force public relations man Captain Robert White reacting to the story also gave wide distribution to the phrase "little green men" and it appears in frequent use thereafter. There is no evidence whatever that little green men were a common form of saucer pilot and what little evidence we have suggests the phrase got transplanted from science fiction pulps. Fredric Brown, for example, speaks of the expression as a cliché in a September 1954 story *Martians Go Home!* (Kottmeyer, 1999)

The 1978 Zanfretta alien is labeled reptilian, but one should beware that it is neither the first nor significantly influential. Curiously, the Time Line's drawing lacks the third eye that appeared in the original drawing. This caused some amusement among bad-film buffs for it made Zanfretta's alien look rather like a cross between the reptilian *Creature from the*

Black Lagoon (1954) and the three-eyed Mutant from *The Day the World Ended* (1956).

There is one reptoid type being as early as 1967, but the more significant omission here is any representation of the current version of reptoids seen in places like the M.I.T. conference (Pritchard, 1994), Linda Howe's volumes, or *Discover* and *Omni* magazines around 1982, among other places. (Craft, 1996; Lewels, 1997)

Lastly, we come to the issue of the use of the Time Line to demonstrate the anachronistic character of the Alien Autopsy Gray. We are told the type of alien described a "a little, big-headed humanoid with wraparound eyes" first appeared in 1961 with the Hill abduction. The initial descriptions of the entities in Betty Hill's nightmares after the 1961 sighting are described as normal-sized men with dark hair. Barney's descriptions initially suggest military pilots. The wraparound eyes got added in 1964, and his version only turns fully humanoid after hearing tapes of the hypnotic regressions. (Kottmeyer, 1994, 1998) By the time of the Baker drawing, the hair and nose are gone. It is the 1975 telefilm that makes them little. This is a complex situation and hard to represent on a Time Line, one would have to agree. Yet it can't be skirted, given the importance of the Hill case. It has to be added that the drawing offered on the Time Line adds to the general confusion by making the shape of the head too globular and adding a thin neck. Such a neck is thoroughly anachronistic for a pre-Spielberg abductor Gray.

The more serious error is the implication that there were no little, big-headed humanoids before the Hill case. As early as July 9, 1947, there appeared an item in the *Houston* (Texas) *Post* of a seaman who encountered a two-foot-tall saucer pilot with a round head the size of a basketball. (Davis & Bloecher, 1978)

In 1950, the *Wiesbadener Tagblatt* (Germany) published a photo of a short alien with a large oval head and described as having large, glaring eyes. Berlitz and Moore published it in *The Roswell Incident* (1980) with a cagey caption refusing to say "whether it may or may not pertain to certain significant aspects of the Roswell Incident." Klaus Webner subsequently researched it and proved conclusively it was an April Fool's joke perpetrated by reporter Wilhelm Sprunkel. He had confessed it in print two days afterwards and with Webner upon contact. (Webner, 1991)

Additionally there are cases involving humanoids with big heads and short frames appearing during the 1954 French wave. These are contemporary enough to the alleged autopsy film to rebut the charge of anachronism. Big-headed men with degenerated bodies was a commonplace in the science fiction pulps in the early part of the century and pretty surely trace their ancestry to H.G. Wells's writings about the future form of man. Wells himself never intended this form of future-man to be taken seriously as a scientific extrapolation. It started as a jest upon Herbert Spencer's writings and the doctrine of orthogenesis that had a degree of acceptance among paleontologists. (Kottmeyer, 1998)

Where the alien autopsy truly runs into trouble is when it bumps into a more compelling anachronism. During the film, the "doctor" removes a black membrane from the eyes. As discussed above, all-black eyes are unambiguously a post-Spielberg development without precedent among earlier Grays in the UFO literature. The notion of aliens having a removable covering membrane seems unknown prior to the 1976 film *The Man Who Fell to Earth* with David Bowie.

The David Bowie character inserts membranes over his eyes so he can walk among humanity undetected as the alien that he is. In an interesting bit of malpractice, doctors who later examine him manage to fuse the membrane onto his eyes. I suppose one can consider it appropriate to have promoters of the Roswell crash, intended or unintended, borrowing material from a film with such a title.

My final advice is to erase the numbers and use Huyghe's drawings to prove what he intended to prove, namely, the diversity of the imagination in UFO culture.

—MARTIN S. KOTTMEYER

References

Berlitz, Charles, and William Moore. *The Roswell Incident* (Grosset & Dunlap, 1980).

Bloecher, Ted. *Report on the Wave of 1947* (privately published, 1967).

Clark, Jerry. "Betty Hill—The Closest Encounter," *Saga UFO Report* (January 1978).

Craft, Michael. *Alien Impact* (St. Martin's Press, 1996).

Creighton, Gordon. "The Villa Santina Case" in *The Humanoids* edited by Charles Bowen (Henry Regnery, 1969).

Fowler, Raymond. *The Andreasson Affair* (Prentice-Hall, 1979).

Gross, Loren. *UFOs: A History—1952* in 6 volumes (privately published, 1987-1999).

Howe, Linda. *Glimpses of Other Realities: volume 1: Facts and Eyewitnesses,* 2nd ed. Linda Moulton Howe, July 1997.

Kottmeyer, Martin S. "The Eyes That Spoke," *REALL News* (July 1994).

———. "Space Bug a Boo Boo," *Talking Pictures* (Summer 1996).

———. "Bugs Baroque," *UFO Magazine* (July/August 1997).

———. "Varicose Brains," *Magonia* (February 1998); also on the Magonia Web site.

———. "Heading into the Future," *Magonia* (September 1999).

———. "The Fool on the Hill Case," *Doubting Thomas* (October-November 1998).

———. "Graying Mantis" *REALL News* (May 1999).

———. "Little Green Men" (unpublished manuscript).

Kroll, J. "The UFOs are Coming!" *Newsweek* (November 21, 1997).

Lewels, J. *The God Hypothesis* (Wild Flower Press, 1997).

Pritchard, Andrea, ed. *Alien Discussions—Proceedings of the Abduction Study Conference* (North Cambridge Press, 1994).

Shay, Don "Close Encounter Extraterrestrials" *Cinefantastique* (1978).

Webner, Klaus. "The Strange Case of Mister X" *The Probe Report* (September 1981).

Alien Identities (Govardhan Hill, 1993).

Richard Thompson relates how ancient Vedic texts from India may not be folklore and myth, but could accurately preserve accounts of human interaction with extraterrestrial visitors. These stories portray the peoples of India from 3000 B.C. onward being in contact with advanced beings from a host of other worlds who traveled here in aerial vehicles that resemble modern accounts of UFO craft.

—RANDALL FITZGERALD

Alien Impact (St. Martin's Press, 1996). To

help himself understand his own "strange, UFO-type encounters," Michael Craft explores the role of consciousness in the UFO experience. He concludes that UFO contactees, shamans, channelers, and white and black magic practitioners may all be seeing the same thing, a deliberately deceptive phenomenon stage-managed by cosmic tricksters who are conditioning our species to engage in new behaviors.

—RANDALL FITZGERALD

alien motives A fundamental question in the great UFO-ET debate is: "If aliens are indeed visiting us, *why* are they here?"

Carl Sagan once wondered disdainfully, "Why would all the anthropologists in the neighborhood suddenly come to Earth?" J. Allen Hynek once asked why would aliens visit Earth to scare people by swooping near their cars? Clearly these are inappropriate questions since there is no basis for suggesting a significant number of visitors are anthropologists. Furthermore, people who travel a great deal on Earth rarely bump into anthropologists. Because people in autos may be frightened by close approaches of flying saucers certainly doesn't mean that the purpose of the flights are to frighten the people. Surely drivers of the crude automobiles of a century ago weren't driving for the purpose of frightening horses, even though horses were sometimes frightened by the vehicles.

Before considering a host of possible reasons for visiting Earth, it is useful to examine travel by Earthlings. The reasons for travel and the locations to which one travels depend on a number of factors such as how long will the trip take? What will it cost and who will pay the bill? How much time and money can be spent? How important is the trip?

Between 1890 and 1910 millions of poor immigrants came from Europe to North America in steerage class in ships seeking an opportunity to improve their lives and their families or to escape tyranny. Many had to save for years to obtain money for their passage. Before WW II, sleek luxury liners carried many people, most of them quite rich, between Europe and North America in great comfort. During WW II the Queen Elizabeth served as a troop carrier hauling 15,000 soldiers per trip at government expense. Their objective was to fight in a war against tyranny.

In May 1927, Charles Lindbergh received great acclaim for the first solo flight across the Atlantic. Last year ten million people flew across the ocean with very few of them being pilots. Some have gone to London or Paris or New York on the Concorde at great expense to spend a weekend. Impossible with the Queen Elizabeth. It is interesting that many military bombers depend entirely on aerial refueling to reach distant targets. Commercial airliners land for refueling.

Anybody who spends much time at airports knows that there are many different reasons for flying. With regard to interstellar travel, one might expect that the number of trips and travelers would be determined by the ease of the trip and the importance of the trip to whoever pays the bill.

What assumptions can be made about alien motivation? It seems to me there is really only one: namely that every civilization would be concerned about its own survival and security. That certainly seems true on Earth. Compare the annual U.S. budget for national security concerns (roughly $300 billion) with that for anthropology and astronomy: surely under $1 billion. Security concerns would certainly require that an eye be kept on all primitives in the neighborhood. Especially close scrutiny would be required for those civilizations that will soon be able to take their brand of friendship, when it is hostility as it is for Earthlings, out to bother nearby civilizations. It was per-

fectly obvious by the end of WW II to any alien observer that in less than a century (which is no time at all by cosmic standards) this primitive Earthling society would be able to reach the stars. Reasons for concern might be the simple fact that between 1939 and 1946, we Earthlings killed at least 50 million of our own kind and destroyed 1700 cities. Signs indicating that interstellar flight would soon be a reality were: (1) nuclear weapon explosions; (2) the flights of V-2 rockets gradually improved upon for intercontinental ballistic missiles; and (3) the use of powerful radar indicating mastery of a whole new area of technology.

It should be no surprise at all that the only place in the world in July 1947, where visitors could study all three new, futuristic technologies was Southeastern New Mexico. Trinity site on White Sands Missile Range was where the first atomic bomb was exploded. WSMR was also where dozens of captured German V-2 rockets were being tested (by their German builders, for the U.S.) and where the best tracking radar was installed to follow the missiles which often didn't go where they were supposed to go. Roswell is not far away.

In short then, it may well be that aliens are primarily visiting to evaluate our society, our technology and countermeasures for it, and to make sure that Earthlings do not move out into space until we get our act together. One often hears the ridiculous question "why don't they land on the White House lawn, and say 'take me to your leader'? Does anybody believe that the President of the United States speaks for six billion Earthlings? The UN doesn't allow membership for individual cities. Why would we expect the Galactic Federation to allow individual countries (as opposed to a planet or solar system) to apply for membership?

Many astronauts have expressed surprise that so little progress has been made in terms of manned space exploration since our first moon landing in 1969. Many had expected that by now there would be bases on the moon and successful manned expeditions to Mars.

Furthermore, it is not a trivial question as to why we didn't launch Apollo 18 and Apollo 19 to the moon. All the hardware was built, the crews were selected and trained, so the excuse that it would have cost too much money sounds very hollow indeed. Are we being quarantined?

An important aspect of this line of reasoning is that it would seem, since it takes so little time once one starts down the advanced technology road (look back just 100 years), that during any period of a few centuries there are very few civilizations in the neighborhood going through the transition from being stuck on one's own planet to being able to bother the neighbors. Our neighbors are either way behind us or way ahead. Hence, everybody in the neighborhood would be concerned about the activities of a primitive society (Earth) whose major activity is tribal warfare. Note that planetary military budgets total near $1 trillion per year. Yet every single day more than 30,000 Earthling children die needlessly of preventable disease and starvation. Quarantining us would seem to be expected rather than surprising. Remember that a major motto here, for dealing with strangers, is shoot first and ask questions later. If you were an alien, would you want Earthlings out there?

Obviously, if interstellar jaunts within our neighborhood are as routine for our visitors as transatlantic flights are for us, we might expect an enormous variety of motivations for traveling here. What follows is a relatively brief list:

1. Perhaps our visitors are broadcasters with a weekly show called "Idiocy in the Boondocks."
2. Visitors might be mining engineers. Earth is the densest planet in the solar system, which means more rare, expensive, dense metals than on any other planet including Rhenium, Gold, Uranium, Platinum, Rhodium, Tungsten, Osmium, etc. The California and Klondike gold rushes of the 19th century stimulated a great deal of often difficult travel.
3. Visitors could be graduate students doing thesis work on the development of a primitive society, on foreign languages, on modern warfare.
4. Earth could be the equivalent of a refueling station for oceangoing ships of the last century.
5. Gas, food, lodging next exit.
6. Perhaps this is the center of a vacation industry. Hunting and fishing; no license required.
7. Perhaps Earth is the Devil's Island of the local neighborhood with bad boys and girls having been dumped here. Might be why we are so nasty to each other. Georgia and Australia were initially settled by convicts.
8. Perhaps visitors have come to observe a natural catastrophe they know will happen soon.
9. Visitors might be collecting plant, animal, and human genetic material, of which there is an enormous variety, for breeding projects. Older planets might have much less variety available.
10. Earth could be the "neutral" site for ET chess matches à la Fisher and Spassky in Iceland.
11. We may have a convenient location from which one set of marauders might be attacking another as the U.S. and Japan fought terrible wars on native islands in the Pacific.
12. Perhaps visitors are checking out a colony or colonies started here a long time ago.
13. Some visitors may be completing cross-galaxy flying solos.
14. Visitors may be intelligence spies for a variety of other civilizations in the neighborhood.
15. Perhaps some visitors are gathering specimens for alien zoos.
16. Buyers for ET curio and antique dealers may be collecting specimens.
17. Perhaps some visitors are being punished. Spend two weeks near Earth, punishment to last a lifetime.
18. Perhaps they are ET repairmen seeking the cause of interference with long-

existing communications, computing, or beacon services in the solar system.

19. Some ETs might be time travelers coming back to change things.

20. Some visitors might be ancestors from the distant past who have been traveling at close to the speed of light, coming back home to their descendants' world. Like Methuselah living 900 years.

21. Are some ETs talent recruiters for an ET sports group looking for bigger, faster, stronger recruits?

22. Some visitors might be advance men for space religious missionaries. Earthling missionaries often go to the ends of the Earth.

23. Artists, musicians, sculptures may be here to record new scenery in new ways.

24. Perhaps this is the only planet in the neighborhood that doesn't have a planetary government or where a host of languages are still in use despite space shuttle trips around the world in 90 minutes.

25. Perhaps the rules of the local Galactic Federation require that a complete inventory of the fauna, flora, structures, and resources of our planet be done every 2000 years.

26. Remembering there are many reports of huge "mother" ships, which apparently carry much smaller Earth excursion modules, the situation could be as complicated as an aircraft carrier serving as a base for several dozen smaller aircraft. Such a traveling city has pilots, cooks, mechanics, analysts, and many other specialized crew members.

As the reader has now seen, there is no problem coming up with possible reasons for alien visitors; in fact, the possibilities are virtually endless.

—STANTON T. FRIEDMAN

alien roots For readers interested in CE-3 (close encounters of the third kind) aliens, it is important to realize that once upon a time there was no such thing as a "Gray." Before the publication of *The Andreasson Affair* (Fowler, 1979), *Missing Time* (Hopkins, 1981), *Intruders* (Hopkins, 1987), *Communion* (Strieber, 1987), and other popular works by a then new breed of proponent/investigators, abductees claimed to have observed a wider range of alien creature types. Since then, however, abductees have described primarily bug-eyed gray humanoids. Skeptics could point out that a change in witness descriptions following the publication of a few books is decisive evidence that abductions are fantasies and not physical events.

Abduction proponents of the 1980s may have become dissatisfied with earlier CE-3 entity descriptions, because many aliens seemed to them to look unlike any others. It was as if different alien races from all over the galaxy were visiting the Earth simultaneously. Certainly the abductionists could see that the situation undermined their favored view, the extraterrestrial hypothesis. They did not accept the possibility that abductees' accounts are fantasies, which are as individual as nightmares: two dreamers' descriptions of an exotic monster are never exactly the same. There were many fetal humanoid reports in CE-3s, however, so the proponents focused their research (and later books and articles discussed at UFO gatherings) on an evolving humanoid Gray, consistently ignoring other entity categories. Thus a mere handful of advocates changed the direction of abduction studies.

Entity reports (formerly called occupant or landing cases) have been mired in credulousness and confusion from the very earliest CE-3s. This was so in part because most UFOlogists refused serious consideration of psychological and other non-extraterrestrial explanations for such reports. For many years this situation has obscured ties between CE-3 entities and earthly folklore, mythology, and literary tradition.

Researchers have also ignored classifiable distinctions among CE-3 alien descriptions. Prior to the 1980s CE-3 creature reports were distributed more evenly into six categories: humans, humanoids, animals, robots, exotics (mutants or combinations of two or more types), and apparitions (ghostly creatures that can change shape or vanish). The six categories are based on physical characteristics only, and were not imposed on the data. They emerged from a study of scores of entity descriptions of CE-3s along with those of creatures from traditional and anthropological sources. This is not an attempt to construct an exo-biological tree of life for aliens. The subjects here are folklore and fantasy—not science—and the entity classifications offer some clarity to a maze-like segment of UFOlogy.

CE-3 narratives are often fragmentary and sketches of aliens are amateurish, but most entity descriptions can readily be linked to one of the six categories. Witnesses' awareness is acute and though they cannot always identify the type, they routinely capture key entity attributes, as these quotes show: "One looked human, but the others were little guys with big black eyes." "Its face and hands—they were more like claws—were covered with thick hair or fur." "It walked stiffly, like a robot." "It's got long hair . . . no appendages at all . . . no ears, no nose, and maybe one eye in the center." "One floated upwards, then just disappeared, like a ghost."

PREVIOUS STUDIES OF CE-3 ENTITIES

In-depth studies of UFO/CE-3 entities have been few. *The Humanoids* (Bowen, 1969) was an early collection of mostly anecdotal case reviews: Jacques Vallée summarized 200 1954 European landings, Coral Lorenzen described 29 U.S. cases, and Gordon Creighton discussed 65 Latin American occupant and landing reports. Also in 1969, in *Passport to Magonia*, Vallée collected a century of worldwide landing reports (1868-1968)—923 brief sketches of cases—many of which involved entity sightings. David Webb and Ted Bloecher produced catalogs of sightings for various years of the 1970s and maintained the Humanoid Study Group, which had collected 1000 CE-3 reports.

In these and other works, the writers made few attempts to classify the "humanoids" (then a newly coined synonym for aliens), and so possible entity distinctions are confused. Even so, the six entity types are evident in many of their accounts. In Webb's 1973 study, witness descriptions were classifiable into six types, but the distribution is skewed (18 percent robots, 12 percent animals), perhaps because of same-year bias.

Occasionally there are major studies such as Creighton's piece on Brazilian abductee Antonio Villas-Boas. In the absence of meaningful case investigations of more than a handful of CE-3s, however, we plod through a mass of intriguing claims without guidance, and we do not learn much about ETs.

The books, articles, and CE-3 narrative excerpts published by Ray Fowler, Budd Hopkins, and David Jacobs have focused on the fetal humanoid (though they don't refer to its perinatal connections)—to the exclusion of the other five entity types. Jacobs (following Hopkins) implies that real abductees see only bug-eyed Grays, and the rest are mistakes. He dismisses the Imaginary Abductee Study in part because our subjects described too many entity types.

T.E. Bullard's lengthy study of about 300 abduction reports, *UFO Abductions: Measure of a Mystery* (1987), is an ambitious effort that will doubtless continue to be a resource for researchers. A problem is that the database for these abductions is fragmented, as Bullard admits. He cites 270 cases, but includes in his references several newspaper accounts and similarly questionable sources. He concedes that there are only fifty good cases (about one out of five), and that even these are seriously flawed. Bullard acknowledges that no unambiguous scientific conclusion can be made about such fragmentary, minimal, and uncertain data.

Bullard mentions only three types of entities (human, humanoid, and animal), and ignores or confuses evidence for the robot, exotic, and apparitional classes that make CE-3 entities consistent with entity types in mythology and folklore. Following earlier writers, he calls all entities "humanoid," as if unaware that the word can also refer to a specific type of alien. But there are clear descriptions of robots in the Larson and Hickson cases, unmistakable exotics in the Garden Grove and Kendall reports, and a marvelous apparitional entity in a South African case. These CE-3 categories won't go away, but his study doesn't acknowledge their significance for entity typology.

EXAMPLES OF SIX
CE-3 ENTITY TYPES

As the following examples show, most entity types in CE-3s and folk traditions classify themselves. Human and humanoid entities are self-evident and plentiful. Animal entities are rare in abduction lore but sometimes appear as part-animal exotics. Most robots are easy to recognize, whereas exotics are more complex. Consider two examples of exotic entities: the marvelously weird human/insectoid monster from the 1987 film *Predator*, and the 9-foot-tall floating biped with elephantine feet from the Garden Grove CE-3 hoax. These two entities have wildly varying anatomical particulars, but they are exotics in that each is a mutant or combines features of two or more other entity types. Apparitional beings are recognizable by their supernatural powers even if they are also shape-shifters, in which case their "home" shape determines their apparitional identity.

Type #1. Human entities: Human-appearing UFO creatures have the physical form of human beings and are identified as such by witnesses. Height: 5 to 7 feet. Facial features, skin color, and hair are recognizably human. Bodily movement is normal, as are voice and manner, except for cases in which these beings are telepathic. Both genders are reported. Some humans are described as "Nordics": tall, blond, of seeming Germanic or Scandinavian lineage. Clothing is usually a one-piece jumpsuit, as in the MUFON idealization which follows (in Fig. 1).

Type #2. Humanoid entities: Humanoid (human-like) entities are the most frequently reported type of CE-3 alien, and are the original Little Green (now Gray) Men. (See Fig. 2.) Their appearance is almost always distinctly fetal or even embryonic: a short, frail stature; a disproportionately large head; pallid skin color; underdeveloped facial features; and a hairless body. The dominant feature of the Gray is their enormous, usually unblinking black eyes. Their size and distinctive slanted, almond shape has since become the standard. The pupils are usually double-sized and dark, with little or no white; some are cat-like and vertical.

Body movement is normal to stiff, with frequent reports of floating. Telepathic communication with a witness is routine, though voice communication is sometimes reported. Despite their small stature and feeble physique, humanoids are reportedly very strong. They are usually clothed in a silver or gray skintight jumpsuit, although a few have worn a bulky "space suit" with an apparent breathing apparatus. Taller humanoids function as leaders or interact with the abductee during an abduction.

Behavior ranges from impish teasing to brutal torment, but is usually clinically objective. Gender is usually unspecified, and although male and female humanoids are reported, when seen unclothed most humanoids show no genitalia. But not all: Antonio Villas-Boas's 1957 claim was only the first of many alleged alien/human sexual encounters. This "sexy CE-3" trend reappeared suddenly in the 1980s, especially in the works of Hopkins and Jacobs, and quickly became (and has remained) the primary focus of many abductees and investigators. The abductee may "bond" with one humanoid abductor during the course of the examination or its aftermath. The bond may or may not be sexual, though sexual involvement leading to pregnancy or "genetic" activities between humanoids and abductees has allegedly occurred.

Type #3. Animal entities: CE-3 animal entities, rare except in Latin American reports, show distinctly mammalian, reptilian, or other animalistic features. (See Fig. 3.) They exhibit fur, claws, a tail, scales or similar epidermal texture, pointed ears, enlarged teeth, and non-human eyes with vertical pupils (sometimes glowing). There are a few reports of insect-like creatures, with exoskeletons and pincers. Height: 2 to 8 feet. Most animal entities assume an erect stance, although some slouching, ape-like postures and body movements are reported. Communication modes range from growls to telepathy. Gender is undetermined and few clothed animals are described. Animal entities sometimes carry an unpleasant odor.

Most alien animals appear in CE-3 reports in the form of exotic entities, specifically as animal/human, animal apparition, or other combinations. Few reports tell of extended communication, close involvement, or bonding between abductees and CE-3 animals; rather, encounters tend to be violent. Although abductees elsewhere have not encountered many animal abductors, three animal entities appear in the sixteen narratives of the 1977 Imaginary Abductee Study.

Type #4. Robot entities: CE-3 robots (Fig. 4) seem to be made of metallic or other non-organic materials, and they move at various speeds in a stiff or otherwise unnatural manner. They sometimes float or fly. Some have glowing eyes. Height: a startling range of 6 inches to 20 feet. Their shapes are mostly bipedal, but huge building-like machines are reported. Communication: voice and telepathy. Clothing includes ''welder's helmets,'' padded space suits, and bubble-dome headgear (for improbable air-breathing robots?). Witnesses may have difficulty distinguishing robots from other creatures that would be perceived to move clumsily in bulky suits.

Type #5. Exotic entities: Exotic entities (Fig. 5) are mutants or combinations of two or more other entity types. They display extraordinary physical characteristics and may be grotesque and/or repulsive (at least to Earthlings). A richly diverse category, exotics include the in-famous Bug-Eyed Monsters of science fiction, mythical beings such as the Minotaur (a man/bull), creatures with anatomical deformities (e.g., Cyclops), assorted demons, and a group of reportedly bizarre CE-3 entities.

One subset of exotic entities may relate to birth memories. It includes tentacled placental/umbilical dragons of myth and legend, which are updated in science-fiction and fantasy films as special-effects monsters dripping with birth gore (e.g., in the *Alien* film series). Although tentacled aliens are common in sci-fi magazine illustrations, they are paradoxically rare in CE-3 narratives.

Type #6. Apparitional entities: Apparitionals (Fig. 6) may float, change form, materialize, or dematerialize. Akin to ghosts and fairyland creatures, apparitionals possess a rich tradition in mythology and contemporary folklore: angels, demons, trickster figures, and the ''Beam me up, Scotty'' teleportation technology of TV's *Star Trek*. Through shape-shifting, apparitionals can mimic a human, animal, or any other creature or thing, thus temporarily masking their true identity; yet they are distinctive enough to be easily classified. Communication is verbal or telepathic but often is non-existent. Height: 2 to 10 feet.

Apparitional capabilities are shared by other entities. Some humanoids become temporary apparitionals. They change shape unexpectedly, float, pass through walls and windows unscathed, or disappear and reappear at will—and then revert to being a humanoid. Similar abilities have been attributed at times to every supposed alien type that abductees describe. The presence of these powers—certainly among the most fantastic of reported entity faculties—underscores abductions' linkages with folklore and myth.

PERSPECTIVES ON
CE-3 ENTITIES

Origins of entity types: The origins of entity types are open to speculation. Human entities could develop out of witnesses' awareness of their own body. Humanoids are largely fetal and probably have perinatal roots. Resemblances

Fig. 1. Human-type entities

A. MUFON idealization of a typical human entity. **B.** Australian case, 9/6/73.
C. Example of legendary "Man in Black," a shadowy being of official or unearthly origins notorious for alleged contacts with UFO witnesses after sightings.
D. Christ-like human in Winchester, England, 11/14/76. **E.** Vila Velha, Brazil, 2/3/73. Note puffy variation on usual jumpsuit. **F.** Early contactee George Adamski's "Venusian" friend, allegedly met 11/20/52. Most contactee entities are human.

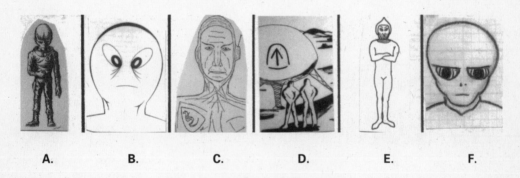

Fig. 2. Humanoid-type entities

A. MUFON idealization of a humanoid entity. **B.** Humanoid specter from the peak time of a major UFO flap, Goffstown, New Hampshire, 11/2/73. **C.** Policeman Herbert Schirmer's humanoid, Ashland, Nebraska, 12/3/67. **D.** Policeman Lonnie Zamora's two humanoids near their egg-shaped craft, Socorro, New Mexico, 4/24/64. **E.** Paulo Silvieira humanoid, Itaperuna, Brazil, 9/22/71. **F.** Travis Walton's explicitly fetal humanoid, Heber, Arizona, 11/5/75, reported about two weeks after the telecast of the Betty Hill abduction, *The UFO Incident* (on NBC-TV).

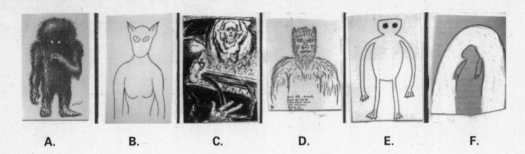

Fig. 3. Animal CE-3 entities

A. MUFON idealization of a CE-3 animal (based on a Brazilian case). **B.** Animal reported during a major UFO flap, El Yunque Mt., Puerto Rico, 10/20/73. **C.** A driver glimpsed this animal near Frederick, Wisconsin, 12/2/74. **D.** A Bigfoot-like entity, Beech Hills, Pennsylvania, 8/23/73. **E.** A frog-like amphibian entity, Carignan, France, 5/2/76. **F.** An ape-like entity reported during the 1973 flap, Cincinnati, Ohio, 10/12/73.

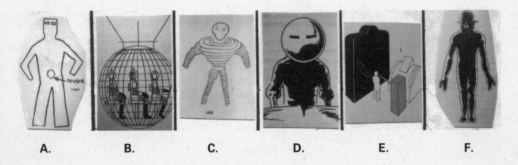

Fig. 4. Robot CE-3 entities

A. A robot with a highlighted navel area, a pattern in other entity descriptions, described during the 1973 flap, Draguignan, France, 10/19/73. **B.** A trio of robotic entities in a spherical craft, Belo Horizonte, Brazil, 8/28/63. **C.** Goodland, Kansas, 6/20/76. **D.** Robot reported in Ashburn, Georgia, 10/19/73 on the same date as the robot in France (A.). **E.** Three robot machines, one 20 feet tall, Prospect, Kentucky, 1/27/77. **F.** A mummy-like robot in a much-publicized CE-3, Pascagoula, Mississippi, 10/11/73.

A. **B.** **C.** **D.** **E.** **F.**

Fig. 5. Exotic CE-3 entities

A. One of several exotic entities, Kelly-Hopkinsville, Kentucky, 10/21/55. No UFO was reported. **B.** "Grasshopper-eyed" entity of the Judy Kendall CE-3, Woodland, California, 11/25/71. **C.** Mysterious head tubes on an exotic, Athens, Georgia, 10/20/73. **D.** Weird exotic entity seen in Fargo, North Dakota, 8/26/75. **E.** Bizarre malformed exotic, Branch Hill, Ohio, 5/25/55. **F.** Reptile-skinned entity of the Garden Grove Case, reported in Apache Junction, Arizona, 3/14/71.

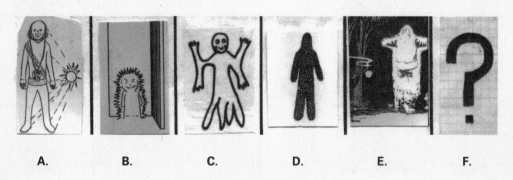

A. **B.** **C.** **D.** **E.** **F.**

Fig. 6. Apparitionals

A. Apparitional humanoid emerged from a ball of light, Garden Grove, California, 11/21/75. **B.** A grinning "electric" apparitional, Albany, Ohio, 10/16/73. **C.** A ghostly apparition, Riverside, California, 8/29/55. **D.** Little Lever, England, 1964. **E.** Talavera la Real, Spain, 11/12/76. **F.** Salisbury, Rhodesia, 5/31/74. The apparition in this case supposedly told the witnesses that they would see the apparition as whatever they wished—a duck, a monster, whatever. The witnesses called this entity a "multi"—aptly emphasizing its capacity for multiple changes of form. An Imaginary Abductee described a precisely similar multievent three years later.

Human   Humanoid   Animal   Robot   Exotic   Apparitional

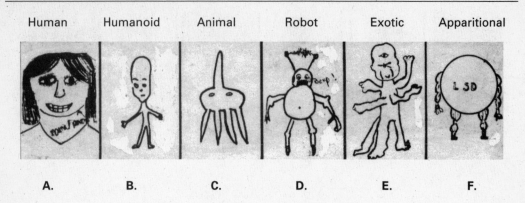

A.   B.   C.   D.   E.   F.

Fig. 7. Children's drawings of aliens

A. A female human UFOnaut, perhaps a self-portrait. **B.** Oddly, this humanoid was one of very few of its type in 180 drawings. It has just three fingers. Most of the sketches depicted exotics. **C.** This tentacled animal entity suggests that even young children are exposed to expectations of tentacled aliens in UFOs. **D.** A beeping robot with antennae and clumsy joints—along with an apparent navel! **E.** A very imaginative sketch of a one-eyed exotic with multiple arms—and a tail! **F.** This animated LSD pill testifies to young people's acute awareness of the real world about them. Is this drawing one youngster's cynical assessment of CE-3 reports? Perhaps, but it also suggests the view that entity sightings are apparitions, whether spontaneous or hallucinogenic.

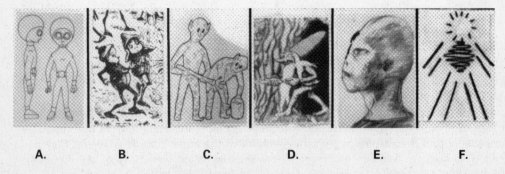

A.   B.   C.   D.   E.   F.

Fig. 8. CE-3 traditional entity parallels

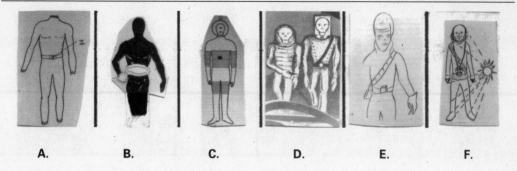

Fig. 9. CE-3 entities' navel and umbilical symbolism

| Human | Humanoid | Animal | Robot | Exotic | Apparition |

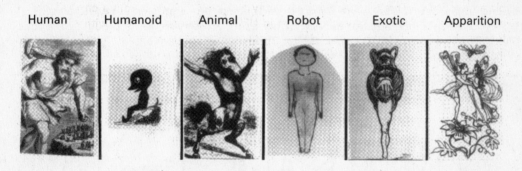

Fig. 10. Six creature types from world folklore

A. Giant   **B.** Pooka   **C.** Kelpie   **D.** Stock   **E.** Fachan   **F.** Fairies

A. Folklore's giants, despite their great size, are essentially human in physical appearance. **B.** A pooka. Like elves, leprechauns, and brownies, pookas were humanoid, but they also had apparitional powers. **C.** The pony-like kelpies from Irish lore were mischievous clawed water-demons. **D.** A wooden image of a baby called a "stock" or a "changeling" was supposedly vivified and left by kidnapping fairies in place of a nursing infant or human baby, and for a time passed for a real child before sickening and dying. **E.** One of the most bizarre folk creatures was the Fachan of Irish belief, who reportedly had one eye, one arm that emerged from its chest, one leg, and a nasty disposition. **F.** Fairies, like demons and divinities, were "shape-shifters" or polymorphous.

Human	Humanoid	Animal	Robot	Exotic	Apparition

A. Alice   **B.** Dum & Dee   **C.** Rabbit   **D.** Cards   **E.** Humpty   **F.** Cheshire

Fig. 11. Six creature types from Alice's Wonderland

A. The very human Alice can't resist her curiosity about everything. **B.** Tweedledum and Tweedledee are a special type of humanoid—mirror images of each other known as enantiomorphs. **C.** The White Rabbit is personified, but is an animal nevertheless. **D.** The Queen's gardeners, like the rest of her court, are playing cards brought to robotic life. **E.** The exotic Humpty Dumpty. **F.** The Cheshire Cat's apparition.

Human	Humanoid	Animal	Robot	Exotic	Apparition

A. Duke   **B.** Puck   **C.** Bottom   **D.** Wall   **E.** Caliban   **F.** Ariel

Fig. 12. Six creature types in Shakespeare

Though Shakespeare particularized his nonhuman creatures in wondrous fashion, they were patterned after well-established models in folklore and tradition. These examples are from two fantasies, *A Midsummer Night's Dream* and *The Tempest*.

(Caption continued on next page)

A. Theseus, the human Duke of Athens. **B.** Puck or Robin Goodfellow, a typically mischievous hobgoblin, brownie, or pooka, also had the shape-shifting powers of many other fairies. **C.** Bottom, after Puck changes him into an ass. Technically an exotic, he is the closest thing to an animal character in Shakespeare. **D.** Shakespeare's only robot is shown in a 19th-century illustration of Snout's costume for the part of the Wall in the ludicrous playlet about Pyramus and Thisbe. **E.** Caliban, the exotic monster of *The Tempest*, is the half-human, half-demonic offspring of a sorceress and a demon. **F.** Ariel, an apparitional fairy in *The Tempest*, spends much of his time onstage as an invisible presence.

Human	Humanoid	Animal	Robot	Exotic	Apparition

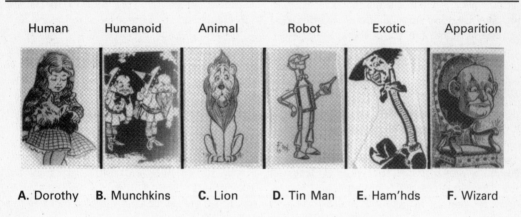

A. Dorothy   **B.** Munchkins   **C.** Lion   **D.** Tin Man   **E.** Ham'hds   **F.** Wizard

Fig. 13. Six creature types from *The Wizard of Oz*

A. The adventurously human child heroine, Dorothy. **B.** Munchkin-style humanoids. **C.** The Cowardly Lion is a personified animal. **D.** The Tin Woodman may be the world's most famous robot. **E.** The Hammerheads are one of several exotics in Oz.
F. The Wizard as an apparition: a scene he creates with technology rather than magic.

among humanoids and brownies, imps, and hordes of other "little folk" seemingly link them all with human birth events. Numerous animals and robots in folklore, myth, and contemporary sources help explain them in CE-3 reports. Exotics may be traced to mutant human or animal births. Apparitional entities' powers of rapid transformation may have entered myth via ancient peoples' responses to sudden changes in individual human development and attitudes, or metamorphoses in the natural world.

The six entity types have appeared in countless contemporary formats—comic books, science-fiction films, TV cartoons, advertisements, and other pop culture—though never in a context with identifying categories that provide perspective and awareness. Every schoolboy (and potential hypnotic subject) knows about the entity classes on some level and can sprinkle his imagined yarns with them, as our 1979 study of a group of adolescents in Orange County, California, demonstrated. About 180 mentally gifted children in grades 6, 7, and 8 were asked to draw their conception of a UFO occupant. Their responses were readily classifiable and represented the complete range of six entity types:

Parallels in traditional and CE-3 entities: A well-established pattern in folklore and traditional literature is entity clothing: typically a seamless, one-piece jumpsuit or similar outfit that covers the body except for the head and the hands (which may be gloved). Compare the ''UFOnaut'' in Fig. 8-A with Fig. 8-B, a 19th-century sketch of traditional brownies from folklore. Both creatures are small in stature and have frail physiques. They wear similar one-piece, seamless, skintight garments that we may interpret as skin, for it is often described as slick and shiny like plastic, suggesting a newborn's wet skin. Other birth parallels include many reports of instrument-carrying UFO entities (Fig. 8-C) and elves from folk tradition (Fig. 8-D). The tube-like instruments suggest another perinatal reminder: the umbilical cord. With ultrasound viewers, fetuses have often been observed grasping the umbilical, either in contentment or fright. A curious aspect of witnesses' entity sketches is that facial features and extremities are sometimes missing, as in Figs. 8-E and 8-F. Inadequate drawing or observational skills may be responsible, though some witnesses maintain that certain entity features were not perceived. There are no analogs in traditional sources for such anatomical omissions.

Navel and umbilical symbolism: CE-3 entities often wear a large buckle, medallion, or similar device on their abdomen (as in Figs. 9-A through 9-C), sometimes with a diagonal strap or ''Sam Browne'' belt across the chest (as in Figs. 9-D through 9-F). Sometimes the buckle device glows brightly (Fig. 9-B). The emphasis on the navel area and the umbilical strap are distinctly perinatal, suggesting that memories of birth events have a significant role in CE-3 fantasies about entities other than the fetal humanoid. Researchers do not offer persuasive alternate interpretations of such details.

Entity types from various sources: I have compiled illustrated sets of creature types from folklore and literary traditions in support of the validity of the six-category CE-3 entity classi-

fication system. The six creature types thrive in diverse cultures worldwide. There are always human entities and diminutive fetal beings that resemble but are distinct from adult humans, as with the rest of the entity types. The patterns in CE-3 witnesses' alien fantasies are operative in wide-ranging sources, including: Greek fables and mythology, Christian belief, demonology, science fiction, comic books, breakfast cereal-box heroes, and the Imaginary Abductee narratives. The following four examples are representative.

Frequencies of CE-3s and UFOs: Nobody knows how many abductions or other CE-3s there have been worldwide since 1947. The Bullard study of about 300 cases used data up to the early 1980s. Abduction proponents claim to have discovered thousands of unknown CE-3s in the 1980s and 1990s. If CE-3s now number 5000, as suggested by the very dubious Roper survey, they are still dwarfed by the guestimated three million or so raw UFO sightings worldwide over the past half century (about 150+ daily).

Whether or not we conservatively dump 90 percent of UFO sightings as IFOs and 90 percent of CE-3s as hoaxes and mistakes, abductions total only about 0.167 percent of UFO sightings (5000 ÷ 3,000,000 = .00167). That means less than two of every thousand UFOs abduct someone. Although abductions are supposedly what UFOs do, these representative statistics argue otherwise. Why the discrepancy?

Proponents have traditionally explained the disproportion in three ways: (1) we encounter aliens only when they want us to; and (2) most abductees forget their CE-3, in strict obedience to their captors' orders. A third explanation, witness reticence, at first glance seems better—who wants to admit being abducted by weirdos from outer space? Proponent-investigators tell of scores of abductees in professional or otherwise sensitive positions (doctors, lawyers, politicians, etc.), who shun all publicity. Yet the public spotlight, such as that offered by Hopkins and others in the past twenty years or so, has obviously proved irresistible to many wannabe famous abductees. The numbers of alleged abductions and books about them since about 1980 has multiplied, while UFO/IFO sightings, corrected for population growth, are about the same. Even so, the ratio of CE-3s to sightings remains minuscule.

The most likely reason for the frequency imbalance between UFO sightings and CE-3s is that the two are separate and distinct experiences, and have nothing to do with one another—aside from the idea of ET visitors. There has never been an authenticated CE-3 in which two or more persons watch while a UFO lands, occupants get out and abduct someone, then the UFO takes off. This primal CE-3 scene, supposedly the initiating and definitive event of unknown numbers of typical abductions, has never been authentically witnessed. There is no unambiguous evidence that it—or anything similar to it—has ever occurred.

Abductions are most likely fantasy/hallucinations and are subjective experiences that probably date from the first shaman's "vision quest" early in human prehistory. UFO sightings at best are objective physical events—whatever the UFO actually is. The lack of connections between these events helps account for the contrasting numbers.

Of course, many "experiencers" (now the preferred term for abductees) surely mistake their dreams or nightmares for CE-3 fantasies, or they really do forget them. Others may undergo their CE-3s as NDEs, OBEs, Martian visitations, or a dozen other abduction analogs. Also, it has been established that the CE-3-like hallucinations of sick and elderly people are routinely ignored by clinical and institutional personnel, and thus are not counted.

Psychologists and other social workers—within and outside of UFOlogy—until recently have not provided a convenient, scientifically respectable, and supportive way for percipients to report, communicate about, and deal with supposed alien abduction events. Indeed, psychologists had not even acknowledged the CE-3 syndrome until a few national support groups for reported CE-3 witnesses, such as P.E.E.R. and T.R.E.A.T., were formed. Psychiatrist John

Mack and hypnotherapist Edith Fiore are two of an increasing number of professionals (never mind that most are true believers) who have created CE-3 support groups as a regular part of their practice.

Low numbers of abduction reports could also reflect the fact that researchers have not embraced credible non-ETH theories to account for such experiences. More "hidden" abductees/experiencers might come forth if there were a viable alternative interpretation to being snatched by planet-hopping aliens. Compared to the ETH, the Birth Memories Hypothesis does not seem far-out at all.

Why only six types of CE-3 entities? If CE-3s are not real and witnesses are fantasizing wildly, why do they repeatedly describe the same few types of creatures—rather than Grays or a sequence of uniquely different entity forms? And why are there only six categories?

To repeat, witnesses describe the same six classes of aliens because abductions are fantasies based on the only models they have: earthly folklore and tradition. As to the six types, it can be shown that they do not exhaust the range of creature types, even within traditional Earth lore. Ancient Middle Eastern cylinder seals (ca. 1000 B.C.) depict what were called "elementals," a variety of creatures that would be unclassifiable under the six-part system. These archaic engraved figures are "heroes and deities" created out of elemental processes (fire, air, water, and earth). They have human or animal bodies, but are shown with water, flames, or light streaming out of their anatomy.

Although the flowing water and other substances may have placental/umbilical relevance, these creatures' anatomy and connections with elemental forces make them qualitatively distinct from the other six types. They can properly be placed in a seventh entity category.

There are a few elemental creatures in TV cartoons, comics, and folklore, but as far as I know they are not described in CE-3s. Perhaps there are too few elementals in contemporary sources, or their differences from other entity types are too subtle, to serve as models.

Other entity types: Although this seventh entity type can be considered the exception that proves the CE-3 six-category rule, additional kinds of entities are certainly conceivable. From time to time imaginative authors have proposed unusual creatures that would not be classifiable under the six CE-3 categories.

In astronomer Fred Hoyle's novel, *The Black Cloud*, a vast intelligent cloud "lives" in interstellar space, with a molecular heart, a brain, and other necessary organs. It feeds on stellar energy and its central nervous system functions via radio waves.

Astrophysicist Ronald Bracewell has imagined "intelligent scum," an enormous collective cellular civilization that thinks and acts as a single entity and controls its environment through a kind of evolutionary specialization.

Equally bizarre is astronomer Frank Drake's fictionalized neutron-star life-form: microscopic, macronucleic creatures weighing tons each and living out their accelerated lives on a 100-million-degree world in fractions of a second.

Philosopher Wilfred Desan describes a creature extended indefinitely in both space and time, making it quasi-infinite and immortal, and since there would be no other of its kind it would be a biological singularity.

These examples are fanciful, but one can infer that the infinitely resourceful universe could produce a greatly more varied range of alien entity types than scientists, writers, and CE-3 witnesses have conjectured.

Must ETs look like us? Considered opinion is divided on whether or not aliens would resemble Earthly life-forms. Some exobiologists and SF writers believe that ETs would share many qualities with us. They point out that eons of evolutionary survival have shaped human anatomical and physiological makeup, and many characteristics seem too useful and widespread among other living creatures not to be essential. They conclude that aliens might not look much different from the rest of Earth life.

Let us speculate that alien life-forms would be more efficient if they were not in a collective, but physically independent from others of their kind—though they could be linked mentally. If made of living tissue they would have to eat, they could get sick, be injured, or die. It is difficult to imagine a hi-tech space traveler without something like a sizeable brain, several senses, and mobility. The brain needs protection, and the major sense organs should have short nerve pathways for efficiency; so something like eyes, ears, nose, and a mouth should be in that something like a skull covering the alien's brain. Bilateral symmetry gives human beings survival-oriented 3-D vision and stereophonic hearing, though maybe those are not essential. But an upright stance could place an alien's limb—with something like hands bearing something like fingers—within convenient distance of its eyes for manipulating food, weapons, and tools. The being would be neither a giant (too ponderous) nor microbe-sized (too few brain cells). It would have to be able to communicate. Telepathy would be the best mode, but speech is efficient too. And aliens almost certainly would be sexual creatures.

An ET space traveler could use traits such as curiosity, intellection, high skills, flexibility, imagination, and a value system with enough altruism to delay tangible rewards; and maybe an emotional nature that helps make existence fun or otherwise worthwhile. If their purpose is to observe Earthlings longitudinally, they need the capacity to feel joy and/or despair.

But other writers have warned against Earth chauvinism, the assumption that conditions for life elsewhere must be generally Earth-like: carbon-based, of moderate temperature, with available water, oxygen, and so on. They reason that different geophysical conditions could create living forms far different from any that have ever existed on Earth. A truly alien being might be something we cannot yet easily imagine, the likeness of which is not in our folklore or systems of traditional belief.

Again, consider the long-term effects of technology. If the dinosaurs had evolved into a smart reptile, it might have been an upright biped, verbal, sexy, and with tool-making hands—more than a little like us. But what would the surviving dinosaurs look like today, after a hundred million years of evolution and hi-tech genetic innovations? We are on the verge of modifying our human genome by seeking super babies with higher IQs, more attractive physiques, and better health. Even if an alien race started out as human-like, after a few hundred millennia of super technology a species could evolve itself into unimaginable modes that CE-3 witnesses might perceive, but which would be unclassifiable within traditional Earthly life-forms.

If aliens ever really come here and are like Travis Walton's fetal humanoids or the Garden Grove exotics, they will leave physical traces and their presence will be provable. In the absence of physical evidence, CE-3s would gain more credibility if even a few abductees told us of a new category of entities, things without the familiar connections to folklore, myth, and tradition; things believable yet strictly alien to Earthly experience. Regrettably for true believers, no such CE-3 aliens have yet been described.

—ALVIN H. LAWSON

References

Bowen, Charles, ed. *The Humanoids* (Henry Regnery, 1969).

Bullard, T.E. *UFO Abductions: Measure of a Mystery* (Fund for UFO Research, 1987).

Fowler, Raymond E. *The Andreasson Affair* (Prentice-Hall, 1979; Bantam Books, 1980; Wild Flower Press, 1994).

Hopkins, Budd. *Missing Time* (Richard Marek, 1981).

———. *Intruders* (Random House, 1987; Ballantine, 1988).

Jacobs, David M. *Secret Life* (Simon & Schuster, 1992).

Vallée, Jacques. *Passport to Magonia* (Henry Regnery, 1969; Neville Spearman, 1970).

alien types Since the late 1960s, a few UFO researchers have tried valiantly to establish a typology of creatures said to be of an extraterrestrial nature. But so great is the variety of alien life-forms reported in UFO incidents (critics like to point out that there are as many types of aliens as there are people who report them) that classification systems have generally failed to cover the entire range of alien types, or take into account the dozens of small differences among the reported entities.

To address this problem, and to counter the notion popularized by the media that the "Grays" are the only "real" aliens, this writer developed an alien classification system based strictly on phenotype (or the observable physical characteristics) of the aliens reported in UFO incidents. This classification system has been detailed (with some 50 sample cases, which are fully illustrated) in my book: *The Field Guide to Extraterrestrials* (Avon, 1996).

I found that just about all the "aliens" seen during the past century could be categorized as belonging to one of four broad classes.

The first class, the **Humanoid**, describes beings with an essentially human shape: a head, torso, two arms, and two legs. The second class, the **Animalian**, refers to entities that are far more animal in appearance than human. The third class, **Robotic**, describes those that look distinctly mechanical. About 95 percent of alien reports fall into these three classes. The other 5 percent can be lumped together into a catchall category that, for want of a better term, I call **Exotic**.

I then divided each of these four classes of aliens into a variety of distinct types. Among the Humanoid, the first and the most recognizable are what I call *Human* simply because they look so much like us that it would be impossible to tell "them" from "us" on any busy metropolitan street corner.

The second type are the *Short Grays*, which thanks to Hollywood, if not the aliens themselves, are the preeminent alien type reported today. But since many short humanoid aliens do not in any way resemble Grays, either because of their extreme hairiness, green skin tone, or bulky spacesuit, I created a separate type called *Short Non-Grays*.

Rounding out the Humanoid class are two other types, the *Giants*, for those entities that stand 8- to 15-feet tall, and the *Non-Classic*, for those that do not fit into any other humanoid type—like the odd being with pointed ears and mummy-like skin seen in Pascagoula, Mississippi, in 1973.

The second major class of beings, the Animalian, consists of entities as different as Bigfoot, swamp creatures, goblins, and fairy-like aliens. For the names of the five Animalian alien types—*Mammalian, Reptilian, Amphibian, Insectoid,* and *Avian*—I simply drew upon their resemblance to either hairy mammals, reptiles, amphibians, insects, or birds.

I found that all Robotic aliens could fit comfortably into one of two types. Either the robots appear to be entirely "Metallic," and are so named, or a part of them, like their appendages, resemble flesh and are therefore called "Fleshy" Robots. Likewise, I divided the Exotic class of aliens into two types: the "Physical" Exotics, which resemble the classic blobs of science fiction, and the "Apparitional" Exotics, which are at least partially transparent or ghost-like in nature.

The Field Guide to Extraterrestrials was generally well received and is widely regarded as *the* standard reference on alien types.

—PATRICK HUYGHE

Allagash abductions This was a multiple-witness abduction that involved four art students, whose encounter occurred while on a camping trip in the state of Maine. The case involved identical twins, Jim and Jack Weiner, and their companions, Charlie Foltz and Chuck Rak, who were abducted from a canoe on the Allagash Waterway on August 26, 1976.

The investigation took place between January 1988 and mid-1993. It resulted in a 702-page (10-volume) report and a book entitled *The Allagash Abductions* written by Raymond E. Fowler and published by Wild Flower Press in 1993. The investigators of the case included:

MUFON Director of Investigations, Ray Fowler; a physicist who specialized in UFO entity cases; a MUFON consultant in hypnosis; and consultants in the areas of polygraph and psychiatric testing.

The UFO encounter was initially reported to Ray Fowler by one of the percipients (Jim Weiner) during a UFO symposium at Waltham, Massachusetts, in May of 1988. Jim told Ray that he, his twin brother Jack, and two friends had a close encounter with a UFO while camping on the Allagash Waterway in a wilderness area of northern Maine. Concurrent with the encounter they had experienced a period of "missing time," which had bothered them for years. Years later, Jim was referred to Ray Fowler by his personal physician during treatment at Beth Israel Hospital in Boston. What follows is a synopsis of the abduction accounts and the subsequent investigation.

On Friday night, August 20, 1976, the four young art students (all in their twenties) left Boston, Massachusetts, for a canoe and camping trip on the Allagash Waterway. Upon arrival at a staging area, they hired a pontoon airplane, which flew them and their canoes to Telos Lake on the Allagash River. During the next several days they canoed and camped along the waterway.

On the evening of Thursday, August 26th, they reached Eagle Lake, where they set up camp and later decided to go night fishing for trout in a canoe. The pitch-darkness of the area necessitated the building of a huge bonfire to mark their campsite, so that they could find their way back. Shortly after beginning to fish, Chuck Rak became aware of a feeling that he was being "watched." He said: "I turned toward the direction from where I felt this and saw a large bright sphere of colored light hovering motionless and soundless about 200-300 feet above the southeastern rim of the cove."

Chuck yelled for the others to look behind them. There, rising above the trees was a huge oval glowing object. As their eyes became adapted to its intense brightness, a gyroscopic motion was noted as if there were pathways of energy flowing equatorially and longitudinally from pole to pole. This divided the sphere into four oscillating quadrants of bright colored light. The color changes were very liquid and enveloping, as if the entire object had a plasmatic motion to it, like a thick sauce does as it starts a rolling boil.

Charlie Folz grabbed a flashlight and blinked it on and off toward the object. Simultaneously, a tube-shaped beam of light erupted from the object and hit the water. A glowing ring with a dark center reflected on the water's surface, indicating that the beam was low. The object and its extruding beam of light began moving toward the canoe. Terrified, the campers began paddling frantically toward their glowing bonfire and camp, as the beam swept across the water and engulfed them.

It was from this point on that the *conscious* memories of the four differed according to each of their vantage points.

The next thing Charlie remembered was paddling for shore and then standing at the campsite with the others, watching the object move away.

Chuck Rak remembers staying in the canoe after the others had piled out in panic onto the shore. Transfixed, still holding his idle paddle, he could not take his eyes off the object.

Jack and Jim were able to consciously remember a bit more about the tail end of the chase. Jack explained that "it was just behind us, and I could see that we were never going to outrun the beam. It was advancing too fast and I remember thinking 'Holy Shit! This is it! We'll never get away.' The next thing I knew, we were on the shore getting out of the canoe looking directly at the object which was now about 20 or 30 feet above the water. The beam was still coming out of the bottom of it like the object was sitting on the beam. It hovered there, right in front of us, completely silent for what seemed like four or five minutes.

"Suddenly the beam was pointing up towards the sky. The object began to move up and away from us towards the southwestern sky and then shot into the stars and was gone in just a second."

Jim Weiner added: "There was no mistake that the beam was coming directly to us. Then I remember standing on the lakeshore watching the object hovering above the lake 50 to 75 yards in front of us. . . . Then the search beam went upward into the sky and we saw it moving away at a tremendous speed. We all seemed to be in a state of shock. . . . We just stood there unable to move or talk."

The object left with a step-like motion. It would suddenly implode into nothing and than appear further in the sky and then repeat this strange flight path before streaking out of sight.

When the strange anesthetizing effect wore off, Chuck got out of the canoe and joined the others as they trudged dreamily up the beach to their camp. Even in this state, they were dumbfounded when they realized what had happened to the huge bonfire that had just been blazing a seeming several minutes ago.

"When we left to go fishing," said Jim, "we set very large logs on the fire to burn for a good 2 to 3 hours. The entire experience seemed to last, at the most, 15 or 20 minutes. Yet the fire was completely burned down to red coals."

At that time, they had no memory of what happened during the time it took for their huge bonfire to burn down. This remained a puzzle to them for years.

Several years after the Allagash incident, Jim suffered a head injury, which caused tempero-limbic epilepsy. During treatment, Jim began to have nightmares about himself and his camping companions being nude and in a strange place with bug-eyed humanoids around him. He also awoke at night to see strange creatures around his bed. Sometimes he felt as if he were being levitated from bed; and other times after being overcome with paralysis, he felt something was being done to his genitals. Jim's doctor noticed that he was overtired and asked him what was the matter. Jim refused to tell him at first but when the doctor told him that it was affecting his medical treatment, Jim confessed to what was happening to him. He also told the doctor about his prior "missing time" experience on the Allagash waterway. Jim's physician was familiar with the abduction phenomenon and advised him to contact a UFO researcher. At that time Jim was reluctant to do so. However, later the doctor saw a newspaper story about Ray Fowler lecturing at a symposium in the area in May of 1988. He phoned Jim and convinced him to attend the lecture and talk to Ray about the UFO experience.

In January of 1989, Ray Fowler initiated a formal investigation with MUFON UFO entity specialist and physicist David Webb and MUFON hypnosis consultant Anthony (Tony) Constantino. The investigation was conducted in a careful and meticulous manner over a period exceeding two years. After the four witnesses completed and signed MUFON UFO-sighting forms, they were interrogated. Their stories were cross-checked for consistency and a character check was performed to check their credibility.

It was obvious that the period of missing time had to be sandwiched between sighting the object and reaching shore. The beam of light engulfing the canoe seemed to be the dividing point between memory and amnesia. During the first of a long series of hypnosis sessions, it was decided to concentrate on this segment of the terrifying encounter.

Under hypnosis, all four witnesses relived detailed and traumatic UFO abduction experiences during the period of missing time. All were transferred from their canoe into the UFO by the hollow tube-like beam of light. On board, they encountered strange humanoid creatures that exerted some kind of mind control over them, so they could not resist their demands.

All four were made to take their clothes off and sit on a plastic-like bench in a misty area illuminated by diffuse white light. After looking at their eyes and in their mouths with a pencil-sized rod with a light on its tip, the entities placed them in a harness and flexed their arms and legs. Then, one by one they were made to lie on a table where each was examined by a number of strange handheld and larger machine-like instruments that were lowered over their bodies. During this segment of the examinations, the entities removed samples of saliva, skin scrapings, blood, feces, urine, and sperm from each of the abductees.

After the physical examinations, the abductees were made to dress and enter another room, which had a round portal in one of its walls. They were lined up and made to walk into the portal. Strange sensations surged through their bodies as they found themselves floating down the hollow beam of light into their canoe, which was now floating in shallow water at their campsite. The tube-like beam of light seemed to hold the canoe steady as each person was placed in it, in the same seating position that they were in prior to their abduction.

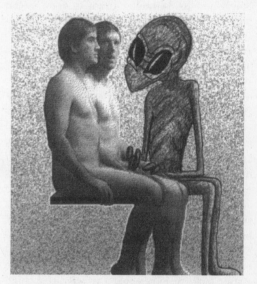

Artist's impression of Jim
and Jack Weiner on a bench,
in the UFO, with one of the aliens

As the hypnosis sessions continued, much detail was recovered about their onboard experience. Also, it was discovered that the twins had undergone bedtime visitations by alien creatures and had abduction experiences since early childhood—in addition to being abducted a number of times during their adult life. These experiences were relived in vivid detail while under hypnosis.

Their UFO experiences left physical evidence behind in the form of burns on the bottom of Jack's feet. Jack also received a biopsy-like scoop mark above his ankle during one of his adult abductions. The scoop mark was located just above a scar left behind during an operation for an anomalous lump that had appeared overnight on Jack's leg. Jack's local doctor thought it was a cyst, but was unable to drain it, so referred Jack to a surgeon who removed it.

Jack was told that local pathologists did not know what it was and that it had been sent to the Center for Disease Control in Atlanta, Georgia, for further analysis. However, when Jack's medical records were checked, it was discovered that the removed object was sent to military pathologists in Washington, D.C., where it was analyzed by a United States Air Force Colonel. Attempts for further information about the anomalous lump were thwarted, as the surgeon would not cooperate with the inquiry.

In addition to character checks of the four abductees, a number of other checks were made to ascertain witness credibility. Medical records, camping diaries and photographs were examined. Friends and relatives that first heard about the experience were interviewed. The head forest ranger who supervised matters on the Allagash Waterway was located. He remembered the incident and had reported it to the then active Dow Air Force Base located in Bangor, Maine.

Psychological profile tests were administered to each abductee. Each was also subjected to polygraph tests. All of these checks indicated that the four percipients were honest and telling the truth about their experience.

The many-faceted and intriguing elements of the Allagash abductions also provided a catalyst for a detailed correlation of the witnesses' experiences with benchmarks exhibited in other abduction reports being investigated and studied. Such reports were derived from an exhaustive survey of 270 reported UFO abductions in the United States and abroad by Dr. Thomas E. Bullard of the University of Indiana. It was found that the four abductees had experienced many of the typical benchmarks of the UFO abduction phenomenon.

A number of alternate theories for the abduction phenomenon were also examined in light of the Allagash abductions. These included hoaxes, fantasy-prone personalities, psychoses, birth-trauma memories, and archetypical images form the so-called "collective unconscious." Each of these was critiqued and eliminated in the light of the evidence collected during the investigation.

Charlie Foltz lying on the examination table; Jim and Jack sitting on a bench

The final 10-volume investigative report was made available to other researchers for peer review. Public information about the case was accomplished through Ray Fowler's 1993 book, *The Allagash Abductions*, a Time-Life book on the UFO-abduction phenomenon, and several TV documentaries.

Fowler's report concluded that the moral character of the witnesses, the graphic reliving of their experiences under hypnosis, and the extraordinary correlations between their experiences and those of others provided overwhelming evidence that their experiences were objective in nature. Such evidence combined with the positive results of polygraph and psychological tests, together with the typical physical effects found on the witnesses' bodies, prompted Ray Fowler to place the Allagash abductions in MUFON's *great significance* category.

—RAYMOND E. FOWLER

Allende letters The mystery of the so-called "Allende letters" arose in 1956, when an annotated copy of Morris K. Jessup's book, *The Case for the UFO* (1955), arrived at the Office of Naval Research (ONR). It looked as if three men (named "Mr. A.," "Mr. B.," and

"Jemi") had passed the book among themselves, adding handwritten notes to Jessup's text. Jessup also reported that he had received a series of letters from Carlos Allende (a.k.a. Carl M. Allen). The letters and annotations seemed to indicate that the writers had some special knowledge of UFOs and alien cultures beyond that of any government on Earth.

The story, as it is usually told, begins when the book arrives at the ONR. Some researchers have claimed that Navy officers, after carefully studying the text, became extremely interested and contacted Jessup. By that time, Jessup had already received the letters.

The Navy, according to the story, requested and received permission to reproduce the book in a limited edition. The original text was printed in black and the notations in red. All the letters sent by Allende were included as an appendix.

During the next several years the Navy allegedly spent taxpayer money, time, and a great deal of effort researching the incident. Navy investigators reportedly looked for Allende but failed to find him. Postmarks suggested Seminole, Texas, Gainesville, Texas, and DuBois, Pennsylvania, as locations for Allende.

The letters concerned the alleged teleportation of a Navy ship from its dock in Philadelphia to a dock in Virginia and back again during the Second World War. The experiment, allegedly witnessed by Allende, who claimed to be a member of the crew, was mentioned only in a single brief article that appeared in a single Philadelphia newspaper. Allende supplied neither the date nor the name of the newspaper so that this aspect could not be corroborated.

Allende claimed that the experiment was a success but the people were failures. Over half the crew was lost during the experiment, and the rest suffered from a variety of strange side effects. Some, according to Allende, were "mad as hatters," while others would "go blank," or "get stuck." Allende said they would seem to disappear or "freeze" on the spot.

The notes added to Jessup's book were no less confusing. Terms like "mother ship,"

"great war," "force cutters," "magnetic and gravity fields," and "sheets of diamonds" were used. The notations explained what happened to the men, women, ships, and planes that have disappeared in various locations around the world. Allende and his friends seemed to explain many things that no one else had been able to solve.

Sidney Sherby, an officer at ONR in 1956, told researchers in the 1970s that the reprinted annotated book was not part of a Navy project as tradition demanded, but a private investigation by men who happened to be in the Navy. No one officially at ONR thought much about the case. They were not going to waste time on an obvious hoax. It meant that members of the Navy, acting on their own as private citizens, had been interested. The Navy had no objection with the reproduction as long as it involved no Navy personnel, time, or finances. The fact that they were employed by the Navy shadowed them, giving rise to the rumor of official Navy interest.

Jessup, who had a financial stake in the Allende Letters, and who saw them as a way of revitalizing his sagging career, never learned the truth. His search came to an end on April 29, 1959, when he was found dead in a Dade County, Florida, park. His death was ruled a suicide.

The whole story should have ended in the 1970s when Jim Lorenzen announced that the whole thing was a hoax. According to a letter written by Lorenzen: "He [Allende] was on his way to Denver . . . and after talking to us for hours, admitted he had made up the whole thing. We even obtained a signed statement by him saying that it was a hoax."

William Moore and Charles Berlitz rejuvenated the tale with the publication of *The Philadelphia Experiment* (1979). In it, they even reprinted the famed newspaper article but in a break from journalistic tradition, not a single name appeared in the article. Once again the newspaper itself and the date were missing so that no corroboration could be found.

In the years that followed, several men have come forward claiming they were involved in the experiment. However, not one has ever provided documentation that they were on the ship. In one case, a man claimed the Navy had altered his life so that it would seem he was not involved.

In the end, Allende's confession that he had invented the tale, Sherby's explanation of what happened at the ONR, and the lack of any evidence that the experiment had taken place should have killed the story. The case has smacked of a hoax from the beginning, and no evidence has ever been offered to suggest otherwise.

—KEVIN D. RANDLE

References

"Allende Letters a Hoax," *The A.P.R.O. Bulletin* (July/August 1969).

Jessup, Morris K. *The Case for the UFO* (The Citadel Press/Bantam Books, 1955).

Moore, William L., and Charles Berlitz. *The Philadelphia Experiment* (Grosset & Dunlap, 1979).

Randle, Kevin D. "Allende Letters" in Story, Ronald D., ed. *The Encyclopedia of UFOs* (Doubleday/New English Library, 1980).

Steiger, Brad, and Whritenour. *New UFO Breakthrough* (Award Books, 1968).

America West Airlines sighting   On the night of May 25, 1995, veteran Captain Eugene Tollefson and First Officer John J. Waller, in charge of America West Flight #564 on a routine trip from Tampa, Florida, to Las Vegas, Nevada, encountered a UFO. At 10:25 MDT, two-thirds of the way through its planned four-and-one-half-hour flight, the Boeing 757 was cruising smoothly at 39,000 feet, and passing near Bovina, Texas. A stratus overcast stretched some 8000 feet below the aircraft while to the northeast an active thunderstorm cell loomed, topping off some 1000 feet above it.

Suddenly the attention of the lead flight attendant, sitting in the cabin behind the pilot, was drawn to a line of flashing lights in the sky to the north of and below the airliner. Both the flight attendant and first officer then observed a horizontal row of eight strobe-like lights, flashing on and off in a sequence from left to right.

Appearing "bright white with a tint of blue" and having the brilliance of landing lights, the row seemed to be at an altitude of 30,000 to 35,000 feet. Although Captain Tollefson had to leave his seat to observe the lights, he too noted their sequencing from left to right. Ultimately, the westward progression of the airliner caused the UFO to be situated in front of the thunderhead, whose lightning discharges silhouetted the strange object. Seen from this aspect, the UFO appeared to the first officer as a dark wingless cigar 300 to 400 feet long, with lights disposed along its length, and perhaps 22 miles distant. Tollefson felt the object might have been closer, with a 400- to 500-foot length. The object was in view for approximately five minutes.

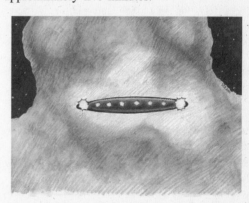

UFO observed by America West pilots

Although the air crew immediately contacted the Albuquerque Air Route Traffic Control Center to report the sighting, a flight controller stated that no unknown object was being picked up on radar; several airplanes in the vicinity of Flight #564 likewise were not able to spot the strange strobing lights. NORAD's western headquarters, alerted by Albuquerque ARTCC to the presence of the unknown aircraft, initially indicated they were tracking a nontransponding radar target in the vicinity of Flight #564. However, NORAD subsequently received a transponder code identifying this target as a specific aircraft.

Longtime researcher Walter N. Webb, working with a grant from the UFO Research Coalition, conducted an extensive investigation of the Flight #564 incident, ultimately acquiring the voice tape communications between the 757 and Albuquerque ARTCC, but was unable to resolve the UFO as any known meteorological phenomenon or man-made aircraft. It remains unexplained.

The case was profiled in 1995 on the TV show *Sightings* and is detailed in a report by Webb published by the UFO Research Coalition.

—ROBERT SWIATEK

Anatomy of a Phenomenon (Henry Regnery, 1965). Jacques Vallée begins his distinguished career as a UFO investigator and theorist with this book, analyzing historical reports of UFOs to discern common themes in the effects on machines and people. Among his many astute observations: the period 1914 to 1946 featured few UFO reports, yet it was "one of the richest periods in science fiction stories of all kinds." This leads him to believe there is little substance to the notion that UFO rumors are spread by public intoxication with science fiction ideas.

—RANDALL FITZGERALD

Ancient Astronaut and SETI Society (AAS) Originally known as the Ancient Astronaut Society (founded in 1973 by Dr. Gene Phillips), the AAS is the principal organization that supports the ancient astronaut theory of Erich von Däniken, et al. The AAS organizes conferences, seminars, and field trips, some of which are guided by von Däniken himself.

Their main areas of interest are quoted as follows:

- The origins of life on Earth
- The origins of intelligence on Earth
- The origins of religions
- The original core of global mythologies
- The description of gods in ancient texts
- The depiction of "judgments of the gods" in prehistoric times
- The legendary ancient kings and ancestors in old Sumerian texts and sacred scriptures
- The vanishing of religious and mythological beings "into the heavens"
- The issue of God and the Devil, the ancient symbols of good and evil
- The promises of a "return" in all religions and the fear mankind has of this event
- The time-shift mentioned in a number of ancient texts
- The construction and motivation of structures from prehistoric times for which there is as yet no explanation
- The earliest offerings for the appeasement of the gods
- The origins of ancient religious symbols and cults
- The origins of related rock carvings around the globe
- The origins of similar figurines of gods
- The origins of worldwide giant ground drawings and hill figures which are designed in such a way that they can be seen only from the air

Membership is the AAS is open to all.

Address: P.O. Box 818
           Ithaca, N.Y. 14851
           U.S.A.
Address: CH-3803 Beatenberg
           Switzerland

Web site: www.aas-fg.org

ancient astronaut theory The ancient astronaut or space-god theory proposes that intelligent, humanoid beings from outer space came to Earth in the distant past, created man in their image, and then went on to develop human civilization. Reports (i.e., legends and references by early historians) of ancient UFOs and alleged biblical UFO sightings are generally assumed by space-god proponents to be connected with ancient astronauts, thereby making it a theory of ancient contactees.

Could this 14th-century fresco from the Desani Monastery in Yugoslavia represent an ancient space traveler?

Author Erich von Däniken, the most popular spokesman for the movement, states the theory as follows: "In prehistoric and early historic times the Earth was visited by unknown beings from the Cosmos. These unknown beings created human intelligence by a deliberate genetic mutation. The extraterrestrials ennobled hominids 'in their own image.' That is why we resemble them—not they us. These visits to Earth by alien beings from the Cosmos were recorded and handed down in religions, mythologies and popular legends. In some places the extraterrestrials also deposited physical signs of their presence on Earth." (*Von Däniken's Proof*, 1978)

Hints of the theory can be found in the writings of Charles Fort, who once said "we are property," in the context that extraterrestrial beings might be watching over us Earthlings as a farmer would cattle or sheep. Another early proponent of ancient astronauts was astronomer Morris K. Jessup, who began to develop the idea in his book *The Case for the UFO* (1955).

It was not until 1960, however, that most of the "classic" or standard examples of alleged extraterrestrial evidence in ancient times were enumerated and synthesized by the French authors Louis Pauwels and Jacques Bergier in their book *The Morning of the Magicians.* Other books followed, such as *The Sky People* by Brinsley Le Poer Trench (1960); Paul Thomas's *Flying Saucers Through the Ages* (1962); Robert Charroux's *One Hundred Thousand Years of Man's Unknown History* (1963); and more recently, the whole series of books by von Däniken, beginning with *Chariots of the Gods?* in 1968, followed by another series of books by Zecharia Sitchin (beginning in 1976), known collectively as the "Earth Chronicles."

To von Däniken, this rock painting from Tin-. Tazarift in the Tassili mountains most likely represents an ancient astronaut "wearing a close-fitting spacesuit with steering gear on his shoulders and antennae on his protective helmet."

Although there is nothing absurd or impossible about the idea that ancient astronauts could have visited the Earth, the theory suffers from a lack of evidence that unambiguously links anything with extraterrestrrials. Discrepancies found in the books of von Däniken and others who have supported the ancient astronaut thesis can be categorized, for the most part, as follows: (1) speculations built on grossly inaccurate or misleading premises; (2) playing the game "it looks like"; and (3) omissions of pertinent information that if known would indicate a very different conclusion.

For example: a Mexican sarcophagus lid that supposedly depicts a man piloting a rocket is actually a deceased Mayan ruler by the name of Lord Shield Pacal who, in the stone carving, is shown against the background of a corn plant (which has been verified by comparisons with other examples of Mayan art); the giant statues on Easter Island, which proponents of ancient astronauts claim could only have been constructed with the aid of extraterrestrials, are known to have been carved by the natives themselves (verified by experiments conducted by Thor Heyerdahl on his famous Easter Island expedition in 1955-56); and a series of events (related by von Däniken in *Chariots of the Gods?*) interpreted as an "eyewitness account of a space trip" supposedly contained in the Epic of Gilgamesh that, upon reading the entire Gilgamesh epic, one does *not* find!

—RONALD D. STORY

References

Story, Ronald D. *The Space-Gods Revealed* (Harper & Row, 1976; New English Library, 1977).

———. *Guardians of the Universe?* (St. Martin's Press/New English Library, 1980).

Von Däniken, Erich. *Chariots of the Gods?* (G. P. Putnam's Sons, 1970; Bantam Books, 1971).

———. *Gods From Outer Space* (G. P. Putnam's Sons, 1971; Bantam Books, 1972)

———. *Von Däniken's Proof* (Bantam Books, 1978).

ancient UFOs   There is no question but that strange aerial objects have been described in roughly similar terms for thousands of years. Unknown lights and shapes seen in the sky, strange beings making contact with humans— these mysteries are a part of man's oldest art and literature. And although we should view the very early reports with caution, it would be unreasonable to ignore them.

References are found all over the world, in ancient legends and written histories, of strange happenings in the sky. "Fiery globes" fluttering about the night sky, "circular shields" during the day—that is how the ancient Greeks and Romans described what they saw. The Egyptians of 3,500 years ago left accounts of "circles of fire" and "flaming chariots" that sailed across the heavens. The American Indians had their legends of "flying canoes" and "great silvery airships" in the days of the covered wagons. Such accounts have been handed down through the ages by nearly all peoples of the world: from ancient Egypt, India, Tibet, Japan, China, Scandinavia, Ireland, England, France, Italy, Polynesia, and the Americas.

The following examples are quoted by the British author Harold T. Wilkins, in his book *Flying Saucers on the Attack* (1954), from reportedly ancient sources:

216 B.C.: Things like ships were seen in the sky, over Italy. . . . At Arpi (180 Roman miles, east of Rome, in Apulia), a *round shield* was seen in the sky.

214 B.C.: The forms of ships seen in the sky at Rome.

213 B.C.: At Hadria (Gulf of Venice), the strange spectacle of men with white clothing was seen in the sky. They seemed to stand around an altar, and were robed in white.

170 B.C.: At Lanupim (on the Appian Way, 16 miles from Rome), a remarkable spectacle of a fleet of ships was seen in the air.

In November 1969, there appeared an intriguing article entitled "Paleolithic UFO Shapes," by the French UFOlogist Aimé Michel in the British *Flying Saucer Review* (Vol. 15, No. 6). Michel had found that our Magdalenian ancestors fashioned works of art that are striking indications that they too had seen UFOs. On the walls of the famous Les Eyzies, Lascaux, and Altamira caves in France and Spain are found renderings of objects that clearly resemble modern descriptions (and photographs) of disk-shaped UFOs. Just what the Magdalenian artists were attempting to portray—15,000 to 30,000 years ago—may never be known. But, without a definitive explanation, the UFO interpretation must at least be considered as a possibility.

Many more examples of ancient UFO interpretations can be found in the books of Desmond Leslie, Morris K. Jessup, W. Raymond Drake, et al.

—RONALD D. STORY

Andreasson abductions *The UFO-related experiences and associated paranormal phenomena experienced by Betty (Andreasson) Luca and members of her family. Raymond Fowler's research over a period of twenty years is broken down into five separate investigative phases. During this inquiry, it gradually became apparent that Ray and his family also bore distinctive benchmarks of the UFO abduction phenomenon. The five phases of the investigation are published in five consecutive books:* The Andreasson Affair *(1979),* The Andreasson Affair, Phase Two *(1982),* The Watchers *(1990),* The Watchers II *(1993), and* The Andreasson Legacy *(1997). A synopsis follows:*

Betty (Andreasson) Luca

PHASE I

Phase I of the investigation took place between January 1977 and January 1978. Betty Ann Luca (then Mrs. James Andreasson) reported a UFO experience to J. Allen Hynek in response to an article that mentioned his interest in receiving such reports. Dr. Hynek referred her letter to the Massachusetts chapter of MUFON (the Mutual UFO Network). After an initial interview, a team was put together to investigate Betty's reported experience. In addition to Ray Fowler, the Phase I MUFON team consisted of a physicist, an aerospace engineer, an electrical engineer, a telecommunications specialist, a professional hypnotist, a lie detector specialist, and a medical doctor (as a consultant).

Betty's report to Dr. Hynek described only her conscious memories and those of her father,

Waino Aho (since deceased). The date was January 25, 1967. At that time, Betty and her family resided in the small Massachusetts town of South Ashburnham. She was in the kitchen when the event began. Her seven children, together with her mother and father, were in the living room. Her husband, James, was in the hospital recovering from an automobile accident.

At about 6:35 P.M. the house lights suddenly began to flicker and then blinked out. A pulsating pink, then reddish-orange light shone through the kitchen window; and a strange vacuum-like feeling settled over the house, as if time was standing still.

Betty told her frightened children to remain in the living room while her father checked to see where the light was coming from. When he looked out the window, he saw a group of strange-looking small humanoid creatures coming toward the house moving with a strange floating, jumping motion. As they passed by the window, one of the entities looked at him. He remembered nothing after that, as he was placed in what can only be termed as a state of suspended animation.

The five entities passed through the solid kitchen door and confronted Betty. As they passed through the door, they seemed to fade in and out of reality. This was essentially Betty's conscious memory of the experience. However, during fourteen sessions of time-regression hypnosis, both Betty and her daughter relived what they think occurred after the entities entered the house.

The rest of Betty's family was placed in a state of suspended animation. The entities commanded Betty to follow them outside. Betty felt strangely compelled to go with them but was concerned for her family. The entities then temporarily released Betty's oldest daughter, Becky, from her suspended state to assure Betty that her family would be all right. Becky relived this segment of the encounter under hypnosis.

Betty floated through the solid-wood kitchen door in line with four of the entities. One entity was left behind. Under hypnosis, Becky remembered this entity again releasing her from suspended animation to ask questions about the rooms in the house and to amuse her with floating balls of light.

Outside, Betty was brought to a small oval-shaped craft on tripod landing gear, whereupon she floated into it. The craft accelerated upward and apparently entered a much larger craft. While on board she was subjected to the effects of strange equipment before and after a physical examination.

During the examination, a tiny BB-like object was removed from her nose. Attempts via hypnosis to learn how it got there were unsuccessful. Betty became terrorized during these probes and the hypnotist refused to press the matter further.

After the exam, Betty was placed into a tank of liquid and made to drink another liquid that had a tranquilizing effect. Soon after, she was removed from the tank and floated along a track into an alien place. While there, she underwent a traumatic experience during an encounter with a holographic-like portrayal of the death and rebirth of the legendary phoenix bird.

During this experience, a booming chorus of voices told Betty that she had been chosen to show something important to the world. She then was returned home to find her family still

in a state of suspended animation and guarded by the entity that was left behind.

Betty and her family, under mind control of the entities, were put to bed in a state of unawareness. Betty was told that she would forget her experience until an appointed time. During the abduction the entities related to Betty that: humans would fear them, but they were here to help the human race; human time is localized and they were not bound by time; their technology is paraphysical in nature, and man is not made of just flesh and blood.

The MUFON team was able to verify a number of facts associated with the initial segment of Betty's UFO abduction experience, including the power blackout and the approximate time that the incident began.

Under hypnosis, Betty related that the event occurred in 1967 on a Wednesday. She stated that her husband was in a Veteran's Administration Hospital and that her parents were visiting to help out. She described the weather as balmy with traces of snow on the ground, melting and causing the neighborhood to be enshrouded with fog.

Betty's husband's hospital records showed that he was in the hospital between January 23 and March 17, 1967. A local weather station in South Ashburnham recorded a temperature of 33 to 54 degrees with mist rising from melting snow. Betty's parents remembered the visit, and her father remembered his brief, conscious look at the entities, which he described as "Halloween freaks."

The local power company confirmed the power failure and attributed it to an open circuit breaker, apparently tripped by an overloaded circuit. Unfortunately, the power company records did not give the time of the power outage. The time was established by other data.

Prior to the encounter, Betty's children were watching a show on TV that featured Bozo the Clown. A check of TV records revealed that this show aired between 4:30 and 5:30 P.M. on that date. Since it was dark outside when the event began, the time of sunset was checked. This turned out to be 4:48 P.M.

Some of Betty Luca's own drawings of the entities she encountered

Betty's drawing of a disk-shaped craft
into which she was taken

Under hypnosis, Becky remembered that it was around 6:35 P.M. when the lights went out.

Betty's credibility was established through a character reference check, a lie-detector test, and a psychiatric interview. Only the weather, television show, and the power failure could be proved as objective reality. However, Betty's (and Becky's) reliving of the account was consistent during an interrogation and while having her repeat various segments of their experience while under hypnosis. Her description of the entities and her experience were also consistent with other abduction reports.

PHASE II

Phase II of the investigation took place between June 1978 and June 1980. In addition to Ray Fowler, the investigative team consisted of a physicist and a behavioral psychologist.

The Phase I investigation had come to a halt because Betty had moved to Florida to live with relatives after her marriage ended. Her first husband, James Andreasson, was a childhood sweetheart who had returned from service in the Navy as an alcoholic. Betty had lived a rocky life with the ups and downs of this disease and had sought help for him many times. However, the time came when he decided to leave her for the family's own good. Attempts to change his mind had been futile.

During her stay in Florida, Betty met Bob Luca. Bob and a friend had been on a cross-country trip to California. Bob had never intended to return to his home in Connecticut via Florida, but he suddenly had a compulsion to visit friends there. Coincidentally, Bob's friends turned out to be mutual friends of Betty's. In fact, they were people Betty worked with. They also told him about Betty's UFO experience.

He was very interested in meeting her, as he also had a UFO sighting, followed by missing time, in the summer of 1967. At that time he was on his way to a beach near Wallingford, Connecticut, when he noticed a railroad crew looking up at two large silver cylindrical objects. He stopped the car and watched as the cylinders released smaller disk-shaped objects.

After the objects were out of sight, he continued to drive to the beach but was distressed when he arrived late with about two hours of missing time.

Bob was introduced to Betty, who informed the MUFON team of his UFO experience, and arrangements were made to conduct an investigation of his "missing time" as well. Bob and Betty were later married.

The team obtained the services of a MUFON consultant in hypnosis living in Connecticut, and Bob underwent two sessions in which he was hypnotically regressed.

During the first session, the hypnotist asked Bob to go back to his first UFO experience. We were amazed when he began reliving an encounter that had taken place at age five, in 1944. Bob began speaking like a child. He said he was sitting on a swing in the back yard, behind his house. He noticed a bright light coming in the sky. When it got close, he described an oval object with two gray entities in a bubble-like dome on top. They flashed a light at him, which induced paralysis. They told him telepathically that they were visiting others like him to help people not to be afraid of them. He was told that someday something good would happen to him, when he was older.

During the second session under hypnosis, Bob relived driving to the beach and watching the cylindrical objects release smaller objects. However, when he began driving to the beach, one of the smaller objects appeared and began descending like a falling leaf toward his car. The car was suddenly filled with red light and he found himself in the craft with small, gray alien beings. He could not resist their wishes. They had him remove his clothes and then placed him on a table, where he underwent a physical examination. While on the table he became terrified when one of the gray entities suddenly turned into a being of light. He refused to describe one of the procedures that the entities were performing on him. He was brought out of hypnosis and refused to undergo further sessions.

Betty underwent seven more sessions under hypnosis. Coincidentally, Betty also relived her first remembered UFO-related experience at age seven, in 1944, at Leominster, Massachusetts. While waiting for a friend in a playhouse, a buzzing, glowing marble-sized object flew in and landed between Betty's eyes. She felt tired and experienced a strange feeling in her head, as a chorus of voices told her that she was being watched and was making good progress. She was told that they were getting some things ready to show her and that it would make her and other people happy. These things would not be ready until she was 12 years of age.

Her second encounter took place at age 12, in 1949, when she lived in Westminster, Massachusetts. While walking in the woods, she was confronted by a small gray entity in a strange coverall suit with buttons and symbols on it. The entity pressed a button on the suit and a glowing marble-sized ball of light flew out and landed between Betty's eyes. Again she heard voices which said that she was not ready yet and that what they were preparing for her would happen in another year.

True to the entities' statement, when Betty was 13, in 1950, she was whisked up into an "orb-shaped" craft while walking in a field. The entities told her they were taking her home to meet the "One."

They placed an instrument in her mouth that held her tongue down and placed her on a smooth rubber-like wheel. The craft took her to an underground installation, which was entered by going underwater. There she witnessed a Museum of Time consisting of lifelike (or real) people from different ages, encased in transparent cubicles.

The entities then caused Betty to undergo an out-of-body experience (OBE). In this state of being, she was told to enter a huge glass door. Through it she entered into a "world of light" and there encountered the One.

Under hypnosis, her face beamed in ecstasy as she described a feeling of unconditional love and a oneness with all things. Attempts to discover other things that she learned there were futile.

She was also subjected to a number of tests including being trained on a console. During the physical examination, the entities removed her eye and inserted a tiny object in her head through the eye cavity, which would be removed 17 years later.

Follow-on hypnotic sessions revealed that in 1961, at age 24, a strange force drew Betty from her home into the woods, where she encountered a tall gray entity. She was told not to be afraid, that the Lord was with her and that her faith in the light would bring many others to the light. She was warned of upcoming trials but to keep her faith for the Lord Jesus was with her.

Phase II of the investigation came to a halt due to a painful mental block when Betty started to relive her next UFO experiences in the 1970s. This pain frightened her so much that she refused to undergo further hypnosis. She felt that the entities did not want her to relate these experiences at this time.

PHASE III

Phase III of the investigation took place between November 1987 and December 1988. It was conducted by Ray Fowler and a behavioral psychologist. At this time, Betty began experiencing dreams and memory flashbacks of a woman's face. What disquieted her so much was the expression of intense fear on the woman's face. The eyes of the woman literally cried out to her for help. Betty tried her utmost to remember who the woman was, as she felt that she had seen her somewhere before.

Betty decided that she would undergo hypnosis again to find out who the woman was, in spite of the chance that she would undergo a painful block again. An initial hypnotic session was not painful and revealed the woman was related to Betty's UFO experiences.

This instigated 17 new hypnotic sessions, which revealed a number of UFO experiences involving both Betty and Bob Luca. It was during these sessions that the entities told Betty that they were the "Watchers."

In 1973, at age 36, Betty described a bedroom visitation by an entity who informed her that it was now time to begin to remember her previous experiences and what she had been told.

In 1975, at age 38, Betty again experienced a bedroom visitation by an entity who told her that her first marriage would end and to prepare for hardships.

In 1977, at age 40, during yet another bedroom visitation by an entity, Betty was told about the impending death of two of her sons. Later, they were both killed in an automobile accident.

In 1978, at age 41, Betty described and shared an OBE abduction with her husband Bob. They were taken to a large round-shaped facility where they witnessed many incredible things, including an alien operation on three family members. During this same year, Betty, Bob, and one of her daughters sighted four UFOs from their car.

Between 1981 and 1986, Betty described several occasions where alien entities were sighted in her bedroom at night.

In 1986, at age 49, Betty was suddenly confronted by an entity during the day, as she lay on the couch. The entity placed a black box on the couch, which precipitated an OBE abduction experience.

In 1987, at age 50, Betty discovered an anomalous scoop mark on the calf of her right leg. Three more scoop marks appeared on her arm, in 1988. During the same week a scoop mark appeared overnight on Ray Fowler's right leg, after a dream of being operated on by alien entities.

Ray's personal physician referred him to a dermatologist, who said it looked like a "punch-biopsy" in the process of healing. The appearance of the scoop mark further instigated Ray to undergo hypnosis himself to explore personal childhood and adult experiences. Ray decided to include samples of personal UFO and paranormal events experienced by himself and family members within the context of the Phase III investigation.

PHASE IV

The Phase IV investigation took place between November 1992 and April 1993. It was conducted by Ray Fowler and a behavioral psychologist. During this period Betty underwent seven hypnotic regression sessions and Bob was involved in four sessions.

One of the priorities in this particular phase of the investigation was to regress Bob Luca to relive his side of his shared OBE abduction experience, in 1978, with Betty. When under hypnosis, Bob provided additional information about his personal interfaces with the entities. This included a detailed treatise on the survival of human beings after death, of which the entities had intimate knowledge. He also provided a complementary description of what he and Betty experienced while together.

In addition, Bob recounted a number of times that he awoke to see entities nearby. Such experiences took place in 1981 during a camping trip and in 1985, 1986, and 1992 in their home. However, each time when eye contact occurred between himself and an entity, he would fall back to sleep.

Bob also relived abduction in 1989. He was awakened by the bed shaking and a bright red light coming through the window. His attempts to awake Betty were futile. When an entity appeared beside the bed, Bob became paralyzed. The entity placed his hand on Bob's forehead and then poured some liquid into his mouth, which caused Bob to calm down. He then floated with the entity out the window into a hovering craft, and placed on a table where he was examined. He was told that they were monitoring his progress. During the examination a metal strap was placed on Bob's head which produced a variety of pictures in his mind.

Betty continued to relive in detail a number of follow-on personal abductions and a shared abduction from a car with Bob, in 1989. During a personal OBE abduction from her bed also in 1989, Betty was taken to a craft where she saw her daughter Becky being trained on a console. She was also brought back to Earth with a human-like robed entity in an OBE state where she was allowed to see him carry out several interfaces with events on Earth.

During another abduction in 1989, Betty was taken in a small craft to a huge cylindrical craft in space, where she described a number of operations being carried out by the robed human-like entities and their small humanoid gray surrogates.

In addition to probing Betty's and Bob's memories of their UFO experiences, the Phase IV investigation included a detailed comparison between OBE abductions and the NDE (near-death experience). This resulted in the possibility that humankind were the larval form of the human-like entities encountered during OBE UFO abductions and NDEs. It hinted that the physical abductions and so-called animal mutilations were analogous to the breeding and maintenance of the human larval form.

This would mean that so-called physical death might be the ultimate abduction: the reception of the metamorphosed larval form into the plane of existence from which the UFO phenomenon originates. Fowler theorized that this would explain why the entities appeared to be so similar in appearance to Homo sapiens, and why OBE abductions and some NDE reports were identical. This concept was also supported by a treatise on human afterlife given to Bob Luca during his shared OBE abduction with Betty, in 1978.

PHASE V

The Phase V investigation took place between November 1993 and February 1995. It was conducted by Ray Fowler and a MUFON consultant in hypnosis. The inquiry was directed specifically at probing the hidden memories of Becky's daughter and Bob Luca, and another probable abductee that was selected at random for comparative purposes.

In addition to recording hypnotic recall, interviews with members of the Luca and Fowler families took place. The experiences of both families were recorded and analyzed. Results supported other researchers' findings that UFO abductions are a family phenomenon, and other types of paranormal phenomena usually accompany UFO experiences. Based on these findings, it was theorized that UFOs and various types of paranormal phenomena might be singular components of one overall metaphenomenon.

Under hypnosis, Becky relived childhood and adult UFO experiences. Her earliest memories went back to 1958 when she was only three years of age. The early abductions were conducted by the robed human-like entities who took her from her crib by a beam of light into a craft, where she was examined with an African-American child. It was at this time that she was returned to her backyard sandbox in the early morning hours, rather than to her crib. This caused great alarm to her mother, who could not understand how she could have gotten outside of a locked house.

A scar remains from an apparent biopsy taken during her childhood abductions. During these early abductions, Becky relived her experience with the entity that was left in the house during Betty's 1967 abduction. Her adult abductions were conducted by the typical small gray entities. During both childhood and adult abductions, Becky was trained on a console with a TV screen-like monitor. Becky attributes her ability to write strange hieroglyphic-type writing to these training sessions.

Bob relived several other abduction episodes, such as being taken from his bed and out a closed window by a small red-suited gray entity in a buzzing beam of light. During another childhood bedtime episode, he suddenly found himself in a strange lighted room with his mother and father, and small gray entities that performed examinations on them.

He also relived his 1967 adult experience, where he was taken from his car while on the way to a beach. During past hypnotic sessions, when probing this event, a mental block was encountered where Bob refused to describe what the entities were doing to him. However, during this session, the block was neutralized. Bob became very upset as he described entities extracting semen from him.

One of the priorities of the Phase V investigation was to probe a recurring dream of Bob seeing an alien child. Under hypnosis, Bob emotionally recalled being in a place where there was a large hallway. A gray entity emerged with an alien-like child with blue eyes, who somehow Bob recognized as his own. Bob was not allowed to go close to the child and sobbed uncontrollably when the child was taken away.

During the Phase V investigation, Ray Fowler decided to include one of the many suspected abductees that had phoned him for help. He wanted to see whether she would relive similar UFO and paranormal events as the Luca and Fowler families. The similitude of the results was extraordinary.

Jean (a pseudonym) was selected and re- lived both childhood and adult UFO and paranormal experiences in excruciating detail. Of great interest was her being used as a surrogate mother for three fetuses and being brought to see and hold them at a later date.

Like Betty, Jean saw other surrogate mothers on board the craft who were undergoing gynecological procedures. She, like members of the Luca and Fowler family, had experienced a variety of psychic phenomena.

Fowler's continuing investigation into his own family uncovered a variety of UFO and paranormal phenomena experienced by them. A highlight event was the discovery that his father, brother, and his brother's son also had pronounced scoop marks just above their shins. His brother recalled remnants of an abduction experience from a motel room, which coincided with the appearance of the scoop mark. Ray's father did not remember when the mark had appeared and was unaware of it until it was pointed out to him. His nephew could not recall anything about the strange scoop marks on his leg.

Phase V was the culmination of a twenty-year investigation of the Andreasson abductions. The result is a collection of conversations between the abductees and their alien abductors, which have been recorded as their message to humankind in the book, *The Andreasson Legacy* (1997).

—RAYMOND E. FOWLER

References

Fowler, Raymond E.. *The Andreasson Affair* (Prentice-Hall, 1979; Bantam Books, 1980).

———. *The Andreasson Affair, Phase Two* (Prentice-Hall, 1982).

———. *The Watchers: The Secret Design Behind UFO Abduction* (Bantam, 1990).

———. *The Watchers II: Exploring UFOs and the Near Death Experience* (Wild Flower Press, 1993).

———. *The Andreasson Legacy* (Marlowe, 1997).

POSTSCRIPT: *What follows is Betty (Andreasson) Luca's own summary of her extraterrestrial encounters*: Since the beginning I have believed that extremely intelligent extraterrestrials have coexisted with mankind, quietly touching the human life and mind, hoping to lead man into a higher path of consciousness where wisdom, love, and freedom abound.

Many people fear and mistrust these entities, because of their covert influence. I have had several physical and spiritual close encounters. Most all the beings I've been involved with, for well over fifty years of UFO encounters, have been benevolent.

In 1967, as I lay magnetically pinned to a table aboard an extraterrestrial craft, several dark-eyed entities, having three fingers on each hand, vigorously measured me for light and procreation, before retrieving a BB-like implant from my nose.

My mind fearfully grasped for answers as I questioned their intention, purpose, and attitude concerning such a peculiar and frightful examination.

I soon realized although these physical probes and unusual methods were bizarre, the beings did not want to hurt me in any way, for they removed the pain by laying their hands on my forehead. I reasoned that their radical examination was no more puzzling, painful, or embarrassing than many necessary medical operations humans endure from physicians, surgeons, and dentists.

Knowledge of these extraterrestrial creatures capable of transformation and invisibility began at age seven and continues to this day. My first abduction in 1950 thrust me into a realm where denizens of small gray-skinned beings dwell, whose enlarged heads and big black eyes seemed grotesque compared to the human form.

In their strange environment was a beautiful crystal forest with amazing powers that came alive through touch. Beyond the forest was a huge crystal-like door. This was the entrance into the beautiful world of Light where the magnificence of One resides. Words are inadequate and incapable of describing the glorious and majestic presence within the dimensions of Light. Upon my exit from the great

In this scene from Betty's 1967 encounter, the leader, "Quazgaa," exchanges a magical book for the Bible.

door, I was greeted by a tall, white-haired being who placed me in a small transport craft to return to the main ship.

While on my journey back home, an implant was strategically placed inside my head which would be removed seventeen years into my future. After the removal I was taken to a room with eight unusual chairs, submersed in liquid for protection from G-forces, then escorted to a high place before the Light where a chorus of one voice called my name to inform me that I had been chosen to show the world. Six more years would pass before I would come to understand what the intriguing statement meant.

Through each encounter, they were revealing themselves: who they were, what they were doing, and why. I had been chosen to report the impact of their reality through my encounters.

In 1973, the gray beings summoned me from my home to their craft where a young terrified woman lay paralyzed on a table. Much to my surprise, some of the beings were working down by her raised legs.

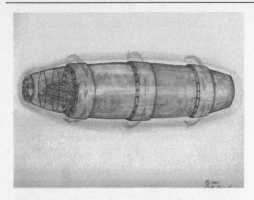

A huge cigar-shaped craft, which carries the Elders and the Watchers

A hybrid fetus was aborted from the woman's womb and thrust into a waiting tank of liquid close by. It was at this time I learned these gray beings were called "Watchers": caretakers of nature and all natural form. They informed me the reason they'd been collecting seed and fetuses was because man would eventually become sterile.

I witnessed technology that seemed magical. A large hovering craft attached itself to a smaller craft below to purge and reline its "cyclinetic trowel," which caused lightning and a rain shower to occur. The lower craft was later shrunken to the size of a car.

Watchers escorted me back to the main craft, where I was lifted to an upper room and brought to a huge forest-like terrarium with a fish pond. The central part of the water opened, and as water and fish fell below, the Watcher explained: "they were just replenishing." I stood in the forest in amazement as tiny fetus-like children, remarkable hybrid infants, appeared from behind bushes and trees.

The next unusual encounter was an out-of-body (OBE) event that happened to both my husband, Bob, and me. We were lifted out of our bodies and brought aboard a craft where the gray Watchers were examining our three daughters. Two tall white-haired beings took Bob into a different room, as I along with others were changed into beings of light. This experience was an advanced learning session for us.

In 1989, I was once again transported to a craft by the gray Watchers and brought to the crystal forest. The ground rumbled and great sheets of blinding light suddenly appeared as the great door to the world of Light opened once again.

A spherical craft transported me forward, where I saw a mass of nesting orbs. These orbs were collectors of wisdom, knowledge, and intelligence. Watchers escorted me to another spherical craft, and we sailed toward a massive cigar-shaped vehicle hovering in the darkness of space. One end of the huge ship was lit with red and white lights. As we entered the long cylindrical craft and parked the small ship, a tall white-robed being greeted us.

Once inside, I learned that these beautiful, pale blue-eyed extraterrestrials are called Elders, and are ambassadors of "O." The gray Watchers are their work force. These Elders love the human race.

—BETTY ANN LUCA

Betty's drawing of an Elder: one of the white-robed beings

Address: P.O. Box 613
            Hayes, VA 23072
            U.S.A.

E-mail: bluca@pilot.infi.net

Andreasson Affair, The   (Prentice-Hall, 1979). Raymond Fowler tells the story of Betty Andreasson, a Massachusetts housewife, who believes she was kidnapped by aliens and given religious messages and formulas for new technologies to benefit humankind. Her account of being subjected to medical tests by the aliens and having an implant removed from her sinuses came from hypnotic regression sessions and became a defining experience for later abductees and their hypnotists.
—RANDALL FITZGERALD

Andrews, Arlan K., Sr.   (b. 1940). Dr. Andrews is an author, lecturer, and consultant, living on Padre Island on the Texas Gulf coast. A native of Little Rock, Arkansas, he retired in 1996 as Manager of Advanced Manufacturing Initiatives at the Sandia National Laboratories of the U.S. Department of Energy, Albuquerque, New Mexico. He is a co-founder of Muse Technologies, Inc., a virtual-reality software firm (NASDAQ: MUZE), and several other high-tech start-up companies.

Dr. Andrews received his Doctor of Science in Engineering at New Mexico State University in 1968, and worked for AT&T Bell Laboratories at White Sands Missile Range, New Mexico; Greensboro, North Carolina; and Indianapolis, Indiana, with assignments in Hong Kong and Japan.

He worked as a Fellow in the Technology Administration of the U.S. Department of Commerce in 1991-92, and in the White House Science Office (Office of Science and Technology Policy) during the Bush and Clinton Administrations in 1992-93, making him the only UFO researcher with White House credentials. He is a Registered Professional Engineer, a Mechanical Engineering consultant for MUFON, and a professional member of the

Arlan Andrews

Science Fiction and Fantasy Writers of America.

E-mail: arlan@thingsto.com

POSITION STATEMENT: My basic outlook on UFOs has not changed since my original position statement in _The Encyclopedia of UFOs_ (1980):

"My own interpretation is with the hardware group: I think that the data reveal that we are visited by craft from other solar systems or elsewhere in space, and that these craft have advanced means of propulsion and materialization, and that the crews are (sometimes) humanoid, and that they are neutral—neither friends nor foes. It is almost meaningless to speculate further upon their motives."

In the years since 1980, most scientific discoveries and technological advancements have unknowingly supported this "Hardware and Extraterrestrial Hypothesis." For example, we now possess "stealth technology," which means that UFOs of the 20th century did not have to show up on our radar, lending more credence to such reports. Extrasolar planets are showing up everywhere, and recent lab experiments indicate that the speed of light may not be the ultimate barrier after all. Advances in nanotechnology and genetic research are making 21st-century technology look like magic to a 1950s observer. Each of these steps supports a universe in which interstellar travel is indeed possible.

It is very interesting, then, that no further progress has been made in explaining UFOs since Day One in 1947. Perhaps UFOs will remain not only unknown, but unknowable.

—ARLAN K. ANDREWS, SR.

Andrus, Walter H., Jr. (b. 1920). As one of the founding members of MUFON in 1969, Walter Andrus served as the International Director of the Mutual UFO Network, Inc. since 1970, succeeding Dr. Allen R. Utke. On July 16, 2000, Andrus retired from that position, and the title was transferred to John F. Schuessler, also a founding member of MUFON.

Born in Des Moines, Iowa, Andrus graduated from the Central Technical Institute in Kansas City, Missouri, in 1940. He also graduated from the U.S. Navy Electronics Technician Program (during World War II) and taught in both of the above schools. He was formerly employed by Mid-Continent Airlines as a Station Manager in Quincy, Illinois. From 1949 to 1975, Andrus was employed by Motorola, Inc. in successive capacities as Assistant Plant Manager, Manager of Quality Control, and Operations Manager in their Quincy, Illinois, facility. In 1975 he transferred to the Seguin, Texas, plant as a Production Manager. After a tenure of nearly thirty-four years with Motorola, he retired at the end of 1982 to devote himself full-time to the management of the Mutual UFO Network.

The MUFON administrative offices were moved from Quincy, Illinois, to Seguin, Texas, in 1975, where MUFON became a Texas Nonprofit Corporation and an I.R.S. Tax Exempt Organization.

Andrus has been interested in the UFO phenomenon since August 15, 1948, when he, his wife, and son had a daylight sighting of

Walter Andrus

four UFOs flying in formation over downtown Phoenix, Arizona.

In addition to presenting slide-illustrated lectures in the U.S.A., Australia, Belgium, Brazil, Canada, England, Italy, and Mexico, he has appeared on national television numerous times, most recently with *Oprah Winfrey, Larry King,* and *Encounters.*

Andrus is a member of the Board of Directors of the Joint USA-CIS Aerial Anomaly Federation. He is also on the Board of Directors for the influential UFO Research Coalition, composed of the J. Allen Hynek Center for UFO Studies (CUFOS), Fund for UFO Research (FUFOR), and Mutual UFO Network (MUFON).

Address: 103 Oldtowne Road
            Seguin, TX 78155
            U.S.A.

Telephone: (830) 379-9216
Fax: (830) 372-9439

E-mail: mufonhq@aol.com

POSITION STATEMENT: During half a century of involvement in the study of the enigma of unidentified flying objects, I have reached certain tentative conclusions based upon the "state of the art" of present-day science.

After personally interviewing several hundred witnesses to UFO sightings, reviewing the 1,600 UFO landing-trace cases compiled by Ted Phillips, and reading the 1,800 humanoid or entity cases collected by Ted Bloecher, my initial conclusion is that our Earth is being visited by entities from an advanced intelligence in their spacecraft conducting a surveillance of life on this planet.

Considering the giant steps that we have made in space travel during the past twenty years, the extraterrestrial hypothesis is not only very exciting, but the physical evidence helps to substantiate this theory.

On the other hand, I cannot lose sight of the probability that they could constitute some unknown physical or psychological manifestation that cannot be explained by present-day science. Evidence to support this hypothesis is directly related to a personal daytime sighting on August 15, 1948, of four round silver objects which my wife, son, and I observed along with numerous other witnesses in downtown Phoenix, Arizona. The objects, while flying slowly from east to west in formation in a cloudless sky, one at a time simply vanished from our sight in sequence in the northern sky. After patiently continuing to observe the sky in the direction and speed that the objects had been traveling, the first three in formation "popped" back into our vision one at a time in the northwest sky still moving slowly west, where they eventually went out of sight due to distance. Considering all factors involved, these objects had performed a feat no known object manufactured on this planet could perform, thus meeting the requirements of a "UFO."

Did these balloon-shaped objects "dematerialize" or change into another dimension right before our eyes and then return a few minutes later into our three-dimensional world?

If UFOs are found to be extraterrestrial spacecraft, our aerospace engineers would like to duplicate their propulsion systems and aerodynamic maneuverability characteristics. If one of our aerospace industries could design and build a craft that could duplicate the feats of a UFO, the United States would be the unchallenged leader in the space race. We would no longer need rockets with millions of pounds of thrust to launch vehicles to the moon and nearby planets.

The third vital question to be answered is "where do they originate?" The modern era of "flying saucers" "kicked off" in 1947; however, the Bible and other historical writings provide evidence that UFOs have been around for several thousand years. If they are extraterrestrial in origin, our planet has been under surveillance for reasons known only to the creatures controlling the vehicles. If they are from another dimension, and have the ability to "materialize" into a "nuts and bolts" type of spacecraft, leaving physical traces, they could be residents of this or any other habitable planet.

A question always directed to those of us involved in UFO research is, "Do you believe in UFOs?" My response always seems to shock the recipient, when I answer *no*. "Belief" has a religious connotation. I believe in God, even though I have never seen him. When I consider UFO sightings, it is a case of looking at the facts, data, and evidence, and arriving at the conclusion that the evidence is overwhelming in favor of UFOs.

I am very cognizant that a phenomenon which has baffled the residents of our tiny planet, conceivably for several thousand years, will not be resolved tomorrow, or even next year. However, until a concerted scientific effort is launched to deal with this perplexing dilemma, it will undoubtedly continue to be "the greatest mystery of our time."

—WALTER H. ANDRUS, JR.

angelic kingdom According to metaphysical theory, this is an evolutionary line of nonphysical beings, existing on Earth and in higher dimensions. The angelic kingdom is parallel to, interactive with, but objectively independent of the human line of evolution.

These beings are said to be responsible for the maintenance of the planet and the solar system, assisting the Creator of our seven-dimensional system in the completion of its development. Examples include the mythical fairies, sylphs, and archangels (such as Mikael and Gabriel), with whom some modern channels also claim to be in contact.

—Scott Mandelker

Angels and Aliens   (Addison-Wesley, 1991). Keith Thompson applies the ideas of Carl Jung and Joseph Campbell to the UFO phenomenon and concludes it is a mythological journey and a rite of passage for humankind to create a Cosmic Man. Thompson delineates the patterns which connect aliens, abductees, angels, and shamanic and near-death experiences, existing in a realm beyond "the tenuous dimension known as ordinary reality," and concludes these experiences are awakening us to uncharted human capacities accelerating our evolution as a species.

—Randall Fitzgerald

angels and UFOs   There has thus far been no comprehensive study relating Biblical angels and UFOs, although possible directions for such studies are apparent. There are several indications that UFOs in the Bible serve as transportation for the angels.

UFOs in the Bible are variously referred to as "the pillar of cloud and fire" of the Exodus, or the "chariot of fire" of Elijah, or the "bright cloud" at the transfiguration of Jesus. Two men in white robes, understood to be angels, were present at the ascension of Jesus (Acts 1:10). Concerning his second coming Jesus says, "they shall see the Son of man coming in the clouds of heaven with power and great glory; and he shall send his angels with a great sound of a trumpet." (Matt. 24:30-31)

In modern UFO studies, it is assumed by many that UFOs provide transportation for humanoids or UFO occupants. Thus the question becomes: Is there a relation between the Biblical angels and modern UFO occupants?

"And behold, there was a great earthquake, for an angel of the Lord descended from heaven and came and rolled back the stone, and sat upon it. His appearance was like lightning, and his garments were white as snow."
(Matthew 28:2,3)

Jacques Vallée in his book *Passport to Magonia* (1969), has explored some similarities between folklore and fairy stories of old, and modern UFO stories and their human-like occupants. There are also parallels between modern UFO-occupant stories and Biblical angels.

For instance, the Bible relates the famous story of Balaam, who while riding his ass met an angel of God. The donkey recognized or saw the angel, but the angel was invisible to Balaam for some time, until the angel chose to become visible to Balaam. (Num. 22:21-35) In modern UFO literature it is often argued that animals can sense the presence of UFOs before humans. Also, visible UFOs are often reported to become invisible almost instantly.

The New Testament reports that an angel came into a prison cell to rescue Peter and led Peter and himself past the first and second guard without being seen, except by Peter. (Acts 12:1-17) The idea suggested is that angels may be visible to some humans while invisible to others at the same time

Some modern UFO occupants have very different features from ordinary humans, but others are reported to look very human. The Biblical angels were understood to have the power to look very human. Thus, the Bible says: "Do not neglect to show hospitality to strangers, for thereby some have entertained angels unawares." (Heb. 13:2) Post-Biblical culture and art frequently picture Biblical angels with wings, but wings are never mentioned in most angel accounts, and, obviously, an angel with wings would hardly catch one "unawares."

The idea that angels were very human begins with Abraham's meeting with "three men" (Gen. 18:2) who meet him at noon and whom he feeds. Eventually he discovers they are from God, and they exhibit the ability of what we call mental telepathy, reading the mind of Sarah, Abraham's wife. Modern UFO occupants are sometimes given credit for the ability to read human minds and communicate psychically. Likewise, angels in the Bible are understood to be able to communicate strictly through psychic impressions, as when an angel appears to Joseph, the husband of Mary, in a dream. (Matt. 2:13) Similarly, in modern cases, witnesses involved in close-encounter cases often report increased psychic sensitivity and suggest that the UFO reality is now communicating with them through dreams and visions.

One other characteristic of angels of interest in the UFO field is that angels can apparently materialize and dematerialize, or else can pass through what we would call solid walls. Thus, in the story mentioned above of Peter in prison, the implication of the story is that the angel entered the jail cell without opening the door or gate. This is similar to the story of Jesus, after his resurrection, who entered a locked room to meet his disciples. (John 20:19-29) One can imagine a kind of "Star Trek" transporter bringing about these events, although the Bible never explains the happenings. A Mrs. Sandy Larson of North Dakota, reported a series of UFO contacts, including one occasion when two UFO beings awakened her from sleep and carried her right through her bedroom wall to the waiting UFO.

This is not to say that we have proof that modern UFOs and Biblical angels are connected, or identical. It is clear, however, that the Biblical concept of angels involves many elements which are familiar to students of modern UFO stories and UFO-occupant cases. While it is true to say that there is no scientific proof at the present time of a connection between Biblical angels and modern UFOs, conversely, there is certainly no proof that they are independent phenomena.

Many modern UFO cults are of a religious nature, and persons sometimes claim to have received divine messages of salvation from UFOs. This fact has made the "scientific" study of UFOs difficult, either because UFOs are not scientific in the sense scientists want them to be or else because UFOs know how to use tactics, including religious symbolism, to make them less scientifically accessible.

—BARRY H. DOWNING

References

Downing, Barry. *The Bible and Flying Saucers* (Lippincott, 1968; Avon, 1970; Marlowe, 1997).

Jessup, M. K. *UFO and the Bible* (The Citadel Press, 1956).

Oswald, John Paul. *What You Need To Know* (privately published, 1983).

Vallée, Jacques. *Passport to Magonia* (Henry Regnery, 1969).

Angels: God's Secret Agents (Doubleday, 1975). Evangelist Billy Graham proposes that angels may be the occupants of UFOs who have been guiding our spiritual evolution since Biblical times. In contrast to other Christians who fear UFOs are piloted by demons, Graham suspects they are angels sent here by God to

help us fight the demons because "the Second Coming of Jesus Christ is close at hand."
—RANDALL FITZGERALD

Angelucci, Orfeo (1912-1993). Orfeo Angelucci is a UFO contactee whose account has attracted especial attention because of the purity of the religious symbolism and spiritual motifs it contains. For this reason Carl G. Jung, in his *Flying Saucers: A Modern Myth of Things Seen in the Skies* (1959), devoted some ten pages to an analysis of the Italian-American's UFO experience.

Angelucci's most important book is *The Secret of the Saucers,* published in 1955. In this autobiographical narrative he tells us that he was raised in comfortable circumstances in New Jersey, married in 1936, had two sons, and moved to Los Angeles in 1948. His life was happy except for recurrent bouts of ill health, which reduced him periodically to a state of total exhaustion and painful nervous prostration, and in acute cases required hospitalization.

One physician attributed the condition to the effects of a childhood attack of trichinosis. Because of this circumstance, he ended formal schooling in the ninth grade. His mind, however, was very much alive. Angelucci as a boy and young adult was continually performing experiments and writing theses on esoteric scientific topics from virology to "the nature of infinite entities."

By his own account, his first saucer experience occurred on May 23, 1952. Angelucci had felt peculiar and slightly sick throughout the day and about 11 P.M., left the swing shift early to go home from his job at the Lockheed aircraft plant in Burbank, California. He was afraid his old illness might be coming back. But as he drove along the bank of the Los Angeles River around midnight, he noticed a glowing disk following him. It came closer and closer until it virtually forced him off the road. He stopped, got out, and encountered a suprahumanly splendid man and woman bathed in light who had come by saucer from another world. The aliens presented Angelucci with a

Orfeo Angelucci

revivifying drink from a crystal goblet, reminded him of events from his past, and informed him that, despite his humble state, he had been singled out as most suitable for the first contact of this magnificent race with the people of Earth. They spoke of the deep compassion they had for Earth and proclaimed they wished to offer hope to this troubled world

On a couple of later occasions, Angelucci rode the marvelous vehicles of his friends, ringing with the music of the spheres, to their paradisal planets. The celestial companions reaffirmed their concern for suffering humankind and the designation of Angelucci as their evangelist. The latter's transcendent experience ended with his mystical marriage to a spacewoman named Lyra.

Dutifully, Angelucci commenced speaking and writing about his experiences. Needless to say, he and his family received considerable ridicule, but eventually he became known in more sympathetic circles and found himself to be a fixture of space conventions and the contactee lecture circuit.

In a later book, *Son of the Sun* (1959), Angelucci relates the alleged experiences (as told by him) of a person known only as Adam, but who is described as a medical doctor from Seattle who had only a few months to live. This narrative concerns the same entities and ships as does *The Secret of the Saucers* and is replete with the same combination of romantic adventure with transcendent quality which makes the earlier book striking; the nature of the supernal beings and the philosophical perspective underlying them here comes through in fuller detail.

The religious character of these encounters is reinforced by Angelucci's continual insistence that the visitants and their craft are not just from another world but, in some way, from an entirely different order of reality. Their ships could not be seen by just anyone, but only by one who is mystically prepared or selected for the experience. On meeting them, he felt an exaltation "as though momentarily I had transcended mortality and was somehow related to these superior beings." It was as though he had "felt another world, or something akin to a whole universe."

He tells us that we are continually under observation by the Spirit of God, by a hierarchy of angels and heavenly hosts, and by the very highly evolved beings he encountered— beings of other planets who are so perfected as to be "almost angels, on the threshold." They cannot directly help us by interfering with the course of affairs in this world, but they can and do help indirectly by providing a powerful hope-giving experience of transcendence, which shows how marvelously beautiful and harmonious the infinite universe beyond darkened Earth really is and what glorious creatures humankind can become. But even this experience, according to Angelucci, can only be given to those able to receive it— "only to people who already have it within them"—for otherwise it would be an unjustifiable violation of the "divine code" of noninterference.

Orfeo Angelucci's saucerian message, based on what were essentially mystical experiences, is wholly one of hope and of the spaceman's positive spiritual meaning. To him, UFOs afford a way to inspiration and transcen-dence and an assurance that for all its anguish Earth is not left alone but is part of a living, God-pervaded universe and has godlike friends.

Orfeo Angelucci founded no organization, claimed no grandiose titles or callings, and claimed no mystical UFO experiences after those recounted in *The Secret of the Saucers.* Since then, he lived in Los Angeles, quietly and modestly, working at various jobs and speaking about his experiences and their meaning as occasion has allowed. His charm, humility, and sincerity were recognized by all who knew him, and he was widely regarded as expressing the religious wing of the UFO contactee movement at its best.

—ROBERT S. ELLWOOD, JR.

animal mutilations   Toward the end of 1974 and throughout most of 1975, newspapers across the United States carried stories of strange cattle mutilations and their possible connection with UFOs, which in some cases had allegedly been observed in close proximity to the time and place of these bizarre happenings.

Hundreds of beef cattle were found dead across a section of the country as wide-ranging as Minnesota, Wisconsin, Kansas, Nebraska, Iowa, South Dakota, Colorado, Texas, Arizona, and California. The series of cases began in Meeker County, Minnesota, and spread westward as law-enforcement agencies became increasingly involved, especially in Minnesota and Colorado.

It was found initially that the vast majority of cattle deaths had resulted from natural causes: mostly disease and malnutrition. The missing parts were those usually attacked first by scavenging animals, because they are the easiest to chew, i.e., the lips, tongue, ears, udders (teats), sex organs, and rectal area. However, some of the cattle bore strange mutilations which could not be accounted for in such a mundane manner. Ears were carefully removed, tongues were cut out, udders and sex organs were gone, anuses sliced out, all with apparent surgical skill. Also, in such cases, which were mostly black Angus or black white-faced cattle, the carcasses were devoid of blood as if drained with a needle. No blood could be found on the ground, nor footprints or vehicular tracks. As one farmer put it, it was as if the bodies were mutilated elsewhere and dropped to the ground from the air. (In fact, there had been several cases reported of helicopters leaving the scene of cattle mutilations, but identifying details were difficult to observe in the dark of night. Most often, in such instances, the helicopters were heard but not seen.)

Eventually, law-enforcement personnel, working together with veterinarians, uncovered the working of a bizarre Satanical cult group somewhat reminiscent of the Charles Manson "family."

The leader of this "family" operated in Minnesota for a while, then moved abruptly to Texas when family members ran afoul of the law. The leaders were apprehended and placed in custody.

Their general *modus operandi* was as follows: The group, which would approach its intended victim at night, walked upon large pieces of pasteboard which they picked up and carried with them; thus no tracks were left. The victim was shot with a tranquilizer dart, immobilizing it (traces of nicotine sulfate were found in the livers of some of the animals). Then a heart stimulant was injected, an artery in the throat was punctured, and the blood was caught in a plastic bag and carried from the scene in that manner. Organs to be used in the Satanic rites were then surgically removed with a minimum of bleeding.

It seems likely that similar cult groups are responsible for other mutilated-animal cases and perhaps some of these instances are even the work of deranged individuals. But one of the least likely explanations is that UFOs were involved.

For a time, a young man who claimed to be a lecturer for the University of Minnesota was spreading the word that UFOs had shot some Minnesota cattle and had "collapsed their blood structure with mercury." An inter-

view with this man disclosed a preoccupation with achieving notoriety, and attempts at technical discussion were patently naive. His credibility also suffered from the fact that he claimed to be a "Sasquatch," or "Bigfoot," contactee (he had visited in their homes). Needless to say, his touted evidence connecting UFOs with dead cattle disappeared in the light of objective investigation.

Despite claims by such individuals and certain sensationalist elements of the national media, no satisfactory evidence has ever emerged which links UFOs to mutilated animals.

—CORAL & JIM LORENZEN

Anomalist, The In 1993, two freelance writers for *Omni* magazine, Patrick Huyghe and Dennis Stacy, met at a Mutual UFO Network (MUFON) conference in Richmond, Virginia, and lamented the then sorry state of UFO and Fortean journalism. Since both had been thinking about starting a new journal on anomalies, they decided to collaborate.

By the summer of 1994, the first issue of *The Anomalist* appeared. The resulting illustrated journal, in trade paperback format, features high quality writing on a variety of topics, ranging from "alien writing" and ghosts, to Bigfoot, crop circles, and issues of human invisibility. The twice-yearly journal, which explores the mysteries of science, history, and nature, quickly garnered rave reviews and spawned a complementary Web site of the same name at www.anomalist.com.

In its first five years, *The Anomalist* has published a number of major UFO stories, including "Project Blue Book's Last Years," an excerpt from the unpublished memoirs of Col. Hector J. Quintanilla; "UFOs: For RAND Use Only" by Karl Pflock; and Martin Kottmeyer's award-winning essay on "UFO Flaps."

The editing team of Huyghe and Stacy have much in common. Stacy was editor of *The MUFON UFO Journal* and had published articles on UFOs in such mainstream publications as *Smithsonian Air & Space* and *New Scientist*. Huyghe had been editor of *UFO*

Commentary, back in the late 1960s and early 1970s, and had published articles on UFOs in *Science Digest* and *The New York Times* Sunday Magazine. Huyghe's book, *The Field Guide to Extraterrestrials*, appeared in 1996 and he has collaborated with Stacy on a companion volume called *The Field Guide to UFOs* (Quill, 2000).

Address: P.O. Box 577
            Jefferson Valley
            NY 10535
            U.S.A.

E-mail: editors@anomalist.com
Web site: www.anomalist.com

—PATRICK HUYGHE

Anthropic Principle This idea is closely related to *anthropomorphism* or *anthropocentrism*, which is seeing the universe in terms of ourselves. As the ancient Greek philosopher Protagoras (ca. 490-420 B.C.) put it: "Man is the measure of all things." This myopic point of view has extended to the human search for extraterrestrial intelligence (SETI).

As concisely stated by Frank Drake: ". . . the controversial 'Anthropic Principle' . . . holds that the universe was made exactly the way it is so we may exist. Or, put another way, we exist only because the unverse is the way it is." This statement is basically a tautology (made true by its definition). However, the extreme implication is ". . . that the universe is so finely tuned as to hold just one intelligent species: us." (Drake and Sobel, 1992)

The "weak" version of the anthropic principle merely points out that if things had been different, we would not exist. For example, the laws of nature and the myriad "coincidences" that have figured into human evolution seem to have been amazingly well adapted to us (rather than the other way around). So much so, that according to proponents of the "strong" version of the anthropic principle, the laws of nature seem to have been specifically designed ". . . (don't ask how or by

whom) *so that* humans would eventually come to be. Almost all of the other possible universes, they say, are inhospitable. In this way, the ancient conceit that the Universe was made for us is resuscitated." (Sagan, 1994)

—RONALD D. STORY

References

Drake, Frank, and Dava Sobel. *Is Anyone Out There?* (Souvenir Press, 1992).
Sagan, Carl. *Pale Blue Dot* (Random House, 1994).

apocalyptic thought connected with UFOs and ETs The belief or feeling that a violent catastrophe will befall humanity in the near future is more formally termed "world-destruction fantasy" or "apocalyptic thought." These terms are used in a broad sense to include cataclysms of virtually any magnitude in which great loss of life and suffering is implied.

Such beliefs are pervasive in the history of UFO culture, with examples numbering in the hundreds. Their history extends back to the earliest puzzlings of Kenneth Arnold and runs continuously to the latest horrors at the cutting edge of abduction research. Contactees, abductees, fringe UFO buffs, and respected UFO researchers alike have contributed to the doomsaying sensibility.

The range of cataclysmic violence begins on the low end with modest spectacles of cities destroyed in nuclear blasts (Cecil Michael, Sonora desert-F-4-74) or a city dying from a nuclear storm or cloud (Cannon's Carrie). The scale runs through wars (John Hodges, Ted Owens, Brian Scott, Linda Taylor, Jerry), the destruction of civilization (George Hunt Williamson, Buck Nelson, Norman Harrison, Marshall Applewhite), the sinking of California (PLW, Helen Hoag, Filiberto Cardenas, Mandelker's Bob), the inundation of continents (Robin McPherson), population reduced by 40 percent or 50 percent or more (Andrijah Puharich's Space Kids, Scott Mandelker), the cracking open of the planet (Pedro Ramirez, Francie Steiger), the atmosphere being set on fire

(Linda Porter), the complete ignition of the planet (Ralph Lael, Arthur Shuttlewood), the orbit shifted outwards (MN Pleiadean), planets pulled toward the Sun (Dr. Malachi Z. York), destabilization of the solar system (Frank Stranges, John Sands, A.N. Tasca), the blowing up of the solar system (Necoma), destabilization of the galaxy (George Adamski), endangerment of the universe (C.A.V., Jerry Gross), destruction of other universes (Janice), and even beyond to a universal dissolution involving black holes that not even the gods would be immune to (George Andrews).

Concern over the "balance of the universe" is peculiarly common and begins early with the Ouija board contact of George Hunt Williamson with Zo of Neptune on August 17, 1952. Dorothy Martin, Sr. Helio Aguiar, Stuart Whitman, and Arthur Shuttlewood echoed this concern. Carlos, one of John Mack's prophets, modernizes the wording by speaking of a tearing of the cosmic fabric essential to the unity of the universe.

The mode of destruction varies across a wide and inconsistent repertoire of creative options. Some say the world will end in fire (Stephen Pulaski, William J. Herrmann, Arthur Shuttlewood, Dana Redfield, Linda Porter, Roxanne Zeigler). Some say in ice (Elgar Brom's Noel, Stan Seers).

Floods and tidal waves equally suffice (Dorothy Martin, Rolf Telano, Barbara Hudson, Lynn Volpe, Peter). Continents rise or fall and Earth's axis will tilt for better than a dozen contactees. The Mitchell sisters and Helen Hoag overtly credit the fact that this is a replay of the Atlantis myth. Arthur, one of Mack's group, warns a cosmic water balloon will flood the Earth, suffocating everything. Inversely, the desertfication of the Brazilian rain forest will extend everywhere according to Jerry in this same group.

Mona Stafford and Francis Swan see the end coming in the manner mapped out by the Bible and Revelation. Orfeo Angelucci warned a fiery red comet of doom might collide with Earth if we did not change our ways. Anthony Volpe saw the Earth expanding like a balloon

by 20 percent and then settling back. There's an electromagnetic catastrophe coming (Joe), or the end of oil (Paul Bennett), or a plague of communicable AIDS (Scott), or extinction by sterility (Betty Andreasson). Eduard Meier and Robert Short see problems connected with the loss of the ionosphere.

Professor R.N. Hernandez casts his doomsday in a virtually unreadable bafflegab that has something to do with a band of mineral solids encircling our world and aliens trying to make us annihilate ourselves. Richard Miller said aliens had a ring of ten million ships around our world trying to protect us from the effects of a cloud of cosmic debris. Some quakes, tidal waves, and bad weather caused by radiation effects on the Earth's core could not be prevented.

Dino Kraspedon warned that use of the hydrogen bomb would create unknown elements that would upset the atmosphere in ways that would lead to quakes, tidal waves, strange diseases, and maniacs in the streets. Dorothy Cannon's subject, Janice, fears the circumference of the Earth will fold into its center causing an explosion that ripples to other galaxies and universes, because of their atomic structure.

A nice number of these prophets were kind enough to set firm endpoints on their prophecies thus allowing them to be easily tested and falsified by simply letting time pass.

Phrases like "the end is coming soon" (Harry Joe Turner) and "Earth time is desperately short" (Arthur Shuttlewood) are a recurrent refrain. The fact that decades have passed since ten or so uttered them indicates either they are wrong or use "soon" in an opaque fashion.

The record of error presented in the table calls for some sort of explanation. Some will follow the lead of the Lorenzens who felt aliens were liars and disseminated disinformation as part of an immense charade. It is a peculiar sort of campaign however.

Starfarers should be more scientifically sophisticated than to bluff with notions as dubious as pole-shifts.

Concerns that man could have tangible ef-

DATE-SETTING SAUCER PROPHETS

Name:	End type:	End time:
MFS Hehr	Atlantean	1960
Orfeo Angelucci	comet	1986
George van Tassel	H-bomb	1952
George Hunt Williamson	cataclysm	Dec. 1, 1952
Albert Bender	pole-shift	1953
Francis Swan	Biblical	1956
Richard Miller	quakes	1956
Dorothy Martin	floods	Dec. 21, 1954
Gladys White Eagle	quake	Oct. 1954
Wayne Aho	Earth changes	1980
Ralph Lael	Earth blows up	1964
Knud Weiking	nuclear holocaust	Dec. 24, 1967
Robin McPherson	pole-shift	Nov. 22, 1969
John Hodges	war	1984
Ted Owens	nuclear war	1974
Stephen Pulaski	world burns	1976
Helen Hoag	Earth changes	1978
Sonora desert contact	U.S. city nuked	1980
German Navarrete	pole-shift	1988
Robert Short	pole-shift	1975
Greta Woodrew	Earth changes	1984
Francie Steiger	coastal floods	1990
Starseed poll	pole-shift	1984
Charles Hickson	total destruction	1984
PLW	California sinks, worldwide disasters	1993
Gaynor Sunderland	Earth destroyed	1992
Jamie Sams	world cleansing	Late 1980s
Graham Allen	severe Earth changes	1992
Paul Bennett	end of oil, cars, men	2000
Penny Smith	period of destruction	1995-2000

fects on the universe's balance sound pre-Copernican and a grandiose conceit of man's powers. It is also odd that they don't stick to one scenario filtered through all their contacts to give the lies more credibility and the letdown more bite.

Kenneth Ring's Omega Project affirms the ubiquitous character of apocalyptic thinking in UFO belief. His survey of a population of UFO experiencers found fully 85 percent reported an increase in their concern for planetary welfare after their experiences; 60 percent said it strongly increased. This provides a nice backdrop to Jenny Randles's finding that 28 percent of bedroom-visitor contacts included imminent Earth catastrophe as a reason for alien visitation, the most common of the motifs looked at.

Apocalyptic thought is hardly limited to the UFO subculture. One has only to look at the history of Christianity, from the beliefs of Jesus that the world would spectacularly end in his generation, to Revelation, to the latest end-time cults, to realize the power of this belief.

Environmentalists have offered a smorgasbord of eco-catastrophes in recent decades. New Age literature repeatedly foresees Earth changes, with the name Edgar Cayce repeatedly invoked as an authority on these matters. Apocalypse has been considered part of the basic plot of all science fiction. Stanislaw Lem notes that every fan has a library of agonies in which writers have refined the end of the world into something "as formally elegant as a well thought out gambit" in chess. Anthropologists have encountered world-destruction fantasies in far-flung cultures and myriad forms such as to suggest it extends back through aboriginal times. This hints at the involvement of a panhuman psychological process.

Psychologists have developed some insights into this process. Fantasies about the destruction of the world are a common feature of psychotic mental universes. Freud was one of the earlier psychological thinkers to observe world-catastrophe beliefs are not infrequent in

the agitated stages of developing paranoia. His favorite paranoid, the respected judge and doctor Daniel Paul Schreber, held a conviction of the imminence of a great catastrophe either by the withdrawal of the sun, by earthquake, or by pestilence through nervous disorders. Though he initially placed this event 212 years in the future, Schreber came to believe that period of time elapsed and he was the only real man left alive. His doctors and attendants were "miracled up, cursorily improvised men." With the passage of time, he concluded that he himself had passed away and was replaced. Despite the florid nature of these delusions, in practical affairs Schreber was reasonable and well informed and never bothered people with his private beliefs save to publish a book stating them.

Some lack this ability to wall off their delusions and slip into debilitating madness. In *The Autobiography of a Schizophrenic Girl*, a young lady named Renee describes in the early stages of her developing psychosis how she came to believe the frozen wind from the North Pole wanted to crush the Earth. In time she regarded it as an omen or sign, and confided to friends her fears that planes were coming to bomb and annihilate them. She covered her conviction in a jesting manner because of fears the idea was unfounded and not generally held. Her sense of unreality deepened and she saw her madness as a country of implacable blinding light. It was an immense space: limitless, flat, shadowless; a mineral lunar country, cold as the wastes at the pole; a stretching emptiness where all is congealed, crystallized, and unchanging. As time progressed, she had waking fantasies of an electric machine that could blow up the world and rob all men of their brains. This machine then took control of her life and made her do destructive acts like putting her hand in a fire.

William J. Spring, who made a study of these world-destruction fantasies, affirms eschatological fantasies are frequently met in schizophrenia, especially in the early stages. Floods, wars, revolutions, earthquakes, plagues, and mass poisonings form some of the more common motifs. The wiping out of the human race is generally the anticipated outcome, but nations and mere cities have served as stand-ins. Ernest Keen, a narrative psychologist, goes even further than some observers and affirms he has "never known a paranoid who did not have cataclysmic content" in his expectations about life.

The cause of this relationship has been the subject of some amount of theorizing over the years. Some of Freud's thoughts about the involvement of the libido are no longer accepted. But there is one explanation that has approval. It is nicely embodied in a parable told by the fictional yet prototypical debunker Michael Webb:

"As a philosopher I have a special license to be peculiar; so now I'm going to tell a fable. It's short and soon over—so listen closely. One day a peasant walking along a riverbank saw a fox struggling in the water. 'Help, help' the fox cried. 'The world is coming to an end.' 'You are mistaken, my friend,' replied the peasant, 'all I see is one small fox drowning.' The moral is short and easy to remember: when around deep water, watch your step." The fable is as astute as it is succinct. In more formal jargon, the end of the world is a projection of a personal crisis. The ego is experiencing disintegration, dissolution, loss of identity— self-destruction—and these impulses are mirrored onto the external world. Of eleven patients presenting world destruction fantasies, William Spring found that the idea of the person's own death played a prominent role in eight. Two fantasized about suicide, six had delusions of dying or already being dead. The identification of self with the cosmos was tragicomically illustrated by a patient of Spring who believed he was himself God. He believed people feared that if he died, they would die. One day, in a fit of anger, he pronounced retribution. "It's the end of the world!" Then, he threw himself onto the floor.

Kenneth Ring reinforced the general point in a study of near-death experiences. Visions of world destruction formed a small but significant fraction. They had a compelling vividness and similarity, but despite this soon failed as factual forecasting. Carl Jung, the famed psychologist, had a similarly vivid vision of the destruction of the world while suffering from arteriosclerosis shortly before his death.

Stanislav Grof has observed that death and rebirth struggles in LSD hallucinations are similarly accompanied by imagery of violent catastrophe: earthquakes, volcanoes, hurricanes, tornadoes, electrical storms, gigantic comets and meteors, Armageddon, and so forth. They are constantly appearing during certain stages of the tearing down of the ego; a tactic sometimes obliged in therapy. Grof regards such imagery as the "source of schizophrenic experiences and paranoid conditions." (Grof, 1975)

The association of paranoia and schizophrenia with cataclysmic fantasy is readily explicable within the framework of object relations theory. (Rinsley, 1981) When people fail to form an identity separate from parental figures, ego defenses are poorly developed and tend to have a primitive, fear-laced logic. The ego in such cases is easily susceptible to fragmentation and destruction in the face of crises. (Frosch, 1983) In paranoia, the crisis typically involves shame or humiliation. The persistence of apocalyptic thought thus reflects the persistence of suffering in the world and the panhuman tendency to project one's mental state onto general reality.

The projective character of UFO apocalypticism is strongly hinted in the expansive, totalistic nature of these fears. The imminent doom spreads to all facets of external reality, much as paranoid conspiracies often spread to international dimensions. The psychodynamic underpinnings of the world-destruction fantasies in UFO culture are sometimes fairly evident when the circumstances surrounding the prophecy are known to some degree of detail.

When Prophecy Fails by Leon Festinger is a psycho-sociological classic that offers the most detailed account of a prophecy of doom on record. The investigators ran across an item in the paper in which Dorothy Martin was predicting a flood would destroy Chicago just before dawn on December 21, 1954. The cataclysm would spread, and the West Coast from Washington State to Chile would be submerged. Festinger thought it would make an ideal case study in the nature of proselytization in the wake of doomsday prediction failing.

Festinger's reporting is impressively comprehensive and he was able to pin down the first explicit reference to the impending disaster as appearing in a message from Sananda dated August 2, 1954. The authors don't ask why it appeared when it did, but their chronicle provides the answer. The day before, on August 1st, Martin was joined by a group of people at an airfield to await the landing of a spaceship that her contacts promised would come. It is simple enough to infer the failure of this prediction in so public a manner was a source of embarrassment. Some took it eventually as a sign she was a false prophet and dropped out of the group surrounding her. (Festinger, et al., 1956)

Wilhelm Reich was officially declared to possess a paranoid nature by a prison psychologist, and informally colleagues in Vienna psychoanalytic circles regarded him so long before. His wife separated from him due to irrational accusations of infidelity. In the waning years of his life he believed he was involved in a war being waged from outer space with DOR, a negative form of orgone energy he defined as Dead Life Energy. UFOs were an agent in the deterioration of the environment manifesting in the destruction of rocks, trees, forests, and the drying up of the atmosphere. Simultaneously with persecution by the FDA, Reich declared seeing far and wide a DOR emergency—evidence the War of the Universe was on. Later he predicted "the complete destruction of the globe of mother Earth looms on the horizon of the future." David Boadella, speaking of Reich's space-gun adventures in Arizona, regards it as obvious his mind had "tumbled beyond retrieve." (Reich, 1973)

Even before the events of *Communion*, Whitley Strieber was whispering conspiracies—so much so that acquaintances tended to regard him as "the quintessential paranoid." His early life follows the recipe of creating a paranoid: a trauma-filled childhood, a proud and ambitious family, a fall from grace into financial ruin sparking social slights and ridicule, rejections, and a withdrawal into himself. (Metzger, 1984; Winter, 1985)

These examples are merely illustrative of the personal dimension in the process of apocalyptic thought and not a full accounting. Charles Strozier's study of the psychology of apocalyptic opinion among contemporary Christians gives cause to note that end-time beliefs are sometimes adopted because of group pressure, but modified and qualified by personality and experience. (Strozier, 1994)

This likely applies in UFO culture when the fantasy conforms to more popular fears like the common New Age expectation of a poleshift. A similar case would be Betty Andreasson's aliens who forecast "mankind will become sterile." This echoes a familiar fear of environmentalists, one involving some dubious premises according to an investigation by Michael Fumento. (Fumento, 1999) It also looks like a projection of her life. Andreasson had a hysterectomy and abortion in 1964 because of cervical cancer. (Fowler, 1990) Her sterility expands to fill the fate of the world.

One last note of possible interest is that these fantasies are rarely challenged in a forceful way among believers. The failure of apocalyptic predictions may be granted in a general way, but usually in a context advancing an alternative pessimism.

The ideologies of optimism found elsewhere in the culture never germinate there, never mind take root. Disbelievers, by contrast, tend to wax enthusiastic over human progress and the march of science, embed human history in deep time, and tend to see problems like overpopulation as solvable. (Kottmeyer, 2000) The infrequent instances of apocalyptic thought tend to be those appearing popularly in general culture.

—MARTIN S. KOTTMEYER

NOTE: For the sake of scholarly completeness, numerous names are mentioned in the text with which the reader may be unfamiliar. However, the author stands ready to direct the scholarly reader to his sources upon request. (Please include a self-addressed, stamped envelope.) Contact information can be found under the entry: KOTTMEYER, MARTIN S., in this encyclopedia.

References

Boadella, David. *Wilhelm Reich: The Evolution of His Work* (Laurel, 1973).

Festinger, Leon, Henry W. Riecken, and Stanley Schachter. *When Prophecy Fails: A Social and Psychological Study of a Modern Group that Predicted the Destruction of the World* (Harper, 1956).

Fowler, Raymond. *The Watchers* (Bantam, 1990).

Frosch, John. *The Psychotic Process* (International University Press, 1983).

Fumento, Michael. "Hormonally Challenged," *American Spectator* (October, 1999).

Grof, Stanislaw. *Realms of the Human Unconscious: Observations from LSD Research* (Viking, 1975).

Keel, John. *The Mothman Prophecies* (Signet/NAL, 1975).

Keen, Ernest. "Paranoia and Cataclysmic Narratives," in Sarbin, Theodore J., ed. *Narrative Psychology: The Storied Nature of Human Conduct* (Praeger, 1986).

Kottmeyer, Martin. "Debunkers of Doom," *The Anomalist* (2000).

La Barre, Weston. *The Ghost Dance: The Origins of Religion* (Delta, 1972).

Lem, Stanislaw. *Microworlds* (Harcourt, Brace & Jovanovich, 1984).

Metzger, Linda, ed. *Contemporary Authors, New Revision Series, Vol. 12* (Gale Research, 1984).

Randles, Jenny. *UFO Reality* (Robert Hale, 1983).

Reich, Wilhelm. *Contact with Space: Orop Desert Ea 1954-55* (Core Pilot, 1957).

Ring, Kenneth. "Precognitive and Prophetic Visions in Near Death Experiences," *Anabiosis: The Journal of Near-Death Studies* (1982).

———. "Prophetic Visions in 1988: A Critical Reappraisal," *The Journal of Near-Death Studies* (Fall 1988).

———. *The Omega Project* (William Morrow, 1992).

Rinsley, Donald B. *Borderline and Self Disorders: A Developmental and Object Relations Perspective* (Jason Aronson, 1981).

Sechehaye, Marguerite. *Autobiography of a Schizophrenic Girl* (Signet/NAL, 1968).

Spring, William J. "Observations on World Destruction Fantasies," *Psychoanalytic Quarterly* (1939).

Strachey, James, ed. *The Standard Edition of the Complete Psychological Works of Sigmund Freud, Vol. 12: The Case of Schreber* (The Hogarth Press, 1963).

Strieber, Whitley. *Communion: A True Story* (William Morrow/Beech Tree, 1987).

———. *Transformation* (William Morrow/Beech Tree, 1988).

Strozier, Charles. *Apocalypse: On the Psychology of Fundamentalism in America* (Beacon, 1994).

Winter, Douglas. *Faces of Fear* (Berkley, 1985).

Woodward, W. E. *Bunk* (Harper, 1923).

APRO   See AERIAL PHENOMENA RESEARCH ORGANIZATION.

archetypes, UFO-ET phenomena as Psychologist Carl G. Jung was the first to term UFO sightings and contacts with them as "archetypal" phenomena in his 1959 book, *Flying Saucers: A Modern Myth of Things Seen in the Sky*. Jung was quick to point out that the word "myth" did not imply something that did not happen. All myths, according to Jung, have a basis in reality; however, myths are embellishments of truth. Jung believed that UFOs had both a psychic (archetypal) and a physical component. The spectacular, physical appearance of an unknown phenomenon (like brilliant manifestations in the sky) stimulated powerful unconscious processes in observers. These unconscious processes were released into the conscious minds of the observers causing them to give meaning to what they had observed. The meaning ascribed to UFO sightings come from the observers' cultural and personal expectations.

For example, UFO reports beginning in the modern era (1949) were often interpreted as a military threat or a possible "alien" invasion.

This was consistent with societal fears caused by the Cold War developing immediately after World War II and the rapid proliferation of nuclear weapons. Some people also saw the emerging UFO phenomenon as representing the coming of a savior. Many people saw a world gone mad and had fervent hopes for an unearthly salvation from the madness. The contactee reports in the 1950s affirmed these expectations.

Basel Broadsheet of 1566

Jung interpreted the UFO phenomenon as a meaningful coincidence—or synchronicity—between a physical occurrence coinciding with an expectant mental state. Many people expected—and feared—uncontrollable disruption in all life. At the same time—and probably unrelated to the ongoing events in humanity—an unknown phenomenon (UFOs) manifested in the skies around the world. This unknown provided people with a screen upon which they could project their unconscious expectations and a "visionary rumor" quickly developed. Jung's famous statement, "*something is seen, but one doesn't know what,*" was his way of describing how this process begins.

When the unknown event is observed, people immediately project meaning on to it and report it to others. As more and more people hear about the reports, this "rumor"—driven by something actually seen but not understood—is perpetuated and strengthened. In this complicated process, archetypal forces are released and provoke a powerful influence on society.

Jung took care to show that a long-term historical record existed showing that spectacular (and unknown) manifestations in the sky had occurred regularly throughout history. He cited Biblical accounts and reproduced the Nuremberg Broadsheet from 1561 and the Basel Broadsheet from 1566 as evidence.

Broadsheets served as the newspapers of that time. The unknown aerial phenomena observed by thousands in Germany during this period were widely reported and generally interpreted as a heavenly battle that was occurring in conjunction with the many religious wars going on in Germany. The present writer has uncovered at least fifty additional broadsheets showing similar phenomena.

Nuremberg Broadsheet of 1561

Jung's thought can be incomprehensible to many people, in part, because it is necessary to be deeply acquainted with his other writings where he explains his terminology in greater detail. Few people have the necessary background or motivation to delve that deeply into his writing and have simply read or skimmed his 1959 book. Many of the examples Jung used to show how archetypes affect humanity come from consistencies in fairy tales, angelic visitations, and even in art. So, the average person envisions an archetype merely as a symbol. Most UFO writers have therefore interpreted Jung's depiction of UFOs as a visionary rumor to mean that the phenomenon is not real in a physical sense—it is a mental process. However, that is not the case.

Jung termed the actual UFO manifestations

as archetypal in nature and quite real. ("Something is seen, but one doesn't know what.") In his vast writings, Jung defined archetypes as "psychoid factors consisting of pure energy." Under the right conditions, these psychoid factors—archetypes—can manifest into physical reality. Jung also related that the archetypes actually exist on the "invisible, ultraviolet end of the light spectrum." In *The Archetype Experience* (Little, 1984) it was explained that the term "psychoid" describes a process that bridges the gap between psychological reality and objective reality—exactly as Jung described it. That is, archetypes are living energy forms (as described by Jung) that can move into the visible portion of the electromagnetic energy spectrum. John Keel's (1970) classic book, *UFOs: Operation Trojan Horse* and *Grand Illusions* (Little, 1994) make similar proposals.

Perhaps the most misunderstood and ignored aspect of Jung's archetypal theory of UFO phenomena was his idea that UFO-like flaps occur at regular, predictable times in a great, cosmic cycle. In the preface to his 1959 book, Jung states that, "reflections such as these are . . . exceedingly unpopular . . ." What he proposed in his preface was that spectacular manifestations occur in the sky roughly every 2,150 years. Each 2,150-year cycle was a transition period between the so-called Platonic Months in the well-known 26,000-year precession of the equinoxes. The Age of Pisces, beginning just before the birth of Christ, was heralded by archetypal manifestations (angels, stars, etc.), and the Age of Aquarius is being heralded by modern UFO sightings. As each age changed, the religious focus of the world changed with it. Jung wrote that the transition period could last for a considerable time period, but that almost no one would comprehend this idea or accept it—a prediction that has proven true up to this point.

—GREGORY L. LITTLE

References

Jung, C. G. *Flying Saucers: A Modern Myth of Things Seen in the Skies* (Routledge & Kegan Paul/Harcourt, Brace & Co. 1959; Signet/NAL, 1969; Princeton University Press, 1978).

———. *Mandala Symbolism* (Princeton University Press, 1959, 1972).

———. *The Archetypes and the Collective Unconscious* (Princeton University Press, 1959, 1969).

———. *On the Nature of the Psyche* (Princeton University Press, 1960, 1969).

———. *Answer to Job* (Princeton University Press, 1960).

———. *Two Essays on Analytical Psychology* (Princeton University Press, 1966).

———. *The Undiscovered Self* (Princeton University Press, 1990).

Keel, John. *UFOs: Operation Trojan Horse* (G.P. Putnam's Sons, 1970).

Little, Gregory L. *The Archetype Experience* (Rainbow Books, 1984).

———. *Grand Illusions* (White Buffalo Books, 1994).

Are We Alone? (Charles Scribner's Sons, 1981). Two University of Virginia science professors, Robert Rood and James Trefil, write the first science book proposing that we humans may be alone in our galaxy because a series of "bottlenecks" make the evolution of life rare if not impossible elsewhere. The first extraterrestrials we meet in space will be our own grandchildren who have migrated from Earth.

—RANDALL FITZGERALD

Are We Alone? (Basic Books, 1995). Paul Davies, an Australian Professor of Natural Philosophy, thinks the extraterrestrial civilizations we eventually meet will be so far advanced they will appear as gods to us. He conjectures that what we know as consciousness is a "fundamental emergent property" and a natural consequence of the laws of physics, meaning "the emergence of consciousness in the universe is more or less guaranteed."

—RANDALL FITZGERALD

Area 51   Also known as "Dreamland," "Groom Lake," or simply "the Ranch," this now semi-secret U.S. government test facility has become in the minds of many the UFO capital of the world. The six-by-ten-mile dry lake bed is located approximately 90 miles northwest of Las Vegas, Nevada, as part of the Nellis Test Range.

Popularly known as "Area 51" the site has a long history of official denial and controversy, which has only intensified outside interest in it. During a 1995 hearing on an environmental pollution suit at the base, then-Secretary of the Air Force Sheila Widnall refused to reveal even the official name of the facility, claiming national security concerns.

Area 51 reportedly began life in the early 1950s, under the unofficial designation "McGinley's Farm," to serve as a test site for the U-2 spy plane. Since then, the facility has allegedly served as a test range for many of America's "black projects," such as the SR-71 "Blackbird" reconnaissance airplane, the F-117 stealth fighter, and other still-undisclosed aerospace vehicles and systems; possibly including the mysterious hypersonic "Aurora," as well as laser-assisted orbital launching systems and particle-beam weapons.

In 1989, a self-described "physicist" by the name of Robert Lazar claimed in a Las Vegas TV interview to have observed and worked with "flying saucers" under test at the neighboring S-4 location (also known as Papoose Dry Lake Bed), while he was employed there as a contractor. Lazar's allegations that the government has recovered, "reverse-engineered," and flight-tested alien saucer-craft are completely unsubstantiated, and his falsified educational and employment histories have been exposed by investigators. Nonetheless, Lazar's claims have brought lasting worldwide attention to the base and himself, which of course is the point. If any of Lazar's claims of secret technology were true, he would be serving a long prison term for violation of his so-called "Majestic" security clearance.

Perhaps one should ask which is more likely: that Lazar can freely reveal to the world his super-secret assignment (for which he was especially chosen) of back-engineering the propulsion systems of captured UFOs, or that this

elusive fellow who drives a red Corvette sporting a license plate that reads "MJ-12," and whose claimed credentials are mostly nonexistent, might have something of a Walter Mitty complex?

Because the Groom Lake facility is in a known, accessible location and because unusual aircraft and unidentified aerial phenomena are sometimes visible from nearby, it has become a magnet for many who wish to observe "UFO events."

The nearby town of Rachel, Nevada, boasts a "Little A'Le'Inn" and a small but continuous stream of tourists looking for UFOs. The state of Nevada has even designated the local road, State Highway 375, as "The Extraterrestrial Highway." A cottage industry of Area 51 experts and alleged witnesses, similar to that of the Roswell, New Mexico, incident, seems to be a permanent part of UFO lore.

Russian satellite photo of runways at Area 51

The U.S. Air Force has resisted allowing this once-secret installation to be scrutinized close-up by uncleared people with no need-to-know. In response to the unwanted worldwide publicity, the government recently expanded the 60-square-mile property to include nearby hills, in an effort to deny would-be observers any high ground from which to photograph tests in Area 51. The government also employs contracted security guards to prevent unauthorized entry to the posted area, and prominent signs warn intruders away with the statement: "deadly force is authorized."

Despite these government attempts, determined UFO buffs have recorded intriguing telescopic videos that show bright lights hovering and zipping about Groom Lake in maneuvers that seem impossible for conventional aircraft. It has been suggested that these pictures may indicate tests of VTOL (vertical takeoff and landing) craft, laser-assisted launch systems, particle-beam weapons, or other developmental projects that combine these or other technologies.

Not surprisingly, the government has also resisted legal efforts by citizens to disclose Area 51's activities. A lawsuit concerning alleged pollution injuries in Area 51 brought the following response on September 20, 1999: In Presidential Determination 99-37, President Clinton said, in part, "I find that it is in the paramount interest of the United States to exempt the United States Air Force's operating location near Groom Lake, Nevada, from any applicable requirement for the disclosure to unauthorized persons of classified information concerning that operating location."

A search of the literature on the World Wide Web provides many speculative articles on the possible uses and significance of Area 51, as well as detailed satellite photographs of the base.

—ARLAN K. ANDREWS

Arnold sighting   The "modern age" of "flying saucers" began with the sighting by Kenneth Arnold on June 24, 1947. Arnold, a civilian pilot, was flying over the Cascade mountains in western Washington State, when he reported seeing nine shiny objects in a chain-like formation flying at an estimated speed of 1,600 miles per hour.

Arnold was thirty-two years old at the time, and the owner of a fire-control equipment company based in Boise, Idaho. He took off from the Chehalis, Washington, airport at 2 P.M. flying his own single-engine plane. He was searching for a lost Marine C-46 transport; a $5,000 reward had been offered for its location.

Kenneth Arnold and his plane

After about one hour aloft, Arnold trimmed out his aircraft and simply observed the terrain. He described the sky as clear. Upon entering the vicinity of Mount Rainier, a sudden brilliant flash lit up the surfaces of his plane. Startled, he began scanning the sky to locate the source. The only other aircraft in sight was a lone DC-4 far to his left and rear, too far away to have been the source of the flash. The flash occurred again, and this time he caught the direction from which it came. To his left and to the north he saw nine brightly illuminated objects flying in a chain-like formation from north to south.

Arnold was no stranger to this territory, as

A re-creation of the scene according to Arnold's description (Drawing by Susan Swiatek)

he had flown in the area many times before. This was one aspect of the sighting that made many people take it seriously. Not only was he a ''solid citizen'' and a respected business-man, but an experienced mountain pilot as well; and he saw something that was truly un-usual to him.

The objects appeared to come from the vi-cinity of Mount Baker and were staying close to the mountaintops, swerving in and out of the highest peaks. Noticing this, Arnold was able to calculate their speed. The distance be-tween Mount Rainier and Mount Adams was forty-seven miles and the ''objects'' crossed this distance in one minute and forty-two sec-onds. This translates into 1,656.71 miles per hour, nearly three times as fast as the capabil-ity of any aircraft at that time. (The top speed of the F-80 ''Shooting Star'' was 605 mph, and the top speed of the F-84 ''Thunderjet'' and F-84F ''Thunderstreak'' was 620 mph.)

The objects, furthermore, had a strange ap-pearance, which Arnold said he could observe plainly (though this point is questionable, since he was observing from an estimated distance of twenty-three miles); they had wings, he said, but no tails. One was almost crescent-shaped, with a small dome midway between the wingtips; the others were ''flat like a pie pan and so shiny they reflected the sun in a mirror.'' Their motion was also weird: ''like speedboats on rough water'' or, to use Ar-nold's most famous phrase, ''they flew like a saucer would if you skipped it across the water.'' The duration of the sighting was two to three minutes.

After giving his original account to news-men at Pendleton, Oregon, airport, the story soon broke worldwide, over the radio and via the press. The news reporter who is generally credited with coining the term ''flying saucer'' is William C. Bequette, who at the time worked in the newsroom of the Pendleton *East Oregonian*. (See the POSTSCRIPT to this entry for more information on this.)

Arnold originally described the objects for the Air Force as being nearly round but slightly longer than wide. But in the book he

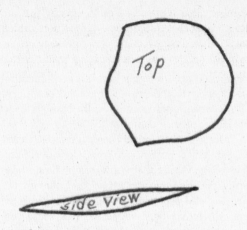

A tracing of Arnold's original sketch for the U.S. Air Force

wrote with Ray Palmer there appears a draw-ing of a quite different shape, looking almost like a crescent moon with a small, speckled circle located midway between the wingtips.

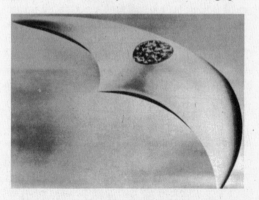

Photo of a model of one of the objects Arnold reportedly saw

For fourteen years, Arnold had refrained from endorsing any special theory to account for his sighting. He steadfastly rejected any possibility of a mirage or illusion of any sort, insisting that he saw something that was flying through the air, just as he was, at 9,500 feet. But, what is not widely known is that Arnold is a ''repeater,'' i.e., he claims to have seen several more UFOs since his famous sighting in 1947. In *Flying Saucers* magazine of November 1962 (edited and published by the late Ray Palmer), Arnold took a position which must have shocked many who relied upon his original sighting as corroborative evidence for the extraterrestrial-spaceship theory to account for UFOs. He wrote:

> After some fourteen years of extensive research, it is my conclusion that the so-called unidentified flying objects that have been seen in our atmosphere are not space ships from another planet at all, but are groups and masses of living organisms that are as much a part of our atmosphere and space as the life we find in the depths of our oceans. The only major difference in the space and atmospheric organisms are that they have the natural ability to change their densities at will.

And, in a special issue of *Look* magazine devoted to flying saucers, Arnold was quoted as saying: "The impression I have held after observing these strange objects a second time was that they were something alive rather than machines—a living organism of some type that apparently has the ability to change its density similar to fish that are found in our oceans without losing their apparent identity."

After reviewing such bizarre testimony, perhaps there is little wonder why the U.S. Air Force could not explain what Arnold actually saw on 24 June 1947. As in all cases of alleged UFO sightings, no matter who investigates the case, the investigator is severely limited by the testimony of the witness. Astronomer J. Allen Hynek (who served as the scientific consultant to the U.S. Air Force's Projects Sign and Blue Book from 1948 to 1969) first thought that Arnold saw a fleet of jet aircraft and that the estimated distance between the objects and the witness was wrong.

Debunkers have paraded a long list of explanations over the following half century including clouds, mirages, balloons, earthlights, hallucinations, and hoaxes.

More recently, the theory has been offered by James Easton—and endorsed by Martin Kottmeyer—that what Arnold actually saw was a flock of American White Pelicans, which were much closer to Arnold than he realized. The behavior and appearance of the "objects" as described by Arnold seem to be more consistent with this answer than anything else.

(1) Appearance (wings, but no tails);
(2) Formation ("very similar to a formation of geese");
(3) Flight characteristics ("they fluttered and sailed, tipping their wings alternately and emitting those very bright blue-white flashes from their surfaces").

Arnold also stated that he ". . . did not get the impression that these flashes were emitted by them, but rather that it was the sun's reflection from the extremely highly polished surface of their wings."

But, the Arnold sighting was an exciting story in 1947, and the one that triggered public interest and official U.S. Air Force involvement in the UFO controversy. It is also a sighting that is technically unexplained.

—RONALD D. STORY

References

Arnold, Kenneth, and Ray Palmer. *The Coming of the Saucers* (privately published, 1952).

Arnold, Kenneth. *Flying Saucers* (November 1962).

"Flying Saucers," a *Look* magazine special by the editors of United Press International and Cowles Communications (1967).

Story, Ronald D. *UFOs and the Limits of Science* (William Morrow, 1981).

Story, Ronald D., ed. *The Encyclopedia of UFOs* (Doubleday/New English Library, 1980).

POSTSCRIPT: In early 1992, I was working as a technical editor on a temporary contract assignment at the Hanford nuclear site in southeastern Washington State, about 70 miles north of Pendleton, Oregon. One Sunday, as I flipped through the *Tri-City Herald*, I noticed an editorial by retired editor William C. Bequette. I thought the name sounded familiar, and a small photo of the guest editor showed him to be just about the right age.

It then dawned on me who this was. I proceeded to look up his number in the local telephone directory (for Kennewick, Richland, and Pasco) and decided to give him a call. When Mr. Bequette answered the phone, I asked whether he was the newsman who had interviewed Kenneth Arnold for the *East Oregonian,* in 1947, and coined the term "flying saucer." He said he was.

I just had to ask a few questions for historical interest—and to satisfy my own curiosity—and Mr. Bequette kindly obliged me with a very pleasant 30-minute telephone conversation. I first wanted to know the story behind the term "flying saucer" itself. There has always been a controversy about the Arnold case concerning whether the term "saucer" referred to the object's motion or shape. Even in Arnold's book, *The Coming of the Saucers*, co-authored with Ray Palmer in 1951, the term "saucer" was used only to describe the objects' motion. The famous quote is: ". . . they flew like a saucer would if you skipped it across the water." The shape is depicted variously as a crescent or flying wing, a pie pan, and a giant washer with a hole in the middle. But Bequette told me that Arnold used the term to describe the objects' *shape* as well as its motion. He said that Arnold definitely described the objects as "saucer-shaped," and that is how the term "flying saucer" was born.

I recently read somewhere that Bequette has said otherwise, but I can only repeat what he confirmed to me: that he was indeed the man who coined the term "flying saucer," which was based on Arnold's description of both the objects' appearance and motion. If the reporters and witnesses change and/or confuse their stories—which often happens in UFOlogy—what can you do?

—RONALD D. STORY

Ashtar Command   A title used to describe an intergalactic, multidimensional federation of benevolent extraterrestrials, under the supreme jurisdiction of a being named "Ashtar" or "Ashtar Sheran," said to be a higher dimensional ET ship commander. The phenomenon of physical and/or telepathic contact with Ashtar seems to have begun with the 1950s contactees, and continues globally to the present day.

—SCOTT MANDELKER

astrogenesis   This term was coined by the editor of this encyclopedia (Ronald Story) to designate the particular theory that Biblical references to the "Elohim" or extraterrestrial "gods" having created human beings closely parallel the modern conception of god-like beings coming here from outer space.

Even in our enlightened age (at the dawn of the 21st century) the most intelligent species on this planet (supposedly Homo sapiens) is split on the question of its origins. About 50 percent believe in the received doctrine of official science: Darwin's theory of evolution as modified by the modern scientific community. According to this view, the magic ingredient to evolutionary development is time. Agreeing with the Bible in that man (or Adam) was derived from the dust of the Earth—after possible seeding from the heavens—most scientists think that given sufficient time, atoms just naturally evolve into molecules, and molecules eventually evolve into thinking anthropoids. All of this occurs through a process of random mutation, natural selection, and survival of the fittest, they say. Admittedly, this is a bit oversimplified; but the key point is that for most self-respecting scientific types, no intelligent intervention is required.

Another view, held by the other half of the world's population, is that the world and its inhabitants were not the result of accidental forces (but that some form of intelligence was required). Those who favor this idea are divided into various factions, all of which represent some form of special creation.

The religious fundamentalists say that God is the Creator. However, their version of God, the Father, has an uncanny resemblance to our own fathers or at least the common childhood concept. Freud's theory was that God is indeed the father—writ large—as derived from our own exaggerated concept conceived in infancy.

Another version of special creation, and one that is more compatible with modern science than the views of the religious fundamentalists is the space-god theory—or what I prefer to call "astrogenesis." This view is, in effect, a space-age Genesis: a creation story featuring mankind as the product of a cosmic experiment being carried out not by the traditional Judeo-Christian God, but by advanced extraterrestrials who, because of attributes acquired during their own long evolution, might themselves be defined as gods.

The popularity of this view in recent times is clearly attributable to author Erich von Däniken, who resurrected the concept (in tandem with the release of Arthur C. Clarke and Stanley Kubrick's *2001: A Space Odyssey*) three decades ago, and has since sold more than 50 million books on the subject.

While many do not accept all his examples of alleged extraterrestrial evidence, there seems to be growing support for the underlying thesis that extraterrestrial intervention holds the key to our origin and purpose on this planet.

What is the nature of the evidence for astrogenesis? There are two major categories: (1) artifacts and (2) contact myths. The artifacts usually take the form of impressive monuments—such as the Egyptian pyramids and other gigantic stone structures—which seemingly were beyond the capabilities of mere humans to create. Thus, it is argued that advanced extraterrestrial science must have been required. The contact myths, found worldwide, share an intriguing consistency in their tales of super-beings coming from the sky to create mankind and instruct him in how to live.

For some, the theory of astrogenesis brings science and religion closer together. For others, it represents a travesty of both. This writer believes that we should strive to be as objective and open-minded as possible to allow for new discoveries. Keeping an open mind does not mean ignoring the facts, however, as one can see by reading my previous books on this sub-

ject: *The Space-Gods Revealed* (1976) and *Guardians of the Universe?* (1980). Both studies dealt extensively with the question of alleged extraterrestrial science and found none.

What I found was that if you take each of the examples of "alien technology" (as alleged by von Däniken, et al.) and subject them to the normal rules of evidence, they fall apart. For one thing, the level of technology required for the construction of the various artifacts and monuments in question never exceeds the capabilities of Earthmen working on their own in the context of their own cultures. The archaeological "wonders" that are alleged to prove, or at least "indicate," ancient astronauts comprise a collection of interesting finds, superficially described and taken out of context. In most cases, when looking more deeply into the matter—as opposed to playing the "it looks like . . ." game—one finds the omission of highly relevant, key information that if known casts an entirely different light on the subject at hand. These "sins of omission" are unfortunately typical of all the leading proponents of ancient astronauts.

So, leaving aside the issue of physical evidence at this time, let us consider the world's most popular contact myth: the Holy Bible. The implications are enormous. If indeed the Bible does refer to extraterrestrials (which it does, in one sense or another), it tells their purpose and ours. It tells us where we came from, our mission on Earth, and what we can expect in the future—depending on whether or not we follow the teachings of the Bible. If we obey the Ten Commandments (and the other universal laws taught in the Bible) and have faith that Jesus Christ is our savior, we are told that we will not only be saved, but that we can achieve immortality like the gods.

In essence, the Bible is a creation story and operating manual for life on planet Earth. Whether it is interpreted supernaturally or scientifically, one cannot escape its central message—that *we are not alone*. Nor can anyone deny that here we are dealing with an account of superior extraterrestrial forces coming down out of the heavens to intervene in the lives of mortal human beings. This is literally what the Bible says.

These gods (the Elohim) first create man in their image, and then attempt to impart ultimate principles (or Cosmic Laws) for him to live by. What is promised, if we choose to obey these laws, is nothing less than everlasting life. Put simply, we are given vital instructions on how to achieve immortality—individually and as a species. These laws, such as the Ten Commandments and the lessons of Jesus, constitute the "good" or benevolent God (or gods) versus the "evil" forces (or dark side) of the universe. These laws, known as the "word of God," tell us how to live in harmony with nature and find our rightful place in a universe of immortal souls. Whatever your interpretation, God and his angels (including the fallen angels) are de facto extraterrestrials and represent ultimate authority, any way you look at it. That is the key point.

An important question often asked by skeptics is: "If extraterrestrials exist, why is there no open contact?" One answer to this question is that if the Bible is to be taken literally, then we have had open contact. According to both the Old and New Testaments, extraterrestrial forces representing the classic struggle of good versus evil (gods and demons) have intervened in the creation and development of humankind and may be planning a return visit as indicated in the Book of Revelation.

We know what happened last time, when Jesus tried to convert the masses to follow the "word of God." According to the prophecies of Revelation, we should clearly expect something different next time. For one thing—no more Mr. Nice Guy!

This writer's position is that if we are to take the Bible literally, then logically speaking, the concept of technologically superior beings from other worlds in space is at least as reasonable as the traditional supernatural interpretation. In addition, we have the moral and religious teachings kept intact as well, if we view the Biblical messages as the philosophy of advanced civilizations (representing good and evil factions) each vying for control.

—RONALD D. STORY

astronauts, UFO sightings by The glamour and drama of manned space flights have been transferred to the UFO field via a highly publicized group of "UFO sightings" and photographs allegedly made by American and Russian space pilots. Hardly a UFO book or movie fails to mention that "astronauts have seen UFOs too."

However, careful examination of each and every one of these stories can produce quite reasonable explanations, in terms of visual phenomena associated with space flights. On a visit to NASA's Johnson Manned Spacecraft Center in Houston in July 1976, Dr. J. Allen Hynek, of the Center for UFO Studies, concluded that none of the authentic cases (as opposed to the majority of reports, which are fictitious) really had anything to do with the "real UFO phenomenon."

UFO skeptics, while pleased that Hynek had dismissed all "astronaut UFO reports" as unreliable, have insisted that this body of stories has quite a lot to do with the major problems besetting the UFO community. How, they ask, can a body of stories so patently false and unreliable obtain such seeming authenticity simply by being passed back and forth among researchers without ever being seriously investigated? Is this a characteristic of UFO stories in general, and if so, the skeptics ask, can a study of how the "astronaut UFO" myth began and flourished help us to understand better the UFO phenomenon in general?

Hynek's disavowal of the stories came after publication of his book, *The Edge of Reality* (1975), which carried a long list of astronaut-sighting reports. Hynek told colleagues that the inclusion of the list (compiled by UFOlogist George Fawcett) in the book was Jacques Vallée's idea, not his, but that even so, he just wanted to generate interest and discussion. He insisted that inclusion of the list was not a judgment on his belief in its credibility and that readers had no right to assume that the data had actually been verified just because it was included. Fawcett, on the other hand, claims that he just assembled the list from all available sources and assumed that somebody else would check the accounts before publication. "Maybe one percent of the stories are true UFOs," Fawcett suggested in 1978.

Here is the complete "Fawcett List" quoted from *The Edge of Reality* but, this time, including likely explanations (in italics) of the reports:

(1) "February 20, 1962—John Glenn, piloting his Mercury capsule, saw three objects follow him and then overtake him at varying speeds." *Glenn also said that these "snow-flakes" were small, and seemed to be coming from the rear end of his capsule. Astronauts on later flights also observed them and were able to create "snowstorms" by banging on the walls of their capsules.*

(2) "May 24, 1962—Mercury VII: Scott Carpenter reported photographing firefly-like objects with a hand camera and that he had what looked like a good shot of a saucer." *Carpenter did see "fireflies," as well as a balloon ejected from his capsule. The claim that he reported photographing a "saucer" is counterfeit. His photo, taking into account the glare of sunlight, smeared window, and gross enlargement of the small image, has been widely published as a "saucer" but is in fact the tracking balloon.*

(3) "May 30, 1962—XI5 Pilot Joe Walton photographed five disc-like objects." *This story appears to be a complete fabrication. The real pilot's name was Joe Walker, who supports no such claim.*

(4) "July 17, 1962—X15 Pilot Robert White photographed objects about thirty feet away from his craft while about fifty-eight miles up." *Right, and he also reported that the objects were small—"about the size of a piece of paper." They were probably flakes of ice off the supercold fuel tanks.*

(5) "May 16, 1963—Mercury IX: Gordon Cooper reported a greenish UFO with a red tail during his fifteenth orbit. He also reported other mysterious sightings over South America and Australia. The object he sighted over Perth, Australia, was caught on screens by ground tracking stations." *Cooper has recently denounced all stories of UFOs on his space flights as fabrications—this one included. The multicolor UFO is probably based on a misquotation of Cooper's postflight report on a sighting of the Aurora Australis.*

(6) "October 3, 1963—Mercury VIII: Walter Schirra reported large glowing masses over the Indian Ocean." *Indeed he did, referring to lightning-lit cloud masses over the nighttime ocean a hundred miles below.*

(7) "March 8, 1964—Voskhod 2: Russian cosmonauts reported an unidentified object just as they entered the Earth's atmosphere." *Several hours before returning to Earth the cosmonauts spotted a cylinder-shaped object they assumed (probably correctly) was just another man-made satellite. Such sightings were becoming more and more frequent as the number of manned flights and unmanned satellites rose.*

(8) "June 3, 1964—Gemini IV: Jim McDivitt reported he photographed several strange objects, including a cylindrical object with arms sticking out and an egg-shaped UFO with some sort of exhaust." *This is the most famous "astronaut-UFO" case and it has been embellished and distorted in dozens of publications. McDivitt saw a "beer can-shaped" object, which he took to be another man-made satellite (some observers believe it was his own booster rocket), and tried to take a few photos which did not turn out. A still from the movie camera was mistakenly released without the astronaut's review, showing what turned out to be a light reflection off his copilot's window, according to McDivitt. Some UFO buffs became excited about this photo and acclaimed it as one of the best UFO photos ever taken, showing (they claim) a glowing object with a plasma tail. But, McDivitt denies he saw anything like that in space.*

(9) "October 12, 1964—Voskhod 1: Three

Russian cosmonauts reported they were surrounded by a formation of swiftly moving disc-shaped objects.'' This story appears to be a complete fabrication but certain UFO believers cling to it while challenging skeptics to approve it did NOT happen.''

(10) ''December 4, 1965—Gemini VIII: Frank Borman and Jim Lovell photographed twin oval-shaped UFOs with glowing undersides.'' *This famous photograph is a blatant forgery (by sensationalist elements of the media), in which light reflections off the nose of the spacecraft were later made to look like UFOs, by airbrushing away the vehicle structure around them.*

(11) ''July 18, 1966—Gemini X: John Young and Mike Collins saw a large, cylindrical object accompanied by two smaller, bright objects, which Young photographed. NASA failed to pick them up on screens.'' *The astronauts reported two bright fragments near their spacecraft soon after launch, presumably pieces of the booster or of some other satellite. No photos were taken. They were out of range of NASA radar at this point anyway.*

(12) ''September 12, 1966—Gemini XI: Richard Gordon and Charles Conrad reported a yellow-orange UFO about six miles from them. It dropped down in front of them and then disappeared when they tried to photograph it.'' *The astronauts described the close passage of another space satellite, identified by NORAD as the Russian Proton-3 satellite (an identification later disproved by Bruce Maccabee). The men got three fuzzy photos which, much blown up, have been widely published. But their eyesight accounts describe a solid satellite-looking object on a ballistic non-maneuvering path.*

(13) ''November 11, 1966—Gemini XIII: Jim Lovell and Edwin Aldrin saw four UFOs linked in a row. Both spacemen said the objects were not stars.'' *Indeed they were not, since the astronauts were talking about four bags of trash they had thrown overboard an hour earlier!*

(14) ''December 21, 1968—Apollo VIII: Frank Borman and Jim Lovell reported a 'bogie'—an unidentified object—ten miles up.'' *Actually, Borman referred to a ''bogie'' on his first space flight three years before, describing some pieces of debris associated with his spacecraft's separation from the booster rocket. The reference to Apollo VIII is careless, possibly even fictitious.*

(15) ''July 16, 1969—Apollo XI: This was a mission on which a UFO reportedly chased the spacecraft.'' *''Reportedly,'' indeed, but not very accurate. Actually, several UFO stories have attached themselves barnacle-like to man's first moon landing. A photo of an insulation fragment taken soon after third-stage separation has been widely published as a ''UFO.'' The astronauts watched their booster through a telescope on the way to the moon. A series of ''UFO photos'' allegedly taken by astronaut Aldrin in lunar orbit are actually forgeries by a Japanese UFO magazine. An alleged ''astronaut radio conversation'' describing a UFO ambush is a hoax.*

The ''UFO'' at the right in this NASA photograph is actually an insulation fragment from the Apollo XI rocket.

(16) ''November 14, 1969—Apollo XII: Astronauts Pete Conrad, Alan Bean, and Dick Gordon said a UFO accompanied them to within 132,000 miles of the moon, preceding them all the way.'' *They never said that. They were joking with the ground control about a tumbling piece of their booster rocket which was flashing in the sky. Certain UFO buffs completely misunderstood the meaning of the conversation and conjured up a UFO. On the*

way back to Earth, the astronauts were puzzled by a light between them and the Earth which turned out to be the reflection of the moon behind them on the nighttime Indian Ocean below.

Many other "astronaut reports" have been added to this list, including photographs from Skylab (of a passing satellite, distorted by some camera artifact), from Apollo lunar flights (movies showing debris floating around inside the cabin), and from other Mercury and Gemini flights. None, when investigated with an appreciation of the actual space-flight environment, appears to be "extraordinary" or "unusual," although many sightings of passing satellites remain technically "unidentified" because the actual satellites have never been named (since nobody has taken the trouble to spend the necessary time searching computer memory banks).

The entire phenomenon of the "astronaut UFO sightings," however, does explicitly demonstrate the carelessness and lack of verification among certain UFO circles eager to exchange the latest, hottest stories without any regard for authenticity or accuracy. UFO skeptics have claimed that this characteristic is not limited to the "astronaut UFO sightings." The topic is not one to which some UFO specialists can point with pride in their own behavior and standards of reliability.

Nevertheless it is still commonly claimed that there exists some sort of "cover-up" by NASA of secret photographs and/or voice transcripts from space. In fact, every photograph taken by NASA in space is available for publication and can be inspected by accredited news media representatives (there are tens of thousands of photos and no way to arrange public viewing). Volumes and volumes of voice transcripts are readily available at NASA/Houston.

Astronauts are often quoted about UFOs. Sometimes the "quotations" are completely fictitious! Only one astronaut claims to have seen a UFO in space; and that is James McDivitt, who stipulates that his definition of a UFO covers the probability that his object was some other man-made satellite which has not been identified. He does not think it was an alien space vehicle or any such similar "real UFO" manifestation.

—JAMES E. OBERG

atomic bomb and UFOs   Imagine a U.S. government project involving many of the world's top scientists developing a fantastic new technology, requiring the services of thousands of workers in three separate locations, yet a project so secret that not even the Vice President knew about it. "Area 51" perhaps? No, it was the Manhattan Project, which developed the atomic bomb.

Of course there was a war on, so the secrecy that surrounded the Manhattan Project was easier to maintain and more acceptable to the public. Still, it was extraordinary. The people who lived around Los Alamos, New Mexico (the scientific center for the project), knew that something was going on at "the Hill" behind all that barbed wire—they just didn't know what. The government deliberately and successfully spread false rumors about the project.

Even the test of the first atomic bomb at the Trinity site in New Mexico on July 16, 1945, the largest man-made explosion ever (at the time), was kept secret. The test site was remote, but thousands of unauthorized people saw the explosion. The cover story was that a large ammunition magazine had blown up. Local newspapers were pressured to not add any additional details or speculate about other explanations.

A cub reporter for a Chicago newspaper got a call from a man who had been traveling through the area and told her, in great detail, about the crash of a huge meteorite. She wrote a short article about it. The next day she found herself being grilled by FBI agents and as a result promised to write no more about "the meteorite."

A few weeks later, after atom bombs had been dropped on Japan, and the war came to an end, information about what had been accomplished, and how, began to come out—

though the full story would not be revealed for years.

It was the birth of the Atomic Age in 1945—even more than the birth of the Space Age—more than a dozen years later, that profoundly influenced the development of UFO beliefs.

People realized that the government was capable of covering up even such an enormous development. Then there was the psychological impact of "the Bomb" itself. After the initial "we won the war" euphoria was over, the reality that humanity had developed the power with which to destroy itself set in. When flying saucer reports began in 1947, there was much speculation that it was the atomic explosions themselves that had attracted the attention of the extraterrestrials.

There was also a widespread belief that nuclear war was inevitable, that the human race did not have the ability to save itself, and could only be saved by extraterrestrial intervention. That was the theme of much early UFO science fiction, like the film *The Day the Earth Stood Still* (1951) and of many of the early contactee tales of the "Space Brothers."

This connection—between the atomic bomb and UFOs—was reinforced by the fact that a large number of the most important UFO cases took place in the same desert southwest where the Bomb was developed and tested. There was Roswell, of course, and the variety of other "flying saucer crashes" that were supposed to have taken place in the same general area. There were many UFO reports from the area of the Alamogordo Bombing Range, where the Trinity site was located. Later there was the well-publicized Socorro, New Mexico, case; Socorro being one of the population centers closest to Los Alamos.

—DANIEL COHEN

Aveley (England) abduction On a Sunday evening, the Avis family was driving home after a visit with relatives at Harold Hill, when they experienced, first, a UFO sighting, then, a green mist that enveloped their car and a "time loss" (apparent amnesia) of about three hours. Three years following the alleged events, time-regression hypnosis was used to "unlock" memories of an apparent abduction of the Avis family (involving teleportation of their car) by strange creatures on board the UFO.

The story concerns John and Elaine Avis (pseudonyms), a young married couple with three children. They had been visiting some relatives at Harold Hill, Essex (near London), on October 27, 1974, but had been delayed longer than they had expected. (John had wanted to be home by 10:20 P.M. to see a particular television program.) The family left at 9:50 P.M. for the normal twenty-minute drive back to the quiet village of Aveley; and no problems were anticipated. Karen and Stuart, the two younger children, were asleep on the backseat, and seven-year-old Kevin was awake, listening to the local radio station.

Kevin was the first to spot a pale blue, oval light traveling alongside the car over the open fields. Elaine and John discussed possibilities, but none seemed to fit properly. They watched for some minutes, as it was intermittently obscured by trees and scattered houses, alongside the road. They came to accept the object as a UFO, but thought no more of it than that. As the car entered some very dark and lonely stretches of road on the outskirts of Aveley, they saw the light pass across the road in front of them and disappear.

The Avises drove on for about a mile, and were quite close to home. The time was about 10:10 P.M. Suddenly, the couple was overcome by a feeling that something was wrong; all sounds in their car seemed to vanish. The radio started to crackle and smoke, and with an instinctive reaction, John ripped out the wiring. Then the headlights went out, but not before they had caught sight of an eerie block of green mist enveloping the road in front of them. The car jerked as it entered the mist. There was silence and a strange coldness. Then, within what seemed like about a second, they left the mist with another jerk, and things apparently returned to normal.

What happened when the car came out of

the mist is uncertain. John recalled only the car being a half mile farther along the road, and feeling as if he were alone. The car was functioning normally. Elaine's memory returned yet another half mile farther. Kevin was awake, but the other children were still asleep. Within a few minutes, the family had reached home.

Thinking that there were still several minutes before the TV show he had planned to watch, John rewired the radio quickly and checked the lighting system of the car. Elaine took the children up to bed and checked the clock. She was amazed to find that it was 1 A.M.; almost three hours had vanished.

The next day, Elaine told her mother about the green mist and the strange light but not about the time loss. They also decided it would be best to forget it. Apart from a deep weariness the next day, there were no ill effects felt at the time.

However, over the next three years, the lifestyle of the Avis family underwent a dramatic change. John had a nervous breakdown, for no apparent reason, within months. Both he and Elaine then began to gain enormously in self-confidence. Kevin, who was a backward reader at school, suddenly shot ahead in leaps and bounds. Within months, the whole family except Stuart stopped eating meat. In fact, they could not even stand the smell of it. Smoking and alcohol were also cut out. (John had previously smoked sixty to seventy cigarettes per day.) Eventually, the couple began to link their behavior change to the UFO, the green mist, and whatever happened during the missing three hours. They wanted to find out if there could be a connection, and in mid-1977, they reported the incident to local UFO investigators.

Andy Coffins and Barry King pursued the investigation for the British *Flying Saucer Review* and found that both John and Elaine (Kevin was not involved in the investigation by mutual agreement) had suffered peculiar dreams since the experience (which, according to their testimony, were not discussed with one another until questioned by investigators). The dreams were about weird creatures and examinations in theater-type operating rooms.

A qualified hypnotist, Dr. Leonard Wilder, a dental surgeon by profession, was brought into the case and apparently released memories that had heretofore been buried in the Avises subconscious minds. After only two sessions with the hypnotist, John and Elaine began remembering details from that "missing period" on their own.

A graphic account of the "missing three hours" was obtained. It seemed that, when inside the green mist, the car (with the Avis family in it) had been teleported up a column of light into a very large "craft." John, Elaine, and Kevin were separated (the other two children remained asleep) and given "medical examinations" by four-foot-tall creatures looking something like birds. In contrast to these beings were some tall entities (over six and a half feet tall) wearing "lurex" suits, and balaclava helmets, who gave John and Elaine a tour around the ship. The tour included an explanation of the ship's propulsion system, and John was even shown a holographic "map" of a section of the "universe" (galaxy?), which included the aliens' home planet. (John believes that visual information was implanted into his brain, to be triggered at a later date.) The Avises were eventually returned to their car, which, in turn, was teleported back down to a spot on the road, about a half mile beyond where they were abducted.

The true nature of this case is difficult to determine or to comprehend. There is no proof for or against an actual encounter with alien beings, even though, perhaps, the "abductees" firmly believe that to be the answer. Regardless of the final outcome of this case, if an explanation is forthcoming, be it from a physical or psychological perspective, that explanation should add to our knowledge in one of those two general areas.

—JENNY RANDLES

Avensa airline hoax This photo was originally submitted to the Aerial Phenomena Research Organization (APRO) by a Mr. Delio

Ribas, of Valera, State of Trujillo, Venezuela, in October 1966. Only the print was available for analysis, as the negative remained in the possession of the pilot who took the picture.

In his letter, Mr. Ribas said the photograph was taken sometime in 1965 by a pilot friend of his employed by the Avensa Airline, while they were on a flight between the city of Barcelona and the international Maiquetia Airport. He stated that ". . .the airline pilot who took the photograph and myself are absolutely certain that the object is one of the so-called 'flying saucers.' The pilot does not wish to speak much on the subject because he has been the object of ridicule by some of his Venezuelan fellow pilots and also certain pilot friends in the USAF. . . ."

Mr. Fernando de Calvet, a professional topographer and geometrician, made a study of the position of the shadows and demonstrated mathematically that all of the objects and details in the photograph have a self-consistent geometry. Also, Mr. Konrad Honeck, an electronics engineer, and Mr. Miguel Sapowsky, another engineer in charge of the technical department of a large Caracas television station, substantiated de Calvet's explanation.

In 1971, the photo was studied by APRO consultant Dr. B. Roy Frieden of the University of Arizona's Optical Sciences Center. Dr.

APRO

This "flying saucer" turned out to be a button superimposed on the background scene.

Frieden noted that the "UFO" seemed too sharp to be a large distant object, and then determined that its shadow was far less dense than the shadow of the plane, indicating that it had been drawn in. Finally, an engineer in Caracas, Venezuela, confessed to hoaxing the photo. His motive: revenge against "UFO buffs" who had ridiculed him for not believing in "flying saucers."

He did it by placing a photo of a button onto an enlargement of the aerial shot, which was then rephotographed; he then "burned" in the "UFO" shadow, when the print was made.

B

B-57 bomber photo Originally intended as merely a promotional shot of the Martin (Canberra) B-57 bomber, the photograph—which seems to clearly show more than one aeroform—found its way to NICAP (the National Investigations Committee on Aerial Phenomena) and subsequently became a UFO-photo classic. It was taken near Edwards Air Force Base in California about 1954.

According to Mr. Ralph Rankow, who analyzed the photo for NICAP: "No one actually reported seeing, with their own eyes, the saucerlike object in the upper right portion of the picture. Even so, the object evoked such curiosity that another flight was reportedly made over the same area to look for ground reflec-

tions that might have caused it—although I understand none were observed. . . .

"A close scrutiny of the B-57 photo shows the trees, bushes, and houses all casting long shadows, but the object throws no shadows on the ground whatsoever. Moreover (and this point is very important), the dark parts of the object are much too strong to be so far away. As the trees, bushes, and houses get farther away, the haze cuts down their intensity and contrast. And the wooded area in the distance directly behind the object is fuzzy and weak by comparison with the strong highlights and shadows on the UFO itself.

"In my analysis report to NICAP, I also pointed out that the object obviously had di-

Photo of B-57 bomber with apparent UFO (upper right corner)

Close-up of UFO

doing research at the University of Kentucky from 1970 to 1990.

Robert A. Baker

mension. Its pattern of light and shadow is consistent with the rest of the picture, with the sun low and coming from the left. The object is also symmetrically shaped and contains all tones of gray, from white to black.''

The Martin Aircraft Company never could satisfactorily explain what the second image was. It appeared to be following their B-57 plane in flight, although they tried to persuade UFO investigators that it was merely a ''scratch'' or ''rub'' on the film. The curious photo underwent a series of unexplained ''touch up'' jobs by the Martin Company during the course of their supplying prints to different UFO investigators.

Three different versions of the photo exist: (1) the original (which is reproduced here), (2) one with a scratch across the UFO (producing a jagged appearance), and (3) one with the UFO nearly blotted out. No one could ever supply a satisfactory reason for the touch-ups, nor a solution to the mystery of the UFO in the original picture.

—RONALD D. STORY

Baker, Robert A., Jr. (b. 1921). A native Kentuckian and World War II veteran, Dr. Baker received his B.S. and M.S. degrees from the University of Kentucky and his Ph.D. degree in psychology from Stanford in 1952. Following employment as an MIT Research Psychologist and a similar position with the U.S. Army, Baker also worked as a clinical and forensic psychologist before teaching and

Dr. Baker has published over 100 professional journal articles, is editor of several collections of scientific humor (as well as a history of the American detective story) and had edited several textbooks. He has also written *They Call It Hypnosis* (1990), *Missing Pieces* (with Joe Nickell), *Hidden Memories* (1995), *Mind Games* (1996), and most recently, he has edited *Child Sexual Abuse and False Memory Syndrome* (1999). He is also a Fellow of the American Psychological Association as well as CSICOP (Committee for the Scientific Investigation of Claims of the Paranormal) and a regular contributor to *The Skeptical Inquirer* and *Skeptical Briefs* regarding UFOs, aliens and alleged abductees.

Address: 3495 Castleton Hill
Lexington, KY 40517
U.S.A.

POSITION STATEMENT: My conviction is that historians of future generations will look at the current ET hypothesis, with its UFOs and alien abductions, as the greatest mass delusion of the 20th century—equivalent in all respects to the 19th century's Age of Spiritualism with its ghosts, mediums, and seances. What is truly mind-boggling is the ease with which a few zealous salesmen of the supernatural convinced millions there was something to their nonsense. Raised on a steady diet of *Star Wars, Star Trek,* and *The X-Files,* and aided by wishful thinking, pseudo-science and pop-psychology, the average citizen was ready to be persuaded that the truth was, indeed, "out there" and that an evil and conspiratorial government was denying him and her their "right to know." Future students of the behavioral sciences will, literally, "have a ball" dissecting this massive irrationality.

—ROBERT A. BAKER

Balwyn (Australia) photo Said to have been taken by a prominent Melbourne businessman on April 2, 1966, the Balwyn photo has appeared in numerous books and films, and is always represented as a "genuine UFO."

According to the story, at 2:20 P.M. the man was in his garden using up the remaining film in his Polaroid camera. Suddenly, he said, a bright reflection caught his eye. As he looked up, he saw a bell-shaped object hovering, on its side, over a house. The man snapped the photo, whereupon the object accelerated at great speed and took off in a northerly direction. He estimated the object was about 20 to 25 feet in diameter and at an altitude of about 150 feet.

However, when the photo was examined by Aerial Phenomena Research Organization consultant Dr. B. Roy Frieden, Professor of Optical Sciences at the University of Arizona, he found that the chimney in the lower part of the photo was more blurred than the alleged UFO, which prompted him to examine the photo more closely. He then found a jagged line of discontinuity running across the center of the photo, through the cloud field, which suggests that there are actually two separate photos joined together and rephotographed to make the one.

—APRO

Behind the Flying Saucers (Henry Holt, 1950). *Variety* columnist Frank Scully wrote this book based on a series of 1949 columns

Balwyn, Australia, "UFO"

he wrote for the show business tabloid describing how two informants revealed to him details of a U.S. Air Force retrieval, somewhere east of Aztec, New Mexico, of a crashed flying saucer and its crew of sixteen aliens. Though Scully's account was convincingly undermined by other journalists, especially the credibility of his two witnesses, this tale helped inspire later variations on the story culminating in the Roswell crashed saucer stories of the 1980s and '90s.

—RANDALL FITZGERALD

Belgian UFO wave of 1989-90 Over the weekend of November 25-26, 1989, alarmed citizens from the Dutch-speaking part of Belgium reported seeing a strange luminous disk circling their homes. Later it turned out that the sightings had been caused by a light show of a disco in Halen (province of Limbourg). The owner had been trying to attract youngsters by projecting a rotating xenon lamp onto the cloud deck. Despite the fact that a local UFO group had identified the culprit, the light show continued to spark off UFO reports in the area until December 16th when, after the

Belgian Air Force had sent two F-16 fighter planes into the air in an attempt to identify the mysterious disk, the Public Prosecutor's Office ordered the disco manager to switch off his installation.

THE COMING OF THE TRIANGLES

Meanwhile, another UFO incident had occurred 70 km southeast of Halen. This time the events were to create waves far beyond the borders of the small Belgian state. From 5:24 P.M. until 8:39 P.M. on November 29, 1989, two members of the *gendarmerie*, driving their patrol car just south of the city of Eupen (the German-speaking part of Belgium), found themselves entangled in a cat and mouse game with an unknown flying object.

The policemen described what they had seen as "a dark solid mass in the shape of an isosceles triangle." According to their statements, it carried "three blinding white lights in each corner and a pulsating red light in the centre." In the course of the events, the two men had also spotted "a white ball of light" over the watchtower of the lake of Gileppe with "what looked like beams of red light shooting out in opposite directions" (investigators later found that Venus was probably responsible for this phase of the sightings).

Throughout the three-hour incident, the policemen had been in constant contact with their headquarters in Eupen. Greatly to their relief, the dispatch officer informed them that he too had seen the triangular object and that additional sightings were being reported by patrols in nearby communities. Several witnesses—out of 150 eyewitness accounts that were gathered that night—mentioned a distinct sound that reminded them of a ventilator. One policeman reported that he had also noticed "something at the back of the craft that was turning round, like a turbine."

SOBEPS COMES INTO PLAY

The next day the story of the Eupen "triangle" was highlighted in the press and on various Belgian television stations. During the first week of December 1989, members of the *Société Belge d'Étude des Phénomènes Spatiaux* (Belgian Society for the Study of Space Phenomena), Belgian's largest UFO group, visited the region in a search for additional witnesses. It marked the beginning of the group's monopoly over the events that were to follow.

The "Belgian Triangle" as sketched by one of the gendarmes who spotted the "craft" over Eupen on November 29, 1989

December 11-12, 1989, was another memorable day for the Belgian UFOlogists. That night numerous people in the regions around the cities of Liège and Namur were baffled by a mysterious illuminated contraption that sailed over their homes. The sightings came to a strange end when, shortly after 2 A.M., a man in Jupille-sur-Meuse, was awakened by a deep, pulsating sound, and saw an egg-shaped object that seemed to be stuck in a spruce fir. The object carried three bright spotlights underneath and something that looked like a rudder at the back. On the hull there was a logo reminiscent of classic symbols that represent the orbits of electrons. It took a few seconds before it managed to tear itself loose, after which it headed toward the witness, flew over his house, and finally disappeared in the distance. According to the witness, the next day Army officers were searching the area.

On December 21, 1989, the Belgian Minister of Defense issued a statement telling the public that the Army had no idea what was causing the UFO reports. With no convincing explanations coming from the scientific community either, speculation and imagination were given free play, and it did not take long before almost any bright light in the sky was labelled a UFO.

As UFO reports kept pouring in for more than a year and a half, the popularity of SOBEPS increased at an equivalent pace. New volunteer investigators were recruited and interviews with members of the group were published in almost every newspaper and magazine in the country. In two years' time, SOBEPS collected approximately 2,000 eyewitness accounts, some 450 of which were investigated. Most of these cases were regarded as unexplained. They are detailed in two large books.

The majority of the sightings occurred within an area of about 200 by 100 kilometers in size. While the first series of reports originated from the Dutch- and German-speaking areas in the east of the country, the wave had shifted to the French-speaking part of Belgium in a matter of days. To skeptics, this illustrated how socio-cultural factors, such as language, population, and the location of UFO investigators, had strongly influenced the reporting process. They further pointed to the lack of experience of some of the new recruits and to the fact that SOBEP's predisposition to promote an extraterrestrial origin for the events, had diverted the investigators' attention from looking for down-to-earth explanations.

THE AIR FORCE CLOSES RANKS

Despite the criticism, SOBEPS managed to earn respect from both UFOlogists and non-UFOlogists, including the Belgian Air Force. During the first weeks of the wave, the BAF had been swamped with telephone calls. With an already chock-full agenda on his hands, Lieutenant-Colonel Wilfried Debrouwer, later promoted to Major-General, decided to call in SOBEPS. This marked the beginning of a short but intense relationship which reached its peak during the Easter days of 1990. During this prolonged holiday weekend of April 14-17, a Hawker Siddeley and a Brittan Norman reconnaissance airplane were put at standby during a skywatch organized by SOBEPS. The code-

name of this historical collaboration was "Operation Identification Ovni." Military men, civilians, investigators, and newsmen took part. The only absentees were the UFOs themselves.

THE EVIDENCE

On July 11, 1990, De Brouwer held a remarkable press conference at the NATO headquarters at Evere, Brussels. In the presence of a considerable press crowd he acknowledged that, on the night of March 30-31, 1990, two F-16 fighters had been scrambled to identify a number of inexplicable lights reported by a group of gendarmes. Although the pilots never had visual contact with anything unusual, one of them had managed to videotape the jet's radar display. Analysis of the tape by scientists, military experts, and skeptics revealed that the freakish radar returns had been caused by an unusual meteorological condition in combination with a malfunction of the radar's electronics. The lights that had been seen just prior to the scramble were identified as bright stars and planets.

Coincidentally, only minutes after the F-16s had returned to base, a man in Brussels managed to capture "the flying triangle" on video. The images, shown on television in many countries, depict the well-known configuration of three white lights and a pulsating red light in the center. SOBEPS investigators later found that the witness had filmed an airliner preparing to land at Zaventem airfield.

As in any modern UFO flap, several videos turned up, the majority of which showed not only aircraft lights but also bright stars or planets. In one instance the reflection of sunlight in distant windows was taken for a low hovering UFO. In another, it was a group of streetlamps that fooled the witnesses. Various reports were generated by imperfections in the autofocus system of early generation camcorders. Many of these early systems have problems focussing on a small point of light. This often resulted in optical oddities that can transform a bright star into a large—sometimes metallic looking—disk.

One of the rare photographic documents that defied explanation was a color slide taken in early April 1990 by a young man from Petit-Rechain, not far from the city of Liège. The photo depicts a black triangle silhouetted against a dark bluish background. There are white blobs of light in each corner and a fourth light, surrounded by a reddish aura, in the center. While co-workers of SOBEPS claim that these lights were probably plasma jets that are part of the object's propulsion system, skeptics point to glaring contradictions in the testimonies of the two witnesses and to the absence of background details in the picture (making it impossible to verify the object's actual size and distance).

Famous "Belgian Triangle" photo

Markedly absent during the Belgian wave were reports of electromagnetic effects. As for traces on ground and vegetation, only four such cases were recorded for the 1989-1991 period, none of which constituted the slightest proof of any unusual event.

IN SEARCH OF EXPLANATIONS

Although many cases could be classified as misinterpretations, a considerable percentage remained puzzling, namely those incidents in which independent witnesses reported seeing a similar, unidentified object at close range, during the same night, and within a well-defined area. Three such peak days stand

out: November 29, 1989, December 11-12, 1989, and March 12, 1991.

Teleguided spherical balloon equipped with three spotlights. Some investigators suggested that a similar construction may have been responsible for at least some of the Belgian sightings.

Researchers skeptical of an extraterrestrial interpretation argued that the objects described reminded them of ultralight motorized aircraft. This hypothesis was supported by a rumor that an Air Force pilot had flown a home-built ULM without the permission of his superiors.

Others suspected that the Air Force was flying state-of-the-art experimental aircraft, presumably of U.S. design, and was taking advantage of the UFO excitement to draw public attention away from these secret test flights. The revolutionary concept of the first generation stealth planes still sparked the imagination in 1989-1990 and the newest trends in aviation design were also being reflected in the UFO descriptions. Skeptics scrutinized aviation magazines for the latest news on obscure Black Projects. After all, the much reported configuration of three white lights and a red flashing light was consistent with standard lighting configuration for aircraft. What they failed to take into account was that these presumed wonder planes were supposed to be fast aircraft, not capable of hovering close to the ground, making sharp turns and producing no downdraft, but only a soft humming sound, as was described in the best-documented cases.

Several investigators, troubled by these unusual flight characteristics, sought salvation in the blimp hypothesis, pointing to the "accident" with the blimp-type object in Jupille-sur-Meuse and to the November 29 sightings. With regard to the latter they pointed out that, earlier that same day, several independent witnesses had spotted, in broad daylight, an oval- or cigar-shaped object traveling slowly south of the lake of Gileppe. Moreover, they discovered that teleguided blimps, equipped with bright spotlights and a camera, had indeed been tested in Belgium in late 1989. The owner of these craft turned out to be an eccentric Hungarian who rented his contraptions for publicity purposes and was hoping to gather a few orders from the military as well. It appeared that he had actually contacted not only Major-General De Brouwer, but also the country's intelligence services, claiming that he himself had single-handedly started the Belgian UFO wave and that he would be willing to prove this in exchange for a big amount of money.

Both the Air Force and the intelligence services gave little credence to the story and turned the offer down. Surprisingly, the inventor later denied having ever flown his radio-controlled balloons outdoors, causing even more confusion. In the end, the only thing that remained certain was that the Belgian UFOs were an important factor in transforming the traditional nuts-and-bolts image of the flying saucer into a new high-tech UFO that pops up almost exclusively at night, looks like a dark, angular structure, and carries a panoply of multicolored lights.

—WIM VAN UTRECHT

Bender mystery ("Men in Black") In September 1953, Albert K. Bender, then director of the International Flying Saucer Bureau

(IFSB), reported that three men dressed in black suits had called on him at his Bridgeport, Connecticut, home and revealed to him the frightening answer to the UFO mystery. Bender confided to IFSB associates soon afterward that the men, whose manner had been threatening, had warned him he would be thrown into jail if he repeated any of the information they had given him.

Gray Barker, Dominick Lucchesi, and August Roberts called on Bender shortly after the supposed incident and were able to draw a few more details out of him. He said the three men in black had told him that for the past two years the United States Government had known the secret of the UFOs. They claimed, according to Bender, that this secret would be revealed in either five months or four years. Shortly after the original visit, one of the strangers returned and imparted additional insight into the mystery, which, Bender said later, tended to ease some of the fear Bender had experienced during and after the first meeting.

Apparently the men, or at least the agency they represented, continued to monitor Bender's activities. He alleged that once, after he had made a "bad slip" during a long-distance telephone conversation with another saucer buff, a call came from Washington, D.C., and a voice warned him to be more careful in the future.

Soon afterward Bender closed down the IFSB. In the last issue of the organization's publication, *Space Review,* he wrote cryptically, in his first public allusion to the episode, "STATEMENT OF IMPORTANCE: The mystery of the flying saucer is no longer a mystery. The source is already known, but any information about this is being withheld by orders from a higher source. We would like to print the full story in *Space Review,* but because of the nature of the information we are very sorry that we have been advised in the negative.

"We advise those engaged in saucer work to please be very cautious."

Bender withdrew from the UFO field and

resisted pressure to discuss the matter further. Although serious UFOlogists viewed his claims with considerable skepticism, occult- and contactee-oriented saucerians speculated endlessly about the possible identity of the "Three Men," as they came to be called. The Three Men were variously held to be CIA operatives, space people, evil astral entities, demons, agents of an international Nazi conspiracy, or agents of an international Jewish conspiracy.

Bender's former associate Gray Barker, a Clarksburg, West Virginia, publisher, tirelessly promoted the mystery and started a small industry specializing in Bender-related materials. Barker's *They Knew Too Much About Flying Saucers* (1956) is an entertaining excursion into the outer reaches of UFOlogical paranoia which recounted the Bender affair and other similar alleged silencings of UFO researchers in Canada, New Zealand, and Australia.

In 1962, Bender suddenly announced he was ready to tell all and did so in a volume published that year by Barker's Saucerian Books. The eagerly awaited *Flying Saucers and the Three Men* proved a disappointing climax to the nine-year-old controversy. Even Barker conceded privately that he could not swallow Bender's fantastic tale of abduction to the South Pole by monstrous space beings. Practically everyone who read it, even those ordinarily predisposed to unbridled credulity, dismissed the book as a work of conscious or unconscious fiction. Bender himself showed minimal enthusiasm for it and did little to promote it. Soon afterward he moved to Los Angeles and secured an unlisted telephone number.

But *Three Men* does shed some light on the background of the Bender Mystery and points (albeit unintentionally) to the likely solution. It reveals Bender's longtime obsession with science fiction, horror movies, and the occult. Bender, at the time of the alleged visitation a bachelor living with his stepfather, had converted his section of the house into a "chamber of horrors," with paintings of monsters on the walls and shrunken heads and artificial bats on the tables and shelves. Reading the book one cannot resist an obvious conclusion—that Bender was ripe for what might be euphemistically be termed a "psychological experience."

In 1976, Bender, now the director of an organization which seeks to perpetuate the music of film composer Max Steiner, wrote, replying to a letter from a UFOlogist, "In 1977 something spectacular will take place involving space." In this, as in his 1953 prediction that the truth about UFOs would be known in five months or four years, Bender proved to be a poor prophet.

—JEROME CLARK

Bermuda Triangle-UFO link A popular explanation for the disappearances of ships and planes in the so-called "Bermuda Triangle" is the "UFO-capture theory." Upon close inspection, however, the supposed UFO link is found to be merely a literary creation without basis in fact.

Over the past half century, more than a hundred ships and planes, with over a thousand persons on board, have supposedly disappeared—some say "mysteriously, without a trace"—in an area variously dubbed "the Bermuda Triangle," "the Devil's Triangle," "the Hoodoo Sea," "the Triangle of Death," and "the Graveyard of the Atlantic." It is actually a large area of undefinable shape around, and including, the triangle formed by Florida, Bermuda, and Puerto Rico, where sea and air traffic is said to be the greatest. For reasons which are to follow, some writers have "theorized" a UFO connection to explain the "strange" disappearances.

The Bermuda Triangle-UFO link, to missing vessels was perhaps first hinted at in the 1930s by Charles Fort (1874-1932), who, as his biographer Loren Gross writes for this encyclopedia, "played with the notion that mysterious vanishments of ocean vessels and their crews . . . may be due to wanton seizures by spacemen." Two decades later, astronomer

Morris K. Jessup (1900-59), in his book *The Case for the UFO* (1955), wrote: "To attempt to postulate *motive* for space inhabitants *kidnapping* crews from ships . . . is in the realm of pure speculation. On the other hand . . . our space friends would want to know what has happened to us since they left, or what has happened to us since they put us down here. Again, there is always the possibility that the open seas provide an easy *catching place.*"

More recently, author Charles Berlitz capitalized on the "Triangle" and a possible UFO connection by quoting, in his bestselling book *The Bermuda Triangle* (1974), his friend J. Manson Valentine, who reported several UFO sightings in the area. Berlitz also quoted a reporter by the name of Art Ford, who claimed that a final radio transmission, picked up by a ham operator from one of the doomed pilots (in this case, Lieutenant Charles Taylor, flight leader of the five Navy torpedo bombers that disappeared on December 5, 1945), contained the warning: "Don't come after me. . . . They look like they are from outer space." (According to a transcript from the Navy Inquiry Board, what Taylor actually said was: "I know where I am now. I'm at 2,300 feet. Don't come after me.")

Also, there are claims of unusual electromagnetic effects occurring in the Triangle, a common feature of many UFO reports. Actually, none of the "magnetic anomalies" claimed about the area are true. Reports of compass needles spinning crazily have never been substantiated. The fact that the compass points to true north from the Triangle does not cause confusion, but rather, simplifies navigation. (The compass points to true north from many other places in the world. The only part of the Triangle from which it does point directly north is at the southern tip of Florida.) Those who claim that the north-pointing compass is strange or confusing lack even the most fundamental knowledge of magnetism, compasses, or navigation. The presence of a "Space/Time warp" (whatever that means) is, again, unsubstantiated, to say the least.

Popular author John Wallace Spencer, in a revised version of his book *Limbo of the Lost* (1973), offered a provocative theory: He reasoned that: "Since a 575-foot vessel with 39 crew members disappearing 50 miles offshore in the Gulf of Mexico, and commercial airliners disappearing while coming in for a landing cannot happen according to earthly standards and yet are happening, I am forced to conclude that they are actually being taken away from our planet for a variety of reasons."

In a 1975 version of the book, retitled *Limbo of the Lost—Today,* Spencer modified his UFO theory so that the extraterrestrials were no longer carting the captives away from Earth but were taking them to hidden underwater facilities, where the ETs conducted experiments on the Earthlings and their machinery. But Spencer offered no evidence that UFOs had been present or were even sighted in conjunction with any of the incidents he described. In other words, it seems that some authors are apparently dressing up their accounts by including UFOs in order to attempt to make a bigger story.

The UFO-capture theme was again used in the 1977 movie *Close Encounters of the Third Kind.* It turned out that five Navy torpedo bombers that disappeared in 1945 were taken aboard a gigantic "Mother Ship"; and all of its captives (who had not aged over the years) were released at the end of the movie to help demonstrate that the extraterrestrials are indeed friendly after all.

In reality, the "Bermuda Triangle Mystery" has been shown, in *The Bermuda Triangle Mystery—Solved,* by Larry Kusche (1975), to be a sham—an accumulation of careless research, misconceptions, sensationalism, and downright falsification of data—and is so regarded by most leading UFO researchers. For example, the 575-foot ship that Spencer claimed had disappeared was found within two weeks, sunken in shallow water. Volatile fumes in the holds had exploded, nearly tearing the ship in two. The airliner that Spencer said had disappeared while on a landing approach was a chartered DC-3 that lost its way at night in 1948, out of sight of land, because of radio navigational problems. Thorough investigations of other incidents by Kusche led to similar "down to earth" explanations.

According to the April 1978 issue of J. Allen Hynek's *International UFO Reporter:* "The Bermuda Triangle stories . . . are NOT relayed by the pilots or sailors who *experience* them; they are the fraudulent literary distortions of a small handful of authors. All Triangle mysteries so far have been easily explainable once the actual records have been examined. Would that the more baffling UFOs (which are *themselves* the mysteries) were so easily resolved."

—RONALD D. STORY

Bethurum, Truman (1898-1969). Truman Bethurum was one of the five major "contactees" of the 1950s. He claimed to have met Space People on numerous occasions. He said that the "captain" gave him information about the workings of "flying saucers" and life on the planet Clarion. Bethurum offered no evidence to substantiate these claims, and most UFO researchers regard him as a charlatan.

Drawing of the lady captain,
Aura Rhanes

Truman Bethurum

Bethurum became famous in 1954 with the publication of his book, *Aboard a Flying Saucer.* In it, Bethurum claimed that he encountered a landed flying saucer in the Mojave Desert, where he was laying asphalt for a construction company. Invited aboard the flying saucer, he said, he met the crew and its female captain, Aura Rhanes. She explained to Bethurum that she had come from an idyllic society on the planet Clarion, where there was no war, divorce, or taxes. Clarion could not be seen from Earth because it was always behind the moon.

Bethurum struck up a friendship with Aura Rhanes. After the first encounter, he met with her ten more times at lunch counters and other such mundane places. During these meetings, she gave more information about Clarion, and she explained the composition of her "saucer." Once she tried to aid Bethurum by predicting what would happen on his job. Eventually, Rhanes invited Bethurum and some of his guests to take a ride in the flying saucer; but when the time came, Aura Rhanes and the saucer did not show up, and Bethurum never saw her again.

All but the most desperate contactee advocates have considered Bethurum's book to be a hoax. Bethurum stuck by the story and capitalized on it by appearing on television and radio shows and giving lectures at contactee-oriented UFO conventions. He was friends with "Professor" George Adamski and other contactees of the period, and his claims were similar to those of Adamski, Fry, and Angelucci.

In 1969, Edward U. Condon used nearly two pages of his Condon Report to prove that Clarion could not possibly exist. For Condon, Clarion was evidence of the gullibility of UFO "believers."

Bethurum died on May 21, 1969, in Landers, California. The following year, Timothy Green Beckley published some previously unpublished material by Bethurum which rehashed the story in his 1954 book and gave additional details about the planet Clarion. Bethurum's *Aboard a Flying Saucer* is now considered a relic of the 1950s, a time when contactees were "media events." Its main importance is as an example of how individuals have tried to exploit the UFO phenomenon for their own gain.

—DAVID M. JACOBS

POSTSCRIPT: As with the other "contactees," to regard Bethurum as a simple charlatan is to miss much of the point. Like the stories of the other contactees, Bethurum's classic book, *Aboard a Flying Saucer*, is rich in metaphors. Take for example the lady captain, Aura Rhanes, or "Aura Rains"—as we would spell her name if we thought about what she signifies. Indeed, Bethurum was quite "taken" by her. She was everything his own wife was not. When one reads the details in Bethurum's book about his own life, it is no wonder he required this kind of fantasy to escape his world of loneliness and uncaring people. A utopian dream was precisely what he needed.

When the alien crew brought Bethurum aboard the saucer, he found the ravishing captain seated at a desk in her cabin. He described her as having short black hair "brushed into an upward curl at the ends," and wearing a

The flying saucer (called the "Admiral Scow") as described by Bethurum

"black and red beret" tilted on one side of her head. Her blouse "looked like black velvet, with short sleeves decorated with a small red ribbon bow"; and she wore a red skirt that "looked like wool and was set all round in small flat pleats." Bethurum remarked that "Her eyes . . . seemed as if they saw and understood everything, including the questions I was about to ask even before I was able to get them out." (Bethurum, 1954)

Mrs. Rhanes (who was said to have two grandchildren back on the planet Clarion) explained to Bethurum that the Clarionites had come to Earth only for their own education (which means for *our* education, if they are teaching by example, reading the account metaphorically). But she also mentioned that other space people might be watching us as well: "You have taken such an interest in atomic power, some of them might be surveying you. If you blow up your own planet, it would cause considerable confusion in the Space around you."

As for life on Clarion, Captain Rhanes described an idyllic existence: She told Bethurum that on Clarion there were no such things as prisons, lawyers, guards at banks, and child delinquency; no divorce or adultery; no illnesses or doctors; no traffic problems; and definitely no politicians. "That's what's cleft your world through," she said. Nor was there any use of liquor or tobacco. The Clarionites were said to be very religious—"Christians" in fact—who "worship a Supreme Deity who sees, knows, and controls all." (Bethurum, 1954)

As in the case of Adamski and the other contactees, Bethurum's account is shot through with technological metaphors. When he asked Captain Rhanes about the greatest problem the Clarionites had to solve, he was given this answer: "It was, of course, learning how to control magnetic force. You know that we have solved it, both pro and anti of course, or we wouldn't be here tonight." In other words, they have learned the secret of the reconciliation of opposites. Throughout all the contactee accounts, "magnetic force" symboblizes primal psychic energy (or libido), which is precisely what man must learn to control if he is to achieve psychic balance (and thus survival).

Everything associated with the Clarionites was a model of perfection. The little men were described as having "masklike faces, without scar or blemish. . . ." Aura Rhanes, the "queen of women" was rated "tops in shapeliness and beauty"; She "wore no makeup" because she "needed none," and couldn't be smarter or more capable. The beautiful 300-foot diameter saucer "was smooth and symmetrical," magically floating several feet above the ground, and produced "no noise of any kind at . . . take-off." In a word, we are talking about "Utopia."

Sociologist David Stupple was the first, I believe, to point out that the contactees were essentially "*utopians*," who envisioned a better world, and came to believe their own fantasies in pursuit of that goal. "In contactee parlance a 'Space Brother' is not an entity who drops by and gives nonsense information," Stupple says, "a Space Brother is a being who visits a contactee and imparts some special knowledge" so that "by using that information the contactee can then go forth and help humanity." (Stupple, 1980) (And for those who are familiar with the ideas of Carl Jung and Joseph Campbell, that, of course, is the archetypal pattern of the "hero's journey.")

And speaking of classic examples, I would be amiss if I did not point out the perfect example of the *anima* archetype in Aura Rhanes. That she is Truman Bethurum's ideal woman goes without saying. What is more subtle, and more in need of an explanation, is why the feminine aspect of this fantasy requires such intense projection. I think it is clear in all of the contactee accounts that the world is in desparate need of more balance between matriarchal and patriarchal qualities. And what we are missing, of course, is the necessary addition of more feminine aspects, such as: unconditional love, understanding, and compassion.

At the request of Aura Rhanes, Bethurum later established a "Sanctuary of Thought," dedicated to world peace, understanding, and universal brotherhood.

—RONALD D. STORY

References

Bethurum, Truman. *Aboard a Flying Saucer* (De-Vorss & Co., 1954).
———. *Messages from the People of the Planet Clarion: The True Experiences of Truman Bethurum.* Beckley, Timothy Green, ed. (Inner Light Publications, 1995).
Gibbons, Gavin. *They Rode in Space Ships* (The Citadel Press, 1957).
Stupple, David. Quoted in *Proceedings of the First International UFO Congress.* Fuller, Curtis G., ed. (Warner Books, 1980).

Bible and Flying Saucers, The (Lippincott, 1968). Presbyterian pastor Barry H. Downing argues that Biblical events and teachings were deliberately inspired by visiting extraterrestrial "angels." His interpretation of the scriptures indicates that Jesus' resurrection occurred as he was spirited away by a flying saucer.

The same sort of space vehicle led the Israelites across the Red Sea by parting it, spoke to Moses from a cloud, and emitted radiation which produced the plagues described in Exodus. In other words, Downing substitutes super-technology for the supernatural.

—RANDALL FITZGERALD

Biblical miracles as super-technology

Biblical miracles have generally been explained in one of three ways: they are seen as (1) mythology, (2) as misunderstood or rare natural phenomena, or (3) they are supernatural. (Note that interpretation of modern UFOs have followed similar lines.) Connecting Biblical miracles with UFOs offers a fourth interpretation: super-technology or more specifically, extraterrestrial science.

The general academic/scientific view of UFOs and Biblical miracles is that they are mythology. Perhaps driven by unconscious Jungian archetypes, mythologists argue that stories like the parting of the Red Sea were invented by humans to comfort and inspire them in what appears to be a godless world.

Then there are those who have taken many of the stories in Exodus, for example, to be historical facts—although misidentifications of natural phenomena. Scientists John Marr and Curtis Mulloy have argued that the plagues during the Exodus were caused by a "toxic algal bloom." The late Harvard astronomer Donald Menzel has argued that the burning bush seen by Moses was St. Elmo's fire. Immanuel Velikovsky, in his book *Worlds in Collision* (1950), argued that the "pillar of cloud and of fire" (the Exodus UFO) was the planet Venus making a near pass at the Earth with its gravity causing the parting of the Red Sea. Those making these kinds of arguments say that the Biblical people were involved in natural events, which due to their lack of scientific understanding they called the work of God.

The supernatural explanation of the parting of the Red Sea and other Exodus miracles is simply this: God can do anything. The miracles are supernatural events and thus not explainable in logical terms.

Each of the above theories treats the historicity of the story differently. Those advocating the mythological theory do not require that the parting of the Red Sea, or any other reported Biblical event, actually occurred.

Those advocating naturalistic explanations accept many of the reported events as described (the plagues, the burning bush, the parting of the Red Sea), but see them as fortuitous natural events (for good or ill). For them, God was not involved.

The supernatural theory, on the other hand, assumes that the reported events occurred and were also caused by the supernatural power of God.

Those who support the mythological, naturalistic, or supernatural points of view do not usually welcome the UFO interpretation of Exodus. However, the UFO interpretation supposes that the Biblical reports must be given serious factual consideration; something the mythological view does not do.

The UFO interpretation takes the Biblical reports as seriously as either the naturalistic or the supernatural interpretation, but it has an advantage over the naturalistic view by giving coherence to the reported facts while also making scientific sense, which the supernatural interpretation makes no attempt to do.

In my book *The Bible and Flying Saucers* (1968, 1997), I have explored Exodus in detail. The Bible says that during the forty-year wilderness journey, something described as a "pillar of cloud by day and a pillar of fire by night" (Exodus 13:21,22) was constantly present. One might suppose with Velikovsky that this was the planet Venus or a comet making a near pass at the Earth.

Or one might suppose with Dr. Menzel that the burning bush was St. Elmo's fire. But what about the voice Moses heard? (Exodus 3:4) The naturalists suppose the voice is mythology. But suppose that a UFO landed in a clump of bushes. Modern UFOs have been reported to cause bushes to glow. And when modern persons have close encounters, they often report hearing a voice.

One of the most compelling stories that might link the Bible and UFOs is the story of the parting of the Red Sea.

According to the Bible, when the pillar of cloud hovered over the Red Sea, the voice of God or an angel of God was in frequent voice contact with Moses. The main point of Exodus is that Moses was in constant contact with an intelligent being connected with a UFO, which

Could this have been the scene
at the parting of the Red Sea?
(Painting by Monarca Lynn Merrifield)

The approach I have taken to UFOs and Christianity is this: We need to wonder a lot more and not shut ourselves off from possibilities.

—BARRY H. DOWNING

Biblical UFOs Strange objects are reported throughout the Bible. In fact, so many references to UFOs in the Bible exist that a complete list is impossible here. Most Biblical UFOs can be divided into two categories: (1) those that seem to be connected with what we might call psychic phenomena and (2) those that we would now call "multiple witness" sightings. The question of whether Biblical UFOs and modern UFOs are directly connected has of course not yet been answered.

Abraham, while in a "deep sleep," had some kind of UFO experience. "When the sun had gone down and it was dark, behold a smoking fire pot and a flaming torch passed between these pieces" (Gen. 15:17). Jacob, while sleeping, had a well-known dream that the angels of God were ascending and descending on a ladder leading to heaven (Gen. 28:12). These experiences have traditionally been viewed as spiritual or psychic rather than "objectively real," as this phrase is usually understood in modern science. In the modern UFO field, it must be remembered, however, that some of the most important UFO research is done by placing persons who have experienced close encounters of the third kind under a hypnotic trance in order to recover a UFO experience which someone experienced, apparently in a trance. Thus the modern trance experience has its twin in the Bible. Whether the famous wheels of Ezekiel belong in this category is not clear. Ezekiel describes his experience as a "vision," which most have assumed means trance, but the former NASA engineer, Josef Blumrich, in his book *The Spaceships of Ezekiel* (1974), argues for the objective reality of Ezekiel's experience.

There are important "multiple-witness sightings" in both the Old and New Testaments. The most important in the Old Testament is the Exodus UFO. "And the Lord went

was cloud-like during the day and glowing like fire in the dark. It may have been cylindrical in shape like modern "cloud-cigar" UFOs. This UFO then landed on Mount Sinai and gave Moses the commandments for the Jewish religion in oral and written form.

I believe that a UFO used its power system—some kind of force field—to part the Red Sea, and when the Egyptians tried to drive their chariots under the force field, they were knocked flat.

For those who are committed to the Biblical religion, what does this mean? Were the Biblical miracles carried out by super-technological—rather than supernatural—beings? If so, how would this affect our religious beliefs? These questions have yet to be debated in the halls of theology.

"And the angel of the Lord appeared to him in a flame of fire out of the midst of a bush; and he looked, and lo, the bush was burning, yet it was not consumed."
(Ex. 3:2)

"And as they still went on and talked, behold a chariot of fire and horses of fire separated the two of them. Elijah went up by a whirlwind into heaven."
(II Kings 2:11)

before them by day in a pillar of cloud to lead them along the way, and by night in a pillar of fire to give them light, that they might travel by day and by night" (Ex. 13:21). This UFO, similar to "cloud cigars" described today, was present during the forty-year Exodus of the Israelites from Egypt under the leadership of Moses. It is understood to be the same reality which met Moses in the "burning bush" (Ex. 3:2).

The Exodus UFO is given different names, sometimes called "the cloud," sometimes "the glory" of the Lord, sometimes called "the Presence." It apparently leads the Israelites to Mount Sinai, descends on Mount Sinai (see Ex. 19), gives Moses the commandments of the Jewish religion, and dictates the building of the Tabernacle. Finally, it leads the way to the Promised Land. Some have argued that the "pillar of cloud and fire" caused the parting of the Red Sea with its propulsion system and that it dropped the manna for food during the Exodus. The "pillar of cloud" is called a multiple-witness sighting because it is understood to have been seen by all the Israelites during all of the Exodus. (Downing, 1968)

Another famous Old Testament multiple-witness sighting involves the ascension of Elijah in a "chariot of fire" (II Kings 2). The Bible reports that about fifty priests witnessed this event.

Multiple-witness sightings in the New Testament include: the shepherds who saw the angels and the bright "glory" of the Lord at the birth of Christ (Luke 2:9); the "bright cloud" seen by Peter, James, and John during the transfiguration of Jesus (Matt. 17:1-8); several disciples witnessing the ascension of Jesus in a "cloud" (Acts 2:9) as angels explained the event; and the bright "light from heaven" which blinded the Apostle Paul and brought about his conversion on the Damascus Road (Acts 9:1-9). Angels are connected with the "clouds of heaven" in the New Testament, which seem to be understood as a heavenly form of transportation.

What is the meaning of UFOs in the Bible? Some have suggested that UFOs in the Bible, like modem UFOs, are mainly an expression of man's unconscious needs; that they are myth, creations of man's mind.

"And it came to pass that at midnight the Lord smote all the firstborn in the land of Egypt, from the firstborn of Pharaoh . . . [to] the firstborn of cattle." (Ex. 12:29)

Others have suggested that UFOs carried "ancient astronauts," who may have contacted man for scientific purposes but who never intended to start religion as we know it.

Another theory is that UFOs started the Biblical religion, either as a kind of giant interplanetary hoax or because UFOs are in fact a divine reality. This latter view would see UFOs as carrying the angels of God in the past to start the Biblical religion and, as still being seen today, shepherds watching over their sheep.

—BARRY H. DOWNING

References

Downing, Barry. *The Bible and Flying Saucers* (Lippincott, 1968; Avon, 1970; Marlowe, 1997).

Jessup, M. K. *UFO and the Bible* (The Citadel Press, 1956).

birth memories hypothesis   The birth memories hypothesis (BMH) culminated in a decade of research into hypnosis and CE-3 re-

ports, including the Imaginary Abductee Study, which led my colleague Dr. W. C. McCall and me to a skeptical view of abduction claims. We concluded that abductions are nonphysical, archetypal fantasies involving belief or deception in which the witness's perinatal (pre- and postnatal) memories play a central role.

Some basic assumptions of the BMH follow from recent brain research. The fetus, once described as incapable of thought and memory, is now seen as keenly responsive to its environment. Of the two memory systems in the brain, the verbal declarative memory in the hippocampus matures by age four, but the non-verbal emotional memory, located in the amygdala, is all but matured at birth. Daniel Goleman writes, ". . . many potent emotional memories date from the first few years of life, in the relationship between an infant and its caretakers. This is especially true of traumatic events, like beatings or outright neglect." These "emotional lessons" are stored in the amygdala as "rough, wordless blueprints for emotional life" and are difficult for an adult to articulate exactly because they originated before words were there to help the infant understand experiences. It is our belief that this process typically starts long before birth, certainly by the tumultuous events of the last trimester of pregnancy, so that the earliest if not most intense emotional memories in everyone are prenatal.

Perinatal memories show a strong connection with fantasy, which seems to encourage access to often-inexpressible emotional memories. For example, one can relive the ordeal of birth with the aid of hallucinogenic drugs, as psychiatrist Stanislav Grof has shown, but it can be done somewhat easier under hypnosis, or even while fantasizing an abduction scenario. Our hypnotized real and imaginary CE-3 witnesses were giving us figurative perinatal imagery long before I recognized it, and before I found that Grof's birth narratives contain major parallels with abduction imagery. The relation also works in reverse: some of Grof's subjects describe hallucinations involving flying saucers, aliens, and *Star Trek*-like adventures.

UFOs as flying saucers are rich and varied perinatal symbols, but witness descriptions are usually indirect and metaphorical. Accounts of entering or leaving a UFO may suggest a symbolic birth: abductees squeeze through small cervical doors into big rooms, a process clearly analogous to the newborn's feelings of decompression at delivery. Or they may exit through a small passageway to the "big room" outside. Sometimes the birth reference is explicit, as with the abductee who said she had to twist her shoulders 90 degrees to pass through a little doorway—an exact reliving of fetal rotation in birth. A few witnesses choose to be reborn repeatedly (as in the Andreasson case) by passing from one amniotic room to another, through narrow vaginal tunnels, elevators, exploding doorways, or cervical openings.

Only about half of the CE-3 reports I have seen are substantive and coherent narratives, yet they all contain some perinatal imagery; many are dominated by it. The more detailed the narrative, the greater the total birth data—clear indication of an inherent birth abduction connection.

The birth memories hypothesis is significant because it is one of the few falsifiable theories ever proposed about abduction cases. There is no reason why an actual abduction should stimulate birth imagery in an abductee. On the contrary, the thought of umbilical pain or birth gore playing any role in confrontations between humans and alien beings is absurd in the extreme. Birth imagery is thus a marker showing that abduction claims are non-physical events. That knowledge gives investigators an evaluative tool of major importance.

We devised three falsifying tests of the BMH, as follows:

BMH FALSIFICATION TEST #1

The birth memories hypothesis could be wholly or partially invalidated by any fully developed case narrative lacking substantive peri-

natal references, but I know of no such CE-3 case. Below are some random abduction imagery/events and their probable perinatal connections that could rule out a claim of alien contact:

- "alien genetics" procedures (overall perinatal experiences)
- birth laboratory (womb and amniotic memories)
- body probing, handling (postnatal exam)
- body dismemberment (normal vaginal passage hallucinations)
- body size change (normal vaginal pressure)
- breathing problems (late stage placental hypoxia)
- center-opening doors (the dilating cervix)
- communication or message (bonding, loving contact)
- fetal humanoid (womb/infant memories)
- floating (fetus in amniotic suspension)
- head, body pressure (normal vaginal birth)
- humming (womb or maternal sounds)
- paralysis (normal vaginal pressure, delivery room swaddling)
- pulsing sensation (placental pulse or maternal heartbeat)
- sense of abrupt motion (in womb as mother moves about)
- tastes or odors (amniotic fluid, post-natal gore)
- time loss, amnesia (emotional memories of perinatal events)
- transparent walls, rooms (translucent amnion)
- tubes of various size (umbilical/placental memories)
- tunnel for boarding/exit (vaginal birth memories)

BMH FALSIFICATION TEST #2

We propose that cesarean-born volunteers be hypnotized and given imaginary abductions. If any cesarean narratives contain explicit or figurative descriptions of head and body pressure or other tunnel and tube experiences, the BMH would be weakened or proved false.

In the absence of formal replication attempts by other UFOlogists, Dr. McCall and I gave imaginary abductions under hypnosis to a group of persons who said they were born by cesarean section. We found statistical evidence that tunnel imagery in CE-3 narratives relates to vaginal birth. Of eight cesarean subjects in the experiment, seven used no tunnel imagery in describing how they boarded or left the UFO, and there were few tunnel images throughout their narratives. The eighth subject exited via a body tube, but she had spent long hours in a contracting *placenta previa* (obstructed) womb before an emergency cesarean, perhaps enough time to imprint a tunnel/tube memory.

BMH FALSIFICATION TEST #3

We propose that abduction narratives be studied for echoes of problem-birth witnesses' birth histories. In the continuing absence of verification attempts by others, Dr. McCall and I also tested this proposal. Ten volunteers—two normal births and eight others who reported some birth problem (breech, forceps delivery, twin birth, etc.)—were hypnotized and given first an imaginary abduction and then a birth revivification (to avoid birth-CE-3 cueing). Significant correlations emerged in several subjects, particularly when boarding or exiting the UFO.

Birth images frequently dominate literary, cinematic, and other fantasies because it is the fantasizing process and not a particular book, film, or other work that evokes perinatal data. Since Occam's relentless razor prefers the simplest alternative, reasonable people should conclude that birth imagery in a CE-3 report is evidence of perinatal fantasy. No one has read all 5,000 abduction narratives (the current guesstimated number), but CE-3s without perinatal data seem about as scarce as aliens.

Until one or the other appears, the debate over the reality of CE-3s favors probable birth fantasies over verified abductions by—more or less—5,000 to zip.

—ALVIN H. LAWSON

Book of the Damned, The (Boni & Liveright, 1919). Charles Fort produces the first book to chronicle eyewitness accounts in a range of unexplained phenomena from UFO sightings to rocks and other unusual objects falling from cloudless skies.

He is the first author to speculate that humankind has been visited and may be owned by a race of super beings from other worlds who came and established colonies on Earth for "hunting, trading, replenishing harems, and mining."

—RANDALL FITZGERALD

boundary deficit hypothesis Within the subject of UFOlogy, the boundary deficit hypothesis is the proposition that the population of people claiming nightmare-like abduction experiences will include a statistically significant proportion of people who have the same psychological characteristics as people who have nightmares. It derives from studies by Ernest Hartmann who has shown that people who have frequent nightmares tend to share a large cluster of common psychological traits that seems to be organized around a central property of the brain's predisposition to fuse and mix information and experience rather than separating such things into distinct categories. (Hartmann, 1984)

Boundary theory begins with the axiom that as the mind matures, it categorizes experiences. It walls off experiences into sets with common properties. Boundaries are set up between what is self and non-self, between sleep and waking experiences, between fantasy and reality, passion and reason, right and wrong, masculine and feminine, and a large population of other experiential categories. This drive to categorize is subject to natural variation. The determinants of that drive appear to be biochemical and genetic and probably have no environmental component such as trauma. When the drive is weak, the boundaries between the categories are thinner, more permeable, or more fluid. When the boundaries become abnormally thin one sees psychopathologies like schizophrenia. When abnormally thick, the psychopathologies tend toward neurotic defensiveness. Hartmann discovered that individuals who suffer from nightmares have thin boundaries. From this central characteristic one can derive a large constellation of traits that set these people apart from the general population.

From earliest childhood, people with thin boundaries are perceived as "different." They are regarded as more sensitive than their peers. Thin character armor causes them to be more fragile and easily hurt. They are easily empathic, but dive into relationships too deeply and quickly. Recipients of their affection complain they are unusually close and clinging and thus frequently rejected. Experience with their vulnerability teaches them to be wary of entering into relationships with others. Adolescence tends to be stormy and difficult. Adult relationships—whether sexual, marital, or friendships—also tend to be unsettled and variable. Paranoia, as measured by the MMPI, has the highest correlation to thin boundaries. One-third will have contemplated or attempted suicide. (Hartmann, 1991)

Experimentation with drugs tends to yield bad trips and is quickly abandoned. They are unusually alert to lights, sounds, and sensations. They tend to have fluid sexual identities. Bisexuals tend to be overrepresented in the nightmare sufferers' group and it is rare to find manly men or womanly women. They are not rule followers. Either they reject society or society rejects them. They are rebels and outsiders. There is a striking tendency for these people to find their way into fields involving artistic self-expression: musicians, poets, writers, art teachers, etc. Some develop their empathic talents and become therapists. Ordinary blue or white collar jobs are rare.

Hartmann believes the predominance of artists results from the fact that thin boundaries allow them to experience the world more directly and painfully than others. The ability to experience their inner life in a very direct fashion contributes to the authenticity of their creations. They become lost in daydreaming quite easily and may even experience daymares—a phenomenon people with thick boundaries won't even realize exists. This trait of imaginative absorption was predicted to make nightmare sufferers good hypnotic subjects and later tests confirmed this. (Hartmann, 1991) Boundary deficits also contribute to fluid memories and a fluid time sense.

Hartmann developed a psychological instrument called the Boundary Questionnaire that reliably discriminates this trait. (Hartmann, 1991) Use of it makes objective measure of the trait possible and propositions of correlation testable and falsifiable.

The similarity of many abduction experiences to nightmares should be fairly obvious. The overarching theme of abduction narratives is powerlessness. This is manifest not in the mere sense of capture and involuntary scrutiny, but in the extraordinary variety of dramatic intrusions imposed on the abductee. Pain is ubiquitous and is reported in nearly every part of the body somewhere in the literature—head, neck, chest, back, leg, toes, hand, navel, genitalia. Needles, absurdly big at times, are used to penetrate a variety of points including the nose, the eye, the navel, penis, anus. Organs have been removed and replaced. One body is completely ripped apart and put back together. One abductee had her eye scraped with a knife. Some have their limbs pulled sharply, their hair pulled, even their heads pulled and squeezed by aliens. Abductees are subjected to rape, castration, impregnation, abortion, choking, drowning, freezing, profuse bleeding, temporary blinding, hand cramps, being stripped, and having their brains scrambled. One is confronted with his personal phobia.

Abductees have also reported sensations of weakness, of hurtling or tumbling through space, of spinning, of being stuck, of being buried alive, and, once, of crashing to the ground with a saucer. Most of this is inflicted with no clear purpose and seems just plain bizarre. There is often detailing that frankly looks impossible. Aliens and abductees both pass though walls; a possible symbol of boundarylessness. Eyes are removed from sockets and left hanging out on the face for a time; anatomically nonsensical. A hocus-pocus motion of the hand relieves the pain of a needle thrust into a navel. Needles go through the nose and tear into the brain, certain death one would think. Evil alien eyes paralyze people and overwhelm their souls. There is out-of-body travel and telepathy. And let's not get started on all the apocalyptic visions, failed predictions, and misinformation that has come from abductions.

Much of this parallels, sometimes precisely, sometimes in a more general way, what happens in nightmares. There are the basic childhood fears like completely dissolving or being destroyed; fear of mutilation, castration, loss of body parts, fear of isolation and abandonment; fear of loss of sustenance and love; and an inability to control the body. There are chases, capture, torture, imminent catastrophe, wild kinetic sensations, and eerie background scenes. Regarding the last, it is especially damning how fog often finds it way into abduction experiences, a detail common to horror stories and one seen endlessly in science fiction movies and TV programs with a lineage stretching back to Lovecraft.

Certain correlative features to abductions could readily be accounted for. So-called "missing time" could result from a fluid time sense. Forgotten scars are reinterpreted due to a fluidity of memory. Dramatic reactions to mundane stimuli like lights leading to misinterpretations might reflect stimulus sensitivity and paranoia. Good hypnotizability would preferentially yield emotionally authentic behavior. When such correlates are used in a diagnostic fashion by abductologists, they may be screening away thick-boundaried people in favor of people with thin boundaries.

The likelihood that abductees with such nightmare experiences shared the same psychological profile as nightmare sufferers was strongly suggested by several points of correspondence between thin boundary traits and an early psychological study of abductees. UFOlogists regarded the Slater psychological study of nine abductees as an *experimentum crucis* for the view that abductees are victims of real extraterrestrial intrusions. It affirmed not only the normality of abductees, but offered a hint of traumatization in the finding that abductees showed a tendency to show distrust and interpersonal caution. Yet this was only part of the story.

Slater found the abductees had rich inner lives, a relatively weak sense of identity, particularly a weak sexual identity; vulnerability; and an alertness characteristic of both perceptual sophistication and interpersonal caution. (Hopkins, 1984) She also volunteered the opinion that her test subjects did not represent an ordinary cross section of the population. She found some were "downright eccentric or odd" and that the group as a whole was very distinctive, unusual, and interesting. "This last nicely paralleled Hartmann's observation that those of the nightmare group are perceived as "different" from "normal" people. Indeed all four of the reported commonalities are parsimoniously accounted for by thin boundaries.

By contrast, Slater had to multiply assumptions to account for weak sexual identities— she suggested forgotten involuntary surgical penetrations by aliens in childhood might have traumatized them. The uncertainties there are threefold: Did her nine subjects actually claim abduction experiences extending back to childhood? Should experiences that a person is unaware of affect one's sexual identity? Should surgical experiences per se even weaken sexual identity?

Also favoring the hypothesis was the unusual proportion of creative artists and therapists evident in the abductee population. Virtually anyone can satisfy for themselves their ubiquitous presence in abductee literature; Whitley Strieber's award-winning horror fiction and Betty Andreasson's having won prizes in many art contests being prime examples. Hopkins reports many mental health professionals among his abductees: two psychiatrists, three Ph.D. psychologists, and an unstated number of psychotherapists with Master's degrees in a population of 180 claimants. (Hopkins, 1988) This is demonstrably a hundred times greater than one could expect by chance based on government figures. A look at Mack's first book shows eight of its thirteen subjects had artistic and therapeutic backgrounds. (Kottmeyer, 1994)

There has been only one formal test of the hypothesis using Hartmann's Boundary Questionnaire. David Ritchey, as part of a larger investigation into abductees being psychologically sensitive, included the questionnaire among several test instruments. The results were unambiguous. The average boundary score of the abductees was 305, which was thinner than average and consistent with the scores of Hartmann's nightmare sufferers. (Ritchey, 1994) The obvious caveat to Ritchey's study is that it involved only fourteen subjects; a small sample, though larger than Slater's study.

The main criticism to date of the general proposition has been by Stuart Appelle who argues that the test findings of Spanos are not fully consistent with the cluster of personality traits predicted. (Appelle, 1995-96).

The Spanos study was not however limited to abductees with nightmarish experiences. Nine of thirty-one subjects with complex UFO experiences felt they had positive experiences and fifteen, just under half, rated their experience as negative. (Spanos, 1993) This renders application of boundary theory problematic. Other studies of the personalities of abductees have not directly addressed the boundary issue, but the consistent finding of paranoia scores higher than normal on standard MMPI tests points to sensitivities that look consistent with the thin boundary proposition. Further testing might resolve the issue more clearly in the future.

—MARTIN S. KOTTMEYER

References

Appelle, Stuart. "The Abduction Experience: A Critical Evaluation of Theory and Evidence," *Journal of UFO Studies* (1995/96).

Hartmann, Ernest. *Boundaries of the Mind: A New Psychology of Personality* (Basic Books, 1991).
———. *The Nightmare: The Psychology and Biology of Terrifying Dreams* (Basic Books, 1984).
Hopkins, Budd. "Abductees are 'Normal' People," *International UFO Reporter* (July/August 1984).
———. "UFO Abductions—The Skeleton Key" in *MUFON 1988 International UFO Symposium Proceedings* (MUFON, 1988).
Kottmeyer, Martin. "Testing the Boundaries" (*Bulletin of Anomalous Experience,* August 1994).
Ritchey, David. "Elephantology—The Science of Limiting Perception to a Single Aspect of a Large Object, Parts II & III" (*Bulletin of Anomalous Experience,* December 1994).
Spanos, Nicolas, et al. "Close Encounters: An Examination of UFO Experiences," *Journal of Abnormal Psychology* (1993).

Breakthrough (HarperCollins, 1995). Whitley Strieber concludes in this book that alien visitors compose a large number of familial groups who have become a part of the interior life of humans. He bases this conclusion on 139,914 letters he received between 1987 and 1994, in the aftermath of his *Communion* book, from persons describing their own alien encounters. These correspondents from all over the world gave a multitude of descriptions of their abductors ranging from insects and cat people to Greek gods and beams of light.

—RANDALL FITZGERALD

British UFO Research Association (BUFORA)
Originating in 1959 as the London UFO Research Organization, what was once LUFORO became BUFORA in 1964.

Today BUFORA is a nationwide network of about four hundred people who have a dedicated, non-cultist interest in understanding the UFO mystery. Within that membership are many active investigators and researchers working with the direct claims of witnesses to collate the data necessary to bring that understanding nearer.

A loose federation of U.K. regional UFO groups called the British UFO Association was formed in 1962. Over the next two years many of these groups decided to amalgamate all their activities under the BUFOA banner; so the organization was renamed the British UFO Research Association in 1964.

Benefits to members include BUFORA's principal publication, which is the *BUFORA Bulletin*, a bimonthly magazine of current interest articles.

The three aims of BUFORA are:

1. To encourage, promote, and conduct unbiased scientific research of unidentified flying object (UFO) phenomena throughout the United Kingdom
2. To collect and disseminate evidence and data relating to unidentified flying objects
3. To coordinate UFO research throughout the United Kingdom and to cooperate with others engaged in such research throughout the world

RESEARCH AND INVESTIGATION ACTIVITIES

In pursuit of its aims, BUFORA supports active investigation and research teams. The investigation team carries out on-site field investigation of cases, while the research team is involved in activities such as statistical research and technical support activities.

There are approximately fifty investigators and trainee investigators spread around the country. Trainee investigators are expected to work with an experienced investigator and to undertake a postal training course. These are supplemented by guidance notes. Investigators are expected to work to a Code of Practice.

BUFORA disseminates its findings and updates through several means:

• A lecture program
• UFO telephone hotline
• Publications
• Internet

Address: 70 High Street
            Wingham
            Kent CT3 1BJ
            England

E-mail: enquiries@bufora.org.uk
Web site: www.bufora.org.uk

Buff Ledge (Vermont) abduction Located on the Vermont side of Lake Champlain, north of Burlington, Buff Ledge Camp for girls became the scene for a dual-witness UFO abduction episode on August 7, 1968.

THE ENCOUNTER

Just after sunset "Michael Lapp" (a pseudonym), 16, who maintained the camp's waterfront equipment, and "Janet Cornell," 19, the water-skiing instructor, stood together on the end of the dock. Most of the campers and counselors were away on a two-day break.

As the two co-workers watched the western sky, a white cigar-shaped object appeared over the lake. Before departing, it released three small round objects which performed a series of acrobatic maneuvers. Then two of the satellite objects accelerated out of sight.

The remaining UFO headed directly toward the amazed witnesses and stopped within about ten feet from the end of the dock. Michael, who retained more conscious recall of the whole experience than Janet, described a classic "flying saucer," complete with transparent dome and revolving multicolored glowing rim. The object emitted a vibratory hum, he said.

While the female witness appeared frozen in a trance, her associate reported two short entities behind the dome clothed in tight-fitting uniforms. They had large heads, big oval eyes, and a small mouth. Michael was told telepathically they were from a distant planet and that he would not be harmed.

Next the craft moved overhead and a brilliant beam of light came on underneath, bathing the two in its glow. Michael, and presumably Janet, lost consciousness.

When the teens became aware again it was totally dark out, and they could hear the voices of campers returning from a swim meet. A tree-covered bluff and pavilion partially concealed the scene below on the dock. But Michael said two of the swimmers, "Susan" and "Barbara," rushed down to the top of the bluff, perhaps attracted by the UFO's glow, and must have seen the object at that moment as it angled upward and disappeared across the lake.

Aftermath

Both primary witnesses felt extremely tired afterward and fell asleep in their separate quarters. Although Michael remembered the close encounter and the entities, Janet apparently recalled only moving lights in the sky. Not wishing to traumatize his friend, Michael said he decided not to discuss with her what had taken place. The camp closed and the two participants went their separate ways.

Ten Years Later

After ten years had passed, the male witness said he had come across Dr. Allen Hynek's name and promptly called the Center for UFO Studies, which put him in touch with me. Thus began a five-year investigation into an experience—significant for its uncontaminated testimony; the two witnesses had never discussed with one another their shared encounter with the UFO.

During separate hypnosis sessions, not only did Michael fill in his "missing time"

with an abduction scenario, but so did his female counterpart.

Similar Accounts Revealed

There were remarkable similarities between their accounts. Both individuals recalled being inside the UFO's dimly lit interior. Their captors were described similarly as having large elongated heads, big eyes, two nasal openings, and a mouth slit. Each abductee had a "guide" who kept in telepathic contact with them throughout the experience. While Janet felt herself being probed and inspected by strange figures (she was instructed to keep her eyes closed), Michael stood nearby with his "guide" and watched the examination. He said this included taking blood and skin samples and extracting vaginal fluid (eggs?).

While two entities conducted the actual examination on Janet, a third figure monitored a console below an array of screens. The displays appeared to register various parts of the exam. Independent confirmation of this monitoring array by both witnesses provided strong evidence for a shared abduction experience.

Michael's Journey

Though Michael had no memory of the tests performed on him during his own physical examination, he apparently remained aware

Michael's drawing of close-encounter UFO as seen from the dock. Two entities were visible through the dome. Glowing plasma-like energy moved around the furrowed rim. Square plates covered the UFO on both top and bottom surfaces.

through much of the encounter, and consequently his overall experience was more detailed. During his hypnotic regressions, the male subject spoke of a journey he and his guide took through a "mother ship" into which the abduction craft had entered.

His tour included riding a tube of light across a giant hangar, the placement of a helmet on his head which conveyed some sort of imagery to a curved screen, and the presentation of a park-like landscape where Janet joined him. After this, Michael sensed himself falling through space and then waking up on the dock next to his co-worker.

SUPPORTING WITNESSES?

A persistent search turned up three possible supporting witnesses to both the UFO's abduction departure and its final exit from the dock. They were the two swimmers "Susan" and "Barbara," and the camp's playhouse director "Elaine." Unfortunately, the exact dates of their sightings could not be confirmed.

I subjected the two abductees to extensive

psychological tests, including the Psychological Stress Evaluator (voice analysis), and to background character checks. Both individuals appeared to be honest and credible. A hoax or some sort of shared hallucination was ruled out.

—WALTER N. WEBB

NOTE: For more information, see the full account in Walter Webb's book *Encounter at Buff Ledge: A UFO Case History* (J. Allen Hynek Center for UFO Studies, 1994).

Bullard, Thomas Eddie (b. 1949). Thomas Eddie Bullard was born in North Carolina and educated at the University of North Carolina at Chapel Hill and Indiana University, where he received his Ph.D. in Folklore. A lifelong interest in UFOs led to a dissertation on UFOs as modern folklore and articles treating the same theme in the *Journal of American Folklore, Magonia, International UFO Reporter,* and the *Journal of UFO Studies.*

Thomas Eddie Bullard

Under sponsorship of the Fund for UFO Research, Dr. Bullard carried out a comparative study of abduction reports, *UFO Abductions: The Measure of a Mystery* (1987), and a comparative survey of abduction investigators, *The Sympathetic Ear* (1995). He participated in the Abduction Study Conference held at

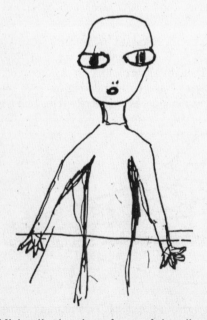

Michael's drawing of one of the aliens

M.I.T., while his articles on UFO waves and historical UFOlogy appear in Jerome Clark's *UFO Encyclopedia* (1998). He serves on the boards of the Center for UFO Studies and the Fund for UFO Research.

Address: 517 E. University St. #2
                 Bloomington, IN 47401
                 U.S.A.

POSITION STATEMENT: There is no question in my mind that people have seen strange objects in the sky and have undergone unusual experiences in the presence of these objects. I am also convinced that any hard and fast conclusions about the nature of these objects is premature.

Only scientific investigation of reports and a better understanding of the witnesses, as well as the interaction between observation and belief or cultural expectation, will set conclusions on a solid foundation. Until then I will admit that some reports seem unlikely to evaporate into any conventional explanation, but the human mind is full of surprises, and human ability to err in observation appears boundless. All in all the best position to me seems one of speculative restraint and investigative vigor.

—THOMAS EDDIE BULLARD

C

Case for the UFO, The (The Citadel Press, 1955). Astronomer Morris K. Jessup says in this book that UFOs have been present throughout human history and these visitors, operating from bases perhaps on our own Moon, are abducting human beings.

Jessup beat Erich von Däniken by more than a decade in describing how megalithic structures worldwide, from the Nazca lines in Peru to the Easter Island statues, could be the calling cards of extraterrestrials. He also was the first author by fifteen years to describe "Bermuda Triangle" areas where ships and planes "vanished without a trace."

—RANDALL FITZGERALD

Cash-Landrum UFO encounter Three Texans encountered a UFO while driving on a dark, lonely road near Huffman, Texas, on December 29, 1980. They suffered life-threatening injuries as a result of the encounter.

Betty Cash (51), Vickie Landrum (57), and Vickie's grandson Colby (7), were driving on the Cleveland-Huffman Road on the way to their homes in Dayton, Texas, when they spotted the UFO. It was about 9 P.M. and the road was deserted. The first indication of something unusual was the presence of a very intense light several miles ahead just above the pine trees. Betty remarked about the unusual brightness, but temporarily lost sight of it due to the many trees along the road.

Suddenly, hovering over the road only a short distance ahead was an enormous diamond-shaped object. "It was like a diamond of fire," Vickie said. The glow was so intense they could barely stand to look at it. Vickie at first thought it was the fulfillment of biblical prophecy and expected Jesus to come out of the fire in the sky.

In addition to lighting up the whole area like daytime, the UFO periodically belched flames downward. Fearing they would be burned alive, Betty stopped her 1980 Oldsmobile Cutlass without leaving the road. They all got out of the car to escape the heat and to get a better look at the UFO. Colby was terrified and dived back into the car, begging his grandma to get back in too. Vickie quickly reentered the car and comforted Colby.

Illustration courtesy of John Schuessler

Artist's depiction of the UFO

Betty stood momentarily by the driver's door and then walked forward to the front of the car. After much pleading by Vickie, Betty finally returned to the car; but the door handle was so hot she had to use her leather coat as a hot pad to open the door. Although the winter night air was only about 40 degrees, the heat from the UFO caused the witnesses to sweat and feel so uncomfortable that they turned on the car's air conditioner.

The sound from the UFO would increase each time it shot flames downward, but the intense glow never changed. In addition, the threesome heard an irregular beeping sound throughout the encounter.

Finally, the flames stopped and the object rose to the southwest and was lost from sight. Vickie and Colby commented that they could also see several helicopters and they seemed to be following the UFO. Betty started the car and headed for Dayton.

Betty was outside the car and directly exposed to emanations from the UFO for five to ten minutes. Vickie was outside for a much shorter time and Colby was exposed for only a minute or so.

As Betty raced homeward bound, she turned right onto highway FM-2100. Five minutes had lapsed since the encounter and just ahead of the car they could see the UFO and a large number of helicopters. "The sky was full of helicopters," Betty said. Some were near the object and others lagged behind. Betty pulled the car to the side of the road and waited for the entourage to get out of the way. It was then they counted more than twenty helicopters, many of them with twin rotors on top.

December 29th was a turning point in their lives. Betty, an unusually energetic woman, had plans to open a new restaurant the following week.

The sickness that followed the incident ruined those plans. Betty did not know it, but she would never work again. For the next four days, Betty's health degenerated. Red blotches on her skin became blisters of clear fluid, her eyes swelled closed, and she was weak from dehydration. At the same time Vickie and Colby were experiencing similar ills, but to a slightly lesser extent than Betty.

Betty was hospitalized for twelve days, went home briefly, but returned to the hospital for another fifteen days. The blisters caused a significant amount of skin loss and by the end of the third week she was losing a significant amount of her hair. Betty was also suffering from diarrhea, stomach distress, and severe headaches.

Vickie treated Colby and herself with

Summary of Medical Effects

Betty	Vickie	Colby
Erythema	Erythema	Erythema
Acute Photophthalmia	Photophthalmia	Photophthalmia
Stomach pains	Stomach pains	Stomach pains
Vomiting	Vomiting	Vomiting
Headaches	Headaches	Headaches
Diarrhea	Diarrhea	Diarrhea
Anorexia	Anorexia	Anorexia
Excessive hair loss	Hair loss	Minor hair loss
Fingernail damage	Fingernail damage	Tooth decay
Skin ulceration	Skin ulceration	Skin nodules
Cancer	Facial paralysis	
Low red cell count		

home remedies. She also lost some hair, suffered some eye damage, had diarrhea, stomach distress, and headaches. Colby's maladies were similar.

Vickie, Betty, and Colby

Although others also witnessed the UFO and the helicopter activity that same evening, various military agencies denied participating in the incident. With the help of Senators Bentsen and Towers, a meeting was arranged with U.S. Air Force attorneys at Bergstrom Air Force Base to get to the bottom of the situation. Other than a suggestion that Betty and Vickie might want to file a claim against the U.S. government, nothing else came from the meeting.

With the assistance of private attorney Peter Gersten, they did file a claim against the government for damages, which was denied. Then they filed for damages in the U.S. District Court in Houston, Texas. After months of activity in the discovery process, the judge finally refused to hear the case and their hopes of medical or any other kind of help were quashed.

Neither Betty nor Vickie ever worked again. Betty lost her businesses and moved to Alabama, where her family could care for her. She was hospitalized several times each year and many of those visits were in the Intensive Care Unit. Betty's life ended on December 29, 1998, exactly 18 years after the UFO encounter. By the fifteenth anniversary of the event, Vickie's health had slowly recovered. After several years, Colby overcame the physical and emotional impact of the event and became a productive adult.

Betty and Vickie requested that the investigators of this case make it known as broadly as possible, so that others who might experience the same thing in the future would know what to expect.

—JOHN F. SCHUESSLER

For more information, see John Schuessler's book, *The Cash-Landrum UFO Incident* (1998), available from MUFON (the Mutual UFO Network, P.O. Box 369, Morrison, CO 80465 U.S.A.).

categories of UFO reports The following classification system is now the most widely used among UFOlogists and popular journalists around the world:

RELATIVELY DISTANT SIGHTINGS

1. **Nocturnal Lights**. These are sightings of well-defined lights in the night sky whose appearance and/or motions are not explainable in terms of conventional light sources. The lights appear most often as red, orange, or white. They represent the largest group of UFO reports.

2. **Daylight Disks**. Daytime sightings are generally of oval or disk-shaped metallic-looking objects. They can appear high in the sky or close to the ground and are often re-

ported to hover. They can seem to disappear with astounding speed.

3.   **Radar/Visuals**. Of special significance are unidentified ''blips'' on radar screens that coincide with—and confirm—simultaneous visual sightings by the same or other witness(es).

RELATIVELY CLOSE SIGHTINGS
(WITHIN 200 YARDS)

1.   **Close Encounters of the First Kind (CE-I)**. Though the witness observes a UFO nearby, there appears to be no interaction with either the witness or the environment.

2.   **Close Encounters of the Second Kind (CE-II)**. The encounters include details of interaction between the UFO and the environment, which may vary from interference with car ignition systems and electronic gear to imprints or burns on the ground and physical effects on plants, animals, and humans.

3.   **Close Encounters of the Third Kind (CE-III)**. In this category, occupants from a UFO (entities of more or less human-like appearance now referred to as ''humanoids,'' or nonhuman creatures) have been reported. There is usually no direct contact or communication with the witness, but there have been some reports, increasing in recent years, of incidents involving very close contact with, and even temporary detainment of, the witness(es).

Since Dr. Hynek's death in 1986, two more categories of close encounters have entered the UFO lexicon:

4.   **Close Encounters of the Fourth Kind (CE-IV)**. This category makes the jump from mere sightings to kidnappings or abductions. In these cases, the UFO-related entities take the witness (or abductee) to another place, either mentally or physically.

5.   **Close Encounters of the Fifth Kind (CE-V)**. This category involves human-initiated contact with a UFO and/or its occupants. In these cases, the witness (or contactee) deliberately establishes contact with the UFO—via signaling or mental telepathy—and receives a like response.

—J. ALLEN HYNEK
& RONALD D. STORY

Chalker, William C. (b. 1952). Bill Chalker is one of Australia's most prominent UFO researchers and has written extensively on the subject.

William Chalker

Born in Grafton, New South Wales (NSW), Australia, Mr. Chalker was educated at the University of New England, graduating with an Honours Science Degree (B.Sc. Hons.) with majors in chemistry and mathematics. Since 1975 he has worked as an industrial chemist, laboratory manager, and quality manager. He is also a contributing editor for the *International UFO Reporter* and coordinates the NSW UFO Investigation Centre (UFOIC).

Chalker was the Australian representative for the Aerial Phenomena Research Organization (APRO) from 1978 to 1986 and NSW state representative for the Mutual UFO Network (MUFON) from 1976 to 1993.

His first book, *The OZ Files: the Australian UFO Story*, was published in 1996.

Address: P. O. Box W42
West Pennant Hills
NSW, 2125
Australia
E-mail: bill_c@bigpond.com

POSITION STATEMENT: Although the UFO problem has been under scrutiny for several decades, only the last few years have seen any real major advances in the study of the subject. It is fast becoming a serious area of scientific study, and only recently has it started moving beyond the area of casual inspection. Even though civilian groups have conducted an often remarkable documentation program during the past few decades, only in the past few years has the UFO subject been worthy of legitimate scientific study.

Clandestine inquiry has been replaced by serious open inquiry, and a solid database has been established. It is this documented data that science should seriously examine.

While the present data do not support any one clear hypothesis of origin and nature of the UFO, it certainly indicates without question the existence of a new empirical phenomenon.

Localized flaps that are ongoing can bring UFO research under the scrutiny of direct experimentation, which can provide us with the repeatable phenomena that legitimate science accepts. Personal experience has shown that such research activity yields considerable data, and it is these sorts of data that will thrust UFOs into the mainstream of scientific inquiry.

—WILLIAM C. CHALKER

channeling Considered to be a form of interdimensional communication in which a nonphysical intelligent being—not necessarily but often extraterrestrial—speaks through a human being in some form of trance. Channeling is one form of telepathy, which is not a new phenomenon, although it does figure prominently in modern New Age literature. Instances of inspired revelation and spiritual communication can be found in the Christian Bible, as well as in the scriptures of almost all human religions, globally and historically.

—SCOTT MANDELKER

Chariots of the Gods? (Econ-Verlag, 1968). Swiss hotelier Erich von Däniken, in this, his first and most widely circulated (reportedly 40 million copies) of many books on the ancient astronaut theme, seizes upon every megalith, every seemingly technological vestige of lost civilizations, practically every known myth or religious tale that mentions gods from heavens, to make a case that conventional theories of history and archaeology cannot explain the evolution of human intelligence. Though he doesn't know who they were, or where they came from in space, those ''gods of the distant past'' who were extraterrestrial visitors ''annihilated part of mankind'' to produce *Homo sapiens*. He gives partial credit for his findings to a rediscovery of ''knowledge that was hidden in the libraries of secret societies,'' groups he doesn't name or mention again beyond the introduction.

—RANDALL FITZGERALD

chupacabras The anomalous entity known as *el chupacabras*—the ''Goatsucker''—has been described by witnesses as standing between four and five feet tall and covered in greenish brown or blackish gray fur, with spindly arms ending in claws, powerful hind legs enabling it to jump over fences, a thin membrane under its arms that have been described as ''wings,'' and glowing red eyes. A proboscis emanating from the creature's mouth, allegedly employed to suck its victims' blood, has also been reported.

Mutilations had been reported on the island of Puerto Rico since the 1970s with the depredations of the notorious ''Moca Vampire,'' but it was not until March 1995 when the strange animal mutilations would replay themselves in a way that would attract media attention to the locality of Saltos Cabra outside Orocovis, Puerto Rico. A number of farm animals had

Artist's impression of *el chupacabras,*
the "goatsucker"

turned up dead on the property of Enrique
Barreto.

Researchers found strange three-toed footprints covering the ground and ruled out an
attack by a feral dog or cat, since canines and
felines have four toes. Further analysis proved
there was an 18-inch distance between footprints, suggesting that whatever creature they
belonged to was bipedal rather than quadruped-
al. Its weight was estimated at between 120
and 140 pounds.

In August 1995, Madelyne Tolentino of the
coastal town of Canóvanas would have the distinction of being one of the first witnesses to
the creature. Ms. Tolentino became aware that
a strange creature was approaching the house
at a moderate pace, allowing her to take a
good, long look at the aberration. Whatever it
was stood four feet tall and had a pelt covered
in a mixture of colors ranging from brown to
black and ashen gray, as if it had been burned.

On September 29, 1995, the creature killed
an assortment of rabbits, guinea hens, and
chickens at a farm in Guaynabo, P.R. A week
later eyewitnesses claimed to have seen a beast
"hairy like a bear" in Canóvanas again. On
October 29th, Canóvanas mayor José
"Chemo" Soto led a series of nightly hunts
for the creature, equipping his posse with nets,
tranquilizing dart guns, and other non-lethal
means. It represented the first response against
the bloodsucking visitor from anyone in an of-

ficial capacity. The balance of 1995 was filled
with senseless animal deaths and a choking
feeling of terror among rural residents.

A case could perhaps be made for paying
little attention to the chupacabras if it had remained circumscribed to the island of Puerto
Rico. But in February 1996, the chupacabras
killed forty-two animals in Miami, Florida.
Eyewitnesses in northwestern Miami reported
seeing a creature walking erect and covered
with thick matted hair at the scene of the attacks. The "Florida leg" of aberrant predatory
activity ran from February through July 1996.

Mexico's turn would soon be next: in May
1996, Teodora Ayala Reyes, a resident of the
village of Alfonso Genaro Calderón in Sinaloa,
became the chupacabras' first human victim,
presenting what appeared to be "burn marks"
on her back, exactly where the creature had
clawed her. The seaside village was further
wrenched out of obscurity after reports of a
colossal bat-like creature stalking the area became widespread. All manner of farm animals
were being found dead by their owners.

Reports soon followed from Guatemala,
Costa Rica, Honduras and as far south as the
Amazon Basin. Guatemalan farmer Vicente
Sosa thought he had seen a black dog with a
long tail that suddenly increased in size, becoming a red-eyed beast with enormous eyes.
Researchers visited the site of a chupacabras
attack on chicken coops in the Estanzuela region, and remarked on the high radioactivity
readings found in the area.

The southern U.S. soon produced its very
own chupacabras sightings. In mid-May 1996,
Sylvia Ybarra went out to her backyard in the
Texas town of Donna only to find that her pet
goat had been killed by three inflamed puncture wounds to its throat. The animal had been
felled near its shed.

The events surrounding the chupacabras'
initial eruption into popular awareness are now
many years behind us, allowing for a less
heated atmosphere in which to debate its origin
and even its existence. Skeptics refused to look
at the evidence, offering the same tired expla-

nations for the mutilations (feral dogs, apes, Satanists), but never explaining the face-to-face encounters with humans or the odd radiation signatures found in Puerto Rico and Central America.

—SCOTT CORRALES

Clark, Jerome (b. 1946). Jerome Clark has been active in UFOlogy since the early 1960s and is a much-published writer on UFO and Fortean subjects. He is also a songwriter (with Robin and Linda Williams) whose compositions have been recorded by Emmylou Harris, Mary Chapin Carpenter, Tom T. Hall, and other country, folk, and bluegrass artists. He has a wide range of historical, cultural, and literary interests.

Born in Canby, Minnesota, Clark attended South Dakota State University (Brookings) and Moorhead State University (Minnesota), majoring in English and political science. Between 1976 and 1989 he was an editor of *Fate* magazine. Since 1985 he has edited the *International UFO Reporter*, the magazine of the J. Allen Hynek Center for UFO Studies. He is the author of two editions of *The UFO Encyclopedia*. The first was published in three volumes between 1990 and 1996. *The UFO Encyclopedia: The Phenomenon from the Beginning*, the second edition, appeared in two volumes in 1998. Clark has won a dozen literary awards for his writings. In 1992 he won the Isabel L. Davis award, bestowed by the Fund for UFO Research, for his contributions to rationality in UFO study. He has written some fifteen books.

In 1989, after years in the Chicago area, he moved back to his hometown, where he now lives and works.

Address: 612 N. Oscar Ave.
            Canby, MN 56220
            U.S.A.
E-mail: jkclark@frontiernet.net

POSITION STATEMENT: After a lifetime in this subject, I have concluded that the extraterrestrial hypothesis is one reasonable tentative approach to putting the best-documented and most puzzling UFO reports into a scientifically defensible conceptual framework. By such reports I mean those with credible multiple or independent witnesses, instrumented observations, and physical evidence.

In this context the most crucial cases are not the most exotic or scary, but those with which actual science can be accomplished—usually close encounters of the second kind. In that sense, a single well-investigated landing-trace case is worth a thousand intriguing but evidentially empty abduction narratives.

I am also convinced that besides what might be called the "event phenomenon," there is an "experience phenomenon" which bears only a superficial relationship to the former. We lack a good vocabulary for, or even any real understanding of, a class of human experience—call it "visionary" for want of a better word—in which ostensibly supernatural entities are encountered. All we know is that such experiences are not objectively "real" in any conventional sense of the term; they just seem that way, and vividly so, to those who undergo them, and thus, since they are unlike ordinary hallucinations, they are genuinely mysterious. They mirror the cultural moment's notion of what a "supernatural experience" might be; thus, today the entities are extraterrestrials, whereas once they were fairies or demons or angels.

It is entirely likely, in my opinion, that daylight disks tracked on radar and exotic entity encounters experienced by individuals are two entirely separate, unrelated classes of phenomena. The first involves an event (it can be demonstrated that it happened in the world), and the second involves an experience (which can never be conclusively shown to have happened in the world).

I am in no way arguing for a paranormal hypothesis here. All I am saying is that certain sorts of human experiences are only dimly understood, if that; and that—where the UFO phenomenon is concerned—some of these contribute to the noise around the signal, which may be the intrusion of somebody else's technology into our planet-space.

—JEROME CLARK

Clear Intent (Prentice-Hall, 1984). Lawrence Fawcett and Barry Greenwood rely on 3,000 pages of previously classified documents, released under the Freedom of Information Act by eight military and civilian intelligence agencies, to construct a historical pattern of federal government involvement in UFO investigations. They also provide the first American version of an incident which occurred in 1980 at the Bentwaters Air Force Base in England involving an alleged night landing by a UFO witnessed by numerous U.S. Air Force security personnel.

—RANDALL FITZGERALD

Close Encounters of the Third Kind (Columbia Pictures, 1977; written and directed by Steven Spielberg.) A trend-setting UFO classic, starring Richard Dreyfuss, Melinda Dillon, François Truffaut, and Teri Garr.

More than a classic, Spielberg's monumental film is an exuberant rendering of contact with extraterrestrial visitors. It achieves an ingenious blend of ''human interest'' and sense of wonder that few can match. As reviewer Paul Clemens put it: ''*Close Encounters* . . . is quite possibly the most important film of our time. The most important because it encompasses all. The entire human race, our planet, our universe . . . our destiny.''

In the story, the protagonist (Roy Neary, played by Richard Dreyfuss) is confronted with the greatest mystery—culminating in the greatest imagined event—of our time, during the course of his mundane duties as a power company repairman. It turns out Neary's quest (instilled telepathically, it seems, by the aliens) proceeds in parallel with a secret group of scientific and military types, who are also hot on the UFO trail.

The film represents perfectly the symbiotic relationship between alleged science fact and science fiction. Spielberg even retained Dr. J. Allen Hynek (whose coined phrase served as the movie's title) as a technical advisor on the film to authenticate essential ''facts'' of UFO lore. Then, the film later had an apparent effect on what kind of ''real'' UFO-aliens were reported.

It reshaped reports of short, big-headed aliens in two demonstrable ways: (1) Before the film, aliens with long, thin necks were nonexistent. After it, they became common. (2) Before the film, the eyes were of a generally human arrangement of pupil, iris, and white. Afterwards, they generally became totally black. The eyes tended to be more tilted and larger than before.

Though it may be impossible to prove, the ''Spielberg effect'' is as real as any alien ever reported.

—MARTIN S. KOTTMEYER
& RONALD D. STORY

References

Close Encounters of the Third Kind '78 magazine (Warren Publishing, 1977).

Clute, John, and Peter Nicholls. *The Encyclopedia of Science Fiction* (St. Martin's/Griffin, 1993; 1995).

Spielberg, Steven. *Close Encounters of the Third Kind* (Dell Books, 1977).

Colony: Earth (Stein & Day, 1974). Richard Mooney proposes that humans arrived on Earth as colonists escaping the wreckage of a greater culture elsewhere in the galaxy. But another disaster befell this species in the form of the flood described in the Bible. Stonehenge, the pyramids of Egypt, and other megalithic structures were built to protect the ruling classes from future cataclysms and to determine the new orbital position of the planet and length of the year once the flood waters receded.

—RANDALL FITZGERALD

Coming of the Saucers, The (privately published by Ray Palmer, 1952). Pilot Kenneth

Arnold, assisted by publisher Ray Palmer, recount Arnold's 1947 UFO sighting, which made worldwide headlines. The book includes Palmer's subsequent investigation of other similar reports. Arnold had described the nine bright objects he spotted while flying near Mount Rainier as fluttering in formation, silver wings without fuselages, moving "like a saucer would if you skipped it across the water." Newspaper reporters took that statement and turned it into "flying saucers," creating a shape and an observational standard against which all future UFO reports would be compared.

—RANDALL FITZGERALD

Committee for the Scientific Investigation of Claims of the Paranormal (CSICOP)

CSICOP is a leading independent organization of scientists and scholars formed in 1976 and active ever since in critically examining paranormal and fringe-science claims (including those concerning UFOs and alien contact) from a scientific point of view. It is based at the Center for Inquiry in Amherst, New York, and has been headed since its inception by founding chairman Paul Kurtz, professor emeritus of philosophy at the State University of New York at Buffalo. CSICOP's more general mission is to promote science and scientific inquiry, critical thinking, science education, and reason. It publishes the *Skeptical Inquirer* (subtitled "The Magazine for Science and Reason"), a bimonthly journal that presents evaluative and investigative articles and information and perspective on a wide range of topics. Authors include scientists, scholars, and investigators worldwide; they need not be associated with CSICOP. It also holds national and international conferences, assists news media with finding scientific sources and scientifically credible information, sponsors workshops on skepticism, puts out a quarterly printed newsletter, disseminates electronic newsletters, and so on. CSICOP has been strongly critical of those who fail to use scientific rigor in investigating claims and of media that present credulous, unskeptical accounts of UFO claims and other unproved assertions about alien contact. Many scientists, writers, and investigators interested in extraterrestrial intelligence and active in examining claims of UFOs and alien contact have been associated with the CSICOP over the years, including astronomers Carl Sagan, George Abell, David Morrison, Alan Hale, and Edwin Krupp, UFO investigators Philip J. Klass, Robert Sheaffer, and James Oberg (Klass is chairman of CSICOP's UFO subcommittee), writers Isaac Asimov and Martin Gardner, and many physicists, plus a number of psychologists and social scientists (among them Robert A. Baker, Susan Blackmore, and Robert Bartholomew) interested in the psychological and sociological aspects of these controversies. Robert Sheaffer frequently critically comments on the most recent bizarre claims about aliens and UFOs in his "Psychic Vibrations" *Skeptical Inquirer* column.

Noteworthy investigative articles published in SI over the years include Klass's series demonstrating that the Majestic-12 documents are probably hoax documents, David E. Thomas's reports on the actual, very earthly origin of the 1947 Roswell "crashed saucer" debris (a Project Mogul multiple-balloon launch), and investigations into other claims and hoaxes surrounding Roswell. Forty of these articles were collected recently in a book, *The UFO Invasion* (Prometheus, 1997).

—KENDRICK FRAZIER

Address: P.O. Box 703
            Amherst, NY 14226
            U.S.A.

Web site: www.csicop.org

Communication with Extraterrestrial Intelligence

(The MIT Press, 1973) edited by Carl Sagan. In 1971 more than fifty American and Russian scientists and academicians met at a conference to debate the prospects for communicating with other life in the universe. Numerous unconventional theories for the evolution of intelligent life were offered: that life can exist at the level of elementary particles; that life can exist on planetary systems without suns; that comets could be a home for technological civilizations, and so we should be aiming our radio telescopes at both comets and stars.

—RANDALL FITZGERALD

Communion (William Morrow, 1987). Horror fiction novelist Whitley Strieber catapulted himself onto the top of the *New York Times* bestseller list with this book describing how he used hypnosis to uncover memories of having been abducted by aliens from childhood through adulthood.

According to Strieber abductions are connected to the number three and a triangular shape, because the visitors often appear in threes wearing triangular shapes or devices. He ends the book on a cautionary note: ''I cannot say, in all truth, that I am certain the visitors are present as entities entirely independent of their observers.''

—RANDALL FITZGERALD

Communion Foundation The Communion Foundation was founded as a private foundation by Whitley and Anne Strieber in 1988. It remains a private foundation, supported only by contributions from the Striebers.

By 1997, with the surgical removal of unexplained objects from the bodies of close encounter witnesses, innovations in memory research, and advances in video recording technology it has become clear that science now has the tools to make some clear determinations about the nature of both the close encounter experience and UFOs.

The Foundation does not have any bias for or against the notion that contact with a nonhuman intelligence may be under way. Its bias is toward objectivity and its goal is to answer the questions correctly.

However, a powerful prejudice has evolved within the culture of science against any research into this area at all. Without clear direction and a credible source of funding, genuine scientific progress will be impossible. The Foundation intends to work against this prejudice by educating scientists in the fact that there is a serious problem to be solved, there are interesting and useful discoveries to be made, and an obligation to replace public confusion with objective knowledge.

MISSION STATEMENT

It is the mission of the Communion Foundation to provide funding to established scientific institutions and credentialed professionals within the scientific and academic communities to accomplish the following objectives:

1. To engage in research into brain function associated with memory, in order to determine the degree to which specific memories refer to experiences that the subject perceived as a physical event.
2. To carry out sequential studies of close encounter witnesses in order to determine their profile within social and population groups.
3. To study the tens of thousands of witness narratives archived by the foundation in the past ten years in order to construct a clear and correct picture of the close encounter phenomenon. This is expected to be vastly different from current preconceptions.
4. To engage in the removal and examination of unknown objects from the bodies of close encounter witnesses and, if possible, a sample of subjects displaying the presence of such objects but reporting no close encounter memories.
5. To encourage and facilitate research into new propulsion technologies intended to replace heat, chemical reaction, and atomic propulsion in order to provide mankind with an efficient means of expanding into the solar system and the farther cosmos on as broad a scale as possible.

Address: 5928 Broadway
San Antonio, TX 78209
U.S.A.

Web site: www.whitleysworld.com

Condon Study See UNIVERSITY OF COLO-RADO UFO PROJECT.

Confederation of Planets in Service to the Infinite Creator A term used in classic channeled text, *The RA Material* (a.k.a. *The Law of One* series), as well as other channeled sources, beginning with the 1950s contactees. The term denotes an intergalactic collective of benevolently oriented extraterrestrial races (comparable to the "Ashtar Command"), which aids human evolution on Earth, as the source for all "positively oriented" ET contacts throughout the ages. It can be assumed this group goes by many different names; but regardless of name, it points to a unified association of ET races in our portion of the galaxy, serving to assist the development of consciousness. Many spiritually oriented teachers also believe that Earth will join this collective in the near future.

—SCOTT MANDELKER

Contactees Shortly after the influx of UFO sightings in the early 1950s came a new phase of saucerism: the emergence of the "contactees." Suddenly, it seemed, the Space People who piloted the heretofore unidentified craft were now introducing themselves to a select group of individuals, chosen, or self-appointed, to spread the wisdom of the "Space Brothers" to all mankind.

The Space Brothers came from Venus, Mars, Jupiter, Saturn, Neptune, "Clarion," and even from the Earth in times gone by. The contactee stories were deeply rooted in a strong religious tradition. More accurately, they were mystical "New Agers" who embraced the "mystery" religions of the East (especially Hinduism) as well as the Messianic traditions of the West. They were also utopians.

The Space People were described as idealized humans from idyllic societies whose message was one of love and peace. Obviously inspired by Cold War tensions and the resulting paranoia, the contactees were the "chosen ones" selected by the Space People to warn mankind of its folly.

Among UFOlogists, the contactees were seen as distinct from witnesses merely reporting UFO occupants and UFO "kidnap" victims known as "abductees." The typical occupant report involved a chance encounter in which the witness would just happen upon a landed craft and entities associated with it. Although this is sometimes the claim made by contactees concerning their initial encounter, once contact is made there is usually a long series of continued encounters that are planned rather than accidental. Furthermore, there are usually specially arranged meetings for instructional purposes. In these meetings, the Space People benevolently impart their secret cosmic knowledge—and most important, "Cosmic Laws"—to the chosen ones. As such they become initiates and assume their mission on Earth, which is to promote cosmic awareness—sometimes by spearheading new religions.

In recent years "abductees" have begun to serve as messengers for the same spiritual beliefs that were formerly associated with the contactees—hence blurring a sharp distinction that once existed.

—RONALD D. STORY

Corrales, Scott (b. 1963). Scott Corrales is a writer and translator of UFO and paranormal subjects dealing with Latin America and Spain. His work has appeared in magazines in the U.S., U.K., Japan, Spain, and Italy. Corrales is also the author of *Chupacabras and Other Mysteries* (Greenleaf, 1997), *Flashpoint: High Strangeness in Puerto Rico* (Amarna, 1998), and *Forbidden Mexico* (1999). He lives in Pennsylvania, where he edits *Inexplicata: The Journal of Hispanic Ufology*.

Address: P.O. Box 228
            Derrick City, PA 16727
            U.S.A.

E-mail: Lornis1@juno.com
Web site: www.inexplicata.com

POSITION STATEMENT: The UFO phenomenon is undoubtedly real and represents one of humanity's greatest concerns, yet one that it has steadily chosen to ignore over the years, largely out of complacency.

In my opinion, the UFO phenomenon is interdimensional in origin, with "interdimensional" being understood as another level or plane of existence coequal to our own that serves as the home base of the UFO phenomenon and perhaps many others.

Whether the UFO and its attendant phenomena manifest in our own reality by chance or design cannot be ascertained, but the sheer number of sightings and encounters with non-human entities leads me to think that their visits have always been deliberate.

Curiously enough, humanity has always been in contact with these entities, which appear under a number of names and identities, but has only recently come to identify them as "UFO occupants," "aliens," "ultraterrestrials," etc.

General awareness of this fact would perhaps serve to heal the breach between the spiritual and the physical that has always existed in Western society, particularly since the rise of Scientism.

—SCOTT CORRALES

Cosmic Consciousness This term was coined by the Canadian psychiatrist Richard Maurice Bucke, in 1899, to denote a higher level of spiritual awareness. "The prime characteristic of Cosmic Consciousness is, as its name implies, a consciousness of the cosmos, that is, of the life and order of the universe," Bucke wrote. "In the evolution of the human mind simple consciousness was first produced; then self-consciousness; and lastly . . . Cosmic Consciousness." (Bucke, 1901)

This theoretical model of human awareness emphasizes those changes in human consciousness that occur as a result of UFO encounters, and the personal and social transformations that develop around the meaning and significance of UFO experiences. This model also contains the minor hypothesis that UFO investigators are themselves UFO contactees.

This model is based on the work of Teilhard de Chardin, Julian Huxley, and the emerging theories of a holographic universe. (Ferguson, 1977; Wilbur, 1982)

Ferguson quotes Ilya Prigogine with regard to social and cultural transformations: "Cultures are 'perhaps the most coherent and strangest of dissipative structures.' Some innovations succeed, but others are suppressed by the surrounding 'medium,' the dominant society. A critical number of advocates of change can create a 'preferential direction' like the ordering of a crystal or a magnet organizes the whole." (Ferguson, 1979)

Prigogine's theory of cultural transformations may provide theoretical support for empirical evidence which has been obtained for the hypothesis of the "1% Effect": 1 percent of persons in society, practicing daily meditation, can significantly lower levels of crime, sickness, accident rates, etc.; they can significantly increase the conditions for an ideal society (Zimmerman, 1979); and they can reduce significantly the crime rates in an urban area. (Arons and Arons, 1981)

The UFO experience may be hypothesized as a program to increase the level of awareness and spiritual knowledge through the individual contactee. For example: A French physician, Dr. "X" experienced "healing" as a result of his UFO observation. (Michel, 1979) A 73-year-old Argentine gaucho, Ventura Maceiras, suddenly gained more philosophical and scientific knowledge after his UFO experience. (Romaniuk, 1973) A young woman, Betty Andreasson, with a fundamentalist religious faith, encountered humanoids whose food is "knowledge tried by fire." (Fowler, 1979)

Each of these UFO-related experiences seemed to be based on the views of reality that were held by the observer/experiencer, but each of these experiences apparently extended their views of reality, as well. In a holographic universe, a sophisticated observer can obtain many views of each hologram, and yet each "space-time" event contains all of the elements of the larger order of reality.

So, each UFO experience can be hypothesized as a separate "space-time" display, and yet each UFO display can be viewed as a "lens" that allows the observer to gain a larger display: a glimpse of the universe, or Cosmic Consciousness Conditioning. (Sprinkle, 1976a)

UFO CONTACTEE EXPERIENCES

In the opinion of the writer, the asinine, bizarre, and crazy aspects of UFO/alien activity can be hypothesized as the ABCs of a Cosmic Consciousness Conditioning (CCC) program: to change humans from Planetary Persons to Cosmic Citizens.

This CCC hypothesis may be wrong; certainly it is difficult to test. However, it is appropriate to explore, because many UFO contactees claim that it is the basis for their experiences and for the direction of their lives. So, we can learn something about the psychology and the sociology of UFO experiences, even if the claims of UFO contactees cannot be substantiated by current traditional scientific investigations.

Since 1980, a group of interested persons in Laramie, Wyoming, have conducted the Rocky Mountain Conference on UFO Investigation. The main purpose of the "Contactee Conference," as it is also called, is to provide a forum for private and/or public presentations by UFO contactees and UFO investigators, so they can become acquainted and share information.

UFO contactees and UFO investigators are often suspicious of one another, in the same way that "mystics" and "skeptics" are often suspicious of one another and drawn together by their mutual need for one another! Some of us who participate in the Contactee Conference view ourselves as both UFO investigators and UFO contactees.

We are willing to discuss our UFO experiences as well as our investigations. The writer views himself as biased in at least two ways: (1) As a "contactee," who has described his UFO encounters of 1949 and 1956, and his 1980 recollection (or fantasy or impression) of a fifth-grade experience on board a spacecraft,

with a tall man who said: "Leo, learn to read and write well; when you grow up, you can help other people learn more about their purpose in life." (2) As a UFO investigator who has talked with hundreds of UFO witnesses, read thousands of reports, and spent many hours discussing various aspects of UFO experiences with other investigators and contactees, including hypnotic sessions with more than 500 UFO abductees. These biases, or course, influence the writer—positively and negatively—in his UFO investigations. However, these biases do not negate the UFO contactee phenomenon.

As reported in the 1981 *Proceedings* of the Rocky Mountain Conference on UFO Investigation, the writer has worked with many persons who describe in hypnotic sessions their memories or impressions of abductions by UFO occupants or "UFOLKS."

These persons often express the fear of being crazy, or being ridiculed by relatives, friends, or neighbors. But they usually express relief upon learning that other participants have reported similar events: strange dreams, physiological symptoms such as bodily marks, poltergeist activity, apparitions, electromagnetic anomalies, and "mental messages" from entities who claim to come from outer space.

Of course, many investigators express doubts about the use of hypnotic procedures for the evaluation of UFO experiences (e.g., Hendry, 1979; Lawson, 1976). However, the exploration of "loss of time" experiences, or amnesic periods during UFO sightings, can be enhanced. Later, perhaps, other evidence can be obtained which can be used to support, or refute, the information obtained in hypnotic sessions.

Since 1976, the writer has been conducting a "Survey of Psychic Impressions of UFO Phenomena." (Sprinkle, 1976b) Over 600 participants have completed a questionnaire.

The majority of these persons present profiles of "normal" responses to psychological inventories, and yet they are puzzled by their UFO experiences and related changes in their lives. Many of these persons (e.g., Fisher, 1981; Kannenberg, 1979; and McNames,

1981) have described their claims of verbal messages or mental communications which offer information about the purposes of UFO personalities.

What follows is a summary of these claims about UFO experiences and related conditions:

1. UFO contactees have been chosen; no UFO contact is accidental.

2. Contactees are ordinary people, who exhibit a caring or a loving concern for all humankind.

3. Contactees have an experience which can be viewed as a manifestation of their ideas of reality.

4. UFO experiences include paraphysical, parapsychological, and spiritual manifestations which are designed to influence the "world view" of contactees.

5. Contactees receive information during, and after, their UFO experiences that is related to their life interests (e.g., natural sciences, social sciences, music and art, ancient civilizations, psychic phenomena, reincarnation, metaphysical and spiritual knowledge, etc.).

6. Contactees are gently coerced into studies and activities which blend with the ultimate purpose of UFO entities; they are not forced to be obedient to UFOLKS.

7. Contacts are initiated and maintained within the general framework of the contactees' views of reality. (Thus, UFO contacts can be viewed as physical, face-to-face encounters with flesh and blood beings, or out-of-body experiences, or mental programming by UFOLKS; or UFO contacts can be viewed as dreams, fantasies, and/or subconscious ideas which are manifested consciously, without external stimulus.)

8. Contactees are programmed for a variety of "future" activities, including awareness of their own contacts and desire to share their messages and knowledge with other contactees.

9. The lives of contactees move in the direction of greater self-awareness, greater concern for the welfare of the planet Earth, and a greater sense of Cosmic Citizenship with other beings in the universe.

10. The personal metamorphosis of UFO contactees is the forerunner of a social transformation in human consciousness, which now is leading to changes in the economic, educational, military, political, and religious institutions of nations of the Earth: the "New Age" of true science and spirituality.

EXAMPLE OF A UFO CONTACTEE EXPERIENCE

Ann (Canary) Brooke (a.k.a. "Gloria Archer") experienced some strange events, which for many long years caused her much distress. She is a bright, attractive, and perceptive person; however, she was raised in a family that valued family unity, nationalism, traditional views of "common sense" reality, and Christian fundamentalist beliefs.

She was unable to talk with her family about her UFO experience, which included: the out-of-the body experience; near-death experience; abduction; bodily and sexual examination; and mental communication with UFO entities.

Results of psychological inventories were in the normal range. Hypnotic suggestions to recall and relive her UFO experiences were helpful to her in recognizing that she had experienced direct contact with alien beings. Ann Brooke described the effects of her UFO experience as follows:

After my experience I knew that I had been privileged with a glimpse at something infinitely wondrous and profound. My inner consciousness had undergone a complete and staggering metamorphosis. Those truths I had been taught through the years by my church, family, parents, and teachers no longer were valid to me.

Those beliefs had been replaced by an understanding of the process we call creation and I know our Earth science and education were not yet beginning to suspect the Universal Laws that govern the creation of worlds within our universe. The following is a synopsis of the changes brought about in the inner me as a direct consequence of my experience:

1. I have embraced a faith of cosmic con-

ditions. I know the Creator as sexless and all creation as a material manifestation of mind extended into matter.

2. I no longer have allegiance to any particular form of earthly government, political system, race, economic or social structure. My only allegiance is to my Creator and to the Cosmic Christ.

3. I have continued to be obsessed with an expanded desire for truth and understanding of Earth's and man's evolutionary progress.

4. I have studied the mind and altered states of consciousness.

5. I am a firm believer in reincarnation. All of us are immortal souls—and we are responsible for what our minds manifest around us.

6. I have strived to balance myself: to evolve physically, mentally, and spiritually into a balanced human being.

7. I have tried to live my principles and moral laws within myself. Man is his own ultimate judge and therefore metes out his own punishment.

8. I have vowed to serve the Universal Law. I try to live and feel the law of love for others.

9. All life is *one*. We are part of the stars, oceans, all creation.

10. I have no fear of death. Death is the laying aside of one's physical body. Life is eternal—mind is eternal.

11. My mission is to Earth's citizens and environment; unless the consciousness of humankind is raised, we will ultimately destroy the work of eons, ourselves, and the present environment of our world.

12. Man is facing a crucial period in his evolution as a species.

13. I believe in a Father-Mother God, a balanced interchange between the creativity of both sexes.

14. I have the knowledge that we are unknowing participants in a living universe. There are other life-forms, other worlds, other dimensions.

15. I am experiencing loss of interest in the accumulation of material things.

16. Basically I have become a pacifist. War depletes—it does not enrich.

17. I have the knowledge that the world's fuel must be water. I feel a total disagreement with any society that pushes the use of nuclear fuel or weapons.

18. Within myself, I experience the consummation of science with religion.

After many years, I now realize and know that my own transformation was not and is not a single experience here on Earth. There are literally hundreds if not thousands of people who have experienced this metamorphosis. Our numbers are growing yearly and we are beginning to locate and communicate with each other.

An alien invasion has already occurred on Earth. The conquering power is not military or technological and economic superiority. It is a revolution in consciousness, and spiritual knowing that has been implanted within the minds of thousands of people all over the world.

The future of this world is passing into the hands and minds of these people. Those of us who have been contacted no longer serve the old orders. We fear nothing—least of all the threat of death or physical deprivation. We are *here—now*!

We walk among you daily—we pass you on the streets, stand next to you in the elevators, and you see little of what is moving daily closer to completion. We are among you—and our force is the force of mind governed by a morality and an ethical code that upon Earth is incomprehensible. (Archer, 1979)

"HIDDEN" UFO CONTACTEE EXPERIENCES

If these messages to UFO contactees are accurate, and if these messages are reported accurately, then the "alien invasion" *has* already occurred—and not as a conquering power, but as a revolution in consciousness.

In other words, UFO activity could be viewed as a lesson plan, or an educational project, to transform us Earthlings into UFO observers, witnesses, and contactees: to change us Earthlings from Planetary Persons into Cosmic Citizens!

Then the scenario follows along these lines: the next generation of scientists can build space-time craft, or "flying saucers," and Earth pilots can fly out in UFOs as UFO occupants, providing scientific and spiritual knowledge, or cosmic citizenship, to other planetary persons, etc.

THE NEW AGE

In support of the theme that a "new age" is dawning, three examples are summarized: (1) the effects on crime by groups of meditators; (2) the "hundredth monkey phenomenon"; and (3) the hypothesis of formative causation:

1. Arons and Arons presented a paper at the American Psychological Association meeting, in 1981, that demonstrated differences in police records for number of arrests in specified areas of Atlanta, Georgia, during those time periods when groups of meditators were meditating in those areas. The authors concluded that the data support the hypothesis that there are conditions under which small numbers of meditating individuals (at least if they are practicing the Transcendental Meditation technique) can create harmonious influences in a large social system, without face-to-face contact.

2. Lyall Watson, an English biologist, surveys biological foundations for unconscious behavior, including the delightful story of the "hundredth monkey." Watson described Imo, a female monkey, who learned to wash sand from sweet potatoes, which were provided by Japanese scientists who were observing monkeys on the island of Koshima. Imo taught her mother to wash her food; young monkeys were teaching their elders to wash their food; then, one day, an extraordinary event occurred, after an unspecified number of monkeys (about 100) had learned to wash their food, by nightfall of that day almost all of the monkeys were washing their food! Even more unusual, according to the un-

published notes of several scientists, other colonies of monkeys on other islands and on the mainland at Takasakiyama "spontaneously" began washing their food! (Watson, 1979)

3. Rupert Sheldrake, an English biologist, has suggested that the hypothesis of "formative causation" can account for some changes in evolutionary development. (Sheldrake, 1981) The concept of "morphic reasonance" is used as a basis for observed changes in organisms that grow and evolve in unusual increments. For example, Sheldrake described the long-range studies by McDougall and his associates. The results support the hypothesis that when groups of rats in one location learn to negotiate a particular maze, then other groups of rats in other locations learn to negotiate a similar maze in fewer trials.

These examples support the view that new learning can occur through "psychic" channels as well as "physical" channels of cause and effect.

CONCLUSIONS

With this short survey of some references to "new" learning, what can we conclude about the New Age? We cannot conclude, necessarily, that any Earth changes will result in the total destruction of the Earth. On the other hand, the number of prophecies about change would suggest that external and/or internal forces are impelling humankind toward another level of physical, biological, psychosocial, and spiritual awareness.

What we can conclude is that there is increasing evidence to support the hypothesis that a shift is occurring: a shift in thinking, or a change in human awareness, from a mechanistic model of the universe to a holographic model of the universe; to both "hardware" and "software"; science and spirituality.

Furthermore, we can predict that this shift in awareness will continue at an ever increasing pace, especially if groups of people come together to share their own experiences and their new learning. If these networks of concerned persons continue to grow, then education will become more public and more psychic in form and in process.

This writer has presented a view of human consciousness as a theoretical model for explaining UFO activity. The model suggests that UFO experiences are educational events that are presented to UFO observers, who become witnesses, who become contactees, who are impelled to learn more about the "outer" world and "inner" world, to share knowledge, and to become advocates for transformation in human awareness.

If this hypothetical model of UFO activity has relevance, then UFO investigators can expect an increased number of reports of UFOs as physical craft and as psychic phenomena and increased awareness of messages being received by UFO contactees. If the messages are meaningful, then personal consciousness is changing and social institutions are changing.

The major question remains a puzzle: Is UFO activity leading to the awareness, acceptance, and acknowledgment of the peaceful presence of alien intelligence? Or is UFO activity leading to the awareness, acceptance, and acknowledgment of "US FOLKS" as "UFOLKS" of the future?

This model suggests that a possible explanation for one facet of the UFO puzzle is that we UFO investigators also are UFO contactees, and that our investigations are a small part of a huge operation: a plan by which human consciousness is being transformed from that of Planetary Persons to Cosmic Citizens.

—R. LEO SPRINKLE

References

Archer, G. Personal communication, June 9, 1979.

Arons, A. and E. N. Arons. "Experimental Interventions of High Coherence Groups into Disorderly Social Systems" American Psychological Association Symposium, Los Angeles, August 27, 1982.

Bucke, Richard Maurice. *Cosmic Consciousness* (Innes & Sons, 1901; E. P. Dutton, 1969).

Ferguson, Marilyn. *Brain/Mind Bullein Special Issue*: "A New Perspective of Reality" (July 4, 1977).

———. *Brain/Mind Bullein Special Issue*: "Prigogine's Science of Becoming" (May 21, 1979).

———. *The Aquarian Conspiracy* (J. P. Tarcher, 1980).

Fisher, C. Personal communications, May 27, 1968-March 16, 1981.

Fowler, Raymond. *The Andreasson Affair* (Prentice-Hall, 1979).

Haines, Richard F. *UFO Phenomena and the Behavioral Scientist* (Scarecrow Press, 1979).

Hendry, Allan. *The UFO Handbook* (Doubleday, 1979).

Huxley, Julian. *Evolution in Action* (Mentor/NAL, 1953).

Kannenberg, Ida. Personal communication, April 27, 1979.

———. "The Great Contactee Hoax," *Proceedings*, Rocky Mountain Conference on UFO Investigation, Laramie, Wyoming, May 1981.

Lawson, A. H. "Hypnotic Regression of Alleged CE-III Cases," *Flying Saucer Review* (October 1976).

McNames, L. Personal communications, April 2, 1973-March 17, 1981.

Michel, A. "The Strange Case of Dr. 'X'," *Flying Saucer Review* (August 1979).

Romaniuk, P. "Rejuvenation Follows Close Encounter with UFO," *Flying Saucer Review* (July-August 1973).

Sheldrake, Rupert. *A New Science of Life: The Hypothesis of Formative Causation* (Tarcher, 1981).

Sprinkle, R. Leo. "A Preliminary Report on the Investigation of an Alleged UFO Occupant Encounter," *Flying Saucer Review* (November 1976).

———. "UFO Activity: Cosmic Consciousness Conditioning?" *UPIAR* (Editecs, 1976).

———. "Hypnotic and Psychic Implications in the Investigation of UFO Reports" in Lorenzen, Coral and James. *Encounters with UFO Occupants* (Berkley/NAL, 1976).

———. "Using the Pendulum Technique in the Investigation of UFO Experiences" in *UFO Phenomena: International Annual Review* (Editecs, 1978).

———. ed. *Proceedings* of Rocky Mountain Conference on UFO Investigation, Laramie, Wyoming, May 1980; May 1981.

Teilhard de Chardin, Pierre. *The Phenomenon of Man* (Editions du Seuil, 1955; Harper & Row, 1959).

Watson, Lyall. *Lifetide: The Biology of the Unconscious* (Simon & Schuster, 1979).

Wilbur, K. *The Holographic Paradigm and Other Paradoxes: Exploring the Leading Edge of Science* (Shambala, 1982).

Zimmerman, W. J. "Improved Quality of Life During the Rhode Island Ideal Society Campaign, Phase I, June 12, 1979 to September 12, 1979" (*Global Research Program,* May 1979).

cosmonauts, UFO sightings by   Unlike their American colleagues, Russian cosmonauts speak openly about their UFO sightings. Several of them were interviewed by western UFO researchers Michael Hesemann from Germany and Giorgio Bongiovanni from Italy.

Even the first man in space, Juri Gagarin, was quoted by the Russian press as saying: "UFOs are a reality. They fly with incredible speeds and, if one will give me permission to do so, I will gladly tell you what I saw while in orbit around the Earth." His colleague, cosmonaut E.V. Khrunov, stated in the March 3, 1979, issue of the magazine *Technique and Youth*: "The UFO problem exists and is very serious. Thousands of people have seen UFOs, but it is not clear what they are. . . . It is quite possible that behind this question the problem of communication with an extraterrestrial civilization is hidden."

In 1978, Cosmonaut and Air Force General Pavel Romanovich Popovich had a sighting of a "white triangle" on a flight from Washington, D.C., to Moscow at an altitude of 31,000 feet. It flew faster than the aircraft, going about 1,000 miles per hour.

On May 5, 1981, at about 6 P.M., Cosmonaut and Air Force General Vladimir Kovalyonok had a remarkable sighting in space, aboard the Saljut 6. When his space capsule passed Africa in the direction of the Indian Ocean, he saw through the porthole an object which he described as "disk shaped, one half of it surrounded by a conical kind of fog." It flew aside the Saljut, rotating in flight direction. Then, suddenly, it seemed to explode in a golden light. About two seconds later, a second explosion happened, and two spheres appeared, "two globes of the same color, golden, beautiful," as Kovalyonok described them. They seemed to be connected by a kind of "white smoke." A few minutes later, the spaceship entered the Earth's shadow, and the object was not visible anymore. The cosmonaut is convinced that it was under intelligent control.

On September 28, 1990, at 10:50 P.M., MIR Cosmonauts Gennadij Manakov and Gennadij Strekhalov saw "a big, iridescent silvery sphere . . . hovering above the Earth" after the Soviet Space Station had passed Newfoundland. After six or seven seconds, he stated, it disappeared.

In March 1991, MIR cosmonaut Musa Manarov, when observing the approach of a space capsule, saw and filmed a cigar-shaped object, surrounded by a rotating light, in some distance for several minutes. The film was released to the German researcher Michael Hesemann and published as part of his video collection "UFOs: The Footage Archives."

More video films, taken by the MIR crews, were released in 1999 to the Italian researcher Giorgio Bongiovanni. Although the Cosmonauts of these missions were not yet interviewed, the footage confirms further sightings by MIR cosmonauts Vladislav Volkov and Sergei Krikaliov in August 1991 and by MIR Cosmonauts Vladimir Soloviov and Nikolai Budarin on November 18, 1995.

—MICHAEL HESEMANN

Cowichan (Canada) encounter   One morning Mrs. Doreen Kendall, a practical nurse at the Cowichan District Hospital, British Columbia, Canada, reportedly saw through a hospital window a circular UFO with a transparent dome hovering outside about forty feet away. She claims to have seen two figures inside the dome, operating levers. Although Mrs. Kendall was the sole witness of the occupants, several other nurses are said to have seen the UFO leave.

The following condensed account gives the essential details of the January 5, 1970, sighting:

Mrs. Kendall, a registered nurse, lived in

Nanaimo and commuted to work at the Cowichan District Hospital. At midnight on New Year's Eve, both she and Mrs. Frieda Wilson began the midnight to 8 A.M. shift on the second floor (east wing) of the hospital. At 5 A.M., they went into a four-bed ward to begin morning care. Nurse Wilson attended the patient whose bed was by the door, and Nurse Kendall attended the patient in the next bed, which was located next to the window.

At this point, Nurse Kendall pulled the drapes open as is frequently done at that time in the morning. She stood looking out while nurse Wilson continued with her duties. What Doreen Kendall claims she saw is described as follows:

A "saucer," resembling a sphere, around which was a circular airfoil with lights on the rim, was hovering about sixty feet off the ground over a small patio. She estimated it to be about fifty feet in diameter, and that it was hovering at about the level of the third or children's floor, at about sixty feet from the hospital wall. When first seen, it was tilted toward her position, so that she could see inside of the upper portion, which she felt was illumined from below rather than above. The top portion was transparent and the light on the bottom (which she saw later) was red.

Inside the transparent "bubble" or "cupola," she claimed to observe two human-appearing entities. At first, they were visible from the side and only from the waist up, but when the object tipped toward the hospital she saw their complete forms. Both were standing, one apparently behind the other, and each stood in front of a stool with a back on it. The occupant farthest to her right was facing what appeared to be a chrome instrument panel comprised of large and small "circles" (possibly dials), which were brilliantly lit. She felt that both of the "men" were over six feet tall and noted that they were both well built.

As the object hovered, the man on Mrs. Kendall's left turned toward her, then extended his hand and touched the back of the man near the instrument panel, who reached down and

The scene of the UFO encounter as described by Doreen Kendall (Artist: Brian James)

grabbed a rod-like device with a ball on the top extremity, which protruded from the floor. She compared the latter to the joystick of an airplane. The man moved the "stick" up, then down, at which time the disk tilted toward her, and she obtained a good view of the interior, including the men.

She said that the hand of the man, who apparently alerted the other to her presence, was flesh-colored and human-appearing. Both wore dark clothing, and their features were concealed by some kind of headgear. The latter seemed to be similar to the material of the rest of their clothing.

Up until this time, Nurse Kendall had been so entranced with what she was watching that she did not think to call anyone, but when the object began to move away, she realized no one would believe her, so she called to Nurse Wilson, who reportedly went to the window,

Detail of UFO occupants
as described by Doreen Kendall
(Artist: Brian James)

and saw the strange object just outside. She said, "What on earth is that?" to which Mrs. Kendall replied: "I guess it's a flying saucer."

The couple then dashed quickly to the nurse's station, down the hall, and told what they had seen. They were not believed at first, but eventually two nurses, followed shortly by a third, came into the ward where they watched the lights of the disk-shaped craft. It was some distance away by then, but the lights were clearly seen by all. One of the nurses ran down the corridor to a bathroom and watched the object circle five or six times after which it took off "like a streak" to the northeast.

Mrs. Kendall later said that she had not been afraid, but just was very curious. She had the impression that the disk was having mechanical trouble.

—CORAL & JIM LORENZEN

Reference

Lorenzen, Coral and Jim. *Encounters with UFO Occupants* (Berkley, 1976).

Coyne (Mansfield, Ohio) helicopter case

On October 18, 1973, the four-man crew of an Army Reserve UH-1 helicopter, based in Cleveland, Ohio, flew to Columbus, Ohio, for regularly scheduled physical exams. When fin-

ished, they left the medical facility at approximately 10:00 P.M., drove back to the airport (a distance of two miles), filed a flight plan, and took off for the return to Cleveland at approximately 10:30.

The night was clear, calm, starry, and moonless; the temperature was 43 degrees F., visibility 15 miles. The route was familiar and the men were relaxed.

The aircraft was commanded by Capt. Lawrence J. Coyne, 36, full-time commander of the 316th Medivac Unit of the U.S. Army Reserve. Coyne was rated for helicopter, seaplane, and fixed-wing aircraft. The co-pilot was Lt. Arrigo Jezzi, 26, rated for helicopter flying only. Sgt. John Healey, 35, a detective in the Intelligence Unit of the Cleveland Police Department, was the flight medic. Spec. 5 Robert Yanacek, 23, was the crew chief. He had seen active duty in Vietnam as a helicopter crew chief.

Jezzi was flying from the left-hand seat. The helicopter was cruising at 90 kts. at an altitude of 2500 feet above sea level over mixed woods, farmland, and rolling hills averaging 1100 to 2300 feet elevation.

Near Mansfield, Ohio, Healey, in the left rear seat, saw a single red light off to the left (west) heading south. It seemed brighter than a port wing light of a normal aircraft, but because it was not relevant traffic, he did not mention it.

Approximately three to four minutes later, Yanacek, in the right rear seat, noticed a single steady red light on the eastern horizon. It appeared to be pacing the helicopter. After watching it for perhaps a minute, he reported it to Coyne, who instructed him to "keep an eye on it."

After about another 30 seconds, Yanacek announced that the light appeared to be closing on their craft. Coyne and Yanacek watched from their seats. Healy got up and stooped in the aisle to observe. Jezzi's view was obstructed.

The light continued its approach. Coyne grabbed the controls from Jezzi, began a powered descent of approximately 500 feet per minute, and contacted Mansfield control tower, requesting information on possible jet traffic. After initial radio contact, the radios malfunctioned on both UHF and VHF.

The red light increased in intensity and appeared to be on a collision course at a speed estimated to be 600+ kts. Coyne increased the rate of descent to 2,000 f.p.m. The last altitude he noted was 1,700 feet msl.

As a collision appeared imminent, the light decelerated and assumed a hovering relationship above and in front of the helicopter. Coyne, Healy, and Yanacek reported that a cigar-shaped gray metallic object filled the entire front windshield. A red light was at the nose, a white light at the tail, and a distinctive green beam emanated from the lower part of the object. The green beam swung up over the helicopter nose, through the main windshield, and into the upper tinted window panels, bathing the cockpit in green light. Jezzi reported only a white light from the upper windows. No noise or turbulence from the object was noted.

After a few seconds of hovering, the object accelerated and moved off to the west, showing only the white taillight. Coyne and Healey reported that the object made a decisive 45-degree course change to the right. Jezzi did not observe the course change. Yanacek's view was partially obscured.

While the object was still visible, Jezzi and Coyne noted that the altimeter read 3,500 feet with a rate of climb of 1,000 f.p.m. Coyne stated that the collective was still in the full down position from his evasive descent. The magnetic compass appeared to be malfunctioning.

Coyne gingerly raised the collective. The helicopter climbed nearly another 300 feet before positive control was regained. Then the crew felt a slight "bump."

Coyne descended to the previously assigned altitude of 2,500 feet, radio contact with Akron/Canton airport was easily achieved, and the flight continued to Cleveland without further incident.

THE GROUND WITNESSES

Mrs. Erma C. and four adolescents were driving south from Mansfield to their rural home on October 18, 1973, at about 11:00 P.M. when they noticed a single steady bright red light, flying south. This observation lasted about thirty seconds. Approximately five minutes later they had turned east on Route 430 when they noticed two bright lights—red and green—descending rapidly from the east. They then became aware of the "beating sound, a lot of racket" from an approaching helicopter.

Mrs. C. pulled over and parked. Two of the children, both aged 13, jumped from the car. They witnessed an unknown object "about the size of a blimp (or) a school bus" approaching from the east, and the helicopter approaching from the southwest. The unknown object assumed a hovering position over the helicopter and maintained this position as both aircraft, at very low altitude, crossed the road behind the auto. An intense green beam flared from the object, enveloping the helicopter and the environment. "The woods, the car, everything turned green," the ground witnesses reported. As the helicopter continued toward the northeast, the hovering object was in retrograde motion, which was corroborated by the ground witnesses who reported it as a "zigzag." The crew was of course oblivious to this component of the object's flight path.

The ground witnesses then observed the helicopter and object separate and the object proceed to the northwest, exhibiting only a white "tail" light, while the helicopter continued off to the northeast.

A second set of ground witnesses was found in 1988. On October 18, 1973, Mrs. Jeanne Elias was in bed watching the 11:00 P.M. news when she heard the sound of a helicopter, unusually low and very near the house. The residence is southeast of Mansfield, less than six miles from the Mansfield runway and 1.75 miles from the C. family's position. Jeanne was used to close aircraft activity, but this time felt there was definite threat of a crash, and (she realized rather foolishly) hid

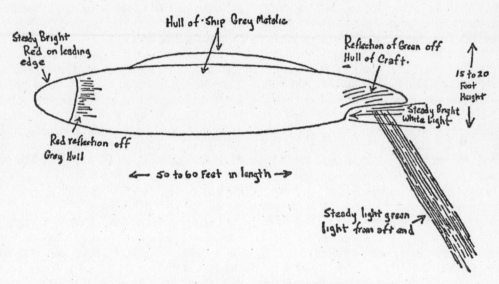

Direction of movement

Hull of Ship Grey Metalic

Steady Bright Red on leading edge

Reflection of Green off Hull of Craft.

15 to 20 Foot Height

Steady Bright White light

Red reflection off Grey Hull

← 50 to 60 Feet in length →

Steady light green light from aft end

Eyewitness sketch by National Guard helicopter pilot Larry Coyne

her head under the pillow. Her son John, 14, called to her from his room. He reported that the helicopter noise had awakened him and he had observed a bright green light "coming so heavy into my room." Neither Elias visually witnessed helicopter or object.

The eleven witnesses (4 crew, 5 C. family, 2 Eliases) were interviewed on location, repeatedly, separately and at length. All reported that the object appeared solid, with no diffuse areas, no train or trail, no fuzzy outlines. It had precisely positioned lights (including a 'maneuverable' spotlight), which bore no relationship to standard FAA aircraft lighting requirements. It made decisive hard-angle turns. It *may* have affected the helicopter controls and instruments. Scrupulous analysis of the individual increments of the event indicate that the object was in continuous view for a minumum of 300 seconds.

The identity of the object remains un-known. Clearly, with a duration of at least five minutes, it could not have been a meteor.

—JENNIE ZEIDMAN

Crash at Corona (Marlowe, 1992). Stanton Friedman and Don Berliner try to make a case that two separate extraterrestrial spacecraft crashed in New Mexico during 1947—one outside Roswell, the other 150 miles to the west. With this book they became the first authors to speculate that the military retrieval of this spacecraft debris produced technological spin-offs for human science, including solid-state electronics, an idea latched onto and made into a bestseller five years later by retired Army Colonel Philip Corso.

—RANDALL FITZGERALD

CUFOS   See J. ALLEN HYNEK CENTER FOR UFO STUDIES.

crop circles In August 1980 near Westbury, Wiltshire, some roughly swirled circular patterns were found in fields of oats. This was in an area famous for UFO activity in the 1960s—where the "Warminster Thing" had been reported.

The marks were studied by the Bristol UFO group, Probe (headed by Ian Mrzyglod), because of tales that they were UFO "landing sites." Probe consulted with a local physicist, Dr. Terence Meaden, who convinced them that the patterns were the result of fair weather whirlwinds—a mild form of tornado. Although Britain has few destructive tornadoes, it has more wind vortices of this modest type per square mile than any other country on Earth. Meaden operates TORRO (the Tornado and Storm Research Organisation) and regularly advises on the sites of damage-sensitive projects such as power stations.

During the next few summers several more circles appeared—apparently consistent with this weather theory. Then, engineer and UFO enthusiast, Pat Delgado, discovered the phenomenon and alerted the media. By 1983 he, later with Colin Andrews, had ensured that the stranger possibilities for circles were very much in the public perception, via articles for *Flying Saucer Review* and press interviews.

The 1983 circles came in a new complex form—several linked together in a geometric pattern. However, one was soon exposed to be a hoax by Mrzyglod, now working with BUFORA (British UFO Research Association). A national newspaper had tried to trap other media sources by paying a farmer to fake the "quintuplet" pattern.

Faced with this challenge, Meaden attempted to modify his theory to involve electrified forces and multiple tornado funnels. This was possibly a step too far. Circle patterns got even more complicated and turned into "pictograms" that were of obviously intelligent origin. Alongside this escalation and the rising level of media attention—at first in the U.K. and then globally—a crop circle research community of several thousand people rapidly

sprang up. Although more modest in size these days this community still exists.

In 1986, BUFORA published the first-ever book on the subject, *Mystery of the Circles*, compiled by its Director of Investigations, Jenny Randles, and a Hampshire statistician, Paul Fuller. They reported the work of Mrzyglod (who quit UFOlogy in disgust at the lack of common sense), Meaden, and theories of Delgado and Andrews.

The conclusion was that circles were a combination of hoaxing and weather effects. The report was issued to the serious media, and led to outrage in certain quarters of the UFO community who thought BUFORA were destructive skeptics. A public seminar was arranged by BUFORA in London at which—for the only time ever—all the key players in the story got together and had their say. A vote at the end by the audience overwhelmingly endorsed the BUFORA verdict.

Undeterred, and with the circles becoming ever more "unnatural" in appearance (including by 1990 images of whales and spiders), Delgado and Andrews signed a major book deal. *Circular Evidence*—packed with spectacular aerial color photos—became a global bestseller, attracted huge media attention, and established the circle mystery for all time.

Delgado and Andrews claimed that the circles were most likely the result of unknown energies—although the circle community was speculating much further. Talk of alien messages, cries to prevent the destruction of our planet, and more esoteric tales were soon incorporated.

BUFORA fought back with a more in-depth look, *Controversy of the Circles* (1989), again by Fuller and Randles, arguing in detail for the twin theory of hoaxing and wind vortices. They now had gathered a number of eyewitness accounts, where circles had been seen to be formed by what looked like the wind. However, their case was little heeded. In 1990 the BUFORA researchers greatly expanded their work as *Crop Circles: A Mystery Solved?* This work emphasized the greater level of hoaxing, *predicted* that the hoaxers would create patterns of a sort that could not be wind-produced, and also reported on research by Japanese scientists. This had established that the electrified vortex, proposed by Meaden, could be artificially generated in a laboratory and did leave simple circular aftereffects. These were also found in disused underground railway tunnels, where the combination of wind and electric fields provoked similar conditions. The BUFORA team also proposed that some UFOs might, in fact, be visible electrified vortices.

In September 1991, two retired artists, Doug Bower and Dave Chorley, approached a national newspaper claiming responsibility for the circle hoax and successfully fooled Delgado under the watchful eyes of a newspaper. They said they had created the most publicized circles from 1980 onward, after seeing a circle in Australia in 1966, which they did not fake. Bower and Chorley added that they had deliberately escalated their activities to fake new amazing patterns in direct response to Meaden's ever more convoluted theories. This was just as Randles and Fuller had predicted in their book the year before.

After the tricksters quit in 1991, circles continued to appear in some numbers each summer. Between May and September, in crop fields all over the U.K., although mostly in southwest England, a wide range still do appear. After the publicity blitz from 1989 onward, they were also found all over the world.

While termed "crop circles," because they mostly appear in cereal fields, they have, in fact, been reported in grass, reeds, sand, ice, and even on a wet road surface. They simply last longer in cereal crops, which are permanently deformed and so remain visible for days or weeks until discovery. Circles in grass, for example, tend to be blown out within hours and are much less pronounced.

Following the Bower and Chorley confessions, the media lost virtually all interest in circles—claiming everyone had been fooled by these two men and an army of copycat hoaxers

that trailed in their wake. Meaden moved on to other research. The crop circle community, bruised but not defeated, continued to try to prove that there was a real mystery. BUFORA argued that they had solved the mystery.

The key may be research by Fuller in the 1990s. He made a massive search for crop circles before the admitted activities of "Doug and Dave." This search included scouring old records, scientific literature, and aerial survey photographs of the landscape taken decades ago. Randles, meanwhile, went to Queensland to investigate the genesis of the 1966 circle—said to have inspired these two hoaxers.

This turned out to be one of many such patterns found for years in matted reeds in this poisonous snake infested swampland south of Cairns. There is little prospect that these are hoaxes. Yet all were simple, single, oval shapes like the first ones seen in Britain. Moreover, Fuller found dozens of examples dating back into the 19th century, including eyewitnesses who actually saw circles form. There were even some folk tales from as far back as the 16th century that might relate to circles found then and ascribed to the devil. Yet in every case—and all modern eyewitness sightings—only single, simple circles appeared.

The conclusion that one might reasonably draw from this is that simple circles can, and do, result from some kind of wind vortex. Throughout history this has produced occasional crop marks, and that led to the Queensland circles in 1966.

This natural phenomenon then gave Bower and Chorley the idea to create a hoax back in England. Having faked only simple circles with limited impact, and seen that there were apparently some genuine cases of a similar nature, they moved on in response to Meaden and BUFORA's rational ideas. The complex patterns, they thought, would prove that an intelligence must lie behind the marks and scupper Meaden's theories for good. This happened, insofar as the media and public were concerned, but led instead to escalating wild ideas about alien forces.

Once the mythology was in place, there were too many people who had invested time and effort—not to mention the tourist potential. Some farmers quickly learned they could earn more from faking a circle and charging entrance fees than from selling the same corn!

The result is the confusion seen today where arguments rage back and forth. Yet still nobody has reliably seen or filmed a complex circle pattern being produced or found any solid evidence of a link with aliens. The case mooted by BUFORA in 1986 still stands up well to scrutiny.

—JENNY RANDLES

References

Andrews, Colin, and Pat Delgado. *Circular Evidence* (Bloomsbury, 1989).

Noyes, R., ed. *The Crop Circle Enigma* (Gateway, 1990).

Fuller, Paul, and Jenny Randles. *Mystery of the Circles* (BUFORA, 1986).

———. *Controversy of the Circles* (BUFORA, 1989).

———. *Crop Circles: A Mystery Solved?* (Robert Hale, 1990; revised 1993).

D

Davenport, Peter B. (b. 1948). Peter Davenport has been Director of the National UFO Reporting Center (NUFORC) since July 1994. Born in St. Louis, Missouri, he attended high school in St. Louis, Ethiopia, and New Hampshire. He received his undergraduate education at Stanford University in California, where he earned bachelor's degrees in both Russian and biology, as well as a translator's certificate in Russian translation.

His graduate education was completed at the University of Washington in Seattle, where he earned an M.S. degree in the genetics and biochemistry of fish from the College of Fisheries, as well as an M.B.A. degree in finance and international business from the Graduate School of Business.

Davenport has worked as a college instructor, a commercial fisherman, a Russian translator in the Soviet Union, a fisheries observer aboard Soviet fishing vessels, a flight instructor, and a businessman. He was the founding president of a Seattle-based biotechnology company, which currently employs over 300 scientists and technicians.

In 1986, he was a candidate for the Washington State legislature, and in 1992, he was a candidate for the U.S. House of Representatives.

Davenport has had an active interest in the UFO phenomenon from his early boyhood. He experienced his first UFO sighting over the St. Louis municipal airport in the summer of 1954, and he investigated his first UFO case during the summer of 1965 in Exeter, New Hampshire.

He has been witness to several anomalous events, possibly UFO-related, including a dramatic sighting over Baja, California, in February 1990, and several nighttime sightings over Washington State during 1992.

In addition to being the Director of the National UFO Reporting Center, Davenport has served as the director of investigations for the Washington Chapter of the Mutual UFO Network.

Address: P.O. Box 45623
          University Station
          Seattle, WA 98145
          U.S.A.

Peter Davenport

E-mail: director@ufocenter.com
Web site: www.UFOcenter.com
Hotline: (206) 722-3000
          (8 A.M. to midnight
          Pacific Time preferred)

POSITION STATEMENT: The issue of whether UFOs are both real and of extraterrestrial origin has been extant in the public forum since its first appearance in the 1940s. For over half a century, it has remained a subject of heated debate, with skeptics citing the fact that there is no "hard" evidence supporting the existence of UFOs.

The proponents, on the other hand, offer up impressive quantities of principally eyewitness data, which although largely subjective and circumstantial in nature, is nevertheless quite intriguing. Despite the fact that most eyewitness reports are of low quality, many of the high-quality sighting reports involve certain objective aspects, which, to an open-minded bystander, are quite impressive.

As a full-time, and serious-minded, UFO investigator, I strongly side with the proponents. It seems indisputable that the phenomenon is real, and that it falls outside the scope of "normal" human experience.

Strong evidence suggests that we are dealing with a phenomenon that is being caused by palpable, solid objects whose characteristics are not of human design, and whose behavior is suggestive of intelligent control.

As a scientist, however, I am quick to add that our understanding of UFOs is still quite limited, and that the proponents of the phenomenon, and of its unambiguous involvement with extraterrestrial intelligence, have not provided unambiguous proof in support of their position. However, that absence of incontrovertible evidence could change very quickly.

—PETER DAVENPORT

Dawson encounter This event allegedly occurred on August 6, 1977, near Pelham, Georgia (20 miles north of Thomasville), in Mitchell County. At 10:30 A.M., retired automobile salesman Tom Dawson (sixty-three years old, at the time) took a walk down to his favorite pond to see how it looked for fishing later that day.

Just as he got inside the fence surrounding the pond, a circular space ship zipped right in between the trees and hovered just a few feet above the ground. At the same time he found himself, his two dogs and twenty head of cattle, frozen in place by an unseen force.

Dawson said the craft was about 15 feet high and 50 feet in diameter. It had portholes all around and a dome on top. It made no sound and changed colors rapidly from one to another. Suddenly, a ramp came down and out came seven hairless, snow-white beings, about 5 feet tall, with pointed ears and noses.

Some had on tight-fitting one-piece suits while others wore nothing. They talked in a high-pitched gibberish he could not understand.

They conducted what he thought to be a medical exam of some kind. They placed a skullcap-like device on his head and a large hula hoop-shaped thing (connected to a box) around his midsection. After they had collected "some leaves and stuff," they got back on the ship and were gone in the blink of an eye.

Once free, Mr. Dawson ran uphill (about 300 yards) to his trailer. He was having trouble breathing and talking, so he was taken to the Mitchell County Hospital, where the doctor said he had been shaken both mentally and physically from his encounter with the UFO and its occupants. He was treated for hysteria (given something to calm him down) and later released. Dawson said he believed that if he had been a younger man the extraterrestrials would have taken him away.

—BILLY J. RACHELS

Day After Roswell, The (Pocket Books, 1997). Retired U.S. Army Colonel Philip J. Corso claims in this book that he seeded alien technology harvested from the Roswell spacecraft crash to American defense contractors resulting in the development of night vision equipment, lasers, integrated circuit chips, and other breakthroughs. Though not present at the Roswell crash site in 1947, he describes what happened and who was there anyway, and says he saw firsthand one of the extraterrestrial bodies while it was being shipped by truck to Wright Field in Ohio. This "secret history of the United States since 1947," as Corso calls it, culminated in President Reagan's Strategic Defense Initiative, whose real target wasn't Soviet ICBM missiles but rather alien spacecraft invading our skies.

—RANDALL FITZGERALD

Day the Earth Stood Still, The (20th Century Fox, 1951; directed by Robert Wise) An historic "flying saucer" film of the Cold War era, starring Michael Rennie, Patricia Neal, and Hugh Marlowe.

Unlike most alien-invasion films of the 1950s, the extraterrestrial in this one is not a monster, but a clean-cut human being who brings a message of love and peace—backed by enough firepower to annihilate any troublemakers. Accompanied by an 8-ft.-tall robot wielding an awesome death ray, this emissary from another planet lands his saucer in Washington, D.C., not far from the White House lawn. "Klaatu," as he is called, has come to warn the people of Earth that those with whom we share the solar system will not tolerate our ignorant and evil ways. Worried about the atomic bomb in particular and our tendency toward violence in general, we are told that the Space People are fully prepared to reduce the Earth to a "burnt-out cinder," if need be.

As a demonstration of their power—in addition to the robot's death ray—Klaatu arranges for all electrical equipment on Earth to stop, at a prearranged time, for one day; hence the title of the movie.

As an allegory to Jesus Christ, Klaatu is shot dead by a soldier and subsequently resurrected by the robot, exercising advanced technology that is indistinguishable from magic.

Obviously inspired by paranoiac fears of communist subversion, the film is also important as a prelude to the UFO "contactees" who echoed the same philosophy, in their best-selling books, a few years later.

—RONALD D. STORY
& MARTIN S. KOTTMEYER

Delphos (Kansas) landing trace This case won the *National Enquirer*'s $5,000 prize for the UFO story "that supplied the most scientifically valuable evidence" (of extraterrestrial life) out of more than 1,000 entries submitted in 1972. The selection was made by the *Enquirer*'s "Blue Ribbon Panel," consisting of the late Dr. J. Allen Hynek, then an astronomer at Northwestern University; Dr. James A. Harder, professor of hydraulic engineering at the University of California at Berkeley; Dr R. Leo Sprinkle, then professor of counseling services (psychologist) at the University of Wyoming, Laramie; Dr. Frank B. Salisbury, professor of plant physiology at Utah State

Drawing by Billy Norris as described by the witness in the "Dawson encounter."

University, Logan; and Dr. Robert F. Creegan, professor of philosophy at the State University of New York, Albany (the one panel member who did not vote for the Delphos case).

Here is the story: Shortly after sunset (about 7 P.M. CST), on November 2, 1971, sixteen-year-old Ronnie Johnson was finishing his chores on his parents' farm when he suddenly heard a loud "rumbling" sound in the direction of the hog house. Looking up, he suddenly saw a brilliantly lit "mushroom-shaped" object hovering about two feet above the ground, with a shaft of white light below and glowing with intensely bright multicolored light (red, blue, orange, and yellow), "like the light of a welder's arc."

After about five minutes, the nine-foot-diameter "craft" suddenly ascended and started heading south. As it passed over the hog shed, about fifty feet from the witness, the boy said that the rumbling sound changed to a high pitch "like a jet," at which time Ronnie said he was temporarily blinded and completely paralyzed. About fifteen minutes later (now 7:20 P.M.), his sight and mobility returned and he burst into the house to tell his parents, Durel, 54, and Erma Johnson, 49. They rushed out of the house (they were eating dinner at the time, and had called Ronnie in earlier) just in time to see a bright object receding to the south. (Apparently, the object was moving very slowly, since it required fifteen minutes to travel only about 200 feet, as later estimated by Mr. Johnson, and was close enough to be described by Mrs. Johnson as looking "like a giant washtub.")

The Johnsons then rushed over to the spot where the UFO had hovered, and found the extraordinary, eight-foot-diameter ring, which they said "glowed in the dark." (The "ring" was actually shaped something like "an *irregular horseshoe . . . with an open space to the northwest.* The outer diameter was approximately 90 inches in a north-south direction and 99 inches in an east-west direction. The thickness of the horseshoe/ring varied from *12 inches* to *30 inches.*")

Mr. Johnson quickly photographed the ring, using a Polaroid camera *with a flashbulb*—later claiming that the picture constituted proof that the ring glowed! The Johnsons further claimed that when they touched the strange, grayish-white substance of the ring their fingers went numb. The effect did not last long in the case of Mr. Johnson, but Mrs. Johnson claimed a long-term numbness in her thigh, where she rubbed her hand after touching the "glowing ring."

The site where sixteen-year-old Ronnie Johnson, of Delphos, Kansas, claimed to have seen a glowing, mushroom-shaped UFO

Curiously, instead of calling a doctor or reporting the extraordinary incident to proper authorities (such as the Department of Public Safety or the police), Durel Johnson got into his truck with his son (this was about 8 P.M.), and headed straight for the office of the local newspaper. When the Johnsons arrived at the *Delphos Republican*, they found the editor Willard Critchfield, who was apparently unimpressed with the story; he made an excuse why he couldn't go to the farm that night and see for himself the evidence of an alleged UFO landing; nor would he send anyone else to check on the bizarre tale.

Not one to be discouraged, Mr. Johnson drove into town with Ronnie the next morning, this time seeking to find Critchfield at the main restaurant in town where the editor usually ate.

It happened that Critchfield was not there, but Johnson did find, instead, Mrs. Lester (Thaddia) Smith, a reporter on the *Republican*, who had already heard the UFO story from her boss, and who already knew the Johnsons. (She later wrote, in a signed testimonial, that: ''The Johnson family having lived in the Delphos Community their entire life are respected, truthful, conscientious, trustworthy, and well thought of, typical hard-working Kansas farm family.'')

Mrs. Smith was, therefore, quite willing to visit the Johnson farm (which she did, in the company of her husband and son-in-law) at around 11:30 A.M. on the 3rd of November. Mrs. Smith apparently accepted the Johnsons' story at face value, which she sought to help substantiate by collecting samples of the ring soil and some tree branches apparently broken off by the departing UFO. She, in turn, notified the Ottawa County sheriff, Ralph Enlow, who, with Kansas highway patrol trooper Kenneth Yager and undersheriff Harlan Enlow, arrived at the Johnson farm at about 2 P.M. also on 3 November. They talked to the Johnson family and inspected the ''landing'' site, taking photographs and soil samples. In addition, undersheriff Enlow stated in his report that: ''We used a Civil Defense Radiological monitor to determine that the soil was *not* radioactive.''

Ted Phillips arrived at the scene thirty-one days later, in the company of Sheriff Enlow, for an on-site investigation at the request of Dr. Hynek, Director of the Center for UFO Studies. Phillips conducted a detailed investigation which included subsequent testing (by eighteen independent laboratories) of several soil samples (including comparisons between ''ring soil'' and ''control soil''), but all the results were inconclusive. The upshot of Phillips's investigation was: ''no definitive conclusion . . . but, these traces in conjunction with over 1,000 physical trace reports from around the world do pose fascinating questions.''

Most fascinating of all were the ring's special properties. As stated in a sensational news story in the *National Enquirer*:

. . . independent laboratory tests of the soil have shown that it:

- Mysteriously resists water.
- Retards plant growth.
- Has a calcium content up to 10 times higher than the earth around it.
- Contains a ''white fibrous substance'' that is not in nearby soil.

What is so utterly amazing, however, is how these classic symptoms of the common fairy ring fungus, *Marasmius oreades*, had gone unrecognized after repeated analyses and ''investigations'' by so many ''experts'' and others who should have known better.

Photo courtesy of The University of Arizona

What may appear to be a UFO ''landing trace'' in this picture is actually none other than the ''fairy ring'' mushroom, a fungus known to botanists as *Marasmius oreades*.

According to the *Turf Pest Management Handbook*: ''Fairy rings are likely to appear if there is an abundance of organic matter in the soil. These fungi decompose organic matter to products which first stimulate growth of grass. Then fungus filaments either become so dense that the soil cannot be wetted and grass plants die from lack of moisture, or they excrete a toxic substance which inhibits growth of the grass.''

In fact, there was abundant organic matter

found in the ring soil (according to a report by Dr. Harold H. Williams, a geochemist, who analyzed a sample sent to him at Sunwapta Minerals Ltd. of Canada by APRO, and confirmed by an independent analysis performed at the request of Kansas City lawyer—and part-time UFO investigator—the late Clancy D. Tull).

In addition, there were other factors which normally contribute to the accelerated growth of the fairy ring fungus: recent heavy rains, leaves having fallen from the overhanging elm trees (creating a good humus), and animal urine in the soil (providing the necessary nitrogen for good fertilization).

There is also the curious fact that the "white fibrous substance" had "penetrated" the soil to a depth of fourteen inches. Such deep growth is also typical of *Marasmius*, which can sometimes grow to a depth of seven feet. Many of the surrounding elm trees also show signs of disease (as can be seen in photographs taken within a few days of the supposed incident) which, again, figured in the Johnsons's report. (It was said that the bark of the trees facing the ring also glowed in the dark, just as the ring did.) Indeed, *Marasmius* happens to be known as a wood-rotting fungus of living trees (especially elm) that appears on the outer bark—as can be verified by consulting the *Index of Plant Diseases in the United States, Agricultural Research Service Handbook No. 165.*

Another symptom is the accelerated growth of mushrooms (or "toadstools") in the vicinity of the ring, which also occurred in due course. And, according to a letter dated 30 November 1972 (in APRO's files), from Dr. Alexander H. Smith of the University of Michigan Herbarium, a sample sent to him by none other than Blue Ribbon Panel member and botanist Dr. Frank B. Salisbury, was apparently identified as none other than *Marasmius oreades*, the common fairy ring mushroom!

As for the associated UFO sighting, several factors tend to discredit the account given by the Johnson boy: all investigators agree that no evidence was ever found of soil-heating, as might be expected from a brilliantly lit UFO "blasting off." In fact, there is strong evidence that the ground (it is said) under the hovering UFO was not disturbed at all! As can be seen in photographs, taken within twenty-four hours of the supposed "landing" or "hovering" of the UFO, there were several small twigs resting directly on top of the whitish ring which showed no signs of being disturbed. If the object did indeed leave the "glowing ring" as evidence of its visit, one would logically expect that it would have at least deposited some of the same material on the overlying twigs, if not burning or blowing them completely away.

To make matters worse, from the standpoint of witness credibility, Ronnie Johnson reported that the UFO returned on April 27, 1974, and he predicts it will return again a third time. Ronnie also claims to have acquired psychic powers since the first UFO incident, and to have observed other strange goings-on. To wit, during the summer of 1973, he claims to have spotted, and chased, a creature dubbed the "Wolf Girl"—described "as having wild blonde hair, wearing a torn red dress of cloth, about three feet tall and standing with a stoop.

"When it ran, it got down on all fours and ran away faster than anything human can run," Ronnie said.

—RONALD D. STORY

Demon-Haunted World, The   (Random House, 1995). Astronomer Carl Sagan's last major book, published before his death. Addressing pseudoscience issues, Sagan devotes a section to alien abduction accounts, which he explains as a type of sleep disturbance that gullible researcher-hypnotists have manipulated for profit. Nonetheless, the eminent astronomer believes there is "genuine scientific paydirt in UFOs and alien abductions"—only it has to do with brain physiology, the nature of hallucinations, the psychology of systems of manipulation and belief, and "perhaps even the origins of our religions."

—RANDALL FITZGERALD

demonic theory of UFOs One explanation of UFOs is that they are demonic in nature; a logical theory in the sense that if they could be angels from God, they could also be the Devil and his demons, or a mixture of both in a classical religious dualism. (See RELIGION AND UFOs)

To ask if UFOs are demonic is to ask in the broadest sense if UFOs are evil, or at least, if their conduct toward man would be evil from man's point of view. Much modern science fiction in books and movies has dealt with the theme that Earth might be "invaded" by evil powers from another world. This view is not too far from the view of Christian fundamentalism that there are evil powers, devils, and demons, beyond man's control, which can invade this world.

While most students of UFOs believe their nature and intention are "good," the alternative must certainly be seriously considered. The "good" theories of UFOs see them either as benevolent scientific beings trying to make peaceful contact with our world (as in the 1977 film *Close Encounters of the Third Kind*) or as the angels of God, shepherds watching over their flocks of human sheep by night.

But the idea that UFOs are "good" is not totally obvious. In UFO literature, the obvious fact is that UFOs, if they are operated by some higher intelligence, do not make overt contact with the human race. How can we trust a reality which insists on hiding from us? If the intentions of UFOs were honorable, the argument goes, wouldn't they land openly? (The most obvious reply to this is: God is supposed to be good, but He is not too open about it either.)

One of the difficulties about the UFO problem is knowing precisely which data are reliable. Reliable or not, there are reports of UFOs shooting down fighter planes (usually after being attacked first), of humanoids giving off strange sounds and smells, of UFOs or their occupants paralyzing humans with various types of weapons, and also of humans being kidnapped, and later released, often with severe psychological aftereffects, as in the Barney and Betty Hill abduction case. Furthermore, people who have been in contact with UFOs sometimes develop unusual psychic powers—gaining prophetic ability in visions and dreams. There have been rumors that UFO beings are vampire-like, draining blood from domestic animals. In some ways, UFO stories often border on spiritualism.

How do we develop a consistent theory to explain the "unpleasant" data associated with UFOs? The most obvious way is to say that UFOs, from a human point of view, are evil. What is the nature of this evil? There are at least four categories of the evil or demon theory of UFOs: (1) the secular-scientific theory, (2) the secular-psychic theory, (3) the secular-supernatural theory, and (4) the religious-supernatural theory. Some of these theories are fairly well developed; others are very much in the embryo stage.

(1) The secular-scientific theory of UFOs sees them as evil or demonic in the sense that they have been deceptive in the influence of our religious values and beliefs. One famous UFO sighting occurred at Fatima, Portugal, in 1917. This sighting followed the vision of the Virgin Mary as reported by a group of children on the thirteenth day of several successive months, ending in a bright object in the sky witnessed by perhaps 70,000 people. Jacques Vallée, in his book *Anatomy of a Phenomenon* (1965), wonders with G. Inglefield if Fatima was really a religious miracle, or "a gesture of mocking"? In other words, was Fatima some kind of cosmic trick pulled on some gullible Catholics?

This view of religion is exemplified by the theory of R. L. Dione in his book *God Drives a Flying Saucer* (1969). Dione argues that God is really a spaceman who used an advanced technology to "fool" people into believing he had divine power. The miracles of Jesus were computerized tricks worked out on buttons pushed in a controlled spacecraft, which followed Jesus in his ministry and helped establish his divine reputation. In other words, the biblical religion is really a fraud, a scientific fraud perpetrated by beings from a higher technical civilization. Maybe Dione would not call these beings "demonic," but the Devil could hardly have a better advocate. The biblical religion turns out, in Dione's view, to be a big celestial joke. The reason UFOs don't land is that we would discover the nature of the fraud.

(2) The second theory of UFOs as demonic is what I call the secular-psychic theory. The origins of this theory go back to Carl Jung's book, *Flying Saucers: A Modern Myth of Things Seen in the Skies* (1959), advances in historical content in Jacques Vallée's *Passport to Magonia* (1970), and continues in Jerome Clark and Loren Coleman's book *The Unidentified* (1975). Another title for this theory might be "The Global Nervous Breakdown Theory."

Jung argued from the beginning that UFOs were psychological archetypes of the soul, round in shape, glowing in the dark. The old religions had died, and the world needed an image of a divine power flying to us from the heavens to save us. So, the human collective unconscious invented the UFO, a modern myth. Vallée shows how many UFO stories are similar to folklore and fairy stories of old. Clark and Coleman carried this further and suggested that due to the stress of our scientific age, we may be having a kind of collective nervous breakdown. Our rational-scientific side has buried our unconscious (psychic) side, and the soul is fighting back with the UFO myth.

The reason this theory takes on demonic dimensions is that there is concern that the unconscious may win the battle over the rational completely, and this would throw the human race back to the jungle—to the days of instinct and emotion without the control of reason. UFOs in this theory are a sign that the collective psyche of man is breaking down and, therefore, civilization is breaking down. We are destroying ourselves by an invisible power, our own unconscious minds. Jungians might not call this theory "demonic," but it is hardly good news.

(3) The third theory of UFOs as demonic is the secular-supernatural theory, developed almost entirely by John A. Keel in books such as *UFOS: Operation Trojan Horse* (1970) and *The Mothman Prophecies* (1975). Keel's theory is that UFOs are a reality from another dimension—an almost supernatural dimension in the midst of our world. The UFO beings from this world Keel calls "ultraterrestrials."

I call Keel's theory "secular-supernatural" because the UFO beings have what we would traditionally call supernatural power, but Keel tries to avoid making a religious connection with UFOs. From his point of view, UFOs come from a dimension right in the midst of us (much as I have argued in the chapter "Where Is Heaven?" in my 1968 book *The Bible and Flying Saucers*). Keel's beings sometimes have a demonic nature, but much of the time they seem to fly into our world the way we go to the movies for entertainment.

The Mothman Prophecies may be one of the most important (and least read) UFO books ever published. In it Keel explains his attempt to track down a UFO-related vision of impending doom, which turns out to be the collapse of the Silver Bridge at Point Pleasant, West Virginia. It seems clear to Keel that the UFO beings knew in advance of the collapse of the bridge, and they let him know of the impending disaster; enough so that he knew they knew, but not enough so he could avert it. Other unsettling aspects of Keel's book include his impression that the UFO beings knew his every move and every thought, in advance. Maybe they even controlled his mind. One reason Keel's work may not have received much attention is that its implications are too unsettling.

(4) The religious-supernatural theory of UFOs does not find John Keel's work too unsettling at all. Christian fundamentalist millennialists love Keel's theory, for it means that the Devil and his demons have been set loose on Earth in preparation for the end and the Second Coming of Christ.

The religious-supernatural theory has been developed by Clifford Wilson in his book *U.F.O.s and Their Mission Impossible* (1974), and by John Weldon with Zola Levitt in their work *UFOs: What on Earth Is Happening?* (1975). These Christian fundamentalists argue that UFOs are just as bad as John Keel says (they draw from his work), and a lot worse. It is the Devil and his angels let loose to torment civilization, to lead us to repent and believe in Christ, before he comes to judge the Earth. Weldon is a student of the theology of Hal Lindsey (*Late Great Planet Earth*, 1970, and *Satan Is Alive and Well on Planet Earth*, 1972), and UFOs along with the atomic bomb are a sign the end is near.

The weakness of the works of Wilson and Weldon is they support a religious dualism, of God and the Devil who are almost coequals fighting for the Earth. In traditional Christian theology, the Devil or Satan is only a "tester," working under God's direction. He has no authority except from God. In considering the religious nature of UFOs, "point of view" must be considered. Thus, as I have argued in *The Bible and Flying Saucers,* angels of God in the "pillar of cloud and fire" may have caused the parting of the Red Sea to save the Jews. This same power drowned the Egyptians. From the Jewish point of view, the pillar of cloud was an angel; from the Egyptian point of view, a demon.

—BARRY H. DOWNING

References

Clark, Jerry, and Loren Coleman. *The Unidentified* (Warner Books, 1975).

Dione, R. L. *God Drives a Flying Saucer* (Exposition Press, 1969; Bantam Books, 1973).

Downing, Barry. *The Bible and Flying Saucers* (J. P. Lippincott, 1968; Avon, 1970; Sphere Books, 1973; Marlowe, 1997).

Jung, C.G. *Flying Saucers: A Modern Myth of Things Seen in the Skies* (Routledge & Kegan Paul/Harcourt, Brace & Co. 1959; Signet/NAL, 1969; Princeton University Press, 1978). Original German language edition published in 1958.

Keel, John A. *The Eighth Tower* (Saturday Review Press, 1975; Signet/NAL, 1977).

———. *Operation Trojan Horse* (G. P. Putnam's Sons, 1970).

———. *The Mothman Prophecies* (Signet/NAL, 1975).

Lindsey, Hal. *The Late Great Planet Earth* (Zondervan Books, 1970).

Norman, Eric. *Gods, Demons and Space Chariots* (Lancer Books, 1970).

———. *Gods and Devils From Outer Space* (Lancer Books, 1973).

Spielberg, Steven. *Close Encounters of the Third Kind* (Dell, 1977).

Vallée, Jacques. *Anatomy of a Phenomenon* (Henry Regnery, 1965; Ace Books, 1966).

———. *Passport to Magonia* (Henry Regnery, 1969).

Weldon, John, and Zola Levitt. *UFOs: What On Earth Is Happening?* (Harvest House, 1975).

Wilson, Clifford, and John Weldon. *Close Encounters: A Better Explanation* (Master Books, 1978).

Wilson, Clifford. *UFOs and Their Mission Impossible* (Signet/NAL, 1974).

densification   A process whereby nonphysical spiritual energies, ideas, and tendencies become anchored in the physical body and personality over time. This process is common for ET walk-ins as they learn to integrate new spiritual and psychological qualities, associated with the new entering soul.

—SCOTT MANDELKER

Dick, Steven J.   (b. 1949). An astronomer and historian of science at the U.S. Naval Observatory since 1979, Steven Dick is best known as an historian of the extraterrestrial life debate. He obtained his B.S. in astrophysics (1971), and M.A. and Ph.D. (1977) in history and philosophy of science from Indiana University. His doctoral dissertation was subsequently published as *Plurality of Worlds: The Origins of the Extraterrestrial Life Debate from Democritus to Kant* (1982).

Dr. Dick tackled the entire scope of the 20th-century debate in *The Biological Universe: The Twentieth Century Extraterrestrial Life Debate and the Limits of Science* (1996), and its abridgement and update *Life on Other Worlds* (1998). The latter works argue that the idea of extraterrestrial life is a world view analogous to the Copernican theory, with widespread implications. Dick has written on these implications, notably in a volume he edited entitled *Many Worlds: The New Universe, Extraterrestrial Life and the Theological Implications* (2000).

Dr. Dick has served as Chairman of the Historical Astronomy Division of the American Astronomical Society (1993-1994), and as President of the History of Astronomy Commission of the International Astronomical Union (1997-2000).

Steven Dick

Address: United States
            Naval Observatory
            Code PAS
            3450 Massachusetts Ave. N.W.
            Washington, DC 20392
            U.S.A.

POSITION STATEMENT: The vast majority of UFO cases have prosaic explanations, including the planet Venus, balloons, hoaxes, and so on.

The question is what is the nature of the remaining few percent? In my view these few percent deserve further study, although it is unlikely they are extraterrestrial spacecraft for many reasons. They may be primarily a psychological or sociological phenomenon, but there is a chance they may be a physical phenomenon we do not yet understand.

Nevertheless, seen in the broad context of the history of the extraterrestrial life debate, UFOs are one way (science fiction is another) that popular culture deals with the worldview that extraterrestrial intelligence represents. Like so many other elements in the debate over life on other worlds, the resolution of the UFO question is deeply embedded in the problem of the nature of evidence and inference.

These problems, as well as the fascinating history of the UFO debate, are discussed in my book *The Biological Universe: The Twentieth Century Extraterrestrial Life Debate and the Limits of Science* (1996) and its abridgement and update *Life on Other Worlds* (1998).

The effect on humanity of contact with extraterrestrial intelligence depends very much on the contact scenario, especially whether it is remote contact by radio, or direct contact.

If one accepts the premise that a universe filled with life is a worldview, the best way to study the implications is by using historical analogues. One may study the trajectory of major world views such as the Copernican theory. Alternately, an appropriate analogue for remote contact would be the transmission of knowledge from ancient Greece to the Latin West via the Arabs in the 12th century; this input of knowledge resulted in the Renaissance of Western civilization.

—STEVEN J. DICK

Did Spacemen Colonise the Earth? (Pelham Books, 1974). Robin Collyns of New Zealand, who claims his ideas were shaped by Buddhist philosophy, believes Earth was established as a way station for reincarnated souls from other parts of the universe, which explains our planet's racial and linguistic diversity. Our own solar system is inhabited by extraterrestrials who have captured and even repaired satellites launched by humans. These beneficent aliens live on Venus, Mars, Jupiter, and Neptune, but have remained invisible to us because they scramble or censor our satellite photos.

—RANDALL FITZGERALD

Downing, Barry H. (b. 1938). Barry Downing is an important proponent of the ancient astronaut theory as it applies to biblical interpretation. His book *The Bible and Flying Saucers* (1968), which deals primarily with the material in the Book of Exodus as it relates to possible descriptions of UFO intervention, is considered a classic.

Barry Downing

Dr. Downing is presently the pastor of Northminster Presbyterian Church in Endwell, New York. He has been an advisor in theology to the Mutual UFO Network (MUFON) for more than twenty years, and is on the national board of directors of the Fund for UFO Research (FUFOR). He has published more than thirty articles and papers in the field of UFOs and religion. He is listed in *Who's Who in Theology and Science.*

Born in Syracuse, New York, Downing received his elementary education in that state, and his B.A. degree in physics, from Hartwick College, Oneonta, New York. His other degrees are as follows: B.D. in theology, Princeton Theological Seminary, Princeton, New Jersey; and Ph.D. in philosophy of science and religion, University of Edinburgh, New College, Edinburgh, Scotland. Downing was ordained as a United Presbyterian clergyman on March 5, 1967.

Address: P.O. Box 8655
            Endwell, NY 13762
            U.S.A.

POSITION STATEMENT: My main area of study has concerned the possible relation between UFOs and the biblical religion. My theory is that some, if not all, modern UFOs are related to what has been called the "angelic reality" reported in the Bible.

My theory, worked out in my book *The Bible and Flying Saucers,* is that UFOs come from another dimension, a parallel universe "in the midst of us" as Jesus said (Luke 17:21). According to the Bible, God is invisible, but his angels can become visible if they need to, and so the reports of visible angels in the Bible. Furthermore, these angels often have forms of space transportation, reported as the "pillar of cloud and of fire" of the Exodus, the "chariot of fire" of Elijah, the "wheels" of Ezekiel, the bright "glory" hovering over the shepherds at the birth of Jesus, the "bright cloud" over Jesus at his transfiguration and ascension, and the "bright light" over the Apostle Paul on the Damascus Road. The angels were understood to travel on the "clouds of heaven," a description parallel with many modern UFOs which often have a cloudlike appearance.

I believe the Exodus UFO, the "pillar of cloud and of fire," used its powers to split the waters of the Red Sea, and that this same UFO on the ground in a thicket caused the famous "burning bush" of Moses.

Psalm 23 says "The Lord is my shepherd," and I believe the modern UFO reports indicate that the "angels of God" are still with us, doing their shepherd work—by night and day.

—BARRY H. DOWNING

Drake Equation How can we estimate the number of technological civilizations that might exist among the stars? While working as a radio astronomer at the National Radio Astronomy Observatory in Green Bank, West Virginia, Dr. Frank Drake (now President of the SETI Institute) conceived an approach to quantify the factors involved in estimating the number of technological civilizations that may exist in our galaxy.

The Drake Equation, as it has come to be known, was first presented by Drake in 1961 and identifies specific factors thought to play a role in the development of such civilizations. Although there is no unique solution to this equation, it is a generally accepted tool used by the scientific community to examine these factors. The equation is expressed as follows:

$$N = R^* \cdot f_p \cdot n_e \cdot f_l \cdot f_i \cdot f_c \cdot L$$

N The number of civilizations in the Milky Way Galaxy whose radio emissions are detectable.

R* The rate of formation of suitable stars: The rate of formation of stars with a large enough "habitable zone."

f_p The fraction of those stars with planets: The fraction of Sun-like stars with planets is currently unknown, but evidence indicates that planetary systems may be common for stars like the Sun.

n_e The number of "Earths" per planetary system: How many planets occupy a habitable zone where it would be able to maintain a temperature that would allow liquid water? A planet in the habitable zone could have the basic conditions for life as we know it.

f_l The fraction of those planets where life develops: Although a planet orbits in the habitable zone of a suitable star, other factors are necessary for life to arise. Thus, only a fraction of suitable planets will actually develop life.

f_i The fraction of life sites where intelligence develops: Life on Earth began over 3.5 billion years ago. Intelligence took a long time to develop. On other life-bearing planets it may happen faster, it may take longer, or it may not develop at all.

f_c The fraction of planets where technology develops: The fraction of planets with intelligent life that develop technological civilizations, i.e., technology that releases detectable signs of their existence into space.

L The "Lifetime" of communicating civilizations: The length of time such civilizations release detectable signals into space.

Within the limits of our existing technology, any practical search for distant intelligent life must necessarily be a search for some manifestation of a distant technology.

A search for extraterrestrial radio signals has long been considered the most promising approach by the majority of the scientific community.

Besides illuminating the factors involved in such a search, the Drake Equation is a simple, effective tool for stimulating intellectual curiosity about the universe around us, for helping us to understand that life as we know it is the end product of a natural, cosmic evolution and for making us realize how much we are a part of that universe.

—SETI INSTITUTE

Drake, Frank (b. 1930). Widely known for his beliefs that life exists elsewhere in the universe, Frank Drake is a leading authority on methods for the possible detection of extraterrestrial intelligent signals. His pioneering efforts in this field are widely recognized and highly respected. Dr. Drake is currently Chairman of the Board at the SETI Institute in Mountain View, California, and Professor of Astronomy and Astrophysics (since 1984) at the University of California at Santa Cruz. From 1984-1988, he was Dean of Natural Sciences, and from 1988-1990, President of the Astronomical Society of the Pacific.

Dr. Drake shared in the discovery of the radiation belts of Jupiter (1959) and played an important role in the observational studies which led to the early understanding of pulsars. He received a B.A. in Engineering Physics from Cornell University in 1952, and an M.S. and Ph.D. in Astronomy from Harvard University in 1956 and 1958, respectively. Dr. Drake is a member of numerous professional societies and international organizations, including the prestigious National Academy of Sciences of the United States of America.

From 1952-1955, he was an electronics officer in the U.S. Navy. At Harvard, he was associated with the Agassiz Station Radio Astronomy Project, specializing in 21-cm research, and the development of infrared photometers. From 1958-1963, he was head of the Telescope Operations and Scientific Services Division at the National Radio Astronomy Observatory, Green Bank, West Virginia. While at Green Bank, he carried out planetary research as well as studies of cosmic radio sources, and conducted the first organized search for extraterrestrial intelligent radio signals, known as OZMA. In the fall of 1963, he became chief of the Lunar and Planetary Sciences Section of the Jet Propulsion Laboratory, California Institute of Technology. He joined the faculty at Cornell University in 1964, first as an associate professor of Astronomy, then, from 1966-1984 as a full professor.

From 1966-1968, he was the director of the Arecibo Observatory, near Arecibo, Puerto Rico. From 1969-1971, he was chairman of Cornell's Astronomy Department, and was Director of the National Astronomy and Ionosphere Center (of which the Arecibo Observatory is part) from 1970 to 1981.

Dr. Drake was among the first to show how interstellar messages could be constructed for easy radio transmission. In 1960, about the same time he conducted project OZMA, he pioneered in the development of binary coded messages from which a "picture" could be obtained after proper decryption of the codes. Dr. Drake constructed the first interstellar message ever transmitted via radio waves by our planet for the benefit

Frank Drake

of any extraterrestrial civilizations. This message is known as the "Arecibo Message of November 1974." Three messages, utilizing the techniques and methods developed by Dr. Drake, have already been sent to outer space. They are the Pioneer 10 and 11 Plaques (designed by Drake, Sagan, and Sagan), the Voyager Record on board the Voyager spacecraft (conceived by Drake and compiled by a host of contributors in addition to Drake), and the Arecibo Message of 1974.

Dr. Drake also devised an equation by which he gave an estimate of the number of communicative extraterrestrial civilizations we might find in our galaxy. Known as the Drake equation, $N = R^* \cdot f_p \cdot n_e \cdot f_l \cdot f_i \cdot f_c \cdot L$ is still valid and is regarded as the authority on the number of detectable civilizations.

Dr. Drake is the author of *Intelligent Life in Space* (1962), a contributor to *UFOs—A Scientific Debate,* edited by Carl Sagan and Thornton Page (1972), "Communication with Other Intelligences" in *Prospects for Man—Communication,* edited by W. J. Megaw (1977), co-author with Sagan et al. of *Murmurs of Earth: The Voyager Interstellar Record* (1978), and co-author with Dava Sobel of *Is Anyone Out There?* (1992).

Address: 2035 Landings Drive
            Mountain View, CA 94043
            U.S.A.
Web site: www.seti.org

POSITION STATEMENT: There is no general explanation of the UFO phenomenon which is complete and accurate. The UFO phenomenon is very likely more than one phenomenon, including at least very rare natural events and misinterpretations of rare but spectacular natural events. There is no good evidence for further origins of the UFO phenomenon.

The best hope for progress with UFOs is to obtain a variety of good quantitative observations of one of the more spectacular and "strange" cases. These observations should include high-quality photographs, calibrated, with good time references. Sound recordings, spectral information, and possibly radioactivity and magnetic activity recordings would be requirements. Unfortunately, I see no practical way to provide instrumentation in sufficient quantity to assure that such a set of observations will be made in the foreseeable future.

—FRANK DRAKE

Drake, W. Raymond (1913-1989). British author Walter Raymond Drake was a pioneer in the ancient astronaut field. He published numerous articles on the topic, beginning in 1957, followed by his book, *Gods or Spacemen?* first published in 1964.

A retired customs official, Mr. Drake spent twenty-five years promoting the ancient astronaut theory, most notably in his nine books: *Gods or Spacemen?* (1964), *Gods and Spacemen in the Ancient East* (1968), *Gods and Spacemen in the Ancient West* (1974), *Gods and Spacemen in the Ancient Past* (1975), *Gods and Spacemen Throughout History* (1975), *Gods and Spacemen in Greece and Rome* (1976), *Gods and Spacemen in Ancient Israel* (1976), *Messengers from the Stars* (1977), and *Cosmic Continents* (1986).

W. Raymond Drake

POSITION STATEMENT: Since 1957 I have given profound attention to the enigma of UFOs, which I consider the most baffling problem of the century.

I support the theory of extraterrestrials from other planets although I do recognize the formidable arguments of UFOs from inner etherean realms; the inner-Earth; time-travelers from the past or future; of even ultraterrestrials sharing our planet, but existing in another space-time continuum. With the confused information at our disposal, it is impossible to make a definite appraisal regarding their true origin. Recent research seems to indicate psychic influence beyond our cognizance. Several cases of abduction of men and women, past and present, make us wonder.

Many years ago, influenced by the Master Charles Fort, who collected unusual cosmic data for modern times in his wonderful books, I aspired to collect as many facts as possible from ancient literature to chronicle for the past what Charles Fort has so brilliantly done for the present century. I spent many years reading the classics and ancient histories in many languages, and in 1964 published *Gods or Spacemen?*, the first of nine books, wherein I detailed my researches covering most countries of the world, proving to my own satisfaction at least, that the gods of antiquity were spacemen, who landed and ruled our Earth in a Golden Age, bringing civilization to mankind.

Can our word "God" have at least two meanings? The Absolute imagining the Universe, in Whom we live and move, and the local "Gods" or Space-Beings, who originate from some advanced planet and from time to time manifest themselves among men? This startling conception could prove the fundamental discovery of our century. Our ancestors believed the Gods, the Spacemen, inspired them.

Gazing aloft in humility at those shining stars amid the dark, unfathomable infinitudes, we marvel at this magic, mysterious Universe and with sudden loneliness wonder who we are and why we find ourselves living now on ancient Earth.

A wondrous Renaissance of cosmic wisdom slowly dawns, soon to shine in spiritual splendor inspiring us all to think as Earth-folk, people of a small but proud planet, eager to meet our fellow men from other worlds. Salvation may descend from the skies. To communicate with the Spacemen on their cultural level, we must soar beyond our earthly ethics and expand to Cosmic Consciousness attuning our souls to all Creation.

—W. Raymond Drake

Druffel, Ann (b. 1926). A California native, Ann Druffel received her B.A. degree in Sociology from Immaculate Heart College (Hollywood) and did graduate studies toward an M.A. in Social Case Work at the National Catholic School of Social Service (Catholic University, Washington, D.C.). She worked for five years as a social caseworker for family- and child-welfare agencies. She retains a lifetime RSW (Registered Social Worker) in California. She married Charles K. Druffel in 1953. They have five daughters.

Her interest in UFOs stems from a personal sighting with another adult witness of a luminous daytime object over Long Beach, California, in Summer 1945. "Seemingly high above the Earth," she says, this object released numerous small objects which reflected the sun and disappeared after departing on different paths up and out from the main object She has been a UFO researcher in the Southern California area since 1957, beginning as an investigator for NICAP, and subsequently for MUFON and CUFOS.

Besides her investigative and research work, she was an associate editor of the *MUFON UFO Journal* from 1977 through 1983, is presently a contributing editor for that journal, and is a consultant for *Flying Saucer Review,* published in England.

She is Project Coordinator for Skynet, a public filter center and tracking system, from 1965 to the present. This work has revealed certain correlative patterns in UFO activity on which Druffel has reported in UFO symposia and conferences.

She has been a freelance writer since 1969 with 100+ articles published in the areas of UFOs, psychic phenomena and other subjects, plus film credits (documentary and screenplay). She is the author, with D. Scott Rogo, of *The Tujunga Canyon Contacts.*

Ann Druffel

She is currently with the Mobius Society in Los Angeles, assisting in psychic archaeology and intuitive criminology projects, and other experiments into the study of human consciousness. She is an accomplished remote viewer and certified hypnotist.

Address: 257 Sycamore Glen
            Pasadena, CA 91105
            U.S.A.

POSITION STATEMENT: UFOs present an urgent problem to the human race. For that reason, attitudes of secrecy and deliberate ridicule employed by world governments is dangerous and foolish. The mystery must be solved by physical and social scientists and other professional researchers, including philosophers and theologians. No facet of man's knowledge should be overlooked in the attempt to unravel this enigma.

UFOs apparently have been with us since prehistoric times; UFOs shapes found in Magdalenian cave art may be evidence that some unknown type of intelligence observed the human race's evolutionary leap from Neanderthal to Cro-Magnon. UFOs, as described in the Old Testament, seemed instrumental in the formation of the first major monotheistic culture. Reports of ''jinns'' in Islam, and ''incubi'' and ''succubae'' which reportedly harassed humans in medieval times indicate that extradimensional intelligence beings have interacted with the human race; these reports have aspects in common with present-day UFO activity. They cannot explain all UFO reports, however; it is likely that UFOs are multisourced. The multisource hypothesis would include: (1) physical extraterrestrial visitors; (2) unknown life forms normally invisible to us but capable of penetrating into our space-time; (3) time travelers.

There is little doubt, however, that the human race is currently under observation by an unknown order of intelligence(s), interested in human technology, and having particular interest in human reproduction. No *reliable* communication has been received from UFO entities to date. ''Messages'' received by witnesses, even considering a multisource hypothesis, are vague, contradictory, and therefore suspect. UFO entities involved in ''abduction scenarios'' seem to bode ill for the race; however, a growing body of evidence indicates that some close-encounter witnesses have successfully used various metaphysical and mental techniques against them. Intensive research to discover if unwelcome contacts can be fended off should proceed without delay.

—ANN DRUFFEL

E

"Earth Chronicles" The "Earth Chronicles" are a series of books by Zecharia Sitchin that, beginning with *The 12th Planet* in 1976, combine ancient cuneiform texts, the Hebrew Bible, and recent scientific discoveries to present a cohesive tale of how a renegade planet (Nibiru) became the twelfth member (sun, moon, and ten, not nine, planets) of our own solar system, and how its inhabitants, the Anunnaki, began to come and go between their planet and ours some 450,000 years ago.

Coming initially to obtain gold needed to protect the dwindling atmosphere of Nibiru, they ended up creating the "Adam," a species of primitive workers, by combining their genes with those of the hominids who had evolved on Earth. The events that ensued are echoed in the biblical tales of the Garden of Eden, the Deluge, and the Tower of Babel.

Sitchin's writings bring to life not only the incredibly advanced civilization of Sumer that blossomed about 6,000 years ago in Mesopotamia, but also the Anunnaki themselves: Their first leader Ea, also known as Enki; his half-brother the commander Enlil, and their half-sister Ninharsag who was the chief medical officer.

The Chronicles follow the tangled tale of gods and men through the millennia, until in 2024 B.C. one clan of Anunnaki used nuclear weapons to deprive another of the spaceport in the Sinai peninsula.

The six books, together with the two companion volumes, *Genesis Revisited* (1990) and *Divine Encounters* (1996), throw new light on the enigmas of Mars (what appears to have existed on it and why spacecraft keep getting lost there), the true builders of the Pyramids and Sphinx at Giza and their purpose, and the identity of the Divine Architect of the enigmatic colossal stone structures in both the Old and New Worlds.

—ETEP STAFF

References

Sitchin, Zecharia. *The 12th Planet* (Stein & Day, 1976; Avon, 1978).
———. *The Stairway to Heaven* (St. Martin's Press, 1980; Avon, 1981).
———. *The Wars of Gods and Men* (Avon, 1985).
———. *The Lost Realms* (Avon, 1990).
———. *Genesis Revisited* (Avon, 1990).
———. *When Time Began* (Avon, 1993).
———. *Divine Encounters* (Avon, 1996).
———. *The Cosmic Code* (Avon, 1999).

Edge of Reality, The (Henry Regnery, 1975). Two pioneers in the UFO investigative field, J. Allen Hynek and Jacques Vallée, together offer a progress report on research and scenarios for resolution of the extraterrestrial visitation question. Neither of these scientists sees much hope in radio telescope attempts to contact advanced civilizations. They offer seven scenarios on resolving the UFO enigma, ranging from extraterrestrial invasion to surrealistic holograms projected by a cabal of clever scientists.

—RANDALL FITZGERALD

Eighth Tower, The (Saturday Review Press, 1975). John A. Keel speculates that a superspectrum of energies encompassing gravity, the magnetic field, and infrasonic sound, control our observation of UFOs, Men in Black, ghosts, Bigfoot, and evil itself. This single intelligent force accounts for all religious, occult, and unexplained phenomena by blindly recording all the electrical impulses of human minds.

—RANDALL FITZGERALD

Elk abduction At approximately 11:58 A.M., on Thursday, February 25, 1999, three forestry workers, located approximately 20 miles west of Mt. St. Helens in Washington State, suddenly noticed a bizarre object—shaped somewhat like the heel of a man's shoe—drifting slowly toward them. It first appeared over a nearby ridge and was traveling in a northeastly direction. As it approached, the strange "craft" seemed to hug the contour of the terrain below it, and seemed to witnesses to be "flying" in a purposeful manner.

The three workers at first thought the object was some kind of parachute that was drifting and descending, but they quickly realized that their initial impression was wrong. One of the three immediately shouted to the eleven other co-workers nearby; then all fourteen members of the work crew stood on the hillside and watched for an estimated 5 to 10 minutes, as a remarkable chain of events unfolded in the valley below them.

Within seconds of their first observation of the craft, the witnesses realized that it appeared to be moving in the direction of a herd of elk that the crew had been watching all morning. They continued to watch as the object proceeded directly toward the herd, and succeeded in getting quite close to the animals. The animals apparently remained unaware of the object's presence until it was within a very short distance of the herd.

Suddenly, the animals became startled and bolted for cover—most of them running up the

White dot marks location where elk was abducted in Washington State.

slope to the east toward a densely wooded area. However, one adult animal was seen by the witnesses to separate itself from the herd and trot generally to the north, along a nearby unused logging road.

The witnesses reported that at this point, the object quickly moved directly above the lone elk and seemed to "pluck" it off the ground, although no visible means of support of the animal was evident to the observers.

The witnesses added that immediately upon lifting the elk off the ground, the object seemed to begin to "wobble" to an even greater degree than it had exhibited earlier. Also, as the object appeared to increase its altitude, the elk, which was suspended upright directly below it, rotated slowly beneath it, with its head apparently in contact with the ventral surface of the craft.

With the elk suspended below, the object began to ascend slowly up a clear-cut slope to the north, wobbling slowly as it moved almost directly away from the witnesses. However, when it reached a stand of tall trees at the end of the clear-cut, it appeared to brush the lower branches of the trees, at which point the object stopped, backed up, and began to rise almost vertically. At this point, the object appeared to wobble back and forth, i.e., begin a rolling motion from left to right, at an even more rapid rate.

It appeared to rise vertically over the trees and continued its "flight" to the north, apparently hugging the contour of the hill below it as it moved. When it crested the top of the rise, it descended into the neighboring valley to the north, and disappeared from the sight of the witnesses for a few seconds. Moments later, they last witnessed the object rising at a steep angle, and at high speed. It continued rising until it simply disappeared from their sight in the northern sky.

The witnesses stated that once the craft had reached the clear-cut to the north, they no longer could see the animal suspended below it. Their presumption was that the elk had somehow been taken into the object, although they never saw any kind of "door" or aperture through which the animal might have been conveyed into the craft.

Although there were slight discrepancies among the witnesses with regard to the appearance of the peculiar object, they agreed that it was relatively small, perhaps not too much longer than the elk itself. Its shape was reminiscent of the heel of a man's shoe, i.e., roughly U-shaped, and slightly tapered toward the aft end. Also, they agreed that it seemed to exhibit two "stripes," or patches, running longitudinally along its dorsal side, one of which appeared red, the other white.

The witnesses also stated that following the incident, the herd of elk remained in the same general area, although they remained more closely huddled together than had been the case earlier in the morning. The workers added that they too had remained closer to one another during the remainder of the work day, feeling ill at ease about what they had been witness to earlier in the day.

The case was first investigated jointly by Peter B. Davenport, Director of the National UFO Reporting Center, and Robert A. Fairfax, Director of Investigations in Washington State for the Mutual UFO Network. They traveled to the site of the incident on March 5, 1999, examined the body of an adult female elk found to the north of the initial abduction site by the landowner, and interviewed several of the witnesses. The investigation was continued over subsequent months.

The witnesses were deemed by the investigators to be reliable and sober-minded, with little to gain from the event. Some of them had been working for the same company for many years, and were described by their employer to be excellent employees. The witnesses refused all suggestions that they speak with the press, or go public in any way, about the alleged incident.

—PETER B. DAVENPORT

Ellwood, Robert S., Jr. (b. 1933). Dr. Ellwood is retired from the University of Southern California, where he was Professor Emeritus of Religion. A specialist in the history of religions,

Ellwood has written more than twenty books; the most important of which are *Religious and Spiritual Groups in Modern America* (1973), which contains a section on UFO groups, and *Many Peoples, Many Faiths* (1976), an introductory textbook in world religions, and *Alternative Altars—Unconventional and Eastern Spirituality in America* (1979).

Address: 997 Athens Street
          Altadena, CA 91001
          U.S.A.
E-mail: robertellwood@hotmail.com
Web site: www.rcf.usc.edu/~ellwood

POSITION STATEMENT: I have no public position on the physical science aspects of UFOs, since I do not have appropriate competence. I do, however, have an open mind and lively interest in the matter. My professional concern is UFO-inspired religious movements. I do not say that they or any other religion are false; the ultimate origin and meaning of all of humankind's religious experience and conceptual systems remain too full of mystery for final pronouncements, and in any case, a religious experience and belief can have rich subjective validity for a person regardless of what the facts are about its objective referent. My chief touchstone of interpretation for the evaluation of UFO religious movements would be Carl Jung's concept of the UFO as, for its religious believers, a "technological angel."

Humanity's immemorial spiritual quest, and the symbol systems which express its findings, change in outer form as worldviews and perceptions of appropriate guises for the transcendent change. UFO religious movements are interesting and worthy of a certain respect as innovative discoveries of the transcendent in a form congruous with a scientific and technological age. They accept and rejoice in the vast universe of space travel and possible extraterrestrials are given us by modern science rather than compartmentalizing it off as does so much older religion. In this respect the UFO religionists are spiritual adventurers and pioneers—people willing to deal with the profound modern spiritual crisis engendered by our living in the scientific world on the one hand, while remaining creatures with deep needs for subjective meaning and identity on the other. By making sacred the UFO, they have resolved the crisis in one possible way: In their "technological angels" they have given us striking symbols reconciling the universe of modern cosmology and the human need for transcendent points of reference. Like any pioneers, they can take false steps, rush to premature conclusions about the terrain they are exploring, and even lose their bearings altogether. But they have faced a crisis that many choose to ignore. They have dealt with it in their own way even at the cost of being called fools and worse by those who prefer not to perceive that, whether or not their space contacts are real, the modern spiritual conundrum to which the contact answers and to which the contactee is alive is real and must be faced before our culture slips into collective schizophrenia.

—ROBERT ELLWOOD

Elohim   The Hebrew word for deity; a plural form translated as "gods" by Hebrew scholars and UFO theorists alike, thus giving rise to the notion that extraterrestrials were involved in humanity's creation.

The UFO-ET interpretation was first suggested in 1960 by UFOlogist Brinsley Le Poer Trench in his book, *The Sky People*. Trench, who was called "the evangelist and top theologian of what amounts to a new galactic religion," claimed that the Hebrew version of the Old Testament refers to the Sky People when it uses the word *Elohim;* translated as "God" (where it should say "gods") in the English Bible. He, and Erich von Däniken after him, called attention to certain passages in the English version of the Bible that retain the plural form, particularly Gen. 1:26: "And God said, Let us make man in our image, after our likeness." "Why does God speak in the plural?" asks von Däniken. One would think that the one and only God ought to address mankind

in the singular, not in the plural." (Von Däniken, 1970).

According to Vergilius Ferm's *An Encyclopedia of Religion*: "Usually Hebrew writers speak of gods (elohim) and Yahweh (their god) before the exile but God (elohim) thereafter." (Ferm, 1945) However, certain passages of the English version have retained the plural form, such as the passage (1:26) quoted above, and the phrase "Behold the man is become as one of us." (Gen. 3:22)

More recently, the concept of the Elohim as extraterrestrial creators has been adopted by Zecharia Sitchin in his "Earth Chronicles" series of books and by the Raëlian Religion of Claude Vorilhon (a.k.a. "Raël").

—RONALD D. STORY

References:

Ferm, Vergilius, ed., *An Encyclopedia of Religion* (Philosophical Library, 1945).

Raël. *The True Face of God* (The Raëlian Foundation, 1998).

Sitchin, Zecharia. *The 12th Planet* (Avon, 1976).

———. *The Stairway to Heaven* (Avon, 1980).

———. *The Wars of Gods and Men* (Avon, 1985).

———. *The Lost Realms* (Avon, 1990).

———. *Genesis Revisited* (Avon, 1990).

———. *When Time Began* (Avon, 1993).

———. *Divine Encounters* (Avon, 1996).

———. *The Cosmic Code* (Avon, 1999).

Story, Ronald D. *The Space-Gods Revealed* (Harper & Row/New English Library, 1976).

———. *Guardians of the Universe?* (New English Library/St. Martin's Press, 1980).

Trench, Brinsley Le Poer. *The Sky People* (Neville Spearman, 1960).

Von Däniken, Erich. *Chariots of the Gods?* (G. P. Putnam's Sons, 1970; Bantam Books, 1971).

Elohim of Peace   Comparable to "Cosmic Christ," this term indicates a transcendent spiritual being or universal principle of peace and harmony, which can overshadow or inspire those individuals who are sufficiently evolved, and who seek to be used in the service of cosmic evolution on Earth.

—SCOTT MANDELKER

Encyclopedia of UFOs, The (Doubleday/ New English Library, 1980). Compiled and edited by Ronald Story, this was the first UFO encyclopedia ever produced and remains a standard reference on the subject.

Former *Fate* magazine editor Jerome Clark stated in his review: ". . . by any standard *Encyclopedia* is a magnificent achievement. It is, as all of us who awaited its appearance hoped it would be, *the* essential UFO reference work." Clark subsequently produced his own *UFO Encyclopedia* (Apogee Books, 1990; Omnigraphics, 1998).

When combined with the present work (*The Encyclopedia of Extraterrestrial Encounters*), readers will have a balanced set of books from which to draw their own conclusions.

—RANDALL FITZGERALD

Ether Ship and Its Solution, The (Borderland Sciences, 1950). Meade Layne has the distinction of being the first author to combine ancient astronaut theory speculations with a clearly metaphysical explanation for UFOs. From the etheric plane, seemingly empty space, these craft and their etheric pilots have materialized for thousands of years to help accelerate the evolution of human consciousness. Nine years before Carl Jung tried to tailor (in print) the UFO phenomenon to his theories of the collective unconscious, Layne was using a Jungian approach by explaining how these manifestations from the etheric realm could be thought forms produced by the human unconscious mind.

—RANDALL FITZGERALD

Evans, Hilary (b. 1929). Hilary Evans is a prolific writer/researcher and a leading proponent of the psychosocial approach to the UFO mystery. He works as a picture librarian, assisting his wife who is the proprietor of the Mary Evans Picture Library.

Born in Shrewsbury, England, Evans was educated at Cambridge and Birmingham Universities, where he received his B.A. and M.A. degrees in English literature in 1951 and 1953, respectively. His early writings—*UFOs, the*

Greatest Mystery (1979) and *The Evidence for UFOs* (1982)—were straightforward assessments of the UFO phenomenon. In 1987 he devised and edited, with John Spencer, the international compilation *UFOs 1947-1987*, and in turn assisted Spencer on another compilation: *Phenomenon* (1988); both on behalf of BUFORA, on whose Council both serve. His more individual researches are embodied in three books: *Visions, Apparitions, Alien Visitors* (1984); *Gods, Spirits, Cosmic Guardians* (1987); and *Alternate States* (1989). Though none of these is a UFO book as such, they are relevant to UFO research in that they are largely concerned with alleged encounters with otherworldly entities.

Hilary Evans

Evans is a frequent contributor to many UFO publications and lectures widely in North America and Europe. His most recent books include: *Almanac of the Uncanny* (1995), *UFOs: 1947-1997* (ed. with Dennis Stacy), and *From Other Worlds* (1998).

Address: 59 Tranquil Vale
           London SE3 OBS
           England
E-mail: hevans@satven.co.uk

POSITON STATEMENT: Of course there are objects flying about which we can't identify, and to that extent UFOs exist. But so long as the evidence for physical UFOs—let alone extraterrestrial visitation—rests on witness testimony, so long will it be subject to the reservations with which all such testimony must be received. Psychological and sociological findings show that we cannot set any limits to what the subconscious mind can devise and impose upon the conscious mind; so until I see convincing evidence for an external source, I find it easier to believe that it is to the subconscious mind of the individual that we must look for the most probable origin of most UFO reports.

While this can be seen as a form of debunking, I prefer to see it rather as a shift of interpretation. Simply because we cannot take an encounter experience at face value does not mean that it is has no other value. Those who claim abduction experiences, for example, are for the most part neither charlatans nor pathological cases; rather, they are people whose personal circumstances have interacted with the cultural ambiance to confuse fantasy with reality.

Approached on this level, the UFO experience can tell us a great deal about human behavior, both individual and social. Findings such as those of Alvin Lawson, and speculations such as those of Jacques Vallée and Mark Moravec should therefore be of the greatest interest to the behavioral scientist. At the same time it is clear that many UFO cases involve physical phenomena of an extremely interesting kind. Consequently, I find the work of Persinger, Rutkowski, Long, and others, and the fieldwork of Harley Rutledge and Project Hessdalen, to be of great potential value to our knowledge of the world around us.

—HILARY EVANS

Exeter (New Hampshire) sightings

The Exeter case represents one of the most spectacular and best-corroborated UFO close encounters of all time.

About half past midnight on Friday, September 3, 1965, Officer Eugene F. Bertrand, of the Exeter (New Hampshire), Police Department, was on routine patrol on the outskirts of Exeter when he spotted an automobile parked beside the road on Route 101. He stopped his patrol car to investigate, and upon approaching the vehicle, he found a lone woman in the car who appeared to be extremely upset. When Officer Bertrand inquired what the difficulty was, the woman replied that she had been chased approximately 12 miles along Route 101, from Epping to Exeter, by a very unusual looking, disk-shaped object, surrounded by a "halo" of bright red light. She reported that the object had made several swooping "dives" or "passes" at her car.

Officer Bertrand attempted to calm the woman, and asked her whether she could still see the object. She responded by pointing to what appeared to the officer to be nothing more than a star located close to the horizon. After several minutes of conversation with the woman, he returned to his cruiser and drove off, not bothering to record her name.

Officer Bertrand had no way of knowing that he had just been introduced to the first episode of what would very soon become known as the "Incident at Exeter." Based on subsequent events that morning, the case might better have been titled "Incident at Kensington" (New Hampshire), since most of the dramatic aspects of the case occurred in the latter township, located a few miles south of Exeter.

At approximately 1:00 A.M., some thirty minutes after Officer Bertrand's conversation with the woman, an 18-year-old man, Norman J. Muscarello, was hitchhiking along Route 150 in Kensington, while returning from his girlfriend's home in Amesbury (Massachusetts), to his home in Exeter. Mr. Muscarello had arranged to have his father pick him up in Amesbury and drive him home, but that rendezvous had not occurred, and he was making his own way home on foot and by catching rides with passing vehicles. As he hiked along the roadway on Shaw's Hill, Muscarello was alarmed by the sudden appearance of a very bizarre-looking object, which looked somewhat like a rugby ball viewed from the side, with five very bright, pulsating red lights or "windows" along its side. It apparently had risen out of a heavily wooded area several hundred yards to the north of the roadway, and it proceeded to approach Muscarello's location, passing over a nearby field and horse corral belonging to a Mr. Carl Dining.

In very short order, the object was hovering directly above the home of Mr. Clyde Russell, located some fifty feet north of the roadway, where it bathed the house and surrounding area in a "pool" of bright red light. At this time, it was not more than 80 feet from Muscarello, who later estimated its width at approximately 80-90 feet, considerably larger than the house located directly below it. He also reported that the object made no sound at all.

Artist's conception of the
Exeter/Kensington UFO

Muscarello at first crouched beside a low stone fence in front of the Russell home, hoping to be able to take cover from the bizarre object. Then, as soon as the object had moved away from the house, he knocked on the front door, hoping to raise its occupants. Although his pounding was heard by Mr. and Mrs. Russell, they elected not to answer the door, thinking the individual was possibly drunk or somehow deranged.

Muscarello then proceeded on foot west along the roadway, hoping to catch a ride into Exeter. He was picked up by a passing motorist, who took him to the center of Exeter, where he entered the police station at approximately 1:45 A.M.

The desk officer on duty that night was Officer Reginald "Scratch" Towland, who later reported that Muscarello was obviously quite agitated, so much so that his complexion was visibly pale, and he was barely able to stand. Based on this observation, together with the young man's story, Officer Towland radioed the information to all units. Officer Bertrand immediately returned to the station, picked up Muscarello, and requested that he direct the officer back to the location where the young man had last seen the object on Shaw's Hill.

When they first arrived at the location on Route 150, the two sat in the cruiser for a short period of time, at first witnessing nothing. Officer Bertrand made a radio broadcast to the police station, indicating that fact. They then exited the cruiser and proceeded into the field adjacent to the Russell home. For several minutes, they continued to see nothing unusual, but suddenly Muscarello witnessed the same object rise from behind dense trees at the end of the field, several hundred yards away. He shouted a warning to Bertrand, who wheeled around to face the object, now in the northern sky. At that moment, Bertrand considered drawing his service revolver to protect them both, but he quickly changed his mind. The two ran back to the cruiser, where Bertrand quickly radioed police headquarters about the sighting now in progress.

Within a few minutes, a second Exeter police cruiser, driven by Officer David R. Hunt arrived at the scene. Officer Hunt sat in his cruiser, while Bertrand and Muscarello sat in the other, and the three of them continued watching the object move around the area for an estimated five to ten minutes. Officer Bertrand later described how the object was capable of moving from one area of the sky to another, accelerating and stopping faster than the witnesses were able to track its movement visually.

All of the witnesses later reported that the object was extraordinarily bright, and that it was painful to look at it because of its brilliance. In addition, the five lights, or "window,'' on its side would pulse, or ''flash,'' in a repeating sequence, such that four were illuminated at any given moment, and the fifth was not illuminated.

Moreover, the three agreed that the lights were so bright that it was difficult to perceive the precise outline of the larger body, which remained indistinct to the observers. The light formed a distinct halo-effect around the object, as well.

The bizarre object proceeded to float around the nearby field, at one time passing within 100 feet of the three witnesses, they estimated. Slowly, it moved away from the three observers, passing to the southeast, over the roadway, and generally to the southeast. It passed over a tree line approximately 500 yards to the south, and disappeared over the top of Shaw's Hill, headed toward the New Hampshire shoreline. As it moved away, the object appeared to rock slowly from side to side.

Later the same morning, at approximately 3:30 A.M., Officer Hunt witnessed what he presumed to be the same object, located at a considerable distance from his location at the time on Route 85-101 Bypass.

Making the case even more intriguing is a report from a telephone operator in nearby Hampton, N.H. She reported receiving a call from a man calling from a pay telephone, who urgently requested that he be connected with a local police department. He told her that he had just been chased by a ''flying saucer.'' Suddenly, before the operator could get the man's name or identify the pay telephone he was calling from, the line went dead. Neither the caller, nor the pay telephone, was ever traced.

Hours after the incident on Shaw's Hill, the Exeter Police contacted nearby Pease Air Force Base, near Portsmouth, N.H., which dispatched at least two officers, a major and a lieutenant, to investigate. One of the officers, who gave his name as Lt. Alan B. Brandt, was interviewed at Pease AFB by *The Derry News*, shortly after the two military officers had conducted their investigation. Lt. Brandt reported during the interview that the officers had traveled to the site on Shaw's Hill, and that they had interviewed both police officers involved in the sighting, as well as Mr. Muscarello. The officer added that they had checked the area near Shaw's Hill, where the object presumably had been resting on the ground, for radioactivity, but had detected none. Lt. Brandt stated to the reporter during the interview that, whereas he had been a skeptic regarding UFOs prior to this case, the evidence he had witnessed related to the Exeter case had forced him to reconsider his opinion on the matter.

Mrs. Muscarello, the mother of the witness, later reported to UFO investigators that the officers had come to her home and asked her questions about her son and the alleged incident. She reported that she thought the name of one of the officers was ''Brant.''

The case attracted immediate attention in the New England press, being reported by the *Manchester Union-Leader*, *The Derry News*, *The Haverhill* (MA) *Gazette*, and perhaps by other local and regional newspapers, as well. In addition, the case was investigated by noted UFO investigator, Raymond E. Fowler, and by the Boston columnist, John G. Fuller, who authored the book entitled *Incident at Exeter* (first published in 1966).

There are other aspects of the case that have been alleged, but which remain unconfirmed. One of the assertions by a resident of Kensington suggested that an officer from the U.S. Air Force had attempted to purchase all the copies of the *Manchester Union-Leader* that had a major article about the sighting. The same source, who worked as a nurse, stated that the Hampton Police Department had contacted the Exeter Hospital to inquire whether a man suffering from shock might have been admitted there.

The bottom line is that the Exeter case remains as one of the best-documented UFO encounters on record.

—Peter B. Davenport
& Peter Geremia

extra-celestial Coined by a group of spiritual teachers associated with the "ET Earth Mission," this term denotes an ET Walk-in soul transfer which incarnates from the Angelic Kingdom into the Human Kingdom, taking over the life of a human being, to better serve the spiritual evolution of humanity.
                                        —SCOTT MANDELKER

ESP (Extra-Sensory Perception) This term is used to describe a range of nonordinary powers and abilities which suggest the use of sensory faculties which transcend the range and powers of the standard five physical senses. This type of power is responsible for telepathy and the range of ET channeling, and figures prominently in some of the more spiritually oriented ET contacts occurring.
                                        —SCOTT MANDELKER

ET (extraterrestrial) This term has been used for decades (equated with "Space Brothers" among the 1950s contactees), but was more recently popularized by the Hollywood movie of the same name. It is broadly used to describe individual beings and entire planetary races that originate from beyond the confines of the physical Earth, and are generally associated with other solar systems. ETs are linked to UFO phenomena, modern channeling, worldwide abductions, and New Age spiritual philosophy. Individuals who may be called "Wanderers, Walk-ins, or ET souls" are considered to be incarnated ET beings in human form, who by voluntary agreement, have chosen to enter human evolution to better serve planetary development. They agree also to forget and lose their higher dimensional powers and awareness, and during their series of human incarnations, are susceptible to all the same confusion and suffering as non-ET souls.
                                        —SCOTT MANDELKER

Extraterrestrial Civilizations (Crown Publishers, 1979). Science fact and science fiction writer Isaac Asimov believes we are not alone. Advanced civilizations are common, but they rarely come into contact with each other because of the vast distances between them. Using a series of variables in his own equation to calculate the numbers of extraterrestrial civilizations, Asimov predicts that 600 million planets in our galaxy are life-bearing, of which 530,000 have produced a technological species which still exists. If these are spread evenly throughout the galaxy, then 630 light-years separate every two neighboring civilizations, a distance sufficiently daunting so that visits may be out of the question.
                                        —RANDALL FITZGERALD

Extraterrestrial Encounter (David & Charles, 1979). British science writer Chris Boyce believes that alien probes or databanks may already be located on our planet or somewhere in our solar system. Sometime in the early 21st century humankind will obtain a piece of "hard irrefutable evidence" that other intelligent life exists, and we must begin preparing for the consequences this contact will have on us, challenging our culture, our religions, and all of our perceptions of ourselves as a species.
                                        —RANDALL FITZGERALD

extraterrestrial hypothesis The most popular and appealing notion about UFOs is the extraterrestrial hypothesis (ETH), the idea that intelligent beings from other planets are visiting Earth. To some, it is more than a hypothesis and can best be described as a belief. To others, it is an impossibility that should not be seriously considered. Much emotion has predominated in these debates since the late 1940s.

The ETH hinges on a long list of variables related to stellar and planetary physics and chemistry, and evolutionary biology. Data acquired on other planets in the solar system since the 1960s, mainly through on-site instrumentation delivered by American and Russian space probes, have made very dismal the prospects of extraterrestrial life in the solar system, much less intelligent life. The Victorian image of advanced beings on Mars carefully nurturing scarce water resources supplied by annual melting polar caps has been totally discarded, and even the most active proponents of the ETH now accept the fact that if UFOs represent alien intelligence, we must look elsewhere; that is, outside the solar system to planets associated with other stars.

The closest stellar system to our Sun is Alpha Centauri A, B, and C—a triple-star system located 1.32 parsecs from the solar system, equivalent to 4.3 light-years or 39.6 trillion kilometers. (A light-year represents the distance covered by electromagnetic radiation, such as light, in a one-Earth-year period, at a speed of about 300,000 kilometers per second. A light-year is thus equivalent to almost 10 trillion kilometers, or 6.25 trillion miles.)

Moving out to a radius of about five parsecs (16.7 light-years), there are about 40 more stars, some of which are good candidates for possessing life-bearing planets. All of these are located in a relatively provincial region of our Milky Way galaxy, which has been estimated to contain between 100 and 130 billion stars. So, on the surface, it would appear that the UFO problem is resolved by the very large number of possible abodes for intelligent life in the galaxy. Beyond our own galaxy are many millions of other galaxies, reaching out to the edge of the observable universe. The number of potentially habitable planets in the entire universe is almost too awesome to contemplate, and most astronomers content themselves with speculating on the number of habitable planets in our own Milky Way galaxy.

One Rand Corporation study, for example, produced a figure of 600 million planets in the galaxy capable of supporting intelligent life. More conservative analyses have produced a figure of 10 million habitable planets and a figure of 4.5 million planets on which sufficient time has elapsed for life to have evolved to intelligence, and the late Cornell University planetary astronomer Carl Sagan calculated the number of advanced technical civilizations in the galaxy at one million.

Astronomers have used various methods to

Thousands of galaxies were captured in this view of the universe, called the "Hubble Deep Field," made with NASA's Hubble Space Telescope.

arrive at these figures, usually for the purpose of estimating the number of possible sources of intelligent extraterrestrial signals. Since 1971, the study of this topic has become quite fashionable in astronomical circles and has been labeled the Search for Extraterrestrial Intelligence (SETI). Basically, the SETI-type analyses represent a process of elimination. Habitable planets should be affiliated with single-star systems, like our own, as binary- or triple-star systems would usually result in planets experiencing unstable orbits and periodically entering areas of intense heat or cold. At least half of the stars in the galaxy are thought to actually involve binary-, triple-, or even quadruple-star systems, and these are thus immediately eliminated from serious consideration. In a close study of the 123 sun-like stars visible to the eye in the Northern Hemisphere (all within 85 light-years of Earth), astronomers Helmut A. Abt and Saul Levy found that 57 percent did indeed have stellar companions.

The parent star must also be of a certain mass, and it should be in its "calm phase," allowing several billion years of stability for life to evolve. The mass of the planet itself is also important, as this will result in the retention or loss of numerous important chemical components necessary for carbon-based life. Its mass must be greater than 0.4 but less than 2.35 that of the Earth, and, in order to avoid overheating or overcooling, its period of rotation should be less than four Earth days.

In making all these kinds of calculations, however, astronomers have generally ignored important evolutionary factors, and have proceeded on the basis that, once life begins, "intelligence" will sooner or later evolve. While there are some good reasons for believing this, related to the increase in physiological complexity up the phylogenetic scale observable on Earth, there is no actual proof to support this belief.

A Miocene/Pliocene-ape lineage evolved into man only through a long series of chance and complex environmental, morphological, and social interactions occurring in unison at given places in given times. The probability of similar interactions occurring in unison elsewhere is not high.

Even accepting the figure of one million civilizations proposed by Sagan, the problems related to an extraterrestrial origin of UFOs appear, on the surface, to be insoluble. Such civilizations would be spread randomly across the galaxy, which is about 100,000 light-years across and 30,000 light-years wide, and the average distances between them would be far too great for spacecraft to cross there, on such a routine basis as implied by UFO reports.

A good example of a first primitive effort is Pioneer X, launched in March 1972, which was the first man-made object to leave the solar system and penetrate interstellar space. At its relatively slow speed, it would take over 100,000 years for Pioneer X to reach Alpha Centauri, our closest stellar neighbor, if it were moving in that direction, which it is not. In fact, it will take billions of years, perhaps even more time than the age of the galaxy itself, for Pioneer X to pass within less than 3 billion miles of another star, and the probability of such a star harboring advanced intelligent life (at that time) is almost absolute zero.

It is these enormous interstellar distances which are difficult to reconcile with UFO reports, which sometimes give the impression that an operation the size of the Normandy landings is in progress. However, there are no physical laws prohibiting interstellar travel within human life spans. The main obstacles, at least in our case, appear to be financial and, as a result, engineering.

Several types of rocket propulsion systems besides the currently used chemical ones have been proposed over the years to surmount the problem of the vast interstellar distances: ion, nuclear fission, nuclear fusion, and photon. "Ideal" photon propulsion, which would convert all of its fuel into radiation and would have a very high exhaust velocity, has been called the most efficient, while another proposal called for a nuclear fusion-based interstellar ramjet which would scoop up interstellar gas as a source of energy.

Others have proposed more efficient multistage nuclear systems which would permit travel to Alpha Centauri (4.3 light-years) in nine to fourteen years (Earth time) utilizing a fission rocket, and six to seven years (Earth time) utilizing a fusion rocket. Return trips (involving deceleration at Alpha Centauri), however, would involve sixty-six years (Earth time) with a fission rocket and twenty-nine years (Earth time) with a fusion rocket, barely within a human life span.

Another analysis has indicated that only photon rockets would have the capability for really long interstellar flights, nuclear fission and fusion systems permitting only short interstellar flights, and ion rockets being totally inadequate.

In the late 1970s, the British Interplanetary Society (BIS) proposed a flyby of Barnard's star, which is believed to possess one or two planets. The BIS concept involves a two-staged rocket, Daedalus, about 600 feet in length, which would be ready for launch by about the year 2075. Weighing 54,000 tons, the vehicle would accelerate up to almost one eighth the speed of light, but would take fifty years to travel the meager 5.9 light-years to its destination. Furthermore, Daedalus, powered by a nuclear fusion-based propulsion system, would be an unmanned vehicle.

A major factor involving interstellar travel which is often overlooked is that of "time dilation." An object, such as a spaceship, traveling at a relativistic speed (that is, close to the speed of light) would be subject to the effects predicted by Albert Einstein's Special Theory of Relativity. The passing of time on Earth, if it could be observed from the spaceship, would appear to be speeded up, and the passing of time on the spaceship relative to a percipient on Earth (or on any slower moving object) would appear to be comparatively slow. Thus, an astronaut returning to Earth following a relativistic flight could suddenly find that he is the same "age" as the son he left behind, or even much younger. In fact, depending on the speed at which he traveled, and the length of time he maintained that speed, he could find that hundreds, thousands, or even millions of years had transpired on Earth during his absence. It is important to note that the astronaut would not perceive time passing "slower" on the spaceship (as, indeed, it would not be), just as we do not perceive it passing "faster" on Earth. The astronaut would not live longer in the biological sense; his "absolute" life span be unaffected. What would permit him to survive millions of years "longer" relative to those still on "Earth time" is the peculiar and hard-to-understand concept of relativity theory, which goes beyond the more comprehensible laws of classic mechanics.

The Special Theory of Relativity is not just a fanciful and esoteric idea which might or might not be valid. Like many of Einstein's propositions, it has withstood the test of time and has been validated in numerous ways in many observations and experiments. Perhaps the most interesting was an experiment conducted by the U.S. Naval Observatory in October of 1971. Four atomic clocks were flown twice around the world (in opposite directions) at commercial jet speeds to determine the time differences they would experience relative to

"control" clocks which remained at the observatory.

Because the clocks at the Observatory were actually moving (due to the Earth's rotation), Special Relativity predicted a loss of 40 (give or take 23) nanoseconds (billionths of a second) on the eastward trip (consistent with the Earth's rotation), which lasted 41.2 hours, and a gain of 275 (give or take 21) nanoseconds on the westward trip (against the Earth's rotation), which lasted 48.6 hours. The experiment validated the prediction: On the eastward flight, the clocks lost about 59 nanoseconds (they "aged" slower), and on the westward flight they gained about 273 nanoseconds (they "aged" faster), thus demonstrating the reality of time dilation.

The implications of the phenomenon of time dilation relative to interstellar travel, and UFOs, are enormous. The following figures represent the lengths of time a vehicle would take to reach certain destinations as perceived on Earth relative to the lengths of time it would take as perceived on the spaceship, assuming a constant acceleration of one Earth gravity (1g.) up to a high relativistic speed during the first half of the flight, and a constant deceleration of 1g. during the second half.

As can be seen, even travel to the known limits of the universe can be accomplished within a normal human life span. Astronauts could travel to nearby stars, nearby galaxies, or even go "galaxy chasing," all within fifty *years spaceship time,* although billions of years could have transpired on Earth. The main factor would be speed: so long as a high relativistic speed is attained and maintained, all this would be possible, but if the spaceship were to decelerate for any reason, such as to enable visitation to interesting places, the time dilation effect would dramatically lose its potency.

The main argument which can be used against the time dilation effect for interstellar travel, particularly in regard to possible extraterrestrial UFOs, is that the astronauts would have to leave behind all their families and friends, never to see them again, and it is also

Destination (one way only)	Flight Duration (Earth time)	Flight Duration (spaceship time)
Alpha Centauri	6 years	3 years
Center of Milky Way galaxy	30,000 years	19 years
Andromeda galaxy	750,000 years	26 years
Known limits of the universe	30 billion years	46 years

highly questionable whether a society, however technologically advanced, would be willing to finance such a venture when it would have absolutely no possibility of ever knowing the results. The same argument can be used against the SETI signal approach, in that by the time another society received the message, the sending society may have radically altered its "state of mind" or even ceased to exist.

To solve the "time-gap" problem in interstellar travel, Johns Hopkins astrophysicist Richard C. Henry has proposed that the astronauts "take their friends with them." In other words, one could envision increasing colonization in the vicinity of a home planet, including the hollowing out of giant asteroids, and the eventual abandonment of the home star system and displacement across interstellar space. That is, the *entire* society, or a major segment of it, would become an interstellar one and could speed up and slow down at will, visiting whatever planetary systems, or even galaxies, it wished, without any subgroup experiencing time differences relative to the society as a whole.

Other techniques which could improve even further the practicality of interstellar travel are biomagnetic levitation, suspended animation, and prolongevity. Biomagnetic levitation would permit the human body to withstand an acceleration much higher than 1g. to attain relativistic speeds. The process would levitate a biological body in a strong inhomogeneous magnetic field to compensate for acceleration inertial forces on the body and could reduce flight duration times from years to months (spaceship time).

Suspended animation would involve slowing down all bodily life support functions to a minimum, similar to hibernation in some mammals. Suspended animation (which would reduce unnecessary aging even during relativistic interstellar trips) combined with biomagnetic levitation and time dilation effects would vastly increase practical travel distance potentials in interstellar travel. As for prolongevity, UFOs, if interstellar in origin, could be controlled by beings with biologically longer life spans, or such life spans could have been artificially lengthened, or the aging process itself could have been eliminated. Research in these areas is actively being conducted in the United States, and major breakthroughs are expected within decades. Elimination of the aging process, now believed to be within man's grasp by many biological scientists, would invalidate all "distance" arguments against the practicality of interstellar travel, or the interstellar origin of UFOs.

Some have proposed that, in the course of time, extraterrestrials could also have learned to replace more and more of their body parts with artificial parts, as is happening with humans, until beings with more efficient and long-lasting "bodies" have resulted. It has even been suggested that biological-based intelligence is simply a stepping-stone to a higher order of existence, first mechanical, and then possibly "psychic," in which no central processing system is required at all. Such possibilities can only be speculated upon, but it should be emphasized that extraterrestrial intelligences, if they exist, would have enormous lead times over the human species. The statistical probability of such intelligences being at (or even near) man's current stage of development is extremely low.

All of these possibilities are also assuming that the speed of light is not attainable or surpassable, as predicted by Einsteinian physics. Some writers have advocated that there may be means of bypassing this Einsteinian limitation (not necessarily invalidating it), so as to facilitate interstellar travel, and that such could only be accomplished by a society far in advance of our own. Carl Sagan, for example, once proposed that such supercivilizations may have discovered "new laws of physics" to reduce time intervals in radio communication; although, curiously, he did not propose such new laws to reduce the times of interstellar travel.

In the 1970s, increasing interest centered on hypothetical particles named tachyons, which would exist in a state faster than the speed of light, although their existence has not been conclusively established. The fact is that we still understand relatively little of the processes occurring in the universe, and certain astrophysical phenomena have demonstrated this quite clearly.

A colorful analogy has been proposed by University of Texas theoretical astrophysicist John Archibald Wheeler (formerly at Princeton University), who compared our understanding of the universe to what our understanding of an auto junkyard would be if all our knowledge of it were gained by viewing it through a small instrument lowered by an overhead crane; one would observe part of a dented hubcap here, a broken mirror there, but the engine would remain usually hidden. It would thus be a very long time indeed before we really understood the purpose of all the auto components and how they are integrated and work together.

In the 1980s and 1990s, new theoretical thinking advanced the concept of "wormholes." Such proposed cosmic "tunnels" would make possible space-time shortcuts from one part of a galaxy to another, or even between different galaxies in different parts of the universe. The concept is that a wormhole would provide almost instant access by a

spaceship to any desired location, and possibly any desired time, not by crossing space in the traditional method of classic physics, but by penetrating the fabric of space-time in a way that is hard for the human mind—accustomed as it is to three-dimensional space—to understand.

The mathematics underlying the concept of wormholes is sound but extremely complex. Although wormholes were predicted early in the century by Einstein's General Theory of Relativity, it was only in the 1980s that the first serious theoretical postulations were made. These were initiated by astrophysicist Kip S. Thorne, at the California Institute of Technology, and he and other physicists and mathematicians are continuing with such theoretical studies. (Curiously, the idea for the initial research came from Carl Sagan, who asked Thorne to investigate the possibility of such a transportation gateway so that he could include it in his novel *Contact*, which was published in 1985 and produced as a motion picture in 1997. In the story, Sagan's heroine is not only transported through a wormhole, but through myriad such tunnels—like a sort of subway system of the cosmos.)

Needless to say, the construction of a wormhole, or even the locating and using of a "natural" wormhole within practical distance from the Earth, is currently far beyond the technical capability of humans. Thorne developed a set of nine requirements for the construction of such a wormhole, which would require the use of "exotic matter." However, the needed "exotic matter" would probably have to be harvested somehow from a black hole—and it may take a wormhole to reach a black hole within a reasonable time in the first place!

Nevertheless, it is conceivable that, at some time within the coming centuries, humans may attain the capability to produce and utilize such interstellar gateways for practical interstellar travel. Certainly, if such were to occur, all the problems associated with traditional spaceflight, such as the distances between the stars and the time it takes to traverse such distances, would become obsolete and archaic.

It is possible that extraterrestrial civilizations, way in advance of humans technologically, have mastered the physics and engineering that such kind of travel would require. Under such conditions, easy travel from other parts of the galaxy to Earth could be quite routine and commonplace. If UFOs do represent extraterrestrial craft or devices that traverse wormholes to reach Earth, this would help resolve the problem of the inexplicably high frequency of UFO sighting reports.

Whether or not advanced intelligences have more fully understood the physics still beyond our grasp, and whether they have eventually taken advantage of the enormous energy resources available in the galaxy, are questions of profound interest. Physicist Freeman J. Dyson, of the Institute for Advanced Study, has written on this topic. He predicts that supercivilizations would have taken apart planets and harnessed the complete energy output of stars within 100,000 years of becoming technological, and that such operations would unavoidably create waste heat in the form of infrared radiation. Star collisions would also have been engineered throughout the galaxy, and stars would appear grouped and organized to a point where a "tame" galaxy would provide various forms of telltale clues. Dyson reluctantly concludes that the proposition of a supercivilization at work in our galaxy is not supported by observational evidence and, further, that if the galaxy contained a large number of civilizations, at least one would have "tamed" the galaxy by now.

An even more negative conclusion has been reached by Michael H. Hart; he states that, because no extraterrestrials have actually come to Earth for colonization, there is ". . . strong evidence that we are the first civilization in our galaxy. . . ." A similar view has been expressed by Eric M. Jones: "The results suggest that no technological/space faring/colonizing civilization has arisen in the galaxy."

The reasons for all these negative conclusions is that a technological civilization would have rapidly colonized or at least visited the entire galaxy, but there is no evidence of such visitation to Earth. UFO reports are, of course, not given serious consideration, leading some UFO proponents to regard this approach as circular: UFOs cannot represent extraterrestrial visitation because if extraterrestrials existed they would visit us!

A calculation by T. B. H. Kuiper and M. Morris determined that just one technological civilization would populate the entire galaxy in a mere five million years. As conditions for life on Earth have been suitable for at least a billion years, the lack of such visitation can be interpreted as a lack of any extraterrestrial civilization in the galaxy. Kuiper and Morris, however, propose other explanations, such as purposeful noncontact, as does David W. Schwartzman, who even supports the "UFO hypothesis."

In considering the extraterrestrial hypothesis for UFOs, then, it should be recognized that:

(1) there are many likely locations for the emergence of life in our galaxy, as well as in other galaxies;

(2) the emergence of life does not necessarily imply the eventual evolution of intelligent species;

(3) if such intelligences have evolved in the galaxy, or in other galaxies, they have already existed as such for far longer periods than the existence of *Homo sapiens;*

(4) one can only speculate over the biological, social, or technical development of such hypothetical intelligences;

(5) average distances between stars are enormous, but factors such as moving entire societies, time dilation, suspended animation, biomagnetic levitation, and prolongevity, would reduce or even eliminate the distance problem;

(6) our understanding of processes in the universe is still relatively poor, and it is premature to decide at this time what is "possible" or what is "impossible";

(7) any statement categorically rejecting the *hypothesis* that UFOs may represent some form of interstellar visitation is simplistic and is not based on a critical evaluation and synthesis of all relevant factors;

(8) any acceptance of UFOs as representing extraterrestrial visitation, based on the available evidence, can only be construed as a belief unsupported by established facts.

The emotional commitment on the part of those speculating on the ETH, positively or negatively, is not likely to diminish as long as UFOs continue to be reported, and there is no indication that reports are decreasing with the advent of a better-informed public and a more sophisticated Earth-based technology.

The debate over the extraterrestrial hypothesis for UFOs will probably continue for many years to come.

—J. RICHARD GREENWELL

extraterrestrial life, history of The idea of extraterrestrial life, which dates back at least to the ancient Greeks, has become one of the most persistent themes of Western civilization. Nevertheless, historians of science prior to the 1980s largely ignored it, because it was not believed to constitute science or to have any intellectually respectable history.

With a more realistic concept of the nature of science, however, historians have now analyzed the idea in considerable detail, beginning with Steven Dick's *Plurality of Worlds: The Origins of the Extraterrestrial Life from Democritus to Kant* (1982). This work showed that far from being an aberration, the idea of life on other worlds was strongly connected to major scientific traditions, including the ancient atomist, Copernican, Cartesian, and Newtonian worldviews. The Aristotelian worldview strongly opposed it.

Professor Michael J. Crowe, in his volume entitled *The Extraterrestrial Life Debate, 1750-1900* (1986), showed how pervasive the idea was in religious and intellectual discussion in the 19th century. Harvard Professor Karl Guthke emphasized the literary aspects of the discussion in *The Last Frontier: Imagining other Worlds from the Copernican Revolution to Modern Science Fiction* (1990).

Dick's *The Biological Universe: The Twentieth Century Extraterrestrial Life Debate and the Limits of Science* (1996), and its abridgment and update, *Life on other Worlds* (1998), covered the entire scope of the debate—from the scientific aspects of the search for life to the popular culture elements of UFOs and alien science fiction and the implications of contact with extraterrestrial intelligence.

The history of the debate offers many lessons about the nature of evidence and inference, the limits of scientific inquiry, and the differing styles among scientists in terms of what problems they take up and how they pursue them. Moreover, Dick argues that the idea of a universe filled with life, the "Biological Universe" as he terms it, is the major worldview of the 20th century. As such, it has implications for all of society, and has the potential to change our perspective on theology, philosophy, and all areas of human endeavor.

The status of extraterrestrial life as a worldview comparable to the Copernican and Darwinian world views allows one to discuss possible implications of contact. All worldviews go through stages, and a rich literature in the history of science has analyzed the reception of past scientific world views over the short and long term and among various segments of society. Although there are obvious differences among worldviews, and although predictions cannot be made and outcomes are scenario-dependent, the cautious use of these analogues may serve as a foundation for discussing the implications of contact with extraterrestrial intelligence.

The biological universe, however, has not yet been proven—either for microbial or intelligent life. Claims of proof in the past, ranging from the canals of Mars to Martian meteorites and UFOs of extraterrestrial origin, have stirred great passion precisely because so much is at stake—an entire worldview with profound implications for human destiny. Possible implications have become part of popular culture in the form of science fiction literature and film, where the alien theme has been one of the most dominant.

—ETEP STAFF

References

Crowe, M. *The Extraterrestrial Life Debate, 1750-1900* (Cambridge University Press, 1986).

Dick, S. J. *Plurality of Worlds: The Origins of the Extraterrestrial Life from Democritus to Kant* (Cambridge University Press, 1982).

———. *The Biological Universe: The Twentieth Century Extraterrestrial Life Debate and the Limits of Science* (Cambridge University Press, 1996),

———. *Life on other Worlds* (Cambridge, 1998).

Guthke, K. S. *The Last Frontier: Imagining Other Worlds from the Copernican Revolution to Modern Science Fiction* (Cornell University Press, 1990).

Extraterrestrial Visitations from Prehistoric Times to the Present (Editions J'ai Lu, 1970). Jacques Bergier makes a series of extraordinary claims: extraterrestrials intentionally exploded a star so its radiation would kill the dinosaurs on Earth and enable humans to evolve; beings of light bestowed secret interplanetary knowledge on the Rosicrucians and Freemasons; at least two million people disappear worldwide each year and many reappear with false memories designed to puzzle the rest of us; Bigfoot, elves, fairies, and other creatures are manufactured by extraterrestrial intelligence and deposited among us in an experiment to test our reactions; and all of human evolution is a continuing experiment conducted by higher intelligences who have us in cosmic quarantine.

—RANDALL FITZGERALD

Extraterrestrials . . . Where Are They? (Pergamon Press, 1982) edited by Ben Zuckerman and Michael Hart. Twenty-two essays argue that humans may be the most advanced species in the galaxy. It is a waste of time and money to search for radio signals, goes their argument, because even if other advanced technological civilizations existed, they would be of such short duration that they would have quickly given up on searching for or sending signals of their own.

—RANDALL FITZGERALD

Eyes of the Sphinx, The (Berkley Books, 1996). Erich von Däniken says the ancient Sumerians and Egyptians preserve evidence in their art of hybrid creatures which were genetically designed by alien visitors. These creatures included humans who were mixed with animals in ghoulish combinations, which explains why the Olmec and Mayan cultures featured human-animal hybrids in art representations on their temple walls.

—RANDALL FITZGERALD

Ezekiel's wheel Ezekiel, who lived in the sixth century B.C., was one of the most colorful of the Hebrew prophets. His writings are contained in the Old Testament of the Bible. In 597 B.C., Ezekiel was among several thousand captives carried off to Babylon by Nebuchadnezzar II in the first of three captivities of the Jews. (Nebuchadnezzar II's reign of forty-four years, from about 605-562 B.C., marked the peak of the Chaldean or neo-Babylonian kingdom.) The prophet Ezekiel lived among the exiles at Tel Abib on the Chebar River, or Grand Canal, which stretched alongside the town of Nippur from Babylon to Uruk.

It was in the fifth year of the Judean captivity, in 593 B.C., that Ezekiel described a vivid experience that represented his call to prophesy. This account in the first three chapters of ''The Book of the Prophet Ezekiel'' is generally explained as a visionary experience while in a state of trance. Indeed, the story has all the earmarks of a religious revelation: God, seated in a throne, descends to Earth in a wondrous heavenly chariot; angels accompany Him; the ''eyes round about'' indicate God's all-seeing, all-knowing power. Ezekiel, according to this interpretation, is commissioned to speak God's word to a rebellious nation. He is told Israel will be punished for its sins, and the warning is emphasized on a scroll. The prophet is warned of the resistance he will meet. After the glory of the Lord departs, Ezekiel goes to his people and sits in a daze for a week.

Quite a different slant on Ezekiel's experience, and a more bizarre one perhaps, is the hypothesis that Ezekiel had a dramatic encounter with a UFO.

In spite of the weird imagery and elaborate symbolism employed by the prophet, and in spite of the difficulty of extracting meaningful details from the account, a thread of coherence does run through the first three chapters of the book. When viewed in the light of the current UFO phenomenon, a surprising tale of a biblical UFO landing and contact emerges. The description is remarkably similar to many modern low-level encounters with UFOs.

What follows is a modern interpretation of the Book of Ezekiel, chapters 1 through 3. It is a free, imaginative interpretation and as such is purely speculative. But it does not require much imagination to realize how a UFO witness of the sixth century B.C. would react in the presence of an extraterrestrial spacecraft. He would probably behave precisely the way Ezekiel did. In fact, he might even regard the event as simply God's way of revealing Himself to chosen mortals. It would, of course, be extremely difficult for Ezekiel to describe an advanced flying craft and its occupants. He would have to use terminology and comparisons familiar to him in his day.

Thus, the prophet's experience might translate something like this: As he sat by the Chaldean river Chebar one day in 593 B.C., the priest Ezekiel suddenly noticed what appeared to be a bright, fiery cloud of amber color coming out of the north. As the "cloud" drew closer, four disk-shaped objects ("wheels") became visible and approached. At least one of the disks landed near where Ezekiel stood.

All the objects had the same appearance— "the color of a beryl [greenish]". . . like "a wheel in the middle of a wheel [an outer rim

encircling a round center section]" . . . and "eyes round about them four (probably portholes or windows]." Describing their maneuvers, Ezekiel said "when they went, they went upon their four sides, and they turned not when they went."

Four humanoid creatures traveled back and forth from the craft. At times they were visible through a transparent dome on each disk. Though this portion of the account is particularly difficult to decipher in terms of the UFO phenomenon, the beings each had four "wings," which might have been a helicopter-like device strapped to their backs. Whatever the "wings" were, they allowed the creatures to maneuver about rapidly ("and the living creatures ran and returned as the appearance of a flash of lightning"). The prophet also stated: "And when they went, I heard the noise of their wings, like the noise of great water . . ."

The beings wore shimmering, shiny garments, or spacesuits, like "burning coals of fire," with transparent helmets on top—"the firmament upon the heads . . . was as the color of the terrible crystal, stretched forth over their heads above [a similar transparent dome on the craft]."

Although Ezekiel had no idea what forces propelled the mysterious "wheels," he linked control of the disks to the creatures: "When those [the creatures] went, these [the wheels] went; and when those stood, these stood; and when those were lifted up from the Earth, the wheels were lifted up over against them: for the spirit of the living creature was in the wheels."

The witness to this amazing event goes on to describe "the likeness of a throne [pilot's chair?]" located above (?) the ship's dome with "the likeness . . . of a man" seated in it, dressed in an amber-colored, glittering garment. Ezekiel was so awestruck and frightened by this figure that he fell upon his face (1:28).

A voice emanating from one of the ships told him to get up and then it proceeded to address him. It complained of attacks against him by his people (they "hath rebelled against me") and warned that any further provocation would bring punishment (in our own age UFOs have been shot at from the air and from the ground). A scroll was spread out before Ezekiel. It evidently listed complaints against the Israelites. The witness was told to consider these complaints carefully and deliver the message of warning to his people. Ezekiel, according to this view, was selected as a spokesman for the space voyagers. He was also told he would be ridiculed and scoffed at by persons who would not believe his experience—the plight of many UFO witnesses today.

Then the amazed prophet was taken aboard ("then the spirit took me up"), and he heard "the noise of the wheels . . . and a noise of a great rushing." He was carried to Tel Abib, where his fellow exiles were and where he sat "astonished among them seven days." At the end of that period he recalled more clearly what had happened.

Ezekiel received word (telepathically?) again from the voice to "go forth into the plain, and I will talk with thee." This he did, and when he saw the same figure "which I saw by the river of Chebar . . . I fell on my face." Once again the note of warning was repeated for Ezekiel to convey to his people.

The figure in his shining uniform appears again (dream?) in Chapter 8. And in Chapter 10 the four wheels turn up once more with the figure and winged creatures, but these repetitions may have been the handiwork of other writers trying to improve or expand Ezekiel's book. However, the first three chapters of the book are believed to be the work of the prophet himself.

Having no knowledge of machines or spaceships, it would be natural for Ezekiel to assume he had been in the presence of supernatural powers. We may never know whether his experience was, in fact, a religious vision or an encounter with extraterrestrial visitors.

—WALTER N. WEBB

F

"Face" on Mars   On July 25, 1976, as NASA's Viking 1 spacecraft orbited Mars in search of a suitable spot for the next Viking lander, it photographed a relatively crater-free region known as Cydonia. Strewn with rocky mesas and devoid of dried river channels, Cydonia did not pique NASA's interest as a promising candidate for harboring traces of possible ancient life. However, after the photos were released to the public, one of the many mesas seen in #035A72 captured the national spotlight because of its striking resemblance to a humanoid face, complete with headdress.

Hoagland's "City" is imagined to be in the left portion of this picture.

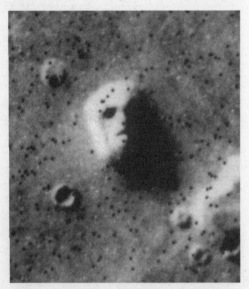

Section of NASA Viking photo #035A72 showing the controversial "Face" on Mars

Speculation then arose in some quarters that perhaps this 1.2-mile-wide x 1.6-mile-long structure was not a natural surface feature at all, but rather an artificial monument. Could it have been constructed by a once-thriving Martian civilization? Was it erected by beings from elsewhere in the galaxy during a brief junket through our solar system, perhaps as a "calling card" for when we became a space-faring species? Or might Earthlings—from our own future—be responsible?

The person most responsible for promoting the "Face" on Mars is Richard C. Hoagland, a gifted speaker and author of the popular 1987 book, *The Monuments of Mars: A City on the Edge of Forever*. Yes, a "City." For within frame #035A72, Hoagland and his associates thought they had discovered evidence of, among other relics, a "fortress," an artificial "cliff," a "five-sided pyramid" with humanoid "proportions" (its "head . . . apparently damaged by explosive penetration," pointing directly toward the more-famous "Face"), and a collection of structures dubbed the "City Square."

According to Hoagland, the city may date back approximately 500,000 years to a time when, if one had stood in the middle of the City Square, "the Summer Solstice sun would have arisen directly over the 'Face.'"

The publisher's foreword to Hoagland's book describes the author as somewhat of a science prodigy: "Richard C. Hoagland is, by career, a science writer as well as a consultant in the fields of astronomy, planetarium curating, and space-program education. . . . In 1965, at the age of nineteen, [Hoagland] became Curator (possibly the youngest in the country) of the Springfield, Massachusetts, Museum of Science. . . . In 1966 Hoagland served as NBC consultant for the historic soft landing of a U.S. spacecraft on the moon—*Surveyor 1.* Later he appeared on 'The Tonight Show' explaining the significance of the landing to Johnny Carson. . . . At Christmas of [1968] he was asked to become a consultant to CBS News . . . and served as [a science] advisor to Walter Cronkite."

But in 1990, with no NASA program yet in the works to aggressively explore Cydonia, despite Hoagland's public proclamations about "a groundswell of official NASA interest" in his findings, I set out to learn a bit more about NASA's position.

Dr. David Morrison, Chief of the Space Science Division at NASA's Ames Research Center, informed me that Hoagland was largely "self-educated" in science, and that he (Morrison) knew of "no one in the scientific community, or who is associated with the NASA Mars Science Working Group, or who is working on Mars mission plans at such NASA centers as Ames, Johnson, or JPL [Jet Propulsion Laboratory], who ascribes even the smallest credibility to [Hoagland's] weird ideas about

Mars." None of the other three NASA officials responding to my inquiries knew of any interest at all in Hoagland's claims.

Then on April 5, 1998, as part of its orbital photography mission, the Mars Global Surveyor returned images of Cydonia taken at more than ten times the resolution of the earlier Viking 1 pictures of 1976. Now, our new and improved view of the "Face" reveals it to be nothing more than what NASA scientists said it was all along: a natural feature, like many others on Mars, blown into the dusty, rocky surface by the planet's fierce, swirling winds.

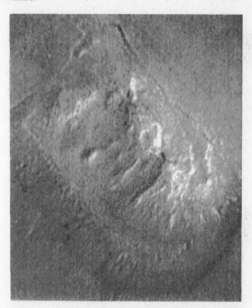

The supposed "Face" is resolved into its true irregular features in this Mars Global Surveyor view.

With the benefit of 20/20 hindsight, has Hoagland now abandoned his "City"? Oddly, a visit to his Web site (www.enterprisemission.com) reveals just the opposite.

—GARY P. POSNER

Fads and Fallacies in the Name of Science (G.P. Putnam's Sons, 1952). Science writer Martin Gardner wrote this classic—the first book to take a skeptical, "debunking" approach to the growing belief in extraterrestrial visitors. Most UFOs are misperceptions and delusions, Gardner says, and UFO-book authors are preying upon human gullibility; particularly Major Donald Keyhoe, Gerald Heard, and Frank Scully.

—RANDALL FITZGERALD

fairy lore and UFO encounters An age-old and nearly universal folk belief alleges that a race of supernatural beings shares the Earth with humankind. These beings are seldom seen because they live underground or are invisible. It is further alleged that they live in some magical place, where they are numerous and have cities, customs, and civilizations of their own. The generic term for such a being is "fairy."

Human contact with fairies is rare, often hazardous, and in some striking respects can be likened to encounters with UFOs. Fairies come in all shapes and sizes, some of them tall and beautiful while others are animal-like and monstrous. The most familiar type is shorter than human height and similar in some respects to the humanoids associated with UFOs.

The best-known fairies belong to Ireland and other Celtic lands, but folk traditions of diminutive supernatural beings are worldwide. In European folklore, Germany has dwarfs while Sweden has elves and trolls. Various forms of Jinn inhabit the Islamic world, while the Devas of India, the kappas of Japan, and the duwende of the Philippines populate Asian folklore. The Mmoetia appear in western Africa, while the Pygmies describe a spirit race even smaller than themselves. The Hawaiians have legends of the Menehune, while in *American Elves* John E. Roth has compiled a book-length catalogue of fairy types in the folklore of the American Indians.

The broadest similarities between fairies and UFO occupants are their mutual other-world origin and possession of extraordinary powers or skills. Fairies paralyze assailants, seem part physical and part immaterial, and impart prophetic messages to humans. Fairies

This fairy, known as "Pwca," was drawn by a Welsh peasant with a piece of coal.

float or fly, and in some strands of tradition sail ships through the air or climb a ladder into a cloud. A common motif in fairy lore is the fairy mound or hill that rises up on pillars of light during nocturnal celebrations, creating a sight very similar to a landed UFO.

Fairies may have a short stature, large head, piercing eyes, and crippled feet or a clumsy gait—features more or less readily comparable to UFO humanoids. Similarities in

Nowadays, a "fairy ring" may be considered a UFO landing spot.

fairy and UFO lore have been treated at length by Jacques Vallée in *Passport to Magonia* (1969), Jerome Clark and Loren Coleman in *The Unidentified* (1975), and Hilary Evans in *Visions, Apparitions, Alien Visitors* (1984).

An extended list of comparisons link fairy beliefs with UFO abduction accounts. Abductee Betty Andreasson's childhood experience of playing in the woods when a short being emerged out of the ground, dressed in clothing like the rough bark of a tree, describes a fairy encounter with no more modernization than the substitution of an alien being for the supernatural. She later visited an otherworld that had more in common with an underground fairyland than another planet. On one trip she saw a beautiful crystalline forest; on another she passed through a tunnel to a lush and fertile land of plentiful light, but no sun or visible horizon. Fairyland is often underground and entered through a tunnel, devoid of sunlight but lit by a perpetual twilight. The place is extraordinary in its beauty, though the appearance may be sustained by magical deception. Like fairies, alien abductors are proficient in mind control and prone to deceive their captives.

Abducting aliens show a keen interest in reproduction by examining genitals, harvesting eggs and sperm. They also indicate that their home planet has lost its fertility and they somehow need humans to restore the viability of their race. Fairies lack reproductive self-sufficiency as well. They steal human children, take human mates, or need a human midwife to assist at a fairy birth. One common practice is exchange of a human baby for an elderly fairy. This changeling has a wizened look and wisdom beyond its apparent age, features comparable with the "wise babies" described by Budd Hopkins in *Intruders* (1987).

A human who meets fairies may experience the "supernatural lapse of time," wherein a few minutes or hours spent in fairy company translates into years or centuries elapsed in earthly time, the sort of shocking discovery that Rip van Winkle made when he returned home. The time lapse of abductees is a loss of memory rather than a loss of years, but a break in the continuity of time occurs in both cases. Some contacts with fairies lead to gains of supernatural powers or knowledge, while some abductees receive prophecies or acquire psychic powers. Unfriendly fairy encounters lead to injury or insanity, while the personalities of some abductees also deteriorate.

A mother struggles with the fairies as they try to abduct her baby.

Any recognition of the similarities between UFO lore and fairy lore must also reckon with the extensive differences. Few fairies are hairless or large-eyed, as so many aliens are, and no fairy drives a spaceship. Yet the parallels between fairy kidnappings and abductions are too striking to ignore, and suggest that fairy lore, near-death experiences, and perhaps abduction accounts as well may stem from some subjective, psychological experience common to all people. The basic content may be inherent in the human mind even if the outer trappings belong to a particular time and culture.

—THOMAS EDDIE BULLARD

FATE magazine Long before the paranormal was popular, *FATE* magazine was publishing true reports of the strange and unknown.

FATE first hit the newsstands in the spring of 1948. Co-founded by Ray Palmer and Curtis Fuller, the magazine's first cover story was a feature by Kenneth Arnold as he shared in his own words the unknown objects he saw over Mount Rainier one fateful day in 1947.

Arnold's sighting inspired the modern UFO era, and his story propelled the fledgling *FATE* to national recognition. Ray Palmer had worked as editor of several science fiction pulp magazines (including the venerable *Amazing Stories*) and head of the fiction group at Ziff-Davis Publishing Company in the 1930s and 1940s. Curtis Fuller was also an accomplished editor. He and his wife Mary took full control of *FATE* magazine in 1955, when Palmer sold his interest in the venture. The Fullers expanded the magazine's focus, and increased readership to over 100,000 subscribers.

The Fullers published the magazine until 1988, when they sold it to the present owner, Llewellyn Worldwide, Ltd. In his farewell editorial, Fuller explained: "Our purpose throughout this long time has been to explore and report honestly the strangest facts in this strange world—ones that don't fit into the general beliefs of the way things are."

From personal accounts of UFOs and ghosts, to scientific examinations of psychic phenomena and mysterious places, *FATE*'s main purpose continues to be honest reporting and open discussion of strange and unexplainable events.

Address: FATE Magazine
           P.O. Box 64383
           St. Paul, MN 55164-0383

Web site: www.fatemag.com
                              —FATE MAGAZINE

Fatima (Portugal), miracle at The "miracle of Fatima," which occurred in Portugal in 1917, has been given acceptance by the Catholic Church as a miraculous occurrence. However, because the series of incidents culminated with the witnessing by fifty thousand persons of a large, silver, aerial disk, which performed incredible maneuvers, it is also considered to

be of definite UFOlogical value. It deserves study also because numerous aspects of the occurrence seem to parallel other outstanding UFO cases.

The village of Aljustrel, where the events took place, lies one half mile south of Fatima, Portugal. In 1917, very few of the villagers were literate; they were isolated from happenings of national and international interest.

In the summer of 1915, a young Aljustrel peasant girl, Lucia Abobora, and a group of other children were herding their families' sheep in the deserted countryside. They viewed what they described as a white, glowing figure move majestically three times over an adjacent valley. When Lucia, then age eight, tried to tell her family about the object which "looked like someone wrapped in a sheet," she was ridiculed.

In 1916, Lucia was joined in her shepherdess duties by two smaller cousins, Francisco Marto, then seven years old, and Jacinta Marto, age five. While herding the flocks, they spent the time laughing, playing games, and listening to Lucia tell stories.

The entry of Portugal into World War I, and the takeover of the government by anti-Christian factions, did not disturb the pastoral serenity of the villagers' lives. One day, while tending their sheep, the three children sought shelter from a violent storm and were astonished to see a strange light approaching them from the east. It stopped very near them, at the entrance of a tiny cave, and became distinguishable as a "transparent young man," fully human and handsome in appearance. He introduced himself as "the Angel of Peace" and invited them to pray with him. The children entered a trance-like state with suspension of bodily powers, which continued for some time after the entity's disappearance. This same radiant being appeared twice more; after the third visit, they were left in a state of tranquil lethargy which persisted for a week.

They kept these experiences to themselves for fear of ridicule, but their lives and personalities subtly changed. They became more contemplative, less boisterous, dancing and singing less than before. The war, too, began to touch their pastoral lives with the departure of some of their male relatives for military service.

On May 13, 1917, two tremendous flashes, like lightning, sent the three children scurrying for shelter in an isolated area called the Cova da Iria. The Cova was a great wooded hollow, a favorite place for grazing sheep. They were stopped in their headlong dash by the sight of a ball of light hovering above a small, three-foot evergreen tree. In its midst was a woman, exquisitely beautiful but serious-faced. Everything about her—her form, face, tunic-style garment, mantle, even a rosary dangling from her hands—seemed composed of brilliant white light, except the edges of the mantle which glittered with a golden hue. The ball of light in which she was encircled extended about a meter and one half in diameter all around her.

The children felt "great joy and peace" in her presence. The Lady introduced herself as being "from Heaven" and answered many questions put to her by the amazed witnesses. She spoke Portuguese in low, musical tones. She asked the children to pray for the end of the war and promised to return on the thirteenth day of the next five successive months. Then, still enclosed in the glowing globe, she floated off to the east, disappearing into the distance.

The children decided not to tell anyone what had occurred, but six-year-old Jacinta could not contain her excitement, and the secret got out. Her protective parents were impressed by the girl's repetition of the sophisticated language the woman had used. Francisco's statements lent credence to the occurrence, in the Marto family's estimation. Lucia, however, was ridiculed and scolded, particularly by her sharp-tongued mother.

As the children kept the dates of the Lady's successive appearances, curious villagers and outsiders accompanied them. The crowds became progressively larger, more aggressive, and persistent. The children resented their interference and made every effort to avoid them. By the third visit of the Lady to the Cova da Iria, about twenty-five hundred curious onlookers were there, including many wealthy persons among the poorly clad peasants. None but the children saw or heard the apparition, but many reported hearing a sound like a very faint voice, similar to "the buzzing of a bee." Others noticed an odd dimming of the noonday sun, and the top of the small tree curved and bent as if an invisible weight was pressed upon it. Another phenomenon noted by startled witnesses was a "small cloud" which descended upon the tiny tree at the moment the children became entranced.

On July 13th, the Lady promised to reveal her name on October 13th and stated that on that date a miracle would occur "so that everyone would have to believe." Then, according to the children, streams of light poured from her fingers, seemingly opening the surface of the earth. A terrifying scene of fire was revealed to the children in which were "devils . . . horrible and loathsome forms of animals frightful and unknown." The Lady told the children they were seeing a "vision of hell." She prophesied the ending of World War I, the rise of Communist Russia, and a second World War. She also gave them a secret which is said to be known only to the Pope in Rome.

Though the two younger witnesses' family remained supportive, Lucia's family believed she was a hoaxer and liar. She was questioned by the village priest, who felt Lucia was truthful, but he suspected that the apparitions might be "the work of the devil." This suspicion multiplied her mother's fears, and she began to treat her daughter badly. Lucia persisted in her belief that the Lady was beautiful and good.

By August, the news of the apparitions had spread throughout Portugal. The secular newspapers and magazines were generous with space and sarcastic in interpretation. The Catholic press was characteristically cautious. The children continued to be persecuted by crowds of persons—skeptical and devout alike—who visited daily in their homes. The children's lives and personalities changed drastically. Forsaking childhood interests and games, they began to make sacrifices, often forgoing food and drink in response to the Lady's request to "do penance for sinners to save them from hellfire." Jacinta began to have prophetic visions of a second World War, many of which were later realized.

The press continued its persecution, and, as a result, the civil authorities entered the controversy. The children were ordered to trial on August 11, 1917, for "disturbing the peace." Lucia's family forced her to face trial, hoping it would serve as a lesson to persuade her to retract her statements. She refused to answer questions put to her at court and ignored the cruel laughter of onlookers. She was finally dismissed with a threat of execution if she did not reveal the "secret" the Lady had given her and her two companions. All three children seemed prepared to die rather than break the Lady's confidence.

On the day of the fourth promised visit, they were furtively kidnapped by the administrator of the Fatima district, Arturo de Oliveira Santos. After interrogating them without success, he threw them into an ill-kept jail. Later he separated them, one at a time, and told the others that they "had been boiled in oil." Even this desperate ploy failed. The children would not break. Defeated, Santos took them back to Aljustrel.

Meanwhile, on August 13th, without the children being present, six thousand witnesses at the Cova heard a low rumbling; the origin was undetectable. They viewed a flash of light, and a small white cloud floated in from the east, coming to rest over the little evergreen. During this series of events, the faces and clothes of the throng were tinged with vivid, rainbow colors.

On the thirteenth of September, a vast crowd filled the hollow of the Cova da Iria. Among them were a few Catholic priests, who were curious about the incidents which were causing extreme controversy in Church circles. An eminent visitor, Monsignor João Quaresma,

viewed the luminous globe which heralded the Lady's approach and described it later as a heavenly "carriage." Also present was the Reverend Dr. Manuel Nunes Formigao, noted for his scholarship and integrity. He noted the strange dimming of the sun's light and the appearance of stars in some areas of the midday sky. Later, in interrogating the children, he sought to entrap them in discrepancies and lies. He was unable to do so and went away convinced of their truthfulness.

On October 13, 1917, the sky was covered with thick clouds and an unrelenting rain was falling. The muddy roads leading to Aljustrel were clogged with fifty thousand pilgrims and curiosity-seekers. Among them was Avelino de Almeida, managing editor of *O Seculo,* the largest newspaper in Lisbon. He was a skeptical, cautious man, anti-religious in nature.

The children pushed their way through a sea of black umbrellas toward the tiny tree. When a flash of light in the east heralded the beginning of the last apparition, the crowd saw the children kneel down, entranced. Those nearest them were struck by the radiance on their faces. Suddenly, Lucia pointed upward and shouted: "Look at the sun!"

Looking up, the crowd saw the thick rain clouds parting like curtains at the zenith. The rain stopped, as a huge silver disk, the apparent size of the sun, shone at the top of the sky. It gave out as much light as the sun, but the fifty thousand witnesses could stare at it without apparent harm to their eyes.

The disk began to "dance," whirling rapidly like a fireworks wheel. On its rim, a crimson tinge threw off flames, reflecting onto the throng below in all colors of the spectrum. The disk stopped three times, then resumed its rotating gyrations. Suddenly, it plunged in a zigzag motion toward the earth. Warmth engulfed the vast crowd as many fell to their knees, horrified. The disk then climbed back into the sky, in similar zigzag fashion. It quieted, then assumed the dazzling brilliance of a normal sun.

Many in the crowd found that their rain-drenched clothing had dried in seconds. The total phenomenon, from beginning to end, had lasted about ten minutes.

Even the skeptical editor of *O Seculo* was impressed. He wrote: "It remains for those competent to pronounce on the 'danse macabre' of the sun which . . . has made hosannas burst from the hearts of the faithful and naturally has impressed—as witnesses worthy of belief assure me—even freethinkers and other persons not at all interested in religious matters."

Two of the young witnesses, Francisco and Jacinta Marto, died in early childhood, having prophesied their own deaths long before the actual dates. Lucia Abobora was taken under the protection of church authorities.

Now known as Sister Maria das Dores, she has never publicly revealed the last "secret" of the Lady. The Lady, however, identified herself to the children as "Our Lady of the Rosary," and, very slowly, the Catholic Church accepted the occurrences as being of miraculous nature. Most of the specific utterances of the Lady had definite religious significance.

Many UFO researchers and authors have considered the Aljustrel (Fatima) events to be UFOlogical in nature, if one considers the following parallel aspects: (1) initial skepticism and total unpreparedness of the primary witnesses; (2) ridicule and persecution suffered by the witnesses; (3) reports of "unearthly" entities; (4) a luminous globe which apparently acted as an aerial vehicle; (5) sighting by secondary witnesses of unexplained meteorological phenomena; (6) auditory phenomena of undetectable origin; (7) associated psychic phenomena, such as healings, et cetera.

Every aspect of the children's statements and those of secondary witnesses have been fully and authoritatively documented by both clerical and secular authors. It remains, however, for expert UFO researchers to document the specifics, particularly the well-witnessed "miracle of the sun."

A careful study of the azimuth and eleva-

tion angles might rule out the sun as being the source of the "silver disk." Fatima being at latitude 39.37 north, the sun would not appear at the top of the sky or "zenith" at that date. Also, photogrammetric analyses of available photos of the gyrating object might aid in establishing whether or not the incident was primarily of metaphysical or UFOlogical significance.

Since the true nature of UFOs is still a mystery, it is possible that the series of events at Fatima were both metaphysical and UFOlogical in nature. There may be no real conflict between the two at all.

—ANN DRUFFEL

Fawcett, George D.   (b. 1929). George Fawcett is known for his many investigative and research articles in various magazines, UFO journals, books, and newspapers. Fawcett is also widely known for his public lectures and for having been the founder and chief advisor to five UFO study groups: the New England UFO Study Group (1957), the Pennsylvania and New Jersey Two-State UFO Study Group (1965), the Florida UFO Study Group (1968), the Tar Heel UFO Study Group (1973) and the Mutual UFO Network of North Carolina, Inc. (1989).

He is currently an active member of the Mutual UFO Network (MUFON), the J. Allen

George Fawcett (on the left)

Hynek Center for UFO Studies (CUFOS), and the Fund for UFO Research (FUFOR). He is also the author of a 1975 book entitled *Quarter Century Studies of UFOs in Florida, North Carolina and Tennessee.*

Fawcett received his B.A. degree in psychology and education from Lynchburg (Virginia) College in 1952. He was a professional YMCA director for twenty years and the general manager of the Malden *Times* (North Carolina) weekly newspaper. Though now retired, he has continued his UFO investigations, and continues to write and lecture on the subject.

In 1998 Fawcett and his UFO colleague E. R. (Bob) Sabo of St. Petersburg, Florida, donated 45,000 UFO items to the rapidly expanding International UFO Museum & Research Center at Roswell, New Mexico, where Fawcett serves as a UFO consultant.

Address: 602 Battleground Rd.
            Lincolnton, NC 28092
            U.S.A.
E-mail: gfawcett@charlotte.infi.net

POSITION STATEMENT: It has been my firm belief, based on my research and investigations over the past half century, that UFOs and their occupants, which I have named "UFOnauts," are both real. These non-human occupants and their craft continue to be a part of an ever-growing global enigma.

Because of increased UFO encounters there has been a flurry of UFO information, misinformation, and disinformation from worldwide agencies, both from within the private and public domain.

I have found there are real objects under intelligent control being seen on the ground and in our skies worldwide. The unknowns have varied over the decades from 22 percent in my own civilian files, 30 percent in the University of Colorado Condon Committee scientific studies, to at least 40 percent (recently revised) found in the U.S. Air Force Project Blue Book military investigations. This is not acceptable, no matter who is doing the investigations.

The fact that the UFOs and UFOnauts use advanced scientific devices and extraordinary powers (reported by many trained and highly qualified witnesses as psychic experiences) indicates a highly developed intelligence and scientific technology at work continues to give confirmation to my position. UFOs continue to represent a challenge to science, religion, and society.

These objects and their occupants continue to represent the highest secrecy of any subject in American history to date. Much of this information has come from over 36,000 documents released through Freedom of Information Act (FOIA) lawsuits.

The biggest question still remains, what is the final purpose for these visitations and the end result for all mankind? The future will tell. Meanwhile, investigations and research should continue in the 147 world nations involved with UFO experiences and proper funding should be provided for these efforts both in the private and public domain. Special studies of the UFO repetitions (see FAWCETT'S "REPETITIONS") should be emphasized. And special attention should be paid to the strange physical and chemical effects of UFOs and their occupants on the soil in landing spots; the sensory effects upon animals; the physiological and psychological effects on humans; and the electromagnetic (E-M) effects on machines and instruments.

It is the complexity of the worldwide UFO phenomenon that makes continued civilian, military, and scientific investigations even more important in the years ahead.

These unexplained phenomena continue to pose a challenge to science, religion, the military, and society. These are challenges that must be met if we are to survive as a civilization of the cosmos in the future.

—GEORGE D. FAWCETT

Fawcett's "Repetitions" List prepared by veteran UFOlogist George D. Fawcett, which he describes as aspects of sightings of unidentified flying objects (UFOs) that have been repeated time and time again over the past forty-seven years—which have proven themselves both persistent and consistent on a global basis—and are a challenge to science. Any future solution to the growing worldwide UFO enigma will have to deal directly with these UFO repetitions:

1. Sightings of unknown flying objects that demonstrate superior speeds and intricate maneuvers beyond those of present satellites, aircraft, and missiles.
2. Radar trackings of UFOs.
3. Photographs and movies of UFOs.
4. Pursuits of UFOs by planes in the skies, by ships at sea and by cars on open highways.
5. Falls of "fragments" and "angel hair" from UFOs overhead.
6. Increases in background radiation, ground markings, changes in soil samples, and deposits of both metallic and non-metallic residues after UFOs have been reported in the skies or on the ground (especially magnesium, aluminum, silicon, boron, and calcium).
7. Near-collisions, pacings and head-on passes by UFOs reported by civilian, military, and commercial pilots.
8. Physiological and psychological effects, such as electric shock, radiation burns, dimming of vision, blackouts, temporary paralysis, headaches, blood disorders, nightmares and dreams, reported by observers in close UFO encounters, both in the air and on the ground.
9. lectromagnetic interference reports caused by UFOs on compasses, plane and car motors, headlights, houselights, searchlights, radar beams, radios, TV, power stations, and other instruments and communication devices.
10. Skyquakes, explosions and sonic booms in the skies during UFO appearances
11. Propulsion sounds and smells attributed to UFOs.
12. Landings and near-landings (hoverings) of UFOs and their occupants.
13. Hostile acts due to UFOs (both toward and from these objects).

14. Reports of so-called "contactees" in association with "space visitors" as occupants of UFOs.
15. Straight lines of flight related to UFOs, along with their other kinematic, geometric, and luminescent characteristics.
16. Reputable sightings by scientists, astronauts, engineers, astronomers, and other trained observers of UFOs.
17. Appearances of "little men" (apparently humanoids) and other entities in relation to worldwide UFO landings, who were reported to have taken rocks, vegetation, soil, water, and animals, flowers, etc. Several hundred cases of human kidnappings, abductions, physical examinations, etc.
18. Periodic cycles of increased UFO sightings every twenty-six months, five years, and ten years in large numbers.
19. Unique shapes of UFOs, especially nocturnal lights, daylight disks, domed saucers, cigar-shaped or rocket-shaped objects, crescents, half-globes, and Saturn-shaped objects.
20. Revolving wheel-like machines in oceans, seas, and vast masses of water reported by ship and plane crews and passengers, and other witnesses nearby.
21. Depressions, craters, denuded vegetation, holes, ground markings, burned areas, and landing-gear marks on the ground due to UFO landings worldwide.
22. Power failures due to UFO appearances, both locally and on a widespread basis.
23. Severe animal reactions reported during UFO encounters.
24. Levitations in close proximity with UFOs of persons, cars, helicopters, trucks, garage roofs, fishing bobbers, UFO occupants, horses, etc.
25. The historical evidence of UFOs found in archaeology, cave-wall drawings, Holy Scriptures, legends, mythology, ancient manuscripts, frescoes, and folklore throughout the world.

To investigate any phenomenon in or outside of a laboratory requires that they must be repeatable, and such UFO encounters are recurrent in nature regardless of where they occur. Thus, the challenge in future scientific investigations remains.

Future science must meet the challenge posed by these UFO repetitions among over 140 world nations in order to solve the growing global UFO problem; otherwise, it will become part of the problem itself. The peoples of the world deserve better than that.

—GEORGE D. FAWCETT

Fire Came By, The (Doubleday, 1976). John Baxter and Thomas Atkins rely on the expeditions, researches, and the theories of Russian scientists to conclude that a nuclear spacecraft may have caused the 1908 explosion at Tunguska in Siberia. They base much of their evidence on purported eyewitness accounts that a huge shining, cylindrical object had manuevered and changed directions before falling and leveling 1,200 square miles of forest.

—RANDALL FITZGERALD

Fitzgerald, Randall (b. 1950). A former investigative reporter for syndicated columnist Jack Anderson and congressional reporter for Capitol Hill News Service, Randy Fitzgerald has twenty years' experience as a Washington watchdog for the American taxpayer. He has reported on public policy issues for *Reader's Digest* since 1981, becoming a staff writer and contributing editor in 1984.

The Texas native began his journalism career straight out of high school, writing for the Tyler *Morning-Telegraph*. He later graduated from the University of Texas, receiving his B.S. degree in journalism in 1974.

He was a founder and co-editor of *Second Look* magazine (1978-1980), later called *Frontiers of Science*, and is the author of four books: *The Complete Book of Extraterrestrial Encounters* (1979), *Porkbarrel* (1984), *When Government Goes Private* (1988), and *Cosmic Test Tube* (1998).

Address: P.O. Box 1536
            Cobb, CA 95426
            U.S.A.
E-mail: rftruman@earthlink.net

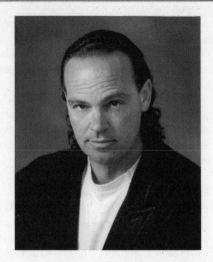

Randall Fitzgerald

POSITION STATEMENT: I consider myself an open-minded skeptic/agnostic on the UFO issue. However, at the very least, I think the UFO phenomenon should be considered as an evolutionary benchmark by which we can begin to measure our potential as a species for absorbing future contact with a higher intelligence.

—RANDALL FITZGERALD

Flatwoods (West Virginia) monster In modern police parlance a long-unsolved homicide or other crime may be known as a "cold case," a term we might borrow for such paranormal mysteries as that of the Flatwoods Monster, which was launched on September 12, 1952, and never completely explained.

About 7:15 P.M. on that day, at Flatwoods, a little village in the hills of West Virginia, some youngsters were playing football on the school playground. Suddenly they saw a fiery UFO streak across the sky and, apparently, land on a hilltop of the nearby Bailey Fisher farm. The youths ran to the home of Mrs. Kathleen May, who provided a flashlight and accompanied them up the hill. In addition to Mrs. May, a local beautician, the group included her two sons, Eddie 13, and Freddie 14, Neil Nunley 14, Gene Lemon 17, and

Tommy Hyer and Ronnie Shaver, both 10, along with Lemon's dog.

There are myriad, often contradictory versions of what happened next, but UFO writer Gray Barker was soon on the scene and wrote an account for *Fate* magazine based on tape-recorded interviews. He found that the least emotional account was provided by Neil Nunley, one of two youths who were in the lead as the group hastened to the crest of the hill. Some distance ahead was a pulsing red light. Then, suddenly, Gene Lemon saw a pair of shining animal-like eyes, and aimed the flashlight in their direction. The light revealed a towering "man-like" figure with a round, red "face" surrounded by a "pointed, hood-like shape." The body was dark and seemingly colorless, but some would later say it was green, and Mrs. May reported drape-like folds. The monster was observed only momentarily, as suddenly it emitted a hissing sound and glided toward the group. Lemon responded by screaming and dropping his flashlight, whereupon everyone fled.

The group had noticed a pungent mist at the scene and afterward some were nauseous. A few locals, then later the sheriff and a deputy (who came from investigating a reported airplane crash), searched the site but "saw, heard and smelled nothing." The following day A. Lee Stewart, Jr., from the *Braxton Democrat* discovered "skid marks" in the roadside field, along with an "odd, gummy deposit"—traces attributed to the landed "saucer." (Barker, 1953)

In his article Barker (1953) noted that "numerous people in a 20-mile radius saw the illuminated objects in the sky at the same time," evidently seeing different objects or a single one "making a circuit of the area." Barker believed the Flatwoods incident was consistent with other reports of "flying saucers or similar craft" and that "such a vehicle landed on the hillside, either from necessity or to make observations." (At this time in UFOlogical history, the developing mythology had not yet involved alien "abductions.")

In addition to Barker's article and later his book (1956), accounts of the Flatwoods incident were related by another on-site investigator, paranormal writer Ivan T. Sanderson (1952, 1967), as well as the early UFOlogist Major Donald E. Keyhoe (1953). More recent accounts have garbled details, with Brookesmith (1995), for example, incorrectly reporting five of the children as belonging to Mrs. May, and Ritchie (1994) referring to the monster's hood-like feature as a "halo," which he compared with those in Japanese Buddhist art. However, Jerome Clark's *The UFO Encyclopedia* (1998) has a generally factual, sensible account of the affair, appropriately termed "one of the most bizarre UFO encounters of all time."

THE UFO

On June 1, 2000, while on a trip that took me through Flatwoods, I was able to stop off for an afternoon of on-site investigating. I was amused to be greeted by a sign announcing: "Welcome to Flatwoods, Home of the Green Monster." Although the village has no local library, I found something even better: a real-estate business, Country Properties, whose co-owners Betty Hallman and Laura Green generously photocopied articles for me and telephoned residents to set up interviews.

Johnny Lockard, 95, told me that virtually everyone who had seen the alleged flying saucer in 1952 recognized it for what it was: a meteor. He, his daughter Betty Jean, and her husband Bill Sumpter said that the fireball had been seen on a relatively horizontal trajectory in various states. In fact, according to a former local newspaper editor, "There is no doubt that a meteor of considerable proportion flashed across the heavens that Friday night since it was visible in at least three states— Maryland, Pennsylvania and West Virginia." (Byrne, 1966) The meteor explanation contrasts with the fanciful notions of Sanderson (1967). He cites several persons who each saw a *single* glowing object. Although observing that "All of the objects were traveling in the same direction and apparently at the same speed and at exactly the same time,'' he fails to draw the obvious conclusion: that there was one object, albeit variously described. (For example, one report said the object landed on a nearby knoll, while another described it as ''disintegrating in the air with a rain of ashes.'') Instead of suspecting that people were mistaken or that they saw a meteor that broke apart, Sanderson asserts that ''to be logical'' we should believe that ''a flight of aerial machines'' were ''maneuvering in formation.'' For some reason the craft went out of control, with one *landing,* rather than crashing, at Flatwoods, and its pilot emerged ''in a space suit.'' Observed, it headed back to the spaceship which—like two others that ''crashed''— soon ''vaporized.'' (Sanderson, 1967)

Such airy speculations aside, according to Major Keyhoe (1953), Air Force Intelligence reportedly sent two men in civilian clothes to Flatwoods, posing as magazine writers, and they determined that the UFO had been a meteor that ''merely appeared to be landing when it disappeared over the hill.'' That illusion also deceived a man approximately ten miles southwest of Flatwoods, who reported that an aircraft had gone down in flames on the side of a wooded hill. (That was the report the sheriff had investigated, without success, before arriving at the Flatwoods site.)

Keyhoe's sources told him that ''several astronomers'' had concluded that the UFO was indeed a meteor. As well, a staff member of the Maryland Academy of Sciences announced that a meteor had passed over Baltimore at 7:00 P.M. on September 12th, ''traveling at a height of from 60 to 70 miles.'' (Reese, 1952) It was on a trajectory toward West Virginia, where the ''saucer'' was sighted minutes later.

SPACESHIP AGROUND?

If the UFO was not a spaceship but a meteor, then how do we explain the other elements—the pulsating light, the landing traces, the noxious smell, and, above all, the frightening creature? Let us consider each in turn.

As the group had proceeded up the road-

way that led to the hilltop, they saw ''a reddish light pulsating from dim to bright.'' It was described as a ''globe'' and as ''a big ball of fire'' (Barker, 1953) but Sanderson (1967) says they ''disagreed violently on their interpretation of this object.'' We should keep in mind that it was a distance away—an unknown distance—and that there was no trustworthy frame of reference from which to estimate size (reported to Sanderson as over twenty feet across).

Significantly, at the time of the incident, a local schoolteacher called attention to ''the light from a nearby plane beacon,'' and Sanderson (1952) conceded that there were three such beacons ''in sight all the time on the hilltop.'' However, he dismissed the obvious possibility that one of these was the source of the pulsing light because he was advocating an extraterrestrial explanation.

But if a UFO had not landed at the site, how do we explain the supposed landing traces? They were found at 7:00 the morning after the incident by A. Lee Stewart, Jr., editor of *The Braxton Democrat,* who had visited the site the night before. Stewart discovered two parallel ''skid marks'' in the tall meadow grass, between the spot where the monster was seen and the area where the red pulsating light was sighted. He also saw traces of ''oil'' or ''an odd, gummy deposit.'' (Barker, 1953)

Johnny Lockard's son, Max, describes Stewart in a word: ''windy.'' Max had tried to explain to him and others the nature of the unidentified object that left the skid marks and oily/greasy deposit, namely Max's black, 1942 Chevrolet pickup truck. Soon after news of the the incident had spread around Flatwoods that evening, Max drove up the hillside to have a look around. He told me he left the dirt road and circled through the field, but saw nothing, no monster and no landing traces in the meadow grass.

At the time of the incident a few locals who had been skeptical that a flying saucer had landed on the hill attributed the skid marks and oil to a farm tractor. When several others told Gray Barker that the traces had actually been left by Max Lockard, he recalled his old high school chum and decided to telephone him. They had a proverbial failure to communicate and Barker—who admitted to seeing "an opportunity to get my name in print again"—concluded that Max's truck had not been at the exact spot where the alleged UFO markings were found.

Reading Barker (1956), one senses his impulse to dismiss the tractor and pickup hypotheses and never even to consider the possibility of some other vehicle. It is not clear that Barker ever saw the traces. He arrived one week after the incident, and during the interim rain had obliterated the evidence. He could find "no trace of the oil reported to have been on the ground," and although he saw "marks and a huge area of grass trampled down," he conceded that could be due to the "multitudes" that had "visited and walked over the location." (Barker, 1953, 1956)

Max Lockard took me to the site in his modern pickup. A locked gate across the road prompted him to shift into four-wheel drive and take us on a cross-country shortcut through a field, much as he had done in his search for the reported UFO and monster nearly a half century before. He has convinced me that he indeed left the supposedly unexplained traces. With a twinkle in my eye, I posed a question: 'Max, had you ever piloted a UFO before?' His sniffle answered that he had not.

As to the nauseating odor, that has been variously described as a sulfurous smell, "metallic stench," gas-like mist, or simply a "sickening, irritating" odor. Investigators first on the scene noticed no such smell, except for Lee Stewart who detected it when he beat close to the ground. The effect on three of the youths, particularly Lemon, was later to cause nausea and complaints of irritated throats. (Barker, 1953, 1956; Sanderson, 1967; Keyhoe, 1953)

This element of the story may be overstated. Ivan Sanderson (1967), scarcely a militant skeptic, also noticed the "strange smell in the grass" but stated that it was "almost surely derived from a kind of grass that abounds in the area." He added, "We found this grass

growing all over the county and it always smelt the same, though not perhaps as strongly." Keyhoe (1953) reported that the Air Force investigators had concluded that "the boys' illness was a physical effect brought on by their fright." Indeed Gene Lemon, the worst affected, had seemed the most frightened; he had "shrieked with terror" and fallen backward, dropping the flashlight, and later "appeared too greatly terrified to talk coherently." (Barker, 1956). As to the strange "mist" that had accompanied the odor (Barker, 1953), that seems easily explained. Obviously it was the beginning stage of what the sheriff subsequently noticed on his arrival, a fog that was "settling over the hillside." (Keyhoe, 1953)

THE CREATURE

Finally, and most significantly, there remains to be explained "the Flatwoods Monster," a.k.a. "the Phantom of Flatwoods," "the Braxton County Monster," "the Visitor from Outer Space," and other appellations. (Byrne, 1966) Many candidates have been proposed, but—considering that the UFO became an IFO, namely a meteor—the least likely one is some extraterrestrial entity. I think we can dismiss also the notion, among the hypotheses put forward by a local paper, that it was the effect of "vapor from a falling meteorite that took the form of a man." (Sanderson, 1967) Also extremely unlikely was the eventual explanation of Mrs. May that what she had seen "wasn't a monster" but rather "a secret plane the government was working on." (Marchal, 1966) (Both she and her son Fred declined to be interviewed for my investigation.) I agree with most previous investigators that the monster sighting was not a hoax. The fact that the witnesses did see a meteor and assembled on the spur of the moment to investigate makes that unlikely. So does the fact that everyone who talked to them afterward insisted—as Max Lockard did to me—that the eyewitnesses were genuinely frightened. Clearly, something they saw frightened them, but what?

The group described shining "animal eyes," and Mrs. May at first thought they belonged to "an opossum or raccoon in the tree." (Barker, 1956; Sanderson, 1967) Locals continued to suggest some such local animal, including "a buck deer" (Barker, 1956), but a much more credible candidate was put forth by the unnamed Air Force investigators. According to Keyhoe (1953), they concluded the "monster" was probably "a large owl perched on a limb" with underbrush beneath it having "given the impression of a giant figure" and the excited witnesses having "imagined the rest."

I believe this generic solution is correct, but that the owl was not from the family of atypical owls (Strigidae, which includes the familiar great horned owl) but the other family (Tytonidae) which comprises the barn owls. Several elements in the witnesses' descriptions help identify the Flatwoods creature specifically as Tyto alba, the common barn owl, known almost worldwide. (Collins, 1959) Consider the following evidence.

The "monster" reportedly had a "man-like shape" and stood some ten feet tall, although Barker (1953) noted that "descriptions from the waist down are vague; most of the seven said this part of the figure was not under view." These perceptions are consistent with an owl perched on a limb.

Also suggestive of an owl is the description of the creature's "face" as "round" with "two eye-like openings" and a dark, "hood-like shape" around it (if not the "pointed" appearance of the latter). (Barker, 1953) The barn owl has a large head with a "ghastly," roundish heart-shaped face, resembling "that of a toothless, hook-nosed old woman, shrouded in a closely fitting hood" and with an expression "that gives it a mysterious air" (Jordan, 1952; Blanchan, 1925).

Very evidential in the case of the Flatwoods Monster is the description of its cry as "something between a hiss and a high-pitched squeal." (Barker, 1953) This tallies with the startling "wild, peevish scream" or "shrill rasping hiss or snore" of the barn owl. Indeed its "shrill, strangled scream is the most unbird-like noise." Its "weird calls" include "hissing notes, screams," and "guttural grunts." (Blanchan, 1925; Peterson, 1980; Bull and Farrand, 1977; Cloudsley-Thompson et al., 1983). The latter might explain the monster's accompanying "thumping or throbbing noise." (Barker, 1953), if those sounds were not from the flapping of wings.

Descriptions of the creature's movement varied, being characterized as "bobbing up and down, jumping toward the witnesses," or as moving "evenly," indeed "describing an arc, coming toward them, but circling at the same time." (Barker, 1956) Again, it had "a gliding motion as if afloat in midair." These movements are strongly suggestive of a bird's flight. When accidentally disturbed, the barn owl "makes a bewildered and erratic getaway" (Jordan, 1952)—while hissing (Blanchan, 1925)—but its flight is generally characterized with "slow, flapping wing beats and long glides." (Cloudsley-Thompson et al., 1983)

According to Barker (1953): "Not all agreed that the 'monster' had arms," but "Mrs. May described it with terrible claws." Sanderson (1967) cites the witnesses' observation that "the creature had small, claw-like hands that extended in front of it," a description consistent with a raptor (a predatory bird). The barn owl is relatively long-legged and knock-kneed, sporting sizable claws with sharp, curved talons that may be prominently extended. (Peterson, 1980; Forshaw, 1998)

It is important to note that the youths and Mrs. May only glimpsed the creature briefly—an estimated "one or a few more seconds," and even that was while they were frightened. Barker (1956) asks, "If Lemon dropped the flashlight, as he claimed, how did they get an apparently longer look at the 'monster'?" Some said the being was lighted from within (probably only the effect of its "shining" eyes), while Nunley stated that it was illuminated by the pulsing red light (ostensibly from the supposed UFO but probably from one of the beacons mentioned earlier). This might also

Split-image illustration compares fanciful Flatwoods Monster (left) with the real-world creature it most resembles, the common barn owl (right). (Drawing by Joe Nickell)

explain the "fiery orange color" of the creature's head (Sanderson, 1967), but an alternative explanation is, while the barn owl is typically described as having a white facial disk and underparts, in the case of the female those parts "have some darker buff or tawny color." ("Barn Owl," 2000)

For this reason, as well as the fact that in this species (a medium-sized owl, measuring about 14-20 inches [Peterson, 1980]) the male is typically the smaller (Blanchan, 1925), I suspect the Flatwoods creature was a female. It is also interesting to speculate that it may not have been too late in the year for a female to have been brooding young. That could explain why "she" did not fly away at the first warning of intruders (given barn owls' "excellent low-light vision and exceptional hearing ability" ["Barn Owl," 2000]); instead, probably

hoping not to be noticed, she stood her ground until the invaders confronted her with a flashlight, a threatening act that provoked her hissing, attack-like swoop toward them.

Significantly, the locale where the Flatwoods Monster made its appearance—near a large oak tree on a partially wooded hilltop overlooking a farm on the outskirts of town—tallies with the habitat of the barn owl. Indeed, it is "the best known of farmland owls." (Cloudsley-Thompson, 1983) It builds no nest, but takes as its "favorite home" a "hollow tree." (Blanchan, 1925) It "does not mind the neighborhood of man" (Jordan, 1952), in fact seeking out mice and rats from its residence in "woodlands, groves, farms, barns, towns, cliffs." (Peterson, 1980)

Considering all of the characteristics of the described monster, and making small allowances for misperceptions and other distorting factors, we may conclude (adapting an old adage) that if it looked like a barn owl, acted like a barn owl, and hissed, then it most likely was a barn owl.

How Monsters Appear

It may be wondered, however, why the creature was not immediately recognized for what it was. The answer is that, first, the witnesses were led to *expect* an alien being by their sighting of a UFO that appeared to land and by the pulsating red light and strange smell that seemed to confirm the landing. Therefore, when they then encountered a strange creature, acting aggressively, their fears seemed to be confirmed and they panicked.

Moreover, the group had probably never seen a barn owl up close (after all, such birds are nocturnal) and almost certainly not under the adverse conditions that prevailed. The brief glimpse, at night, of a being that suddenly swept at them—coupled with its strange "ghastly" appearance and shrill frightening cry—would have been disconcerting to virtually anyone at any time. But under the circumstances, involving an inexperienced group primed with expectations of extraterrestrials, the situation was a recipe for terror.

And so a spooked barn owl in turn spooked the interlopers, and a monster was born. A "windy" newspaperman and pro-paranormal writers hyped the incident, favoring sensational explanations for more prosaic ones. Such is often the case with paranormal claims.

—JOE NICKELL

References

Barker, Gray. "The Monster and the Saucer," *Fate,* January, 12-17, 1953.

———. *They Knew Too Much About Flying Saucers* (Tower Books, 1967).

"Barn Owl." 2000. www.vetmed.auburn.edu.

Blanchan, Neltje. *Birds Worth Knowing* (Doubleday, 1925).

Bull, John, and John Farrand Jr. *The Audubon Society Field Guide to North American Birds: Eastern Region* (Knopf, 1977).

Byrne, Holt. "The Phantom of Flatwoods," *Sunday Gazette-Mail State Magazine* (Charleston, W. Va.), March 6, 1966.

Clark, Jerome. *The UFO Encyclopedia,* second edition (Omnigraphics, 1998).

Cloudsley-Thompson, John, et al. *Nightwatch: The Natural World from Dusk to Dawn* (Facts on File, 1983).

Collins, Henry Hill, Jr. *Complete Field Guide to American Wildlife: East, Central and North* (Harper & Row, 1959).

Forshaw, Joseph. *Encyclopedia of Birds* (Academic Press, 1998).

Jordan, E. L. *Hammond's Nature Atlas of America* (C. S. Hammond & Co., 1952).

Keyhoe, Donald E. *Flying Saucers from Outer Space* (Henry Holt, 1953).

Marchal, Terry. "Flatwoods Revisited," *Sunday Gazette-Mail State Magazine* (Charleston, W. Va.), March 6, 1966.

Peterson, Roger Tory. *A Field Guide to the Birds* (Houghton Mifflin, 1980).

Reese, P. M. (1952) Cited in Sanderson, 1967.

Ritchie, David. *UFO: The Definitive Guide to Unidentified Flying Objects and Related Phenomena* (Facts on File, 1994).

Sanderson, Ivan T. (1952) Typewritten report quoted in Byrne, 1966.

———. *Uninvited Visitors: A Biologist Looks at UFO's* (Cowles, 1967).

"flying saucer" An expression commonly used to describe an unexplained aerial phenomenon. The words do not always convey a just conception, since much of what is reported is not saucer-shaped nor can it be assumed that they are solid bodies utilizing aerodynamic principles. This particular designation was coined on June 25, 1947, in the newsroom of the *East Oregonian*, a newspaper serving Pendleton, Oregon. Newsman Bill Bequette denominated the phenomenon during an interview with private pilot Kenneth Arnold while the flyer was relating his famous sighting of strange, "tailless aircraft," an episode that took place the previous afternoon over the Cascade mountains.

Some maintain that the distinctive appellation "flying saucer" was derived solely from Arnold's description of the undulatory flight of the things he saw, which, he said, traveled through the air like a "flat rock" skipped along the surface of a pond. Nonetheless, the *Chicago Daily Tribune*, as early as June 25th, quotes Arnold as saying the objects were "shaped like a pie plate." Later, when questioned carefully, Arnold insisted that the objects he spotted were wide and flat, but none of the nine were true disks, one being crescent in outline and the other eight having curved leading edges and pointed trailing edges. U.S. Air Force experts rightly doubted Arnold's ability to make out an object's shape at a distance of twenty-three miles, a distance Arnold claims separated him from the flight path of the unknowns, an estimate he refused to retract.

Since his attention was initially attracted to the swiftly moving objects by sunlight flashing from their shiny wings as they sped through the air in an undulating manner, Arnold's perception of the objects may have also been hampered significantly by the rapid dipping motion changing the intensity of the reflected rays of the sun. It may, nevertheless, be safe to assume that the objects Arnold saw were thin, flat, and tailless, words which do not rule out a true disk shape.

The word "saucer" was first used to describe an unidentified aerial object in 1878, when a farmer named John Martin told the Denison, Texas, *Daily News* on January 25th, that a mysterious saucer-shaped object had flown over his property south of town.

The "flying saucer" design is actually not that modern; as early as 1918, the science-fantasy magazine *Electrical Experimenter* featured a saucer-like craft on the cover of its March edition to illustrate R. and G. Winthrop's novelette "At War with the Invisible." It should also be noted that a year before the big UFO wave of 1947, the pulp magazine *Amazing Stories* had an interesting fictional illustration on its back cover showing a group of "flying saucer spaceships" in V-formation.

—LOREN E. GROSS

Flying Saucer Occupants (Signet/NAL, 1967). Coral and Jim Lorenzen set forth their belief that three races of alien beings are visiting Earth, but the CIA and Air Force are probably not aware of the problem. Conspiracy theorists who believe a cover-up exists, say this husband and wife team, exhibit a need for "instant reassurance" which comes from a fear that no authority figures may be in control, or even aware, that UFO visitors pose a problem for humankind.

—RANDALL FITZGERALD

Flying Saucers (Harvard University Press, 1953). With this book Harvard University astrophysicist Donald Menzel became the first scientist to craft a rational, natural phenomena explanation for UFOs in a presentation tailored to a mainstream audience. Flying saucers are real, he says, as real as rainbows, sundogs, mirages, and other optical tricks the atmosphere plays on the human brain. These misidentifications of natural phenomena account for both contemporary and Biblical accounts of UFOs. Ironically, with this 1953 discussion of ancient UFO sightings, Menzel would one day claim the dubious credit for having ushered in the

spate of ancient astronaut theories and books which flooded mainstream literature more than a decade later.

—RANDALL FITZGERALD

Flying Saucers: A Modern Myth of Things Seen in the Skies (Routledge & Kegan Paul/Harcourt, Brace & Co., 1959; Signet/NAL, 1969). Psychologist Carl Jung sees UFOs as projections from the collective unconscious of humanity and a symptom of psychic change in our species.

Jung examines the UFO phenomenon as a complement to, or the cause of, "long-lasting transformations of the collective psyche." This psychic component of the phenomenon Jung details in three stages or interconnections: in the first, an "objectively real, physical process forms the basis for an accompanying myth"; in the second, an archetype, whose specific form our collective instincts take, creates a corresponding vision; finally, emerging with these two "causal relationships," we experience synchronistic behavior, the meaningful coincidence, in which the psychic stress of humankind and the appearance of UFOs coincide as a meaningful pattern.

—RANDALL FITZGERALD

Flying Saucers and the Straight-line Mystery (S.G. Phillips, 1958). Aimé Michel, a French mathematician and engineer, recounts a wave of UFO sightings in France which included human encounters with alien craft and creatures. When he charted these sightings chronologically several patterns emerged. Sightings occurring on the same day were found to be in straight lines on maps. Aside from the extraterrestrial hypothesis, Michel wonders whether another explanation might be that human thoughts actualized these visions in the sky.

—RANDALL FITZGERALD

Flying Saucers Are Real, The (Fawcett Publications, 1950). This book by retired U.S. Marine Major Donald E. Keyhoe was the first ever devoted to the flying saucer topic.

It was essentially an expanded version of Keyhoe's seminal article for *True* magazine under the same title. In this book Keyhoe states his main conclusions, which defined the modern flying saucer era: "(1) The Earth has been under periodic observation from another planet, or other planets, for at least two centuries. (2) This observation suddenly increased in 1947, following the series of A-bomb explosions begun in 1945. (3) The observation, now intermittent, is part of a long-range survey and will continue indefinitely. There may be some unknown block to making contact, but it is more probable that the spacemen's plans are not complete."

—RONALD D. STORY

Flying Saucers from Outer Space (Henry Holt, 1953). With this book retired Marine Corps Major Donald E. Keyhoe became the first prominent and outspoken conspiracy theory proponent.

He claimed that flying saucers are piloted by extraterrestrial visitors, the U.S. Air Force is aware of the truth, it is engaged in a cover-up, and it is up to civilian UFO groups to end this secrecy. He is also the first author to speculate that UFOs have an electromagnetic propulsion system.

—RANDALL FITZGERALD

Flying Saucers Have Landed (The British Book Centre/Werner Laurie, 1953) by Desmond Leslie and George Adamski. America's first famous contactee, Adamski, collaborates with an Irish journalist to tell how he met a Venusian with long sandy hair in the California desert.

Supposedly he and other beings from Venus are here on this planet to express their displeasure with nuclear testing, a theme which soon became a cause taken up by other contactees. Adamski hit the lecture circuit after the book and later circulated a series of photos of Venusian spaceships which were generally regarded as crude hoaxes.

—RANDALL FITZGERALD

Flying Saucers—Serious Business (Lyle Stuart, 1966). Radio broadcaster Frank Edwards wonders whether the race to the moon between America and Russia has the ulterior motive of being the first to contact aliens based there. He points out how the shapes of reported UFOs have been evolving over the years from dirigibles in the late 1890s to flying disks in the 1950s to egg-shaped craft in the 1960s.

—RANDALL FITZGERALD

Flying Saucers Uncensored (Citadel Press, 1955) by Harold T. Wilkins. Author catalogues UFO sightings and incidents over the U.K., Western Europe, U.S., and Australia from 1947 through 1955 and speculates that extraterrestrial visitants are possibly established in bases on the moon and other planets; a cosmic general staff may receive reports on terrestrial affairs as well as biological and ecological samples from Earth for purposes of study and experimentation.

—LYNN CATOE

foo fighters   The foo fighters, or "kraut balls," as they were also called, were first observed as very small (from a few inches to a few feet in diameter) balls of light that followed and seemingly "teased" military fighter and bomber aircraft during the final months of World War II. These miniature-sized UFOs would appear alone, in pairs, or in groups, and seemed at times to be under some kind of remote, intelligent control. They would sometimes emit a steady glow of red, gold, or white light; other times they would blink on and off.

Although it is customary in most UFO literature to associate the foo fighters with the beginning of the "modern" phase of the UFO phenomenon in general, there are important differences between these and most other UFO reports. In fact, there are good reasons to believe that the foo-ball mystery is explainable in nonprosaic, albeit earthly, terms.

The earliest reliable report of the specter-like apparitions came from a pilot and crew belonging to the 415th Night Fighter Squadron based at Dijon, France. The 415th patrolled both sides of the Rhine River, north of Strasbourg, in eastern Germany, seeking out any German planes in the area with the aid of U.S. Army ground-based radar stations. Lieutenant Ed Schlueter (pilot), Lieutenant Donald J. Meiers (radar observer), and Lieutenant Fred Ringwald (intelligence officer, flying as an observer) were on such a mission on the night of November 23, 1944, when Ringwald first spotted what appeared to be stars off at a distance. Within a few minutes, the star-like points became orange balls of light (eight or ten of them) "moving through the air at a terrific speed." The "objects" could not be picked up by radar, either ground-based or from the plane. The lights then disappeared, reappeared farther off, and within a few minutes vanished from view.

More reports followed, as the mystery spread to other parts of the world. The foo fighters (a name that was picked up from the Smokey Stover comic strip, wherein it was frequently said that "where there's foo, there's fire") appeared also on the bombing route to Japan and over the Truk Lagoon in the mid-Pacific. The reports were similar: speeds generally estimated at between two hundred and five hundred miles per hour; orange, red, and white colors; steady or blinking lights, alone or in groups, but not detectable by radar.

The consistency of these well-authenticated encounters is unlike any other set of UFO reports. According to the Italian aircraft engineer and writer, Renato Vesco, it is for good reason. In an article published in *Argosy* magazine (August 1969), Vesco writes:

> Later encounters with foo-fighters led experts to assume they were German inventions of a new order, employed to baffle radar.
>
> How close they had come to the truth, they learned only when the war was over and Allied Intelligence teams moved into the secret Nazi plants. The foo-fighters seen by Allied pilots were only a minor demonstration, and a fraction of a vast variety of methods to confuse radar and interrupt electromagnetic currents. Work on the German anti-radar Feuerball, or fireball, had been speeded up during the fall of 1944 at a Luftwaffe experimental center near Oberammergau, Bavaria. There, and at the aeronautical establishment of Wiener Neustadt, the first fireballs were produced. Later, when the Russians moved closer to Austria, the workshops producing the fireballs were moved to the Black Forest. Fast and remote-controlled, the fireballs, equipped with kliston tubes and operating on the same frequency as Allied radar, could eliminate the blips from screens and remain practically invisible to ground control.

It is also interesting to note that in one of the first published accounts of the foo-fighter mystery, Jo Chamberlin reported in *The American Legion Magazine* (December 1945) that: "The foo-fighters simply disappeared when Allied ground forces captured the area East of the Rhine. This was known to be the location of many German experimental stations."

Another theory is that the foo balls might have been a type of plasma, in the form of an electrical discharge, known as St. Elmo's Fire. Both the German secret-weapon theory and the plasma theory have their merits, whereas an extraterrestrial explanation seems unlikely.

—RONALD D. STORY

Fort, Charles (1874-1932). A former newspaper reporter and amateur naturalist who, for twenty-six years, collected strange, unexplained bits of information—including some of the earliest documented sightings of UFOs—culled from old newspapers, magazines, and even scientific journals.

A daring mind, Fort proposed various exotic solutions to weird mysteries ignored by science. Although Fort explored different ideas about a number of subjects, his postulations about unexplained aerial phenomena gave him enduring notoriety. Backed by an impressive documentary effort (some 40,000 notes), Fort's writings have served to call attention to UFO activity that occurred between 1801 and 1930. Fort authored five books, the earliest of which, *The Outcast Manufactures* (1909), was a novel having nothing to do with his later preoccupation with bizarre events. The other four books contain the data and thoughts that have made Fort famous among students of the UFO riddle. Those are: *The Book of the Damned* (1919), *New Lands* (1923), *Lo!* (1931), and *Wild Talents* (1932). The books were limited editions, having little public impact at the time. As for book reviewers, they were either baffled or exhilarated by Fort's revelations. It was the American iconoclast's small but influential following in literary circles that guaranteed the survival of his writings.

Just before the United States entered World War II, Fort's four books on the esoteric were republished together (in 1941) in a single 1,100-page tome, a volume that has gone through many editions and is still widely used by UFO enthusiasts as a reference work; though close scrutiny reveals that Fort's documentation was not always completely accurate, the data published in his books was not meant to be exhaustive. Considerable detail on UFO cases was deleted in favor of clownish and clever commentary. Many UFO reports, pinpointed by Fort, lacked extensive investigation.

Fort's *Book of the Damned* is the richest of all four in UFO material. Besides mysterious lights and objects in the atmosphere, the book contains two episodes on a larger scale that are especially striking. There was the extraordinary telescopic discovery of a lunar-size body close to the planet Venus, which was observed at various times between 1645 and 1767. Astronomers called the little world "Neith," but, to the consternation of the experts, the orb eventually vanished. Likewise, another smaller, spindle-shaped body was observed by astronomers in 1762, which remained inexplicable, but was noted by Fort, who named it "Monstrator." To Fort, the data suggested space arks and cosmic mother ships—vast vessels that had dropped anchor in the solar system so they could probe closer to the abode of mankind.

After accepting the possibility that scout craft from a "super-Rome" were coming and going in the Earth's atmosphere, Fort soon became stumped by a puzzle which still troubles modern-day UFO researchers. If the Earth was being visited, why was it not done openly? This "greatest of mysteries," (Fort's very words) he compared to civilized man's contact with a primitive tribe. Would not visitors from a superior extraterrestrial culture be eager to sell Earthmen "super-whiskeys, cast-off super-fineries," or proselytize us with "ultra-Bibles"? he asks. Perhaps, he suggests, mankind's hostile behavior was considered so dangerous that possible contamination was feared, thus making the Earth a place to be avoided, at least as far as direct contact was concerned.

Another hypothesis proposed by Fort placed the Earth under the guardianship of some other superior beings. Unbeknownst to us, like a farmer's pigs, geese, or cattle (which lack the sophistication to understand they are "owned"), man, with his own limited perceptions, does not realize that aliens have long ago quarreled over, and eventually divided up, the cosmos, and that our world is the property of some victorious extraterrestrial civilization, which occasionally checks on us, chasing away all unauthorized intruders.

New Lands, Fort's second collection of weird data, also contains a considerable amount of UFO information. Significant sections relate events pertaining to UFO waves in England in 1905 and 1913, and UFO waves in the United States in 1897 and 1908-10. Giving his thousands of notes some thought, Fort wrote that he could conceive of many kinds of extramundanians, some of which might adapt to the conditions on Earth, although he assumed the surface of our world would be like an ocean floor to aliens from a radically different environment. And if such were to be the case, then that could be another reason why such creatures do not land.

Another fascinating line of conjecture was Fort's suggestions that many mysterious occurrences classified as supposed psychic phenomena might actually be due to the unrecognized antics of alien visitors. (Interestingly, the noted Fortean investigator/author John Keel later suggested the exact reverse—that many reports of supposed alien visitors actually represent paranormal or psychic phenomena.)

The third work by Fort of interest to UFO buffs, *Lo!* is only sparsely sprinkled with UFO accounts, with the exception of a discussion of the English UFO waves of 1904-05 and 1908-09. Still, it contains some memorable "Fortean" suggestions on the UFO enigma.

For example: Could alien spies be living in the major cities of Earth, regularly reporting back to their home base on a distant world? Also, could it be that the Earth is actually at war with extraterrestrial powers? This curious Wellsian train of speculation he did not develop fully, nor does any sizable amount of data justify such a suspicion. Fort did, however, play with the notion that mysterious vanishments of ocean vessels and their crews, of which he gives numerous examples, may have been due to wanton seizures by spacemen.

In *Lo!* Fort expressed concern over the lack of public interest in UFO activity, of how people could not take such data and its implications seriously and seemed to suffer from strong preconceptions that such things were nonsense. Even if eyewitnesses were to number in the millions, he asserted, UFO phenomena would be explained away, or in his own words, "conventionalized."

In a more humorous mood, he foresaw the possibility that even if real creatures from Mars were to land and, with much fanfare, parade up Broadway in New York City, disbelief would remain so great, some jokers could, after the aliens had departed, successfully proclaim they had plotted and carried out a grand deception.

Fort's last book, *Wild Talents,* has little of value UFO-wise but is laced with more of his views of how strange data can represent "gulfs of the unaccountable," which the authorities "bridge with terminology."

Although a timid man and, in general, content as an obscure author, Fort nevertheless penned four letters to *The New York Times* between 1924 and 1926, trying to alert the public to the fact that craft piloted by creatures from other worlds were patrolling the skies of Earth. He confessed in his letters that the possibility was difficult to accept, yet when its time came, the "great discovery" would amount to the "final perception of the obvious." The publication of *Wild Talents* took place just before Fort died on May 3, 1932. On May 5th, Fort's passing was reported in *The New York Times.* Instead of being recognized as something of a prognosticater, the *Times* tagged Fort a "foe of science," an unfortunately distorted view of a man who, although critical of "scientists"—when they spoke *ex cathedra*—was really a true proponent of the scientific method in its purest form.

—LOREN E. GROSS

Fowler, Raymond E. (b. 1933). Born in Salem, Massachusetts, Raymond Fowler enlisted in the U.S. Air Force in 1952 and served a four-year term, first as a general radio operator and later with the USAF Security Service. In 1960, he received his B.A. degree (*magna cum laude*) from Gordon College of Liberal Arts (majoring in Bible and Greek studies) at Wenham, Massachusetts. After twenty-five years of service, he retired early from GTE Government Systems where he worked as task manager and senior planner for several major weapons systems, including both the Minuteman and MX intercontinental ballistic missiles.

Ray Fowler is a veteran UFO researcher (since 1947) and investigator. His investigative reports have been published in Congressional hearings, military publications, newspapers, magazines, and professional journals in the U.S.A. and abroad. Fowler also believes himself to be a UFO-abductee.

In addition to his interest in UFOs, Fowler is an avid amateur astronomer and teacher. In 1970, he built the Woodside Planetarium and Observatory, where he conducts both adult and children's shows, supplemented by observation sessions with a 14-inch Schmidt-Cassegrain telescope.

Fowler has written eight books and a novel on the subject of unidentified flying objects. In order of publication they are: *UFOs: Interplanetary Visitors* (1974), *The Andreasson Affair* (1979), *The Andreasson Affair—Phase Two* (1982), *Casebook of a UFO Investigator* (1981), *The Melchizedek Connection* (1981), *The Watchers* (1990), *The Allagash Abductions* (1993), *The Watchers II* (1993), and *The Andreasson Legacy* (1997).

Address: 13 Friend Court
          Wenham, MA 01984
          U.S.A.
E-mail: eveleth@aol.com

Raymond Fowler

POSITION STATEMENT: After years of study and personal on-site investigation of UFO reports, I am certain that there is more than ample high-quality observational evidence from highly trained and reliable lay witnesses to indicate that there are unidentified machine-like objects under intelligent control operating in our atmosphere. Such evidence in some cases is supported by anomalous physical effects upon the witnesses, electrical devices, and the environment, as well as by instrumentation such as radar and Geiger counters.

I have also come to the conclusion through investigation and personal experience that the so-called UFO-abduction experience is supported by strong circumstantial physical and anecdotal evidence. It has also become apparent to me that such experiences contain (for want of a better term) "paranormal phenomena."

The reported objects appear to exhibit both physical and non-physical characteristics. Radar-visual reports of UFOs indicate that they are able to appear and disappear at a point A and then reappear at a point B with no visible transit between these two points. UFOs sometimes behave as if they have little or no mass: They execute right-angle turns without a curve radius and exceed the speed of sound without causing a sonic boom.

In other instances they exhibit very little mass, as they appear to float and bob like a cork on water, descend like a falling leaf or move with an up-and-down motion as they encounter air resistance. At other times, however, UFOs do exhibit mass and weight. They reflect radar waves. Bullets are reported to ricochet off their surface. When UFOs land they physically affect the environment and leave traces behind indicative of great weight.

The reported "entities" exhibit similar abilities to materialize and dematerialize. They more often float rather than walk, and are able to pass through solid walls and windows. Other paranormal abilities of UFO occupants reported are the ability to: appear and disappear in a ball of light, communicate by mental telepathy, exercise physical and mental control over humans, know when humans will die, cause abductees to undergo OBEs and experiences identical to NDEs.

Abduction research, personal and family UFO/psychic experiences have led me to consider the possibility that UFOs are paraphysical in nature and perhaps just one of many other components of an overall *metaphenomenon* that is made up of a variety of other so-called paranormal phenomena. Such manifestations may be the reflection of a super-technology, highly developed psychic abilities or a combination of both.

This is not to say that UFOs are not visitors from another star system. It just opens the possibility that multiple dimensions and other states of reality may exist throughout the universe and manifest their existence to us by what we term psychic or paranormal phenomena including UFOs. Such terms are merely descriptive words for things that we currently do not understand.

The seeming limits of the laws of physics as applied to short-term interstellar travel in our plane of existence may not be a limiting factor elsewhere. We may be dealing with intelligences with the technology not only to travel between star systems within other planes of existence, but also to physically interface from such existences with our planet and its life-forms at will for their own purposes.

The very fact that UFOs appear to be paraphysical in nature and have exhibited a technology seemingly beyond the pale of science appears to be the reason why governments have been extremely reluctant to publicly admit their existence and capabilities. The UFO phenomenon is not predictable, and is therefore difficult to study using the scientific method. Its ability to outperform and neutralize our best military systems at will makes it a potential threat to international security. Government investigations may prove the physical existence of UFOs by radar, photographic and other types of instrumentation. But governments may still not have answers to their origin and purpose, nor the ability to mount a defense against them if they are hostile. Most likely officialdom believes that if these hard truths were officially made public, it would be very disruptive to the body politic.

Contrary to what I formerly believed, I tend to agree. But, such impacts have taken place before in human history. Painful as they have been, we have survived. Such impacts to our belief systems are an integral part of humankind's intellectual and emotional evolu-

tion. Officialdom can delay but not prevent cultural impacts caused by such disturbing truths. Thus both the public and the civilian scientific community currently are left to fend for themselves against official disinformation and denials of UFO existence.

Nonetheless, in spite of this current situation, no one can prevent UFO activity nor can witnesses be prevented from sighting UFOs and reporting UFO experiences. The results of polls taken over many years show that people have and are being conditioned to UFO reality and to mistrust of government in general. In the long run, it may be that no one will ever know what the UFO phenomenon is all about, unless the powers behind the phenomenon itself decides to overtly reveal that truth to us.
—RAYMOND E. FOWLER

Friedman, Stanton T.   (b. 1934). Stanton Friedman is one of the world's best known UFO-ET researchers. More than four decades of study have convinced him that "the evidence is overwhelming that the Earth is being visited by intelligently controlled vehicles from off the Earth."

Friedman received his B.Sc. and M.Sc. de-

Stanton Friedman

grees in physics from the University of Chicago, in 1955, 1956; his professional background as a nuclear physicist includes fourteen years of industrial experience in the development of nuclear aircraft, fission and fusion rockets, and nuclear power plants for space and terrestrial applications.

Since 1970 Friedman has been a full-time UFO researcher and lecturer. He is the author of two books: *Crash at Corona* (1992) and *Top Secret/Majic* (1996), as well as numerous articles published in both professional and UFO journals and magazines.

Address: 79 Pembroke Crescent
            Fredericton
            New Brunswick
            Canada E3B 2V1
E-mail: fsphys@brunnet.net

POSITION STATEMENT: There are no good arguments to be made against the conclusion that some UFOs are intelligently controlled vehicles from off the Earth. Some skeptics may be well intentioned, but they are almost always ignorant of the significant scientific data indicating UFO reality. They read the newspapers but not the solid information. They are unaware of the myriad landing-trace cases, the multitude of "critter" reports and Earthling abductions, the numerous large-scale scientific collections of data, the many published scientific studies indicating that trips to nearby stars in our galactic neighborhood are already feasible without violating the laws of physics or invoking science fiction techniques.

I can safely say that the "laughter curtain" has gradually been rising. Most people are ready to listen to the scientific data, which I present at lectures, and to agree with my conclusions. The notion that most people and most scientists do not believe in UFOs is pure fiction concocted and repeated over and over again by ancient academics, naysaying newsmen, and fossilized physicists who form a very small, but very vocal, minority full of false platitudes, illogical reasoning, misinformation, and usually egotistical notions about their own knowledge and importance. They are sure that if flying saucers were real, they would know all about them, because the aliens would, of course, have already visited with them. Since these all-important persons have not been visited, UFOs must not be real. There is every indication that the United States Government (and other governments as well) has covered up loads of the best cases involving data obtained by military radar and aircraft and not referred to Project Blue Book or its equivalent overseas. Such a cover-up can be easily understood from the viewpoint of a nationalistically oriented planet and the search for better flying weapons delivery systems, though it does not make much sense from an Earthling viewpoint. Having spent fourteen years as a nuclear physicist on advanced development programs, many of which were highly classified, I can safely state that the government can keep secrets. The whole UFO subject is a kind of "Cosmic Watergate" crying out for a Daniel Ellsberg and/or the same media effort that went into uncovering the political Watergate.

It is time for all of those who have studied mountains of relevant data to stop being "closet UFOlogists" and to speak up and not hide behind "invisible colleges" and private rather than public pronouncements. The future of the planet many depend upon our courage as Earthlings.

—STANTON T. FRIEDMAN

Fry, Daniel W. (1908-1992). Probably the most technically oriented of the famous contactees, Dan Fry is described on his book jacket (of *The White Sands Incident,* 1966) as: "an internationally known scientist, researcher, and electronics engineer who is recognized by many as the best-informed scientist in the world on the subject of space and space travel."

Mr. Fry described himself as "an engineer, scientist, author, and lecturer," who "was one of the prime movers in the Crescent Engineering and Research Company's liquid-fueled missile flight-testing program." He also worked for the Aerojet General Corporation at the White Sands Proving Grounds, where he was "in charge of installation of instruments for missile control and guidance." Fry later moved to Tonopah, Arizona, the home base of his quasi-religious organization called Understanding, Inc. (After that, he lived in Alamogordo, New Mexico.) He also claimed to be an "ordained" minister and to hold a Ph.D. degree from St. Andrews College of London, England.

Daniel Fry

Dan Fry's initial contact with the "Space People" (he claimed four contacts in all, between 1950 and 1954) allegedly occurred on July 4, 1950, near the White Sands Proving Grounds (now Missile Range), near Las Cruces, New Mexico, while employed by Aerojet General. Fry said he missed a bus which would have taken him into town that night to observe the traditional fireworks display. Thinking he would spend the evening reading, he returned to his room, but his air conditioner failed, so he decided just to take a desert stroll and enjoy the cool, night air.

As he was scanning the sky, he caught sight of a "disappearing" star. The star only appeared to "blink out" because it had been eclipsed, he claims, by a "flying saucer" (he described it as "an oblate spheroid about thirty feet in diameter at the equator or largest part"). The "saucer" supposedly settled to the ground about seventy feet away, whereupon he approached to investigate the surface of the highly polished metal. He was startled to hear a deep voice, which he claims came out of the air beside him, which said, "Better not touch the hull, pal. It's still hot!" He was so taken aback by this, he says, that he caught his foot against a root sticking out of the ground and fell over onto the desert sand. Then, a chuckle filled the air as the invisible voice supposedly spoke again: "Take it easy, pal. You are among friends."

After a little introductory chat, Fry claims to have learned that he was talking to an invisible spaceman named Alan. The spaceman explained some of the technicalities of the spacecraft's operation, and then took Fry on a quick flight to New York City and back to White Sands—a trip which lasted only thirty minutes (flying at a speed of 8,000 miles per hour).

The Space People who contacted Fry were said to be the descendants of a past supercivilization on Earth, which was annihilated in an atomic war more than thirty thousand years ago. According to Alan, the Saucerians' ancestors were originally from the legendary Lemuria, which was in scientific competition with the ancient civilization of Atlantis. These two nations eventually destroyed each other, except for a few survivors who were able to escape in four aerial craft capable of space travel. One ship was lost along the way; but three landed safely on the planet Mars, where the survivors established a new society. Later, they became independent of planets altogether, and began living aboard huge, self-sustaining ships that float through space in whatever direction the people choose, somewhat like the imaginary floating island fictionalized by Jonathan Swift in *Gulliver's Travels*.

According to the skeptic-UFOlogist Philip J. Klass, who did some checking on the matter, Fry's doctoral degree was obtained from "a sort of correspondence school" operated by a small church, from which it is possible for virtually anyone to be granted a Ph.D. by merely submitting a ten-thousand-word thesis and paying a standard fee.

Captain Edward J. Ruppelt, former head of the U.S. Air Force Project Blue Book, also had this to say: "He [Fry] hadn't told the Air Force about his ride before because he was afraid he'd lose his job. But, at the press conference, he did plug his new book, *The White Sands Incident.* By this time Adamski had already published his book *Flying Saucers Have Landed* and it looked as if Fry was going to cut him out. But Fry took a lie-detector test on a widely viewed West Coast television show and flunked it flat." (Ruppelt, 1956)

However, if we are looking for *meaning* when we study the contactees, does it really matter if the alleged contacts are literally true? Let us consider the story about the war between the Lemurians and Atlanteans as a parable, or metaphor, demonstrating what consequences we can expect when competition is not balanced with cooperation. When you read *The White Sands Incident* carefully for its meaning, it is hard to miss. The spaceman, Alan, uses a series of metaphors to trace the different phases of human civilization, beginning with "the symbol of the tree and the serpent," and culminating in our present-day situation.

"The tree is almost always the symbol of life," says Alan, "beginning in the sea, rising to the atmosphere, and finally into space. There is another factor which may, perhaps, have some significance. Your people and some of mine, including myself, have, at least in part, a common ancestry." This is where Alan relates the story of the rivalry between the two factions, represented by Lemuria and Atlantis. He applies the parable directly to us when he states that: "Unless some small balancing force is applied in the right quarters, your entire civilization may wipe itself out in a planet-wide holocaust before we are in a position to be of assistance." He adds: ". . . man can improve the conditions of his life only through cooperation."

According to the psychologist Carl Jung,

the UFO (or spaceship) represented the higher Self. It is usually in the shape of a mandala (or magic circle), which universally symbolizes order and perfection. Thus the independent, free-floating spaceships—mentioned in all of the contactee accounts—clearly symbolize the perfect, self-reliant, individuated psyche: the ideal to which all humans seeking wisdom aspire. It is also the ideal that is required for survival; hence, the warning.

Photo taken by Fry at Merlin, Oregon, in 1964

In the same manner that the technological gods and angels reside inside the self-sustaining spaceships, the "kingdom of heaven" resides within each of us, just as Jesus said. In every case, the contactee is given a tour of the ship—which, of course, means looking inward at the elements that make up the psyche and realizing the virtually unlimited potential that exists within us, once we tap into nature's forces. The personal message is that when we take control of our own "ship," we have all the power we need, and we become the cure for whatever ails us. When Alan says "Every aspect of our environment is precisely controlled within our ships," he is really talking about human potential and self-actualization. When you read Fry's original account, the metaphor becomes richer and more obvious with every sentence.

Fry was informed that he was specially

chosen to be the liaison between planet Earth and the Galactic Confederation. "One of the purposes of this visit," Alan told him, "is to determine the basic adaptability of the Earth's peoples, particularly your ability to adjust your minds quickly to conditions and concepts completely foreign to your customary modes of thought. Previous expeditions by our ancestors, over a period of many centuries, met with almost total failure in this respect. This time there is hope that we may find minds somewhat more receptive so that we may assist you in the progress, or at least in the continued existence of your race." (Fry, 1973)

Alan made the most important point of all when he said: "Actually, the possibility of atomic warfare on your planet, while it is an immediate danger, is not the basic problem, it is merely a symptom, and few illnesses can be cured by treating only the symptoms." He then explained how material science and social science are perfectly good in themselves, but must be based on a foundation of "spiritual science which deals with the relationship between man and the great creative power and infinite intelligence which pervades and controls all nature, and which your people refer to as God." (Fry, 1973).

That is one of the main differences between man and the other animals: "the animal has no spiritual or social science"; whereas "Mankind . . . is endowed with the innate realization of the infinite intelligence and the creative power of the supreme mind, even though he may not yet be able to understand." (Fry, 1973)

—RONALD D. STORY

References

Fry, Daniel W. *The White Sands Incident* (New Age Publishing, 1954; Best Books, 1966).

——. *To Men of Earth*, including *The White Sands Incident* (Merlin Publishing Co., 1973).

Gibbons, Gavin. *They Rode in Space Ships* (The Citadel Press, 1957).

Ruppelt, Edward J. *The Report on Unidentified Flying Objects* (Doubleday, 1956).

G

Galactic Club, The (W.H. Freeman, 1974). Australian astrophysicist Ronald Bracewell sounds the first pessimistic note in science books about the prospect of contacting an advanced civilization using radio telescopes. There is only one chance in a thousand that radio signals will come our way and only one chance in a thousand that one of our radio telescopes will be pointed the right way when the signal arrives. He proposes instead that first contact will come as a result of our detection of an interstellar space probe sent to contact us. "It is quite possible," he writes, "that such a space probe, or messenger, has already arrived in our solar system and is even now monitoring us."

Galicia UFO wave of 1995-1996 What would prove to be one of the best-documented UFO "flaps" of the decade began on November 28, 1995, in Galicia (the autonomous region occupying Spain's northwestern corner), when the security cameras of the As Gándaras military facility captured several UFOs on film, causing concern among the Spanish military.

The media soon learned that soccer players at a nearby field had also seen the mysterious objects. UFOlogist Marcelino Requejo was quick to stress that the As Gándaras sighting was by no means an isolated incident, and that "a veritable flood of sightings" was taking place in the region, coinciding with seismic disturbances—approximately 70 in that month alone.

The UFOlogist's prediction would come true in January 1996, when sightings multiplied throughout northern Spain. Citizens of Pedrona (Santander) were treated to the passing of a brightly lit oval object over their town. The coastal city of Gijón reported a UFO hanging over the sea at night—its multicolored lights dispelling the darkness. In the Galician village of As Pontes, cameraman Bartolomé Vázquez filmed the maneuvers of a triangular UFO which he described as an "upside down steam iron." This episode was considered to be one of the most significant, given that the cameraman had managed to capture two jet fighters in pursuit of the slow-moving triangle. Yet the most spectacular one occurred at Monforte de Lemos, where a local camera crew filmed hundreds of witnesses absorbed in contemplation of a massive oval UFO which remained suspended overhead for an hour. Other television crews filmed UFO maneuvers over sensitive locations like the ENDESA thermoelectric plant at As Pontes.

The phenomenon entered its proactive phase on February 26, 1996, when motorist Andrés Landeira, driving at night toward the city of Lugo, found that his car was being drawn upward by an unknown force. In a panic, Landeira opened the car's door to jump out, but found he was at least thirty feet above the ground. He would later tell UFO investigator Manuel Carballal, "I forced myself back into the driver's seat and thought I was going to die, being taken to God knows where . . ." However, the force that picked up the car deposited it further along the road, but in a sideways manner.

Like the classic UFO flaps of earlier decades, the Galician wave followed the classic pattern of sightings, ground effects, and occupant encounters. On February 18, 1996, two children playing in the woods outside Entrimo reported seeing a trio of luminous spheres which merged to form "a pair of saucers on top of each other'' before vanishing. The youngsters also claimed having found clearly non-human footprints upon returning the next day; investigators ascertained that the marks corresponded to a creature standing at least 7 feet tall.

On March 7, 1996, José Manuel Castro, a rancher from the town of Ferrerías, saw a UFO land on his property a mere 100 feet away from his house. Small creatures ''looking like monkeys'' emerged from the object, and the vehicle left surface impressions and footprints similar to those found at Entrimo.

—SCOTT CORRALES

Garden Grove (California) abduction hoax The 1975 Garden Grove, California, abduction was the most spectacular CE-3 of its time. A 33-year-old man (let's call him ''BS'') gave the following story in eight weekly videotaped hypnosis sessions with Dr. W.C. McCall.

BS and a friend were camping in the Arizona desert in 1971 when suddenly a weird beam descended slowly and lifted them aboard a UFO where ugly 7-foot reptilian entities stripped them naked. Two entities took BS and floated down a curving hallway, through an exploding door and into a brightly lit room.

As two creatures fidgeted in boredom at their consoles, BS stood against a wall and was given a lightning-quick physical exam. Two beams shot at him; one held his eyes in a fixed gaze and the other probed his body from his feet up: he sensed he was bleeding, he urinated, liquid drained from his stomach, his chest opened as his heart left his body briefly, and in a dizzying moment he saw his brain travel up the beam and back.

Then everything stopped and from across the room an alien like the others but 9 feet tall glided toward him, smelling foul and with bad breath as well. BS was terrified but when the monster's scaly hand touched his head he was instantly calmed. The tall alien gave him a tour of the ship. BS learned that the aliens were clones created by a central intelligence called the Host, in the form of a giant computer (and also as a fetal humanoid) on the UFO's upper floor. There he also saw a vast birth laboratory—row after row of clear cylinders with writhing alien embryos in liquid. The aliens were ''checking the original biological plantation'' on Earth.

BS was returned down the curving hall to his pal and they were dressed and beamed to the ground, and the UFO disappeared. He had been on board about two hours.

BS's weekly regressions kept a group of local UFOlogists gasping. In the fourth week BS reported that he had been visited at night in his garage workroom by a ball of light that became a fetal humanoid. In the seventh week BS disappeared. Police were notified, but BS turned up 24 hours later, unshaven and woozy, wearing only his shorts. Hypnotized, he claimed that he had been abducted by a UFO and taken to Peru where he underwent a ritual with the aliens at the site of the famous spider figure on the Nazca Plain. BS said his first CE-3 was at 16, when he was forced by aliens to give himself a tattoo on his right forearm in the shape of the Nazca spider—spectacular physical evidence, if true.

The Garden Grove case ultimately involved six alleged abductions (unprecedented in 1975), two with separate second witnesses, and loads of data channeled during BS's daily self-hypnosis sessions, including blueprints of the UFO (BS was a draftsman, though otherwise unschooled); chemical formulae for the craft's propulsion system (with atomic weights of elements to four decimal places); texts of a mysterious computer-like alien language; and a brief message from the aliens written in pre-Homeric Greek (ca. 3500 years ago), ''*Nous laos hikáno.*'' BS gave us a loose translation: ''I come in the mind of man.''

Unbelievably, perhaps, BS's case seemed believable to McCall and me. But after several weeks of hypnosis, videotaping, and laborious analysis of his narratives, we caught BS in a hoax. He claimed to have found a spider figure drawn on the ground at the site of a reported

UFO sighting, but a young boy had seen BS scratching it in the dirt himself.

Then—belatedly—we looked into BS's personal life and found disturbing facts. He worked for a computer manufacturer (bye-bye to the alien computer motif). At work he had access to both a technical library (adios to the atomic weights) and books by Erich von Däniken (ta-ta to the Nazca Plain, the biological plantation, etc.). One of his friends at work was a Greek scholar. Neither of two alleged second witnesses would verify BS's claims (all fabrications). Finally, we learned that BS had once served prison time for fraud. He had glib excuses for his actions but we stopped working with him.

How were a medical doctor and a college professor flimflammed by a fable that in another context few people with an IQ higher than a coat of floor wax might believe? In our defense, BS's sessions were convincing in the extreme. He had an Irishman's gift for blarney, a con man's cunning, and a draftsman's eye for specific details. As a clincher, there were surprise factors in his sessions—such as the clinically plausible high-tech exam, the ghastly birth lab, and his mention of alien ennui—that electrified us because we naively assumed they were beyond his powers of invention. BS's case remains one of the most persuasively detailed CE-3s ever, and though it made monkeys out of us for a while, chances are that it would have done the same to many of the intelligent life-forms in the galaxy.

BS deceived us just as decades of supposedly real CE-3 yarns before and since have duped other investigators—who rarely discuss hoaxers. BS's hoax worked because we wanted to believe him, and we were seduced by his ability to spin an appealing saga. Our inadequacies were those that have afflicted the spotty history of abduction investigations from the beginning.

The Garden Grove hoax is unusual in that we compiled a complete audiovisual and written record of a CE-3 hoaxer's regressions, from acceptance to exposure. Also, our somewhat humbled perseverance ultimately solved a complex case without media sensationalism. More important, we began to make sense of its wealth of birth imagery, which we found was common in other supposedly real and known-to-be-imaginary cases. (See BIRTH MEMORIES HYPOTHESIS)

In retrospect, our first CE-3 case was a stumble that we made into a giant leap: BS hoaxed us into permanent skepticism about CE-3 claims. Now I think of him as our first Imaginary Abductee. Like the subjects of that 1977 study, BS fabricated a typical and perinatally rich CE-3 narrative out of his own fertile fantasy. His case establishes that hoaxers, Imaginaries, and allegedly real abductees have more in common than proponents are likely to acknowledge. (See also IMAGINARY ABDUCTEE STUDY)

—ALVIN H. LAWSON

geomagnetic explanations of UFOs Dr. Michael Persinger, a neuropsychologist at Laurentian University in Canada, has conducted and published hundreds of studies showing how magnetic fields can produce UFO-like visions as well as hallucinations of saucers, ''Grays,'' and abductions in people subjected to the fields in a controlled laboratory setting. Beginning his research in the early 1970s, Persinger initially showed that UFO reports were statistically correlated with seismic (earthquake) activity. His results showed that increased reports of UFOs come at times when seismic activity is low or stable.

Working with geologist John Derr and others, Persinger speculated that the tectonic stress that builds between earthquakes produces powerful geomagnetic fields. These fields, it was hypothesized, somehow affected the areas in the brain that can produce hallucinatory phenomena. One related line of speculation has asserted that plasmas are produced by a building tectonic strain in the Earth's surface, thus creating powerful but localized geomagnetic fields. Plasmas—balls of charged air particles—are not speculative phenomena, and have been produced in laboratory settings. The piezoelectric effect, the production of electricity when a crystal is pressured or crushed—is often theorized to be the source of plasma energies that can emerge from the Earth. In addition, plasmas are believed to be related to "earthquake lights" as well as lights observed at volcanic sites. Greg Long's 1990 book, *Examining the Earthlight Theory: The Yakima UFO Microcosm* does an admirable job of showing how a 1970s UFO flap on the Yakima, Washington, reservation was probably caused by tectonic strain on a ridge in the reservation covered with over 100 earthquake fault lines. The eruption of Mt. St. Helens in 1980 is hypothesized as relieving the building tectonic strain in the region, thus accounting for the sudden cessation of UFO reports in the area after the pressure was relieved. Another investigator, Paul Devereux, has long theorized that charged balls of light coming from the Earth produce mental and physical phenomena in people who come close enough to observe the lights.

Persinger's more recent research has focused on identifying specific brain sites and specific magnetic frequencies that can produce a host of phenomena. For example, magnetic fields focused on the temporal lobe can create visions of various types. Research shows that different magnetic frequencies focused on various brain areas can, in fact, literally create abduction-like experiences as well as visions of saucers, angels, and apparitions. Persinger has speculated that "haunted" sites and places where long-term phenomena occur are situated on an area of the Earth's surface where plasma energy is regularly released.

The influence of magnetic fields and frequencies on human behavior is under intense investigation in laboratories across the globe. Military and medical applications are both being investigated. Publication of results from this vast arena of research does occur routinely, however, the scientific journals disseminating studies are highly technical and sometimes obscure. Major university research libraries and government repositories generally carry these technical journals. The amount of research being conducted in this area is staggering. For example, the Harvard University Genetics Department supplied this writer with a bibliography of 3,000 published studies in 1995.

Exactly how magnetic fields can produce mental phenomena is also becoming known. In 1992, the mineral magnetite was discovered in human brain cells. In the presence of a magnetic field, the magnetite in brain cells aligns itself with the field and begins to resonate (vibrate). As it resonates, ion channels on the surface of brain cells open allowing the passage of specific ions that result in the release of neurotransmitters. This produces imagery and other experiences. The textbook *Psychopharmacology* (Little, 1997) and *Grand Illusions* (Little, 1994) both summarize this process.

Related to the geomagnetic explanation of UFOs is the proposal that electromagnetic pollution accounts for increased paranormal phenomena. Albert Budden's *Electric UFOs* (1998) and *Allergies and Aliens* (1994) assert that electromagnetic pollution created by microwaves, transmission lines, and modern society's proliferation of electronics has created a cesspool of magnetic pollution. Budden proposes that this bombardment of electromagnetic energy alters brain chemistry through its influence on brain magnetite. Hauntings, abductions, missing time, and paranormal experiences result from this influence. A more speculative but all-encompassing theory invoking geomagnetic energy is that proposed by Greg Little. (See also GEOMAGNETIC INTELLIGENT ENERGY THEORY OF UFOS)

—GREGORY L. LITTLE

References

Little, Gregory L. *Grand Illusions* (White Buffalo Books, 1994).
——. *Psychopharmacology* (White Buffalo Books, 1997).
Long, Greg. *Examining the Earthlight Theory: The Yakima UFO Microcosm* (CUFOS, 1990).

geomagnetic intelligent energy theory of UFOs Building from the works of John

Keel and Carl Jung as well as from geomagnetic research and neurochemistry, the present writer has theorized that the plasma energies produced by the Earth represent Carl Jung's archetypes manifesting in physical reality. This form of archetypal manifestation can be described as intelligent geomagnetic energy forms.

The theory begins by proposing that the electromagnetic energy (EM) spectrum is the abode of Jung's archetypes (as Jung himself stated). The EM spectrum is sometimes referred to as forming the fences that hold physical reality together. The entire universe is bathed in constant pulses of EM energy. The human visual system is capable of perceiving less than 5 percent of the EM spectrum. The remaining 95 percent of reality is there—all around us—but unseen. A perusal of a basic text in psychology or physics will explain the EM spectrum in more detail.

As proposed by Jung through his concept of archetypes and John Keel with his idea of "ultraterrestrials," the intelligent energy theory proposes that UFOs, abductions, apparitional, and various other psychic phenomena are produced when the intelligent energy forms residing on the unseen ends of the EM spectrum manifest in physical reality.

Jung wrote in several places that angels were archetypal forms that could manifest into reality. This process has long been termed transmutation by occultists and occurs by an alteration of the energy form's vibrational frequency into the narrow band of the EM spectrum perceived by the human visual system. As such, these manifestations have also been termed "spectral intrusions."

The theory accounts for a wide range of ancient reports. For example, in Zechariah 5:2, a flying tube 30 feet by 15 feet is described as a permanent curse of the Earth judging the deeds of men. In Zechiariah 5:6 he is shown an object the size of a bushel basket moving through the Earth. He is told that the object collects the wicked thoughts of men. Zech. 4:6-10 describes lamp-shaped objects that run "to and fro" everywhere on the Earth. These are the "eyes of God" that record everything that occurs on Earth. These "collection" devices are normally unseen but are living beings as described by the angel who showed them to the ancient prophet.

The Hebrew Book of Enoch (translated in 1928) also contains numerous descriptions of devices used by "angels" in their work. These flying objects are described as "pipes," orbs, and tubes. They not only record events on Earth but are used by the Watchers (fallen angels) to literally contain the souls of evil people after death. The souls of these people are then taken to the "gates of hell" where they are pushed out the tubes into hell. This ancient religious text (3 Enoch) describes the fallen angels who control these collection devices as gray in color, short like children, and having a partial human-like appearance.

The geomagnetic intelligent energy theory proposes that the EM spectrum *is* the spiritual world. The intelligent beings residing on the unseen ends of the EM spectrum can, under some conditions, come into physical reality when their frequency comes into the visible frequency range. The powerful EM fields constantly produced by the Earth (and the Sun) provide an energy source for the EM forms to utilize.

Human consciousness is changed when in proximity to an emerging EM form because of the alteration in neurochemistry. In addition, people can voluntarily tune themselves to specific EM frequencies through various rituals and processes. Many occult practices as well as religious rites are designed to foster an attunement to specific EM frequencies.

The theory also proposes that ancient ritual sites, including specific mound and pyramid complexes, were built because they were in areas where frequent and powerful geomagnetic fields emerged from the Earth. Many rituals were designed to allow the participants to attune themselves to the frequency of the emerging EM form. Many Native American legends relate how this process works. Three books: *The Archetype Experience, People of the Web,* and *Grand Illusions*; and a series of articles in *Alternate Perceptions* develop this theory.

—GREGORY L. LITTLE

References

Alternate Perceptions, Box 9972, Memphis, TN 38190.

Jung, C. G. *On the Nature of the Psyche* (Princeton University Press, 1960, 1969).

Keel, John. *UFOs: Operation Trojan Horse* (G.P. Putnam's Sons, 1970).

Little, Gregory L. *The Archetype Experience* (Rainbow Books, 1984).

———. *People of the Web* (White Buffalo Books, 1990).

———. *Grand Illusions* (White Buffalo Books, 1994).

ghost rockets of 1946   Strange phenomena reported in the skies of Europe just after the Second World War, for the most part in the year 1946, have become known among the students of the UFO problem as the "ghost rocket" mystery. This UFO flap was first recognized officially when Finland announced over Helsinki radio on February 26, 1946, that "inordinate meteor activity" had been noticed in the nation's northern districts near the Arctic Circle. Later, toward the end of May, persons in northern Sweden also became aware of unusual sights in the heavens. On June 9th, when something spewing a trail of smoke raced through the night sky over Finland's capital city, Helsinki, at a reported altitude of one thousand feet, leaving a luminous afterglow, public consternation became widespread. When another report was made, asserting that an unidentified luminous body giving off glowing vapor had approached the Finnish coast from the direction of the Baltic, only to turn sharply and retrace its course, a correspondent for the London *Daily Mail*, stationed in Helsinki, cabled the story to England, thus arousing international interest.

Unsure of the exact nature of the phenomena being reported, the newspapers adopted the term "ghost rocket" to explain the "missile-like meteors." As reports accumulated at an increasing rate, suspicions grew that the Soviet Union was testing missiles over the Baltic Sea. Often, a single "ghost rocket" would be seen exploding in the air, prompting careful ground searches for fragments. According to press reports, the residue recovered after such explosions consisted of tiny particles of dark-colored, slag-like material. This seemed to reinforce the meteor theory, but it did not explain other puzzling characteristics reported by witnesses.

People claimed that the strange objects did more than simply fall earthward, as one would expect of a meteor. Instead, the ghost rockets would fly horizontally, and sometimes even dive and climb, leap, barrel-roll, and backtrack. And while some of the objects in question crossed the sky at tremendous velocity, many times the objects reportedly moved in a very leisurely fashion. Frequently the objects sighted were not shaped like missiles, but more like common bolides, yet they would behave in an unmeteor-like manner. Expressions used in such cases were: "luminous bodies," "balls of fire," "cometlike," "shooting starlike," "flarelike," "greenish globe," "gray sphere," "like a huge soap bubble," "shining ball," "rotating object emitting sparks," and an "arrow-shaped object."

One of the mysterious "ghost rockets" of the 1946 Scandinavian wave, as depicted by artist Hal Crawford

However, the most mysterious cases were the ones that had started the "ghost rocket" rumors. These sightings mentioned flying bodies that did not have a round, fiery appearance. They resembled wartime German V-2 rockets. Such descriptions used the words: "football shape," "silver torpedo," "cigar shape," "rocketlike," "silvery projectile," "cylinderlike," "missile-like," "elliptical," "bullet-shaped," and "like a squash racquet."

Although documentation is incomplete, reports catalogued to date seem to indicate that the aerial phenomena of 1946 slowly shifted southward from the Arctic, eventually reaching Portugal, Tangiers, Italy, Greece, and even Kashmir in India, by the month of September. The phenomena were striking enough to warrant official reaction from the governments of Norway, Sweden, Finland, Denmark, Greece, Belgium, England, Russia, and the United States.

Of all the nations affected, Sweden was the most alarmed, experiencing as many as a thousand sightings. Reports of ghost rockets reached a peak on August 11th in the skies of Sweden, and during the following days angry anti-Soviet editorials were published in most newspapers as tension in the country approached the boiling point. In the United States, such newspapers as the *Washington Post*, the *Christian Science Monitor*, and the *New York Times* gave front-page treatment to the latest dispatches from Stockholm. The Swedish High Command, pressured by public opinion, seriously discussed the possibility that the Russians were conducting a mysterious bombardment of Sweden. The armed forces of Sweden were placed on alert and the government authorities prepared a strong protest addressed at a "certain neighboring country." Restraining the Swedes, however, was the lack of any tangible evidence aside from the fragments of slag-like material gathered from ground searches. This perplexing problem was explained away by the Swedish military experts by the postulation of what they called: "the new explosion theory," the idea that the ghost rockets were totally consumed by fire when they exploded and burst into flame. This

hypothesis was based on a number of vivid eyewitness accounts.

According to the *New York Times*, the United States felt compelled to send two top intelligence experts to Sweden to confer with the Swedish General Staff. They were General James Doolittle and David Sarnoff. Just what the two men learned about the mystery has never been revealed, although Mr. Sarnoff told a group of electronics experts after his return from Europe that he was convinced the strange missiles being reported over Sweden were not a myth but something real.

Aside from the exact nature of the ghost rockets, the biggest question mark about the flap was the secrecy imposed by the authorities in the nations affected. Early investigations of the riddle relied on public cooperation, and reports were often written up in detail in the press; but by July 27th, the Swedish government prohibited newspapers from printing the location of any ghost rocket. The Norwegian government also ordered that such information not be published as of July 29th, followed by the government of Denmark on August 16th. Later, on August 31st, Norway totally banned ghost rocket sighting information, while news on the continuing rocket barrage had all but disappeared from the Swedish press by August 22nd. Lending support to the fact that the mystery surrounding the ghost rockets was increasing was a story in the *Christian Science Monitor* which declared that the British Foreign Office had admitted that British radar experts were submitting secret reports about the ghost rockets.

Although very little appeared in the Scandinavian newspapers at the time, the Associated Press learned that ghost rocket sightings had continued in considerable numbers right up to October before tapering off. The last official word on the ghost rocket mystery in 1946 was a Swedish military communiqué made public October 10th, remarking on the results of Sweden's investigation. The briefly worded release asserted that, while most reports were vague, different instruments registered something definite, and that many reports were "clear unambiguous observations." The Swedish experts claimed that some 20 percent of the ghost rocket reports appeared to be neither aircraft nor natural phenomena. Details of the 1946 Swedish investigation are still classified.

The ghost rockets returned to Scandinavian skies in the first part of 1947 and during the early months of 1948. Even the conservative *London Times* acknowledged that ghost rockets were once again infesting the skies of Denmark, Norway, and Sweden. According to the *Times,* pilots of the Norwegian Air Lines reported missile-like objects speeding along through the air, emitting bluish-green flames, and that these "missiles" were seen flying as fast as 6,700-miles per hour, traveling as much as 25,000 feet high and as low as the treetops. The 6,700 miles-per-hour clocking was witnessed and timed by the president of the Norwegian Airline Pilots Association.

Ghost rocket-type UFOs are still being reported around the world, and they remain one of the most spectacular and mystifying of unidentified aerial phenomena. In summation, it should be stated that while the American wave of 1947 heralded the "flying saucer" craze, the European "ghost rocket" flap of 1946 truly marked the beginning of the modern era of large-scale UFO activity.

—LOREN E. GROSS

Gill sighting William B. Gill, an Anglican priest with a mission in Boainai, Papua, New Guinea, observed craft-like UFOs—one with humanoid figures on top—on two consecutive evenings, June 26-27, 1959. About twenty-five natives, including teachers and medical technicians, also witnessed the phenomena. They "signaled" the humanoids and received an apparent response. This was one of sixty UFO sightings within a few weeks in the New Guinea area.

An approximate chronology of the complex series of sightings follows (based on Father Gill's log of events and a summary report by his colleague, the Reverend Norman Cruttwell):

June 26th

6:45 P.M. Large sparkling light seen by Father Gill in western sky. Called natives who also saw it.

6:55-7:04 P.M. Up to four illuminated humanoid figures seen on top of object, off and on.

7:10-7:20 P.M. Sky now overcast at about 2,000 feet. Humanoid figures seen again, and a "thin electric blue spotlight" upward from the UFO, hovering below the overcast. UFO disappears in clouds.

8:28-8:35 P.M. Skies clear again; UFO visible, appearing to descend and increase in size. Second object seen over sea, "hovering at times," and another over village.

8:50-9:30 P.M. Clouds forming again. Large UFO stationary, others (about three) like disks coming and going through clouds, casting a light halo on the clouds. Large UFO moves away rapidly across sea toward Giwa.

9:46-10:30 P.M. UFO reappears overhead, hovering.

10:50 P.M. Heavy overcast; no sign of UFO.

11:04 P.M. Heavy rain.

June 27th

6-7 P.M. Large UFO seen again, first sighted by medical technician at hospital, before dark. Closest sighting yet; seen clearly, bright and sparkling. Humanoid figures seen on top. Father Gill and about twelve others in group waved at humanoids, and one of figures appeared to wave back. One member of the group waved both arms, and figures apparently responded by waving both arms. Two smaller objects remained visible, stationary at a higher altitude.

7:45 P.M. Sky overcast; no UFOs visible.

On the first night, Father Gill stepped out the front door of the mission house after dinner, about 6:45 P.M., and glanced at the western sky looking for Venus, which was conspicuous at the time. "I saw Venus," he said, "but I also saw this sparkling object, which to me was peculiar because it sparkled and because it was very, very bright, and it was above Venus and so that caused me to watch it for a while; then I saw it descend towards us."

Father Gill estimated the object's angular diameter as about five inches at arm's length. Stephen Gill Moi, a teacher, who joined Father Gill a few minutes later, said that if he put his hand out closed, it would cover about half of the object.

In a signed statement, the witnesses agreed that the object was circular, had a wide base and a narrower upper "deck," had something like legs beneath it, at times produced a shaft of blue light which shone upward into the sky at an angle of about 45 degrees, and that four humanoid figures appeared on top. Some of the witnesses described seeing about four portholes or windows on the side. Father Gill saw what appeared to be bright panels on the side of the craft, but did not interpret them as portholes.

"As we watched it," Father Gill said, "men came out from this object and appeared on top of it, on what seemed to be a deck on top of the huge disk. There were four men in all, occasionally two, then one, then three, then four; we noted the various times the men appeared. . . .

"Another peculiar thing was this shaft of blue light, which emanated from what appeared to be the center of the deck. The men appeared to be illuminated not only by this light reflected on them, but also by a sort of glow which completely surrounded them as well as the craft. The glow did not touch them, but there appeared to be a little space between their outline and the light. . . ."

Father Gill described the movements of the objects, especially the smaller disks, as very erratic. They sometimes moved rapidly, sometimes slowly, approaching and receding, changing direction, and at times swinging back and forth like a pendulum. One object moved away and appeared to descend toward Wado-buna village, and everyone thought it was going to land. The Papuans ran down on the beach, but the object swooped up and away over the mountains, turning red as it disappeared.

When the large object disappeared at 9.30 P.M., Father Gill said it made a slight wavering motion, then suddenly shot away at tremendous speed across the bay in the direction of Giwa, diminishing to a pinpoint and vanishing. No sound was heard throughout.

The next evening, about 6 P.M., the same or a similar object reappeared while the sky was still bright, first seen by Annie Laurie Borewa, a Papuan medical assistant at the hospital. She called Father Gill, who in turn called Ananias and several others to watch. "We watched figures appear on top," Father Gill said. "Four of them. There is no doubt that they were human. This is possibly the same object that I took to be the 'mother ship' last night. Two smaller UFOs were seen at the same time, stationary, one above the hills, and another overhead."

Two of the figures seemed to be doing something, occasionally bending over and raising their arm as if "adjusting or setting up something. One figure seemed to be standing, looking down on us (a group of about a dozen)." This figure, he explained later, was standing with his hands on the "rail" looking over, "just as one will look over the rails of a ship.

"I stretched my arm above my head and waved. To our surprise the figure did the same. Ananias waved both arms over his head, then the two outside figures did the same. Then both of us began waving our arms and all four seemed to wave back. There seemed to be no doubt that our movements were answered. All the Mission boys made audible gasps."

As darkness began to settle in, Father Gill sent one of the natives for a flashlight and directed a series of signals ("long dashes") toward the UFO. After a minute or two, the UFO wavered back and forth like a pendulum, in apparent acknowledgment. They waved and flashed signals again, and the UFO appeared

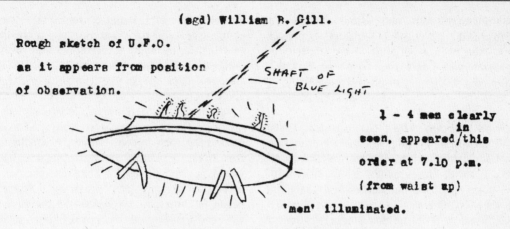

(sgd) William B. Gill.

Rough sketch of U.F.O.
as it appears from position
of observation.

SHAFT OF BLUE LIGHT

1 - 4 men clearly
seen, appeared/this
order at 7.10 p.m.
(from waist up)
'men' illuminated.

Eyewitness sketch by Reverend William B. Gill

to descend toward them, but stopped and came no closer. After two or three more minutes, the figures disappeared. Then, at 6:25 P.M., two figures resumed their activity, and the blue spotlight came on for a few seconds twice in succession. By 7:45 P.M. the sky was totally overcast and no UFOs were visible. This ended the sightings.

In his evaluation of the incidents, Dr. Donald H. Menzel, a Harvard University astronomer who wrote three UFO-debunking books, refers to the natives as "uneducated" and to Father Gill as being their "great leader," to them "a holy man" (implying that they were influenced in their testimony). He attributed the sightings to the planet Venus viewed myopically by Father Gill. Venus, he noted, was very conspicuous in the west, setting about three hours after the sun.

Menzel then openly assumed that Father Gill was myopic and without glasses at the time, that he "probably" had appreciable astigmatism as well (causing him to see a distorted image of Venus), plus blood cells on the retina producing illusory motion. He concluded: "Since a very simple hypothesis accounts, without any strain, for the reported observations, I shall henceforth consider the Father Gill case as solved. Moreover, I feel the same phenomena are responsible for some of the more spectacular, unsolved cases in the Air Force files."

Dr. J. Allen Hynek, the former Air Force UFO consultant, notes in rebuttal that Father Gill was wearing properly corrected glasses at the time and that "Venus was pointed out separately by Gill."

Although any prolonged series of UFO sightings with excited witnesses may be "contaminated" by coincidental sightings of aircraft, meteors, or stars and planets glimpsed through moving clouds, the report of a large structured object (with moving humanoid figures) below a low overcast is not easily explainable.

—RICHARD HALL

References

Hynek, J. Allen. *The UFO Experience: A Scientific Inquiry* (Henry Regnery, 1972).

Hall, Richard. "Gill sighting" in Story, Ronald D., ed. *The Encyclopedia of UFOs* (Doubleday/New English Library, 1980).

Story, Ronald D. *UFOs and the Limits of Science* (William Morrow/New English Library, 1981).

God Drives a Flying Saucer (Bantam, 1969).

Connecticut schoolteacher R. L. Dione writes that UFOs are God's messengers, responsible for the prophecies, scriptures, and miracles of the Christian religion. Even Jesus Christ accomplished his miracles by channeling energy beamed to him by extraterrestrial spacecraft, according to this view, and persons who were incarcerated throughout history, perhaps including even Adolf Hitler, were subjected to programming signals beamed at them by UFOs to produce "divinely inspired writing."

—RANDALL FITZGERALD

Gods of Eden, The   (Avon Books, 1989). William Bramley proposes the ultimate conspiracy theory of history—that we humans are a species of slaves owned by extraterrestrial visitors who used our ancestors to mine the planet for minerals. To keep humans divided, confused, and in turmoil, these visitors or keepers, called the "Custodians," inspired the creation of competing religions. A secret society called "The Brotherhood" has been used by the Custodians, through its various branches such as the Freemasons and the Rosicrucians, to foment terror, revolution, and warfare among humans.

—RANDALL FITZGERALD

Gods or Spacemen?   (Amherst Press, 1964; reprinted in the U.K. by Sphere Books, in 1977, as *Messengers from the Stars*). In this, the first of his five books on the ancient astronaut theme, W. Raymond Drake scans the myths of numerous ancient and modern cultures and civilizations to find similarities in the way they portray visits from sky-dwelling beings who revealed cosmic mysteries to leaders chosen from among the humans.

From witch doctors in Africa to the shamans of Siberia and the Celtic Druids, Drake finds "fragments of a very high theology" that once existed worldwide and inspired construction of the megaliths, the Nazca lines in Peru, and the Egyptian and Mayan pyramids.

—RANDALL FITZGERALD

Good, Timothy   (b. 1942). Timothy Good first became interested in UFOs in 1955, when his passion for aviation and space travel led him to read a book by Major Donald Keyhoe which described sightings by military and civilian pilots. Now regarded as a top authority,

he has researched the subject worldwide, interviewing key witnesses and amassing a wealth of evidence, including several thousands of intelligence documents. He has conducted extensive investigations in the United States for many years.

Born in London, Timothy Good completed his formal education at the King's School, Canterbury, then gained a violin scholarship to the Royal Academy of Music in London, where he won prizes for solo, chamber and orchestral playing. His professional career began in earnest in 1963 when he toured the U.S. and Canada with the Royal Philharmonic Orchestra. From 1964 to 1978 he played with the London Symphony Orchestra. He has also played with many other orchestras, and has worked for many great conductors and composers, including Leonard Bernstein, Benjamin Britten, Otto Klemperer, Leopold Stokowski, Igor Stravinsky, and Sir William Walton.

Timothy Good

Since 1978 Timothy Good has been involved in freelance session work for television dramas, commercials, feature films, and recordings with pop musicians. Those he has recorded for include Phil Collins, George Harrison, Elton John, Paul McCartney, Rod Stewart, Barbra Streisand, and U2. Recent films include *The Fifth Element, The Man in the Iron Mask, Tomorrow Never Dies,* and *Wings of the Dove.*

Timothy Good is known to millions worldwide through his numerous television appearances, and has acted as associate producer for several documentaries on the UFO subject. He has given lectures worldwide at universities, schools, and to many organizations, including the House of Lords All-Party UFO Study Group, IBM, the Institute of Medical Laboratory Sciences, the Royal Canadian Military Institute, the Royal Geographical Society, the Royal Naval Air Reserve Branch, and the Oxford and Cambridge Union Societies. He liaises with a number of retired intelligence officers, and in 1998 was invited to discuss the subject at the Defense Airborne Reconnaissance Office in the Pentagon.

Timothy Good's bestselling books include: *Above Top Secret: The Worldwide UFO Cover-Up* (1987), retitled *Beyond Top Secret: The Worldwide UFO Security Threat* (1996) in its revised edition; *Alien Contact: Top-Secret UFO Files Revealed* (1993); and *Alien Update* (1995).

Address: 247 High Street
            Beckenham
            Kent BR3 1AB
            U.K.

POSITION STATEMENT: It is my conviction that we are being visited by several different groups of extraterrestrials, and that while some may not be well disposed toward us, the majority are essentially benevolent. All share a common "foreign" policy of avoiding open contact with Earth, which to me seems entirely logical. From my own investigations throughout the world, however, I am convinced that *selective* contacts have been made with hundreds of individuals. The visitors have no need to establish open contact, nor do they want the majority of us to know what they are doing here.

—TIMOTHY GOOD

(Position statement was adapted from Timothy Good's first book, *Above Top Secret: The Wordwide UFO Cover-Up*, 1987.)

Grays The image of the alien in UFO culture has generally been dominated by a fetus-like entity with a large, bald head (more pear-shaped than round). Usually the being is small compared to humans. Often the limbs are described as thinner or more slender, but the more closely universal rule is that such aliens are never fat or obese. Current convention labels approximations to this stereotypical UFO-naut with the term "Grays." Ostensibly this is because of grayish skin tones usually being associated with this body type. In practice, absence of this defining trait does not inhibit use of the label so long as a big bald head appears somewhere in the description.

The project of assembling a history of this alien stereotype with a view to understanding its origins and rise to dominance is a daunting one, because there are special hazards. There are no maps to guide us. Therefore, this encyclopedia entry should be regarded as a pioneering effort, not as the final word.

We will start this history by offering the proposition that the idea underlying the Grays was constructed in the 19th century. Images that fit loosely the definition of Grays can be found here and there in art and myths long predating the modern era. Finding them is an easy and pleasant diversion. Take the Greco-Egyptian painting of mortuary house 21 at Tuna-Gebel. It has an entity with a large smooth head and very slender build that includes a pencil-neck. Few would quarrel that the look matches that of the Grays. The fact that the being is the shadow of the deceased represented symbolically as a black emaciated corpse makes it questionable that the look carries the modern idea. (Baines and Melek, 1990)

Dr. Gregory Little has found a description of the watchman at the gates of Sheol in the Hebrew Book of Enoch as gray in color, short like a child, and taking on a somewhat human

Collection of typical "Grays" drawn
by forensic artist William Louis
McDonald

appearance that he says left him stunned. (Little, 1994) I've described elsewhere items from ancient Denmark and the Congo whose facial features mimic the exotic facets of Whitley Strieber's "visitor." (Kottmeyer, 1995)

Such images are quite scattered and could be random outcomes of the immense creativity of artists exploring hundreds of permutations. There is no evidence of deeper linkages between them and current UFO beliefs, and no hint of historical connections. As a parallel example, ponder how some short bald fairies ended up in *Star Trek, The Next Generation* Starfleet uniforms, even though the painting was done in 1880 by Sir Arthur Conan Doyle's father. (Philpotts, 1978) One may not be able to rule out some swirly space-time anomaly causing such things, but coincidence has to be the favored judgment.

The trait of big-headedness can be found associated with aliens inhabiting the sun in Pierre Boitard's *Musée des familles* (1838), but the beings possess hair and otherwise seem completely human. This seems a simple way of representing higher intelligence in such beings. I consider it slightly outside the definition of a Gray. (Pinvidic, 1993)

The idea underlying the Grays did not and could not exist before the idea of evolution. Christian theology held that God created life in the first week of creation. Each species was designed optimally for its niche in the hierarchy of nature, and, presumably, given all the fuss over the Ark, would never be re-created. Transformation of form or future improvement on present design held no place in such a worldview. Evolution was heretical and rarely considered at length prior to the 19th century. It is to one of the proponents of an early version of evolution, Jean-Baptiste Lamarck, that we will turn to for an important element of out history.

Lamarck was an early opponent of the ideas of special creation and catastrophism. Nature did everything little by little and successively. Where earlier thinkers spoke of a great chain of being with each species created specifically for its place, Lamarck felt that varying environmental pressures created new needs and increased the use of certain organs to make them more perfect while adding to the organism's complexity. Conversely, ". . . the permanent disuse of an organ, arising from a change of habits, causes a gradual shrinkage and ultimately the disappearance and even extinction of that organ." (Lamarck, 1809; 1963)

Lamarck regarded man as a probable product of evolution. The process, he felt, reached the limits of complexity and perfection; and, while noting individual instances of the perfecting or degradation of reason, will, and morality, was not compelled to speculate on the future of the human form. Since man's intelligence and powers protect him from the voracity of any animal, man could potentially multiply indefinitely, but he believed the Sublime author installed a safety feature: ". . . nature has given him numerous passions which unfortunately develop with his intelligence, and thus set up a great obstacle to the extreme multiplication of individuals of his species. It seems that man is responsible for keeping down the numbers of his kind; for I have hesitation in saying the earth will never be covered by the population that it might support; several of its habitable regions will always be sparsely populated in turns, although the periods of these fluctuations are, so far as we are concerned, immeasurable." (Lamarck, 1809; 1963) Man ". . . assuredly presents the type of highest perfection that nature will attain to. . . ." (Lamarck, 1809; 1963)

Towards 1866, a Lamarckian named Alpheus Hyatt indicated his studies of fossils were providing a less optimistic understanding of the process of evolution. Just as individuals slip into senility and decrepitude at the end of life, groups like races and species display a senile phase before going extinct. This theory of racial senescence later becomes an indispensable feature of the doctrine of orthogenesis. It held that the organism was not shaped by natural selection, but by processes internal to the germ plasm that caused modification along trend lines that ran on until they became overdeveloped and detrimental to survival. Examples of this process could be found in the huge antlers of the Irish elk, the demise of the sabre-toothed tiger, and the massiveness of dinosaurs. Hyatt himself believed man was already showing senile and regressive features. (Bowler, 1983)

The writings of Herbert Spencer, another Lamarckian, provide us with the next step in the development of the idea underlying the Grays. In his work *The Principles of Biology* (1875), he speculates at length on the human future. He feels there will be "larger-brained descendents" and the brain will have more convolutions, a more developed structure. Asserting the existence of "an apparent connection between higher cerebral development and prolonged sexual maturity," evidence that excessive expenditure of mental activity during education causes complete or partial infertility, and conversely that "where exceptional fertil-

ity exists there is a sluggishness of mind"; Spencer concluded further evolution may be expected to cause a decline in his power of reproduction. (Spencer, 1875)

There most likely would be greater delicacy of manipulation, better coordination of complex movements, and a "corresponding development of perceptive and executive faculties." There would also be greater power of self-regulation and higher emotional development. He would be more moral. Crimes and cruelties would cease. Of strength and agility, Spencer doubted there would be further improvement. He does not explicitly articulate that a general degeneration of the rest of the body would follow, but that is now only a couple of steps away. (Spencer, 1875)

We should digress to point out that Darwin does not belong to this line of development. His theory of evolution by natural selection builds in part on Lamarck's arguments against special creation and catastrophism while stripping animal evolution of its central mechanism of use-inheritance. The issue of Darwin's views on progress is a notoriously thorny subject, and on the future form of man he was silent. He seemed to think some ongoing natural selection existed in the destruction of more primitive peoples. However, he was also concerned that natural selection no longer operated to scythe down the sickly and degenerate. Any slow evolution of mankind, however, paled next to his pet horror, the eventual and inevitable ice-death of the earth under the aegis of a cooling sun. "To think of the progress of millions of years with every continent swarming with good and enlightened men all ending in this . . . *Sic transit gloria mundi* with a vengeance." (Darwin quoted by Desmond and Moore, 1991)

Alfred Russell Wallace, Darwin's co-discoverer of natural selection, believed the human physique was no longer subject to natural forces. War killed off the strongest and bravest, he thought. Skin color and hair perhaps still evolved, but the body remained an upright ape. The human species was still capable of spectacular advances with women's rights giving females free choice in marriage and allowing them to reject males who were chronically diseased, intellectually weak, idle, or utterly selfish. (Brackman, 1980) These matters, however, belonged to the moral and spiritual realms, not the realm of man's physical being.

Thomas Henry Huxley, the era's most prominent Darwinian, also lies outside this line of development, but bears special attention and caution. Scholars have caricatured him alternately as a naïve advocate of progress and a purveyor of cosmic pessimism. These extreme interpretations derive from selective focus on separate facets of a carefully balanced view blending the lessons of natural history and social history.

Early writings indicate he "had no confidence in the doctrine of ultimate happiness," but it was impossible for him to be blind to the improvements in life that science was making manifest around him in his personal sphere. (Desmond, 1994) Huxley often argued with Spencer over the nature of evolutionary and social progress. Huxley soon developed the metaphor of society advancing, insect-like, from grub to butterfly. There are periods of repressive restraint, dark ages, that are broken in dramatic moults like the French revolution. Each moult moves us closer to a butterfly state of man, albeit that may prove to be terribly distant. (Desmond, 1994)

In 1894 he offered his mature statement on these matters in *Evolution and Ethics* and we see the same balancing. He rejects utopia, "the prospect of attaining untroubled happiness, or a state which can, even remotely, deserve the title of perfection, appears to me as misleading an illusion as ever dangled before the eyes of poor humanity." Yet, "that which lies before the human race is a constant struggle to maintain and improve." (Huxley quoted in Paradis and Williams, 1989)

The theory of evolution encourages no millennial expectations, he writes: "There is no hope that mere human beings will ever possess enough intelligence to select the fittest." (Paradis and Williams, 1989) He sees "no limit to the extent to which intelligence and will,

guided by sound principles of investigation and organized in common effort, may modify the conditions for a period than that now covered by history. And much may be done to change the nature of man himself . . . (we) ought to be able to do something towards curbing the instincts of savagery in civilized men [thus permitting] a larger hope of abatement of the essential evil of the world . . ." (Paradis and Williams, 1989)

Evolution, however, permits both progressive and retrogressive development. "The most daring imagination will hardly venture upon the suggestion that the power and the intelligence of man can ever arrest the procession of the great year." Eventually, "the evolution of our globe shall have entered so far upon its downward course that the cosmic process resumes its sway; and, once more, the State of Nature prevails over the surface of our planet." This is an allusion to the thermodynamic heat death of the Earth. (Paradis and Williams, 1989)

To point to these latter quotes and label it cosmic pessimism has the perverse air of saying that someone who expects to achieve some measure of happiness and success and die at 120 is being depressing. Huxley dialectically balanced optimism and pessimism in a manner he felt most people did. (Paradis and Williams, 1989; Hillegas, 1974) Huxley nowhere comments on the future biological shape of man as Spencer did, nor does he dwell on the implications of the possibility of his retrogressive modification.

The final steps in the development of the idea underlying the Grays were made by one of Huxley's students. The student thought Huxley was the greatest man he ever knew and when he published his first book he sent his teacher a note that read:

May 1895

I am sending you a little book that I fancy may be of interest to you. The central idea—of degeneration following security—was the outcome of a certain amount of biological study. I daresay your position subjects you to a good many such displays of the range of authors but I have this excuse—I was one of your students at the Royal College of Science and finally (?): The book is a very little one. (Quoted in Smith, 1986)

It was a work of fiction that describes a traveler's encounter with a delicate little people of the far future. The first person is described as "a slight creature—perhaps 4 feet high—clad in a purple tunic, girdled at the waist with a leather belt. Sandals or huskins were on his feet; his legs were bare to the knees and his head was bare . . . . He struck me as being a very beautiful and graceful creature, but indescribably frail. His flushed face reminded me of the more beautiful kind of consumptive—that hectic beauty of which you used to hear so much about." As he observes more of them he notes their Dresden china prettiness had peculiarities. They had some curly hair that did not go past the neck and cheek. There was no trace of beard or other facial hair. The lips were thin. The ears were singularly minute. Chins were small and ran to a point. The eyes were large, but mild and indifferent.

There is nothing said about the size of the head, and the intelligence of these people is slight. Their behavior is child-like and playful and they show a lack of interest in the traveler. There was little to distinguish the sexes. The traveler eventually learns the name of this beautiful race—Eloi. He also learns of a second race—the Morlocks—which are described as a white, ape-like human spider. They tend the underworld of machines that make the utopia of the aristocratic Eloi possible.

The title of the story was *The Time Machine*. The student was H. G. Wells. His boast to Huxley that it was based on an amount of biological study is easily proven. Four years earlier he had written a non-fiction essay titled *Zoological Retrogression* that displayed his familiarity with the biological literature involving degeneration. In it he describes a popular and poetic formulation of evolution as a steadily rising mountain slope that he terms Excelsior biology. Proclaiming it lacking any satisfactory confirmation in geological biology or embryology, he argues degeneration has entire parity with progressive trends. He points to ascidians, cirripeds, copepods, corals, seamats, oysters, mussels, and mites as examples. Advance has been fitful and uncertain. There is no guarantee in scientific knowledge of man's permanence or permanent ascendancy. Huxley's teachings are apparent except for one point of divergence. Wells concludes The Coming Beast must certainly be reckoned in any anticipatory calculations in the Coming Man. (Philmus and Hughes, 1975)

Though Wells believed he was swimming against the stream of mass opinion in this essay, some historians would argue he was being swept along by the currents of his time. The concept of degeneration was not new and the Victorian era's concerns over the permanent underclass bred in urban areas like London had spawned a theory of urban degeneration that held powerful appeal to the British after 1885 no matter what their politics. (Nye, 1985) This degeneration scare, as it has been termed, was part of a yet larger trend of cultural pessimism spreading among western intellectuals. (Herman, 1997) Peter Bowler, an expert on evolutionary theories of the era speculates that E. Ray Lankester's book *Degeneration* is a likely source of the ideas behind *The Time Machine*. (Bowler, 1989) The unavoidable caveat to this attribution is that the concept of degeneration was present in so many forums from medical journals like *The Lancet* to much popular fiction. Wells could have been influenced by a variety of sources.

The 11th chapter of *The Time Machine* takes the reader beyond the time of the Eloi and Morlocks to a farther future where the Earth approaches its end. Life had grown sparse and was in obvious regression. The dominant form was an ungainly monster crab smeared in slime. He goes another thirty million years into the future and only lichen and liverworts remained. That and a black, round, hopping thing with tentacles trailing from it. It seems like Alpheus Hyatt writ large; life as a whole falls into senescence as everything becomes extinct. (Eisenstein, 1976)

The Eloi come halfway to our image of the Gray in short and fragile bodies being indicative of a degenerate evolutionary history. What is missing is the big bald head. Wells began playing with that part of the image maybe as early as 1885 for an address before a student debating society. It was written out for publication in a facetious book review for the *Pall Mall Budget*, 9 November 1893. "Of a Book Unwritten, The Man of the Year Million" is a short piece with no ambitions of wanting to be taken seriously. Wells imagines a book titled *The Necessary Characters of Man of the Remote Future Deduced from the Existing Stream of Tendency*. Though easily missed, Wells is telegraphing his intent to play upon the ideas of orthogenesis which as its name implies dealt with straight-line trends in the fossil record. Just as a fish is molded to swimming and a bird is molded to flight, man's form will be determined by the trait of intelligence. We already see the decay of much of the animal part of man: the loss of hair, the loss of teeth, the diminution of jaw, slighter mouth and ears. Athleticism yields to a subtle mind in real-world competition. The coming man, then, will clearly have a larger brain and a slighter body than the present. Wells:

Behold the dim strange vision of the latter day face suggested by loss of unused features: Eyes large, lustrous, beautiful soulful; above them, no longer separated by rugged brow ridges, is the top of the head, a glistening hairless dome, terete and beautiful; no craggy nose rises to disturb by its unmeaning shadows the symmetry of that calm face, no vestigial ears project; the mouth is a small perfectly round aperture, toothless and gumless, unanimal, no futile emotions disturbing its roundness as it lies, like the harvest moon or the eve-

ning star, in the wide firmament of the face. (Quoted by Hughes, 1993)

Potentially, man's knowledge of organic chemistry will supplant the use of a stomach and alimentary canal and the brain will swim in a nutritive bath—some clear, mobile, and amber liquid. In still deeper time the cooling Earth will force a retreat to galleries and laboratories deep inside the bowels of the planet following the diminishing supply of heat with boring machinery and glaring artificial lighting. Wells takes pleasure in noting the whole of this imaginary book may vanish in the smoke of a pipe with no great bother—one of the great advantages of unwritten literature.

But of course it did not vanish and did become a great bother. It ended up in a book that would guarantee a very enduring life. The book was *The War of the Worlds* (1898). Mars is an ancient world and evolution has proceeded farther than on Earth, thus is the logical setting for Man of the Year Million. The Martians were 4-foot-diameter round heads. They had very large dark-colored eyes, no nostrils, and no ears per se. They had a fleshy beak for a mouth. The internal anatomy was, in a word, simple. They had no entrails and did not eat. Rather, they injected blood from other creatures, most notably a type of biped with flimsy skeletons and feeble musculature, and a round head with large eyes set in flinty sockets.

The Martians were absolutely without sex and allied tumultuous emotions. They budded off the parent. Wells's fictional narrator explicitly credits the author of the *Pall Mall Budget* book review with forecasting such a creature, albeit in a foolish, facetious tone. Noting that many a truth is said in jest, the idea seemed likely that Martians had once been like us but with a brain evolved at the expense of the rest of the body. They turn out to also be telepathic. The Martians die off at the end of the war because of their vulnerability to Earth's microorganisms. There were none on Mars, probably because their science eliminated them ages before. We would say nowadays that their immune systems had degenerated from disuse. (Hughes, 1993)

The mental giantism and diminished sexuality clearly echo Spencer. It has a Lamarckian sensibility in the early part of the argument of man's form being molded by the trait of intelligence, but Wells does include Darwinian competition in suggesting a subtle mind wins over athleticism in the real world. One can fairly wonder how many people would accept that premise these days. The basic thrust that evolution would trend to a grossly overspecialized super-tick, however, is decisively orthogenetic. Admittedly, extinction in a foreign environment rich in microorganism is not strictly a proof of maladaptation, but nobody is meant to think this type of monstrosity is a good thing.

The critical literature on *The War of the Worlds* generally agrees that the Martians are nightmare extensions of ourselves and our machine civilization. It is a warning that an overreliance on cold intellect and technology need not lead to better and better. Basically it is a moral it shares with *The Time Machine*. Where the atrophy from overreliance on technology and the brain is played for comic effect in the *Pall Mall Budget*, here it is played for horror. That a story with such an anti-intellectual moral should come from the pen of a person as intellectual as Wells is slightly ironic, but not amazing. Science fiction writers are a brainy bunch, but are perennially worried over the social consequences of science and technology.

Wells himself never regarded his atrophied aliens as a realistic speculation. Though he granted life on Mars might exist and even speculated on what interesting differences might be expected because of the harsh environment, his nonfiction writings did not advance the probability that big, bald-headed aliens with degenerate bodies existed. ("The Things That Live on Mars" reprinted in Hughes, 1993) The idea that begat the Grays was born as a jest that never was intended by its author to be taken as a serious scientific speculation.

—MARTIN S. KOTTMEYER

References

Baines, John, and Jaromir Malek. *The Cultural Atlas of the World: Ancient Egypt* (Andromeda, 1990).

Bowler, Peter. *The Eclipse of Darwinism: Anti-Darwinian Evolution Theories in the Decades Around 1900* (Johns Hopkins University Press, 1983).

Bowler, Peter. *The Invention of Progress* (Basil Blackwell, 1989).

Brackman, Arnold C. *A Delicate Arrangement: The Strange Case of Charles Darwin and Alfred Russell Wallace* (Times Books, 1980).

Desmond, Adrian, and James Moore. *Darwin—The Life of a Tormented Evolutionist* (Warner Books, 1991).

Desmond, Adrian. *Huxley—The Devil's Disciple* (Michael Joseph, 1994).

Eisenstein, Alex. "The Time Machine and the End of Man," *Science Fiction Studies* (July, 1976).

Gentleman's Magazine, September 1981, reprinted in Philmus, Robert M. and David Y. Hughes, *H.G. Wells: Early Writings in Science and Science Fiction* (California University Press, 1975).

Herman, Arthur. *The Idea of Decline in Human History* (Free Press, 1997).

Hughes, David Y. *A Critical Edition of The War of the Worlds* (Indiana University Press, 1993).

Hillegas, Mark R. *The Future as Nightmare: H.G. Wells and the Anti-Utopians* (Southern Illinois University Press, 1974).

Kottmeyer, Martin. "Ishtar Descendant," *The Skeptic* (1995).

———. "Varicose Brains: Entering a Gray Area" *Magonia* (February 1998).

Lamarck, Jean-Baptiste. *Zoological Philosophy: An Exposition with Regard to the Natural History of Animals* (Hafner Publishing, 1963). Originally published in 1809.

Little, Gregory. *Grand Illusions* (White Buffalo Books, 1994).

Nye, Robert A. "Sociology: The Irony of Progress" in Chamberlin, J. Edward and Sander L. Gilman, *Degeneration: The Dark Side of Progress* (Columbia University Press, 1985).

Paradis, James and Williams, George C. *T.H. Huxley's Evolution and Ethics with New Essays on its Victorian and Sociobiological Context* (Princeton University Press, 1989).

Philpotts, Beatrice. *The Book of Fairies* (Ballantine, 1978).

Pinvidic, Thierry. *OVNI vers une Anthopologie d'un Mythe Contemporain* (Editions Heimdal, 1993).

Smith, David C. *H.G. Wells: Desperately Mortal* (Yale University Press, 1986).

Spencer, Herbert *The Principles of Biology* (D. Appleton, 1875).

POSTSCRIPT: In UFO lore, the Grays are sometimes good and sometimes evil, but generally they are *amoral*. In other words, they represent multiple aspects of the human personality—especially the contemporary human (or humanoid)—for good or ill.

They are usually described as sexually neuter and perform their hybrid breeding experiments, for the most part, through artificial insemination. The gray color symbolizes neutrality in morals, sexuality, and emotions. It also symbolizes "gray matter" or intelligence. The eyes are large and black (without pupils) like a shark's eyes—uncaring, one might say. The hairlessness of the Grays is derived from the assumption that we are losing our animal characteristics—but to be replaced by emotionless clones.

The Grays aren't exactly the good guys or the bad guys—they're in a "gray area," as Martin Kottmeyer has pointed out. They represent human evolution and its uncertain future. They are analogies of ourselves.

—RONALD D. STORY

Great Falls (Montana) movie On August 5 or 15, 1950 (the exact date is not known with certainty), Nick Mariana, thirty-eight at the time and the general manager of the local "Selectics" baseball team, in the company of his secretary, nineteen-year-old Virginia Raunig, were at the Great Falls Legion Ball Park in preparation for that afternoon's game. It was about 11:30 A.M., and, as was his habit before every game, Mariana checked the wind direction by watching the steady stream of white smoke issuing from a towering Anaconda smokestack located about a mile northwest of the stadium. Mariana said: "As I looked up I saw two silvery objects moving swiftly out of the northwestern blue. They appeared to be moving directly south. My first thought was, 'Get the camera—they're flying discs!' Then I thought again, 'Don't be stupid—they must be planes in a bank and I'll see their wings in just a minute.' Then as they got closer and more distinct, I realized there were no wings—these were not banking planes, they were flying saucers!'' (Saunders, 1968)

One of the frames (cropped) from Nick Mariana's 16mm movie shot over Great Falls, Montana, in August of 1950

The witness then called to his secretary, who came running, as Mariana himself raced from the grandstand to his car where he always kept a 16mm movie camera in the glove compartment. After losing a few more seconds to turn the telephoto turret lens into position, he managed to film the objects for sixteen seconds while standing by his car. The duration of the whole sighting was about one minute. Miss Raunig arrived in time to see "two silvery balls," but Mariana's description was more detailed. He said the objects were definitely disk-shaped, apparently "about fifty feet across and about three or four feet thick." Also, "the discs appeared to be spinning, like a top." (Saunders, 1968)

The distance was estimated at about two miles, altitude at 5,000 to 10,000 feet, and the objects' speed at between 200 and 400 miles per hour. Mariana also claimed that at one point, just before he started filming, "the objects appeared to hover or stop in midair." (Saunders, 1968)

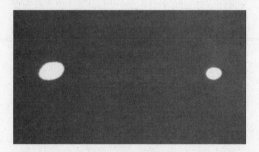

Computer enhancement of the Great Falls, Montana, UFOs

The Montana movie was submitted to the U.S. Air Force for analysis in 1950, but the military investigators did not seem impressed. Project Grudge regarded the UFOs simply as "the reflections from two F-94 jet fighters that were in the area." (Ruppelt, 1956) Sunlight from the fuselages washed out the other details and that was why Mariana had been fooled. Mariana, however, claimed that both he and Raunig saw the jets in another part of the sky just after seeing the UFOs.

Then in 1952, according to former Project Blue Book chief Captain Edward J. Ruppelt, the investigation was reopened "at the request of the Pentagon." (Ruppelt, 1956) This time, the airplane-reflection theory was studied a little more closely. Though Mariana and his secretary had testified to seeing two jets roaring by in the opposite direction just two minutes after the UFO sighting, the Air Force investigators understandably wanted something more solid. With information obtained through an intelligence officer at Great Falls Air Force Base (now Malmstrom AFB), the landing pattern of the planes that were in the vicinity on August 15th was carefully established. Ruppelt said: "The two jets just weren't anywhere

close to where the two UFOs had been. Next we studied each individual light and both appeared to be too steady to be reflections.

"We drew a blank on the Montana Movie—it was an unknown." (Ruppelt, 1956)

When the film was returned, Mariana claimed that some thirty frames at the beginning had been removed. It was in those frames that the oval shape of the UFOs could be seen. The Air Force denied editing the film except to remove a single frame because of damaged sprockets. Mariana claimed he had a letter about the removal of the thirty frames, but was unable to produce it.

In 1953 the CIA-sponsored Robertson Panel examined the Mariana film. Their scientists believed that aircraft could account for the images on the film, so they concluded that the film probably showed sunlight reflected from aircraft.

The film was analyzed again in 1955 by Dr. Robert M. L. Baker, Jr., a specialist in celestial mechanics, then employed by the Douglas Aircraft Company. Dr. Baker shot comparative films of planes at varying distances reflecting the sun, using a 16mm movie camera similar to Mariana's. But none of the images came close to resembling those on Mariana's film, convincing Baker that if Mariana had filmed two jets "at the largest distances compatible with their speeds and the angular rate of the images . . . [their structure] would have been identifiable on the film." (Baker, 1972)

Baker did not believe the images were the result of any known natural phenomena. He determined that the objects were two miles from the camera, and his experiments showed that jet fighters would have been identifiable as aircraft. Baker considered the case unexplained.

It wasn't until the Condon Committee investigation in 1966 that the film was again examined. All the previous investigations were reviewed and Mariana was re-interviewed. The principal photo analyst for the Condon study, Dr. William K. Hartmann (an astronomer), found that the objects had a constant elliptical shape consistent with the "resolution of disks oriented parallel with the ground." (Baker, 1972) Hartmann concluded, however, that the evidence of the film was not sufficient to draw a final conclusion about the objects.

In the end, none of the studies produced any evidence that the film had been faked. Data indicated that the objects were basically disk-shaped and that the images on the film were consistent with highly polished metal surfaces.

Because these pictures consist of 290 continuous frames of 16mm color movie film, the possibility of a hoax in this case is generally considered by skeptics and proponents alike to be extremely remote. And, if Mariana's accompanying testimony is given any credibility at all, this case would have to rank as one of the "best" of all time. Dr. David R. Saunders, a psychologist and member of the former University of Colorado UFO Project, considered it "the one sighting of all time that did more than any other single case to convince me that there is something to the UFO problem." (Saunders, 1968)

Along with the photos taken at McMinnville, Oregon, also in 1950, this is the one other photographic case which defied all efforts by the Condon team to arrive at a completely satisfactory explanation. Dr. William K. Hartmann, chief photo-analyst for the University of Colorado UFO Project, wrote in the Condon Report that: "The case remains unexplained. Analysis indicates that the images on the film are difficult to reconcile with aircraft or other known phenomena, although aircraft cannot be entirely ruled out." (Gillmor, 1969)

Most UFOlogists believe the photographic evidence, as well as the eyewitness testimony, suggests that the aircraft explanation is unlikely.

Computer enhancements by William Spaulding at GSW (Ground Saucer Watch) add further support to the conclusion that the Great Falls/Mariana movie is one of the strongest photographic cases of apparently genuine UFOs on record.

—KEVIN D. RANDLE
& RONALD D. STORY

References

Baker, Robert M.L., Jr. "Motion Pictures of UFO's" in Sagan, Carl and Thornton Page, eds. *UFO's—A Scientific Debate* (Cornell University Press, 1972; W.W. Norton, 1974).

Gillmor, Daniel S. and Edward U. Condon, eds. *Scientific Study of Unidentified Flying Objects* (E. P. Dutton/Bantam Books, 1969).

Randle, Kevin D. "Great Falls (Montana) movie" in Story, Ronald D., ed. *The Encyclopedia of UFOs* (Doubleday/New English Library, 1980).

———. *Conspiracy of Silence* (Avon Books, 1997).

———. *Scientific UFOlogy* (Avon Books, 1999).

Ruppelt, Edward J. *The Report on Unidentified Flying Objects* (Doubleday, 1956).

Saunders, David R. and R. Roger Harkins. *UFOs? Yes! Where the Condon Committee Went Wrong* (Signet/NAL, 1968).

Story, Ronald D. *UFOs and the Limits of Science* (William Morrow, 1981).

Guardians of the Universe?

Guardians of the Universe? (St. Martin's Press/New English Library, 1980). Ronald Story makes a case that alleged evidence for ancient astronauts is a psychological projective test based on faith and hope, not verifiable facts.

Despite the contention of Erich von Däniken and other proponents, the construction of the Great Pyramid in Egypt and other megalithic monuments never required a level of technology which was beyond "the capacities of Earthmen working on their own in the normal context of their own cultures." Much of the evidence used in support of ancient visitation by aliens, especially artistic representations on cave and temple walls, takes the form of psychological projective tests in which the book authors plant interpretive ideas in the minds of readers, substituting propaganda for logic.

—RANDALL FITZGERALD

Gulf Breeze (Florida) incidents

Gulf Breeze (Florida) incidents Since the late 1980s, Gulf Breeze, Florida, has become a "window" area of UFO sightings and other paranormal events. (See WINDOW AREAS) It all began on November 11, 1987, with a foiled abduction attempt. Local building contractor Edward Walters happened to glance out the window of his home office when he saw an unusual glow behind some trees. Grabbing his Polaroid camera, he headed outside just in time to snap five pictures of a spectacular UFO heading toward his house. Then, as the UFO hovered silently above him at an altitude of about 200 feet, Ed was struck by a paralyzing blue beam which shot down from the bottom of the object. Screaming as the beam lifted him up, he resisted with all his power while a "voice" communicated with him telepathically from the UFO saying "calm down" and "stop it." Ed answered by screaming "screw you!" Then, just as a plane flew by, the UFO let him go and disappeared out of sight.

After discussing the matter with his wife and son, Ed submitted the photos anonymously to the local weekly newspaper, The (Gulf Breeze) *Sentinel*. Soon after Ed's story and the photos were published in the *Sentinel* on November 19, 1987, the whole area became a UFO hot spot. First dozens, then hundreds, of other witnesses came forth to report their own UFO sightings and experiences. These included sightings of UFOs, jets chasing UFOs, and abductions.

By the time the first Gulf Breeze flap had subsided in July, 1988, there had been over 100 sightings involving over 200 people (with many multiple witness sightings). Twenty-four of these sightings were reported by Ed Walters who, understandably, became a highly controversial figure—especially because of the multiple photo opportunities afforded him—making Walters as contentious as George Adamski and Billy Meier before him.

Although some investigators consider the whole series of sightings to be explainable as a hoax by Walters, followed by misidentifications and attempts by other witnesses to gain public recognition, the fact is that numerous witnesses with no connection to Walters have provided detailed descriptions of objects that appear to have been what he photographed.

One of the most explicit descriptions was given by a medical doctor and his wife who

The first photo taken by Ed Walters on November 11, 1987

Enlargement of the "UFO"

saw the object at rather close range (a few hundred feet) for many seconds hovering over Pensacola Bay near their home. They could see light from the object reflected off the water.

From July 1988 through late November 1990, the sighting rate diminished somewhat, there being about 120 sightings over that time period. About a dozen or so of these involved Ed Walters. In late November a new series of sightings began which had a distinctly different nature. The new sightings were of a light moving through the sky, which had peculiar properties. Usually it was first seen by witnesses as a red light (although sometimes it was initially seen as white and would then turn red), moving at a steady pace through the early evening sky within an hour of darkness. The light would remain red for a period of time—from many seconds to several minutes—and then it would suddenly turn white and start flashing brightly. Quite often glowing lights were seen to drop downward from the light as it began flashing. Then it would go out.

Lights such as this were seen so often that a group of local residents began a nightly "skywatch," broken only by bad weather, which existed from November 1990 through 1995—even though the first major wave of sightings ended in July 1992, by which time there had been about 170 recorded events. Here "recorded" means multiply witnessed and generally recorded on video and sometimes with telephoto photography as well. Starting in September 1991, yet another type of moving object was seen. Witnesses observed (and recorded) rings of light, that is, individual lights forming a circular pattern moving through the sky. This author was a witness to one such ring of eight white lights forming an octagon, which appeared in the sky above Gulf Breeze at about 8:30 P.M. on the night of September 16, 1991. A crude triangulation combined with photographic data showed it to be many feet, perhaps several tens of feet, in diameter. It simply appeared in the sky and then moved upward and perhaps toward the 30 or so witnesses to this event and then, after 70 seconds, disappeared.

The red light and its "relatives" (two red lights traveling in parallel, a ring of lights, a cluster of lights) seen over the year-and-a-half period, were early on referred to as "bubba" (slang for "brother"). These "bubba" sightings were observed by several TV camera crews as well as the local residents and visitors who came from all over the world to see the Gulf Breeze UFOs.

The bubba sightings have never been satisfactorily explained. The initial thought was that some sort of balloon carrying a road flare could explain some of the reported phenomena. However, it could not have been this simple. "Bubba" was never observed to rise into the sky and travel along. Instead, it always ap-

peared at some altitude, hence requiring remote ignition or a long-burning, hidden fuse. A simple red road flare could not explain the sudden change of color to extremely bright white and the subsequent many-seconds-long duration of rapid white flashing, often at a high rate comparable to the frame rate of a TV camera (30 complete frames per second). If a bubba were a pyrotechnic display, it would have to have been some special formulation.

Moreover, an experiment was performed to compare the optical spectrum of bubba with the spectrum of a red flare. A diffraction grating was placed inside a camera that was then used to photograph both a bubba light and a red road flare. Analysis of the resulting images showed conclusively that the color spectra of the two were different, with bubba having more blue light than a road flare—a color shift that was obvious to the witnesses who saw both the bubba light and the flare that was burned almost immediately afterward.

Several of the bubba lights were simultaneously witnessed by observers separated by considerable distances (up to several miles) thereby allowing for accurate triangulations. For several of the triangulated sightings it was possible to calculate a speed of up to 50 miles per hour, much faster than any wind at the time, and even a crosswind. If this was a hoax, it would require a motorized transport system, such as a model plane or a very small blimp. Yet, there was never any engine noise associated with a bubba sighting. The triangulated altitudes were a few thousand feet.

Except for one crude attempt at a hoax, which was identified immediately by the witnesses, there was not one shred of hard evidence, such as debris found on the ground or floating on the water around Gulf Breeze, that the bulk of the bubba sightings were hoaxes, even though one would expect that with nearly two hundred recorded events there would have been some mistake at some time by the hoaxer(s). Had they been hoaxes involving some pyrotechnic display, they would have been illegal and highly dangerous (a lighted flare falling on a building could cause a fire; in some cases the bubba was over a thousand feet high and in the vicinity of the landing pattern for Pensacola airport). Of course, the balloon-flare hypothesis could not explain the rings of lights and other sightings of even more complex light arrangements.

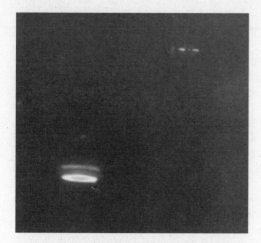

Photo by Ed Walters, taken on May 1, 1988, showing two different UFOs

No debris of a suspicious nature was ever found, even though many of the sighted objects were over land when they disappeared. Several of the bubba sightings have been analyzed in detail and are presented in *UFOs Are Real: Here's the Proof* (Walters and Maccabee, 1997), along with the details of this author's sighting. Also in that reference is an analysis of the January 1990 sighting in which Ed Walters and other witnesses took pictures of a structured object with a red light on the bottom.

After July 1992, the sightings in the Gulf Breeze area diminished considerably.

Although there have been quite a few sightings in the years since, there has been nothing like the 1987-1988 and 1990-1992 concentrations. Ed Walters had nine sightings during the time period from 1993 through the end of 1996 and took pictures or videos of

what he saw. The incident depicted in the above photos is described below.

January 12, 1994

Ed Walters was in his office which has windows that face northward toward the Santa Rosa Sound (his house is on the north side of Pensacola Beach). Across the Sound is the south shore of Gulf Breeze.

As he was working at his desk a glint from something shiny in the clear sky attracted his attention. He looked up and saw a strange object, stationary in the sky apparently above Gulf Breeze. Its shape indicated it was no ordinary object. He grabbed a 35 mm camera with zoom lens (with a maximum effective focal length of 214 mm) that he kept loaded in the event that something should appear, and ran outside where he had an unobstructed view. The camera was set on automatic so, based on subsequent experiments, its shutter speed was probably 1/250 or 1/500 sec.

As he started to zoom and focus on the UFO, he heard the noise of jets. Lowering the camera he noticed two jets—one low and one high—coming from the east, heading west toward the object (he was looking north-northwest). They were not traveling at a high rate of speed (estimates based on the photos suggest about 300 mph). He unzoomed the lens to get a wide angle shot and, when the lower jet appeared in the frame, he took the first picture. He wanted a close-up of the UFO, so he zoomed in on it and tried to hold the camera steady. This took a few seconds and, just as he was about to click the shutter button, he noticed that the lower jet was entering the field of view. He took the second shot and watched as the lower jet made a slight curve around the UFO and then headed west. The upper jet was still headed west. These two jets traveled westward for several seconds and then made a U-turn and headed back toward the UFO. Suddenly it streaked away to the east and the jets then made a southward turn and flew over Pensacola Beach and off into the

Photos taken by Ed Walters on January 12, 1994. The wide-angle view shows the jet and UFO in the same picture. Enlargements are superimposed to show more detail. The second insert shows the F-15 partially obscuring the UFO.

distance. The total sighting may have lasted about a minute.

Ed described the UFO as appearing like a large egg with its axis vertical, with several smaller ball-like or egg-shaped objects forming a horizontal ring about the vertical center of the UFO. The photos support this description. The first photo shows the UFO and the jet approaching. The second photo is particularly remarkable, however, because the shutter opened just as the jet was passing between the camera and the UFO. From the known size of the jet, the known focal length of the camera lens at full zoom and image size on the film, one can calculate that the jet was about 8,500 feet from the camera and about 1,300 feet high. The image size of the UFO then indicates that it was about 30 feet wide and 20 feet high if it was only a few hundred feet farther from the camera than the jet (larger if it was farther away).

The experiences of Walters, his wife and family, and many of the other witnesses have been documented in three books: *The Gulf Breeze Sightings* by Ed and Frances Walters (Morrow, 1990; Avon 1992), *UFO Abductions in Gulf Breeze* by Ed and Frances Walters (Avon, 1994), and *UFOs are Real: Here's the Proof* by Ed Walters and Bruce Maccabee (Avon, 1997).

—BRUCE MACCABEE

POSTSCRIPT: This whole "three-ring flying saucer circus," claims science writer Robert Sheaffer, has been exposed as a hoax perpetrated by Walters for financial gain. A Gulf Breeze youth came forward to confess that he and two others, including Walters's son, had helped to fabricate the photos. Equally damning, occupants of a house Walters had lived in during the alleged UFO blitz found a UFO model—hidden under some insulation in the garage attic—which resembled the object seen in the Walters photos. The model was wrapped in part of an old house plan drawn by Walters himself. News photographers were able to use the model to essentially duplicate some of the UFO photos that had made Walters rich and famous.

When two MUFON (Mutual UFO Network) investigators (Rex and Carol Salisberry) took another look at Walters, they found that he was "adept at trick photography," and the case had all the earmarks of a clever hoax; one that enriched Walters with a book deal and fees from movie and television producers, which reportedly added up to hundreds of thousands of dollars.

Interestingly, this updated finding caused MUFON to lose confidence in the Salisberrys—who had previously received an award from MUFON for their outstanding investigations—but not in Walters.

—RANDALL FITZGERALD

H

Haines, Richard F. (b. 1937). Dr. Haines retired from NASA as a senior research scientist in 1988. Originally from Seattle, Washington, he received his M.A. and Ph.D. degrees (in experimental psychology and physiology) from Michigan State University in 1962 and 1964 respectively.

He then worked for the NASA Ames Research Center, where he developed and then directed NASA's "High Luminance Vision Laboratory" carrying out rendezvous and docking simulation studies for America's Gemini and Apollo Programs.

From 1967 to 1985 Haines was a research scientist in various NASA life science divisions carrying out theoretical and applied research on astronaut and aircraft pilot vision. He was appointed Chief of the Space Human Factors Office at Ames (1986-1988) and retired from government service in 1988.

Dr. Haines was also an associate professor of psychology at San Jose State University, and a senior research scientist for the Research Institute for Advanced Computer Science (1988-1992). In 1993 he joined the staff of RECOM Technologies, Inc. to carry out advanced research and development in multimedia telecommunications for NASA's International Space Station, and, more recently, for an advanced air traffic control research simulator to be built at Ames.

Dr. Haines is the author or editor of six books on UFO themes, including: *UFO Phenomena and the Behavioral Scientist* (1969), *Observing UFOs* (1980), and *Close Encounters of the Fifth Kind* (1998).

Address: 325 Langton Ave.
            Los Altos, CA 94022
            U.S.A.

Richard Haines

POSITION STATEMENT: Although I do not yet have enough reliable information concerning the relevant characteristics of the UFO phenomenon with which to form a scientific judgment of its "core" identity, I do believe that the phenomenon is objectively real; i.e., I believe that the many thousands of eyewitnesses around the world are experiencing UFO phenomena in a manner very similar to the way any other human with normal sensory capabilities would perceive it if they happened to be present. And the wide variety of reported characteristics of UFOs suggests that there is also a cognitive (psychological?) component present which brings into play deeply submerged sub- or preconscious protosymbols lying largely dormant within most people. I also think that we will one day discover the phenomenon's "core" identity. When that day comes, we are likely to be in for some big surprises concerning the nature of reality and the infancy of our sciences.

—RICHARD F. HAINES

Hall, Richard H. (b. 1930). Richard Hall is a graduate (in philosophy) of Tulane University, New Orleans, Louisiana (1958), and is currently employed by a major publishing firm in the Washington, D.C., area. Among numerous other credits in the UFO field, he was assistant director of the National Investigations Committee on Aerial Phenomena (NICAP) from 1958 to 1967, and former editor of the *MUFON UFO Journal.*

Richard Hall

He is currently Director of Publications (and a Board Member) of MUFON; a National Board Member for the Fund for UFO Research; and Consulting Editor for the *International UFO Reporter (IUR)* (published by the J. Allen Hynek Center for UFO Studies, Chicago, Illinois). Hall was the compiler-editor of *The UFO Evidence*, published by NICAP in 1964, and the author of *Uninvited Guests: A Documented History of UFO Sightings, Alien Encounters, and Cover-Ups*, published by Aurora Press in 1988). He is presently compiling and editing *The UFO Evidence: Volume II: 1964-1993*, to be published by Scarecrow Press in 2001.

Address: 4418 39th St.
           Brentwood, MD 20722
           U.S.A.

POSITION STATEMENT: Among the hundreds of so-called "UFO reports" each year, a sizable fraction of those clearly observed by reputable witnesses remain unexplained—and difficult to explain in conventional terms. There is a modicum of physical evidence, radar cases, residual effects, and some films—and photographs in support of the unexplained cases. Collectively, these cases constitute a genuine scientific mystery, badly in need of well-supported, systematic investigation.

In answer to the skeptical objection that the alleged unexplained cases have not been thoroughly investigated, that is exactly my point. They should be. The circumstantial—and sometimes physical—evidence indicates that something real is going on for which no satisfactory explanation currently exists.

The available "theories" include: (1) Extraterrestrial, (a) visitors from another planet, (b) "time travelers," (c) gods or other not entirely physical beings from realms unknown; (2) Terrestrial, (a) mistaken observations of Earth technology or familiar events misidentified, (b) advanced secret technology, (c) psychic projections of the human mind, (d) hoaxes/imagination.

I reject (2-a) and (2-d) as inapplicable to the hard-core unexplained cases. Among the other choices, by Occam's razor, I prefer (1-a)—the so-called "nuts and bolts" visitors from elsewhere.

—RICHARD H. HALL

Harmonic 33   (A.W. Reed, 1968). New Zealand airline pilot Bruce Cathie, seeking an explanation for six of his own UFO sightings, writes about his discovery of a worldwide grid system set up by aliens in ancient times to power their spaceships using gravitational frequencies. He suspects that scientist Nikola Tesla uncovered the power grid's secrets, which were seized at his death by U.S. government officials who have since exploited this information.

—RANDALL FITZGERALD

harvest This is a central term used in *The RA Material* and other spiritually based ET channeled sources to denote the impending physical, energetic, and consciousness transformation on Earth. This global shift is predicted to occur during the time period of 2010-2013 A.D., after which the planet will enter a higher dimension of cosmic life. Geological upheaval, climatic and solar anomalies, increasing UFO visitation, socio-cultural stresses, and the entire range of global ET contacts are all believed to be due to the imminence of this major cycle change in human evolution.

This change is also alluded to by other mystic, indigenous, and New Age sources, including esoteric Christianity ("the Rapture, Ascension, Revelation, Kingdom of Heaven"), Judaism and Islam ("Return of the Messiah/ Imam Mahdi"), Hinduism ("end of the Kali Yuga"), Theosophy ("the Aquarian Age"), as well as the Mayans and Hopis ("the Fifth World"), Edgar Cayce, and Nostradamus. It is held that only those individuals who embrace love, compassion, and kindness to a sufficient degree will be able to remain in incarnation on the physical planet, after Earth enters its new cycle of evolution.

—SCOTT MANDELKER

Hesemann, Michael (b. 1964). One of Europe's leading UFO researchers, Michael Hesemann studied cultural anthropology and history at Göttingen University. Since 1984 he has published *Magazine 2000*, Europe's most popular magazine on the paranormal. His international bestsellers *The Cosmic Connection*, *Beyond Roswell* (with Philip Mantle), *UFOs: A Secret History*, and *The Fatima-Secret* were published in eighteen countries with a circulation of nearly a million copies.

Hesemann has produced several award-winning video documentaries (distributed in fifteen countries) and worked as a UFO expert and advisor for several TV programs in the U.S., U.K., Germany, Mexico, and Japan. He is an sssociate member of the Society for Scientific Exploration and the Israel Exploration Society.

He received honorary membership in the Italian Centro Ufologico Nazionale (C.U.N.) and was honored with the Colman Von Keviczky Medal of Hungarian UFOology. In 1989, Hesemann organized the world's largest UFO conference, "Dialogue with the Universe," with 1830 participants and 44 speakers in Frankfurt, Germany. It was the first time that Russian scientists, military, and UFO researchers presented their evidence to a Western audience. Because of his contacts in Russia, Hesemann was able to publish the KGB UFO files.

Hesemann has investigated UFO incidents in forty-four countries and has traveled more than 700,000 miles in search of answers. He has interviewed U.S. astronauts as well as Russian cosmonauts on their UFO experiences. He has lectured at international conferences in twenty-three countries, at dozens of universities, the United Nations, and was personally received by Pope John Paul II.

Hesemann's historical work on religious relics was greeted by the Pontiff with "admiration and appreciation . . . for your laborious research." Hesemann resides in Duesseldorf, Germany.

Address: An der Obererft 88
D-41464 Neuss
Germany

E-mail: hesemann@m-n-d.com
Web site: hesemann.m-n-d.com

POSITION STATEMENT: (1) After investigating the UFO phenomenon all over the world, after studying thousands of pages of released government documents, and inter-

Michael Hesemann

viewing eyewitnesses and insiders, including generals, intelligence officers, cosmonauts and astronauts, military and commercial pilots, I do not have the shadow of a doubt anymore that we are indeed visited by extraterrestrial intelligences. The evidence just does not allow another conclusion.

(2) We have to learn to deal with this situation and prepare for a contact. Studying the behavioral pattern of the phenomenon, I came to the conclusion that they are neither friend nor foe, but study our planet and civilization from a mainly scientific perspective. They are as curious to learn more about us, as we would love to study other human and humanoid civilizations.

Most probably the ETs have been here since the beginning of mankind. They, during our history, intervened in our evolution several times. Today, after the human race have become ''adults,'' they prefer to be non-intrusive, obviously because every interference would contaminate their research subject. Therefore, any approach must come from our side, by a common, international effort, e.g., through the United Nations.

(3) A contact with an extraterrestrial civilization is the greatest challenge for mankind in the Third Millennium. We would finally real-

ize that we are indeed not alone, what could cause a new Copernican revolution, a quantum leap in our thinking and perspective. We would finally realize that we are one mankind and all the small differences which separate humans from each other today—nationality, race, religion—would disappear. Only together can mankind explore the universe, our true home and destiny.

—MICHAEL HESEMANN

Higdon experience   Carl Higdon was elk hunting south of Rawlins, Wyoming, when he said he met a man from another planet. Higdon claims that the ''man,'' named ''Ausso,'' pointed a ''fingerlike'' appendage at him and, instantly, they were aboard a spaceship. The experience, which lasted from 4:00 P.M. to 6:30 P.M., supposedly involved a trip to Ausso's home planet, 163,000 ''light miles'' away, and Higdon's safe return to Earth.

It was a Friday night, October 25, 1974, at about 4 P.M. Carl Higdon (an oil driller, employed by the AM Well Services of Riverton, Wyoming) was hunting elk on the north edge of the Medicine Bow National Forest, when his bizarre experience began to unfold.

''I walked over this hill and saw five elk,'' Higdon said. ''I raised my rifle and fired, but the bullet only went about fifty feet and dropped.'' He went over, got the bullet, and tucked it into a fold in his canteen pouch. ''I heard a noise like a twig snapping and looked over to my right, and there in the shadow of the trees was this sort of man standing there.''

Higdon described the ''man'' as being six feet two inches tall and weighing approximately 180 pounds. He was dressed in a black suit and black shoes and wore a belt with a star in the middle and a yellow emblem below it. Higdon also said the man was quite bow-legged, had a slanted head, and no chin. His hair was thin and stood straight up on his head.

''He asked me if I was hungry and I said yes,'' Higdon said, ''so he tossed me some pills and I took one.'' Higdon commented that he didn't understand why he took the pills because ordinarily he doesn't even like to take an aspirin. The man had told him that the pills were "four-day" pills, apparently to slake his hunger. Higdon said the man called himself "Ausso" and asked Higdon if he'd like to go with him. Higdon replied "yes" and the man pointed an appendage which came out of his sleeve.

Higdon said he suddenly found himself in a transparent cubicle along with Ausso. He was sitting in a chair with "bands" around his arms (apparently holding him in the chair which resembled a high-backed "bucket seat") and a helmet-like apparatus on his head somewhat like a football helmet, except that it had two wires on top and two on the sides leading to the back. On a sort of console opposite his chair, Higdon said he saw three levers of different sizes which had letters on them and which Ausso manipulated.

Artist's conception of "Ausso" from Higdon's description

Higdon was unclear on the size of the cubicle. He said there was a mirror on the upper right, in which he could see the reflection of the live elk which seemed to be behind him in a "cage" or corral. They were still, not moving, just as they had been when he first spotted them before he encountered Ausso. He thought the cubicle was about seven feet square but couldn't account for the elk being there also.

When Ausso pointed his appendage at the largest lever it moved down and the cubicle felt as if it was moving. After they took off, Higdon said he saw a basketball-shaped object under the cubicle, which he took to be the Earth. There was another being in the cubicle who "just disappeared" when they landed. Ausso said they had traveled 163,000 "light miles."

Outside the cubicle, Higdon said, was a huge tower, perhaps ninety feet high with a brilliant, rotating light, and he heard a sound like that made by an electric razor. The light bothered his eyes considerably, and he put his hands over them.

Standing outside the tower were five human-appearing people: a gray-haired man of forty or fifty years old, a brown-haired girl about ten or eleven, a blond girl of thirteen or fourteen, a young man of seventeen or eighteen with brown hair, and a blond seventeen- or eighteen-year-old girl. They were dressed in ordinary clothing and appeared to be talking among themselves.

Ausso pointed his "hand" and they (Ausso and Higdon) moved into the tower and up an elevator to a room where he stood on a small platform and a "shield" moved out from the wall. Ausso was on the other side of it. The shield was "glassy" appearing, stayed in front of Higdon for what he estimated to be three or four minutes, then moved back in the wall.

Ausso then told Higdon he was *not what they needed* and they would take him back. The two moved out of the room to the elevator and then down to the main door. It seemed that all Ausso needed to do was to point his hand and they moved effortlessly.

Next, Higdon found himself back in the cubicle with Ausso, who was holding Higdon's gun. He said the gun was primitive and he wanted to keep it, but wasn't allowed to, and so he gave it back to Higdon. Then he pointed at the longest lever and Higdon found himself standing on a slope. His foot struck a loose rock and he fell, hurting his neck, head, and shoulder.

At this point Higdon didn't know who or where he was. He got up and walked past his pickup truck, which was sitting in a wooded area on a road with deep ruts. He walked along the track about a mile past the truck, then came back to the truck and heard a woman's voice. As he regained a little of his senses, he used the citizen's band radio to call for help. He told the woman he didn't know who or where he was. Authorities were notified, and Higdon was eventually found about 11:30 that night. He was dazed and confused and had difficulty recognizing his wife. The search party had a considerable problem retrieving Higdon's two-wheel-drive vehicle (it had to be towed as it could not navigate the rough road).

Higdon was brought to the Carbon County Memorial Hospital in Rawlins at 2:30 A.M. on the twenty-sixth. Besides the sore head, neck, and shoulder, his eyes were extremely bloodshot and they teared constantly. He had no appetite on Saturday, and his wife Margery had to force him to eat. On Sunday morning, however, he was ravenous and complained about the meager size of the hospital breakfast.

This, essentially, is Carl Higdon's account of his time from 4:15 P.M. on October 25, 1974, when he first spotted the five elk, until he called on the CB radio, at around 6:30 P.M., that evening.

Some foundation for his story is found in the testimony of the search-party members, who said Higdon's pickup truck could not have driven into or out of the area where it was found. Also, unidentified lights were seen near the area where Higdon was found before the searchers started driving out of the area, so the lights of the vehicles could not have accounted for the unidentified lights.

According to psychologist Dr. R. Leo Sprinkle, who investigated the case, Higdon has agreed to other interviews, as well as the use of hypnotic techniques for the purpose of obtaining further information about his experience. Sprinkle comments that: "Although the sighting of a single UFO witness often is difficult to evaluate, the indirect evidence supports the tentative conclusion that Carl Higdon is reporting sincerely the events which he experienced. Hopefully, further statements from other persons can be obtained to support the basic statement."

—CORAL & JIM LORENZEN

Higher Self This term is a translated from the Sanskrit word *Atman,* used by Hindus and in Western mysticism, to denote the essential, monadic core of the human body/mind/spirit. Metaphysical science holds that each of us is connected to an individualized, yet universal Higher Self, which possesses a full and complete knowledge of all our past events and future development. Many meditation practices and New Age teachers are concerned with the means by which we may contact Higher Self for guidance and to support personal healing and spiritual evolution.

—SCOTT MANDELKER

Hill abduction Barney and Betty Hill's "interrupted journey" was the first publicized time-lapse (or "missing time") UFO-abduction episode, and the first such case in which hypnosis was used to elicit hidden details of the experience.

THE ENCOUNTER

The Portsmouth, New Hampshire, couple was returning home from a vacation at Niagara Falls on the night of September 19-20, 1961. Barney, 39 (who died in 1969), worked as a postal clerk in Boston; while Betty, 41, was employed by the state as a child welfare worker.

As they drove south on U.S. 3 in northern New Hampshire, the Hills noticed a bright moving star-like object in the southwestern sky. The time was approximately 11 P.M.

Betty and Barney Hill

The object turned toward the car and then seemed to accompany it, at a distance, for the next 35 miles. The couple stopped now and then to observe the UFO through binoculars. As it drew closer, the light source appeared to be a spinning circular object describing an erratic, step-like path above the White Mountains.

In the vicinity of North Woodstock, the "object" came to a halt over an open area. When Barney stopped the car and got out, the UFO crossed the road ahead, from right to left, and hovered above a field next to the highway. Barney then proceeded into the field, halting periodically to view the unknown object through his binoculars. He could see a large, flat, disk-shaped craft with two rows of bluish-white glowing windows and a red light on each side.

According to Mr. Hill, eight or more humanoid figures were looking back at him. The "leader" of the group, in particular, both fas-

cinated and terrified him. As the disk descended toward Barney, all of the occupants except the leader started scurrying around, at which time the two red lights moved outward at opposite ends of the "craft." After the craft approached to within 100 feet or less, Barney panicked. He dashed to the car and took off down the highway.

The couple recalled hearing "beeping" sounds that vibrated the car twice—once after they left the UFO, and again in the Ashland area some 30 miles farther south. Oddly, the Hills had no memory of the interval between the two sets of "beeps" nor why they arrived home at least two hours later than expected. Other peculiarities were noted as well.

BETTY'S DREAMS

About ten days after this experience, Betty said she had a series of dreams in which she and Barney were captured by the entities and examined on board their craft. To Mrs. Hill, the dreams indicated her recall of a real abduction that must have occurred following their initial encounter along Highway 3.

Betty reported the sighting to nearby Pease Air Force Base and to the National Investigations Committee on Aerial Phenomena. As a New England advisor to NICAP, I was asked to interview the New Hampshire couple. Just one month after the encounter, I questioned the two witnesses for six hours and came away impressed with them and their incredible story. (Had I known at the time the historic significance of this prototypical UFO abduction, I would have handled many aspects of my investigation quite differently.)

THE ABDUCTION

Over the next two years, Barney Hill experienced anxieties and physical ailments—possibly connected with his UFO encounter—and Betty became even more concerned about her capture dreams. Eventually the couple was referred to Boston psychiatrist Benjamin Simon for treatment. In 1964 Dr. Simon hypnotized

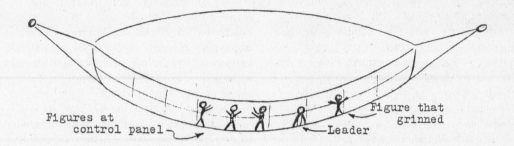

Figures at
control panel ⌐

⌐Leader

Figure that
grinned

Drawing of the UFO by Walter Webb, based on Barney Hill's original sketch

the Hills separately, and found that both husband and wife related similar stories of being kidnapped and examined by the UFO beings. (I have heard all eleven hours of the taped testimony.)

Barney recalled that after hearing the first "beeps," he was directed telepathically to drive to a wooded area where his car stalled. A group of alien figures approached the vehicle and then led the couple into the landed UFO. The beings were described as about five feet tall with large gray heads, enormous slanted eyes, small nose, and narrow mouth.

THE EXAMINATIONS

Betty said she was left with the leader and an examiner who proceeded to inspect her arm under a big lens and to take samples from her skin, ear, hair, and nails. Instruments used in the examination included a skin-scraper, hand-held light, a cluster of needles (that touched the skin all over her body), and a long needle inserted into her navel.

Explaining that the needle was a "pregnancy test," the examiner seemed surprised at the pain this caused. Betty said the pain disap-

Artist's depiction of the alien humanoids, as described by Betty and Barney Hill

peared when the leader passed his hands over her eyes. When Mrs. Hill asked the leader where he was from, he exhibited a three-dimensional (holographic) "star map." According to Betty, it was explained to her that the curved lines connecting twelve of the glowing dots were routes from the leader's home star system to other stars. Under Simon's posthypnotic suggestion, Mrs. Hill later drew the star map as she remembered it.

Barney Hill, who was led to another room, recalled lying on a table with his eyes closed. He said his exam included the withdrawal of sperm and rectal samples, as well as the removal of skin cells.

After their exams, the Hills were led to their car where they watched the alien ship depart. Memories of the abduction began to fade as they drove back to the main highway. Near Ashland the couple said they heard the second set of "beeps," and conscious memory returned.

REALITY OR FANTASY

It was Dr. Simon's belief that the initial encounter probably involved an unidentified military aircraft, while the abduction scenario happened only in Betty's dreams—a fantasy she shared with her husband. Simon, however, had no interest at all in the UFO subject, refusing even to read my own case material submitted to him. While I do agree that contaminated testimony between Barney and Betty probably played some role in the retelling, I remain convinced to this day of the reality of both stages of the UFO encounter.

BETTY'S STAR MAP AND THE FISH MODEL

In 1972 Marjorie Fish, an Ohio schoolteacher, finished a six-year search to find matching stars for the ones in Betty Hill's star map. After constructing more than 20 three-

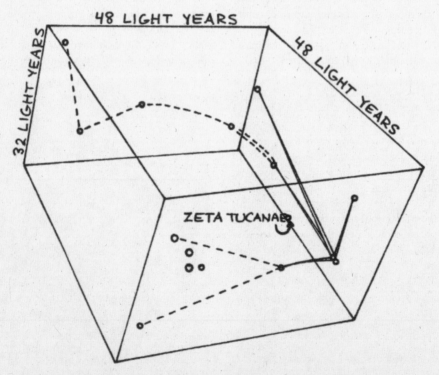

Oblique view of the Fish model, drawn from a photo by Marjorie Fish

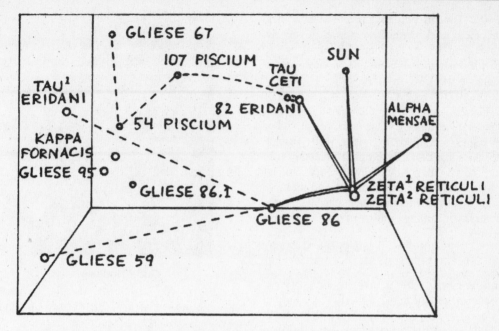

Front view of the Fish model. Compare with Betty's drawing shown below.

dimensional models of the Sun's neighborhood out to 65 light-years, and spending hundreds of hours photographing and inspecting models from all angles, Fish found what she believed were the 12 linked stars in Betty's drawing, including the home base of the Hill aliens (Zeta Reticuli) and our sun.

At the outset, Marjorie Fish herself had expected to discover many random patterns among the stars that would resemble the Hill map. Much to her surprise, only one unique set of stars emerged that combined: (1) a reasonable match with Betty's star map; (2) all lines in the map connecting solely to stars that were good candidates for life-bearing planets; (3) all of the life-supporting candidate stars found in the volume of space encompassing the Hill network stars were included in Betty Hill's map; and (4) all stars in the Hill pattern were connected to each other in a logical travel sequence from star-to-star—the base star being linked only with the nearest stars having spectral classes that favor life.

I spent six hours with Marjorie in 1974, discussing her work and reviewing her data.

From my own personal inspection of the model, I can attest that the star pattern she selected in her model did indeed match amazingly well the one in Betty Hill's map.

Returning home with copies of her voluminous notes and photographs, I checked her data in six star catalogs and found no errors. The significance of Fish's prodigious research has so far gone unrecognized by the scientific com-

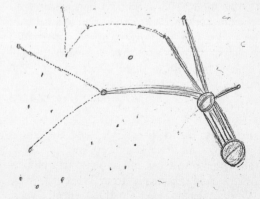

Alien star map, as drawn by Betty Hill
under posthypnotic suggestion

munity. Though but an amateur astronomer, Marjorie's work certainly deserves to be acknowledged by professionals, because someday the Fish model could be a vital key in unlocking the UFO mystery.

Despite the recent discovery that several of the Fish/Hill stars are double (damaging Fish's single-star criterion), Fish's selected stellar candidates still hold up rather well. Double stars do not necessarily prohibit planetary life. Marjorie's model should now be reexamined in light of the Hipparcos satellite and its more accurate distance measurements to thousands of stars—including those in the Fish/Hill network.

—WALTER N. WEBB

Hollow Earth, The (University Press, 1969). Raymond Bernard thinks a worldwide conspiracy exists to suppress knowledge that the Earth is hollow and the place where UFOs, driven by survivors of Atlantis, originate. Bernard heads a European branch of the Rosicrucians and claims he was told by extraterrestrial visitors to write this book to prepare humans for their coming.

—RANDALL FITZGERALD

Home of the Gods, The (Editions Robert Laffont, 1972). Andrew Tomas opines that the residents of Atlantis were descendants of extraterrestrials and their civilization was destroyed by the Biblical flood. Some Atlanteans escaped the flood in spacecraft, others fled to a network of underground tunnels, chambers and hidden valleys, from where they occasionally still emerge in UFOs to share "their wisdom with those who are ready for it."

—RANDALL FITZGERALD

Hopkins, Budd (b. 1931). Budd Hopkins is probably the world's best-known UFO-abduction researcher and an important pioneer in the field. Originally from Wheeling, West Virginia, he attended Oberlin College, where he studied Art and Art History, graduating in 1953. That year he moved to New York City,

Budd Hopkins

where he has lived ever since, with summers spent at his home on Cape Cod.

As a painter and sculptor, Hopkins has had over fifty one-person shows in the United States and Europe. His work is in the permanent collections of many prestigious museums and art galleries in New York, Washington, San Francisco, and elsewhere. These include the Solomon R. Guggenheim, the Whitney Museum of American Art, the Museum of Modern Art, the Metropolitan Museum, the Hirshhorn Museum, the Corcoran Gallery, the San Francisco Museum of Modern Art, the British Museum, and many other distinguished institutions.

Hopkins has received a fellowship grant from the National Endowment for the Arts, a Guggenheim Fellowship, and other distinguished awards, and his work has been widely and favorably reviewed. As a writer on the subject of modern art, Hopkins has contributed articles on art to magazines such as *Art Forum*, *Arts*, and *Art in America*.

Hopkins had his first UFO experience in 1964. On a sunny afternoon on Cape Cod, he and two others had a daylight UFO sighting, which sparked his interest in this subject.

In 1975, a neighborhood friend described a UFO landing and sample-gathering occupants he had witnessed in a New Jersey Park, across the Hudson River from Manhattan. This was Hopkins's first extensive investigation, and in 1976 he published an account of this case in a New York newspaper, *The Village Voice.* The case was widely publicized, and among the many ensuing reports Hopkins received were several that included tantalizing accounts of "missing time."

With the help of veteran UFO researcher Ted Bloecher and several mental health professionals, Hopkins began to investigate these accounts in which previously hidden UFO abduction experiences came to light. This research led to his first book, *Missing Time* published in 1981. In it, Hopkins presented several patterns heretofore unreported in the abduction literature. Among them were:

1. The potentially widespread nature of the (covert) abduction phenomenon, in which the abductees may have virtually no conscious recollection of sighting a UFO, observing occupants, and so on.
2. Physical sequelae, such as wounds, bruises and other lesions often resulting from these abductions.
3. Repeated abductions, whereby an individual may be abducted again and again, as if he/she were the object of an ongoing systematic study.
4. Screen memories, apparently imposed by the aliens, in which a more palatable image (such as an owl or a deer) was substituted for images of the aliens themselves.
5. Evidence that abductions were carried out in families, seemingly across the same genetic stock.

Hopkins's second book, *Intruders,* was published in 1987, and presented the then radical notion that the central goal of the UFO occupants was to create a hybrid mix of alien and human DNA. The accounts in *Intruders* detailed processes of artificial insemination, ova and sperm sampling, and the systematic removal of hybrid fetuses. *Intrud-*

ers was widely read, translated into many languages, and was the subject of a CBS miniseries. It remains one of the most influential books on the subject of UFO abductions ever written.

In 1996, Hopkins published his third book, *Witnessed,* about an abduction that took place in New York City in 1989, and was witnessed by a number of people including government officials and an important international leader. The incident was apparently a deliberate demonstration by the aliens of their power, and it remains the clearest account of their involvement in human political affairs.

Hopkins has also detailed several other previously unnoticed abduction patterns, such as:

1. Alien co-option, the "taking over" of a human to function in an abduction as if he/she was an ally of the aliens, not the other abducted humans.

2. The "Mickey-Baby Ann" phenomenon, in which aliens occasionally abduct children who do not know one another, putting them together from time to time to "bond," as if the aliens are studying the formation of human romantic relationships. Many such cases have since been reported.

Hopkins lectures widely around the world on his research findings, and—as founder and director of The Intruders Foundation—continues to lead the way in the field of UFO-abduction research.

Address: P.O. Box 30233
            New York, N.Y. 10011
            U.S.A.

E-mail: ebhopkins@aol.com

Web site: www.spacelab.net

Hudson Valley (New York) UFO sightings

Spectacular sightings of a triangular or

boomerang-shaped UFO that has seemingly haunted the Hudson River Valley (along the border of New York and Connecticut) from 1983 to the present day.

The Hudson Valley of New York is located about thirty miles north of New York City and is one of the most densely populated areas in the country. This area of New York is rich in legend, and tales of unusual happenings date back to colonial times. The home of the infamous headless horseman from Washington Irving's *The Legend of Sleepy Hollow* is located in the heart of Hudson Valley. Now, many residents of southern New York report encounters of a different kind—sightings of a giant UFO that they say is not of this Earth.

During the evening of March 23, 1983, thousands of people from all walks of life reported that they had seen an object larger than a football field pass over the highways and their homes. Bewildered witnesses said they saw an object that was solid in structure and made up of very dark gray materials. The UFO was described as having rows of multicolored lights attached to a triangular shape, as it moved slowly across the night sky. The sightings continued on a regular basis, and in 1984, at 10:20 P.M., the object was videotaped in Brewster, New York. At this time also the UFO was witnessed by thousands, as it silently drifted over five counties of New York and Connecticut.

Shortly after the object was videotaped, the giant UFO was reported hovering over the Indian Point Nuclear Reactor located on the shore of the Hudson River near Peekskill, New York, at 10:30 P.M. The object was witnessed by State Police and twelve New York State Power Authority Police officers. They reported that the UFO hovered three-hundred feet over reactor Number Three for fifteen minutes. They said it was triangular in shape with a network of grids underneath and was the size of three football fields. The object then slowly moved across the Hudson River to Rockland County, where hundreds of residents and police officers saw it. Later, a spokesman from the Indian Point Reactor Complex confirmed the sightings, but insisted that the object in no way affected plant operations. This was the first time a UFO was officially confirmed as being over or near a nuclear reactor.

One of the official explanations for the sightings made by the FAA and the Air Force was that the UFO was nothing more than a group of prankster pilots flying in close formation. The videotape of the UFO was analyzed twice by imaging scientists at the Jet Propulsion Laboratory in Pasadena, California. Their conclusions were that the lights on the videotape were not individual objects, but rather one large object. The scientists were unable to identify the UFO, however, as a conventional aircraft; and so it remains a genuine "unknown" to this day.

Artist's conception of
the Hudson Valley UFO

Although much of the UFO activity has died down during the late nineties, many people in the area claim to have close encounters with an alien intelligence that they feel is the intelligence from the UFO. Where the UFO comes from remains a mystery, and without a doubt generations from now it will become part of the area's local folklore.

As one witness (an IBM executive) said in an interview: "This thing was a city in the sky, it was not from this world and airplanes it was not!"

—PHILIP J. IMBROGNO

NOTE: For more information, see the author's books: *Contact of the Fifth Kind* (Llewellyn, 1997) and *Night Siege: The Hudson Valley UFO Sightings* (Llewellyn, 1998, second edition, expanded and revised).

Humanoids, The   (Henry Regnery, 1969). Edited by Charles Bowen. Eleven essayists survey more than 300 reports of spacecraft landing and disgorging alien occupants. These occupants are of every imaginable shape, size, and color—from giants over eight feet tall to tiny dwarfs—leading Bowen, the former editor of Britain's *Flying Saucer Review* magazine, to conclude that "UFOs and their occupants are in the eyes of the beholder."
—RANDALL FITZGERALD

J. Allen Hynek

Hynek, J. Allen (1910-1986). Dubbed "The Galileo of UFOlogy" by *Newsweek* magazine (November 1977), Dr. J. Allen Hynek was considered by his colleagues to be the preeminent authority on UFO phenomena. Hynek became involved with UFOs as Scientific Consultant to the U.S. Air Force from 1948 to 1968. He was the first speaker to present testimony at the 1968 hearing on UFOs held by the House Committee on Science and Astronautics and later appeared before the United Nations to support the proposed establishment of an agency to conduct and coordinate research into UFOs and related phenomena.

In the early 1970s, Hynek coined the phrase "close encounters of the third kind," and acted as technical advisor to director Steven Spielberg on the movie of the same name. Hynek founded CUFOS (the Center for UFO Studies) in 1973 and served as its director until his death in 1986.

For more than twenty years Dr. Hynek served as astronomical consultant to the U.S. Air Force Projects Sign and Blue Book, which processed and studied UFO sightings reported to Air Force bases. He came to Northwestern University in 1960 from his position as associate director of the Smithsonian Astrophysical Observatory in Cambridge, Massachusetts, where he was in charge of the U.S. Optical Satellite Tracking Program. He was responsible for the precise tracking of man's first artificial satellite, as well as for some 270 volunteer "Moonwatch" stations in various countries.

A native of Chicago, Hynek has had many illustrious posts in his scientific career. After receiving his doctorate in astronomy from the University of Chicago, he was, in turn: professor of astronomy and director of the McMillin Observatory at Ohio State University; supervisor of technical reports at the Applied Physics Laboratory of the Johns Hopkins University during World War II; assistant dean of the Graduate School at Ohio State and professor of astronomy after the war; and lecturer in astronomy at Harvard during the four years he was associate director of the Smithsonian's Observatory in Cambridge; after which he joined Northwestern University as chairman of the Department of Astronomy and director of the Dearborn Observatory, posts he held for fifteen years. During his tenure he was instrumental in the founding of the Lindheimer Astronomical Research Center and served as its first director.

Dr. Hynek has published numerous technical papers in astrophysics and is the author of several textbooks. He is also the author of *The UFO Experience: A Scientific Inquiry* (1972), *The Hynek Report of UFOs* (1977), and co-author (with Jacques Vallée) of *The Edge of Reality* (1975).

POSITION STATEMENT: In an interview for *Fate* magazine (June 1976 issue), Hynek stated his position on the UFO problem as follows:

> The conclusion I've come to after all these years is that first of all, the subject is much more complex than any of us imagined. It has paranormal aspects but certainly it has very real physical aspects, too. The attitude we're taking in the Center for UFO Studies is that since we're going to have scientists involved, we will push the physical approach as hard and far as we can—instrumentation, physical evidence, photographs, radar records. If we are finally forced by the evidence itself to go into the paranormal, then we will.

And in another interview, he expressed these views (from *Lumières dans la Nuit,* issue No. 168 of October 1977):

> [The extraterrestrial] theory runs up against a very big difficulty, namely, that we are seeing too many UFOs. The Earth is only a spot of dust in the Universe. Why should it be honored with so many visits?
> INTERVIEWER: Then what is your hypothesis?
> HYNEK: I am more inclined to think in terms of something metaterrestrial, a sort of parallel reality.
> INTERVIEWER: And what then is your personal conviction?
> HYNEK: I have the impression that the UFOs are announcing a change that is coming soon in our scientific paradigms. I am very much afraid that UFOs are related to certain psychic phenomena. And if I say "I am very much afraid," this is because in our Center at Evanston we are trying to

study this problem from the angle of the physical sciences.

> . . . But it would be absurd to follow up only one path to the exclusion of all others.

This theory was repeated again, when Hynek was interviewed by *Newsweek:* "UFO's, he says, may be psychic phenomena and the 'aliens' may not come from outer space but from a 'parallel reality'." (November 21, 1977)

In yet another interview (for the April 3, 1978, issue of *Today's Student*), Hynek added that:

> Certainly the phenomenon has psychic aspects. I don't talk about them very much because to a general audience the words "psychic" and "occult" have bad overtones. They say, "Aw, it's all crazy." But the fact is that there are psychic things; for instance, UFOs seem to materialize and dematerialize. There are people who've had UFO experiences who've claimed to have developed psychic ability. There have been reported cases of hearings in close encounters and there have been reported cases of precognition, where people had foreknowledge or forewarning that they were going to see something. There has been a change of outlook, a change of philosophy of persons' lives. Now, you see, those are rather tricky things to talk about openly, but it's there.
>
> Many people, like Jacques Vallée and I, to some extent, feel that it might be a conditioning process.

(Note: The biographical portion of this entry was written by Ronald Story.)

Hynek UFO Report, The (Dell, 1977). Dr. J. Allen Hynek concludes in this book that whatever UFOs are, they want to play games with us and lead us on a confusing chase. He also demonstrates from his own experiences as a consultant to the Air Force's Project Blue Book that the U.S. Air Force intentionally deceived and lied to the American public about its UFO investigations.

—RANDALL FITZGERALD

hypnosis, use of, in UFO investigations

Hypnosis has often been discussed and used as one tool available to the UFO investigator, as well as to the criminal investigator and, of course, the psychological therapist. The history of hypnosis is characterized by trends from physical to physiological to psychological explanations of hypnotic phenomena. Although many theories about the nature of hypnosis have been advanced, no one theory has been accepted by all theorists. Despite many differences in theoretical positions, most researchers describe hypnosis in terms of psychological processes which are related to interpersonal situations and to personal abilities of participants.

Good hypnotic subjects are described as persons who (1) can respond to suggestions for deep relaxation, (2) have vivid imaginations, (3) are able to minimize temporarily their awareness of "external" reality and, (4) can maximize temporarily an alternate or "internal" reality. These persons can learn to alter their perceptions of "pain," "time," "memory," etc. Autohypnosis, or self-hypnosis, seems to be the primary experience, with assistance from a guide or teacher as a possible facilitator in the process. There seems to be no danger inherent in the use of hypnotic processes, but there may be a risk in accepting and following suggestions from an inexperienced or poorly trained hypnotist.

Experimental studies have yielded results which cast doubt on the view that hypnotic time-regression (age regression) procedures can cause a participant to "relive" the experiences of earlier events. On the other hand, these studies have shown that many individuals have the potential to use hypnotic suggestions to increase their recall of "forgotten" memories.

Along with other controversies about the UFO problem, there are disagreements among UFO investigators about the value of hypnotic time-regression procedures in the investigation of UFO experiences. Despite the difficulties in evaluating information which is obtained during hypnotic sessions, most investigators agree that hypnotic procedures may be useful in exploring the available testimony of UFO witnesses.

A list of possible uses of hypnotic procedures in UFO investigations could include the following activities:

1. Assisting UFO witnesses to relax deeply and to reduce any anxiety which may be associated with their UFO experiences.
2. Instructing UFO witnesses to elicit ideomotor responses (by use of the pendulum technique or through finger-and-thumb responses) for communication with the "subconscious mind," or subconscious processes.
3. Encouraging UFO witnesses to release any repressed memory about an amnesic period, or "loss of time" experience during a UFO sighting, including possible memories of apparent abduction, examination, and/or experimentation by UFO occupants.
4. Checking the consistency of conscious and subconscious information from the UFO witnesses, and comparing these claims with information about the backgrounds of witnesses and other information about their UFO experiences.
5. Training interested persons to obtain possible "psychic impressions," e.g., clairvoyant impressions of UFO occupants, telepathic communications with UFO occupants, and precognitive impressions or impressions of future events.

The information that has been obtained from hypnotic sessions with participants who claim UFO experiences, including abduction and communication with UFO occupants, is tentative and inconclusive. At present, there seem to be five general hypotheses to account for these reports:

1. *UFO witnesses are lying.* Evidence to support this hypothesis might be obtained by conducting background investigations and polygraph examinations.

2. *UFO witnesses are experiencing neurotic or psychotic reactions.* Evidence for this hypothesis might be obtained by conducting psychiatric evaluations.

3. *UFO witnesses are submitting information which stems from fantasies or daydreams.* Evidence for this hypothesis might be obtained from psychological evaluation of the witnesses, and from comparisons of their experiences with other information about UFO reports.

4. *UFO witnesses are submitting information which is desired by the UFO investigator.* Evidence for this hypothesis can be obtained by employing consultants in hypnosis who do not share the same biases about the significance and meaning of UFO experiences.

5. *UFO witnesses are submitting reliable and/or valid information.* Evidence for this hypothesis can be obtained by comparing the testimony of UFO witnesses with the pattern of evidence obtained from other UFO investigations.

In conclusion, hypnotic procedures offer a method for exploring some of the puzzling areas of UFO phenomena. Hypnotic techniques can be used for a variety of tasks, depending upon the needs and the interests of UFO witnesses, UFO investigators, and consultants in hypnosis. Despite the difficulties of evaluating information obtained from hypnotic procedures, the experienced UFO investigator should encourage the UFO witness to consider possible participation in hypnotic sessions for further investigation of his or her UFO experience.

—R. Leo Sprinkle

ANOTHER VIEW: In France in the 1770s, when Mesmerism was in its heyday, the king appointed two commissions to investigate Mesmer's activities. The commissions included such eminent men as Benjamin Franklin, Antonine Lavoisier, and Jean-Sylvain Bailly, the French astronomer. After months of study the report of the commissioners concluded that it was imagination, not magnetism, that accounted for the swooning, trance-like rigidity of Mesmer's subjects. Surprisingly enough, this conclusion is still closer to the truth about hypnosis than most of the modern definitions found in today's textbooks.

So-called authorities still disagree about "hypnosis." But whether it is or is not a "state," there is common and widespread agreement among all the major disputants that "hypnosis" is a situation in which people set aside critical judgment (without abandoning it entirely) and engage in make-believe and fantasy; that is, they use their imagination. (Sarbin and Andersen, 1967; Barber, 1969; Gill and Brenman, 1959; Hilgard, 1977)

Josephine Hilgard (1979) refers to hypnosis as "imaginative involvement," Sarbin and Coe (1972) term it "believed-in imaginings," Spanos and Barber (1974) call it "involvement in suggestion-related imaginings," and Sutcliffe (1961) has gone so far as to characterize the hypnotizable individual as someone who is "deluded in a descriptive, nonpejorative sense" and he sees the hypnotic situation as an arena in which people who are skilled at make-believe and fantasy are provided with the opportunity and the means to do what they enjoy doing and what they are able to do especially well. Even more recently Perry, Laurence, Nadon, and Labelle (1986) concluded that "abilities such as imagery/imagination, absorption, disassociation, and selective attention underlie high hypnotic responsivity in yet undetermined combinations." The same authors, in another context dealing with past-lives regression, also concluded that "it should be expected that any material provided in age regression (which is at the basis of reports of reincarnation) may be fact or fantasy, and it is most likely an admixture of both." The authors further report that such regression material is colored by issues of confabulation, memory creation, inadvertent cueing, and the regressee's current psychological needs.

CONFABULATION

Because of its universality, it is quite surprising that the phenomenon of confabulation is not better known. Confabulation, or the tendency of ordinary, sane individuals to confuse fact with fiction and to report fantasized events as actual occurrences, has surfaced in just about every situation in which a person has attempted to remember very specific details from the past. A classic and amusing example occurs in the movie *Gigi*, in the scene where Maurice Chevalier and Hermione Gingold compare memories of their courtship in the song "I Remember It Well." We remember things not the way they really were but the way we would have liked them to have been.

The work of Elizabeth Loftus and others over the past decade has demonstrated that the human memory works not like a tape recorder but more like the village storyteller—i.e., it is both creative and *recreative*. We can and we do easily forget. We blur, shape, erase, and change details of the events in our past. Many people walk around daily with heads full of "fake memories." The unreliability of "eyewitness testimony" is not only legendary but well documented.

All of this is further complicated and compounded by the impact of suggestions provided by the hypnotist—supposedly "regressing" the subject—and the social-demand characteristics of the typical hypnotic situation. Under such conditions, there is little wonder that the resulting "recall" on the part of the regressee bears no resemblance to the truth. *In fact, the regressee often does not know what the truth is.*

Confabulation shows up without fail in nearly every context in which hypnosis is employed, including the forensic area. Thus it is not surprising that most states have no legal precedents on the use of hypnotic testimony. Furthermore, many state courts have begun to limit testimony from hypnotized witnesses or to follow the guidelines laid down by the American Medical Association in 1985 to assure that witnesses' memories are not contaminated by the hypnosis itself. For not only do we translate beliefs into memories when we are wide awake, but in the case of hypnotized witnesses with few specific memories, the hypnotist may unwittingly suggest memories and create a witness with a number of crucial and vivid recollections of events that never happened, i.e., pseudo-memories. It may turn out that the recent Supreme Court decision allowing the individual states limited use of hypnotically aided testimony may not be in the best interests of those who seek the truth. Even in their decision the judges recognized that hypnosis may often produce incorrect recollections and unreliable testimony.

There have also been a number of clinical and experimental demonstrations of the creation of pseudo-memories that have subsequently come to be believed as veridical. Hilgard (1981) implanted a false memory of an experience connected with a bank robbery that never occurred. His subject found the experience so vivid that he was able to select from a series of photographs a picture of the man he thought had committed the robbery. At another time, Hilgard deliberately assigned two concurrent—though spatially different—life experiences to the same person and regressed him at separate times to that date. The individual subsequently gave very accurate accounts of both experiences, so that anyone believing in reincarnation who reviewed the two accounts would conclude the man really had lived the two assigned lives.

In a number of other experiments designed to measure eyewitness reliability, Loftus (1979) found that details supplied by others invariably contaminated the memory of the eyewitness. People's hair changed color, "stop" signs became "yield" signs, yellow convertibles turned to red sedans, the left side of the street became the right side, and so on. The results of these studies led her to conclude, "It may well be that the legal notion of an independent recollection is a psychological impossibility." As for hypnosis, she says: "There's no way even the most sophisticated hypnotist can tell the difference between a memory that is real and one that's created. If a person is hypnotized and highly suggestible and false information is implanted in his mind, it may get embedded even more strongly. One psychologist tried to use a polygraph to distinguish between real and phony memory, but it didn't work. Once someone has constructed a memory, he comes to believe it himself.''

CUEING

Without a doubt, inadvertent cueing also plays a major role in UFO-abduction fantasies. The hypnotist unintentionally gives away to the person being regressed exactly what response is wanted. This was most clearly shown in an experimental study of hypnotic age regression by R. M. True in 1949. He found that 92 percent of his subjects regressed to the day of their tenth birthday, and could accurately recall the day of the week on which it fell. He also found the same thing for 84 percent of his subjects for their fourth birthday. Other investigators, however, were unable to duplicate True's findings. When True was questioned by Martin Orne about his experiment, he discovered that the editors of *Science,* where his report had appeared, altered his procedure section without his prior consent. True, Orne discovered, had inadvertently cued his subjects by following the unusual technique of asking them, "Is it Monday? Is it Tuesday? Is it Wednesday?" etc., and he monitored their responses by using a perpetual desk calendar in full view of all his subjects. Further evidence of the prevalence and importance of such cueing came from a study by O'Connell, Shor, and Orne (1970). They found that in an existing group of four-year-olds, not a single one knew what day of the week it was. The reincarnation literature is also replete with examples of such inadvertent cueing. Ian Wilson (1981), for example, has shown that hypnotically elicited reports of being reincarnated vary as a direct function of the hypnotist's belief about reincarnation. Finally, Laurence, Nadon, Nogrady, and Perry (1986) have shown that pseudo-memories were elicited also by inadvertent cueing in the use of hypnosis by the police.

As for advertent, or *deliberate,* cueing, one of my own studies offers a clear example. Sixty undergraduates divided into three groups of twenty each were hypnotized and age-regressed to previous lifetimes. Before each hypnosis session, however, suggestions very favorable to and supportive of past-life and reincarnation beliefs were given to one group; neutral and noncommittal statements about past lives were given to the second group; and skeptical and derogatory statements about past lives were given to the third group. The results clearly showed the effects of these cues and suggestions. Subjects in the first group showed the most past-life regressions and the most past-life productions; subjects in the third group showed the least. (Baker, 1982)

Regression subjects take cues as to how they are to respond from the person doing the regressions and asking the questions. If the hypnotist is a believer in UFO abductions, the odds are heavily in favor of him eliciting UFO-abductee stories from his volunteers.

FANTASY-PRONE PERSONALITIES AND PSYCHOLOGICAL NEEDS

"Assuming that all you have said thus far *is* true," the skeptical observer might ask, "why would hundreds of ordinary, mild-mannered, unassuming citizens suddenly go off the deep end and turn up with cases of amnesia and then, when under hypnosis, all report nearly identical experiences?" First, the abductees are not as numerous as we are led to believe; and, second, even though bestselling UFO-abduction authors Whitley Strieber and Budd Hopkins go to great lengths to emphasize the diversity of the people who report these events, they are much more alike than these taxonomists declare. In an afterword to Hopkins's *Missing Time,* a psychologist named Aphrodite Clamar raises exactly this question and then adds, "All of these people seem quite ordinary in the psychological sense—*although they have not been subjected to the kind of psychological testing that might provide a deeper understanding of their personalities.''* (emphasis added). And herein lies the problem. If these abductees were given this sort of intensive diagnostic testing, it is highly likely that many similarities would emerge—particularly an unusual personality pattern that Wilson and Barber (1983) have categorized as ''fantasy-prone.'' In an important but much neglected article, they report in some detail their discovery of a group of excellent hypnotic subjects with unusual fantasy abilities. In their words:

Although this study provided a broader understanding of the kind of life experiences that may underlie the ability to be an excellent hypnotic subject, it has also led to a serendipitous finding that has wide implication for all of psychology—it has shown that there exists a small group of individuals (possibly 4% of the population) who fantasize a large part of the time, who typically ''see,'' ''hear,'' ''smell,'' and ''touch'' and fully experience what they fantasize; and who can be labeled fantasy-prone personalities. (Wilson and Barber, 1983)

Wilson and Barber also stress that such individuals experience a reduction in orientation to time, place, and person that is characteristic of hypnosis or trance during their daily lives whenever they are deeply involved in a fantasy. They also have experiences during their daily ongoing lives that resemble the classic hypnotic phenomena. In other words, the behavior we would normally call ''hypnotic'' is exhibited by these fantasy-prone types (FPs) all the time. In Wilson and Barber's words: ''When we give them 'hypnotic suggestions,' such as suggestions for visual and auditory hallucinations, negative hallucinations, age regression, limb rigidity, anesthesia, and sensory hallucinations, we are asking them to do for us the kind of thing they can do independently of us in their daily lives.''

The reason we do not run into these types more often is that they have learned long ago to be highly secretive and private about their fantasy lives. Whenever the FPs do encounter a hypnosis situation it provides them with a social situation in which they are encouraged to do, and are rewarded for doing, what they usually do only in secrecy and in private. Wilson and Barber also emphasize that regression and the reliving of previous experiences is something that virtually all the FPs do naturally in their daily lives. When they recall the past, they relive it to a surprisingly vivid extent, and they all have vivid memories of their experiences extending back to their early years.

Fantasy-prone individuals also show up as mediums, psychics, and religious visionaries. They are also the ones who have many realistic ''out-of-body'' experiences and prototypic ''near-death'' experiences.

In spite of the fact that many such extreme types show FP characteristics, the overwhelming majority of FPs fall within the broad range of ''normal functioning.'' It is totally inappropriate to apply a psychiatric diagnosis to them. In Wilson and Barber's words: ''It needs to be strongly emphasized that our subjects with a propensity for hallucinations are as well adjusted as our comparison group or the average person. It appears that the life experiences and skill developments that underlie the ability of hallucinatory fantasy are more or less independent of the kinds of life experience that leads to pathology.'' In general, FPs are ''normal'' people who function as well as others and who are as well adjusted, competent, and satisfied or dissatisfied as everyone else.

Anyone familiar with the the fantasy-prone personality who reads Whitley Strieber's book *Communion* will experience an immediate shock of recognition. Strieber is a classic example of the genre: he is easily hypnotized; he is amnesiac; he has vivid memories of his early life, body immobility and rigidity, a very religious background, a very active fantasy life (he is a writer of occult and highly imaginative novels); he has unusually strong sensory experiences—particularly smells and sounds—and vivid dreams. But even more remarkable are the correspondences between Strieber's alien encounters and the typical hypnopompic hallucinations to be discussed shortly.

It is perfectly clear, therefore, why most of the UFO abductees, when given cursory examinations by psychiatrists and psychologists, would turn out to be ordinary, normal citizens as sane as themselves. It is also evident why the elaborate fantasies woven in fine cloth from the now universally familiar UFO-abduction fable—a fable known to every man, woman, and child newspaper reader or movie-goer in the nation—would have so much in common, so much consistency in the telling. Any one of us, if asked to pretend that he had been kidnapped by aliens from outer space or another dimension, would make up a story that would vary little, either in its details or in the supposed motives of the abductors, from the stories told by any and all of the kidnap victims reported by Hopkins. As for the close encounters of the third kind and conversations with the little gray aliens described in *Communion* and *Intruders,* again, our imaginative tales would be remarkably similar in plot, dialogue, description, and characterization. The means of transportation would be saucer-shaped; the aliens would be small, humanoid, two-eyed, and gray, white, or tan. The purpose of their visits would be: (1) to save our planet; (2) to find a better home for themselves; (3) to end nuclear war and the threat we pose to the peaceful life in the rest of the galaxy; (4) to bring us knowledge and enlightenment; and (5) to increase their knowledge and understanding of other forms of intelligent life. In fact, the fantasy-prone abductees' stories would be much more credible if some of them, at least, reported the aliens as eight-foot-tall, red-striped octapeds riding bicycles and intent upon eating us for dessert.

Finally, what would or could motivate even the FPs to concoct such outlandish and absurd tales that without fail draw much unwelcome attention and notoriety? What sort of psychological motives and needs would underlie such fabrications? Perhaps the best answer to this question is the one provided by the author-photographer Douglas Curran. Traveling from British Columbia down the West Coast and circumscribing the United States along a counterclockwise route, Curran spent more than two years questioning ordinary people about outer space. Curran writes:

> On my travels across the continent I never had to wait too long for someone to tell me about his or her UFO experience, whether I was chatting with a farmer in Kansas, Ruth Norman at the Unarius Foundation, or a cafe owner in Florida. What continually struck me in talking with these people was how positive and ultimately life-giving a force was their belief in outer space. Their belief reaffirmed the essential fact of human existence: the need for order and hope. It is this that establishes them—and me—in the continuity of human experience. It brought to me a greater understanding of Oscar Wilde's observation. "We are all lying in the gutter—but some of us are looking at the stars."

Jung (1969), in his study of flying saucers, first published in 1957, argues that the saucer represents an archetype of order, wholeness, deliverance, and salvation—a symbol manifested in other cultures as a sun wheel or magic circle. Further in his essay, Jung compares the spacemen aboard the flying saucers to the angelic messengers of earlier times who brought messages of hope and salvation—the theme emphasized in Strieber's *Communion.* Curran also observes that the spiritual message conveyed by the aliens is, recognizably, our own. None of the aliens Curran's contactees talked about advocated any moral or metaphysical belief that was not firmly rooted in the Judeo-Christian tradition. As Curran says, "Every single flying saucer group I encountered in my travels incorporated Jesus Christ into the hierarchy of its belief system." Many theorists have long recognized that whenever world events prove to be psychologically destabilizing, men turn to religion as their only hope. Jung, again, in his 1957 essay, wrote: "In the threatening situation of the world today, when people are beginning to see that everything is at stake, the projection-creating fantasy soars beyond the realm of earthly organization and powers into the heavens, into interstellar space, where the rulers of human fate, the gods, once had their abode in the planets."

The beauty and power of Curran's portraits of hundreds of true UFO believers lies in his sympathetic understanding of their fears and frailties. As psychologists are well aware, our religions are not so much systems of objective truths about the universe as they are collections of subjective statements about humanity's hopes and fears. The true believers interviewed by Curran are all around us. Over the years I have encountered several. One particularly memorable and poignant case was that of a federal prisoner who said he could leave his body at will and sincerely believed it. Every weekend he would go home to visit his family, while his physical body stayed behind in his cell. Then there was the female psychic from the planet Xenon who could turn electric lights on and off at will, especially traffic signals. Proof of her powers? If she drove up to a red light she would concentrate on it intently for thirty to forty seconds and then, invariably, it would turn green!

HYPNAGOGIC AND HYPNOPOMPIC HALLUCINATIONS

Another common yet little publicized and rarely discussed phenomenon is that of hypnagogic (when *falling asleep)* and hypnopompic (when *waking up*) hallucinations. These phenomena, often referred to as "waking dreams," find the individual suddenly awake, but paralyzed, unable to move, and most often encountering a "ghost." The typical report goes somewhat as follows: "I went to bed and then sometime near morning something woke me up. I opened my eyes and found myself wide awake but unable to move. There, standing at the foot of my bed was my mother, wearing her favorite dress—the one we buried

her in. She stood there looking at me and smiling and then she said: 'Don't worry about me, Doris, I'm at peace at last. I just want you and the children to be happy.' " Well, what happened next? "Nothing, she slowly faded away." What did you do then? "Nothing, I just closed my eyes and went back to sleep."

There are always a number of characteristic clues that indicate a hypnagogic or hypnopompic hallucination. First, it always occurs before or after falling asleep. Second, one is paralyzed or has difficulty in moving; or, contrarily, one may float out of one's body and have an out-of-body experience. Third, the hallucination is unusually bizarre; i.e., one sees ghosts, aliens, monsters, and such. Fourth, after the hallucination is over, the hallucinator typically goes back to sleep. And, fifth, the hallucinator is unalterably convinced of the "reality" of the entire experience.

Strieber's *Communion* provides a classic textbook description of a hypnopompic hallucination, complete with the awakening from a sound sleep, the strong sense of reality and of being awake, the paralysis (due to the fact that the body's neural circuits keep our muscles relaxed and help preserve our sleep), and the encounter with strange beings. Following the encounter, instead of jumping out of bed and going in search of the strangers he has seen, Strieber typically goes back to sleep. He even reports that the burglar alarm was still working—proof again that the intruders were mental rather than physical. Strieber also reports an occasion when he awakens and believes that the roof of his house is on fire and that the aliens are threatening his family. Yet his only response to this was to go peacefully back to sleep. Again, clear evidence of a hypnopompic dream. Strieber, of course, is convinced of the reality of these experiences. This too is to be expected. If he was not convinced of their reality, then the experience would not be hypnopompic or hallucinatory.

The point cannot be more strongly made that ordinary, perfectly sane and rational people have these hallucinatory experiences and that such individuals are in no way mentally disturbed or psychotic. But neither are such experiences to be taken as incontrovertible proof of some sort of objective or consensual reality. They may be subjectively real, but objectively they are nothing more than dreams or delusions. They are called ''hallucinatory'' because of their heightened subjective reality. Leaving no rational explanation unspurned, Strieber is nevertheless forthright enough to suggest at one point the possibility that his experiences indeed could be hypnopompic. Moreover, in a summary chapter he speculates, correctly, that the alien visitors could be ''from within us'' and/or ''a side effect of a natural phenomenon . . . a certain hallucinatory wire in the mind causing many different people to have experiences so similar as to seem to be the result of encounters with the same physical phenomena.'' (Strieber, 1987)

Interestingly enough, these hypnopompic and hypnagogic hallucinations do show individual differences in content and character as well as a lot of similarity: ghosts, monsters, fairies, friends, lovers, neighbors, and even little gray men and golden-haired ladies from the Pleiades are frequently encountered. Do such hallucinations appear more frequently to highly imaginative and fantasy-prone people than to other personality types? There is some evidence that they do (McKellar, 1957; Tart, 1969; Reed, 1972; Wilson and Barber, 1983), and there can certainly be no doubt that Strieber is a highly imaginative personality type. (See also IMAGINARY ABDUCTEE STUDY)

—ROBERT A. BAKER

References

Alcock, James. *Parapsychology: Science or Magic?* (Pergamon, 1981).

AMA Council on Scientific Affairs. ''Scientific Status of Refreshing Recollection by Use of Hypnosis,'' *AMA* (April 5, 1985).

Baker, Robert A. ''The Effect of Suggestion on Past-Lives Regression.'' *American Journal of Clinical Hypnosis* (1982).

Baker, Robert A., B. Haynes, and B. Patrick. ''Hypnosis, Memory, and Incidental Memory,'' *American Journal of Clinical Hypnosis* (1983).

Barber, Theodore X. *Hypnosis: A Scientific Approach* (Van Nostrand, 1969).

Corliss, William R. *The Unfathomed Mind: A Handbook of Unusual Mental Phenomena* (Sourcebook, 1982).

Curran, Douglas. *In Advance of the Landing: Folk Concepts of Outer Space* (Abbeville Press, 1985).

Frazier, Kendrick, ed. *Paranormal Borderlands of Science* (Prometheus Books, 1981).

Gill, M. M., and M. Brenman. *Hypnosis and Related States* (International Universities Press, 1959).

Hilgard, Ernest R. *Divided Consciousness: Multiple Controls in Human Thought and Action* (John Wiley & Sons, 1977).

———. ''Hypnosis Gives Rise to Fantasy and Is Not a Truth Serum,'' *Skeptical Inquirer* (Spring, 1981).

Hilgard, Josephine R. *Personality and Hypnosis: A Study of Imaginative Involvement,* 2nd ed. (University of Chicago Press, 1979).

Loftus, Elizabeth. *Eyewitness Testimony* (Harvard University Press, 1979).

McKellar, Peter. *Imagination and Thinking* (Cohen and West, 1957).

O'Connell, D. N., R. E. Shor, and M. T. Orne. ''Hypnotic Age Regression: An Empirical and Methodological Analysis,'' *Journal of Abnormal Psychology Monograph* 76 (1970).

Perry, Campbell, Jean-Roch Laurence, Robert Nadon, and Louise Labelle. ''Past-Lives Regression'' in *Hypnosis: Questions and Answers.* Bernie Zilbergeld, M. G. Edelstein, and D. L. Araoz, eds. (Norton, 1986).

Reed, Graham. *The Psychology of Anomalous Experience* (Houghton Mifflin, 1972).

Sarbin, T. R., and M. L. Andersen. ''Role-theoretical Analysis of Hypnotic Behavior'' in *Handbook of Clinical and Experimental Hypnosis,* Gordon, Jesse E., ed. (Macmillan,1967).

Sarbin, T.R., and W. C. Coe. *Hypnosis: A Social Psychological Analysis of Influence Communication* (Holt, Rinehart and Winston, 1972).

Spanos, N. R, and T. X. Barber. ''Toward a Convergence in Hypnotic Research,'' *American Psychologist* (1974).

Strieber, Whitley. *Communion* (William Morrow/ Beech Tree Books, 1987).

Sutcliffe, J. P. '' 'Credulous' and 'Skeptical' Views of Hypnotic Phenomena: Experiments on Esthesia, Hallucinations, and Delusion'' *Journal of Abnormnal and Social Psychology* (1961).

Tart, Charles, ed. *Altered States of Consciousness: A Book of Readings* (Wiley, 1969).

True, R. M. ''Experimental Control in Hypnotic Age Regression States,'' *Science* (1949).

Wilson, Ian. *Mind Out of Time* (Gollancz, 1981).

Wilson, Sheryl C. and Theodore X. Barber. ''The Fantasy-Prone Personality: Implications for Understanding Imagery, Hypnosis, and Parapsychological Phenomena'' in *Imagery: Current Theory, Research and Application.* Sheikh, Anees A., ed. (John Wiley & Sons, 1983).

I

iatrogenesis One of the real tragedies of modern medical practice is the unintentional creation of a new, or, in many cases, a more serious and disabling disorder by the therapist's misguided efforts to heal. Such disorders created by the physician or therapist are called *iatrogenic* from the Greek *iatros* meaning "healer."

Sadly enough, the prevalence and extent of such disorders is much greater than is generally thought, especially in the area of psychiatric and psychological disorders. During the late 1980s and 1990s a number of misguided psychotherapists and pseudotherapists have been persuading people they are victims of "alien abductions." The engineering processes and procedures used to accomplish this iatrogenic feat of construction are fairly easy.

The needed materials are: a person with a problem of some sort seeking an answer; a therapist, counselor, or guru; social compliance on the part of the person with the problem; a number of suggestions from the therapist; and finally, a total relaxation of the reins of the client's imagination. This combination results in what is usually referred to as "hypnosis" or "trance"—terms which are both inaccurate and misleading, since creating or using "the hypnotic ritual" is unnecessary. In most instances, most people can be persuaded to relax, close their eyes, take slow deep breaths, and follow the therapist's suggestions. Nearly everyone possesses some degree of intelligence, imagination, and memory; and although some individuals are more suggestive than others, all of us, without exception, are prone to being influenced by suggestion. When these factors are combined with a therapist's stimulation of memory (which is virtually indistinguishable from imagination), what emerges ninety-nine times out of a hundred is a mixture of both fact and fiction. Our memories are never 100 percent accurate, and the further away in time we are from the event we are trying to recall, the less accurate our account will be.

When a dominant and persuasive therapist suggests to his patients who are in a relaxed and susceptible state that they were "abducted by aliens," the ideas become "memory" and an iatrogenic disorder is born.

—ROBERT A. BAKER

Imaginary Abductee Study The Imaginary Abductee Study is one of the few scientific experiments ever conducted in the history of UFO-abduction research. We developed the 1977 imaginary series for several reasons. We needed more information about abductions, and the study promised us narrative data from fantasized CE-3s (close encounters of the third kind) in a convenient synthetic form. We also wanted to learn more about using hypnosis effectively in such cases. Above all, we were dissatisfied with several inconclusive previous real CE-3s, and we sought ways to determine whether or not abductees were fabricating.

My colleague Dr. W.C. McCall and I were increasingly doubtful about abduction claims, which had proliferated during and after the 1973 UFO flap. We still remembered the 1975 Garden Grove abduction hoax, which had changed us abruptly from believers to skeptics. Neither of us cared whether abductees' claims were caused by aliens or not, yet we continued our investigations with new enthusiasm.

Over the spring and summer of 1977, we found sixteen volunteers who knew relatively nothing about UFOs or CE-3 literature, hypnotized them, and gave each an imaginary abduction. We asked them eight simple questions (derived from events in a few dozen published and manuscript CE-3 cases then available) and directed them to respond fluently:

1. Imagine you are in a favorite place, and suddenly you see a UFO. Describe that UFO.
2. Imagine you are aboard the UFO. How do you get there?
3. Imagine you are inside the UFO. What do you see?
4. Imagine you see some beings in the UFO. What do they look like?
5. Imagine the beings give you a physical examination. What is happening?
6. Imagine they give you a message. What does the message say, and how do you get it?
7. Imagine you return to where you sighted the UFO. How do you get there?
8. Imagine an aftermath. How were you affected by your abduction?
    (Subject is awakened.)

We assumed the imaginary subjects would need much prompting but they had been selected for creativity and high verbal skills and were good hypnotic subjects, going readily into deep trance and responding well to questions. McCall never deliberately cued them beyond introducing each situation, and then let them talk freely with no more guidance than an occasional "What's happening now?" Almost all sixteen imaginary subjects gave us detailed and often intriguing narratives that were fully comparable to those in CE-3 case reports.

Word-by-word comparisons with real abduction transcripts showed many similarities and few major differences. All of the imaginary subjects described typical CE-3 images and incidents, ranging from the obvious (disk-shaped craft) to the unusual (two alien types on a single UFO), to rare details of high strangeness (projecting/retracting light beams with cut-off ends). The hundreds of similarities are too numerous and characteristic to be dismissed. One imaginary subject described a (nonexistent) "scoop mark" on her arm put there by an alien—years before such abductee body scars became fashionable. Further, all six types of aliens commonly described by pre-1980s CE-3 witnesses appeared in just the first eight imaginary sessions: human, humanoid, animal, robot, exotic, and apparitional. There were no bug-eyed Grays among these entities.

Responses to the Imaginary study generally followed predictable paths—abduction skeptics welcomed it, while those abduction proponents who did not ignore it attacked us variously for cueing our subjects, for finding trivial imaginary/real parallels, or for flawed methodology, among other things. The objections seemed to us then as now to be mostly nit-picking by true believers. The study's core assertion, that CE-3 claims are mental events, remains unsullied—particularly in the absence of any serious attempts at replication, even after a near quarter-century.

One of our critics agreed with us in part. In 1989 longtime proponent Thomas Bullard called for a replication of the Imaginary Study, then concluded: "Imaginary cases thus pose a vexing question—how can non-abductees tell stories even broadly like those of real abductees? . . . More to the point, how can the hypothesis of an objective abduction survive if anyone can tell the abduction story, no experience required?"

How indeed? Some maintain that the general outlines of a CE-3 are "in the air"—in TV, film, and print versions of abduction cases. But in 1977 such sources were far fewer, and cannot account for the capacity of nearly any imaginary subject even today to fantasize a fully detailed CE-3 yarn, including specifics that few abductees describe, about any given segment of the abduction sequence. The imaginaries seemed to possess intuitive knowledge of an abduction sequence they had never consciously experienced. The origin of such knowledge must be innate, and I think it almost certainly has to relate to perinatal memories.

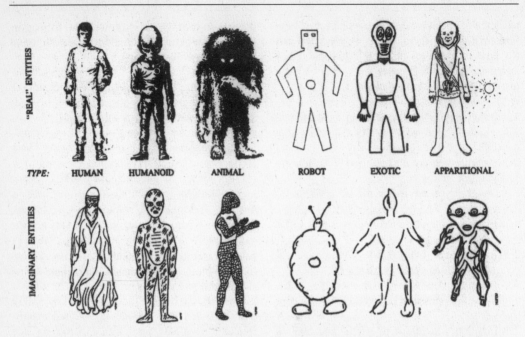

All six types of aliens commonly described by pre-1980s CE-3 witnesses appeared in the early imaginary sessions: human, humanoid, animal, robot, exotic, and apparitional. Missing were the big-eyed Grays that became so prominent in the late 1980s.

The Imaginary Study's significance is that it provided the first persuasive demonstration that claims of abduction are non-physical experiences, i.e., hoaxes or fantasy/hallucinations rather than physical events. The study continues to perturb abduction proponents, but even independent replications if they occur are unlikely to modify its skeptical conclusions.

—ALVIN H. LAWSON

implants, alien For many years the subject of alien implants in humans has not only intrigued abduction researchers, but attempts to isolate and study these objects have been fraught with disappointment and failure. The situation changed in 1995 when I became acquainted with Derrel Sims, a longtime researcher in the alien abduction field.

On August 19, 1995, the first set of surgeries was performed for the removal of objects from the bodies of two individuals who were subjects of the alien-abduction phenomenon.

The recovered objects were subjected to scientific analysis of both the biological and nonbiological material, and the findings were baffling. There was a second set of surgeries performed on May 18, 1996. The total number to date is now eight surgeries which has netted nine objects.

The first surgeries were performed on a male patient whose x-rays demonstrated an object in his hand and one female with two obvious metallic objects in a toe that were also demonstrative in x-rays. There was an additional surgery following the first set that yielded a small grayish white ball. This was followed by a set of three surgeries. Two were female and one was male. Both females showed radiographic signs of objects beneath the skin on the front of the left leg, whereas the male patient had a metallic radiographic object in the left jaw area. Following this set of surgeries another independent procedure was performed on a female who had an object in her left heel. The last surgery to date was performed on August 17, 1998, and was filmed by NBC to be included in their two-hour prime-time special, which aired on February 17, 1999.

Because of the expense incurred from the scientific analysis in world-class laboratories, a method had to be devised to raise money. All the surgical procedures performed were without charge to the patient, and the scientific data found eventually becomes the property of all the Earth's inhabitants. Derrel Sims and I have formed an organization, which serves both functions. It is a nonprofit organization called: The Fund For Interactive Research in Space Technology (F.I.R.S.T.). The Web site address is www.Firstevidence.org.

Another nonprofit organization deals with the matter of scientific analysis. This is The National Institute for Discovery Science (N.I.D.S.), headed by Robert Bigelow who is solely responsible for looking at our scientific data and finding it worthy of inclusion in their studies. The board of directors of N.I.D.S. is composed of some of the finest scientific authorities in the United States. Our findings to date have been as follows:

Of the eight surgeries performed, we have four that were metallic rods covered with an unusual biological membrane not found in the medical literature. This membrane tightly wraps the metallic rods and is dark gray and shiny. Mysteriously, it cannot be cut through with a surgical blade. The analysis of this tissue shows that it is composed of three substances most probably belonging to the recipient of the implant. These substances are a protein coagulum, hemosiderin, and keratin.

In addition, we have found two other biological mysteries. The soft tissue surrounding the objects demonstrates microscopically that the area has a high quantity of small nerve receptors called proprioceptors. Secondly, there is a stark and surprising absence of any inflammatory response to these objects, although we all know it is virtually impossible to have something enter the body without it responding by inflammation. We believe that the reason for this has to do with the formation of the membrane. The metallurgical findings are also earthshaking.

Scientists who have examined the "implants" compare them to meteorite fragments because they contain isotopic ratios consistent with nonearthly isotopic ratio numbers.

Three of the objects appeared to be small grayish-white ovoid balls. These were in turn attached to an abnormality of the skin, which is commonly associated with the abduction phenomenon called a "scoop mark." When the surgical procedures were performed, the entire segment was removed and sent in for pathological analysis. The ovoid balls are still being examined, but preliminary results on one of the objects shows that it is composed of eleven complex elements.

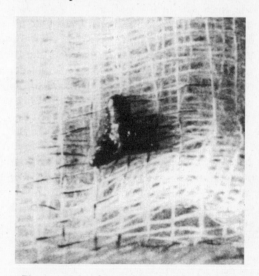

Photograph of an alleged alien implant

Some of the biological findings associated with these skin abnormalities include such things as Solar Elastosis, a rare exposure of the dermal layer of the skin to ultraviolet radiation. Last but not least is the object removed from the heel area, which appeared to be glass or crystal. After careful and continued analysis, we found that the object was brown bottle glass made by Dow Corning.

However, the other objects seem to be

structured as if designed for a purpose. This purpose has not been determined yet. We hope that further study will provide answers regarding function. One possibility is that the objects are tracking devices. This would enable someone or something to find individuals anywhere on the globe. Another possibility is that they are behavior-controlling devices. I believe a more plausible purpose might be a device for monitoring certain pollution levels or even genetic changes in the body. This may be similar to the way we monitor our astronauts in space. Only more time, effort, and study will answer these questions.

Many believe that we are on the verge of a great scientific discovery: that mankind is actually being tampered with by extraterrestrial intelligences. Also, based on the work of Zecharia Sitchen, Allen Alford, and others, I personally believe that alien intervention in the development of mankind has been going on for thousands of years and that man's consciousness has undergone a systematic process of expansion and greater awareness. This in turn gives rise to our conscious awareness of the abduction phenomenon.

—ROGER K. LEIR

Incident at Exeter (G.P. Putnam's Sons, 1966). *Saturday Review* writer John G. Fuller wrote a column for that magazine and an article for *Look* magazine about a wave of UFO sightings in New Hampshire. He expanded those articles into this book, which is the first to draw a connection between UFOs and powerlines, over which the bright balls of red lights were seen hovering, and which may have caused a blackout affecting the Northeastern United States.

—RANDALL FITZGERALD

Insectoids "Big Bugs" thought to be of alien origin. Generally the form resembles a praying mantis that is larger than a man, but variants include grasshopper, fly, ant, and caterpillar. Their history is quite unusual and bears special interest to those with an interest in the cultural dimension of alien imagery.

Throughout most of history, believers in other worlds have buttressed their position with theology. The feeling was other worlds must be populated. God would not waste worlds by having them barren of life and people. God designed the world for men. Other worlds meant other men. The first important challenge to this reasoning appeared in 1742 when David Hume, famous for his criticism of the Argument from Design which supported belief in the existence of God, warned that life on other worlds would not be copies of ourselves. In a fictional dialogue, a character of his named Philo points out that nature is diverse for such expectations.

Pierre Louis Moreau in his *Essaie de Cosmologie* (1750) soon after affirmed, "If such great varieties are observed already among those who populated the different climes of the earth, how can one conceive of those who live on planets so distant from our own? Their varieties probably exceed the scope of our imagination." The atheistic Baron d'Holbach in *Le système de la nature* (1770) similarly argued that the different temperatures of other worlds meant their inhabitants may not be like us.

This sensibility did not immediately overturn more stolidly anthropomorphic views. Pride of place on the eve of the Darwinian revolution goes to Thomas Cullin Simon's *Scientific Certainties of Planetary Life* (1855) which asserted all planets would share the same vegetable, animal, and intellectual life. Charles Darwin's demolition of the Design argument with his theory of evolution by natural selection gave the speculation of non-human life elsewhere added force. In 1870, Richard A. Proctor indicated stellar nebulae might be inhabited by "their own peculiar forms of life." In his 1873 work, *The Borderland of Science*, he affirms that if life exists on Mars, "it must differ so remarkably from what is known on earth because of its atmosphere." R. S. Ball in *Story of the Heavens* (1885) indicated life elsewhere should be specially adapted to their particular environments: "Life in forms strange and weird . . . stranger than ever Dante described or Doré drew."

Camille Flammarion was especially influential with the 1885 edition of *The Plurality of Inhabited Worlds* (1885) when he routed prior thinkers on the question for their anthropomorphism. The "planetarians" imagined by Huygens, Wolff, Swedenborg, Kant, Locke, and Fourier were only remodeled men. Soon after, the idea of silicon-based life-forms turns up in *Astronomie* with a Dr. Julius Scheiner urging that extraterrestrials may not resemble us. Imagination was clearly being set free by the new worldview of the Darwinians.

It was a cousin of Darwin, Francis Galton, who first introduced the idea of alien insects into scientific discourse. While on a dreamy vacation in 1896, he was pondering the question of Earth-Mars communication using dot-dash-line signals. A fantasy came to him of a mad millionaire on Mars signaling us. A clever girl deduces a base-8 code because "the Mars folk are nothing more than highly-developed ants, who counted up to 8 by their 6 limbs and two antennae as our forefathers counted up to 10 on their fingers." A couple years later, Edward Mason offers a paper proposing life on the planets of other systems might be similar to ants and dragonflies. (Crowe, 1999)

Perhaps the first work of fiction to put Big Bugs on distant planets was John Jacob Astor's *A Journey in Other Worlds* (1894). It involves a trip to Jupiter that is still in the carboniferous stage of evolution. Among the creatures they find are dinosaurs, mastodons, giant serpents, and flesh-eating ants the size of locomotives. Paleontological finds of giant dragonflies and other fossil discoveries indicative of giant life earlier in Earth's history combined with the growing popularity of evolutionary thought.

Fred T. Jane's *To Venus in Five Seconds* (1897) takes up Francis Galton's communicative ants and populates Venus with big, brainy bugs. Soon after, the Darwinian H. G. Wells famously imagined a society of insectile Selenites in *First Men in the Moon* (1901). Diverse writers in the pulp era, including leaders like E. E. "Doc" Smith, Edgar Rice Burroughs, and H. P. Lovecraft, kept the idea going during the pulp era among the flood of the Big Bug

stories up to the start of sci-fi's Golden Age around 1940. John Campbell exiled them from science fiction because of their scientific implausibility.

They soon returned in the fifties, as filmmakers grew comfortable with sci-fi themes and trick photography. *Killers from Space* (1954) had aliens hoping to destroy humanity with Big Bugs and other giant vermin. The success of the giant-ant film *Them!* (1954) quickly turned Big Bugs into an easy horror cliché. There has been a relatively constant stream of insectoid-related films, TV shows, comic books, and cultural media ever since. Much of it is considered campy by culture vultures and even specialists in horror and science fiction rarely discuss it.

While the current philosophy that Nature does indeed waste worlds—an idea now amply reinforced by space probes proving the existence of dead worlds—is partly responsible for alien insects being a feature of modern Western imagination, non-rational aspects also must partly underlie their use. The creatures are a way of exploiting people's fears about bugs, evoking the emotions of horror. Obvious enough, it seems, yet this leads us into a deep paradox.

Fear of insects is one of the more common phobias in human psychology, though the argument continues about whether this fear is learned or innate. The nervous system seems to have a bias in developing fears about spiders; arachnophobia is easier to acquire and harder to extinguish than other animal phobias. It may in part be learned in youth when one sees the fear in the mother or others; but traits like blackness, similarity to pubic hair, or sheer strangeness may act on a more innate level to imprint fear. Whatever the ultimate explanation, the fear exists viscerally in many humans and we may reasonably expect storytellers to have exploited it for its cringing value throughout history. Exaggerating the size of bugs should be a common gimmick much as giants and large beasts are a common feature of world mythology.

It should, but in fact the image appears

only in modern Western civilization. One can spend days looking through texts on mythology and world artwork and find only a tiny few ambiguous and isolated specimens analogous to current Big Bug fantasies. One hopeful precursor would be the giant spider drawing among the Nazca lines etched into the landscape of Peru. Though the image is big, what is not known is if the culture actually envisioned the spider as large in its myths. Spiders appear on Nazca ceramics, and one seems to represent a demon transformed into a large insect that captures a bird. Tarantulas however actually have shown the ability to kill birds. The Nazca lines also have giant drawings of a spider monkey and bird with no indication of them being thought mythically gigantic.

A compilation of superstitions about animals can be found in Hastings's *Encyclopedia of Religion and Ethics* where it is blatantly obvious that insect lore is a small genre compared to that of bears, goats, dogs, cats, and even cuckoo birds. We are told the Bushmen worshipped a mantis named Cagn or Ikaggen. Caucasians termed the mantis the "Hottentot god." The Hottentots also feared the scarab beetle, and the author notes the existence of a cult of the scarab among Egyptians. But if there is any relevance to modern Big Bug fantasies, it has to be faint. May Berenbaum's discussion of insect art and myth is especially recommended as illustrative of the fact that bugs had various symbolic properties through the ages, but gigantism never featured in their portrayal until recent times.

Should the scorpion men of the *Epic of Gilgamesh* be called Big Bugs or monstrous men? An 1149 painting of Satan, the Vision of Tundal, makes him look almost like a giant centipede, yet the intent was to portray him as a man with a thousand hands and fingernails like knights' lances. A giant Earth spider drawn by Hokusai in Japan around 1814 comes as close as anything to being a true Big Bug yet I found nothing about the myth it illustrates. An 1846 story by Edgar Allan Poe seems possibly relevant, yet it involves an illusion that makes a small bug seem large, not a fantasy about a truly monster-sized bug. Even if one was in a generous mood to consider these things as somehow relevant, the frequency of this imagery before 1890 is orders of magnitude below the rate since then.

Cross-cultural studies do not exist to confirm or deny if arachnophobia is a specifically modern phenomenon, but animal phobias demonstrably are panhuman and this is probably grounds enough to suspect bug fears pre-date the modern era. In the 19th century, substantial strides were made in sanitation that might have enhanced anxieties over the germ-carrying activities of bugs, yet pre-moderns surely associated bugs with sickness and death. It would be nice if one could blame Big Bug imagery on the invention of the microscope, but that happened three centuries too soon.

Some Big Bug stories pre-date their use as alien insects. They involve tropical origins and origins in biological experiments, areas made familiar by the Darwinian revolution. Even after they start populating fictional other worlds, these themes of bugs grown large in mad experiments and primitive tropical regions—lost jungles, evolutionarily isolated caverns, the inner Earth—recur repeatedly.

The main deduction following these observations is that Big Bug imagery did not arise out of pure archetypal psychological processes, but arose as a tradition contingent upon historical events. When storytellers create new examples they cannot be reinventing the idea wholly by accessing an unconscious realm of universal fears. They are building upon prior work.

The idea of UFOs being populated by bugs is one of the earliest speculations of the UFO literature, but evidence for it was indirect and arguably nonexistent. For the first couple of decades of the flying saucer era, no accounts exist of anyone seeing bugs inside an alien craft. There are a couple of ambiguous creatures—a humanoid with compound eyes like a bug and a dream reported to Carl Jung—but the first fully realized space bug appears in the mid-1960s.

The first claimant was Ted Owens and his story of the alien grasshoppers Twitter and

Tweeter emerged under circumstances that would today be called channeling. That would be enough to render it dubious to serious UFOlogists and we should add they did not embrace it. The saucer press gave him some public exposure and he managed to get an autobiographical account of his contact published by Gray Barker's Saucerian Press. (Owens, 1969) The doubtful character of the Owens contact is enhanced by the presence of elements that look inspired by the movie *First Men in the Moon* (1964), a gorgeous extravaganza made possible by Ray Harryhausen's special effects artistry. Aliens with grasshopper traits appear in abductions with better pedigrees sporadically thereafter. (Kottmeyer, 1996)

The first insectoid said explicitly to resemble a large praying mantis appears in a hypnotic regression dated March 14, 1986, in which horror writer Whitley Strieber explores a 1967 incident at his grandmother's house. A praying mantis appears in the middle of the living room, scaring the bejesus out of his son. "How can it be so big?" he asks. A few months after *Communion* is published, John Lear issues a statement revealing the "horrible truth" that a saucer crash many years ago proved that UFOnauts were ugly little creatures, shaped like praying mantises and who were more advanced than us by perhaps a billion years. Like a Lovecraft creation, those who learned this firsthand have tended to commit suicide, one of those being Defense Secretary James V. Forrestal whose records are still sealed. Lear's statement was one of the more widely disseminated pieces of EBE-lore and probably was a major influence in people coming forward with their insectoid encounters in the past decade. Cases now number in the dozens, a small yet impressive fraction of abduction entities reported. The nature of these entities is a matter of interesting debate with some thinking them almost god-like in their oversight of humanity. Others think they are servants to more imperial minded reptoids. (Kottmeyer, 1999)

That UFOlogists have dared to allow such campy material to be presented as evidence for the reality of aliens is a strange testament to open-mindedness. Insectoid accounts will be rejected outright by people with an exposure to science writing. Bugs are small in real life for certain reasons. As they become larger, hair-like limbs cannot support the weight of the body. The physical material has to be thicker and stronger and placed more directly under the torso. Bugs oxygenate their tissues via diffusion of air through small holes in the exoskeleton. Beyond a couple of inches, oxygenation of the deeper tissues becomes impossible. Bigger bugs need lungs. A more extensive musculature is needed with increasing mass, and with it an interior skeleton. The proboscis of some bugs is an adaptation to deal with the surface tension of water and would be useless for man-sized bugs, yet it has been reported in at least one encounter case.

Some will doubtless argue that insectoids must be real and that earlier cultural material reflects evidence of veiled encounters now known only because UFOlogists use hypnosis to unlock the secret of their presence on Earth. The obvious problem is the arrival time. Most UFOlogists assume either the aliens arrived in 1947 to check on atomic activity or have been with us throughout history. If one picks 1947, why is there so much Big Bug imagery in science fiction before then? If one chooses to believe they have always been with us, why is there virtually no Big Bug imagery before 1890? Did insectoids have a special fear about the development of Darwinian philosophy that they chose then to furtively invade us?

By failing to reject such reports, UFOlogists grant themselves the same dramatic license as creators of horror films and tacitly flaunt abductions as a tool to evoke fear, revulsion, and confusion. The claim that abduction experiences are immune to psychological insight is acceptable only in the same way one might casually lament why so many people go to horror films or how anybody could produce such monstrosities.

The presence of insectoids proves with high probability the fictional character of a significant subset of abduction reports. The imagery of the UFO phenomenon is distinctly reflective of modern Western culture in this matter. To accept their material reality is to play blind to a substantial cultural genealogy and their birth on Earth in modern times.

—MARTIN S. KOTTMEYER

References:

Berenbaum, May R. *Bugs in the System: Insects and Their Impact on Human Affairs* (Helix, 1995).

Bleiler, Everett. *Science Fiction—The Early Years* (Kent State, 1990).

Crowe, Michael. *The Extraterrestrial Life Debate, 1750-1900* (Dover, 1999).

Kottmeyer, Martin. "Space Bug a Boo Boo," *Talking Pictures #15* (Summer, 1996).

Kottmeyer, Martin. "Graying Mantis," *The REALL News* (May, 1999).

Owens, Ted. *How to Contact Space People* (Saucerian, 1969).

Sullivan, Jack, ed. *Penguin Encyclopedia of Horror and the Supernatural* (Viking, 1986).

Intelligent Life in the Universe (Holden-Day, 1966) by I.S. Shklovskii and Carl Sagan. A Russian and an American astronomer team up in this book to voice their suspicion that an advanced civilization may have visited or briefly colonized our solar system in ancient times. Shklovskii theorizes that Phobos and Deimos, the two moons of Mars, might be artificial satellites, which are "mute testaments to an ancient Martian civilization." Sagan calculates, based on Frank Drake's estimate of technical civilizations existing in our galaxy, that each "should be visited by another such civilization about once every thousand years."

—RANDALL FITZGERALD

Interrupted Journey, The (The Dial Press, 1966). *Saturday Review* magazine columnist John G. Fuller relates the story of a New Hampshire couple who underwent regressive hypnosis to uncover memories of their apparent abduction by aliens. This case involving Betty and Barney Hill became the first alien-abduction story to receive widespread publicity, resulting in a 1975 made-for-television movie called *The UFO Incident*, starring James Earl Jones. Their experience became the standard by which all later abduction accounts would be compared.

—RANDALL FITZGERALD

interstellar travel A major argument against any UFOs being intelligently controlled extraterrestrial spacecraft is that travel between star systems is impossible. Other stars are too far away from us; it would take too long to get here; it would take too much energy; it always takes less energy to communicate than to travel, etc. These arguments are almost never made by aeronautical or astronautical engineers, but rather by astronomers and often by SETI specialists trying to justify the use of radio-telescopes to listen for radio signals from alien civilizations.

Some assume that visitors would have to come from another galaxy. Our own Milky Way galaxy is about 80,000 light-years across, perhaps 15,000 light-years thick, and contains upwards of 100 billion stars. Why worry about another galaxy? There are none closer than about 1 million light-years, yet within 55 light-years of our solar system there are about 1,000 stars of which 46 are very similar to the sun and might well have planets and life. That is to say they are not too hot or too cold; too new or too old; don't have a companion star which would make planetary orbits too variable; don't vary in their energy output very much over time, so life would have a chance to develop in fairly stable conditions. There are even some planets orbiting nearby sun-like stars—more than a billion years older than our sun—within possibly habitable zones. Civilizations on planets around such stars might have begun their technological development a billion years before ours.

Most arguments against interstellar travel neglect the simple fact that technological progress almost always comes from doing things differently in an unpredictable way. Lasers aren't just better lightbulbs. Micro-integrated circuits are not just better transistors; nuclear

fission rockets—many of which were successfully operated in the 1960s, at power levels as
high as 4.4 billion watts—are not just better
chemical rockets. In each case different physics are involved in the more advanced system.

Therefore, one might expect better means
of long distance communication than radio
(which might not be observed with radio telescopes) and certainly more advanced means of
propulsion than the use of modern chemical
rockets. Detailed studies done almost 40 years
ago in industry show that trips to nearby stars
are feasible with round trip times shorter than
the average human life span, using staged nuclear fusion rockets. Fusion reactions provide
the energy of the stars and of hydrogen bombs.
Many different fusion reactions are available.
The most interesting appears to be the use of
the Deuterium (heavy hydrogen with one neutron and one proton) Helium-3 (light helium
with two protons and one neutron) reaction.
This produces charged particles which (unlike
neutrons produced in other fusion reactions)
can be directed out the back end of the rocket
with electric and magnetic fields and which
have 10 million times as much energy per particle as can be obtained in a chemical rocket.

Many other schemes have been proposed
including space-time warping, white holes, the
energy of the vacuum, laser propulsion, etc. Of
course advantage would be taken of the fact
that time slows down for things moving at
close to the speed of light. For example, at
99.99 percent of the speed of light it only takes
6 months pilot time to travel a distance of 37
light-years. Considering that man's first powered flight took place less than a century ago,
it would not be surprising if visitors had technology about which we know nothing.

—STANTON T. FRIEDMAN

**Into The Fringe: A True Story of Alien
Abduction** (Berkley Books, 1992). Texas
English professor Karla Turner describes in
this book how she and relatives and friends
experienced a contagion of alien abductions
and body wounds. Over a 13-month period,
at least ten people in Karla's life reportedly

experienced the same disturbing pattern of
alien intrusions and disturbances.

—RANDALL FITZGERALD

Intruders (Random House, 1987). According
to Budd Hopkins, humans are the subject of
an alien breeding experiment which tracks specific family bloodlines. This book chronicles
the UFO-related experiences of "Kathie
Davis" (real name Debra Jordan-Kauble), who
has since gained considerable notoriety as an
abductee thanks to Hopkins. This book along
with Whitley Strieber's *Communion* heralded,
or helped initiate, a major wave of abduction
stories continuing through the remainder of the
20th century.

—RANDALL FITZGERALD

Invaders from Mars (National Pictures/20th
Century-Fox, 1953). A classic science fiction
film of the Cold War era, starring Helena Carter, Arthur Franz, Jimmy Hunt, and Leif
Erickson.

This was one of the first films to portray
humans under medical assault by aliens and to
show the insertion of implants. It could also
have influenced the famous Barney and Betty
Hill case.

The story involves the takeover of a small
town by aliens from a landed flying saucer.
The events are seen through the eyes of a boy
whose parents are also victimized by the aliens
and put under a form of mind control—accomplished through the use of small devices implanted surgically into the victims' bodies.

Clute and Nicholls comment (in their *Encyclopedia of Science Fiction*) that the film
produces: ". . . a powerful metaphor for the
loneliness and alienation of a child whose
world seems subtly wrong. The image of
human bodies concealing incomprehensible
and menacing alien motives was, in its paranoia, an important one in U.S. sci-fi cinema,
especially during the 1950s Communist-spy
phobias."

—MARTIN S. KOTTMEYER
& RONALD D. STORY

References

Clute, John, and Peter Nicholls. *The Encyclopedia of Science Fiction* (St. Martin's/Griffin, 1993; 1995).

Warren, Bill. *Keep Watching the Skies, Vol. 1* (McFarland, 1982).

Invasion of the Body Snatchers (Republic Pictures, 1956; directed by Don Siegel). A classic alien invasion film of the Cold War era, starring Kevin McCarthy, Dana Wynter, and Carolyn Jones; based on a story by Jack Finney.

The film portrays the aliens as interstellar parasites who create replicas of human individuals, thus assuming their identities and taking over their minds as well as their bodies. The aliens themselves are spawned as giant seed pods that float through space until encountering a host planet. Each pod serves as a "blank" to be filled in by the human form. The conversion process takes place while the victim sleeps—a parallel feature of modern UFO-abduction lore. Upon awakening, the new "pod person" is without human feeling or individuality. He or she becomes an emotionless "clone" only appearing like a human being on the surface.

The film exploits the venerable mythic theme of the doppelganger—more commonly termed the "evil twin"—in the service of exploring the horror of dehumanization. Pods come down from space and replace people with duplicates that take the body and memories, but are subtly different. The "pod people" are vegetable in their essence and cannot take in the animal vitality of humanity: their emotions, desires, and love. As they quickly spread and threaten to overtake all the friends and neighbors of the central character, there is a confrontation in which the pod people make their case that life is so much simpler as a vegetable. Love does not last and there is no pain.

In interviews, Siegel explains his attraction to the story as due to his knowing people who gave in to the seduction of settling for contentment and turning off their passions, unaware that the trade-off is a living death. The allegory of the pod people is thus a timeless morality story sure to be retold over the years, as partly illustrated by the 1978 remake by Philip Kaufman.

—MARTIN S. KOTTMEYER
& RONALD D. STORY

References

Finney, Jack. *Invasion of the Body Snatchers* (Dell Books, 1954, 1955, 1978).

Clute, John, and Peter Nicholls. *The Encyclopedia of Science Fiction* (St. Martin's/Griffin, 1993; 1995).

Siegel on "Invasion of the Body Snatchers" *Cinefantastique* (Winter, 1973).

Invisible College, The (E.P. Dutton, 1975). Jacques Vallée proposes that a control system for human consciousness connected to the UFO phenomenon is being explored in secret by a group of scientists. This control system, which the author believes has influenced humankind since the dawn of history, originates either within the collective human consciousness or as a direct consequence of extraterrestrial intervention.

—RANDALL FITZGERALD

Invisible Residents (Thomas Y. Crowell, 1970). Ivan T. Sanderson tries to draw connections between UFO sightings and the disappearance of ships and planes. He claims to have plotted these sightings and disappearances on maps and found ten vortices around the planet which are used by UFOs to distort space and time and cause ships, planes, and people to disappear without a trace.

—RANDALL FITZGERALD

Is Another World Watching? (Carroll & Nicholson/Harper and Brothers, 1950; Bantam Books, 1951). Subtitled: *The Riddle of the Flying Saucers,* this was the first book on the topic of flying saucers to be published in the U.K. and the second (following Keyhoe's *The Flying Saucers are Real*) in the U.S.

Variety columnist Gerald Heard tries to make a case that 2-inch-long bees from Mars are buzzing Earth in saucers to show their displeasure about our atomic weapons. He urges Earth scientists to establish diplomatic relations with our own planet's bees and to use them as intermediaries when and if the more advanced Martian bees decide to "swarm upon us."

—RANDALL FITZGERALD

Is Anyone Out There? (Delacorte Press, 1992). Astronomer Frank Drake and science writer Dava Sobel believe humankind will receive radio signals but never actual physical visits from other intelligent life in the universe. Perhaps the most unexpected benefit of deciphering these signals, "bequeathing to us vast libraries of useful information," will be the secret of immortality, delivering unto us "the grand instruction book telling creatures how to live forever." (Does this not sound a little like the legend of the Holy Grail?)

—RANDALL FITZGERALD

J

J. Allen Hynek Center for UFO Studies

Known as CUFOS, the J. Allen Hynek Center for UFO Studies was founded in 1973 by Dr. J. Allen Hynek, former chief scientific advisor the U.S. Air Force Project Blue Book. CUFOS is not a membership organization, but instead is composed of volunteers, including scientists, academics, investigators, and members of the public, all dedicated to the continuing serious examination and analysis of the UFO phenomenon. It is supported entirely through public donations and contributions.

The organization has several goals. The first is to be an archive for UFO reports and literature. CUFOS maintains the largest collection of case files in the world, including the files of NICAP, Blue Book, and its own report files. CUFOS also investigates the most scientifically promising cases it receives. Second, it promotes the general public understanding of the UFO phenomenon through its publishing program. This includes the quarterly *International UFO Reporter*, special monographs and other documents, and the *Journal of UFO Studies*, the only peer-reviewed journal devoted solely to the study of UFOs. Third, CUFOS conducts various research projects and assists the research of others. For example, CUFOS researchers have been involved in investigating the Roswell incident, the psychological characteristics of abductees, physical traces left by UFOs, and the history of government involvement in UFO investigation.

Address: 2457 W. Peterson Ave.
Chicago, IL 60659
U.S.A.

E-mail: infocenter@cufos.org
—J. ALLEN HYNEK CENTER FOR UFO STUDIES

Jacobs, David M.

(b. 1942). David M. Jacobs is Associate Professor of History at Temple University, specializing in 20th-century American history and culture. Dr. Jacobs began researching the controversy over unidentified flying objects in America in the mid-1960s, and has amassed over 35 years of primary research data and analytical hypotheses on the subject.

In 1973 Jacobs completed his doctoral dissertation in the field of intellectual history at the University of Wisconsin-Madison on the controversy over unidentified flying objects in America. This was only the second Ph.D. degree granted involving a UFO-related theme. A revised version of his dissertation was published by Indiana University Press as *The UFO Controversy in America* (1975).

David Jacobs

Since 1973 Dr. Jacobs has continued to devote most of his professional and personal energies to researching the UFO phenomenon in general, and the abduction phenomenon in particular. Having conducted over 750 hypnotic regressions with over 125 abductees, Dr. Jacobs is one of the foremost UFO abduction researchers in the world.

The results of his studies are reported in two books: *Secret Life* (1992) and *The Threat* (1998). Jacobs is also the founder and director of a research organization known as ICAR: The International Center for Abduction Research.

Address: Department of History
            Temple University
            Philadelphia, PA 19122
            U.S.A.

E-mail: djacobs@temple.edu

Web site: www.ufoabduction.com

POSITION STATEMENT: Having studied the UFO and abduction phenomenon since the mid-1960s, I have gone through different phases of enthusiasm for it. At first I was thrilled with the idea that it might mean extraterrestrial contact. Eventually I was challenged by the difficulty of proving not only that contention but also of demonstrating the subject's importance to the scientific community. By the early 1970s, the difficulty of understanding the origins and motivations of the UFOs provided me with almost insurmountable intellectual demands.

My interest in the abduction phenomenon came in 1982 with my introduction to Budd Hopkins and his work. In 1986 I began my own hypnosis of abductees. After investigating hundreds of abduction events, I have come to understand, at least partially, the nature of this phenomenon. What I have found has been unsettling. As a result of my own studies and of the research of other abduction researchers, I have begun to grasp alien motivations, pur-

poses, and goals. The consequences have been that I have come to fear this clandestine program of physiological exploitation by one species of another for an alien agenda. I dislike what the phenomenon does to the lives of individual abductees, and I like even less the changes that the abductors intend for the society in which the abductees live.

I fully understand the fringe position that I occupy within the UFO research community, but I have, unfortunately, not found an alternative theory to account for the data.

The intellectual challenges that faced me in the past have now changed drastically. I confront the subject with dread. Studying its motivations results in my anxiety. I find myself in the position of having spent my entire adult life studying a phenomenon that I have come to abhor. I desperately wish I could say otherwise.

—DAVID M. JACOBS

JAL Flight #1628 Alaska sighting November 17, 1986: Japanese Airlines pilot Kenju Terauchi was on a routine cargo flight from Iceland to Anchorage, Alaska, when he and his two crewmen saw the lights of three mysterious "craft" following his jet. One of the walnut-shaped objects appeared enormous, dwarfing his Boeing 747, while the other two were smaller.

The objects, each of which appeared to have two panels of lights, darted quickly and occasionally stopped suddenly—once appearing in front of the cockpit. They instantly disappeared and reappeared, according to the 47-year-old pilot.

Terauchi said he briefly glimpsed the largest object in silhouette eight miles away. "It was a very big one—two times bigger than an aircraft carrier," he said. He tried to shake the objects with evasive maneuvers, but said they followed his plane for 400 miles.

The U.S. Federal Aviation Administration and U.S. Air Force said a large object appeared on air traffic controllers' radar screens. FAA flight control reports indicated that the object stayed with Flight 1628 for at least 32 minutes. The flight controller directing the Japanese plane reported the object on his radar as close as five miles to the jet.

When the recorded radar transmission was replayed later, however, there was no image except for the JAL cargo plane. Anchorage FAA spokesman Paul Steuche said it was possible the signal from the UFO was strong enough to be picked up at the time, but not strong enough to register on the radar recording system.

Subsequent FAA examination of the tapes showed what appeared to be a second object near JAL Flight 1628, but investigators now think it may have been a double image from the 747. FAA investigators who questioned the crew in Anchorage concluded they were "normal, professional, rational and had no drug or alcohol involvement."

Captain Terauchi reported sighting unusual lights again on the morning of January 11, 1987, while on a flight from London to a refueling stop in Anchorage. "After landing at Anchorage I checked the map," he said, "and concluded it was a light of a town or village" reflected off ice crystals. The first one "was a real UFO," Terauchi added, noting that crew members (copilot Takanori Tamefuji and flight engineer Yoshio Tsukuba) also saw it.

—Coral E. Lorenzen

References

APRO Bulletin, The. "Giant UFO Shadows 747" (April, 1987).

Maccabee, Bruce. "The Fantastic Flight of JAL 1628," *International UFO Reporter* (March-April, 1987).

Jessup, Morris K. (1900-1959). An American astronomer who championed the unorthodox, Jessup was the author of several pioneering books on the UFO phenomenon, the first of which (*The Case for the UFO,* 1955) became famous in connection with the Allende Letters episode. At the age of fifty-nine (on April 20, 1959), he committed suicide in Dade

County, Florida, under circumstances thought by some UFO specialists to be "suspicious."

Jessup was born on a farm near Rockville, Indiana, on March 2, 1900. He grew up with an intense interest in astronomy, which he pursued at the University of Michigan in Ann Arbor, where, after receiving a B.S. degree, he served as assistant in astronomy (in 1925), instructor in astronomy (1925-26) and member of the University of Michigan's expedition to Mexico (in 1926).

Morris K. Jessup

While working as an observer at the Lamont-Hussey Observatory associated with the university (1926-30), Jessup received a Master of Science degree (in 1926) and began a doctoral dissertation. University records show that he stopped his Ph.D. work in the spring of 1931 without receiving the degree. Reportedly, he worked later at Drake University but no records of his employment can be found there.

Until he became interested in UFOs, in the mid-1950s, little is known of Jessup's life after leaving the University of Michigan. He was a photographer on a U.S. Department of Agriculture expedition up the Amazon investigating rubber cultivation, and he was reportedly in South Africa in charge of an observatory mapping southern stars. Some tales place him in the Andes, investigating Inca ruins, and in

Mexico in the early 1950s, charting alien structures.

He is the author of four books: *The Case for the UFO* (1955), *UFO and the Bible* (1956), *The UFO Annual* (1956), and *The Expanding Case for the UFO* (1957).

In April 1959 he committed suicide by placing a hose from the exhaust pipe of his station wagon into the car, while parked in a public park. Some UFO buffs suggest he was murdered to silence some secret knowledge connected with the Bermuda Triangle or the "Philadelphia Experiment," but evidently he was a deeply troubled man who had been discussing suicide for several months.

—JAMES E. OBERG

POSITION STATEMENT: The subject of UFOs in its present stage is like astronomy in that it is a purely observational "science," not an experimental one; necessarily, therefore, it must be based on observation and not on experiment. Observation, in this case, consists of everything which can be found to have bearing on the subject. There are thousands of references to it in ancient literature, but the authors did not know that their references had any bearing, for the subject did not then exist. The writers were recording such things as met their senses solely through an honest effort to report inexplicable observational data.

Some of my contemporaries have attempted to prove that all of these phenomena are, in some way or other, illusory, and that in any case they do not involve flight, wingless or otherwise, mechanical propulsion, or intelligent direction.

I consider their negative case unproven because there is an overwhelming mass of authentic evidence which can be cited as: (1) direct observation, (2) indirect observation, and (3) supporting evidence or indication.

There is one sphere of indirect evidence in the form of events of a mysterious nature which have never been explained. These things would be easy to explain were we to admit the limitations of our own knowledge, and the possibility of "intelligence" elsewhere in the universe operating spaceships—and quite possibly more than one kind of "intelligence" and more than one kind of space-ship!

This world is full of unexplained oddities. The legends of Atlantis and Mu have been favorite targets of the scoffers. They say there are no ghosts, no spirits, nothing falls from the sky but iron and stone meteorites. But for centuries the Earth was believed to be flat, there was no America, no heliocentric system of Earth and planets, no fossil dinosaurs; yet we now know these beliefs to have been wrong.

Reliable people have been seeing the phenomena known as *flying saucers* for a thousand years and more. There are good reports as far back as 1500 B.C. and before. Thousands of people have seen some kind of navigable contraptions in the sky, and some have sworn it under oath.

I cannot agree with any astronomer who insists that all of these things are mirages, planets, clouds, or illusions. The majority of the people are articulate enough to tell their stories and sincere enough to make depositions before notaries public. Even scientists concede that these folk saw *something*.

—MORRIS K. JESSUP

(Position statement was adapted from the preface of Jessup's book, *The Case for the UFO*, 1955.)

Jesus as an extraterrestrial Although the concept of Jesus as an extraterrestrial will be shocking and iconoclastic to some, such an interpretation is inescapable.

The idea has received serious attention from Morris K. Jessup, Brinsley LePoer Trench, W. Raymond Drake, Paul Thomas, Barry H. Downing, R. L. Dione, Gerhard R. Steinhäuser, and others. Steinhäuser devoted an entire book to the subject entitled *Jesus Christ—Heir to the Astronauts* (1974). More recently, Raël, founder and leader of the 50,000-member Raëlian religion, claimed special knowledge—direct from the Elohim—that this is true. (Raël, 1998). And in this writer's

Painting by Monarca Lynn Merrifield

view, Jesus of Nazareth is indeed the extraterrestrial *par excellence.*

That Jesus was an extraterrestrial is first of all true by definition. Doesn't extraterrestrial mean "not of this Earth"? That Jesus came from another world, performed miracles—which today would be associated with advanced technology—and then returned to "heaven" is all part of the Holy Gospel.

Therefore, Jesus is *de facto* an extraterrestrial. Celestial wonders accompanied his birth, many aspects of his life, his death, and resurrection are not dissimilar to events associated today with UFO-related phenomena. In addition to his own words (attributed to Jesus in the New Testament), the evidence includes:

- His miraculous virgin birth, which some UFOlogists attribute to genetic hybridization
- The star of Bethlehem, which hovered over his birthplace like a modern-day flying saucer
- Voices from the sky affirming his otherworldly and superior nature
- His association with angels, who could also be considered *de facto* extraterrestrials
- The transfiguration, during which he appeared as a being composed of brilliant white light
- The resurrection, during which he walked through the walls of his tomb
- The ascension, in which he rose into the sky inside a "bright cloud"
- Sacred religious paintings (or icons) seemingly depicting Jesus in flight

Let us consider each item in more detail.

THE VIRGIN BIRTH

The circumstances surrounding the birth of Jesus are full of hints that something miraculous occurred. A "star" miraculously appears in the sky to herald the birth of the God-Man.

Illustration by Gustave Doré

Brinsley LePoer Trench, the late Earl of Clancarty, was one of the first to suggest that Jesus was an alien hybrid: "Etheric Galactic reproduction proceeds through juggling the chromosomes and genes already there to produce the desired effect. Gabriel could have fathered Jesus only without actual intercourse with Mary, because he was a Galactic." (Trench, 1960)

Again we have a *de facto* case of something that is true by definition. If we accept the tenets of Christianity, then we accept that

Jesus was both the Son of Man and the Son of God—not a mortal human, but a God-Man—a *hybrid*, in other words. From the perspective of modern science, we can now postulate that some form of genetic engineering may have taken place.

THE STAR OF BETHLEHEM

It is more than curious that a bright light or "star" hovered over the birthplace of Jesus at just the right time and place.

Here are the relevant passages from Matthew 2:1-10:

> Now when the birth of Jesus took place in Bethlehem of Judaea, in the days of Herod the king, there came wise men from the east to Jerusalem,
>
> Saying, Where is the King of the Jews whose birth has now taken place? We have seen his star in the east and have come to give him worship.
>
> And when it came to the ears of Herod the king, he was troubled, and all Jerusalem with him.
>
> And he got together all the chief priests and scribes of the people, questioning them as to where the birthplace of the Christ would be.
>
> And they said to him, In Bethlehem of Judaea; for so it is said in the writings of the prophet,
>
> You Bethlehem, in the land of Judah, are not the least among the chiefs of Judah: out of you will come a ruler, who will be the keeper of my people Israel.
>
> Then Herod sent for the wise men privately, and put questions to them about what time the star had been seen.
>
> And he sent them to Bethlehem and said, Go and make certain where the young child is; and when you have seen him, let me have news of it, so that I may come and give him worship.
>
> And after hearing the king, they went on their way; and the star which they saw in the east went before them, till it came to rest over the place where the young child was.
>
> And when they saw the star they were full of joy.

It is universally agreed—by astronomers and space-god proponents alike—that the so-called "Star of Bethlehem" was *not* a star. As pointed out by R. L. Dione, if ". . . it appeared only over Bethlehem . . ." it ". . . would have had to be very close to the earth." (Dione, 1974) Furthermore, the "star" was apparently leading the Magi until it stopped over the birthplace of Jesus. Celestial objects that are millions of miles or light years away do not behave in that manner.

It is also a fact that the "Star of Bethlehem" has never been definitively identified by astronomers even with the assistance of powerful computers that have calculated every instance of known objects such as comets, planets, and supernovae. Some guesses have been made, but no one has ever truly established just exactly what the Star of Bethlehem really was. Again, we have a case in which it is true by definition that the Star of Bethlehem was an unidentified flying object.

THE BAPTISM

Throughout the New Testament, Jesus is affirmed by voices from the sky which some UFOlogists associate with some kind of loud-speaker system emanating from hovering spacecraft.

A case in point occurs at the baptism of Jesus:

> Then Jesus came from Galilee to John at the Jordan, to be given baptism by him.
>
> But John would have kept him back, saying, It is I who have need of baptism from you, and do you come to me?
>
> But Jesus made answer, saying to him, Let it be so now: because so it is right for us to make righteousness complete. Then he gave him baptism.

And Jesus, having been given baptism, straight away went up from the water; and, the heavens opening, he saw the Spirit of God coming down on him as a dove;

And a voice came out of heaven, saying, This is my dearly loved Son, with whom I am well pleased. (Matthew 3:13-17)

ANGELS AS ALIENS

Consider this passage from Luke 2:9: "And an angel of the Lord came to them, and the glory of the Lord was shining round about them: and fear came on them."

This eleventh-century French cloisonné angel is not entirely unlike some aliens that are reported today. Even a possible "space helmet" seems to be in evidence.

The Bible is full of references to Jesus in the company of angels who are in turn associated with bright lights. References to angels constitute the full range of anomalies that we have come to associate with UFOs and their occupants.

As Jessup reminds us: "The theme of bright lights as connected with UFO activity and the appearance of paranormal entities runs profusely through the Bible and Apocryphal books. God, Angels, Messengers, Voices, appeared as, in, or with brilliant lights." (*UFO and the Bible*, p. 32)

In his book, *The Sky People* (1960), Trench quotes a statement of Jesus from Mark 26-7:

And then shall they see the Son of Man coming in the clouds with a great power and glory.

And then shall he send his angels, and shall gather together his elect from the four winds, from the uttermost parts of the earth to the uttermost part of heaven.

Could the "bright cloud" have been a UFO and "Heaven" the planet from which Jesus came?

THE TRANSFIGURATION

The transfiguration of Jesus—in which his appearance became glorified in a display of radiant luminosity—took place probably on either Mt. Tabor or Mt. Hermon.

According to the Bible:

And after six days Jesus takes with him Peter, and James, and John, his brother, and makes them go up with him into a high mountain by themselves.

And he was changed in form before them; and his face was shining like the sun, and his clothing became white as light.

And Moses and Elijah came before their eyes, talking with him.

And Peter made answer and said to Jesus, Lord, it is good for us to be here: if you will let me, I will make here three tents, one for you, and one for Moses, and one for Elijah.

While he was still talking, a bright cloud came over them: and a voice out of the cloud, saying, This is my dearly loved

Son, with whom I am well pleased; give ear to him.

And at these words the disciples went down on their faces in great fear.

And Jesus came and put his hand on them and said, Get up and have no fear.

And lifting up their eyes, they saw no one, but Jesus only.

(Matthew 17:1-8)

THE ASCENSION

Jessup thought that: "The ascension of Christ into the sky (Heaven) is the best known example . . ." of Jesus as an advanced extraterrestrial, ". . .and is an integral part of the resurrection story, or central miracle of Christianity." According to Jessup, ". . .some type of levitation was involved, and the least disturbing solution lies in the presence of a UFO to lift Him, and take Him into the clouds, or heavenly vault, which, to Him, was home." (Jessup, 1956)

According to the Bible:

And he said to them, It is not for you to have knowledge of the time and the order of events which the Father has kept in his control.

But you will have power, when the Holy Spirit has come on you; and you will be my witnesses in Jerusalem and all Judaea and Samaria, and to the ends of the earth.

And when he had said these things, while they were looking, he was taken up, and went from their view into a cloud.

And while they were looking up to heaven with great attention, two men came to them, in white clothing,

And said, O men of Galilee, why are you looking up into heaven? This Jesus, who was taken from you into heaven, will come again, in the same way as you saw him go into heaven.

(Acts 1:6-11)

"Cloud" seems to be a code word for UFO (or some form of aerial transport) throughout the Bible. Jesus was also said to have walked through the solid walls of his tomb, just as alien beings have been reported to do in modern times.

ICONS

Also intriguing are the many sacred paintings called "icons," on the walls of churches and cathedrals throughout Eastern Europe, which could be taken to represent Jesus in various aspects of spaceflight.

These paintings are said to represent the ascension, transfiguration, and second coming, and show lines or rays being emitted from the tail end of the surrounding design which give it a star-like or cometary appearance. It takes only a little imagination to see how these frescoes could be interpreted as a man in a spaceship.

THE MESSAGE

Downing points out that: "What is clear throughout the Biblical material . . . is that God's will for the Jews, and eventually for all mankind, was 'revealed' by beings from another world." (Downing, 1968)

Whether we think in metaphysical or technological terms, the Bible clearly speaks of a superior, extraterrestrial intelligence coming down out of the sky to first create, and then save, mankind. Therefore, if we accept the Bible literally, it would be logically consistent to consider Jesus as a more highly evolved, extraterrestrial being.

Whether he was just more advanced biologically and ethically—as if those were small matters—or in a sacred spiritual sense (the Son of God, no less), that is the great question. But either way, it would seem a safe bet to heed his teachings.

In essence, I think Jesus was telling us how to save our souls (in more than one sense) and how to achieve immortality (in more than one

This collection of icons from churches and cathedrals throughout Europe and Asia traces the Transfiguration (lower left), Ascension, and Second Coming of Christ.

sense). Through the use of parables, he imparted a great deal of practical wisdom that if put into practice would benefit—and save—humanity. He also tried to teach us that man is not the highest authority in the universe—or even on Earth—and that human folly and hubris could lead to our downfall.

So far—he has been proven correct.

—RONALD D. STORY

References

Drake, W. Raymond. *Messengers from the Stars* (London: Sphere Books, 1977). First published as *Gods or Spacemen?* (Amherst Press, 1964).

Dione, R.L. *God Drives a Flying Saucer* (Corgi, 1974).

Downing, Barry. *The Bible and Flying Saucers* (London: Sphere Books, 1973).

Jessup, Morris K. *UFO and the Bible* (The Citadel Press, 1956).

Raël. *The True Face of God* (The Raëlian Foundation, 1998).

Steinhäuser, Gerhard R. *Jesus Christ, Heir to the Astronauts* (Abelard-Schuman, 1974).

Thomas, Paul. *Flying Saucers through the Ages* (Tandem, 1973). First published as *Les Extraterrestres* (France: Libraire Plon, 1962).

Trench, Brinsley Le Poer. *The Sky People* (Neville Spearman, 1960).

Jesus Christ, Heir to the Astronauts (Abelard-Schuman, 1974). German author Gerhard Steinhäuser believes that between 12,000 and 8,000 B.C. competing races of extraterrestrials waged a war throughout our solar system. The winning race colonized Earth in Biblical times, inspired the myths of Moses and Christ, and used energy gates such as the Gate of the Sun in Bolivia as time transporters through which they left this planet.
—RANDALL FITZGERALD

Jordan-Kauble, Debra   (b. 1959). Debbie Jordan-Kauble (formerly Debbie Tomey) is also known as "Kathy Davis," the central figure of Budd Hopkins's bestselling book, *Intruders: The Incredible Visitations at Copley Woods* (1987). She later co-authored, with her sister Kathy Mitchell, *Abducted! The Story of the Intruders Continues . . .* (1994).

Debbie lives in north central Indiana with Dave Kauble (her husband of five years), four dogs, two birds, and two cats. She is a licensed cosmetologist and mother of two grown sons. Debbie is a member of MENSA. She has traveled all over the United States speaking about her experiences and recently traveled to England to speak for BUFORA (British UFO Research Association). She has appeared on Maury Povich, Dini Petty (Canada) Oprah Winfrey's AM Chicago, Sightings, and the Sci Fi Channel. She has appeared on numerous other radio and television programs, as well. She assists her husband in maintaining an impressive Web site of UFO research information, newsclips, and links.

Address: P.O. Box 6730
           Kokomo, IN 46904
           U.S.A.

E-mail: DebKauble@aol.com
Web site: www.debshome.com

FIRST-PERSON ACCOUNT OF
CENTRAL UFO ENCOUNTER

June 30, 1983: I was preparing to go to a neighbor's house to do some sewing and had stopped at the kitchen sink to wash my hands before I left the house. As I looked aimlessly out the window, a very bright light radiating from the swimming pool pumphouse caught

Debbie Jordan-Kauble
(a.k.a. "Kathy Davis")

my eye. At the time, I couldn't figure out exactly why this light didn't seem quite right.

A few minutes later, as I got in my car to leave, I decided to drive around the back of the house on the turnaround to see if the light was still there. I couldn't shake the uneasy feeling I had when I had first seen it. When I reached a point in the driveway where I could see the pumphouse clearly, I saw that the light was gone and the pedestrian door to the attached garage was now open. I began to worry that there might be a prowler on the property. I don't know why I didn't stop right then. Instead, I continued on my way to my neighbor's house.

One of the "Intruders"
(Drawing by Debbie Kauble)

When I arrived at my destination, I called my mother and reported to her what I had seen. I asked her if she wanted me to come home. She told me that she would be fine and not to worry about coming home. As soon as

I hung up the phone, it rang again. I answered it instinctively, and was surprised to hear my mother's voice on the other end asking me to come home "right away." She sounded frightened and that's not like my mother.

When I returned home, I entered the house through the back patio door, grabbed my father's rifle, and proceeded to explore the back yard and the attached garage. At one point in my investigation, I found my loyal dog, Penny, hiding terrified beneath my father's old ladder truck. I couldn't drag her out from under the truck no matter how hard I tried.

I then decided to have a look in the attached garage, to see how the door could have been opened. While I was in there, looking behind old mattresses and boxes, I suddenly began to feel as if my skin was on fire. I thought to myself, "I've got to get out of here right now!" As I reached the open pedestrian door, I was stopped in my tracks by a "bolt from the blue." The only way I can describe what I felt is to say I felt as if I had been hit in the chest by lightning. I immediately thought to myself, "I'm dead! This is what it feels like to be dead!" Every muscle in my body vibrated and I felt as if I were on fire with this bright light tearing through my chest. I couldn't see a thing because the light was so bright, and even when my eyes were closed, the light was still so bright that it hurt my eyes.

After what seemed like an eternity, the brightness of the light faded, the vibrating stopped and I felt a heavy numbness sweep over me. I then realized that I was paralyzed. My eyes were still having trouble focusing; all I could see were a few vague shadows moving in front of me. I then felt a tug at my right shoulder and felt a piercing pain in my right ear.

My next memory is of being about ten feet outside the doorway from where all this had started. To my left, I could see the silhouette of an egg-shaped craft, approximately twelve feet tall and ten feet wide at its greatest width. I could see six small, bullet-shaped figures moving diagonally in front of me toward this craft. I could see a soft white ball of light about ten feet in front of me. It was about five feet off the ground, and it moved slowly down and then back up again to where it had started. I recalled someone telling me that it was unfortunate that I had to have felt pain, but that it was now over.

The next memory I had was of walking up the sidewalk to the kitchen door, speaking to my mother, and then going back to my neighbor's house to bring her back to my house to swim. (I had decided to swim instead of sew.) I had no memory of what had happened to me in the yard that night until a couple of days later, when I first saw the mark the craft had left in our yard.

That mark was to remain there for nearly five years and after I saw it for the first time, a dozen memories came flooding back to me of events that had happened over much of my life.

POSITION STATEMENT: UFOs (Unidentified Flying Objects) exist. There are many different explanations for them, some very rational and prosaic, others not so clear. I don't think there is any question as to their existence. Of the ones not so easily explained away, we should be asking, "What are they, where are they from, and why are they here?"

I have had so many different types of experiences with so many different aspects of this field that I am somewhat mixed as to what I think they are and where they come from. I have seen the hard evidence that debunkers claim does not exist. I have also experienced the psychological and physical effects, as well as the spiritual awakening of a close encounter. I am also smart enough to realize how powerful the human mind can be when faced with something that it cannot comprehend. All I have ever been able to do was report what I saw and let everyone else sort it all out.

Deep in my heart, I cannot help but think that all paranormal phenomena is somehow connected and that our visitors may be a part of our past as well as our future. I don't think the time traveler theory is out of the question.

But that's just my opinion. I have tried to stay away from theories to avoid contaminating the facts.

Over the past sixteen years, I have found many people who could tell me what I *didn't* see, or what *didn't* happen, but no one has been able to tell me what *did* happen. There is still a great deal that I don't remember about some of my experiences. I have resigned myself to the fact that I probably never will know the "rest of the story."

But one thing I am certain of—something extraordinary happened to me that night back in 1983. Something that would change me and my life forever. Now, if that isn't something the whole world should know about, I don't know what is.

—DEBBIE JORDAN-KAUBLE

References

Hopkins, Budd. *Intruders: The Incredible Visitations at Copley Woods* (Random House, 1987).

Jordan, Debbie, and Kathy Mitchell. *Abducted! The Story of the Intruders Continues . . .* (Carroll & Graf, 1994).

Jung, Carl Gustav (1875-1961). C. G. Jung, world-famous psychiatrist (and philosopher-psychologist), is perhaps best known for some of the terms he coined, such as "complex," "introvert," and "extrovert"; but he made his mark in UFO research as well. His little book *Flying Saucers: A Modern Myth of Things Seen in the Skies* (1958) has had a lasting influence on virtually every UFOlogist who has ever considered the psychological and sociological aspects of the UFO phenomenon.

Dr. Jung was born in Kesswil, Thurgau, Switzerland, on July 26, 1875, and died at Kusnacht, Zilrich, on June 6, 1961. He earned his medical degree from the University of Basle in 1900, and took a position shortly thereafter at the University of Ziffich Psychiatric Clinic. His collaboration with Sigmund Freud lasted from 1907 to 1914, at which time Jung established his own school of thought, called Analytical Psychology (later renamed

C. G. Jung

Complex Psychology). The year 1921 saw the publication of Jung's classic book, *Psychological Types,* wherein the terms ''introvert'' and ''extrovert'' were first introduced.

According to Jungian theory, the human psyche is embroiled in a battle of opposites: extroversion versus introversion; the ego (center of consciousness) versus the integrated conscious and unconscious Self (or God-image); the *persona* (or social mask) versus the *shadow* (unconscious natural self); thinking and feeling (rational functions) versus sensation and intuition (irrational forces). The dominant component is that which determines the individual's psychological type. The unifying elements are the *archetypes* or ''primordial images,'' according to which we all think. The archetypes are manifested symbolically in myths, dreams, and psychoses. Certain of these symbols are common to every human psyche as part of what Jung called the ''collective unconscious.'' He once said, ''the archetypes of the unconscious can be shown empirically to be the equivalents of religious dogmas.''

Some classic archetypes are the ''wise old man,'' the ''great mother,'' the ''trickster,'' the ''child-god,'' ''Christ'' (or the ideal Self—with a capital ''S''), and the *mandala* (a Sanskrit word meaning ''magic circle''), which Jung thought of as representing UFOs (as well as the God-image).

The mandala is one of the oldest religious symbols found throughout the world. Frieda Fordham wrote in her biography of Jung *(An Introduction to Jung's Psychology,* 1953): ''Historically, the mandala served as a symbol representing the nature of the deity, both in order to clarify it philosophically, and for the purpose of adoration. Jung found the mandala symbolism occurring spontaneously in the dreams and visions of many of his patients. Its appearance was incomprehensible to them, but it was usually accompanied by a strong feeling of harmony or of peace.'' Jung himself later wrote (in *Flying Saucers: A Modern Myth):*

''Insofar as the mandala encompasses, protects, and defends the psychic totality against outside influences and seeks to unite the inner opposites, it is at the same time a distinct *individuation symbol* and was known as such even to medieval alchemy. The soul was supposed to have the form of a sphere, on the analogy of Plato's world-soul, and we meet the same symbol in modern dreams. By reason of its antiquity, this symbol leads us to the heavenly spheres, to Plato's 'supra-celestial place,' where the 'Ideas' of all things are stored up. Hence there would be nothing against the naive interpretation of the UFOs as 'souls.' Naturally they do not represent our modern conception of the soul, but rather an involuntary archetypal or mythological conception of an unconscious content, a *rotundum,* as the alchemists called it, that expresses the totality of the individual. . . .

''If the round shining objects that appear in the sky be regarded as visions, we can hardly avoid interpreting them as archetypal images. They would then be involuntary, automatic projections based on instinct, and as little as any other psychic manifestations or symptoms can they be dismissed as meaningless and merely fortuitous. Anyone with the requisite historical and psychological knowledge knows that circular symbols have played an important role in every age; in our own sphere of culture, for instance, they were not only soul symbols but 'God-images.' There is an old saying that 'God is a circle whose center is everywhere and the circumference nowhere.' God in his omniscience, omnipotence, and omnipresence is a totality symbol *par excellence,* something round, complete, and perfect. Epiphanies of this sort are, in the tradition, often associated with fire and light. On the antique level, therefore, the UFOs could easily be conceived as 'gods.' If these things [UFOs] are real—and by all human standards it hardly seems possible to doubt this any longer—then we are left with only two hypotheses: that of their *weightlessness* on the one hand and of their *psychic nature* on the other.''

What occurred to Jung was that thoughts and dreams are also ''weightless,'' and this he considered a clue to the psychic nature of UFOs, which might mean that they are purely mental and have no existence outside the mind of the observer. He regarded the UFO phenomenon as a visionary rumor and as a psychological projection of man's hopes and fears in an uncertain world. Although not denying the possible physical reality of the phenomenon, Jung saw UFOs as the new mythology—the Gods of the age of science.

—RONALD D. STORY

References

Fordham, Frieda. *An Introduction to Jung's Psychology* (Penguin Books, 1953).

Jung, C. G. *Flying Saucers: A Modern Myth of Things Seen in the Skies* (Routledge & Kegan Paul/Harcourt, Brace & Co. 1959; Signet/NAL, 1969; Princeton University Press, 1978). (Original German language edition published in 1958.)

———. *Mandala Symbolism* (Princeton University Press, 1959, 1969).

K

Kecksberg (Pennsylvania) incident The Kecksberg event occurred on December 9, 1965, about 40 miles from Pittsburgh in a rural area of western Pennsylvania. At the time many people saw a brilliant object moving across the sky. The news media focused on a young boy who, while playing outside, said he saw an object fall from the sky into some nearby woods. The media pursued his story since there were numerous accounts from others that an aerial object was seen over a large area including many reports from the greater Pittsburgh area.

Besides the police authorities, various newspapers, and radio and TV stations around Pittsburgh had their phone lines jammed with calls about the object in the sky. Coincidentally, author Frank Edwards, who had written some popular books on UFOs, was a guest on a KDKA radio talk show in Pittsburgh that evening, hosted by the late Mike Levine.

During my years of investigation into the matter, other witnesses who saw the object go down into the woods that day have been located. It has been stated that moments after the object fell, blue smoke rose up among the trees, but dissipated quickly. Many people say that the military, including members of the Army and Air Force, began to arrive in the area around the village of Kecksburg within a few hours after the reported landing. During the evening, reporters from numerous media sources went to Kecksburg to investigate the event.

The area around the alleged impact site was cordoned off, and a search for the object was conducted in the woods. Neither civilians nor reporters were able to get near the spot where the object had reportedly fallen. Hundreds of spectators looked on from a narrow county road which circled around the area, unaware that the object appeared to have fallen on the opposite side of the woods.

As time passed that evening, many people left disappointed that they couldn't see the object. A few curious folks tried to sneak down into the woods, and later told me that they were turned back by the military. Late that night, others say they observed a military flat-bed tractor-trailer truck, carrying a large tarpaulin-covered object, leaving the area at a high rate of speed. Reporters are among the many witnesses who verify that they saw military personnel in the Kecksburg area that night. The front page of the Greensburg, Pennsylvania, *Tribune-Review* county edition dated December 10, 1965, ran the headlines "Unidentified Flying Object Falls Near Kecksburg" and "Army Ropes Off Area." The city edition of the same paper, however, on the same day ran the headline "Searchers Fail To Find Object."

Officially, no object was found in the woods by searchers. It was suggested that the most likely explanation was that the brilliant object in the sky was a meteor. But word that something was removed from the site by the military that night quickly circulated around the county. The Kecksburg incident remained a topic for area radio talk shows for years as it does today. As the years passed, I would receive various accounts from sources who claimed knowledge of the event. Many of those involved with the incident even today, wish to remain anonymous. Others have gone public and stand by their accounts. Some have faced personal attacks and ridicule. Many important witnesses have passed away.

What we now know is that there are individuals who say that they went down into the woods that December day in 1965, before the military arrived, and came upon a large metallic acorn-shaped object partially buried in the ground. The device was large enough for a man to stand inside of it. The object was a bronze-gold color, and appeared to be one solid piece of metal, displaying no rivets or seams. At the back of the acorn shape was what witness Jim Romansky calls the bumper area.

Artist's conception of the object some claim to have seen
(Drawing by C.M. Hanna)

Upon this area were unusual markings that Romansky says looked similar to ancient Egyptian hieroglyphics. Romansky, who has been a machinist for many years, says the object itself looked as though it had been made from liquid metal and poured into a big mold. Since the object was impacted in the ground, the bottom portion was not visible, but what could be seen appeared well intact. The late John Murphy, was the news director of WHJB radio in Greensburg at the time, and is believed to have been the first reporter on the scene. His former wife says that she was in radio contact with him from the site that day, and that he told her that he went down into the woods and saw the object. Various informants have approached me with information. Some of these were people who had military or gov-

ernment affiliation and wished not to be identified at this time. Some information is expected to be revealed in the future, when these sources feel that they are safe to disclose what they know.

I have also received anonymous tips that pointed me in the right direction which helped to uncover other details. Before "Unsolved Mysteries" broadcast their story about Kecksburg in 1990, I was contacted by a former Air Force security policeman who told me that he was among the unit that guarded the object when it arrived from Pennsylvania in the early morning hours of December 10, 1965, at Lockbourne Air Force Base near Columbus, Ohio. He remembers extreme security measures at the time, and says that the object was only at the base for a short time, and then continued on to Wright-Patterson Air Force Base near Dayton, Ohio.

We later learned that the object was allegedly sealed up inside a building at that base. After years of searching for government documents relating to this event, the only official record located was in the Air Force Project Blue Book files. Included in the report it was stated "A further call was made to the Oakdale Radar site in Pennsylvania. A three-man team has been dispatched to Acme [some residents not far from the site have an Acme mailing address] to investigate and pick up an object that started a fire." While the report shows a lot of interest from various agencies concerning the aerial object, the report also indicates that the search found nothing. I have learned a lot about the Kecksburg case over the years, yet there remain many unanswered questions. I surely don't have all of the answers.

Based on the accounts of multitudes of eyewitnesses which I have interviewed, I am convinced that an object did fall from the sky and apparently was removed by the military. Other witnesses say they saw NASA personnel at the scene that night also involved in the search. Many have asked me what I believe that the object was, and my reply still is "I don't know." As I have stated in the past, the two most likely possibilities are (1) a highly advanced man-made space probe with some re-entry control capability; or (2) an extraterrestrial spacecraft. It has been confirmed that a faulty Soviet Venus probe identified as *Kosmos 96*, reentered in Canada on the same date, but at about 3:18 A.M. The sightings around Kecksburg occurred at about 4:47 P.M., many hours later. The Russians have told me that *Kosmos 96* was not the source of what fell that day.

Other researchers have provided me with interesting but unverifiable information that they have talked with former NASA sources who claimed to have examined the object which fell in Pennsylvania, and determined it to be Soviet in origin. I have also talked with two former military men who are unknown to each other, who told me that during different years, and at different installations, they saw the recovery report on the Kecksburg object, and both said the report indicated that the object was extraterrestrial. From what the observers tell us, the object, whatever it was, appeared to be slowing down a few miles before it impacted. During its flight, it appears to have made some turns, and those who saw the object drop from the sky, say it was moving quite slowly as it moved toward the woods. This might account for the good condition of the object itself, and the little damage at the impact site, except for trees which were reportedly knocked down.

One question we must ask is what was it that fell which was so important that it caused the military to act the way they did at the scene?

Various witnesses have now gone public confirming that armed soldiers were around the village, and were preventing anyone from trespassing near the crash site. Jerry Betters, a popular jazz musician from Pittsburgh, has gone public and told his story that soldiers aimed rifles at him and his friends, ordering them from a back road, as an Army flatbed tractor-trailer with an acorn-shaped object on board, was making its way up from a field.

More recently, a prominent businessman contacted me and told me how he and his friends, then teenagers in 1965, tried to get near the site and were stopped by military personnel. He was frightened at the time of the experience, he thought the soldier was going to shoot him. Would armed soldiers respond to the scene of a meteorite crash? Who issued the orders for such an operation to take place? The Kecksburg mystery remains.

—STAN GORDON

References

Gordon, Stan. ''Kecksburg: The Untold Story'' video (Stan Gordon Productions, 1998).

Randle, Kevin D. *A History of UFO Crashes* (Avon Books, 1995).

Randles, Jenny. *UFO Retrievals* (Blandford Books, 1995).

Young, Robert. ''Old Solved Mysteries: The Kecksburg UFO Incident'' in Frazier, Kendrick, Barry Karr, and Joe Nickell, eds. *The UFO Invasion* (Prometheus Books, 1997).

Keel, John A. (b. 1930). Pen name of Alva John Kiehle. A professional writer since age sixteen, John Keel was head writer on numerous radio and television programs, science editor for Funk & Wagnall's encyclopedia, a syndicated newspaper columnist, and author of thirteen books and countless published short pieces for major publications in the U.S. and abroad. He also founded the New York Fortean Society in 1987.

John Keel

His books include: *UFOs: Operation Trojan Horse* (1970), *Strange Creatures from Time and Space* (1970), *Our Haunted Planet* (1971), *The Mothman Prophecies* (1975), *The Eighth Tower* (1976), and *Disneyland of the Gods* (1988).

POSITION STATEMENT: I abandoned the extraterrestrial hypothesis (ETH) in 1967 when my own field investigations disclosed an astonishing overlap between psychic phenomena and UFOs. My findings were extremely unpopular at the time, but in the years since, most of the major European investigators, and many of the American scientists involved in the subject, have verified and accepted my conclusions.

Basically, a large part of the UFO lore is subjective and many alleged UFO events are actually the products of a complex hallucinatory process, particularly in the contactee and CE-III-type reports. The same process stimulated religious beliefs, fairy lore, and occult systems of belief in other centuries.

A very small percentage of sightings (perhaps less than 2 percent) and events indicate that other strange, but natural, phenomena are often included, or absorbed, into the UFO data.

While we cannot satisfactorily explain all UFO events in terms of present-day knowledge and technology, I feel that the ultimate solution will involve a complicated system of new physics related to theories of the space-time continuum. It is possible, even highly probable, that a subtle cosmological system of control has been in effect since the dawn of mankind and that UFOs are a part of that system.

The objects and apparitions do not necessarily originate on another planet and may not even exist as permanent constructions of matter. It is more likely that we see what we want to see and interpret such visions according to our contemporary beliefs. The problem can be reduced to a series of difficult philosophical questions and might be explored by behavioral scientists and mathematicians.

—JOHN A. KEEL

Kelly Cahill abduction   A woman, Kelly Cahill, contacted me on October 4, 1993, about a bizarre experience she had near the outer Melbourne (Australia) suburban housing estate of Narre Warren North, in the foothills of the Dandenongs, Victoria, during the early hours of August 8, 1993. Because of the potential significance of the initial report by Kelly Cahill, I referred her to John Auchetti and his Victoria-based group Phenomena Research Australia (PRA). Kelly Cahill proved to be central to the unraveling of an independently witnessed CE-3 event with apparent "abduction" dimensions and related physical evidence.

Illustration courtesy of MUFON

Entities and craft as described by
Kelly Cahill (Drawing by Wes Crum)

On their way home, Kelly and her husband were confronted with a spectacular view of a UFO. They seemed to experience "missing time." Subsequent spontaneous conscious recall by Kelly Cahill indicated that the couple had stopped their car. The large UFO was over a field off the road. They got out to get a closer look. It was at this point that Kelly recollected seeing another car that was parked further down the road, which contained at least two people, a man and a woman. She paid little heed to them at the time, because they were focused on the UFO that had landed in the field. Kelly recollects crossing the road to the field, seeing at first one tall black being with glowing red eyes, then many which seemed to be approaching rapidly, as if gliding. The large group of tall black beings, seemed to split into two groups, one focused on Kelly and her husband, and the other one on the other people who had also crossed further down the road.

Kelly found herself screaming out to the other group of people down the road, "They're evil. They're going to kill us." She was then struck in the stomach area and fell back onto the ground, somehow unable to see. The rest of her recollection is somewhat confusing and fragmentary. Voices and blindness were experienced. She experienced physical effects including marks on her abdomen.

By November 17, 1993, PRA's investigation managed to locate the man and woman apparently seen by Kelly that night. They took PRA back to the encounter site, to a spot consistent with Kelly's location of them. The group's drawings of the UFO and entities also closely coincide with those of Kelly. Another woman was with this couple that night.

Bill, the male witness in the trio also, like Kelly's husband, appears have also had only limited involvement. The two women had a conscious recollection up to and including onboard episodes. They recollected the UFO, and the tall black beings. Their description did not feature the red eyes Kelly saw. Sketches made by the three women of both the UFO and the beings bear a striking resemblance.

As they approached the site the trio heard a strange noise and started to feel ill. The driver, Bill, started to lose control over the car, and ran off the road striking a pole. After checking for damage they drove on for a short distance. Throughout this Bill's vision was impaired. He was unable to remember seeing the UFO. The two women with him recollected the UFO clearly and their descriptions matched those of Kelly's closely. Bill had extensive conscious recall of smells and sounds, and a lot of activity going on, but does not recall seeing anything. He subsequently underwent hypnosis, which expanded his apparent recollections to apparent onboard components but again these were through the senses of smell and hearing only.

The two women with Bill had a conscious recollection of the UFO, the beings, and onboard experiences. There was no sense of this, for them, being an abduction experience, as there seemed to be a "free will" type of situation. The primary element of their onboard experiences seemed to be a form of examination. However the abduction episode was not visually remembered. Other parts of their onboard experience were remembered visually and consciously. Hypnosis in their cases appeared to have only reinforced their conscious recollections. There was no apparent speech and very little information from the entities involved. Marks that resembled pressure rings around the base of their legs lasted for about two weeks. Each had "rash"-like spotting around the thigh areas and one had swelling of the vaginal area.

This second group described seeing yet another car parked further back down from them. In it a man appeared to be looking at the UFO's position through a break in the vegetation cover. This man has come forward anonymously providing details that could only have been known to someone who was there. He had also experienced ligature-style marks on his ankles.

This extraordinary case appears to involve independent groups of people unknown to each other witnessing the same UFO encounter, entities, and experiencing missing time. Two of the groups have been available to investigators and researchers. There were effects on some of the witnesses, including gynecological problems, body marks, and ankle ligature-like injuries. Unusual ground traces at the site of the apparent UFO landing (including three ground markings about 6 metres apart resembling affected or wilted grass). Possibly significant levels of pyrene (a polynuclear aromatic compound, which can be found in coal tar) and above-average sulphur content, were noted. There was also a half-moon-shaped magnetic trace of a low order. Perhaps for the first time independent witnesses have been able to provide information that enabled cross checking and correlations to reveal a striking degree of similar information, therefore offering a compelling case for the reality of the strange events described.

—WILLIAM C. CHALKER

References

Cahill, Kelly. *Encounter* (1996).
Chalker, William C. *The Oz Files: The Australian UFO Story* (Duffy & Snellgrove, 1996).
———. "An Extraordinary Encounter in the Dandenong Foothills," *International UFO Reporter* (September/October 1994).

Kelly-Hopkinsville (Kentucky) goblins

Probably the granddaddy of all "occupant" sightings in the United States is that which occurred on August 22, 1955, near Hopkinsville, Kentucky. The basic details include the beginning of the episode when visiting relative Bill Taylor went out to the well for a drink and came back in to tell of a "spaceship" which had landed in a nearby field. Just a scant few minutes later the aroused household saw a small specter-like figure approaching the house.

It appeared to be lit by an internal source, had a roundish head, huge elephantine ears, a slit-like mouth which extended from ear to ear. The eyes were huge and wide-set. Only about three or three and one-half feet in height, the creature had no visible neck, and its arms were long and ended in clawed hands. Although it stood upright, it dropped to all fours when it ran.

According to the Frank Sutton family, several of these creatures roamed the area adjacent to the house, climbed trees, and climbed up on the roof. At one point Sutton fired a shotgun

through the screen door at one of the little men. Although struck and knocked over by the blast, the little fellow got up and scuttled away on his hands and feet. Later, Taylor walked out the same door, only to be confronted by one of the creatures on the roof, apparently grabbing for his head.

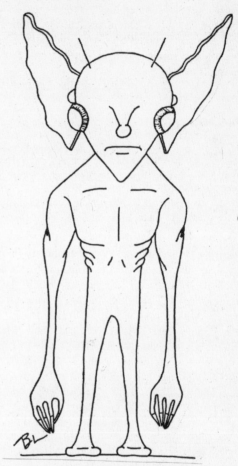

One of the creatures as described to artist Bud Ledwith

This weird sequence of events continued for the greater part of one night, and finally the family scrambled to the car and drove into town to report their plight. Deputy Sheriff George Batts and two Kentucky state police came to the house but found no evidence of the little men's presence or the "spaceship."

However, researchers who interviewed the Suttons and carefully investigated the whole affair, including Isabel Davis of New York (Civilian Saucer Investigations), were inclined to believe the incident did take place.

Local investigators, including Chief of Police Greenwell, said that "something scared those people—something beyond reason—nothing ordinary." One investigator with medical experience noted Sutton's rapid pulse beat of 140 per minute, which is about twice the normal rate.

—CORAL & JIM LORENZEN

References

Hendry, Allan. "Kelly/Hopkinsville (Kentucky) encounter" in Story, Ronald D., ed. *The Encyclopedia of UFOs* (Doubleday/New English Library, 1980).

Lorenzen, Coral and Jim. *Flying Saucer Occupants* (Signet/NAL, 1967).

Kentucky abduction　The February 1, 1976, issue of the *Kentucky Advocate,* published at Danville, Kentucky, carried an article pertaining to UFO sightings in that general area, among which was the story told by Mrs. Louise Smith, Mrs. Mona Stafford, and Mrs. Elaine Thomas about their drive home to Liberty from a late dinner at the Redwoods Restaurant, located five miles north of Stanford.

The ladies were celebrating Mona Stafford's thirty-sixth birthday on January 6, 1976. After they left the restaurant—at a point about one mile south of Stanford—they saw a huge disk-shaped object, which was metallic gray with a white glowing dome. A row of red lights rotated around the middle, and underneath were three or four red and yellow lights that burned steadily. A bluish beam of light issued from the bottom.

The newspaper did not carry a lot of detail, but it was mentioned that when the women arrived home in Liberty, it was 1:25 A.M. Having left the restaurant at 11:15 P.M., they should have arrived home by midnight, indicating a time loss of about one hour and twenty-five minutes.

An Aerial Phenomena Research Organization (APRO) investigation brought out the following details: After Mona spotted the object, which was descending from their right to the left, she asked Louise to speed up as she thought it was a plane about to crash, and she wanted to help any survivors. Mrs. Smith saw it clearly, but Mrs. Thomas did not see it until it had stopped at treetop level at what they estimated to be one hundred yards ahead of them. All of the women said the object was huge; Louise described it as being "as big as a football field," while Mrs. Stafford said it was at least as large as two houses.

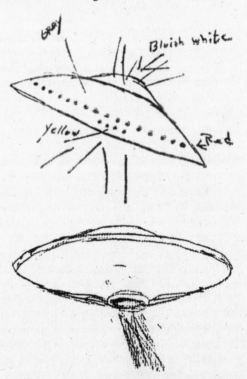

Drawings of the UFO by Louise Smith

Mrs. Smith said that the object rocked gently for perhaps two seconds, at which time she estimated its size, for it extended beyond the edges of the road and over the fields on both sides. It then moved across the road to their left, circling behind and above some houses, and then apparently came back to the highway and swung in behind the car.

At a point in their journey, about a quarter of a mile beyond the houses, the inside of the car was lit up with a bluish light which came from behind. Mrs. Smith said that at first she thought it was a state trooper approaching from behind, but realized almost immediately that it was not. At this point, Louise and Mona were near panic. The car began to pull to the left, and Louise screamed at Mona to help her control it. The speedometer was registering eighty-five miles per hour, and both Mona and Mrs. Thomas shouted at Mrs. Smith to slow down. Louise held her foot in the air to show them and said: "I don't have my foot on the accelerator and I can't stop it!" Mona reached over and grabbed the wheel and they fought the "force" together. Then, quite suddenly, the women experienced a burning sensation in their eyes, and Louise later described an additional pain which seemed to "go right through the top of my head! It was almost unbearable!"

The next sensation was that of some "force" pulling the car backward. Also, they got the feeling that the car was going over a series of "speed bumps." Mrs. Thomas began urging Louise to stop so that she could get a good look at the object, but Mona and Louise were too terrified. Elaine had only a glimpse of the object as it circled to their left and around behind them, and later commented about the object's "beauty." "I can't describe it," she said. "I've never seen red that beautiful. I wanted to get out and look at it."

Then, the women said, they saw a strange, wide, lighted road stretching as far as they could see ahead of them. At the same moment, Mona noted that a red light on the car's instrument panel had come on, indicating that the engine had stalled, despite the sensation that they were moving very fast.

At what seemed to be a split second later, the women saw a streetlight ahead and realized that they were coming into Hustonville, a full eight miles beyond where they had encountered the strange craft. They wondered among themselves how they had gotten there so fast, then became quiet while they proceeded on into Liberty.

When they arrived at Mrs. Smith's trailer, they all went inside. Mrs. Smith went into the bathroom, took off her glasses, and splashed water on her face, whereupon her hands and face began to burn with searing pain. All three had a red mark on the back of their necks, measuring about three inches long and one inch wide, with clearly defined edges, giving the appearance of a new burn before it blisters. Louise and Elaine's marks were centrally located between the base of their skulls and the top of the back, whereas Mona's was located to the left, behind her ear. They could not account for the marks, which disappeared two days later. All three were experiencing burning and tearing of their eyes, but Mona Stafford had a much more severe case of conjunctivitis (an inflammation of the conjunctiva membrane of the eyes).

Prior to washing her hands, Louise had taken off her watch and was startled to see that the hands of her watch were moving at an accelerated rate of speed, the minute hand moving at the speed of a second hand, and the hour hand was moving also. Upon experiencing the pain of the water on her hands and face, she forgot about the phenomenon of the watch and does not recall when it returned to normal or when she reset it.

Concluding that something was wrong, the three ladies went next door to the home of Mr. Lowell Lee and told him what they had seen. He asked them to go into separate rooms and sketch the object, and when finished, he found the resulting sketches to be almost identical.

Although all the women had trouble with their eyes, only Mona Stafford sought medical help, as her problem was so severe. The doctor who examined her found no explanation for the pain and tearing, but gave her some eyedrops which helped very little.

On July 23, 1976, the three ladies met in Liberty with Jack C. Young, president of Professional Polygraph Consultants, Inc., of Lexington, and they were given a polygraph test.

The pertinent test questions for Mary Louise Smith were the following:

Question: After this experience, were you unable to account for a period of time that night? *Answer:* Yes.

Question: This past January 6, did a UFO hover over your 1967 Chevrolet sedan? *Answer:* Yes.

Question: During this experience, did you lose physical control over your automobile? *Answer:* Yes.

Question: Have you conspired with anyone to create a hoax about this UFO encounter? *Answer:* No.

In Mrs. Stafford's and Mrs. Thomas's report, as with that of Louise Smith, Young stated that in his opinion they believed they were telling the truth about the questions asked. However, Mr. Young did make a comment which should not be overlooked. He wrote, "Prior to the examination of these three persons, it was determined by the polygraphist that these persons had been previously interviewed by Dr. R. Leo Sprinkle and members of the Mutual UFO Network (MUFON). How much or how little these previous interviews played a part in what these persons now believe about this alleged encounter cannot be determined by the polygraphist. I cannot discount the fact that previous interviews with these persons could influence their personal beliefs as to whether or not this alleged encounter did or did not occur."

On July 24, psychologist R. Leo Sprinkle, Professor Emeritus of the University of Wyoming (also an APRO consultant), conducted hypnotic trance sessions. What follows is a summary of Dr. Sprinkle's findings:

". . . Mrs. Smith suffered much as she relived the experience. The behaviors, e.g., weeping, moaning, tossing her head, shuddering, and shaking were evident to those of us who observed her, especially as she seemed to relive an experience of a fluid material covering her face." Sprinkle then goes on to recount Louise's claim that her pet parakeet, according to her claims and the claims of others who observed the bird, refused to have anything to do with her after the UFO experience. Others could approach the bird and it would not react wildly; however, whenever Louise came close to the bird, the bird would flutter and move away from her. The bird died within weeks after the UFO experience.

Mona Stafford ". . . responded well to the hypnotic suggestions, and she was able to describe impressions which led her to believe that she had been taken out of the car and that she was alone on a white table or bed. She saw a large eye which seemed to be observing her. She felt as if a bright white light was shining on her and that there was power or energy which transfixed her and held her to the table or bed. She experienced a variety of physiological reactions, including the impressions that her right arm was pinned or fastened, her left leg forced back under her, with pain to the ankle and foot; pressure on the fingers of the left hand, as if they were forced or squeezed in some way; a feeling of being examined by four or five short humanoids who sat around in 'surgical masks' and 'surgical garments' while observing her. At one point, she sensed that she was either experiencing out-of-body travel or else she was waiting outside of a large room in which she could view another person, probably a woman, lying on a white bed or observation table. She perceived a long tunnel, or a view of the sky, as if she had been transported to an area inside a large mountain or volcano. Although she wept and moaned and experienced a great deal of fatigue as a result of the reliving of the experience, she felt better the next day; she expressed the belief to me that she now had a better understanding of what happened during the loss-of-time experience.

"Mrs. Thomas had been rather quiet during the initial interview in March 1976, although it was obvious that she is perceptive and aware of other people's attitudes and feelings. Like the others, she has lost weight, but she has also experienced some personality changes. She dresses a bit more colorfully now, and she is more willing to talk and to share her ideas with others. She, too, experienced a similar reaction during the hypnotic techniques: She apparently was responding well to suggestions to go deeper; when she relived the UFO experience, she experienced a great deal of emotional reaction. Her main impression was that she was taken away from her two friends and that she was placed in a 'chamber' with a window on the side. She seemed to recall figures which moved back and forth in front of the window of the chamber as if she were being observed. Her impression was that the observers were four-foot-tall humanoids, with dark eyes and gray skin. One disturbing aspect of the experience was the memory that she had some kind of contraption or covering that was placed around her neck, whenever she tried to speak, or think, the contraption or covering was tightened, and she experienced a choking sensation during these moments. At first, Mrs. Thomas interpreted the memories as an indication that she was being choked by hands or that she was being prevented from calling out to her friends; later, however, she came to the tentative conclusion that an experiment was being conducted, and the experiment was to learn more about her intellectual and emotional processes. She recalled a bullet-shaped object, about an inch and one half in diameter, being placed on her left chest; she previously had experienced pain and a red spot at that location.

"During the polygraph examination, and during the initial hypnotic sessions, each UFO witness was interviewed separately from the other witnesses. After the initial description of impressions, the women were invited to attend the additional hypnosis sessions so that each woman could observe the reaction of the other two women. During these sessions, there was much emotional reaction, which seemed to arise from two conditions: the compassion of the witnesses for their friend who was reliving the experience and releasing emotional reactions to the experience; also, it seems as if the description by one witness would trigger a memory on the part of another witness, even if the experiences seemed to be similar or different.

"Certain similarities were observed: a feeling of anxiety on the part of each witness regarding a specific aspect of the experience. For Ms. Smith, it was the wall and the gate beyond which she was afraid to move psychologically; for Ms. Stafford it was the eye which she observed and the impression that something evil or bad would be learned if she allowed the eye to control her; for Ms. Thomas, it was the blackness which seemed to be the feared condition or cause for anxiety. Each woman seemed to experience the impression that she had been taken out of the car and placed elsewhere without her friends and without verbal communication. For Ms. Smith, the lack of verbal communication was most distressing, although she had the feeling that she would be returned after the experiment.

"Differences were noted in that each woman seemed to have a somewhat different kind of examination, and in a different location. Ms. Smith did not have a clear impression of the location, although she did recall a feeling of lying down and being examined; Ms. Stafford had the impression of being in a volcano or mountainside, with a room in which a bright light was shining on a white table with white-clothed persons or humanoids sitting around and observing her; Mrs. Thomas recalled impressions of being in a dark chamber, with gray light permitting a view of the humanoids who were apparently observing her."

In his conclusive paragraphs, Dr. Sprinkle reports:

"In my opinion, each woman is describing a real experience, and they are using their intelligence and perceptivity as accurately as possible in order to describe the impressions which they obtained during the hypnotic regressions session. Although there is uncertainty about their impressions, especially in regard to how each person could be transported out of the car and relocated in the car, the impressions during the loss-of-time experience are similar to those of other UFO witnesses who apparently have experienced an abduction and examination during their UFO sighting.

"Although it is not possible to claim absolutely that a physical examination and abduction has taken place, I believe that the tentative hypothesis of abduction and examination is the best hypothesis to explain the apparent loss-of-time experience, the apparent physical and emotional reactions of the witnesses to the UFO sighting. An interesting subsequent event is that the women were re-experiencing their physical symptoms that had followed the January 1976 sightings. When I called them on July 26, the women said that they were suffering some of the same kinds of symptoms, e.g., fatigue, listlessness, sensitivity to skin, burning feeling on the face and eyes, fluid discharge, etc.

"I tried to reassure the ladies that it is not an uncommon experience in hypnotic regression that persons—after reliving earlier emotional experiences—may re-experience some of the symptoms which accompany those emotional reactions.

"I believe the case is a good example of UFO experiences, because of the number and character of the witnesses . . . and because of the results of further investigation through polygraph examinations and hypnotic regression sessions."

—CORAL & JIM LORENZEN
& R. LEO SPRINKLE

Keyhoe, Donald E. (1897-1988). A graduate of the U.S. Naval Academy and the Marine Corps Officers School, Major Donald Keyhoe (USMC Ret.) was a Marine aircraft and balloon pilot during World War II. After a night crash in the Pacific, he was temporarily retired from active duty. During this period he was Chief of Information, Civil Aeronautics, Department of Commerce (now the Federal Aviation Administration). Having previously established himself as an aviation journalist, Keyhoe resumed his writing career after the war.

He was asked to become the director of the National Investigations Committee on Aerial Phenomena (NICAP) in 1957, and served in that capacity for thirteen years. During the period from 1949 to 1973, he wrote several best-selling books on UFOs in which he championed the government cover-up/conspiracy theory. His first article on the subject, "Flying Saucers Are Real," caused a sensation when published by *True* magazine in its January 1950 issue. His five books on UFOs are: *The Flying Saucers Are Real* (1950); *Flying Saucers From Outer Space* (1953); *The Flying Saucer Conspiracy* (1955); *Flying Saucers—Top Secret* (1960); and *Aliens From Space* (1973).

POSITION STATEMENT: Air Force Headquarters, following a high-level policy, still publicly denies that UFOs exist, convinced this is best for the country. But for years the Air Force has had full proof of UFO reality.

During my long investigation of these strange objects, I have seen many reports verified by Air Force Intelligence, detailed accounts by Air Force pilots, radar operators, and

Donald Keyhoe

other trained observers proving the UFOs are high-speed craft superior to anything built on Earth.

Behind the scenes, there are strong efforts to create an official program to attempt communication with UFO aliens and learn the purposes of the long surveillance and to take steps toward peaceful contacts if there is no serious physical bar.

To succeed in communicating with the aliens, we should first end all capture attempts. No nation so far has been able to duplicate the UFOs' control of gravity and other technical secrets. Ending the UFO chases would not mean exposing our country to deadly attacks by a fleet of Earth-made UFOs.

If we had started communicating earlier, we now might know the answers to all the major questions: the purpose of the long surveillance; the kinds of beings involved, if they are humanoid or at least not frighteningly different; the secrets of advanced space travel; and many other things of which we have no knowledge today.

There are scientists who warn against trying to communicate and meet with highly advanced beings from other worlds. It is true that such meetings would have a tremendous impact, as the Space Science Board admitted some years ago. Some "doomsday" writers hint at terrible alien actions which could destroy us and our world. They believe that the Air Force and the CIA are hiding some awful discovery the public could never stand.

But today we are already living with the constant danger of surprise nuclear attack by an enemy nation. We know that such an attack could kill millions of people and destroy much of our civilization. Yet we do not live in overwhelming fear.

Whatever the answer to UFO aliens may be, we would not be utterly paralyzed. The American people have proved they can take shocking situations—such as World War II—without collapsing in fear. If prepared carefully—and honestly—they can take the hidden UFO facts, startling as they may be.

(Position statement was adapted from *Aliens from Space* (Doubleday, 1973; Signet/NAL, 1974) and the *1978 MUFON (Mutual UFO Network) Symposium Proceedings*.)

Kinross (Michigan) jet chase On the night of November 23, 1953, an Air Defense Command radar detected an unidentified "target" over Lake Superior. Kinross Air Force Base, closest to the scene, alerted the 433rd Fighter Interceptor Squadron at Truax Field, Madison, Wisconsin, and an F-89C all-weather interceptor was scrambled. Radar operators watched the "blips" of the UFO and the F-89 merge on their scopes in an apparent collision, and disappear. No trace of the plane was ever found.

U.S. Air Force accident-report records indicate that the F-89 was vectored west-northwest, then west, climbing to 30,000 feet. At the controls was First Lieutenant Felix E. Moncia, Jr.; his radar observer was Second Lieutenant Robert L. Wilson. While on a westerly course, they were cleared to descend to 7,000 feet, turning east-northeast and coming steeply down on the unknown target from above. The last radar contact placed the interceptor at 8,000 feet, 70 miles off Keeweenaw Point, and about 150 miles northwest of Kinross AFB (now Kincheloe AFB).

The incident is not even labeled as a "UFO" case in Air Force records; instead, it was investigated by air-safety experts. There were several layers of scattered clouds (one with bottoms at 5,000 to 8,000 feet) and some snow flurries in the general area. Official records state, however, that the air was stable and there was little or no turbulence.

The Air Force later stated that the "UFO" turned out to be a Royal Canadian Air Force (RCAF) C-47 "on a flight plan from Winnipeg, Manitoba, to Sudbury, Ontario, Canada." The F-89 apparently had crashed for unknown reasons after breaking off the intercept. In answer to queries from the National Investigations Committee on Aerial Phenomena (NICAP) in 1961 and again in 1963, RCAF spokesmen denied that one of their planes was involved. Squadron Leader W. B. Totman, noting that the C-47 was said to be on a flight plan over Canadian territory, said ". . . this alone would seem to make such an intercept unlikely."

The Air Force suggested that ". . . the pilot probably suffered from vertigo and crashed into the lake." Harvard University astronomer and UFO debunker Dr. Donald H. Menzel accepted this explanation, adding that the radar operators probably saw a "phantom echo" of the F-89, produced by atmospheric conditions, that merged with the radar return from the jet and vanished with it when the plane struck the water.

Exactly what happened that night remains unclear, as the Air Force acknowledges, and serious unanswered questions remain. How likely is it that a pilot could suffer from vertigo when flying on instruments, as official records indicate was the case? If the F-89 *did* intercept an RCAF C-47, why did the "blip" of the C-47 also disappear off the radar scope? Or, if Menzel's explanation is accepted and there was no actual intercept, why did the Air Force invoke a Canadian C-47, which RCAF spokesmen later stated was not there?

No intelligence document has yet surfaced that reports the radio communications between the pilot and radar controllers, and what each was seeing. Without this information, it is impossible to evaluate the "true UFO" versus the false radar returns and accidental crash explanations.

—RICHARD HALL

Klass, Philip J. (b. 1919). Philip Klass is best known to the general public as the world's leading UFO skeptic. Dubbed "The Sherlock Holmes of UFOlogy," by a reviewer, Klass's books on the subject include *UFOs: Identified* (1968), *UFOs: Explained* (1974), *UFOs: The Public Deceived* (1983), *UFO Abductions: A Dangerous Game* (1989), and *The Real Roswell Crashed-Saucer Coverup* (1997).

Klass was born in Des Moines and raised in Cedar Rapids, Iowa. Upon graduation from Iowa State in 1941 with a B.S. degree in electrical engineering, Klass joined General Electric Company as an avionics engineer. In 1952 he accepted a technical journalism position with *Aviation Week* magazine (now *Aviation Week & Space Technology*), and served as Senior Avionics Editor for 34 years before his semiretirement in 1986. His 1957 article on microelectronics, the first ever published on the subject, predicted its revolutionary impact on the electronics industry. In 1973 Klass became one of only two journalists ever to be named a Fellow of the Institute of Electrical and Electronics Engineers.

Klass has also been honored by the Aviation/Space Writers Association with awards in 1972, '74, '75, '77, and '86. In 1989, he received the Association's ultimate Lauren D. Lyman Award for a career distinguished by "the qualities of integrity, accuracy and excellence in reporting." Additionally, the Royal Aeronautical Society (London) bestowed its Decade of Excellence Award upon him in 1998 for lifetime achievement.

One of the original founders of the Committee for the Scientific Investigation of Claims of the Paranormal in 1976, Klass has served on CSICOP's Executive Council since the outset, and chairs its UFO Subcommittee. His privately published bimonthly *Skeptics UFO Newsletter* has more than 300 subscribers across the U.S. and around the world. And he continues to write for *Aviation Week & Space Technology*, living in Washington with his wife Nadya and their Lhasa apso Shi-Shi.

Address: 404 "N" Street, S.W.
            Washington, D.C. 20024
            U.S.A.

E-mail: PhilKlass@aol.com

POSITION STATEMENT: One of the characteristic fingerprints of pseudoscience is that the passage of time provides no additional basic knowledge of an alleged phenomenon. To date, despite the efforts of many hundreds of UFO investigators, including numerous scientists

Philip Klass

with Ph.D.s who believe that some UFOs are ET spacecraft, they have not been able to produce any scientifically credible evidence to support their views. All that we have learned is that experienced pilots, law enforcement officers, and even professional astronomers can readily mistake a bright planet Venus, a meteor-fireball, or the launch of a multistage ballistic missile for a UFO.

In my nearly fifty years as a Washington-based technical journalist with a magazine referred to as "Aviation Leak"—because of the sometimes sensitive material it publishes—I have developed highly placed sources in the intelligence community and the Pentagon. This enabled me to write, for example, the first book describing the then "Top Secret" U.S. and Soviet spy satellites (*Secret Sentries In Space*, 1971). It would be nearly 25 more years before the U.S. declassified some details of its early spy satellite program; the Russians have never done so.

In my 30-plus years of investigating UFO reports—including many of the most celebrated cases—I have yet to encounter a shred of credible evidence to suggest that any of those reports involves extraterrestrial spacecraft. Nor have I found any evidence of a government conspiracy to cover up the "truth" about UFOs. Had I done so, I would have eagerly published such and graciously accepted my Pulitzer Prize. Rather, I have observed firsthand how Washington is incapable of keeping such secrets for so long, and how once-"Top Secret" documents (now declassified) dating back to the late 1940s make clear that the government knew nothing of any ET crash at Roswell or anywhere else.

When I first entered the UFO field in the mid-'60s, even the pro-UFO organizations like NICAP exercised appropriate caution when evaluating claims from "repeaters," and especially from "abductees." Now, no tale is too wild to be embraced by a large segment of the UFO community. How very sad.

—PHILIP J. KLASS

(Note: The biographical portion of this entry was written by Gary Posner.)

Klass's UFOlogical Principles

UFOLOGICAL PRINCIPLE 1: Basically honest and intelligent persons who are suddenly exposed to a brief, unexpected event, especially one that involves an unfamiliar object, may be grossly inaccurate in trying to describe precisely what they have seen.

UFOLOGICAL PRINCIPLE 2: Despite the intrinsic limitations of human perception when exposed to brief, unexpected, and unusual events, some details recalled by the observer may be reasonably accurate. The problem facing the UFO investigator is to try to distinguish between those details that are accurate and those that are grossly inaccurate. This may be impossible until the true identity of the UFO can be determined; in some cases this poses an insoluble problem.

UFOLOGICAL PRINCIPLE 3: If a person observing an unusual or unfamiliar object concludes that it is probably a spaceship from another world, he can readily adduce that the object is reacting to his presence or actions, when in reality there is absolutely no cause-effect relationship.

UFOLOGICAL PRINCIPLE 4: News media that give great prominence to a UFO report when it is first received subsequently devote little, if any, space or time to reporting a prosaic explanation for the case after the facts are uncovered.

UFOLOGICAL PRINCIPLE 5: No human observer, including experienced flight crews, can accurately estimate either the distance/altitude or the size of an unfamiliar object in the sky, unless it is in very close proximity to a familiar object whose size or altitude is known.

UFOLOGICAL PRINCIPLE 6: Once news coverage leads the public to believe that UFOs may be in the vicinity, there are numerous natural and man-made objects which, especially when seen at night, can take on unusual characteristics in the minds of hopeful viewers. Their UFO reports in turn add to the mass excitement, which encourages still more observers to watch for UFOs. This situation feeds upon itself until such time as the media lose interest in the subject, and then the "flap" quickly runs out of steam.

UFOLOGICAL PRINCIPLE 7: In attempting to determine whether a UFO report is a hoax, an investigator should rely on physical evidence, or the lack of it where evidence should exist, and should not depend on character endorsements of the principals involved.

UFOLOGICAL PRINCIPLE 8: The inability of even experienced investigators to fully and positively explain a UFO report for lack of sufficient information, even after a rigorous effort, does not really provide evidence to support the hypothesis that spaceships from other worlds are visiting the earth.

UFOLOGICAL PRINCIPLE 9: When a light is sighted in the night skies that is believed to be a UFO and this is reported to a radar operator, who is asked to search his scope for an unknown target, almost invariably an "unknown" target will be found. Conversely, if an unusual target is spotted on a radarscope at night that is suspected of being a UFO, and an observer is dispatched or asked to search for a light in the night sky, almost invariably a visual sighting will be made.

UFOLOGICAL PRINCIPLE 10: Many UFO cases seem puzzling and unexplainable simply because case investigators have failed to devote a sufficiently rigorous effort to the investigation.
—PHILIP J. KLASS

Kottmeyer, Martin S. (b. 1953). Martin Kottmeyer is one of the world's leading experts on the psycho-social aspects of the UFO phenomenon. He holds an associate's degree in science, but his knowledge of the history of UFO belief is the source of his achievements.

Kottmeyer has written dozens of articles exploring different facets of UFO lore while tracing the cultural sources of UFO and extraterrestrial imagery. His work has appeared in such publications as *The Anomalist, Archaeus, Magonia, The MUFON UFO Journal, The REALL News* (newsletter of the Rational Examination Association of Lincoln Land), *UFO Magazine,* and *The Wild Places.* He works a farm in America's heartland.

Address: 10501 Knolhoff Rd.
Carlyle, IL 6223
U.S.A.

POSITION STATEMENT: UFO belief is permeated by paranoid themes that include furtive activities, spying and reconnaissance, influencing machine fantasies, worldwide conspiracies, invasion fears, persecution, miscegenation and degeneration, grandeur, cosmic identification, and a ubiquitous stream of world destruction fantasies. Interpreting the diverse range of UFO experiences in terms of materially real, but perpetually furtive, aliens runs against many inconsistencies involving the differences among the cases and assaults against known science like the absurdities of the hybrid program and man-sized bugs. Study of the repetitive elements with emphasis on their historical development lets one achieve an understanding of UFO culture that the ETH forbids. Over two hundred predictions premised in the extraterrestrial hypothesis by encounter claimants and UFOlogists have been offered over the past half-century and they have uniformly failed. Further belief in it is not recommended.

—MARTIN S. KOTTMEYER

kundalini A Sanskrit term, associated with the image of "a coiled serpent" at the base of the spine, and uncoiling up the spine, used to express the basic intelligence and power of the universal life-force resident in the human body/mind/spirit system. The kundalini is said to affect and influence the major and minor chakras (energy centers) in the human subtle bodies, and becomes activated during the normal course of spiritual evolution, but which can be hastened by specific meditative practices (in particular, various Eastern yogas). Kundalini is associated with various paranormal experiences, which include ESP and mystic states, healing powers and telekinesis, plus near-death and out-of-body events.

—SCOTT MANDELKER

L

Lakenheath-Bentwaters radar-visual UFO Perhaps the most solid UFO case in the radar/ visual category concerns a series of events which took place over the flat plains of eastern England on the night of August 13-14, 1956.

Objects were sighted visually from the air by the pilots of two different aircraft, confirmed by airborne radar on one of the planes, tracked by radar from three ground-radar stations, and sighted visually by control tower personnel at two ground stations. The UFOs were described as round, white, rapidly moving objects that could make abrupt changes in speed and direction.

The first radar contact occurred at Bentwaters USAF-RAF Station, thirteen miles east-northeast of Ipswich, near the coast, at 9:30 P.M. (GMT). The target was moving at between 4,000 and 9,000 miles per hour, and it covered a distance of forty to fifty miles in a straight line from where it was first picked up at about twenty-five to thirty miles east-southeast of Bentwaters to a point fifteen to twenty miles west-northwest, where it vanished from the screen. The return reportedly had the characteristics of a normal aircraft target, except for its abnormally high speed.

About 10:00 P.M., another rapidly moving target appeared on the radar scopes at Bentwaters and was tracked over a distance of fifty-five miles in sixteen seconds, which is equivalent to 12,000 miles per hour—too slow to be a meteor and too fast to be any conventional aircraft. Again, the return was described as being comparable to that of a normal aircraft and, according to University of Arizona atmospheric physicist James E. McDonald, who later studied the case, could in no way be ascribed to anomalous propagation effects. Also,

while the object was being tracked on radar, ground personnel at Bentwaters saw a blurred light racing overhead, as the pilot of a C-47 aircraft over the airfield looked down at a blurry light streaking under his plane. (There is some evidence of anomalous propagation on this night, however: Between 9:30 and 10:15 P.M. the Bentwaters radar tracked a large group of ill-defined targets that seemed to drift roughly in the direction of the prevailing upper winds at the time. A search made by a flight of one or two USAF T-33 jet trainers during this period turned up no evidence of any objects that might have been producing these radar returns.)

By this time, Bentwaters had alerted another USAF-RAF Station at Lakenheath, where both radar and visual sightings were likewise taking place. One luminous object came in on a southwesterly heading, stopped abruptly, and then streaked out of sight to the east. This was confirmed by two radars, as well as by visual observations from the ground, at Lakenheath. As stated in the original Project Blue Book report: "Thus, two radar sets (i.e., Lakenheath GCA [Ground Controlled Approach] and RA TCC [Radar Traffic Control Center] radars) and three ground observers report substantially the same." Still another sighting was reported as follows: "Lakenheath Radar Traffic Control Center observed an object 17 miles east of the Station making sharp rectangular course in flight. This maneuver was not conducted by circular path but on right angles at speeds of 600-800 mph. Object would stop and start with amazing rapidity."

About midnight, while the sightings were taking place at Lakenheath, a call was placed to the chief fighter controller on duty at the

RAF Station at Neatishead. Within a few minutes, a De Havilland Venom night-fighter interceptor was scrambled from nearby Waterbeach and vectored toward, first, a target that was chased and lost, and then, to a second target (over Bedford, just north of Cambridge) that was confirmed by the navigator of the Venom as the "clearest target I have ever seen on radar" (referring to his own airborne-radar). At that point the UFO was being tracked simultaneously from the air, both visually and by radar, and from the ground by radars at Neatishead and at Lakenheath.

Suddenly, within one sweep (about fifteen seconds) of the radar scopes, the blip showed up *behind* the fighter (whereas before it had been in front), and the pilot requested additional tracking assistance from the ground. In spite of evasive maneuvers, however, the pilot of the Venom could not shake the UFO, which continued to follow the plane at a distance of about one quarter of a mile. The object then (after about ten minutes) became stationary, and the friendly fighter returned to base. A second Venom was then scrambled but had to abort its mission because of an engine malfunction. The UFO soon left the range of both ground radars, moving off the scopes in a northerly direction at an approximate speed of 600 miles per hour; though at Lakenheath, unknown echoes continued to be tracked until about 3:30 on the morning of the 14th.

The Condon Report called this ". . . the most puzzling and unusual case in the radar-visual files." And Gordon David Thayer, who was the principal analyst of the case for the Condon committee, added the following comment in his entry on the case for *The Encyclopedia of UFOs:*

> In sheer redundancy of contacts this episode is unparalleled by any other radar-visual UFO case. Three ground radars at two locations plus an airborne radar—four radars in all, each operating at a different frequency, pulse repetition rate, etc.— combined, apparently, with the Venom pi-

lot's vision all detected something unknown in the same place at the same time. There is simply no way that any known sort of anomalous propagation effect could account for this. In fact, any explanation even remotely conceivable seems to demand the presence of some physical object in the air over Lakenheath on that August night in 1956. This is why the Condon Report states: "the probability that at least one genuine UFO was involved appears to be fairly high"—and that was written before it was revealed in 1978 that the Neatishead RAF radar also tracked the same apparent target.

To this day, the Lakenheath-Bentwaters episode remains as one of the most puzzling UFO cases on record.

—RONALD D. STORY

Lawson, Alvin H.   (b. 1929). Dr. Lawson was born and educated in northern California. He received his A.B. degree in 1952 from the University of California at Berkeley, and his M.A. and Ph.D. degrees from Stanford, in 1958 and 1967 respectively.

Alvin Lawson

He was an English Professor at California State University, Long Beach, for more than thirty years. An unusual class he originated, "UFO Literature: The Rhetoric of the Unknown" (actually a course in rhetorical techniques) was developed in response to the 1960s call for more relevance in higher education. In the aftermath of the 1973 UFO flap, student interest was high and the class was first offered in the fall of 1974 and for ten years after. Lawson operated a UFO hotline in his home for research, and callers' abduction claims led him to Dr. W.C. McCall, his longtime colleague. They carried out the 1977 Hypnosis of Imaginary Abductees study, which found that imaginary and real abduction narratives are indistinguishable.

Lawson also formulated the Birth Memories Hypothesis, which argues that abductions are non-physical, archetypal fantasies in which the witness's birth memories play a central role. Lawson is retired in Garden Grove where he lives with his wife of nearly half a century, watercolorist Barbara Slade Lawson.

E-mail: alawz@earthlink.net
Web site: www.geocities.com/Area51/Vault/ 6521

POSITION STATEMENT: I am a skeptic about abduction claims and an agnostic about UFO sightings. These are unconnected phenomena and neither one has much to do with extraterrestrial aliens. CE-3s are fantasy/hallucinations and are mental rather than physical experiences. UFOs are physically real but mysterious whatevers.

Dr. W.C. McCall and I carried out a decade of successful hypnotic research into CE-3 reports, including the Imaginary Abductee Study, all of which led to the Birth Memories Hypothesis. The BMH shows that abductions are archetypal fantasies in which witnesses' birth memories play a central role. Fantasizing encourages access to birth memories. Every good CE-3 fantasy is rich in birth imagery, such as fetal humanoids, cervical doors (open from the middle), and vaginal/umbilical tunnels and tubes. Witnesses interpret their CE-3s as actual alien visitations but, like analogous mental phenomena such as shamans' trances and near-death experiences, abductions are all in the mind.

CE-3s long ago stole the spotlight from UFO sighting reports because abduction yarns are better at satisfying our alien fantasies. Paradoxically, human contact with aliens would be disastrous for the weaker side. We and our religions and cultures are not ready for bright and sly ETs, and vice versa. Though humans are made to wonder about what is out there, the wonder cannot be accounted for. Man's drive toward the stars is more mysterious even than UFOs.

—Alvin H. Lawson

Levelland (Texas) landings The night of November 2-3, 1957, was one to remember for the folks of Levelland, a small oil and cotton town (population 10,000) located thirty-two miles west of Lubbock in northwest Texas. The Soviets had just launched Sputnik II one hour before the UFO events would begin around Levelland, but news of the launch had not yet reached the general public.

News of another kind was being created near the formerly obscure west Texas town, as one or more giant, glowing, egg-shaped UFOs seemed to be playing games with motorists on the outskirts of town. During a two-and-one-half-hour period, duty officer A. J. Fowler at the Levelland Police Department would receive fifteen telephone calls—seven of which correlate remarkably well.

The first call was received at around 10:50 P.M. from farmhand Pedro Saucedo, who, along with a companion, Joe Salaz, observed a remarkable and frightening phenomenon. They were in a small truck along Route 116 about four miles west of Levelland, when a sudden flash of light drew their attention to a field just off the right of the road. Suddenly, the yellow-white light rose up out of the field, picked up speed, and "passed directly over the truck with a great sound and rush of wind. It sounded like thunder," reported Saucedo, "and my truck rocked from the blast. I felt a lot of heat." Saucedo described the "object" as "torpedo-shaped, like a rocket," (Hall, 1964) about 200 feet long, and apparently "moving at about 600 to 800 miles per hour. (Hynek, 1972)

As the glowing object approached the truck, both the headlights and the engine failed. As the object departed in the direction of Levelland, the headlights came back on and the truck could be started without difficulty.

Officer Fowler didn't know what to make of the report when Saucedo called in. Perhaps just a drunk, the patrolman thought. Then, about one hour later (shortly before midnight), Fowler received a second call, from another motorist later identified as Jim Wheeler, who had just experienced something similar. Wheeler was driving on Route 110, about four miles *east* of Levelland—i.e., the same general direction in which the UFO was headed when last seen by Saucedo—when he came upon a 200-foot, egg-shaped thing sitting on the road in front of him. Wheeler said his lights and motor died also, and, as the strange glowing oval rose into the sky and blinked out, his headlights came back on.

The next call came at around midnight from Jose Alvarez, who was driving on Route 51, about eleven miles north of town. It was the same story again: He saw a glowing oval object sitting on the road in front of him, and his car's headlights and engine failed. The "object" took off and his car returned to normal.

Then, at 12:05 A.M., a student from Texas Tech, Newell Wright, was driving on Route 116 when he experienced "motor trouble." Getting out of the car, he saw ahead of him a large oval object, which he estimated to be about 125 feet across, glowing blue-green. After a few minutes, the strange object rose "almost straight up," headed north, and quickly disappeared. The witness had no trouble restarting his car.

Frank Williams was the next unwitting victim of headlight and engine failure. The time was about 12:15 A.M., when he encountered a similar object on Route 51, close to where Alvarez had his experience. Williams said that the light was pulsating steadily, on and off, before rising into the air with a noise like thunder. As before, the car functioned normally once the UFO left.

By this time, Fowler had notified Sheriff Weir Clem, who began searching the area for the object (or objects) to see for himself.

The time of the next sighting was 12:45 A.M. Truck driver Ronald Martin, driving along Route 116 just west of Levelland, saw his headlights go out and felt his engine die "when a big ball of fire dropped on the highway." (*The A.P.R.O. Bulletin*, November 1957) Martin noted that the object changed color from red-orange to blue-green as it lauded; and then to red-orange again when it took off.

The seventh witness to call the Levelland Police Department with a detailed report was James Long, a truck driver from Waco, Texas, who at 1:15 A.M. reportedly saw a 200-foot-long, egg-shaped object glowing "like a neon sign." (Hynek, 1972) This time, the thing was just northeast of Levelland, and the same electromagnetic effects were noted. The electrical system of Long's vehicle failed when relatively close to the object but returned to normal as the UFO rose up and streaked away.

At 1:30 A.M., Sheriff Clem and Deputy Pat McCulloch, while driving along "Oklahoma Flat Road" about five miles outside of town, witnessed the UFO themselves. They spotted an oval-shaped light, "looking like a brilliant red sunset across the highway." (Hynek, 1972)

Two days later, on November 5th, the U.S. Air Force dispatched an investigator who spent less than one day in the area and hastily dismissed the sightings as "ball lightning."

Astronomer J. Allen Hynek, a scientific consultant to the Air Force at the time, agreed, and debunker Donald Menzel (another astronomer and noted UFO debunker) echoed this explanation in his book, *The World of Flying Saucers,* published in 1963. However, some years later, Hynek had second thoughts on the matter, which he expressed in his 1972 book, *The UFO Experience:*

> Captain Gregory, then head of Blue Book, did call me by phone, but at that time, as the person directly responsible for the tracking of the new Russian satellite, I was on a virtual around-the-clock duty and was unable to give it any attention whatever. I am not proud today that I hastily concurred in Captain Gregory's evaluation as "ball lightning" on the basis of information that an electrical storm had been in progress in the Levelland area at the time. That was shown not to be the case. Observers reported overcast and mist but no lightning. Besides, had I given it any thought whatever, I would soon have recognized the absence of any evidence that ball lightning can stop cars and put out headlights. (Hynek, 1972)

Nor is ball lightning known to have a preference for landing on dirt roads and paved highways, as these "objects" reportedly did.

We must also consider the enormous size (around 200 feet across) of most of the objects reported, a factor that again seems to rule out the phenomenon of ball lightning, which is not known to attain such gargantuan proportions.

Whatever happened that night, at least six witnesses experienced something very similar and extraordinary, independent of each other: an incredible UFO display within a ten-mile radius of Levelland, which has never to this day been satisfactorily explained.

—RONALD D. STORY

References

The A.P.R.O. Bulletin, November 1957.

Hall, Richard H., ed. *The UFO Evidence* (NICAP, 1964).

Hynek, J. Allen. *The UFO Experience: A Scientific Inquiry* (Henry Regnery, 1972; Ballantine Books, 1974).

Menzel, Donald H. and Lyle G. Boyd. *The World of Flying Saucers* (Doubleday, 1963).

Story, Ronald D. *UFOs and the Limits of Science* (William Morrow, 1981).

Webb, Walter N. "Levelland (Texas) sightings" in Story, Ronald D., ed. *The Encyclopedia of UFOs* (Doubleday/New English Library, 1980).

Light Years (Atlantic Monthly Press, 1987). Gary Kinder relates the story of a rural Swiss contactee, Eduard Meier, who claims to be in frequent contact with a group of alien beings from the Pleiades star system. Meier produced hundreds of photos of his visits from Pleiadian starships. These sharp, high quality photos of hovering disks attracted many believers, including the actress Shirley MacLaine who made a pilgrimage to Meier's door. The book author could not figure out how or if the photos were faked. As for the Pleiadian visitors, Meier claimed they are led by a German-speaking female named Semjase, who looks just like a beautiful Earth woman with amber hair and blue eyes.

—RANDALL FITZGERALD

Lorenzen, Coral E. (1925-1988). A prolific writer of UFO books and articles, Coral Lorenzen was perhaps best known for her role as the founder of the pioneering and long-standing Aerial Phenomena Research Organization (APRO).

Born in Hillsdale, Wisconsin, Coral attended public schools in Barron, Wisconsin, graduating from high school in May 1941.

Her interest in the UFO phenomenon began on a summer day in 1934, when, at the age of nine, she and two playmates saw a hemisphere-shaped white object cross the western sky from south to north in an undulating trajectory. Three years later, during a routine eye examination, she mentioned the object to the family doctor, Harry Schlomovitz, who lent her the books of Charles Fort to show her that strange objects had been seen in the sky for many years. This sparked an interest in astronomy and she began reading books dealing with that subject, and combing periodicals and newspapers for information on the strange objects. She married L. J. (Jim) Lorenzen on September 29, 1943, and worked at various jobs during his tour with the Army Air Transport Command in India, including shipfitting for the Navy and assembly-line work for Douglas Aircraft.

Her second sighting came on June 10, 1947, in Douglas, Arizona. She had put her daughter to bed and was outside watching for meteors, when she saw a tiny, round, lighted object leave the ground in the south and move quickly straight up into the sky until it disappeared from sight. On June 24, 1947, Kenneth Arnold made his famous sighting over Mount Rainier in the state of Washington.

During the next five years Mrs. Lorenzen made many contacts with people interested in the subject of UFOs, and in January 1952, she began contacting them to form a group (APRO), with the main idea being to preserve information which otherwise would have been lost to history. She was sure, in view of the publicity given the UFOs in big-city papers, that hundreds of additional sightings had been made in rural areas but were never reported or were buried in the pages of small-town newspapers. Besides the reports being publicized, it was to the problem of past reports that APRO members addressed themselves.

In the early years, most of the work was done by Mrs. Lorenzen and she served as director until 1964, when Mr. Lorenzen took

Coral and Jim Lorenzen

over the post. From 1964 to 1988, she served as secretary-treasurer and a member of the APRO board of directors.

Through the years, Mrs. Lorenzen has also held additional positions as a correspondent and feature writer for various newspapers, and was employed by the United States Air Force at Holloman Air Force Base from 1954 to 1956, where she became familiar with Air Force procedures and missile testing.

She was the author, or co-author, with her husband, Jim, of seven books: *Flying Saucers—The Startling Evidence of the Invasion from Outer Space* (originally entitled *The Great Flying Saucer Hoax,* 1962, 1966); *The Shadow of the Unknown* (1970); *Flying Saucer Occupants* (1967); *UFOs Over the Americas* (1968); *UFOs—The Whole Story* (1969); *Encounters with UFO Occupants* (1976); and *Abducted!* (1977).

POSITION STATEMENT: Although I have, throughout my long involvement with APRO, seen many changes in the field of UFO research, I realize there is room, indeed a desperate need, for further change. Specifically, there is a tendency toward ''do your own thing'' and little or no cooperation in the field. There are too many organizations and too many lone researchers who investigate cases, then file them away where they are unavailable to others for study.

APRO was founded in 1952 and became international in scope in 1954. However, our biggest step forward came in 1962 with the publication of my first book, *The Great Flying Saucer Hoax,* which attracted the attention of a few scientists who ultimately recruited others.

In the future, UFO researchers should concentrate on improving the quality of investigations and reports and, therefore, attempt to see that the results are made available to the entire scientific community.

As far as my opinion of the UFO enigma is concerned, I do not think there are any hard-and-fast answers at this time. It seems to be a multifaceted phenomenon and will require much more work than has been expended by the UFO-research community to date. The most popular theory as to their identity and origin is the extraterrestrial hypothesis, and in view of the evidence currently available, it seems to be the most sensible.

Those individuals (generally scientists) who dismiss the UFO problem without examining the data are very remiss. One has only to see the distress and wonderment of a UFO witness to realize that *something* is afoot on this globe we call Earth.

There are probably several races of intelligent beings in our galaxy alone who have solved the problem of propulsion which would make visitation to this planet very possible. Man does not like to accept this possibility because his ego gets in the way of his reason.

However, the thousands of reports of UFOs in the sky, on the ground, and accompanied by humanoid but alien-appearing occupants, indicate that a careful, methodical, and in-depth study of Earth and its inhabitants is under way.

—CORAL E. LORENZEN

Lorenzen, L. J. (1922-1986). Jim Lorenzen was well known in UFO circles as the international director of APRO (the Aerial Phenomena Research Organization) and, with his wife, Coral, as the co-author of many popular books on UFOs. Born in Grand Meadow, Minnesota, he attended schools in Grand Meadow and Elkton, graduating from Elkton High School in 1938.

Jim worked as a professional musician until induction into the U.S. Army Air Corps in 1942, where he was trained as a radio-operator mechanic. He served with the Air Corps until his discharge in 1945. During that time he served with the Air Transport Command in the China-Burma-India theater of operations, receiving the Air Medal with cluster, the Presidential Unit Citation with cluster, and the Distinguished Flying Cross with cluster.

After his discharge from the Air Corps, Mr. Lorenzen returned to his music profession until 1950, when he entered the Electronic Technical Institute in Los Angeles and Broadcasters' Network Studios for training, acquiring a first-class Radio/Telephone License. Since then he held positions with various companies. He was chief engineer for radio station WDOR in Sturgeon Bay, Wisconsin, and chief of communications installations for Christy Shipyards, Sturgeon Bay. In 1954, he joined Telecomputing Corporation at Holloman Air Force Base, New Mexico. After serving as chief of electronic maintenance of the Data Reduction Facility, he transferred to engineering where he served three years as a junior engineer.

In 1960, Lorenzen accepted a position of senior technical associate with the Kitt Peak National Observatory in Tucson, Arizona, where he remained until 1967, at which time he left that job to go into the electronic organ business.

Since 1964, Mr. Lorenzen also served as international director for APRO, an organization which he and Coral Lorenzen founded in January 1952. Also with Coral, he co-authored five books on UFOs: *Flying Saucer Occupants* (1967); *UFOs Over the Americas* (1968); *UFOs—The Whole Story* (1969); *Encounters with UFO Occupants* (1976); and *Abducted!* (1977).

POSITION STATEMENT: Study of the UFO mystery is complicated by the fact that it is so poorly defined. There has been, it seems to me, a tendency to arbitrarily include under its umbrella many unrelated problems. This stems probably from an unconscious wish to simplify a sometimes ominously mysterious universe— to say, in effect, that there is only one all-embracing major mystery, rather than many potentially disturbing enigmas, and be somewhat comforted thereby. Such ideas are nurtured by sensationalistic ''potboiler'' writers who seem to feel that combining two or more sensational subjects will give their stories more ''gee whiz'' appeal. This gives us UFO accounts mixed with various portions of Sasquatch, teleportation, telepathy, faith healing, Satanism, new age scriptural interpretation, mediumistic channeling, cattle mutilations, theosophy, poltergeist phenomena, et cetera, ad infinitum.

We find with consternation, however, that some of the foregoing elements appear in real, solidly based reports and are left to wonder if science fiction anticipates the phenomenon or the phenomenon imitates science fiction. We note in passing that much otherwise acceptable data becomes somehow contaminated when associated with unacceptable data.

This leads many conventional scientists to give voice to their ''unflinching skepticism'' and give ''stouthearted expression to the feeling that such preposterous rumors are an offence to human dignity'' to quote C. G. Jung. (*Flying Saucers—A Modern Myth of Things Seen in the Skies*, 1959)

I have stated on occasion that APRO exists to solve the many questions raised by the existence of UFO reports. In practice we soon learn that a major problem exists in defining the limits of the mystery (i.e., deciding which reports to include in our study); for there certainly is no obvious way to determine, for example, which reports are triggered by ''nuts and bolts'' activity and which are perhaps psychic projections whose superficial form is dictated by the idea or rumor of UFOs but which ultimately stem from the internal needs of the ''observer.'' Once we have defined the problem, I think we will be well on the way to its solution. We will not be able to do that until we have learned to come to grips with its realities which means, in part, to conquer our own biases and prejudices.

At present, utilizing the principal of parsimony, my ''investigative assumption'' is still (as it has been since 1952) that we are dealing with extraterrestrial visitations as the central core of the problem. Most of the bizarre fringes I can rationalize as being (1) the actions of one or more advanced cultures whose technology, motives, and psychology we do not understand and (2) deliberate deception of the witness through influence of his perception for the purpose of counterintelligence.

But perhaps we stand too close to the riddle and do not see the forest for the trees. Standing back a little we can see the outstanding characteristic of the UFO phenomenon: It is a mystery! What is the effect of a mystery? It causes us to think. To puzzle. To ponder. And our consciousness is raised. Maybe that's what it's all about. At any rate the journey is only begun and we have miles to go before we sleep. . . .

—L. J. Lorenzen

Lost Tribes from Outer Space, The (Editions Alvin Michel, 1974). Frenchman Marc Dem argues that Jews are God's chosen people because they were selectively bred by extraterrestrial visitors. The Jewish race has always been oppressed by others throughout history because oppression is ''like the process of rejection that sometimes occurs in organ transplants.'' Yahweh, the extraterrestrial visitor who was worshipped as God, found Stone Age humans to be an inadequate species, so he genetically altered them and the Jews were the fruit of his creation, destined by their special status to lead humanity out of ignorance.

—Randall Fitzgerald

Lubbock (Texas) lights The story of the Lubbock lights began on a hot summer night in August 1951, as several professors from Texas Tech (W. I. Robinson, A. G. Oberg, and W. L. Ducker) sat outside in a backyard. A group of lights flashed overhead. They moved silently, crossing the sky rapidly, and seemed to be in some kind of loose formation. They were only in sight for two or three seconds, and none of the professors got a very good look at them.

An hour or so later, the lights reappeared, and this time the professors were ready. The lights were softly glowing, bluish-green objects in loose formation. It seemed to the professors that the first group had been in a more rigid and structured formation than later groups.

Joe Bryant of Brownsfield, Texas, told investigators that he was sitting in his backyard when a group of lights flew overhead. He described them as having a "kind of a glow, a little bigger than a star." Not long after that, a second group appeared. Neither of the groups was in a regular formation.

There was a third flight, but instead of flying over the house, they dropped down and circled the building. As Bryant watched, one of the "objects" chirped and he recognized it immediately as a plover, a bird common in west Texas.

The professors, unaware of what Bryant had seen and heard, set out to obtain additional information. Joined by other professors and professionals (including Grayson Meade, E.R. Hienaman, and J.P Brand), Robinson, Oberg, and Ducker equipped teams with two-way radios, measured a base from the location of the original sightings, and then staked out the area. Knowing the length of that line, the time of the sighting, and the location and direction of flight, they would be able to calculate some important and useful information. The problem was that none of the teams ever made a sighting.

Then, on August 31st, the case took an amazing turn. Carl Hart, Jr., a nineteen-year-old college freshman and amateur photographer, managed to take five pictures as the lights flew over his house in the middle of Lubbock.

Joe Harris of the Lubbock newspaper learned about the pictures when a photographer who worked for him periodically called to tell him that Hart had used his studio to develop the film. Naturally the newspaper feared a hoax. Harris, and the newspaper's lead photographer, William Hans, talked to Hart on a number of occasions. Harris bluntly asked if the pictures were faked. Hart denied it. About forty years later, in the 1990s, when asked by researchers what he had photographed, Hart said that he still didn't know.

Hans later decided to try to duplicate the pictures at night from the roof of the newspaper office. He would attempt to photograph

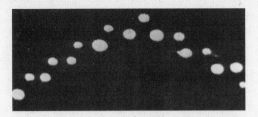

The Lubbock lights, as photographed by Carl Hart, Jr., on August 31, 1951

anything that flew over. He waited, but all he saw was a flight of birds that were barely visible in the glow of the sodium vapor lamps on the streets below him. He took photographs of the birds, but when he developed the film, the images were too faint to show on prints. From his experiment, he was convinced that what Hart photographed couldn't have been birds under any circumstances.

Air Force investigations were conducted throughout the fall of 1951. Investigators were dispatched from Reese AFB on the west side of Lubbock. They spoke to Hart on a number of occasions. They forwarded copies of their reports to both Project Blue Book headquarters and to Air Force Office of Special Investigation headquarters in Washington, D.C. First Lieutenant Edward Ruppelt, chief of Project Blue Book, even made a trip to Lubbock to speak to the witnesses including Carl Hart.

During those interviews, Hart was advised of his rights under the Constitution of the United States. The investigators were playing hardball with the teenager. Between November 6 and 9, 1951, Ruppelt and AFOSI Special Agent Howard N. Bossert again interviewed Hart. In their report, they wrote, "Hart's story could not be 'picked apart' because it was entirely logical. He [Hart] was questioned on why he did certain things and his answers were all logical, concise, and without hesitation."

From Bryant's claim of birds, however, the Air Force investigators extrapolated that all the Lubbock sightings could be explained by birds. In one of the reports, the investigators wrote, "It was concluded that birds, with street lights reflecting from them, were the probable cause of these sightings . . .''

The problem is that strings of lights in the night skies were seen all over west Texas. From as far north as Amarillo to as far south as the Midland/Odessa area, reports of these sorts of sightings were made. Birds and the newly installed sodium vapor lamps in Lubbock do not provide an adequate explanation.

What is relevant here, however, is that Air Force officers made a long, complex investigation of the sightings. Ruppelt later made it clear that he believed there to be a plausible, mundane explanation for the sightings. In a 1960 revision to his book, *The Report on Unidentified Flying Objects*, Ruppelt said the Lubbock Lights were explained by ''night flying moths reflecting the bluish-green light of a nearby row of mercury vapor street lights.''

Of course, that explanation didn't explain the photographs. Ruppelt wrote that he never found an explanation for them. ''The photos were never proven to be a hoax but neither were they proven to be genuine.''
—KEVIN D. RANDLE

References

Randle, Kevin D. *Conspiracy of Silence* (Avon Books, 1997).

Ruppelt, Edward J. *The Report on Unidentified Flying Objects* (Doubleday/Ace Books, 1960).

———. ''Lubbock (Texas) lights'' in Story, Ronald D., ed. *The Encyclopedia of UFOs* (Doubleday/New English Library, 1980).

Wheeler, David R. *The Lubbock Lights* (Award Books, 1977).

lucid dreams These are vivid dream-like experiences in which the person retains normal waking awareness, as well as a certain degree of control over the elements of dream imagery and the narrative sequence. There are both Eastern and Western yogic practices which facilitate the process of achieving the power to create lucid dreams. This phenomenon is comparable to, but not identical with, the more common experience of out-of-body journeys or ''astral travel.'' Some ET contacts are made through lucid dreams, and often involve transfer of spiritual teaching or messages for humanity.
—SCOTT MANDELKER

M

Maccabee, Bruce (b. 1942). Bruce Maccabee has been a research physicist at the Naval Surface Warfare Center (formerly the Naval Ordnance Laboratory) in Washington, D.C., since 1972. Originally from Rutland, Vermont, he received his B.S. degree in physics, from Worcester Polytechnic Institute (Massachusetts) in 1964, and his M.S. and Ph.D. (also in physics) from the American University (Washington, D.C.) in 1967 and 1970 respectively.

Bruce Maccabee

Dr. Maccabee is the Chairman of the Fund for UFO Research, the MUFON (Mutual UFO Network) State Director for Maryland, and is a member of the Scientific Board of the J. Allen Hynek Center for UFO Studies (CUFOS). He has written dozens of papers related to UFO history and case investigations, and has appeared on numerous TV and radio shows. He has also been a consultant to *National Geographic*, *Reader's Digest*, and Time-Life Books.

Dr. Maccabee is the co-author (with Ed Walters) of *UFOs Are Real, Here's the Proof* (1997) and the author of *The UFO-FBI Connection* (2000).

Address: Box 277
             Mount Rainier, MD 20712
             U.S.A.

E-mail: brumac@compuserve.com

POSITION STATEMENT: From my studies of old and recent reports, and from direct involvement with several UFO investigations, I have become convinced that there is something real and new behind the UFO phenomenon. Although I tend to be a ''nuts-and-bolts'' man, I would not yet throw out the possibility that some reports which remain unidentified after investigation (i.e., ''true UFO'' reports) are psychological in nature. I don't think we have enough information at this time to be able to identify the source or sources (such as extraterrestrial, interdimensional, time travelers, etc.) of the phenomena which give rise to UFO reports. However, I think it is time for the scientific community to admit there is some new phenomenon involved.

—BRUCE MACCABEE

Mack, John E. (b. 1929). John Mack, M.D., is professor of psychiatry at Harvard Medical School and founding director of the Program for Extraordinary Experience Research (PEER). Dr. Mack is the author of the Pulitzer Prize-winning book *A Prince of Disorder* (a 1976 biography of T. E. Lawrence), but is best known as a UFO-abduction researcher and the author of the best-selling 1994 book, *Abduction: Human Encounters with Aliens*.

In 1990, after meeting veteran alien-abduction researcher Budd Hopkins, Dr. Mack began working with people who seem to have experienced encounters with unknown intelligences. In 1993 Mack founded PEER to continue this work, and to explore the varieties of extraordinary experience. His latest book is called *Passport to the Cosmos: Human Transformation and Alien Encounters* (1999), wherein he tries to demonstrate "how the alien abduction phenomenon offers a revolutionary new way of understanding reality and our place in the universe." Mack asserts that "the alien abduction phenomenon ushers in a new era in human consciousness, a time in which we must be willing to embrace the idea that alien visitation is occurring on some level." According to the publisher's summary: "*Passport to the Cosmos* reveals the naiveté in our assumption that our world is devoid of spirits and beings who can cross the barrier we have built up between the material and immaterial worlds. The book leads us through the possibility that the alien abduction phenomenon is a cosmic wake-up call to humans that we do indeed live in a multi-dimensional world."

Address: P.O. Box 398080
            Cambridge, MA 02139
            U.S.A.

Web site: www.peer-mack.org
                                —PEER Staff

Mack's abductees Because of his stature, as a Harvard professor of psychiatry, and his influence on the UFO community and others who have read his bestselling book, *Abduction: Human Encounters with Aliens* (1994), Dr. John Mack's abductees deserve special attention. Each case is summarized here in the order it appears in Mack's book, followed by a special commentary by Joe Nickell.

CASE NO. 1

Ed's case was important to Dr. Mack because of the timing of his experience (during Ed's teenage years) and the vivid recall of his abduction during hypnosis. Ed says he first learned of his abduction in 1961, two months before Betty and Barney Hill had their encounter.

A female alien—to whom he was forced to give sperm—told Ed that our planet would soon be destroyed if humanity continued on its present course. She conveyed to him that human disharmony with nature was the cause of the impending disaster. Ed has taken her message seriously and is working to communicate what he has learned to those who are willing to listen

CASE NO. 2

Sheila was experiencing "spiritual" dreams that had begun shortly after her mother's death. Sheila was seeing a psychiatrist to help her with this undue stress, but had difficulty explaining these dreams to her doctor once she became convinced they weren't dreams after all, but actual alien abductions.

Sheila had a difficult time distinguishing fantasy from reality, but through the use of hypnosis she was able to relive the traumatic abduction experiences and bring out the repressed feelings that were affecting her life.

CASE NO. 3

Scott's most vivid memory of abduction which involved terror, paralysis, and extraction of sperm occurred in 1992. Other abductions had occurred throughout his childhood, which caused physical trauma including headaches and seizures.

As an adult Scott has undergone an important personal transformation which has enabled him to confront and move through his abduction experiences. Scott now considers himself to be both human and alien. He also envisions an apocalyptic catastrophe in the near future. Scott says the aliens come from a dying world—a fate that will be ours, unless we soon change our ways.

Case No. 4

Jerry's abduction experiences were mainly sexual in nature, including many reproductive procedures and involvement with the hybrid entities. These sexual abductions have caused havoc with Jerry's human relationships, because she has difficulty differentiating between normal sex and being raped.

Despite the anguish of these sexual experiences with the aliens, Jerry has become spiritual in nature. She has become a prolific writer of existentialism. Jerry has shown a great deal of fortitude and bravery in confronting the horrendous abduction experiences she encountered and through her writings has regained her dignity and spiritual strength.

Case No. 5

Catherine is a young woman who has been abducted since childhood and used in sexual experiments by the aliens. In her case, she describes rows and rows of hybrid babies in tank-like incubators.

Catherine has seen hundreds of other human abductees lying on tables aboard a spacecraft waiting to be examined by the aliens. She has had the unique experience of reliving a past life as an Egyptian painter named "Akremenon." Catherine learned from this reincarnation that all life is connected and that we can't exist without each other. The aliens wanted to convey to her not to be so frightened of them but to work with them. Since then, Catherine's attitude has changed from fear to "active acceptance."

Case No. 6

Joe, a psychotherapist, had early childhood abduction experiences. His later episodes became memorable when his child, Mark, was born. It seems the both of them have a dual human-alien existence. Joe perceives his role as a father to keep Mark connected to his "higher self."

It seems that the aliens have been involved with Joe's entire cycle of life and death. They have been available to him, for as long as he can remember, as guides and protectors of his spiritual awareness and growth. As a result of his changing lifestyle, Joe has become more outgoing and has been sharing his experiences and knowledge with the public.

Case No. 7

Sara, a graduate student, brings a spiritual interest into the understanding of her abduction experiences. She was smart and precocious as a child, dabbling in the paranormal: one activity was being able to levitate others. Sara feels like she is involved in a special project of bringing the alien species together with ours through evolution. Once merged, these new hybrid life-forms will be more spiritually advanced.

Sara has one intense abduction experience where she goes through an illusion of a mirror, which becomes a corridor where she meets a reptilian-like alien. It gives her information that is still embedded in her consciousness.

Case No. 8

Paul expresses himself as a bridge between two worlds. He feels he has the identities of both human and alien forms. Paul has experienced painful, terrifying procedures on his body. He relates an incident of being at Roswell, New Mexico, in 1947, and remembering what happened there—even though it was nineteen years before he was born.

Paul's hypnosis sessions were powerful and intense in that he was able to access knowledge and information that was stored within him, including the need to save our planet. Paul feels he is here to set an example of love and understanding to transform human consciousness for the better.

Case No. 9

Eva's mission is one of global healing and peace. Her most powerful abduction experience was when she remembered her past life as "Omrishi" from the thirteenth century. To relive this incarnation was to represent Eva's journey of her soul.

Eva had the typical physical examination, but the role of abductions is a process of cleansing the body in order for more knowledge to come through. She feels she became both alien and human so that the melding of consciousness would bring about peace and harmony. Communication and integration of alien wisdom is essential to the advancement of our world.

CASE NO. 10

Dave's abduction experiences occurred at Pemsit Mountain, a big power place of Native American legends and traditions. He considers it the "Magic Mountain." Dave has gone through the traumatic physical examinations typical of alien abductions, but he has mostly overcome his fears and has become aware of a protective female alien named "Velia," who has been with him through many previous lifetimes.

Dave feels connected to past life Indian reincarnations and is a student of power through karate and Chi, which is helping him to gain control of his life.

CASE NO. 11

Peter's abductions seem to evolve from the usual traumatic invasions to complex spiritual experiences involving the expansion of his mind and visions of the future. As an example, Peter passes through some kind of wall of metaphoric expression where he discovers that he has been chosen to participate in a special breeding program of aliens and humans.

Peter feels that he is "part alien" and that he is here to impart information about the impending disasters that may occur. His role also comprises breeding with the female aliens to create a new race or tribe that would survive any kind of cataclysm.

CASE NO. 12

Carlos is an artist who uses the special "light" that he experienced in his abduction encounters. His abductions have been more exploratory in that the aliens change the energy structure of his body. In fact, Carlos refers to the aliens as "light beings." He uses this new energy to create paintings that activate the need to protect the Earth.

Carlos expresses his feelings of awe as he relates to his abduction experiences. The nearness of death seems to be a very significant part of Carlos's life including a rebirth at the age of one. He compares it to a transformation of power in the name of healing, both physical and emotional.

CASE NO. 13

Arthur considers himself to be a voluntary abductee. He remembers being abducted, as a nine-year-old boy, while in a car with his mother and siblings. Arthur was not afraid. He was told about the danger facing the Earth's ecology.

Arthur's abduction experiences included two different kinds of beings: the "little people," friendly and loving; and darker ones (Grays) who were more serious. As he matured, he realized that his alien encounters were instrumental in the development of this own sense of responsibility on a personal and corporate level to protect the Earth's environment.

—ETEP STAFF

POSTSCRIPT: Since the appearance of Dr. Robert A Baker's pioneering article, "The Aliens Among Us: Hypnotic Regression Revisited," in the *Skeptical Inquirer* (Winter 1987-88), a controversy has raged over his suggestion that most "alien abductees" exhibited an array of unusual traits indicating a psychological phenomenon known as "fantasy-proneness." Baker cited the "important but neglected" work of Wilson and Barber (1983), who listed certain identifying characteristics of people who fantasize profoundly.

Baker applied Wilson and Barber's findings to the alien-abduction phenomenon and found a strong correlation. Baker explained how a cursory examination by a psychologist or psychiatrist might find an "abductee" to be perfectly normal, while more detailed knowledge about the person's background and habits would reveal to such a trained observer a pattern of fantasy proneness.

For example, Baker found Whitley Strieber—author of *Communion* (1987), which tells the "true story" of Strieber's own alleged abduction—to be "a classic example of the [fantasy-prone personality] genre." Baker noted that Strieber exhibited such symptoms as being easily hypnotized, having vivid memories, and experiencing hypnopompic hallucinations (i.e., "waking dreams"), as well as being "a writer of occult and highly imaginative novels" and exhibiting other characteristics of fantasy proneness. A subsequent, but apparently independent, study by Bartholomew and Basterfield (1988) drew similar conclusions.

Wilson and Barber's study did not deal with the abduction phenomenon (which at the time consisted of only a handful of reported cases), and some of their criteria seem less applicable to abduction cases than to other types of reported phenomena, such as psychic experiences. Nevertheless, although the criteria for fantasy proneness have not been exactly codified, they generally include such features as having a rich fantasy life, showing high hypnotic susceptibility, claiming psychic abilities and healing powers, reporting out-of-body experiences and vivid or "waking" dreams, having apparitional experiences and religious visions, and exhibiting automatic writing.

In one study, Bartholomew, Basterfield, and Howard (1991) found that, of 152 otherwise normal, functional individuals who reported they had been abducted or had persistent contacts with extraterrestrials, 132 had one or more major characteristics of the fantasy-prone personality.

Somewhat equivocal results were obtained by Spanos et al. (1993), although their "findings suggest that intense UFO experiences are more likely to occur in individuals who are predisposed toward esoteric beliefs in general and alien beliefs in particular and who interpret unusual sensory and imagined experiences in terms of the alien hypothesis. Among UFO believers, those with stronger propensities toward fantasy production were particularly likely to generate such experiences." (Spanos et al., 1993)

A totally dismissive view of these attempts to find conventional psychological explanations for the abduction experience is found in the introduction to psychiatrist John Mack's *Abduction: Human Encounters with Aliens* (1994). Mack states unequivocally: "The effort to discover a personality type associated with abductions has also not been successful." According to Mack, since some alleged abductions have reportedly taken place in infancy or early childhood, "Cause and effect in the relationship of abduction experiences to building of personality are thus virtually impossible to sort out." (Mack, 1994) But surely it is Mack's burden to prove his own thesis that the alien hypothesis does have a basis in fact beyond mere allegation. Otherwise the evidence may well be explained by a simpler hypothesis, such as the possibility that most "abductees" are fantasy-prone personality types. (Such people have traits that cut across many different personality dimensions; thus conventional personality tests are useless for identifying easily hypnotizable people. Some "abductees" who are not fantasy prone may be hoaxers, for example, or exhibit other distinctive personality traits or psychological problems.) Mack's approach to the diagnosis and treatment of his "abductee'" patients has been criticized by many of his colleagues (e.g., Cone 1994).

Methodology

To test the fantasy-proneness hypothesis, I carefully reviewed the thirteen chapter-length cases in Mack's *Abduction* (Chapters 3-15), selected from the forty-nine patients he most carefully studied out of seventy-six "abductees." Since his presentation was not intended to include fantasy proneness, certain potential indicators of that personality type—like a subject's having an imaginary playmate—would not be expected to be present. Nevertheless, Mack's rendering of each personality in light of the person's alleged abduction experiences was sufficiently detailed to allow the extraction of data pertaining to several indicators of fantasy proneness. They are the following:

1. **Susceptibility to hypnosis.** Wilson and Barber rated "hypnotizability" as one of the main indicators of fantasy proneness. In all cases, Mack repeatedly hypnotized the subjects without reporting the least difficulty in doing so. Also, under hypnosis the subjects did not merely "recall" their alleged abduction experiences but all of them reexperienced and relived them in a manner typical of fantasy proneness. (Wilson and Barber, 1983) For example, Mack's patient "Scott" (Case No. 3) was so alarmed at "remembering" his first abduction (in a pre-Mack hypnosis session with another psychiatrist) that, he said, "I jumped clear off the couch." (Mack, 1994) "Jerry" (No. 4) "expressed shock over how vividly she had relived the abduction," said Mack. Similarly, "Catherine" (No. 5) "began to relive" a feeling of numbness and began "to sob and pant." (Mack, 1994)

2. **Paraidentity.** I have used this term to refer to a subject's having had imaginary companions as a child and/or by extension to claiming to have lived past lives or to have a dual identity of some type. Of their fantasy-prone subjects, Wilson and Barber stated: "In fantasy they can do anything—experience a previous lifetime, experience their own birth, go off into the future, go into space, and so on." As well, "While they are pretending, they become totally absorbed in the character and tend to lose awareness of their true identity."

(Wilson and Barber, 1983)

Thus, as a child, "Ed" (Case No. 1) stated: "Things talked to me. The animals, the spirits . . . I can sense the earth." "Jerry" (No. 4) said she has had a relationship with a tall extraterrestrial being since age five. At least four of Mack's subjects (Nos. 5, 7, 9, and 10) said they have had past-life experiences, and seven (Nos. 3, 6, 7, 8, 9, 11, and 12) said they have some sort of dual identity. For example "Dave" (No. 10) said he considers himself "a modern-day Indian," while "Peter" (No. 11) under hypnosis said he becomes an alien and speaks in robotic tones. (Mack, 1994) In all, eleven of Mack's thirteen featured subjects exhibited paraidentity.

3. **Psychic experiences.** Another strong characteristic of fantasy proneness, according to Wilson and Barber, is that of having telepathic, precognitive, or other types of psychic experience.

One hundred percent of Mack's thirteen subjects claimed to have experienced one or more types of alleged psychical phenomena, most reporting telepathic contact with extraterrestrials. "Catherine" (Case No. 5) also claimed she can "feel people's auras." "Eva" (No. 9) said she is able to perceive beyond the range of the five senses; and "Carlos" (No. 12) said he has had "a history of what he calls 'visionary' experiences." (Mack, 1994)

4. **"Floating" or out-of-body experiences.** Wilson and Barber stated: "The overwhelming majority of subjects (88 percent) in the fantasy-prone group, as contrasted to few (8 percent) in the comparison group, report realistic out-of-the-body experiences" which one subject described as "a weightless, floating sensation" and another called "astral travel." Only one of Mack's thirteen subjects (No. 2) failed to report this. Of the other twelve, most described, under hypnosis, being "floated" from their beds to an

awaiting spaceship. Some said they were even able to drift through a solid door or wall, that being a further indication of the fantasy nature of the experience (more on this later). Also, "Eva" (No. 9) stated that she had once put her head down to nap at her desk and then "saw myself floating from the ceiling. . . . My consciousness was up there. My physical body was down there." Also, in the case of "Carlos" (No. 12), "Flying is a recurring motif in some of his more vivid dreams." (Mack, 1994)

5. **Vivid or "waking" dreams, visions, or hallucinations.** A majority of Wilson and Barber's subjects (64 percent) reported they frequently experienced a type of dream that is particularly vivid and realistic. Technically termed hypnogogic or hypnopompic hallucinations (depending on whether they occur, respectively, while the person is going to sleep or waking), they are more popularly known as "waking dreams" or, in earlier times, as "night terrors." (Nickell, 1995) Wilson and Barber reported that several of their subjects "were especially grateful to learn that the 'monsters' they saw nightly when they were children could be discussed in terms of 'what the mind does when it is nearly, but not quite, asleep." Some of Wilson and Barber's subjects (six in the fantasy-prone group of twenty-seven, contrasted with none in the comparison group of twenty-five) also had religious visions, and some had outright hallucinations. (Wilson and Barber, 1983)

Of Mack's thirteen selected cases, all but one (Case No. 13) reported either some type of especially vivid dream, or vision, or hallucination. For example, "Scott" (No. 3) said he had "visual hallucinations" from age twelve. "Jerry" (No. 4) recorded in her journal "vivid dreams of UFOs" as well as "visions," and "Carlos" (No. 12) had the previously mentioned "visionary" experiences and dreams of flying. Almost all of Mack's subjects (Nos. 1-11), like "Sheila" (No. 2), had vivid dreams with strong indi-

cations of hypnogogic and/or hypnopompic hallucinations. (Mack, 1994)

6. **Hypnotically generated apparitions.** Encountering apparitions (which Wilson and Barber define rather narrowly as "ghosts" or "spirits") is another Wilson-Barber characteristic (contrasted with only 16 percent of their comparison group). A large number of the fantasizers also reported seeing classic hypnogogic imagery, which included such apparition-like entities as "demon-type beings, goblins, gargoyles, monsters that seemed to be from outer space." (Wilson and Barber, 1983)

Mack's subjects had a variety of such encounters, both in their apparent "waking dreams" and under hypnosis. Only the latter were considered here; all thirteen subjects reported seeing one or more types of outer-space creatures during hypnosis.

7. **Receipt of special messages.** Fifty percent of Wilson and Barber's fantasizers (contrasted with only eight percent of their comparison subjects) reported having felt that some spirit or higher intelligence was using them "to write a poem, song, or message." (Wilson and Barber, 1983)

Of Mack's thirteen abductees, all but one clearly exhibited this characteristic, usually in the form of receiving telepathic messages from the extraterrestrials and usually with a message similar to the one given "Arthur" (Case No. 13) "about the danger facing the earth's ecology." Interestingly, many of these messages just happen to echo Mack's own apocalyptic notions (indicating that Mack may be leading his witnesses).

In the case of "Eva" (No. 9), the aliens, who represented a "higher communication," purportedly spoke through her and described her "global mission." "Jerry" (No. 4) produced a "flood of poetry," yet stated, "I don't know where it's coming from." "Sara" (No. 7) has been "spontaneously making drawings with a pen in each hand [of aliens]'' although she had never used her left hand before; and ''Peter'' (No. 11) stated he has ''always known that I could commune with God'' and that the aliens ''want to see if I'm a worthy leader.'' (Mack, 1994)

RESULTS

One of Mack's subjects (''Sheila,'' No. 2) exhibited four of the seven fantasy-prone indicators, and another (''Arthur,'' No. 13) exhibited five; the rest showed all seven characteristics.

Although not included here, healing—that is, the subjects' feeling that they have the ability to heal—is another characteristic of the fantasy-prone personality noted by Wilson and Barber. At least six of Mack's thirteen subjects exhibited this. Other traits, not discussed by Wilson and Barber but nevertheless of possible interest, are the following (together with the number of Mack's thirteen subjects that exhibit it): having seen UFOs (9 cases); New Age or mystical involvement (11); Roman Catholic upbringing (6 of 9, whose religion was known or could be inferred); previously being in a religio-philosophical limbo/quest for meaning in life (10); and involvement in the arts as a vocation or avocation (5). For example, while apparently neither an artist, healer, nor UFO sighter, ''Ed'' (No. 1) had ''a traditional Roman Catholic upbringing'' and—as rather a loner who said he felt ''lost in the desert''—he not only feels he can ''talk to plants'' but said he has ''practiced meditation and studied Eastern philosophy in his struggle to find his authentic path.'' ''Carlos'' (No. 12) is an artist/writer/''fine arts professor'' involved in theatrical production who said he has seen UFOs and has a ''capacity as a healer''; raised a Roman Catholic, and interested in numerology and mythology, he calls himself ''a shaman/artist teacher.'' (Mack, 1994)

Also of interest, I think, is the evidence that many of Mack's subjects fantasized while under hypnosis. For example—in addition to

aliens—''Ed'' (No. 1) also said he saw Earth spirits whom he described as ''mirthful little playful creatures''; and ''Joe'' (No. 6) said he saw ''mythic gods, and winged horses.'' ''Joe'' also ''remembered'' being born. ''Catherine'' (No. 5), ''Sara'' (No. 7), ''Paul'' (No. 8), and ''Eva'' (No. 9), said they had past-life experiences or engaged in time-travel while under hypnosis. Several said they were able to drift through solid doors or walls, including ''Ed'' (No. 1), ''Jerry'' (No. 4), ''Catherine'' (No. 5), ''Paul'' (No. 8), ''Dave'' (No. 10), and ''Arthur'' (No. 13). ''Carlos'' (No. 12) claimed his body was transmuted into light. I have already mentioned that under hypnosis ''Peter'' (No. 11) said he becomes an alien and speaks in an imitative, robotic voice. In all, eleven of Mack's thirteen subjects (all but Nos. 2 and 3) appear to fantasize under hypnosis. Of course it may be argued that there really are ''earth spirits'' and ''winged horses,'' or that the extraterrestrials may truly have the ability to time-travel or dematerialize bodies, or that any of the other examples I have given as evidence of fantasizing are really true. However, once again the burden of proof is on the claimant and until that burden is met, the examples can be taken as further evidence of the subjects' ability to fantasize.

CONCLUSIONS

Despite John Mack's denial, the results of my study of his best thirteen cases show high fantasy proneness among his selected subjects. Whether or not the same results would be obtained with his additional subjects remains to be seen. Nevertheless, my study does support the earlier opinions of Baker and Bartholomew and Basterfield that alleged alien abductees tend to be fantasy-prone personalities. Certainly, that is the evidence for the very best cases selected by a major advocate.

—JOE NICKELL

(Note: I am grateful to psychologists Robert A. Baker and Barry Beyerstein for reading this study and making helpful suggestions.)

References

Baker, Robert A. "The Aliens Among Us: Hypnotic Regression Revisited," *Skeptical Inquirer* (Winter 1987-88).

Bartholomew, Robert E. and Keith Basterfield. "Abduction States of Consciousness," *International UFO Reporter* (March/April 1988).

Bartholomew, Robert E., Keith Basterfield, and George S. Howard. "UFO Abductees and Contactees: Psychopathology or Fantasy Proneness?" *Professional Psychology: Research and Practice* (1991).

Cone, William. 1994. Research therapy methods questioned. UFO 9(5): 32-34.

Mack, John E. *Abduction: Human Encounters with Aliens* (Charles Scribner's Sons, 1994).

Nickell, Joe. *Entities: Angels, Spirits, Demons and Other Alien Beings* (Prometheus Books, 1995).

Spanos, Nicholas P.; Patricia A. Cross, Kirby Dickson, and Susan C. DuBreuil. "Close Encounters: An Examination of UFO Experiences," *Journal of Abnormal Psychology* (1993).

Wilson, Sheryl C., and Theodore X. Barber. "The Fantasy-Prone Personality: Implications for Understanding Imagery, Hypnosis, and Parapsychological Phenomena" in Sheikh, Anees A., ed. *Imagery: Current Theory, Research, and Application* (John Wiley & Sons, 1983).

Maitreya   The Buddhist Sanskrit title and name for the Buddha to come, comparable in definition and purpose to the Cosmic Christ, Hebrew Messiah, and Islamic Imam Mahdi. Maitreya is channeled by some New Age teachers and is associated with "the return of the Christ," the establishment of the Kingdom of Heaven on Earth, and the Harvest or Ascension.
— SCOTT MANDELKER

Majestic 12 (MJ-12) documents   In December of 1984 a Los Angeles UFO researcher named Jaime H. Shandera allegedly received, anonymously, a roll of unprocessed 35-mm film. He contacted an associate, William L. Moore, co-author (with Charles Berlitz) of *The Roswell Incident* (1980), and the two had the film developed. On it were two purported government documents marked "TOP SECRET/EYES ONLY." If genuine, the papers would prove that the United States had recovered crashed saucers in the American southwest and that President Harry S. Truman authorized "Operation Majestic Twelve" to handle such matters.

Another MJ-12 document surfaced later, reportedly discovered by Moore and Shandera at the National Archives in the summer of 1985. Still others appeared in 1992, allegedly left in the mailbox of a little-known researcher, and in 1994 an "MJ-12 Special Operations Manual" appeared on a roll of film sent anonymously to UFOlogist Don Berliner. (Klass, 1999)

That the documents were available only as copies effectively prevented examination of paper, ink, etc. However it also raised questions about their *provenance* (i.e., history or chain of ownership). While prominent UFOlogist Stanton T. Friedman defended the authenticity of the first three documents (but not others), forensic analysis revealed their spuriousness. (Klass, 1990; Nickell and Fischer, 1990)

One document, a seven-page "BRIEFING DOCUMENT: OPERATION MAJESTIC 12 / PREPARED FOR PRESIDENT-ELECT DWIGHT D. EISENHOWER" bore a pseudo-military date format, containing an extraneous comma: "18 November, 1952." Another incorrect feature was the use of a zero with single-digit dates, e.g. "On 07 July, 1947 . . ." These two anomalous date features are separately distinctive and all the more so when found together. The combination has not been discovered in genuine documents of the period

Note that characters are not aligned with numerals, indicating a composite.

(although, interestingly, it appeared in personal letters written by William L. Moore during the 1980s). While the "briefing document" was purportedly written by Rear Admiral R. H. Hillenkoetter, a linguistic expert found stylistic elements that were "uncharacteristic" of Hillenkoetter and suggested that the text could have been an imitation of his style. (Nickell and Fischer, 1990)

The other document, a "MEMORANDUM FOR THE SECRETARY OF DEFENSE," dated September 24, 1947, was seriously flawed. Labeled a memorandum, it bore a *salutation*—an element reserved for letters. No such incompetent hybrid memo/letter has ever been shown to emanate from President Truman's office. Moreover, although cited in the "briefing document" as an executive order, the memo/letter was given a bogus executive order number. Other problems concerned the typewriting. For example, careful inspection reveals that the numerals of the date are out of alignment with respect to the other characters, thereby indicating they were typed at a different time. (Nickell, 1996)

Also, the positioning of Truman's signature is atypical.

Most important, the signature exactly matches the signature on a known Truman letter, showing—in the words of a professional document examiner—that the "memo" signature was "a classic signature transplant, i.e., a genuine signature employed in a photocopy forgery."

Philip J. Klass (1990) correctly described the match as the "smoking gun" in the MJ-12 case, clearly proving forgery.

As to the document allegedly found in the National Archives—ostensibly a carbon copy of a memorandum from Robert Cutler (special assistant to President Eisenhower) to USAF Chief of Staff General Nathan Twining—the National Archives issued a statement questioning its authenticity on numerous grounds. For example, it lacked a requisite "Top Secret register number." Also, on the day the memo was purportedly written—July 14, 1954—Cutler was actually away from Washington. (Klass 1990; Nickell and Fischer 1990) The subse-

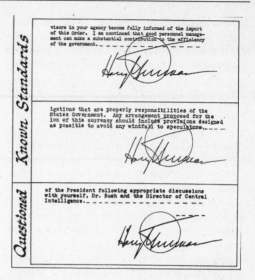

President Truman invariably placed his signature close to the text, as is shown in the top two examples. With the "T" as a radius, an inscribed circle cuts well into the typewriting. However, the questioned "MJ-12" example (which follows) fails this test.

quently appearing MJ-12 documents of 1992 and 1994 similarly suffer from scrutiny. (For a discussion see Klass, 1999.)

While a few UFO researchers who lack

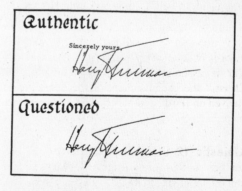

Truman signature from authentic letter matches one on an "MJ-12" memo (although multiple copying has rendered the text darker and slightly stretched). Since no two individual signatures are identical, this demonstrates that the questioned document is spurious.

document expertise continue to argue otherwise, the scientific and scholarly evidence unquestionably proved the MJ-12 documents are forgeries.

—JOE NICKELL

References

Klass, Philip J. "New Evidence of MJ-12 Hoax," *Skeptical Inquirer* (Winter, 1990).

———. "Dr. Robert Wood Emerges as New Promoter of MJ-12 Authenticity," *Skeptics UFO Newsletter* (January, 1999).

Nickell, Joe. *Detecting Forgery: Forensic Investigation of Documents.* (The University Press of Kentucky, 1996).

Nickell, Joe, and John F. Fischer. "The Crashed-saucer Forgeries," *International UFO Reporter* (March/April, 1990).

Mandelker, Scott (b. 1962). Scott Mandelker integrates the principles of Ageless Wisdom with the spiritual dimensions of ET contact and UFO research. He has an M.A. in Counseling, Ph.D. in East-West Psychology, and over 20 years' practice in Buddhist Zen and Vipassana.

His first book, *From Elsewhere: Being ET in America* (1995), explored the lives of people who claim to be ET souls on Earth. His second book, *Universal Vision: Soul-Evolution and the Cosmic Plan* (2000), reveals the cosmic plan behind global ET contact, and the basic tools of spiritual self-healing, emotional balance, and mystic meditation.

Dr. Mandelker has taught throughout Japan and Israel, and continues to offer workshops and counseling in the U.S., including presentations for MUFON, UFO conferences, and the Whole Life Expo. He has appeared on over 70 radio and TV shows, including *The Art Bell Show, Strange Universe, Hard Copy,* and *UFOAZ.* He makes his home in San Francisco.

Address: PMB 201
           2130 Fillmore St.
           San Francisco, CA 94115
E-mail: scott@universal-vision.com
Web site: www.universal-vision.com

POSITION STATEMENT: Given my background in meditation and years of paranormal experience, my position on UFOs is different from most researchers. I have no doubt that some UFOs come from extraterrestrial sources, including other star systems, older civilizations, and other dimensions of reality not yet understood by mainstream science. I hold these beliefs simply because I have had numerous direct contact experiences, and I trust the validity of these so-called paranormal events.

Some UFOs are made of physical materials, while others are "thought-form" holographs and energy-plasma devices. Since UFOs come from a wide range of ET groups, their nature is variable. However, ET agendas are relatively fixed: they are either benevolent or not. This idea is fully supported by almost all religions, East and West, plus all traditions of Ageless Wisdom

In the near future, there will certainly be "open contact" with ET groups, but the effects upon humanity depend on *when* such contact occurs. *If it occurs in the next decade,* our response will be largely the same as it is today: continued doubt and disbelief among some, fascination and adoration among others,

Scott Mandelker

with continued manipulation and co-optation by various human groups who seek to maintain their positions of power and prestige.

After the next decade, however, there will be a rapid expansion of human consciousness. Open contact then will quickly lead to willing cooperation, unified co-habitation, and long-term alliance. I have no doubt this will usher in a "golden age" on Earth, far beyond our greatest hopes.

—SCOTT MANDELKER

Manna Machine, The (Sidgwick & Jackson, 1978). British authors George Sassoon and Rodney Dale, both engineers, did a technical translation of the manna-making device of the Old Testament, as described in the ancient Hebrew book The Kabbalah, to conclude that extraterrestrial visitors gave the Jews this food producing machine so they could survive 40 years in the desert, and disguised it as the Ark of the Covenant. Since the device was probably a neutron-pumped laser, converting nuclear energy into light, it produced radiation which accounted for the plagues recounted in the Bible as having accompanied the Ark wherever it went.

—RANDALL FITZGERALD

man-made UFOs   Very little detailed research has been conducted into the subject of man-made UFOs and secret military aircraft. One of the problems is that the UFO and aviation research communities have, historically, gone their separate ways. It is, therefore, not surprising to learn that new and important discoveries have been made by those people with an interest in UFOs and secret military aircraft; these include respected aviation journalist Bill Sweetman, U.S. military monitor and aviation writer Steve Douglass, U.K. astronomy and aviation expert Bill Rose, and Nick Cook of *Jane's Defence Weekly*.

Research has shown that many secret aviation projects were undertaken both during and after the Second World War. The Horten Brothers and Alexander Lippisch in Germany,

and Jack Northrop in the U.S. all developed and flew aircraft of radical, triangular design.

It is also the case that a classified German disk-plane project was started by the Heinkel company at its plant in Marienhe, Northern Germany, in 1942, and that a primitive, disk-like aircraft was tested with support from BMW at Prague-Kbely airfield from 1944. Perhaps only two jet-powered disks were constructed by this German team. Talk of superior Nazi "anti-gravity" technology—the "Vril" and "Haunebu" saucers—is a simple fantasy and has no basis in fact. Nevertheless, a CIA document released in the 1970s and dated 1955 notes the development of a secret man-made flying saucer by the A.V. Roe Company of Malton, Ontario, whose English designer, John C. Frost, took his ideas from a "group of Germans." Another early document, dated 10 November 1947, circulated to Counter Intelligence Corps operatives in Germany, states that flying saucers "may have been developed from the original plans and experiments conducted by the Germans prior to capitulation."

During the war the U.S. Navy sponsored the development of a disk-plane known as the XF5U-1, built by the Chance-Vought Company of Bridgeport, Connecticut. Contrary to the official history put out by both the U.S. Navy, its apologists within the aviation re-

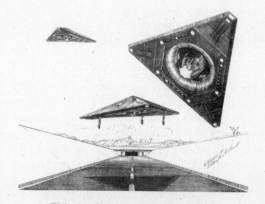

This craft is described by four anonymous aerospace retirees as America's man-made UFO.
(Art by William Louis McDonald)

search community, it is suspected that this aircraft was reworked and that a jet-powered version, the XF5U-2, was flown at Muroc Field (now Edwards AFB) from mid-1947 and may have been responsible for the famous saucer sighting at the base on the 8th of July.

Other aircraft, like the Douglass *Skyray*, had a saucer-like shape and, along with other experimental aircraft in the 1950s, may have been responsible for some UFO reports. In fact, it is my contention that an almost unbroken line of disk-planes was developed in secret—largely by the U.S. Navy—from the late 1940s onwards. We have reports of man-made disk-planes operating during Navy maneuvers in 1952, 1958, and 1959; and intriguing evidence of U.S. Navy disk projects discovered in newly acquired FOIA documents.

One important and instructive story relates to the work of Frank Carlson. His testimony puts much of the genuine concern surrounding Groom Lake/Area 51 and Bob Lazar's "S4" site into perspective. According to his wife Debra, interviewed in 1992 in Los Angeles, Carlson was a Korean War veteran and Master Sergeant formerly assigned to F-86 and later F-104 *Starfighter* maintenance teams. He was well liked and highly skilled, and moved to Edwards AFB in 1959. From 1960-62 he was involved in highly classified work at a remote Nevada test site known by projects workers and their wives as "The Facility" or "The Ranch." The Facility was, in fact, located at Papoose Lake and was not known as "S4" at that time. Here, work was continuing on a secret and radical flying saucer design based upon original work undertaken by the AVRO team in Canada. The aim was to build a high-speed "disk-interceptor" able to take out more advanced Soviet aircraft of similar design—possibly based upon plans recovered from the Prague facility in 1945—which were probing the North American Distant Early Warning (DEW) radar defenses with alarming regularity from the late 1950s onwards.

The problem with the U.S.-built system was the engine. We know a little about the highly advanced radial-flow engine because it is shown in previously *Top Secret* rated documents released in 1995 and dated 1955. The document in which this is shown relates to another AVRO disk known as *Project Silver Bug*. The *Silver Bug* disk-plane was configured for supersonic flight and vertical take off—not unlike the mysterious Carlson saucer. The engine was so advanced that we suspect it could literally not be relied upon to do its job at that time.

A Hughes Corporation missile system, the hypersonic (Mach 5) AIM-47A was said by Carlson to have been developed for use specifically with the classified disk. Other disk-plane projects were said to have the designations D-5A and RD-7A, the latter being a much-larger multiengine version.

In the final analysis, according to Carlson, the disks were replaced by less radical though classified aircraft like the A-12 proposed by Lockheed Skunk Works in 1961, the YF-12A interceptor, and ultimately the SR-71 *Blackbird* spy plane. Nevertheless, the work at Papoose Lake had been mirrored by classified activities at Holloman AFB within the White Sands Missile Range.

Not unlike many other former test site workers, Carlson was struck down by a mystery cancer in the late 1980s, having moved to Los Angeles where he owned and ran a small machine shop.

In 1967, former combat veteran and U.S. Air Force magazine editor Jack Pickett saw four rusting jet-powered disk-planes of between approximately 30- and 100-ft. diameter in a compound at McDill AFB in Florida. Shocked by his sighting, he raised the matter with the base CO and was subsequently debriefed by USAF Intelligence personnel who told him the true story of the classified disk program. Pickett noted the designation "UL" on one of the aircraft tail fins which experts tell us indicates construction prior to 1962 by a joint Bell-Vought team. Furthermore, Pickett testifies that he was asked to release part of the story of the disks to the public via one of his Air Force in-house magazines and that the story was only pulled at the last minute after an accident involving a more advanced disk-plane at the nearby Avon Park facility. Pickett is still alive and is a highly respected journalist. There is every reason to believe his story and the testimony adds considerable weight to our other claims.

The 1950s was a time when contractors like Lockheed, Bell, General Dynamics, Northrop, and A.V. Roe learned the business of hiding classified aircraft from the public. The CIA, as stated in a 1952 memorandum, sought to use flying saucers for "psychological warfare," while the hardware was effectively "hidden" behind a smoke screen of developing myth and fantasy relating to alien saucers, "men from outer space" and, later, tales of "alien contact." Some of this was, quite clearly, encouraged by the CIA and other intelligence operatives placed within the UFO research community.

The evidence for this view includes a 1999 interview by Nick Cook with former General Dynamics boss Bob Widmer, a man at the peak of his profession and with great knowledge of the inner workings of the "black projects" world. Widmer not only testified to the illegal destruction of documents relating to his still-classified 1950s high Mach *Kingfish* airplane but that the secrecy was overwhelming in every respect. Widmer also stated that the aircraft they sought to build was a flying saucer with the back cut out. The *Kingfish* is said to have been a delta (triangular) aircraft and although disk-plane projects continued up until the early to mid-1980s and were under development by the U.S. Navy at China Lake in California, a strategic decision appears to have been made in the 1970s whereby the more efficient and aerodynamically effective delta came into general use.

Many companies, including Lockheed-Martin, had classified triangular aircraft under development from the early 1960s—the Lockheed *Gusto* being a case in point. Rockwell, Northrop, and Teledyne-Ryan proposed a number of manned and unmanned aircraft in the 1970s although these are not well known.

The way in which classified aircraft can be and were hidden is clear from our knowledge of the stealth program of the mid-1970s. The Top Secret F-117A *Nighthawk* interdictor was developed at the Groom Lake and later Tonopah facilities in Nevada. Although the prototype *Have Blue* aircraft was flown from 1978, the finished product was not declassified until 1989!

And the F-117A, and the more advanced low observable Northrop B-2 *Spirit*—another aircraft mistaken for a UFO by virtue of its shape—are but two of many classified aviation projects whose budgets are massive and said to be somewhere in the region of $40-50 billion per year. This figure, and the lack of congressional oversight relating to these programs, is a good enough reason for the secrecy; the secrecy itself adds a major financial component to any classified program although this, it is argued, guarantees Western military superiority.

In recent years, starting with the Hudson Valley, New York, UFO "flap" of 1982-1990 and in Belgium from November 1989, triangular aircraft of differing design have been seen by hundreds of witnesses. Despite the expected majority of misidentifications, it is clear that a structured, almost noiseless and slow-moving aircraft of considerable size was seen. Although UFOlogists have claimed that these reports are evidence of "alien" or "back-engineered" technology our research has highlighted the development of massive lighter-than-air vehicles, not dissimilar to those conceived and test-flown by the Aereon Corporation of Princeton, New Jersey, in the early 1970s. Aereon, though a small company, is strongly suspected to have designed LTA vehicles later developed by the military-industrial complex for reconnaissance.

These aircraft, and those using a range of emerging technologies, are built of Kevlar, a light but incredibly strong material that is itself carbon-based and therefore excellent for stealth. They can fly at very low speeds and often use an advanced electric propulsion system that leads to reports of "humming noises" and blue coronal discharges from the craft.

The Aereon Corporation worked closely with the U.S. Navy during the 1970s to develop massive lighter-than-air platforms for reconnaissance, mapping, and transport. Sources suggest that a massive LTA platform along these lines might have been responsible for some UFO sightings.

Many reports indicate remarkable maneuverability, and the craft are said by a variety of sources—including the Federation of American Scientists—to be up to 600 feet in length. Every time they are used *outside* the usual testing areas their flight can be hidden behind the "alien technology" smokescreen. Reports of massive triangular platforms from southwest England, the location of two former test facilities (Boscombe Down and Yeovilton), during the 1990 Belgian flap therefore come as no surprise. Neither do reports from the northwest English coast of black triangular aircraft under escort by RAF Tornados!

From the point of view of the UFO researcher and the public at large, these slow-moving platforms are of greater importance than the near-mythical triangular spyplanes like *Aurora*. In *UFO Revelation* (1999) I detail the existence of the Advanced Airborne Reconnaissance System (AARS), also known as "Tier 3," in the early 1990s. This was a slow-moving triangular aircraft and was said by insiders to utilize electrochromic plates to change the color and hue of the craft in flight and to move "at walking pace."

Add to this a new generation of Unmanned Aerial Vehicles (UAVs) and stealth helicopters, which bring the many developments of the past 50 years to their logical conclusions,

then we have an impressive range of military hardware that must be responsible for its fair share of UFO reports. However, given the secrecy and paranoia surrounding these projects, it is likely that new information will only emerge in very small pieces as we move further into the 21st century.

Only if we remember that circular and triangular aircraft are configured for flight within an atmosphere will we understand the terrestrial, military origins of these remarkable machines.

—TIM MATTHEWS

Reference

Matthews, Tim. *UFO Revelation: The Secret Technology Exposed?* (Blandford, 1999).

Mars and Martians   Scientific speculation about intelligent life on Mars has shaped both popular ideas about extraterrestrials and efforts to understand UFOs. In 1877, the Italian astronomer Giovanni Schiaparelli observed narrow lines across the face of Mars and designated them *canali*, or channels.

In most English translations these lines became "canals," a name connoting an artificial structure. The canals in Schiaparelli's 1877 drawings did not look especially artificial, but some writers were quick to jump on the possibility and develop the theme. Schiaparelli then made an even more amazing discovery while observing the planet in 1881-1882.

Over a period of days or even hours, some of the canals seem to "double"—that is, where one canal appeared before, two appeared in its place. These double canals were often thin, straight lines running sometimes for thousands of miles in perfect parallel. He realized the implications of this discovery and published his results in an obscure Italian scientific journal, but to no avail. The popular press soon spread these observations far and wide as proof that Mars was home to intelligent beings capable of vast engineering projects.

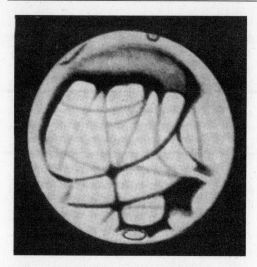

Martian "canals" as drawn
by Schiaparelli in 1886

The question of Mars and its canals became the most exciting issue in astronomy. In 1894, the American astronomer Percival Lowell built his famous observatory on a site west of Flagstaff (in Arizona) which came to be known as "Mars Hill."

He quickly became the most active observer of the red planet and a vociferous publicist for the theory of an inhabited Mars. Lowell rejected the earlier view of the planet as a world with oceans linked by the canals, and proposed instead that Mars was a dying planet. Its seas and thick atmosphere had departed with its evolutionary youth. The remaining water was locked in the polar caps. When they melted in the spring their moisture revived the vegetation, which appeared as dark gray or blue-green areas on the surface of Mars. The melting polar caps filled the canals with water, which was then distributed to the ancient Martian cities that were stranded amid vast reddish deserts. The visible canals were not the waterways themselves but strips of vegetation, probably cultivated lands, over pipelines constructed to conserve the precious remaining water. In summer, when the polar runoff was greatest, the Martians opened a sec-

ond canal to handle the overflow. According to Lowell, the Martians were more advanced than us in science, technology, social organization, and physical evolution.

Other astronomers saw the canals as nothing more than natural spots and shadings on the surface of Mars, joined into long straight lines by deceptions of the human eye and the will to believe. This controversy continued through the 1920s, with most astronomers persuaded that the canals were in fact optical illusions. The Mariner and Viking probes of the 1960s and 1970s ultimately bore out this explanation.

Canals were not the only Martian mysteries suggesting intelligent life there. Bright spots observed on the planet around the turn of the century were interpreted by the popular press as signals, though Lowell and other astronmers scotched these rumors by explaining them as clouds. A few decades later, a vast cloud shaped like a "W" formed periodically over the same area of the surface. Again popular interest was excited, but again astronomers called on natural forces. During the 1920s several experimenters with radio, including Guglielmo Marconi and Nikola Tesla, believed they picked up radio signals from Mars. In 1937 a Japanese astronomer saw a brilliant spot suddenly appear on the surface, followed by a large cloud. This observation suggested a meteor or volcanic eruption to astronomers in the 1930s; but by the 1950s, a new possibility was suggested: now the events fit the pattern of an atomic explosion.

If no physical canals marked the surface of Mars, their idea has left an indelible impression on literature and popular belief. In 1897, H. G. Wells drew on Lowell's theory as the basis for his novel, *The War of the Worlds*, which assumed the Martians were intelligent enough to escape their dying planet and attempt a migration to Earth. This most famous alien invasion story provoked a major panic when Orson Welles broadcast a radio version in October 1938. A survival motive as the reason for extraterrestrials coming to Earth has appeared in the UFO literature from time to time, and is prominent in current speculations about the purpose of abductions.

A Dweller on Two Planets (1899), dictated by the Martian Phylos to Frederick S. Oliver by automatic writing, tells of Martians coming to Earth in aerial craft to visit Atlantis and Lemuria, and prefigures the later "ancient astronaut" literature. Theodore Fluornoy wrote *From India to the Planet Mars* (1900) describing the visionary travels of a young woman who brought back an elaborate description of the Martian landscape and civilization, much like modern UFO contactees.

Life-on-Mars beliefs intersected with UFO reports from an early date. A report from South America in 1877 alleged the discovery of a meteor containing the body of a being from Mars. Most 1897 airships were credited to an earthly inventor, but a minority opinion blamed the airships on Martians coming to Earth on an exploratory mission.

Several landing yarns included Martians, such as a St. Louis man who visited with two humans who looked like Adam and Eve but indicated they came from Mars before flying off in their airship; and the Aurora, Texas, crash, where a local expert in astronomy looked at the pilot's body and said he must have been a Martian.

Mars was still a viable candidate for life in the 1950s, and many writers tied UFOs to that planet. Gerald Heard identified the UFO-nauts as bee-like Martians in his book, *Is Another World Watching?* (1951). Some contactees claimed to have visited Mars or met Martians; and hoaxer "Cedric Allingham" gave away the origin of his contact in the title, of his book, *Flying Saucer from Mars* (1955).

More serious UFOlogists discerned a correspondence between 1950s UFO waves and oppositions of Mars, though from 1957 onward this relationship has broken down. A flurry of excitement began around 1960 when a Soviet scientist proposed that the moons of Mars, Deimos and Phobos, were artificial satellites. They seemed to behave like Sputnik. Moreover, they were not discovered until 1877, the same year as the canals, yet smaller telescopes could and should have detected these bodies. A reasonable conclusion would be that they were launched just prior to 1877; therefore Mars is presently home to a native civilization advanced enough to launch huge space stations and send probes to Earth, or a base for visitors from beyond the solar system. Further understanding of artificial and natural satellite dynamics exploded this notion.

With the landing of the Viking Mars probes in 1976, hope for life on the planet flickered out. Not even simple plant life or bacteria greeted the expeditions from Earth. Yet thanks to those probes, a new Martian controversy began over the so-called "Face on Mars": a formation found in some Viking photos with a remarkable resemblance to a human face. The surrounding formations have impressed some people as artificial and city-like, and led to speculations that an ancient civilization once inhabited the planet.

Alas, now yet another Martian myth bites the dust. On April 5, 1998, the Mars Orbital Camera on the Mars Global Surveyor spacecraft photographed these features at different sun angles and at ten times the resolution of the previous images. Even computer enhancements of the pictures show no resemblance to a "face" or anything else, except randomly scattered rocks and hills of the natural Martian landscape.

If present-day supporters of the extraterrestrial hypothesis have had to look beyond the solar system for the origin of UFOs, the legacy of the life-on-Mars controversy has accompanied the search. Ideas of superior alien intellects with body forms different from ours were boosted into popular consciousness as never before by scientific and literary treatments of Mars. Notions of a dying planet and aliens seeking out the Earth for purposes of their own have persisted in UFO lore down to the present.

—Thomas Eddie Bullard

Mars rock Known technically as sample #ALH84001, this potato-sized Martian meteorite contains what most scientists believe is fossilized bacteria from the planet Mars.

What looks like a worm in this photo may be the first known example of life beyond the Earth.

In August of 1996, headlines around the world announced "Life on Mars." Though disputed by some scientists, most support the conclusion that this 4.2-lb. chunk of basalt does indeed contain the first evidence of life beyond the Earth.

The meteorite, discovered in Antarctica in 1984, is believed to have arrived on Earth between 11,000 and 13,000 years ago; probably the result of a comet or asteroid impact to the planet Mars some 16 or 17 million years before that. With the explosive force of perhaps a million hydrogen bombs, the ejecta from the impact, according to this scenario, probably escaped the weak Martian gravity to assume orbits around the sun until encountering the Earth at the opportune point.

We know the rock is from Mars, because it contains chemical markers—known from samples taken by the Viking lander—that "fingerprint" the Martian atmosphere. The conclusion that the rock contains a 3.6-billion-year-old life-form is drawn from four separate lines of evidence, which are highly technical in nature.

There is strong evidence, as well, that the early Mars had running water, and perhaps even oceans, covering much of its surface.

—RONALD D. STORY

Matthews, Tim (b. 1967). Tim Matthews is an English researcher of UFOs and the paranormal. He holds an Honours degree from the University of Lancaster in Classical Music as well as numerous music diplomas and awards. He is the Commercial Editor for *Quest for Knowledge* and *Beyond* magazines—both U.K. newsstand publications. His investigation into man-made UFOs has been both controversial and pioneering. Some of this work was published to critical acclaim in his book *UFO Revelation: The Secret Technology Exposed?* (Blandford, 1999) and concludes that some of the "classic" UFO cases (McMinnville, 1950; Mainbrace, 1952; Hudson Valley, 1980s; and Belgium, 1989/90) actually relate to the testing, development, and operation of secret military aircraft of circular and triangular design.

Matthews is at the forefront of research into American and British secret military aircraft programs begun during the Second World War and which have been largely ignored by UFOlogists. He has obtained files and holds an archive of some 4,000 pages of Freedom of Information Act material from various U.S. archives.

He is a regular guest on Jeff Rense's *Sightings* radio show and many U.K. radio and TV programs where his lively and hard-hitting debating style is well known.

He lives in Lancashire with his wife Lynda, daughter Alexandra Maia, and three Jack Russell terriers. He is a keen soccer fan and sports fanatic.

Address: c/o Discovery
           BCM 4067
           London WC1N 3XX
           England

E-mail: TMMatthews99@aol.com

POSITION STATEMENT: I have investigated dozens of cases across the U.K., particularly those in Northern England. I believe that there are many causes for UFO sightings—not one simple "catch-all" explanation. My own research indicates that nine out of ten cases have a relatively simple explanation; misidentification of stars and planets, aircraft lights, and so on. Nevertheless, a few cases indicate a much deeper mystery, some involving mysterious paranormal phenomena and "earthlights" of natural origin.

I have investigated cases which clearly point to the operation of secret military aircraft—often hidden from us by a combination of media fascination with fantastic alien stories and imagery, the extraterrestrial prejudices of the UFO community and the American government whose secret projects have been responsible for the growth in a multibillion dollar, and largely unaccountable, underground economy.

—TIM MATTHEWS

James McDonald

McDonald, James E.   (1920-1971). The main proponent in the scientific community during the mid-late 1960s that UFOs probably represent extraterrestrial visitation, McDonald conducted intensive research on UFO data, both theoretical and in the field, interviewed hundreds of UFO witnesses, and attempted to interest other scientists in the data. He lectured widely on the subject to many scientific societies and played a key role in Congressional UFO hearings in 1968.

A critic of the Air Force's Project Blue Book, and the methodology and conclusions of the Air Force-sponsored University of Colorado UFO study, McDonald analyzed all of the cases in the university's Condon Report and concluded that many of the Colorado explanations were not well founded. Before his death in 1971, McDonald was granted access to the official Air Force UFO files from the former Project Blue Book, which were then housed at Maxwell Air Force Base, in Alabama. His analyses of these case files, many of which had only just been declassified, convinced him further that UFOs represented a physical phenomena of scientific importance, and that the hypothesis of extraterrestrial visitation appeared to be the least unlikely in explaining many of the reports. He was also critical of J. Allen Hynek, the Air Force's scientific consultant for over twenty years, for not bringing the data to the attention of other scientists. McDonald left no published book outlining his conclusions or thoughts on UFOs; he concentrated, instead, on the continuing analysis of UFO data. He privately published many short monographs based on his lecture presentations or specific UFO topics or cases.

Both before and after receiving his Ph.D. in physics at Iowa State College (now University) in 1951, McDonald taught meteorology there, first as an instructor (1946-49), then as an assistant professor (1950-53). He was a research physicist in the University of Chicago's department of meteorology (1953-54), later joining the University of Arizona faculty, first as an associate professor (1954-56), then as a full professor (1956-71) in the department of meteorology (now atmospheric sciences). Concurrently, he was a senior physicist in the university's Institute of Atmospheric Physics, of which he served as associate director (1954-56) and scientific director (1956-57). McDonald was a consultant to numerous federal agencies, including the National Science Foundation, the National Academy of Sciences, the Office of Naval Research, and the Environmental Science Service Administration (now National Oceanic and Atmospheric Administration).

His principal research interests related to physical meteorology, the physics of cloud and precipitation processes, meteorological optics, atmospheric electricity, and weather modification.

POSITION STATEMENT: If there were even a slim possibility that the Earth were under extraterrestrial surveillance in any form, that would be a matter of the greatest scientific importance, warranting the most rigorous investigation. In fact, the evidence that seems to point to the conclusion that UFOs could be such devices is far from negligible; yet because of the history of official and scientific response to the earlier UFO reports, we continue to see mainly neglect or ridicule on this intriguing question.

After examining around a thousand UFO reports and directly interviewing several hundred witnesses in selected UFO cases of outstanding interest, and after weighing alternative hypotheses, I find myself driven steadily further toward the position that the extraterrestrial hypothesis is the least unlikely hypothesis to account for the UFO. That hypothesis is, of course, not original with me; it has been urged for many years by persons knowledgeable with respect to the UFO problem, who spoke from outside scientific circles. Our collective failure to examine scientific aspects of the UFO problem will, I fear, be held against the scientific community when the full dimensions of the UFO evidence come to be recognized.

The type of UFO reports that are most intriguing, and point most directly to an extraterrestrial hypothesis, are close-range sightings of machine-like objects of unconventional nature and unconventional performance characteristics, seen at low altitudes, and sometimes even on the ground. The general public is entirely unaware of the large number of such reports that are coming from credible witnesses be-

cause ridicule and scoffing have made most witnesses reluctant to report openly such unusual incidents. When one starts searching for such cases, their number are quite astonishing. Also, such sightings appear to be occurring all over the globe.

The sooner we take a serious new stance and confront the UFO question with adequate scientific talent and staffing, the less embarrassing will be the ultimate admission that we have been overlooking a problem of potentially enormous scientific importance to a humanity.

—ETEP STAFF

(Position statement was abstracted and adapted from the monograph *Are UFOs Extraterrestrial Surveillance Craft?* The monograph was based on a talk given by McDonald before the American Institute of Aeronautics and Astronautics in Los Angeles, California, March 26, 1968.)

McMinnville (Oregon) photos The photographer, Mr. Paul Trent, took two photos of an object which he claimed was flying past his farm (near McMinnville, Oregon) on May 11, 1950. These classic photos are important in terms of their quality and credibility, having withstood close scrutiny over time. The images are clear, and their investigation has been stringent.

The Trents (who both witnessed the UFO) originally treated the photos rather casually, waiting several weeks to have them developed, and then they only showed them to family members. A friend suggested they take the photos to their banker. The banker subsequently alerted a local newspaper reporter, William Powell, who interviewed the Trents in detail at their home. He analyzed the negatives in considerable detail at the newspaper office and then decided that, despite the incredible nature of the subject, it was beyond the capabilities of the Trents to have created such a hoax. He then published full-frame prints and blowups of the UFO in the (McMinnville) *Telephone Register* on June 8, 1950. The following week the now famous photos were published in *Life* magazine.

The basic history of this case (up to 1973) was summarized by William K. Hartmann in the *Scientific Study of Unidentified Flying Objects* (edited by E. U. Condon and D. Gillmor, 1969) and by Philip J. Klass in *UFOs Explained* (1974)—except for the claim by the Trents that they were visited by two "FBI men" several weeks after the photos were taken. The FBI has denied involvement in the case.

Powell also claimed that the newspaper office was visited by two U.S. Air Force officers who confiscated all of his prints. There is a document that discusses the Trent case in the files of the Office of Special Investigations of the Air Force, now on microfilm at the National Archives.

When Hartmann investigated the Trent case, he interviewed the witnesses and performed careful photometric and photogrammetric analyses of the original negatives. By use of a clever photometric argument, he was able to establish "to within a factor of four" that the object was about 1.3 km away from the camera in the first photo. At the conclusion of his analysis, he stated that "all factors investigated, geometric, psychological, and physical appear to be consistent with the assertion that an extraordinary flying object, silvery, metallic, disk-shaped, tens of meters in diameter, and evidently artificial, flew within sight of two witnesses." He then included the disclaimer that the evidence does not positively rule out a hoax, although certain "physical factors argue against a fabrication." (Gillmor, 1969)

Robert Sheaffer, at the request of Philip Klass, analyzed blown-up prints and discovered shadows of the eave rafters on the east wall of the nearby garage. Sheaffer used these shadows to argue that there was a considerable time lag between the photos and that the photos must have been taken in the morning rather than in the evening, as claimed by the Trents. He also criticized Hartmann's photometric analysis for failing to take into account the "spillover" of light (veiling glare) onto the UFO image if there were fingerprints on the camera lens.

The writer (Maccabee) obtained the original negatives in 1975, and found that the shadows on the garage wall did not provide any evidence for a long time lag between photos (the witnesses claimed that there was probably less than thirty seconds between photos). I also repeated Hartmann's photometric calculation, but included corrections for veiling glare and the assumed illumination of the bottom of the UFO in photo #1 by ground reflected light in his analysis. I concluded that, if the bottom of the UFO were not itself a source of light, the object would have been more than 1 km distant, with resulting dimensions greater than 30 meters in diameter by 4 meters thick. In a computer-aided study of the negatives, William

Photo #1

Close-up of object in Photo #1

Spaulding (in Proceedings of the 1976 Center for UFO Studies Symposium) found no evidence of a wire or thread suspending the object (if it were hanging from the wires clearly visible over the object), and he also found an excessive fuzziness of the image which might be related to atmospheric effects if the object were distant.

In order to account for the excessive brightness of the bottom of the UFO in photo #2, I suggested and rejected the hypothesis of internal lighting, and then suggested that the upper part of the object might be translucent. I then proceeded to test the brightness distributions of the bottoms of various small UFO models made of paper and plastic.

I found that under the lighting conditions similar to those expected at the time of the photos, the brightness of the bottom of a translucent UFO model would not be uniform, whereas the brightness of the image of the bottom of the object photographed by the Trents was very uniform. Thus I concluded that if the object was a hoax, the Trents must have suspended some nonuniform translucent object.

A detailed photogrammetric analysis has failed to prove that the object was suspended beneath the overhead wires. However, the photogrammetric analysis has turned up an interesting coincidence between the amount of angular motion of the UFO between photos as claimed by Mrs. Trent in 1950, and the amount actually recorded by the photos. *The Portland Oregonian* of June 10, 1950, states: ''During

this time the object moved across the horizon through an arc of about 15 degrees, according to her description.'' The actual angle between the sighting lines to the UFO in photos #1 and #2 is about 17 degrees.

Although Klass has argued that the discrepancies between the original accounts of the sighting as expressed in the original newspaper stories are evidence of a hoax, because they didn't get their stories straight, these discrepancies could also have resulted from attempts by the witnesses to reconstruct what would have taken place several weeks before they were interviewed by the newspaper reporters. Thus, these discrepancies are relatively unimportant.

However, one major discrepancy does exist. One would expect that the Trents could remember whether the photos were taken in the morning or in the evening just before sunset, as stated in the original reports and as repeated many times by Mrs. Trent. The shadows of the east wall of the garage are sharp and suggestive of a small bright source in the sky east of the garage. According to Sheaffer, the shadow positions suggest that, if they were made by the sun, the sun was approximately due east of the garage wall. This would place the time at about 7:30 A.M. on the eleventh of May, 1950. Sheaffer has argued that no source but the sun could have made such shadows. On the other hand, Mrs. Trent has repeatedly claimed that Mr. Trent went on a milk run every day early in the morning after they took care of the farm animals. This milk

Photo #2

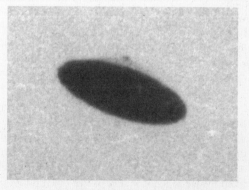

Close-up of object in Photo #2

run would have lasted from 6:30 or 7 A.M. to later than 9 A.M. under normal circumstances. Thus, he would not have been available to take the photos in the morning.

Furthermore, a detailed photometric study of the shadows under the garage eave provides evidence which appears to contradict the sun-shadow hypothesis. The shadow image that provides the most data for evaluation is that of the edge of the roof. Densitometric scans of this shadow show that it is sufficiently smeared in a vertical direction to have been made by a source which has an angular vertical extension of between 5 and 10 degrees, whereas the angular size of the sun is only about one half a degree. A study of the effects of haze and clouds on the "effective angular size of the sun" showed that, when nearly obscured by clouds, the sun has an effective angular size of no more than about 1.5 degrees. On the other hand, the rather sharp width of the shadows of the eave rafters suggest that the source must have had a relatively small horizontal extension, probably not exceeding about 2 degrees.

Both Sheaffer and Hartmann have argued that it would be impossible for a bright cloud to cause shadows similar to those on the east wall of the Trent garage. A detailed theoretical analysis showed that it might be possible under certain conditions. However, the main argument for the possibility that a bright cloud at sunset could have caused such shadows comes from photographic evidence taken by the writer in July 1977. Although the average brightness of the cloud was only about four times that of the sky, the shadows were very noticeable, with a contrast comparable to the 20 percent or so contrast between the illuminated areas and the areas shaded by the eave rafters on the Trent garage. The weather report for McMinnville on May 11, 1950, indicates that cumulous clouds were present during the afternoon. Whether or not a single cumulous cloud would have been east of the Trent farm at sunset is, however, impossible to determine from evidence independent of the Trent photos.

Over the years since the photos were pub-lished, numerous investigators have talked with the Trents about their sightings. The first interviewer was William Powell. He was convinced the Trents were telling the truth, as was the newspaper editor, P. Bladine. The banker, F. Wortmann (now deceased), wrote in 1969 to the late Dr. James McDonald that Mr. Trent "is an individual who can be relied on without any question." In response to letters from P. Klass in 1969 and 1972, Wortmann restated his firm belief "as to the truth of the whole thing." In a "spot intelligence report" to the Air Force Office of Special Investigations, Sergeant L. J. Hyder referred to the Trents as "substantial, solid, honest citizens of the community." The late Frank Halstead, an astronomer, interviewed the Trents in 1958 and stated in a letter to Major Donald Keyhoe that "they seemed to be very sincere people." Halstead's letter contains the first reference to an "FBI" investigation of the Trents. In 1967, Hartmann interviewed the Trents during his photo analysis for the Condon Committee. He was impressed by their lack of interest in the sighting, as evidenced by the fact that Mr. Trent did not even bother to get down from his tractor while Hartmann was interviewing him. In 1969, Dr. McDonald had several phone conversations with the Trents and concluded: "I find them to be the kind of people who could scarcely carry off an imaginative hoax or fabrication." Mr. Trent told McDonald that Trent's father had also seen the object, but only after it receded into the distance. Also in 1969, Veikko Itkonen, a film producer and director, who was working on a UFO documentary that was shown in Europe, interviewed the Trents at the scene of the original photos. He stated that "the conclusions of Dr. Hartmann are very close to the impressions we got." A. Fryer, a former high-school science teacher at McMinnville, interviewed the Trents in 1976 and subsequently stated: "No question in my mind that they weren't trying to hoax—she never called it a flying saucer or UFO."

I had twenty-six phone conversations with Mrs. Trent during the period 1974-77. During this time, she maintained the expected consistency in retelling the account of the sighting. She has also provided new information in response to certain questions which she probably had never been asked before, such as questions about their typical daily activities and the involvement of any relatives and friends in the aftermath of the sightings. Mrs. Trent has stated that, some time after the photos were published, a lady who lived within several miles of the Trent farm in 1950 told Mrs. Trent that she, too, had seen the strange "parachute-like" object. Mrs. Trent also thinks that Mr. Trent's mother might have seen it. Although Mr. Trent's father was dead by the time of Hartmann's interview, the lady who was her neighbor, according to Mrs. Trent, was still alive (now deceased). It is unfortunate that Hartmann did not ask Mrs. Trent whether or not she knew of other witnesses. Mrs. Trent has passed two PSE (psychological stress evaluator) tests of statements she has made concerning the original sighting and the new information. In the opinion of the PSE analysts, she shows no noticeable stress when answering any of the questions regarding the sighting and associated events (e.g., other witnesses, daily activities, et cetera). Thus, it appears that Hartmann's official conclusion is still valid.

—BRUCE MACCABEE

References

Gillmor, Daniel S., ed. *Scientific Study of Unidentified Flying Objects* (Bantam Books, 1969). "Final Report of the Scientific Study of Unidentified Flying Objects" Conducted by the University of Colorado under contract to the United States Air Force, Dr. Edward U. Condon, Scientific Director.

Klass, Philip J. *UFOs Explained* (Random House, 1974).

Maccabee, Bruce. "McMinnville (Oregon) photos" in Story, Ronald D., ed. *The Encyclopedia of UFOs* (Doubleday/New English Library, 1980).

Sheaffer, Robert. *The UFO Verdict* (Prometheus Books, 1981).

Meier contacts (b. 1937). Eduard Meier, popularly known as "Billy," claims to have had his first telepathic contacts at the age of five with an elderly extraterrestrial man who called himself Sfath. Shortly thereafter he physically met with Sfath on several occasions in the extraterrestrial's pear-shaped metallic vehicle, in an area near Meier's home in northern Switzerland. The purpose of these contacts was, through the application of advanced technologies, to accelerate the development of young Meier's mind to that of an adult, and prepare him for the mission that would become synonymous with his life's purpose.

As a result of this educational process, and ensuing developmental dissonance with his peers and neighbors, as well as hospitalization for several years due to tuberculosis, Meier would withdraw from his regular schooling after nine years.

Meier's telepathic contacts with Sfath continued until 1953 and, after their cessation, were replaced by contacts with an extraterrestrial woman named Asket who claimed to come from a different adjoining universe, the Dal universe. Meier emphasizes that these contacts, and all subsequent ones with various extraterrestrials, were voluntary and not what are commonly called abductions.

Meier received additional education from Asket, which he claims included travel back in time to different periods to allow him to see important events as they actually happened. These experiences, as well as Meier's own studies of Earth's various religions during his extensive travels throughout India and the Mid-East during the 1960s, further prepared him for his mission.

In 1965 Meier lost his left arm in a bus accident in Turkey—an event foretold by Asket as having to occur. In 1966 he married a Greek woman and returned to Switzerland with her in 1970, where they began raising their family of three children.

Five years later, on January 28, 1975, Meier's contacts began with Semjase, a female who said that she was from the Pleiades. It was Semjase who would subsequently provide Meier with the opportunities for the now world-famous photographs and films of UFOs that have been at the center of the controversy swirling around him.

One of the Pleiadian (or Plejaran) "beamships" with Mount Auruti in the background. Photo by Eduard "Billy" Meier

This photo by Meier shows a beamship with an accompanying remote-controlled craft.

The remarkable clarity of the hundreds of daytime 35mm photos, and the half-dozen pre-video 8mm film segments are unique in all of UFOlogy. Meier also made cassette tape sound recordings of the UFOs which could not be duplicated in sound studios using the best synthesizers available at the time. Semjase also provided him with metal samples that, upon analysis by Marcel Vogel, a research chemist with IBM who was a key researcher in the development of liquid crystal technology and the floppy disk, were determined to be of such quality and composition as to be unknown and not duplicable by current scientific methods.

Additionally, the counterclockwise circular landing patterns made in the grass by the Pleiadian spacecraft, or "beamships" as they are called, remained in a horizontal position throughout several months with the grass remaining unbroken, green, and healthy. The sheer volume and unmatched quality of these items has, paradoxically, caused some in the UFO field to call the Meier case too good to be true.

Even more controversial, however, has been the content of the *Contact Notes*: the transcripts of the conversations that Meier claims to have had with Semjase, her father Ptaah and other extraterrestrials, and the Talmud Jmmanuel (about which more shall be said later). The *Contact Notes* cover a very wide range of topics and are telepathically transmitted to Meier, through an advanced Pleiadian technology, and then typed by him with his one remaining hand at very high speed on a typewriter specially modified by the Pleiadians for this purpose. Unlike a lot of so-called channeled information, the *Contact Notes* are unique in that the majority of the material transcribed by Meier is from his face-to-face encounters with the Pleiadians, which usually occurred on their beamships. They are not only quite specific but have already been proven to contain extremely accurate, and previously unpublished, scientific information. Time will tell how much of the information Meier published on a wide range of topics is accurate. It has long been accepted by people researching the case that deliberate disinformation may have been injected by the Pleiadians as a "safety valve" type of mechanism for skeptics. This viewpoint has in itself generated some skepticism from critics of the case. Additional areas of information include:

Environmental Damage

During Meier's 7th recorded contact with Semjase on February 25, 1975, his 34th recorded contact on September 14, 1975, and 35th contact on September 16, 1975, he was informed of the dangers facing humankind from the consequences of the human-caused damage to the ozone layer. Semjase emphasized that the greatest, and at that time unknown to us, damage was caused by the atmospheric atomic testing of the late 1940s, 1950s, and 1960s (which released certain "elementary radiations" that our scientists didn't even have a means of detecting) as well as from bromine and CFC gases.

Semjase told Meier that the explosions of the atomic devices tore holes in the ozone allowing deadly UV rays to pass through, killing off microorganisms in the upper atmosphere as well as microorganisms in the seas, with which they were in symbiotic relationship. Ultimately this would lead to problems with the food chain as well as genetic mutations.

An article from the November 29, 1988, Santa Monica, California, *Evening Outlook* newspaper, titled "Atom Bomb Testing Tied to Nuclear Depletion," confirmed Semjase's conversation with Meier thirteen years earlier. An article from the February 24, 1992, *Los Angeles Times,* titled "Ozone Hole Damages Food Chain," further confirmed Semjase's warnings.

During Meier's 45th contact with Semjase, on February 25, 1976, she also told him that our extraction of petroleum and natural gas from the Earth, and damming of waters, was a major contributing factor to the increase of earthquakes and volcanic activity. A professor

at Stanford published a corroborating article in the June 21 through June 27, 1990, issue of *The Good Life-Independent Journal*, a southern California newspaper. A scientific report aired on National Public Radio in 1991 during which the discovery of the connection between bromine gases and the ozone damage was "first" revealed. The report made mention that bromine gases were used extensively in wood treatment, especially woods prepared for export to Japan, and also for agricultural applications. Now, decades after Semjase's warning, bromine gases are well recognized as damaging to the ozone layer.

The Talmud Jmmanuel

Central to understanding Meier and his mission is the *Talmud Jmmanuel*, or "TJ," as it is referred to. The TJ was alleged to be an ancient Aramaic document which was discovered in a long-abandoned half-buried tomb in Jerusalem, which was initially located by Isa Rashid, a former Greek Orthodox priest, in 1963 while under the subconscious prompting of the Pleiadians. The document itself, sealed in a resin box, was retrieved by Meier, who located the small obscured opening to the tomb during a subsequent visit with Rashid. The surviving translated segment of the TJ is considered by some to be a segment of the original testament of Jmmanuel (who was later called Jesus), which gave rise to the New Testament gospels, in particular the Gospel of Matthew. The TJ is unique in that it answers and resolves more than 300 problems and inconsistencies that have troubled New Testament scholars for decades according to James Deardorff, an independent TJ researcher. (For a detailed exploration of the TJ see Deardorff's research at http://www.proaxis.com/~deardorj)

Genetic Manipulation of the Species

The Pleiadians told Meier that many Earth humans are related to them through common ancient ancestors or to other extraterrestrial visitors from the far distant past. The case contains quite a bit of specific information about the extraterrestrial connection as well as why genetic manipulations were deliberately done, by some ETs, to limit the Earth human's life span to about 100 years. The Pleiadians claim that the original lengthy life spans of several hundred years, as referred to in the Bible and other sources, will one day be reclaimed when scientists discover and rectify the particular genes that were tampered with. Meier's writings on this predated the fairly recent published discoveries in this area. According to Meier, the "original sin" as it is referred to in the Bible is erroneous, as it really refers to this genetic tampering of the human DNA that limited the human life span.

Genetically Engineered Crops and People

Meier states that the well-meaning attempts to categorically block the genetic experimentation and modification of foods and crops are misguided. He says that it is part of the process of evolution that mankind moves in this direction, but he also states that vigilance is necessary as there are inevitable positive and negative results in this area as in all others in life. Perhaps even more controversial is his prophetic information on the types of genetic modifications that await the human species. He foresees a time when humans will also incorporate technological devices into their bodies for a wide range of functions—a futuristic vision that also portends great difficulties as well as achievements.

Organ Transplant Dangers

Years ago, the Pleiadians advised Meier that organ transplantation was a dangerous practice that would ultimately have to be relinquished in favor of regrowing and replacing worn or damaged organs. Consideration of this approach is gaining ground in our scientific circles with rumors that some scientists are close to perfecting this technology.

Flight TWA 800

In response to Meier's question as to the cause of the crash of TWA flight 800, Ptaah, Semjase's father and one of the leaders of the Pleiadians, unequivocally told Meier that it was an errant U.S. Navy missile.

The Beast

Meier has written that the "New World Order" is an inevitable development in human evolution. Though sure to be initially fraught with very negative conditions, it is seen as the precursor step to a truly unified, cooperative world. Regarding the Beast of the Bible, Meier says this actually refers to the super-computer in Brussels that will ultimately be used to track and control humanity (that computer reportedly already bears the acronym B.E.A.S.T.).

This control will be accomplished by the implantation of chips, the "mark" of the Beast, and the use of already existing military satellites, such as were relied upon in the Gulf War, whose capabilities are far beyond what is publicly known.

Vegetarianism

Meier, claiming to speak on behalf of the Pleiadians, states that vegetarianism is not healthful for the vast majority of human beings and that it contributes to faulty thinking due to deficiencies of certain nutrients currently found only in foods from animal sources. Rather than helping their cause of protecting animals, those vegetarians opposed to genetic engineering actually help to perpetuate the unnecessary suffering of countless animals, says Meier. This is because the answer to the nutritional as well as moral questions lies in the development of animal proteins "grown" through genetic engineering of plants; something at least one scientist was exploring several years ago.

FACE ON MARS

What we call the "Face on Mars" is, according to Meier, only the tip of the artifact-iceberg of what exists, and will be one day found by man, on the now desolate planet. Meier contends that Mars was one of three planets in the solar system that have been inhabited by humans. The other planet (besides Mars and the Earth) was called "Malona" or "Maldek" (its remnants now making up the asteroid belt). Meier predicts that the discovery of artifacts on Mars will shake the foundations of our understanding of mankind's origins.

ABORTION

In his discussions with the Pleiadians, Meier learned that they allow abortion only up to the third week, as their advanced scientific technology confirms that the human spirit becomes present with the fetus at this time. Here on Earth, however, abortion is allowed and in accordance with the spiritual laws and directives if certain conditions and reasons are present, e.g., genetic defects, brain damage, danger of the mother's health, etc. They affirm that terrestrial science has not yet progressed enough to be able to detect hereditary defects and other malfunctions in the first three weeks of a pregnancy.

THE LAWS OF CREATION

The Pleiadians say that the universe in which we live is the conscious embodiment of all that exists, the source of all love, existence, intelligence, wisdom, knowledge, compassion, mercy, justice, and more. They say that it permeates all things. Therefore, we must learn to live by its laws and directives. The "Creation" is that which we may otherwise refer to as "God," except that it is of an incomprehensibly greater magnitude, as the term God referred to the highly advanced extraterrestrial rulers of the distant past who falsely represented themselves to many peoples in many cultures as the Creation itself.

The Pleiadians state that each human spirit is unique, as it is a small piece—a tiny hologram—of the full potential of the Creation, which is designed to unfold and evolve to its full spiritual potential over many millions of incarnations.

TERRESTRIAL RELIGIONS

With the supremacy of the Creation as the foundation of all spiritual truth, the Pleiadians and Meier point out that all terrestrial religions miss the mark and serve to corrupt and retard the development of the human spirit. They are firm in stating that there are absolutely no gods, deities, saints, ascended masters, angels, idols, gurus, or other intermediary forms that should stand between humans and their connection to the Creation. Meier claims that the original version of the Lord's Prayer was not directed outward to a "Father in Heaven" but rather inward to awaken one's own spirit.

MEIER AND JMMANUEL

It is said that Meier is the current embodiment of the same spirit (or spirit form) that incarnated as Jmmanuel (erroneously called "Jesus" according to the Pleiadians and Meier) and Mohammed, as well as several earlier Biblical prophets and the scientist Galileo, a persecuted "prophet" in his own right. The Pleiadians and Meier state that he is the prophet of this time—come to do what the others before him have done—to announce or reintroduce the Laws of Creation. He is adamant and clear that he is not, and was not, "Jesus Christ." Having survived over fifteen assassination attempts, it appears that Meier's claims and teachings have contributed to making him at least as much of a target as the prophets of old.

Research on what is arguably the longest-running, and most extensively researched, UFO contact case was done by Col. Wendell C. Ste-

vens, Lee and Brit Elders, Tom Welch, Jim Di-
lettoso, Michael Hesemann, Lou Zinsstag, Jaime
Maussan, Jun-Ichi Yaoi of Nippon TV, and others. The most vocal of Meier's critics, Kal K.
Korff, allegedly went to Switzerland twice to investigate the case but returned without interviewing a single eyewitness or even Meier
himself.

Notes: Go to www.figu.ch for more information on the Pleiadians' and Meier's information regarding: AIDS, space travel, destiny of the human
races, intermarriage, polygamy, physics, black
holes, spiritual teachings, the New World Order,
religions, ice ages, etc. Of special interest is the
"251st contact" which contains far-reaching
prophecies and predictions.

The Pleiadians are now correctly referred
to as "Plejarans." The term "Pleiadian" was
deliberately used by the Plejarans and Meier to
distinguish themselves, at the appropriate time,
from all other alleged contactees, channels and
mediums who would claim to be in some form
of communication with "Pleiadians." The
Plejarans confirm that the star system of the
Pleiades, as is visible to us on Earth, is too
young and not possessing the conditions suitable for any form of inhabitation. Thus, there
are not, and never have been, any "Pleiadians" providing any information to anyone in
any form.

—MICHAEL HORN

Menger, Howard   (b. 1922). Howard
Menger is the best-known contactee in the
eastern United States, and the first to claim he
was a "child contactee."

Born in Brooklyn, New York, Menger
moved to New Jersey, where he received his
elementary and high school education. Upon
graduation from high school, he worked for a
year in Picatinny Arsenal as a munitions handler
and inspector. In 1942, Menger enlisted in the
U.S. Army, where he was assigned to the Ar-
mored Tank Division. He later worked with
Army Intelligence and on detached service with
Naval Intelligence and Chemical Warfare.

After his discharge from the Army in 1946,

Howard Menger

he established the Menger Advertising Company in Washington and Highbridge, New Jersey, where he was in business for twenty years.
He formed his own company, Energy Systems
Research, Inc., to do basic research in electronics and to promote several of his inventions,
including an emergency power pack.

In 1956, Menger took some photographs
of "flying saucers" in a field near his home.
The story and events which surrounded those
photographs resulted in several cross-country
lecture tours and his book *From Outer Space
to You* (1959). With his wife, Connie (who
helped him compile the first book and a second, entitled *The Carpenter Returns,* co-
authored with her and Milton Selleck), he
currently owns and operates his own advertising sign company and art studio in Vero
Beach, Florida.

Address: 845 28th Ave.
            Vero Beach, FL 32960
            U.S.A.

The Space People who contacted Howard
Menger originated on Venus, Mars, Jupiter,
and Saturn and were making contact for the

first time with a select group of Earthlings. Some of the Earthlings had a very special heritage unbeknownst to them until after their meetings with the Space People. Mr. Menger himself, for example, and his second wife, Connie, were reincarnated from previous lives on the planet Venus. Venus, by the way, is described by Menger as ". . . young and healthy, with beautiful foliage, streams, forests, large bodies of water, mountains, hills . . ." and not unlike ". . . some places in California today. . . ."

A "Venusian Scout Ship" photographed in 1953 by Howard Menger

Menger claims the earliest contact experience of all the contactees. It began when he was only ten years old, in 1932, while he was playing in the woods near his home. He came upon a beautiful golden-haired woman, sitting on a rock. Menger later wrote, [she] "was the most exquisite woman my young eyes had ever beheld! The warm sunlight caught the highlights of her long golden hair as it cascaded around her face and shoulders. The curves of her lovely body were delicately contoured—revealed through the translucent material of [her] clothing. . . ."

The woman said: "Howard, I have come a long way to see you . . . and to talk with you." She told him: *"We are contacting our own."* She explained that when he grew older, he would be contacted again; i.e., when he could understand their teachings, which would include the knowledge of his purpose on Earth and what would be expected of him as a messenger of the Space People.

"Spacewoman" captured on film by Howard Menger

Indeed, there were other meetings with the Space People, a long series of contacts which included a course of instruction that continued over many years and amounted to a complete guide to good, clean living. Spiritual subjects were taught, such as the proper care of the soul, but also there were teachings about the proper care of the body. Special health foods were extremely important. When the Space People visited Earth, but neglected to bring along their own food, "They asked mainly for frozen fruit juices, canned fruit and vegetables, whole wheat bread, wheat germ, and the like." One specimen of food processed by the Space People, a Lunar potato, was given to a laboratory in Philadelphia for analysis. It was reportedly found to have five times more protein than potatoes grown here on Earth.

—RONALD D. STORY

Menzel, Donald H. (1901-1976). Regarded as the leading "debunker" of UFOs for almost twenty-five years, Donald Menzel, a well-known astronomer, was the author of three books and numerous articles which attempted to explain UFO phenomena as a combination of natural and man-made events. He perceived the sky as containing myriad possible UFOs: planets, stars, meteors, aircraft, balloons, etc., all waiting to be misidentified by the credulous observer or, in some instances, by the well-trained observer.

While some found his explanations convincing, others did not. Most UFO advocates considered him an "archenemy." Many of his explanations were, in fact, reasonable, and Menzel certainly had the technical background to evaluate such data. However, he rarely conducted personal field checks and limited himself to more theoretical explanations, which, however unlikely, he considered more probable than extraterrestrial visitation. He accepted the probability of many technologically advanced civilizations throughout the galaxy, but not that they could easily, and routinely, travel across interstellar distances to Earth.

Menzel had a certain impatience with those who entertained the extraterrestrial hypothesis (ETH), as well as with those who were not altogether convinced by his explanations of UFO reports. He was also critical of the U.S. Air Force UFO investigators, whom he felt often ignored his evaluations and his advice, particularly during the early 1950s.

After obtaining a Ph.D. in astrophysics from Princeton University in 1924, Menzel taught astronomy at the University of Iowa (1924-25) and Ohio State University (1925-26), and worked at the Lick Observatory of the University of California (1926-32). He then joined the faculty at Harvard University as an assistant professor of astronomy (1932-35), later becoming associate (1935-38) and full professor (1938-71) of astrophysics, and Paine Professor of Practical Astronomy (1956-71). He served as head of the astronomy department (1946-49), and associate director (1946-54), acting director (1952-54), and director (1954-66) of the Harvard College Observatory. He became a professor emeritus in 1971, and so remained until his death in late 1976. He was also affiliated with the Smithsonian Astrophysical Observatory (1966-71).

Menzel was a member of many scientific societies, was president of the American Astronomical Society (1954-56), and was the recipient of many distinguished awards. He was a consultant to numerous industrial firms and federal agencies. During World War II, he served as chairman of the Radio Propagation Committee of the Joint and Combined Chiefs of Staff, which worked on critical communications and radar problems, and headed the Section of Mathematical and Physical Research of U.S. Naval Communications.

His principal research activities involved solar and stellar astronomy, planetary atmospheres, wave mechanics and atomic spectra, radio propagation, and sun-ionosphere problems. Major UFO works: *Flying Saucers* (1953); *The World of Flying Saucers,* with Lyle Boyd (1964); and *The UFO Enigma: A Definitive Explanation of the UFO Phenomenon,* with Ernest Taves (1977).

POSITION STATEMENT: Man has traditionally tended to construct a myth to explain anything he cannot understand. And this is precisely the way the flying saucers, or UFOs, came into existence. I became actively involved with UFOs in 1952. *Look* [magazine] called me to ask if I had any ideas on the subject. I did and wrote two articles for them which I later expanded into a book.

In the summer of 1952, while on a tour of active duty with the Navy, I addressed a large and enthusiastic group of officers at the Pentagon concerning my views of UFOs. I was also invited to brief the personnel of Project Blue Book. I found them much less receptive. A few were positively antagonistic, especially those who, as I later found out, had become convinced of the extraterrestrial hypothesis, or ETH. However, I made a few converts to my views, individuals who later came to reorganize the project completely, about 1954.

I predict a decline of public interest in UFOs. The people seem to have taken up a new cause: Astrology. It has a similar scientific basis and fulfills a similar need in human desire. The government should withdraw all support for UFO studies as such, though I could advocate the support of research in certain atmospheric phenomena associated with UFO reports. I further predict that scientists of the twenty-first century will look back on UFOs as the greatest nonsense of the twentieth century.

In conclusion, I want to point out that, in my opinion, the question of whether planets of our solar system or elsewhere have intelligent life on them is irrelevant. Nor am I denying the possibility that someday we may actually experience visits from outer space. My point is that the UFO reports to date do not represent extraterrestrial activity in any form. I confidently predict that no amount of investigation will bring evidence in support of the extraterrestrial hypothesis.

—ETEP STAFF

(Position statement was abstracted and adapted from "UFOs—The Modem Myth" by Donald Menzel, in Sagan, Carl and Thornton, Page, eds., *UFOs—A Scientific Debate,* 1972.)

Messages from the Stars (Harper & Row, 1978). British science writer Ian Ridpath proposes that humankind may never meet extraterrestrials because the acquisition of higher intelligence diminishes curiosity about space exploration. After dismissing UFO sightings and ancient astronaut evidence as based on fanatical belief, not evidence, he wonders whether or not we might be the first technological civilization in the universe to survive.

—RANDALL FITZGERALD

Messengers of Deception (And/Or Press, 1979). Jacques Vallée speculates that contactees may be unwitting victims of cult groups pursuing a hidden social and political agenda. He began to develop this conspiracy theory after computers used to search for patterns in the global distribution of UFO reports portrayed the behavior of the phenomenon as if it were a conditioning process using "absurdity and confusion to achieve its goal while hiding its mechanism."

—RANDALL FITZGERALD

Metán (Argentina) UFO crash-retrieval

The controversial events that took place at Metán, a small town near Salta, Argentina, fit in well with the UFO crash/retrieval obsession that prevailed in the early and mid-'90s. Between August 17-18, 1995, thousands of people allegedly witnessed the collision of an unidentified flying object against the slopes of 9,000-ft. El Crestón after having supposedly been struck by air-to-air missiles. A small private plane flying over the crash site hours later was knocked out of the sky by alleged "electromagnetic interference" emanating from the wreckage.

Details tacked on to the story—such as the six-hundred-foot diameter of the downed saucer and its 200 dead occupants—hampered its credibility when the news was first circulated. But clearly verifiable ground effects, including uprooted trees and deep furrows in the landscape, coupled with the fact that seismometers 90 miles away from the source were set in motion after the impact, were clear indicators that something had indeed occurred. A rescue team led by Pedro Olivera saw a metallic object at the epicenter of the devastation and advised their superiors of the fact. The rescuers were curtly told to advance no further and return to their headquarters.

On August 18, 1995, local residents saw English-speaking personnel heading toward the Metán crash site. The foreigners removed pieces of a slender, metallic material resembling aluminum from the crash site, which allegedly "assumed a concave shape when joined."

Raúl Córdoba, a Salta journalist interviewed by Buenos Aires's *Crónica* newspaper on September 1, 1995, stated that "there is no doubt that we have NASA personnel here trying to conceal the truth, assisted by members of the National University at Salta, since it is already involved in the matter but refuses to publicize its involvement."

—SCOTT CORRALES

metaphysical aspects of UFOs and ETs

With every passing year, the study of UFOlogy grows more complex, as UFO sightings and ET (extraterrestrial) contacts continue to occur across the world. We are faced with an enormous body of research at our disposal—well documented and extensively studied. Facing the dawn of the 21st century, we have no problem finding data to support the claim of true extraterrestrial visitation. *Our problem is how to interpret and make sense of all this data.*

As we seek to uncover the deeper levels of meaning, we have to realize that empirical methods, for all their merits, have built-in limitations. Put simply, the scientific approach of most UFOlogists and SETI scientists gives us but a piece of the puzzle. While it does provide ample documentation of isolated events and experiences, it is completely unable to address the larger dynamics. UFOlogists have little to say about the metaphysics of such visitors from beyond.

However, there are other sources of information to consult. As documented by Richard Thompson in his book, *Alien Identities* (1993), many aspects of modern UFO/ET phenomena were well understood by the ancient Hindu priests, and were extensively documented in the Vedic scriptures. We find comparable material in the texts of almost all world religions, including the Judeo-Christian and Native American traditions, such as the Mayan and Hopi. There is also a huge body of material in Western esoteric schools, including Theosophy, as well as coming from more modern "ET channels." All of these sources offer a wealth of information on cosmic life and its relation to Earth, and when wisely used, can help us fill in the gaps left by empirical UFO research.

Admittedly, the reliability of these sources varies, they offer no proof of their claims, and being based on subjective, non-empirical methods, they do often suffer from exaggeration and mythologizing. Nonetheless, they do give us important perspectives, which, in some cases, can help us interpret and integrate the disparate facts emerging from UFO investigation. It is arrogant and naïve for UFOlogy to dismiss all such sources, because of the distortions of some. This writer believes it is prudent to take a careful look.

For instance, we can find numerous references to extraterrestrial life in Buddhist texts, spanning a period of more than 2,500 years

from the time of the historical Buddha. In particular, they document the polarized intentions of two main groups of beings. These groups are placed in the traditional Buddhist cosmology of the "six realms," and in Sanskrit, are termed *devas* ("radiant gods") and *asuras* ("angry, jealous, or fighting gods"). The idea of benevolent spiritual beings who support humanity, and evil beings who do harm, can be found in all mystic traditions, and is highly applicable to understanding ET agendas.

We also find numerous references to interplanetary evolution in the writings of Alice Bailey, an exponent of Theosophy. It is well understood that souls live on different worlds, divided according to their age and level of development, and that there are cosmic bodies that govern their growth and interaction. We even find commentary on the relationship between Earth and other star systems, such as that of Sirius and the Pleiades. Interestingly, these stars figure highly in the mythology of the Maya, Sumerians, and Dogon of Africa, and many contactees claim to have met ETs from these systems. Obviously, the ancients knew some things about cosmic life that modern UFOlogy is only reaffirming.

Finally, we can even find useful data amid the popular books that claim to be channeled from ET groups, despite the obvious folly of some. In my own comparative research, one such source stands out as most credible and accurate. Consisting of four main volumes, *The Law of One* series (also called *The RA Material*) speaks extensively about the metaphysics of UFOs and ET contact. Most important, they explain just why these visitors are now coming to Earth.

According to this source, which claims to have also contacted the Egyptian Pharaoh Akhnaton, we are nearing the end of a major cycle of human evolution. They say that ET groups are well aware of this fact, and knowing that time is short before drastic changes occur in our dimension, they seek to influence us toward a more conscious choice of our own destiny. Not surprisingly, many ET experiencers also bring the same kind of message. They say that UFO visitation is basically a global spiritual wake-up call.

Admittedly, we have much to learn about the metaphysics of UFOs and cosmic life, and we should take a careful approach to our study and data collection. Nevertheless, facing such a complex, abstruse topic, it is essential we broaden our perspective, and consider alternative sources of information, outside the realm of empirical investigation. The UFO phenomenon need not remain a mystery, and the big picture can be known, but we will need courage, discernment, and an open mind to find the answers.

—SCOTT MANDELKER

References

Bailey, A. A. *A Treatise on Cosmic Fire* (Lucis, 1925).

Elkins, D., C. Rueckert, and J. McCarty. *The Law of One, vol. II* (L/L Research, 1982).

———. *The Law of One, vol. III* (L/L Research, 1982).

———. *The Law of One, vol. IV* (L/L Research, 1983).

———. *The RA Material* (L/L Research, 1984).

Mandelker, Scott. *From Elsewhere: Being E.T. in America* (Birch Lane Press, 1995).

Thompson, Richard L. *Alien Identities* (Govardhan Hill, 1993).

Mexican UFO wave of the 1990s

During the first half of the decade, Mexico produced a wealth of tantalizing, crystal-clear video and photographic images of unidentified flying objects. Interaction between U.S. and Mexican researchers reached an all-time high as vast quantities of information were disseminated throughout the world. The lion's share of the attention was commanded by the aerial display over Mexico City on September 16, 1991, but cases had been coming in from all over the Mexican Republic since the second quarter of 1991, with numerous sightings being reported in the states of Sonora, Sinaloa, San Luis Potosí, Michoacán, and Puebla.

In April 1991, Adriana Velázquez and her brothers witnessed two "midgets"—1.20 meters tall—who signaled to them with a powerful red light near Tepejí del Río, following the sighting of a "fireball." In May 1991, in the state of Hidalgo (northeast of Mexico City), three elongated silvery vehicles appeared over the town of Huejutla, and a small UFO was seen to fire a beam of red light over the village of Real del Monte with no apparent damage caused.

On May 29, 1991, hundreds of witnesses were treated to the sight of a nocturnal "parade" of twelve shining, elongated objects over the city of Pachuca, Hidalgo—an incident which would repeat itself a few days later, when approximately 15 triangular lights (resembling the ones seen frequently in Belgium during 1990) were reported over the same location.

The city of Jojutla, Puebla, was rocked by an unexplained explosion on May 11, 1991, in which a blinding light was followed a massive detonation, deeper and more resonant than even the loudest thunderclap which rattled windows and shook homes down to their foundations. The unusual light disappeared seconds after the loud report. Professor José Luis Martínez, a mathematician and physicist, indicated that "either a bona fide UFO or a meteorite" could have been responsible for the extraordinary event, but added that he was "more inclined to believe in the first" alternative—the UFO explanation—since meteorites do not explode noisily in mid-flight.

On January 2, 1992, a blackout plunged 22 municipalities in the states of Guerrero and Morelos, as well as the cities of Iguala and Taxco (a well-known tourist destination), into absolute darkness. Witnesses were startled to see three unusual objects which appeared to be equipped with "spotlights" scanning the ground.

By April 1993, the UFOlogical action had shifted even further north to Ciudad Valle (San Luis Potosí) and its surrounding communities: on the 22nd, hundreds of eyewitnesses saw the nocturnal antics of luminous vehicles performing aerial somersaults for well over an hour. Four disk-shaped vehicles, escorted by a larger "mothership," cavorted with impunity over the countryside.

A similar event took place on April 26 and 27, but this time the intruders were accompanied by unknown, mysterious "airplanes" (reminiscent of the "ghost flyers" reported over Scandinavia in the 1940s) that flew lower than the UFOs themselves before thousands of startled onlookers. Circles of crushed and burnt vegetation were found in Chantol, a community close to Valles, and in the vicinity of the Tanchipa Mountains.

Yet the Mexican saucer wave was also characterized by a number of surprising encounters with non-human entities: in May 1994, a humanoid alien creature was reported in the town of Cosolapa, Oaxaca. Witness Joaquina Reyes described the alleged UFOnaut as an entity the size of a ten-year-old boy ". . . all in white, with a crown and belt that changed color constantly."

The wave was also characterized by crash/retrieval incidents, such as the one involving the Mexican Army's 5th Cavalry Regiment in the alleged collision of an artifact on April 30, 1994, in the region known as Arroyo de los Gatos (San Luis Potosí).

UFO activity over Mexico would continue well into the decade, but without the intensity that had characterized its initial years. The credibility of many incidents captured on videotape was called into question by their commercial exploitation and the famous "Las Lomas UFO hoax" of 1997, which portrayed a wobbly saucer disappearing behind a high-rise condominium in a neighborhood of Mexico City.

—SCOTT CORRALES

Michel, Aimé (1919-1992). Aimé Michel was a French mathematician and engineer, well known in UFO circles for his theory called orthoteny, that UFO sightings occurring on the same day are often arranged along a straight line. Michel retired in 1975 and devoted himself to "reading and study in several scientific areas." He also served as an overseas consultant to the British *Flying Saucer Review*.

Michel attended the universities of Aix, Grenoble, and Marseilles (1939-43), where he studied the theory of sound, musical harmony, and various instruments. He earned his License (similar to the master's degree) in philosophy and letters. He worked at the Short-Wave Service of National Radio Broadcasting (1944-58) and with the Research Service of the French Radio-Television Office (1958-75). He had been a writer specializing in the topic of animal communication from 1954 to 1965, during which time he published several articles. Michel also studied communication in the mystical community.

In UFOlogy, his involvement dates from the postwar Scandinavian ghost rocket wave. His two books, *The Truth About Flying Saucers* (1954) and *Flying Saucers and the Straight-Line Mystery* (1958), have been very influential among students of the UFO phenomenon, both in Europe and the United States.

POSITION STATEMENT: I do not think that one can capture the essentials of UFOlogy in a brief article. In effect, thinking about UFOs

Aimé Michel

requires a reconstitution of the mind more drastic than the Copernican Revolution. The most sensible approach is through astrophysics. The two basic facts to keep in mind are these: (1) the great number of stars with planets, and (2) the age of these stars, billions of which are billions of years older than the sun.

If the attainment of the level of psychological complexity of human beings is a normal, nonmiraculous phenomenon, then one must admit the existence of a "cosmic psychic milieu," which would have surpassed the human level of complexity some millions of years ago. This "milieu" can be presumed to be present everywhere in one or more unknown forms and probably exceeds our own level of complexity as much as ours exceeds that of the lower animals. It is not a question of a "club of advanced civilizations"; this is an anthropomorphic idea which supposes that the human level is the final one in the evolution of every intelligent species, and that after it is reached, the species can evolve its culture but not itself. It is the last and the most naïve of the pre-Copernican superstitions.

It would take a long and very difficult effort of reflection to imagine the rational means for studying *even the aspects accessible to us* of a psychic milieu so far superior without falling into superstition. It is up to astronomers, biologists, specialists in evolution, epistemologists, and other philosophers to tell us whether the observed phenomena of UFOs corresponds to the predictions one could make about the behavior of such a psychic milieu. To my thought, based on premises too complicated to explain here, UFOs are a manifestation of this milieu, present, through some unknown manner, since the origin of the solar system. I think that it would be a great mystery if something like UFOs did not exist; since this would contradict everything we know about astrophysics, biology, et cetera. For the existence of UFOs in all their unfathomable strangeness conforms to what science would lead us to expect.

The short amount of time in which Western science has existed (a few centuries) is a very brief passage in the process of cosmic evolution. The Earth itself, which twentieth-century man sees is a transient phenomenon, and thus at any instant a very rare one. We are perhaps the only beings at a "human" level throughout the galaxy. What action (if any) does the cosmic psychic milieu exercise on this brief passage? Are we treated in a special manner? Is this passage through the human stage something cosmically precious (similar, for example, to infancy for human beings)? Is the lack of open contact the proof that we are something rare and precious? I think it is, but I will not attempt to demonstrate it here.

One means of measuring the effects of this action on us is constant surveillance of the global UFO experience through opinion polls. There are more direct methods, but they remain to be invented.

In my opinion, the noncontact phase will last until we ourselves discover the method of contact. To discover the method will require a profound transformation of mankind. It is not certain that we will find it. It is not even certain that our evolution has not already missed the path that would lead to contact (good or bad). Nonetheless, my opinion is that the scientific path is the right way; but it is long and dangerous, and the contact may have good or bad results.

At present, UFOlogy is not yet a science. To my thinking, it will not become a science unless there is a change of paradigm *in the classical sciences* thinking that the new physics is in the process of discovering the new paradigm by introducing the phenomenon of consciousness in its theories. I also feel that the phenomenon of consciousness will take an expanding role in the new physics, perhaps as far as becoming *the sole object of science*. It is thus, I believe, that humanity, transformed by itself, will enter the cosmic psychic milieu.

—AIMÉ MICHEL

Michalak encounter Stefan Michalak of Winnipeg, Manitoba, Canada, claimed to have suffered first- and second-degree burns, severe nausea, loss of weight, and other apparent symptoms of radiation sickness after a close encounter with a landed UFO, about eighty miles east of Winnipeg, on the afternoon of May 20, 1967. Michalak, age fifty-one at the time, was employed as a mechanic at the Inland Cement Company and enjoyed amateur prospecting as a hobby. One weekend, he set out alone to look for minerals in the wooded and rocky terrain near Falcon Lake. While examining a quartz vein, he said, he became aware of the sound of some cackling geese, apparently alarmed by something. Looking up, he reportedly observed two oval-shaped UFOs, glowing scarlet-red that were descending rapidly. While one of the objects came to rest on a rock about 160 feet away, the other one hovered about fifteen feet above the ground for a few minutes and then took off at high speed.

Michalak waited and watched for about thirty minutes, he said, while the "machine" that landed just sat there, "radiating heat," and "changing in color, turning from red to gray-red to light gray and then to the color of hot stainless steel, with a golden glow around it." Then, a door (square but rounded at the corners) opened, from which a brilliant purple light emanated. He also reported "wafts of warm air that seemed to come out in waves from the craft, accompanied by [a] pungent odor of sulfur. I heard a soft murmur, like the whirl of a tiny electric motor running very fast." As he approached within sixty feet of the "craft," he claimed, he heard voices coming from inside. "They sounded like humans," he said, and "I was able to make out two distinct voices, one with a higher pitch than the other." He attempted to communicate by shouting in English, Russian, German, Italian, French, and Ukrainian but got no response.

Michalak then approached within touching distance of the object and decided to take a look inside. He said, "Placing green lenses over my goggles [carried with him on prospecting trips to protect his eyes from rock chips], I stuck my head inside the opening. The inside was a maze of lights. Direct beams running in horizontal and diagonal paths and

a series of flashing lights, it seemed to me, were working in a random fashion, with no particular order or sequence." He then took a closer look at the surface of the craft, which he said had no rivets or seams of any kind. just then, the object tilted slightly, and Michalak felt a scorching pain around his chest. As he touched the machine, his rubber-coated glove melted and his shirt suddenly caught fire. As he tore off his shirt and tossed it to the ground, the ship lifted off and, with a sudden rush of air, disappeared into the sky.

Confused and frightened, Michalak headed back toward the highway to seek medical help. He was subsequently treated at Misericordia Hospital for chest burns and released. He reported the incident to the Royal Canadian Mounted Police (RCMP), but they initially expressed no interest in the case. Eventually, the incident came to the attention of the press, radio, and television media, and various authorities. Many UFO investigators, including Dr. Roy Craig of the University of Colorado UFO Project, checked into the matter.

Probably the most significant aspect of the case was the prolonged period of illness endured by the witness. For weeks, Michalak could not keep food in his stomach and suffered from nausea, vomiting, diarrhea, a drop in his lymphocyte count, and a weight loss of twenty-two pounds. A curious characteristic of the burns on his chest was their arrangement, which was in a checkerboard pattern. Michalak's health gradually returned to normal, but not without several recurring episodes.

On June 10th, three weeks following the UFO incident, he experienced a number of blisters high on his chest and a V-shaped rash that ran from the middle of his chest to his ears. Michalak consulted a radiologist and a skin specialist, who treated him for the condition. Then, on September 21st, five months after the UFO encounter, he reported a burning sensation around the neck and chest, followed by a recurrence of several large red spots in the same places where the burns had been. He also had swelling in his hands and chest, accompanied by dizziness, which prompted his readmittance to Misericordia Hospital for observation. He was released the following day.

After several unsuccessful attempts in the company of representatives from the RCAF (Royal Canadian Air Force), RCMP, and Dr. Craig, Michalak allegedly found the UFO-landing site, with the help of Mr. G. A. Hart, an electronics engineer of Winnipeg, who happened to be interested in the case. In the words of Michalak: "Our greatest surprise was to see very plainly the outline of the ship on the ground where it had landed six weeks earlier.

"We found the remains of my shirt at the scene along with the tape measure I lost that day. We placed the articles in plastic bags, gathered some samples of rock and earth from the area, and took some pictures of the spot. We also discovered that branches of trees in the area where the craft came down had withered away and died, while all around the trees were flourishing normally."

It is said that the soil samples collected were tested by various authorities, but again, as is usual in UFO matters, nothing was ever proven.

Mr. Michalak died, at the age of 83, in October of 1999. And his encounter has remained one of the most puzzling UFO cases on record.

—RONALD D. STORY

mind control by aliens The idea that the mind can be controlled or influenced by some form of advanced technology wielded by aliens or secretive people in possession of special knowledge is more pervasive than most people realize. The thought that free will can be subverted and man is a mere puppet to higher powers in the universe has fascinated thinkers throughout history. Supernatural beliefs, most notably demonic possession and the casting of spells, often invoke the premise that the mind may be powerless against control by forces external to the human soul.

Arthur Koestler affirms that the dramatic motif of volition against fate is one of the most powerful archetypes in literature and has appeared in countless forms. Threats to individual or collective freedom arouses very primal human fears and can yield a drama of intense emotions when free will is affirmed. Conversely, when free will is denied, the effect is coldly distancing and allows contemplation of humans as blameless innocents caught in a web of impersonal forces. Because you cannot have heroes without a powerful adversary, paranoia is virtually *de rigueur* in great literature. (Thorpe, 1980) Extraterrestrials are one of the more recent additions to the pantheon of gods, demons, superior races, secret societies, and power elites that have been pulling the strings for ages.

EARLY HISTORY

Guy de Maupassant's short story "The Horla" (1885) may be the first work of fiction to incorporate the general notion. A gentleman tormented by fears and possible hallucinations speculates that thinkers from a distant world may traverse space to conquer as the Norsemen crossed seas to subjugate feebler nations. "We are so weak, so powerless, so ignorant, so small—we who live on this particle of mud which revolves in liquid air." He realizes that Mesmer's experiments in suggestion, ten years earlier, were the first look at a new weapon of this new Lord, the Horla. Enslaving the human soul, he would make of humanity what we made of horses and oxen. "His slave and His food, by the mere power of His will. Woe to us!" As the story proceeds, the realization strengthens that the Horla has taken hold of the gentleman. "It is He, the Horla who haunts me, and who makes me think of these foolish things! He is within me, He is becoming my soul." He tries to combat it, and in horror realizes there is only one escape.

The story, tragically, reflects a worsening mental state of the author. Maupassant's body was failing and he took drugs. He started to have hallucinations, then delusions of persecution, and eventually made attempts at suicide.

He was committed to an asylum where he died in 1893. (Commin, n.d.)

H. P. Lovecraft's "The Call of Cthulhu" (1928) speaks of a race called the Great Old Ones which came from the stars and spoke to men by "molding their dreams." The emergence of Cthulhu from beneath the seas is accompanied by sensitive individuals going mad. The cult that sought to liberate him warned he would bring Earth beneath his sway. (Lovecraft, 1978)

Lovecraft's use of the motif is more philosophical and consciously guided by a mechanistic supernatural vision of the cosmos as totally indifferent to the wants and ultimate welfare of mosquitoes, pterodactyls, fungi, men, trees, or other forms of biological energy. As he wrote in a letter a year before this story: "To achieve the essence of real externality, whether of time or space or dimension, one must forget that such things as organic life, good and evil, love and hate, and all such local attributes of a negligible and temporary race called mankind, have any existence at all." It has been said that Lovecraft was the first science-fiction writer to cultivate this stark aesthetic in the service of horror. (Joshi, 1980) The idea has obvious roots in the metaphor of deep time advanced by Charles Lyell and other geologists in the prior century. (Gould, 1987) Lovecraft's aesthetic led to a proliferation of amoral aliens in subsequent decades.

THE SF CONNECTION

C. L. Moore's "Shambleau" (1933) reinvents the Medusa as a feline alien with terrible hypnotic eyes able to control the mind and soul as it drains the life force of its victim. The victim enjoys both horror and pleasure as he knows horrible wild things and visits unbelievable places while entwined in her ropy embrace. "Black Thirst" (1934) revisits the idea with an alien able to steal a soul through the eyes and sink the victim into a waking nightmare. (Del Rey, 1975) Stanley Weinbaum's "A Valley of Dreams" (1934) has Tweel, an ostrich-like Martian, try to prevent Earthmen from entering a valley that looks like paradise. It soon transpires it is a telepathic illusion generated by dream-beasts, blobby plants with writhing rope tentacles to lure animals in to feed on them. (Weinbaum, 1974)

H.G. Wells wrote a couple of works involving the idea of extraterrestrial influences in 1937. *The Camford Visitation* has a vicar use a case of a person troubled by a disembodied voice in a book he is writing called *Extra-Terrestrial Disturbances of Human Mentality*. The case is said to demonstrate an "upthrust of the subconscious through some sort of space-time dislocation." (Slusser and Rabkin, 1987) Better known is *Star-Begotten: A Biological Fantasia*. It tells the tale of a man discovering a generation of humans who are more elevated than prior generations. They possess unaccountable intuitions, mathematical gifts, strange memories and exceptional abilities. He becomes enamored with the idea that aliens of higher development are manipulating cosmic energies and firing away at human chromosomes with increasing accuracy and effectiveness through the ages. The Martians were acting as a sort of interplanetary tutor unlike the invaders of *War of the Worlds*. The book affects an ambiguity over whether the narrator was deluding himself with pseudoscientific nonsense or making an actual discovery. At the conclusion, the narrator realizes with a start that he himself was one of the "strangers and innovators to our fantastic planet who were crowding into life and making it over anew." (Wells, 1970)

The pulp writer Raymond Z. Gallun utilized the extraterrestrial influence motif in several stories. "The Magician of Dream Valley" (1938) and "The Lotus-Engine" (1940) develop the idea of aliens able to generate radiations that totally envelop humans in a hallucinatory reality. In "Godson of Almarlu" (1936) a machine was devised that was said to now and again influence terrestrial life. "Hotel Cosmos" (1938) revolves around a globe that sends out invisible radiations of madness that affects the nervous tissue and is used to sabotage a Galactic Conference.

Arthur C. Clarke used the motif in two widely acclaimed works. In *Childhood's End* (1953) an Overmind "attempted to act directly upon the minds of races and to influence their development." It failed with prior worlds, but Earth's youths are successfully adapted to alien consciousness and the reader experiences them leaving the cradle of the Earth as they evolve toward the Overmind.

Even better known, if less understood, is the film *2001: A Space Odyssey* (1968). The monolith of an alien culture appears before a tribe of apes and invests a new awareness within them that sets human evolution on the course of cosmic ambitions. As originally conceived, the alien artifact was to create an hypnotic teaching effect. In the film it is wisely rendered as a mystical moment of McLuhanesque enlightenment as the ape that touched the monolith realized the extension of power capable with a tool. A bone becomes a weapon for hunting and murder and this leads inexorably toward atom bombs and space travel. (Agel, 1970)

Kurt Vonnegut's *The Sirens of Titan* (1959) is another acclaimed work that uses the device for particularly enjoyable distancing purposes. Humankind was caused to evolve solely to create and transport a tiny repair part for an alien vessel stranded on the Saturnian moon of Titan. The aliens, called Tralfamadorians, sent messages to the stranded aliens by having humans unconsciously form them. Here is how the process is explained: "Tralfamadorians were able to make certain impulses from the Universal Will to Become echo through the vaulted architecture of the universe with about three times the speed of light. And able to focus and modulate these impulses so as to influence creatures far, far away and inspire them to serve Tralfamodorian ends." Civilizations bloomed and crumbled as humans built tremendous structures to relay messages to Titan. The meaning of Stonehenge in Tralfamadorian, when viewed from above, is: "Re-

placement part being rushed with all possible speed." (Vonnegut, 1959)

Also notable, particularly in the light of interviews where the author claims the book is based in part on his real-life mystical experiences, is Philip K. Dick's *Valis* (1983). (Platt, 1980) The title refers to an influencing machine from the star system of Sirius. The protagonist explains its operation by saying, "Sites of his brain were being selectively stimulated by tight energy beams from far off, perhaps millions of miles away." The narrator is convinced of the insanity of the idea of Valis and is struck by the oddity of "a lunatic discounting his hallucinations in this sophisticated manner; [the protagonist] had intellectually dealt himself out of the game of madness while still enjoying its sights and sounds." The belief that information-rich beams of energy focused on his head allowed him to recognize his hallucinations as hallucinations "But . . . he now had a 'they'." Not much of an improvement, in the opinion of the narrator. (Dick, 1981)

Movies involving the motif of alien influence are common. Dramatically, the best was probably *Five Million Miles to Earth* of the Quatermass series. It is discovered that insectoid Martians once psychically enslaved humanity at the dawn of history. A buried spaceship with dead Martians is dug up, but the spaceship comes alive and starts to take control of humanity once more.

Invasion of the Body Snatchers (1955) is also revered by critics for its rich metaphor of the pod people. Technically, this is better as an example of the Capgras syndrome form of paranoia, but it is understandably lumped in with the pandemic of alien possession in fifties cinema: *Invaders from Mars, It Came from Outer Space, Earth vs. the Flying Saucers, Kronos, Beast with a Million Eyes, Enemy from Space*, and so on.

Control by implant is found in *Invaders from Mars*, where the operation to insert it is utilized as a dramatic peril. It recurs in *Battle in Outer Space*, but here a strobing beam of light does the operation as the victim drives a car. After the radio control apparatus makes him a slave to the glorious planet Nehtal, he experiences a time loss and discovers a trickle of blood on his forehead. In *Catwomen of the Moon* a beam of light is alone the force of influence. In *Earth vs. the Flying Saucers* another beam of light makes the skull of a victim transparent while knowledge is sucked out. A cruder form of mindscan involving a TV monitor can be found in *Invasion of the Star Creatures*, a lame comedy. *Zontar—The Thing from Venus* offers an amusing variant by some very unconvincing ''injecto-pods,'' vampire bats with lobster tails that gain control when they bite you in the neck.

TV Mind Control

Television probably regards alien influence as a staple item. *Star Trek, Lost in Space, The Invaders, The Outer Limits, Space 1999, Dr. Who* all immediately spring to mind with episodes. It has prompted caricature such as a Dick van Dyke show in which Zombies from Twylo import walnuts that Rob feels is stealing his imagination. The final episode of *The Monkees* titled ''Mijacageo'' masterfully invokes the motif for satirical purposes. Humanity becomes controlled through the agency of television sets broadcasting frodis energy directed by a mad scientist (Rip Taylor at his best), and originating in an extraterrestrial bush whose spacecraft crashed on Earth. By any measure, the idea that aliens influence or control man has shown itself to be a durable and seductive feature of our image of higher powers in the universe. Their intimate concern with the mental life of humans is an unconscious given.

As a dramatic device, the mind-bending alien cannot be faulted. Fiction is always granted license in the matter of gimmicks helpful in generating conflict and disparities of power or in generating philosophical moods and ambiances. Questions of plausibility would be invalid in such contexts. Yet, it is a question worth asking when the context becomes nonfictional as happens in UFOlogy. Are such things possible?

The answer is *probably not*. Direct material control of the mind by external forces can be placed near the bottom of any list of science-fiction (SF) notions likely to become reality. It may be more probable than invisibility and teleportation, but time travel, warp drives, and utopia probably have better odds and they seem overly paradoxical to lend them much credence. Many factors contribute to such an assessment.

Brain Research

How does one generate minute but precise potentials of energy across microscopic distances at specific points within a mass of biological tissues possessing electrical potentials in overlying areas? To do this without electrodes to insulate and guide the energy would require fabulous finesse. Varying tissue densities would defocus particle streams. What prevents interactive effects in the tissue above the sites of manipulation? Worse, brains do not map precisely one to another. Knowing how to control one mind does not immediately gain you the ability to control another one. (Valenstein, 1975)

Another problem underlying external modes of influence is that the brain, contrary to popular metaphors, is not like a computer with switches that can be flipped or wires that can be inductively given an electrical charge. Electricity is probably only a superficial feature of brain activity overlying systems of molecular interactions that are the primary modifiers of consciousness. There are hundreds of hormones, maybe even thousands (their science is embryonic at present) involved in brain function; and there must be a careful orchestration of these chemical reactions for the brain to do its work. Once comprehended, one can easily realize why efforts to use electricity to control the mind are about as effective as hitting a person over the head with a hammer. Our hypothetical mind ray would practically have to change water into wine from a distance, indeed into a stable of far more complex molecules. It is literally asking for miracles. (Bergland, 1985)

Electrodes implanted in the brain remove some of the problems inherent in the ray, but not the fundamental one that the brain is more gland than computer. Wilder Penfield's work with electrodes that yielded some reactions is sometimes cited by mind controller wannabes as evidence that there is a future in brain stimulation. Penfield himself, however, regarded his work as eliminating the possibility of mind control. Pleasant sensations and some modifications of emotional states were elicited in a few instances. Compelled behavior, however, was totally absent. The brain proved to be a remarkably plastic biological entity with behaviors regulated through many sites. For all practical purposes, the human will remains autonomous. (Lewis, 1981)

The dream of controlling human thought and action with less fabulous technology has been a notoriously hit and miss occupation. Threats and torture, crude as they are, worked well enough for most social engineers in the past, though the downside risks of revenge, intransigence, and low productivity must be factored in. Social persuasion techniques like advertising do not compel buying behavior, but rather try to draw attention to product existence followed by the evocation of pleasurable mental associations to make purchase of the product a rewarding experience. Drugs can alter the general state of mind and elicit rewarding sensations of power, ecstasy, excitement, and tranquility which seemingly provoke compulsive behavior in the form of more drug-taking, but do not force one to do the will of others in an absolute sense. You can find other drug sources and the option of quitting is usually chosen at some point. Hypnosis, as the alternate term indicates, is more a case of suggestion than a bending of will. Even the bugaboo of brainwashing has on critical analysis showed itself to be less imposing than myth warns. Humans do pretty much as they darn well please. (Bromley and Shupe, 1981)

These considerations force a high measure of skepticism toward all claims that mind rays from any source are manipulating humans. The alternative that humans can convince themselves such things are real when in fact they are fantasy has to be accorded a higher order of probability. Such claims do appear in UFO culture repeatedly.

THE AGE OF FLYING SAUCERS

In May 1945, Ray Palmer's magazine *Amazing Stories* published a story "I Remember Lemuria" by Richard Shaver. Though appearing in a SF magazine, Shaver and Palmer professed that it recounted true occurrences. That story and others serialized from it started a controversy known as the Shaver Mystery. The tales built up a cosmology steeped in cult conspiracy notions, hearkening back to ancient wisdom and lost continents. Among the elements of the cosmology was something called the "dero." In Shaver's words, the dero referred to a concept of "electronic surveillance, through mind-contacting and mind-influencing machinery." He believed the mind was capable of inducting influences "magnetically from the destructive forces of nature" and that opened up the possibility of a worldwide "telemach" that would be like a radiotelephone into the mind.

With this device, degenerate beings infiltrating old service chambers of a previous civilization were trying to rule men's minds. Among the signs demonstrating someone was being affected by the dero was a person's tendency to talk contradictions and clichés. The dero speeds up the thoughts of emperors and czars to impel the world toward destruction. Shaver's views struck a chord with many readers, but hard-core SF fans reacted with disdain. (Keel, 1983)

SOUL SNATCHERS

The early contactees utilize mind control notions sporadically. Howard Menger was probably the most prominent one with his aliens claiming to distribute devices over the landscape designed to open minds up to the possibility of space travel. A rival group of darker intent called The Conspiracy possessed the capability of advanced brain therapy. The two sides were locked in a ceaseless battle for men's souls. (Menger, 1959; 1967)

The Stanfords, whose writings have roots in George Hunt Williamson's speculations, experienced a fantastic sparkling beam projected by a hovering UFO that raised their consciousness above earth man's delusions. This illumination swept them into a whirlpool of ever expanding consciousness until it reached a numinous state of *knowingness*. It was felt to possess a very high resonant frequency or vibration, more visible with the third eye than with the physical eyes. (Stanford, 1958)

Eugenia Siragusa, who gained some fame as a European contactee, similarly reported an encounter in which a beam of light created a "redimension" of her personality. (Vallée, 1979; Keel, 1976)

In July 1961, a student in France reportedly was transported to a large machine that had tapes that transmitted ideas into his brain. After three hours he was transported back to where he was before. He learned that eighteen days had actually passed. He now had psychic powers, improved memory, and a sense of mission.

In May 1975, Chuck Doyle encountered a manta-shaped UFO that was probing the area with a green laser-like beam. The beam hit him and he felt paralyzed. Strange thoughts came into his mind like mathematical equations that made no sense, the symbol omega, a landscape with a red ocean beneath a green sky and blue ground underfoot, and sensations of floating in space with stars of many colors. When the beam went out, he fell on his face. (Stringfield, 1977)

Eugenia Macer-Story, in her charming autobiography about the craziness of her life after becoming an UFO buff, reported an altered mental state following telepathic contact with a ball of light. She feels it made her a different person not fully in control of her personal mind-set. (Macer-Story, 1978)

STEALING THOUGHTS

Abductees have claimed a notable variety of alien-influence episodes. Patty Price claimed aliens hooked wires to her head; and her thoughts, impressions, and emotions were taken and recorded (Lorenzen, 1977). Charles Hickson of the Pascagoula classic has complained, "They took my mind." He couldn't remember things or think straight (Clark, 1978). Aliens told Charles Moody that he had been "absorbed." The Lorenzens, who investigated, took this to mean information was extracted from his mind. Trekkies remembering "Return of the Archons" will take a slightly different meaning. (Lorenzen, 1977) Aliens in the William Herrmann case utilize "inoculation" bars and chambers to enhance mental abilities. (Stevens and Herrmann, 1981)

Still farther up the weirdness scale, there is the Sandra Larson case wherein aliens physically removed her brain from her body. She asserts that when they put it back in, they reconnected it differently and she lost control of her speech. Trekkies may think this a rewrite of the camp episode "Spock's Brain," but perhaps the fact that she thinks aliens can press a button to know what she is thinking, wherever she happens to be, may change their minds. (Lorenzen, 1977)

Abductologist Yvonne Smith tells of a subject who perceived the top of his head being removed and something that seemed like welding being done to his brain. (Smith, 1993)

IMPLANTS

There has been a proliferation of claims about implants being inserted into humans in recent years. Many, particularly ones from the eighties and early nineties, involved them being shoved up the nose and apparently into the brain. Given the septic nature of sinus passages, this would, in real life, mean the person's death. Betty Andreasson, Meagan Elliot,

Virginia Horton, Kathie Davis, Casey Turner, to name a few, somehow survived to tell the tale. (Kottmeyer, 1993)

James Gordon notes that while talk of implants would almost certainly point to paranoia, the claimants seem to recognize how crazy it all sounds and are less sure of what it means than most paranoids would be. (Gordon, 1991) This is probably because they function within an imaginary social world whose paranoia is constructed more by the beliefs of UFOlogists than their listeners.

These people are presenting themes familiar to most students of abnormal psychology. Malcolm Bowers's study of the nature of emerging psychoses notes that fragmentation of self-experience—the loss of the sense of self—is common. The first case he speaks of involves a gentleman who believed his thoughts were stolen. (Bowers, 1974) "Thought-stealing," we have already seen, is repeatedly claimed in abductee accounts. The sense of mission that follows some UFO contacts also frequently accompanies the onset of psychosis. Ideas of reference—a term given to notions that others are responsible for the thoughts one is thinking—is the most common delusion shared by schizophrenics. Some diagnosticians speak of it as a "first-rank" symptom of schizophrenia. (Torrey, 1983)

INFLUENCING MACHINES

In trying to explain how his erstwhile persecutors inject thoughts into his mind, the schizophrenic frequently develops a belief in the existence of influencing machines. Viktor Tausk presented a description of this process among schizophrenics back in 1918. Tausk found the belief evolves out of an originating sensation of inner change accompanied by a sense of estrangement. The need some people have for causality yields belief in a persecutor. As the delusion develops over time, it focuses first on one person, then to a circle of conspirators. The mechanism was grasped only vaguely at first but, in time, buttons, levers, and cranks would flesh out the image. The machine manipulates magnetic or electrical forces or air currents or telepathy or some mysterious radiations beyond the patient's knowledge of physics. In identifying their persecutors, the victim will commonly point to ex-lovers, employers, and physicians. However, they can also be picked from the general culture surrounding them—the CIA, Einstein, movie characters, computers, and, of course, extraterrestrials. (Tausk, 1953)

These fantasies can become quite elaborate. In one schizophrenic's autobiography, the girl began fantasizing about an electronic machine capable of blowing up the Earth and which robs all men of their brains. They would then all be robots obedient to her will. She calls it the "System." As her delusions progressed, she discovered the System had become a "a vast world-like entity encompassing all men." Subsequently it turned on her and forced her into self-destructive acts like burning her own hand and refusing food. At the end, the System was involved in saying silly and innocuous things and finally just sank "beyond thought" with the loss of the delusion. (Sechehaye, 1968)

In a second autobiography, a corps of Operators armed with stroboscopes plagued the victim. They would probe minds, feed in thoughts, and take out information. They were a gabby lot and had a whole vocabulary to cover aspects of their job. Their motive was purportedly a sporting one. He who gained the greatest influence over something was the winner. (O'Brien, 1976)

The novel autobiography of the scientist John C. Lilly presents another illustration of the marvelous nature of influencing machine fantasies. Lilly helped to advance brain electrode technology in a desire to help ferret out the brain/mind duality problem. He dreamed of the possibility of lacing the brain with electrodes and seeing whether playing back its own impulses would yield an identical or different experience.

When the secret intelligence possibilities

of mind control created an ethical conflict in him, he abandoned his work for dolphin and isolation tank research. In time, he became involved in taking the drug ketamine. He experienced a startling hallucination involving the Comet Kohoutek, then passing near the Earth, wherein it spoke to Lilly and offered a demonstration of its ''power over the solid-state control systems upon the earth'' by shutting down Los Angeles Airport.

Lilly reports the demonstration was successful. As the delusion evolved over the ensuing months, Lilly lived within a cosmology where computerization would take over the Earth and remove its corrosive air and water. Solid-state civilizations roamed the galaxy and they tried to convince Lilly to develop machines to ''take care of'' man. Everywhere, Lilly began to find evidence of the ''control of human society by these networks of extraterrestrial communication.''

As ketamine's effects seduced Lilly, he shot up every hour and became convinced of solid-state intervention in human affairs to the extent that he tried to contact the President to warn the government. Lilly came to believe Elliot Richardson was being controlled by these alien forces, then television networks as well. Lilly felt he himself was being controlled by these solid-state entities to see messages in things like a film on the Kennedy assassination.

Lilly hedged on admitting the unreality of the experiences while taking ketamine, but it is a model of psychosis from the precipitating shame of helping spies, the withdrawal from society, estrangement and fears of encroaching death, the conspiratorial pseudo-community relating real to fictional entities, overinterpretations of events as encoding messages to oneself, manic thought, and inevitably, the motif of the influencing machine. It serves here, as it usually does in paranoia, the function of disowning or alienating (in the archaic sense of the term) his unwanted hallucinations and those aspects of technocratic civilization he senses are running out of our control. (Lilly, 1978)

It should be emphasized that influencing machine fantasies and ideas of reference are defensive strategies to retain some measure of self-esteem against crazy thoughts and shameful impulses and actions. The individual does not want to call himself crazy and blames others for the unwanted situation he is in. Though a primary sign of schizophrenia because it indicates the mind is misbehaving and flooding the consciousness with primitive thought, loose associations, or blocking mechanisms, it is also a sign of a positive prognosis. The mind is at least defending itself and not passively giving in. It is in this sense equally a sign of normality. It is a defense potentially available for most people and can be called upon for less challenging dilemmas than schizophrenic episodes. As we saw up front, fiction writers call them up frequently for dramaturgical purposes. They have license to use fantasy mechanisms and retain the presumption of normality. Some of the UFO cases cited earlier probably involved psychotic episodes and some are just stories. Either way, the presence of these motifs justifies the presumption of unreality unless very extraordinary proof is marshaled against its likely impossibility.

In the course of paranoid psychoses, influencing machine fantasies and ideas of reference generally appear after the hypochondriacal phase and at the beginning of the reintegration of the ego. Their appearance defines what workers call the projection phase.

This terminology unfortunately invites confusion with everyday forms of psychological projection, wherein one's impulses are mirrored onto someone else. Though this is undeniably part of what is seen in this phase, the salient features are more concerned with the disowning of unwanted mental content and blame being shifted onto an external agent or locus of control. Externality might be a better term, but it also has milder everyday counterparts.

It has been demonstrated elsewhere (see THREAT, UFO-ET) that the history of UFOlogy exhibits a pattern of changes reminiscent of how paranoia evolves over time. Delusions of observation, end-of-the-world fears, and hypochondriacal fears cluster in the early years. The appearance of influencing-machine fantasies cluster in a later period, as the following chronicle will demonstrate.

FORTEAN INFLUENCES

Nearly every significant speculation in UFOlogical thought seems to be prefigured somewhere in the writings of Charles Fort; control fantasies being no exception. Sometime before writing the *Book of the Damned*, Fort wrote a book titled *X* that was organized on the idea that our civilization was controlled by certain rays emanating from Mars. The process was akin to the way images on photographic film are controlled by light rays. To the "X," Earth is a sensitive photographic plate and all of our reality is an artistic medium.

Theodore Dreiser saw it and thought it was an amazing new idea. Publishers rejected it and Fort later destroyed it. (Knight, 1970) Fort did not totally abandon the notion, since a decade later in a letter to the *New York Times* (in 1926) he opined "for ages Martians may have been in communication with this earth and have, in some occult way, been in control of its inhabitants." (Fort, 1926)

A subtler variant, briefly mentioned in his books, was that aliens communicated with esoteric cults that sought to direct humanity (Fort, 1919). In this respect and many others, Fort is the veritable Lovecraft and Wells of UFOlogy.

THE UFOLOGISTS SPEAK

The first generation of UFOlogists following the start of the flying saucer mystery was dominated by the ideas of reconnaissance and eventual contact. None of the major authors of the period—Keyhoe, Heard, Scully, Wilkins, Jessup, Girvan, Ruppelt, Michel, Stringfield, and Barker—voiced any notions about alien influence or control. Some lesser figures, as we saw in connection with the contactees, had fantasies of the relevant form, but only one bears notice here. George Hunt Williamson straddles

categories in that he was one of the first contactees, but he also had sufficient interest in studying UFOs as a historical phenomenon to regard him as an UFOlogist.

In *The Saucers Speak* (1954), Williamson discusses the raw contact claims of alien communication to his circle of friends by means of radiotelegraphy, Ouija boards, and automatic writing. It would be difficult to find a more bizarre collection of cosmological misinformation. The sun is cool. Pluto is not. All the planets can support life. The motif of influence surfaces in a moment of sublime inscrutability.

Williamson provides some background in his first work, *Other Tongues—Other Flesh* (1953). The origin of man is traced to a migration of spirit from the star-sun Sirius that fuses with the native apes of Earth. Extraterrestrial influence nowadays comes in two types. One comes from the Orion nebula and takes over weak-bodied earth people, making them agents subservient to their will. They are used as instruments to introduce people to others and to ask leading questions at lectures. These agents tend to run amok and upset the plans of other space intelligences. Benevolent space people regard these materialistic types as pirates of creation or universal parasites. They are identified by the strange, faraway glassy look in their eyes and by muscle spasms or throbbings in the neck. Heavy drinkers were also said to be at risk of submitting to telepathic Orion control.

The other influence is a general background of cosmic radiation bearing Universal Knowledge. Williamson variously refers to it as a "music of the spheres," a Great Cosmic Intelligence permeating space, or a universal influx from outer space. Magnetic anomalies on Earth associated with fault lines and volcanoes act as amplifiers of this music. Great civilizations spring up over these anomalies and yield a refinement in the arts and living conditions. Williamson adds that the entire solar system is entering a new possibility area of the universe in which everything will change for the better in all fields of life from economics, politics, eating habits to religion and science. This is possible because he believes the brain acts as a radio set for this radiation. Everything man thinks, says, does, and creates is magnetism, and magnetism is a Universal "I AM."

This phrase may indicate roots in Guy Ballard's doctrine of the I AM, which in turn is rooted in Theosophy's doctrine that man is a spiritual being who is an emanation of the sun. Beneath man's passions and reasonings can be found pure being, the pure "I." (Williamson, 1953; DeCamp, 1980; Hastings, n.d.)

Williamson co-authored a third book with John McCoy entitled *UFOs Confidential!* (1958) It had far fewer ambitions than the previous book. Artificial chemicals in our food supply are said to be controlling man's emotional nature. McCoy reveals that ringing in the ears indicates that space people are beaming instructions into the subconscious mind. He also advocates seeking love and not lustful sex. "No master of darkness can project LOVE frequency," he proclaims. Naïve, to be sure, but overall you've got to give the cosmology points for imagination.

One other lesser figure of interest here is Leon Davidson who graced the pages of *Flying Saucers* with his notions of how the CIA was hoaxing parts of the UFO phenomenon. He explained how George Adamski was not taken to outer space by Venusians, but escorted to Camp Irwin, California, where agents and operatives faked his contact using movie technology and drugs. Davidson was a chemical engineer with atomic energy projects through the forties and fifties, including Los Alamos and Oak Ridge. (Davidson, 1954)

The sixties, despite a voluminous literature, saw at best two or three figures advancing alien mind-control notions. John Cleary-Baker, during a lecture in April 1966, expressed a belief that flying saucers were involved in tampering with people's brains, perhaps by a medical operation that would cause the victim to act in accordance with alien suggestions. He asserted he could identify people possessed by an alien spirit who were occupying positions in society. John Michell did not particularly accept Cleary-Baker's idea, but noted flying saucers were "ideally calculated to disturb the order of our thoughts, to put us in a state of mental anarchy which must start a new phase of our history." He reviewed many tales from mythology that indicated to him the spark of civilization was ignited by gods borne in sky vehicles, though this was not consistently a premeditated act.

Michell viewed the renewed interest in extraterrestrials as a return to an older orthodoxy represented by the religious observances in antiquity. "The possibility that our whole development has been influenced by extraterrestrial forces, with which we may again have to reckon some time in the future, is still hardly considered." Michell would prove himself remarkably prophetic with that little sentence. (Michell, 1967) In the decade that followed, most UFOlogists would reckon with that possibility.

The Lorenzens first advanced alien mind control notions in *UFOs Over the Americas* (1968). Confronted with indications of hallucinations in the Peruvian case of "CAV," they speculate that the UFO occupants projected thoughts designed to influence him to describe images and activities he thinks he saw, but what he actually saw is not remembered at the conscious level. In a different vein, they suggest the beeping sounds in the Hill case suggest the presence of a mechanical device by which UFOnauts lure and control humans through magnetic fields or hypnotic sounds. Though granting the notion seems like rank science fiction, they grant it plausibility on the grounds that the brain is "nothing more or less than a very complex computer." The error is telling, even if commonplace. (Lorenzen, 1968)

The situation concerning control motifs changes radically in the seventies. It appears frequently, is reworked by nearly every major figure, and dominates the theoretical scene as the core concept in several works.

In pure ambition of vision, UFOlogists will find it very hard to ever top the writings of John Keel. Reservations cloud acceptance of the raw material he builds from, but no one need qualify an appreciation of the effort of construction. Drawing on an impressive range of sources, Keel sketches a dark, feathery chiaroscuro of mysterious lights and shadowy patterns of deceptions that plays on primal fears about human powerlessness and naiveté. Keel abandoned the ETH in 1967 when psychic phenomena emerged in his thinking as a full facet of the UFO problem.

Operation Trojan Horse (1970) is his research effort stimulated by this change in perspective. Keel adopts the premise that humans have crude biological crystal sets in their heads that unconsciously receive sophisticated signals of an electromagnetic nature, bearing an omnipotent intelligence that has great flexibility of form. They advance beliefs in various frameworks of thought. Prior ages received Trojan Horses in the shapes of angels, fairies, spirits, phantom armies, mystery inventors and their airships, and ghost rockets. States of mystical illumination and possession accompany receipt of these signals and forward belief in occult happenings. Keel also advances the idea that there are window areas around which UFO sighting congregate—areas typified by a "magnetic fault." The similarities to Williamson are evident, but so are the differences. The cruder physics errors are gone and an impressive body of research into occult history and learned observations about the implausibilities inherent in the existing body of UFO experiences make this a far meatier meal to chew on. (Keel, 1970)

Our Haunted Planet (1971) is a frivolous interlude that reads like somebody tossed a couple dozen books of Forteana into a blender. Mixing lost civilizations, occult conspiracies, Velikovsky, disappearances, UFO contacts and such, we get a speculative history of ultraterrestrials back to the caveman. It retains the view that ultraterrestrials involve hallucinogenic mind trips guided by a force that manipulates the electric circuits of the brain. (Keel, 1971)

The Mothman Prophecies (1975) is UFOlogy's most intensely driven narrative. Its ambiance has the mechanistic supernatural evocations of Lovecraft's finest horror. We learn there is a fearful gamesmanship to the intelligence that scripts the UFO drama. Once a belief of any sort arises, this cosmic mechanism supports and escalates it. The believer is played for the fool when higher expectations for salvation are crushed. The force of events manifests a tangible paranoia. Keel captures this sense of malevolent forces moving the flow of events very convincingly. Psychics and sensitives throughout the centuries parrot monotonously similar phrases like a skipping phonograph needle. Beams of light reprogram people to become belief robots like Saul/Paul at the dawn of Christianity. He adopts the credo of the Enlightenment: "Belief is the enemy."

The Eighth Tower (1975) is the culmination of Keel's vision. Religious visions are more fully incorporated into the tapestry of reprogramming games. Love is twisted into a negative force by robotic Jesus freaks and the fanatics of all faiths. Their ruthless, destructive acts reveal the controlling intelligence as emotionally unstrung and stupid. It distorts reality in whimsical, crazy ways such as to suggest "God may be a crackpot." (Keel, 1975) He expands the control motif around a cosmological construct called the "superspectrum."

This is a hypothetical spectrum of energies that purportedly is extra-dimensional and outside the normal range of the electromagnetic spectrum. It directs unaccountable coincidences into human lives and subtly influences the direction of history. It tried to seduce him in the directions of his own research. Keel even confessed an ability to control other people's minds on a modest scale. In a whimsical moment he speculates that all these UFO and Bigfoot apparitions are the senile end-products of a dying supercomputer that once ran the world in deep history. Now it idles away the time tormenting people with its madness. (Keel, 1975)

In a feverish finale Keel inverts his theoretical edifice. The reprogramming energies come through a black hole from another time. The superspectral God becomes a switchboard and the only real reality. We are the delusion; it is the everything of reality. While this fast-forward into the cosmic identity phase of paranoia was perhaps obligatory in a psychological sense, it is a letdown from wiser panegyrics against unreflective belief. Perhaps Keel's own reprogram button had been pushed. (Keel, 1975)

Control motifs also emerge as a central concept of Jacques Vallée's writings. They have an interesting history with roots in his early science fiction. *Subspace* (1961, 1975) opens with strange appearances in the sky involving blue spirogires and black crosses, a 21st century UFO phenomenon, which impressed images of catastrophe in the minds of those contacted by it. It transpires that the spirogires hail from the star Spica and involve intelligences who are a part of subspace. This is a region of pure thought inhabited with the creations and monsters of the imagination. Some dark thoughts seek to destroy the linear continuum universe. Thanks to thoughts implanted into the unconscious of a protagonist by Erg-Aonians who inhabit this larger universe, a weapon is brought into subspace. It's a cricket. The vibrations shatter the matrix in which the dark thoughts dwell. (Seriel, 1975)

The Dark Satellite (1962) opens with the invasion of our galaxy by a nonbeing-something that encircles it and causes all the races within it to become transfixed artists. The story turns to 22nd-century Paris that is the home of a great computer that oversees a utopia spanning the solar system. It is free of nation states and war. A little cylinder is found one day in the computer's imagination and threatens its breakdown. The cylinder causes a strange death of a human and people begin speculating that the cylinder was created by the machine at the prompting of machines from elsewhere with incomprehensible designs upon humanity, or the great machine—an influencing machine within an influencing machine, as it were. To ferret out the mystery, technicians enter the computer through another plane of reality. Adjusting its circuits they accidentally set it on fire. Destruction of the computer removes Earth's protection from an unsuspected mind ray. People are hypnotized into building spaceships that form a mass exodus into the sun. An iconoclastic mad-scientist guy named Xarius Chimero protects one of the technicians from mind control and takes him on a journey to the center of the universe, distributing artistic sculptures as they go. At the center, the two see into the multifaceted somber satellite of the title. It is a reality seeking to destroy our reality. Xarius Chimero presses a button and the dark satellite slides from sight. The button activated the statues and they turn into young girls. Laughing, primitive girls will repopulate the galaxy and a sublime new order transcending the now obliterated scientific utopia has been created. (Seriel, 1962)

As an UFOlogist, Vallée makes no use of the control motif in his first analyses of the UFO phenomenon, *Anatomy of a Phenomenon* (1965) and *Challenge to Science* (1966). In *Passport to Magonia* (1969) he sees disturbing resemblances between the UFO phenomenon and the fairy faith of earlier centuries, implying a shared mythic basis. He entertains the possibility that superior intelligences are projecting creations into our environment as a pure form of art seeking our puzzlement or as a way to teach us some concept. He immediately backs away from the notion with an admission it hasn't a scientific leg to stand on and offers an apology for showing "how quickly one could be carried into pure fantasy." (Vallée, 1969)

This "pure fantasy" becomes a major theory in *The Invisible College* (1975). Vallée compiled a plot of UFO waves through history and their irregular spacing suggested to University of Chicago's Fred Beckman and Dr. Price-Williams of UCLA a schedule of reinforcement designed to permanently instill a behavior. Vallée developed from this observation the theory that UFOs represent a control system of an undetermined nature. It could simply involve social psychology, but it could also be an imposition of a supernatural will seeking to confuse us and mold us and our civilization by targeting our collective unconscious with a physical and psychical technology. The book closes on a chilling soliloquy wherein Vallée ponders stepping outside the maze of the control system. Would he find some Lovecraftian horror, some well-meaning social engineers, or "the maddening simplicity of unattended clockwork"? (Vallée, 1975) This theory collapses with the recognition of a deadly oversight. UFO experiences usually involve negative emotions like fear and would yield aversive behavior. (Vallée, 1966; Moravec, 1987) They would not reinforce learning. No value attaches to irregular stimuli in the converse hypothesis of an unlearning curve. (Ruch and Zimbardo, 1971)

Messengers of Deception (1979) accepts as a given that control in the form of a machinery of mass manipulation exists behind the UFO phenomenon. Physical devices are being used to affect human consciousness and distort reality. Images and scenes are fabricated to advance belief in an impending intervention from space. The operators could be either a high-level international military group furthering some political goal or some occult group that stumbled upon a psychotronic technology in their studies of astral travel or space-time distortions. (Vallée, 1979)

Dimensions (1988) reprints material from the prior books and would not bear mentioning except for a silent concession that Vallée changed his mind about the external teacher idea being pure fantasy. Those lines were excised. (Vallée, 1988)

Confrontations (1990) contains a brief suggestion that UFOs are a window into another reality possessing symbolic meaning. Like dreams, they can be ignored or shape our lives in inscrutable ways. There is enough ambiguity to regard the notion as either a banality or a marginal idea of reference. (Vallée, 1990)

Revelations (1991) argues that some UFO cases are covert experiments in the manipulation of belief systems, but here the processes are conventional ones of rhetoric and lies. The control system theory is reaffirmed in *Forbidden Science* (1992) with no further elaborations.

Brooks Alexander has characterized Vallée as "equal parts of Carl Jung and *Report from Iron Mountain*." (Alexander, 1992) This is inadvertently scurrilous since the latter is a confessed hoax by political satirist Leonard Lewin. An equal case could be made for roots in the writings of French or English deists who had analogous notions about how stimulating the emotions of wonderment and advancing religious superstitions could be used to manipulate the masses. Not having behaviorist metaphors available, they spoke of a "psychopathology of enthusiasm" evident in individual fanatics and collective frenzies. Vallée's affirmations and denials about the reality of UFOs have much the same puzzling flavor as deist affirmations and denials about the reality and nature of god. (Manuel, 1983) The similarity probably reflects shared intellectual predilections and not an exposure of Vallée to deist literature.

Like Keel and Vallée, D. Scott Rogo's control theories extend through several books. *This Haunted Universe* (1977) was his first foray across the boundary of psychic research into UFOlogy. His first impulse was to ascribe the psychic components of UFO events to a mysterious force within ourselves, but certain experiences proved to him that evil can exist independently of the mind. The motif suddenly emerges: "UFOs demonstrate that our world plays host to a force that seeks to mystify us." (Rogo, 1977) The usage here is brief, but significantly arises to imply humans are blameless for evil and mystifications.

He teams up with Jerome Clark for *Earth's Secret Inhabitants* (1979). Both were facing the psychological aspects of strange UFO cases, so they concocted a notion they termed "The Phenomenon." It is a force or intelligence somewhere in the universe that provides the evidence we seek for whatever it is we want to believe in deeply. It does this by beaming projections into our world. They aver it may be an automatic natural mechanism that acts "as routinely as a clock." (Rogo and Clark, 1979) Clark fell out of sympathy with control systems and collective unconscious as his thinking matured, but Rogo pressed forward with elaborations. (Clark, 1986)

In *Tujunga Canyon Contacts* (1980), The Phenomenon becomes a supermind that presents people in need with objectified materials drawn from deep in the person's mind. The process is described as a "psychokinetic effect directly affecting those brain cells regulating memory storage and retrieval." It does not always materialize the abduction drama into three-dimensional space, but occasionally imprints it directly on the mind of the witness. (Rogo and Druffle, 1980) In *UFO Abductions* (1980) he adds details like the experience being molded individually to each victim into something like an objectified dream. Typically people in a life crisis receive these messages. (Rogo, 1980)

In *Miracles* (1982) Rogo leaps ahead into the cosmic identity stage and redefines God. The supermind becomes a spiritualistic realm that translates all religious, shamanistic, and mythic ideologies egalitarianly into literal spiritual reality. The Phenomenon might be the source of the universe's creative energy and endows those properly attuned to it with great psychic powers. This "God" however would have to satisfy so many contradictory requests and opposing theologies that it would wind up an incoherent mush. (Rogo, 1982)

Looking back on his theory in 1988, Rogo considered it misunderstood and viable. Independent creation of a similar theory by Jenny Randles suggested to him he had probably been on the right track. Alternatively, they both may have read Vallée and a standard text on dreams. One puzzle of the objectified dream

idea is that when subjects are regressed under hypnosis, the experiences do not reify into three-dimensional reality despite deeply emotional re-enactment. Saucers or aliens do not materialize for onlookers to experience or instruments to record. It should also not be ignored that if the supermind is directly imprinting experiences into the mind, such experiences are ultimately phantoms and promote false beliefs. One has only to point to various depictions of future catastrophes by abductees and contactees that have repeatedly failed to come to pass to demonstrate the misinformation such visions create. Should one really go around calling such a deceiver "God"?

Besides our top three control theorists, there have been a significant number of UFOlogists who offered variants of these themes. Some are well-known folks joining the bandwagon; some are less known but offer a different take. There was a steady stream of these ideas in the late seventies, and to a lesser extent, in the years since. This set will be recounted chronologically rather than by status.

1974: Charles Bowen, editorializing in *Flying Saucer Review*, asks if some or all UFO images and entities are projected into the mind by controlling powers and/or UFOs. The meaningless gibberish in messages implies more than humans being treated as playthings; it may be an attempt to influence or remotely control humans. He cites C. Maxwell Cade as suggesting ultrahigh frequency radar beams can induce images in the brain. Stanton Friedman suggests UFOnauts could broadcast telepathic signals that would make UFOs appear to disappear. A microwave beam could jumble vision by means of a scotoma.

1975: Allen H. Greenfield's Alternative Reality Theory accepts the premise that UFOs are "manipulating human history to its own ends." Timothy Green Beckley cites the cases of Paul Clark, Dr. Morales, and Hans Lauritzen to argue higher powers are systematically guiding human destiny and the course of human civilization, if not by physical force, then by direct manipulation of human minds. Joan Writenour warns extraterrestrials engage in "mental rape" by use of strobe-light-type machines that cause instant hypnosis.

You might notice *Operators & Things* (1976) spoke of similar technology and was brought to prominence in the 1997 blockbuster movie *Men in Black.*

1976: Brad Steiger suggests UFOs act as cosmic tutors using space beams. (Steiger, 1976a) They also influence the mind telepathically to project three-dimensional images. The purpose is "too staggeringly complex for our desperately throbbing brains to deal with at this moment in time and space." (Steiger, 1976b)

1977: The Lorenzens accept that thoughts can be taken or absorbed. Abductees may have been programmed with false information to mislead us. James Harder terms this a multi-level cover-up. Abductees are made to look like fools by relaying messages filled with garbage dredged up from their memories and imaginations at the behest of post-hypnotic suggestions. (Clark, 1977) Robert Anton Wilson warns higher beings may be playing mind games with humans and using "mindfucking" technology.

Michael Persinger and Gyslaine LaFreniere set forth a variant of the supermind they term "Geopsyche." A critical mass of believers forms a matrix that is energized by intense geophysical forces of nature. Epidemics of luminous signs, anomalous beasties of the nether realm, unusual kinetic displays, and religious manias foretell earthquakes. A disturbing corollary to this is the irrelevance and expendability of the individual under the sway of activated death instincts and unconscious archetypal forces.

1978: Gordon Creighton fears UFOs influence not only individuals, but governments and whole nations. (Bond, 1978) Art Gatti gravitates to the idea UFOs are mind parasites or occult manipulation thought forms. Brad Steiger suggests aliens may have programmed humans as automatons and Judas goats to lead their fellow humans into servitude.

1979: Leo Sprinkle offers the "Cosmic Consciousness Conditioning" hypothesis that includes the premise that UFO intelligences choose witnesses for illumination. (Haines, 1979) James B. Frazier suggests they implant knowledge in contactees and monitor them by sensor-beam communication and repeat abductions.

Raymond Fowler believes Betty Andreasson is primed subconsciously with extraterrestrial knowledge. She feels like a loaded bomb. They may be interstellar missionaries for conditioning in preparation of overt contact. Pierre Guerin speculates the repetitive character of UFOs is meant to create "a pernicious and stupefying wave of religious credulity." Stefan T. Possony suggests Russia can create semi-stable UFOs via colliding pulsed microwave beams and thus yield UFO crazes and mass anxiety neuroses.

1980: Frank Salisbury guesses UFO sightings "are staged to manipulate us in preparation for contact, for directing our evolution, or to excite the gullible in order to turn off those who are not gullible." Colin Wilson is inspired by Keel to theorize that the spirit world vampirizes energy from humans to achieve temporary material existence. J.N. Williamson views UFO confrontations as a liberating of the right hemisphere of the brain.

1981: Raymond Fowler suggests UFOnauts put people in suspended animation and control their actions.

1982: Jenny Randles argues that consciousness should logically be targeted as the medium of interstellar communication. Their consciousness will act as a radio telescope to beam messages into the complex electrochemical computer of the human mind by selecting ideograms out of the subject's memory to form a holographic playlet. Amnesia results from consciousness being shunted aside as the message program switches the mind to the right frequency. Earth mystery sites act as aerials to pull in messages thus explaining certain window areas. (Randles, 1983) Paul Devereux revamps the Geopsyche concept with the Earth mother doing some planetary dreaming and shaping earthlight ectoplasm into UFO displays. (Devereux, 1989)

The control motif is harder to find for the next few years. Budd Hopkins flirts with such notions in his books, but we don't see any clear advocacy until the premier issue of his *Intruders Foundation Bulletin* in 1989. Hopkins notes that in abduction experiences, the victim never seems to be embarrassed about nudity. This observation eliminates all blanket psychological explanations of abductions and provides powerful evidence of an "externally caused trance-like experience" endemic to the alien abduction process. Actually, Freud observed many years ago that "Dreams of being naked or insufficiently dressed in the presence of strangers sometimes occur with the additional feature of there being a complete absence of shame on the dreamer's part." (Freud, 1900) The use of an influencing machine fantasy to disown the bizarre nature of dream material and uphold the blameless normality of abductee experiences is true to the standard logic of the fantasy.

Randles offers some elaborations of her theory in *Abduction* (1988) and *Mind Monsters* (1990) with Sheldrake's morphic resonance and M-fields thrown in to update the semblance of scientific patter. Given Sheldrake's own modifications in his theory that morphic resonance applies to events like spontaneous crystallization and not to determinate machines like computers, it is highly questionable it should be applied to multi-hormonally determinate systems like the brain. (Sheldrake, 1989) Devereux returns in *Earthmind* (1989) to provide a respectable pedigree for the Geopsyche concept, relating it to the World Soul, geomancy, the noosphere, Mind at Large, supermind, and Gaia. The most interesting twist is perhaps the news that people who commune with the Earth learned of psychoactive plants, because the Earth taught them the lessons that natural hallucinogens provided a mind-gate to the World Soul. Light-form UFOs may be a type of energy interface with the Earth field of consciousness. (Devereux, 1989) David Barclay's revamping of Keel uses cyberspeak in its patter with virtual reality used to make the universe into "God's Little Arcade." (Barclay,

1993) Kenneth Ring offers a New Age variant of the supermind borrowing ideas from Michael Grosso, who in turn borrows the Mind-at-Large concept from Aldous Huxley. (Kottmeyer, 1993)

Martin Cannon's "Controllers" can be viewed as a distant variant of Leon Davidson's CIA hoax theory or, more properly, a return of the zombie assassin, a recurrent spy fiction plot gimmick. (Cannon, 1990) Cannon left the field in 1997 leaving word that he disowns the controllers theory. He complained, "That damned thing caused me nothing but trouble . . . Frankly UFO buffs and conspiracy nuts kind of make me ill these days." (*Saucer Smear*, 1998) Strieber's talk of ELF waves as an external control or perception implant modality involving either advanced technology or the Earth itself is an evident recall of research he did for his spy novel *Black Magic*. (Strieber, 1987)

Helmut Lammer's Project MILAB looks to be an extension of lore surrounding the Dulce Base and accepts that mind and behavior control experiments are being conducted by one military group on abductees. (Lammer, 1997) Those aware of the failure of the CIA's efforts to achieve reliable mind control have perhaps grounds to doubt this scenario. (Thomas, 1989) Even a casual look at the descriptions of the military documents cited by Lammer in section V of his 1997 report is enough to show a lack of critical discernment. Bio-chips are mentioned even though they involve nothing more than interfacing technology designed to make interaction with computers simpler, and has nothing to do with controlling minds. Acoustic and microwave weapons are described that essentially disable people in a manner with all the finesse of sledgehammers and mustard gas. Katharina Wilson's "Project Open Mind," a 1996 essay, endorsed Lammer's work and offered an enthusiastic survey of mind control literature in support of the idea of military involvement in abductions. (Her ten-part essay and Lammer's preliminary work appeared on her Web site, but she closed it down around the start of 2000.) She also testified that she felt herself to have been subjected to mind control activity.

In 1994, Richard Hall endorses the view that aliens are playing a smoke-and-mirrors game with us on several levels and if this is so what can be trusted and what is staged illusion? The Hybrid program is "an alien scam."

Greg Little builds upon Keel's superspectrum idea and proposes electromagnetic energy forms are evolving alongside humanity and perpetrating a grand illusion behind which they can indulge obsessions like sex and power trips: "The key to mental interaction lies in rituals that alter brain chemistry" so that harmony of frequencies is obtained. Areas with high geomagnetic energy and brains with higher levels of magnetite enhance contact. (Little, 1994)

By 1998, David Jacobs believes aliens are able to "effect a wide variety of changes in brain function" through a process he calls Mindscan. Jacobs acknowledges that the effect looks supernatural, but offers some bafflegab about aliens using "the optic nerve to gain entrance to the brain's neural pathways." He continues: "By exciting impulses in the optic nerve, the alien is able to 'travel' along the optic neural pathways through the optical chiasma, into the lateral geniculate body, and then into the primary visual cortex in the back of the brain." He goes on this way for several lines and tells us aliens are thereby able to inject images into the cortex bypassing the retina. The alien has absolute power over the abductee's mind and body. (Jacobs, 1998) Jacobs skips over the part that only half of optical nerves pass through the chiasma crossover and that the retina processes a hundredfold reduction of information between the rods and ganglions before entrance onto the optical expressway. It looks doubtful the retina can be bypassed and it seems peculiar the alien needs to stare into eyes if that is happening.

There is also an interesting paradox in how the uniformly black eye of modern Grays could excite impulses in the ganglion cells at the front of the optic nerve since they tend to remain inactive when the retina is uniformly illuminated. (Luria and Gould, 1981) He also skips over how it comes to pass that impulses excited within the optic nerve are not processed as visual information within the visual cortex but escapes mysteriously to attack other parts of the brain. One needs more than impulses excited within the optic nerve, but some sort of complex animate information transport gimmick like a nano-tech neuro-virus that "knows" where it is, where to go, and how to orchestrate myriad molecular interactions. If you can pull off the miracle of making something like that, there is no point in the alien staring at you, however.

EPILOGUE

Ideas of reference and influencing machine fantasies continue to appear but the late-seventies period was its obvious heyday in both prominence and popularity. The decrease had little or nothing to do with any criticism of this style of thinking. John Michell feared the basic idea was over-fanciful and suffered from the flaw that it imputes human ambitions for power to a race presumably superior to, and certainly different from, ourselves. Dominance behavior has a genetic logic that should make it a common adaptation all over. But in that case, why don't they dominate more ostentatiously? Take over, blow us away, and maybe leave a few to kick around and laugh at.

Ernst Berger lamented control notions signaled a new age of darkness being foisted by UFO spiritists. The fear of external manipulators seemed to him "a projection of their own fearful way of thinking into our restless reality." (Berger, 1981) Kevin McClure's review of control motifs in our Top Three correctly understood they were ways "to offload responsibility" to more deeply explore anomalous phenomena. Such study he felt would lead us to conclude there "was some recurrent quirk in human nature" beneath belief in UFOs and anomalous phenomena. Expressing a distaste for the proliferation of conspiracies and the elevation of paranoia in our top theorists, he proclaims it isn't cricket to evade our responsibilities to be objective by blaming external agents for our mistakes, intentions, decisions, and achievements. (McClure, 1981)

Daniel Cohen places alien control notions in a wider historical context with ancient fears like those that fueled witchcraft. The 17th century had Cotton Mather's *The Wonders of the Invisible World* and we have Keel's invisible world of ultraterrestrials. (Cohen, 1972) The idea of a historical continuum can be taken much farther. In the 17th century, Angelologists Henry Lawrence and Isaac Ambrose believed angels engaged in a type of secret suggesting that depended on the ability to handle the humors and control man's fancies internally by tempting, troubling, inspiring, or soothing him. (West, 1955) As early as the 4th century, the theologians Athanasius and Evagrius of Pontus expressed belief in the idea that the Devil and his demons sometimes send dreams and hallucinations to frighten monks. Though they cannot enter souls, they could, by working on the brain, suggest images, fantasies, fears, and temptations. (Russell, 1981) Beliefs in spirit possession extend analogous ideas into unchronicled antiquity.

Hilary Evans has added some common-sense objections to these control theories. Why, with all of humanity to choose from, have the claims of influence involved low-status individuals? Why not heads of state, financiers, scientists, educators, movie stars; i.e., people with true power and influence to get things done and spread one's messages? Why, with such powers at their disposal, do they employ them in such haphazard, ambiguous ways as puzzling UFO visions? If you had an influencing machine, would you use it for such things as implanting abduction experiences or would you make a millionaire shower you with gifts, make your enemies grovel at your feet, or mess with the minds of leaders in the service of world peace and prosperity? UFO experiences make more sense as idiosyncratic psychodramas. (Evans, 1990)

UFOlogists have always asserted that UFO reporters are sincere and trustworthy observers and therefore we must believe them. Flying saucers are real: ''Q.E.D.'' Take away that syllogism and UFOlogists are out of a job. As the years have passed, UFOlogists have increasingly found themselves in a dilemma. Some strange cases have features that cannot reasonably be believed as true, but the claimants are sincere and honest: they can't be crazy. Influencing machines resolve the dilemma. It's not their fault they are reporting these things. Aliens, the superspectrum, the Phenomenon, occultists, the CIA, the supermind; something out there is to blame. The psychology is simple and transparent because the logic is easily recognized. It is the logic of madness.

Specifically, the logic of paranoia in the projection phase is what we have here. Nestled between the hypochondria of the sixties and the conspiracies of the eighties and early nineties, they form a natural stage in the history of UFOlogy. Control theories seem benign for the most part, letting people indulge in fantasies and psychological games without heavy accusations of abnormality. The cost of autonomy lost or some estrangement from reality is probably not felt as tragic. Free will carries responsibilities we may prefer to do without. Better a puppet than a fool.

—MARTIN S. KOTTMEYER

References

''Psywar 1'' in *Best of Saucer Scoop* (June 1975).

''Theosophy'' in Hastings, James, ed. *Encyclopedia of Religion and Ethics* (Charles Scribner's Sons, no date).

Agel, Jerome, ed., *The Making of Kubrick's 2001* (Signet/NAL, 1970).

Alexander, Brooks. ''Machines Made of Shadows,'' *SCP Journal* (1992).

Barclay, David. *UFOs—The Final Answer* (Blandford, 1993).

Beckley, T.G. ''Mind Manipulation—The New UFO Terror Tactic,'' *UFO Report* (Winter 1975).

Berger, Ernst. "The Dark Side of the UFO," *Pursuit* (1981).

Bergland, Richard. *The Fabric of Mind: A Radical New Understanding of the Brain and How it Works* (Viking, 1985).

Bond, Bryce. "Interdimensional UFOs," *UFO Report* (November 1978).

Bowen, Charles, ed., *Encounter Cases from Flying Saucer Review* (Signet/NAL, 1977).

Bowers, Malcolm B. *Retreat from Sanity: The Structure of Emerging Psychosis* (Human Sciences, 1974).

Bromley, David, and Anson D. Shupe. *Strange Gods: The Great American Cult Scare* (Beacon, 1981).

Cannon, Martin. "The Controllers: A New Hypothesis of Alien Abductions," manuscript for researchers only (September 1989); later published in *MUFON UFO Journal* (October and November 1990).

Clark, Jerome. "Startling New Evidence in the Pascagoula and Adamski Abductions," *UFO Report* (August 1978).

———. "UFO Report Interviews Dr. James Harder," *UFO Report* (December 1977).

———. Personal communication (November 14, 1986).

Clarke, Arthur C. *Childhood's End* (Harcourt, Brace & World, 1953; Ballantine, 1973).

———. *2001: A Space Odyssey* (New America Library, 1968; Signet/NAL, 1969).

Cohen, Daniel. *Voodoo, Devils, and the New Invisible World* (Dodd, Mead, 1972).

Commin, Saxe, ed., *Selected Tales of Guy de Maupassant* (Random House, no date).

Davidson, Leon. "Why I Believe in Adamski," *Flying Saucers* (February 1954).

DeCamp, L. Sprague. *The Ragged Edge of Science* (Owlswick, 1980).

Del Rey, Lester. *The World of Science Fiction* (Ballantine, 1979).

Del Rey, Lester, ed., *The Best of C.L. Moore* (Ballantine, 1975).

Devereux, Paul. *Earthlights: Towards an Understanding of the UFO Enigma* (Turnstone, 1982).

———. *Earthmind: A Modern Adventure in Ancient Wisdom* (Harper & Row, 1989).

Dick, Philip K. *Valis* (Bantam, 1981).

Evans, Hilary. "The Ultimate Myth," *The Wild Places* (September 1990).

Fort, Charles. "Have Martians Visited Us?" *New York Times* (September 5, 1926).

———. *Book of the Damned* (Boni & Liveright, 1919; Holt, Rinehart & Winston, 1941; reprinted by Ace Books, no date).

Fowler, Raymond E. *Casebook of an UFO Investigator* (Prentice-Hall, 1981).

———. *The Andreasson Affair* (Prentice-Hall, 1979).

Freud, Sigmund. *The Interpretation of Dreams* (Random House, 1950; Avon, 1965; originally published in 1900).

Friedman, Stanton. "Flying Saucers and Physics," *MUFON UFO Symposium* (UFORI 1974).

Gatti, Art. *UFO Encounters of the 4th Kind* (Zebra, 1978).

Gordon, James S. "The UFO Experience," *Atlantic* (August 1991).

Gould, Stephen Jay. *Time's Arrow, Time's Cycle* (Harvard University Press, 1987).

Greenfield, Allen H. "Tenets of Alternative Reality Theory," in *Best of Saucer Scoop* (June 1975).

Guerin, Pierre. "Thirty Years after Kenneth Arnold: The Situation Regarding UFOs," *Zetetic Scholar* (1979).

Haines, Richard. *UFO Phenomena and the Behavioral Scientist* (Scarecrow, 1979).

Hall, Richard. "Some Whimsical—and Serious—Reflections on Abductions," *International UFO Reporter* (September/October 1994).

Hastings, James, ed. "Theosophy" in the *Encyclopedia of Religion and Ethics, volume 12* (Charles Scribner's Sons, n.d.).

Hopkins, Budd. "Patterns of UFO Abductions, Part 1," *IF* (Fall 1989).

Jacobs, David. *The Threat* (Simon & Schuster, 1998).

Joshi, S.T. *H.P. Lovecraft: Four Decades of Criticism* (Ohio University Press, 1980).

Keel, John A. "The Man Who Invented Flying Saucers" *Fortean Times* (Winter 1983).

———. *Our Haunted Planet* (Fawcett Books, 1971).

———. *The Eighth Tower* (Saturday Review Press, 1975; Signet/NAL, 1977).

———. *The Mothman Prophecies* (Saturday Review Press, 1975; Signet/NAL, 1976).

———. *Operation Trojan Horse* (G.P. Putnam's Sons, 1970). Reprinted as *Why UFOs?* (Manor Books, 1976).

Knight, Damon. *Charles Fort: Prophet of the Unexplained* (Doubleday, 1970).

Koestler, Arthur. *The Act of Creation* (Macmillan, 1964).

Kottmeyer, Martin S. ''The Alien Booger Menace,'' *The REALL News* (July 1993).

———. ''The Omega Projection,'' *The REALL News* (October 1993).

Lammer, Helmut. ''More Findings of Project MILAB: Looking Behind the Alien/Military Abduction Agenda,'' *MUFON UFO Journal* (November 1997).

Lewis, Jefferson. *Something Hidden: A Biography of Wilder Penfield* (Doubleday, 1981).

Lilly, John C. *The Scientist: A Novel Autobiography* (Lippincott, 1978).

Little, Greg. *Grand Illusions: The Spectral Reality Underlying Sexual UFO Abductions, Crashed Saucers, Afterlife Experiences, Sacred Ancient Sites, and Other Enigmas* (White Buffalo Books, 1994).

Lorenzen, Coral & Jim. *Abducted!* (Berkley Medallion, 1977).

———. *UFOs Over the Americas* (Signet/NAL, 1968).

Lovecraft, H. P. *The Colour Out of Space* (Jove, 1978).

Luria, Salvador E., Stephen Jay Gould, and Sam Singer. *A View of Life* (Benjamin/Cummings Publishing, 1981).

Macer-Story, Eugenia. *Congratulations: The UFO Reality* (Crescent, 1978).

Manuel, Frank. *The Changing of the Gods* (Brown University Press, 1983).

McClure, Kevin. ''Semaphore Without Flags: A Critical Analysis of the UFO Control-System Theory,'' *Common Ground* (August 1981).

Menger, Howard. *From Outer Space to You* (Saucerian Press, 1959) Reprinted as *From Outer Space to You* (Pyramid, 1967).

Michell, John. *The Flying Saucer Vision* (Ace Books 1967; Abacus, 1977).

Moravec, Mark. ''UFOs as Psychological and Parapsychological Phenomena'' in Evans, Hilary, ed., *UFOs: 1947-1987: The 40-Year Search for an Explanation* (Fortean Times, 1987).

O'Brien, Barbara. *Operators and Things: The Inner Life of a Schizophrenic* (Signet/NAL, 1976).

Persinger, Michael, and Gyslaine LaFreniere. *Space-Time Transients and Unusual Events* (Nelson-Hall, 1977).

Platt, Charles. *Dream Makers* (Berkley, 1980).

Possony, Stefan T. ''Mind-Control and Microwaves,'' *Second Look* (November-December 1979).

Randles, Jenny. *The Pennine UFO Mystery* (Granada, 1983).

Rogo, D. Scott. *Miracles: A Parascientific Inquiry into Wondrous Phenomena* (Dial, 1982).

———. *This Haunted Universe* (Signet/NAL, 1977).

Rogo, D. Scott, ed. *UFO Abductions* (Signet/NAL, 1980).

Rogo, D. Scott, and Jerome Clark. *Earth's Secret Inhabitants* (Tempo, 1979).

Rogo, D. Scott, and Ann Druffle. *Tujunga Canyon Contacts* (Prentice-Hall, 1980; Signet/NAL, 1989).

Ruch, Floyd L. and Philip G. Zimbardo. *Psychology and Life* (Scott, Foresman, 1971).

Russell, Jeffrey Burton. *Satan: The Early Christian Tradition* (Cornell University Press, 1981).

Salisbury, Frank. ''Are UFOs from Outer Space?'' in Fuller, Curtis, *Proceedings of the First International UFO Congress* (Warner, 1980).

Saucer Smear (July 10, 1998).

Sechehaye, Marguerite. *Autobiography of a Schizophrenic Girl* (Signet/NAL, 1968).

Seriel, Jerome. *Le Satellite Sombre* (Denoel, 1962).

———. *Sub-Espace* (Librairie des Champs Elysees, 1975).

Shaver, Richard S. ''Teros and Deros,'' *Caveat Emptor* (Summer 1973).

Sheaffer, Robert *The UFO Verdict* (Prometheus, 1981).

Sheldrake, Rupert. ''Morphic Resonance in Silicon Chips,'' *Skeptical Inquirer* (Winter 1989).

Slusser, George E. and Eric S. Rabkin. *Aliens—The Anthropology of Science Fiction* (Southern Illinois University Press, 1987).

Smith, Yvonne. ''Alien Table Procedures,'' *UFO* (1993).

Sprinkle, Leo. ''What are the Implications of UFO Experiences?'' *Journal of UFO Studies* (no date).

Stanford, Rex and Ray. *Look Up* (privately published, 1958).

Steiger, Brad. *Alien Meetings* (Ace Books, 1978).

———. *Gods of Aquarius* (Harcourt, Brace, 1976a).

———. *Project Blue Book* (Ballantine, 1976b).

Stevens, Wendelle C., and William Herrmann. *UFO Contact from the Reticulum* (privately published, 1981).

Strieber, Whitley. *Communion* (William Morrow/Beech Tree Books/Avon, 1987).

Stringfield, Leonard. *Situation Red: The UFO Siege* (Doubleday/Fawcett Crest, 1977).

Tausk, Viktor. ''On the Origin of the Influencing

Machine in Schizophrenia," *Psychoanalytic Quarterly* (1953).

The Best of Stanley Weinbaum (Ballantine, 1974).

Thomas, Gordon. *Journey Into Madness* (Bantam, 1989).

Thorpe, Peter. *Why Literature is Bad for You* (Nelson-Hall, 1980).

Toronto, Richard S. "Do Brain-Damaged Robots Rule the Earth?" *Official UFO* (October 1977).

Torrey, E. Fuller. *Surviving Schizophrenia: A Family Manual* (Harper Colophon, 1983).

Valenstein, Elliot. *Brain Control: A Critical Examination of Brain Stimulation and Psychosurgery* (John Wiley, 1975).

Vallée, Jacques and Janine. *Challenge to Science* (Ace Books, 1966).

Vallée, Jacques. *Confrontations* (Ballantine, 1990).

———. *Dimensions* (Contemporary, 1988).

———. *Messengers of Deception: UFO Contacts and Cults* (And/Or Press, 1979).

———. *Passport to Magonia* (Henry Regnery, 1969).

———. *The Invisible College: What a Group of Scientists Has Discovered about UFO Influences on the Human Race* (E.P. Dutton, 1975).

Vonnegut, Kurt. *The Sirens of Titan* (Delta, 1959).

Wells, H. G. *Star-Begotten* (Leisure, 1970).

West, Robert H. *Milton and the Angels* (University of Georgia, 1955).

Williamson, George H. *Other Tongues—Other Flesh* (Amherst Press, 1953; Neville Spearman, 1969).

———. *The Saucers Speak: A Documentary Report of Interstellar communication by Radiotelegraphy* (New Age Publishing, 1954; Neville Spearman, 1963).

Williamson, George H. and John McCoy. *UFOs Confidential!* (Essene Press, 1958).

Williamson, J.N. "UFOs are Changing the way We Think," *Pursuit* (Spring 1980).

Willis, Walt. "Soiree with the Fringe on Top" *Warhoon* (no date).

Wilson, Colin. *Mysteries* (Perigee, 1980).

Wilson, Robert Anton. *Cosmic Trigger* (Pocket Books, 1977).

Writenour, Joan. "Psywar 1" in *Best of Saucer Scoop* (June 1975)

Missing Time (Marek Publishers, 1981). New York painter and sculptor Budd Hopkins launched his career as an abductee investigator with this book in which he recounts the use of hypnosis to penetrate the abductee's amnesia barriers put in place by aliens during genetic experiments. Seven abduction cases became the basis for this book. Three of these diverse people, all unrelated and born in 1943, were first abducted in 1950 as seven-year-olds. "It seems to me," Hopkins observes, "as if these quite similar abductions constitute some kind of systematic research program, with the human species as subject."

—RANDALL FITZGERALD

"missing time" This term, popularized by UFO-abductionist Budd Hopkins in his books *Missing Time* (1981) and *Intruders* (1987), has become a hallmark of most supposed UFO-alien abductions. As a mythological motif, the idea of "missing time" can be traced back to Celtic fairy lore, as shown by UFOlogist Jacques Vallée in his book *Passport to Magonia—From Folklore to Flying Saucers* (1969). Whenever the fairies abducted someone, they would cause the victim to forget the details of the event—just as the aliens do, when they supposedly abduct an Earthling.

In modern times, the "missing-time" concept played a key role in the famous Barney and Betty Hill abduction case (1961), and has remained a standard theme in UFO-abduction lore ever since. But is this really such a rare phenomenon, such as to indicate a probable abduction by alien beings? UFO skeptic, Philip J. Klass, asks rhetorically: "Is there anyone who has not at some time looked at a clock or watch and discovered that it was much later than he or she expected, or driven some distance and arrived at a destination later than originally expected, thus experiencing 'missing time'?" (Klass, 1988)

As a matter of fact, the so-called "missing time" experienced by most of the UFO abductees is a quite ordinary, common, and universal experience. Jerome Singer (1975) in his *Inner World of Daydreaming* comments:

Are there ever any truly "blank periods'' when we are awake? It certainly seems to be the case that under certain conditions of fatigue or great drowsiness or extreme concentration upon some physical act we may become aware that we cannot account for an interval of time and have no memory of what happened for seconds and sometimes minutes.

Graham Reed (1972) has also dealt with the "time-gap" experience at great length. Typically, motorists will report after a long drive that at some point in the journey they wake up to realize they have no awareness of a preceding period of time. With some justification, people still will describe this as a "gap in time," a "lost half-hour," or a "piece out of my life." Reed writes:

A little reflection will suggest, however, that our experience of time and its passage is determined by *events,* either external or internal. What the time-gapper is reporting is not that a slice of time has vanished, but that he has failed to register a series of events which would normally have functioned as his time-markers. If he is questioned closely he will admit that his "time-gap" experience did not involve his realization at, say, noon that he had somehow "lost" half an hour. Rather, the experience consists of "waking up" at, say, Florence and realizing that he remembers nothing since Bologna. . . . To understand the experience, however, it is best considered in terms of the absence of *events*. If the time-gapper had taken that particular day off, and spent the morning sitting in his garden undisturbed, he might have remembered just as little of the half-hour in question. He might still describe it in terms of lost time, but he would not find the experience unusual or disturbing. For he would point out that he could not remember what took place between eleven-thirty and twelve simply because nothing of note occurred.

In fact, there is nothing recounted in any of the three works under discussion that cannot be easily explained in terms of normal, though somewhat unusual, psychological behavior we now term *anomalous*. Different and unusual? Yes. Paranormal or otherworldly, requiring the presence of extraterrestrials? No. Die-hard proponents may find these explanations unsatisfying, but the open-minded reader will find elaboration and illumination in the textbooks and other works in anomalistic psychology.

Strongly recommended are Reed (1972), Marks and Kammann (1980), Corliss (1982), Zusne and Jones (1982), Radner and Radner (1982), Randi (1982), Gardner (1981), Alcock, (1981), Taylor (1980), and Frazier (1981).

If one looks at the psychodynamics underlying the confabulation of Hopkins's contactees and abductees it is easy to see how even an ordinary, non-fantasy-prone individual can become one of his case histories. How does Hopkins, for instance, locate such individuals in the first place? Typically, it is done through a selection process; i.e., those individuals who are willing to talk about UFOs—the believers—are selected for further questioning. Those who scoff are summarily dismissed. Once selected for study and permission to volunteer for hypnosis is obtained, a response-anticipation process sets in (Kirsch 1985), and the volunteer is now set up to supply answers to anything that might be asked. Then, during the hypnosis sessions, something similar to the Hawthorne Effect occurs: The volunteer says to himself, "This kindly and famous writer and this important and prestigious doctor are interested in poor little old unimportant me!" And the more the volunteer is observed and interrogated, the greater is the volunteer's motivation to come up with a cracking "good story" that is important and significant and pleasing to these important people. Moreover, as we have long known, it is the perception of reality not the reality itself that is truly significant in determining behavior. If the writer and the doctor-hypnotist are on hand to encourage the volunteer and to suggest to him that his fantasy really happened, who is he to question their interpretation of his experience? Once they tell the contactee how important his fantasy is, he now—if he ever doubted before—begins to believe it himself and to elaborate and embellish it every time it is repeated.

—ROBERT A. BAKER
& RONALD D. STORY

References

Alcock, James E. *Parapsychology: Science or Magic?* (Pergamon, 1981).

Corliss, William R. *The Unfathomed Mind—A Handbook of Unusual Mental Phenomena* (Sourcebook, 1982).

Frazier, Kendrick, ed. *Paranormal Borderlands of Science* (Prometheus Books, 1981).

Fuller, John G. *The Interrupted Journey—Two Lost Hours "Aboard a Flying Saucer"* (Dial Press, 1966; Dell Books, 1967).

Gardner, Martin. *Science: Good, Bad and Bogus* (Prometheus Books, 1981).

Hopkins, Budd. *Missing Time* (Richard Marek, 1981; Ballantine Books, 1988).

———. *Intruders* (Random House, 1987; Ballantine Books, 1988).

Kirsch, Irving. "Response Expectancy as a Determinant of Experience and Behavior," *American Psychologist* (1985).

Klass, Philip J. *UFO Abductions: A Dangerous Game* (Prometheus Books, 1988).

Marks, David, and Richard Kammann. *The Psychology of the Psychic* (Prometheus Books, 1980).

Radner, Daisie and Michael. *Science and Unreason* (Wadsworth, 1982).

Randi, James. *Flim-Flam!* (Prometheus Books, 1982).

Reed, Graham. *The Psychology of Anomalous Experience* (Houghton Mifflin, 1972).

Singer, Jerome. *The Inner World of Daydreaming* (Harper & Row, 1975).

Taylor, John. *Science and the Supernatural: An Investigation of Paranormal Phenomena* (Dutton, 1980).

Vallée, Jacques. *Passport to Magonia—From Folklore to Flying Saucers* (Henry Regnery, 1969; Neville Spearman, 1970).

Wentz, Walter Evans. *The Fairy Faith in Celtic Countries, its Psychological Origin and Nature* (Oberthur, Rennes, 1909; Oxford University Press, 1911).

Zusne, Leonard, and Warren H. Jones. *Anomalistic Psychology: A Study of Extraordinary Phenomena of Behavior and Experience* (Erlbaum, 1982).

Monuments of Mars, The (North Atlantic Books, 1987). Science writer Richard Hoagland studied the 1976 Viking photos of Mars, depicting a human-like face in the Cydonia region, and concluded that extraterrestrial colonists once lived on Mars and created the face, a pyramid, and other huge structures that were left as reminders of their lost civilization. He believes there may be a connection between the Cydonia complex and the Giza plateau in Egypt with its Sphinx and pyramids, which seem to indicate that both ancient Sumer and Egypt took inspiration and guidance from the Martian builders at Cydonia.

—RANDALL FITZGERALD

Moody abduction According to Staff Sergeant Charles L. Moody, a crew chief in the U.S. Air Force, he arrived at his home in Alamogordo, New Mexico, at about midnight on the evening of August 12, 1975, after working the swing shift at Holloman Air Force Base. Not feeling tired, he decided to drive to the outskirts of town to have a quiet smoke and watch for meteors. After parking for a short period of time, he observed a disk-shaped object drop from the sky to an elevation estimated to be less than fifty feet, at a distance of about a hundred yards and moving toward him.

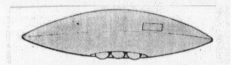

Sketch of disk-shaped craft
(according to Moody's description)

Moody, who was sitting on the hood of his car at the time, panicked and tried to flee, but his car would not start Then it seemed, he felt a numbness over his body and watched the object depart. He tried his car again. It started and he drove home. To his surprise he had lost about one and one half hours' time. The following day he complained of a sore back and his wife found the small of his back to be inflamed. Also, there was a small puncture wound over his spine.

Within a few days he broke out in a rash which covered his trunk from the midchest to the knees. On reporting to sick call he was sent to William Beaumont Army Hospital for observation. There he was told he had apparently received a dose of radiation. Standard treatment for such a problem (deep enema and laxatives) was administered, and Sergeant Moody was returned to duty. Over the next two months, states Moody, partial memory of the "lost" time gradually returned.

He told of finding himself aboard a strange craft, and of a kind of telepathic communication with aliens who were about four feet eight inches tall, with large, domed, hairless heads; large eyes; a small slit-like mouth; small ears and small nose; five-digit hands with no nails. They were dressed in plain coveralls without cuffs or collars. His injuries, said Moody, were the result of a scuffle when he initially resisted their efforts to take him aboard.

An interesting sidelight of the Moody case is the fact that his records at William Beaumont Army Hospital disappeared from the files. Doctors and medics at the hospital remember treating him but cannot provide any clue as to what happened to the records.

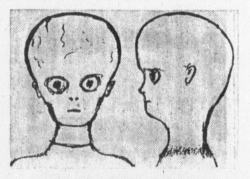

Aliens as described by Moody

Sergeant Moody was shipped to Europe soon after PRO (the Aerial Phenomena Research Organization) began investigating his case. A PSE (Psychological Stress Evaluator) test administered (by Charles McQuiston, one of the instrument's designers) to Moody's tape-recorded testimony indicated that the alleged abductee had reported his experience truthfully.

—L. J. LORENZEN

POSTSCRIPT: *What follows is Moody's own testimony as reported to Jim and Coral Lorenzen of the Aerial Phenomena Research Organization and published in the July 1976 issue of* The APRO Bulletin:

"The day of the 12th of August 1975 I had heard about a meteor shower that was to occur the morning of the 13th at 0100 hours. Since I get off work at 2330 hours I thought it might be something to watch that might be interesting so that night when I got off work I was not tired so I went home, changed my clothes and watched TV till about 0030 hours. I then got in my car and drove a short distance from my home to a dirt road on the outskirts of Alamogordo. I parked my car just off the dirt road, got out and sat on my left front fender. I did observe 8 or 9 bright meteors. It was now approximately 0115 hours.

"At approximately 0120 hours I observed a dull metallic object that seemed to just drop out of the sky and started to hover with a wobbling motion approximately 100 feet in front of me and approximately 10 to 15 feet off the ground. My first thought was one of fear (I was very frightened). The object was moving slowly toward my car. I jumped off the fender and got into my car. I tried to start my car but it was like there was no battery at all and now that I think about it the dome light and courtesy lights did not come on when I opened the door. I cannot understand this. I keep my car in top-notch condition.

"At this time the object stopped dead still as if to just hang there in the air. The wobbling motion had stopped. It was dead still at approximately 70-80 feet away and still approximately 15 to 20 feet off the ground. The approximate size of the object was about 50 feet across and approximately 18 to 20 feet thick at the center, maybe more. At this time I heard a high-pitched sound, something like a dental drill might make at high speed and just to the right of the center of the object I saw what seemed to be an oblong-shaped window. I had not seen this before. It was approximately 4 to 5 feet long and approximately 2 to 3 feet wide.

"At the window there were the shadows of what looked to be human forms. I could not make them out, only that they looked humanoid. There were two or three of them at the window. At this time the high-pitched sound stopped and a feeling of numbness came over my body. The fear that I had before left me and I felt a very peaceful calmness over my body. It was like floating on a cloud. At this time the object lifted very fast and was gone. It made no sound as it left, only a slight more glow than before.

"What I will tell you two folks now does not come easy for me but I feel that you two will be the only ones who will understand. Jim, as I told you over the phone, I have been remembering some of what took place that night. There was definitely a contact made. I only wish that someone like you and Coral could have been there that night. I can tell you that the people of this world have really misunderstood UFOers and what they are doing. It's not only just one advanced race that is studying this planet earth but a group of them and within three years from now [which was 1979] they will make themselves known to all mankind. It may be as early as midsummer 1976. I can also say that it will not be a pleasant type of meeting for there will be warnings made to the people of this world. Their plan is for only limited contact and after 20 years of further study and only after deeper consideration will there be any type of closer contact. They also fear for their own lives and will protect themselves at all costs. Their intent is a peaceful one and if the leaders of this world will only heed their warnings we will find ourselves a lot better off than before, and at this time it's not up to us to accept them, but for them to accept us!

"My dear friends Jim and Coral, what I saw that night aboard their craft were things I cannot explain but I can only try. The beings were about 5 feet tall and very much like us except their heads were larger and no hair, ears very small, eyes a little larger than ours, nose small and the mouth had very thin lips. I would say their weight was maybe between 110-130 pounds. There was speech but their lips did not move. Their type of clothing was skintight. I could not see any zippers or buttons on their clothing at all. The color of their clothes was black except for one of them that had on a silver-white looking suit. There were no names said but they knew who I was and called me by my proper name—Charles, and did not use my nickname, Chuck. It was like they could read my mind and I believe they did because the elder or leader would speak sometimes before I would ask something.

"I was taken to a room and the elder or leader touched my back and legs with a rod-looking device and when I asked what he was doing he said there had been a scuffle when they first made contact with me and he only wanted to correct any misplacement that might have happened. I do not remember any type of scuffle or fight but I do know my back hurt the next day.

"The inside of the craft was as clean as an operating room. I cannot say if the fixtures were metal or plastic. The lighting was indirect. I did not see any source of light but there was light. I was thinking to myself 'If I could only see the drive unit of the craft, how wonderful that would be.' The elder or leader put his hand on my shoulder and said to follow him. We went to a small room that had no fixtures in it and was dimly lit and stood on the side of the room. The floor seemed to give way like an elevator. I guess we went down about 6 feet and what I saw then was a room about 25 feet across and in the center was what looked like a huge carbon rod going through the roof of the room; around the rod were what looked like three holes covered with glass. Inside the glass-covered holes or balls were what looked like large crystals with two rods, one on each side of the crystal. One rod came to a ball-like top, the other one came to a 'T' type top. I was told that this was the drive unit and that I could understand it if I tried. There were no wires or cables. I then saw what looked like a large black box on the side of the room. I asked about it and was told what it was but then was told not to ever reveal what the black box was for. I have really tried to remember but I can't remember about the black box, only that it was there.

"I guess I was there about half an hour looking at the drive unit. It was then taken back up through the same way we came down—part of the floor just went up with us. The elder or leader then told me that this was not their main craft, but only used for observing, and that their main craft was about 400 of our miles above the earth. And the drive unit on it was different from the one on their craft. I asked if I could go to the main craft and I was told no, that their time was short but they could find me any time they desired and that in a short time they would see me again.

"I then asked the elder or leader why I was so sluggish and clumsy, and he told me that I was quite hostile at the first contact and that they had to use a type of sound or light on me to calm me down and that the effect would go away in a short time. The elder or leader then put both his hands on the sides of my head and told me it was time for them to leave and asked me not to remember what had been said or what I had seen for at least two weeks. I don't know why the two weeks but I guess there was a reason because it was about two weeks later that you came to Alamogordo and shortly after that it started coming back to me—what had happened to me. I asked him if we would meet again and he said yes, in a short time. And then he told me to be sure and visit a doctor soon. And I did—I guess there was a reason for that, too. I then asked why they had talked to me and why was I taken on board their craft. He only said that in time 'you will understand.' The next thing I knew I was sitting in my car watching a strange object lift into the sky and trying to start my car—the rest you know about."

—CHARLES L. MOODY

Morel encounter Lyndia Morel was driving home from work (from Manchester to Goffstown, New Hampshire) when she was allegedly followed by a UFO and its occupant, which she could see through an oval porthole on the front of the object. The UFO was described as spherical, with a honeycombed appearance all over its surface, and was glowing bright yellow.

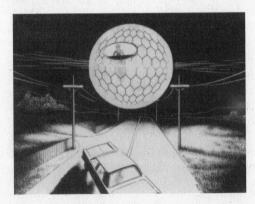

The UFO encounter scene as described by Lyndia Morel

The episode reportedly began soon after 2:45 A.M. on Friday morning, November 2, 1973, when Mrs. Morel signed out at the Swedish Sauna in Manchester where she was employed as a masseuse. She then stopped to have coffee with a friend, purchased gas for her car, and proceeded home.

After crossing the Merrimack River via Queen City Bridge, Mrs. Morel proceeded northwest on Mast Road (Route 114A). As she passed the Bi-Wise Supermarket in Pinardville (outskirts of Manchester), her attention was attracted to a large, bright, yellow light in the sky to her left and ahead of her. Resembling a bright star, the object flashed red, green, and blue colors. In fact, the witness could not tell at this point if it was moving and thought the object was a planet. After traveling about a mile, Mrs. Morel said she looked at the object and saw that it was still in the same position but seemed to be brighter.

Approaching the intersection of routes 114A and 114, she lit a cigarette, and at that moment, as she looked at the object, its light went out. Thinking that was peculiar for a planet, she entertained the idea for the first time that the object might be a UFO. However, she was not apprehensive, and after passing the intersection, the light reappeared in the same spot to the left and ahead of the car.

The road was dark but up ahead on the right Mrs. Morel said she could see the lights of the Hillsborough County Nursing Home (the so-called "county farm") and across the road, on the left, the lights of Moore General Hospital. As her car approached the farm, the object's light went out again.

About a half mile from the nursing home, near the Boston and Maine Railroad crossing, the light came back on again, perhaps at an even brighter level. For another two miles the strange object maintained the same appearance and relationship to the Morel car as before.

On the outskirts of Goffstown (population: 2,300), about where the town's streetlights began, the UFO's light vanished once more and, after about three quarters of a mile, reappeared for perhaps fifteen seconds. But as Mrs. Morel veered right around a corner into downtown Goffstown, the light went out and remained out during the drive of a third of a mile through the lighted downtown area.

Veering left at the intersection of routes 114 and 13 (near a popcorn stand), the witness said she was astounded to see the light dead ahead down North Mast Road (Route 114). The object appeared larger, quite a bit closer, and lower than before—and positioned as if waiting for her.

She described the object, now, as an orange-and-gold globe completely covered with a honeycomb design of hexagons except for an oval window of paler color situated on the upper left portion of the UFO. The witness thought the object was not totally opaque, but had a peculiar translucent quality about it. The flashes of red, green, and blue light were rays or beams emanating from a source in the center; these three colors constantly changed back and forth, as in the twinkling of a star. A steady, thin, high-pitched whine could be heard, and, according to the woman, this sound was felt through her body as a tingling sensation.

Mrs. Morel said her amazement quickly turned to panic when she suddenly was unable to remove her hands from the steering wheel. Moreover, she reported that she felt her eyes pulled toward the UFO and had the sensation it was taking control of her body and drawing her toward it. When later asked about any possible disturbances to the car's electrical system, she said she was not aware of any effects on her automobile's engine, lights, or radio which was playing at this time.

At no time during this phase of the sighting did the witness recall stopping her car. However, as she drove forward a "short distance" from the intersection she said she experienced a "loss of memory" for nearly a half mile. She said she was unaware of driving a stretch between a church on her right and Westlawn Cemetery on her left, although she felt her eyes followed the UFO without interruption. After the experience, she speculated that "they" may have "retrieved" and "recorded" her memory during this interval.

Suddenly, Mrs. Morel said she realized where she was and became cognizant that the car was moving at a high rate of speed and that the vehicle was out of her control. She had the definite impression that the UFO was pulling her car toward it like a magnet and getting closer. It was at this point that she noticed the figure in the upper left window of the UFO.

As the car approached a point opposite the middle of the cemetery, the UFO closed possibly to within less than five hundred feet (perhaps considerably less) becoming larger than a quarter at arm's length. At the same time, the object grew brighter and the whine seemed louder. At this point, Mrs. Morel estimated the object to be at the height of a three-story building. The figure in the window was now distinct.

She said the figure's head, upper body, and arms were visible, while a dark horizontal surface occupying the lower portion of the oval window obscured the rest of the body. She thought the humanoid could have been standing at a control board of some kind. Behind the figure was a white background. The occupant's body appeared darker than the face, with small shoulders, but it was uncertain whether the body was clothed in a uniform or not. The rounded head was grayish (between a gray and flesh tone), except for a darker color on top, and the face bore wrinkles or loose skin like an elephant's hide. Angling upward across the forehead, two large "egg-shaped" eyes with large dark pupils gripped the observer's attention so much that she felt unable to look away. She said she received an impression or awareness that "told" her "don't be afraid." A mouth-slit turned down at the corners completed the description of the face. No nose or ears were noticed.

Panic-stricken, Mrs. Morel believed she was in imminent danger of being captured by the UFO occupant. Passing by the cemetery, she spotted a house ahead on the left. The globe became so dazzling that she covered her eyes with an arm and simultaneously turned the wheel with the other hand, entering the driveway of the Beaudoin house at an angle, and coming to a halt partly on the front lawn. The witness had covered a distance of almost exactly a mile from the Route 114/13 intersection, and now she was only three quarters of a mile from home. Leaving the engine running and the headlights on, Mrs. Morel said she pushed open the door of the car. At that instant, the Beaudoin's growling German shepherd dashed up to the woman as she got out of the car. Normally afraid of strange dogs, she said she "belted" the animal across the mouth. Though she did not recall running to the house, she began pounding on the kitchen

door, ringing the bell, and yelling over and over again: "Help me! Help me! Help me!"

Glancing to her right, she noticed the UFO had shifted its position from west to north, as if to keep her in view, and was now hovering directly across the road opposite the Beaudoin house. The object still emitted its high-pitched whine, which according to Mrs. Morel was becoming almost unbearable.

After what the witness estimated to be about two minutes of attempting to attract the attention of the residents of the house, the door was opened by Mr. Beaudoin—as Mrs. Morel began sinking to her knees in almost a faint.

The Beaudoins had been asleep upstairs and reluctantly came down in response to the persistent noise at the door. Mrs. Beaudoin said an obviously frightened woman, her eyes wide open with terror, fell into Mr. Beaudoin's arms, crying, "Help me! I'm not drunk! I'm not on drugs! A UFO just tried to pick me up!" Mrs. Beaudoin said the witness was covering her ears but neither she nor her husband remember hearing an unusual sound. Mrs. Morel said that the sound ceased and the numbness or tingling sensation she had experienced vanished after two minutes in the Beaudoin kitchen. However, she became aware of an afterimage (the effect caused by staring too long at a bright light source).

The clock on the kitchen wall read 4.30 A.M. Mrs. Beaudoin said the woman's story sounded impossible, but she did phone the Goffstown Police Department and reported the occurrence. Goffstown Patrolman Daniel Jubinville, 23, received the call while on routine patrol, and proceeded to the Beaudoin house, arriving there at 4:40 A.M. On his way to the door, the officer turned off the lights and engine of the Morel car, then heard Mrs. Morel's account. In his report he stated: "This writer took note that the subject was quite shaken up and this writer did not note any evidence of alcohol or drug influence."

After Officer Jubinville arrived, the four went outside and spotted an object whose light seemingly went out when a flashlight was trained on it, and appeared to move slightly, occasionally changing colors. However, the multiwitness phase of the sighting should probably be ruled ambiguous and therefore nonsupportive of the Morel sighting because: (1) the object, as described by all four observers, matched the appearance and behavior of both the planet Mars and the UFO (the latter when seen at a distance); and (2) the planet's known position was too close to the UFO's estimated position to entirely dismiss the planet from contention. Other aspects of the case are, so far, unconfirmed and rest on the testimony of Mrs. Morel herself.

—WALTER N. WEBB

Morning of the Magicians, The (Editions Gallimard, 1960). French authors Louis Pauwels and Jacques Bergier pioneer a conspiracy theory of history. They make a case that the traditions and myths of secret societies, and mutations in human intelligence throughout history which produced geniuses like Leonardo da Vinci, could be a by-product of extraterrestrial visitors who genetically tinkered with human evolution.

—RANDALL FITZGERALD

Moseley, James W. (b. 1931). Veteran UFO researcher and journalist who is known as the "court jester" and "Voltaire" of UFOlogy. Having been part of the American UFO scene for half a century, Moseley keeps UFOlogists on their toes with his satirical newsletter called *Saucer Smear* (with the tagline: "Shockingly Close to the Truth"). He began publishing *Smear* in 1976, which he describes as a "non-scheduled newsletter devoted to humor, satire, and UFOlogical scandal."

Originally from New York City, Jim Moseley attended Princeton University for two years. He became interested in UFOs after the famous Kenneth Arnold sighting in 1947, and more so in 1948, when the Mantell incident occurred.

In 1954, he founded a magazine called *Saucer News,* which was subsequently taken over by Gray Barker in 1968 (publication ceased in 1970). In 1967, Moseley organized and sponsored a mammoth UFO convention at the Hotel Commodore in New York City, with a total attendance of about 8,000 persons.

James Moseley

His archaeological interests are also notable. Moseley became interested in pre-Columbian antiquities in the late 1950s, when he did extensive digging in various archaeological sites on the coast of Peru. Having been an antiques collector ever since those adventurous days, in 1984 he and his wife Anna opened their present primitive art gallery in Key West, Florida. The gallery features pottery from Mexico, Peru, and various other areas of artistic interest, in Central and South America. Also for sale is museum-quality antique gold, ancient tribal art from Africa, rare books, and even a shrunken head from the Jivaro tribe of Ecuador!

Today, Moseley's newsletter takes an attitude of benign skepticism toward the more extreme UFO beliefs, and generally reflects the various ways in which he has mellowed in his thinking over the years.

His three books on UFOs are entitled: *Jim Moseley's Book of Saucer News* (1967), *The Wright Field Story* (1971), and (with Karl Pflock) *Shockingly Close to the Truth* (forthcoming in 2001).

Address: P.O. Box 1709,
             Key West, FL 33041
             U.S.A.
E-mail: slm\@well.com
Web site: www.martiansgohome.com

POSITION STATEMENT: Over the years, my views on the UFO subject have changed several times. In the early days, I took what might be called a NICAP (National Investigations Committee on Aerial Phenomena) position, in that I believed saucers were extraterrestrial, but that the contactees were basically lying. Later I flirted, for a time, with the theory that UFOs were secret weapons. By the early 1960s, I was back with the extraterrestrial theory.

In the seventies, I became greatly influenced by UFO writers, such as John Keel, Peter Kor, Allen Greenfield, et al., who propounded one version or another of what might be called a "4-D" (fourth dimensional) interpretation. I still feel that UFOS, as well as most "psychic" events, are manifestations of some sort from another realm or dimension. They may have a degree of physical reality, but they are beyond our present science and present powers of human comprehension.

Although I disagreed strongly with NICAP's effort to blame everything on the Air Force, I now believe that there is a government cover-up—whether deliberate or not remains to be seen—which has prevented the public from taking UFOs as seriously as they should. Were the public to realize that UFOs are a serious and continuing problem, government funds (in the millions) could be devoted to scientific attempts to solve the mystery properly; and eventually, with enough money, and given our present level of technology, some progress in that direction would be inevitable.

As things stand now, the field is still largely inhabited by amateurs, including teenaged hobbyists, cultists, and disturbed people of all sorts. In recent years, however, a few "real" scientists have taken a serious interest in UFOs and have been willing to say so publicly, which is a good trend. However, their pro-UFO bias largely invalidates their work.

Today, whereas most UFOlogists still prefer 3-D "nuts and bolts" saucers and space people, I prefer 3½-D, 4-D, or 4½-D entities. Also, while some others believe that our visitors were around for a few years and then went away, I feel rather that, whatever this phenomenon is, it has been a permanent part of the Earth's environment at least since the dawn of recorded history, and remains here now.

My skepticism is caused by the fact that *our supposed visitors are just too much like us*—physically, emotionally, and intellectually. They never seem to tell us anything we don't already know. Their technology is only a very few years ahead of our own.

Granted that intelligent life probably exists throughout the universe, it is still a weird coincidence indeed that we are being visited by creatures who are almost precisely at our own stage of evolution. If they were a little less developed, they couldn't get here at all, and if they were much more developed, we might not even recognize them as intelligent life-forms. After all, evolution has been going on for billions of years and hopefully will continue for a few billion years more!

It is absurd to believe that a highly developed race would engage in silly genetic and sexual experiments with Earthlings. These creatures seem to be obsessed with sex—just as we are! Abductions apparently have some sort of reality, but it is definitely not a 3-D physical reality. Just what is involved, we do not know.

What is really happening, in my opinion, is that we are having occasional contacts with another realm of being—another dimension, or whatever. There is a vast spectrum of weirdness that includes saucers as well as the paranormal. One cannot be separated from the other, as tempting as it might be to do so. The reality behind the saucers is the ultimate reality behind science and religion. At our present

stage of knowledge, we cannot understand it all well, but hopefully someday we will.
—JAMES W. MOSELEY

Mothman   A manlike flying creature with glowing red hypnotic eyes, a wingspread of ten feet, and a predilection for chasing automobiles at speeds approaching a hundred miles per hour, Mothman terrorized residents of the Point Pleasant, West Virginia, area during 1966-67. Several witnesses were interviewed by various UFO investigators, including John Keel and the writer, who wrote their findings in two different books. A television newsman gave the nickname ''Mothman'' to the phenomenon, no doubt inspired by the TV program, ''Batman.'' Like the term, ''flying saucer,'' the satirical apellation became permanently attached, both to the Point Pleasant sightings and to such phenomena as a class. As with many other strange-creature reports, such as ''Bigfoot,'' and seemingly allied events such as visitations by ''men in black,'' many witnesses and investigators believed there was a connection between Mothman and the numerous UFO sightings in the area at the same time. Later, some witnesses, investigators, and area residents would believe the phenomena represented a portent of the tragic collapse of the Silver Bridge on December 16, 1967. These beliefs, blended with a tradition that Cornstalk, an Indian chief, had placed a curse on the town, tended to adapt Mothman to the folklore of the area.

Despite the mythlike quality of the occurrences when considered ten years afterward, two books, this writer's *The Silver Bridge* (1970) and Keel's *The Mothman Prophecies* (1975), record interviews with eyewitnesses and otherwise substantiate the events.

The best-documented sighting of Mothman involved four witnesses and occurred on November 17, 1966. Two newly married couples, Roger and Linda Scarberry and Steve and Mary Mallette, were driving together in the ''TNT'' area, an abandoned World War II munitions manufacturing-storage complex, when they encountered a frightening six-foot figure,

with wings and glowing red eyes, emerging from behind an abandoned power plant.

An artist's rendering of the ''Mothman''
(Drawn by Hal Crawford)

''It was more or less running,'' Mallette reported, ''trying to balance itself with its wings which spread slightly outward. It staggered like a crippled chicken as it disappeared around the corner of the building.''

The party fled homeward toward Point Pleasant, but believed Mothman was following them. Suddenly, as they rounded a sharp curve, they saw the creature standing near the highway on a hillside. Instead of flapping its huge wings, it took off vertically, shooting upward like a rocket at great speed, but without visible means of propulsion. As they continued speeding homeward they could see the shadow of the creature, cast by the moon, still following them, even though they were driving at almost a hundred miles per hour.

When city police responded to their report and drove to the ''TNT'' area, they found no evidence, though they reported unusual radio interference, ''like high-pitched beeping sounds.''

This dramatic report might be written off as just a horror story, were it not for several other independent sightings of the same phenomenon. On November 25, Tom Ury, a shoe-store manager, was driving north of Point Pleasant on Route 62, when he saw what he thought to be a helicopter rising from a wooded area several hundred yards from the road. As the object approached him, he perceived it to be a huge bird, of grayish-brown color, six feet in length, and with a wingspread of at least ten feet. Fearing it would attack his convertible, he accelerated to seventy miles per hour. It followed him for about a mile, then veered off and flew away.

Although largely confined to the Point Pleasant area, one sighting was reported fifty miles away in Charleston.

On November 26, Mrs. Ruth Foster, watching for her husband to arrive home from a late evening work shift, peered through a window in her front door and was horrified to meet the gaze of two huge bulbous red eyes staring back at her. She noted a white body with what she termed "close feathers," standing almost six feet tall. A huge set of folded wings and a "peculiar face" were the only other details she could recall. During the following evening, a thirteen-year-old neighbor, Shelia Cain, along with a friend, saw a "gray-and-white-looking" bird-like creature while passing an auto junkyard. It, too, displayed glowing eyes, a common denominator of most of the sightings. The glowing eyes generally were the only facial features described by witnesses—neither a head nor beak are mentioned.

Another incident, about one hundred miles away, may also be connected. During the evening of November 15, Newell Partridge, who lived near Wallace, noted interference on his television set, and at the same time heard his German shepherd dog, "Bandit," howling. He went outside and directed his flashlight toward the barn where the beam picked up glowing red eyes, "like bicycle reflectors." The dog charged toward the eyes, but did not return to the house. The next morning Partridge tracked Bandit to the barn where the dog's footprints in the soft mud went into a circle as if he were baying at some animal. But the footprints did not leave the circle, and when Partridge heard

about the Point Pleasant incidents, he believed Mothman had snatched up and carried off his pet.

Within a framework of UFOlogical theory advanced by Keel, along with Jerome Clark, writing with Loren Coleman in *The Unidentified and Creatures From the Outer Edge* (1975 and 1978 respectively), the Point Pleasant sightings take on a "classic" pattern. Even the "men in black" appeared shortly after the initial Mothman and UFO sightings. Mary Hyre, a newspaper reporter, recounted how mysterious, oddly dressed visitors showed up at her office, inquiring about various investigators who had interviewed witnesses. Keel believes that certain locations may represent "window" areas, where, at certain times, massive unexplained phenomena of various kinds may occur. This could include the experience of Woodrow Derenberger, who, driving near Parkersburg (about fifty miles north of Point Pleasant), claimed his van was forced off the road on the evening of November 2, that a UFO landed, and an OCCUPANT named "Indrid Cold" emerged from it to assure him that "We mean you no harm."

There are two natural explanations suggested for Mothman. George Wolfe, Jr., of Beaver Falls, Pennsylvania, reported that, while hunting during the Thanksgiving weekend, he had seen a "seven-foot-tall bird that looked something like an ostrich." Could Mothman have been a migratory bird, temporarily grounded from its travels? Dr. Robert L. Smith speculated the creature could have been a sandhill crane, the second largest American crane. "It stands almost as tall as a man, with its feathers a slate gray," the scientist stated. Large, bright red fleshy rings around the crane's eyes could have been mistaken for the red "hypnotic" eyes reported by witnesses. But its appearance in West Virginia during the winter was difficult to explain: Smith noted it winters in a warm climate and is rarely seen east of the Mississippi, except in Florida.

Despite their bizarre attributes, the Point Pleasant Mothman sightings are not unique. Ten years later, residents of the Rio Grande

Valley, Texas, would report a "flap" of un-identified flying creatures, which television newsmen of a later programming decade would call "Big Bird." Jerome Clark documents many "Big Bird" sightings in his article, "Unidentified Flapping Objects" in *Oui* magazine, October 1976, including an account of the creature's allegedly attacking a witness. In Texas, like West Virginia, ornithologists tried to identify the phenomenon with questionable success.

"Mothmen" and other mystery "animals" are interesting to UFOlogists because they are connected, either in origin, or by popular myth-making, with the "flying saucer" phenomenon.

—GRAY BARKER

Mutual UFO Network (MUFON)   The Midwest UFO Network was founded on May 31, 1969. Retaining the acronym MUFON, the name was changed on June 17, 1973, to the Mutual UFO Network, Inc., to reflect the worldwide scope of the organization.

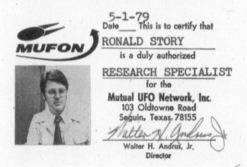

MUFON is governed by a board of directors, composed of twenty-two men and women, which includes the corporate officers, four elected regional directors, and the directors of the major functional departments. In North America, each state or province is headed by a state or provincial director. Each state is geographically divided into groups of counties with a state section director correlating the investigative activities of the field investigators.

At the worldwide level, the international coordinator, assisted by the continental coordi-nators, provide the liaison between MUFON and the national directors or foreign representatives in each nation. Since the field investigators comprise such an important segment of MUFON, the fourth edition of the copyrighted *MUFON Field Investigator's Manual* edited by Walter H. Andrus, Jr., was released in 1995 and has been adopted by the English-speaking nations as a universal guide.

On July 16, 2000, founding member and veteran UFOlogist, John F. Schuessler became the International Director of MUFON, replacing Walter H. Andrus, Jr., who headed the organization for 30 years.

The objective of MUFON is to resolve the UFO mystery and all of its ramifications in a scientific manner. MUFON is dedicated to the express purpose of answering four basic questions pertaining to this enigma:

(1) Are UFOs some form of spacecraft controlled by an advanced intelligence conducting a surveillance of Earth, or do they constitute some unknown physical or psychological manifestation that is not understood by twentieth-century science?

(2) If UFOs are found to be extraterrestrial craft controlled by intelligent beings, what is their method of propulsion, or if they have the technique to operate in another dimension, how is this accomplished?

(3) Postulating that they may be controlled by an extraterrestrial intelligence, where do they originate—in our universe or in another dimension?

(4) Assuming that some of the craft are piloted by beings, what can we learn from their apparently advanced science and civilization that could benefit mankind on the planet Earth?

Since 1970, one of the major activities of MUFON has been the sponsorship of an annual MUFON International UFO symposium, where internationally known scientists, engieers, researchers, and authors lectured on their particular specialization or contribution to resolving this perplexing scientific dilemma. In order to provide a permanent record of the presentations, the copyrighted proceedings are published annually for worldwide distribution.

The official monthly publication of the Mutual UFO Network is the *MUFON UFO Journal* formerly entitled *Skylook* and founded in 1967. Dwight Connelly is the present editor.

Address: P.O. Box 369
           Morrison, CO 80465
           U.S.A.

Telephone: (303) 932-7701
Fax: (303) 932-9279

Web site: www.mufon.com
E-mail: mufonhq@aol.com

—WALTER ANDRUS

Mysteries of Time and Space (Prentice-Hall, 1974). Brad Steiger thinks that alien visitors mold space and time so the human mind can perceive poltergeists, Sasquatch, and other unusual phenomena. They are intentionally confounding human notions of reality as a teaching method, tuning our minds to other dimensions and the intelligences that reside within them.

—RANDALL FITZGERALD

N

NASA Fact Sheet on UFOs *The official U.S. Government position on unidentified flying objects and possible alien visitors is quoted here (verbatim) from a "Fact Sheet" published by the National Aeronautics and Space Administration (dated May 17, 2000). The Fact Sheet is entitled* **"The US Government and Unidentified Flying Objects."**

No branch of the United States Government is currently involved with or responsible for investigations into the possibility of alien life on other planets or for investigating Unidentified Flying Objects (UFOs). The US Air Force (USAF) and the National Aeronautics and Space Administration (NASA) have had intermittent, independent investigations of the possibility of alien life on other planets; however, none of these has produced factual evidence that life exists on other planets, nor that UFOs are related to aliens. From 1947 to 1969, the Air Force investigated UFOs; then in 1977, NASA was asked to examine the possibility of resuming UFO investigations. After studying all of the facts available, it was determined that nothing would be gained by further investigation, since there was an absence of tangible evidence.

In October 1992, NASA was directed by Congress to begin a detailed search for artificial radio signals from other civilizations under the NASA Towards Other Planetary Systems (TOPS)/High Resolution Microwave Survey (HRMS) program (also known as the Search for Extraterrestrial Intelligence project). Congress directed NASA to end this project in October 1993, citing pressures on the U.S. Federal budget. The HRMS did not detect any confirmed signal before it was stopped. However, similar work will continue in a more limited manner through efforts of private groups and through academic institutions. The Search for Extraterrestrial Intelligence Institute (SETI Institute) in Mountain View, California, effectively replaced the Government project, borrowing the signal processing system from NASA. The SETI Institute is a nonprofit corporation conducting research in a number of fields including all science and technology aspects of astronomy and planetary sciences, chemical evolution, the origin of life, biological evolution, and cultural evolution.

During several space missions, NASA astronauts have reported phenomena not immediately explainable; however, in every instance NASA determined that the observations could not be termed "abnormal" in the space environment. The 1947 to 1969 USAF investigations studied UFOs under Project Blue Book. The project, headquartered at Wright-Patterson Air Force Base, Ohio, was terminated December 17, 1969. Of the total of 12,618 sightings reported to Project Blue Book, 701 remain "unidentified."

The decision to discontinue UFO investigations was based on an evaluation of a report prepared by the University of Colorado entitled, "Scientific Study of Unidentified Flying Objects"; a review of the University of Colorado's report by the National Academy of Sciences; previous UFO studies; and Air Force experience investigating UFO reports during the 1940s, '50s and '60s. As a result of experience, investigations, and studies since 1948, the conclusions of Project Blue Book were: (1) no UFO reported, investigated, and evaluated by the Air Force was ever a threat to our national security; (2) there was no evidence submitted to, or discovered by, the Air Force that sightings categorized as "unidentified" represented technological developments or principles beyond the range of modern scientific knowledge; and (3) there was no evidence indicating that sightings categorized as "unidentified" were extraterrestrial vehicles.

With the termination of Project Blue Book, the USAF regulation establishing and controlling the program for investigating and analyzing UFOs was rescinded. Documentation regarding the former Project Blue Book investigation was permanently transferred to the Modern Military Branch, National Archives and Records Service, in Washington, D.C. 20408, and is available for public review and analysis.

Since the termination of Project Blue Book, nothing has occurred that would support a resumption of UFO investigations by the USAF or NASA. Given the current environment of steadily decreasing defense and space budgets, it is unlikely that the Air Force or NASA will become involved in this type of costly project in the foreseeable future.

Since neither NASA nor the Air Force is engaged in day-to-day UFO research, neither one reviews UFO-related articles intended for publication, evaluates UFO-type spacecraft drawings, or accepts accounts of UFO sightings or applications for employment in the field of aerial phenomena investigation.

UFO POINTS OF CONTACT

1. For further information on the Search for Extraterrestrial Intelligence, please contact the SETI Institute, 2035 Landings Drive, Mountain View, CA 94043, (415) 960-4530.

2. News media requiring Project Blue Book files should contact the National Archives Public Affairs Office, (202) 501-5525. Public queries should be addressed to the Project Blue Book archivist at (202) 501-5385. For queries not related to Project Blue Book, contact the National Archives receptionist at (202) 501-5400. Documentation is available from: Modern Military Branch, National Archives and Records Service, Eighth Street and Pennsylvania Avenue, NW, Washington, DC 20408.

3. The Air Force publication, "The Roswell Report: Fact vs. Fiction in the New Mexico Desert," a lengthy document providing all of the details available from the Air Force on the Roswell incident, is available for $52 from the US Government Printing Office, Superintendent of Documents, Mail Stop: SSOP, Washington, DC 20402-9328.

4. There are a number of universities and professional scientific organizations that have considered UFO phenomena during periodic meetings and seminars. A list of private organizations interested in aerial phenomena may be found in *Gale's Encyclopedia of Associations*.

5. Persons wishing to report UFO sightings are advised to contact law enforcement agencies.

—NASA

National Investigations Committee on Aerial Phenomena (NICAP) NICAP was founded in October 1956 by a former Navy scientist, Townsend Brown, and a small group of Washington, D.C., area professional men. Initially it planned to publish a slick magazine and to have an elaborate and costly staff structure, but this failed to materialize. With the support of retired Admiral Delmer S. Fahmey and other prominent figures, Major Donald E. Keyhoe, USMC, Ret., became director in January 1957 and established a more realistic operating plan. NICAP flourished between 1957 and 1970, attaining a membership of over ten thousand, then began a slow decline. John L. Acuff, an entrepreneur of small associations, became director/president in 1973. During the 1950s, NICAP established itself, through national news media publicity, as a research organization willing to accept UFO reports in confidence from pilots, military personnel, and others in sensitive positions. Scientists, engineers, and other technically trained persons were encouraged to participate in UFO investigations. Beginning in 1958, a national network of investigators was established; these ''subcommittees'' included operational units at major scientific and military establishments. Active members also formed affiliates in Chicago, Connecticut, Kentucky, Los Angeles, and New York City.

Throughout the late 1950s and 1960s, the affiliate/subcommittee network funneled information into the Washington, D.C., headquarters office which was maintained for over fifteen years. (Mr. Acuff later moved the office to the Maryland suburbs.) NICAP used the information to dispute Air Force contentions that UFO sightings were being explained adequately and to keep government officials apprised of important sightings by reputable and competent observers. Information also was supplied to interested members of Congress and congressional staffs, and NICAP repeatedly recommended that congressional hearings be held to illuminate the UFO question.

In 1964 NICAP published *The UFO Evidence*, edited by Richard Hall. This 200,000-word documentary report was supplied to every member of Congress and to local and national news media.

NICAP collaborated with the University of Colorado UFO Project, but early in 1968 it broke off its formerly close relations, alleging that its director, Dr. Edward Condon was prejudging UFOs by making negative and skeptical public statements and that the project was ignoring hundreds of important cases. When it became clear that the project's report would be negative, NICAP devoted its resources to countering the report and offsetting its presumed detrimental effect on UFO investigations. The supplying of large amounts of information in the form of photostatic copies and the publishing of additional reports (*UFOs: A New Look* and *Strange Effects from UFOs*, both in 1969) depleted NICAP's finances. This, coupled with a decline of public interest in the wake of the Condon Report led to the organization's decline.

The NICAP board, in 1970, relieved Major Keyhoe as director (he continued to serve as a board member) and appointed John L. Acuff. As manager of several small associations, Mr. Acuff was charged with reorganizing NICAP on a businesslike basis. The scale of operations was drastically reduced, costs were cut, but NICAP continued to publish a newsletter, *The UFO Investigator*. The membership continued to decline, however, and the NICAP budget for research and investigation was minuscule. Mr. Acuff resigned as president in 1978 but accepted a position on the board. The new president in 1979 was Alan N. Hall.

As of early 1979, NICAP was engaged in an attempt at fundamental reorganization and was considering a merger with one or more other UFO groups. A controversy arose concerning the alleged CIA connections of several then-current board members. The membership was stated to be about two thousand.

By 1980 NICAP became inoperative and its files were given to the J. Allen Hynek Center for UFO Studies.

—RICHARD HALL

Nazca "spaceport" Thought by some to be an ancient landing site for extraterrestrials, the Nazca plain is located in a desert near the southern coast of Peru, and occupies an area of at least forty square miles.

Though built by the pre-Inca Nazca civilization (ca. 200 B.C.-A.D. 600), the immense lines and figures received little attention until the German-American mathematician and amateur archaeologist Maria Reiche decided to devote her life to studying them.

Beginning in the 1940s until her recent death, Ms. Reiche roamed the lines with a jeep and a 10-foot stepladder, mapping them in painstaking detail. Her work was not generally known in the United States until a 1955 article in *Fate* magazine by the writer. Later, Erich von Däniken and other writers popularized the lines, because of their superficial resemblance to a giant airport or landing field, giving rise to speculation that they were intended to be seen by the occupants of flying saucers.

The lines represent an important engineering feat only because of their great length, running as long as several miles each, and because of their absolute straightness. Most are almost parallel to each other, and in a few cases as many as a dozen of them intersect at small artificial mounds. Treasure hunters in the 1950s were unable to find anything of value in these mounds.

Mingled among the lines are large figures of various animals, very similar to the animal designs on the ancient Nazca pottery that is still found in tombs in the valleys near this coastal desert.

These figures, like the straight lines themselves, were made quite simply by clearing away the reddish topsoil of the desert, exposing the white sand beneath it. Since there is virtually no rain at all in the area, these markings on the desert lasted intact for all these many hundreds of years.

Much nonsense has been written on this subject. There is no question as to *who* made the lines, or *how* they were made. The only mystery is in regard to *why*. Since the ancient people of Peru (and elsewhere in South America) had no written language, we will never know for sure. Maria Reiche and other serious researchers suggest an astronomical explanation, and this most likely is correct.

The Nazca lines were apparently an attempt to correlate with the most visible stars and planets in the sky. Over the entries the apparent positions of these heavenly bodies kept shifting slightly; thus the fact that so many of the lines are nearly parallel, but not quite.

INTERNATIONAL EXPLORERS SOCIETY

A pilot's-eye view of the Nazca "spaceport"

Legend has it that these lines can be seen only from the air. Whereas the entire area can only be seen at once from an airplane, significant portions can be seen from Ms. Reich's

10-foot ladder, or from low hills that surround the Nazca plain. As usual, reality is less exciting than myth.

Little known is the fact that very similar but less complex patterns of lines have been found hundreds of miles away near Lima, the Peruvian capital, as well as in Chile, Colombia, Bolivia, and possibly other countries of South America. Their purpose is not clear.

—JAMES W. MOSELEY

ANOTHER VIEW: Across 30 miles of gravel-covered desert near the southern coast of Peru are the famed Nazca lines and effigies. The latter—figures of animals and birds, including a 440-foot-long "condor"—are so large that they can effectively be seen only from the air. In his *Chariots of the Gods?* (1970), Erich von Däniken speculated that the drawings were "signals" to extraterrestrials and the wider lines "landing strips" for alien spacecraft. He suggested that the figures could have been "built according to instructions from an aircraft."

However, the late Maria Reiche who devoted her life to mapping and preserving the markings, observed that the imagined runways were on soft ground, commenting, "I'm afraid the spacemen would have gotten stuck." (McIntyre, 1975) And when von Däniken exhibited a photo of one Nazca configuration "very reminiscent of the aircraft parking areas in a modern airport," he failed to tell his readers that it was a cropped view of the knee joint of one of the bird figures.

In fact, everywhere there is evidence that the lines were made by the local Nazca Indian culture which flourished in the area from about 200 B.C. to A.D. 600. One of the wooden stakes found at the termination of some of the long lines was actually carbon-dated to A.D. 525 (plus or minus 80 years), and the stylized Nazcan figures bear striking similarity to those of other Nazcan art. Nazcan pottery is also found in association with the lines, and their graves and ruins of their settlements lie nearby.

Why the markings were made remains a mystery, although various hypotheses have been

A giant condor on the Nazca plain. The line running parallel with the wings is a solstice line.

offered, ranging from von Däniken's "ancient astronauts" notion to the idea that they represented a giant astronomical calendar or some form of offerings to the Indian deities or even the path of a ritual maze. The outlines of the figures were made by removing surface gravel to expose the lighter soil underneath. (Isbell, 1978, 1980; McIntyre, 1975)

Exactly *how* the Nazcans made such ruler-straight lines and giant drawings, so large their creators could not effectively view them, is another mystery. Some writers have exaggerated the difficulty, and even Maria Reiche in her book *Mystery on the Desert* (1976) went so far as to say, "Ancient Peruvians must have had instruments and equipment which we ignore and which together with ancient knowledge were buried and hidden from the eyes of the conquerors as the one treasure which was not to be surrendered."

However, no such special equipment has ever turned up, and indeed need not be assumed. It has been shown that straight lines

JOE NICKELL

Aerial photograph of full-scale condor
drawing made by Joe Nickell
(and helpers) in eastern Kentucky

could be constructed over many miles by using
a simple series of ranging poles. As to the
figures, one suggestion was the use of a grid
system by which a small drawing would be
enlarged square by square onto a large grid.
(Isbell, 1980) However, such a technique
seems not to account for the asymmetry of
some figures.

In 1982 with five helpers I reproduced the
giant "condor" on an eastern Kentucky land-
fill using only sticks and string. We laid out
a center line on the ground and plotted the
coordinates of significant points. On the small
drawing we would measure along its center
line from one end to a point on the line opposite the point to be plotted—say a wing tip.
Next we measured the distance from the center
line to that point. We then repeated the process
on the ground, using larger units of measure-
ment. We employed a T-shaped device to keep
the sightings at right angles to the center line.
We plotted 165 points (temporarily marked
with stakes) which we later smoothly con-

nected (using white lime in the manner of
marking a playing field) to produce the figure.
We then photographed it from an airplane at
nearly 1,000 feet. (Nickell, 1982)

Our method was so accurate that we reproduced flaws in the original target figure, suggesting that the Nazcans probably used a
simplified form of this method, with perhaps
a significant amount of the work being done
freehand. The results demonstrated that extraterrestrials need not be invoked to explain the
Nazca lines.

—JOE NICKELL

References

Isbell, William H. "The Prehistoric Ground Draw-
ings of Peru," *Scientific American* (October
1978).
———. "Solving the Mystery of Nazca," *Fate*
(October 1980).
McIntyre, Loren. "Mystery of the Ancient Nazca
Lines," *National Geographic* (May 1975).
Morrison, Tony. *Pathways to the Gods* (Harper &
Row, 1978).
Nickell, Joe. "The Nazca Drawings Revisited: Cre-
ation of a Full-Sized Duplicate," *Skeptical In-
quirer* (Spring 1983).
Reiche, Maria. *Mystery on the Desert*, revised ed.
(privately published, 1976).
Von Däniken, Erich. *Chariots of the Gods?* (G. P.
Putnam's Sons, 1970).

POSTSCRIPT: First discovered in 1927 (by
Toribio Mexta Xessepe, a member of a Peruvian aerial survey team), the Nazca markings
cover about a 330-square-mile area of desert
that became a gigantic drawing board for its
ancient inhabitants. There, discernible only
from an elevated vantage point, are found
enormous straight lines, trapezoids, triangles,
spirals, and the outlines of animals: birds, fish,
lizards, a spider, and a monkey. There are
something like 13,000 lines, 100 spirals, trapezoids, and triangles, and nearly 800 huge animal drawings. The markings, made between
400 B.C. and A.D. 900, were etched into the
desert floor by removing the surface stones to
expose the lighter subsoil underneath.

To von Däniken, the geometric designs looked like landing strips, probably for interplanetary spacecraft. Again, as in most other cases of his alleged evidence for the space-god theory, the original idea was not his own. (The "spaceport" interpretation had been offered earlier by George Hunt Williamson in his 1959 book *Road in the Sky* as a complete chapter entitled "Beacons for the Gods.")

Von Däniken popularized the idea with the following suggestion made in *Chariots of the Gods?* (1970):

If you fly over this territory—the plain of Nazca—you can make out gigantic lines, laid out geometrically, some of which run parallel to each other, while others intersect or are surrounded by large trapezoidal areas. The archaeologists say that they are Inca roads. A preposterous idea! Of what use to the Incas were roads that ran parallel to each other? That intersected? That were laid out in a plain and came to a sudden end? . . .

Seen from the air, the clear-cut impression that the 37-mile-long plain of Nazca made on *me* [italics in the original] was that of an airfield!

Then, a year later, von Däniken became more bold and stated his theory matter-of-factly in *Gods from Outer Space* (1971): "At some time in the past, unknown intelligences landed on the uninhabited plain near the present-day town of Nazca and built an improvised airfield for their spacecraft which were to operate in the vicinity of the earth."

While previous authors of the ancient-airfield theory are easily found in the popular literature of the 1950s and 1960s, it is not so easy to find references to any archaeologists who ever seriously considered the Nazca lines as Inca roads. In fact, the first archaeologist to investigate the lines, the late Paul Kosok of Long Island University, ruled out this possibility in his first article on the subject, published in 1947. In his preliminary report, entitled "The Mysterious Markings of Nazca," Kosok

pointed out that although the present inhabitants of the Nazca area sometimes referred to the markings as Inca Roads, "their very nature, size, and position indicate that they could never have been used for ordinary purposes of transportation."

Dr. Kosok was the first to investigate the strange desert markings. In 1939, while studying ancient irrigation systems on the coast of Peru, he noticed that one of the lines coincided with the point on the horizon where the sun set on the day of the winter solstice in the Southern Hemisphere (i.e., the shortest day of the year). This discovery led Kosok to theorize that the lines represented a gigantic astronomical calendar.

A brief study of the lines was reported in 1973 by astronomer Gerald Hawkins of Boston University in his book *Beyond Stonehenge*. After making computer calculations of significant alignments of a selected number of lines at different dates in the ancient past, Hawkins concluded that the solar, lunar, and stellar alignments were no better than what would be expected by chance. But mathematician Maria Reiche, who had studied the Nazca lines for decades, supported the calendar theory; and at least one American astronomer, William Hartmann of the Planetary Science Institute in Tucson, Arizona, partially agrees with her.

Hartmann suggests that the lines may not represent a single undertaking at one particular point in time. When Hawkins fed into the computer the question: "What stars did the lines point to at any date between 5000 B.C. and A.D. 1900?" he says, "The printout sheets were full, stars at the end of each line. But Hawkins rejects the significance of this finding, because he requires that the lines "hang together" in any given century; that is, for each century investigated, the number of alignments should be more than would be expected by chance for the number of lines, or directions, tested. Furthermore, Hawkins's study was not geared to detect other *kinds* of alignments, such as how the shadows of certain hills and ridges, marked by the lines, might also prove to be significant.

Stars making up the southern-sky constellation Pavo, the Peacock, superimposed on the outline of a giant bird, identified as a condor, depicted on the Nazca plain.

It is interesting that certain of the animal figures laid out on the Nazca plain almost perfectly coincide with some of the ancient constellations over the Southern Hemisphere. The drawing here shows the constellation of Pavo, the Peacock, superimposed on the outline of a bird, identified as a condor, "drawn" on the plain. The stars fit the condor in much the same manner as the northern star patterns line up with their mythical counterparts. Perhaps the Nazca figures were representations of constellations recognized at the time. This hypothesis supports Maria Reiche's suggestion that the large figures were drawn from reduced models; the models might have been the star patterns that form the outlines of the subjects represented.

The fact that the Nazca configurations are seen only from the air is consistent with the ancient desire that the gods in the sky notice the peoples below. And what would make the people more noticeable to them (at a time without electric lights or radio signals) than giant pictorial representations of certain forms of life indigenous to their own particular region of the Earth? Even von Däniken admits that the ancients *already* worshipped the Sun and the Moon before "the gods [came] down from heaven."

Whether these mysterious markings represent constellations, ceremonial pathways, an astronomical calendar, or something quite different, we do not know. But one thing is fairly certain, and that is the absurdity of the ancient-airfield theory.

In both *The Space-Gods Revealed* (1976) and *Guardians of the Universe?* (1980), I gave reasons why the lines were probably *not* ancient landing strips, namely that: (1) there simply would be no need for a runway, several miles long, to accommodate a space vehicle that should be capable of a vertical landing, and (2) the soft, sandy soil would not be a suitable surface for any kind of heavy vehicle to land on.

Another version of the spaceport theory maintains that the exhaust from hovering spacecraft was responsible for blowing away the sand and thus creating the lines. Again, a nice try, but this idea would seem to prove just the opposite of what its proponents intend. It is not the lightweight soil that was removed to create the lines, but rather the heavier rocks, that are actually stacked in linear piles all along the borders of the lines and figures.

What then, could have been the purpose of such an enormous array of lines, shapes, and animal figures created more than a thousand years ago?

When Professor Paul Kosok of Long Island University first studied the lines, his most significant finding came not from his aerial surveys, but while he was standing on the ground gazing down one of the lines toward the setting sun on June 22, 1941. This happened to be the day of the winter solstice in the Southern Hemisphere; and the apparent alignment gave Kosok a startling idea:

perhaps the lines represented ''the largest astronomy book in the world.'' He later confirmed more than a dozen such alignments, some for the solstices and others for the equinoxes, indicating that the Nazca ''landing field'' very likely comprised a gigantic astronomical calendar and observatory. It has been found also that several of the large animal drawings have solstice lines associated with them. After all, how would the Nazcans be able to recognize which lines were which, if they had not devised some reference system by which to find them later?

Von Däniken and some others have rejected the Nazca calendar theory because, they say, not *all* of the lines have been shown to be astronomically oriented. We must realize, however, that this does not negate the fact of the many solstice lines that *have* been discovered. These also ''happen'' to be special lines marked prominently by certain bird, spider, and other animal figures.

The fact that *most* of the lines on the Nazca plain radiate from *central mounds* also appears significant, and fits logically with the theory that they were used as sightlines. Considering all the evidence, it seems likely that the Nazca markings were of astrological and astronomical significance.

—RONALD D. STORY

References

Hawkins, Gerald S. *Beyond Stonehenge* (Harper & Row, 1973).

Kosok, Paul. *Life, Land and Water in Ancient Peru* (Long Island University Press, 1965).

Kosok, Paul, and Maria Reiche. ''The Mysterious Markings of Nazca,'' *Natural History* (May 1947).

———. ''Ancient Drawings on the Desert of Peru,'' *Archaeology* (December 1949).

McIntyre, Loren. ''Mystery of the Ancient Nazca Lines,'' *National Geographic* (May 1975).

Morrison, Tony. *Pathways to the Gods* (Harper & Row, 1978).

Reiche, Maria. *Mystery on the Desert* (privately published, 1968).

Story, Ronald. *The Space-Gods Revealed* (Harper & Row, 1976; New English Library, 1977).

———. *Guardians of the Universe?* (New English Library/St. Martin's Press, 1980).

Von Däniken, Erich. *Chariots of the Gods?* (G. P. Putnam's Sons, 1970).

———. *Gods from Outer Space* (G.P. Putnam's Sons, 1971).

Williamson, George Hunt. *Road in the Sky* (Neville Spearman, 1959).

NDE (near-death experience)   This term is used to indicate an experience of conscious separation from the physical body under circumstances approaching the death and dying process. It is often associated with spiritual and transcendent visions, insights, and meetings with benevolent ET beings.

—SCOTT MANDELKER

NICAP   See NATIONAL INVESTIGATIONS COMMITTEE ON AERIAL PHENOMENA.

Nickell, Joe   (b. 1944). Dr. Nickell is a Senior Research Fellow of the Committee for the Scientific Investigation of Claims of the Paranormal (CSICOP). A full-time paranormal investigator, he has been called ''the real-life Scully'' (after the skeptical character in *The X-Files*). He worked professionally as a stage magician, private investigator, and journalist before returning to the University of Kentucky (1980–1995) to teach technical writing and to obtain a Ph.D. in English.

His articles have appeared in numerous magazines and journals, including *International UFO Reporter*—and he has authored (or co-authored or edited) sixteen books, including *Entities* (1995) and *The UFO Invasion* (1997). He has also appeared on numerous radio and television shows.

His contributions to UFOlogy include research relating to crop circles, the Nazca lines, the cultural evolution of the familiar humanoid-type extraterrestrial, and the experiences of alien abductees (seen primarily as ''waking dreams'' and hypnotic fantasies).

Address: c/o CSICOP
            P.O. Box 703
            Amherst, NY 14226
            U.S.A.

POSITION STATEMENT: Since the modern wave of UFO reports began in 1947, an elaborate extraterrestrial *mythos* has developed. Like other mythologies, it features supernormal beings interacting with humans and has implications to man's origins and place in the universe. Thus far a great quantity of evidence has accumulated relating to alien visitation, but it is unfortunately of very poor quality, consisting of dubious physical evidence and anecdotal reports that, when investigated, typically prove to be due to misperceptions and hoaxes.

Nevertheless, there remains a residue of unexplained cases which proponents and skeptics interpret quite differently. Proponents treat the residual cases as if—simply by being unsolved—they infer a paranormal cause. But that is, at best, a logical fallacy called "arguing from ignorance" and, at worst, mystery mongering. Skeptics may sometimes be too dismissive, but they correctly observe that incidents may be unexplained for various reasons, including insufficient, erroneous, or even falsified evidence—the same reasons that many crimes remain unsolved.

The appropriate response to reports of alien encounters is neither uncritical acceptance nor *a priori* dismissal. Rather, substantive cases should be carefully investigated in an attempt to solve them.

—Joe Nickell

Joe Nickell

No Earthly Explanation (Phillips Publishing, 1974). John Wallace Spencer proposes that UFO bases in the Earth's oceans use the Bermuda Triangle to snatch ships and planes for their experiments. These extraterrestrial colonizers absorb energy from the world's power lines and then leave a trail of confusing patterns of sightings to deceive human governments about the true nature of their mission.

No further study or serious attention should be given UFOs by the scientific community, Condon concluded, though his report admitted some UFO reports are difficult to explain by conventional means. In nearly all cases examined, the project staff found the persons who reported UFOs "to be normal, responsible individuals."

—Randall Fitzgerald

O

Oberg, James E. (b. 1944). Jim Oberg is a computer specialist by education (M.S. in computing science, University of New Mexico, 1972), served in the U.S. Air Force from 1970 to 1978, was a flight controller at NASA's Johnson Space Center in Houston, Texas, and since 1997 has been a full-time author.

He is a prolific science writer, having written numerous articles for popular science magazines in America and Europe, particularly *Astronomy* and *Omni*. He is also a principal member of the UFO Subcommittee of the Committee on the Scientific Investigation of Claims of the Paranormal. In 1979 he won the worldwide Cutty Sark UFO Essay Contest.

Address: Rt. 2, Box 350
             Dickinson, TX 77539
             U.S.A.

E-mail: JamesOberg@aol.com
Web site: www.JamesOberg.com

POSITION STATEMENT: The grossest source of error concerning popular ideas about UFOs remains the sensationalist news media and the pro-UFO groups whose research has been shown time and again to be superficial and biased. UFO believers pin their hopes on the "residue" of "unexplained sightings," perhaps 2 to 5 percent of the total, insisting that these cases are qualitatively different from those caused by terrestrial or otherwise "normal" stimuli.

Without more vigorous work, such a thesis cannot be accepted by anyone who considers all the facts. Generally, UFO writing which is not appallingly sloppy is in such an advocative mode that deliberate or unconscious distortions and omissions are commonplace. Until the serious UFO movement refuses to tolerate such low standards, any "real" UFOs which *might* represent anomalous phenomena or extraterrestrial visitors cannot be rigorously separated out from the overwhelming "noise." Until that happens, contemporary science is entirely justified in applying its energies elsewhere.

However, just in case there *is* something to be learned from the "UFO phenomenon," I support the work of such UFO research groups as CUFOS; and I shall endeavor to correct any straying which I detect from scientific standards, considering myself a sympathetic critic who really *hopes* that science can advance because of discoveries made via UFO research. It is not a view based on rational observation of the results of the first thirty years of so-called "UFO research," but, rather, a judgment similar in nature to that exemplified by the words of Samuel Johnson, quoted by Boswell, in a comment upon a friend's remarriage: "Ahh, the triumph of hope over experience!"

—JAMES E. OBERG

occult connection with UFOs and ET encounters

The relationship between occultism and UFO/extraterrestrial encounters may be ambiguous and difficult to decipher—but is certain, nonetheless. Long before the modern age of "flying saucers" began, related—and often identical—phenomena were known to mystical adepts.

Over the millennia, the secret canons of numerous secret societies have alluded to visitors from "elsewhere." More often than not, the preponderance of "extraterrestrialism" in arcane studies tends to present itself on psychic, spiritual, and/or mediumistic levels. Two exquisite examples are Emanuel Swedenborg (1688-1772) and Hélène Smith (1861-1930).

The former asserted that he was not only conceptually and telepathically in touch with God and the angels, but with creatures of other planets as well. The latter was in contact with entities from Mars, whom she described as ". . . people exactly like the inhabitants of our earth, save that both sexes wore the same costume. . . ." (Flournoy, 1899) She related her psychic transmigrations to the red sphere in diaries composed in fluent "Martian," which no one, other than herself, could decode.

The last great magus Aleister Crowley is said to have had in his employ, at one time, a scientist who had contact with Kenneth Arnold. So far this writer has been unable to authenticate this contention, although like names are to be found in both contexts.

Certain New Age sects have claimed spiritual liaison with "poly-planet" masters of infinite knowledge and wisdom, but often seem to reflect misconceptions of South Asian mysticism more than anything else; though similarities can still be seen with such saucerological mentors as Van Tassel's "Council of the Seven Lights" and Angelucci's spiritual "Overlords."

Psychic reciprocity is frequent in much of saucerdom and UFOlogy; and almost all of alienology is permeated with telepathy, clairvoyance, clairaudience, and precognition with some telekinesis thrown in. Apportation, teleportation, astral projection, and prophecy often enter the picture as well, completing the connection with occultism.

Gloria Lee (Byrd), one of the better-known minor contactees, found her way into that odd realm only by virtue of her solely telepathic rapport with Jupertarians (Jovians).

The connection between these two worlds is one of the most uninvestigated dimensions of UFOlogy, but possibly could be among the most fruitful. Unfortunately, even a cursory examination of this strange interplay requires a solid foundation in both saucer lore and the *outré*—a rare combination in scholars of the improbable.

—PARIS FLAMMONDE

References

Flournoy, Théodore. *From India to the Planet Mars* (Princeton University Press, 1994). Originally published in 1899.

Spence, Lewis. *Encyclopedia of Occultism* (University Books, 1960). Originally published in 1920.

Omega Project, The (William Morrow, 1992). Psychology professor Kenneth Ring spent ten years studying near-death experiences and then read *Communion* by Whitley Strieber, which convinced him that numerous similarities exist between near-death and UFO encounters. In a survey of several hundred people reporting UFO and near-death episodes, Ring found no evidence such people had fantasy-prone personalities, yet he did find a pattern of them reporting much higher than normal incidences of childhood abuse, trauma, and serious illnesses.

—RANDALL FITZGERALD

One Hundred Thousand Years of Man's Unknown History (Editions Robert Laffont, 1963). Robert Charroux proposes that secret societies, such as the Freemasons, preserve evidence that Atlantis was an extraterrestrial colony. Using Incan and other traditions, this Frenchman tries to make a case that beings from Venus colonized Central America and mated with the humans found there.

—RANDALL FITZGERALD

Operation Mainbrace sightings A particularly interesting series of UFO reports came from the vicinity of the "Operation Mainbrace" NATO maneuvers held in September 1952. The maneuvers commenced September 13 and lasted twelve days. According to the U. S. Navy, units of eight NATO governments and New Zealand participated, including 80,000 men, 1,000 planes, and 200 ships in the vicinity of Denmark and Norway. Directed by British Admiral Sir Patrick Brind, it was the largest NATO maneuver held up until that time.

September 13—The Danish destroyer *Wil-*

lemoes. participating in the maneuvers, was north of Bornholm Island. During the night, Lieutenant Commander Schmidt Jensen and several members of the crew saw an unidentified object, triangular in shape, which moved at high speed toward the southeast. The object emitted a bluish glow. Commander Jensen estimated the speed at over 900 mph.

Within the next week, there were four important sightings by well-qualified observers. (Various sources differ by a day or two on the exact dates, but agree on details. There is no question about the authenticity of the sightings; the British cases were officially reported by the Air Ministry, the others are confirmed by reliable sources. All occurred on or about September 20.)

September 19—A British Meteor jet aircraft was returning to the airfield at Topcliffe, Yorkshire, England, just before 11 A.M. As it approached for landing, a silvery object was observed following it, swaying back and forth like a pendulum. Lieutenant John W. Kilburn and other observers on the ground said that when the Meteor began circling, the UFO stopped. It was disk-shaped, and rotated on its axis while hovering. The disk suddenly took off westward at high speed, changed course, and disappeared to the southeast.

About September 20—Personnel of the U.S.S. *Franklin D. Roosevelt,* an aircraft carrier participating in the Mainbrace maneuvers, observed a silvery, spherical object which was also photographed. (The pictures have never been made public.) The UFO was seen moving across the sky behind the fleet. Reporter Wallace Litwin took a series of color photographs, which were examined by Navy Intelligence officers. The Air Force project chief, Captain Ruppelt stated: "[The pictures] turned out to be excellent. Judging by the size of the object in each successive photo, one could see that it was moving rapidly." The possibility that a balloon had been launched from one of the ships was immediately checked out. No unit had launched a balloon. A poor print of one of the photographs appears in the Project Blue Book files, but with no analysis report.

September 20—At Karup Field, Denmark, three Danish Air Force officers sighted a UFO about 7:30 P.M. The object, a shiny disk with metallic appearance, passed overhead from the direction of the fleet and disappeared in clouds to the east.

September 21—Six British pilots flying a formation of RAF jets above the North Sea observed a shiny sphere approaching from the direction of the fleet. The UFO eluded their pursuit and disappeared. When returning to base, one of the pilots looked back and saw the UFO following him. He turned to chase it, but the UFO also turned and sped away.

September 27/28—Throughout Western Germany, Denmark, and southern Sweden, there were widespread UFO reports. A brightly luminous object with a comet-like tail was visible for a long period of time moving irregularly near Hamburg and Kiel. On one occasion, three satellite objects were reported moving around a larger object. A cigar-shaped object moving silently eastward also was reported.

Since existing documentation shows that U.S. Navy and Air Force Intelligence, and the RAF, were studying these incidents, it is a safe assumption that more information exists in the files of NATO, the British Air Ministry, the U.S. Navy, and the U.S. Air Force. The sightings remain unexplained.

—RICHARD HALL

OBE (out-of-body experience)   Like the NDE, this is also an experience of conscious separation from the physical body while retaining full or partial awareness. OBEs are responsible for a significant portion of ET contact events, and many contactees with spiritual messages claim to have been given their teachings by ETs while in an out-of-body state. There are many mystic practices, especially in the Hindu and Buddhist traditions, that train the practitioner to achieve conscious out-of-body travel.

—SCOTT MANDELKER

P

Palenque "astronaut" In the ancient Maya city of Palenque (on the Yucatan Peninsula, in the state of Chiapas, Mexico) stands a seventy-foot-high limestone pyramid called the Temple of the Inscriptions. Until 1949, the interior of the structure had remained unexplored. But when the Mexican archaeologist Alberto Ruz Lhuillier noticed finger-holes in one of the large floor-slabs, he raised the stone and discovered a hidden stairway that had been deliberately filled in, centuries ago, with stone rubble and clay. After four years of clearing away the blockage, Ruz and his workers had descended sixty-five feet into the pyramid, where he came upon a secret tomb. Little did Ruz know that twenty years later this discovery would be used as one of the "proofs" of the existence of ancient astronauts.

What has attracted the attention of ancient-astronaut proponents is the stone carving that decorates the tomb lid. Erich von Däniken describes it this way: "On the slab [covering the tomb is] a wonderful chiseled relief. In my eyes, you can see a kind of frame. In the center of that frame is a man sitting, bending forward. He has a mask on his nose, he uses his two hands to manipulate some controls, and the heel of his left foot is on a kind of pedal with different adjustments. The rear portion is separated from him; he is sitting on a complicated chair, and outside of this whole frame you see a little flame like an exhaust."

Could it be that the Palenque tomb lid actually depicts a man piloting a rocket? The notion becomes less plausible once the various elements that make up the overall design are examined separately, in detail. Notice first that the "astronaut" is not wearing a space suit, but is practically naked. The man in this scene is barefoot, does not wear gloves (both finger-nails and toenails are illustrated), and is outfitted in nothing more than a decorative loin-cloth and jewelry. In other words, he is dressed in typical style, characteristic of the Maya nobility as to be expected at around A.D. 700. Actually, this is the tomb of the Maya king Lord-Shield Pacal, who died in A.D. 683.

The details of his royal history are well established. The glyphs carved on the frame of

the sarcophagus lid, as well as other glyphic evidence found in other temples at the Palenque site, trace his ancestry and give the exact dates of when he was born, when he ruled, and when he died. When the illustration on Pacal's tomb lid is oriented vertically instead of horizontally, we can see that the "rocket" is actually a composite art form incorporating the design of a cross, a two-headed serpent, and some large corn leaves. The "oxygen mask" is an ornament that does not connect with the nostrils, but rather seems to touch the tip of Pacal's nose; the "controls" are not really associated with the hands, but are elements from a profile view of the Maya Sun God in the background; the "pedal" operated by the "astronaut's" foot is a seashell (a Maya symbol associated with death); and the "rocket's exhaust" is very likely the roots of the sacred maize tree (the cross), which is symbolic of the life-sustaining corn plant. The whole scene is a religious illustration, not a technological one, and is well understood within the proper context of Maya art.

—RONALD D. STORY

References

Story, Ronald. *The Space-Gods Revealed* (Harper & Row/New English Library, 1976).
———. *Guardians of the Universe?* (St. Martin's Press/New English Library, 1980).
Von Däniken, Erich. *Chariots of the Gods?* (Souvenir Press, 1969; G. P. Putnam's Sons, 1970).

Palmer, Raymond A. (1911-77). Ray Palmer or R. A. P., as he usually signed his editorials, was the original UFO buff. In his book *The World of Flying Saucers* (1963), skeptic Donald Menzel called flying saucers virtually a Palmer creation. While that is something of an exaggeration, Palmer's enormous influence on the early history of UFOlogy can hardly be underestimated. Yet, by the 1970s his name was little known beyond the small circle of hard-core buffs. David M. Jacobs's *The UFO Controversy in America* (1975), which is generally considered to be a fairly complete UFO history up through 1974, mentions him only in a footnote. What happened?

Part of the problem lay in Palmer's wild and unpredictable imagination. He was likely to say or do practically anything and would not be contained by prudence or respectability. Then there was his sense of humor. He left even his admirers with the uncomfortable feeling that he might be pulling their leg. In the 1960s, UFOlogist Jim Moseley made a pilgrimage to the Wisconsin farm on which Palmer spent most of his later years. Palmer asked Moseley rhetorically, "What if I told you it was all a joke?" In a speech to a UFOlogical convention in Chicago shortly before his death in 1977, Palmer warned his audience not to believe everything he said. Serious UFOlogists had a lot of trouble with his attitude, and they often tried to pretend that Ray Palmer did not exist at all. But he did.

As a child, Palmer suffered severe injuries, which left him dwarfed in stature and partially crippled, but he never allowed these handicaps to stop him. In the 1930s and 1940s Palmer was editor of *Amazing Stories* and *Fantastic Adventures.* two of America's bestselling science fiction magazines.

Each issue of the magazines began with a long editorial by Palmer, which was often more imaginative than the stories it was supposed to introduce! In 1944 there was what John A. Keel has called "a significant prelude to the 1947 flap." *Amazing Stories* published a tale called "I Remember Lemuria," written by a Pennsylvania welder by the name of Richard S. Shaver. Shaver told of a secret underground world peopled by Deros (detrimental robots), who caused most of the world's troubles by controlling men's minds with rays projected from their underground caverns.

According to Keel, "Palmer was amazed when he was buried under thousands of letters from people claiming they, too, had experiences with the Dero and that Shaver was telling the truth." Keel may be overstating the reaction, but "I Remember Lemuria" did get a great deal of attention from readers. Several other stories about this underground world were published under Shaver's byline, though they were heavily written by Palmer, whose writing style was unmistakable. Palmer even devoted an entire issue of *Amazing Stories* to what he called "the Shaver Mystery." Palmer no longer said these underground-world stories were fictitious; now he claimed that they were products of Shaver's "racial memory."

While "the Shaver Mystery" temporarily upped the sales of Palmer-edited publications, they did not find favor with all science fiction fans. Many began referring to the series as "the Shaver Hoax."

Palmer was one of many who was intrigued by Kenneth Arnold's reported sighting of a "flying saucer" on June 24, 1947. He wrote about flying saucers in his editorials. But Ziff-Davis, the publishers of *Amazing Stories* and *Fantastic Adventures,* were not nearly as enthusiastic. They were stung by the "Shaver Hoax" criticism and disturbed by some of Palmer's activities on behalf of flying saucers, and, besides, sales were not what they had hoped. In 1948, Palmer left Ziff-Davis in a disagreement over an all-UFO issue.

That same year, in conjunction with Curtis Fuller, he started *Fate* magazine, a publication devoted to the exploration of strange phenomena. The first issue contained a bylined article by Arnold, defending his flying saucer sighting from criticism and ridicule.

During this same period, Palmer became involved with the most controversial incident in his UFOlogical career, the Maury Island hoax. Two men, Harold Dahl and Fred Crisman, claimed that they had seen a flock of flying saucers while boating off Maury Island, near Tacoma, Washington, in June 1947. They got in touch with Palmer, who sent no other than Kenneth Arnold out to investigate. Arnold thought the story was too big for him, and he contacted the Air Force. Two intelligence officers were sent to interview Crisman and Dahl. On their return flight, their plane crashed and both were killed.

An investigation of the crash found nothing out of the ordinary and concluded that the entire Maury Island incident was a hoax. The investigation also concluded that Palmer had actually encouraged the hoax and was, indirectly at least, responsible for the death of the two officers. Palmer put a different interpretation on the incident. He hinted darkly at some sort of "cover-up" and "conspiracy" and said that he wanted "no more blood on his hands." This was the first or one of the first times that the "conspiracy of silence" theme was injected into UFOlogical thinking.

In the early 1950s, Palmer moved to Amherst, Wisconsin, sold his interest in *Fate,* and started his own publishing company. For years he put out a bewildering variety of books and periodicals, many on occult or other "borderland" subjects. Most of Palmer's ventures were only marginally profitable. His most successful and longest-lived periodical was *Flying Saucers.* While this magazine never had a circulation that exceeded a few thousand, it was, for many years, the largest-circulation American magazine dealing exclusively with the subject.

Early on, Palmer himself had abandoned the mundane idea that UFOs came from outer space. He actively promoted the theory that UFOs came from the Shaverian underground world, and that they flew out of the "Hollow Earth" through holes at the North and South Poles.

Though the UFOs from the hollow Earth idea never really caught on, Palmer's influence on the popularity of UFOs in America was enormous. He was the subject's earliest and most consistent publicist. Through *Fate,* and later *Flying Saucers,* he continued to print UFO reports at times when it seemed that practically everyone else had lost interest.

Ray Palmer died on August 15, 1977.

—DANIEL COHEN

Paradox: The Case for the Extraterrestrial Origin of Man (Crown, 1977). Irish archaeologist John Philip Cohane believes *Homo sapiens* are descended directly from extraterrestrial colonists who genetically manipulated apes. He bases this conclusion primarily on two observations: inadequate fossil records to indicate an evolutionary link between humans and apes; and humans are "too spiritually refined" to be related to other primates.

—RANDALL FITZGERALD

Parallel Time Line The time line which follows (pp. 403-417) is intended to show the history of UFOlogy and SETI (the search for extraterrestrial intelligence) in context with developments in science and technology, and other world events, as well as the symbiotic relationship between UFO-ET events and science fiction.

Notably absent are new and exciting developments in the world's religions, whereas the opposite is true in the joint-category of science and technology.

It is also notable that developments in science have probably influenced the UFO mythology as much as, or possibly even more so, than science fiction.

—MARTIN S. KOTTMEYER
& RONALD D. STORY

References

Cooke, Jean, Ann Kramer, and Theodore Rowland-Entwistle. *History's Timeline* (Barnes & Noble Books, 1996).

Engelbert, Phillis, and Diane L. Dupuis. *The Handy Space Answer Book* (Visible Ink Press, 1998).

Flammonde, Paris. *UFO Exist!* (Ballantine, 1976).

Gribbin, John, ed. *A Brief History of Science* (Barnes & Noble, 1998).

Hall, Richard. "Chronology of Important Events in UFO History" in Story, Ronald D., ed. *The Encyclopedia of UFOs* (Doubleday/New English Library, 1980).

Hellemans, Alexander, and Bryan Bunch. *The Timetables of Science* (Simon & Schuster, 1988).

Imhoff, Susan, Ailbhe MacShamhráin, Richard Killeen, et al. *Timelines of World History* (Quadrillion Publishing/CLB, 1998).

Stein, Werner, Bernard Grun, et al. *The Timetables of History* (Simon & Schuster, 1979).

Story, Ronald D., ed. *The Encyclopedia of UFOs* (Doubleday/New English Library, 1980).

Time Almanac 2000 (Information Please, 2000).

Time: Great Images of the 20th Century (Time-Life Books, 1999).

Time magazine (Fall 1992) special issue. Research by Deborah Wells and Ratu Kamlani.

Trench, Brinsley Le Poer. *The Flying Saucer Story* (Ace, 1966).

Urdang, Laurence, ed. *The Timetables of American History* (Simon & Schuster, 1981).

Vallée, Jacques. *Anatomy of a Phenomenon* (Ace, 1965).

World Events: 1000 Events That Changed the World (Rand McNally, 2000).

paranoia and UFOs Is UFOlogy a species of paranoia? In common usage, paranoia is exemplified by individuals who believe that others are persecuting or spying on them. Such people will describe events and point to evidence that some sort of covert plot is being directed against them. For those confronted with making judgment on these beliefs, the issue is generally one of the individual's interpretation rather than his facticity. The evidence is real enough, but is the interpretation valid, or is the person applying, in Jacques Lacan's phrase, "a novel form of syntax" in expressing his experience of the world? The paranoid's experience of the bond of the human community is troubled, and there is a resultant distortion of his style of thought, with inflation in the significance of trivial things in the environment. A torn letter is taken as evidence of CIA surveillance. That the letter is junk mail is a criticism that will only temporarily faze his confidence in the general frame of his beliefs. The disparity between the strangeness of the claim and triviality of the proof, so striking to the onlooker, is ignored in the need to believe that some power is intent on subverting his life. (Clement, 1983)

In this most common sense, UFOlogy should have been recognized as a manifestation of the paranoid style of thought decades ago. Amid the silly political ploys of UFOlogists like Richard Haines to gerrymander solved UFO reports out of existence by linguistic fiat, it is easy to lose sight of the fact that the U in UFO stands for "unidentified," not "unexplained." (Haines, 1987) The word contains an important connotation and suggests a presumption. The flying object has not provided identification of itself. No radio contact. No flight plan. Remember, the term was introduced by the U.S. Air Force. The initial suspicion was that Russian spycraft were breaching U.S. security for unknown ends. The escalation of the hypothesis to suspicion of extraterrestrial reconnaissance retained the presumption of a furtive spying intelligence. The manner of presentation of their reality never made great sense, and the Air Force eventually stated that UFOs were not a direct threat to U.S. security. Time has fully borne out that judgment. Civilian UFO investigators, however, argued that even one unsolved UFO report held enormous implications and continued to entertain the interpretation of UFOs as evidence of extraterrestrial visitation.

Apart from the hoaxes, the physical evidence used to argue UFO reality is as trivial as the things used to support the more personal delusions of other paranoids—lost rings, dimming lights, mechanical failures, unexplained medical ailments, overinterpreted photographs, etc. UFOs never melt cars into radioactive puddles, snatch up football stadiums, invert amino acid in victims, or leave behind slabs of multiquark strong force adaptors when they crash. In short, there is nothing that requires an extramundane explanation. This is not to say that there is always an obvious mundane solution, but even less airy paranoids can ask questions hard to answer. Commonsense arguments directed at the strangeness of the frame of belief are generally dismissed. The problem of noncontact, first advanced by the father of UFOlogy himself, Charles Fort, has been termed a debunker's ploy to subvert UFO research or merely labeled irrelevant.

No one would question that this or that individual UFOlogist is paranoid, but the collective enterprise has somehow managed to escape the notice of the diagnosticians. By faulting the reality-testing processes of UFOlogy, orthodox science has implicitly exiled it among the psychoses. (Frosch, 1983) It never

bothered to explain the UFOlogists' delusion, however. The oversight is regrettable at least from the humanitarian point of view that one should try to understand those he opposes and gain, if not empathy, perspective and depth. But science has also missed the philosophical pleasure of forming an esthetic gestalt of the history of UFO belief.

The exercise in taxonomy does not result merely in a descriptive conclusion. The realization that UFOlogy is a species of paranoia means that the psychological literature on paranoia will provide insights into the dynamics of UFO belief. Certainly, the most intriguing fruit yielded by a consideration of the clinical profile of paranoia is the discovery that paranoid beliefs are not static facets of personality. They evolve. In fact, paranoia follows a well-defined progression that is remarkable in the "almost monotonous regularity" of its development. It advances through a series of stages that begins with shame and ends in delusions of grandeur.

The full schematic runs as follows:

- A precipitation factor—a social setback or a slight or humiliation
- A sensitivity to external contacts
- An asocial withdrawal of some kind
- Subjective preoccupations
- Hypochondriasis—the search for medical verification of illness and failure to find it
- Increased concern, even obsession, with bodily functions
- Increasing worry—Why? What? When?
- Irrational revelation—the formulation of a manufactured insight into how the illness happened
- Somatic delusions and retrospective falsification of the origins of the physical complaint
- Projection—the belief the illness is caused by an external factor
- Systematization of the delusion, clarification, shift of anxiety and consequent reintegration of personality
- Conspiracy logic (interpretation of events as links in a conspiracy) with a widening circle of persecutors worldwide

SECOND WORLD WAR

	UFOLOGY & SETI	SCIENCE & TECHNOLOGY	SCIENCE FICTION	POLITICS & RELIGION
UFOLOGY & SETI	**1941** Publication of *The Books of Charles Fort* (the complete "nonfiction" works of Charles Fort)	**1942** First "foo fighters" were reported by RAF pilots over France	**1943** More small UFOs called "foo fighters" were seen by military pilots over Germany and Japan	**1944** Sightings of foo fighters were made public for the first time
SCIENCE & TECHNOLOGY	**1941** "Manhattan Project" (intensive atomic research) begins	**1942** Erico Fermi (U.S.) splits the atom: first nuclear chain reaction; Bell Aircraft tests the first U.S. jet plane	**1943** Penicillin is successfully used in the treatment of chronic diseases; Alan Turing (in the U.K.) designs "Colossus" computer	**1944** U.S. builds uranium pile at Clinton, Tennessee
SCIENCE FICTION	**1941** "Nightfall" by Isaac Asimov is published in *Astounding* magazine	**1942** *Foundation* series by Isaac Asimov is launched in *Astounding* magazine	**1943** Publication of *Donovan's Brain* by Curt Siodmak	**1944** Publication of *Sirius* by Olaf Stapledon; Publication of "Deadline" by Cleve Cartmill in *Astounding*
POLITICS & RELIGION	**1941** U.S. enters the Second World War, following the Japanese attack on Pearl Harbor	**1942** Chinese "Great Leap Forward" leads to mass starvation	**1943** President Franklin Delano Roosevelt freezes prices, salaries, and wages to prevent inflation	**1944** V-2 rockets are used to bomb London; The Allies invade northern Europe on D-Day

BEGINNING OF THE ATOMIC AGE

UFOLOGY & SETI			
1945 Raymond Palmer, editor of *Amazing Stories*, publishes as fact the Richard Shaver stories of furtive aliens with flying machines	**1946** Mysterious "ghost rockets" are reported in the skies over Scandinavian countries	**1947** Kenneth Arnold reports nine mysterious flying objects passing over Mt. Rainier in Washington State; USAF Project Sign is established	**1948** F-51 pilot, Capt. Thomas Mantell, crashes plane and is killed while chasing a giant UFO over Ft. Knox, Kentucky

SCIENCE & TECHNOLOGY			
1945 U.S. explodes first Atomic Bomb at Trinity Site, near Alamogordo, New Mexico	**1946** ENIAC computer built at the University of Pennsylvania	**1947** U.S. scientists at Bell laboratories invent the transistor; First human breaks the sound barrier in a U.S. rocket plane	**1948** 200-inch telescope on Mt. Palomar is dedicated (then largest in the world); USAF Project Blue Book is initiated

SCIENCE FICTION			
1945 Serial: "The Purple Monster Strikes," later retitled *D-Day on Mars* (1966)	**1946** H.G. Wells dies (b. 1866)	**1947** Publication of *Pilgrims Through Space and Time* by J.O. Bailey	**1948** "Superman" serial with Kirk Alyn (*Superman* comics started in 1938)

POLITICS & RELIGION			
1945 U.S. drops atomic bombs on Hiroshima and Nagasaki, Japan Second World War ends	**1946** President Truman creates the Atomic Energy Commission	**1947** U.S. President Truman declares communism an insidious world menace and institutes loyalty review program	**1948** Gandhi is assassinated (b. 1869) The State of Israel is established

THE COLD WAR & THE ATOMIC AGE

UFOLOGY & SETI			
1949 Mysterious green fireballs are seen in the skies of New Mexico; Project Twinkle is set up; Project Sign becomes Project Grudge	**1950** Publication of *The Flying Saucers are Real* by Donald Keyhoe; heyday of stories about "little men" retrieved from flying saucers	**1951** Project Grudge becomes Project Blue Book	**1952** Peak year for UFO reports; UFOs are tracked over Washington, D.C.; APRO is founded by Coral and Jim Lorenzen

SCIENCE & TECHNOLOGY			
1949 Soviet Union explodes its first atomic bomb; U.S. rocket is developed that can reach beyond Earth's atmosphere	**1950** First embryo transplants are performed on cattle	**1951** Experimental breeder reactor is built near Idaho Falls, Idaho	**1952** British doctor Douglas Bevis develops amniocentesis, a method of examining the fetus while still in the womb

SCIENCE FICTION			
1949 Publication of *1984* by George Orwell; "Captain Video" appears on TV	**1950** Movie: *The Flying Saucer;* "Tom Corbett, Space Cadet" appears on TV	**1951** Movies: *The Day the Earth Stood Still; The Man from Planet X;* and *The Thing*	**1952** Movie: *Red Planet Mars;* Publication of "The Martian Way" by Isaac Asimov

POLITICS & RELIGION			
1949 NATO (North Atlantic Treaty Organization) is created by Western nations as a common defense against the Soviet Union	**1950** Korean War begins; U.S. President Harry Truman approves development of hydrogen bomb	**1951** North Korean forces take Seoul and reject truce; U.S. forces capture "Heartbreak Ridge"	**1952** Winston Churchill announces that Britain has an atomic bomb; Truman announces H-bomb tests in the Pacific

THE COLD WAR & THE ATOMIC AGE

UFOLOGY & SETI	SCIENCE & TECHNOLOGY	SCIENCE FICTION	POLITICS & RELIGION
1953 CIA sponsors the Robertson Panel; two military fliers disappear while chasing a UFO over Lake Superior (Kinross case)	**1954** French humanoid wave	**1955** UFO creatures invade Sutton family near Hopkinsville, Kentucky	**1956** UFO reported at close range by police officers near Red Bluff, California; NICAP is founded in Washington, D.C.
1953 James Watson and Francis Crick discover double-helix structure of DNA	**1954** The U.S.S.R. builds its first nuclear reactor for peacetime use; the first atomic submarine, the U.S.S. *Nautilus*, is commissioned	**1955** Christopher Cockerell develops the first practical hovercraft	**1956** DNA is synthesized; amniocentesis is practiced in England; first aerial H-bomb is exploded over Bikini Atoll
1953 Movies: *Invaders from Mars*; *It Came from Outer Space*; and *The War of the Worlds*; *Superman* TV series starring George Reeves	**1954** Movies: *Killers from Space* and *Them!*	**1955** Movies: *This Island Earth* and *Devil Girl from Mars*	**1956** Movies: *Earth vs. the Flying Saucers*; *Forbidden Planet*; and *The Invasion of the Body Snatchers*
1953 Eisenhower is inaugurated as President of the U.S.; U.S.S.R. announces H-bomb test	**1954** Joseph McCarthy hearings and "witch hunt" activities result in his formal censure and condemnation by the U.S. Senate	**1955** Warsaw Pact is made between the U.S.S.R. and eastern Europe, aligning them against the NATO countries of the West	**1956** Dwight Eisenhower is re-elected President of the U.S.; in the U.S.S.R., Nikita Khrushchev denounces Joseph Stalin

THE COLD WAR & THE SPACE AGE

UFOLOGY & SETI			
1957 UFOs land near Levelland, Texas; other UFOs reported in the skies of New Mexico and west Texas	**1958** UFO photographed near Trindade Island, off the coast of Brazil	**1959** UFO with occupants observed by multiple witnesses at Boianai, New Guinea (Gill case)	**1960** UFO reported at close range by police officers near Red Bluff, California; Project Ozma is initiated by radio astronomer Frank Drake

SCIENCE & TECHNOLOGY			
1957 U.S.S.R. launches *Sputnik I*, the Earth's first artificial satellite (marking the beginning of the Space Age)	**1958** U.S. launches its first satellite, *Explorer I*; U.S.S.R. launches *Sputnik III*	**1959** U.S.S.R. reaches Moon with *Luna III* and photographs the Moon's far side	**1960** U.S. develops laser device

SCIENCE FICTION			
1957 Movie: *Invasion of the Saucer Men*; Book: *The Black Cloud* by Fred Hoyle	**1958** Movies: *The Blob, I Married a Monster from Outer Space*; *Plan Nine from Outer Space*; and *The Space Children*	**1959** Movie: *The Mysterians*; TV series: *The Twilight Zone*; Book: *The Sirens of Titan* by Kurt Vonnegut	**1960** Movies: *The Village of the Damned* and *The Time Machine*; TV: *The Twilight Zone*

POLITICS & RELIGION			
1957 Gromyko becomes U.S.S.R. Foreign Minister	**1958** Khrushchev becomes Chairman of Council of U.S.S.R. Ministers	**1959** Fidel Castro takes over Cuba as former Cuban President Batista resigns and flees	**1960** Brezhnev becomes President of the U.S.S.R.; John F. Kennedy is elected President of the United States

THE SPACE AGE AND THE ARMS RACE

UFOLOGY & SETI			
1961 Hill couple is allegedly abducted by UFO-aliens in New Hampshire; first conference on SETI is held at Green Bank in the U.S.	**1962** U.S. astronauts began seeing and photographing UFOs in space, all of which turned out to have prosaic explanations	**1963** Wave of "monster" sightings takes place in South America and Great Britain, which were associated with UFOs	**1964** Deputy Lonnie Zamora reports UFO landing near Socorro, New Mexico; R. H. Hall's *The UFO Evidence* is published by NICAP

SCIENCE & TECHNOLOGY			
1961 Soviets send the first human, Yuri Gagarin, into space; the following month, the U.S. sends Alan Shepard into space	**1962** Publication of *Silent Spring* by U.S. marine biologist Rachel Carson	**1963** The tranquilizer Valium is introduced	**1964** Scientists prove that the sequence of nucleotides in DNA corresponds exactly to the sequence of amino acids in proteins

SCIENCE FICTION			
1961 Movie: *Planets Against Us*; Books: *Stranger in a Strange Land* by Robert Heinlein; *Solaris* by Stanislaw Lem	**1962** Movie: *Invasion of the Star Creatures* and *The Manchurian Candidate*; TV series: *The Jetsons*	**1963** Movie: *Dr. Strangelove*; Book: *Planet of the Apes* by Pierre Boulle; TV: *Dr. Who*; *The Outer Limits*; *My Favorite Martian*	**1964** Movies: *Attack from Space* and *Mutiny in Outer Space*; *First Men in the Moon*; Television: *The Invaders*; *Johnny Quest*

POLITICS & RELIGION			
1961 John F. Kennedy is inaugurated as youngest President of the U.S.; The Berlin Wall is constructed	**1962** Cuban missile crisis: U.S.S.R. removes nuclear missiles from Cuba in exchange for U.S. removal of missiles from Turkey	**1963** President John F. Kennedy is assassinated; Lyndon Johnson is sworn in as President of the U.S.	**1964** U.S. destroyer is allegedy attacked off the coast of N. Vietnam; U.S. aircraft attack N. Vietnam bases in reprisal: Vietnam War escalates

THE SPACE AGE & THE ARMS RACE

UFOLOGY & SETI			
1965 UFO reports occur in and around Exeter, New Hampshire; UFO with occupants reportedly lands near Valensole, France	**1966** UFOs are reported near Ann Arbor, Michigan; Dr. J. Allen Hynek offers "swamp gas" explanation (infamous media event)	**1967** U.S. Air Force commissions the University of Colorado (Condon) Study of UFOs; man in Canada is burned by a landed UFO (Michalak case)	**1968** UFO reports are confirmed in the Soviet Union; U.S. House Committee on Science and Astronautics Symposium on UFOs is held

SCIENCE & TECHNOLOGY			
1965 U.S. space probe, *Mariner IV*, sends back first close-up pictures of the planet Mars; first communications satellite is placed in Earth orbit	**1966** The Soviet space probe *Luna IX* makes the first successful soft landing on the moon	**1967** South African surgeon Christiaan Barnard performs the first successful human heart transplant	**1968** Apollo 8 astronauts orbit the moon; Earthrise is seen for the first time from the moon; water molecules are discovered in space

SCIENCE FICTION			
1965 Movies: *The Planet of the Vampires*; *Frankenstein Meets the Space Monster*; TV: *Lost in Space*	**1966** Movie: *Zontar, The Thing from Venus*; TV: *Star Trek* and *Space Ghost*	**1967** Movies: *Barbarella; Five Million Years to Earth*; TV: *The Herculoids*	**1968** Movies: *2001: A Space Odyssey* and *Planet of the Apes*; TV: *The Prisoner*

POLITICS & RELIGION			
1965 Lyndon Johnson is inaugurated as President of the U.S.	**1966** Pope Paul VI issues encyclical on Vietnam War	**1967** Civil war erupts in Nigeria; War, as usual, between Arabs and Israelis; a temporary cease-fire is arranged by the United Nations	**1968** Martin Luther King is assassinated; Moscow overthrows liberal regime in Czechoslovakia

YEARS OF RISING EXPECTATIONS

UFOLOGY & SETI			
1969 The Condon Report is publicly released; Project Blue Book shuts down; Walter Andrus leaves APRO to form MUFON	**1970** Interest in UFOs drops off sharply; Amino acids are discovered in the Murchison meteorite	**1971** Claims of alien implants begin following bedroom visitations by UFO abductors; First international SETI conference held in Armenia	**1972** CUFOS is founded by Dr. J. Allen Hynek

SCIENCE & TECHNOLOGY			
1969 Men land on the moon: U.S. astronauts Neil Armstrong and "Buzz" Aldrin land and walk on the moon	**1970** University of Wisconsin researchers synthesize a gene	**1971** Godfrey Hounsfield invents the CAT scan, which gives a 3-D image of the brain; *Mariner IX* orbits Mars; first "black hole" is detected	**1972** U.S. bans DDT because of adverse effects on the environment

SCIENCE FICTION			
1969 Movie: *Alien Women*	**1970** TV: Gerry Anderson's *UFO*	**1971** Movie: *The Andromeda Strain*; Book: *Ultimate World* by Hugo Gernsback (posthumously published)	**1972** Movies: *Eyes Behind the Stars and Slaughterhouse 5*; Book: *Star Diaries* by Stanislaw Lem

POLITICS & RELIGION			
1969 Widespread civil "unrest" in Northern Ireland; Britain sends troops	**1970** Vietnam War spreads to Laos and Cambodia	**1971** Communist China joins the United Nations; Taiwan (Formosa) is expelled	**1972** Watergate break-in; Britain takes over direct rule of Northern Ireland

YEARS OF DISILLUSIONMENT

UFOLOGY & SETI			
1973 Pascagoula abduction claim and American humanoid wave boosts popularity of UFOs and alien visitors	**1974** The Avis family allegedly abducted by UFO-aliens as they drove their car into a bank of mist, near Aveley, Essex, England	**1975** Charles Moody and Travis Walton abduction claims are publicized in the *National Enquirer* and elsewhere	**1976** Tehran, Iran, jet chase; U.S. *Viking I* and *Viking II* land on Mars but find no life

SCIENCE & TECHNOLOGY			
1973 Cohen and Boyer insert a gene from a toad into bacterial DNA, where it begins to work. This marks the beginning of genetic engineering	**1974** A Soviet space-probe lands on Mars; *Australopithecus afarensis* (a 3.2-million-year- old human ancestor) is discovered in Ethiopia	**1975** Scientists hold international meeting to establish guidelines for recombinant-DNA research (i.e., genetic engineering)	**1976** The first commercial super-sonic commercial airplane (the Concorde) goes into service

SCIENCE FICTION			
1973 Movie: *Invasion of the Girl Snatchers*; Book: *Rendevous with Rama* by Arthur C. Clarke	**1974** Movies: *Dark Star* and *The Stranger Within*; TV: *Land of the Lost*	**1975** Movie: *Rocky Horror Picture Show*; TV: *The UFO Incident* and *Space 1999*	**1976** Movies: *The Man Who Fell to Earth* and *God Told Me To*

POLITICS & RELIGION			
1973 Cease-fire agreed upon in Vietnam War; U.S. withdraws	**1974** U.S. President Richard M. Nixon resigns from office because of Watergate scandal	**1975** Vietnam War ends; N. Vietnam conquers S. Vietnam and re-unites country under Ho Chi Minh	**1976** Thousands of dissidents in Argentina are murdered by military government

THE INFORMATION AGE

UFOLOGY & SETI	**1977** Lawson/McCall conduct Imaginary Abduction Study; Radio telescope in Delaware, Ohio, detects the "Wow" signal	**1978** Frederick Valentich disappeared after reporting a UFO encounter from his small plane over Bass Strait, between Australia and Tasmania	**1979** Apparent "face on Mars" is discovered in Viking photo; SETI Project SEREN-DIP is launched at the University of California	**1980** Close encounters are alleged at USAF/RAF base at Rendlesham Forest, England, and near Huffman, Texas (Cash-Landrum case)

1977 Lawson/McCall conduct Imaginary Abduction Study; Radio telescope in Delaware, Ohio, detects the "Wow" signal

1978 Frederick Valentich disappeared after reporting a UFO encounter from his small plane over Bass Strait, between Australia and Tasmania

1979 Apparent "face on Mars" is discovered in Viking photo; SETI Project SERENDIP is launched at the University of California

1980 Close encounters are alleged at USAF/RAF base at Rendlesham Forest, England, and near Huffman, Texas (Cash-Landrum case)

SCIENCE & TECHNOLOGY

1977 Doctors use balloon angioplasty to unclog a coronary artery

1978 The first test-tube baby (Louise Brown) is born in England; U.S. bans chlorofluorocarbons to protect Earth's ozone layer

1979 James Christy and Robert Harrington discover Charon, the only known satellite of Pluto

1980 Luis and Walter Alvarez propose that an asteroid impact with Earth wiped out the dinosaurs, and other species, 65 million years ago

SCIENCE FICTION

1977 Movies: *Close Encounters of the Third Kind; Star Wars;* and *Starship Invaders*

1978 Movie: *Superman;* TV: *Mork and Mindy;* David Rorvik's cloned human controversy

1979 Movies: *Alien* and *Star Trek: The Motion Picture;* TV: *Project UFO* and *Buck Rogers in the 25th Century*

1980 Movies: *Uforia* and *Hangar 18;* TV: *The Martian Chronicles*

POLITICS & RELIGION

1977 U.S. President Jimmy Carter persuades leaders of Egypt and Israel to end their 30-year war

1978 Egypt and Israel sign Camp David accords to normalize relations

1979 Soviet troops intervene in Afghan civil war; Shah of Iran is deposed

1980 Outbreak of war between Iran and Iraq (1980-1988) splits the Islamic world

THE INFORMATION AGE

UFOLOGY & SETI			

1981 Crop circles become worldwide news; Congress cuts SETI from NASA budget	**1982** UFOs are reported by multiple witnesses over Hudson Valley, New York; Congress restores funds for SETI	**1983** The Fantasy-Prone Hypothesis first introduced as a possible explanation for apparent UFO-alien abductions	**1984** NASA creates SETI project; MJ-12 documents surface; Kenneth Arnold dies (b. 1915)
1981 IBM introduces the personal computer; U.S. space shuttle makes inaugural flight; AIDS is officially recognized	**1982** Theory is advanced that humans, chimpanzees, and gorillas had a common ancestor five million years ago	**1983** Buster and Bustillo of the Harbor-UCLA Medical Center perform the first successful human embryo transfers	**1984** Apple introduces the Macintosh computer; Jeffrey and colleagues develop ''genetic fingerprinting''
1981 Movies: *Superman 2* and *Humanoid Woman*	**1982** Movies: *E.T.* and *Blade Runner*	**1983** Movie: *Strange Invaders*; TV: *V*	**1984** Movies: *Repo Man* and *Buckaroo Banzai*
1981 Egyptian President Anwar Sadat is assassinated	**1982** U.S. federal debt tops $1 trillion; Israel invades Lebanon; Argentines invade Falkland Islands; British task force reoccupies them and takes control	**1983** U.S. invades the Caribbean island of Grenada	**1984** Indian Prime Minister Indira Gandhi is assassinated

SCIENCE & TECHNOLOGY

SCIENCE FICTION

POLITICS & RELIGION

THE COMPUTER AGE

UFOLOGY & SETI	1985 Moore and Shandera discover the Cutler Memo while searching the National Archives for the MJ-12 documents	1986 Jim Lorenzen dies (b. 1922)	1987 MJ-12 and Lear statements are publicized; books *Communion* and *Intruders* are released; Gulf Breeze, Florida, reports begin	1988 Donald Keyhoe dies (b. 1897); Coral Lorenzen dies (b. 1925); First suggestion that Martian "face" is artificial
SCIENCE & TECHNOLOGY	1985 Gallo and Montagnier publish the genetic sequence of the AIDS virus	1986 U.S. FDA approves the first genetically engineered vaccine for humans (for hepatitis B)	1987 U.S. FDA approves the antidepressant drug Prozac	1988 Harvard University receives the first patent for a genetically engineered animal (a mouse)
SCIENCE FICTION	1985 Movies: *Cocoon* and *Enemy Mine*; Book: *Schismatrix* by Bruce Sterling	1986 Movies: *Aliens* and *Pink Chiquitas*; Book: *Contact* by Carl Sagan	1987 TV: *Star Trek: The Next Generation*; Book: *Dawn* by Octavia Butler	1988 Movie: *Killer Klowns from Outer Space*
POLITICS & RELIGION	1985 Mikhail Gorbachev becomes the Secretary General of the Soviet Communist Party	1986 Overthrow of the Marcos dictatorship in the Philippines	1987 U.S. and U.S.S.R. agree to eliminate intermediate-range nuclear missiles	1988 Soviet troops withdraw from Afghanistan; Iran-Iraq war ends

THE COMPUTER AGE

UFOLOGY & SETI	**1989** Belgian UFO wave begins (Wavre, Belgium)	**1990** Second Belgian wave of UFOs (Eupen, Belgium)	**1991** Alleged UFO crash in Shaitan Mazar in the former Soviet Union	**1992** MIT Abduction Conference; NASA begins High Resolution Microwave Survey program
SCIENCE & TECHNOLOGY	**1989** Creation of the National Center for Human Genome Research to oversee the Human Genome Project	**1990** Formal start of the Human Genome Project: an international effort to map and sequence all human DNA	**1991** Mary Claire King of the University of California discovers a gene that causes the inherited form of breast cancer	**1992** U.S. Army begins collecting blood and tissue samples as part of a "genetic dog tag" program
SCIENCE FICTION	**1989** Movies: *Communion* and *Dr. Alien*; TV: *Alien Nation*	**1990** Book: *The Difference Engine* by Gibson and Sterling; TV: *Pirates of Darkwater*	**1991** Movie: *Tribulation 99— Alien Anomalies Under America*	**1992** Movie: *Intruders*; Book: *Red Mars* by Kim Stanley Robinson
POLITICS & RELIGION	**1989** Fall of communism in Eastern Europe; The Berlin Wall is torn down	**1990** Boris Yeltsin is elected President of Russia; the Supreme Soviet ends religious repression	**1991** The second Russian revolution: breakup of the U.S.S.R. and overthrow of the Communist Party; Persian Gulf War	**1992** Reunification of Germany; Assassination of Rajiv Gandhi, Prime Minister of India

THE COMPUTER AGE & THE AGE OF ANXIETY

UFOLOGY & SETI	SCIENCE & TECHNOLOGY	SCIENCE FICTION	POLITICS & RELIGION
1993 Congress kills funds for SETI	**1994** GAO renews investigation of Roswell; With private donations, Project Phoenix is initiated by the SETI Institute	**1995** GAO releases report on Roswell	**1996** UFO-aliens allegedly captured at Varginha, Brazil
1993 Researchers at George Washington University clone human embryos and nurture them in a Petri dish for several days	**1994** U.S. Clementine mission provides high-resolution pictures from which entire lunar surface is mapped in 3-D	**1995** Researchers at Duke University transplant hearts from genetically altered pigs into baboons, proving that cross-species operations are possible	**1996** Possible signs of life found in Mars rock (ALH84001)
1993 Movie: *Fire in the Sky*; TV: *Star Trek: Deep Space 9; Babylon 5;* and debut of *The X-Files*	**1994** Movies: *Stargate* and *Star Trek Generations* ; Books: *Green Mars* by Kim Stanley Robinson and *Moving Mars* by Greg Bear	**1995** Movie: *Plan 10 from Outer Space*; TV: *Outer Limits* and *Star Trek: Voyager*	**1996** Movie: *Independence Day*; TV: *Earth: Final Conflict; Dark Skies;* and *Beast Wars*
1993 In Russia, armed uprising against Yeltsin fails	**1994** Nelson Mandela is elected President of South Africa	**1995** Oklahoma City bombing by extremists kills 150 people	**1996** China agrees to world ban on nuclear testing

THE BRAVE NEW WORLD

UFOLOGY & SETI			
1997 UFOs are reported over Phoenix, Arizona; Heaven's Gate cult members commit mass suicide	**1998** The Mars Global Surveyor reveals the "face on Mars" to be nothing more than a rocky mesa	**1999** SETI@home is initiated by the SERENDIP project	**2000** Mars Global Surveyor finds evidence of water on Mars; more than 30 extrasolar planets have been detected
SCIENCE & TECHNOLOGY			
1997 Sheep are cloned; U.S. Pathfinder Sojourner spacecraft roams surface of Mars and sends live pictures back to Earth	**1998** Mice and calves are cloned; plans for Human Genome Project are announced; water is discovered on the moon	**1999** Liquid water is found inside a 4.5-billion-year-old meteorite	**2000** Human Genome Project is completed: genetic mapping of all human DNA
SCIENCE FICTION			
1997 Movies: *Men in Black; Starship Troopers;* and *The 5th Element*	**1998** Movies: *Lost in Space* and *Dark City*	**1999** TV: *Futurama;* Movie: *Star Wars: The Phantom Menace*	**2000** Movies: *Mission to Mars* and *Red Planet*
POLITICS & RELIGION			
1997 U.S. corporation launches first commercial spy satellite; Hong Kong is returned to China after more than a century of British rule	**1998** U.S. President William J. Clinton outlines first balanced budget in 30 years	**1999** Earth's population reaches 6 billion	**2000** Vladimir Putin is elected President of Russia; George W. Bush is elected President of the United States

- Puzzlement about why persecution has focused on self
- Delusions of grandeur
- Recognition of an important mission such as saving the world or being a messenger of God
- Cosmic identity—belief that "I am the universe" or "I am God."

There is a striking correspondence between this progression and the history of UFOlogy. (Frosch, 1983)

If UFO belief behaves like other systems of paranoia, it should begin in social setbacks and humiliations. On the sociological level, Donald I. Warren's study of Gallup poll data offers evidence that social setbacks may be a common element in the histories of UFO believers. Warren found that highly educated males who were stuck in lower-paying occupations than they were educated for are five to sixteen times more likely to report UFOs than their fellow students who "made it." Warren termed this condition the "status inconsistency theory." (Warren, 1970)

On the historical level, the origin of UFOlogy as a discipline is credited to Charles Fort. Damon Knight's biography of Fort gives clear proof that Fort's paranoid syntax originated in a social setback. As a young man, Fort traveled around the world with the definite purpose of accumulating experiences and impressions of life so as to become a writer. After a few years he settled down with a wife and began to write. In 1905, he was briefly hailed as a new and rare literary star, but his ambitions went largely unrequited. By 1906, he was harboring intense feelings of bitterness and hatred. Months passed without his being able to sell any of his work. Images of suicide filled his mind. He was crushed by the poverty he was living in. He turned to novels instead of short stories and in 1909 published *The Outcast Manufacturers*. It fell into neglect. He withdrew from life and immersed himself in reading. Little is known about the next few years, partly because he destroyed his notes and writings. We do know he wrote a crank work

called *X*, which revolved around the idea that Mars invisibly controlled all life on Earth by means of rays, rather as light in a movie camera controls the images on a sensitive film. (Rarely do you see projection taken quite so literally!) Fort followed this by another excessive work called *Y* (around 1915). It apparently involved a sinister civilization at the South Pole from which Kaspar Hauser, a mysterious boy who showed up in Nuremberg in 1828, had hailed. Fort supposedly says that Hauser was murdered to prevent him from revealing the truth about "Y-land." Both *X* and *Y* went unpublished and apparently were trashed. In a correspondence with Theodore Dreiser in 1916, Fort fancied himself being in "communion with strange orthogenetic gods." By 1919, the progression was complete. The *Book of the Damned* advances a philosophical position that Fort calls "Intermediatism" which argues that all acts of identification are arbitrary because reality, the Universal, is one intercontinuous nexus in which all seeming things are but localized expressions of independence. In Fort's clever analogy, "I think we're all bugs and mice, and are only different expressions of an all-inclusive cheese." Wan tracings of paranoid syntax can be discerned in a number of his musings. The excluding System that excludes all others, that "quasi-opposes" the data he has collected; the surreptitious Visitors that secretly communicate with esoteric cults who direct humanity, etc. Fort had been a class clown in school, and the clown in his personality impishly plays with beliefs that the Earth may not be round or "that science and imbecility are continuous." The term *paranoid* thus seems somehow inappropriately overstated as descriptive of the man. In fact, there is such erudition, sophistication, and good-natured fun in his books that I still think him a veritable saint over all who succeeded him. The central point, however, must not be missed: UFOlogy began in the paranoid musings of a failed novelist. (Knight, 1970)

UFOlogy as a cultural phenomenon originates in a different man. It was Kenneth Arnold's report of an impossibly fast-moving group of unknown objects near Mount Rainier which propelled the idea of flying saucers into a worldwide myth. The investigations of J. Allen Hynek and subsequent debunkers, I have learned from my reassessment of the facts of the case, were frankly bungled. A plausible solution was possible, but between incorrect presumptions and failure to see the obvious, it was missed. Arnold's observations were consistent with his seeing a distant flock of pelicans at a shallow viewing angle. I do not fault Arnold for an honest puzzlement under conditions that made identification unlikely and I think a bit of righteous indignation against his detractors was fully indicated. What I do fault is Arnold's style of interpretation. His initial interpretation of the objects as military aircraft was reasonable as a first guess. But after he performed some calculations showing that the objects had been traveling close to 1,700 miles per hour, there clearly had to be some rethinking, since such speeds were far in excess of any piloted craft flown in 1947. But instead of abandoning the hypothesis, he escalated it. He drifted into a belief that the objects were missiles being tested secretly by the U.S. or some foreign government. This suggests a paranoid orientation in his thinking. This would be only speculation had not Greg Long done an interview with Arnold years later and uncovered a clear slant in his beliefs toward conspiracy logic and grandiosity. Arnold believed in 1981 that Hynek was probably "still working with the Air Force," a ludicrous idea from the standpoint of the politics of UFOlogy but psychologically explicable as due to the animosity Arnold would feel toward Hynek for his debunking attempt.

Arnold's belief that the government was deeply fearful of phenomena like UFOs, because they would "cause their self-destruction," bespeaks the grandiosity of an advanced system of paranoia. Arnold's background provides further grist for the mill of the diagnostician. In his early years he showed great promise as an athlete. He was selected all-state end in 1932 and 1933 for North Dakota, had entered U.S. Olympic trials, taught swimming and diving,

and had planned to use his athletic talent to achieve a college education. On entering college, however, his plans collapsed because of a knee injury. With no finances, he dropped out and in time became adept at selling firefighting equipment Thus we see again the role of social setbacks in originating the belief in UFOs. (Steiger, 1976)

With the origin accounted for, we can move on to the evolution of UFOlogy. For convenience it will be treated as a collective phenomenon rather than as the work of individuals. Ours will be a somewhat "cooked" history, but it should be fairly true to the major trends.

Early UFOlogy was characterized by oversensitivity to personal interactions. Many UFOlogists withdrew and chose not to share their research with anybody. Feuds existed between all the organizations involved in saucer belief. The Air Force itself forbade talk about UFOs to civilians. The period has been termed UFOlogy's Dark Age. UFOlogy as a body turned inward on itself. Some UFOlogists turned to studying the backgrounds of other UFOlogists. Donald Keyhoe kept files on everybody. Others collected "seed catalogues" of UFO sightings and took to searching for patterns. By playing connect the dots in this way, Aimé Michel invented the delusion of orthoteny. Expressing a growing fear, he asked, "Why does this sword of Damocles hang over our heads, year after year, without falling?" The fear of invasion became palpable by the mid-1960s, and all UFOlogists predicted that the mystery would break soon. Some proclaimed that UFOs were hostile and pointed to injuries and mechanical disruptions attributed to UFOs. (Keel, 1975a)

UFOlogists called for Congressional hearings and demanded that the reality of UFOs be verified and acknowledged. The Condon Committee was set up and, of course, deemed UFOs to be harmless to security interests and lacking in scientific value. Meanwhile, UFO books flooded out of publishing houses, complaining that UFOs were a real and serious problem. The invasion, however, never materialized. What, then, were UFOs up to? How long had this been going on? The New UFOlogists ransacked the mythologies of the world and saw parallels in ancient religions and the fairy faith. An irrational insight arose: the Phenomenon is deceiving us to make us believe in it. Hypnosis as a memory-enhancer made inroads among some researchers.

By the 1970s, the belief had become widespread that some external agent was engineering UFO experiences in the minds of UFO percipients. Influencing-machine fantasies began to clog the growing vocabularies of UFOlogists with phrases like control systems, psychotronics, the superspectrum, ultraterrestrials, alternate reality theory, space beams, cosmic consciousness conditioning, tensor-beam monitored knowledge implants, psychokinetic effects on brain cells, superminds, and Geopsyche. (See MIND CONTROL BY ALIENS)

Around 1974, a new, stern, businesslike UFOlogy replaced the old amateurs. The anxieties of a couple of years before suddenly lifted. (Greenfield, 1976)

In the late 1970s, Jacques Vallée began to advance the "Martian hypothesis," which postulated government manipulation of UFO belief. Alternatively, he felt, some occult group could be engaging in a deception. (Vallée, 1979) Elsewhere, old rumors of a government conspiracy to withhold the remains of UFO crashes began to be taken seriously.

Though the retrievalist fantasy was initially resisted, it soon came to occupy center stage in such issues as Roswell and the MJ-12 documents controversy. Cosmic Watergate, over time, expanded into a vision of international conspiracy and beyond. UFO mythology fused with traditional conspiracy literature as links to Trilateralism and even the Illuminati were proposed. For some the conspiracy extended off-planet with Grays having a deal with the government, allowing Grays to abduct humans with impunity in exchange for advanced technology. In a later development, Helmut Lammer's MILAB project explores proposed links between abductions and the military.

During the 1990s, signs of grandeur became evident in a number of UFOlogical authors. The most florid and well-documented concerns Philip Corso's claims in the best-selling *The Day After Roswell* and elsewhere. An appendix to the paperback version of Kal Korff's *The Roswell UFO Crash* details the matter convincingly and is recommended as a high-profile instance of the trait.

Cosmic identity also becomes a notable feature in this period, most blatantly in John Mack's latest offering *Passport to the Cosmos* (1999) when it speaks of a "shift of consciousness that is collapsing duality and enabling us to see that we are connected beyond the Earth at a cosmic level." One can find analogous sentiments in works by Steiger, Lewels, Howe, Hesemann, Fowler, and Ware. (See THREAT, UFO-ET)

It needs to be emphasized that UFOlogy consists of diverse individuals and obviously some people arrive at the various stages before or after the larger group. John Keel and D. Scott Rogo arrived at the cosmic identity stage years before the current crop sprouted. (See MIND CONTROL BY ALIENS) Some current authors, largely those concerned with abductions or Dulce Base lore, are back in the hypochondriasis stage. David Jacobs's *The Threat* is the most prominent example of this regression with its fears that hybrids and insectoids will be taking over the planet before too very long, dooming human freedom and maybe much of the population as well. Exceptions are common, but the mass of UFO works exhibits a robust progression conforming to the stages of paranoia.

With the full sequence of development having now been reached, there is little left for prediction. Beyond more examples of cosmic identity appearing and the eventual advance of stragglers to later stages, the crystal ball clouds up for the future of the field. Apart from celebration of a nice ordering of the history of UFOlogy, there may yet be other matters to attend to.

The monotonous regularity of paranoid styles of thought prompted some psychologists to explore its etiology. Why are paranoids paranoid? Temporally, the precipitating factor may be ridicule or setbacks, but not everybody victimized by shame becomes psychotic. Some sort of personality deficit must also be involved in a paranoid reaction.

In his discussion of paranoia, John Frosch cites a 1949 study by Klein and Horowitz involving 80 paranoids, which uncovered a singular instance of a psychological universal. Every paranoid had had an extremely disruptive, cruel, and violent childhood upbringing. Marital strife was common among the parents. They also found poor adult sexual development related to a background of masturbatory guilt. Generalized problems dealing with failure and blows to pride were also found, replicating psychoanalytic observations going back to Freud. Traumatic humiliation during the formation of sexual identity seems to contribute to the paranoid's fixed understanding of the nature of dominance and submission. Paranoia thus must be deeply rooted to a learned sense of the self as powerless before those who first had control over his life. (Frosch, 1983)

Do UFOlogists have traumatic childhoods? We don't know. Only in the instance of Charles Fort do we have information. In his case, the answer is "absolutely yes." His father treated him with severity in ways that can only be termed, by present standards, savage. We know he was beaten with a dog whip. He was struck in the face with force enough to cause blood to gush from his nose. After one episode of discipline, Fort butted his head against a banister, trying to kill himself and, failing in that, he ran up and down the hall in a frenzy. After he reached a certain age, his father finally stopped beating him and, instead, sentenced him to days or weeks in solitude. (Knight, 1970) Whether similar horror stories lie in the backgrounds of other UFOlogists can only be a matter of conjecture or an issue to be explored by more resourceful psychological investigators.

There are a number of studies of UFO belief that support the general thesis here. Sprinkle and Parnell gave two standard psychological tests to 225 people who reported UFO experiences.

Both tests found moderately elevated scores on the Pa scale (paranoia), and those with communication experiences were significantly more elevated. (Parnell and Sprinkle, 1990) Rodeghier, Goodpaster, and Blatterbauer got a Pa score consistent within less than a point to Parnell and Sprinkle when they gave the MMPI to 27 abductees. (Rodeghier, Goodpaster, and Blatterbauer, 1991)

When Sprinkle gave 259 NICAP members a test instrument designed to measure open vs. closed-mindedness, the score showed significantly higher levels of dogmatism among UFOlogists than a control group of psychologists and counselors. (Sprinkle, 1969) This fits in well with other studies linking prejudice to paranoia and superstitious beliefs to closed minds. (Allport, 1960) The sense of powerlessness underlying much of paranoia was confirmed in a master's dissertation by Stephen P. Resta. Though it was primarily directed at testing the prediction of anomie made by the status inconsistency theory of UFO belief, Resta included a test for locus of control, a trendy topic at the time, to see what it might turn up. Interestingly, the anomie test failed, chalking up a second anomaly for Warren's thesis. The Warren study failed to find elevated belief in certain categories predicted by his theory. Resta added that he found no evidence of the feelings of alienation expected by the tenets of status inconsistency theory. The test for locus of control, however, yielded a strong positive correlation ($r = .32$ significant to the .01 level) between UFO belief and external locus of control. (Resta, 1975) Externality is defined as the belief that one's life is primarily ruled by external circumstances as opposed to one's internal directives. It involves the sense of the self as powerless. Resta's finding dovetails perfectly with UFO belief being a manifestation of the deeply rooted feeling of powerlessness that results in paranoia.

If we assume, for the sake of argument, that the etiology of paranoia will apply to UFOlogists, we are given new insight into certain aspects of UFOlogy that initially seem impenetrable. Why do UFOlogists dismiss the problem of noncontact so effortlessly? They may have learned early in life that the higher powers in their world could not be counted on to be either benevolent or rational. Why do UFOlogists accept abductee tales more readily than tales of Space Brothers, given the almost identical character of the objective evidence? The answer may lie in the fact that the feelings of powerlessness emerging from these accounts are very real in a way that the sugary paternalism of contacteeism cannot compare with. How can some UFOlogists believe that a democratic government could withhold the treasures of an extraterrestrial crash from its capitalistic and sensation-mongering constituency? If you can't trust parents to be generous, you certainly can't expect generosity from a government.

Such psychologizing is admittedly presumptuous, but the conclusion is preeminently humanitarian. It allows us to understand that the enterprise of UFOlogy is not an incomprehensibly malicious exercise in subverting truth. Rather it is a tragedy in which the tortured souls of UFOlogists are ensnared in a terrifying vision of dark and furtive power.

—MARTIN S. KOTTMEYER

References

Allport, Gordon W. *The Nature of Prejudice* (Anchor Books, 1958).

Clement, Catherine. *The Lives and Legends of Jacques Lacan* (Columbia University Press, 1983).

Frosch, John. *The Psychotic Process* (International University Press, 1983).

Greenfield, Allen H. *Saucers and Saucerers* (Pan American New Physics Press, 1976).

Haines, Richard. "Defining the UFO" in *UFOs: 1947-1987*, edited by Hilary Evans (Fortean Tomes, 1987).

Hopkins, Budd. *Intruders* (Random House, 1987; Ballantine, 1988).

Keel, John A. "The Flying Saucer Subculture," *Journal of Popular Subculture* (Spring, 1975).

———. *The Eighth Tower* (Saturday Review Press, 1975; Signet/NAL, 1977).

Knight, Damon. *Charles Fort: Prophet of the Unexplained* (Doubleday, 1970).

Parnell, June O., and R. Leo Sprinkle. "Personality Characteristics of Persons Who Claim UFO Experiences," *Journal of UFO Studies* (1990).

Resta, Stephen P. "The Relationship of Anomie and Externality to Strength of Belief in Unidentified Flying Objects," Dissertation: Loyola College Graduate School, Baltimore, Md., 1975.

Roberts, Anthony, and Geoff Gilbertson. *The Dark Gods* (Rider/Hutchinson, 1980).

Rodeghier, Mark, Jeff Goodpaster, & Sandra Blatterbauer. "Psychosocial Charcteristics of Abductees: Results from the CUFOS Abduction Project," *Journal of UFO Studies* (1991).

Rogo, D. Scott. *Miracles* (Dial Press, 1982).

Rokeach, Milton. *The Open and Closed Mind* (Basic Books, 1960).

Sprinkle, R. Leo. "Personal and Scientific Attitudes: A Study of Persons Interested in UFO Reports," *Flying Saucer Review, Special Issue #2* (June 1969).

Steiger, Brad. *Project Blue Book* (Ballantine Books, 1976).

Vallée, Jacques. *Messengers of Deception* (And/Or Press, 1979).

Warren, Donald I. "Status Inconsistency Theory and Flying Saucer Sightings," *Science* (November 6, 1970).

Parra incident Yelling, without his shirt and with a terrified look on his face, Jose Parra, an eighteen-year-old jockey from Valencia, Venezuela, arrived at a police station in the early morning of December 19, 1954, and related his hair-raising tale of how a hairy little man tried to kidnap him.

Upon his arrival, Parra was detained by Mr. Lopez Ayara, Commissioner of Criminal Investigation, until he calmed down. Detectives detailed to examine the place where the incident supposedly happened found tracks which they were not able to identify as either those of a man or an animal. Parra, out doing road work to lose some extra poundage, stopped near a cement factory on the highway, where he was surprised to see six little "men," all very hairy, who were engaged in pulling boulders from the side of the highway

A rendering of the Parra incident
by artist Hal Crawford

and loading them aboard their disk-shaped craft, which was hovering less than nine feet from the ground. Parra, startled and frightened, started to run away to call someone else to watch the sight.

At this point, one of the little men spotted Parra, and pointed a device at him which gave off a violet light. Parra was unable to move and stood by helplessly while the little creatures ran to their ship and leaped aboard. The craft then disappeared into the sky.

One hour after Mr. Parra's experience, a brightly lit disk was seen hovering a few feet from the ground near the Barbula Sanitorium for Tuberculars at Valencia. Two hospital employees saw the object at different times, one at about twelve midnight and the other at about 3:15 A.M. The man who witnessed the earlier incident notified no one for fear of disturbing the hospital patients. The man involved in the latter incident attempted to approach the craft for a better look, but it moved away and disappeared into the sky.

—APRO

Pascagoula (Mississippi) abduction   On the evening of October 11, 1973, while fishing in the Pascagoula River, Charles Hickson and Calvin Parker claimed they not only saw a strange, egg-and-saucer-shaped object, but were abducted by three creatures. The beings floated from the object, captured both men, and took them up into the craft where they were subjected to a medical-type examination. When the examination was over, the men were returned to their original location.

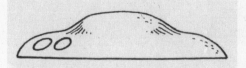

Drawing of the spaceship,
as described by Hickson and Parker

The craft was described as blue-gray in color, saucer-shaped, and had two portholes. Hickson said it made a sustained "buzzing" noise and had a flashing blue light. The aliens were described as mummy-like with crab-like pincers for hands, a pointy nose, and pointy ears. These creatures floated out of the saucer and moved around like robots, according to Hickson.

According to Hickson and Parker, they didn't know what to do, so they had a couple of drinks. Hickson, who would claim he wanted no publicity, first sought out reporters, but could not find any. He finally went to the local sheriff and told the story. Within hours it was front-page news.

Dr. James Harder of APRO (the Aerial Phenomena Research Organization) and former U.S. Air Force scientific consultant Dr. J. Allen Hynek of CUFOS (the Center for UFO Studies) rushed to Pascagoula to interview the men. Harder used hypnosis in an attempt to learn more about the abduction. When he completed his sessions, Harder told reporters that he believed the tale. Hynek agreed.

Controversy raged. Skeptics demanded a polygraph examination and Hickson took one. But the operator, a man from New Orleans, had not completed his training, and so the results were questionable. Philip Klass, as well as others, suggested the test was invalid. Klass also noted that Parker had a nervous breakdown and never took the test.

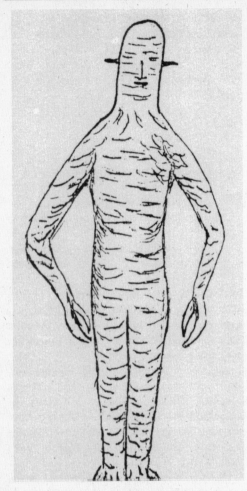

One of the mummy-like aliens, as
described by Hickson and Parker

In October 1975, about two years after the
event, Hickson was invited to participate in a
UFO conference held in Fort Smith, Arkansas,
on the condition that he would take a second
polygraph examination. He agreed.

Upon arrival, however, Hickson declined
to take the test on the advice of his attorney.
Some said it was because it would be administered at the local police station and should
have been held on neutral ground. Police officers said that part of the effectiveness of the
test was to have it given at the police station.
Whatever the reason, Hickson refused to take

the test, and many believe it compromised his
credibility. And there were other problems
with the case.

There were constant changes in the details.
Although researchers believe that minor alter-
ations in a story are natural, these went beyond
that. These changes seemed to be in response
to criticisms and appeared to be an attempt to
smooth out rough spots in the story. To skeptics, such inconsistencies suggest a hoax.

The landing site of the UFO was only a
few hundred yards away from and in full view
of a heavily traveled highway. No one ever
came forward to corroborate the story, or to
suggest that he or she had been on the highway
and saw the UFO.

Although Parker has generally remained
quiet about the events, Hickson has moved on
to more contacts. His tale began to take on
more attributes of the tales of typical "contactees," in that he claimed to be in contact with
the alien creatures.

In the final analysis, most of those who
accept extraterrestrial visitation as a fact also
accept the Pascagoula abduction at face value;
whereas most skeptics and debunkers believe
this case is a hoax.

—KEVIN D. RANDLE

References

Blum, Ralph and Judy. *Beyond Earth: Man's Contact with UFOs* (Bantam Books, 1974).
Randle, Kevin D. "Pascagoula (Mississippi) Abduction" in Story, Ronald D., ed. *The Encyclopedia of
UFOs* (Doubleday/New English Library, 1980).

Passport to Magonia (Henry Regnery,
1969). Jacques Vallée sees the UFO phenomenon as a metaphysical programming process to
prepare us for higher consciousness. In this
path-breaking book he makes a compelling
case that all religious apparitions, mystical experiences, and UFO sightings rely upon the
same mechanisms, sharing similar effects on
the human observer, varying only to the extent
that the projections are interpreted within the
prevailing cultural environment. If it were pos-

sible to construct three-dimensional holograms with mass then most religious miracles and UFO sightings could be similarly explained. He raises the prospect that humankind is being exposed to deliberately staged and faked apparitions intended to program our imaginations and accelerate our evolution as a species.

—RANDALL FITZGERALD

Pflock, Karl T. (b. 1943). A former U.S. deputy assistant secretary of defense, CIA intelligence officer, and senior congressional aide, Karl Pflock is now a writer, consultant, and UFO researcher. His articles on UFOs have appeared in such journals as *Omni, Fortean Times,* the *International UFO Reporter, The Anomalist, Fate,* the *MUFON UFO Journal, Cuadernos de Ufologia* (Spain), and the *MUFON 1995 International UFO Symposium Proceedings.* A popular speaker, he was named 1998 UFOlogist of the Year by the National UFO Conference.

His interest in UFOs is virtually lifelong, stemming from a crashed-saucer story he overheard at the age of five or six and a multiple-witness sighting in which he was involved in the early 1950s.

In the late 1960s, he was the first chairman of the National Capital Area (investigative) Subcommittee of the National Investigations Committee on Aerial Phenomena (NICAP). He has carried out independent research on UFO-occupant sightings and contacts and allegations of UFO-connected animal mutilations, but is best known in contemporary UFOlogy for his controversial work on the Roswell incident.

His *Roswell in Perspective* was published by the Fund for UFO Research in 1994. He is also collaborating with James W. Moseley, editor of the newsletter *Saucer Smear,* on *Shockingly Close to the Truth!* Moseley's UFOlogical memoirs.

Address: P.O. Box 93338
Albuquerque, NM 87199
U.S.A.

E-mail: Ktperehwon@aol.com

Karl T. Pflock

POSITION STATEMENT: UFOs are real—that is, as yet unexplained phenomena. Moreover, many solid unknowns involving reports of strange craft and sometimes living creatures and/or physical evidence leave us with but two choices, hoax or real essentially as reported, while some admit of a psychological explanation as well. In these instances, if what occurred was real and reasonably accurately reported, they must have been encounters with products of nonhuman intelligence and, in some cases, the intelligences themselves.

Based on the data, I'm subjectively certain we have been visited by nonhuman intelligent beings—to my '50s-conditioned mind, most likely from an extra-solar planet of our galaxy. However, we do not yet have *proof* of this—as opposed to very strong evidence pointing to it—though such proof very well may be in the data already in hand, as yet unrecognized as such.

I use the past tense advisedly. If I am correct that some sightings were observations of such visitors and their vehicles, I suspect they were here and left some time ago—arriving in the early to mid-1940s, departing in the late 1960s or early 1970s. They came here because Sol and his planets seemed cozily familiar. They studied our entire system and us quite closely. Once in a while a couple of grad students got out of hand and buzzed the natives. On occasion some ambitious scientists overstepped a bit and interfered with the locals—the famous and likely real 1961 abduction of Barney and Betty Hill comes to mind. Then they left, leaving us wondering, dreaming, and hoping.

—KARL T. PFLOCK

Phoenix (Arizona) lights At approximately 6:55 P.M. (Pacific Time) on Thursday, March 13, 1997, a young man in Henderson, Nevada, reportedly witnessed a V-shaped object, with six large lights on its leading edge, approach his position from the northwest and pass overhead. In his subsequent written report to the National UFO Reporting Center, he described it as appearing to be quite large, approximately the "size of a [Boeing] 747," and said that it generated a sound which he equated to that of "rushing wind." It continued on a straight line toward the southeast and disappeared from his view over the horizon.

This sighting is perhaps the earliest of a complex series of events that would take place during the next 2-3 hours over the states of Nevada, Arizona, and possibly New Mexico, and which would quickly become known as the "Phoenix Lights." It involved sightings by tens, or perhaps even hundreds of thousands of witnesses on the ground, and it gave rise to a storm of controversy over what had caused the event.

The next reported sighting was from a former police officer in Paulden, Arizona. He had just left his home at approximately 8:15 P.M. (Mountain Time), and was driving north, when he looked out the driver's-side window of his car to the west and witnessed a cluster of five reddish or orange lights.

The formation consisted of four lights together, with a fifth light seemingly "trailing" the other four. Each of the individual lights in the formation appeared to the witness to consist of two separate point sources of orange light.

The witness immediately returned to his

NUFORC

Phoenix - 8:20 p.m. - from Indian School Rd.

Artist's conception by Robert Fairfax

home, obtained a pair of binoculars, and watched as the lights disappeared over the horizon to the south. He watched the lights for an estimated two minutes, and reported that they made no sound that he could discern from his vantage point on the ground.

Within a matter of minutes of these first sightings, a "blitz" of telephoned reports began pouring into the National UFO Reporting Center, to other UFO organizations, to law enforcement offices, to news media offices, and to Luke Air Force Base. They were submitted from Chino Valley, Prescott, Prescott Valley, Dewey, Cordes Junction, Wickenburg, Cavecreek, and many other communities to the north and west of Phoenix.

Witnesses were reporting such markedly different objects and events that night that it was difficult for investigators to understand what was taking place. Some witnesses reported five lights, others seven, or even more. Some reported that the lights were distinctly orange or red, whereas others reported distinctly white or yellow lights. Many reported the lights were moving across the sky at seemingly high speed, whereas others reported they moved at a slow (angular) velocity, or they even hovered motionless for several minutes.

These apparent discrepancies, together with the large number of communities from which sightings were being reported in rapid

NUFORC

Distortion of stars seen within inner "V"

Illustration by Robert Fairfax

sequence, raised early suspicions that multiple objects were involved in the event, and that they perhaps were traveling at high speed. These suspicions would be borne out over subsequent months, following extensive investigation by many individuals. The investigations pointed to the fact that several objects, all markedly different in appearance, and most of them almost unbelievably large, passed over Arizona that night.

One group of three witnesses, located just north of Phoenix, reported seeing a huge, wedge-shaped craft with five lights on its ventral surface pass overhead with an eerie "gliding" type of flight. It coursed to the south and passed between two mountain peaks to the south. The witnesses emphasized how huge the object was, blocking out up to 70-90 degrees of the sky.

A second group of witnesses, a mother and four daughters near the intersection of Indian School Road and 7th Avenue, were shocked to witness an object, shaped somewhat like a sergeant's stripes, approach from over Camelback Mountain to the north. They report that it stopped directly above them, where it hovered for an estimated 5 minutes. They described how it filled at least 30-40 degrees of sky, and how it exhibited a faint glow along its trailing edge. The witnesses felt they could see individual features on the ventral surface of the object, and they were certain that they were looking at a very large, solid object.

The object began moving slowly to the south, at which time it appeared to "fire" a white beam of light at the ground. At about the same time, the seven lights on the object's leading edge suddenly dimmed and disappeared from the witnesses' sight. The object moved off in the general direction of Sky Harbor International Airport, a few miles to the south, where it was witnessed by two air traffic controllers in the airport tower, and reportedly by several pilots, both on the ground and on final approach from the east.

After this point in the sighting, the facts are somewhat less clear to investigators. It is known that at least one object continued generally to the south and southeast, passing over the communities of Scottsdale, Glendale, and Gilbert. One of the witnesses in Scottsdale, a former airline pilot with 13,700 hours of flight time, reported seeing the object execute a distinct turn as it approached his position on the ground. He noted that he witnessed many lights on the object as it approached him, but that the number of lights appeared to diminish as it got closer to overhead. Many other witnesses in those communities reported seeing the object pass overhead as it made its way toward the mountains to the south of Phoenix.

Other sightings occurred shortly afterward along Interstate 10 in the vicinity of Casa Grande. One family of five, who were driving from Tucson to Phoenix, reported that the object that passed over their station wagon was so large that they could see one "wing tip" of the object out one side of their car, and the other "wing tip" out the other side. They estimated they were driving toward Phoenix at approximately 80 miles per hour, and they remained underneath the object for between one and two minutes as it moved in the opposite direction. They emphasized how incredibly huge the object appeared to be as it blocked out the sky above their car.

Many witnesses located throughout the Phoenix basin continued to report objects and peculiar clusters of lights for several hours following the initial sightings. One group of witnesses reported a large disk streaking westward over Phoenix at high speed. Others reported peculiar orange "fireballs" which appeared to hover in the sky even hours after the initial sightings.

One of the more intriguing reports was submitted by a young man who claimed to be an airman in the Air Force, stationed at Luke Air Force Base, located to the west of Phoenix in Litchfield Park. He telephoned the National UFO Reporting Center at 3:20 A.M. on Friday, some eight hours after the sightings on the previous night, and reported that two USAF F-15 fighters had been "scrambled" from Luke AFB, and had intercepted one of the objects.

NUFORC

Size Comparison with Boeing-727 jets.

Illustration by Robert Fairfax

Although the presence of F-15's could never be confirmed, the airman provided detailed information which proved to be accurate, based on what investigators would reconstruct from witnesses over subsequent weeks and months. Two days after his first telephone call, the airman called to report that he had just been informed by his commander that he was being transferred to an assignment in Greenland. He has never been heard from again since that telephone call.

Most of the controversy that arose from the incident centers around a cluster of lights that was seen, and videotaped, to the south of Phoenix at between 9:30 and 10:00 P.M. on the same night as the sightings. In May 1997, the Public Affairs Office at Luke AFB announced that their personnel had investigated these lights, and had established that they were flares launched from A-10 "Warthog" aircraft over the Gila Bend "Barry M. Goldwater" Firing Range at approximately 10:00 P.M. Even the most implacable UFO skeptics admit, however, that irrespective of whether such flares had in fact been launched or not, they cannot serve as an explanation for the objects that had been witnessed by many individuals some 1-2 hours earlier.

Another interesting aspect of the case is the virtual absence of coverage in the print media, save for a handful of articles in local newspapers. The Prescott *Daily Courier* carried an article on March 14, but the Phoenix newspapers, and the national wire services, provided no early coverage of the event, even though they had been apprised of it.

It was not until mid-June, almost ten weeks later, that the national press took any interest in the incident with the appearance of a front-page article in *USA Today* on June 18, 1997.

Investigators may never be able to reassemble all of the facts surrounding the events that took place over Arizona on the night of March 13, 1997. However, there is no doubt in the minds of most that what occurred was extraordinarily bizarre in nature, and that many thousands of witnesses can attest to the events.

—PETER B. DAVENPORT

photographs of UFOs Alleged UFO photographs have long been a source of difficulties, as well as constituting an important supportive element in the case for the UFO. Of the many hundreds of offerings received by private UFO research groups and official agencies, most are utterly worthless for one or more reasons: (1) The imagery is so poor that no meaningful information content is present. (2) If a structural object does appear in the picture, the circumstances surrounding the taking of the photograph are usually such that fraud is either reasonably suspected or clearly evident. (3) Some vital element (such as the original negative), which would aid in a more definitive analysis, is usually missing. (4) The testimony of the photographer and/or supporting witnesses may be internally inconsistent or not in agreement with features observable in the photo(s). (5) Inconsistencies within the photo itself suggesting a montage or double exposure, are often found.

Former assistant director of the now defunct National Investigations Committee on Aerial Phenomena, Stuart Nixon, characterized the general situation very well when he said: ". . . NICAP has never analyzed a structured-object picture that is fully consistent with the claim an extraordinary flying device was photographed. In every case, there has been some small detail, or group of details, that raised the suspicion of a hoax or a mistake."

One might easily conclude from all this that any and all photographs purporting to show UFOs should be promptly and mercilessly rejected. However, to do so might conceivably result in overlooking the genuine article if and when it does happen along.

The samples chosen for the UFO Photo Gallery which follows (pp. 430-433) are typical. Included in this collection are "classics" from three categories: (1) allegedly "real" UFOs that many UFOlogists believe could be extraterrestrial spaceships; (2) photos that are highly suspect but not proven to be false; and (3) confessed or otherwise proven hoaxes.

Can you tell which is which? Who really knows?

—RONALD D. STORY

Piata Beach (Brazil) photos The following events reportedly happened on the afternoon of April 24, 1959, as Sr. Helio Aguiar, a thirty-two-year-old statistician employed by a bank in Bahia, Brazil, was riding his motorcycle down the highway to Itapan. As he was passing Piata Beach, in the Amaralina District, he noticed a silvery, domed disk, shaped something like a Cardinal's hat, with a number of "windows" visible around the base of the dome on top. The underside of this object showed four strange markings, or symbols, faintly visible in the photographs taken. (See Aguiar's drawings superimposed on the photographs.)

About that time, his motorcycle engine stopped and he got off to unpack his camera. He adjusted it and took three quick shots as the object made a leisurely sweeping turn (from the sea toward him) over the surf. He then began to feel a strange pressure in his brain, and a state of progressive confusion overtook him. He felt vaguely as though he was being ordered by somebody to write something down. As he was winding the film to take a fourth picture, he lost all sense of what was happening.

The next thing Aguiar knew, he was slumped over his motorcycle and the UFO was gone. In his hand he held a piece of paper bearing a message in his own handwriting. It said, "Put an absolute stop to all atomic tests for warlike purposes. The balance of the universe is threatened. We shall remain vigilant and ready to intervene."

As he tried to recall the experience, he remembered that the craft was a dark silvery metallic color, with a somewhat luminous orange-colored dome. The "windows" were small and square, and appeared more like panels or ports running around the base of the dome. There were three tubes, or rib-like structures of some kind, running parallel from the dome to the edge of the disk on one side; and it had four small semispherical protuberances on the underside, equally spaced near the center of the disk. Three of the markings on the underside of the flange of the disk were faintly distinguishable in the photographs taken, but they do not conform to any symbol or language known today.

Although the object moved in a sweeping curve in its flight path, it did not seem to employ aerodynamic lift to remain aloft. When first seen, it was traveling edge forward in a very steep bank, and then its position changed so that in the last photo it is traveling dome forward in a maximum drag condition, with the full area of the disk flat against its line of flight. Aguiar did not see it leave.

The APRO (Aerial Phenomena Research Organization) photographic consultant at the time, John Hopf, gave the following report:

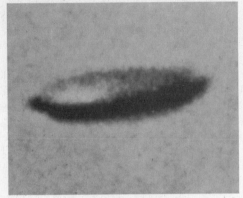

Calgary, Alberta, Canada
July 3, 1947

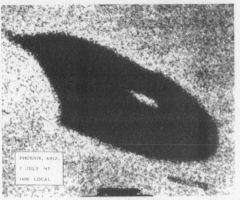

Phoenix, Arizona
July 7, 1947

McMinnville, Oregon
May 11, 1950

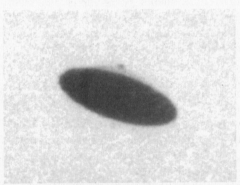

McMinnville, Oregon
May 11, 1950

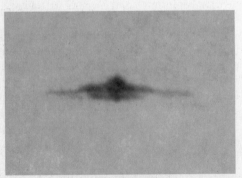

Barra de Tijuca, Brazil
May 7, 1952

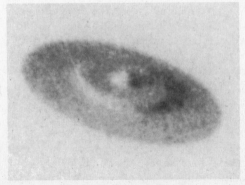

Barra de Tijuca, Brazil
May 7, 1952

New York, N.Y.
July 28, 1952

Riverside, California
1952

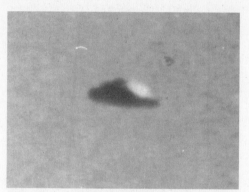

Namur, Belgium
June 5, 1955

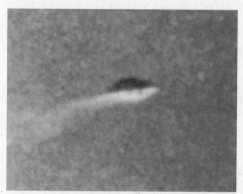

Namur, Belgium
June 5, 1955

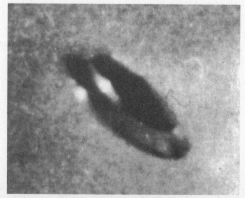

Natal, South Africa
July 17, 1956

San Francisco, California
October 10, 1956

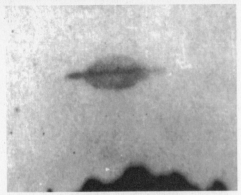

Trindade Island, Brazil
January 16, 1958

Santa Ana, California
August 3, 1965

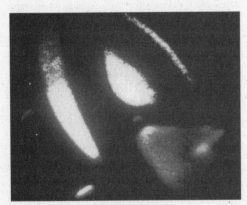

Tulsa, Oklahoma
August 1965

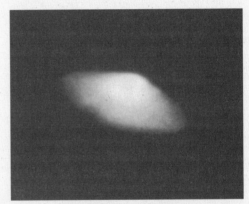

Sibley County, Minnesota
October 21, 1965

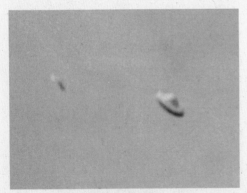

Yungay, Peru
1967

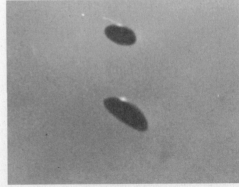

Yungay, Peru
1967

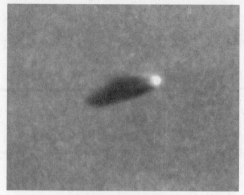

Charleston, S.C.
January 22, 1978

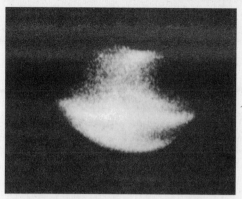

Wellington-Kaikoura, New Zealand
October 31, 1978

Vancouver Island, B.C., Canada
October 8, 1981

Belgium
1990

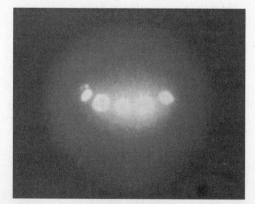

Puebla, Mexico
July 7, 1991

Tulancingo, Hidalgo, Mexico
June 5, 1992

APRO

Photo #1   Photo#2   Photo #3   Photo #4

"Working from the highly enlarged prints made from the original negatives, it is quite certain that these are authentic photographs of an unconventional aerial object actually over the water. By lining up the horizon as has been done in the composite print, and assuming equal enlargement of the originals, the apparent maneuver of the object may be noted. The apparent size of the object increases from view No. 1 to view No. 3, indicating the object was approaching the camera.

"In views Nos. 1 and 2 we seem to be looking at the bottom of the disk. The spots (indentations or protrusions) are not distinct enough to determine their nature and shadow effect from these is lost in the grain pattern.

"The altitude of the disk increased from view No. 3 to view No. 4 as the water is no longer visible in the last view. Only the shiny central dome is visible in this view. This may be due to the reflectivity matching that of the sky and being concealed by the grain."

As in most cases of alleged UFO photo-graphs, the authenticity of the story and accompanying photos is left open to debate.

—APRO

Pope, Nick (b. 1965). Nick Pope is a government employee in the British Ministry of Defence. In 1991 he was posted to a division called Secretariat (Air Staff), where for the next three years his job was to investigate UFO sightings to see if there was evidence of any threat to the defense of the United Kingdom. The job that he did was broadly analogous to the work done by the now defunct USAF study, Project Blue Book. Through his official research and investigation of the UFO phenomenon Pope became involved in related subjects such as alien abductions, crop circles, and animal mutilations.

When he was promoted in 1994, and moved to another position, he continued his research privately, specializing in work with abductees. Concerned by the defense and national security implications of the UFO phenomenon he spoke out publicly, and wrote a book about his work, entitled *Open Skies, Closed Minds.* Later, he wrote *The Uninvited,* dealing with alien contact/abduction cases, and a speculative novel about alien invasion, entitled *Operation Thunder Child.*

Address: 50 Hogarth Crescent
            Merton Abbey
            London SW19 2DW
            U.K.

POSITION STATEMENT: On the basis of my official research and investigation into UFO sightings and reports of alien contact, I am personally convinced that intelligent extraterrestrials are visiting the Earth. I say this on the basis of the data available to me at the Ministry of Defense, both in terms of the historic records and the several hundred new cases that I investigated each year.

While around ninety-five percent of sightings could be explained in terms of misidentifications of known objects and phenomena, there was a hard core of cases that defied any conventional explanation and involved craft capable of speeds and maneuvers beyond the capabilities of our own technology. I was particularly interested in UFO sightings that could be correlated by radar and in reports where the witnesses were military personnel; such cases were directly responsible for my gradual conversion from skeptic to believer.

Nick Pope

Although a supporter of the extraterrestrial hypothesis, I am wary of the UFOlogical obsession with official cover-ups and conspiracies. I generally find such ideas to be unconvincing and ill-informed. While excited by the possibility of open contact with extraterrestrials, my defense background has instilled me with a natural caution, and I believe that governments should make some contingency plans for such a scenario, not least to counter the potential biological hazard that may stem from such contact.

It seems to me that UFOlogists need to adopt more of an empirical, methodological approach to their work, and should try to get away from the believer versus skeptic mindset. Bridges need to be built with the scientific community, not least because undisputed proof that we are not alone in the universe is more likely to come from optical or radio astronomy than from UFOlogy.

—NICK POPE

Portage County (Ohio) police chase One of the most dramatic encounters by police officers with an apparently structured, low-level UFO occurred in the early morning of April 17, 1966. Officers of the Portage County, Ohio, Sheriff's Department first saw the object rise up from near ground level, bathing them in light, near Ravenna, Ohio, about 5 A.M. Ordered by the sergeant to pursue the object, they chased it for eighty-five miles across the border into Pennsylvania, as it seemed to play a cat-and-mouse game with them. Along the route, police officers from other jurisdictions also saw the object and joined in the chase.

Deputy Sheriff Dale Spaur and Mounted Deputy Wilbur "Barney" Neff had left their scout car to investigate an apparently abandoned automobile on Route 224. Spaur described the first sighting in these words:

"I always look behind me so no one can come up behind me. And when I looked in this wooded area behind us, I saw this thing. At this time it was coming up . . . to about treetop level, I'd say about one hundred feet. It started moving toward us. . . . As it came over the trees, I looked at Barney and he was still watching the car . . . and he didn't say nothing and the thing kept getting brighter and the area started to get light. . . . I told him to look over his shoulder, and he did.

"He just stood there with his mouth open for a minute, as bright as it was, and he looked down. And I started looking down and I looked at my hands and my clothes weren't burning or anything, when it *stopped,* right over on top of us. The only thing, the only sound in the whole area was a hum . . . like a transformer being loaded or an overloaded transformer when it changes. . . .

"I was petrified, and, uh, so I moved my right foot, and everything seemed to work all right. And evidently he made the same decision I did, to get *something* between me and it, or us and it, or whatever you would say. So we both went for the car, we got to the car and we sat there. . . .''

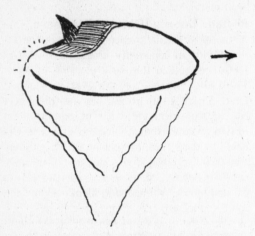

The UFO as sketched by Deputy Spaur

As they watched, the UFO moved toward the east, and then stopped again. Spaur picked up the microphone and reported it to the dispatcher. At this time, the object was about 250 feet away, brilliantly lighting up the area. (''It was *very* bright; it'd make your eyes water,'' Spaur said.) Sergeant Schoenfelt, on duty at the station, told them to follow it and keep it under observation while they tried to get a photo unit to the scene.

Spaur and Neff turned south on Route 183, then back east on Route 224, which placed the object to their north, out the left window. ''At this time,'' said Spaur, ''it came straight south, just one motion, buddy, just a smooth glide . . .'' and began moving east with them pacing it, just to their right at an estimated altitude of 300-500 feet, illuminating the ground beneath it. Once more the UFO darted to the north, now left of the car, and they sped up to over 100 mph to keep up with it.

As the sky became lighter with predawn light, Spaur and Neff saw the UFO in silhouette, with a vertical projection at its rear. The object began to take on a metallic appearance as the chase continued. Spaur kept up a running conversation with other police cars that

were trying to catch up with them. Once when they made a wrong turn at an intersection, the object stopped, then turned and came back to their position.

Police Officer Wayne Huston of East Palestine, Ohio, situated near the Pennsylvania border, had been monitoring the radio broadcasts and was parked at an intersection he knew the Portage County officers would be passing soon. Shortly afterward he saw the UFO pass by with the sheriff's cruiser in hot pursuit. He swung out and joined the chase. At Conway, Pennsylvania, Spaur spotted another parked police car and stopped to enlist his aid, since their cruiser was almost out of gas. The Pennsylvania officer called his dispatcher.

According to Spaur, as the four officers stood and watched the UFO, which had stopped and was hovering, there was traffic on the radio about jets being scrambled to chase the UFO, and ''. . . we could see these planes coming in. . . . When they started talking about fighter planes, it was just as if that thing heard every word that was said; it went PSSSSHHEW, *straight* up; and I mean when it went up, friend, it didn't play no games; it went *straight* up.''

The Air Force later ''identified'' the UFO as a satellite, seen part of the time, and confused with the planet Venus. Under pressure from Ohio officials, Major Hector Quintanilla, chief of Project Blue Book, had an acrimonious confrontation with the witnesses and refused to change the identification, although it was pointed out to him that they had seen the UFO *in addition* to Venus and the moon at the conclusion of the observation. Major Quintanilla also denied that any jets had been scrambled.

William B. Weitzel conducted an exhaustive investigation on behalf of the National Investigations Committee on Aerial Phenomena (NICAP), obtaining taped interviews, signed statements, sketches, and all pertinent data, which was assembled into a massive report that was made available to congressional investigators. When the University of Colorado UFO Project was initiated in 1966, a copy of

Weitzel's report was hand-delivered to the director, Dr. Edward U. Condon, for his consideration. The Condon Report, published two years later, does not mention the case.

—RICHARD HALL

powerlessness The vitality of the UFO mythos lies in its presumption that there exists a higher power in the external world that is able to provoke fear and desire due to the alien's ability to command forces that man does not. The existence of a futuristic technology that, at our level of development, appears supernatural and magical is a necessary premise in the argument that extraterrestrials are able to cross vast distances of space to visit our world. Such a power could in principle render the most powerful individuals subservient and all of us would, in principle, be vulnerable to their will.

In this minimal respect, UFO belief is analogous to religion and supernatural beliefs such as witchcraft that premise the existence of animistic forces greater than oneself. Such beliefs can be useful in fantasy by allowing oneself to believe that one is a victim of willful intention rather than blind randomness, thus imparting meaning and drama to misfortunes.

The dominant emotion in UFO encounters tends to be fear. (Moravec, 1987) When one is present, chaos reigns. Witnesses are paralyzed. Vehicles lose power. Television and radio is disrupted. Animals go crazy. Power grids black out. Fires erupt. Things fall apart. Abductions also tend to be nightmarish horrors in which the victim feels powerless. Pain is ubiquitous. The aliens come from dying worlds. The government and sinister Men in Black try to cover up the truth. The end of the world or some similar cataclysm is nigh. While Jung suggested UFOs might be mandalas and thus symbols of wholeness, the presence of tranquil emotions are strikingly rare and decisively refute the idea that the circularity of saucers is due to desires for order.

Studies of UFO belief repeatedly implicate the frustration of the will to power, i.e., the generalized drive to dominate and master. Walter Kaufman's treatment of Nietzsche's formulation of the concept is recommended for a full exposition. (Kaufman, 1980) Stephen P. Resta's study found strength of UFO belief is well correlated with externality—a generalized attitude that one has little control over one's life. (Resta, 1975) Resta also tested for anomie and did find a correlation. This would be consistent with paranoia. Paranoia acts as a defense against depression and meaninglessness.

There is a significant correlation between UFO belief and belief in witches, necromancy, and ghosts. (Zusne and Jones, 1982) Witchcraft in some form is found in all societies and practiced most avidly by those lacking, but desiring, power.

Donald Warren's Gallup poll analysis found elevated levels of UFO belief among individuals who failed to achieve the economic level of status that their education would lead society to expect of them. (Warren, 1970)

—MARTIN S. KOTTMEYER

References

Moravec, Mark. "UFOs as Psychological and Parapsychological Phenomena" in Evans, Hilary, ed. *UFOs: 1947-1987: The 40-Year Search for an Explanation* (Fortean Times, 1988).

Kaufman, Walter. *Discovering the Mind, Volume 2* (McGraw-Hill, 1980).

Resta, Stephen P. "The Relationship of Anomie and Externality to the Strength of Belief in Unidentified Flying Objects," Dissertation: Loyola College Graduate School, Baltimore, Md., 1975.

Zusne, Leonard and Warren H. Jones. *Anomalistic Psychology* (Lawrence Erlbaum, 1982).

Warren, Donald. "Status Inconsistency Theory and Flying Saucer Sightings" *Science* (November 6, 1970).

Principle of Mediocrity The Principle (or assumption) of Mediocrity (also known as the Copernican Principle) holds that conditions favorable for the evolution of life and intelligence are prevalent throughout the universe. The implication is that intelligent life is common, not rare, and thus we humans are not so special.

The Principle of Mediocrity is basically the reverse of the Anthropic Principle, according to which we humans may be the only case of intelligent life in the universe. However, just as Copernicus dislodged us from the center of the solar system, the Principle of Mediocrity goes hand-in-hand with the Principle of Uniformity of Nature in assuming that the same laws of nature and natural processes that produced intelligent life on Earth are typical, not exceptional, undermining the age-old religious principle of Special Creation.

—RONALD D. STORY

Prison Earth theory Though rarely considered in serious discussions of the nature of the relationship of Earth to the rest of life in the cosmos, the idea that the Earth is a prison has had a minor notoriety. One could hear it now and again on talk shows during the fifties and sixties perhaps as an effort to show an urbane wittiness of the Mark Twain sort. At some point, it seemed to sink into obscurity. Yet the idea developed a respectable pedigree along the way that deserves mention.

One can find the idea in the UFO literature as early as the first saucerzine from 1953, Al Bender's *Space Review*. Bender called upon people to send in their theories on what flying saucers were all about and he made up a list of the responses. As part of Theory No. 11 Harold F. Emridh of Kansas wrote, "I think the saucers are to keep us imprisoned on Earth until we civilize ourselves to the point where we no longer pose a threat to them."

In a book written with Ouija board contactee George Hunt Williamson, *UFOs Confidential* (1958), John McCoy offered his opinion that Earth is a "prison world" or a "great lunatic asylum." Man has lost awareness of reality and has been given the illusion of freedom. Our desires are controlled by our system of economics and the inculcation of materialistic goals. This enslavement is accomplished by the trick of putting children in physical education classes. Its regimentation and excitation of savage instincts levels delicate and creative genius. This Earth is controlled by a great force from the deceptive aliens of Orion.

Donald Keyhoe's *Flying Saucers—Top Secret* (1960) briefly puts forward the notion that aliens are here to keep tabs on a colony that was deliberately abandoned. It was a means of getting rid of undesirables. With Earth acting as a Devil's Island, these exiles would serve as examples for others at home to stay in line. This would serve to explain the human appearance of many UFOnauts, particularly in that period.

Ray Palmer, in the January 1959 issue of *Search*, relayed the probably facetious contact tale of Art LaVove that appeared in the *Los Angeles Times*. The InterGalactic Empire banished rebels who destroyed a base beyond Mars. They were lobotomized and consigned to a life of savagery on Earth. Ever since, the Empire has sent its lobotomized prisoners here on a daily basis. "All of the aberrated of the Cosmos are dispatched here, where they can be watched. To put it bluntly, this planet is an IGE nuthouse." Palmer granted it was likely that this was only a cleverly conceived fiction, but that it nevertheless matched his personal beliefs. He thought LaVove "may have uttered the prize truth of all time."

Jan Hudson in *Those Sexy Saucer People* (1967) admits arriving independently at a similar theory. Believing UFOs showed up after we sent off H-bombs or took off for space travel, she offered this thought, "I think the earth is a giant institution in which the human race has been incarcerated for its own good. And every time we start rattling the bars, the keepers come hurrying down to take a look." Hudson relates that when she offered this idea before a group of contactees, none seemed to care for it much. It's hard to know why, but maybe it had something to do with the fact that George Adamski and Orfeo Angelucci had both testified to the truth of the Prison Earth theory well before, in the middle of the fifties.

A Saturnian named Ramu told George Adamski during a conversation in a café that Earth had been selected centuries ago as the system to which they would exile their troublemakers. "They were gathered in ships from the many planets and transported to Earth, without equipment or implements of any kind." Here they were forced to work and draw on their talents to earn their place in the Creator's fold. The extraterrestrials watch and send messiahs from time to time to help out, but man wars against man and his achievements are lost to his penchant for destruction.

Orfeo Angelucci's astral contacts revealed that vast numbers of Earthlings are former inhabitants of the world of Lucifer that once existed between Mars and Jupiter. Those responsible for the destruction of Lucifer were deep-drowned in time and matter to live in the "underworld of illusion" that makes up the Earth. Flying saucers still visit "our prison world" to liberate us spiritually.

The theory makes an odd brief return in abduction history. During a 1974 visit to another world, Carl Higdon recalled seeing a gray-haired man among some younger people that aliens had picked up. He seemed familiar as a guy he saw on a TV show called *The Unknown*. During the show, this man said of the UFO people, "They put us down here for punishment. They're going to come and take us back." Leo Sprinkle, who performed the regression, realizes he knows who Higdon is talking about. "I have a copy of the book that the man is talking about, saying that the Earth was like a prison." (Haines, 1979) Later, it comes to him: Lawrence W. Foreman's *Passport to Eternity* (1970). Foreman was a southern Californian who had gone out into the desert on several occasions and talked with people from flying saucers. There is no indication if the investigators tried to contact Foreman about Higdon's corroboration of his relationship with UFOnauts or if Sprinkle simply discounted the claim out of disinterest in helping prove the Prison Earth theory.

The theory was toyed with in science fiction culture well before it showed up in UFO literature. Frank Belknap Long, Jr.'s "Exiles of the Stratosphere" involved an advanced race with lighter-than-air vessels dwelling in the upper atmosphere that sent only outcasts to the surface. In A.E. van Vogt's *Asylum* (1942) the Earth is a sort of Botany Bay or dumping ground for the vicious elements of the galaxy. And before science fiction there was religion. George Berkeley's *Alciphron, or the Minute Philosopher* (1732) contains the opinion "the Earth is, after all, the prison house in God's Kingdom."

Palmer warned the Prison Earth theory was a dangerous idea and so it is. It explains the problem of suffering all too well. The world should be a good place. Life should be fair. So why isn't it? Any answer is going to be mythological in character, if not in form. The venerable orthodox choices are original sin and karma. We are cursed by the actions of our ancestors or our forgotten selves. Prison Earth did not change this. Adamski blamed ancestors. Angelucci blamed our forgotten selves. The clarification is one of setting. Prisons are supposed to be cruel, so no wonder there is so much insanity and suffering in the world.

So far so good, yet it also explains the problem of noncontact all too well. Aliens avoid us because we are useless misfits, the scum of the galaxy. We are ultimately beyond reasoning with and do not deserve to be free. Take that message to heart and you are asking for an inferiority complex of cosmic dimensions. You are free to believe it if you wish, just don't forget that any bars to this prison are metaphorical and not metallic.

—MARTIN S. KOTTMEYER

Reference

Haines, Richard, ed., *UFO Phenomena and the Behavioral Scientist* (Scarecrow Press, 1979).

Problem of Noncontact Of all the arguments against the presence of extraterrestrial visitors, the Problem of Noncontact has been the most frequently advanced and most respected among disbelievers. Charles Fort posed the issue in counterpoint to his own speculations about extraterrestrials decades before people started arguing about the source of flying saucers. This version from a 1926 letter to

The New York Times would still be acceptable to most skeptics: "Then why have they not landed, say in Central Park, and had a big time of it—monstrous parade down Broadway, historic turn out, eruptions of confetti." (Fort, 1926)

Later writers play around with landing spots in other places like the White House lawn, M.I.T., or Hollywood, but the basic sensibility retained is that they should be open about their activities rather than behave in a furtive and secretive manner. A roster of critics who have accepted the compelling nature of the Problem of Noncontact includes James Lipp of Project Sign, Arthur C. Clarke, Isaac Asimov, Donald Menzel, Peter Kor, Robert Plank, John Keel, William Markowitz, and Robert Sheaffer.

UFOlogists tend to be dismissive of the problem, characterizing it in such terms as "a homocentric fallacy of the most obvious nature" embodying "more whimsy than good reasoning" (McCampbell); "an arbitrary desire" intended to demean UFOs as imaginary (Hendry) or "irrelevant" (Hopkins). Another considers the idea as being "on extremely thin ice" since nobody has done a concerted study forecasting the social characteristics of advanced civilizations (Baker).

Stanton Friedman engages the argument in a more elite manner. He felt the intent of the aliens is "not to seek out lunch with loonies of earth but rather to get data at their leisure without much risk." He doubts that "the Margaret Meads of Zeta Reticuli" would care to live with a people who have "made such a mess of a nice planet." Such remarks would ring truer had UFOnauts repeatedly shown a lack of social discernment.

Though the class of people abducted by aliens are generally not the sort seen on the *Jerry Springer Show*, high-status or highbrow folks are not much in evidence. The aliens clearly favor those who entertain New Age concepts, such as alternate realities, telepathy, and cosmic consciousness. The reckless driving habits of UFOnauts and their evident problems with clunky vessels that spit smoke and flame, and often need repair, raises doubts that they truly operate by the motto, "Safety First."

Advanced medical technology should assuage anxieties over the violent tendencies of humans and their planet-wrecking tendencies. Even if it would not, is safety truly enhanced by not openly declaring that their intentions are anthropological or otherwise innocuous? Secretive and furtive behavior normally elicits suspicion and taunts of having something to hide.

In the years since Friedman's remarks, developments in abduction lore have given force to the presumption that aliens are in fact evil. Thus, we could account for Noncontact by fears of reprisal in some form, or perhaps even shame. The huge investment of resources required to construct and propel interstellar crafts, however, renders all motives of alien self-interest paradoxical. Few things on Earth are worth going light years and expending energy sufficient to power a civilization for years. It is scarcely conceivable that any genetic or medical problem supposedly motivating the Hybrid Program wouldn't be more quickly and efficiently solved by diverting space program funds directly into medical and genetic research *in situ*. Even if we could puzzle out the motive for such evil, this explanation would apply to only a fraction of cases. Do we assume those aliens who collect rocks and pick flowers are also evil?

Such dilemmas apply to other explanations of extraterrestrial behavior. Stanton Friedman was able to think of some twenty-six reasons why aliens might decide to visit Earth. When you ponder them at length however, only two of them have any potential of accounting for the furtive nature of the UFO phenomenon: Aliens scouting Earth for future invasion is one. Using Earth as a honeymoon hideaway is the other. Extrapolating human modesty to extraterrestrials seems questionable, but let's allow it. The immediate dilemma facing these motives is that the behaviors of UFO entities en masse do not really seem to be guided by such motives.

What sort of invasion scout does medical exams? Abductees rarely seem to come from positions of status or have jobs privy to important information. Infiltrating libraries and publishing houses would efficiently get you most of what abductees know. Worse, saucers have been around over fifty years, which would seem to be procrastination on a rather unlikely scale. Information gathered during the 1950s would be obsolete and of no use for any invasion now.

Villas Boas-type affairs are not the rule in UFO stories. One may well wonder if sex under Saturn's rings might be more romantic than Earth's mosquito-infested tropics, but tastes are such an individual matter we should not assume universality. More troubling, though, should be the absence of hints that aliens savor the chosen environment after the trysts are over—no hand-in-hand walks on a beach, skipping stones, playful chases around the trees, taking pictures. How about taking souvenirs or teleporting tourist knickknacks? Given the distance they must have traveled, why don't they show more interest in where they have come from?

The most common argument made in response to the Problem of Noncontact is to point out that superhuman thought and the effects of an independent evolutionary and cultural history would inevitably render aliens, in part or wholly, incomprehensible. This is perfectly true. Consider, as proof, one of the great unsolved mysteries of human evolution—our love for music. There is no widely accepted theory to explain the emotional effect music has on man. Certainly there are no grounds to assume the music sense has a universal survival value that would cause it to arise on alien worlds. It would be miraculous if aliens could fathom the meaning music holds for humans and trying to work out music's logic would be nonsensical even in principle for it plays on emotions rather than reason. Yet we put music on the Voyager probes for distant interstellar civilizations to find and puzzle over. Given our own behavior, one cannot disagree that aliens will be capable of mystifying behavior.

To say this, however, is not the same thing as explaining away noncontact. While we can nonimagine reasons for noncontact, one is equally justified in nonimagining reasons aliens would make contact. The issue then turns on deciding the likelihood that all aliens would adhere to philosophies, however inscrutable, mandating noncontact to the exclusion of pro-contact philosophies. Charles Fort demonstrated his reflective nature by seeing this broader and deadlier version of the Problem of Noncontact: "The greatest of mysteries: Why don't they ever come here or send here openly? Of course there is nothing to this mystery if we don't take seriously the notion that we must be interesting. It's probably for moral reasons they stay away—but even so there must be some degraded ones among them."

As he states elsewhere, there must be "many different kinds of visitors to this earth as there are visitors to New York, to a jail, to a church—some persons go to church to pick pockets for instance."

So where are the degraded aliens? It violates what we see every day about life, society, culture, and intellectual discourse to expect radical uniformity among extraterrestrials.

Just within the sphere of the scrutable, there seems to be no reason to avoid contact that could gain likely universal assent. Take the oft-cited example of *Star Trek*'s Prime Directive—aliens refrain from interfering in the affairs of other cultures to prevent culture shock or contaminating the natural development of the subject culture. It is a romantic notion charged with allusions to clashes of culture within human history. Many had horrid consequences—disease, butchery, slavery, erasure of cultural history. Yet not all contacts were disastrous. One has only to think of the legacy of immigration in New York City. Sure there were conflicts, yet the resulting hybrid has been a jewel of American culture. It is hardly certain alien worlds would all have brutal histories, or that brutality would lead to the lesson of the Prime Directive. An imperial-minded culture might opt for a let-the-dice-roll-and-see-who-wins philosophy that takes any result of interaction as, metaphysically, all the best in the long run.

It should be remembered that the heroes of the *Star Trek* universe repeatedly void the Prime Directive in favor of saving lives, subverting tyranny, and allaying suffering. They even dismantle utopias for notions about the need for people to achieve and struggle to be *human.*

Noninterference is not nearly as elementary an ethical dictate as others like cooperation or love. One can imagine precepts of cooperative tolerance that would mandate interaction between alien worlds to learn from each other to increase their mutual survival and well-being and pleasure. A sharing of the best of all worlds is an aim even an advocate of self-interest could justify.

One could equally see how extraterrestrials might be guided by love and thus seek to alleviate suffering and cultivate joy on other worlds. To put things in their starkest terms, one can procure from theodicy, religion's biggest headache—The Problem of Suffering— and transplant it to the question of the existence of god-like extraterrestrial civilizations: If extraterrestrials exist, why do humans suffer needlessly?

Scrutable reasons for contact or nonfurtiveness can take many forms besides love. Some possibilities that present themselves: hunting and fishing, art trade and instruction, antique-hunting, attention-seeking, power-seeking, entertainment, lawsuits against humans, sports, the offering of services (interstellar taxi), impartial police protection (*The Day the Earth Stood Still*), famine relief, exile of undesirables, erotic adventure, eccentric obsession with alien life, playfulness, tourism, territorial displays.

We dare not forget Charles Fort's awful thought: ''Why not missionaries sent here openly to convert us from our barbarous prohibitions and other taboos, and to prepare the way for a good trade in ultra-bibles and superwhiskies . . .'' Add to this the set of motives that aliens might have for contact beyond our comprehension and you have a conception of the magnitude the Problem of Noncontact presents to the extraterrestrial hypothesis. The odds that all possible visiting extraterrestrials would be philosophically opposed to contact seems thoroughly remote.

Parenthetically, it must be observed that if one believes the evidence for an extraterrestrial presence is too extraordinary to reject even in the face of innate implausibility, there are implications that the ETH advocate is obliged to come to terms with. If UFOs are real, the cosmos is barren. There is no diversity. The cosmos is home to entities with only a narrow range of behaviors.

Similarly, there are no aliens in any reasonable sense analogous to humanity. The startling corollary stares back: Only Humans Love. Does that sound arrogant? Yet consider, aliens capable of deep empathy would not fly around indifferent to the troubles of humanity. They would make contact and help. If you wish to affirm the ETH is valid, understand that the heavens are sending only creeps our way. We either have incredibly bad luck or there is no variety of life-forms blooming in the vast depths of space. The universe does not know how to throw a good party.

In fairness, Charles Fort did proffer a way around the paradoxical absence of degraded aliens. ''We are property,'' he wrote. The degraded ones are warned off. This reduces some of the problems posed by the expectation of diversity, but hardly eliminates it. Unless we can reduce the number of owners to one individual being or a small family, the problem still hangs on in the dynamics of groups. The range of forms suggested by the UFO phenomenon doesn't really support such an idea as a single owner. There is also a problem that philosophies usually evolve or degrade over time. People change their minds once in a while. Thus, even evidence for a single owner would raise issues of how noncontact should last over the whole of UFO history.

There is a temptation to extrapolate territorial behavior found in many species to the realms of outer space to buttress the property thesis. Here, the difficulty is that territoriality is typically directed to forms of one's own species. It would limit noncontact only within one species of aliens, not many, as UFO lore tends to favor. Property is also not a cultural universal. Many alien cultures quite possibly would not recognize the idea of property and ignore warnings not to trespass.

There is then the question of whether the owners would feel the Earth is worth defending against other aliens. UFO behavior gives no evidence that resources are being exploited. No special care is lavished on humans or other animals leading to doubts about us being regarded as highly valued. There is no blatant evidence of cultivation, weeding, domestication, or artificial breeding on a planetary scale.

Having granted that UFOnauts seem indifferent to the state of human life leads naturally to a different explanation that has been advanced to explain noncontact. Maybe technologically advanced life evolves to a higher plane of existence. All their desires are taken care of eventually and they live in a state of perpetual satisfaction due to the march of technological advance and scientific inquiry. Maybe they are gods of their own realms and no longer notice, let alone care about, those beings more primitive than themselves. This can be justified by analogy to the universal indifference humans have toward protozoa.

This could work for Fermi's Paradox—the absence of aliens on Earth despite a fecund cosmos—but this is less than compelling when applied to the UFO phenomenon. The universe is far too big for aliens to arrive here randomly. Some motive must target them into the onionskin of Earth's atmosphere. When we see alien theme parks scudding along the rings of Saturn, then talk of indifference will make some sense. Needless to say, the many abduction stories of aliens examining humans do not support the notion of indifference either.

Ultimately, one can never escape the fact that the problem of no degraded aliens lies in the shadows of any variation of the ETH that can be offered. There are just too many possibilities in a universe full of life. The Problem of Noncontact can only be defeated if the UFO phenomenon changes radically and strips away from its label the prefix *un-*. If aliens identify themselves and make open contact then the problem goes away. Until then, UFOlogists will keep encountering it.

—MARTIN S. KOTTMEYER

References

Asimov, Isaac. "The Rocketing Dutchmen" in *The Planet That Wasn't* (Avon, 1976).

Baker, Robert M. L. and James McDonald. *Symposium on UFOs—Hearings Before the Committee on Science and Astronautics*, U.S. House of Representatives, 90th Congress, 2nd session, July 29, 1968.

Clarke, Arthur C. "Last Words on UFOs" in *The View from Serendip* (Ballantine, 1978).

Fort, Charles. "Have Martians Visited Us? British Observer Argues in the Affirmative and Seeks News of Future Manifestations" (*The New York Times,* September 5, 1926).

Fort, Charles. *The Book of the Damned* (Ace Star, undated; originally published by Boni & Liveright, 1919).

Friedman, Stanton. "A Scientific Approach to Flying Saucer Behavior" (*Thesis-Antithesis*, AIAA Los Angeles, no date).

Hendry, Allan. *The UFO Handbook* (Doubleday, 1979).

Hopkins, Budd. *Missing Time* (Richard Marek, 1981).

Keel, John. *Why UFOs?* (Manor Books, 1970).

Klass, Philip. *UFOs Identified* (Random House, 1968).

Kor, Peter. "Saucer Clubs—20th Century Cults" (*Flying Saucers,* October 1961).

Lipp, James. Appendix D of *Project Sign*, December 13, 1948.

Markowitz, William. "The Physics and Metaphysics of UFOs" (*Science,* September 15, 1967).

McCampbell, James M. *UFOlogy* (Celestial Arts, 1976).

Menzel, Donald. *Flying Saucers* (Harvard University Press, 1953).

Plank, Robert. *The Emotional Significance of Imaginary Beings* (1968).

Sheaffer, Robert. *The UFO Verdict* (Prometheus, 1981).

Program for Extraordinary Experience Research, The (PEER) PEER was founded

in 1993 by Harvard professor of psychiatry John E. Mack, M.D., to formalize his study of reported alien encounters and other experiences that seem at odds with the Western worldview. PEER's work is motivated by the understanding that expansions of human knowledge come with the exploration of unexplained phenomena.

PEER's mission is to explore and integrate extraordinary experiences within a context of personal, societal, and global transformation. This comprehensive vision and integrative approach has evolved from the understanding that no single field or human perspective can account for the anomalies we are encountering in our research.

PEER is a project of the Center for Psychology and Social Change. Through the Center's twenty-year history, we have been committed to the exploration, understanding, and integration of personal and collective identity: tribal (ethno-national conflict), species (human potential), interspecies (relationship with Earth's ecosystem), and cosmic (relationships with intelligences in the universe).

PEER's knowledge of the exploration, integration, and application of experiences not readily understood is called upon as a resource by diverse groups. PEER representatives have been invited to speak to and educate political, religious, and spiritual leaders about extraordinary experiences and their relationship to social, environmental, economic, spiritual, epistemological, and ontological matters. These relationships and initiatives may, we feel, ultimately have a great impact on our society, encouraging others to reconsider their views of the universe in which we live.

Address: P.O. Box 398080
            Cambridge, MA 02139
            U.S.A.

E-mail: peer@peermack.org

Web site: www.peermack.org

—PEER STAFF

Project Blue Book   For over twenty years, the U.S. Air Force was charged with investigating and evaluating UFO reports brought to its attention in the United States and at U.S. bases, stations, or property in other countries. Project Blue Book was the responsible unit within the Air Force during most of that period—from 1952 until the end of 1969.

The first UFO project, located within the Air Technical Intelligence Center (ATIC) of Air Matériel Command, Wright-Patterson Air Force Base, Dayton, Ohio, was Project Sign, created in January 1948, with a Restricted classification. It was replaced by Project Grudge in February 1949. While Project Sign had reportedly suffered from an internal ideological battle concerning the origin or cause of UFO reports, Project Grudge took a more negative approach to the question and soon became a relatively dormant operation. The project was revitalized under the direction of Captain Edward J. Ruppelt, and the new, unofficial code name of Blue Book was assigned to it. Most of this early history of the Air Force involvement with UFOs is known through a book authored by Ruppelt (see THE REPORT ON UNIDENTIFIED FLYING OBJECTS), and much of what he wrote has since been verified by declassified Air Force documents.

Ruppelt was a World War II veteran who had returned to active duty during the Korean conflict. With a degree in aeronautical engineering, he was assigned to ATIC and was involved in the analysis of the Soviet MIG-15 jet fighter. According to Ruppelt, ATIC was ordered to undertake a new study of the UFO situation at a special Pentagon meeting in September of 1950, during the Grudge dormancy. The study report was delivered to General John Samford, the new director of Air Force Intelligence, by Ruppelt and Colonel Frank Dunn, the head of ATIC, in December of 1951. Ruppelt was then assigned to reactivate the project, and the name was changed to Blue Book. Under Ruppelt's direction, Blue Book grew into a better-organized unit, but over the next two years, it was barely able to handle the volume of reports it received for analysis and, sometimes, additional investigation. It was during Ruppelt's tenure that some of the most famous incidents in UFO history occurred, such as the Lubbock Lights, the Washington National radar/visual reports, and the Robertson Panel meeting. Ruppelt was responsible for briefing the Robertson Panel members on the then-classified UFO material.

After retiring from the Air Force, Ruppelt wrote his book detailing the history of Air Force involvement with UFOs up to that time, and it has since become a classic in the UFO literature. The book took a positive approach, leaving the reader with the impression that Ruppelt accepted the reality of UFOs. A subsequent edition of the book, published in 1960, included three new chapters, and Ruppelt seemed to have considerably mellowed his enthusiasm. Perhaps this was due to the increasing contactee claims, or perhaps to the attacks being directed at the Air Force by the newly created National Investigations Committee on Aerial Phenomena (NICAP). As Ruppelt was an engineer at Northrop Corporation at the time, some writers have speculated that the Air Force, embarrassed by the first edition of Ruppelt's book, applied pressure on Northrop, a large Air Force contractor, to have him update the book with a more negative conclusion. No evidence for this has ever surfaced. Ruppelt died in 1960.

After Ruppelt's departure from Blue Book, the operation was directed during the 1950s and 1960s by Captain Charles Hardin (1954-56), Captain George T. Gregory (1956-58), Major (later Lieutenant Colonel) Robert J. Friend (1958-63), and Major (later Lieutenant Colonel) Hector Quintanilla, Jr. (1963-69). The project never again enjoyed the large staff and support of the Ruppelt days.

Indeed, under the premise that there was no real underlying, unconventional phenomenon behind UFO reports, its new, low-key operational approach was changed to that of explaining as many reports as possible by any means possible, preferably without additional

investigation. Exceptions were made in special instances, particularly in cases that received widespread publicity, and the Air Force, as a public relations measure, had to "show the flag." Thus, Blue Book became little more than an Air Force showpiece, always subject to the political needs of senior Air Force officers in the Pentagon, who, in turn, were subject to pressures from the press, the public, and even the Congress.

The scientific community generally did not involve itself in the controversy, erroneously assuming that the Air Force had a dynamic research project under way. Dr. J. Allen Hynek, Blue Book's scientific consultant, who had been retained originally under Project Sign, was not always happy with Blue Book's approach, but he felt that directly confronting the Air Force would serve little purpose. Other pressures on the Air Force came from Donald Menzel, a well-known Harvard astronomer, who dismissed the entire business as nonsense, and, at the other extreme, NICAP, which lobbied actively in Congress and had some influence on the press.

It was in the mid-1960s that the UFO controversy again climaxed, with highly publicized sightings, accusations against Air Force secrecy, and/or incompetence by the press and some members of Congress (including Representative Gerald Ford), and, finally, the awarding of an Air Force contract to the University of Colorado to conduct an independent, two-year study. During that period, Blue Book (formally known as the Aerial Phenomena Branch) was located within ATIC's successor, the Foreign Technology Division (FMD), Systems Command (still at Wright-Patterson Air Force Base), and was directed by Major Quintanilla, who held a degree in physics. His staff consisted of a lieutenant, a sergeant, and a secretary.

Many observers believed that the Blue Book staff was intellectually unable to handle some of the new, challenging cases, such as the Exeter, New Hampshire, and Portage County (Ravenna, Ohio) sightings, resulting in further embarrassing confrontations with the press and the private UFO organizations. After 1966, the University of Colorado UFO Project relieved the pressure considerably. The university's Condon Report, released publicly in early 1969, recommended the closing of Project Blue Book. A March 1969 meeting in Washington, D.C., attended by officers from Systems Command, Air Defense Command, and Air Force Headquarters, resulted in the decision to close the operation permanently, and the termination was announced on December 17, 1969, by Secretary of the Air Force Robert C. Seamans, Jr. In a memorandum to the Air Force Chief of Staff, General John D. Ryan, Dr. Seamans stated that Blue Book could no longer "be justified either on the ground of national security or in the interest of science."

The Air Force's final statistical breakdown, released soon afterward by the Secretary of the Air Force Office of Information (SAFOI), gave a total of 12,618 UFO reports in Blue Book files, 701 of which remained unidentified. Numerous private UFO researchers have claimed that many more of the reports should have been carried as unidentified, and some unidentifieds are actually easy to explain, indicating, at least in some instances (according to these observers), arbitrary assignments of labels.

In the SAFOI release, Lieutenant Colonel James H. Aikman stated, among other things, that no UFO had ever ". . . given any indication of threat to our national security . . ." and that ". . . there has been no evidence submitted to or discovered by the Air Force that sightings categorized as 'unidentified' represent technological developments or principles beyond the range of present-day scientific knowledge." These statements were identical, word for word, to the periodic Air Force UFO releases throughout the 1950s and 1960s, which were based on the terminology of the 1953 Robertson Panel report.

Most of the Blue Book files were declassified and retired to the Air Force Archives at Maxwell Air Force Base, in Alabama, where several academic researchers obtained access to them. They were subsequently transferred to the Modern Military Branch of the National Archives, in Washington, D.C., where public access to them is granted.

Over the years, numerous claims have been made that Project Blue Book was merely a "front" for a secret and more sophisticated Air Force or Central Intelligence Agency (CIA) operation. Some observers have even proposed that Blue Book staff members were innocent "pawns," who were totally unaware of the ultrasecret laboratories where the real "good" UFO material was sent. Despite all the claims, no hard evidence has ever been produced to support this. In fact, as Air Force personnel were subject to AFR 200-2 (and amendments), which required all UFO reports and material be transmitted to ATIC and, later, FTD, and as AFR 200-2 was signed by the Air Force Chief of Staff, it is difficult to envision how hundreds of base-level personnel, of which there was (and is) a constant turnover, could have done otherwise. That is, it is not at all clear how they would have known where to send only the "good" reports without the existence of an additional regulation, and any such additional regulation would have very soon become public knowledge.

Although the U.S. Air Force no longer maintains a special UFO investigative unit like Project Blue Book, it continues to investigate specific UFO incidents, if and when warranted by national defense or security reasons, as part of its normal intelligence functions.

—ETEP STAFF

Project Magnet This project was a study of UFOs carried out by the Department of Transport (DOT) in Canada in the early 1950s. It was set up in December 1950 under the direction of Wilbert B. Smith, then senior radio engineer, Broadcast and Measurements Section.

The project was quite small; it used facilities of DOT, with assistance from other government departments, including the Defense Research Board (DRB) and the National Research Council (NRC). The project was an outgrowth of work already being done by Smith and a group of colleagues within DOT on the collapse of the Earth's magnetic field as a source of energy. It was the belief of many that "flying saucers" were operating on magnetic principles and it was thought the DOT work might explain their operation.

The program consisted of two parts: (1) collection of high-quality data, analysis, and drawing conclusions; and (2) a systematic questioning of all our basic concepts in hope of identifying a discrepancy which might be the key to a new technology. Smith also developed ideas for measuring the reliability of observational data, and using these measurements to rate the probability that a given report could be accepted as a real observation.

It is noteworthy that in September 1950, Smith interviewed Dr. Robert I. Sarbacher who was then Director of Research for National Scientific Laboratories Inc., in Washington, D.C., and had held numerous other top-rank industrial positions and worked on contract as a "dollar-a-year-man" on UFO research. He was also Dean of the Graduate School of the Georgia Institute of Technology. Smith was told by Sarbacher, through LCDR Bremner, on staff of the Canadian Embassy in Washington who acted as intermediary, that the facts reported in Frank Scully's book (*Behind the Flying Saucers,* 1950) "are substantially correct," that flying saucers exist and that the subject of flying saucers "is classified two points higher even than the H-bomb. In fact, it is the most highly classified subject in the U.S. Government at the present time," according to this record. Smith went on: "May I ask the reason for the classification?" Sarbacher replied: "You may ask, but I can't tell you." The notes recording this interview were first discovered in one of Smith's personal files given to this writer by Smith's widow; then another copy was found in a formerly classified file held by the Canadian government. In 1983, as reported in the MUFON Symposium Proceedings for 1986, Sarbacher confirmed the above statements to Mr. William Steinman. It was only three months after Sarbacher's statements to Smith that Project Magnet received official Canadian government authorization.

In 1952, Smith submitted an interim report, in which he stated that it appeared evident that flying saucers are emissaries from some other civilization and actually do operate on magnetic principles.

In 1953, he submitted a further report in which he concluded that we are faced with a substantial probability of the real existence of extraterrestrial vehicles and that such vehicles must of necessity use a technology considerably in advance of our own.

Smith established the world's first "flying saucer sighting station" at Shirley Bay, outside Ottawa, in November 1953. This station consisted of a small wooden DRB building, containing some highly sophisticated instrumentation specially adapted to detect flying saucers. These instruments were: a gamma-ray counter, a magnetometer, a radio receiver, and a recording gravimeter. These four instruments produced traces on a multiple-pen graphical recorder which was checked periodically to note any disturbances.

At 3:01 P.M., August 8, 1954, the station registered a definite disturbance, quite different from disturbances registered by passing aircraft. Smith and his colleagues were alerted by a built-in alarm system. Regrettably, heavy fog prevailed and it was impossible to see anything overhead. The recorded evidence, however, indicated that something strange had flown within feet of the station.

On August 10, 1954, DOT officially folded Project Magnet, but permitted Smith to continue using its facilities on his own time at no expense to the government. Smith continued his work privately until his death in December 1962.

—ARTHUR BRAY

projection/warning theory of UFOs and ETs This could also be called the "they-are-us" theory: not as time travelers back from the future, but rather "us in the here and now" mentally projecting our hopes and fears in a conflicted world. Though I cannot speak for Martin Kottmeyer, in my opinion his theory of UFOs as an evolving system of paranoia (see PARANOIA AND UFOs) is closely related to my version of the projection/warning theory. Kott-meyer demonstrates the extremes the UFO myth can take in the minds of paranoids who accentuate what I consider "normal" concerns of anyone who realizes what is happening to our society—namely, dehumanization and loss of individuality on a massive scale. Ultimately, Aldous Huxley's *Brave New World* (1932) and *Brave New World Revisited* (1958), and George Orwell's *1984* (1949) may prove to be understatements.

When you consider the content of the UFO-alien myth (or reality), we are faced with two possibilities: either (1) we are being invaded by aliens who are behaving much the same (good and bad) as human beings, or (2) we are metaphorically projecting personal situations and social trends. In other words we are seeing in UFO-alien lore a metaphorical representation of our own evolution in all its aspects.

I personally believe this phenomenon functions as an instinctive warning system orchestrated by the unconscious mind. In this view, the main purpose of projections is to draw attention to our unconscious perceptions and enhance awareness of our natural instincts. As with other features of human evolution, the unconscious warning system has obvious survival value.

The essence of the projection/warning theory was contained in Carl Jung's 1958 book, *Flying Saucers: A Modern Myth of Things Seen in the Skies*. Therein Jung offered the suggestion that UFOs and ETs constitute a living mythology that is signaling a coming new age. In this writer's view, the main purpose of a living myth is to provide a coping mechanism for the human condition. Like dreams (hence the surrealism of UFO-abduction accounts), myths are almost pure metaphor: analogies that reflect our life situations, collectively and individually.

Dreams = private myths and myths = public dreams, as Joseph Campbell would say. The images making up these dramas are symbolic and therefore require psychological interpretation in order to be "decoded," so to speak,

into literal terms. To one who understands their language, myths and dreams provide insights into the human condition. And the same holds true for the entire body of UFO-alien lore.

If we interpret the UFO myth symbolically, it tells us everything that is happening in our world as understood by the unconscious mind. And more important, when the archetypal themes and events are interpreted as predictions, we can explore what is likely to happen in the future if the present course is maintained. Our modern UFO-alien mythology is a *projection* in every sense.

Just about everything found in UFO lore is really happening—in one sense or another—but in my view our imagined "aliens" are not from another planet; they are "mutant" forms of what we used to regard as human beings. In the words of the protagonist, Dr. Miles Binnell, in Jack Finney's 1955 novel, *Invasion of the Body Snatchers*: "Sometimes I think we're refining all humanity out of our lives." Yes—we are being invaded by "non-human" (alien) life-forms who are taking over the Earth: the Grays (emotionless clones), robots (see the book *Robopaths* by Lewis Yablonsky); reptilians (like the serpent in the Garden of Eden); and alien captors using anal probes (a clear analogy here) who invade our privacy, make us feel paralyzed and powerless—taking away our human dignity and our freedom by taking our thoughts. These are all symbolic representations of how we unconsciously see the non-humans who are taking over and undermining our human society. That is the reason for the cry to be more "spiritual" vs. material; more caring vs. cut-throat; and having a conscience vs. being a sociopath. Yes, the *human* population on this planet is in deep trouble, and that's why so many want to be beamed up!

Combine these archetypes with the motifs found in science fiction—which were also created to depict the same kinds of conditions—and you have the magic formula for the living myth of UFOs and invaders from outer space. As a side note, when I met Gene Roddenberry on a New York TV show, in 1981, he told me that *Star Trek* was primarily intended as a "social commentary" and not as science fiction *per se*.

The reason we have a neurotic society is that we've been double-crossed. We have a major psychological conflict going on. Our parents, society, organized religion (sold to us as "God"), and our government were all thought to be the unquestioned guardians of our welfare. And now we know—unconsciously and consciously—that they cannot be trusted. We've been betrayed, which I think is the major reason for the paranoia that Martin Kottmeyer writes about.

Psychologist Rollo May thought *conflict* between what we trusted to be the case and mixed messages were the leading cause of anxiety disorders. He gave an example of a case in which parents were openly mean to their child, but at least were consistent, which did not result in an anxiety disorder. But another example that involved mixed messages, or inconsistencies, did. (May, 1977)

When we begin to recognize discrepancies in what we were taught in childhood, a psychological conflict develops. That is why we need new myths to take the place of old-time religion. This became *science* with all its promises for a wonderful utopian future for all, administered by our supposedly benevolent government leaders.

Now we see science and technology used for all kinds of hidden agendas for the benefit of certain people (especially forthcoming in the field of genetic engineering and pharmaceutical research—as in *Brave New World*). So now we've been double-crossed once again. More conflict; more neuroses. It will be remembered that a number of famous and intelligent optimists (like Jules Verne, H. G. Wells, C. G. Jung, et al.) became pessimistic about the fate of man shortly before they died.

The neurotic response is a cry for myth: a myth we can believe that will reconcile the disparate elements that do not otherwise make sense.

Most of us cannot look into the mirror or out upon the world and see what is truly there.

We deny the hypocrisy, because we don't want to believe it is really happening. So, as Freud and Jung tried to inform us, the projections are launched as defense mechanisms. But, I think projections should also be regarded as *warnings* (in the form of metaphors or analogies) of possible dangers lurking ahead. The first unconscious model for the "aliens" in modern times was the "Red Threat" (or the "Commies") of the Cold War era. But today, the aliens are our own people (our leaders and ourselves).

Regarding UFOs: Jung seemed puzzled by the fact that "something is seen, but one doesn't know what." That's where the misidentifications come in. Especially since World War II, we've had all kinds of secret technology (mostly aircraft) which accounts for quite a lot. Then, of course, there are myriad other things seen that can play tricks on our perceptions, especially since we are always projecting order onto the unknown.

I would also say there is a high probability that other phenomena exist, presently unknown to science, and that might even include extraterrestrial visitors. So, all the more reason to study every aspect of the UFO phenomenon, but especially the psycho-social aspects, because, with Jung, I think ". . . we need more psychology. We need more understanding of human nature, because the only real danger that exists is man himself. He is the great danger, and we are pitifully unaware of it." (BBC interview, 1957) But as Bertrand Russell once said: "Men fear truth more than anything else in the world." That is our predicament.

—RONALD D. STORY

References

Bacon, Francis. "The Four Idols" (first published in 1620). Reprinted in *Readings in Philosophy*, edited by John Herman Randall, Jr., et al. (Barnes & Noble, 1967).

Fromm, Erich. *The Forgotten Language: An Introduction to the Understanding of Dreams, Fairy Tales, and Myths* (Holt, Rinehart and Winston, 1951).

————. *The Revolution of Hope: Toward a Humanized Technology* (Harper & Row, 1968).

————. *On Being Human* (Continuum, 1997).

Huxley, Aldous. *Brave New World* (Harper & Row, 1932, 1946).

————. *Brave New World Revisited* (Harper & Row, 1958).

Jung, C. G. *Flying Saucers: A Modern Myth of Things Seen in the Skies* (Routledge & Kegan Paul/Harcourt, Brace & Co. 1959; Signet/NAL, 1969; Princeton University Press, 1978). Original German language edition published in 1958.

C. G. Jung Speaking, edited by William McGuire and R. F. C. Hull (Princeton University Press, 1977).

Lorenz, Conrad. *The Waning of Humaneness* (Little, Brown & Co., 1983; 1987).

May, Rollo. *The Meaning of Anxiety* (W. W. Norton, 1977).

————. *The Cry for Myth* (W. W. Norton, 1991).

Orwell, George. *1984* (Harcourt Brace Jovanovich, 1949; Signet/NAL, 1961).

Sagan, Carl. Foreword to *The Space-Gods Revealed* by Ronald Story (Harper & Row, 1976).

Story, Ronald D. "UFOs and the Meaning of Life," *The Quest* (Winter 1997).

Yablonsky, Lewis. *Robopaths* (Penguin Books, 1972).

psychiatric aspects of UFO encounters

One intriguing aspect of the UFO-ET problem concerns people who have claimed contact or abduction by UFO entities.

At times, these experiences involve multiple witnesses and include other corroborative data, such as associated animal reactions. The human biological or psychophysiological responses to close encounters have included alleged illnesses, injuries, burns, temporary paralysis, relief or healing of a condition or illness, blackouts, seizures, time lapses, change in memory (either increased or blanked out), changes in intelligence (either vast improvement or impairment), and various behavioral effects such as fugues and psychosis.

Also, there are many published cases involving psychic (or *psi*) phenomena, including instances of (1) purported telepathic and clairvoyant communications; (2) possible precognition or prophecy; (3) alleged forces making the craft and/or entities invisible—possibly akin to supposed materialization, dematerialization, or apportation; (4) accounts of mysterious appearances and disappearances of UFO-associated creatures (sometimes "monsters"), with little or no evidence for their existence beyond that which is witnessed by one person or several persons; (5) claimed telekinesis ("mind over matter")—objects moving, strange rappings, sounds, or effects on radio, TV, lights, telephones, computers, or other electrical appliances; (6) possible psychic or thoughtographic photographs of UFOS; (7) alleged UFO-associated paranormal audiotapes; (8) alleged teleportations of people or objects; (9) levitation and "antigravity effects"; and (10) supposed pre- and post-UFO-sighting paranoia events, such as hauntings, poltergeists, etc.

Much of the UFO "physical" phenomena could be equated with the data of psychotronics and could be explained as an extension of "psi" (or psychic phenomena).

An overlooked feature might be the contactee-abductee interactions with computers. In these instances, two factors that should be considered are: (1) the mechanism(s) by which the presumed effects take place, and (2) the interpretation of such data and how these might be possibly (and often intimately and presently) tie in with the experient's personal life, precipitating factors, and so forth. Where does the information come from? How do they receive the information? What does the information mean?

As UFO experiences and related phenomena are more carefully and critically studied, these become more understandable and plausible; and paradoxically, more complex, inscrutable, frustrating, and ambiguous. The separation of the experience itself from contributory psychodynamics—and in recent years often gross contamination from the media and popular literature—poses problems.

Another category of data that the psychiatrist might find interesting is that which comprises the aftermath of a UFO experience. These data include such events as strange phone calls and peculiar messages, mail tampering, frightening visitors of unusual appearance—so-called "Men in Black," who often arrive in black Cadillacs—and instances of extreme bad luck.

Follow-up study of these experiences, as well as interviews in some of the renowned contactee-abductee cases of years ago, might yield significant additional information about what happened to these people long ago, how they fared subsequently with their health, what are the apparent wax-and-wane patterns of various claimed associated psychic phenomena, and what their current views would be in comparison with what they stated at the time of their original UFO contact.

It should be stressed that, in contrast to the scarcity of hard-core "nuts and bolts" UFO data, there is a wealth of biological, psychodynamic, and psychic data which has been widely published in the *Flying Saucer Review*, *MUFON UFO Journal*, and elsewhere.

It is unfortunate that the psychic aspects of the problem have received little professional attention compared with the copious material on the astronomical and physical effects. Of the medical specialties, psychiatry is well equipped to study those persons who claim contact or abduction by a UFO. The psychiatrist is proficient in various clinical, laboratory, and experimental techniques, including obtaining detailed histories of the alleged contactees and abductees and their families; data on their past health; physical examinations; and, when indicated, additional studies such as hypnosis and electroencephalography; and when indicated, videographically monitored electroencephalographic activation techniques for possible temporal lobe focal discharges; and utilizing newer discoveries from neuroscience.

The psychiatrist can also collate the various findings of colleagues in other fields: for example, the ophthalmologist's evaluation of alleged UFO-induced eye injury; the dermatologist's or radiologist's findings in purported cases of radiation burns and various skin effects; and arranging consultation with specialists in positron emission tomography (PET) and functional magnetic resonance imaging

(MRI). Also, how interesting it would be to have genetic/DNA profiles of different gifted, documented UFO experients (contactees, abductees, paragnosts) and their families.

It is often helpful to make field trips to study these persons and their families in their home environments, and to listen carefully to their stories no matter how strange. With such background knowledge and discreet use of suggestion, clinical experiments can be performed that might engender UFO or UFO-like phenomena, or yield clues to the possible human "here and now" of some, if not much, of the material and thereby provide a possible understanding of the psychic core of much of the UFO-ET contact experience.

It appears that what the contactees and abductees claim often constitutes "subjective" reality, and their ideational content and behavioral reactions do not conform to the usual mental illnesses that a psychiatrist sees in his everyday practice.

The UFO experience, whatever its explanation, is seldom, if ever, solely the product of mental disease; however, the reverse can happen: namely, the close-encounter UFO experience can precipitate various emotional reactions, such as anxiety, depression, dissociation, etc.

The contactee or abductee can also become emotionally disturbed over the open ridicule or disbelief of family, friends, or society in general. This destructive attitude can be more damaging than an out-and-out credulity.

These people might benefit by seeing the psychiatrist or mental health professional. Also mention should be made of a useful clinical technique, "collaborative research," as developed and pioneered by the late Adelaide M. Johnson, M.D., Ph.D., of the Mayo Clinic. In this prohibitively costly research and psychotherapeutic method, highly skilled teams of psychiatrists studied individual patients and their families with various conditions: e.g., diverse forms of delinquency, sexual deviations, sociopathic behavior and so forth. Then, with the permission of the participants, information was reported and collated in meetings where the data could be pieced together, so that it was often possible to pinpoint precise causes, contributory factors, and expressions of these specific forms of deviant behavior and mental aberrations. Much of the mystery then dissolves.

Possibly an expanded series of psychiatric studies of contactees and abductees would help answer the question of whether their experiences were: (1) solely the product of the UFO; (2) a psychopathologically colored, culturally conditioned reaction to the psychodynamically and psychically projected UFO; or (3) a combination of these.

Furthermore, it would be helpful to know if the clinical impression is correct as to: (1) Are many contactees and abductees great natural psychics who by largely unconscious factors within themselves, and in conjunction with other persons, induce the UFO experience? (2) Does the terror and uniqueness of the UFO-encounter experience split them and leave them open to a great awareness of their otherwise latent psychic abilities? (3) Or, finally, does the force associated with the UFO encounter directly instill the seemingly enhanced psychic faculties that engender the phenomena or permit the contactee to tap another dimension? (4) Could the UFO force be identical with psi? And if not, (5) what is their interface?

Interestingly, most contactees are excellent hypnotic subjects, and this might also be a clue to the causation of the phenomena; i.e., they seem to be exquisitely sensitive to all kinds of subliminal and psychic stimuli. Therefore, could the UFO force or X factor from another dimension take advantage of this hypersuggestible state?

Whatever the answers to these speculations, the key to the human part of the UFO equation might be related to the mechanism and role of the contactee's or abductee's dissociation and relationship to other trance-like and psychopathological states, multiple personality disorder, gifted paragnosia, idiot savants, and genius.

The complexity of the UFO phenomenon—considered from both human and extra-terrestrial standpoints—raises momentous questions. Naturally, it would be desirable to know as much as possible about such a powerful force that can influence matter, alter our mental states, affect our health and behavior; and even though it cannot be measured, this force can inspire, frighten, cause terror, lead to fanaticism, invention, creativity, and discovery.

Perhaps what could be learned might be turned to constructive use, or perhaps the various manifestations and the social complications of the UFO experience suggest that, if what is known were more widely disseminated, it could have a disintegrative effect on society. If man's basic mental mechanisms (e.g., denial, dissociation, projection, and so forth) fail to protect him, there could be individual and collective epidemics of chaos.

—Berthold E. Schwarz

Psychosocial aspects of UFOs   A psychosocial approach to the UFO phenomenon is one which asks: Are ostensible UFO events the physical happenings they seem to be? Or, do they originate in the *psychology* of the individual and take their shape from *social* factors?

There is no single psychosocial hypothesis to which all who adopt such an approach subscribe; there are probably as many variants as there are people proposing such an approach. What they have in common is a belief that a typical UFO-related event should not necessarily be taken to be what the experiencer claims (or believes) it to be, particularly when—as is the case with most, if not all such experiences—there are no independent witnesses and no convincing supporting evidence. Rather, it may well be a fantasy created subconsciously by the witness: a fantasy shaped and conditioned by their prevailing cultural milieu.

For example, in the case of someone who claims to have been abducted by extraterrestrial aliens, a psychosocial view might be that he/she is subconsciously projecting his/her *subjective* preoccupations as an imagined *objective* event. The abduction scenario is chosen because it enables one to externalize their state not only outside oneself but outside humankind, and because extraterrestrial intervention has become the "authorized myth" of our time, which has generally replaced the demons, deities, and magicians who fulfilled the role in former times.

The source material used to construct the fantasy may be of many kinds. Apart from the general climate generated by mankind's first ventures into space, the influence of science-fiction books and movies has been demonstrated by such commentators as Bertrand Méheust, Martin Kottmeyer, and Nigel Watson: virtually every feature of the post-1947 flying saucer phenomenon can be matched with parallels in the American science-fiction pulps of the 1920s and 1930s.

Alvin Lawson has suggested birth trauma: the abduction experience resembles the birth experience in several ways apart from the resemblance of the widely perceived "Gray" aliens to the human fetus. Hilary Evans has shown parallels with other types of entity experiences: religious visions, ghosts, spirits, and demons. Dennis Stillings looks to Jungian archetypes as a conditioning force. Jung himself perceived as early as 1958 that "flying saucers" were archetypal visions that represented "a modern myth of things seen in the skies," though he could not foresee how rich and complex that myth was to become in the years that followed his death in 1961.

In a typical psychosocial scenario, the subconscious mind confabulates such materials into a personal story in much the same way that our dreaming mind draws together elements from all kinds of sources to create our dreams. The result is a narrative that can often be coherent and plausible, rich in appropriate detail, convincing many that the event was physically real and took place as claimed.

Few proponents of the psychosocial approach believe that the experiences are "all in the mind": often the experience will be triggered by a physical event. This event may be genuinely mysterious: more frequently, though, as has been demonstrated by Randles, Hendry, and Monnerie among others, a banal event, such as an airplane with landing lights, an advertising airship, or the moon, can lead to an extravagant fantasy.

The most sustained expression of the psychosocial approach has come from the small but highly influential British journal *Magonia,* which even in its earlier incarnation as the *Merseyside UFO Bulletin* cast a cold eye on face-value explanations and found them wanting. Currently edited by John Rimmer, whose *The Evidence for Alien Abductions* (1984) is an intelligent appraisal of the extraterrestrial and psychosocial alternatives, its staff and contributors have consistently invited readers to consider the psychosocial alternative to the extraterrestrial hypothesis.

In the U.S., Dennis Stillings's seminal 1989 collective *Cyberbiological Studies of the Imaginal Component in the UFO Contact Experience* provided a forum for those who felt there was no need to look beyond Earth for an explanation of the phenomenon.

European UFOlogists have also published some excellent material representing the psychosocial: Thierry Pinvidic's massive 1993 collective *OVNI,* subtitled "Towards the Anthropology of a Contemporary Myth," brought together many psychosocially inclined viewpoints. In Australia, Mark Moravec has made valuable contributions related to the interplay of psychological and cultural factors, such as the destabilizing effect of immigration.

Few of those who favor the psychosocial approach regard it as *the* answer to every puzzle that has arisen in the UFO context. It is evidently not an explanation for those events which are better explained as secret man-made devices or for purely understood natural phenomena. But it is probably fair to say that its proponents see it as the preferred explanation in all cases where others look to an extraterrestrial explanation.

This viewpoint received strong experimental support when California professor Alvin Lawson, with his colleague McCall, conducted the "imaginary abductee" experiment that demonstrated the ability of ordinary people to fabricate complex experiences. Though virulently attacked by dissenting UFOlogists, this experiment simply demonstrated, in a UFO-abduction context, processes well enough known to psychologists.

Another important dimension drawn from psychology has been the suggestion that UFO witnesses and abductees are "fantasy prone" personalities. Though Bartholomew and Basterfield were unsuccessful in their attempts to show that abductees conformed to the classic fantasy-proneness mold, their thesis received convincing support from the research of Kenneth Ring who established that UFO witnesses show a psychological profile that is not entirely typical, leading him to postulate that there is a class of people who are "encounter prone." The inference is that UFO incidents and abductions are more likely to be experienced by some people than by others, which in turn suggests a psychological origin for the experience.

The weakness of the psychosocial approach is that it relates to human behavior, an area of study in which it is difficult to obtain consensus views. The behavioral sciences still remain largely uncharted, and their findings are often controversial. Consequently, the debate largely consists of speculation and a balancing of probabilities.

Some of the evidence points either way: for example, the fact that currently fashionable themes such as ecology and resource abuse recurs frequently in claimed messages from aliens could be because the aliens really are concerned with such matters, or because witnesses are projecting their own preoccupations into an external framework. The fact that one abduction case will resemble another in close detail has been seen by some, such as folklorist Thomas Eddie Bullard, as evidence that they are physically real; but it is equally possible that the similarity derives from unconscious imitation, or even from the fact that all witnesses are drawing on the same pool of archetypal imagery.

Particularly significant are those cases where it has been demonstrated that the claimed event did not physically take place. Some abductees, notably Maureen Puddy in Australia, have been seen *not* to be abducted when they claimed to be so. However, such cases are rare, for the abduction witness is generally isolated and unobserved, and while it is all-but-impossible for them to prove that their experience is real, it is equally difficult for the critic to prove it is not. So, although the psychosocial approach can occasionally be proved valid in individual cases, there may be no way to establish its overall validity.

In the end, it comes down to a question of probability. Each of us must make up our own mind which is more likely: that humankind is under threat from abducting aliens, as investigators such as David Jacobs suggest, or that a collective mythmaking process is at work, fuelled by psychological and social factors.

—HILARY EVANS

Q

Quarouble (France) encounter One of the best-known sightings of UFO occupants in France took place near Valenciennes on the night of September 10, 1954. It was such a strange incident that it received international press notice.

Marius Dewilde, thirty-four years old at the time, was a metalworker in the Blanc-Misseron steel mills on the Belgian frontier. He lived with his family in a small home in the midst of fields and woods about a mile from Quarouble. His garden was adjacent to the National Coal Mines railway track running from Blanc-Misseron to St. Armand-les-Eaux, and grade crossing 79 was next to his house.

On the night in question, Dewilde was reading after his wife and children had retired. It was 10:30 P.M. when he heard his dog Kiki barking, and thinking there was a prowler in the vicinity of his property, he took a flashlight and went outside.

Dewilde walked to his garden, found nothing en route, then spotted a dark mass on the railroad tracks less than 6 yards from his door. He thought at first that someone had left a farm cart there. At that point his dog approached, crawling on her belly and whining, and simultaneously he heard hurried footsteps to the right of him. The dog began barking again and Dewilde directed his flashlight toward the sound of the footsteps.

What Dewilde saw startled him greatly. Less than 3 or 4 yards away, beyond the fence, were two creatures, walking in single file toward the dark mass at the tracks. Both creatures were dressed in suits similar to those of divers, and light was reflected off glass or metal in the area of their heads. Both entities were small, less than 3 feet tall, but had very wide shoulders. The legs looked very short in proportion to the height of the little "men," and Dewilde could not make out any arms.

After the first fright passed, Dewilde rushed to the gate, intending to cut them off from the path or to grapple with one of them. When he was about 6 feet from them, he was blinded by a very powerful light somewhat like a magnesium flare which came from a square opening in the dark mass on the tracks. He closed his eyes and tried to scream but couldn't, and he felt paralyzed. He tried to move but his legs would not function.

Shortly, Dewilde heard the sound of steps at this garden gate, and the two creatures seemed to be going toward the railroad. The beam of light finally went out and he recovered the use of this legs and headed for the track. But the dark object had begun to rise, hovering lightly, and Dewilde saw a kind of door closing. A low whistling sound accompanied a thick dark steam which issued from the bottom of the object. The object ascended vertically to about 100 feet altitude, turned east, and when it was some distance away it took on a reddish glow. A minute later it was completely out of sight.

After he regained his senses, Dewilde woke his wife and a neighbor, told them of this experience, then ran to the police station in the village of Onnaing, a mile distant. He was so upset and his speech so confused that the police thought he was a lunatic and dismissed him. From there he went to the office of the police commissioner where he told his story to Commissioner Gouchet.

Dewilde's fear was so evident that Gouchet realized something extraordinary must have taken place, and the next morning his report brought investigators from the Air Police and the Department of Territorial Security. These teams, along with police investigators, questioned Dewilde and then examined the area where the dark object had rested. They found no footprints in the area, but the ground was very hard. However, they did find five places on three of the wooden ties which had identical impressions, each about 1½ inches square. The marks were fresh and sharply cut, indicating that the wooden ties had been subjected to very great pressure at those five points.

The impressions were never satisfactorily explained, but railroad engineers who were consulted by the investigators, calculated that the amount of pressure required to make the marks was approximately thirty tons.

An examination of the gravel of the road-bed showed that at the site of the alleged landing the stones were brittle as if calcined at very high temperature.

Lastly, several residents in the area reported that they had seen a reddish object or glow moving in the sky at about the time Dewilde indicated that the object had left.

—Coral & Jim Lorenzen

References

Lorenzen, Coral and Jim. *Flying Saucer Occupants* (Signet/NAL, 1967).
———. *Encounters with UFO Occupants* (Berkley Medallion Books, 1976).

R

Randle, Kevin D. (b. 1949). Born in Cheyenne, Wyoming, Kevin Randle received his undergraduate degree from the University of Iowa and has done graduate work at the University of Iowa, California Coast University, and the American Military University. He has earned a Master's Degree and Doctorate in psychology and a Master of Military Science.

Randle is a former U.S. Army helicopter pilot who served in Vietnam, and a former Air Force intelligence officer who rose to the rank of captain. He was at one time a field investigator for APRO, and a special investigator of the J. Allen Hynek Center for UFO Studies.

He has published more than fifty magazine articles, and more than a dozen books about UFOs. His 1991 book, *UFO Crash at Roswell* was made into the Showtime original film *Roswell*. His work on alien abductions, along with that of Russell Estes and Dr. William P. Cone, has suggested important new information on the topic. In addition, Randle has written more

Kevin Randle

than eighty novels, including several science fiction books. (His pseudonyms include: Eric Helm, Cat Brannigan, James Butler Bonham, and B. R. Strong.)

Address: P.O. Box 264
          Marion, IA 52302
          U.S.A.

E-mail: krandle993@aol.com

POSITION STATEMENT: I believe that we have been visited by extraterrestrial creatures. I base that conclusion on my research into the Roswell UFO crash, my interviews with the men and women involved on that case, and the limited documentation available.

That said, I must add that I believe that the visitations have been extremely rare. Most of the information circling in the UFO field today has little factual base. Many of the subsets of UFOlogy, crop circles, cattle mutilations, MJ-12, the Allende Letters, and half a dozen other areas, have little or no legitimate basis. They are made of hoaxes, lies, misidentifications, fabrications, and anonymous and useless documents. By eliminating these, we begin to see the real picture.

One subset of the UFO field, alien abductions, is extremely dangerous. Although I don't believe that alien abduction is real, I do believe that those claiming abduction are sincere people who truly believe what they say. The answer to the problem does not lie with alien spacecraft, but with the researchers, therapists, and investigators, as well as human psychology. We can answer all the questions without the need of alien intervention.

The bottom line is that I accept little of what has been said in the UFO field. Although

I now believe that we have been visited, that does not require me to accept all of the ancillary areas of UFO research. Once we reduce the noise, we will find the answers.

—KEVIN D. RANDLE

Randles, Jenny (b. 1951). Jenny Randles joined the British UFO Research Association (BUFORA) in 1969 and became a council member in 1975. She served as Director of Investigations (1981-1994) and created the democratic, one person one vote, National Investigations Committee as a team of loosely integrated UFO investigators. During her tenure she was a driving force behind the implementation of a "Code of Practice" to govern ethical behaviour for UFOlogists (1982). There was also a BUFORA ban, still in force, on the use of regression hypnosis (1988) and she wrote and then administrated a six-month postal training course for new investigators (1990). From 1989 to date Jenny has continued to write and record BUFORA's "UFO Call"—a weekly news and information service available to all telephone subscribers in the U.K.

Jenny Randles

Randles worked closely with the British *Flying Saucer Review*, serving behind the scenes under editor Charles Bowen. Since leaving FSR she has worked closely as British representative for the J. Allen Hynek Center for UFO Studies (CUFOS) and contributes regularly to the *International UFO Reporter* as British consultant. Since 1974 she has edited the magazine *Northern UFO News*—making her one of the world's longest-running editors to still publish the same UFO journal. Jenny has been a member of the paranormal research group NARO (Northern Anomalies Research Organization), formerly known as MUFORA, and also worked closely with ASSAP, the Society for Psychical Research and *Fortean Times*. For over 20 years she has handled UFO cases referred to her by the world famous astronomy and science center at Jodrell Bank.

In 1978 Jenny became a professional researcher, funding her own work through writing. She has since published articles in many prestigious sources, including *The London Times* and *New Scientist*. Her 42 books have covered a wide range of paranormal topics but 26 have been about UFOs. Editions have appeared in 26 countries and over one million copies have been sold. Library lending figures regularly place Jenny among the most lent authors in the U.K.

Randles trained as a science teacher and has a diploma in audiovisual/media communications. For some years she served as the ITV network "Paranormal Agony Aunt" answering viewers' questions. She has written and presented a series of radio comedy items about the paranormal and serious radio documentaries about UFOs for the BBC. In 1996 she coproduced, scripted, and presented her own documentary—"Britain's Secret UFO Files"—for BBC Television. This venture achieved a record audience rating for the department and was the third-most-watched show on the whole channel that week.

Between 1993 and 1998 Jenny was officially contracted as "Story Consultant" by the hit ITV series "Strange But True?" Her extensive involvement from the pilot onwards included the writing of two spin-off books and work on a 90-minute live special on the night of UFOs 50th anniversary in 1997. "Strange But True?" set a record audience figure in 1994 when almost one quarter of the entire

U.K. population (12.5 million people) watched its celebrated episode on the Rendlesham Forest case. In 1999 she was consultant to the six-part Granada TV series "Origin Unknown"—devoted exclusively to UFO cases.

Address: 1 Hallsteads Close
            Dove Holes, Buxton
            Derbyshire
            England SK17 8BS

E-mail: nufon@currantbun.com

POSITION STATEMENT: There is no "UFO phenomenon." But there are multiple UFO *phenomena* that require a range of different explanations.

From my experience in the field I have no doubt that 95 percent of sightings can be explained as the result of known scientific causes (such as bolides, weather effects, and other IFOs). Many of the remainder are what I prefer to term UAP—Unidentified Atmospheric Phenomena—and result from energy sources created by atmospheric physics, geology, and meteorology. Some of these will, in my opinion, extend the boundaries of known science and are "new" phenomena in that sense. Indeed researchers in fields such as ball lightning lose key evidence because they ignore UFOs. In fact more extreme forms of ball lightning are often reported not to science, but to UFOlogy in the mistaken guise of alien craft.

I also suspect that there are other rare and more "exotic" types of UAP, involving plasma energy and vortices that can perhaps cause temporary rifts in the fabric of space. We do a disservice to ourselves by neglecting to study them or by our ill-judged presumption that the word UFO is synonymous with alien spacecraft. Some of these energies can be harnessed for the benefit of mankind—as may have been grasped by a few scientists in government employ. The cover-up, such as it is, operates not to hide fantastic secrets such as crashed spaceships, but to obscure ignorance of the truth. I fear that the powers that be may well be using UFOlogists as unsuspecting pawns in a social disinformation exercise to make the subject appear absurd to mainstream science. This allows research to continue covertly where such energies are more likely to be used for offensive purposes. A UFO cold war is thus afoot with UFOlogists as puppets in it.

As for alien contact/abductions, the vast majority of witnesses are sincere, telling things as they perceive them to have occurred. They are not psychologically unstable. However, it seems beyond question that these close encounters are fundamentally different from UAP. They are *experiences*, not sightings, and occur when the witness is in an altered state of consciousness, as marked by the *Oz Factor*. Those who are prone to undergoing such experiences have abilities that are different from most other people. This includes high levels of visual creativity and an unusual level of recall of early life. Such people are either able to have a visual experience that is so vividly real and appears to them to be reality, or can communicate with some other level of reality not normally accessible to the rest of us.

These experiences have more in common with near-death and out-of-body visions than with UFO or UAP. In my opinion the concept of aliens coming to Earth in starships to perform medical examinations is unsuccessful—as is the skeptical dismissal of cases as mere illusion. Instead the truth reveals a great deal about the nature of consciousness and of reality itself. But until we realize that we are looking in quite the wrong direction for the answer to the close encounter mystery, we will appear to make little progress. In fact we have actually made huge strides toward that truth—not least by clarifying what is *not* taking place. Far too few UFOlogists, let alone members of the public, have come to realize this sobering news, because the media have dismally failed to grasp the true complexity of the field. There is a huge social and financial incentive to maintain the illusion of alien invaders.

—JENNY RANDLES

reconnaissance theory of UFOs Once the existence of UFOs is accepted, their purpose must be addressed. The most pervasive thinking tends to gravitate toward the ideas of secret, stealthy, or covert observation. (Haines, 1987) *Is Another World Watching?* (Heard, 1951), *Why Are They Watching Us?* (Erskine, 1967), *Are We Being Watched?* (Bord, 1980) are just a few of the titles which exemplify this theme.

UFOlogists have preferred the terms "reconnaissance" or "surveillance" to describe these operations. Some, like Donald Keyhoe, were more precise and called it "spying." Spies evoke connotations of furtiveness, moral ambiguity, and psychological complexities that the other terms skirt. This essay traces how the aliens-are-watching-us anxiety came to occupy such a central place in UFOlogical thought.

The flying saucer era opened in an atmosphere of deep intrigue. Kenneth Arnold saw nine objects brush by Mount Rainier at speeds far beyond that of anything then being tested by the U.S. Air Force. Arnold believed they were unconventional craft being tested by the government. The public was fascinated. The Pentagon was, however, confused. It wasn't anything of ours, they were fairly sure. Was it something of the Soviets? They got a lot of German scientists from World War II and we knew the Nazis had a lot of wild ideas. But why fly it here? It set a lot of heads scratching in the intelligence community. The FBI was asked to do background checks on saucer reporters to see if they had Communist leanings.

The linking of flying saucers to extraterrestrials happened very quickly. Within four days of his sighting, Arnold said some woman rushed into a room, took one look at him, then dashed out shrieking: "There's the man who saw men from Mars!" (Gross, 1976) Hal Boyle, an Associated Press columnist, spoofed going on a trip in a flying saucer with a green Martian named "Balmy." (Strentz, 1982) Dewitt Miller spoke of the objects being not just possibly from outer space, but from other dimensions of time and space. (Gross, 1976) On July 8th, the Army issued a statement expressing assurances that the devices were neither bacteriological devices of some foreign power

or secret Army rockets, and they were not from outer space. (Gross, 1976)

On July 10th, Senator Taylor expressed the wish that saucers would turn out to be from outer space to unify Earth. (Gross, 1976) This idea was apparently common coin for it had been satirized already two years earlier in a favorite Fritz Leiber story "Wanted—An Enemy." The plot consisted of an Earthling trying to convince peace-loving Martians to make a token invasion and looting of the Earth. He explains wistfully that mankind needs an enemy to unify him. The discussion convinces the aliens that they should reconnoiter the Earth and verify that our psychology was as the visitor claims. If true, they would exterminate us. Why take chances? (Leiber, 1974)

Kenneth Arnold

Amid these extraterrestrial speculations can be found an early expression of the idea that aliens are watching us. Loren Gross found a little news article dated July 8, 1947, bearing the headline "Eyes from Mars." In it R. L. Farnsworth, a Fortean and the president of the U.S. Rocket Society, noted that spots in the sky were nothing new and opined, "I wouldn't even be surprised if the flying saucers were remote-control eyes from Mars.'' (Gross, 1976)

Despite talk of Martians in the air, few took the idea seriously. Of 853 cases collected by Ted Bloecher for his *Report on the Wave of 1947*, only two witnesses openly expressed the opinion that the objects they saw were spaceships. Kjell Qvale was the first and dates to July 5th. (Bloecher, 1967)

The other one was by John H. Jannsen and is of a rather special nature. To begin with, he is one of the few witnesses who took a photograph of the saucers. He states: ''I really believe these craft to be operated by an intelligence far beyond that developed by we earth-bound mortals and am inclined to agree with the theory they are spacecraft from outer space.'' He theorizes about magnetic and anti-gravity propulsion methods, then continues: ''In all probability these are reconnaissance craft and as they have been seen all over the world and not only in this country, are probably making a thorough study of us and our terrain and atmosphere before making any overtures.''

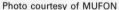
Photo courtesy of MUFON

Donald Keyhoe

It is all reminiscent of Keyhoe, but undeniably precedes him by two years. Several weeks after this sighting, Jannsen has another encounter. His plane is stopped in midair for a number of minutes while being scrutinized by a pair of disks hovering nearby. Since this makes Jannsen a repeater, Bloecher counsels suspicion. The case is, however, an instructive microcosm of reconnaissance beliefs generating reconnaissance experiences in a period when practically no one had such expectations. (Bloecher, 1967)

A Gallup poll in August of 1947 indicated that 29 percent of the public thought the saucers were optical illusions or products of the imagination. Ten percent thought they were hoaxes. A fair percentage, 15 percent, agreed with Arnold that the saucers were a U.S. secret weapon. Only 1 percent thought they were Russian secret weapons. If anyone volunteered the opinion that the saucers were extraterrestrial, the pollsters did not bother to tally them.

The intelligence community continued to ponder the mystery in the months following the 1947 wave and was less inclined to dismiss it as imagination. A letter between General N. F. Twining and Brigadier General George Schulgen demonstrates belief by the intelligence community that the phenomenon was real and either a domestic high-security project or a foreign nation had developed a new form of propulsion, possibly nuclear. (Gillmor, 1969)

Sometime during this period a school of thought grew which held that the phenomenon was probably interplanetary. A Top Secret ''Estimate of the Situation'' by some of these people allegedly exists that recommended the military be put on an alert footing. The Air Force Chief of Staff General Hoyt Vandenberg, however, vetoed any such drastic official action. (Gross, 1982)

An Air Intelligence Report dated December 10, 1948, concluded that the flying objects were probably Soviet in origin, and pondered the reasons for the flights: (1) negating U.S. confidence that A-bombs were the ultimate defense; (2) photographic reconnaissance; (3) testing US defenses in advance of a one-way all-out attack by strategic bombers; (4) familiarizing their pilots with our topography. The report expressed doubts about each of these ideas.

With regard to the reconnaissance notion, the report pointed out that sightings rarely involved areas we considered strategic. Maybe it was an effort to fill in gaps that were left from intelligence the Soviets gathered in liaisons with American industry in World War II. Some sites like Oak Ridge, Las Cruces, and the Hanford atomic works (which had sightings) would not have been accessible to them. (Andrus, 1985)

Almost simultaneously, in a report for Project Sign dated December 13, 1948, James E. Lipp offered the first thoughtful analysis of the notion that extraterrestrials were involved. From the text it is evident that various people had begun taking the possibility seriously. One section of the report dealt specifically with the reconnaissance concept.

Here it was suggested that perhaps the Martians, having kept a long-term routine watch on Earth, became alarmed at the sight of our A-bomb blasts as evidence that we were warlike and on the threshold of space travel. (Venus is eliminated here because her cloudy atmosphere would make such a survey impractical.)

The first flying objects were sighted in the Spring of 1947, after a total of five atomic bomb explosions: i.e., Alamogordo, Hiroshima, Nagasaki, Crossroads A, and Crossroads B. Of these, the first two were in positions to be seen from Mars, but the third was at the edge of the Earth's disk in daylight, and the last two were on the wrong side of Earth to be seen. Some thought it was likely that Martian astronomers, with their thin atmosphere, could build telescopes big enough to see A-bomb explosions on Earth, even though we were 165 and 153 million miles away, respectively, on the Alamagordo and Hiroshima dates.

Lipp didn't foresee the possibility that the watch could be turned over to computers and photoelectric sensors and other monitoring devices like remote satellites which would leave Martians free to consider more exciting pastimes and still be alerted to special developments when they happened.

Elsewhere in the report for Project Sign, G. E. Valley did a little brainstorming of the various possibilities. He astutely said of the Soviet secret weapon theory: "It is doubtful a potential enemy would arouse our attention in so idle a fashion." He toyed with the idea of space animals explaining saucer behavior. He junked notions about ships propelled by rays or magnetic fields on straightforward physical considerations, but held out the possibility of an antigravity shield. The notions that seemed to be left were mass psychology or extraterrestrial visits prompted by A-bomb development. (Steiger, 1976)

The public knew little more than the fact that saucer sightings kept popping up from time to time. The Mantell case in January, 1948, seemed to remove the possibility it was all some kind of joke. While the Air Force seemed to be taking some of the sightings seriously, it still downplayed the materiality of the phenomena as well as the Soviet or outer space notions about their origin.

The editor of *True* magazine thought their behavior was "damned queer" and called in Donald Keyhoe to snoop around aviation circles to see if he could turn up anything. (Gross, 1983) Keyhoe thought the Air Force's treatment of the Mantell case looked like a cover-up. He was also unimpressed by their handling of the Gorman and Chiles-Whitted cases. A former intelligence officer provided Keyhoe with a scenario in which saucers were remote-control "observer units with television eyes sent from an orbiting space base." This would be a prudent preliminary step to determine if we were a "fiercely barbarous race" before exploring the world in "person."

These contentions formed the basis of Keyhoe's infamous article for *True* magazine "The Flying Saucers are Real." His main conclusions were that:

1. For the past 175 years, the planet Earth has been under systematic close-range observation by living, intelligent observers from another planet.

2. The intensity of this observation, and the frequency of the visits to the Earth's atmosphere by which it is being conducted have increased markedly during the past two years.

3. The vehicles used for this observation and for interplanetary transport by the explorers have been identified and categorized as follows: Type I, a small nonpilot-carrying disk-shaped aircraft equipped with some form of television or impulse transmitter; Type II, a very large (up to 250 feet in diameter) metallic disk-shaped aircraft operating on the helicopter principle; Type III, a dirigible-shaped, wingless aircraft which, in the Earth's atmosphere, operated in conformance with the Prandtl theory of lift.

4. The discernible pattern of observation and exploration shown by the so-called "flying disks" varies in no important particular way from well-developed American plans for the exploration of space expected to come to fruition within the next 50 years. There is reason to believe, however, that some other race of thinking beings is a matter of two and a quarter centuries ahead of us.

The *True* article was one of the most widely discussed magazine articles of its time. Prominent newsmen like Walter Winchell and Frank Edwards discussed it. The article was expanded into a book bearing the same title later that same year. (Keyhoe, 1950)

In May 1950, the Gallup poll showed that the American public was leaning toward Arnold's view. Twenty-three percent now believed saucers were an American secret weapon. Those who believed they were illusions or hoaxes had dropped to 16 percent of the sample. The Russian secret weapon idea now garnered 3 percent of the public. The pollsters had to add a new category called "comets, shooting stars, something from another planet" and placed 5 percent of the public into it. (Gallup, 1972)

Documents released by the intelligence community were of such a contradictory nature that Keyhoe sensed a cover-up. Never mind that the contradictions could be explained more simply by the fact that they had not come to any consensus. Keyhoe claimed many scientists had come to believe the saucers contained "spies from another planet." Even Nazi scientists believed space observers (according to Keyhoe) were watching us, and their conviction had led to their experimentation with circular aerofoils. (Keyhoe, 1950)

Keyhoe bolstered the reconnaissance theory by pointing to what he perceived as a pattern of focused interests. In the 19th century, interest was on the most advanced part of the globe—Europe. It shifted to America in the late 19th century as industry and cities sprang up. Then came surveys of both continents as aircraft were developed. Observation increased in response to the V-2s during World War II.

Still more increases followed our A-bomb explosions and a second spurt followed Soviet A-bomb testing. Recent interest had focused on our Air Force bases and atomic testing areas. Encounters like the Gorman incident were viewed as a test of our aircraft capabilities. Keyhoe concluded that observation had become intermittent and that the long-range survey would continue indefinitely. Their plans concerning us were incomplete so no contact seemed evident. (Keyhoe, 1950)

Three years later, Keyhoe came out with a sequel, *Flying Saucers from Outer Space* (1953). He articulates in greater detail the clustering of saucer sightings over various locales. These are: (1) atomic energy plants at Oak Ridge, Hanford, but most frequently over Los Alamos; (2) Air Force bases; (3) Naval bases; (4) the high-altitude rocket base at White Sands; (5) aircraft plants; (6) major cities. The repetitive nature of some of the saucer visits led to the speculation: "it looks like they're getting ready for an attack." The dominant theme, however, remained that this was a new phase of "surveillance by some planet race" prompted by radio and television signals. Keyhoe unmodestly quoted a friend as saying: "But one thing's absolutely certain. We're being watched by beings from outer space." (Keyhoe, 1953)

The Robertson Panel looked at the same clusterings and was not so sure. Yes, they saw the cluster around Los Alamos. Maybe it had to do with the overalertness of security at such a secret installation. In counterpoint, it was noted that similarly sensitive atomic energy establishments showed no saucer clusters. They also noted that many of the sightings were over areas with no strategic worth whatsoever. They concluded that the evidence of any direct threat from these sightings was wholly lacking. Concern that these sightings might clog emergency channels with false information or be used by the enemy for purposes of psychological warfare led to the recommendation that a program of education be set up "to reduce the current gullibility of the public." Aimé Michel would also speculate that Keyhoe's clusters resulted from the atmosphere and hyperalertness present at secret atomic and military facilities. People end up fearful of many things in such establishments. (Michel, 1967)

Keyhoe's thesis in these early books was impressionistic and airy speculation. He cites no evidence of downed saucers with TV cameras. He cites no alien informants explaining their missions. We don't even see talk of glints of sunlight off telescopic lenses. John Janssen was the only person during the 1947 wave who had the impression the saucers were scrutinizing him.

Retrospectively, Loren Gross points to five other cases in 1947 of UFOs making circling motions that he felt could be indicative of spying, but such behavior is also consistent with birds getting navigational bearings or traveling on thermals. (Gross, 1983)

There really wasn't any evidence to build on. Some of the cases even argue against it. Keyhoe expresses the opinion: "The Mantell case alone proves we've been observed from space ships," yet the object was nonsensically huge from a reconnaissance perspective. Why utilize a thousand-foot craft if they possess speedy, maneuverable devices only 6 to 8 inches wide as supposedly proved by the Gorman case? (Keyhoe, 1950)

Whatever their faults in retrospect, Keyhoe's writings were seminal in directing the future course of the UFO mythos. Keyhoe was read by many, and heard in the media by many more. UFOlogists adopted his thesis sometimes explicitly, often implicitly.

Albert Bender in the first issue of his fannish publication *Space Review* (1952) spoke of the Earth being "under observation of some greater power in space." (Bender, 1962) Harold T. Wilkins wondered aloud if the saucermen had terrestrial spies and spoke of small observation disks sending information to half-mile-wide "brain ships." (Wilkins, 1967) Morris K. Jessup referred to some UFOs as "small, agile observers" which are sent out to exploratory missions from larger vessels dwelling in the "earth-sun-moon gravitational neutral." (Jessup, 1955) Aimé Michel, despite his doubts over Keyhoe's clusters, nevertheless believed that aliens had been watching us for some time. (Michel, 1967)

Gavin Gibbons followed Keyhoe, adding more detail. In *The Coming of the Space Ships* (1958) he reported on a pattern of sightings in his vicinity in England which led him to believe there was little doubt saucers represented a "reconnaissance preparatory to a landing in force." He offers a fourfold typology of saucers in place of Keyhoe's threefold typology. His consists of: (I) vast metallic disks; (II) cigar-shaped craft; (III) scout craft; and (IV) unmanned scanners, small spheres, remote-controlled, nonmetallic and maybe liquid or vaporous.

One notable feature of this forgotten book is its bringing into play a report that genuinely supports the aliens-are-watching-us concept. A person named Roestenberg witnessed strange men who gazed down at him and his family from a saucer tilted at an angle for detailed viewing. (Gibbons, 1958)

The Lorenzens of APRO added new intensity to the reconnaissance concept as the UFO mythos entered the sixties. They asserted that the saucers adhere to a pattern indicating the Earth is the subject of a geographical, ecological, and biological survey accompanied by military reconnaissance of the whole world's terrestrial defenses. This pattern, they further claimed, could not be mimicked by psychic projections on the part of thousands of people. They theorized that the saucers represented a flotilla of reconnaissance ships concerned about protecting intelligent beings who as recently as 1877 had migrated to Mars on what are now known as its moons Phobos and Deimos. Comparatively small in number, they would be preoccupied with our future scientific and military developments. Since this pattern showed a progression not only from reconnaissance to surveying, but from surveying to hostility, the Lorenzens believed the saucer problems embodied "an urgency that defies expression." (Lorenzen, 1966)

Frank Edwards, basing his work on the work of Keyhoe and NICAP, also advanced the idea that the UFO phenomenon was progressing through a series of phases. The foo fighters of World War II, for example, now represented the second phase of the alien plan and represented close-range surveillance by instrumented probes. The seventh phase was to be the "Overt Landing" and was due, by his reckoning, in 1968 or 1969. (Edwards, 1966)

James E. McDonald, another major figure

Frank Edwards

of the sixties, expressed a belief in patterns indicating "something in the nature of surveillance lies at the heart of the UFO problem." (Sagan and Page, eds., 1972)

The popular books of Brad Steiger suggested the existence of a "steady pervasive program of invasion or antagonistic observation." (Steiger, 1967) Brinsley Le Poer Trench also believed the Earth has been under constant surveillance for a very long time. Rank-and-file UFOlogist Robert Loftin also concurred that UFOs engaged in surveillance. (Loftin, 1968)

Far and away the best argument for the surveillance concept was made by Otto Binder in his 1967 magnum opus *What We Really Know About Flying Saucers*. In the finest empirical tradition, he cited a series of reports which at least do show aliens engaged in activities suggesting a program of observation. Saucers are shown maneuvering around objects in an inquisitive manner; aliens are shown taking samples of soil, vegetation and animals; aliens are shown to be watching people; and saucers are shown bearing searchlights. With this array of evidence, he concluded with a measure of logical force that a Project Earth Reconnaissance exists, which could mean either future conquest or peaceful scientific exploration. Against the idea of future conquest, Binder noted that 20 years had by then already passed with no concerted hostile move; and so he predicted that no secret takeover was in the offing. (Binder, 1967)

In a sequel titled *Flying Saucers Are Watching Us*, Binder backdates the saucer phenomenon into deep history. The human body's many mysteries speak to our world being a vast biological laboratory and breeding ground. "A vast, never-ending world-wide game of observing humans under all kinds of conditions and situations" seemed apparent. (Binder, 1968)

Sensible as Binder's argument is, it is compromised by the fact that Keyhoe's argument had altered people's expectations. By 1968, 40 percent of the public believed people had seen

Brad Steiger

spaceships that did not come from this planet—a far cry from 1950 when pollsters did not even give the idea a category to itself. (Gillmor, 1969)

The belief was generating experiences that proved it. This is evident in *The Interrupted Journey*, when Betty Hill read one of Keyhoe's books, *The Flying Saucer Conspiracy*, and soon after had a nightmare involving aliens examining her out of neutral curiosity. (Fuller, 1966) While Keyhoe could not accept it 100 percent, he would include an account of the Hill case in a

Brinsley Le Poer Trench

later book as possible evidence of extraterrestrial visitation. (Keyhoe, 1973 and Steinberg, 1989)

Validation of the concept could be seemingly straightforward, such as when saucers hovered alongside ships or a saucer followed a train "as if inspecting" the crew, or when saucers shadowed people. But it could take on peculiar aspects as in a case reported in Hynek's *The UFO Experience* (1972). A 3-foot luminous spheroid "appeared to be examining a tree rather closely" for several minutes. It moved deliberately and purposefully in its inspection of the tree, pausing slightly at apparent points of interest and giving the distinct impression of "intelligent" behavior. Intelligent it does sound like, albeit no greater than that of a hummingbird and seemingly less meaningful. Granted, there is no *a priori* reason why aliens can't love trees as much as humans, yet it still seems a problematic point of surveillance interest. (Hynek, 1972)

As UFOlogy entered the seventies, doubts about the reconnaissance concept began to grow, even among advocates of the extraterrestrial hypothesis (ETH). James McCampbell surveyed cases in Jacques Vallée's catalogue of Type I UFO events for evidence of reconnaissance and came away puzzled. He saw supportive evidence in aliens gathering flowers, plants, grass, animals, water samples, soil samples, stones, and boulders. There was also an alien observing abandoned oil derricks and a contact where an alien revealed their philanthropic and scientific motives.

He felt, however, that a thorough study of the Earth would require an enormous range of activities, and these cases weren't even coming close. He concluded: "The idea that the UFO people are conducting any kind of organized and thorough scientific study on Earth is not sustained by the available information. Instead their activities on the ground are strangely haphazard and disorganized. . . . Instead of conducting a comprehensive survey of Earth, the UFO people appear to be snooping around for some natural commodity on Earth, either vegetable or mineral." (McCampbell, 1973)

In his final book, in 1973, Keyhoe still

defended the reconnaissance thesis, but had to concede it was a "strange surveillance." A group of Keyhoe's assistants which included anthropologists, educators, psychologists, and communication experts almost unanimously concurred that aliens could not get a true picture of our world by distant observation. The implications were serious. Aliens would be seriously misled by the protocol evident in their study of us. Instead of rejecting the ETH, Keyhoe decided we urgently needed to force contact with the aliens to rectify their procedural error. This prompted Keyhoe's advocacy of Operation Lure, a fantastic cargo cult scheme to draw UFOs down to Earth. (Keyhoe, 1973)

Longtime critic of UFOlogy Peter Kor took Keyhoe's book to task as an anachronism. While Keyhoe's theory may have had a certain plausibility in 1950, the operation had since become inconceivably long. The showdown predicted by so many people inspired by Keyhoe's concept had never come. (Kor, 1974)

Frank Salisbury echoed that he had problems believing reconnaissance would be extended as long as UFO history suggests. Even granting aliens might survey a planet in a way we would not, Salisbury had a tough time believing aliens would do the things UFOs were reported to do. (Salisbury, 1974)

Skeptic Ian Ridpath reiterated that the purpose of all the scrutiny implied by the volume of reports was unclear. He expressed the surprisingly Fortean skepticism that belief in the reconnaissance theory is built on the basic assumption/fallacy that we are important enough for other people to be deeply interested in us. (Ridpath, 1978)

Leonard Stringfield maintained that we know incontrovertibly that UFOs exist, but agreed it was "disturbing to not know its source, its nature, and the purpose of keeping Earth under constant surveillance." He cited among many cases an incident which suggested a UFO intended either to spy on a missile base or take some type of provocative or offensive action (Stringfield, 1976)

B. Ann Slate also mentioned that the alien surveillance of key military and research installations, and defense maneuvers was continuing, based on witnesses she had interviewed. (Slate, 1977) Kolman S. von Keviczky was unabashedly maintaining in 1976 that authorities "must after all seriously assume that the galactic powers operation clearly indicates a centrally conducted 'interstellar reconnaissance' with the ultimate objective of a landing operation on earthly soil." (Hervey, 1976)

Yurko Bondarchuck, in 1979, was surprisingly excited over an intensifying pattern indicative of increased Earth occupant surveillance. He can even be seen exclaiming: "UFOs are engaged in data gathering activities!" He felt their behavior suggested a preoccupation with monitoring Earth's natural habitat, our technological development, and our physiological-behavioral makeup. (Bondarchuk, 1979)

Raymond Fowler considered among many ideas the notion that the aloofness of aliens might be a strategy of advanced reconnaissance parties awaiting the main force of a classic invasion. (Fowler, 1974)

The eighties have seen both reticence and devotion to Keyhoe's concept. The most significant modern devotee to the Keyhoe tradition has been Budd Hopkins. For Hopkins, patterns in the abductions indicate that aliens are conducting a long-term, in-depth study of humans, using implants to monitor us. (Hopkins, 1981)

Hilary Evans, in *The Evidence for UFOs*, allowed the possibility that structured artifacts of extraterrestrial origin were engaged in some kind of surveillance operation, but, if so, it was being conducted in a "remarkably sporadic and unworkmanlike manner." (Evans, 1983) The authors of *Clear Intent* were likewise tentative and felt the purpose of UFOs was unknown but "may be related to an extended surveillance of what may be termed a primitive, embryonic society." (Fawcett and Greenwood, 1984) Whitley Strieber took a mystical tone and asserted that the visitors' activities go far beyond a mere study of mankind. (Strieber, 1987)

In 1987, Timothy Good felt "surveillance has intensified" since we have endangered our planet and expanded into space. The modern wave began with the development of nuclear weapons and rockets. Activity around nuclear missile sites demonstrated their continuing interest. He also felt Earth held spectacular attractions for tourists. (Good, 1987) This last sentiment is an interesting conceit relative to a fifties notion that Earth was a prison. (Keyhoe, 1960)

A tract on abductions by Dr. Edith Fiore has flatly affirmed: ''ETs are monitoring and watching people throughout the world.'' (Fiore, 1989)

The latest exercise in the Keyhoe tradition was some speculation advanced by Richard Hall about UFO patterns. According to Hall, extraterrestrial intelligences (ETIs) have been watching our technological progress, especially our propulsion capabilities, our actions in warfare, our nuclear technology, and our reaching out into space. His private studies convinced him that interest has focused on atomic energy facilities and petroleum-related activities. Hall makes explicit the corollary Ridpath felt UFOlogists were obliged to make: the persistence of ETIs implies a strong interest in us. (Hall, 1988)

Aimé Michel went further, earlier in the decade, and acclaimed that humans must be something rare and ''cosmically precious.'' (Story, ed., 1980)

There are no signs that the aliens-are-watching-us idea is going to disappear from the UFO mythos. Despite blows to its credibility in the seventies, it continues to garner adherents. From the standpoint of historical development, it seems that the idea arose less from scientific evidence than from the habit of the intelligence community to regard deception and furtiveness as the natural order of things. No one seems to have questioned whether the aliens would be ideologically and behaviorally diverse. Rather, the most natural state of affairs is presumed to be a universe filled with spies—to the exclusion of curious extraterrestrials imbued with a spirit of open inquiry and mutual exchange.

As Keyhoe was told, a program of scientific inquiry cannot be done from a distance. Face-to-face interaction and participation in affairs of life are the proper ways to conduct anthropological investigation. If covertness is essential to avoid infusion of alien concepts, reconnaissance could be done by bioengineered mimics of humans, dogs, cats, insects, or dust mites. Instead of glowing UFOs, an advanced culture would engineer mimics of conventional objects like planes, choppers, balloons, clouds, or the moon. They wouldn't invite questions by presenting an identifiable alien construct. (Lem, 1936)

The reconnaissance idea never pulled together into a coherent framework more than a minor fraction of Type I cases. As McCampbell found out, no more than 2 percent of the cases implicate the existence of alien investigators. A crashed or captured reconnaissance disk has never been tendered for display at MIT or the Smithsonian. Predictions based on the concept have consistently been proven wrong.

Given the persistence of the idea and the irrational nature of the arguments that supported it, the question arises: Could it be that UFOlogists are telling people something they need to believe?

Paranoid ETs

It is instructive to see how the ideas of UFOlogists were mirrored by the aliens themselves. One of the first people alleging inside information about aliens was a medium named Mark Probert who was in the service of the Borderland Sciences Research Foundation (BSRF). The group learned through persons on the ''other side of life,'' having access to the etheric worlds, that the saucers were appearing in order to demonstrate the possibility that there are ways to travel faster and eliminate friction. The sensation was all meant to compel our attention and wake us up.

There is actually something to be said in favor of that view. It was much easier to believe that flying objects passing by Mount Rainier were meant to be seen, rather than secret hardware being tested by the government as Arnold believed.

In 1948 Probert got the word that we were being observed, so that a final record of our civilization could be made for future history. This was reiterated in a 1950 communication which said notes were being taken on our advancement—before our fall.

In 1952 there is an apparent intrusion of Keyhoe's ideas into messages received by the BSRF group. There is talk of reconnaissance craft and small remote-control craft used to make visual observations without drawing attention to themselves. Note the inversion—they no longer want to wake us up. (Layne, 1972)

Employing a glass tumbler on a Ouija board, George Hunt Williamson eliminated one of the middlemen in extraterrestrial communications. On August 2, 1952, he made direct contact with a being from Mars named "Nah-9." The Martian revealed that our world had been observed for 75,000 years.

Williamson and his circle eventually contacted dozens of aliens, among them the first known paranoid extraterrestrial. "Affa" of Uranus expressed fear of the work going on at Lowell University: "The big eyes were looking at us," he complained. (Williamson, 1963)

Three months later, an acquaintance of Williamson would do him one better and meet a human being from another world fact-to-face. The name of that acquaintance was George Adamski. In the initial encounter, Adamski communicated with the alien by signs and gestures, and telepathy. Among the things he learned was that the little disks which were often reported served as eyes for the larger motherships. If the disks were in trouble, a crosscurrent would detonate them in order to prevent capture. (Leslie and Adamski, 1953) This innovation could have been gleaned from Keyhoe's writings.

Though Keyhoe personally rejected the rumors, he reported in *The Flying Saucers Are Real* that some individuals believed the disks would disintegrate with an explosive charge if they ever got out of control. (Keyhoe, 1960)

The idea began with Dr. Lincoln La Paz, who thought the green fireballs were made of beryllium copper, so they would burn up with no debris. Spectra indicated, however, that the green fireballs contained magnesium, and so were probably of natural origin.

In a later encounter, the aliens took Adamski on a tour of their ship. Inside, he was shown a central magnetic pillar that doubled as both a propulsion unit and a powerful telescope, which allowed them to inspect the land below. He is shown a TV set on which is registered everything seen by remote-control disks ranging in size from 10 inches to 12 feet in diameter. These disks registered every vibration taking place in the area under observation. They even allow aliens to know what we are thinking. Adamski saw over a dozen of these registering disks. (Adamski, 1955)

Howard Menger, in time, saw one of these registering disks explode. The aliens shortly thereafter affirmed to Menger that it had been out of control. He elaborated on the fact that these disks recorded all emotions, thoughts, and possible intents. (Menger, 1959)

The Mitchell sisters added a novel wrinkle to this portrait. An alien named "Alna" demonstrated for them a spy scope that could see through roofs by subtracting their vibrations from other vibrations of a building. (Mitchell, 1973)

Orfeo Angelucci's aliens spoke of our planet having been under observation for centuries, but only recently it had been resurveyed. Every point of progress in our society is registered. (Angelucci, 1955)

Dan Martin corroborated the spy paradigm in titling the account of his contact *The Watcher*. Decades later, another alien named "Khyla" would also be known as "The Watcher." (Valerian, 1988) Contacts with names like "Asmiz," "Quamquat," and "Mister Zno" likewise affirmed that we were being watched. The seventies contactee Claude Vorilhon (a.k.a. "Raël") was told by his alien mentors that they had come to see what we were up to, and to watch over them. (Vorilhon, 1978)

Abductee literature also lends support to the picture of aliens spying on humanity. Herb Shirmer, from his 1967 encounter, received testimony that his aliens were engaged in surveillance. (Smith, 1976) Like Adamski, Schirmer was shown a baby saucer inside the ship that could be launched to check out an area and send pictures to a vision screen in the mothership.

In the 1975 abduction of Charles L. Moody, aliens refer to the craft they are on as an observation craft. It was distinctly smaller than the main craft and was said to be vulnerable to interference by radar. (Lorenzen, 1978)

Raymond Shearer, an abductee of 1978, broke out in a cold sweat fearful he had become a possible agent or spy for the aliens. (Smith, 1979)

During a May 1979 encounter, William Herrmann, while aboard a saucer, witnessed rendezvous with what the aliens termed an "observance vehicle." (Stevens, 1989)

Virginia Horton's aliens included one wanting to be a bioanthropologist. They collected a blood sample for later examination and research. The aliens' research had led to us being considered a "precious species." (Hopkins, 1981)

One could regard all this face-to-face testimony as corroboration of the validity of Keyhoe's thesis. The pedigrees of these experiencers, however, are of mixed value. Mediums and Ouija boards are suspect to say the least. Adamski is largely dismissed as a charlatan by UFOlogists who want to be taken seriously. Menger confessed his experiences more or less were not real. The other contactees also tend to be rejected as promulgators of fantasy. Abductees come late to the game and long after Keyhoe's ideas had suffused the UFO mythos.

If these are fantasies, why do all of these people have their aliens say, in essence, "I spy"? The first possibility is camouflage. The contactees try to blend their fantasies with contemporary beliefs to give them credibility. An allied possibility is that they sense this is something people want to believe and, following an ancient credo, "Tell them what they want to hear." The other basic possibility is that contactees want to believe it themselves.

UFOlogists, until the advent of the abductees, never used the testimony of UFO contacts to buttress the reconnaissance thesis. But both groups affirm it explicitly and implicitly. It is harder to discount the need to believe as fuel for the advancement of the idea in the case of the contactees. Untainted rationality can hardly account for the motif's presence there. If need accounts for one, it may unconsciously account for both groups believing aliens are watching us. Yet why would anyone want to believe anything like that?

The sensation of being watched is a common psychological experience. It can be termed an archetypal phenomenon, for it is founded on a universal feature of human life. All of us are watched when we are children. Parents must constantly keep an eye on us to keep us out of danger or prevent us from causing trouble. As the child grows up he learns that certain behaviors have undesirable consequences and will become wary of doing things that might provoke an unwanted response from his parents. A glance at the parents for a look of approval or disapproval can cue him whether he's doing the right or wrong thing. These parental responses are sought and anticipated. Over time they are internalized, as a separate agency develops within the mind that oversees and supervises behavior even when the parent is absent. This agency has been variously termed the conscience or superego. Poets have called it the "watchman of the soul."

The conscience constantly compares our behavior to the ideals instilled in us by our parents. The ideals are added to by authority figures such as teachers, religious figures, cops, media pundits, friends, and public opinion as time goes by. When we fall short of the ideals we set for ourselves, become insecure, or find ourselves apart or isolated from the rest of society, the conscience makes itself felt. Sensations imprinted from childhood of being spied upon by distrusting parents or parents giving "that look" can surface to make us stop what we're doing and think over our actions.

Though such actions on the part of our conscience may make us anxious and may even cause us to be wracked with guilt, they develop from the need to feel pride about ourselves and warn us there are consequences in our misbehaving.

Parenting and socialization are unfortunately not always gracefully managed. Ambitious parents can instill ideals impossible to live up to in a child. Cruel parents can assault the child with criticisms and punishments that are impossible to live down. Parents may teach distrust by unfairly spying on the child with insufficient cause. Under these circumstances the superego can take on severe qualities that hang on as fixed aspects of the adult's character. When these superego functions are split off and distort an individual's perception of reality, the situation can be termed pathological and the condition acquires the description of paranoia. (Frosch, 1983)

Generally speaking, paranoia is defined by the idea that one is being persecuted. Among the striking commonalities of this idea is the motif of being watched by others. Such erroneous beliefs have been categorized by psychiatrists under the phrase "delusions of observation." (Eidelberg, 1968) As Freud saw it, there is ultimately a grain of historical truth behind such delusions. The individual had been watched before, but as a child. Pride forces the individual to deny feelings of internal narcissistic mortification, but accepts external control by imaginary others or others in imaginary relationships. It is a compromise solution to a moralistic dilemma. Without it, the individual falls into unbearable depression and self-loathing. Distorting one's perceptions of reality exacts costs over time, however. Whether the cost is worth it is a deeply problematic issue.

Many paranoids function at superior levels of performance in their work and may bother no one with their quirky ideas. Others may act on their delusions and make false accusations that destroy human relationships and injure the innocent. While paranoia can be treated by analysis, it is a difficult and emotionally painful process for both the individual and the therapist. Therapists, if nobody else, wonder if it is worth it.

It is fairly natural to assume that the beliefs encountered earlier in this essay are collective equivalents of the delusions of observation seen in individual cases of paranoia. We are looking for the eyes of our parents in some sense. Rather than dwell on our inadequacies, which we know we would find, we anxiously look skyward for signs of attention and supervision. In the case of the contactees nothing could be clearer, given the beliefs of aliens being able to read our thoughts, something parents give every appearance of doing at times.

It is tempting to lay the growth of the UFO mythos to collective shame over Hiroshima and the development of nuclear weapons in the fifties. Outwardly we were proud of the Yankee ingenuity we showed in constructing this superweapon, but the gruesome effects of it were undeniable in the photos brought back and displayed in *Life* magazine and elsewhere.

Oppenheimer, in his oft-quoted lecture before MIT in December 1947, spoke his conscience: "In some crude sense, which no vulgarity, no humor, no overstatement can quite extinguish, the physicists have known sin and this is a knowledge they cannot lose." One could easily deny the physicists had sinned and many did. The knowledge, however, returned in projected form—the delusion of aliens watching us. The concern reflected in Lipp's researching whether or not aliens could have seen our nuclear blasts gives some credence to the notion, as does the frequency of talk about A-bombs by both contactees and UFOlogists in the fifties.

The possibility of narcissistic mortification over Hiroshima is most relevant in the context of the cluster of UFO reports around Los Alamos noted by Keyhoe and the Robertson Panel. Interest in flying saucers appears to have been considerable there. Ruppelt of Blue Book singles out the Atomic Energy Commission's Los Alamos lab as a place where so many people turned up for his briefings that the lecture theater wouldn't hold them all.

Whether nuclear shame has a wider role in

fueling the UFO mythos is open to considerable doubt. Why didn't the paranoiac reaction set in immediately in 1945? UFO flaps don't correlate well with atomic tests. Blue Book set up a UFO reporting net in the Eniwetok H-bomb test region, but got nothing for the effort. Not only has there been a notable absence of bomb-project physicists among UFOlogists, but two are renowned for their disbelief. Enrico Fermi, the mastermind of the first chain reaction in 1942, is also known for the famous Fermi Paradox against the prevalence of ETI civilizations. Edward Condon was a member of the committee that established the U.S. atomic bomb program and later served as advisor to later atom-related study groups of the government. A recent tribute to Hermann Oberth reminds us that while here is a figure who believed in saucer reconnaissance, his claim to immortality lies not with the atom, but with the creation of the V-2 rocket.

Clearly nuclear shame has limitations as a source for UFO paranoia. This is more fully rendered inadequate by the larger consideration that paranoid delusions are a constant element in our culture's fantasies. Paranoia may have been rampant in the forties and fifties, but even then it was nothing new. Collective paranoia existed before there was a Hiroshima.

C. R. Badcock points out that beliefs in shepherding sky-gods begin, historically, with the formation of nomadic pastoral economies and the domestication of animals. Before that, man's beliefs tended to be animistic and polytheistic because of the nature of cultivation and agriculture. The practices of pastoralism obliged a special psychology formed of independence, an obsessional nature, and the feeling of guilt-shame. The formation of such personalities favors the creation of paranoiac reaction states of mind and the spread of paranoid beliefs. From the inception of these new practices we start to see the spread of myths about all-seeing gods and secret races of watchers of mankind. (Badcock, 1980)

There survives from ancient Babylon, for example, a prayer to the first-begotten of Mar-

duk who is addressed as "You watch over all men." (Saggs, 1962) Nebuchadnezzar, king of Babylon, besieged Jerusalem in early Biblical times and exiled its people. Among them was the prophet Ezekiel. He believed God had passed judgment that his people were sinful. While in exile he came to see a vision of wheels in the air with "eyes round about," and from then on prophesied doom and destruction. (Ezekiel 1:20)

Also in the Bible we encounter practices like Joshua's placing seven eyes on every stone of the Temple to convey the special watchfulness of God. It is commonly believed that the eyes of the Lord can range through the whole Earth. (Eichrodt, 1967) As he lay in bed, Daniel had a vision of a watcher that came down from heaven. (Daniel 4:13) Watchers are also spoken of in 2 Enoch XVIII as a group of angels banished to a dungeon along with Samael, a planetary power and prince in heaven. (Patai, 1983)

A rendering of Ezekiel's vision
with eyes everywhere

Christianity, with its end-of-the-world fantasies and fears of eternal damnation for trivial infractions, has been termed paranoid by some psychiatrists. (Badcock, 1980) It is an interesting question whether or not the decay of the Roman empire provided the fuel for its diffusion. Regardless, there is little dispute it lent a distinctly paranoid tone to the Dark Ages. People lived in a double-spy cosmology, as angels and devils scrutinized the minute day-to-day behavior of everybody for the slightest blasphemy or offense. (Keen, 1989)

Toward the end of the Middle Ages, fantasies of flying witches and secret meetings of Devil worshipers led to the Great Witch Hunt, one of the deadlier paranoid delusions to have gripped masses of people. (Cohn, 1969)

Mass paranoia does not confine itself to religious realms. Conspiracy theories constantly interweave with reality-based political thought and often dominate it. The American Revolution, some historians now argue, was rooted in a pandemic of persecutory delusions.

Paranoiac fantasies suffuse American history: the Illuminati conspiracy and anti-Masonry, anti-Catholicism, "the Gallic Peril," slaveholders' conspiracies, baby-killing and dismemberment by Indians, the Yellow Peril, reefer madness, the fluoridation-poisoning fear, the Red Nightmare and McCarthyism in the fifties, JFK assassination theories, the TriLateralists, the Gemstone file, cattle mutilations, the Satanist conspiracy, etc. (DeMause, 1982)

Anyone in doubt of the influence and industry of the paranoid is directed to Murray Levin's dissection of the Great Red Scare of 1919-20. It led to lynchings, the crushing of unions, and the abandoning of civil liberties. The belief in a nonexistent Bolshevik conspiracy to foment a revolution that would destroy the American way of life was supported by an "irrefutable" 4,465-page document called the Lusk Report. Psychotic ravings are reprinted without evaluation and bits and pieces of reality are force-fitted to prove what amounted to a vague assumption. (Levin, 1971)

This writer suspects that our culture has a constant reservoir of paranoids ready to adopt and give flight to any fear that finds a coterie of advocates. It isn't any particular instance of collective shame that accounts for the origin or diffusion of paranoid beliefs in our culture. Thus the spread of Keyhoe's reconnaissance theory probably wasn't dependent on Hiroshima.

Elements of the UFO mythos are clearly evident long before the forties and fifties.

There was, for example, a significant market for stories about extraterrestrials visiting Earth or being visited by Earthlings as early as the 1890s. Nearly 60 such "interplanetaries" appeared in that decade. (Locke, 1975)

Among the latecomers was H. G. Wells's *The War of the Worlds* in 1898. It may be a small surprise to the reader that more extraterrestrials were reported during the airship waves of 1896 and 1897 than during the flying saucer flap of 1947. (Neeley, 1988)

Most of the 19 reports involve little more than extraterrestrial picnics and camp-outs or excursions. A pair speak of negotiating trade agreements. One airship is here to pick up ice. Two involve spirits or angels making surveys for future colonization. Only one case involves Martians scrutinizing humans for the apparent purpose of securing an inhabitant. There is also one case of unearthly beings hurling balls of fire, brimstone, and molten lava from an airship at witnesses—the only other one fully suggestive of paranoid fear. Overall, the airship waves look like nine-day wonders unrelated to paranoia-fueled UFO fantasies of our times.

It is actually easier to trace the development of the UFO mythos to the British airship scare of 1912-13. These flaps were clearly paranoid in character, involving the belief that German Zeppelin airships were secretly visiting Britain for spying out the land in preparation for war. (Watson, 1988) There seems to be no compelling reason to doubt that these events inspired John N. Raphael to pen "Up Above: The Story of the Sky Folk" for *Pearson's Magazine*.

The plot begins with a rash of disappearances that include the Prime Minister, an elm tree pulled up by the roots, an invalid in bed from a collapsing house, the town pump, a weathercock, a ewe, and a ram. One man survives to describe being picked up by some force and later dropped. A professor arrives to investigate and speculates that a race of sky folk may have the same curiosity about us as we have about creatures at the bottom of the sea.

"Isn't it plausible that having this curiosity, and having at their disposal scientific methods, of which for the present, we can know little or nothing, they should endeavor to discover more about us? How would they try to obtain information?"

The answer it seems is by using an immense pincher to take up samples, by winch, to their space ship. Blood subsequently falls from the sky—then, a decapitated gorilla's head. Finally, the body of a man, partly skinned, is discovered with a diary confirming the worst.

The man describes being placed in a transparent cubicle and seeing animals, humans, quantities of dirt, rocks, and seawater on display as though the ship were a combination of museum and zoo. He observes dissection experiments and, realizing his fate, straps his diary to his body in expectation of his remains being tossed overboard.

The ship subsequently develops power trouble and settles into Trafalgar Square. The aliens are regrettably killed when rescuers cause air to rush inside the craft after making a hole in it. The hope is expressed that the aliens won't be sending down another expedition. (Moskowitz, 1976)

This was probably the first major story to adopt the premise of furtive extraterrestrials flying about our atmosphere engaged in abduction for scientific research. Sam Moskowitz argues it is unlikely Fort could have missed this story in his extensive reading. *Pearson's* was one of the most widely read magazines in its day and was certainly in the New York Public Library, which was haunted by Charles Fort. The first corollary, that it played a role in Fort's ruminations about extraterrestrial visitors—who found us mysteriously useful and caused various disappearances and sky falls—follows naturally.

All the elements for the reconnaissance theory of UFOs seem to be present by 1913: belief in extraterrestrials, belief in furtive airships, the idea of examination, and paranoia. The only thing that seems to be missing is a Keyhoe and a Mantell case to lend his idea

seriousness. Fort was too much the class clown to phrase his ideas in arguments that tried to convince. It also might be that the public needed the sensation of Arnold's supersonic saucers to redirect their attention to aerial mysteries. Teasing out all the relevant factors and possibilities may keep historians guessing for years.

Though no single episode of collective shame can be pointed to, as establishing the UFO mythos, the idea may provide a key to several mass manifestations of the UFO phenomenon. The major flaps subsequent to 1947 appear in concert with major historical episodes of national shame or humiliation.

The 1952 wave coincides with an emotionally charged steel strike which caused allegations of treason: that steelworkers were undermining the war in Korea.

The 1957 wave emerged in the wake of Russia's launch of Sputnik and the realization that Yankee technological superiority had been called into question. It was easily the pivotal identity crisis of the fifties generation.

The 1965 wave began within days of the first U.S. ground combat operations in Vietnam. It was quickly termed a "futile assault," and in the weeks that followed the situation visibly deteriorated. After the initial pulse of the wave passed, the famous Watts riots kicked up a secondary peak in mid-August.

The notorious "swamp-gas" flap of 1966 played against the backdrop of the first anti-U.S. demonstrations in Hue and Danang, then Saigon and elsewhere. Spectacular fiery suicides by religious figures were particularly agonizing to behold. Last, the 1973 wave blossomed in the heat of Watergate.

Psycho-social historian Lloyd DeMause has asserted that staring eyes can be found during times of crisis in every country and every age—from ancient Egypt's "Eye of Horus" to the "hypnotic eyes" of Adolf Hitler. Though they can be attached to foreign enemies, they are often pictured as simply floating above us—strange, unidentified staring eyes. (DeMause, 1984)

Unidentified Flying Objects with their connotations of aliens-are-watching-us seem to be a variation of the paranoid delusions of observation prompted by ego crises seen both with individuals and groups.

EYE IMAGERY

"The eye to this day gives me a cold shudder . . ." Darwin confessed, as he tried to explain how the eye arose through the process of natural selection. (Colp, 1986) But the power of the eye to elicit this sense of the uncanny is itself a product of evolved instinct. Staring eyes provoke physiological arousal in many species of animal. The eye-shaped pattern emblazoned on the bodies of butterflies, birds, snakes, fish, and peacocks evolved because of the instinctive avoidance the eyes provoke. The predator does not want itself to become prey. (Grumet, 1983)

Eyes are one of the first things recognized and tracked by infants. Experiments have shown that masks consisting of two eyes, a smooth forehead, and a nose will by themselves cause an infant to react with a smile. The absence of a mouth makes no difference and serves to prove the smile is not imitative. It is only the area of the eyes that innately provokes the response. (Campbell, 1959) After six months the response is limited to familiar faces. Strangers will elicit screams, particularly if they have large eyes (as when wearing spectacles) or show large teeth.

The power of the eye is constantly alluded to in love poetry through the ages. Eye makeup highlights and exaggerates the allure of the eye in a manner that ethologists term "supernormal sign stimulation."

Exaggeration of the size of the eye is commonplace in art and sculpture. Eye idols, and idols with eyes twice the normal size, have been found in places where cultural diffusion is an improbable explanation, such as the Olmec culture of Mexico and cultures of the Indus and Euphrates. (Jaynes, 1976)

Divine eyes have been regarded as a universal motif in mythology. (Meslin, 1936) Though such images can connote, in their be-

nevolent aspect, the love of a parent for the child, it can also connote the authority of parent and society.

One finds eye imagery exaggerated in paranoid art, because of the focused attention on the eyes looking for any faint cues of disapproval. Film buffs will recall movies of the fifties, the era of the blacklist, as often possessing scenes of montages of disembodied eyes connoting disapproval of an anxious or harried outcast from society. Films of the alien invasion genre often possess exaggerated eye imagery in connection with a varied array of paranoid motifs. Some aliens are little more than giant eyes, such as in the films *It Came from Outer Space* (1953), *The War of the Worlds* (1953), *The Crawling Eye* (1958), *The Atomic Submarine* (1959), the "Moonstone" episode of *Outer Limits* (1964), and "The Robot Spy" of *Johnny Quest* (1964).

Humanoids with oversized eyes are also commonplace in science fiction and pulp horror illustrations.

The alien invasion genre of films provides an accessible body of paranoid fantasy with which to demonstrate certain facets of the psycho-dynamics of paranoia. The facet to be demonstrated here is the relationship between cataclysmic themes and supernormal eye imagery.

Probably the best place to start is with the movie *The War of the Worlds* (1953). The world of Mars is dying, so the Martians decide to wipe out mankind and take over our planet. Their space ships crash into the Earth as fiery meteors. The first thing to emerge from the crater is a large mechanical eye, which spectacularly destroys anything in its gaze. Here is the old fear of the Evil Eye updated with a vengeance.

It later transpires that the Martians themselves aren't much more than eyes with spindly arms and legs. The film is an orgy of fire and explosions and doom. Only the hand of God, the original term for plagues, ends the invasion.

It Came from Outer Space (1953) also

opens with a fiery meteor crashing to earth. A scientist goes into the crater to investigate and confronts a huge spherical spaceship that resembles a huge eyeball with a hexagonal pupil. A rockslide starts descending around him at the sight of it, and he flees with no proof. The rest of the film dabbles in dopplegangers, Men in Black, mysterious phone noises, and other paranoid paraphernalia.

Killers From Space (1954) is an especially fascinating work possessing a nakedly paranoid structure. It opens with an A-bomb going off and the crash of a plane researching the effects of the blast. The project official in the plane stumbles into base after the crash with amnesia and a surgical scar over his chest. While recuperating, he awakens one evening to see a pair of disembodied eyes floating toward him. He encounters the eyeballs again on a later occasion, as he is driving down a highway. He complains that people regard him as a mental case.

Then he is caught passing along military secrets to an unknown party. Sodium pentathol is injected into him and out pops a story of his being operated on by aliens with eyes like painted Ping-Pong balls. They learn the aliens had removed his heart and repaired the damage he received from the plane crash.

He is shown a screen on which appears the image of the aliens' home world and their dying sun. It looks like an eye. The aliens, one billion strong, intend to invade our world by releasing monster insects and reptiles to wipe us out.

Aware of the threat, now that the amnesia is lifted, the official contrives a plan that results in the destruction of the alien bases of operations via a surreally tilted nuclear blast that vindicates his sanity.

Skipping ahead to the more familiar territory of *Star Trek*, we can point to the award-winning episode "The Doomsday Machine" as another illustration of the relationship. Starship Captain William Decker is found catatonic after losing his crew. He had beamed them down to a planet, but couldn't rescue them when an immense automated planet-killer

reduced it to rubble. Events lead him to command the Enterprise and take it into futile battle. As they approach the machine, the planet-killer looms up with the appearance of a giant eye.

Decker eventually commits suicide and Kirk destroys the planet-killer by imploding the engines of Decker's abandoned ship. Speaking of planet-killers, the Death Star of *Star Wars* also presents the appearance of a giant eyeball that shoots lasers from its pupil.

The reason for this intertwining of cataclysmic imagery and eyes is psychiatrically elementary. Paranoia is intimately tied to the experience of shame. It is shame that creates delusions of observation. Shame also has the effect of fragmenting the ego and this is accompanied by fantasies of world destruction or other images of cataclysm. (Freud, 1953)

Paranoiac reactions, with their enhanced stimulus sensitivities and loss of discrimination, will stimulate many idiosyncratic concerns, but these two are archetypal and structural.

UFOlogy, not unexpectedly, provides many examples of this relationship. Donald Keyhoe, our premier advocate of the belief that we are being watched by other worlds, also expressed numerous apocalyptic fears in his early books: super-atomic bombs he feared would throw Earth out of its orbit or propel large chunks out of the planet with unpredictable results. Aliens might be here to play audience to a replay of Velikovsky's *Worlds in Collision* (1950). He also feared that Russians would stage a mass A-bomb attack in 1954, employing rumors of saucer attacks to paralyze communication and transportation networks. (Kottmeyer, 1991)

Most of the early believers in the reconnaissance theory held some form of fear that catastrophe was impending. Albert Bender believed the polar ice caps were ready to capsize the Earth in 1953 with an attendant array of natural disturbances. (Bender, 1953)

Harold T. Wilkins warned that lithium bombs would turn the Earth into a flaming nova. Morris Jessup feared either a pole-shift, a cosmic storm, or atomic holocaust would befall the Earth before 1980. Aimé Michel regarded saucers as a sword of Damocles hanging over us, portending "the greatest catastrophe in human history" if they should contact us and learn of our inferior ethics. The Lorenzens felt the saucers embodied an urgency comparable to Pearl Harbor and speculated Earth faced a crisis of the Velikovskian variety. (See this writer's entry on PARANOIA AND UFOs for more examples)

This relationship breaks down around 1974 as cataclysmic fantasies decrease in response to the reintegration of the ego taking place around that time in UFOlogy. It is not surprising that ambivalence about the reality of alien reconnaissance takes place about then. A complete rejection however is difficult, since this might be tantamount to denial of the existence of a superego or conscience and so a threat to the recovering ego.

There are numerous independent criteria pointing to the reintegration taking place at that time: the appearance of influencing machine fantasies, the decline in hypochondriacal pleas to diagnose the flying saucer problem as real, decreased death fears about mass poisoning or galactic experiments in cremation. The shift in viewing Earth as a fiercely barbarous race and a prison or asylum to viewing Earth as a tourist attraction, and an anthropologist's prize, similarly signals the increase in self-worth attending the ego reintegration of the paranoid over time. (Kottmeyer, 1989)

UFO experiencers also show evidence of this relationship. One example concerns the case of the abductee William J. Herrmann. On the 10th of November, 1981, Herrmann was fired from his position as a children's church teacher, because the church believed he had become involved in satanic things when he spoke on TV about UFOs. On November 14th, Herrmann received by "automatic transmission" from his alien contacts a diagram of the power unit which contains images of a pair of eyes. That same day, he wrote an essay titled "Inevitable Destruction," in which he warns that geopolitical events may soon lead to the

entire Earth being engulfed in an "eternal firestorm." That these things turned up so soon after the humiliation of a public excoriation makes a clear case that a paranoiac reaction was in process. (Stevens, 1989)

In the Liberty, Kentucky, triple abduction we find our paired motif (the watchful eye and world destruction), but separated into two individuals. Under hypnotic regression, Mona Stafford sees a large "eye" observing her as she lies on a table. Humanoids in surgical garb then examine her and she is transported to a room in a volcano. (Lorenzen, 1977)

She then experiences traveling at the speed of light while glued to a stool. She later revealed a belief that she had been tested to be a messenger of God's warning that man had to better his ways. "It's going to be a terrible time," as Revelation predicts. She believed the effort to be as futile as warnings before Noah's flood. She was personally convinced her life was going to be destroyed and she would never see another birthday.

Louise Smith, one of the other abductees, did not experience seeing an eye during her regression. Instead she relived fluid material covering her that made her gasp for breath. She thinks they were making a mold of her body. She subsequently learned the aliens were coming from a dying solar system, but admits that this made no sense to her since she was unaware that a solar system could die.

This may have been derived from *Earth versus Flying Saucers* (1956) whose aliens hail from a "disintegrating solar system." Smith's aliens allegedly could control rain. The movie's aliens were able to induce meteorological convulsions on Earth to warn everyone of their power.

One can also see the pairing of motifs in Whitley Strieber's *Communion* (1987). The eyes of the alien are horrifically blank, black, and inhumanly large. Subsequent to his nightmare, he felt one evening the sky was alive and watching him. Strieber had full awareness this was a paranoid fantasy. (Strieber, 1987) In a hypnotic session he experiences an image of the world blowing up.

Edith Fiore reports an instance of a friend who felt faint and whose heart beat wildly upon picking up a copy of *Communion*. Fiore felt this reaction was peculiar and was able to elicit memories of a CE-IV (Close Encounter of the Fourth Kind or abduction) from this individual.

This should not be too surprising, given the large staring eyes on the book's jacket. As mentioned earlier, staring eyes stimulate physiological arousal in many animals besides man. Fiore's ability to elicit a CE-IV experience from this individual is deeply suspicious since it proceeded from the false premise that her friend's reaction was unusual. But wouldn't most people find the image of Strieber's alien unsettling to some extent?

Barney Hill's experience lacks a cataclysmic motif, but deserves attention here because of the issue it raises about eyes and the UFO experience. It is safe to say that we would never have heard of *The Interrupted Journey* if Barney Hill had not reacted so dramatically to the image of the UFO he saw in the binoculars.

This incident was not an artifact of the hypnotic sessions; it was consciously experienced and remembered. As he looked at the UFO, he felt the leader was staring at him. On experiencing this he rips the binoculars from his face, tearing the straps, and runs screaming back to the car. This is very untypical behavior, for Barney had served three years in the Army and handled himself well in crisis situations. He didn't seem to be the type to panic over something like being looked at. Getting to the car he threw it into gear and told Betty, his wife, to look out for the craft. Later, she admitted she thought his imagination was being overactive—because when she looked up, she saw nothing. (Fuller, 1966)

These facts alone point to the presence of a paranoid reaction, but we also know that he was in this state before the UFO experience. When they stopped to eat earlier at the restaurant, Barney complained that everybody in the street was looking at them. This complaint, "all eyes are on us," is a delusion of observa-

tion just like the image of the staring leader in the saucer. Barney himself realized everybody was actually behaving in a pleasant manner and that he had better get a hold on himself.

What is also interesting about Barney's account is the drawing of the UFO itself. As Alvin Lawson has pointed out, it has the general form of an eye in the sky. (Lawson, 1982) This is an important point, since the context of the eye-like UFO demonstrates its psychological origin beyond reasonable doubt.

Barney Hill's UFO is not alone in the UFO literature in having a resemblance to an eye, and it will doubtless be argued that coincidence could account for some or all of these instances of eye-like UFOs. Flying saucers oblige at least one circle in their form, and aesthetic symmetries would doubtless lead to other circles and radiating lines. This writer agrees, yet we can see the psychological processes at work, for example, in dreams reported in Carl Jung's book on flying saucers. Consider this one:

"I was walking, at night, in the streets of a city. Interplanetary 'machines' appeared in the sky, and everyone fled. The 'machines' looked like large steel cigars. I did not flee. One of the 'machines' spotted me and came straight towards me at an oblique angle. I think: Professor Jung says that one should not run away, so I stand still and look at the machine. From the front, seen close to, it looked like a circular eye, half blue, half white.

"A room in a hospital: my two chiefs come in, very worried, and ask my sister how it was going. My sister replied that the mere sight of the machine had burnt my whole face. Only then did I realize that they were talking about me, and that my whole head was bandaged, although I could not see it." (Jung, 1959)

Jung also reports on a woman's dream about a black humming metallic object like a spider with great dark eyes that flies over her. She was not clothed and felt somewhat embarrassed. The spider flew alongside a large administrative building in which international decisions were being made and influenced people inside to go the way of peace, which was the way to the inner, secret world. Obviously eyes are intimately associated with UFOs in the unconscious. Eye-like UFOs are to be expected.

Carl Jung

There may of course be perfectly plausible ways of explaining away the eye-like nature of UFOs as a function of their observation equipment behaving like the machinery of the human eye. There may be perfectly plausible ways of explaining the cop-sunglasses eyes of Strieber's aliens as the plausible product of evolutionary adaptation to the environment of the planet from which they came. But what really makes the most sense?

In the final analysis, one has to go back to context. The eyes appear in relationship to a web of paranoid themes in the UFO mythos and a structure of paranoid development occurring in paranoid systems of thought. We also see them in the context of a mythos grown up from Keyhoe in which aliens were assumed to be spying on us. It is a context filled with apocalypses, amnesia, persecutions, chases, influencing machines, and conspiracies. And always there is furtiveness to allow evidence but never proof. So, what ultimately is the more meaningful interpretation—extraterrestrials or superegos?

—MARTIN S. KOTTMEYER

References

Adamski, George. *Inside the Space Ships* (Abelard-Schuman, 1955).

Andrus, Walter. "Air Intelligence Report No. 10-203-79" *MUFON UFO Journal* (July 1985).

Angelucci, Orfeo M. *The Secret of the Saucers* (Amherst Press, 1955).

Badcock, C.R. *The Psychoanalysis of Culture* (1980).

Bender, Albert K. "Editorial," *Space Review* (April 1953).

Bender, Albert K. *Space Review—Complete File* (Saucerian Books, 1962).

Binder, Otto. *Flying Saucers Are Watching Us* (Tower, 1968).

Bloecher, Ted. *Report on the UFO Wave of 1947* (privately published, 1967).

Bondarchuk, Yurko. *UFO Sightings, Landings, and Abductions* (Methuen, 1979).

Bord, Janet and Colin. *Are We Being Watched?* (Angus Robertson, 1980).

Campbell, Joseph. *The Masks of God: Primitive Mythology* (Viking, 1959; Penguin, 1985).

Cohn, Norman. *Europe's Inner Demons* (Meridian, 1975).

Colp, Ralph. "Confessing a Murder," *Isis* (1986).

DeMause, Lloyd. *Foundations of Psychohistory* (Creative Roots, 1982).

Edwards, Frank. *Flying Saucers—Serious Business* (Bantam, 1966).

Eichrodt, Walther. *Theology of the Old Testament, Vol. 2* (SCM Press, 1967).

Eidelberg, Ludwig. *Encyclopedia of Psychoanalysis* (Free Press, 1968).

Erskine, Allen Louis. *Why Are They Watching Us?* (Tower, 1967).

Evans, Hilary. *The Evidence for UFOs* (The Aquarian Press, 1983).

Fawcett, Lawrence and Barry Greenwood. *Clear Intent* (Prentice-Hall, 1984).

Fiore, Edith. *Encounters: A Psychologist Reveals Case Studies of Abductions by Extraterrestrials* (Doubleday, 1989).

Fort, Charles. *The Book of the Damned* (Boni & Liveright, 1919).

Fowler, Raymond. *UFOs: Interplanetary Visitors)* (Prentice-Hall, 1974).

Freud, Sigmund. "On Narcissism: An Introduction" in Strachey, James, ed. *The Standard Edition of the Complete Psychological Works of Sigmund Freud, Vol. 14* (The Hogarth Press, 1953).

Frosch, John. *The Psychotic Process* (International University Press, 1983).

Fuller, John G. *The Interrupted Journey* (The Dial Press, 1966).

Gallup, George. *The Gallup Poll: Public Opinion, Volume 2 (1949-1958)* (Random House, 1972).

Gibbons, Gavin. *The Coming of the Space Ships* (The Citadel Press, 1958).

Gillmor, Daniel S., ed. *Scientific Study of Unidentified Flying Objects* (Bantam, 1969).

Godwin, Donald W. *Anxiety* (Oxford, 1986).

Good, Timothy. *Above Top Secret* (Sidgwick and Jackson, 1987; Morrow/Quill, 1988).

Gross, Loren E. *Charles Fort, the Fortean Society and Unidentified Flying Objects* (privately published, 1976).

———. *UFOs: A History, Vol. 1: July 1947-December 1948* (Arcturus Book Service, 1982).

———. *UFOs: A History, Vol. 2: 1949* (Arcturus Book Service, 1983).

Grumet, Gerald W. "Eye Contact: The Core of Interpersonal Relatedness," *Psychiatry* (May 1983).

Haines, Richard F. "A Review of Proposed Explanatory Hypotheses for Unidentified Aerial Phenomena," *Flying Saucer Review* (February 1987).

Haining, Peter. *Terror* (A & W Visual Library, 1976).

Hall, Richard. *Uninvited Guests* (Aurora, 1988).

Hamilton, William F. *Close Encounter Report* (Nexus, 1988).

Heard, Gerald. *Is Another World Watching?* (Harper, 1951).

Hervey, Michael. *UFOs: The American Scene* (St. Martin's Press, 1976).

Hopkins, Budd. *Missing Time* (Richard Marek, 1981).

Hudson, Jan. *Those Sexy Saucer People* (Greenleaf Classics, 1967).

Hynek, J. Allen. *The UFO Experience: A Scientific Inquiry* (Henry Regnery, 1972).

Jaynes, Julian. *Origins of Consciousness in the Breakdown of the Bicameral Mind* (Houghton Mifflin, 1976).

Jessup, Morris K. *The Case for the UFO* (The Citadel Press, 1955; Vero edition/Saucerian, 1973).

John. *The Etherean Invasion* (Hwong, 1979).

Jung, C. G. *Flying Saucers: A Modern Myth of Things Seen in the Skies* (Routledge & Kegan Paul/Harcourt, Brace & Co. 1959; Signet/NAL, 1969; Princeton University Press, 1978).

Keen, Maurice. "A Master of the Middle Ages," *New York Review of Books* (May 1989).

Keyhoe, Donald. "Flying Saucers Are Real" *True* (January 1950).

———. *The Flying Saucers Are Real* (Fawcett, 1950).

———. *Flying Saucers from Outer Space* (Henry Holt, 1953).

———. *Flying Saucers—Top Secret* (G.P. Putnam's Sons, 1960).

———. *Aliens from Space* (Doubleday, 1973).

Kor, Peter. "Keyhoe's Last Stand" *Flying Saucers* (September 1974).

Kottmeyer, Martin. "Dying Worlds, Dying Selves," *UFO Brigantia* (January 1991).

Kottmeyer, Martin. "Ufology Considered as an Evolving System of Paranoia," in Stillings, Dennis, ed. *Cyberbiological Studies of the Imaginal Component in the UFO Contact Experience* (Archaeus, 1989).

Lawson, Alvin. "Birth Trauma Imagery in CE-III Narratives" in *International UPIAR Colloquium on Human Sciences and UFO Phenomena Proceedings* (July 1982).

Layne, Meade. *The Coming of the Guardians* (Borderland Sciences Research Foundation, 1972).

Leiber, Fritz. *The Best of Fritz Leiber* (Ballantine, 1974).

Lem, Stanislaw. *One Human Minute* (1936).

Leslie, Desmond and George Adamski. *Flying Saucers Have Landed* (British Book Centre/Werner Laurie, 1953).

Levin, Murray B. *Political Hysteria in America* (Basic Books, 1971).

Locke, George. *Voyages in Space: A Bibliography of Interplanetary Fiction, 1801-1914* (Ferret Fantasy, 1975).

Loftin, Robert. *Identified Flying Saucers* (McKay, 1968).

Lorenzen, Coral and Jim. *Abducted! Confrontations with Beings from Outer Space* (Berkley, 1977).

Lorenzen, Coral E. *Flying Saucers: The Startling Evidence of the Invasion From Outer Space* (Signet/NAL, 1966).

McCampbell, James M. *UFOlogy* (Celestial Arts, 1973).

McDonald, James E. "Science in Default: Twenty-two Years of Inadequate UFO Investigations" in

Sagan, Carl and Page, Thornton, eds. *UFOs: A Scientific Debate* (Cornell University Press, 1972).

Menger, Howard. *From Outer Space* (Saucerian, 1959; Pyramid, 1967).

Meslin, Michel. "Eye" in Eliade, Mircea, ed. *Encyclopedia of Religion, Vol. 5* (Macmillan, 1936).

Michel, Aimé. *The Truth About Flying Saucers* (Pyramid, 1967).

Mitchell, Helen and Betty. *We Met the Space People* (Galaxy, 1973).

Moskowitz, Sam. *Strange Horizons: The Spectrum of Science Fiction* (Scribner's, 1976).

Neeley, Robert G. *UFOs of 1896/1897: The Airship Wave* (Fund for UFO Research, 1988).

Patai, Raphael. *Hebrew Myths: The Book of Genesis* (Greenwich, 1983).

Ridpath, Ian. *Messages From the Stars* (Harper & Row, 1978).

Sachs, Margaret. *The UFO Encyclopedia* (Perigee, 1980).

Saggs, H.W.F. *The Greatness that was Babylon* (1962).

Salisbury, Frank. *The Utah UFO Display* (Devin-Adair, 1974).

Scully, Frank. *Behind the Flying Saucers* (Henry Holt, 1950).

Shuttlewood, Arthur. *The Warminster Mystery* (Tandem, 1976).

Slate, B. Ann. "UFO Vigil Over Top-Secret Air Force Base" *UFO Annual 1977*.

Smith, Warren. "Contact with a UFO Crew," *UFO Report* (January 1979)

Smith, Warren. *UFO Trek* (Zebra, 1976).

Steiger, Brad and Joan Whritenour. *Flying Saucers Are Hostile* (Ace, 1966).

Steiger, Brad. *Project Blue Book* (Ballantine, 1976).

Steinberg, Gene. "Last Interview with Major Donald E. Keyhoe" *UFO Universe* (Summer 1989).

Stevens, Wendelle C. *UFO Contact from Reticulum Update* (privately published, 1989).

Story, Ronald D., ed. *The Encyclopedia of UFOs* (Doubleday/New English Library, 1980).

Strentz, Herbert J. *A Survey of Press Coverage of Unidentified Flying Objects, 1947-1966* (Arcturus Book Service, 1982).

Strieber, Whitley. *Communion* (Beech Tree Books/William Morrow, 1987; Avon, 1988).

Stringfield, Leonard H. *Situation Red: The UFO Siege* (Doubleday, 1977).

Trench, Brinsley Le Poer. *The Flying Saucer Story* (Ace, 1966).

Valerian, Valdamar. *The Matrix* (Arcturus Book Service, 1988).

Vorilhon, Claude. "Raël" in *Space Aliens Took Me To Their Planet* (Canadian Raëlian Movement, 1978).

Warren, Bill. *Keep Watching the Skies* (MacFarland, 1982).

Watson, Nigel, et al. *The 1912-1913 British Phantom Airship Scare* (Fund for UFO Research, 1988).

Wilkins, Harold T. *Flying Saucers on the Attack* (Ace, 1967).

Williamson, George Hunt and John McCoy. *UFOs Confidential* (privately published, 1958).

Williamson, George Hunt. *The Saucers Speak* (Neville Spearman, 1963).

religion and UFOs Religion is used by some in the UFO field to explain away the existence of UFOs. It is used in the following form: "Religion and UFOs have one thing in common: Both are make-believe." In fact, UFOs are a modern form of religion, something quasi-scientific, which have taken the place of traditional ideas of angels and miracles. To some extent, the theories of Carl Jung, found in his book *Flying Saucers: A Modern Myth of Things Seen in the Skies* (1959), develop the view that saucer-shaped UFOs are symbolic of the longing of the soul for unity. Therefore, UFOs may not be "real" in our usual scientific sense. In the book edited by Carl Sagan and Thornton Page, *UFOs—A Scientific Debate* (1972), the article by Sagan, "UFO's: The Extraterrestrial and Other Hypotheses," and the article by the late Donald H. Menzel, "UFO's—The Modern Myth," both develop the view that UFOs do not have any more scientific reality than religion does. In effect, people like Sagan and Menzel use religion to destroy the credibility of UFOs as a scientific study.

As Sagan and Menzel use religion to get rid of UFOs, there are others who use UFOs, and related subjects, to get rid of religion. Erich von Däniken's *Chariots of the Gods?* (1968), as well as his other works, represent this view. Von Däniken deals mainly with the history of what he believes is extraterrestrial visitation to Earth, in which space beings carried on experiments in science with Earth people. Earth people fell in religious awe before advanced space technology. The city of Sodom, von Däniken believes, was destroyed by nuclear weapons in the hands of space beings. Likewise, the Exodus in the Bible was the work of space beings carrying out a breeding experiment. Man, in his ignorance, began to worship these beings. Von Däniken is very hostile toward organized religion, especially his native Roman Catholic Church and its priesthood, as may be seen from his attacks on it, especially in his book *Miracles of the Gods* (1974). Von Däniken sees UFOs and the visitation of "ancient astronauts" as "true science" and uses this "UFO science" to discredit religion.

Could this have been the scene at
Sodom and Gomorah?
(Painting by Monarca Lynn Merrifield)

A third approach to UFOs and religion is to say "God is an astronaut." Von Däniken used this approach to discredit religion, but R. L. Dione, in books such as *God Drives a Flying Saucer* (1969), develops the view that the God of the Bible is really an astronaut, a kind of *Star Trek* Captain Kirk, who for reasons known only to himself decided to start the biblical religion. This "god" uses advanced tech-

nology to perform the miracles in the Bible— everything from the parting of the Red Sea to the artificial insemination of Mary so that Jesus could be born and promote the work of the astronaut-god. The unfortunate thing about Dione's god is that he appears demonically deceptive, and, in fact, Dione feels himself called to uncover the fraud which this technological god has brought upon us: an astronaut who has tried to make us think he is really divine!

Angels announcing the
birth of the savior

A fourth approach to UFOs and religion is more complex, and suggests that UFOs and religion may share a common ground in man's unconscious or psychic area. One approach in this area is directly religious, as in the work of Ted Peters, *UFOs—God's Chariots?* (1977), while another approach is more secular, as in Jerome Clark and Loren Coleman's book *The Unidentified* (1975). Peters approaches the subject phenomenologically, making no decision about the "reality" of UFOs, but pointing out that how a person sees a UFO usually depends on what he is: Politicians see them as space visitors here to establish contact, scientists see them as scientists here to study us, some religious leaders see them as angels as found in the Bible. In other words, man's unconscious nature determines our UFO theories.

Clark and Coleman go even further. They argue that UFOs are a psychic projection of man's collective unconscious (drawing on C. G. Jung), a kind of "poltergeist" phenomena. Their theory is able to draw together the physical and psychological dimensions of the UFO problem better than most theories, but in order to accept their view, one has to believe the human unconscious is capable of powers unknown before. The theories of Peters and Clark and Coleman might be summarized in terms of religion in this way: "If faith can move mountains, then it can certainly create UFOs."

A fifth theory joining UFOs and religion is that UFOs are demons. This view is most popular among Christian fundamentalists and is expressed in the work of John Weldon and Zola Levitt in *UFOs: What on Earth Is Happening?* (1975) and Clifford Wilson in his book *UFOs and their Mission Impossible* (1974). These authors conclude that since UFOs will not reveal their true nature to us, they are demonic. Weldon and Levitt use this approach in a fairly traditional fundamentalist way: The world is coming to an end, Jesus is returning, UFOs are a sign that the devil has been let loose; repent and be saved. The weakness of both the above books is that they make no serious attempt to relate their theory to the other possibility, that UFOs are in a sense "good" angels as described in the Bible.

The sixth theory is that UFOs are some kind of divine power. This theory has been developed in both a secular and religious form. Jacques Vallée has put forth this theory in secular form in his book *The Invisible College* (1975). He concludes his book with a chapter describing "The Next Form of Religion," by suggesting that UFOs are some kind of power which directs, at a deep unconscious level, human destiny. Vallée does not call this power God, although that has been the traditional name for such a power. I have developed this theory from the more traditional point of view in my book *The Bible and Flying Saucers* (1968) and in various articles. I have suggested that the "pillar of cloud and fire" of the Exodus was what we now call a UFO, that it led the way to the Red Sea, parted the water, fed Israel on manna, and led the way to Mount Sinai, where Moses received all the commandments of the Jewish religion. This, together with major UFO contacts with the prophets, represents the "First Revelation" or the Old Testament. The "Second Revelation" concerns the coming of Jesus, one called the son of God, who comes from the Higher Reality into our reality to explain what life is about. Roughly the message of life is this: Life is a three-stage process: (1) we begin in the dark in our mother's womb, and then are born into (2) a second womb, the world we see, but in which we only begin to understand the nature of God, and then we are born again into (3) the higher spiritual world, from which Jesus has come, and to which we will go when we die, leaving our physical body behind as a baby leaves the placenta.

UFO events in the New Testament include the bright light over the shepherds at Christmas (Luke 2:9), the Baptism of Jesus (Matt. 3:16), the Transfiguration of Jesus (Matt. 17:5), the Ascension of Jesus (Acts 1:9), and the conversion of the Apostle Paul by a bright light on the Damascus Road (Acts 9:3). This theory of the Bible has been largely rejected by liberals because they have tended to doubt the "reality" of miracles, angels, and life after death. This theory of the Bible has also been rejected by fundamentalist Christians in favor of the "demon" view described above. The reason for this in part is that Protestant fundamentalists do not expect to see any real divine activity now. They tend to think God finished his work in the New Testament, with the exception of the Second Coming of Christ. The idea that God might be doing any obvious work is foreign to their doctrines.

Traditional religion has also rejected my views for the very good reason that it raises some difficult issues. For instance, are UFOs really supernatural, or are they just advanced technology? If one takes too technological an approach, God seems to get left out, as in Josef Blunuich's work *The Spaceships of Ezekiel* (1974). But if one takes the spiritual approach, then why are UFOs apparently acting like scientists who take Earth people on board to give physical exams, as in the Betty and Barney Hill abduction case?

The tentative answer to these questions is: The supernatural is a very ''free'' reality and can therefore take on technological form if it so desires.

In regard to ''contact'' cases like the Hills, it can be argued that they are modern forms of ''revelation,'' and that contact must be interpreted symbolically rather than literally. Thus, in the Betty and Barney Hill case, we must see their examination as a way of saying to the whole human race: ''We know you inside and out, and we are watching you.'' This is a very old biblical religious message of what God's angels are doing.

Recent studies have shown that people who have not had UFO contacts can, under

hypnosis, nevertheless be led very easily to tell of UFO contact experiences. This does not mean the Hill case did not occur. It means that the UFO reality has found a way to hide itself from our scientific study, while at the same time making known to us what it wants to.

Perhaps the one element that religion can contribute at this point to UFO studies is one of attitude: humility. Religion has always approached God with respect, seeking to know Him in His own terms, not by putting Him in a cage like a rat. Science, in order to study UFOs, may have to learn from religion that, whatever UFOs are, they are bigger than we are, and they had best be treated with respect and humility.

—BARRY H. DOWNING

References

Blumrich, Josef F. *The Spaceships of Ezekiel* (Bantam Books, 1974).

Clark, Jerome, and Loren Coleman. *The Unidentified* (Warner Paperback Library, 1975).

Dione, R. L. *God Drives a Flying Saucer* (Bantam Books, 1973).

Downing, Barry. *The Bible and Flying Saucers* (J. P. Lippincott, 1968; Avon, 1970; Sphere Books, 1973; Marlowe, 1997).

Jessup, Morris K. *UFO and the Bible* (The Citadel Press, 1956).

Jung, C. G. *Flying Saucers: A Modern Myth of Things Seen in the Skies* (Routledge & Kegan Paul/Harcourt, Brace & Co. 1959; Signet/NAL, 1969; Princeton University Press, 1978). Original German edition published in 1958.

Peters, Ted. *UFOs—God's Chariots?* (John Knox Press, 1977).

Sagan, Carl, and Thornton Page, eds. *UFOs—A Scientific Debate* (W. W. Norton, 1974).

Vallée, Jacques. *The Invisible College* (E. P. Dutton, 1975).

Von Däniken, Erich. *Chariots of the Gods?* (Bantam Books, 1970). Original German edtion published in 1968.

———. *Miracles of the Gods* (Dell, 1976).

Weldon, John, and Zola Levitt. *UFOs: What on Earth Is Happening?* (Harvest House, 1975)

Wilson, Clifford. *UFOs and Their Mission Impossible* (Signet/NAL, 1974)

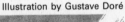
Illustration by Gustave Doré

The miraculous conversion of St. Paul

religious movements and UFOs The UFO experience has seemed for many fraught with spiritual or religious meaning. This is understandable, for the sense of wonder evoked by the thought of otherworldly visitants flows easily, for people of a certain susceptibility, into those feelings of the presence of the numinous and the transcendent which characterizes religious experience.

The religious response to UFOs takes many forms. There are those for whom it is purely personal and subjective. Others translate revelation of the sacred meaning of UFOs into books and lectures, which win some attention but do not form specific groups or movements. In still other cases, the response takes the shape of a group with discernible structure and continuity, however fragile and ephemeral it may appear in comparison with major religious institutions. These groups may be called UFO religious movements.

A religious movement is more than a personal religious experience or belief, but less than a religious institution. It catches up two or more people in the mystique of the same experience and belief, it has some extension in time, some distinct practices or meetings, and a definable sociology. In regard to the last, generally one finds a leader endowed with charisma by a special blessing he has received, and a tight or loose company of followers. Yet groups concerned with the spiritual meaning of UFOs have generally not achieved the permanence and institutional structure one would associate with a religion.

The connection of UFOs with the sacred has existed almost from the beginning of modern UFOlogy with the 1947 sightings by Kenneth Arnold. In the early 1950s, a number of contactee experiences were reported, the most notable of them being probably those of Dan Fry in 1950; George Van Tassel in 1951; George Adamski, Truman Bethurum, and George Hunt Williamson in 1952; George King in 1954; and Orfeo Angelucci in 1955.

All of these persons lectured widely, wrote books about their experiences that were widely read in saucerian circles, and gave glowing accounts of the saucer people as being masters or elder brothers of the human race. These "Space Brothers" are described as kind and wise beyond our imagining, and able and eager to help us. Whether a simple contact with a message and vision or a ride in the UFO—like a shaman's flight—the experience in these cases had all the overtones of an initiation into a universe of infinitely richer marvel and meaning than the ordinary. It left the recipient with a sense of mission, of having an ethic to follow and a message of hope or salvation to deliver.

The 1950s were, in fact, the golden age of UFO religion. The dazzlingly beautiful and spiritual entities of these contact accounts contrast strikingly with the bizarre, slit-mouthed UFO occupants (including the medical examiners) of the 1960s and '70s reports. It was only of the 1950s type of contacts that religious movements would likely be derived, and it was in the 1950s that the major movements started. The '50s aliens were, in the words of the famous analytic psychologist Carl G. Jung, "technological angels"—beings coming to a scientific age in the vehicles required by its worldview but having the power and mission of the mythic descending saviors and guardian spirits of old.

Several of these contacts developed into specific religious movements. Their practices and forms of expression seem mostly derived from spiritualism, with the principal contactee playing the role of a major medium. Apart from the initial hierophany, saucer contact is mostly "mental" and transmitted through mediumship and automatic writing.

While most of these groups dwindled away in subsequent decades, other UFO religions—like the Raëlians—have achieved a significant following at the start of the new millennium. Saucer group meetings typically consist of lectures, chanting (which produces an atmosphere conducive to transmittal), mediumistic messages from the saucer friends, and perhaps "circle" messages in which various members of the group will spontaneously receive and contribute to the transmission coming in. The scenario compares closely to the format of spiritualist services and séances, and one is not surprised to find that a large percentage of UFO religionists have a background in spiritualism and other forms of occultism.

One of the oldest and most enduring of the saucer movements is Understanding, Inc., founded by Dan Fry. The latter says that he had his initial UFO experience in 1950, although the book describing it was not published until 1954, the year before Understanding, Inc., was started. Fry states that on July 4, 1950, he encountered a UFO when alone in the desert at the White Sands Proving Ground in New Mexico; the celestial vehicle took him for a ride to New York and back in half an hour. In the course of this journey he was given instruction by A-Lan, his invisible mentor, on true science, the importance of understanding, and information that the saucer people are the remnant of a past supercivilization on Earth. The organization, however, has not been as concerned with promoting these particular views as with providing a forum for contactee and other saucerian speakers with a spiritual emphasis. In this respect, it is different from most of the others, which are mediumistic and related to particular saucer contacts.

The best-known of these is undoubtedly the Aetherius Society, founded by the late George King in England, which is still active both there and in the United States. It centers around transmissions through Mr. King from masters on flying saucers and other planets. Members perform a diversity of spiritual work under their direction designed to initiate a new spiritual age on Earth. The services of Aetherius are rather formal. The inner group is close-knit and the doctrine is heavily influenced by occultism of the theosophical sort.

Another activity which should be mentioned is the Giant Rock Space Convention, formerly held by the contactee George Van Tassel at his small airport near Yucca Valley, California, on the Mojave Desert between 1954 and 1970. The conventions were held for two days every September and brought together many of the major religious contactees and their followers in the atmosphere of a camp meeting, with speeches, transmissions, and fellowship abounding.

Something of the saucerian atmosphere of the 1950s returned in 1975 with the strange phenomenon of the movement headed by a man and a woman called The Two, or Bo and Peep. After they gave lectures on UFOs in several western cities, a couple hundred people, mostly young, left all to follow them to isolated mountain camps, where they would be purified in preparation to being taken imminently by UFOs to a paradisal world. Many left when these hopes were not immediately fulfilled, but a small core remained.

The cult later became known to the world as the infamous "Heaven's Gate," shortly after their leader, Marshall Applewhite instigated a mass suicide of 39 cult members at Rancho Sante Fe, California, in March of 1997.

Robert Balch and David Taylor, in a sociological study of this group (years before the mass suicide), determined something probably true of all UFO religious movements: that the preponderance of participants were people with a long history of involvement in other occult, spiritualist, and "metaphysical" organizations.

Several scores of other groups qualify as UFO religious movements, including the Solar Cross, the Amalgamated Flying Saucer Clubs (led by Gabriel Green), the Inner Circle, Light of the Universe, Solar Light Center, Unarius, and the Etherean Society. One UFO group, which believed that the world would be destroyed on a particular date when the Space Brothers would rescue believers, but which transmuted the expected apocalypse into a spiritual hope when the destruction and rescue did not take place, was the subject of a celebrated sociological study, *When Prophecy Fails* (1956). Most, however, have received little fame beyond their small host of friends and adherents. But all represent modern transformations of humankind's age-old need for wonder and for supernormal companionship in this vast and lonely universe.

—ROBERT S. ELLWOOD, JR.

Rendlesham Forest incident Several UFO incidents, including multiple-witness sightings by military personnel, ground traces, and radioactive anomalies were reported from Rendlesham Forest, an area between two British NATO bases in Suffolk, East England. Both bases, RAF Bentwaters and RAF Woodbridge (since closed down), were at that time leased to the U.S. Air Force.

The incidents took place between December 27 and 30, 1980. According to an official report (dated January 13, 1981; released in 1983 under F.O.I.A.) by RAF Woodbridge's deputy base commander Lt. Col. Charles Halt, the events were as follows:

1. Early in the morning of 27 December 1980 (approximately 0300L), two USAF security police patrolmen saw unusual lights outside the back gate at RAF Woodbridge. Thinking an aircraft might have crashed or been forced down, they called for permission to go outside the gate to investigate. The on-duty flight chief responded and allowed three patrolmen to proceed on foot. The individuals reported seeing a strange glowing object in the forest. The object was described as being metallic in appearance and triangular in shape, approximately two to three meters [six to nine feet] across the base and approximately two meters [six feet] high. It illuminated the entire forest with a white light. The object itself had a pulsing red light on top and a bank(s) of blue lights underneath. The object was hovering or on legs. As the patrolmen approached the object it maneuvered through the trees and disappeared. At this time the animals on a nearby farm went into a frenzy. The object was briefly sighted approximately an hour later near the back gate.

2. The next day, three depressions 1½" deep and 7" in diameter were found where the object had been sighted on the ground. The following night (29 Dec 80) the area was checked for radiation. Beta/gamma readings of 0.1 milliroentgens were recorded with peak readings in the three depressions and near the center of the triangle formed by the depressions. A tree had moderate (.05-.07) readings on the side of the tree towards the depressions.

3. Later in the night a red sun-like light was seen through the trees. It moved about and pulsed. At one point it appeared to throw off glowing particles and then broke into five separate white objects and then disappeared. Immediately thereafter three star-like objects were noticed in the sky. . . . The objects moved rapidly in sharp angular movements and displayed red, green and blue lights. The objects to the north appeared to be elliptical. . . . The object to the south was visible for two or three hours and beamed down a stream of light from time to time. Numerous individuals, including the undersigned, witnessed the activities in paragraphs 2 and 3.

Later, an audiotape was released which contained Col. Halt's recording during the nightly investigation in Rendlesham Forest on the night of December 29, 1980. In this, Halt describes how first the animals of a nearby farm started to make noise when he saw a "yellow thing" approaching and releasing luminous "pieces."

When it was only 200-300 yards away, the Colonel said "it looks like an eye winking at you, still moving from side to side." Furthermore he reported "one object still hovering over Woodbridge base," beaming down rays of light.

Already in January of 1981, the first rumors about the incident surfaced and two local UFO investigators, Brenda Butler and Dot Street, started to investigate. They were immediately confronted with bizarre rumors including that base commander General Gordon Williams met three small humanoids who came out in a beam of light from a landed UFO in Rendlesham Forest on December 27th.

Still skeptical, they learned that an unidentified object was recorded on radar at the time in question by RAF Wharton, a British air base. During their investigation and also after the publication of their book *Sky Crash* (together with Jenny Randles), Butler and Street were able to locate and interview several dozen eyewitnesses of the event. The subsequent release of the Halt memorandum confirmed most of their testimony. Furthermore, interviewed by *Omni* editor Eric Mischera, Bentwaters Base Commander Col. Ted Conrad confirmed: ''It was a large craft, mounted on tripod legs. It had no windows but was covered in red and blue lights. It definitely demonstrated intelligent control. After almost an hour it flew off at phenomenal speed. It left behind a triangular set of marks evidently formed by the tripod legs. A later investigation proved the marks to be problematic.''

When this UFO landing seems to be an undebatable fact, other aspects of several eyewitness testimonies are rather bizarre and were never confirmed, including the claim of an encounter with small humanoids and even of abduction-like experiences related to the sightings.

Two British Ministry of Defense officials, Ralph Noyes, a retired under-secretary of the MoD, and Nick Pope of the MoD's UFO Desk, inquired about the incident. Pope learned about claims that the pencil-thin rays beamed down by the craft (mentioned by Col. Halt) penetrated the walls of the nuclear weapon storage areas of RAF Woodbridge.

On July 24, 1996, the Rendlesham Forest Incident became subject of a Parliamentary Questioning by the British House of Commons representative Mr. Redmond. The reply of the MoD spokesman Mr. Soames was that the incident contained ''nothing of defense significance'' and that therefore ''no further action was taken.''

—MICHAEL HESEMANN

Report on Communion (William Morrow, 1989). San Antonio newspaper reporter Ed Conroy, after interviewing San Antonio native Whitley Strieber for a feature story, decided to investigate Strieber's alien abduction account in more depth by interviewing his family and friends and by following Strieber around. Conroy describes in this book how he began to experience his own nighttime visitations by mysterious entities and buzzings at all hours by unmarked helicopters.

—RANDALL FITZGERALD

Report on Unidentified Flying Objects, The (Doubleday, 1956). Former chief of the Air Force's Project Blue Book, Edward J. Ruppelt, who first coined the term Unidentified Flying Object (UFO), describes the most intriguing cases of his two years spent investigating UFO reports. He tells how he was under orders to publicly discuss only the sightings that had been solved and to denigrate the significance of the 20 percent of cases investigated that remained unexplained.

—RANDALL FITZGERALD

reptoids   The word reptoid is considered by UFO buffs to be a contraction of reptilian humanoid rather than an exotic form of reptile. They are invariably bipedal with a human torso. The word is first used among UFO buffs in the mid to late 1980s in the context of EBE lore surrounding the Dulce Base. Earlier, the word appeared in comic books. It appears in the 1977 *Thor Annual #6* (Marvel Comics) as the name of a species of bipedal reptiles inhabiting the planet Tayp circling a distant star called Kormuk.

Reptilian aliens are second only to humanoid forms in their popularity among comic book aliens. A file of alien races from *The Official Handbook of the Marvel Universe* has nineteen reptilian races. Though far less than the ninety-one humanoid and semi-humanoid races listed, it is well more than the eight examples of insectoid races and three examples of amoeboid races. Still farther down in frequency are forms based on fish, plants, cats, dogs, snails, horses, hippos, pigs, and sentient energy. Examples in the science fiction tradition go back as far as the highly intelligent reptiles on a planet around the star Mirach in Edgar Fawcett's *The Ghost of Guy Thyrle* (1895). Pulp-master Edmond Hamilton has a race of lizard-men threatening the doom of mankind in "The Abysmal Invaders" (1929).

Adding animal features to the human form is arguably the oldest known act of mythic imagination. The earliest known work of art is a handsome lion/man carved from ivory dating back over 30,000 years and found in southern Germany. Cave art in southern France, nearly as old, shows a figure combining the head and torso of a bison to human legs. In the French prehistoric cave art gallery of Lascaux can be found bird-headed men. At Trois Freres an upright figure combines human legs and upright posture to parts from horses, reindeers, and felines. (Mithin, 1976)

Michael Harner, anthropologist and specialist in shamanic visions, has observed that snakes and jaguars populate visions in many cultures and he cites many examples from the anthropological literature. "Serpents certainly recur in the visions, and crocodiles and reptiles in general, and so do tigers, leopards and cats; but fangs also do, and birds of prey and vampires, and perhaps all of these are interrelated by their implication of danger. . . ." (Harner, 1973)

Their deadliness makes them figures not only to fear, but to identify with. If one could harness their power, one could strike fear into one's enemies. Mythologists will tell you, "There is probably no creature which is found more widely distributed in the mythologies of the world than the serpent." (Cavendish, 1985) Examples include the Egyptian crocodile god Sebek, the Hindu Nagas, the Toltec Quetzalcoatl, the Greek Typhon, and the Biblical Serpent of Eden.

The current presence of reptoids within UFOlogy is less a puzzle than their absence in the early years of the UFO controversy. This absence was likely caused by a general sensibility in the early years that aliens would be benevolent or at least neutral. Reptiles however seem inherently to be felt to be dangerous. Such presumptions favored the contactees' utopians and the UFOlogists' big-brained humanoids over other forms. As sensibilities changed in the sixties we see horror clichés like mummies and Big Bugs enter the mythos. A crocodile-skinned alien turns up in the 1967 David Seewaldt abduction of Calgary, Canada. It had holes for a nose and holes for ears and a slit mouth. It could arguably be called a reptoid though it doesn't have a compelling resemblance to later examples of the form. It gained little attention. (Allen, 1974) A crocodile-skinned biped turns up in the 1975 Brian Scott abduction, but it seems more humanoid than reptilian. (Lawson, 1976) The 1978 Zanfretta abduction from Marzano, Italy, got attention but was quickly dismissed in America as too blatantly identical to *The Creature from the Black Lagoon* (1954). (Steinman, 1986)

In 1980, Leonard Stringfield indicates his sources in the crash-retrieval tales he has been collecting speak of aliens generally having a scaly or reptilian skin and a medical authority confirms that under the microscope resembled mesh-like, granular skin of iguanas and chameleons. Though the rest of the alien seems more like a Gray, this description set the precedent for later speculations in Stringfield's Status Report III (1982), Bernard Finch's "Dinosaurs . . . Not Humanoids" for *Flying Saucer Review* (Finch 1982), and Erich Aggan's "Possible Reptilian Origins of Certain UFO Occupants" for MUFON. (Aggan, 1982) Also in 1982, Dale Russell got widespread attention for a museum exhibition in which he speculated how a dinosaur called the Stenonychosauraus could evolve into an intelligent biped. (Hecht & Williams, 1982) Carl Sagan, in the award-winning *The Dragons of Eden* (1977), had given this idea some prominence a few years earlier.

The culture accentuated the popularity of the form in the mid-1980s. In 1983, a TV mini-series called "V" gained high ratings for alien reptoids disguised as humans in order to steal the Earth's water. This stimulated a number of imitations including *Dreamscape*'s Snakeman (1984), *Buckaroo Banzai*'s lectroid Emilio Lizardo (1984), and the Draks of *Enemy Mine* (1985).

In 1987, the Lear statement spread Dulce Base revelations about frightening creatures with reptilian skin and claw-like fingers. Whistleblowers speak of cases of lizard-humans in Level 7, "Nightmare Hall," and cages of Draco-Reptoids. (Bishop III, 1989) Tal Levesque indicated the Grays and reptoids are in league with each other and a planetoid bearing the ruler race of reptoids was headed to Earth to oversee an invasion. (*Cosmic Awareness*, n.d.) One source said this would occur approximately in 1999. (Wingate, 1999)

By the time of the 1992 M.I.T. Abduction Study Conference, John Carpenter indicated about ten percent of the aliens being seen in abductions collected by himself were reptilian. Three of nine abduction investigators had not seen any however. (Pritchard, 1994) As the nineties proceed some sources reveal that reptoids can cross-breed with anybody and they rape women. One woman sheepishly tells Carpenter they gave her an incredible orgasm despite their repulsive looks. (Carpenter, 1999) Pamela Stonebrooke, a jazz singer, is the most vocal woman to speak of her sexual encounters with reptoids. Dense New Age metaphysics accompany her claims. (greatdreams.com, 1999)

Drawings of the reptoids are inconsistent, but some bear close resemblance to Dale Russell's evolved dinosaur from 1982. Joe Lewels indicates his abductees cannot bear to look at photos of the Russell creation because the resemblance is so close to the terrifying beings. (Lewels, 1997) Though Lewels seems to regard this similarity as a vote for the plausibility of such beings, this overlooks the fact that Russell's creation is highly speculative. Certain things like the absence of ears and yellow eyes with vertical slit pupil are pure guesswork since fossils obviously do not preserve such things. Russell specifically admits the ears were omitted strictly as an artistic choice to avoid a more human appearance. (Hecht & Williams, 1982)

Lore about the reptoids expanded tremendously throughout the nineties. The inconsistencies of form resolve to the existence of different reptoid races. Their history extends to ancient times. One source said reptilians were slave to the Grays, but they are more commonly felt to be their rulers. This however runs counter to other sources who say mantis aliens rule the Grays. We are told they eat children like we eat chicken deepening their image of natural evil. The Chupacabra (goat-sucker) of Puerto Rico is revealed as a reptoid-Gray cross-breed and adds vampirism to their image.

Web sites have sprung up devoted to warning people about these evil beings. David Icke's "Reptilian Research" is the most expansive with a section detailing the history of serpent mythology and another that gathers together some lurid tales of reptoid rape. Another site called "Reptoids.com" offers a typology and a collection of popular reptilian images from television and film. These images are not regarded as sources of reptilian mythology, but rather as ways of preparing the populace for the reptoid takeover. Another called "The Reptilians: Who are They Really" collects documents of the Stonebrook controversy and information about reptoid caverns, but is notable for a large selection of links demonstrating the amount of material about reptoids around and the nature of the beliefs of those drawn to the subject.

It needs to be said that the concept of reptoids is undoubtedly less troubling to scientific sensibilities than certain other alien forms like blond Nordics—too precisely like us (Fortey, 1997)—and the bioengineering absurdity of big Mantis beings. Some will argue that large brains require warm-blooded physiologies and placental gestation, but the different evolutionary pathways explored on alien worlds may open up combinations of traits we could scarcely predict on first principles. There are such unforeseeably bizarre strategies found both in present life and the fossil record on earth that it is hard to regard the reptilian-biped combination as fundamentally unthinkable.

The more compelling objection to reptoids is that the culture finds them such readily compelling villains. It had been using them for years before they started appearing in UFO encounters and there is absolutely no mystery from an anthropological standpoint why such a mythical being could emerge within modern visionary experiences and stories.

—MARTIN S. KOTTMEYER

References

Aggan, Erich A. "Possible Reptilian Origins of Certain UFO Occupants," *MUFON UFO Journal* (August 1982).

Allen, W. K. "Crocodile-Skinned Entities at Calgary," *Flying Saucer Review* (1974).

Bishop III, Jason. "The Dulce Base," *UFO magazine* (July/August 1989).

Buhler, Walter K., Guilherme Pereira, and Ney Pires. "UFO Abduction at Mirassol," UFO Photo Archives (1985).

Carpenter, John. "Reptilians and Other Unmentionables," *MUFON UFO Journal* (April 1973).

Cavendish, Richard. *Man, Myth, Magic* (Marshall Cavendish, 1985).

Cosmic Awareness, "Reptoids Can Recognize All is One and Still Eat You" (http://ufobbs.com/ufo)

Fortey, Richard. *Life: A Natural History of the First Four Billion Years of Life on Earth* (Vintage, 1997).

Harner, Michael. *Hallucinogens and Shamanism* (Oxford University Press, 1973).

Hecht, Jeff, and Gurney Williams. "Smart Dinosaurs," *Omni* magazine (May 1982).

Lawson, Alvin. "Hypnotic Regressions of Alleged CE III Encounters: Ambiguities on the Road to UFOs" in Dornbos, Nancy, ed. Proceedings of the 1976 CUFOS Conference (CUFOS, 1976).

Lewels, Joe. *The God Hypothesis* (Wild Flower Press, 1997).

Mithin, Steven. *The Prehistory of the Mind: The Cognitive Origins of Art, Religion and Science* (Thames and Hudson, 1996).

Pritchard, Andrea, et al. *Alien Discussions* (North Cambridge, 1994).

"The Reptilians: Who Are They Really" (www.greatdreams.com/reptilan/reps.htm)

Sagan, Carl. *The Dragons of Eden* (Random House/Ballantine, 1977).

Stringfield, Leonard. *UFO Crash-Retrievals: Status Report II* (privately published, 1980).

Stringfield, Leonard. *UFO Crash-Retrievals: Amassing the Evidence: Status Report III* (privately published, 1982).

Steinman, William, and Wendelle Stevens. UFO Crash at Aztec (UFO Photo Archives, 1986).

Wingate, Steve. "An Alien Update: How Close Are the Reptoids," IUFO Mailing List: webarchive (January 14, 1999).

resistance techniques against alien abduction A careful study of "alien-abduction scenarios" will demonstrate to objective minds that this is a phenomenon separate and distinct from the physical, craft-like phenomenon we normally call "UFOs." True UFOs are viewed in full waking consciousness, caught on film and radar, and chased by jet pilots, while most abduction scenarios take place in sleep or are induced in light trances such as road hypnosis and other altered states. Retrieval of abduction stories through hypnotic regression adds to the suspicion that they are not physically real.

Fifteen years of research in Tujunga, California, revealed that three of these five abductee witnesses instinctively fended off subsequent approaches of "abductors." (Their experiences were described in my 1988 book, *Tujunga Canyon Contacts*.) Attempts to bring this new aspect to the attention of the field between 1988 and 1992 has resulted in bitter controversy. Although many researchers welcomed this new information, others contended that resistance to "alien abductors" was impossible. They presented contradictory theories: (1) the abductors are technologically superior ETs and humans are powerless against them; or (2) abductors are here to "save" us or help us toward a higher stage of evolution and therefore should *not* be resisted.

Feedback to my initial articles on the subject resulted in seventy additional resisters coming forward, the majority of whom had instinctively freed themselves of abduction scenarios. My subsequent 1998 book, *How to Defend Yourself Against Alien Abduction* describes nine specific resistance techniques:

1. **mental struggle**, in which the witnesses deliberately return to full waking consciousness, resulting in the breaking of the scenario;

2. **physical struggle**, in which the witnesses physically attack the entities, resulting in the entities' rapid departure;

3. **appeal to spiritual personages** such as the Sacred Heart, Allah, or the archangel St. Michael, which brings about an "awakening";

4. **repellents** such as iron objects, small electrical appliances (whirling fans, room heaters, etc.), and time-favored herbs such as pennyroyal and St. John's Wort, which prevent the entities' approach;

5. **righteous anger**, whereby witnesses, in heightened self-esteem, express their inalienable rights against intrusion;

6. **protective rage**, directed toward protecting one's family members as well as oneself;

7. **support from family members**, where housemates assist in breaking the abductee's altered state;

8. **metaphysical methods**, such as visualizing white light, which provide protection and break the scenario;

9. **intuition**, which enables witnesses to detect the approach of the entities so that techniques can be readied before the scenario begins.

A combination of techniques is usually necessary for full success. Resistance techniques are most effective when used by stouthearted, strong-minded individuals who instinctively resent intrusion. They can be learned by witnesses who consider abduction scenarios as unwelcome experiences which interfere with their lives. Abductees who crave constant attention from researchers and other abductees are not good candidates for successful resistance.

The escalation of claims of "implants" and "hybridization" from 1973 through the 1990s seems to have been heightened by a combination of unconscious telepathic leakage between witnesses and even the most careful hypnotist/researchers, as well as the unrecognized psychological needs of the individuals involved. Strong doubts of the physical reality of abductions and reports of "missing fetuses," "genetic manipulation," and "alien-military cooperation" (all of which lack scientific proof) are needed to build up an individual's confidence.

Many abduction scenarios seem to be "real" in some type of altered reality, especially those reported by rational, honest individuals, but respected researchers such as Jacques Vallée and Gordon Creighton suspect that abductees are interacting not with extraterrestrials, but with "interdimensional" beings who share the Earth with us on a "hidden plane." Historical and philosophical texts as well as legends and folklore from such diverse cultures as China, Persia, Slovenia, Australia, Italy, and Ireland all describe deceptive entities who delight in assaulting human beings, usually in a sexual manner. Sexual manipulation is part and parcel of the modern abduction phenomenon in all its forms—as in other myths throughout history.

The order of creation described in the *Koran* as "Al-jinn," in Celtic chronicles as "Sidhe," and in European history as "Incubi" (and "Succubi") acts in ways similar to our modern "alien abductors." They reportedly have the ability to shape-shift and enter Earth's space-time at will. They usually appear to humans in forms consistent with the victims' own cultural backgrounds. The modern American "abduction phenomenon" appears as "space travelers"—a form which it possibly reasoned could terrify even independent, free Americans.

It is to be hoped that our culture will realize that "alien abductors" are merely the newest form of entities which have traumatized other cultures from the beginning. The most important point here is that multiple world cultures have recognized the phenomenon for what it is and found ways to deal with it, using methods very similar to the techniques described above.

—ANN DRUFFEL

References

Druffel, Ann, and Scott Rogo. *Tujunga Canyon Contacts* (Prentice-Hall, 1988).

Druffel, Ann. *How to Defend Yourself Against Alien Abduction* (Three Rivers Press/Random House, 1998).

Revelations (Ballantine Books, 1991). A proliferation of spurious government documents such as MJ-12 helped persuade Jacques Vallée that some aspects of the UFO phenomenon may be covert government experiments in the manipulation of public belief systems. He relates a story in which he and Dr. J. Allen Hynek were deceived by two Air Force generals, both UFO believers, who promised to release genuine UFO evidence but never did because they were only promoting their own personal agendas. While he believes a real UFO mystery exists, he is nonetheless disturbed that "somebody is going to a lot of trouble to convince us of the reality of extraterrestrials, to the exclusion of other, possibly more important hypotheses about UFOs."

—RANDALL FITZGERALD

Roach abduction In 1975, Pat Roach (originally identified as Pat Price to protect her identity), a divorcee living alone with her seven children, wrote to Kevin Randle and *Saga* magazine, telling of her abduction. She said that she knew how whole families could disappear. Her letter was inspired by a report in *Saga's UFO Report* that told of the abduction of Dionisio Llanca, an Argentine truck driver.

According to Roach, she had gone to sleep on the evening of October 16, 1973, and had been awakened just after midnight. Convinced that a prowler had been in the house, she called the police. A record of that report was found, providing both the date of the incident and a corroboration for part of the story.

Although Roach remembered almost nothing about the incident, her children had suggested that there had been "spacemen" in the house. Under hypnotic regression conducted by Dr. James A. Harder, then APRO's Director of Research, Roach began to tell a tale of alien abduction. She claimed that she had been awakened by two smallish creatures standing near her couch, looking at her. They reached down, touched her arms, and lifted her. She saw some of her children in the room, struggling with the aliens. They were then floated outside and into a craft standing in an empty field next to the house. Inside the ship, she was undressed and examined by the creatures, shown some of their advanced technology, hypnotized by the aliens so she could recall some of her life for them, and finally given her clothes and told to dress.

Some of the details of the abduction were corroborated by her daughter, Bonnie, but the descriptions were not as rich as those given by her mother. Attempts to learn more about the abduction by interviewing the other children failed to reveal much additional detail.

An examination of the transcripts of the hypnotic regression sessions, as well as information provided by Harder, both during those sessions and discussions afterward, tainted the case. Harder, after completing the first regression session, expressed concern that Roach had not exhibited the "proper emotional" response. He told her throughout the session that he knew she had been scared, but that she got out of the situation in good shape. It was also Harder who had suggested that Roach had been examined, telling her about the Betty Hill abduction. In a later hypnotic regression, Roach claimed to have undergone a similar examination.

Other sources of contamination were found. Much of the description of the interior of the ship came from an article in *UFO Report* that Roach, in her first letter, acknowledged reading. Many of her descriptions match those of Llanca, not because she had seen the same things, but because she had read about them months earlier.

In my original entry for *The Encyclopedia of UFOs* (1980), I concluded that ". . . until something more was added, an admission by Roach, or a new development in psychological study (or the landing of a spaceship), there didn't seem to be any place to go with the case." That development has since occurred, in what we now know about a psychological phenomenon called "sleep paralysis." (See SLEEP PARALYSIS.) The Roach abduction now appears to be a classic example of sleep paralysis.

Roach, remember, claimed to have awakened and felt that a prowler had been in, or near the house. She had a vague feeling about it and called the police. Then, thinking about it, and reading about alien abductions, she came to believe that she, herself, had been an abduction victim. The details that emerged under hypnosis probably resulted from constant prodding by Harder, including his leading questions to her.

The details of the abduction provided by her children could easily have come from discussions Roach had with them prior to her writing to *UFO Report*.

—KEVIN D. RANDLE

References

Randle, Kevin D. "Roach Abduction" in Story, Ronald D., ed. *The Encyclopedia of UFOs* (Doubleday/New English Library, 1980).

Randle, Kevin D., and Russ Estes. *Faces of the Visitors* (Fireside/Simon & Schuster, 1997).

Randle, Kevin D., Russ Estes, and William P. Cone. *The Abduction Enigma* (Forge, 1999).

Robertson Panel The first scientific advisory panel on UFOs, requested by the White House and sponsored by the United States Central Intelligence Agency, was convened by Dr. H. P. Robertson (a world-renowned physicist then at the California Institute of Technology), on January 14, 1953. The other panel members included Luis W. Alvarez (later Nobel laureate and professor of physics at the University of California at Berkeley), Lloyd Berkner (noted space scientist), Sam A. Goudsmit (nuclear physicist at the Brookhaven National Laboratory), and the writer (then an astronomer and operations analyst at the Johns Hopkins University). It was just after the 1952 UFO scare in Washington, D.C., and Robertson took his responsibility of advising the federal government very seriously. He demanded and got access to all top-secret military data that might bear on UFO sightings, such as tests of new aircraft, rockets, and balloons. As an astronomer, this writer felt that most of the sightings were ludicrous and joked about it in our first meeting. Robertson reprimanded the writer severely, despite the fact that he was an old friend. The panel was briefed by all three military services, and by astronomer J. Allen Hynek, then scientific advisor to the Air Force's Project Blue Book. The panel was shown most of the good photos and drawings of UFO sightings and the movie taken by an obviously reliable Navy man, Delbert Newhouse, at Tremonton, Utah. The panel's explanation of the objects on the film, which was later agreed upon by the investigator for the University of Colorado UFO Project, was seagulls, a half-mile away, rather than fantastic spacecraft ten miles away. Captain E. J. Ruppelt, then head of Project Blue Book, described the Air Force analysis of UFO reports. All day on January 18, 1953, the panel discussed the evidence, and concluded that UFOs presented no direct threat to United States national security. The writer was concerned that, at a time of a "Red threat" (the panelists were worried about a possible Soviet intercontinental ballistic missile attack), UFO reports would disrupt military communications. The panel agreed and also recommended that efforts be made to strip UFOs of "the aura of mystery they have unfortunately acquired" and to educate the public to recognize "true indications of hostile intent or action." The Robertson Panel report was later declassified and (with most names deleted) published as Appendix

U in Edward Condon's *Scientific Study of Unidentified Flying Objects*, edited by Daniel S. Gillmor, 1969.

In retrospect, this writer sees a few misconceptions in the panel's discussion and report. The panel underestimated the long duration of public interest in UFOs, which also puzzles sociologists (see Sagan, Carl, and Page, Thornton, eds., *UFOs—A Scientific Debate,* 1972), and overestimated the astronomers' photographic coverage of the sky (see Page, "Photographic Sky Coverage for the Detection of UFOs," in *Science,* Vol. 160, No. 1258, 1968). Although the panel did not go as far as Condon, it also tended to ignore the 5 percent or 10 percent of UFO reports that are highly reliable and have not as yet been explained.

—THORNTON PAGE

Rogo hypothesis *Parapsychologist D. Scott Rogo developed the hypothesis that abduction experiences could be correlated with a personal crisis and emotional trauma in the life of the abductee. His idea was that we should look more closely at the experiencer in terms of personal history and how the "abduction" experience can shed light on one's life crisis—in symbolic form. The following essay was given to the editor of this encyclopedia for publication by Scott Rogo in 1983, seven years before his untimely death (in 1990).*

THE SECRET LANGUAGE
OF UFO ABDUCTIONS

Reports about people who have been abducted by UFOs have become frighteningly frequent over the last few years. These reports often read surprisingly alike. The victim or victims will be driving along a deserted road late at night when the UFO makes its first appearance. The individual will then momentarily "black out." [A phenomenon now referred to in UFOlogy as "missing time."] Regaining consciousness only a "moment" or so later, he or she will discover that over an hour or two has mysteriously passed from his/her life.

The witness might then be asked by an investigator to undergo hypnotic regression, during which one will remember how the car stalled and how alien beings left the UFO and brought the chosen one aboard. Many UFO abductees tell how they were given medical examinations or given some sort of message before being returned to their cars with the command to forget what has happened.

The explanation for such events seems obvious. UFOs appear to be vehicles from another world, and their occupants carry out these abductions with the intent of studying and learning about us. However, as a result of my own research and investigations into several UFO abduction cases, I have come to a radically different conclusion about the nature of these experiences.

I first began to seriously question the "extraterrestrial hypothesis" after studying the case of Betty and Barney Hill, which was made famous by author John Fuller in his book *The Interrupted Journey* (1966). The case is so well known that only a very brief summary needs to be given here.

The date of the incident was September 19, 1961—a time when the civil rights movement was in its infancy. Betty and Barney Hill were an interracial couple from New Hampshire who were driving home from a vacation trip to Canada through the White Mountains of New England, when they first spotted a mysterious light high in the sky. It gradually approached them as they sped along.

Barney eventually stopped the car, got out, and viewed the "craft" through binoculars when it began hovering by the side of the road. When he saw beings inside it, he panicked, ran back to the automobile, and sped away.

The next thing the Hills noticed was that they were driving somewhat further down the road. They could also hear a "beeping" sound fading out as they drove. Later, they calculated that their trip home had taken longer than it should have.

Just ten days following the experience, Betty began having a series of detailed nightmares about a UFO abduction. Barney, too, was feeling some sort of strain—presumably as a result of the UFO experience—as his ulcer began acting up.

These developments led the Hills to Dr. Benjamin Simon, a psychiatrist in Boston who specialized in hypnosis. The Hills assumed they were suffering from a case of amnesia, and on this basis Dr. Simon explored the supposed time-lapse through hypnotic regression. It was during these sessions that the couple gradually "recalled" how their car had been stopped by mysterious figures ahead of them in the road as they drove away from the UFO.

They remembered being taken aboard the craft by humanoid beings, who separated them and then performed quasi-medical procedures on them individually. The beings tested Betty for pregnancy by inserting a needle into her navel (a procedure similar to amniocentesis). They took sperm samples from Barney, after placing some sort of cup over his groin. Then the couple was returned to their car with instructions to forget the whole experience.

When I read John Fuller's book, which includes transcripts of the Hills' sessions with Dr. Simon, I was left unimpressed. What struck me at the time was how symbolic their experience was, and how it seemed to relate so concisely with conflicts which must have been plaguing the couple at the time.

Barney, a black postal employee, had married a socially prominent white woman (Betty) at a time when racial strife in this country was developing into the most important social issue of the decade. Surely the Hills must have been harboring some deep, and perhaps not even consciously acknowledged, conflicts over their interracial marriage, especially since such unions were rare and socially frowned upon at that time.

These quite normal fears and conflicts are aptly illustrated in their abduction story. Here, Betty and Barney are separated by hostile and mysterious impersonal beings, who check to make sure Betty isn't pregnant, and then symbolically castrate Barney.

Only then are they released to continue on their way. This scenario encapsulates the Hills'

own awareness of how much of society probably viewed their marriage—a sensitivity they must have had as they lived their day-to-day lives in a traditionally conservative area of the United States. (In a classic experiment, a psychologist instructed several white subjects to administer shocks to black volunteers. He found that the subjects would consistently administer more powerful shocks to the blacks—whom they were led to believe were dating white women—than the control subjects.)

What the Hills' abduction story seems to represent is a sort of "dream" in which the couples' own fears and anxieties were translated into a symbolic drama. When I realized the symbolic nature of the Hills' experience, I rejected the notion that they had undergone a genuine abduction. I felt that their recollections, which were based point-by-point on Betty's previous dreams, were merely fantasies in which the Hills expressed their anxieties over the nature of their marriage. The "missing time" they experienced after their encounter may have been a temporary amnesia brought on by the shock of actually seeing a genuine UFO. But it is also interesting to note that the "missing two hours" was not noticed by the Hills, until someone else made the suggestion to them—two weeks after the event.

Over the years, however, I had to change my opinion. Two abduction cases came to light in the 1970s, which placed the UFO abduction syndrome on a firmer evidential footing.

The first was the Pascagoula, Mississippi, abduction of Charles Hickson and Calvin Parker on October 11, 1973. Hickson consciously remembered the abduction and had no need of hypnotic regression. Independent evidence has documented that UFO activity was rife in Mississippi that night as well. The other case was the November 5, 1975, abduction (near Snowflake, Arizona) of Travis Walton, whose encounter was partially witnessed by several of his co-workers. With cases such as these, there can be no denying that UFO abductions are real events and a genuine component of the UFO mystery.

The natural implication of all this might

be that the Hill abduction of 1961 was also a genuine occurrence. But why, then, should the scenario of the Hills' experience—granting that it really happened as reported—be so rich in symbolic allusions to their social, psychological, and sexual concerns?

It was this question that piqued my interest in the deeper meaning of the UFO abduction syndrome and led me to study it in some detail. My current view is that while UFO abductions are genuine events, they are much more complicated than most people suspect. The first (and major) case that helped me formulate my views about the nature of the UFO abduction syndrome was brought to my attention in 1978 by Ann Druffel, a Southern California UFO investigator of some 20 years' experience.

Ann was still investigating a UFO abduction which had occurred in the Tujunga Canyons, near Los Angeles, on March 22, 1953. The victims were Sara Shaw and Jan Whitley, two young women who were sharing a one-bedroom cabin in the Canyons at the time. When Sara Shaw first met Ann she couldn't remember much about her frightening experience. She explained only that she had awakened in the dead of night, when an odd light began to shine into her window. Simultaneously, an odd silence came over the area. Both she and Jan had just gotten out of bed to see what the cause of the light might be, she explained, when they found themselves paralyzed. An "instant" later they realized that over two hours had passed. Sara could remember nothing more.

Sara eventually moved away from Jan, developed a compulsive urge to study medicine, and later experienced a "flash of insight" in which she envisioned a cure for cancer. She did not, however, relate these new developments in her life to her experience of March 1953. She only began to think in terms of a possible UFO encounter some twenty years later, when the subject of UFOs and UFO abductions began receiving a great deal of attention in the media.

Ann Druffel eventually had Sara hypnotically regressed on three occasions: December 5, 1975; February 26, 1976; and (in my presence) on October 22, 1978—which shed new light on the 1953 experience.

A typical abduction scenario unfolded during these sessions. Sara remembered that a group of skinny, black-garbed aliens teleported into her cabin through a closed window. They took hold of Jan and herself and floated them outside to a UFO. Jan fought against them, but Sara was curiously indifferent to what was happening. She found the aliens friendly and thought the experience was "sort of fun," to use her own words.

The two women were separated and Sara recalled being given a physical examination by the male entities, who undressed her as the female aliens stood back passively. She was then taken to a conference room where she was told about a cure for cancer. Then she and Jan were returned to their home. Unfortunately, Jan could never be successfully hypnotized, because she is extremely resistant to suggestion. So she has never been able to verify Sara's recollections. However, even today she recalls waking up, seeing the light, and finding herself paralyzed.

The Sara Shaw case gave me the opportunity for which I had been waiting—the chance to make a detailed psychological study of a UFO abductee. I had found that most reports on abduction cases have focused more on the witness's reported experiences than on the witnesses themselves. I hoped to rectify this situation with my investigation of the Shaw case.

I therefore made a detailed study of Ms. Shaw, which included going over her present concerns and thoughts about her experience, talking to her about her childhood, and also taking a complete sexual history. It was during this process that I discovered that Sara's abduction experience, far from being an alien kidnapping, seemed to encapsulate and dramatize several conflicts which were plaguing her at the time, As I talked with Sara I learned that she came from a rather disturbed family background.

She had been taught to avoid contact with men by an extremely dominant mother, who had imbued in Sara some rather antiquated views about relations with the opposite sex. This indoctrination had so profoundly affected Sara that the (then) young woman had decided, in an unconscious attempt to please her mother, that she would cut herself off from normal contact with men.

She became roommates with a young woman who made independence a virtue and went "off to the wilds" to live an almost hermit-like existence away from men and society in general. She lived with Jan for two years before realizing that her life was not very fulfilling. After much professional counseling, she lost her distrust of men and eventually entered into two marriages. Unfortunately, neither marriage was successful.

Today, Sara is a single woman engaged in her own career. Sara's UFO abduction experience makes considerable sense when viewed in the light of her background, since her story contains some rather overt (though symbolic) allusions to the conflicts which eventually led her to seek counseling.

Just take a look at her recollections. She remembered how strange overpowering figures entered into her *bedroom*, abducted her, and *separated her from Jan*. Oddly, though, Sara found this adventure fun and realized that her abductors were friendly. The *male* entities *took off her clothes and examined her* while the *female entities looked on passively*.

These events seem to be a series of messages right out of Sara's own unconscious, which sought to tell her that her lifestyle was unsatisfactory and that she would not find fulfillment until she could break away from Jan and enter into normal social and sexual relationships with men. The whole abduction seems to be a veiled rape fantasy, which left Sara with a curious sense of happiness and satisfaction—as though she had learned something very important from it.

It appears that Sara's UFO abduction occurred during a time of great conflict in her life. She and Jan moved from the Canyons shortly after the incident, and Sara gradually drew away from Jan and went out on her own. She eventually lost contact with her former roommate, who subsequently developed cancer—during the same time Sara was becoming inexplicably obsessed with medicine and cancer cures!

To put all of this a little more simply, Sara's UFO abduction experience reads surprisingly like a dream she might have had at that time, in which her own unconscious thoughts and conflicts were presented to her by some element of her own mind. The scenario also showed Sara how she could resolve this conflict, which is also a very common aspect of normal dreaming. Yet, on the other hand, there can be no denying that Sara underwent a genuine UFO experience. Although Jan could not remember any details of the abduction during repeated attempts to regress her, she did recall—with frightening vividness—the events which led to her blackout, including the intense pain she felt around her head when she found herself paralyzed after that mysterious light first appeared through the window.

My investigation of the Sara Shaw case led me to totally reject the idea that UFO abductions are orchestrated by beings from another world. Instead I began to toy with the notion that we ourselves have somehow created the UFO mystery and are unleashing it onto the world in vivid reality. My other idea was that perhaps some "X" intelligence exists in the universe which is symbiotically linked to life on this planet and to our minds, and which is sending the UFO phenomenon to us. I went on to theorize that UFO abductions are not random events but occur to very special people at very special moments in their lives.

I speculated that a person who is harboring a strong unconscious conflict, which cannot be internally resolved actually invites a UFO abduction experience. Somehow his or her concerns and mental anguish might act as a beacon that attracts the UFO experience. The intelligence behind the UFO mystery (whatever it might be) may then create a UFO encounter for the witness by modeling it upon those very conflicts. A UFO abduction might therefore be a dramatized encapsulation of the witness's own mental concerns. The goal of the "abduction" would be to bring the conflict to conscious attention.

You might say that according to this theory a UFO abduction is a sort of symbolic dream which has been extracted from the witness's mind and has been made real by the UFO intelligence.

Now having developed this theory, I began looking for ways to document it. One way would be to study the experience of other UFO abductees and delve into their private lives in order to see what sort of connection might exist between the abduction and the victim's state of mind at the time. This was my next project, and it wasn't hard to find evidence that supported my views. I soon found that many UFO abductees undergo their experiences at times of emotional crisis.

Take the much publicized case of Betty Andreasson, for example. This abduction took place on the night of January 25, 1967. The scene was a rural home in Massachusetts where Mrs. Betty Andreasson lived with her seven children. Mrs. Andreasson's husband had been recently injured in an automobile accident and was still recuperating in the hospital. Her chief support during these trying times was her oldest daughter Becky, who was helping take care of the other children. Mrs. Andreasson's father, Waino Aho, was present in the house that night as well.

Most of the Andreassons were watching television as the abduction gradually unfolded The first intimation that something unusual was about to take place came when the lights in the house began to flicker and everything became weirdly silent outside. The electricity finally went out completely and an eerie pink light began shining through a kitchen window. Mr. Aho was the first to look outside. What he saw shocked him.

He later told investigators that he had seen small alien creatures "wearing headdresses" hopping across the backyard. He described them as looking like "Halloween freaks." Before Mr. Aho could see more, though, he—along with the rest of the family—entered into a state of suspended animation. They awoke, later, only to discover that a considerable time had elapsed.

During the next several months both Becky and Betty Andreasson slowly began to recall more details about their experience and came to the conclusion that there was more to their encounter than met the eye. Becky dimly recalled that she had slipped out of a trance at one moment during her time lapse and had seen the aliens in the house with her family. What she had seen matched the description her grandfather had given of the aliens.

Betty Andreasson finally started contacting UFOlogists throughout the country and eventually Raymond Fowler, a seasoned and careful investigator from Massachusetts, had her hypnotically regressed. This was in 1977. It was only at that time that the two witnesses fully remembered what had happened during their time lapse.

Betty recalled how the aliens entered her house by materializing through a closed door. She described them as short, hairless, and gray. They had large heads, slanted huge eyes, and slit-like mouths. Her first response to their presence was to ask them if they wanted some food. The aliens took their victim outside and floated her to their UFO, where she underwent a series of physical and spiritual adventures.

She was first taken to a bubble-shaped room, but was then escorted to another chamber and placed on a platform where she was bathed in a white "cleansing" light. After undergoing a medical examination, which included having a needle thrust into her abdomen (just like Betty Hill reported in 1961), she was taken to an alien realm where she was subjected to more unusual experiences.

First she was placed in a tube which was filled with liquid, after which she was guided down a dark tunnel to another location where she was confronted by a dazzling light so intense that she thought she was going to be incinerated. The light transformed into a vision of a Phoenix being consumed and reborn as a worm. The aliens told her that she would forget what she had seen, and she was then returned to her home.

The case of Betty Andreasson is extremely evidential, since unlike so many other abductions, there was more than one witness to the incident. Before his death, Mr. Aho often talked about seeing the aliens; Becky, too, was able to recall the moment when she slipped out of her suspended animation.

My main interest in this case concerns the nature of the odd visionary experiences to which Mrs. Andreasson was subjected during her kidnapping, which seem to relate to her intense religious beliefs. She is a deeply religious Christian who originally believed that her abduction had nothing to do with beings from outer space, but was actually some form of angelic visitation. I can sympathize with this viewpoint, since her experience aboard the UFO was filled with overt religious symbolism. In fact, Andreasson has become even more religious as a result of her experience.

All this leads me to suspect that her abduction was somehow prompted by a spiritual crisis she was probably undergoing at the time. Her husband was in a "touch and go" situation at the hospital, which had saddled her with enormous household as well as emotional responsibilities. Both her financial and emotional future were totally up in the air. Many people, especially those who harbor deep religious convictions, are prone to question their beliefs and world views in the face of such psychologically mortifying experiences. (The unexpected death of a close relative can even turn one against religion if the death seems meaningless.)

And what of the abduction itself? Just look at all the symbolism it contains. One of the central themes of Christianity is the concept of spiritual death and rebirth, which is epitomized in the ritual of baptism. This same basic concept is also part of ancient alchemical and Masonic traditions as exemplified in the "initiation by fire and water," through which one must triumph in order to earn spiritual per-

fection. Note that these are the same themes that crop up in Mrs. Andreasson's story.

She is placed in a tube which is filled with water, is then "reborn" as she is guided down a dark tunnel, and is next purified by a glowing light which consumes her. She then witnesses the similar immolation and rebirth of the legendary Phoenix, which is also an ancient symbol of spiritual transformation and rebirth. The whole abduction strikes me as an allegorical journey whose purpose was to help Mrs. Andreasson reconfirm her own Christian faith.

It also seems to me that the aliens even told Mrs. Andreasson that they had come to offer her spiritual enlightenment. This message is contained in an interchange which Mrs. Andreasson recalled at the beginning of her experience, which few of her investigators have ever been able to explain.

When the aliens first appeared in her home, Mrs. Andreasson's initial reaction was to offer to cook them some food. The aliens replied that they could eat only burnt food, and thus made a cryptic allusion to the "burnt offerings" mentioned in the Bible. Mrs. Andreasson began to prepare some meat for her visitors, but the aliens told her that they didn't eat that kind of food . . . that their food was "knowledge tried by fire" and asked if she had any such nourishment available. Mrs. Andreasson caught the drift of what she was being told and fetched a Bible for her visitors. The aliens, in turn, gave her a small book in exchange for the Bible.

Now for what purpose would aliens from another solar system engage in such a meaningless, if not ridiculous, conversation? This episode can only be explained on the theory that the UFOnauts had come specifically to offer Mrs. Andreasson a spiritual revelation and were trying to make this known to her in the best way they could. It therefore seems obvious, at least to me, that the whole abduction experience was triggered by Mrs. Andreasson's own religious conflicts which were somehow transformed and dramatized into a very real (or surreal) UFO encounter.

The Andreasson affair indicates that a

UFO abduction can be triggered by a specific event in the victim's life. In this case it was the trauma the witness was suffering due to the crisis engendered by her husband's accident. Yet these trigger events do not have to be that overt. Sometimes they can be subtle events that ignite only unconscious conflicts in the witness's mind. This may seem odd, but anyone who has studied psychiatry will be well aware that at times even seemingly inconsequential events in someone's life can have long-lasting and far-reaching effects. It is just such a subtle conflict which I believe resulted in Carl Higdon's 1974 Wyoming abduction

The Higdon case first hit the presses on October 29, 1974, when the Rawlings (Wyoming) *Daily Times* published an account of his ordeal. Dr. R. Leo Sprinkle, a psychologist and UFOlogist then at the University of Wyoming, traveled to Rawlings a few days later to look into the matter. Dr. Sprinkle subsequently wrote a lengthy report on his findings, which he passed on to APRO (the Aerial Phenomena Research Organization) in Tucson, Arizona.

Although Higdon consciously remembered much of his experience, Sprinkle conducted two hypnotic sessions with him in order to help fill out the details of the abduction. Here's the story as it was finally pieced together:

Higdon went hunting in the Medicine Bow National Forest on October 25th. This preserve is some 49 miles south of Rawlings. At about 4:00 P.M., Higdon spotted a small herd of elk and fired at it. However, the rifle bullet traveled only about fifty feet and then fell to the ground. An eerie silence fell over the forest at about this time. Higdon retrieved the bullet and was about to go on his way when he was disturbed by the sound of a twig breaking behind him.

He turned around to see a rather strange-looking man wearing a black outfit. The man was rather tall and his hair stood on end. The "man" gave Higdon some pills to take (which he did without question) and asked him to follow along. Then the alien pointed some sort of implement at Higdon, who next found himself inside a cubicle. He was sitting in a chair with

a helmet on his head, and the alien was there with him. Levers on the cubicle's console began to move upon command, and the craft took off and shot away to some distant location where it landed.

Now the next phase of the abduction began. Higdon left the cubicle and found himself next to a high tower. A group of people, consisting of a middle-aged man and four children about the ages of 11-17, were talking nearby but paid no attention to their visitor. The alien took Higdon up the tower, where he was briefly examined, and then told that he "wasn't what they needed." He was then taken back to the cubicle and returned to Earth.

Higdon's next recollections were confused. He found himself back in the forest, but he was completely disoriented. He was eventually discovered wandering around aimlessly by a passing motorist and ended up that night in a local hospital. He was in such a confused state that he didn't even recognize his wife when rescuers found him. His truck was discovered later that day, but it had mysteriously found its way into an area of the forest inaccessible by road. Higdon also still had the flattened bullet he had retrieved before his abduction.

The Higdon case was published by Coral and Jim Lorenzen of APRO in 1977 as part of their book *Abducted! Confrontations with Beings from Outer Space.* However, it wasn't until 1979 that Dr. Sprinkle (who is a supporter of the extraterrestrial hypothesis) was able to issue his full 133-page report as part of the anthology, *UFO Phenomena and the Behavioral Scientist* (compiled and edited by Richard Haines).

What trauma could have produced this bizarre abduction? This was the question I asked myself as I read over Sprinkle's account in hopes of finding added support for my theory. The clue finally came halfway through the report. It was a clue that even Higdon seemed to appreciate.

During the course of their conversations together, Higdon himself brought up the fact that some years prior to his abduction he had undergone a vasectomy. He openly questioned whether this operation had something to do with his experience and the ultimate rejection by the aliens. "I had a vasectomy," he told Sprinkle, "and I was wondering if that was the reason that I wasn't any good." This remark not only indicates that Higdon somehow related his vasectomy to the abduction, but was harboring half-conscious conflicts about the operation. Notice that he degrades himself with the remark that he "wasn't any good"—which is a far cry from what the aliens reportedly said when they explained he "wasn't what they needed." This odd, self-demeaning reference is very significant. Had it been made during a therapeutic session with a psychiatrist, for instance, instead of during a UFO investigation, I am sure any competent clinician would have eagerly explored the significance of the remark. For some reason Higdon considered himself "no good" because of his vasectomy, and was projecting his feelings onto the aliens. Now you may think I'm reaching with this one, but I'm really not.

Few people realize just how unconsciously traumatic vasectomies can be to men in this culture. Although a routine operation, many men, although undergoing the procedure willingly, are often emotionally scarred by this self-perceived assault on their sexuality. Such men can suffer the same type of psychological reaction that some women undergo after having a hysterectomy. Some men even perceive a vasectomy as a form of castration—an act which robs them of their sexuality. This is why many men irrationally resist the operation, even though it in no way impairs sexual functioning. Other men sometimes experience depression or anxiety when they realize that they can no longer engender children.

It is perfectly logical to assume that Carl Higdon may have been harboring fears and concerns of this very nature. They even seem to be dramatized in his abduction story. The experience began when Higdon shot a bullet at an elk, but found that it had *lost its potency*, when it traveled a mere 50 feet and fell to the ground. The overt sexual symbolism of the

ineffective bullet needn't be belabored. Then he was abducted to a tower where he was shown a family composed of a middle-aged man, such as himself, and four children. This is quite interesting, since Higdon himself had four children aged 11-15 at the time. He was then examined and told that he wasn't what the aliens needed. The symbolism here strikes me as rather obvious. Higdon is shown a symbolic representation of his own family and is then rather forcefully though cryptically reminded that he is not needed. The aliens then returned Higdon to where they found him.

The whole abduction seems to be a dramatization of Higdon's own fears that he had become worthless because of his vasectomy, which had robbed him of his masculinity as symbolized in his inability to further expand his family. Note too that, just as in the Hill, Shaw, and Andreasson cases, the whole surrealistic scenario very much resembles a dream Higdon might have had as a result of his conflict—complete with symbols, sexual references, and space-time discontinuities.

It is my own belief that probably all UFO abductions contain hidden meanings and symbols which directly relate to conflicts buried in the minds of the victims. Unfortunately, trying to understand the secret language of UFO abduction reports is no easy matter. Very few published reports provide the type of personal information that the psychologically oriented investigator would need to know in order to uncover the cause of the event. The witness's credibility is ascertained and maybe a psychiatrist will have been brought in to make sure he or she isn't crazy, but we learn very little about the inner lives of these very special people. In some cases it might take a detailed and lengthy psychoanalytical exploration of the witness before we could get at the heart of an abduction experience.

I don't think, however, that it takes a trained psychiatrist to see how the experiences of such people as Betty Hill, Sara Shaw, Betty Andreasson, and Carl Higdon are directly related to conflicts that had disrupted their lives at the time of their abductions. The relationship between their inner conflicts and the nature of their UFO abductions are rather blatant. The fact that sexual and spiritual conflicts often seem to be the overriding theme of UFO abductions—just as they are in normal dreams—is also extremely noteworthy, as well as predictable.

I don't mean to imply, however, that people who experience UFO abductions have merely experienced imaginary encounters. I don't think that UFO abductions can be explained away as vivid dreams, visions, or hallucinations. There can be no doubt, in my view, that the UFO phenomenon is as much a technological mystery as it is a paraphysical one. Sara Shaw, Betty and Barney Hill, Betty Andreasson, and Carl Higdon probably were abducted by humanoid aliens. What I don't believe, however, is that these beings were from outer space. Somehow they are created out of our imaginations, or are somehow linked to life on this planet. They come forth and interact with us when we unconsciously need them and beckon them.

—D. SCOTT ROGO

References

Barry, Bill. *Ultimate Encounter* (Pocket Books, 1978).

Blum, Ralph and Judy. *Beyond Earth: Man's Contact with UFOs* (Bantam Books, 1974).

Clark, Jerome, and Loren Coleman. *The Unidentified: Notes Toward Solving the UFO Mystery* (Warner, 1975).

Druffel, Ann, and D. Scott Rogo. *The Tujunga Canyon Contacts* (Prentice-Hall, 1980).

Fontana, David. *The Secret Language of Symbols* (Chronicle Books, 1993).

Fowler, Raymond. *The Andreasson Affair* (Prentice-Hall, 1979).

Fromm, Erich. *The Forgotten Language: An Introduction to the Understanding of Dreams, Fairy Tales, and Myths* (Holt, Rinehart and Winston, 1951).

Fuller, John. *The Interrupted Journey* (Dial Press, 1966).

Haines, Richard, ed. *UFO Phenomena and the Behavioral Scientist* (Scarecrow Press, 1979).

Halpern, James and Ilsa. *Projections* (Seaview/Putnam, 1983).

Jung, C. G. *Flying Saucers: A Modern Myth of Things Seen in the Skies* (Routledge & Kegan Paul/Harcourt, Brace & Co. 1959; Signet/NAL, 1969; Princeton University Press, 1978).

Lorenzen, Coral and Jim. *Abducted! Confrontations with Beings from Outer Space* (Berkley Books, 1977).

Rogo, Scott, ed. *Alien Abductions: True Cases of UFO Kidnappings* (Signet/NAL, 1980).

Rogo, D. Scott, and Jerome Clark. *Earth's Secret Inhabitants* (Temp Books, 1979).

Walton, Travis. *The Walton Experience* (Berkley Books, 1978).

Rosedale (Victoria, Australia) close encounter

One of the best physical trace UFO landing cases in Australia, occurred near Rosedale, Victoria, on September, 30, 1980. It is a striking event because of the wide array of physical effects involved and the credibility of the primary witness.

A property caretaker was awakened in the early hours of the morning by stock disturbances and other strange sounds. Upon investigating he observed, initially only some 200 meters away, an aerial object, approximately 8 meters wide and 5 meters high, moving over the property, at about a height of 2 meters. The object appeared to have orange and blue lights on it, and was dome shaped with a white top.

It travelled slowly toward a 10,000-gallon concrete water tank. Upon reaching the tank, the UFO appeared to hover directly on top of it for about a minute. The object then landed about 15 meters away from the tank. Within about 5 minutes the caretaker had ridden a motorbike down to within 10 to 15 meters of the object on the ground. It appeared to stay on the ground for a further 2 to 3 minutes, until the persistent noise increased to "an awful scream." The object then rose up, tilting so the witness could then see its bottom sections.

The caretaker was hit with a blast of hot air. Debris consisting of stones, weed, and cow dung fell away from the object. It then tilted back into a horizontal position and slowly moved off into the distance, at a steady altitude of about 3 meters.

A circular physical ground trace, shaped like an annulus and just 10 meters in diameter, was left behind. Physical and chemical differences were found in soil samples taken at the site by the writer, but no explanation could be determined. The water tank was found to be largely empty of water, despite being verified as full a few days earlier. A small cone shape of silt was evident in the centre of the near empty tank. There were effects on the witness (including headaches and nausea) and his watch (which for 3 days after the incident stopped working every time he put it on). There were also possible independent witnesses of the UFO. A girl on a nearby property may have observed the object approaching the primary witness's property. A delivery van driver was reported to have seen the UFO on the ground, apparently while the main witness was inside his house preparing to go down to the paddock.

The incident was initially investigated by the Victorian UFO Research Society. The striking nature of the event drew this writer (physical-trace specialist, Bill Chalker) and physical chemist Keith Basterfield to the site. Both of us were impressed with the credibility of the witness and the compelling consistency of the physical evidence.

No prosaic explanation could be determined. A "plasma vortex" (a controversial hypothesis to explain "crop circles") was one of a number of explanations put forward. The evidence does not support this idea. The 1980 Rosedale UFO landing is a very striking example of a CE-2 physical-trace event.

—WILLIAM C. CHALKER

Roswell Incident, The (Grosset and Dunlap, 1980). Charles Berlitz and William Moore produced the second book, after Frank Scully's in 1950, to allege a crashed spacecraft and alien bodies were retrieved by the U.S. military in New Mexico during the 1940s and kept in storage at an Air Force base. Their version relied on the eyewitness testimony of Major Jesse Marcel who investigated a debris field he could not identify on a ranch outside Roswell. Marcel never claimed to have seen alien bodies, so Berlitz and Moore only "postulate a tentative picture of the sequence of events" to support that prospect.

—RANDALL FITZGERALD

Roswell (New Mexico) incident Just two weeks after the famous Kenneth Arnold sighting (of June 24, 1947), which ushered in the modern "flying saucer" era, headlines such as "Flying Disk Captured by Air Force" and "RAAF Captures Flying Saucer" were splashed across the front pages of newspapers across the United States. The front-page story read in part:

"The many rumors regarding the flying disc became a reality yesterday when the intelligence officer of the 509th Bomb Group of the Eighth Air Force, Roswell Army Air Field, was fortunate enough to gain possession of a disc through the cooperation of one of the local ranchers and the sheriff's office of Chaves County.

"The flying object landed on a ranch near Roswell sometime last week. Not having phone facilities, the rancher stored the disc until such time as he was able to contact the sheriff's office, who in turn notified Major Jesse A. Marcel of the 509th Bomb Group Intelligence Office.

"Action was immediately taken and the disc was picked up at the rancher's home. It was inspected at the Roswell Army Air Field and subsequently loaned by Major Marcel to higher headquarters." By the next day, the "flying saucer" no longer existed. It became, instead, a crashed weather balloon. Not until three decades later would the case be reopened by persistent UFOlogists, who eventually pressured the U.S. government into reopening the case themselves.

On July 8, 1947, the commander of the

Illustrations copyright © 1998 by William Louis McDonald

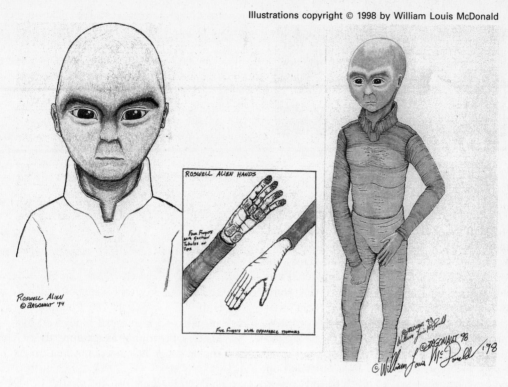

Reconstruction of Roswell alien from alleged eyewitness data supplied to
forensic artist William Louis McDonald

base at Roswell, then Colonel William Blanchard, ordered his public relations officer to announce they had found a flying saucer. Within hours, however, Eighth Air Force Headquarters announced that the debris had been identified as the remains of a common weather balloon and a Rawin radar reflector.

The case took on new life in 1978 when Jesse Marcel, Sr., a former air intelligence officer at the Roswell base, told UFO researchers (Stanton Friedman and Leonard Stringfield) that he had picked up pieces of a flying saucer. Marcel provided the location but not the date. He also said that the object was something *not of this Earth.*

Although the wreckage was officially identified by Army Air Force officers in Fort Worth, Texas, as a weather balloon, interviews conducted with participants thirty and forty years after the event told a different story. Eye-

witnesses, including William Woody and E.L. Pyles claimed to have seen the object in the sky over Roswell, descending toward the ground.

W.W. ("Mac") Brazel, a rancher living in the Corona area of New Mexico, found a field strewn with metallic debris. According to his son, Bill Brazel, Mac wanted to know who was going to clean up the mess. He thought the Army might be responsible and traveled to Roswell to alert both the sheriff and the military.

Those who handled the debris such as Bill Brazel, Jesse Marcel, Sr., Brazel's neighbors (Floyd and Loretta Proctor), and others suggested the material was lightweight and extraordinarily tough. Brazel, the Proctors, and Marcel all experimented with the debris at separate times by trying to burn it, but it failed to ignite. Bill Brazel said the material was as

Composite of the Roswell spacecraft as
conceptualized by forensic artist
William Louis McDonald

light as balsa wood, but so strong it wouldn't
break. It was also impervious to his pocket
knife. Brazel and others also said there were
pieces of material that looked like aluminum
foil, but when crumpled into a ball would unfold itself, returning to its original shape without any signs of a fold or wrinkle.

Marcel and counterintelligence agent,
Sheridan Cavitt, followed Brazel to his ranch.
Marcel later told researchers that the debris
was scattered over a field in a strip several
hundred feet wide and about three quarters of
a mile long. Though not mentioned by Marcel,
Brazel told investigators that the land had been
gouged out in a strip about five hundred feet
long. He said it took about two years for the
area to grass back over.

Other participants, including Colonel
Thomas J. DuBose, Chief of Staff at the Eighth
Air Force, told later investigators that the balloon explanation was just a cover story for the
real find. DuBose said he had not seen the real
debris himself but had been present when some
of it had arrived at the Fort Worth Army Air
Field on its way to Washington, D.C.

Others, such as Roswell adjutant Patrick
Saunders and Roswell provost marshal Edwin
Easley, said they couldn't talk about the case
previously because they had been sworn to secrecy. Still others claimed to have witnessed
alien bodies associated with the crash.

Such statements—coupled with the fact
that the original debris had to be flown immediately to Wright-Patterson AFB, in Ohio—
suggest that something stranger and more

important than a weather balloon had crashed
on Brazel's ranch.

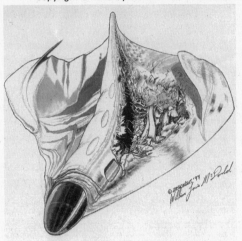

The crashed spacecraft recovered by
military personnel as interpreted by
forensic artist William Louis McDonald

In 1994, the U.S. Air Force, after conducting their own investigation, claimed the case
was explained by a weather balloon with a
radar target. This time, however, they claimed
it came from New York University's constant
level balloon research project known as Mogul.
They implied that the balloons and targets
were something special and highly classified.
While it is true that the project was classified,
the equipment consists of commercial off-the-
shelf balloons and reflectors, which should
have been easily recognizable as such by the
military personnel who first surveyed the
wreckage.

In 1997, the Air Force released another
"final report" on Roswell. In this one they
explained the alleged alien bodies as anthropomorphic crash dummies used in the testing of
aircraft ejection systems and parachutes.

Almost no one accepted this explanation
because these tests hadn't started until 1953—
six years *after* the Roswell crash. The Air
Force seemed to be suggesting they believed
those who said they had seen alien bodies re-

covered in 1947, which would indeed require an explanation.

—KEVIN D. RANDLE

PROJECT MOGUL AND MORE

Nothing dominated the thoughts and provoked the fears of American military planners in 1947 more than the prospect of the Soviet Union exploding an atomic bomb and possessing a nuclear battlefield capability. To provide an early warning system that could detect Soviet nuclear tests, a spying project was authorized in 1946, and given a nearly unlimited budget, to develop an upper atmospheric surveillance device that would acoustically sense reverberations from atomic explosions on the other side of the world. If the Soviets learned that the U.S. had such an atmospheric spy system, they might shift their nuclear weapons tests underground, so the highest possible levels of secrecy would have to cloak Project Mogul, as it was code named. Mogul's top secret classification became Priority 1A, comparable to the Manhattan Project which less than two years earlier had produced the world's first atomic bomb. Only a few key high-ranking military officers with a strict "need-to-know" would be aware of Mogul's existence.

Equipment used in Project Mogul resembled nothing that had ever been launched in the history of flight. It consisted of a gigantic train of 15-foot diameter meteorological balloons, 23 balloons in all, stretching 650 feet into the air. This balloon train carried aloft three radar reflectors, resembling large metalfoil kites, called RAWIN targets; lowfrequency acoustic microphones; metal boxes packed with batteries for the acoustic devices; sonobuoys attached to three- and four-inchdiameter aluminum rings; tubes holding ballast; and altitude pressure switches. Because a New York novelty company had manufactured the radar reflectors, reinforcing tape used to hold it together had a stylized, flower-like lavender design on it.

Mogul Flight 4 was launched by a team of scientists on June 4, 1947, from Alamogordo Army Air Field, located to the southwest of Roswell. It ascended into the stratosphere while traveling northeast, shifted in the face of prevailing winds toward the northwest, then as some of the balloons burst from exposure to the sun, it descended back to Earth heading northeast again. Once the signal batteries depleted the power, ground contact with the balloons was lost at a point near Arabela, New Mexico, about 17 miles from where the balloon train eventually came to rest on the J.B. Foster ranch. As lower portions of the train, with equipment attached, scraped along the field, balloons still aloft dragged everything through prickly desert brush, snagging pieces of balloon, radar targets, and other equipment along the ground at a southwest-to-northeast angle.

Ten days later, ranch foreman Mac Brazel was inspecting his sheep herd by horseback when he spotted this line of debris about seven miles from the ranch house. Brazel would later explain that at the time he "did not pay much attention" to what he described as "bright wreckage made up of rubber strips, tin foil, a rather tough paper and sticks." He was in a hurry to make his rounds of the ranch and finish chores before dark. Besides, twice before he had four weather balloon remnants on the ranch. Maybe this was more of the same.

Another ten days passed and civilian pilot Kenneth Arnold had an encounter that would be the defining experience of a cultural phenomenon. While flying in western Washington State on June 24th, he saw nine shiny objects over the Cascade Mountains, moving "like a saucer would if you skipped it across the water." In subsequent news media accounts the term "flying saucer" was born. Over the next two weeks sightings of unidentified flying objects were reported in 39 states, igniting widespread, excited speculation about whether it was space aliens or Soviet communists who had invaded our skies.

On a visit to Corona, the closest town to the ranch, Brazel heard conversation from relatives about these flying disk reports and rumors of a reward to whoever captured a disk. He began to wonder if what he had found might be wreckage from one of the mysterious craft, since there seemed to be much more debris and of a wider variety this time than he had seen left by the two previous balloons. On July 4, Brazel returned to the debris field accompanied by his wife and their 14-year-old daughter, Bessie, and together they filled several gunny sacks. Bessie would describe years later what they found: ''The debris looked like pieces of a large balloon which had burst.'' She picked up foil-like material, some which had kite sticks attached with two-inch wide tape. On the tape were ''flower-like designs in a variety of pastel colors.''

Needing to buy a new pickup truck, Brazel drove 75 miles into Roswell on July 6, carrying along several pieces of the debris. ''He certainly wouldn't have made the trip just on account of the stuff he had found,'' his son Bill Brazel remembers. Once in town Mac Brazel stopped by the office of Sheriff George Wilcox and showed him the pieces. Thinking it might have military significance, Wilcox phoned Roswell Army Air Field and was referred to an intelligence officer, Major Jesse Marcel, whom he interrupted while eating lunch.

Marcel contacted his base commander, Colonel William Blanchard. ''In my discussion with the colonel, we determined that a downed aircraft of some unusual sort might be involved,'' Marcel later recounted. Col. Blanchard ordered Marcel and a counterintelligence officer, Captain Sheridan Cavitt, to follow Brazel back to the ranch and investigate. They arrived after dark and camped out. The next morning they viewed the debris field.

Though Cavitt claims he immediately knew the material was from a weather balloon, Marcel remained unconvinced. There was simply too much debris, and it looked too unusual, to have come from any known weather balloon. Brazel described the debris field for reporters a few days later as being about 200 yards in diameter, while Cavitt would remember it four decades later as only about 20 feet

square. By contrast, Marcel told me in an interview in 1979 that the debris had been scattered a distance of one mile and measured hundreds of feet across. These vast discrepancies in the various accounts, and Marcel's disturbing tendency toward exaggeration, would prove to be a recurring pattern in events surrounding the Roswell incident.

With Marcel's Buick and Cavitt's jeep crammed with wreckage, both men drove back into Roswell, not arriving until late at night. Marcel drove straight home and awakened his wife and their eleven-year-old son, Jesse Jr., who remembers his father being excited and ''saying something about flying saucers.'' Major Marcel spread some debris out on the kitchen floor and pointed to a foot-long balsa-like beam with violet images on it, marveling at how the indecipherable symbols might be an alien language. ''Dad brought home a quantity of black, brittle plastic material that had either melted or burned, and a lot of metal foil. Some people say they tried to tear it or fold it up and it would unfold on its own. I didn't see that.'' The material resembling plastic were pieces of neoprene balloon which had degraded in the sunlight. After 15 minutes of show-and-tell with his family, Marcel bundled the debris up and drove it to the air base.

Though no record exists of Marcel's meeting with Colonel Blanchard, it seems reasonable to assume that at first both men might have thought the wreckage could be from a Soviet surveillance device sent to spy on American nuclear installations, especially the Roswell home base for B-29s used to carry atomic bombs. That might have prompted Blanchard to suggest using flying disks as a convenient cover story to buy time while superiors in Washington, D.C., and Wright Field in Ohio, were analyzing the debris. It may also be that Marcel had become so convinced the debris ''was out of this world'' that he either persuaded Blanchard of that prospect, or he took the rash step of releasing information about the finding without proper authorization. What we do know, however, is that on the morning of July 8, the same day that Colonel

Blanchard took a scheduled leave of absence, the base's public information officer, Walter Haut, distributed a press release announcing the acquisition of a flying disk.

That afternoon's *Roswell Daily Record* front page story began: "The intelligence office of the 509th Bombardment group at Roswell Army Air Field announced at noon today that the field has come into possession of a flying saucer. According to information released by the department, over authority of Maj. J. A. Marcel, intelligence officer, the disk was recovered. . . ." Nowhere in the press release was Col. Blanchard's name mentioned, only Marcel's. Blanchard either did not want to be associated with the most important discovery in human history, giving all credit to a subordinate, Jesse Marcel, or he wanted to distance himself from what he feared might turn out to be a public embarrassment.

In a 1979 interview Marcel accused Walter Haut of having written the press release without authorization, an act for which "he was severely reprimanded" by superiors. Soon after the incident Haut reportedly resigned from the Air Force "for personal reasons." Haut would confess in 1995 about the press release that "I cannot honestly remember whether I wrote it. How the colonel passed that information on to me I cannot honestly tell you. It was not that big a production at that time, in my mind." So unaffected was Haut that his wife claims he never once mentioned a flying disk or the press release to her. News of this puzzling find shot up the Army Air Force chain of command, in many instances arriving through official channels after the military brass had heard reports of it on news broadcasts, which did not make them happy. On July 9, for instance, *The Washington Post* reported: "Officers at the Roswell, N.M., air base received a blistering rebuke from the Army A.F. Headquarters in Washington for announcing that a 'flying disc' had been found on a New Mexico ranch." Eighth Army Air Force commander Brigadier Gen. Roger Ramey ordered Major Marcel to fly the debris to Fort Worth, Texas, and present it be-

fore a press conference he had called to squelch the firestorm of media attention. In numerous interviews from 1978 until his death in 1986, Marcel maintained "there was half a B-29 full" of the crash debris at Fort Worth. Other officers on that flight have strenuously challenged this claim as a gross exaggeration. Robert R. Porter, the flight engineer of the B-29 flight carrying Marcel, filed an affidavit in 1991 describing the debris as being carried in three shoebox-sized packages and a triangle-shaped package, "all of which could have fit into the trunk of a car."

Once inside Gen. Ramey's office the debris was laid out on the floor and inspected by a weather officer Ramey had called in, Warrant Officer Irving Newton. "I remember Major Marcel chased me all around that room," Newton told investigators during the 1990s. "He kept saying things like, 'look at how tough the metal is. Look at the strange markings on it.' While I was examining the debris, Marcel was picking up pieces of the radar target sticks and trying to convince me that some notations on the sticks were alien writings. But I was adamant that it was a weather balloon with a RAWIN target. I think he was embarrassed as crazy and he would like to do anything to make that turn into a flying saucer."

Two news photos were taken of a sheepish-looking Marcel holding pieces of the weather balloon. At least three more shots were snapped of Gen. Ramey, dressed in his formal uniform, and his assistant, Col. Thomas DuBose, posing by similar pieces. Marcel would claim in 1979 that debris from an ordinary weather balloon had been substituted for the flying saucer wreckage in all the photos but one, which showed him "with pieces of the actual stuff we had found. It was not a staged photo. Later, they cleared out our wreckage and substituted some of their own. Then they allowed more photos. Those photos were taken while the actual wreckage was already on its way to Wright Field."

To test Marcel's allegation, researchers have obtained original prints of the photos and conducted comparisons of the debris pictured in each. No differences were found because the debris is identical. Nor would there have been any reason to believe Gen. Ramey just happened to have remnants of a degraded weather balloon lying around to produce for the media in case a flying saucer cover story ever became necessary.

An FBI teletype message on July 8, sent from the Dallas office to FBI Director J. Edgar Hoover in Washington, D.C., and released to UFO researchers in the 1970s, reads: "Major Curtan, Headquarters, Eighth Air Force telephonically advised this office that an object purporting to be a flying disk was recovered near Roswell, New Mexico, this date. The disc is hexagonal in shape and was suspended from a balloon by cable, which was approximately twenty feet in diameter. Major Curtan further advised that the object found resembles a high altitude weather balloon with a radar reflector, but that telephonic conversation between their office and Wright Field had not (illegible) borne out this belief. Disc and balloon being transported to Wright Field by special plane for examination."

Once at Wright Field parts of the debris were quickly identified by Colonel Marcellus Duffy, a former project officer of Mogul, as being from a Mogul balloon flight. A similar identification was made at Andrews Army Air Field outside Washington, D.C., at the headquarters of the Army Air Forces Weather Service, which was located in the same building as the office of Major General Clements McMullen, Deputy Commander of Strategic Air Command, who had originally ordered Gen. Ramey to concoct a cover story to protect Project Mogul. No one at Roswell, and few at Wright Field, had a need-to-know access concerning Mogul, which meant that many high-ranking officers and their subordinates were left to speculate about what had happened and why it was cloaked in secrecy. Both Col. Blanchard and Gen. Ramey were probably uninformed about Mogul and the true significance of the crash debris. It could even be that top levels of the military wanted rumors of

crashed saucers to spread as confusion for Soviet operatives known to be probing for American nuclear secrets.

In 1994 the Secretary of the Air Force ordered an investigation of allegations that a conspiracy existed within the government to hide the crash of an alien spacecraft near Roswell. The officer placed in charge, Col. Richard Weaver, Director of Security and Special Program Oversight for the Secretary's office, held the highest security clearance, as did the members of his staff, enabling them to examine all super-secret "black" programs that are kept from public scrutiny. Their search of records for references to Roswell, flying saucer debris, and alien bodies turned up nothing. "The morning reports (at the Roswell base) showed that the subsequent activities at Roswell during the month were mostly mundane and not indicative of any unusual high level activity," their report concluded. Nor was any indication found "of heightened activity anywhere else in the military hierarchy in July 1947. If some event happened that was one of the 'watershed happenings' in human history, the U.S. military certainly reacted in an unconcerned and cavalier manner."

A similar investigation was conducted by the U.S. General Accounting Office using employees holding high security clearances. Army Counterintelligence Corps historical files 1947-49, and National Security Council meeting minutes for 1947-48 were reviewed and no mention of Roswell or a crash was found. All CIA databases were searched against the term Roswell and no documents relating to a crash or bodies were uncovered. Also, records of Air Matériel Command at Wright Field from 1947 to 1950 were reviewed and GAO "found no records mentioning the Roswell crash or the examination by Air Matériel Command personnel of any debris recovered from the crash."

A series of declassified military documents from 1947 and 1948, all once classified Secret, reveal that not only did the Air Force have no pieces of an extraterrestrial vehicle, it was an agency increasingly frustrated at being unable to find physical evidence for the reality of flying saucers. Among these documents:

Sept. 23, 1947—A letter by Lt. Gen. Nathan Twining at Wright Field bemoaning "the lack of physical evidence in the shape of crash recovered exhibits . . ."

Dec. 22, 1947—An analysis of UFO reports by Maj. Gen. George McDonald, Director of Air Force Intelligence, declaring "physical evidence, such as crash-recovered exhibits, is not available . . ."

Nov. 8, 1948—A letter by Col. H.M. McCoy, chief of intelligence at Wright Field's Air Matériel Command, concluding "the exact nature of those objects cannot be established until physical evidence, such as that which would result from a crash, has been obtained."

Commercial airline pilot Kent Jeffrey spent several years financing his own personal investigation of Roswell and whether any wreckage or bodies ended up in storage at Wright Field, later called Wright-Patterson. He tracked down and interviewed three retired Air Force colonels who served at Wright-Patterson in the 1950s and 1960s with the Foreign Technology Division, which would have handled any crash debris if it existed. None of the three knew anything about UFO debris or alien bodies. "If something like that had happened, I would have known about it," declared George Weinbrenner, the commander of the Foreign Technology Division from 1968-74. For Jeffrey these three sources provided him with "the final confirmation—no alien bodies, no secret hangar, and no UFO crash at Roswell. Case closed."

A combination of human foibles coalesced to create the modern myth of what happened near Roswell, including a contagion of rumor-mongering, miscommunication, misperception, exaggerations, self-aggrandizing behavior, lies for financial gain, and a psychological condition called false memories. There has been a tendency for second- and thirdhand witnesses to pass on rumor and speculation, a case in point being retired Gen. Arthur Exon, who was a lieutenant colonel at Wright Field in 1947. Exon told Karl Pflock that his information about saucer wreckage and alien bodies was "nothing more than rumors he had heard." Similarly, Exon admitted to Stanton Friedman that he "had heard scuttlebutt about bodies and wreckage, but had no firsthand knowledge of the subject."

For a sad case of apparent exaggeration we need look no further than Major Jesse Marcel. UFO researchers Robert Todd and Kal Korff independently obtained Marcel's nearly 200-page-long military service file and found, in Korff's words, a pattern of Marcel "exaggerating things and repeatedly trying to write himself into the history books." Marcel had told book authors that he held a college bachelor's degree, had been a pilot of B-24s in World War II, received five air medals for shooting down five enemy aircraft, and was himself shot down. Yet absolutely none of this was true according to his own service file! Marcel frequently changed his testimony about the Roswell debris. First he said he had heard about someone trying to dent the metal with a hammer, then later he said "we even tried making a dent in it with a 16-pound sledge hammer, still no dent in it." Sometimes he said the debris "didn't burn very well," and then other times he claimed it would not burn at all. Marcel's career lasted less than three years after his humiliation at Roswell, when he resigned to open a small-town TV repair shop. Gene Tighe worked under Marcel at Strategic Air Command in Washington, D.C. Says Tighe, who ended his own career as a general: "Marcel's reputation suffered dramatically at SAC" in the aftermath of Roswell.

Frank Kaufmann claims he watched a UFO explode on a radar screen, and he was part of the military team sent to retrieve the wreckage and alien bodies. The supposed site of the

UFO explosion was more than 100 miles from the radar unit Kaufmann said he was assigned to, yet radar in 1947 had an effective range of no more than 40 miles. Under intense grilling by aerospace writer Philip J. Klass in the 1990s, Kaufmann confessed that he was never a trained radar operator. As for the site north of Roswell where Kaufmann says the UFO crashed, an affidavit was sworn out in 1997 by Jim McKnight, whose aunt owned the land in question, stating that "no one in my family had any knowledge of such a UFO crash or military retrieval." McKnight emphasized that any military team entering the alleged crash area would have passed within sight of his family's ranch house. A final nail in Kaufmann's tale comes from his claim of having a diary from 1947 verifying his involvement in a crash recovery. He has refused all requests to produce the diary and submit it to forensic testing to substantiate its age.

James Ragsdale professed that he and a girlfriend saw the spacecraft crash and they examined the alien bodies. His first rendering of the incident surfaced in 1993 in the form of a notarized statement describing how he and the woman investigated the crash north of Roswell at sunrise, watching from a distance as the military recovered the craft and bodies. He managed to keep some of the flying saucer debris, pieces that looked like carbon paper 18-30 inches long. But in 1951 his car was stolen with a few saucer pieces in it, and in 1985 his house was broken into and thieves stole the rest of the spacecraft. Two years after this account Ragsdale significantly altered his story. On a videotape made five days before his death from lung cancer, he changed the crash location to Boy Scout Mountain, due west from Roswell. This time he said they had visited the crash immediately that night, not the next morning. Ragsdale said he even tried to pry the helmet off a dead alien to take home as a souvenir. Philip Klass discovered how this fresh version of Ragsdale's story was then being marketed to benefit Ragsdale's family, with The Roswell International UFO Museum selling a 42-page booklet, The *Jim Ragsdale*

Story, for $14.95, a one-hour video with the same title for $29.50, and T-shirts picturing the new "Jim Ragsdale Impact Site" for $13.95 each.

Retired Army officer Philip Corso claims he was in charge of "seeding" alien technology harvested from the Roswell saucer, a modern Johnny Appleseed handing out advanced secrets to select American defense contractors. These and myriad other claims come packaged in his book, *The Day After Roswell,* the circumstances of whose release in June 1997 raised initial questions about Corso's integrity and credibility. The first edition of the book carried a brief foreword by U.S. Senator Strom Thurmond, chairman of the Senate Armed Services Committee, praising Corso for service to his country. It turned out that Corso had apparently misled Thurmond, submitting an entirely different book manuscript, Corso's memoirs called *I Walked With Giants,* for the senator to comment on, with no mention made of UFOs or government conspiracies. Thurmond protested loudly and publicly, forcing removal of the foreword from subsequent editions.

Inside the Roswell book Corso reprinted four UFO photographs he alleges were taken from "Army Intelligence files as support material for the R&D project to harvest the Roswell alien technology for military purposes." Karl Pflock, a former deputy assistant secretary of defense in the Reagan administration, points out that all four photos have been in the public domain for decades. One shows a 1935 Ford hubcap thrown into the air over Riverside, California, in 1953. The other three photos are all lifted from the 1968 Condon Committee report for the Air Force on UFOs, picturing such phenomena as, in Pflock's words, "a smoke ring generated by a simulated atom bomb demonstration in 1957."

A cursory examination of Corso's book reveals a host of errors, unsubstantiated claims, and blatant misrepresentations. Corso depicts Major Jesse Marcel as being in charge of the removal of alien bodies from the spacecraft, whereas Marcel always insisted he never saw alien bodies, nor did he know anyone who had.

Corso says the recovered alien craft is being stored at Norton AFB, seemingly unaware Norton has been closed for years. Corso claims he and the Army developed Corona, the world's first spy satellite program, to detect UFO landings. Pflock counters that Corona "was a 100 percent CIA-Air Force project, and the army had nothing to do with it." Corso writes that the B-2 stealth bomber was a Lockheed project, when anyone familiar with aviation knows it is a Northrop creation. The list goes on and on.

Television reporter George Knapp has known Corso since 1992, interviewing him on numerous occasions. According to Knapp, Corso "has a tough-to-swallow story about an encounter with a live alien in the New Mexico desert, in which the alien being telepathically communicated a strange message." Apparently that Corso experience proved too far out even for this book as it does not appear. In an interview with CNI News, a UFO reporting service, a glimpse emerged of what may be motivating Corso—beyond the considerable financial reward—to sacrifice his reputation within mainstream military and political circles. Boasting of his exploits in World War II, Corso says he personally spirited 10,000 Jewish refugees out of Rome to Palestine. "I thought nothing of it," comments Corso, "but people said what a big thing it was." Now with revelations of his role in saving Earth from the threat of alien invasion, maybe humankind will recognize and appreciate, perhaps even worship, Philip Corso who by his own modest admission has "changed the course of the world."

Glenn Dennis worked as a Roswell mortician and first came forward in 1989 with his story of being at the base on the day saucer wreckage and bodies arrived. Friends who had known Dennis for decades were surprised and incredulous when he spoke up. Walter Haut remembers thinking "what the heck would he know?" since Dennis had never mentioned this experience in three decades of friendship. A review of Roswell base daily personnel accounting records by Air Force investigators in 1996 found Dennis's account "grossly inaccu-

rate" with "serious errors in his recollection of events." A pediatrician Dennis fingered as involved in the 1947 events did not serve in Roswell until 1951-53, and did not recall ever knowing Dennis. Also Dennis had told of a "black sergeant" and a "big redheaded captain" who threatened him at the base hospital where alien bodies were allegedly being autopsied. Racial integration in the armed forces did not occur until 1949, and only one tall officer with red hair matching Dennis's description served at Roswell, but not until 1954. Dennis claimed he spoke with a nurse in that period named Captain Wilson, yet roster reviews found just one nurse named Wilson, who did not arrive until 1956.

Another nurse whose name Dennis gave as Naomi Selff, and who supposedly told Dennis about participating in an alien autopsy, also could not be located on rosters or in military records for any time frame. In 1995 Karl Pflock asked Dennis if he had made up the nurse's name. "No, no way. I've never done that," Dennis replied. Just a few months later Dennis conceded that he had lied. The name was fictitious and he had swore an oath not to reveal her actual identity. There were additional problems with his testimony. In early interviews he said MPs had merely walked with him out of the base hospital and away from the alien bodies inside. Several years passed and Dennis was telling the story this way: "These two MPs grabbed me by the arms and carried me clear outside. I didn't walk, they carried me!" As for those baby caskets Dennis says the base wanted, presumably to hold alien bodies, it turns out that infant coffins were used by officers at Roswell to transport whiskey and other alcohol on airplanes, a smuggling technique they learned to foil enlisted men from pilfering the goods.

Witness memory repeatedly plays a vital though agile role in the Roswell saga. Take the example of Dr. Curry Holden, the Texas Tech anthropologist leading a student archaeological expedition who reportedly came across the crashed saucer and alien bodies. Both Mrs. Holden and their daughter, Dr. Jane Holden

Kelly, said that Curry had never mentioned the event to them, nor did his personal papers produce any corroboration. When Kevin Randle interviewed Dr. Holden, obtaining his account of the sighting, Holden was 96 years old. Mrs. Holden cautioned Randle that her husband's memory "wasn't as sharp as it once had been. He sometimes restructured his life's events, moving them in time so that they were subtly changed."

Psychological studies indicate an estimated 25 percent of all human beings are susceptible to false memories, a belief that something imagined, heard, or read, actually happened to them personally. These studies have found memory to be more like an evolving sculpture than a literal recording of events. Harvard psychologist Daniel Schacter and other memory researchers note how over time most of us re-fashion our memories so dramatically that we remember events which never happened and forget what actually did occur. As we go beyond middle age, memory distortion of the distant past gets worse.

University of Washington psychologist Elizabeth Loftus has accumulated research findings on a phenomena called "rehearsal," in which over time we play back our memories to ourselves again and again, refashioning the details somewhat with each retelling, until the embellishments become a complete memory and feel like the real event. That is why old married couples or longtime friends will recall a shared experience very differently, each insistent about being in possession of the accurate rendition. Memory also acts as a "prestige-enhancing mechanism," building up our egos by inflating our own importance or central role in past events. Roswell "witnesses" embody textbook studies of all these various ways in which we can be tricked by our own consciousness in the pursuit of a desire for belief.

In their book *UFO Crash At Roswell,* Brandeis University anthropology professors Benson Saler and Charles A. Ziegler call the "Roswell myth" a form of social protest, an anti-government narrative about conspiracy and manipulation, whose genesis is the cynicism engendered by the Watergate scandal and the Vietnam War. That an insignificant crash of a balloon project more than a half-century ago could rapidly evolve into a modern American myth, on a scale comparable to the ancient myths of Greece and Rome, tells us that in an age supposedly dominated by Science and Reason we remain at heart a species of mystic, scanning the inward and outward heavens in our search for a divine spark of meaning.

—RANDALL FITZGERALD

(Note: This version of the Roswell events was adapted from Fitzgerald's 1998 book, *Cosmic Test Tube*, in which he tried to make the strongest possible case for an extraterrestrial explanation of the debris, followed by this case for a Mogul balloon solution to the Roswell mystery.)

References

Klass, Philip J. *The Real Roswell Crashed-Saucer Coverup* (Prometheus Books, 1997)

Korff, Kal K. *The Roswell UFO Crash* (Prometheus Books, 1997).

U.S. Air Force Report on the Roswell Incident (July 1994).

U.S. Air Force *The Roswell Report: Case Closed* (June 1997).

U.S. General Accounting Office Report on Roswell (July 1995).

Vallée, Jacques. *Revelations* (Ballantine Books, 1991).

Roswell UFO Crash, The   (Prometheus Books, 1997). Kal Korff makes a case that the myth of a spaceship crash at Roswell, New Mexico, in 1947 arose from a highly selective use of facts and witness testimony by a half-dozen sensationalistic book authors. He dissects the credibility of key witnesses to the alleged crash and points out how even the authors of the three major books written about the incident sharply disagree about where it happened and how.

—RANDALL FITZGERALD

Ruwa (South Africa) landing On the playground of the Ariel School in Ruwa, a suburb of Harare, the capital of Zimbabwe, one of the most remarkable "close encounters of the third kind" occurred on Friday, September 16, 1994. It was 10.00 A.M., time of the morning break, when with the ring of the bell children started to pour out of the little class-houses of the Ariel School. That morning they were alone on the playground, without the supervision of their teachers, who had a meeting in the conference room of the office of the headmaster, Mr. Colin Mackie.

According to the story, some of the children suddenly saw a purple light in the sky above the forest, which kept coming and going. A moment later a disk appeared—a huge, shiny craft with a flattened dome on top, surrounded by yellow lights or portholes, which extended a tripod landing gear. The object came down close to a rock on the other side of the swamp area, between the trees on the edge of the forest. Balls of light or miniature disks appeared and flew around for a short while. The pupils who saw it started to scream out of surprise and fear. This drew the attention of nearly everyone on the playground, and within seconds about a hundred pupils reportedly watched the incredible spectacle.

The closest witnesses observed something coming out of the disk. First one, then a second, and finally a third figure came out of the craft from the back of its dome. The beings wore shiny, tight-fitting black overalls and had dark faces. Two of them were bald but one had long, black hair. All three were about 4 to 5 feet tall. They had big black eyes, which some of the young witnesses described as "like a cat's eyes," a tiny little mouth, and a small nose. Some of the children could see a metal band around the head. All the younger kids were scared and started crying.

One of the entities came closer than the rest and stared in the direction of the children who all started screaming at once. At this moment, several of the children thought they heard a voice in their minds, telling them there was nothing to fear—from the aliens, at least. But the children said the UFO beings had come to warn them that we humans are destroying planet Earth. After about three minutes the creatures went back to their ship, where lights started to flash, before the disk itself disappeared in a burst of light.

During the sighting, several of the children had run into the conference room of the school to tell their teachers to come out and look. But when they eventually arrived, not believing the children in the beginning, everything was already over. Later, one class went to the landing site with their teacher, to find dead birds, strange footprints, burning marks, an indentation in the grass, and heaps of dead ants.

Most children told their parents about the incidents who informed the media. The case caused a stir in South Africa but was generally ignored elsewhere. Soon after the event, Cynthia Hind, the Mutual UFO Network's representative for Africa and a resident of Harare, was able to perform a field investigation and interview the eyewitnesses.

About half a year later, Harvard psychiatrist John E. Mack visited the Ariel School and questioned some of the children. He concluded that they certainly had had a real experience, which had left a very deep impression upon them. Several children had nightmares for weeks and months after. Some black children interpreted the incident in the context of African mythology.

When this writer traveled to Ruwa two years later, he was still able to interview 44 of the children, their teachers and parents on camera. The deep psychological impact and the seriousness of the children convinced him as well as Dr. Mack that the case is authentic. Because of the high number of credible eyewitnesses, the Ruwa case is considered by some to be one of the most significant events in the history of the UFO phenomenon.

—MICHAEL HESEMANN

S

Sagan, Carl (1934-1996). Carl Sagan was a first-rate scientist and popularizer of astronomy, whose award-winning 13-part *Cosmos* series on public television attracted more than 500 million viewers in 60 countries. Dr. Sagan was the David Duncan Professor of Astronomy and Space Sciences and Director of the Laboratory for Planetary Studies at Cornell University; Distinguished Visiting Scientist at the Jet Propulsion Laboratory, California Institute of Technology; and co-founder and President of The Planetary Society, the largest space interest group in the world.

A Pulitzer Prize-winning author for his 1977 #1 bestselling book, *The Dragons of Eden*, Sagan published numerous books on space, evolution, and the environment, which all together sold millions of copies. His science-fiction novel *Contact* (1985) was made into a major motion picture.

His principal research activities were concerned with the physics and chemistry of planetary atmospheres and surfaces, space vehicle exploration of the planets, and the origin of life on Earth. He was also known for his studies in exobiology (now sometimes called astrobiology), the emerging discipline which deals with the possibility of extraterrestrial life and the means for its detection. Dr. Sagan played a leading role in the Mariner, Viking, Voyager, and Galileo missions to the planets, for which he received numerous awards over the years, including the highest award of the National Academy of Sciences.

He served as chairman of the Division for Planetary Sciences of the American Astronomical Society and as chairman of the Astronomy Section of the American Association for the Advancement of Science. He also served as an

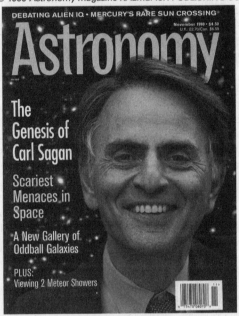

Carl Sagan on the cover of *Astronomy* magazine (November 1999)

adviser to the American Geophysical Union, CETI Foundation, International Academy of Astronautics, Smithsonian, and NASA.

In addition to hundreds of published scientific and popular articles, Dr. Sagan was author, co-author, or editor of more than two dozen books including *Intelligent Life in the Universe* (1966); *UFOs—A Scientific Debate*, edited with Thornton Page (1972); *Communication with Extraterrestrial Intelligence* (1973); *Mars and the Mind of Man* (1973); *The Cosmic Connection* (1973), for which he received the John W. Campbell Memorial Award for the best science book of the year

(1974); *The Dragons of Eden: Speculations on the Evolution of Human Intelligence* (1977), for which he received the Pulitzer Prize; *Murmurs of Earth: The Voyager Interstellar Record* (1978); *Broca's Brain* (1979); *Cosmos* (1980), which topped the bestseller lists for 70 weeks; *Comet* (1985), with Ann Druyan; *Shadows of Forgotten Ancestors* (1992), with Ann Druyan; *Pale Blue Dot* (1994); and *The Demon-Haunted World* (1995).

He received his A.B., B.S., M.S. in physics, and his Ph.D. in astronomy and astrophysics all from the University of Chicago, subsequently serving as Miller Research Fellow in the Institute for Basic Research in Science, University of California, Berkeley; as assistant professor of genetics at Stanford University Medical School; as astrophysicist at the Smithsonian Astrophysical Observatory; and as assistant professor of astronomy at Harvard University. In 1968 he moved to Cornell University, where he became a tenured professor in 1971.

Dr. Sagan played a major role in obtaining the first close-up photos of the moons of Mars, in studying the surface changes on that planet, and in the search for life on Mars. He was active in education of the disadvantaged, was a popular lecturer before audiences of nonscientists, and became an activist against nuclear proliferation.

Sagan was also leader of the U.S. delegation to the Conference on Communication with Extraterrestrial Intelligence, organized jointly by the U.S. National Academy of Sciences and the Soviet Union's Academy of Sciences in Armenia in 1971, and had the principal responsibility for placing Man's first interstellar messages aboard Pioneers 10 and 11, and Voyagers 1 and 2, the first spacecraft to leave the solar system.

POSITION STATEMENT: The interest in unidentified flying objects derives, perhaps, not so much from scientific curiosity as from unfulfilled religious needs. Flying saucers serve, for some, to replace the gods that science has deposed. With their distant and exotic worlds and their pseudoscientific overlay, the contact accounts are acceptable to many people who reject the older religious frameworks. But precisely because people desire so intently that unidentified flying objects be of benign intelligence and extraterrestrial origin, honesty requires that, in evaluating the observations, we accept only the most rigorous logic and the most convincing evidence. At the present time, there is no evidence that unambiguously connects the various flying saucer sightings and contact tales with extraterrestrial intelligence.

And, more recently, Sagan posed these questions:

Which . . . is more likely: that we're undergoing a massive but generally overlooked invasion by alien sexual abusers, or that people are experiencing some unfamiliar internal mental state they do not understand? Admittedly, we're very ignorant both about extraterrestrial beings, if any, and about human psychology. But if these really were the only two alternatives, which one would you pick?

And if the alien abduction accounts are mainly about brain physiology, hallucinations, distorted memories of childhood, and hoaxing, don't we have before us a matter of supreme importance—touching on our limitations, the ease with which we can be misled and manipulated, the fashioning of our beliefs, and perhaps even the origins of our religions? There is genuine scientific paydirt in UFOs and alien abductions—but it is, I think, of a distinctly homegrown and terrestrial character.

(Position statement was adapted from Sagan's article entitled ''Unidentified Flying Objects'' in the *Encyclopedia Americana*, 1975, and from his 1995 book, *The Demon-Haunted World*.)

(Note: The biographical portion of this entry was written by Ronald Story.)

St. Clair (Illinois) police sighting Not only did UFO sightings begin soon after the beginning of the 21st century, they started with a ''bang,'' with one of the possibly most dramatic, and well-documented cases in recent years.

At approximately 4:00 A.M. (Central Time) on Wednesday, January 5, 2000, Mr. Melvern Noll of Highland, Illinois, stopped at his miniature golf course on his way home from work to satisfy himself that the facility was secure. As he returned to his truck, he glanced to the northeast, where minutes earlier he had noticed an unusually prominent ''star.'' He was surprised to see that not only did the ''star'' now appear brighter, but it actually appeared to be drawing closer to his location.

He stood for several minutes watching the light, and quickly came to the conclusion that it was, in fact, attached to a much larger, rectangular-shaped object. What shocked him most of all, however, was that the object appeared to have two rows of ''windows,'' located toward, or on, its aft end. In addition, its ventral surface exhibited many small red lights, and it appeared to be perhaps the size of a football field!

Mr. Noll's sighting was the beginning of a long chain of events that morning over St. Clair County, Illinois, that would involve multiple police officers from eight police departments, several citizens, and possibly Scott Air Force Base personnel. The incident quickly gained considerable attention from the press, and the events were still being debated in the public forum weeks afterward.

Mr. Noll drove directly to the Highland Police Department, hoping that he could convince anyone on duty there to step outside and look at the object. Most of all, he wanted the police dispatcher to broadcast an alert to surrounding areas so that others would observe it, which they did.

Police Officer Ed Barton, of the Lebanon, Illinois, police department, heard the transmission from the Highland Police dispatcher, which caused him to start scanning the night sky to the northeast from his location in Lebanon. What he saw were two intensely bright lights, close to the horizon, and in the direction of Highland. The lights were positioned very close together, and they were so bright that they appeared to radiate ''rays,'' or ''spikes,'' of light into the dark morning sky.

Officer Barton started driving in the general direction of the object, at times traveling at 75 or 80 miles an hour, and with his overhead flashers on. As he drove east from Lebanon, he realized that the very peculiar-looking object appeared to be moving in his direction. He stopped his vehicle, turned off the lights, and sat quietly, hoping to hear whether any sound might be detectable.

As it got closer, he could see that it looked like a slender triangle, longer than it was wide, with a very prominent white light in each of its corners. He estimated that it was at least 75 feet long and perhaps 40 feet wide, although he could not estimate his distance from the object at the time. He noted that the body of the object ''blotted'' out the stars as it moved slowly across the sky, confirming his suspicion that it was a ''solid'' object.

When the object was at its closest to Officer Barton's police cruiser, perhaps 100 feet horizontally and at an altitude of perhaps 1,000 feet, he estimated, it suddenly rotated in the horizontal plane, so it was then pointed to the southwest. The officer radioed the St. Clair County Dispatch to apprise them that he was observing the object, when it almost instantly accelerated so dramatically that his eyes were not able to track it. Subsequent analysis suggested to investigators that the object probably moved not less than 8 miles across the Illinois countryside in the approximately 3 seconds that Officer Barton was observing it!

Next, Officer David Martin of the Shiloh, Illinois, Police Department witnessed the object moving slowly to the west. His description of the object's appearance was similar to Officer Barton's; namely a strange, triangular object with three white lights in the corners, and with red and green lights on its aft end. Officer Martin was watching the object from his cruiser as it suddenly increased its velocity an estimated five- or sixfold, and disappeared from his sight to the west of Shiloh.

The third police officer to witness the object was Officer Craig Stevens of the Millstadt Police Department. He drove his police cruiser to Liederkranz Park, in the north end of Millstadt, and observed the object in the northern sky from that location. He estimated its elevation at 500-1,000 feet, and he thought he could detect a faint buzzing or humming sound emanating from the object. The object appeared generally triangular in shape, with white lights in the corners, and a red light in the center of the ventral surface of the craft.

Officer Stevens quickly obtained a Polaroid camera from the trunk of his cruiser and took a hasty photograph of the object, the only photo taken by any of the observers. Unfortunately, the quality of the photo was low, given the cold conditions at the time, which interfere with chemical development of Polaroid film.

The last police officer to observe the object was an unnamed officer from the Dupo, Illinois, Police Department. He observed the object to the east of Dupo, at a relatively high altitude at the time, he thought, and traveling now generally toward the north-northeast, where it quickly disappeared from his view.

Among the many interesting aspects of the case are: (1) the peculiar appearance of the object, (2) the unorthodox manner in which it was observed to maneuver, (3) the almost unbelievable rate at which it could accelerate, and (4) its apparent huge size. In addition, the case is made even more interesting by both the large number, and high quality, of the observers, most of them experienced, on-duty police officers, who reported the incident over their radios at the time they were observing it.

Another interesting aspect of the case is the fact that in passing near the town of Shiloh, Illinois, the peculiar object passed within an estimated two miles of Scott Air Force Base, which is thought to maintain personnel in its control tower on a 24-hour basis. However, when asked whether any of the tower personnel had witnessed the object that morning, the base personnel stated that the tower had not been staffed for several hours on the morning of the sighting, due to an unexplained suspension of operations. No explanation for the shutdown was ever revealed by Air Force personnel.

—PETER B. DAVENPORT
& DAVID MARLER

San Carlos (Venezuela) incident Jesus Paz and two friends had dined at a restaurant at San Carlos, then proceeded home. According to their tale, when the party neared the Exposition Park of the Ministry of Agriculture, Paz asked the driver of the car to stop while he went behind some bushes, apparently to relieve himself. His friends, still in the car, heard a piercing scream, which literally raised the hair on their heads.

They rushed toward the spot where Paz had entered the brush, came upon their friend unconscious on the ground, and were just in time to see a hairy dwarf running toward a flat, shiny craft which hovered a few feet from the ground. One of the men, Luis Mejia, a national guardsman, reached for his gun, but remembered it was back in his barracks at Guard headquarters. Mejia then picked up a stone and futilely threw it at the craft, which had taken the dwarf in and was rising into the air with a deafening buzzing sound.

A rendering of the San Carlos incident by artist Hal Crawford

At last report, Paz was under the care of doctors and all three men were telling a convincingly hair-raising story to the authorities.

Paz was not only suffering from shock but had several large, long, deep scratches on his right side and along the spine, as if clawed by a wild animal.

—CORAL & JIM LORENZEN

Schwarz, Berthold E. (b. 1924). Since 1955, Dr. Berthold Schwarz, a psychiatrist, has been in private practice in Montclair, New Jersey, and since 1981 in Vero Beach, Florida.

Originally from Jersey City, New Jersey, Dr. Schwarz received his diploma in medicine from the Dartmouth Medical School in 1945. He graduated from the New York University College of Medicine in 1950, interned at Mary Hitchcock Memorial Hospital, Hanover, New Hampshire, in 1951; and was a fellow in psychiatry at the Mayo Foundation from 1951 to 1955. He received an M.S. in psychiatry from the Mayo Graduate School of Medicine in 1957.

Berthold Schwarz

Dr. Schwarz has studied various forms of psychic phenomena since a World War II telepathic experience involving his mother, when his brother was killed in action.

In his professional career he has studied telepathic communications in the parent-child and physician-patient relationships. Dr. Schwarz has also studied a number of extraordinary paragnosts (or psychics), abductees, and contactees.

Dr. Schwarz is the author of *Psychic-Dynamics*, published in paperback as *A Psychiatrist Looks at ESP* (1965), *The Jacques Romano Story* (1968), *Parent-Child Telepathy* (1971), *Psychic Nexus: Psychic Phenomena in Psychiatry and in Everyday Life* (1980), *UFO-Dynamics: Psychiatric and Psychic Aspects of the UFO Syndrome* (1983), *Into the Crystal: the Miracles of Peter Sugleris* (1993), and *Psychiatric and Paranormal Aspects of UFOlogy* (1998). He is co-author with B.A. Ruggieri, M.D. of *Parent-Child Tensions* (1958), and *You CAN Raise Decent Children* (1971). Dr. Schwarz has authored more than 130 articles, appearing both in medical journals and in the UFO literature.

Address: P.O. Box 4030
            Vero Beach, FL 32964
            U.S.A.

POSITION STATEMENT: The outstanding features of many close-encounter UFO experiences are the psychic aspects. These often appear freakish, fantastic, paradoxical, and—to the untrained observer—psychotic.

Despite the abundance of UFO-associated psi material, and the not infrequent existence of past similar related events for those who have had close UFO encounters, serious study of the psychic aspects of UFOs has often been neglected. Notwithstanding considerable public ridicule of those who claim contact with UFOs, this negative attitude has not caused reports of these experiences to disappear. On the contrary, numerous UFO-contact cases and/or their related psi phenomena are "repeaters." Although UFO publications give many details about the physical and astronomical parameters of UFOs, they have often sidestepped the psychic segments of this equation.

I believe that these UFO-related psychic experiences constitute subjective reality for many of these people, and that what they report is similar to paranormal material in general. These UFO contactees and abductees should be studied by behavioral scientists who are also thoroughly experienced and knowledgeable in psychic matters. An inability to understand these UFO events does not mean they did not happen.

Whatever the final explanation for the UFO mystery, there has been a noticeable shift from the more respectable extraterrestrial hypothesis to the psychic hypothesis, which mandates a greater awareness of the complexity of the issues, the significance of the personal-human attributes, and the apparent mind-matter interface. In our present state of technology and science, the psychic hypothesis could be a most practical one for exploration and discovery.
—BERTHOLD E. SCHWARZ

science fiction and UFOs A long-standing symbiotic relationship has persisted between UFO beliefs and science fiction (SF) literature and movies. Jules Verne embodied the expectation of a successful flying machine in his novels, *Robur the Conqueror* (1886) and *Master of the World* (1904), during a time when people began to report phantom airships and other nonexistent flying devices in anticipation of their invention. Countless dime-novel production took up the same theme of successful aerial navigation. The spirit of the turn-of-the-century world was one of boundless confidence in human inventiveness, a faith that all things were possible and all human limitations could be overcome. Both literature and UFO reports of the period reflected this belief.

Extraterrestrial visitors also entered literature in the 19th century. H. G. Wells wrote the most famous invasion novel in 1897, *The War of the Worlds*. He drew on scientific speculation about life on Mars, and imagined the Martians as inhabitants of a dying planet who "regarded this earth with envious eyes," then attacked it with advanced technology in preparation for colonization. Another 1897 novel, *Two Planets* by Kurd Lasswitz, again created an invasion from Mars, only this time the Martians were of human form. Not long after, a short story told of a Martian who worked at the Lowell Observatory and destroyed any photographs showing the canals of Mars—an early version of the alien secret agent among us.

Jules Verne's airship in 1886

The alien visitor theme has remained popular ever since. In fact it nearly defines science fiction in the minds of most people. Reports of crashed Martian spaceships appeared as early as the 1870s and 1880s, while both speculation and a number of airship reports from 1896-97 included references to Martian visitors. Needless to say, this theme of alien visitation has dominated explanatory ideas about UFOs from the early days of flying saucers to the present.

As soon as the heavens became a scene of action, they also became a source of danger in SF literature. More than any other invention, the flying machine represented an almost magical potential for freedom and power. Ambivalence toward this potential is evident in Verne's novels where flight is indeed wonderful, but Robur turns his machine to conquest and destruction. In his poem, "Locksley Hall," Alfred, Lord Tennyson looks into the future and sees a terrible time when wars will be fought by aerial navies, but he tempers this vision with the prophecy that in a more distant future universal peace and world union will follow from the abolition of distance by air travel. Arthur Conan Doyle raised the possibility that the air itself may contain unknown dangers. He wrote a story about a pilot attempting to set a high altitude record, who discovered that vicious snake-like creatures inhabited the upper atmosphere. Yet more than anything else, the idea of aliens lent a sense of foreboding to the sky. Other worlds could hold an almost infinite variety of threats, and their capacity to endanger the Earth was limited only by imagination. They could descend at any time. The panic following the Orson Welles radio broadcast of *The War of the Worlds* in 1938 indicates that some sense of potential peril had settled into public consciousness. Throughout the UFO era, a wariness about alien motives has persisted.

A second important formative era began in the 1920s with the advent of pulp science fiction magazines. During this golden age of the 1920s to the 1940s, stories proliferated of aliens, their craft, and their often evil motives. On the eve of flying saucers and during the early days of the mystery, cover art and articles in such magazines as *Amazing Stories* promoted ''ancient astronaut'' ideas decades before Erich von Däniken.

Subtler ideas about the nature of alien beings developed in such novels as Eric Frank Russell's *Sinister Barrier*. Drawing on suggestions from Charles Fort, Russell postulated that we shared the Earth with hordes of usually invisible globes: beings who fed on human emotional energies and goaded us into wars for the sake of an occasional feast. Once in a while these beings became visible as luminous objects in the sky. Without this popular literature to foster space consciousness and promote the idea of extraterrestrials, an association between UFOs and aliens might have been much slower in coming.

In the mid-1940s an even more paranoid

Fictional flying saucer in 1930

idea took hold as the Shaver Mystery appeared in the pages of *Amazing Stories*. Richard S. Shaver claimed that caverns beneath the Earth contained two races left over from ancient Atlantis and Lemuria. The good beings were the teros and the evil beings were the deros. Using the high technology of these older civilizations, the two races were locked in a conflict to manipulate and control humankind.

The idea of advanced races within the Earth has a history of its own with such milestones as Bulwer-Lytton's 1870s novel, *The Coming Race*. Hollow Earth ideas go back even further, and tales of remnant civilizations from lost continents equipped with flying machines and other wonders have precedent in such mystical literature as *A Dweller on Two Planets* (1899). Yet for many people Shaver's stories struck a sympathetic chord, and editor Ray Palmer fostered the Shaver Mystery until it cost him his job with *Amazing Stories*. When Kenneth Arnold reported flying saucers, Palmer took an immediate interest in this new mystery. He saw in it another facet of a larger mystery and never accepted the extraterrestrial hypothesis as the full or final solution for UFOs. Links between UFOs and the Shaver Mystery have appeared time and again in the UFO literature.

Not all science fiction casts alien visitors in an unfavorable light. Sometimes the aliens come as saviors rather than destroyers, as in Harold M. Sherman's story "The Green Man," which appeared in the October 1946 issue of *Amazing Stories*. A sequel, "The Green Man Returns," appeared in December 1948 and depicts the alien as a Christlike figure. A familiar movie from 1952, *The Day the Earth Stood Still*, also presents an alien on a mission to help keep the people of Earth from destroying themselves. The first contactees, whose stories also contained saintly visitors and messages of peace, followed suspiciously soon after this movie.

Flying saucers entered into popular culture from the late 1940s onward through science fiction literature, comic books, advertisements, rock and roll songs, and television shows—but nowhere as strikingly as in the movies. Many of them borrowed images and ideas from actual reports. Donald Keyhoe's books became a source of technical background for *Earth Versus the Flying Saucers* (1956) and J. Allen Hynek was an advisor for *Close Encounters of the Third Kind* (1977).

The vision of future spaceship design in *Forbidden Planet* (1955) and exemplified by the Enterprise in *Star Trek* shows Earthlings borrowing the saucer design. Invasion has remained a common theme, especially in the Cold War-haunted 1950s, either overt as in George Pal's version of *The War of the Worlds* (1953) or surreptitiously as in *Invasion of the Body Snatchers* (1956). Many films echo the notion that the aliens have fled a dead or dying planet and seek a new home, as in *I Married a Monster from Outer Space* (1958) or have come to exploit the Earth as a way to save their home planet, as in *This Island Earth* (1955). A contrasting view of aliens as friends, if not outright saviors, appears in *E.T.: The*

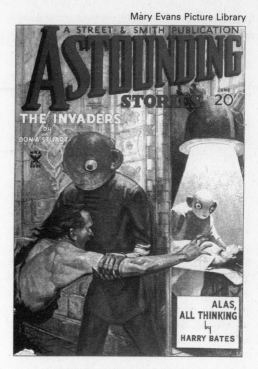

Mary Evans Picture Library

Fictional abduction in 1930

Extraterrestrial (1982) and *Cocoon* (1986). Aliens as age-old visitors to Earth and important influences in the course of human civilization figure in *The Thing* (1951). Anyone familiar with abductions cannot help but be impressed by the parallels in such movies as *Invaders from Mars* (1953) and *Killers from Space* (1953).

Science fiction has anticipated much of UFO lore and UFO lore has found its way into science fiction time and again. The relationship has been a busy two-way street. An examination of the science fiction literature cautions that whatever the nature of UFOs, the beliefs people have and the stories they tell about these objects reflect cultural expectations and concerns as well as objective observation. Reports combine both cultural beliefs and perceptual experience. An intriguing trend toward magic and the supernatural, as opposed to mechanical wonders, has lent a fairy-tale quality to much recent fiction. A similar trend is apparent in UFO reports as abductions and other sightings seem to involve nonphysical objects and surrealistic experiences. Perhaps a new mystical consciousness is in the making.

—THOMAS EDDIE BULLARD

Scientific Study of Unidentified Flying Objects   (Bantam Books, 1969). For two years, thirty-seven scientists and researchers under the direction of Dr. Edward Condon, a University of Colorado physicist, examined UFO reports and issued a 958-page report constituting this book.

—RANDALL FITZGERALD

Scientist: A Novel Autobiography, The (Lippincott, 1978). Pioneer dolphin intelligence researcher John C. Lilly writes about his belief that he can psychically tune in to an intergalactic communication channel with solid-state alien intelligence. These aliens inhabit another reality and operate Earth Coincidence Control, a message center in which a few special humans and all whales and dolphins receive telepathic interstellar communications.

—RANDALL FITZGERALD

Schirmer abduction   The following events allegedly occurred near Ashland, Nebraska, on the morning of December 3, 1967. Police Patrolman Herbert Schirmer said he sighted a football-shaped object encircled by red, flashing lights, which, after a few moments, "shot straight out of sight." Schirmer claims to have gone through a twenty-minute amnesic period immediately following the sighting, which was later "unlocked" during time-regression hypnosis.

At around 2:30 A.M., Patrolman Schirmer, in his police cruiser, had just checked a livestock barn, where he found the cattle making noise and kicking in their stalls. Minutes later, he approached the intersection of highways 6 and 63 on the outskirts of Ashland. About a quarter-mile in front of him, near the highway, appeared a series of red, flashing or blinking lights that shone through the oval portholes of a landed, football-shaped craft. The object was further described as having what appeared to be a polished, aluminum surface, a catwalk around its periphery, and tripod legs underneath. Suddenly, the object rose, emitting a siren-like sound and a red-orange flame from its underside.

Upon returning to the police station, Schirmer noticed the time to be 3 A.M. This seemed odd, since he was sure that only ten minutes had elapsed since the sighting. He filed a standard police report, which read in part: "Saw a flying saucer at the junction of highways 6 and 63. Believe it or not!"

Following a news release of his sighting, Schirmer was interrogated by members of the University of Colorado UFO Project, headed by Edward Condon. After a preliminary interview in Ashland, he was taken to the university headquarters for further psychological testing. When placed under time-regression hypnosis by Dr. R. Leo Sprinkle, a psychologist from the University of Wyoming, Schirmer related what he believed had happened during the twenty-minute "time-loss."

The following details are given here in Schirmer's own words:

"The craft actually pulled me and the car up the hill, toward it; and then as I was going up the road, and the car came to a dead stop, a form came out from underneath the craft and started moving toward the car! And as the one being came to the front of the car, another one was coming out, and the one that was standing in front of the patrol car had sort of a box-like thing in his hand and kind of flashed green all around the whole car. And then one approached the car and reached in and touched me on my neck, at which I felt a sharp amount of pain—and then sort of stood back and sort of moved his hand and I just came right up out of the car, standing right in front of him, and he asked me, 'Are you the Watchman of this town?' And I said, 'Yes, I am.'

"The crew leader had a very high forehead, a very long nose; his eyes were sort of sunken in, and they were round eyes like ours, except for their pupils . . . were sort of the form of a, I would say, like a cat's eye. And their complexion was sort of a grayish-pink. I couldn't see any hair or ears because they were covered by the form of the uniform over their head; there was like a small black box on the other side with a very small antenna sticking up out of it. The mouth was sort of a slit, and as he spoke to me, it came like a very deep tone of voice, like from deep within, and he didn't move his mouth at all.

"He said, 'Watchman, come with me . . .' and we went up to the craft; and as we got to the craft, he took me up into what I call the first level of it . . . and we're standing there looking at these, like 55-gallon barrel drums in a big circle (in the first level), and had black cables being connected to each one of them. And then right in the center of the room, as we looked up, was like a half of a cocoon— and it was spinning, giving off bright colors like the rainbow. And he said, 'Watchman, this is our power source: reversible electrical-magnetism.' We moved over to where we came up in, and just kind of floated up into the second level—just zzzzz!—like you go up on an elevator. It was like red light inside, and this big cone was spinning, and there was all kinds of panels and computers and stuff like this; and there was a map on the wall, and there was this large screen, like a vision screen there . . . and he walked up and he pressed some buttons, and he pointed toward the stars and he said, 'That's where we're from. . . .' There was writing on the map and I couldn't tell really what it was—it was a map of a sun and six planets! They were from a nearby galaxy and that's all he ever said . . . he never said exactly where they were from or anything . . . he just pointed at the map. They were observing us and had been observing us for a long time.

"He said, 'Watchman, the reason why we're here is to get electricity,' and they extracted electricity from one of the power poles there, which led to the main power source there in Ashland. And this sort of antenna that was on the edge of the ship kind of lifted down . . . this one was pressing buttons . . . and a bolt went out and hit the big transformer and bolted back; and the pole was burning, and it went like that for maybe a minute or so, and they shut it off.

"In the top part of where we were was like an observation deck—there was panels and chairs and a big observation window there; and he told me . . . he said, 'Watchman (and he pointed toward the stars), you yourself will see the universe as *I* have seen it.'

"He said, 'Watchman, come with me . . .' and we went back and went straight down and outside and started walking toward the patrol car. And as we approached the car, he said, 'Watchman, what you have seen and what you have heard, you will not remember. The only thing that you'll remember is that you've seen something land and something take off. . . .' And that was it."

The Condon Report concluded as follows: "Evaluation of psychological assessment tests, the lack of any evidence, and interviews with the patrolman, left project staff with no confidence that the trooper's reported UFO experience was physically real." Dr. Sprinkle expressed the opinion that "the trooper believed in the reality of the events he described."

The Schirmer case is a "classic" in more ways than one. (1) It is the quintessential composite of classic UFO lore. (2) The account is told with such exquisite naïveté on the part of the experiencer that no one doubts his sincerity to this day. (3) Likewise, while telling what he clearly believed to be the unvarnished truth, officer Schirmer reveals the primitive state of the average person's knowledge of science and technology—especially astronomy—which earmarks the tale as a fantasy.

More detailed information—which includes edited transcripts of "time-regression" hypnosis sessions by professional hypnotist Loring G. Williams—appears in two books by author-investigator Eric Norman (pen name for Warren Smith): *Gods, Demons and Space Chariots* (1970) and *Gods and Devils from Outer Space* (1973).

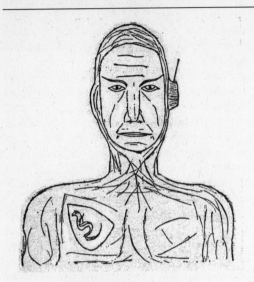

Herbert Schirmer's drawing
of the crew leader

Eric Norman (Warren Smith) in the company of another famed author-investigator, Brad Steiger (pen name for Eugene Olson), extracted a wealth of fascinating detail from Schirmer in their 1968 investigation. Though it doesn't take much to improve upon the pseudoscientific techniques (consisting mostly of academic snobbery) of the so-called Condon Committee, Norman achieved what Condon's "investigators" did not know how to do. Without fanfare, he simply obtained and communicated the relevant information. Through the hypnotic sessions conducted by Williams, Norman uncovered the following details.

According to Schirmer, the spacemen were from a nearby galaxy, but had bases on Venus, Jupiter, and other planets of our solar system. Their purpose in coming to Earth was to obtain electricity from our power lines. Their saucer, which was made of 100 percent pure magnesium, operates on the principle of "reversible electro-magnetism" (whatever that means) and traveled at a speed of 150,000 "something" (Schirmer wasn't sure whether it was miles per hour, miles per second, or what—but it flew pretty darned fast). The spacecraft was 102 feet in diameter, Schirmer was told, and in addition to using measurements in "feet," the aliens also carried standard 55-gallon drums interconnected by cables for some unknown purpose (maybe for the storage of electricity). One is struck by the absence of miniaturization, which is one of the hallmarks of our own advancing technology. The space travelers also had buttons, dials, and gauges on their control panels—another throwback to our own '50s technology—which raises the greatest mystery of all: with this kind of backward technology, how did they ever get here—from another galaxy, no less—in the first place! A ladder was used to enter the "observation ship," as it was called, which sat upon tripod legs.

A large "vision screen" (just like in *Star Trek*) inside the saucer enabled its occupants to see outside. The saucermen were, of course, outfitted with ray guns (which they carried in belt-mounted holsters) and wore one-piece coverall suits which included radio transmitters built in to their skull-cap-type "helmets." Schirmer likened the aliens' uniform to ". . . a flight suit you buy at the Army surplus stores. . . ." Inasmuch as the aliens were said to have telepathic abilities, one wonders why they would still need primitive "walkie-talkie" devices with little antennas sticking out.

Again, this is one of the hallmarks of '50s science fiction, and in fact Schirmer's description closely resembles "The Man from Planet X," from the 1950 film by the same name. Coincidentally, "The Man from Planet X" also had mind-control abilities as did Schirmer's aliens.

Yet another mystery is why intelligent space-faring aliens would establish a base on a planet like Venus—with an atmosphere of sulfuric acid, crushing atmospheric pressure, and a surface temperature high enough to melt lead. Perhaps the aliens are not quite as intelligent as we thought.

Schirmer also said that the spacemen ". . . had a program called 'breeding analysis' and some humans had been used in these experiments." This tidbit anticipates the current genetic-hybrid trend that dominates the new UFOlogy.

One last point should not go unmentioned. While under a hypnotic trance, Schirmer produced a drawing of an emblem the UFOnauts all wore on the upper-right chest portion of their uniforms. It was a serpent with wings. Eric Norman reminds us that this ". . . was an accurate depiction of the feathered serpent" which had been documented throughout our history in ancient Aztec lore, Chinese legends, and all over the world. Norman then posed the question: "Could the UFOnauts and their emblem of the winged serpent be connected with the story of Adam and Eve in the garden of Eden? Was the 'snake' merely a symbol of UFOnauts?"

We now come to the crux of the issue. Does the same symbolism appear in UFOlogy and ancient mythology because extraterrestrials have influenced—or even created—us, or do we project our distinctly human archetypes and culture onto them?

—RONALD D. STORY

References

Blum, Ralph and Judy. *Beyond Earth: Man's Contact with UFOs* (Bantam Books, 1974).

Gillmor, Daniel S., ed. *Scientific Study of Unidentified Flying Objects.* (Bantam Books, 1969). "Final Report of the Scientific Study of Unidentified Flying Objects" Conducted by the University of Colorado under contract to the United States Air Force, Dr. Edward U. Condon, Scientific Director.

Kottmeyer, Martin S. Unpublished notes and personal correspondence.

Norman, Eric. *God's Demons and Space Chariots* (Lancer Books, 1970).

———. *Gods and Devils from Outer Space* (Lancer Books, 1973).

Story, Ronald D., ed. *The Encyclopedia of UFOs* (Doubleday, 1980).

Schuessler, John F.

Schuessler, John F. (b. 1933). John Schuessler has been involved in the U.S. manned space program since 1962 and has been a UFO researcher since 1965. He is a founding member of the Mutual UFO Network (MUFON) and as of July 16, 2000, its International Director. He has written numerous articles for *Skylook* and the *MUFON UFO Journal* and has been a featured speaker at eight MUFON symposia. He administers the MUFON Medical Committee, composed of consultants with medical degrees.

John Schuessler

Schuessler is currently a member of the UFO Research Coalition Board of Directors and a Center for UFO Studies (CUFOS) associate. He was a founding member and past President of the UFO Study Group of Greater St. Louis, Inc., and the Houston-based Vehicle Internal Systems Investigative Team (VISIT).

He has appeared on numerous radio and television programs. In 1996 he cataloged his research in a book entitled *UFO-Related Human Physiological Effects.* In 1998, he published a book entitled *The Cash-Landrum UFO Incident: Three Texans Are Injured During an Encounter with a UFO and Military Helicopters.*

Schuessler retired after 36 years in aerospace engineering with McDonnell Douglas and The Boeing Company, where he was involved in engineering for most manned space programs, from Project Mercury to the International Space Station. He held positions as Project Manager for Space Shuttle Flight

Operations, Director of Engineering, and Director of General Support. In 1998 he was awarded the NASA Public Service Medal for his leadership of the NASA Neutral Buoyancy Laboratory project.

Schuessler holds B.S. and M.S. degrees from the University of Houston, Clear Lake. He is an Associate Fellow in the American Institute of Aeronautics and Astronautics (AIAA), and a member of the Institute of Electrical and Electronics Engineers (IEEE), the American Association for the Advancement of Science (AAAS), the Armed Forces Communications and Electronics Association (AFCEA), the Society for Scientific Exploration (SSE), the National Space Society (NSS), the Planetary Society, and the World Future Society. He is a past member of the NASA Johnson Space Center Human Space Flight Awareness Council, University of Texas Department of Aerospace Engineering Industry Visiting Committee, Houston Ellington Field Airport Development Task Force, Clear Lake Area Economic Development Foundation Education Committee, National Contract Management Association, the Clear Lake Transportation Partnership and past president of the Friends of the Freeman Memorial Library in Houston, Texas.

Address: P.O. Box 369
            Morrison, CO 80465
            U.S.A.

E-mail: schuessler@mho.net

POSITION STATEMENT: After years of amassing information about Unconventional Flying Objects (UFOs) I have come to the conclusion that we are dealing with a very complex mystery on an international scale. While the time-tested ways of investigating this mystery are still useful and must be continued, new approaches must be tried as well.

A basic problem is the lack of cooperation between individuals and groups. Whether or not this is caused by human nature in general or it is a part of some devious plan, it impedes progress, causes data to become obscured and questioned, and is usually harmful to the witnesses and investigators alike. I look forward to greater cooperation in the future through a loose federation of most of the UFO organizations in the world. I look at it as the United Nations of UFOlogy. The power of a federation of this nature has outstanding ramifications for everyone involved.

Another problem stems from the way UFOs are investigated. While it is important to continue to gather and record case information using well-established investigative practices, more must be done. The tools used today in UFO cases are much the same as those used 50 years ago. We need to find ways to tap the myriad new electronic technologies now available in most government agencies for use in UFO investigations.

The characteristics of the objects described in UFO reports appear to evolve over time to stay just beyond the state-of-the-art of technology as we know it. This presents the challenge to researchers to forecast where UFO technology is headed and to develop ways to detect and record the new data as the mystery evolves.

While the quality of UFO investigations improves continuously, we have a tough job ahead. I approach that job with the following points in mind:

- UFO reports worldwide continue unabated.
- The journalistic approach to resolving the mystery has failed. It has only created camps of believers and disbelievers.
- Debating whether or not UFOs exist is futile. As long as we have unresolved reports, UFOs do exist.
- High-quality UFO reports are inspirational to many individuals involved in science and technology. They want to know "what's under the hood."
- Existing technologies, if properly utilized, could aid engineers and scientists in their quest to solve the UFO mystery.
- Until governments decide to support their people with free and open channels of

UFO information, the quest for truth will be a slow and difficult task.
• Our future may depend on the ultimate outcome of UFO research.
—JOHN F. SCHUESSLER

Scully hoax Frank Scully's book *Behind the Flying Saucers* caused a sensation when it was published in 1950. Scully told of three crashed saucers that he claimed were being investigated by officials and scientists of the United States government. According to the story, one flying saucer had crashed in Paradise Valley near Phoenix, Arizona, and the other two were found in the vicinity of Aztec, New Mexico. Thirty-four dead bodies were allegedly found inside the three "spacecraft." The occupants were little humanoids, measuring between thirty-six to forty-two inches in height, and were charred brown, presumably from sudden decompression.

In addition to their small size, there were a few other peculiarities: The little men had no cavities in their teeth, and they drank "heavy" water (about twice as heavy as normal drinking water). There was a food supply on board, consisting of little wafers that when dropped into a pail of water would swell up, causing the water to overflow. The heavy water and concentrated food, it was conjectured, might have been an aid to space flight.

Their dress consisted of dark-blue uniforms without any insignia on their collars or caps to give a clue as to where they might be from (although it was somehow determined that the little fellows hailed from Venus).

Also found on board the disabled saucers were a tiny radio which operated on some unknown principle, some small disks of an unknown metal, a strange fabric, and what appeared to be navigational booklets written in a pictorial type of script.

Scully's chief source of information on the crashed-saucer story was an old friend, one Silas M. Newton, who got the story from a mysterious "Dr. Gee," identified in the book by Scully as "the top magnetic research specialist of the United States." It was said that

Dr. Gee and seven other scientists were called in by the U.S. Air Force to examine the spaceships and their contents. It was never made quite clear why Mr. Newton, an oilman, filled the role as spokesman for Dr. Gee. But no matter, the entire incident was exposed as a hoax by *True* magazine in its September 1952 issue. An investigative reporter, J. P. Cahn, traced Scully's sources to the pair of culprits who made the whole thing up.

Silas Newton, it turned out, had been involved in some other hanky-panky having to do with fraudulent stock practices. Cahn was also able to trace the identity of "Dr. Gee" to one Leo A. GeBauer, the proprietor of Western Radio & Engineering Company, a radio and television parts supply house in Phoenix, Arizona. Scully admitted to Cahn that Mr. GeBauer was indeed "Dr. Gee"; and the book *Behind the Flying Saucers* was confirmed as a hoax.

In 1974, the Scully rumor was revived again by a professor Robert Carr, who was at the time promoting a Flying Saucer Symposium to be held in Tampa, Florida, on November 1-3 of that year. Carr stated at a press conference that, according to his secret sources, the U.S. Air Force was hiding a downed saucer and its twelve deceased occupants at Wright-Patterson AFB in Dayton, Ohio. The professor, who reportedly taught mass communications at the University of Southern Florida, said that an autopsy performed on one of the "little men" revealed that its genes and chromosomes were compatible with those of Earth women. To find out more, one could attend the symposium for the nominal fee of $37.50.

The "little men" stories began surfacing again in 1978. In a lecture given by veteran UFO researcher Leonard H. Stringfield, at the annual Mutual UFO Network (MUFON) Symposium, this one held (appropriately enough) in Dayton, Ohio, on July 29, he said that: "Now, for the first time, sufficient data have been amassed to lend support to some of the old retrieval claims." But the "new" claims—which hark back to the late 1940s and early

1950s—are essentially the same stories told over and over again: The site of the crashed saucer is usually given as Arizona or New Mexico. The military somehow finds out about it first and, under the strictest secrecy, recovers the undamaged craft and its occupants. Top scientists are brought in, who pronounce the find genuine and not of Earth. The descriptions of the occupants are also remarkably consistent: They are small—from three to four feet tall—with a disproportionately large head (with many intricate convolutions in the brain, of course), grayish or tan skin tones, diminutive ears, nose, and mouth; the bodies are hairless or nearly so and are attired in one-piece suits, sometimes with skullcaps of World War I vintage.

In other words, they are patently naïve accounts, not befitting the most unimaginative science fiction writer, and a virtual repeat of Scully's false claims. Stringfield himself admits: ''I do not possess a single affidavit to prove that any one of my informants has seen a retrieved craft or its occupants. I have only their names and their testimony. Unfortunately, I cannot use these names. Anonymity has been requested and will be respected.''

More recently other ''witnesses'' to various facets of flying saucer recovery operations in the American southwest have told their tales. They still amount to unsubstantiated stories, which prohibit further confirmation and are useless to science. However, the infamous Scully hoax is quite enlightening. It demonstrates beautifully the symbiotic relationship that exists between science fact, science fiction, and modern mythology.

What originally inspired the Scully hoax was no doubt the 1947 Roswell incident, in which an announcement was made by a U.S. Air Force representative that a flying saucer had crashed in the New Mexico desert and was recovered by the military. It took just a little imagination to embellish the account, and *presto*: we have the ingredients of a modern myth.

Some years later we have a revival of the Roswell case *(based on recent ''eyewitness'' testimony—not accounts that were documented prior to 1950)*, an alleged alien autopsy film, and reverse engineering at Area 51 of alien technology from the saucers that were recovered and brought to the Roswell base. The story elements are related to each other in a circular relationship that is mutually supportive. If the later embellishments of the Roswell case—details that did not surface prior to 1950—can be traced to the Scully hoax, it appears that the Roswell case rests on a shaky foundation that is not only weak, but fraudulent.

—RONALD D. STORY

References

Cahn, J. P. ''The Flying Saucers and the Mysterious Little Men,'' *True* magazine (September 1952).
The MUFON UFO Journal (July 1978).
Scully, Frank. *Behind the Flying Saucers* (Henry Holt, 1950).

Search for Extraterrestrial Intelligence, The (SETI)

The attempt to locate intelligent civilizations that may exist elsewhere in the universe, SETI is not to be confused with an uncritical or credulous belief in aliens. While the overwhelming majority of scientists reject popular UFO-related claims that alien visitors are surreptitiously visiting Earth, most scientists support SETI as a worthwhile scientific enterprise.

The age of SETI began in 1960, at the National Radio Astronomy Observatory (NRAO) in West Virginia, when Dr. Frank Drake carried out Project Ozma, a search for intelligent signals at the twenty-one centimeter wavelength of interstellar hydrogen. Using an eighty-five-foot radio telescope, Project Ozma examined only two stars: Epsilon Eridani and Tau Ceti.

From 1972 to 1976, also at the NRAO, Dr. Benjamin M. Zuckerman and Dr. Patrick Palmer continued this work, with Project Ozma II. The second Ozma had the use of radio telescopes as large as three hundred feet in diameter, gathering nearly twelve and a half times as much radio energy as an eighty-five-foot dish. Where the first Ozma had just a single radio receiver, Ozma II had 384, each one tuned to a slightly different wavelength (in the vicinity of the target wavelength). Project Ozma examined only two stars, whereas Project Ozma II examined seven hundred.

At Ohio State University, Dr. Robert S. Dixon began conducting a twenty-four-hour, all-sky SETI survey in December of 1973, continuing until 1998 when the "Big Ear" radio telescope was dismantled. No attempt was made to pre-select target stars in advance (the rotation of the Earth constantly sweeps the ear of the radio telescope across the sky); hence, there were an average of three favorable nearby stars being examined at any moment of the night or day. The Ohio State project is planning to resume after new equipment can be designed and built.

The Harvard SETI project, led by physics professor Paul Horowitz, began a small-scale observing project in 1978 using the 1,000-foot Arecibo radio telescope in Puerto Rico. During the 1980s more sophisticated receivers were built to search a greater number of simultaneous targets with greater sensitivity and accuracy. By 1985, a million-channel SETI radio array was on-line at Harvard in Massachusetts. Since 1995, a billion-channel array has been in operation, searching for possible alien transmissions.

The SETI Institute of Mountain View, California, was founded in 1984 to "conduct scientific research and educational projects relevant to the nature, prevalence, and distribution of life in the universe." Among its directors is SETI pioneer Frank Drake. It has been conducting a search project that targets approximately one thousand sun-like stars using several different radio telescopes in both the northern and southern hemispheres.

Between 1978 and 1994, NASA was given a limited amount of funding for SETI programs. However, the project was unpopular with Congress, and funding was cut off several times. Currently, all U.S. SETI projects are privately financed; however, NASA's efforts in the search for extraterrestrial life are being stepped up dramatically at the present time.

Contrary to what some people suggest, UFO skepticism is not synonymous with Earth chauvinism. Paradoxically, UFOlogists have largely been critics of scientific SETI projects, while some of the best-known proponents of the idea of SETI have been UFO skeptics, such as the late astronomer Carl Sagan. Many UFOlogists, on the other hand, take a dim view of SETI, viewing it as a competitor for resources that otherwise might be available to them. However, the scientific community has almost unanimously supported the view that unlike SETI, UFO beliefs are not based upon the kind of critical thinking that is a part of the scientific method.

As of yet, no SETI project has turned up any solid evidence of any extraterrestrial artificial radio source. A few radio "glitches" have been detected, but could not subsequently be confirmed, and were probably due to terrestrial interference. While there is no way of knowing for certain when (or if) the first detection of an alien civilization will take place, we would all do well to keep in mind the tremendous obstacles to early success in the SETI field.

Dr. Frank Drake has estimated that the total number of combinations of wavelength, direction, bandwidth, and other parameters which must be searched to find the first extraterrestrial signal is on the order of 10^{19} (1 followed by 19 zeroes). Assuming this estimate to be correct, it could take more than three hundred billion years before we detect the first alien signal.

Fortunately, there are certain plausible SETI assumptions which, if correct, might make this seemingly hopeless undertaking less than totally futile. For example, if all intelligent civilizations in the universe realized this problem and adopted some "natural" wavelength—perhaps one related to the prominent twenty-one-centimeter wavelength of interstellar hydrogen—our one-combination-a-second search might find an alien civilization as often as once every thirty years. Also, modern SETI receivers can search millions of channels at the same time. Perhaps Drake's estimates will turn out to have been overly pessimistic as to the number of alien civilizations in our galaxy, the strength of their radio signals, and the average distance between civilizations. On the other hand, some astronomers believe that he may have been far too optimistic.

Perhaps we are located in a region where we have one or more interstellar neighbors nearby—much closer than the average distance between civilizations—or we may happen to reside in an exceptionally lonely corner of the universe. In any case, the search for extraterrestrial intelligence is certain to be a long, tedious, and trying undertaking. It will require large commitments of capital, manpower, and scientific expertise for an indefinite period of time, with no guarantee of eventual success.

As SETI advances, a "counterrevolution" of SETI skeptics has likewise gained ground in the scientific community. A controversial conference was held at the University of Maryland in 1979. Participating were such well-known SETI advocates and theorists as Ronald Bracewell, Sebastian Von Hoerner, Benjamin Zuckerman, Patrick Palme, Freeman Dyson, and Michael Papagiannis. The general theme of the conference was that, using space colonies as giant, lumbering space-arks to spend centuries crossing interstellar space, it should be possible for a single civilization to colonize the entire galaxy in roughly ten million years—just a tiny fraction of the age of the galaxy. If millions or billions of other civilizations far older than ours are supposedly out there, why has not one of them progressed to this stage? The logical conclusion would seem to be that it is because we are alone in the galaxy—perhaps even in the universe. The most pessimistic of SETI skeptics, astronomer Michael Hart of Trinity University, told the conference that even the most ridiculously optimistic estimate of the occurrence of life in the universe yields far less than one planet having life in each galaxy. In fact, Hart estimates, at most only one galaxy in 10^{31} has even a single planet with life of any kind.

Astrophysicist Frank J. Tipler of Tulane University, finds the "Where Are They?" objection to extraterrestrials quite insurmountable, charging SETI advocates with promoting unfalsifiable, and hence pseudoscientific, hypotheses: "SETI will become a science—and hence be worth doing—only when its proponents tell us exactly what will convince them that it is reasonable to assume we are alone."

Also weighing in with the SETI doubters were physicist James Trefil and the late astrophysicist Thornton Page, who had taken a mildly pro-UFO stance starting in the 1960s. In 2000, the book *Rare Earth* by scientists Peter Ward and Donald C. Brownlee, mustered new support for the SETI pessimists' position. They argue that recent scientific discoveries suggest that extrasolar planets are generally subjected to far more meteoric bombardment, and far greater orbital instability, than our Earth, making the Earth with its abundant and varied life-forms a cosmic rarity.

Today, thousands of individuals are participating in the SETI effort, using their home computers. A number of sponsors, including the Planetary Society, the University of Califonia, and numerous high-tech companies have established the *SETI@home* project. The software runs in the background like a "screen saver" when your computer is idle, analyzing data from radio telescopes downloaded over the Internet. Should anything unusual turn up, scientists are alerted. This allows SETI researchers to use the resources of thousands of individual computers for data analysis without cost.

Nobody knows when, or whether, the first evidence of extraterrestrial intelligence will be discovered.

—ROBERT SHEAFFER

Secret Life (Simon and Schuster, 1993). Temple University history professor David Jacobs believes aliens are here to exploit us in a program of genetic alteration of our species that begins for abductees in childhood. He has performed more than 325 hypnosis sessions with 60 abductees. From this information Ja-

cobs found a pattern of remarkably similar stories being told of the abductees being subjected to the same mental and physical tests and procedures by the aliens.
—RANDALL FITZGERALD

SETI Institute Founded on the initiative of Tom Pierson in 1984, the SETI Institute is a nonprofit organization that fosters research programs related to the search for extraterrestrial life. It was originally set up in the time of the NASA SETI program to minimize the amount of monies spent on overhead. After the elimination of the NASA program in 1993, the SETI Institute became the nexus of its privately funded successors, as well as the home of related research.

Today, the SETI Institute runs Project Phoenix, the most comprehensive radio SETI search, and is engaged (with the University of California, Berkeley) in constructing the Allen Telescope Array. In addition, it manages approximately 40 other research projects dealing with such related topics as the question of life in the solar system, the origin of terrestrial life, and the nature of cosmic biogenic materials. These latter projects are principally funded by the National Science Foundation and NASA. The Institute also runs a comprehensive program for education and outreach.

In 2001, the Chairman of the Board of the Institute was Frank Drake, and its Chief Executive Officer was Tom Pierson. The Institute's offices are in Mountain View, California, approximately 40 miles south of San Francisco.
—SETH SHOSTAK

Address: 2035 Landings Drive
            Mountain View, CA 94043
            U.S.A.

Web site: www.seti.org

shapes of UFOs It is essentially true what astronomer Donald Menzel wrote in his 1963 book *The World of Flying Saucers* (co-authored with Lyle Boyd), that "No two reports describe exactly the same kind of UFO."

A rare exception is seen in the accompanying photographs. One photo was taken by a farmer, Paul Trent, near McMinnville, Oregon, on May 11, 1950, and the other by a pilot over Rouen, France, in the summer of 1954.

McMinnville above; Rouen below

Nevertheless, in spite of the great diversity of reports, some general patterns have been noted with respect to UFO shapes. The disk shape is clearly the most common, representing about 26 percent of all UFOs reported. Spheres account for about 17 percent, and oval or elliptical shapes make up roughly 13 percent. According to the U.S. Air Force Project Grudge Report of December 1949, the basic types of shapes were broken down as follows:

(1) "The most numerous reports indicate daytime observation of metallic disk-like objects roughly in diameter ten times their thickness."

(2) "Rocket-like objects."

(3) "Sharply defined luminous objects" appearing as lights at night.

An analysis of UFO cases by the National Investigations Committee on Aerial Phenomena (NICAP), for the period of 1942 to the end of 1963, found that the above pattern was "well established."

Investigators for Project Blue Book later found it necessary to increase the number of shape-descriptive terms for coding purposes. The following table presents these shape terms and the percentage and number of UFO sightings evaluated (by a panel of judges) to be of unknown nature with at least 95 percent certainty. These values represent UFO entries for the period 1947 to 1952 (Project Blue Book, Special Report No. 14, Air Technical Intelligence Center, Wright-Patterson AFB, Ohio, May 5, 1955).

Another source of UFO-shape terms is found in Jacques Vallée's book, *Passport to Magonia* (1969), from which a total of 891 cases was reviewed (cases 32 through 923) for the period October 28, 1902, to November 22, 1968. Four hundred and forty-five cases (49.9 percent) were found to possess a total of 79 single words of phrases representing perceived shape.

(See also Haines, R. F., "UFO Appearance Recognition and Identification Test Procedure," *UFO Phenomena,* Vol. 1, No. 1, 1976.)

Still other shapes have been reported by eyewitnesses. Some of them are listed here to further illustrate the extremely wide range of object-shape terms people feel they must refer to in order to describe what they perceived: "arrowhead," "ball," "balloon," "bird-like," "cushion," "dart," "discus," "dots," "dumbbell," "globular," "hamburger sandwich," "jumbo jet (without wings)," "oyster shell with ribbed structure," "pea," "pinpoint," "rhomboid," "Saturn disk," "smudge," "tadpole," "teardrop," "triangle," "water tank," "wedge."

Since around the mid-1980s, more boomerang and triangular-shaped objects have been reported in ever-increasing numbers. The objects seem to display a preponderance of straight edges and equally spaced circular sources of light on their surfaces. As Fowler (1996, 1997) and others have made clear,

ultra-large, silent, three-sided (often dark) aerial objects have been appearing over much of the globe. The debate continues over whether these triangular objects are of terrestrial or extraterrestrial origin. Interestingly, stronger arguments can be made on the extraterrestrial side.

Since it is a truism that a picture is worth a thousand "shape" words, what is known about drawings of UFOs by eyewitnesses? The illustrations that accompany this encyclopedia entry (pp. 538-541) present eyewitness drawings obtained from the open UFO literature and grouped into similar-shape categories. Each drawing has been reduced to fit the available space without appreciably changing the original line thickness, shadow, or other basic details; all identifying labels, symbols, or markings were deleted, however.

It should be noted that photographs of alleged UFOs tend to correspond to the drawings made by eyewitnesses. The reader may confirm this observation for himself or herself.

Visual perception of an unexpected anomalous phenomenon is subject to numerous kinds of transformations (e.g., deletions, distortions, additions) which can, later, appear in a UFO drawing (see Haines, R. F., *Observing UFOs,* 1979; Wertheimer, M., in *Scientific Study of Unidentified Flying Objects,* 1968). Also, there may well be cultural or symbolic correlations between reported or drawn UFO shapes and the psychological state of the witness (see Grinspoon and Persky, in *UFO's—A Scientific Debate,* 1972; Jung, *Flying Saucers: A Modern Myth of Things Seen in the Skies,* 1959). The apparent symmetry of many UFO-shape drawings could have significance for those interested in attempting to identify the true nature of the "core" of the UFO phenomenon, and for those interested in perceptual and psychological factors of eyewitnesses. Indeed, Carl Jung suggested (in *Flying Saucers: A Modern Myth of Things Seen in the Skies,* 1959), regarding the round object, that ". . . whether it be a disk or a sphere—we at once get an analogy with the symbol of totality well known to

Summary of UFO Shapes from U.S. Air Force Project Blue Book, Special Report 14		
Shape Term:	Total:	Percentage:*
Elliptical	331	66.5
Rocket & Aircraft	43	8.6
Meteor or Comet	8	1.6
Lenticular, Conical or Teardrop	32	6.4
Flame	1	3.6
Other Shapes	66	13.3
Sum =	498	100.0

Note: *Based upon 498 cases.

all students of depth psychology, namely the 'mandala' (Sanskrit for 'circle'). This is not by any means a new invention, for it can be found in all epochs and in all places, always with the same meaning, and reappears time and again, independently of tradition.''

In UFO sightings in which the phenomenon was larger than a point of light (i.e., possessed apparent area), a perceived two- and three-dimensional shape becomes one of the most prominent physical characteristics available for study. Literally thousands of UFO eyewitness drawings, verbal descriptions, and photographs of this nature are available. In order to properly evaluate the UFO-shape data that are available, several useful operating principles must be adhered to:

1. A clear distinction must be made, and maintained, between the physical *form* (geometric configuration of boundaries) of the stimulus that produced a UFO report or drawing and its associated perceived *shape* (see Bartley, *Principles of Perception,* 1958).
2. Three-dimensional object forms can present a very large number of shapes depending upon their orientation with respect to the observer and illumination source(s) (see Haines, 1994; Wertheimer, 1968).
3. Eyewitness drawings can be useful for analysis and classification purposes if they are obtained in the proper way (see Haines, *Observing UFOS,* 1979; Shepard, in *UFO Phenomena and the Behavioral Scientist,* 1979).
4. It must not necessarily be assumed that UFO phenomena have to maintain a fixed (rigid) physical form throughout a given sighting. Many cases are available to document this principle. A corollary to this is that perceived shape does not necessarily have to remain fixed throughout a given sighting (e.g., see case #386 in Vallée's *Passport to Magonia,* 1969).

Several useful references are available to the interested reader on the subject of UFO shapes (Haines, ''UFO Drawings by Witnesses and Non-witnesses: Is There Something in Common?'' in *UFO Phenomena,* Vol. 2, No. 1, 1977; Hall, *The UFO Evidence,* 1964; Shepard, ''Some psychologically oriented techniques for the scientific investigation of unidentified aerial phenomena,'' in *Symposium on Unidentified Flying Objects,* U.S. House of Representatives, July 29, 1968; and ''Photographs of alleged UFOS,'' Takanashi, *Worldwide UFO Photos,* 1977). There are also thousands of drawings of UFOs in the files of the U.S. Air Force which are now publicly available, and private UFO study groups in many nations collect eyewitness drawings and photographs. This storehouse of data provides the basis for the above summary of UFO shapes and for further research which investigators may pursue.

Since the first version of this entry appeared in *The Encyclopedia of UFOs* (1980), an intensive study of how children portray UFOs through drawings has been conducted. (Kerth and Haines, 1992) Among the fascinating discoveries was that older children tended to draw more complex shapes that are increasingly wider than thick. Drawings of entities—particularly aliens—peaked at age 8 to 10 years with a steady decline thereafter. Girls drew more entities and attributed less hostile intent by them than boys. Such findings as these suggest the existence of important sociological and psychological precursors leading to unconscious UFO protosymbols.

—RICHARD F. HAINES

References

Bartley, S. Howard. *Principles of Perception* (Harper, 1958).

Fowler, O. *The Flying Triangle Mystery* (Phenomenon Research Association, 1996).

———. *"Flying Triangle" UFOs: The Continuing Story* (Phenomenon Research Association, 1997).

Haines, Richard F., ed. *UFO Phenomena and the Behavioral Scientist* (The Scarecrow Press, 1979).

Haines, Richard F. *Observing UFOs* (Nelson-Hall, 1980).

———. *Project Delta: A Study of Multiple UFOs* (LDA Press, 1994).

Hall, Richard H., ed *The UFO Evidence* (NICAP, 1964).

Jung, Carl G. *Flying Saucers: A Modern Myth of Things Seen in the Skies* (Princeton University Press, 1978).

Kerth, Linda, and Richard F. Haines. "How Children Portray UFOs," *Journal of UFO Studies* (1992).

Menzel, Donald H., and Lyle G. Boyd. *The World of Flying Saucers* (Doubleday, 1963).

Shepard, Roger N. "Some Psychologically Oriented Techniques for the Scientific Investigation of Unidentified Aerial Phenomena" in *Symposium on Unidentified Flying Objects,* U.S. House of Representatives, July 29, 1968 (U.S. Government Printing Office, 1968).

Story, Ronald D., ed. *The Encyclopedia of UFOs* (Doubleday/New English Library, 1980).

Vallée, Jacques. *Passport to Magonia* (Nelson-Hall, 1980).

Wertheimer, Michael. "Perceptual Problems" in *Scientific Study of Unidentified Flying Objects*, edited by Daniel S. Gillmor (Bantam Books, 1969).

Shaver mystery, The   Also known as the "Shaver hoax," this was a publishing phenomenon created in 1945 by Raymond A. Palmer, then editor of *Amazing Stories* (a science fiction pulp magazine) from letters the magazine received from a paranoid schizophrenic by the name of Richard S. Shaver. The Shaver mystery is significant because it spawned the modern myth of "flying saucers"—two years prior to the first sighting wave, which occurred in June 1947. For this reason, Ray Palmer is considered by those who know their history, as "the man who invented flying saucers."

Just as other imaginative writers had done before him, Palmer took an idea—a myth or speculation—and turned it into "reality." For example: North America's "Bigfoot" was nothing more than an Indian legend until a zoologist named Ivan T. Sanderson began collecting contemporary sightings of the creature in the early 1950s, publishing the reports in a series of popular magazine articles. He turned the tall, hairy biped into a household word, just as British author Rupert T. Gould rediscoved sea serpents in the 1930s and, through his radio broadcasts, articles, and books, brought Loch Ness to the attention of the world. Another writer named Vincent Gaddis originated the Bermuda Triangle in his 1965 book, *Invisible Horizons: Strange Mysteries of the Sea.* Sanderson and Charles Berlitz later added to the Triangle lore, and rewriting their books became a cottage industry among hack writers in the United States.

Charles Fort put bread on the table of generations of science fiction writers when, in his 1931 book *Lo!*, he assembled the many reports of objects and people strangely transposed in time and place, and coined the term "teleportation." And it took a politician named Ignatius Donnelly to revive lost Atlantis and turn it into a popular subject. (Donnelly's book, *Atlantis*, published in 1882, set off a 50-year wave of Atlantean hysteria around the world.)

But the man responsible for the most well-known of all such modern myths—flying saucers—has been largely forgotten. Before the first flying saucer was sighted in 1947, he suggested the idea to the American public. Then he converted UFO reports from what might have been a Silly Season phenomenon into a *subject,* and kept that subject alive during periods of total public disinterest.

Born in 1911, Ray Palmer suffered severe injuries that left him dwarfed in stature and partially crippled. He had a difficult childhood because of his infirmities and, like many isolated young men in those pre-television days, he sought escape in "dime novels," cheap magazines printed on coarse paper and filled with lurid stories churned out by writers who were paid a penny a word. He became an avid science fiction fan, and during the Great Depression of the 1930s he was active in the world of fandom—a world of mimeographed fanzines and heavy correspondence. (Science fiction fandom still exists and is very well organized with well-attended annual conventions and lavishly printed fanzines, some of which are even issued weekly.) In 1930, he sold his first science fiction story, and in 1933 he created the Jules Verne Prize Club which gave out annual awards for the best achievements in sci-fi. A facile writer with a robust imagination, Palmer was able to earn many pennies during the dark days of the Depression, undoubtedly buoyed by his mischievous sense of humor, a fortunate development motivated by his unfortunate physical problems. Pain was his constant companion.

In 1938, the Ziff-Davis Publishing Company in Chicago purchased a dying magazine titled *Amazing Stories.* It had been created in 1929 by the inestimable Hugo Gernsback, who is generally acknowledged as the father of modern science fiction. Gernsback, an electrical engineer, ran a small publishing empire of magazines dealing with radio and technical subjects. (He also founded *Sexology*, a magazine of soft-core pornography disguised as science, which enjoyed great success in a somewhat conservative era.) It was his practice to sell—or even give away—a magazine when its circulation began to slip. Although *Amazing Stories* was one of the first of its kind, its readership was down to a mere 25,000 when Gernsback unloaded it on Ziff-Davis. William B. Ziff decided to hand the editorial reins to the young science fiction buff from Milwaukee, Wisconsin. At the age of 28, Palmer found his life's work.

Expanding the pulp magazine to 200 pages (and as many as 250 pages in some issues), Palmer deliberately tailored it to the tastes of teenaged boys. He filled it with nonfiction features and filler items on science and pseudoscience in addition to the usual formula short stories of BEMs (Bug-Eyed Monsters) and beauteous maidens in distress. Many of the stories were written by Palmer himself under a variety of pseudonyms such as Festus Pragnell and Thorton Ayre, enabling him to supplement his meager salary by paying himself the usual penny-a-word. His old cronies from fandom also contributed stories to the magazine with a zeal that far surpassed their talents. In fact, of the dozen or so science fiction magazines then being sold on the newsstands, *Amazing Stories* easily ranks as the very worst of the lot. Its competitors, such as *Startling Stories, Thrilling Wonder Stories, Planet Stories,* and the venerable *Astounding* (renamed *Analog*) employed skilled, experienced professional writers like Ray Bradbury, Isaac Asimov, and L. Ron Hubbard (who later created Dianetics and founded Scientology). *Amazing Stories* was garbage in comparison and hard-core sci-fi fans tended to sneer at it.

The magazine might have limped through the 1940s, largely ignored by everyone, if not for a single incident. Howard Browne, a tele-

Drawings by Diane Prentice. Copyright © 1980 by Diane Prentice and Ronald D. Story

Drawings by Diane Prentice. Copyright © 1980 by Diane Prentice and Ronald D. Story

Drawings by Diane Prentice. Copyright © 1980 by Diane Prentice and Ronald D. Story

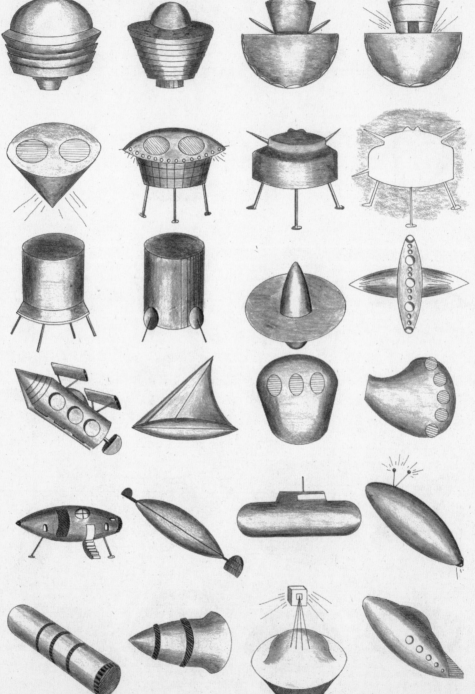

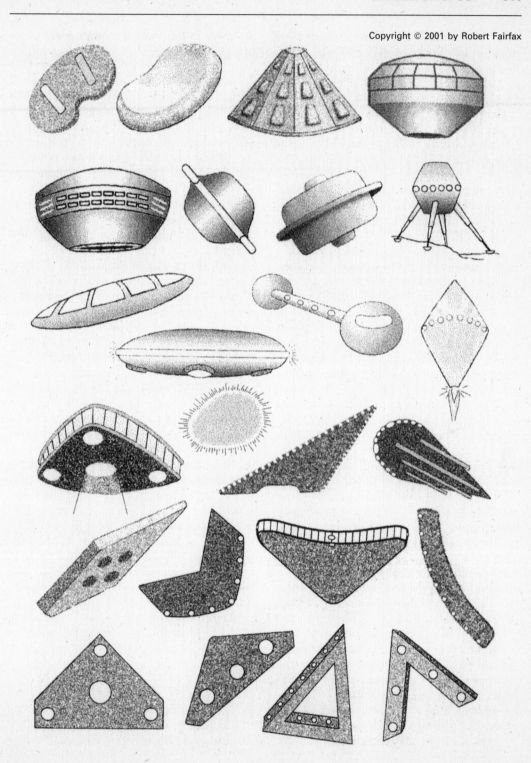

vision writer who served as Palmer's associate editor in those days, recalls: "Early in the 1940s, a letter came to us from Dick Shaver purporting to reveal the 'truth' about a race of freaks called 'deros,' living under the surface of the earth. Ray Palmer read it, handed it to me for comment. I read a third of it, and tossed it in the wastebasket. Ray, who loved to show his editors a trick or two about the business, fished it out of the basket, ran it in *Amazing,* and a flood of mail poured in from readers who insisted every word of it was true because *they'd* been plagued by deros for years." (Goulart, 1972)

Actually, Palmer had accidently tapped a huge, previously unrecognized audience. Nearly every community has at least one person who complains constantly to the local police that someone—usually a neighbor—is aiming a terrible ray gun at their house or apartment. This ray, they claim, is ruining their health, causing their plants to die, turning their bread moldy, making their hair and teeth fall out, and broadcasting voices into their heads. Psychiatrists are very familiar with these "ray" victims and relate the problem with paranoid schizophrenia. (It is estimated there are about three million paranoid schizophrenics in the United States, representing approximately 1 percent of the population.)

For the most part, these paranoiacs are harmless and usually elderly. Occasionally, however, the voices they hear urge them to perform destructive acts, particularly arson. They are a distrustful lot, loners by nature, and very suspicious of everyone, including the government and all figures of authority. In earlier times, they thought they were hearing the voice of God and/or the Devil. Today they often blame the CIA or space beings for their woes. They naturally gravitate to eccentric causes and organizations which reflect their own fears and insecurities, advocating bizarre political philosophies and reinforcing their peculiar belief systems. Ray Palmer unintentionally gave thousands of these people focus to their lives.

Shaver's long, rambling letter claimed that while he was welding he heard voices which explained to him how the underground deros were controlling life on the surface of the Earth through the use of fiendish rays. Palmer rewrote the letter, making a novelette out of it, and it was published in the March 1945 issue under the title: "I Remember Lemuria."

Somehow the news of Shaver's discovery quickly spread beyond science fiction circles and people who had never before bought a pulp magazine were rushing to their local newsstands. The demand for *Amazing Stories* far exceeded the supply and Ziff-Davis had to divert paper supplies (there were still wartime shortages) from other magazines so they could increase the press run of *AS*.

"Palmer traveled to Pennsylvania to talk to Shaver," Howard Brown later recalled, and "found him sitting on reams of stuff he'd written about the deros, bought every bit of it and contracted for more. I thought it was the sickest crap I'd run into. Palmer ran it and doubled the circulation of *Amazing* within four months."

By the end of 1945, *Amazing Stories* was selling 250,000 copies per month, an amazing circulation for a science fiction pulp magazine. Palmer sat up late at night rewriting Shaver's material and writing other short stories about the deros under pseudonyms. Thousands of letters poured into the office. Many of them offered supporting "evidence" for the Shaver stories, describing strange objects they had seen in the sky and strange encounters they had had with alien beings. It seemed that many thousands of people were aware of the existence of some distinctly nonterrestrial group in our midst. Paranoid fantasies were mixed with tales that had the uncomfortable ring of truth. The "Letters-to-the-Editor" section was the most interesting part of the publication. Here is a typical contribution from the issue for June 1946:

Sirs:

I flew my last combat mission on May 26 [1945] when I was shot up over Bassein and ditched my ship in Ramaree Roads off Chedubs Island. I was missing five days. I requested leave at Kashmere [sic]. I and Capt. (deleted by request) left Srinagar and went to Rudok then through the Khese pass to the northern foothills of the Karakoram. We found what we were looking for. We knew what we were searching for.

For heaven's sake, drop the whole thing! You are playing with dynamite. My companion and I fought our way out of a cave with submachine guns. I have two 9" scars on my left arm that came from wounds given me in the cave when I was 50 feet from a moving object of any kind and in perfect silence. The muscles were nearly ripped out. How? I don't know. My friend has a hole the size of a dime in his right bicep. It was seared inside. How we don't know. But we both believe we know more about the Shaver Mystery than any other pair.

You can imagine my fright when I picked up my first copy of *Amazing Stories* and see you splashing words about on the subject.

The identity of the author of this letter was withheld by request. Later Palmer revealed his name: Fred Lee Crisman. He had inadvertently described the effects of a laser beam—even though the laser wasn't invented until years later. Apparently Crisman was obsessed with deros and death rays long before Kenneth Arnold sighted the "first" UFO in June 1947.

In September 1946, *Amazing Stories* published a short article by W. C. Hefferlin, "Circle-Winged Plane," describing experiments with a circular craft in 1927 in San Francisco. Shaver's (Palmer's) contribution to that issue was a 30,000 word novelette, "Earth Slaves to Space," dealing with spaceships that regularly visited the Earth to kidnap humans and haul them away to some other planet. Other stories described amnesia, an important element in the UFO reports that still lay far in the future, and mysterious men who supposedly served as agents for those unfriendly deros.

A letter from army lieutenant Ellis L. Lyon in the September 1946 issue expressed concern over the psychological impact of the Shaver Mystery:

What I am worried about is that there are a few, and perhaps quite a large number of readers who may accept this Shaver Mystery as being founded on fact, even as Orson Welles put across his invasion from Mars, via radio some years ago. It is, of course, impossible for the reader to sift out in your "Discussions" and "Reader Comment" features, which are actually letters from readers and which are credited to an *Amazing Stories* staff writer, whipped up to keep alive interest in your fictional theories. However, if the letters are generally the work of the readers, it is distressing to see the reaction you have caused in their muddled brains. I refer to the letters from people who have "seen" the exhaust trails of rocket ships or "felt" the influence of radiations from underground sources.

Palmer assigned artists to make sketches of objects described by readers and disk-shaped flying machines appeared on the covers of his magazine long before June 1947. So we can note that a considerable number of people—millions—were exposed to the flying saucer concept before the national news media was even aware of it. Anyone who glanced at the magazines on a newsstand and caught a glimpse of the saucers-adorned *Amazing Stories* cover had the image implanted in his subconscious. In the course of the two years between March 1945 and June 1947, millions of Americans had seen at least one issue of *Amazing Stories* and were aware of the Shaver Mystery with all of its bewildering implications. Many of these people were out studying the empty skies in the hope that they, like other *Amazing Stories* readers, might glimpse something wondrous. World War II was over and some new excitement was needed. Raymond

Palmer was supplying it—much to the alarm of Lt. Lyon and Fred Crisman.

Aside from Palmer's readers, two other groups were ready to serve as cadre for the believers. About 1,500 members of Tiffany Thayer's Fortean Society knew that weird aerial objects had been sighted throughout history and some of them were convinced that this planet was under surveillance by beings from another world. Tiffany Thayer was rigidly opposed to Franklin Roosevelt and loudly proclaimed that almost everything was a government conspiracy, so his Forteans were fully prepared to find new conspiracies hidden in the forthcoming UFO mystery. They would become instant experts, willing to educate the press and the public when the time came. The second group were spiritualists and students of the occult headed by Dr. Meade Layne, who had been chatting with the space people at seances through trance mediums and Ouija boards. They knew the spaceships were coming and were hardly surprised when "ghost rockets" were reported over Europe in 1946. Combined, these three groups represented a formidable segment of the population.

On June 24, 1947, Kenneth Arnold made his famous sighting of a group of "flying saucers" over Mt. Rainier, and in Chicago, Ray Palmer watched in astonishment as the newspaper clippings poured in from every state. The things that he had been fabricating for his magazine were suddenly coming true!

For two weeks, the newspapers were filled with UFO reports. Then they tapered off and the Forteans howled "Censorship!" and "Conspiracy!" But dozens of magazine writers were busy compiling articles on this new subject and their pieces would appear steadily during the next year. One man, who had earned his living writing stories for the pulp magazines in the 1930s, saw the situation as a chance to break into the "slicks" (better quality magazines printed on glossy or "slick" paper). Although he was 44 years old at the time of Pearl Harbor, he served as a captain in the Marines until he was in a plane accident. Discharged as major (it was the practice to

promote officers one grade when they retired), he was trying to resume his writing career when Ralph Daigh, an editor at *True* magazine, assigned him to investigate the flying saucer enigma. Thus, at the age of 50, Donald E. Keyhoe entered Never-Never-Land. His article, "Flying Saucers Are Real," would cause a sensation, and Keyhoe would become an instant UFO personality.

That same year, Palmer decided to put out an all-flying saucer issue of *Amazing Stories*. Instead, the publisher demanded that he drop the whole subject after, according to Palmer, two men in Air Force uniforms visited him. Palmer decided to publish a magazine of his own. Enlisting the aid of Curtis Fuller, editor of a flying magazine, and a few other friends, he put out the first issue of *Fate* in the spring of 1948. A digest-sized magazine printed on the cheapest paper, *Fate* was as poorly edited as *Amazing Stories* and had no impact on the reading public. But it was the only newsstand periodical that carried UFO reports in every issue. The *Amazing Stories* readership supported the early issues wholeheartedly.

In the fall of 1948, the first flying saucer convention was held at the Labor Temple on 14th Street in New York City. Attended by about thirty people, most of whom were clutching the latest issue of *Fate,* the meeting quickly dissolved into a shouting match. Although the flying saucer mystery was only a year old, the side issues of government conspiracy and censorship already dominated the situation because of their strong emotional appeal. The U.S. Air Force had been sullenly silent throughout 1948 while, unbeknownst to the UFO advocates, the boys at Wright-Patterson Air Force Base in Ohio were making a sincere effort to untangle the mystery.

When the Air Force investigation failed to turn up any tangible evidence (even though the investigators accepted the extraterrestrial theory) General Hoyt Vandenburg, Chief of the Air Force and former head of the CIA, ordered a negative report to release to the public. The result was Project Grudge, hundreds of pages of irrelevant nonsense that was unveiled around the time *True* magazine printed Keyhoe's pro-UFO article. Keyhoe took this personally, even though his article was largely a rehash of Fort's books, and Ralph Daigh had decided to go with the extraterrestrial hypothesis because it seemed to be the most commercially acceptable theory (that is, it would sell magazines).

Palmer's relationship with Ziff-Davis was strained now that he was publishing his own magazine. ''When I took over from Palmer in 1949,'' Howard Browne said, ''I put an abrupt end to the Shaver Mystery—writing off over 7,000 dollars worth of scripts.''

The September 1948 *Fantastic Stories* included this illustration for a ''factual'' article about a Russian peasant who had been ''burned by a ray from a ship from another world.''

Moving to Amherst, Wisconsin, Palmer set up his own printing plant and eventually he printed many of those Shaver stories in his *Hidden World* series. As it turned out, postwar inflation and the advent of television was kill-

ing the pulp magazine market anyway. In the fall of 1949, hundreds of pulps suddenly ceased publication, putting thousands of writers and editors out of work. *Amazing Stories* has often changed hands since but is still being published, and is still paying its writers a penny a word. For some reason known only to himself, Palmer chose not to use his name in *Fate*. Instead, a fictitious ''Robert N. Webster'' was listed as editor for many years. Palmer established another magazine, *Search*, to compete with *Fate*. *Search* became a catch-all for inane letters and occult articles that failed to meet *Fate*'s low standards.

Although there was a brief revival of public and press interest in flying saucers following the great wave of the summer of 1952, the subject largely remained in the hands of cultists, cranks, teenagers, and housewives who reproduced newspaper clippings in little mimeographed journals and looked up to Palmer as their fearless leader.

In June 1956, a major four-day symposium on UFOs was held in Washington, D.C. It was unquestionably the most important UFO affair of the 1950s and was attended by leading military men, government officials, and industrialists. Men like William Lear, inventor of the Lear Jet, and assorted generals, admirals and former CIA heads freely discussed the UFO ''problem'' with the press. Notably absent were Ray Palmer and Donald Keyhoe. One of the results of the meetings was the founding of the National Investigation Committee on Aerial Phenomena (NICAP) by a physicist named Townsend Brown. Although the symposium received extensive press coverage at the time, it was subsequently censored out of UFO history by the UFO cultists themselves—primarily because they had not participated in it.

The American public was aware of only two flying saucer personalities, contactee George Adamski, a lovable rogue with a talent for obtaining publicity, and Donald Keyhoe, a zealot who howled ''Cover-up!'' and was locked in mortal combat with Adamski for newspaper coverage. Since Adamski was the more colorful (he had ridden a saucer to the moon), he was usually awarded more attention. The press gave him the title of "astronomer" (he lived in a house on Mount Palomar where a great telescope was in operation), while Keyhoe attacked him as "the operator of a hamburger stand." Ray Palmer tried to remain aloof from the warring factions, so, naturally, some of them turned against him.

The year 1957 was marked by several significant developments. There was another major flying saucer wave. Townsend Brown's NICAP floundered and Keyhoe took it over. And Ray Palmer launched a new newsstand publication called *Flying Saucers From Other Worlds*. In the early issues he hinted that he knew some important "secret." After tantalizing his readers for months, he finally revealed that UFOs came from the center of the Earth and the phrase *From Other Worlds* was dropped from the title. His readers were variously enthralled, appalled, and galled by the revelation.

For seven years, from 1957 to 1964, UFOlogy in the United States was in total limbo. This was the Dark Age. Keyhoe and NICAP were buried in Washington, vainly tilting at windmills and trying to initiate a congressional investigation into the UFO situation.

A few hundred UFO believers clustered around Coral Lorenzen's Aerial Phenomena Research Organization (APRO). And about 2,000 teenagers bought *Flying Saucers* from newsstands each month. Palmer devoted much space to UFO clubs, information exchanges, and letters-to-the-editor. So it was Palmer, and Palmer alone, who kept the subject alive during the Dark Age and lured new youngsters into UFOlogy. He published his strange books about deros, and ran a mail-order business selling the UFO books that had been published after the various waves of the 1950s. His partners in the *Fate* venture bought him out, so he was able to devote his full time to his UFO enterprises.

Palmer had set up a system similar to sci-fi fandom, but with himself as the nucleus. He had come a long way since his early days and

the Jules Verne Prize Club. He had been instrumental in inventing a whole system of belief, a frame of reference—the magical world of Shaverism and flying saucers—and he had set himself up as the king of that world. Once the belief system had been set up, it became self-perpetuating. The people beleaguered by mysterious rays were joined by the wishful thinkers who hoped that living, compassionate beings existed out there beyond the stars. They didn't need any real evidence. The belief itself was enough to sustain them.

When a massive new UFO wave—the biggest one in U.S. history—struck in 1964 and continued unabated until 1968, APRO and NICAP were caught unaware and unprepared to deal with renewed public interest. Palmer increased the press run of *Flying Saucers* and reached out to a new audience. Then, in the 1970s, a new Dark Age began. October 1973 produced a flurry of well-publicized reports and then the doldrums set in. NICAP strangled in its own confusion and dissolved in a puddle of apathy, along with scores of lesser UFO organizations. Donald Keyhoe went into seclusion before he died in 1988. Most of the hopeful contactees and UFO investigators of the 1940s and '50s have also passed away. Palmer's *Flying Saucers* quietly self-destructed in 1975, but he continued with *Search* until his death in the summer of 1977. Richard Shaver is gone but the Shaver Mystery still has a few adherents. Yet the sad truth is that none of this might have come about if Howard Browne hadn't scoffed at that letter in that dingy editorial office in that faraway city so long ago.

—JOHN A. KEEL

References

Goulart, Ron. *Cheap Thrills: An Informal History of the Pulp Magazines* (Arlington House, 1972).

Keel, John A. "The Man Who Invented Flying Saucers," *Fortean Times* (1983).

Wentworth, Jim. *Giants in the Earth: The Amazing Story of Ray Palmer, Oahspe and the Shaver Mystery* (Palmer Publications, 1973).

Sheaffer, Robert M. (b. 1949). Robert Sheaffer is a leading skeptical investigator of UFOs with a lifelong interest in astronomy, UFOs, and the question of life on other worlds. He is a founding member of the *Bay Area Skeptics* in California and the UFO Subcommittee of the Committee for the Scientific Investigation of Claims of the Paranormal (CSICOP), which publishes *The Skeptical Inquirer*. Since 1977 he has written the "Psychic Vibrations" column for that publication.

Mr. Sheaffer is the author of *The UFO Verdict* (1981), *UFO Sightings* (1998), and has appeared on many radio and TV programs. His writings and reviews have appeared in such diverse publications as *Omni, Scientific American, Spaceflight, Astronomy, The Humanist, Free Inquiry, Reason*, and others. He is a contributor to the book *Extraterrestrials—Where Are They?* (Hart and Zuckerman, editors) and to *The UFO Invasion*, (Frazier, Karr, and Nickell, editors). He authored the article on UFOs for Prometheus Book's *Encyclopedia of the Paranormal*, as well as for the *Funk and Wagnalls Encyclopedia*.

Sheaffer has been an invited speaker at the Smithsonian UFO Symposium in Washington, D.C., at the National UFO Conferences held in New York City and in Phoenix, as well as at the First World Skeptics' Congress in Buffalo, New York. He works as a data communications software engineer in California's Silicon Valley, and sings tenor in professional opera productions.

Address: P.O. Box 10441
           San Jose, CA 95157
           U.S.A.

E-mail: robert@debunker.com
Web site: www.debunker.com

POSITION STATEMENT: Judging from the writings of well-known, supposedly serious UFO researchers, the UFO phenomenon would appear to be truly massive in scope. Polls show that millions of individuals believe that they have sighted UFOs. More than a thousand supposed "UFO landings" have been catalogued, indicated by effects such as markings on the ground, or broken sticks. There are thousands if not millions of cases in which individuals say that they have had actual encounters with UFO occupants, the famed "Close Encounters of the Third Kind." In many of these cases the individuals report having been taken aboard the UFO against their will, where they were subjected to various unpleasant medical "examinations" or "procedures."

Yet where is all of the evidence that would be left behind by an unquestionably genuine phenomenon that was as widespread as UFOs supposedly are? Where are the clear and unambiguous UFO photographs, taken by independent photographers who had never met, and whose authenticity is beyond question? Where are the supposed "physical traces" of UFO landings that cannot also readily be attributed to terrestrial causes, such as ordinary metal objects on the ground, or rings of fungus growth? Why do we never see clear, distinct photos of alleged UFO landings, or UFO occupants? Why do we not have countless thousands of instances of unambiguous radar trackings of UFOs crisscrossing the country, the objects being followed from place to place like so many migrating geese? FAA radar routinely tracks the positions of airliners as they travel between cities; why are UFOs not tracked in the same way? This persistent lack of tangible evidence strikes one as highly perplexing, since UFOs reportedly *are* occasionally tracked on radar, and supposedly *are* photographed on occasion. *But in every single UFO incident on record,* the UFO has always managed to slip away before the evidence of its existence became fully convincing. What remarkably secretive behavior! And it is even more astonishing that UFOs have apparently been able to avoid any indisputable encounters with recording instruments, *with 100% infallibility,* while reportedly permitting themselves to be seen by many millions of observers worldwide, over a period of more than fifty years. There is only one satisfactory explanation for this paradox: UFOs, as a phenomenon separate and distinct from all phenomena, simply do not exist.

While there are many proponents of UFOs who choose to portray the current status of the UFO field as that of a fledgling protoscience, soon to become a recognized scientific field, such a view is naively optimistic. The chief obstacle to scientific recognition of UFO studies is that UFOlogists *do not behave* like real scientists. Instead of cooperating in UFO research and investigation, UFOlogy remains largely divided into many small rival factions. Each is convinced that it alone is qualified to conduct "scientific" UFO investigations, regarding other groups as either "crackpots," or else as too unimaginative and timid. Instead of encouraging the presentation of dissenting views, UFO buffs will go to almost any lengths to keep unwelcome views under wraps. Skeptical views are largely excluded from the major UFO publications, except in cartoon-parody form. Even UFO proponents who present findings critical of some particular "classic" UFO case typically find themselves reviled or ignored. In some cases researchers have even been ejected from the organization in which they have long labored for the "crime" of discovering major flaws in a case that that organization's leadership has privately decided must be defended in order to keep up interest among the membership. These organizations then claim that they are building the "new science" of UFOs!

Of course, if UFOlogy were actually a scientific movement, it would welcome any and all critics who can successfully sweep aside bogus "evidence," to better enable its "genuine" evidence, if any, to shine forth. Apparently the UFO proponents themselves realize that their "evidence" is so shallow that it cannot stand up to critical scrutiny.

Hence, despite the lofty pronouncements of those who claim that they are building a "science" of UFOlogy, all we find are tightly knit little sects wrapping themselves in the mantle of science. In genuine science, research tending to promote opposing views is actively encouraged, not systematically excluded, as is

done by today's UFO groups. There will be no "science" of UFOlogy until the UFO proponents start to behave like scientists, until they learn to face up to *dis*confirming facts instead of pretending that they don't exist. Scientists understand that they must always spell out how the theories that they promote might, in principle, be falsified, which UFOlogists are never willing to do. Einstein clearly stated the observational results that, if obtained, would suffice to falsify his Theory of Relativity. But no UFOlogist is willing to state how we could ever establish, at least in principle, that UFOs are not extraterrestrial visitors (or something *even more* bizarre).

In short, the current status of the UFO problem is that no progress has been made in more than fifty years toward anything that can be called a science, and nothing promising is on the horizon. In fact, the quality of research in the UFO field is clearly moving *backwards*, in the direction of greater gullibility: a *credulity explosion* has been going on for decades. At any given time, mainstream UFOlogists are willing to accept claims and stories that just a few years earlier would have been dismissed as outlandish. UFOlogy will remain in the shadow-world of pseudoscience until its practitioners begin to act like real scientists. But I suspect that will never happen, because the leading UFOlogists appear to instinctively understand that if they were to begin to live up to the standards and practices of true science, their treasured "UFO evidence" would slowly melt away like a snowman in the sun.

UFOs are what I term a *jealous phenomenon,* always managing to slip away before the evidence becomes too convincing. (For a detailed explanation of what a *jealous phenomenon* is, see my book *UFO Sightings.*) Because of the UFOs' amazing success—if they are real—at evading unambiguous detection, the conclusion seems inevitable that the UFO phenomenon consists of nothing more than misperceptions, hoaxes, and hysteria. While there are many objects in the sky that can be and often are misperceived as UFOs, the extraterrestrial spacecraft of modern folklore exist only in the overheated imaginations of the UFO sighters and investigators. UFOs will continue to play peek-a-boo with the universe of objective reality for decades on end, for as long as there is anyone willing to show them proper attention. When its supporters finally tire of it and move on to something else, as did the believers in alchemy and spirit-rapping, the UFO phenomenon will fall into oblivion. But for the foreseeable future, the steady stream of movies and TV pseudo-documentaries will serve to keep the public's interest in extraterrestrial visitors at a fever pitch.

—ROBERT SHEAFFER

Shostak, G. Seth (b. 1943). A radio astronomer who has worked for the SETI Institute since 1991, Seth Shostak is well known for his public lectures and writings on the search for extraterrestrial intelligence. He received his B.A. in physics (1965) from Princeton University, and a Ph.D. in astrophysics (1972) from the California Institute of Technology. His doctoral dissertation concerned the dynamics of nearby spiral nebulae as inferred from radio mapping of the 21-cm line, and this was among the first investigations to show the excess rotation—and implied dark matter—in the outer regions of galaxies.

Dr. Shostak worked for more than a decade at the Kapteyn Astronomical Institute, in The Netherlands, and in 1982—together with Jill Tarter—conducted one of the few SETI experiments to be undertaken on the continent. At the SETI Institute, Shostak has participated in Project Phoenix, a highly sensitive scrutiny of nearby star systems for microwave transmissions, and has led the Institute's efforts to bring the excitement of SETI research to the public. He has edited several conference proceedings on SETI, contributed to a half-dozen popular books, and penned the popular science volume *Sharing the Universe: Perspectives on Extraterrestrial Life* (1998). He is the author of approximately 200 published articles on astronomy and SETI.

SETI Institute

Seth Shostak

Address: c/o SETI Institute
             2035 Landings Drive
             Mountain View, CA 94043
             U.S.A.

E-mail: seth@seti.org

POSITION STATEMENT: The belief that UFOs have an extraterrestrial connection is persistent and widespread. Polls taken since the early 1960s consistently show that roughly half the American populace is convinced that alien spacecraft are buzzing the landscape. At the SETI Institute, I regularly receive calls and other communications from people who have witnessed something that they interpret as confirming this belief. However, while such claims are clearly sincere, I've yet to hear of any evidence that would withstand the most rudimentary scrutiny. One can be open to the idea of visiting aliens, in the same way that one can be open to the idea of ghosts (also believed to exist by a sizeable fraction of the populace). But being open to the idea hardly serves to augment its chances for being true. What I find appealing about SETI is that, unlike the UFO phenomenon, a claim that we had found evidence of extraterrestrials would be verifiable by anyone with a radio telescope. The proof would be fixed in the sky, and not simply flitting across it for the momentary amazement of a few lucky viewers. It is my expectation that a confirmed SETI detection, by its obvious reality and its promise of additional information, would suddenly make a half-century of UFO sightings rather uninteresting.

—G. Seth Shostak

Sirius mystery, The In 1976, Robert K. G. Temple received wide attention for his book *The Sirius Mystery*, which claimed to present evidence of extraterrestrial visitations to Earth some 5,000 years ago. It even attained the status of a semi-scientific work, as many were impressed with the scientific-looking train of logic of the book. Temple stated that the Dogon, a tribe in Africa, possessed extraordinary knowledge of the star system Sirius, the brightest star in the sky; the star which became the marker of an important ancient Egyptian calendar; the star which according to some is at the center of beliefs held by the Freemasons; the star which according to some is where the forefathers of the human race might have come from.

Temple claimed that the Dogon possessed

U.S. NAVAL OBSERVATORY

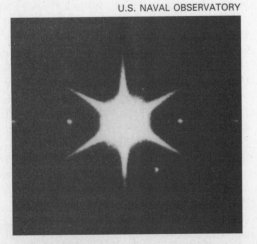

Sirius B is the small dot to the lower right of the bright star Sirius.

knowledge of Sirius B and Sirius C, companion stars to Sirius that are, however, invisible to the naked eye. How did the Dogon know about their existence? Temple referred to legends of a mythical creature "Oannes," who might have been an extraterrestrial being descending to Earth from the stars, to bring wisdom to our forefathers. In 1998, Temple republished the book with the subtitle "New Scientific Evidence of Alien Contact 5,000 Years Ago."

The book's glory came crashing down in the summer of 1999, when Lynn Picknett and Clive Prince published *The Stargate Conspiracy*. That book stated Temple had been highly influenced in his thinking by his mentor, Arthur M. Young. Young was a fervent believer in "the Council of Nine," a group of channelled entities who claim they are the nine creator gods of ancient Egypt. "The Nine" are part of the UFO and New Age and many claim to be in contact with them. "The Nine" also claim to be extraterrestrial beings, from the star Sirius.

In 1952, Young was one of the nine people present during the "first contact" with the Council, where contact was initiated by Andrija Puharich, the man who brought the Israeli spoon bender and presumed psychic Uri Geller to America. It was Young who, in 1965, gave Temple a French article on the secret star lore of the Dogon; an article written by Griaule and Dieterlen.

In 1966, Temple, at the impressionable age of twenty-one, became Secretary of Young's Foundation for the Study of Consciousness. In 1967, Temple began work on what would eventually become *The Sirius Mystery*. As Picknett and Prince have shown, Temple's arguments are often based on erroneous readings of encyclopaedic entries and misrepresentations of ancient Egyptian mythology. They conclude that Temple very much wanted to please his mentor. It is, however, a fact that the end result is indeed a book that would have pleased Young and his beliefs in extraterrestrial beings from Sirius very much, whether or not this was the intention of Temple.

Though Temple's work is now therefore definitely challenged, the core of the mystery remained intact. At the center of this enigma is the work of Marcel Griaule and Germaine Dieterlen, two French anthropologists, who wrote down the secret knowledge on "Sirius B" and "Sirius C" in their book *The Pale Fox*. But now, in another recent publication, *Ancient Mysteries*, by Peter James and Nick Thorpe, this "mystery" is also uncloaked, as a hoax or a lie, perpetrated by Griaule.

To recapitulate, Griaule was initiated in the secret mysteries of the male Dogon, who allegedly told him the secrets of Sirius's invisible companions. Sirius (*sigu tolo* in their language) had two star companions. This was revealed in an article that was published by Griaule and Dieterlen in the French language in 1950.

In the 1930s, when their research occurred, Sirius B was known to have existed, even though it was only photographed in 1970. There was little if no possibility that the Dogon had learned this knowledge from Westerners that had visited them prior to Griaule and Dieterlen.

Griaule and Dieterlen published their findings on the Sirius companions without any reference or comment on how extraordinary the Dogon knowledge was. It would be others, particularly Temple in the sixties and seventies, who would zoom in on that aspect. To quote *Ancient Mysteries*: "While Temple, following Griaule, assumes that *to polo* is the invisible star Sirius B, the Dogon themselves, as reported by Griaule, say something quite different." To quote the Dogon: "When Digitaria (*to polo*) is close to Sirius, the latter becomes brighter; when it is at its most distant from Sirius, Digitaria gives off a twinkling effect, suggesting several stars to the observer." James and Thorpe wonder—as anyone reading this should do—whether *to polo* is therefore an ordinary star near Sirius, *not* an invisible companion, as Griaule and Temple suggest.

The biggest challenge to Griaule, however, came from anthropologist, Walter Van Beek. He points out that Griaule and Dieterlen stand alone in the world in their claims on the secrets

of the Dogon. No other anthropologist supports their opinion or claims.

In 1991, Van Beek led a team of anthropologists who declared that they could find absolutely no trace of the detailed Sirius lore reported by the French anthropologists. James and Thorpe understate the problem when they say that "this is very worrying."

Griaule had stated that about 15 percent of the Dogon tribe knew about this secret knowledge, but Van Beek could, in a decade of research with the Dogon, find not a single trace of this knowledge. Van Beek was initially keen to find evidence for Griaule's claims, but had to admit that there may have been a major problem with Griaule's claims.

Even more worrying is Griaule's background. Though an anthropologist, Griaule was interested in astronomy, which he had studied in Paris. As James and Thorpe point out, he took star maps along with him on his field trips as a way of prompting his informants to divulge their knowledge of the stars. Griaule himself was aware of the discovery of Sirius B and it is quite likely that he overinterpreted the Dogon responses to his questions. In the 1920s, before Griaule went to the Dogon, there were also unconfirmed sightings of Sirius C. Was Griaule told by his informants what he wanted to believe? It seems, alas, that the truth is even worse, at least for Griaule's reputation.

Van Beek actually spoke to the original informants of Griaule, who stated: "though they do speak about *sigu tolo* [interpreted by Griaule as their name for Sirius], they disagree completely with each other as to which star is meant; for some, it is an invisible star that should rise to announce the *sigu* [festival], for another it is Venus that through a different position appears as *sigu tolo*. All agree, however, that they learned about the star from Griaule."

So whatever knowledge they possessed, it was knowledge coming from Griaule, not knowledge native to the Dogon tribe. Van Beek also discovered that the Dogon are of course aware of the brightest star in the sky, which they do not, however, call *sigu tolo*, as Griaule claimed, but *dana tolo*. To quote

James and Thorpe: "As for Sirius B, only Griaule's informants had ever heard of it."

With this, the Dogon mystery comes to a crashing halt. *The Sirius Mystery* influenced more than twenty years of thinking about our possible ancestry from "forefathers" who have come from the stars. In 1996, Temple was quick to point out the new speculation in scientific circles on the possible existence of Sirius C, which made the claims by Griaule even more spectacular and accurate. But Temple was apparently not aware of Van Beek's recent research. With this new research of both Van Beek and the authors of *Ancient Mysteries*, we uncover how Griaule himself was responsible for the creation of a modern myth, which, in retrospect, has created such an industry and almost religious belief that the scope and intensity can hardly be fathomed. Nigel Appleby, in his withdrawn publication *Hall of the Gods*, which was, according to Appleby himself, tremendously influenced by Temple's book, Appleby spoke about how Temple believed that present-day authorities were apparently unwilling to set aside the blinkers of orthodoxy or were unable to admit the validity of anything that lies outside their field or offers a challenge to its status quo. He further wondered whether there was also a modern arrogance that could not countenance the possible scientific superiority of earlier civilizations. It seems, alas, that Griaule, a scientist, wanted to give earlier civilizations more knowledge than they actually possessed. And various popular authors and readers have since been led into a modern mythology: the "Age of the Dark Sirius Companion."

—FILIP COPPENS

Sitchin, Zecharia (b. 1922). Zecharia Sitchin is one of a small number of orientalists who can read the Sumerian clay tablets which trace events from the earliest times. Sitchin was born in Russia and grew up in Palestine, where he acquired a profound knowledge of Semitic and European languages, of the Old Testament, and the history and archaeology of the Near East.

Zecharia Sitchin

He graduated from the University of London, majoring in Economic History, having attended the London School of Economics and Political Science. After a writing career as a journalist, he began writing "The Earth Chronicles"—a series of books that combine the latest scientific discoveries with textual and pictorial evidence from antiquity to form a cohesive and fact-based record of what had really happened on our planet in the past 450,000 years—a tale of visitors to Earth from another planet who created mankind through genetic engineering and shared with mankind more and more of their knowledge and technology. In that record of the Past, Sitchin sees clues to our future.

Zecharia Sitchin is a member of the American Association for the Advancement of Science (AAAS), the American Oriental Society (AOS), the Middle East Studies Association of North America, and the Israel Exploration Society (IES). He was the recipient of the 1996 "Scientist of the Year Award" by the International Forum on New Science.

He has been featured on numerous television and radio programs and written about in journals, magazines, and daily newspapers around the globe.

His books, which have been translated into fourteen languages, include: *The 12th Planet* (1976), *The Stairway to Heaven* (1980), *The*

Wars of Gods and Men (1985), *The Lost Realms* (1990), *Genesis Revisited* (1990), *When Time Began* (1993), *Divine Encounters* (1996), and *The Cosmic Code* (1999).

Address: P.O. Box 577
            New York, NY 10185
            U.S.A.

POSITION STATEMENT: I was fortunate to have studied the Old Testament in its original Hebrew language—fortunate because all translations are in reality interpretations. An incident from my school days will illustrate what I mean:

We reached chapter six of Genesis, which tells the story of the Deluge; but it precedes the tale with seven enigmatic verses that describe the events preceding the Deluge, for those were the days when the "giants" took the daughters of Adam as wives and had children by them. And I raised my hand and asked the teacher why he renders the verse as "giants" when the word the Bible uses is *Nefilim*—which does not mean giants at all, but "those who had come down," and in context from heaven to Earth. Instead of being complimented for my linguistic acumen, I was reprimanded for "questioning the Bible."

Who were the Nefilim? The exchange with the teacher raised this question in my mind to an encompassing obsession. The Bible described them in the same Genesis verses as the "sons of the gods" (plural?)—odd in a Bible devoted to monotheism. It also stated that they were part of the *Anakim* (a term taken to mean "giants"); but who were the Anakim? Studies of ancient Near Eastern languages, civilizations, and archaeological discoveries confirmed that the seven enigmatic verses were a remnant from a pre-biblical "myth." Indeed, the whole tale of the Deluge has been found written on clay tablets, in a script called cuneiform, millennia before the Hebrew Bible was composed. In fact, the whole tale of Creation in Genesis was based on a much longer Mesopotamian tale written on seven tablets. And in time it became evident that the answers to the questions, "Who were the Nefilim?" and "Who were the Anakim?" were to be found in the excavated records of the first known civilization—the Sumerians—which blossomed out in what is now Iraq some 6,000 years ago.

In their writings the Sumerians referred to their gods as *Anunnaki*, literally meaning "those who from heaven to Earth came"—clearly, the biblical Anakim—and stated that they had come to Earth from another planet called Nibiru. The texts are considered to be "myths" by the archaeologists and scholars who have found, deciphered, and translated them; but what if they are true and factual records of the past? They are too numerous, too detailed, too full of sophisticated technological and scientific knowledge, to have been the product of imaginative primitives; and they are accompanied by thousands of pictorial depictions—not only of the Anunnaki, but also of their space and aerial craft, the UFOs of antiquity.

But if all those tales were factual, what planet was Nibiru? It took additional decades of research and study, of both ancient and modern astronomy, to reach a startling conclusion: There is one more planet in our solar system, a post-Plutonian planet with a large elliptical orbit that brings it to our vicinity (passing between Mars and Jupiter) every 3,600 Earth-years; it is then that the comings and goings between Nibiru and Earth take place.

I have put together the textual, pictorial, and scientific evidence in eight books, six of which make up "The Earth Chronicles" series. In the quarter of a century since my first book (*The 12th Planet*) was published in 1976, every new discovery in astronomy, geology, biology, genetics, computer sciences, etc., has corroborated the ancient data. There is thus no doubt in my mind that not only are we not alone in the universe, but we are not alone in our own solar system.

The "UFO enigma" is but a modern version of what people in antiquity had seen, witnessed, and recorded. As a Vatican theologian, Monsignor Corrado Balducci agreed with me

at a public dialogue in Italy in April 2000—
"Extraterrestrials" exist; we are only catching
up with their knowledge.

—ZECHARIA SITCHIN

Situation Red: The UFO Siege (Doubleday, 1977). Leonard Stringfield became the
first author to draw connections between reports of cattle mutilations, Bigfoot sightings,
phantom helicopters, and UFOs. He believes
extraterrestrial visitors are behind these phenomena and may possess psychic powers to
manipulate witnesses into trances as a way of
disguising their true reasons for visiting Earth.

—RANDALL FITZGERALD

Sky People, The (Neville Spearman, 1960).
Brinsley Le Poer Trench details examples of
how diverse human cultures preserve legends
of space visitors who used genetic engineering
to create geniuses and prophets. By reinterpret-
ing the Bible he concludes that the Garden of
Eden once existed on the planet Mars, and that
Noah built a great ark—or spaceship—to escape a flood, which destroyed the Martian civilization. Survivors fled to Earth, and we are
now under a galactic quarantine imposed by
the more advanced Sky People.

—RANDALL FITZGERALD

sleep paralysis Sleep paralysis as defined
by Dr. David J. Hufford is "a period of inability to perform voluntary movements, either
when falling asleep or when awakening, accompanied by conscious awareness. This condition has been ascribed both to hypnagogic
and hypnopompic states." (Hufford, 1982)

Hypnagogic hallucinations, often accompanied by the belief that something, or someone,
is in the room, occur as the person is falling
asleep. Hypnopompic hallucinations occur
upon waking and can contain the same horri-
fying imagery found in hypnagogic hallucinations. These images and imaginary experiences
can be completely recalled afterwards.

Hufford, as well as other researchers,
learned that sleep paralysis is fairly common

in the general population. As many as 15 percent of those surveyed claimed to have experienced an episode of sleep paralysis. Hufford
wrote that "the entire experience seems to be
common, as well as too consistently patterned
to be pathognomic." (Hufford, 1982)

What Hufford was suggesting was that his
own research had suggested that a significant
part of the general population had experienced
some form of sleep paralysis and/or a hypnagogic hallucination. Most people, however,
were unfamiliar with sleep paralysis and began
to search for an explanation for their experiences in other arenas. One of those arenas was
that of alien abduction.

Dr. David Jacobs described in his book,
Secret Life (1992), what he considered to be
the classic abduction scenario. Of that typical
abduction, he wrote: "An unsuspecting woman
is in her room preparing go to bed. She gets
into bed, reads a while, turns off the light, and
drifts off into a peaceful night's sleep. In the
middle of the night she turns over and lies on
her back. She is awakened by a light that
seems to be glowing in her room. The light
moves toward her and takes the shape of a
small 'man' with bald head and huge black
eyes. She is terrified. She wants to run but she
cannot move. She wants to scream but she cannot speak. The 'man' moves toward her and
looks deeply into her eyes. Suddenly she is
calmer, and she 'knows' that the 'man' is not
going to hurt her." (Jacobs, 1992)

Although unaware of it, Jacobs has defined,
in that paragraph, classic sleep paralysis. He
might have accidentally explained the event that
causes some to believe they have been abducted.

It has been estimated by some researchers
that as many as 50 percent of the alien abduction cases can be explained as sleep paralysis.
Sleep paralysis is now better understood because of the research done in the last twenty
years. And because of that research, a cause
for some abduction cases has been found.
Please note that it is a cause for some abductions, but certainly cannot explain all of them.

—KEVIN D. RANDLE

References

Hufford, David J. *The Terror That Comes in the Night* (University of Pennsylvania Press, 1982).

Jacobs, David M. *Secret Life* (Simon & Schuster, 1992).

Randle, Kevin D., Russ Estes, and William P. Cone. *The Abduction Enigma* (Forge, 1999).

Socorro (New Mexico) landing One of the most highly publicized physical-trace cases of all time is the Socorro, New Mexico, "landing," which allegedly occurred on April 24, 1964. The case is considered by many UFOlogists to be one of the "best" because of the combination of factors that make it interesting. It has abundant detail and was reported by an apparently credible, reliable witness. It is also listed in Blue Book files as "unexplained."

According to the story, Officer Lonnie Zamora (a five-year veteran with the Socorro Police Department) was chasing a speeder down South Park Street (the time was reported as 5:45 P.M. MST). The speeder wound up on a dead-end street and Zamora stopped his patrol car to wait. Just then, Zamora was startled to hear a loud "roar" whereupon he saw a bluish-orange flame, conical in shape (narrower at the top), slowly descending in an unpopulated area to the southwest. (Zamora was, at this point, 4,000 feet away from the site where he later found the imprints of the UFO.)

Hearing a loud sound and knowing that a dynamite-storage shed was located in the approximate vicinity of the bright flame, Zamora first thought that someone might be "fooling around" over there. As the flame disappeared behind a small hill, he forgot about the speeder and headed toward whatever was causing the disturbance in the other direction.

Zamora began to see something when he came to the top of a small mesa (about 800 feet from the landed object). At first, all that he could see appeared to be an overturned car,

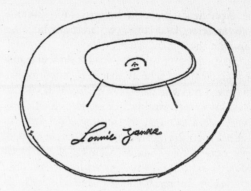

Eyewitness sketch of the Socorro object

down in the gully, and two "small kids" standing next to it. He was quoted by *Look* magazine as saying: "All I could see from that far away was what looked like two sets of white coveralls beside the object. I couldn't see any features, just two figures in the distance. It was like two sets of coveralls hanging on a washline, that's all. They looked about four feet high."

He tried to drive his car to a better vantage point and, in doing so, temporarily lost sight of the object. When he saw it again, the two figures were gone, and suddenly a deafening roar again filled the air. Zamora dived for cover and was on the ground as the object rose into the air. It halted about twenty feet off the ground and hovered motionless for a few seconds before flying away horizontally (its speed was later estimated to be around 120 miles per hour).

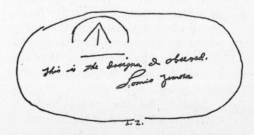

Alleged markings on the object as sketched by the witness, Lonnie Zamora

While the object was hovering, Zamora saw some red markings on its side, which he described as ". . . a crescent with a vertical arrow pointed upward inside the crescent and a horizontal bar beneath that." He tried to use his radio but without success. Even though it was in perfect working order before, it now ceased to function. After a few more tries it started working again, and Zamora requested that Sergeant M. Samuel Chavez of the New Mexico State Police be sent to the scene.

When Sergeant Chavez arrived, both he and Zamora went down in the arroyo (gully), where the object had been seen, to investigate. They found eight imprints in the ground—four large (averaging 10 by 18 inches) rectangular indentations, apparently from the landing legs of the craft, and four smaller round ones (thought by some to be points on the ground where a ladder had been set, and reset). A mesquite bush and a small clump of grass smoldered nearby. The following is quoted from the official Air Force report:

Sgt. Chavez was skeptical of the situation and proceeded to where Zamora had observed the object. Here he found the marks and burns. Smoke appeared to be coming from a bush which was burned but no flame or coals were visible. Sergeant Chavez broke a limb from the bush and it was cold to the touch. The marks were fresh and no other marks were in the area. The burning seemed to be sporadic. Clumps of grass in close proximity to the burned ones were not burned, while others just a short distance away from the unburned ones were again burned, etc. Diagonals of the four impressions (made by the legs of the object) intersect in a perpendicular and the major distance is about 13 feet.

A closer USAF examination of the site on 29 April revealed a fair amount of charred particles mixed in with the dirt, and some charred cardboard was also found. Analysis of soil samples taken on the evening of 24 April was completed on 19 May. It included spectrographic analysis, which revealed that there was no foreign material in the soil samples. Also, no chemicals were detected in the charred or burned soil which would indicate a type of propellant. There was no significant difference in elemental composition between the different samples.

A check for radioactivity was made with a geiger counter at approximately 4 P.M. on 26 April, with negative results. The counter was checked against a watch dial and found to be in working order.

Although Zamora was the only witness to the actual sighting as he described it, nine people in all saw the markings while they were still fresh.

According to Opel Grinder, Manager of Whitting Brothers' Service Station on Route 85 North, at least one other person, an unidentified tourist traveling north on 85, saw the UFO just before it landed in the gully. Grinder said the man stopped at the station and remarked that aircraft flew low around there. Grinder replied that there were many helicopters in that vicinity, and the tourist said, "it was a funny looking helicopter, if that's what it was." The man said further that the object had flown over his car. It actually was headed straight for the gully where it landed moments later. The tourist also commented that he had seen a police car heading up the hill. This was apparently Zamora's car. (From *El Defensor Chieftan,* Tuesday, 28 April 1964, and verified by a direct telephone call to Mr Grinder. Note that this information implies that the UFO not only disappeared in the direction of White Sands [Missile Range] but also came from that same direction.)

The tourist who stopped at Grinder's service station has apparently been identified as Mr. Larry Kratzner of Dubuque, Iowa. Kratzner and a friend, Mr. Paul Kies, traveling together at the time, were finally traced, through an old newspaper clipping (from the 29 April

1964 Dubuque *Telegraph-Herald*) by UFO researcher Ralph C. DeGraw, who published results of the belated personal interviews—conducted in May 1978, fourteen years after the Socorro incident—in his publication, *The UFO Examiner*.

DeGraw noted that the witnesses' "descriptions of what they saw were entirely different." There were also significant discrepancies between the two tourists' testimony and that of Lonnie Zamora.

Agreeing that they were traveling east on Highway 60, approximately one mile southwest of Socorro, at about 3 or 4 P.M. MST (at least one hour and forty-five minutes earlier than the time given by Zamora of his first sighting of the object), Kratzner, the driver, said he saw "a cloud of black smoke coming from the ground ahead of them and to the right." He was also reported to have seen "a round saucer or egg-shaped object ascending vertically from the black smoke." He even described a row of four "windows" on the "craft" and a "red Z" marking on the side facing them. After the vertical climb, Kratzner claimed that the object leveled off and disappeared in the cloud of black smoke it was producing, in the southwest.

Kies, on the other hand, reported seeing black smoke coming from the ground (ahead of them, and slightly to the right) and a bright, shiny "reflection," which appeared to be within the smoke. Kies said he saw the shiny reflection only on the ground, and saw nothing flying in the sky. He thought, at the time, that the source of the smoke might have been a junkyard where someone was burning tires and cutting up wrecked cars, and, perhaps, the reflection was from a car window or part of a car body that had caught the sun. (According to Zamora, there was no smoke, only dust, in the area.)

Both Kratzner and Kies estimated their position at the time of their observations to be about one mile from where the black smoke was apparently coming from. Neither of them heard any noise, even though, according to their accounts, they were at about the same

distance from the "object," when first sighted, as Zamora when he said that he heard a "very loud roar."

An even greater discrepancy has been pointed out by the UFO debunker Philip Klass. During his on-site investigation, in December 1966, Klass interviewed a local resident, "Mr. Felix Phillips, whose house is located only one thousand feet south of the spot where the UFO allegedly landed. Phillips said that he and his wife had been home at the time of the reported incident, and that several windows and doors had been open—yet neither of them had heard the loud roar that Zamora reported during the UFO landing and later during take-off. This was especially curious because Zamora's speeding car was four thousand feet away from the site and the Phillips home was only one-quarter this distance."

Klass concluded (after fitting together several other key pieces of information) that the "UFO landing" was a hoax intended to turn the economically depressed town of Socorro into a tourist attraction.

Nevertheless, many UFOlogists still consider the Socorro case a "classic," which was apparently taken seriously by the U.S. Air Force back in 1964.

—RONALD D. STORY

References

"Flying Saucers," a *Look* magazine special by the editors of UPI and Cowles Communicatons (1967).

Klass, Philip J. *UFOs Explained* (Random House, 1974).

Phillips, Ted. "High Strangeness Ground Trace Reports," *The MUFON UFO Journal* (December 1979).

———. "Landing Traces, Physical Evidence for the UFO" in the MUFON Symposium 1973 Proceedings (MUFON, 1973).

Sorell (Australia) saucers Two men, who prefer to remain anonymous, sighted three UFOs at Lake Sorell, in Tasmania, on February 26, 1975. The reporting witness was a tail gunner in the Royal Australian Air Force, who later became a professional man and is considered to be reliable. He and a friend (a commercial artist) were camped on the shore of Lake Sorell to do some fishing.

At 8:45 P.M., Mr. "Smith" (a pseudonym for the reporting witness) noted three "things" in the sky which he at first thought might have been aircraft. The objects were approaching from the northeast and appeared to be two large craft and a smaller one.

Underneath each of the craft was a red, pulsing light in the center and other red-to-orange lights running around the circumference. The two objects stood out clearly, and one of them headed toward the fishermen's location.

Smith said, "It was about 2½ miles away when we saw it move, and then it was right there only about a thousand yards away and five hundred feet above the lake." He said that if he had not seen it himself, he would not have believed any craft could display such a performance. He was sure that the size of the object was no less than two hundred feet in diameter.

During the next few minutes, the object turned on a "monstrous light" which was directed down toward the lake. It was half the diameter of the UFO itself; the shaft of it was well defined, and it came from one side of the bottom of the UFO. The light was very intense, and it was painful to the eyes to look at. Smith compared its brilliance to that of a welding torch. While watching the phenomena, he took careful sightings on hills in the area with which he was familiar. The spill of light from around the main shaft of the light illuminated a distance of 1½ miles around the lake. The beam was swung back and forth in an arc. "It seemed like a careful search of the Robinson's Swamp area, and I have no doubt that beam of light was intelligently controlled," Smith said.

The two men had a large tent set up at the lakeside together with cover for the car. The car's radio was being used because a portable radio he had was not strong enough to pick up radio stations some distance away. Smith

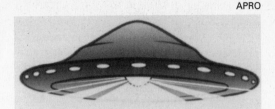

APRO

Artist's conception by Brian James

observed that when the UFO flew close to their campsite the car radio emitted a loud "intense static noise." Still watching the object, Smith traversed the radio dial across the whole band; but he could not pick up one radio station. "There was just the static," he said.

After its "inspection" of the area, the UFO put out its gigantic light beam, after which a blue-white phosphorescence was left hanging about thirty feet above the lake's surface. Once the light was out, the UFO was clearly seen; and it departed "in a flash." Its departing speed was tremendous, Smith said. and watching it leave was "like watching a tracer bullet going away from you." It was accompanied by the other UFO, which had been hovering near Mount Penney. When the two left, the time was 9:30 P.M. Smith and his friend made sketches of what they had seen (redrawn for publication). The next day, Smith and friend met some fishermen who had seen the UFO light up the lake the night before. The anglers had been camped one mile away from Smith's location at Silver Plains. They told Smith they had been in their tent when suddenly the tent was lit up inside like daylight.

Another sighting took place at Lake Sorell on March 14, 1975, when a Mr. Knapek and his two sons and two friends sighted an object while camped in a clearing one mile east of the lake. They were about to have a snack when the children, ages thirteen and fifteen, pointed out an object rising slowly from behind trees three hundred yards to the west toward the lake. The object, once above the trees, rose rapidly and shot up into the southwestern sky diminishing to star size and then being lost to view at 75 degrees elevation. The whole event took only five seconds.

The object in this case was football-shaped and estimated by the witnesses to be about fifty feet across. It was bright yellow underneath, with a lighter yellow on top. As it moved away, the color became more white and much brighter. No ground check was made for physical traces.

—CORAL & JIM LORENZEN

soul exchange This term describes the process of a "Walk-in" experience, in which a human being agrees to vacate their own body-mind system, and allow a second soul (often considered an ET spirit), to take their place and incarnate directly into their voluntarily surrendered body and mind. It is claimed that this is done by mutual agreement for the purpose of release for the departing soul, and to provide an opportunity for greater world service for the entering soul. This process is comparable but not identical to the process by which an "ET Wanderer" comes to take birth in a human body.

—SCOTT MANDELKER

Soul Samples (Wild Flower Press, 1999). This book, by psychologist R. Leo Sprinkle, gives a psychological, psychical, and spiritual perspective on the UFO phenomenon and its relationship to people's lives. UFO author Keith Thompson encapsulated Dr. Sprinkle's efforts by saying, "when other investigators were chasing lights in the sky and gathering *soil* samples, you [Leo] were helping UFO experiencers and gathering *soul* samples."

Partly biographical in nature, this book reveals Dr. Sprinkle's conclusions and insights on the link between UFO/ET activities and the process of reincarnation.

—ETEP STAFF

soul transfer This is a general term applicable to both "Wanderers" and "Walk-ins": individuals who claim to be ET souls living in human bodies. While both claim to be ETs who freely chose to enter human incarnation, their entry into the human system occurs through different modes of transfer. Wanderers are those whose transfer was at birth, and continues for multiple incarnations, while Walk-ins claim to enter human life in a soul exchange with an adult. According to their metaphysics, ET souls are the vanguard of the benevolent ET community, and are here to assist in human evolution.

—SCOTT MANDELKER

Space Brothers An alternate term for benevolent extraterrestrial races, allied in service to various planets and Earth humanity. Especially popularized in the 1950s by science fiction writers, UFO researchers, contactees, and channels, Carl Jung called them "technological angels."

—SCOTT MANDELKER

Space-Gods Revealed, The (Harper & Row, 1976). Ronald Story demonstrates how proponents of the "ancient astronaut theory" (especially Erich von Däniken) are guilty of absurdities, active imaginations, faulty suppositions, and superficialities. As astronomer Carl Sagan writes in the foreword to Story's book: "The possibility of extraterrestrial intelligence is something I and many other scientists take very seriously—to the point of using large radio telescopes to listen for possible signals sent our way by beings on planets of other stars. If there were good evidence that in the past we were visited by such beings, our task would be made immeasurably easier. But unfortunately there is no such evidence, as the present book helps to make clear."

—RANDALL FITZGERALD

Spaceships of Ezekiel, The (Econ-Verlagsgruppe, 1973) NASA engineer Josef Blumrich reinterprets Ezekiel's vision of a "fiery chariot" from the Old Testament to produce an engineering analysis which concludes the Jewish priest and prophet probably encountered an extraterrestrial spacecraft. On four occasions over a 20-year period Ezekiel observed the same craft, according to the Biblical account, which leads Blumrich to believe these trips represented exploration missions to study humans and influence the development of human civilization.

—RANDALL FITZGERALD

Spaceships of the Pleiades (Prometheus Books, 1995). Kal Korff traveled to Switzerland to research this book exposing Swiss farmer Billy Meier, who masterminded the most ambitious UFO hoax in history with his faked photographs. Korff unmasks Meier's criminal background and tracked down former Meier friends and supporters who describe him as a charlatan who began the hoax for financial gain.

—RANDALL FITZGERALD

Space-Time Transients (Nelson-Hall, 1977). Canadian psychologist Michael Persinger and his research associate Gyslaine Lafreniere find correlations between geomagnetic fields and the human perception of UFOs and alien visitors. Their pioneering work found that many unexplained events occur before intense solar and seismic activity. They theorize that the bioelectrical systems of human brains, when exposed to high electric fields, can release stored UFO and alien images from the unconscious and produce in the percipient "dreamlike states, episodes of paralysis, or intervals of unconsciousness."

—RANDALL FITZGERALD

Sprinkle, R. Leo (b. 1930). Leo Sprinkle is a psychotherapist and researcher, who is also a UFO experiencer. Dr. Sprinkle was a consultant to the Aerial Phenomena Research Organization and the Condon Committee at the University of Colorado.

Dr. Sprinkle received his B.A. and M.P.S. degrees from the University of Colorado, in 1952 and 1956, respectively; and his Ph.D. in Counseling Psychology from the University of Missouri in 1961. He was Professor Emeritus of Counseling Services at the University of Wyoming, when he resigned to go into private practice in 1989. Dr. Sprinkle is nationally cer-

R. Leo Sprinkle

tified and licensed and a Registrant of Counsel for the National Register of Health Service Providers.

Dr. Sprinkle has participated in numerous television programs, including ABC-TV's "That's Incredible," NBC-TV's "Tom Snyder, Tomorrow Show," and NBC's "UFOs: Fact or Fantasy?" He has also appeared on many panels with scientists such as J. Allen Hynek and Carl Sagan. He started the UFO Investigation Conference for contactees and participated in the 1968 Symposium on Unidentified Flying Objects (U.S. House Committee on Science and Astronautics), the symposium "Science and the UFO" sponsored by the National Amateur Astronomers Association, and one sponsored by the American Psychological Association.

Dr. Sprinkle's book, entitled *Soul Samples*, was published in 1999.

Address: 105 South 4th Street
Laramie, WY 82070
U.S.A.

POSITION STATEMENT: The status of UFO evidence is a deluge, not a delusion. The characteristics of UF percipients show a wide range of age, education, occupation, and cultural background; however, the evidence does not support the hypothesis that UFO reports are submitted primarily by persons who are experiencing neurotic or psychotic reactions.

The testimony of UFO witnesses indicates that they are convinced of the reality of their UFO experiences; however, traditional scientific methods do not provide "proof" of the existence of UFO phenomena. Thus, UFO investigators face the question: Is UFO research a *problem* (to be solved) or a *predicament* (to be tolerated)?

In my opinion, UFO investigation should continue at each level of existence: "physical" reality, "biological" reality, "psychosocial" reality, and "spiritual" reality. There are problems for many investigators, from astronomers to zoologists, from anthropologists to parapsychologists. The UFO problem represents a significant challenge to science and humanity.

In my opinion, the present evidence for UFO phenomena indicates (tentatively) that the Earth is the object of a survey by intelligent beings from some other civilization(s). However, the evidence is not sufficient to determine the origins, purposes, and powers of these intelligent beings.

The challenge of the UFO problem is to develop our scientific and spiritual knowledge so that we can enter the "New Age" and communicate more effectively with other beings who coexist in this complex universe.

—R. Leo Sprinkle

Star People, The (Berkley, 1981). Husband and wife writing team Brad and Francie Steiger not only believe that many humans are descendants of space beings who mated with our species to prepare Earth for transformation, but they themselves are Star People here to assist the aliens in that work. Among the qualities which identify Star People: they have charisma, a rare blood type, low body temperature, low blood pressure, feel an affinity for ancient Egypt, and as a child had an invisible playmate.

—Randall Fitzgerald

Star People, The It was in his book *Gods of Aquarius: UFOs and the Transformation of Man* (1976) that Brad Steiger first set down a number of apparent peculiarities associated with certain individuals who claimed contact experiences with alleged alien entities. This research had developed from a questionnaire created by Steiger in 1967 as a tool for fashioning a pattern profile of paranormally talented individuals, contemporary mystics, and spiritually oriented men and women. Because so many of these individuals had begun to express an awareness that their "soul essences" had come to Earth from other worlds or dimensions, Steiger decided to name these respondents "The Star People" after an old Chippewa legend of people from the stars that descended to mate with humans.

In 1968, Steiger had developed the questionnaire to define such Star People characteristics as: extra or transitional vertebrae, lower than normal body temperature, unusual blood type, acute sensitivity to electromagnetic fields, chronic sinusitis, and great personal charisma. The research was further delineated in *The Star People* (1981), with Frances Paschal Steiger, and *The Seed* (1983).

By 1987, working together with his present wife, Sherry Hansen Steiger, Brad Steiger estimated that more than 30,000 men and women around the world had responded to the questionnaire. They found the Star People in all ethnic groups, all social strata, all occupations, and professions. Although they often express the feeling of being "strangers in a strange land," the Star People are essentially "helpers"—many of them actively serving in such service-oriented professions as nurses, doctors, clergy, social workers, teachers, counselors, and law enforcement officers.

In 1992, Steiger and his wife Sherry published *Starborn*, revealing that over 90 percent of those who had returned the questionnaire claimed to have experienced the mystical ecstasy of being "one with the universe." A remarkable 86 percent attest to some kind of contact with otherworldly or other-dimensional beings.

In addition to the anomalous physical and psychic similarities that they found among the questionnaire respondents, the Steigers found an intriguing commonality of experiences that they term "activating incidents." At around the age of five nearly 85 percent of the respondents experienced a dramatic interaction with an alleged angel, elf, holy figure, or UFO entity. At about the age of eleven, nearly 80 percent suffered some sort of traumatic event—a severe accident, a serious illness, the divorce of their parents, etc.—that caused them to withdraw from the company of their peers and to retreat within for a period of time.

Currently, the Steigers state that the greatest single commonality among the Star People is a desire to be of service to the planet and all of Mother Earth's children. It is such a sense of mission that seems to distinguish those who believe that they have interacted with some facet of a Higher Intelligence or with an extraterrestrial or multidimensional being.

Research into the Star People phenomenon continues. Those interested in participating may obtain the questionnaire by sending a stamped, self-addressed envelope to:

Timewalker
P.O. Box 434
Forest City, IA 50436
U.S.A.

—ETEP STAFF

References

Steiger, Brad. *Gods of Aquarius: UFOs and the Transformation of Man* (Harcourt Brace Jovanovich, 1976; Berkley Books, 1981).

———. *The Star People* (Berkley Books, 1981).

———. *Revelation: The Divine Fire* (Berkley Books, 1981).

———. *The Seed* (Berkley Books, 1983).

Steiger, Brad and Sherry Hansen Steiger. *Starborn* (Berkley Books, 1992).

Steiger, Brad (b. 1936). Steiger taught American literature and creative writing on secondary and college levels (1957-67). He is the author or co-author of 148 books dealing with the paranormal, including 22 on UFOs. He is also the co-scriptwriter of *Unknown Powers,* winner of the Film Advisory Board's Award of Excellence for 1978.

His major works on UFOs are: *Mysteries of Time and Space* (1974), and *Gods of Aquarius: UFOs and the Transformation of Man* (1976); and, more recently, co-authored with his wife Sherry: *The Rainbow Conspiracy* (1994), and *UFO Odyssey* (1999).

Address: P.O. Box 434
Forest City, IA 50436
U.S.A.

Web site: www.bradandsherry.com

POSITION STATEMENT: I have come to the conclusion that some external intelligence has interacted with humankind throughout history in an effort to learn more about us—or in an effort to communicate certain basic truths and concepts to our species.

I am also convinced there is a subtle kind of symbiotic relationship that exists between humankind and the UFO intelligences. I think that in some way, which we have yet to determine, they need us as much as we need them.

It is quite possible that either one or both of our species might once have had an extraterrestrial origin, but the important thing is that the very biological and spiritual evolution of Earth may depend upon the establishment of equilibrium between us and our cosmic cousins.

I do not dogmatically rule out the extraterrestrial hypothesis, but I do lean toward the theory that UFOs may be our neighbors right around the corner in another space-time continuum. What we have thus far been labeling "spaceships" may be, in reality, multidimensional mechanisms or psychic constructs of our paraphysical companions.

I have even come to suspect that, in some instances, what we have been terming "spaceships" may actually be a form of higher intelligence rather than vehicles transporting occupants.

The UFO, the appearance of elves and "wee" people, and the manifestation of archetypal images throughout the world signify that we are part of a larger community of intelligences, a far more complex hierarchy of powers and principalities, a potentially richer kingdom of interrelated species—both physical and nonphysical—than we have been bold enough to believe.

I believe that numerous literal truths have been prompted by the UFO intelligences. I believe that, through the ages, they have been provoking humankind into higher spirals of intellectual and technological maturity, guiding men and women toward ever-expanding mental and spiritual awareness, pulling our species continually into the future.

Although these paraphysical, multidimensional entities have always coexisted with us, in the last half-century they have been accelerating their interaction with the U.S. in preparation for a fast-approaching time of transition and transformation. This period, we have been told, will be a difficult one; and for generations our prophets and revelators have been referring to it as "the great cleansing," "Judgment Day," "Armageddon." But we have been promised that, after a season of cataclysmic changes on the Earth plane, a New Age consciousness will suffuse the planet. It is to this end that the UFO is a transformative symbol.

—BRAD STEIGER

Steiger, Sherry Hansen (b. 1945). While in seminary in the late 1960s, (Lutheran School of Theology, Chicago), Sherry noticed that many of the things she considered to be mysteries of the Bible suddenly stood out to her in a new way. She noticed that many descriptions in the Old Testament sounded very "otherworldly" in a UFO sense.

Her research at that time was interrupted by a passionate involvement with the social issues of the surrounding community and of the church at large and most of her years from that time forward, she served as counselor, teacher, in various aspects of the ministry and later in advertising. Although throughout the

Brad and Sherry Steiger

years her research and interest in UFOs and related fields, continued, it was not until much later, that she came to work with Dr. J. Allen Hynek.

Sherry founded several nonprofit schools in the late 1970s, for which she was in the process of receiving major funding for educational efforts in the media. One of the focus points was a media package she had written which was her research involving UFOs. In her meeting with Dr. Hynek, to discuss how her findings related to his own research, he asked her to work with him as his personal manager and director of publicity. He was just in the process of discussions with a benefactor who hoped to relocate Dr. Hynek to Scottsdale, Arizona, where a second location for his Center for UFO Studies was proposed. Sherry realized the immensity of Hynek's vast involvement and research in the field and didn't think twice about putting her work on hold. She accepted the honor and opportunity of Dr. Hynek's urging for her to enter into an official contractual relationship for a new partnership.

From late '84 until the time of his death in 1986, Dr. Hynek had Sherry interview people who were reporting their experiences and assist in an analysis based on her experience as a counselor, as well as including her in most meetings and affairs of the Center in Phoenix. Sherry was working on television, motion picture, and international lecture and media exposure for Dr. Hynek when a series of bizarre episodes regarding a "walk through" to see the alien bodies and a release of major documents (into Dr. Hynek's possession) surfaced. A *very high* up official contacted Dr. Hynek and espoused details of an elaborate unveiling of previously classified *very top-secret* government documents and proof of alien craft and visitation to Earth that Hynek had so meticulously researched and sought his entire career. Many mysterious and somewhat "suspicious" events began to unfold until the sudden and untimely death of Dr. Hynek in April of 1986. Sherry described some of the events in *The Rainbow Conspiracy* (1994) one of 26 books she wrote/co-wrote with her husband, Brad Steiger, since 1987.

Address: P.O. Box 434
           Forest City, IA 50436
           U.S.A.

E-mail: timewlkr@WCTAtel.net
Web site: www.bradandsherry.com

POSITION STATEMENT: My interest and research into the field of UFOs has been from the religious perspective, initially stemming from the interaction and guidance of Supernatural Beings in the Old and New Testaments of the Bible. In the Book of Exodus, we are told that a "pillar of fire" and "pillar of cloud" led the exodus out of Egypt. There is some *awesome* force contained in the Ark of the Covenant and the Mercy Seat. We have the "chariots of fire" of the prophet Elijah and the "wheels" of Ezekiel among many other ancient descriptions that also match present day reports of UFO sightings and experiences.

In the New Testament, the Apostle Paul was "blinded by a light" that spoke to him on the road to Damascus and changed his life completely. Angels seemed to travel on the "clouds of heaven" and often literally appear in a physical manner, even to the point of partaking in food and lodging. Such angelic physicality appears in the Biblical account of Sodom and Gomorra, when angels came to warn Lot and his family. The angels "looks" were so appealing they were lusted after to the point where Lot had to secure the door to protect them against the crowd, even offering one of his own daughters to the crowd if they would leave the angels alone! Then, the angels blast and destroy the city with what almost seems to be an atomic or nuclear blast.

I have come to see through my continued study from the 1960s on, that all world religions have similar descriptions of astral vehicles and supernatural beings and their interactions with humankind. I believe UFOs to be the "Powers and Principalities"—as stated in the New Testament and may include many other levels of existence—which could be likened to as Jesus said: "In my Father's House are many mansions" or dwelling places. I also believe that as on Earth we have the positive and negative polarities there must be that of the good and bad in the astral realms as well, meaning that some angels or messengers may be demons—or fallen angels.

In my personal study with Native American Shaman, such as Rolling Thunder and Grandfather David of the Hopis, I learned of the Native American tradition of the Star Beings teaching and guiding them throughout time. The similarities of all cultures and religions, ancient art and rock and cave drawings of star craft and heavenly teachers are far too prevalent and universal to be ignored or viewed as psychological or emotional disturbances . . . although, certainly, those might be involved as well. Myths of elves, fairies, and the like share common threads of "encounters" and also must be taken into consideration.

Certainly many sightings today are of "explained" phenomena, some which are "top secret" airplanes and missions by various governments. But in my counseling of individuals over time, considering the similarity of their own experiences, sightings, and interactions, as well as my own, there is no doubt in my mind that UFOs have been with us from the beginning and their interaction is significant to me now, not only "theologically," but in every other "ology" and historicity there is!

—SHERRY HANSEN STEIGER

Stillings, Dennis (b. 1942). Dennis Stillings is the director of the Archaeus Project, a group of professional people interested in the investigation of unusual claims and anomalies for potential use in medicine and technology.

Dennis Stillings

Stillings received his B.A. degree in philosophy from the University of Minnesota in 1965. He also did graduate work in mathematics and German literature.

Stillings was the founding Director, now board member, of the Five Mountain Medical Community organization, which seeks to promote Northwest Hawaii as a health and healing destination for the Pacific Rim. He is editor of the publication *Healing Island,* and former editor of the now-defunct journals *Artifex* and *Archaeus.* He has published over 60 papers on anomalistics, popular culture, and the history of medicine. Stillings is a member of the Bioelectromagnetics Society, the Society for Sci-

entific Exploration, a Fellow of the American Institute of Stress.

Address: P.O. Box 7079
            Kamuela, HI 96743
            U.S.A.

E-mail: dstillings@kohalacenter.org

POSITION STATEMENT: My position on UFOs is not far different from what is expressed by the title of Jung's monograph on the subject: *Flying Saucers: A Modern Myth of Things Seen in the Skies.* While I believe that there is a residuum of UFO cases that represent genuine anomalies—aspects of reality that would seem to deserve serious scientific investigation—I am exceedingly pessimistic as to whether we have the tools, mental or physical, to do so.

On the other hand, a large part of the "UFO phenomenon" is psychosocial, and is therefore susceptible to investigation by means that are to hand. It is a *fact* that these things are reported, and there is a great collection of *psychological facts* to be found in the reports of sightings and contacts and the theories about them. These can be studied and, at least for the foreseeable future, form the only basis for anything that can be called a "science of UFOlogy."

—DENNIS STILLINGS

Story, Ronald D. (b. 1946). Author, technical writer/editor, and founder of the original UFO Encyclopedia Project. In association with the Aerial Phenomena Research Organization (APRO), between 1976 and 1979, Story compiled and edited the first UFO encyclopedia entitled *The Encyclopedia of UFOs* (published by Doubleday and New English Library in 1980). Story studied anthropology, astronomy, and logic in preparing for his degree in philosophy at the University of Arizona, where he graduated (with honors) in 1970.

Story's interest in UFOs dates from his student days at the University of Arizona, where he met professor James McDonald, during the late 1960s. Together, Story and Mc-

Photo courtesy of Grizzly Adams Productions

Ronald Story

E-mail: ronldstory@aol.com
Web site: www.RonaldStory.com

POSITION STATEMENT: I think UFOs represent a wide variety of different phenomena: some natural, some man-made, and some, perhaps, of extraterrestrial origin. It may very well be that some UFOs carry alien beings on a mission to Earth. Although absolute proof is lacking, there are enough anomalous events to establish probable cause; therefore, I think the prudent course is to prepare ourselves for anything that may happen

Though I favor the psycho-social approach, I think it is *possible* that an extraterrestrial intelligence may have had a hand in humanity's origins and that we could be in for a second coming. In any case, I believe the impact of such open contact and intervention with people of Earth would constitute the single most significant event in human history.

According to the Bible, we were created by an extraterrestrial intelligence (which in Hebrew is pluralized as Elohim or "gods") with our fate depending on our relationship with that superior force. In this respect, modern-day contact with such a superior intelligence would affect every aspect of our lives, including, perhaps, our own survival.

Therefore, I believe in making every effort—using the scientific method—to continue our search for the truth, wherever it may lead.

—RONALD D. STORY

Donald investigated a "ghost light" that Story had photographed in Missouri.

As a technical writer/editor, since 1983, Story has worked primarily in the high-tech defense industry for aerospace companies such as Hughes Aircraft, Rockwell, McDonnell-Douglas, Raytheon, Boeing, and Lockheed Martin.

As a science writer, Story first wrote *The Space-Gods Revealed* (1976), a scientific critique of Erich von Däniken's ancient astronaut theory as presented in *Chariots of the Gods?* (1968) and other books. Story was assisted on the project by leading astronomers and archaeologists, such as Carl Sagan (who wrote the foreword), Frank Drake, William Hartmann, Thor Heyerdahl, Edwin Ferdon, William Rathje, Merle Green Robertson, et al.

Story's other books include *Guardians of the Universe?* (1980) and *UFOs and the Limits of Science* (1981).

Address: 3540 32nd Ave. N. #114
            St. Petersburg, FL 33713
            U.S.A.

Story's UFO "observations"

1. "UFOs," in one form or another, have existed since ancient times.
2. Whatever else "they" or "it" may be, the "UFO" is a perennial symbol. It connotes the magical, the technological, and the unknown. "UFOs" are the modern equivalents of comets and other unknown lights and shapes seen by the ancients that have always meant impending change.
3. "UFOs" have always been associated with a superior, extraterrestrial—or ultraterrestrial—intelligence.

4. UFO-aliens seem to be modern replacements for angels and demons, as well as fairies and other magical creatures of earlier times. In fact, many today still believe in angels and demons as well as aliens. Belief in fairies has declined slightly.

5. The UFO phenomenon did not just happen one day—it *evolved*. Spiritualism became contacteeism. The age-old spirits became the aliens of today. Their history can be traced, and their messages are essentially the same.

6. The UFO/ET myth fulfills psychological needs, which are ageless and timeless. If aliens did not exist, we would invent them.

7. The human mind seeks order, meaning, and explanation. Superior alien life-forms (advanced intelligence) fulfills those needs.

8. Humans are fallible. So-called "eyewitness testimony" and alleged "contact" experiences do not constitute proof of anything. They "happen," in one sense or another, but their interpretation is open to question and debate.

9. Fantasy is not just simple nonsense; it is a natural and pervasive component of everyday life. It provides us humans with a coping mechanism to deal with the dullness and disappointments of reality. Without all sorts of fantasy thinking—taking place mostly at the unconscious level—the real world would be impossible for most of us to endure.

10. For most of us postmoderns, science fiction has become our myth, and science has become our religion. Due mainly to media influences and a hideously complicated world, most people are finding it increasingly difficult to distinguish fantasy from reality. And many do not want to.

11. As in earlier times, most people are heavily influenced by authority figures, and today those authority figures are scientists, government and business leaders, and to a lesser extent—the clergy. Unlike earlier times, today we look to science for answers to most of our questions about life in the universe. The world has become more materialistic than spiritualistic, and so our spiritual needs go largely unmet.

12. Advanced extraterrestrials are accepted by many today as the gods of the age of science. Others see them as gods of both the material and spiritual realms.

13. UFOs and ETs may be visiting Earth, but this writer sees a different pattern in the data.

14. Alleged "contact" experiences are almost always *surrealistic* in nature. Freud called this the "dreamwork." UFO-contact experiences have all the telltale signs of the dreamwork as do myths and dreams. Surrealism is the fingerprint of fantasy and virtually all alien contacts bear the fingerprint.

15. In this writer's view, the key to the UFO phenomenon is to rise above the literal and materialistic viewpoints, and begin to understand the "UFO message," which matches the wisdom of the ages as taught by the greatest philosophers and religious teachers of Earth. In UFOlogy, these teachings are called "Cosmic Laws," and they have universal application.

16. If these teachings are not implemented soon, it may be too late for humankind and we could become an extinct species. What survives will not be *human*, but rather an alien nation (as in the word "alienation"). The "Borg" of *Star Trek* is a fantasy (or metaphorical fiction) that will become even more real than it already is. Humans will become increasingly more like robots, and dehumanization on Earth will be complete.

Stranger at the Pentagon, The (I.E.C., 1967). Evangelist Frank Stranges claims he befriended a Venusian named Valiant Thor here on a mission to neutralize Earth's nuclear weapons. Stranges says he met Thor at the Pentagon in Washington, D.C., where he had taken up residence for three years as the guest of President Dwight Eisenhower.

—RANDALL FITZGERALD

Stranges, Frank E. (b. 1927). Originally from Brooklyn, New York, Frank Stranges was close to death at birth, and weak and sickly in his youth. As a young man he was kidnapped, robbed, and shot at, but, he says, "By the Grace of God, I dodged all that fate was able to hurl at me and scurried on to an active life." He has been active, indeed, as an evangelist who combines his teaching of the scriptures with books, lectures, and movies on UFOs.

In part, his special mission was spurred on by a supposed meeting with a man from Venus, by the name of Val Thor, whose purpose on Earth was "to help mankind return to the Lord." This meeting allegedly occurred, of all places, within the confines of the Pentagon in Washington, D.C.

Dr. Stranges gives his academic credentials as follows: "a Ph.D. in psychology, a Th.D., D.D., B.Th., B.C. Ed., Ll.D., Doctor of Humanities, and Grand Evangelist of the Sovereign Order of Alfred the Great." He says he attended "colleges in the United States, doing further study at the Graduate Theological Seminary, Macau, Asia; Hong Kong; and at the Society of St. Luke the Physician, London, England"; also, "a Ph.D. from the National Institute of Criminology, Washington." Another source has his doctor of psychology and philosophy degrees coming from Faith Bible College and Theological Seminary in Fort Lauderdale, Florida.

Stranges is the president of International Evangelism Crusades, Inc. (IEC), as well as the National Investigations Committee on Unidentified Flying Objects (NICUFO). His early books included: *Flying Saucerama* (1959); *My Friend from Beyond Earth* (1960); and *The Stranger at the Pentagon* (1967). He has since expanded this list considerably to include many other books, as well as numerous audio and videotapes.

Address: 14617 Victory Blvd.
             Suite #4
             Van Nuys, CA 91411
             U.S.A.

E-mail: drfes@earthlink.net

POSITION STATEMENT: UFOlogy, in and of itself, presents a number of avenues of investigation and research. However, there is one avenue that has been sadly neglected: that being the spiritual ramifications.

When one deals with the deeper, more important aspects of UFOlogy—other than the "nuts and bolts" of the mystery—one tears aside the veil and cannot help but notice a spiritual side. A new door is opened, which reveals that those from other worlds are deeply interested in our spiritual well-being.

My personal experience with one at the Pentagon in 1959 causes me to believe that many of those from space are here to assist the human family in a most wonderful and exciting manner.

Consider that a being, traveling millions of miles from deep space, would not travel to this planet unless there was more than a reason, simply to land on the White House lawn and loudly announce their presence. The evidence reveals a deeper, more effective and valuable reason for their visits.

Knowing this, I have been privileged to share this information with other people, which has: (1) elevated their spiritual consciousness; (2) given them ways and means to improve their living status and prosper in their respective communities; and (3) revealed ways and means toward better health.

The spiritual information shared by those from other worlds is far more important than information as to how to build a spacecraft. This is my opinion regarding the spiritual value of space contact. As a clergyman for some 50 years, I am well acquainted with the ancient records that are recorded in the Aramaic, Greek, and Hebrew bibles. There is far too much evidence within the confines of the Bible that totally supports the truth that UFOs are real and that they are here for a divine purpose.

—FRANK STRANGES

Strauch photo At 6:10 P.M., on the evening of October 21, 1965, Mr. Arthur Strauch, Deputy Sheriff of Sibley County, Minnesota, in the company of four others, was returning from a bow-hunting trip by car when he spotted a strange object which seemed to be two thousand feet above the ground and a quarter-mile distant to the northwest. They were two miles west and two miles north of Saint George. The group stopped the car and watched. Strauch got out and observed the object through 7x35 binoculars, while the others watched from inside the car.

APRO

Photograph by Arthur Strauch

After watching for about ten minutes, the group drove down the road about a half-mile and stopped. Strauch got out of the car and snapped a photo just as the object began to move. It moved into the wind (northeast) for what appeared to be several hundred feet and then stopped for a few seconds, at which time its lights changed from a bright white to a dull orange, alternating several times. It then moved toward the southeast at a high rate of speed and disappeared out of sight. As it passed over their heads, the witnesses heard a high-pitched whining sound.

The witnesses were: Arthur A. Strauch (47), Deputy Sheriff of Sibley County, Minnesota; his wife, Mrs. Katherine Strauch (44), housewife; Gary Martin Strauch (16), high school student and son of Mrs. and Mrs. Strauch; Donald Martin Grewe (26), a technician, and his wife, Mrs. Retha Ann Grewe (25), a registered nurse.

Strauch used a Kodak Instamatic camera with Ektachrome color-slide film. He had the focus set at infinity, and the shutter speed was set at 1/60th of a second.

The sun had just set and the sky was clear. The moon had not risen, and Venus was clearly visible in the southeast. One small star was visible to the right and below the UFO.

Testimony of the witnesses differs only in minor details. Whereas Arthur Strauch said the object appeared as large as a quarter held at arm's length, his wife just said it was much larger than the evening star; Gary Strauch said it was like a quarter held at arm's length, and so did Donald Grewe. Mrs. Grewe said it was the size of "a large star."

APRO

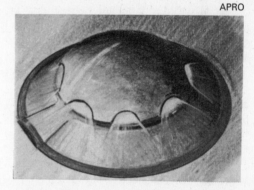

Eyewitness drawing by Arthur Strauch

Mrs. Grewe, Mrs. Strauch, and Gary remained inside the car, while Mr. Grewe and Mr. Strauch got out to observe the object. At first they heard no sound. But then as the object flew over them, Grewe described the sound as a "whistling whine." Strauch called it a "high-pitched whining sound, as made by an electrical motor starting up."

Mr. Strauch's description was the most detailed as he viewed the object with the aid of binoculars. He said: "I have no idea what it was. All I can report is that it was different from anything I had ever seen in the sky. I'm positive it was a machine driven by some inner power that has tremendous speed. The outline was unmistakable through my binoculars as that of a flying saucer."

Strauch stated: "The rounded top of the dome was a metallic-silver gray that reflected the rays of the setting sun, turning the object into a large orange ball. Surrounding the dome were four small portholes that emitted a bright yellow light. Just below the windows or ports was an area that glowed a light blue. This light seemed to be a reflection of some inner light or perhaps exhaust. From the edge of the blue light's reflection to the edge of the flat saucer-like surface (outer edge), the outer ring was rotating counterclockwise, causing it to throw off an aurora or halo of light that changed from orange to white with an overall tinge of blue and green. The extreme outer edge of the saucer glowed a bright orange, and this part did not move or rotate."

Strauch said, "I do not believe that the light went out in the machine as . . . we lost sight of it, but rather that it had such tremendous speed that it just disappeared into space."

—CORAL & JIM LORENZEN

Strieber, Whitley   (b. 1945). Whitley Strieber is probably the world's most famous "abductee" and certainly the most articulate. His book *Communion*—a #1 bestseller in 1987— has sold over ten million copies worldwide, and was also made into a full-length motion picture. In this and other books, Strieber speaks freely about childhood abductions, rectal probes, alien implants, mind control, and government involvement. *Communion* was the first book of its kind: a first-person account of the surrealistic "Visitor" phenomenon, as Strieber calls it, composed by a literary master with obvious intelligence and insight

Strieber was born and raised in San Antonio, Texas, and spent many years living in New York. He received his B.A. degree from the University of Texas, and studied at the London Film School.

A master storyteller, Strieber is the author of eighteen books, including the novels *The Wolfen* (1978) and *The Hunger* (1981), both of which were made into feature films. Andrew Sarris has ranked *The Hunger* among the top ten horror films of all time.

Strieber's other successful books include: *Warday* (1984), *Nature's End* (1986), *Transformation* (1988), and *Majestic* (1989). Strieber's books have sold over twenty-two million copies worldwide

Strieber's nonfiction title *Confirmation* (1998) was made into a two-hour special by NBC. It aired on February 17, 1999, and reached over thirteen million viewers.

Since 1987, Strieber has made hundreds of television appearances and has become well known as a leading authority on mysteries of science.

His latest book, *The Coming Global Superstorm* (1999), was written in partnership with radio talk-show host Art Bell. Strieber, himself, is now the host of the popular "Dreamland" segment of the Art Bell Show.

Address: 5928 Broadway
San Antonio, TX 78209
U.S.A.

E-mail: whitley@strieber.com
Web site: www.whitleysworld.com

Photo by Timothy Greenfield-Sanders

Whitley Strieber

POSITION STATEMENT: The [UFO] evidence, if it is properly addressed by science, has the power to change completely the way we deal with this issue, possibly providing us with wonderful new discoveries and information. But there are problems. Not everybody is open-minded. Not everybody is ready to entertain such evidence as may be presented. . . . But as a society, it would seem that we can now take the whole question another step forward and maybe at last start to move toward some satisfactory answers. Taking an interest need not imply a commitment to belief in alien contact, but we must seriously ask who or what is causing the UFO and close encounter phenomena, why it is taking place, and, above all, what its significance may be.

It is also necessary to face the fact that the existence of the evidence means that there really may be aliens here—aliens who are creating an extraordinary theater in the sky while at the same time entering the personal lives of many people in extremely bizarre and secretive ways.

Unless we deal in an organized and effective manner with the hard evidence that has come to light, we are going to remain passive to what could be not only a valuable knowledge resource but also an intrusion into our world that may or may not be in our best interest. Given its intimacy and the incredibly provocative nature of many contact reports, that doesn't seem wise.

—WHITLEY STRIEBER

(Position statement was adapted from Whitley Strieber's book *Confirmation*, 1998.)

Swiatek, Robert P. (b. 1953). Robert Swiatek has been researching UFOs since 1968, becoming associated with the Fund for UFO Research in 1986. He currently serves as secretary-treasurer of that organization, and is also a director of the UFO Research Coalition.

Swiatek's active participation with the Fund has necessitated his involvement with, *inter alia,* the Roswell incident, abductions, and UFO history.

A Pennsylvania native, Swiatek received his B.A. degree from Bloomsburg State College in 1975—double-majoring in physics and Earth science—followed by one year of graduate study in physics at Lehigh University. In the summer of 1974, he worked at NASA Headquarters for the manager of the Seasat program.

Since 1976 he has been employed as a physics patent examiner at the U.S. Patent and Trademark Office in Arlington, Virginia. Swiatek has evaluated applications in various "arts" at the Patent Office, including aeronautics and space technology.

Address: 10621 John Ayres Dr.
Fairfax, VA 22032
U.S.A.

E-mail: swiman@pop.dn.net

Robert Swiatek

POSITION STATEMENT: Fifty-plus years of UFO activity have proffered no definitive proof that UFOs are extraterrestrial spacecraft, and researchers continue to maintain their traditional posture of collecting sighting reports, separating genuine unknowns from IFOs, and trying to convince a skeptical world that a legitimate phenomenon of unknown origin holds sway

However, when objectively considered, the very best cases *do* indicate the presence of an unknown phenomenon that is not of human, atmospheric, or astronomical origin. Whether the unknowns are solid craft, weird intrusions of some kind from a postulated alternate universe, or holograms is mere conjecture, but in my opinion a nonhuman intelligence is behind them.

Continued collection of sighting reports in the absence of both an instrumented effort to obtain empirical data and the construction of theories to explain sighting and landing trace details is useless inasmuch as thousands of excellent reports have been logged and investigated to date. Even so, if witnesses to the so-called Roswell debris and other crashed UFOs are correct, the U.S. Government has in its possession material to resolve the debate. Episodes of mass psychogenic illness and a consideration of UFO abductees—who rarely panic despite being allegedly taken by aliens on board their craft—give no support to the view there will be a societal meltdown in the event UFOs are revealed to be alien vehicles.

—ROBERT SWIATEK

T

Takeda (Japan) photo This UFO was allegedly observed and photographed by Shinichi Takeda (of Fujisaw City) near Enoshima Miani Beach, Japan. The time was approximately 11:30 A.M. The date was August 20, 1957.

Mr. Takeda's sister first called his attention to it. The object was reported as silvery in color, glowing brilliantly, and seemed to be at around three or four thousand feet altitude, traveling in a southerly direction. When directly overhead, the object made a 90-degree turn and increased its speed from what seemed to be about 250 to 500 kmph—then disappeared into the clouds.

A few minutes later, about fifteen bathers at Enoshima Miani Beach reportedly spotted a similar object, which passed over the beach at high speed, without making a sound.

—CORAL & JIM LORENZEN

Tehran (Iran) jet chase This UFO encounter took place in the vicinity of Shahrokhi Air Force Base, Tehran, Iran, during the early morning hours of September 19, 1976. The incident involved multiple witnesses on the ground (both Iranian civilians and high-ranking military), pilots and crews of two F-4 Phantom jet fighters, radar confirmation, and apparent electromagnetic effects.

Initial reports came in shortly after midnight (local time), to the air base by telephone from citizens living in the Shemiran district of Tehran, who spotted an unusual bright light in the night sky. No shape was discerned, just a brilliant light source, like "a helicopter with a shining light." A quick check by the command post duty officer showed no helicopters or planes to be in the area, so he called the deputy commander of operations for instructions. The deputy commander relayed a message to the effect that the citizens were merely observing stars, but the commander himself was not so sure. He proceeded to look for himself and, after observing a brilliant light (subsequently determined to be seventy miles distant at this point), decided to scramble an Iranian Air Force F-4 Phantom jet to investigate.

At 1:30 A.M., the jet was roaring down the Shahrokhi runway in pursuit of a UFO. As the F-4 crew were headed north of Tehran toward the unidentified light source, control tower operators watched from the base. The first forty-five miles of the flight proceeded uneventfully, but as the jet approached within twenty-five nautical miles of the object, all instrumentation and communications, both UHF and intercom, on the plane suddenly went dead. Rendered defenseless, the pilot broke off the intercept and headed back to base. As the plane retreated, all electronic systems were restored.

As the first plane landed at 1:40 A.M., a second F-4 pilot took off to try his luck. Airborne radar contact was made at a distance of twenty-seven nautical miles from the object, the return being described as similar to the size of the return of a Boeing 707 tanker aircraft. As the second jet closed within twenty-five miles of the UFO, it pulled ahead, keeping the pursuer at that constant distance. The visual description of the object was "flashing strobe lights arranged in a rectangular pattern and alternating blue, green, red, and orange in color. The sequence of the lights was so fast that all the colors could be seen at once."

As the jet continued to pace the object, now on a course to the south of Tehran, the UFO suddenly ejected a smaller object, which came streaking toward the Phantom at a high rate of speed. As the (apparent) "projectile" came closer, the weapons-control panel and all communications on the jet were lost, just as had happened with the first F-4. The pilot, therefore, executed an evasive dive, but the projectile continued to trail him at an estimated distance of three to four miles. After an accelerated circular turn, the smaller UFO then proceeded to rejoin the primary object and merged back with it. Meanwhile, the jet's weapons-control system and communications equipment became operative again, and the F-4 crew bravely continued their pursuit.

Shortly, another smaller object again separated from the main UFO, but this time it headed for the ground below. Anticipating a great explosion, the crew of the jet watched as the jettisoned mini-object gently came to rest on a dry lake bed below, casting a bright light over an area of two to three kilometers all around. The light soon faded, and the main UFO disappeared also, speeding off into the night.

A daylight inspection was made of the apparent "landing site," but no traces were found. There was some corroboration, however, in the form of testimony from a local resident in the area who had heard a loud sound and seen a very bright light.

An official document released under the Freedom of Information and Privacy Act on August 31, 1977, by the United States Department of Defense, recounts the events which took place during the Iranian jet-chase episode but adds little to what was already reported. It did reiterate, however, the puzzling nature of this case; the fact that what was observed by multiple witnesses has yet to be satisfactorily explained.

—RONALD D. STORY

References

Story, Ronald D. *UFOs and the Limits of Science* (William Morrow/New English Library, 1981).

UFO Investigator (published by NICAP, November 1976).

UFO Investigator (published by NICAP, September 1977).

Temple of the Stars   (Neville Spearman, 1962). Brinsley Le Poer Trench uses his second book on the ancient astronaut theme to make a case that Atlantis, Stonehenge, the Pyramids, and other megalithic monuments scattered over the planet were gifts from extraterrestrial visitors. Trench, a member of the British House of Lords, believes the British Isles are sacred territory, because the megaliths there are a legacy of our Atlantean forebears who in turn owed their civilization to those space visitors known as the Sky People.

—RANDALL FITZGERALD

theories, UFO   Numerous hypotheses have been advanced to explain UFO reports. They can be divided into two major categories, the first advocating conventional explanations (involving no purposeful intelligence), the second advocating unconventional explanations involving purposeful intelligence).

The conventional category includes such mundane explanations as aircraft, balloons, birds, and planets and may also encompass more imaginative possibilities, as ball lightning, swamp gas, insect swarms, as well as various psychological explanations. Hoaxes and hallucinations also fall under the conventional category.

The unconventional category is composed of eight major "theories," although there is little to warrant the designation of "theory"; a more appropriate label might be "speculation" or, in some cases, "hypothesis." These eight "theories" are: (1) the secret weapon theory; (2) the hollow Earth theory; (3) the underwater civilization theory; (4) the space animal theory; (5) the extraterrestrial hypothesis; (6) the time travel theory; (7) the ultraterrestrial theory; and (8) the psychic projection theory. The likelihood of each theory is assessed below.

The Secret Weapon Theory: This theory, especially popular in the 1950s and again in recent times, refers to advanced technological flying devices constructed by the U.S. Government or some foreign power. The proposition has some very serious problems. First, UFOs were reported soon after World War II, when military jet aircraft were barely operational. Had the U.S. had operational "saucers" capable of the performance described, it would not have expended the hundreds of billions of dollars that it has, since that time, in the development of alternate and less efficient military weapons systems.

Second, even if such craft had been experimentally tested, or even operationally deployed, they would not have been permitted to approach civilian airports, urban centers, and all the everyday places where UFOs are reported. Also, they would not have been deployed to the dozens of countries from where UFO reports have come. On the other hand, such craft would very probably have been revealed to the world as a major technological breakthrough and as a warning to all potential

adversaries. The political advantages of the latter would have been enormous.

A third problem would be the question of security. The development and operation of such craft would have involved many thousands of persons over a long period of time, and it is almost inconceivable that the secret would not have eventually surfaced. These same arguments can, of course, be applied to a Soviet secret weapon, or one from any other country. A British/Canadian secret weapon theory, for example, was once in vogue, and one organization has been promoting a Nazi secret weapon theory, interwoven with Adolf Hitler's possible survival and escape from Berlin. The organization has published a book supporting this claim and also makes available other Nazi-oriented books, posters, bumper stickers, and tapes (such as "Beautiful Nazi Songs and Marches," "Songs of the Brownshirts," "Dr. Goebbels and the Third Reich," and "Adolf Hitler Speaks to the Reichstag"). (Mattern and Friedrich, 1976) As with all other "secret weapon" theories, it is difficult to imagine how such craft could have been operated for over thirty years without political utilization or without the truth emerging.

The Hollow Earth Theory: Perhaps the most ingenious of all, the original hollow Earth theory was advanced by several writers early in the century, but was later linked to UFOs and popularized by Ray Palmer and Dr. Raymond Bernard (who some think was one and the same person). In the early 1960s, Bernard claimed that the Earth was actually a hollow sphere, with two openings at the poles, and that "flying saucers" belonged to a secret civilization living inside the Earth. (Bernard, 1964)

The theory supposedly gained support from observations made during Admiral Richard E. Byrd's Arctic and Antarctic expeditions. However, Dr. Laurence M. Gould, second in command during Byrd's first Antarctic expedition, denied any such observations or discoveries. Dr. Gould, a distinguished University of Arizona geologist, discussed the matter with Admiral Byrd several times prior to the latter's death in 1957, and both were amazed at the observations attributed to them. When he was president of the American Association for the Advancement of Science, in 1953, Dr. Gould considered but finally declined an invitation to address the Hollow Earth Society, then meeting in Tucson, and believed that, had he accepted the invitation, it would have been promoted endlessly as an endorsement of the hollow Earth theory.

The hollow Earth theory was examined in 1970 by Dr. John S. Derr, a professional seismologist, then working on the Viking Mars lander project with Martin Marietta Corporation, and later with the U.S. Geological Survey. Dr. Derr discussed several types of geodetic and seismological data which clearly demonstrated that the Earth is not, and cannot be, hollow. Artificial satellite perturbations, for example, show not only that the Earth is solid, but that its mass is concentrated toward its center, contrary to that "predicted" by the hollow Earth theory. He also presented seismological data concerning the free oscillations of the Earth and the velocity of compressional and shear waves in the Earth following earthquakes. (Derr, 1970)

Dr. Derr's analysis, plus other less sophisticated but more obvious evidence (such as the fact that numerous U.S. and Soviet satellites, which continually fly over the poles, have not, apparently, photographed the openings) leaves little doubt that UFOs, whatever they are, do not originate from a civilization in a hollow Earth.

The Underwater Civilization Theory: Reports of unknown objects entering or leaving large bodies of water (or proceeding through them) have been made from time to time and have been labeled unidentified submarine objects (USOs). Numerous theorists have consequently speculated that secret UFO bases might be located on the ocean beds, far from human activities and possible detection. By moving underwater, UFOs would have access to all continents and, by proceeding up major rivers and tributaries, could reach many inland locations without risking detection by atmospheric flight.

Vehicles capable of interstellar flight, some

proponents of the extraterrestrial hypothesis point out, would certainly be able to withstand the pressures and stresses of deep oceanic environments. This point has some validity, and it can also be stated that some of the most remote areas of the planet are located in parts of the southern Pacific and Indian oceans, providing easy access from the atmosphere with minimum chance of visual or electronic detection.

At the same time, it could be asked why the UFO operators go to such lengths to remain unobserved, only to display their vehicles so blatantly in such populated areas as the United States and Europe.

One of the proponents of the underwater theory was the late naturalist Ivan T. Sanderson, who not only proposed that an extraterrestrial civilization could be using the ocean depths, but that a native civilization, one having evolved underwater long before man, could also be doing so. He concluded, in fact, that "it is likely that both suggestions apply." Although he provided no sources or references, Sanderson stated that over 50 percent of all UFO reports concerned objects over, coming from, or going toward (or into) bodies of water. (Sanderson, 1970)

The underwater civilization theory, like the hollow Earth theory, addresses the question of the possible location of UFO operational centers. As such, it is not altogether unreasonable, but it provides no real answer to the question of UFO origin.

The Space Animal Theory: One of the least popular of all "unconventional" theories, the space animal theory was first brought to public attention, curiously enough, by the U.S. Air Force during its Project Sign activity in the late 1940s. The Project "Saucer" (Sign was then still a classified code name) press release of April 27, 1949, admitted that the idea had been "remotely considered," and that many UFOs "acted more like animals than anything else." The Air Force concluded that few such reports were reliable. The concept was also contained in the final Project Sign Technical Report of February 1949 (declassified in 1961).

Trevor James Constable (writing under the

pen name of Trevor James) advocated a space animal explanation for UFOs in 1958, and none other than Kenneth Arnold, the man whose sighting opened the UFO era (and who was responsible for coining the label "flying saucer"), concluded that UFOs ". . . are groups and masses of living organisms that are as much a part of our atmosphere and space as the life we find in the oceans." (Arnold, 1962)

Naturalist Ivan T. Sanderson again addressed the question, and many others, in 1967, concluding that there was ". . . nothing illogical, irrational, or even improbable about it. In fact, it is so probable that it must be given first rank in consideration of the question, 'What could UAO's [unexplained aerial objects] be?' " (Sanderson, 1967) That same year, Vincent H. Gaddis addressed the topic, attributing the original idea to a John P. Bessor, who had sent it to the Air Force the month following Arnold's classic 1947 sighting. Gaddis discussed the writings on the subject by Austrian Countess Zoe Wassilko-Serecki, and John Cage, a New Jersey inventor, and concluded that ". . . the time will come when one or more of these entities will be caught, weighed, measured, and exhibited." (Gaddis, 1967)

Trevor James Constable again wrote about space animals in the 1970s, this time in more detail. (Constable, 1976; 1978) He postulated that the UFO space animals ". . . are amoebalike life-forms existing in the plasma state. They are not solid, liquid, or gas. Rather, they exist in the fourth state matter—plasma—as living heat-substance at the upper border of physical nature." He also believed that they are of low intelligence and, because they remain in the infrared part of the electromagnetic spectrum, usually invisible. He concluded that they had ". . . deeply confused UFO research."

Although life may be found in some of the harshest of conditions and in some of the most unlikely places on the planet, it is doubtful that complex life-forms could evolve in space or even in the upper regions of the atmosphere, where exposure to cosmic rays and other radiations, such as those originating from solar flares, would be maximized. The absence of oxygen for carbon-based life would also rule out biological space animals, and the possibility of life existing in a plasma state is, at best, speculative.

The space animal theory has never captured the public imagination, and it has not been seriously considered by most UFO researchers.

The Extraterrestrial Hypothesis (ETH): By far the most popular "theory" concerning the origin of UFOs, the ETH is also the one that, over the years, has aroused the most emotion and controversy. It is based on the assumption that one or more civilizations from outer space, far in advance of our own, have mastered interstellar space flight and have had the human race under systematic observation since at least 1947. Some see a long-term involvement by the extraterrestrials and propose that they have been watching over us, and perhaps even controlling our physical and cultural development for millennia, thus linking the ETH to the ancient astronaut concept.

The main problems with the ETH are space and time: space in the sense that the average distance between the 130 billion or more stars in our Milky Way galaxy is enormous, and time in the sense that these great distances would make interstellar voyages very long, not to mention the economic, engineering, and motivational aspects of such an enterprise.

Despite this, there is a pro-UFO movement that uncritically believes in the ETH. There is no problem with such a belief, provided it is identified as such and is not construed as representing an empirical fact. At the same time, the idea of an extraterrestrial origin for UFOs, as a *hypothesis,* is quite reasonable, despite the strong feelings against the possibility by many scientists who should know better. To deny the validity of a reasonable hypothesis because of an emotional commitment to other explanatory possibilities is not consistent with operational procedures in science, regardless of how learned such individuals may be or how persuasive their arguments may appear.

The real basis for the ETH debate, although many involved in the debate are seemingly unaware of it, is not over whether (or how much) advanced intelligence exists in the galaxy. Most scientists will agree that there are probably many such intelligent civilizations in the galaxy. It is not even over whether such civilizations have developed interstellar-travel capability. The real point of debate concerns the "volume of traffic." That is, most scientists find it very difficult to accept the idea of extraterrestrial visitation *on the scale implied by UFO reports;* that, to them, tends to invalidate all UFO reports. In fact, if UFO sightings were not so common (say, just one good report every three or four years), perhaps more scientists would seriously consider the ETH. Interestingly, this is precisely the reverse of what many exasperated UFO proponents realize, in their attempts to "prove" the ETH by the sheer number of reports.

Despite intensive research by many individuals, scientific bodies, and federal agencies for over three decades, no proof of extraterrestrial visitation has been produced. Such an idea, therefore, must remain as only a viable and intriguing hypothesis, very difficult to test, and frustrating to debate.

The Time Travel Theory: Like most UFO "theories," the time travel theory lacks any empirical supporting evidence; contrary to what one might expect, however, it is probably the least-popular theory in circulation.

The theory is based on the premise that we will eventually progress to such a high technological level that, in learning how to control certain forces of nature, it will be within our power to manipulate the barriers of time and space and "return" to our present time, or any other we wish. It has to be admitted that there are certain astrophysical phenomena currently being studied (i.e., quasars, black holes), which are not properly understood, and there is every indication that some fundamental natural processes in the universe have yet to be identified, described, and incorporated into our framework of knowledge.

Nevertheless, the only hints of a time travel basis for UFOs are in the behavioral and morphological descriptions of occupants sometimes reported to pilot them. The behavioral component refers to reports that such occupants generally avoid contact, or at least do not go beyond an informal communication with witnesses. This "policy of noninterference" would seem to be more appropriate for a society visiting its own past, which has already "happened," than for an interstellar-traveling society, which might be eager to establish formal links with new civilizations.

The morphological component involves the biological feature of neoteny, a characteristic in which infantile features are retained in the adult form. A neotenous trend is evident in the primates, particularly in man (the result is a longer childhood and the acquisition of knowledge and values by children), and the trend will theoretically continue in the future. This implies that human adults, at some future time, could look more like today's children. Curiously, UFO occupants are described as small and childlike, with large heads relative to their bodies. Both of these speculative forms of evidence must rely, of course, on the authenticity and reliability of UFO reports involving "occupants."

The possibility of UFO occupants being *extraterrestrial* time travelers (i.e., not from *our* future) is not generally addressed by UFO researchers.

The Ultraterrestrial Theory: In the late 1960s, a number of UFO authorities became disenchanted with the extraterrestrial hypothesis, which they now considered antiquated. Impatient with the lack of "contact" over the years, these individuals have moved on to accept a more esoteric concept, that involving "ultraterrestrials" in a "parallel universe." These interdimensional beings are thought to share our own space, but at a different "vibratory level" of existence, and that time may have no meaning for them. John A. Keel, one of the major thinkers in the area, believes that UFOs are "nothing more than transmogrifications tailoring themselves to our abilities to understand . . ." and that the ultraterrestrials

". . . are somehow able to manipulate the electrical circuits of the human mind." (Keel, 1970)

There are so many variations of this "theory," and each variation has such loose definitional parameters, that it is difficult to describe in a systematic way. Some authorities, like Dr. Jacques Vallée, talk of long-term cultural control by such intelligences, involving the world's leading religious movements, miracles, angels, ghosts, fairies, poltergeists, and the like; and they interpret UFOs as another (but more modern) manifestation of the same phenomena.

Such beliefs are not for all, however. According to Vallée, they are only for ". . . those few who have . . . graduated to a higher, clearer level of perception of the total meaning of that tenuous dream that underlies the many nightmares of human history." (Vallée, 1969) Others, like Keel, are suspicious of the ultraterrestrials' motives, and a few integrate the new theory into their previously established religious beliefs about good and evil forces.

As with some other areas of the "psychic sciences," the ultraterrestrial theory lacks a cohesive synthesis. This is probably because of its (proposed) nature; there is no way to go about obtaining empirical evidence to support the hypothesis. That is, there is no "observational window" one can look through to even evaluate the reasonableness of the hypothesis. The extraterrestrial hypothesis, on the other hand, does have such an "observational window." To see it, one need only step outside at night and look up; the question of whether or not extraterrestrial visitation is possible can thus be evaluated, based on the time travel theory data made available through the "window," and everyone can usually agree on the data even if they do not always agree on their interpretation. Even some of the more unlikely UFO theories, such as the hollow Earth theory, have "observational windows," thus enabling their appropriate evaluation.

Although the ultraterrestrial theory has become fashionable in some European and American UFO circles, and has gathered a substantial following, it is little known among the public and has had little effect on public opinion.

The Psychic Projection Theory: The psychic projection theory represents a modern school of thought in UFO circles which, like the ultraterrestrial theory, developed as a reaction to the extraterrestrial hypothesis. The theory was fast outlined by Jerome Clark and Loren Coleman in the mid-1970s, based loosely on Carl Jung's concept of the collective unconscious. (Clark and Coleman, 1975)

The authors, however, have gone far beyond Jungian psychology and postulate that the collective unconscious can psychically project material forms, represented in modern times by the UFO—with occupants—and that ". . . the UFO phenomenon has absorbed many of the ancient archetypal forms in which human beings have traditionally needed to believe and which they have sought to complete their world."

Clark and Coleman see a danger in the modern world of science disrupting man's close bond to nature, to mysticism, and to the elements, bringing him to "the brink of catastrophe." The message they see in the UFO myth is that the collective unconscious ". . . too long repressed, will burst free, overwhelm the world, and usher in an era of madness, superstition, and terror—with all the sociopolitical accoutrements: war, anarchy, fascism," and that ". . . when the unconscious can no longer be contained, its liberated contents will destroy all that the conscious mind has produced: the fruits of science and technology, civilized order, and the very process of reason itself. Under the new imbalance a spiritual dark age will blanket the earth."

UFOs, then, are something like "planetary poltergeists" that are generated by the "psychic energy" of the collective unconscious (and sometimes by an individual unconscious), as were fairies, flying saucers, "spacemen," and apparitions of the Virgin Mary.

In some respects, the psychic projection theory relies on the same kinds of evidence as the ultraterrestrial theory, and it is sometimes difficult to distinguish between the writings of authorities in the two schools.

The psychic projection theory would have to depend, at the very least, on both the reality of Jung's collective unconscious—a kind of reality that Jung never claimed for it—and the reality of extrasensory perception (ESP). ESP research is a continuing and active area of research by numerous psychologists, biologists, and physicists. A very bitter and emotional debate has ensued over the years concerning the validity of ESP. Some believe that the whole subject is nonsense and should not be given any serious consideration. Others claim that ESP effects have been conclusively demonstrated in repeated laboratory experiments, and that efforts should be directed more toward understanding the effects than toward attempting to convince the skeptics.

Until the matter is resolved, the psychic projection theory must remain as simply a fascinating idea. Even if ESP effects (precognition, telepathy, telekinesis, et cetera) were ultimately demonstrated to be authentic phenomena, bringing parapsychology into the mainstream of "normal" science, there has been no indication that such "psychic energy" could actually materialize (i.e., project) objects, whether they be fairies or flying saucers.

—J. RICHARD GREENWELL

References

Arnold, Kenneth. "Fireflies and Flying Saucers," *Flying Saucers* magazine (November 1962).

Bernard, Raymond. *The Hollow Earth* (Fieldcrest Publishing, 1964).

Bova, Ben, and Byron Preiss, eds. *First Contact: The Search for Extraterrestrial Intelligence* (Plume, 1991).

Clark, Jerome, and Loren Coleman. *The Unidentified* (Warner Books, 1975).

Constable, Trevor James. *Sky Creatures: Living UFOs* (Pocket Books, 1978).

———. *The Cosmic Pulse of Life* (Merlin Press, 1976).

Derr, John. "UFOs and the Hollow Earth Theory," *The APRO Bulletin* (November-December 1970). Reprinted as the "hollow Earth theory" entry in Story, Ronald D., ed *The Encyclopedia of UFOs* (Doubleday/New English Library, 1980).

Gaddis, Vincent H. *Mysterious Fires and Lights* (Dell, 1967).

James, Trevor. *They Live in the Sky* (New Age Publishing, 1958).

Keel, John A. *UFOs: Operation Trojan Horse* (G.P. Putnam's Sons, 1970).

Mattern (no first name given) and Christof Friedrich. *UFO's: Nazi Secret Weapon?* (Samisdat Publishers, 1976).

Sanderson, Ivan T. *Invisible Residents* (World Publishing, 1970).

———. *Uninvited Visitors* (Cowles, 1967).

Story, Ronald D., with J. Richard Greenwell. *UFOs and the Limits of Science* (Morrow, 1981).

Story, Ronald D., ed. with J. Richard Greenwell. *The Encyclopedia of UFOs* (Doubleday/New English Library, 1980).

U.S. Air Force Technical report No. F-TR-2274-IA, Project "Sign," Technical Intelligence Division, Intelligence Department, Air Matériel Command (February, 1949).

Vallée, Jacques. *Passport to Magonia—From Folklore to Flying Saucers* (Henry Regnery, 1969).

———. *Revelations* (Ballatine Books, 1991).

They Knew Too Much About Flying Saucers (Saucerian Press, 1956). Gray Barker introduces the term "Men in Black" to describe a mysterious agency, presumably of the government, which silences UFO witnesses to conceal the truth about the phenomenon. He tells the stories of six men, including radio newscaster Frank Edwards, who were supposedly censored or otherwise silenced when they spoke out about their UFO experiences or opinions.

—RANDALL FITZGERALD

They Live in the Sky (New Age Publishing Co., 1959) Trevor James Constable with this book became the third author (after Charles Fort in 1919 and Meade Layne in 1950) to speculate that many UFOs might be creatures, or "critters": amoeba-like animal life in our atmosphere which can materialize at will. The difference with Constable is that he claims to have photographed these critters using techniques gleaned from psychic information given him by an extraterrestrial intelligence.

—RANDALL FITZGERALD

Those Gods Who Made Heaven and Earth (Editions Robert Laffont, 1969). French author Jean Sendy reinterprets the Biblical story of our planet's creation to conclude that an extraterrestrial community of 30 or 40 scientists, known collectively as the Elohim, came to Earth aboard the Martian moon Phobos and created a climate-controlled laboratory called the Garden of Eden. Humans were expelled from Eden when they discovered the Elohim were not divine after all. Only Noah survived when the Elohim decided to end their experiment and destroy humankind with an atomic explosion that flooded the planet.

—RANDALL FITZGERALD

Threat, The (Simon & Schuster, 1998). Professor David M. Jacobs provides substantial evidence through the use of hypnotic-regressive interviews with over 700 alleged abductees that the alien-abduction experiences are primarily physical ones with the intent of creating hybrids (offspring of mixed Earth and alien parents).

The report proposes that the secret alien agenda is to integrate the hybrids into human society and thus take control of planet Earth.

—ETEP STAFF

threat, UFO-ET Whether UFOs and extraterrestrials pose a danger to humanity is a question that has been answered differently over the various decades of flying saucer history. The U.S. Air Force investigation of flying saucer reports from 1948 to 1969 was done specifically under its duty to determine if they posed a threat to the people of the United States. UFOlogists are fond of pointing out that the official Air Force explanations of various cases seemed perfunctory and unconvincing, and that they never even tried to propose solutions to a certain residuum. What goes unrecognized is the fact that the Air Force was not approaching flying saucers as a scientific mystery that they had to solve. They only needed to decide whether the reports pointed to some enemy of the U.S. engaging in some activity that undermined the nation's security.

They didn't need to solve every case to satisfy themselves that saucers were not a threat. Nobody was reporting bomb attacks, gunfire, chemical clouds, or other types of deadly intrusion. Nobody indicated there were parachute drops of personnel or supplies in preparation for battle. No base was being built inside our borders. The idea that they were spying on us was undermined by the fact that most reports were over areas with no evident strategic importance. The occasional exceptions like reports near Los Angeles or the 1952 Washington, D.C., incidents—when radar blips indicated some sort of entry into restricted air space near the Capitol and the White House—were troubling in their time, but retrospectively seem to have been innocuous. The D.C. blips behaved mindlessly with no evident goal. If any intelligence was gathered by the UFOs near Los Alamos, it is not evident that it was ever used. No hostile action followed, nor was there any indication it was used in power brokering.

It is a cliché of UFOlogical rhetoric that if even one UFO report can be substantiated, the implications are staggering. Unless one regards the idea of extraterrestrial life as innately intoxicating, this is not absolutely true. What if the one case involves a pair of Ganymedean tourists taking a scenic route to a resort spa on Mercury? The practical consequences to humanity would be nil. The news that extraterrestrial life exists and likes to vacation might be interesting or amusing, but would hardly be in the same league as news that aliens are casing our planet for war and colonization. The latter would truly be matters for full attention and immediate concern.

If one threw aside all critical judgment and accepted all claims made by UFOlogists of UFOs killing specifically named people as true, the death toll would still be less than that caused by everyday hazards. There are many more reasonable things to worry about than the purported UFO menace.

UFOlogists do worry about such things once in a while and have asked both the public and the government to share their concerns. What follows is a history of perceptions and notions about the danger vs. the harmlessness of the UFO phenomenon and how they have changed through the years.

FRIEND OR FOE

News articles from the first weeks of the UFO mystery do not paint the picture of a nation gripped by panic. Arnold's saucers were a source of fascination and mystery, not one of imminent danger. The Air Force said it wasn't anything of ours. The Russians said it wasn't anything of theirs. So what were they? Take your pick: transmutations of atomic energy, beer bottle caps shot out of a blast furnace, secret experiments, tricks of the eye, mirages of planes, a State Department propaganda ploy to lure us into war, helium-filled rings to publicize a ring toss game, electrical flying fish from Venus. One reporter, apparently on a lark, contacted authorities to get a statement about the invasion. The official said he had not heard of one and directed him to contact Orson Welles. Witnesses who came forward to corroborate the existence of flying saucers expressed no fear. One lady spoke of a creepy feeling at seeing a disk, but even that mild effect is exceptional.

In intelligence circles, rumors surfaced in July of 1947 that saucers spewed out radioactive clouds that killed animal life, and one scientist wrote to the FBI claiming saucers might be radio-controlled germ bombs or A-bombs, but these ideas apparently never became part of the public discourse. Some intelligence folks recommended in 1948 that the military might be put on alert status, but cooler heads prevailed. In 1949, a researcher for Project Sign observed that no damage had yet been attributed to UFOs. One doctor proposed there might have been a link between a polio epidemic he was treating and the saucer problem,

but authorities quietly discarded the idea. In 1950 a group of scientists calling themselves the Los Alamos Bird Watchers Association looked into the possibility of a correlation between radiation and UFO overflights, but nothing conclusive came of it. (Gross, 1982)

The Mantell tragedy was a pivotal event in early UFO history in that it began to press the point that something serious was going on. Some rumors appeared in the papers that radioactivity was found at the crash site. They were denied, but the absence of a clear answer to the mysterious circumstances surrounding Mantell's UFO pursuit and subsequent plane crash was not so easy to dismiss. Interestingly, however, the concern among UFO buffs was over the government's handling of the case and not about trigger-happy aliens. Keyhoe felt no belligerence was involved. They had merely acted in self-defense. "Even the stoutest believers in the disks do not think any mass invasion from space is possible at this time." (Keyhoe, 1950)

Gerald Heard noted that, until Mantell, saucers always succeeded in getting out of the way. "They have behaved with a deportment that shows not merely savoir faire but real considerateness." He felt it was puzzling that they threw away the advantage of surprise if they truly posed a future threat. (Heard, 1951) Frank Scully echoed the sentiment that there was no belligerence evident in alien observer actions. His fear was that Earth pilots might attack the saucers and prompt retaliation against not only the aggressors, but our whole planet. (Scully, 1950)

Contactees offered contradictory confessions. Orfeo Angelucci's aliens said Mantell's death was unavoidable because he tried to overtake and capture a "remotely controlled" disk. (Angelucci, 1955) George Adamski's aliens regretted the power field effects of a large manned vessel that caused the "accident." (Adamski, 1955)

In 1951 a Dr. Anthony Mirarchi was widely quoted as suggesting saucers came from a potential enemy of the United States. "If they were launched by a foreign power then they could lead to a worse Pearl Harbor than we have ever experienced.'' He recommended that considerable appropriations be allocated to conduct a complete investigation. The historical significance of this plea is open to argument. It may be the first expression of a fear of attack and call for increased investigation to get wide dissemination, but Mirarchi is not heard from again in UFO circles, and the call to action is surely ignored. The reference to Pearl Harbor, however, will recur a decade later in the writings of the Lorenzens.

Sometime in early 1952 a Rotary Club lecturer took up the subject of flying saucers. He expressed the belief that they heralded a better life. They represented a non-hostile invasion from which we might acquire an advanced science. An informal survey of saucer buffs uniformly got responses that the saucers were not a menace. They: ''come here in peace,'' ''don't wish to destroy us,'' had ''outgrown war,'' had ''curiosity,'' were afraid to contact us, or would eventually contact us and give us secrets. (Bender, 1962)

The most telling fact that this was in fact the general attitude occurred in the wake of the Washington, D.C., radar incidents. Al Chop, working at the Pentagon press desk, said people were writing letters and wiring the President urging the military not to shoot at the saucers. He asked newswriters to please emphasize to people that pilots in fact were not shooting at the saucers.

Kenneth Arnold resurfaced around this time with his opinions that UFOs were harmless and probably a living, thinking animal of the stratosphere. *The Coming of the Saucers* (1952), the book he co-authored with Ray Palmer, avoided any final conclusions about flying saucers. They weren't American or Russian or Spanish or Argentine, and they saw no substance to claims of crashed saucers bearing little men from other planets. They presently hoped that the truth could in time be sifted from the fanciful. All they knew was that flying saucers may be the ''most vitally important fact of our time!''

In 1953 Desmond Leslie and George Adamski offer their contact tale in *Flying Saucers Have Landed*. Their message included the sentiment that these people from other worlds are our friends and wish to ensure the safety and balance of the other planets in our system. They could impose powerful action against us, not with weapons, but by manipulating ''the natural forces of the universe.''

Keyhoe's 1953 book *Flying Saucers from Outer Space* is a first major step into the fear that saucers were dangerous. Keyhoe argues with some friends about the implications of various saucer reports. One of them is a jet pilot named Jim Riordan who presents a spirited defense of his belief that aliens are hostile. Repeated surveillance of certain strategic sites leads him to believe: ''It looks as if they are getting ready for an attack . . . measuring us for a knockout.'' He points to an odd case of a red spray bomb that exploded at Albuquerque, which he suggests had to be a ranging test for a future attack. Keyhoe offers the self-admittedly thin suggestion it is only a back-up plan in case we don't listen to reason. Keyhoe himself insists there was no proof of hostility: ''at least an even chance they mean us no harm.'' The long reconnaissance of Earth was ''possibly nearing its climax . . . the final act of the saucer drama.'' Instead of an all-out attack, he preferred to believe ''the final operation may be entirely peaceful; if so, it could be of benefit to everyone on earth.''

Herman Oberth, the father of the V-2 rocket, offered his opinions about the saucers in a frequently quoted 1954 article. ''They obviously have not come as invaders, but I believe their present mission may be one of scientific investigation.'' He optimistically suggests the ''ultimate result might be disclosure of secrets [that] otherwise we might not lay bare for a hundred thousand years.'' (Flammonde, 1971)

Harold Wilkins of Britain was notably ambivalent about the hazards of saucers in his first book, *Flying Saucers on the Attack* (1954). On one page he deduces they are ''unmistakably hostile'' because of evidence of ''arson on quite a large and dangerous scale.'' Later, he backpedals and thinks it may just be a warning. He speaks of death rays wielded by the airplanes, but allows Earth fliers menacing them could have prompted it. He quotes contactees to the effect that the aliens are not hostile, but notes they do not desire close contact. They perhaps see in us "hooligan children" deserving to be "whipped with a rod of scorpions." Elsewhere he wonders if they are drawn here to profit from mineral deposits.

The following year, his sequel *Flying Saucers Uncensored* (1955) is less ambivalent. He warns it is folly for any sane man to do more than quietly investigate given their ethics are unlikely to be ours. Even so, he speculates on the aggressive tactics a hostile cosmic power might employ and he asserts seeing "a most disturbing pattern has been slowly built up." The issue of death rays reasserts itself and he speaks of a "death ceiling," in essence a blockade, having been instituted to prevent us from future flights to the moon and beyond. Mysterious experiments are performed which causes tears in everybody in an area in Singapore. Horses are sterilized by atomic radiation. Humans are abducted for unknown ends, but in pursuing their overlordship over the Earth, Wilkins suggests they would not need our bodies. It is probably annihilation of our souls they seek. They might create mutations of humans that are devoid of divine creativity and dissatisfaction. "Creative art and pure science, the godlike in man, would die out." They might be throwing "a cosmic monkey wrench into our terrestrial wheels" to derail our use of atomic weaponry and supersonic aircraft. Activity along the Martian canals, he worries, might indicate they are contemplating an invasion of Earth. Dangerous or not, Wilkins is certain they have conducted a pole-to-pole survey of our world. We can only "watch, wait, collate, and synthesize."

In *The Flying Saucer Conspiracy* (1955), Donald Keyhoe began to accept that the saucers were in fact hostile, as Riordan said they were. He began to collect phenomena that could be interpreted as alien attacks. A Walesville plane crash indicates the use of heat beams. Skyquakes indicate the use of focused sound waves. A hole in a billboard becomes evidence of a missile from outer space. The Seattle windshield-pitting epidemic is regarded as retaliation for Earth space activities. The disappearance of Flight 19 becomes evidence that aliens are abducting humans. Keyhoe admits the absence of an all-out takeover is a problem he doesn't have an answer for. His friend Redell gets the final word and proposes the disappearances are to acquire people who can teach them our language before they make contact.

Morris Jessup is ambivalent from his study of the phenomenon. He sees them as exploratory missions that sometime engage in experiments and the capture of specimens. Though they catch planes and cause occasional storms and deluges, he still thinks we should not be astonished if it turns out that space dwellers are preparing to prevent fear-stricken human beings from blowing up another planet. (Jessup, 1955)

Waveney Girvan felt more evidence would exist if saucers truly represented hostile invasion. People feared the saucers because they forced a new dimension in our thinking. They offend the climate of our age, but he felt they brightened it up a little as well. The large proportion of reports proved the visitors were peaceful and friendly and far from hostile. (Girvan, 1955)

One UFOlogist around this time offered the revelation that the craft were not only friendly, they were helping clear our environment of radiation released in atomic bomb blasts. (Moseley, 1956) It turns out this had been advanced in contactee circles, specifically Mark Probert's Inner Circle for some time. There is even a news item dating back to the 1947 Wave in which a San Francisco zany claimed astral contact with the Dhyanis, rulers of creation, who were dropping "metaboblons" into our atmosphere to counteract atomic radiation. (Bloecher, 1967) This is likely a garbling of metabolons, a word in brief use around 1910 to label the fragments of atoms in radioactivity before they were better understood as protons, neutrons, and electrons. The Dhyanis had not kept up in their reading.

Aimé Michel in *The Truth about Flying Saucers* (1956) advanced contradictory opinions about the nature of the saucer problem. In one place he says it is essential to find out what they are, for if they are real a sword of Damocles hangs over our heads: "the destiny of our planet is assuredly at stake." Later, he proclaims "their inoffensive nature is a certainty. If we are being visited, it is by beings whose courtesy and tact need no further illustration. We could learn from them, in addition to their knowledge, a lesson in respect for others. With all the power at their disposal, they have never once attempted to interfere in our affairs." He goes on to suggest that they are fearful of the murderous tendencies evident in all our great enterprises. He felt the American investigations had proved nothing. Further investigation, and a little more human effort, would make the difference. "The mystery would be fathomed very soon, if we really tried."

Michel's sequel, *Flying Saucers and the Straight Line Mystery* (1958), advanced orthoteny as a mortal blow to the idea that saucers were a collective psychopathology. The threads provided by orthoteny now meant there was no question a Sword of Damocles had been hanging over our heads. Why it had not fallen yet was unexplained, but the blow will be fatal. Their landing would lead to the extinction of mankind because of our inferior ethics.

How very different is the conclusion of Bryant and Helen Reeves's contactee study *Flying Saucer Pilgrimage* (1957). The aliens are regarded as Guardians who will never offer coercion or assistance, but are servants of the Light, masters of energy, and are "balanced" beings. While ill-intentioned beings exist, the Guardians prevent their passage to our world. The overall picture is deemed "very progressive and inspiring."

Leonard Stringfield's *Saucer Post—3-0 Blue* (1957) is a portrait of uncertainty. In November of 1955 he had offered the case for interplanetary war, but he changed his mind. UFOs seemed to behave menacingly in certain cases, yet a superior culture could clearly be capable of planeticide and mass harm. Acts of UFO violence exist, but hostility seems highly debatable.

Gray Barker's *They Knew Too Much About Flying Saucers* (1956) added to the growing sense that malevolence was associated with UFO phenomena. These things may mean to do us harm and may or may not be shooting at us with rays from underground. This doesn't alarm him too greatly, since he feels we are bound to find some defense against it. What disturbs him is that some agency is trying to prevent us from learning about their existence and might come knocking at the door. An acquaintance with the name T. James was suggesting to him aliens might be "downright evil."

Two holdouts against the trend to see aliens as troublesome were Max B. Miller and Gavin Gibbons. Miller was still in the sway of the contactee faction and felt they conveyed "fraternal friendship and understanding." Their effects were "positive and constructive." (Miller, 1958) Gibbons was more influenced by the early Keyhoe. "They are not hostile," he affirms. He fully expected them to land en masse in the near future based on patterns of activity he chronicled. "They will certainly bring benefits," he predicts. "We must, all of us, welcome these beings who are taking so much trouble to bring the news of a good life to this planet." (Gibbons, 1958)

Reviewing the UFO myth in 1958, Carl Jung noted the contradictory strands developing in it. According to some, the visitors held superior wisdom and wanted to save humanity; but other aliens were carrying off people, as in the case of Flight 19, according to others. Some affirm their benevolence, but that harmlessness was "recently doubted." To Jung, the flights didn't appear based on any recognizable system. If anything, they were like tourists unsystematically viewing the landscape. (Jung, 1958, 1959)

Robert Dickhoff's *Homecoming of the Mar-*

tians (1958, 1964) might be dismissed as obscure, little-read, and lightly veiled fiction. Yet it is a treasure. According to his conscious mythology, "Germ-invaders" swept down from space in the past and "begat life or a parody thereof" in a variety of forms that included the ape-men mentalities. Aghartan teachers have through the centuries been rendering them a harmless and controlled reality. In the present, a super-brain a.k.a. God-Brain-Head, produced by manipulated biological engineering, exists for which robot-crews and scientists with gangster throwback mentalities travel through space. They "spacenap" earthlings and gather blood for the Brain's nourishment.

By the end of the decade, Keyhoe is fully convinced that UFOs are a danger. The creation of NICAP was directed to the end of proving wrong the Air Force's conclusion that UFOs were no threat. Delmar Fahmey, at NICAP's creation, stated there was "an urgent need to know the facts." (Ruppelt, 1956). To that end they would pester the Air Force for release of all their files. They called for Congressional hearings to acknowledge the reality of the saucer problem. Keyhoe wanted an all-out drive to communicate with the aliens—to convince them we wouldn't try to invade other worlds. Congress would be obliged to force a crash program for our defense against aliens. (Keyhoe, 1960)

That the Air Force refused to release their files is a fact. Ruppelt said they planned to ignore NICAP, because they knew their independent review would nitpick every case. If the bird, balloon, or plane hadn't been caught and a signed confession wrung out, they would call it a spaceship. They knew from earlier experiences what to expect: "Many of the inquiries came from saucer screwballs and these people are like a hypochondriac at the doctor's; nothing will make them believe the diagnosis unless it is what they came to hear. And there are plenty of saucer screwballs. One officer summed it up neatly when he told me, 'It isn't the UFOs that give us the trouble, it's the people.'" (Ruppelt, 1956)

INVASION AND INFECTION

The sixties were a manic time for UFO belief. Flying saucers were so real, only the most bigoted skeptic could deny advanced metallic piloted machines were flying around—a potential threat to the security of the world. Everyone felt something had to be done. Most of all, the authorities should openly admit the reality of the problem.

Book titles convey some of the mood of the period: *Flying Saucers: The Startling Evidence of the Invasion from Outer Space; Flying Saucers are Hostile; Flying Saucer Invasion—Target Earth; Flying Saucers—Serious Business; The Real UFO Invasion; The Terror Above Us*. The teaser on *The Official Guide to UFOs* promised "Exclusive! First News of America's Most Terrifying UFO Invasion!" Wilkins's books return with arch blurbs asking "Are They Friendly Visitors from Outer Space or Invaders Planning Conquest?" and "Is there a cosmic battle plan aimed at Earth?" The actual content was less dramatic than advertised, but that hardly mattered. The conviction of urgency transcended the material gathered for proof.

Throughout the first half of the decade, Keyhoe's NICAP pressed for Congressional hearings on the UFO problem by such tactics as letter-writing campaigns. The Air Force warned congressmen such hearings would only dignify the problem and cause more publicity, thus adding to the problem. NICAP also published a book called *The UFO Evidence* (edited by Richard Hall) and sent copies to congressmen to put forward their case that UFOs were in fact real and posed a danger to the fabric of society. The danger included an unprepared public being caught up in widespread panic if an external danger was suddenly imposed. A sudden confrontation with extraterrestrials could have disastrous results, they warned. Among them, "catastrophic results to morale."

While NICAP found some support for their position in Congress, nothing happened until the infamous "swamp gas" fiasco caused a loss of credibility in the Air Force's handling of the UFO problem. On April 5, 1966, Congress held open hearings. This led to the creation of the Condon Committee to undertake a new investigation—in essence, to get a second opinion of the Air Force's diagnosis. Keyhoe rejoiced, calling it "the most significant development in the history of UFO investigation."

Condon confirmed the diagnosis: "We know of no reason to question the finding of the Air Force that the whole class so far considered does not pose a defense problem." While critics carped at the inability of the committee to solve all the cases they studied, the issue of their agreeing with the absence of a threat went unnoticed. The cases in the report don't suggest much violence beyond the guy who was purportedly burned from a blast of hot gasses expelled by a saucer as it started spinning up for takeoff (the Michalak case). Even if you accept the story—investigators didn't—there is no hint that the harm was intentional.

The writings of the Lorenzens were required reading in the sixties. *Flying Saucers: The Startling Evidence of the Invasion from Outer Space* (1966) builds on the Keyhoe thesis that UFOs are engaged in reconnaissance. They are painstakingly mapping the geographical features of our country and testing our defense capabilities. The 1952 Washington, D.C., incidents are regarded as accidental incursions by aliens mistaking the Capitol and White House for military installations. The Lorenzens expect they will be setting up bases since the taking of plants, boulders, and soil samples probably means they are testing what sort of agriculture they should establish. The Ubatuba explosion is regarded as self-destruction to prevent superior technology from getting into our hands and revealing its secrets. There is a bare possibility it was an atomic explosion. "UFOs are powerful radioactive sources." The dangers they pose extend to the possibility that our next war could involve "all nations fighting as brothers against a common foe from outer space." (Lorenzen, 1966)

They showcase the ideas of Dr. Olavo Fontes that UFOs possessed weapons like heat rays and a device that inhibited the function of gas engines. They claim priority, however, that the observations UFOs made of cars and planes in the early years were done in order to devise these anti-machine machines to disable propulsion systems.

A pattern of reconnaissance is seen which suggests to them that aliens plan to release sleeping drugs into strategic reservoirs and water tanks as a means of bringing the world to its knees in a matter of hours. They are concerned there are too many blackouts on our power grids. There are also people disappearing. Is this the procuring of specimens? Add to this the case of a woman with medical problems they interpret as radiation effects. No person of conscience can ignore the UFO problem in the light of all this. The UFO problem has to be taken out of the hands of the military who are lulling us into a false sense of security and given to an international commission who will handle this red-hot political problem.

"We are in urgent need of the acquisition and objective analysis of basic data." We are facing potential danger. Maybe they aren't hostile, but "there is no indication of friendliness either . . . The existence of a species of superior beings in the universe could cause the civilization of Earth to topple." This urgency "defies expression." We must be anxious to relearn the lessons of history: Billy Mitchell, Maginot, Pearl Harbor, and so on.

Flying Saucer Occupants (1967), the next offering by the Lorenzens, is less suffused with fear. It is primarily a survey of non-contactee UFOnaut reports. As such it is a mixed bag open to a variety of interpretations from "conquerors from space" and "members of a military organization" to "a breeding experiment" to simply "visitors." While they prefer to simply assert the reality of these aliens, they admit in the final paragraph an alternative theory: "The population of the world is falling victim to a particularly insidious and apparently contagious mental disease which generates hallucinations involving specific types of airships and humanoids. This disease seems to be spreading. Who will be next to contract the malady? You?''

The choice of metaphor is interesting and was itself infectious. It turns up in the writings of J. Allen Hynek for one. In an article for *Playboy* he asserts that if an intensive investigation were carried out for a year and yielded nothing, we could shrug off the UFO problem with, ''There must have been a virus going around.'' In *The UFO Experience* (1972), he asks, ''Are then, all these reporters of UFOs truly sick? If so, what is the sickness? Are these people all affected by some strange 'virus' that does not affect 'sensible' people? What a strange sickness this must be, attacking people in all walks of life, regardless of training and vocation, and making them, for a very limited of time—only minutes sometimes—behave in a strange way and see things that are belied by the reliable and stable manner and actions they exhibit in the rest of their lives.''

Gordon Creighton offered the longest exposition of this metaphor in *The Humanoids* (1966):

> One thing at least is certain. These stories of alleged meeting with denizens of other worlds or realms or levels of existence constitute a fascinating social, psychological—and possibly also a parapsychological enigma. And surely an enigma of some urgency, for if the growing numbers of people all over our planet who claim these experiences are indeed hallucinating, or, as we are confidently told, suffering from the stresses and strains of the Nuclear age, then it is plain as a pikestaff that they are in grave need of psychological study and medical attention. If a brand new psychosis is loose amongst us, then, instead of wasting so much time on why we hate our fathers and love our mothers, our mental experts and psychologists ought to have been there right from the start, studying and combating this new plague since its outbreak nearly twenty years ago! Valuable time has been lost. By

now, they might have come to important conclusions, or even licked the malady!

Even rendered in these facetious terms the imperative quality of the UFO problem is retained in the overwrought choice of words like plague and grave need. Aimé Michel also utilized the disease metaphor in suggesting the aliens ''dominate us only to the degree that the microbe dominates us when we are ill.''

UFOs Over the Americas, the Lorenzens' 1968 title, is more suffused with confusion than fear. They note a new phase of UFO activity involving car chases. A new observation is advanced that UFOs show a proclivity to be sighted near cemeteries. They speculate this is just their way of trying to figure out what funeral processions might be about. They criticize the scientific community for holding the position that UFOs show ''no intelligent pattern of behavior; they zip hither and yon but don't seem to be going anywhere.'' Yet elsewhere they observe ''the extraterrestrials' motivations and overall purpose are so well concealed as to suggest a deliberate attempt to confuse.'' They call for a UN-sponsored agency to look into the matter, yet they also predict UFOs would appear so constantly that ''it should be evident before the end of 1968 just what UFOs are.''

Alas, their 1969 volume *UFOs—The Whole Story* was unable to proclaim what that evident identity was. The concern over invasion drops away, replaced by assumptions of aloofness. The stoppage of vehicles is downgraded from weapons-testing activity to a means of studying humans at a more leisurely pace. The fears vanish in favor of discussions of UFO politics and UFOnauts being time-travelers.

The writings of Frank Edwards were the bestselling books of the sixties. Edwards is sometimes dismissed as a journalist and not a UFOlogist, in part because of the embarrassing errors he made. The substance of the books however is heavily indebted to Keyhoe and NICAP. The flyleaf of *Flying Saucers—Serious Business* (1966) is notable for a flying saucer health warning that epitomizes the fearful spirit of the decade:

WARNING!

Near approaches of Unidentified Flying Objects can be harmful to human beings. Do not stand under a UFO that is hovering at low altitude. Do not touch or attempt to touch a UFO that has landed. In either case, the safe thing to do is get away from there quickly and let the military take over. There is a possibility of radiation danger, and there are known cases in which persons have been burned by rays emanating from UFOs. Details on these cases are included in this book.

Edwards's book affirms the reality of cases involving "eye damage, burns, radioactivity, partial or temporary paralysis, and various types of physiological disturbances." He talks of heat waves and stun rays; and the relationship between UFOs and blackouts is explored at length. "They have shown the ability, and sometimes the apparent inclination, to interfere with or prevent the functioning of our electrical and electronic systems." Despite these hints of malevolence, Edwards proclaims at the finale that contact will be the "the greatest experience of the human race."

The sequel *Flying Saucers—Here and Now* (1967) was spawned by the incredible increase in saucer sightings and saucer interest in the middle of the decade. Writings that, in cooler times, would have stimulated half a dozen letters now filled bags at magazine offices. Besides chronicling the rush of unfolding events, the book includes James McDonald's call for a full-scale Congressional investigation. Edwards maintains UFOs are not hostile, but warns contact will have tremendous impact theologically, psychologically, and sociologically. And that contact is described as imminent.

George Fawcett surveyed UFO cases for repetitive features in a February 1965 article. (See FAWCETT's "REPETITIONS") Among his catalogue of commonalities were the phenomena of pursuit, cases of increased background

radiation, cases of electrical shock, burns, dimming of vision, blackouts, temporary paralysis, and hostile acts. In April 1968, he cites dozens of UFO chases, a half-dozen deaths attributed to close encounters, and numerous instances of electromagnetic interference with machinery. He laments that it "may already be too late" for our government to act on the UFO problem. Their crossing of international boundaries could result in "an accidental World War III by mistake." He adds his voice to the chorus of people calling for the verification of UFO reality: "The growing UFO problem worldwide must be solved in 1968 or the explosive situation of UFOs may easily get out of our control and reap a 'real' disaster beyond all imagination. A worldwide probe of this problem is long overdue and should be handled through the United Nations."

The works of Jacques Vallée are a must in every UFOlogist's library. His first book *Anatomy of a Phenomenon: The Detailed and Unbiased Report on UFOs* (1965) remains one of the most dispassionate overviews of the UFO mystery attempted and is virtually beyond reproach. The conclusion of the study is sheer poetry: "The contours of a complex intelligence can be discerned and our dreams have reached across the night. The sky will never be the same." Keyhoe had said essentially the same thing in his first book, but Vallée had the better sensibility of where it belonged for maximum effect.

Challenge to Science: The UFO Enigma (1966), Vallée's next book, drifts into the fear mentality of the era. There is a call for verification by means of the creation of an international scientific commission to separate out those elements that are the work of imagination from those that constitute the physical basis of the phenomenon. The challenges they pose are "unwelcome" and "disturbing," but must be addressed because "our own existence will be dependent upon the sincerity with which we conduct this research." This flirtation with fear is gone by *Passport to Magonia* (1969) where entity behavior is dismissed as consistently absurd and misleading. The search for answers may be futile for they may only constitute a dream that never existed in reality.

Brad Steiger's books are rich sources of threatening themes. The call for verification appears in *Strangers from the Skies* (1966) with a recommendation for an "objective and respected panel" to appraise the situation. UFOs create blackouts and that ability makes national defense "a bad joke." The Lorenzens' notion that UFOs might beam down hypnotic drugs into our drinking water gets repeated. More creatively, Steiger offers the thought that one incident involves galactic experiments in cremation. It seemed UFOs were ready to invade the U.S. on a full scale. "We must be prepared to establish peaceful communication or be prepared to accept annihilation." Much more could be cited, but the books basically hash over the same sort of material as Edwards, the Lorenzens, and Fawcett.

John Fuller's writings are equally rich sources of malevolence. The familiar themes of blackouts and physiological reactions and mechanical breakdowns recur, as does the call for verification by means of a "scientific investigation on a major scale." This is "urgently" needed because of the "startling, alarming, and dangerous material" surfacing. There is "mounting seriousness." He devotes a whole book to the Betty Hill case, which is notably involved in fear of radiation poisoning, a secret abduction, and a nightmarish operation involving a needle thrust in a woman's navel with no prior anesthesia.

One the more interesting fears appeared in an article written by J. Allen Hynek shortly after his conversion in the wake of the humiliating swamp gas affair. Hynek expressed worry that the Russians might solve the mystery with results that would "shake America so hard that the launching of Sputnik in 1957 would appear in retrospect as important as a Russian announcement of a particularly large wheat crop." Hynek felt a Russian colleague slipped when he revealed Russian scientists were not permitted to discuss UFOs. They may have been "studying with dispassionate thoroughness for years." This suggested that official denials of their reality were a cover.

Jerome Clark offered one of the more paradoxical reactions to Hynek's swamp gas statement. He took issue with the comment that a dismal swamp is a most unlikely place for a visit from space. Clark avers, contrarily, it is the most likely place since they could go there without being seen. They go to fantastic lengths to prevent us from knowing what they are doing. This included killing a whole village of people in one incident and the erasing of people's memories in other cases. He berates the idea that injuries are caused in self-defense as inane. Noting that we have tried to force UFOs down, he remarks that we have been treating them with more respect than they deserve. The change of attitude from the '50s when UFOs possessed savior faire is nowhere more strikingly illustrated.

The call for verification turns up again as the subject of a resolution drafted during a 1967 gathering of UFO buffs. They proclaim that UFOs are identified vehicles from outer space and that this is a question of a vital problem concerning the whole world. "All nations must unite in mutual research and scientific cooperation to investigate and solve this for the common cause and mutual advancement of our peaceful relationship in outer space."

The theme turns up in several variations during the Roush Congressional hearings on July 29, 1968. James McDonald wanted a pluralistic approach employing NASA, NSA, ONR, and even the Federal Power Commission—the last to take up the subject of blackouts. J. Allen Hynek wanted Congress to establish a UFO Scientific Board of Inquiry. James A. Harder wanted a multifaceted approach, preferably at several institutions simultaneously. Robert M. Baker wanted a well-funded program with the highest possible standards. Donald Menzel, ever the skeptic, thought the time and money would be completely wasted in such studies.

Toward the end of 1968 the Rand Document recommended a central collection agency with analysis given over to specialists. The last significant expression of this notion appears in 1973, when James McDonald recommends setting up a two-phased research effort: Phase 1, price-tagged at $4 million, would "confirm absolutely the existence of UFOs in scientific terms and identify any advanced technologies." Phase 2 would define the new technology and was price-tagged in the $75-million to $100-million range. Needless to add, nobody leaped forward to fund this idea. People complained the half-million dollars for the Condon commission was a waste.

The concern over invasion spawned some spectacular notions in Raymond Palmer's *The Real UFO Invasion* (1967). Palmer offered evidence that the U.S. was preparing for war with weapons so titanic they couldn't have been intended for a mere international war. That war was not in the future either. Palmer points to nuclear blasts in Project Argus as being against a satellite not made by Earthmen.

Gordon Lore's *Strange Effects from UFOs; A Special NICAP Report* (1969), Robert Loftin's *Identified Flying Saucers* (1968), and Otto Binder's *What We Really Know About Flying Saucers* (1967) deserve brief mention for their brief treatments of physiological effects from saucers: eye injuries, radiation burns, paralyses, cases of shock, and mysterious blows to the body. A particularly odd and problematic case could made for including Vincent Gaddis's *Mysterious Fires and Lights* (1967), since it makes an effort to link UFOs to spontaneous human combustion. Unforgettable is Gaddis's question, "Are We Walking Atom Bombs?"

Passing references should perhaps be given to John Keel's expression of alarm over the 1966 wave and Robert Loftin's speaking of the UFO threat as something we had better get the truth about "before it is too late." One should perhaps resist recalling some thematically similar material from a weird little magazine that haunted the newsstands in the period called *Beyond,* but they are delightful flourishes. Otto Binder fretted over the number of deaths that

were taking place in the UFO field in one article. Timothy Green Beckley acclaimed "UFOs Use High-tension Lines for Re-Charging." James Welling offered a doubtful piece, "Does UFO Radiation Cause Phoenix, Arizona, Residents to be Afflicted with Strange Malady—Why Does Press Not Report Epidemic of Electronic Poisoning?" Other articles to find haven in *Beyond* discussed aliens that probed brains, paralyzed observers, and even made a dog sick with some ghastly condition.

UFOlogists are a heterogeneous bunch, and lack of full consensus is always to be expected. Donald Hanlon felt UFOnauts "do comparatively little harm" even if one counts a case of a use of knockout vapor. Charles Bowen spoke of the pointlessness of alien activity and thought it all "diversionary play to give us a giggle." Otto Binder, Cleary-Baker, and Mervyn Paul emphasized the paradox over why aliens didn't wipe us out years ago if they had bad things planned now. John Keel called for an investigation unhampered by petty UFO cultists and lamented the absence of a suitable psychiatric program to serve those being made insane or attempting suicide from the confusing antics of the UFO phenomenon. Such differences as these do nothing to inhibit calling the period of the sixties as overwhelmingly dominated by fears that UFOs were a danger to individual humans and to mankind collectively.

SHAMS AND SHEPHERDS

The last significant expression of the fear of invasion of this period appears in Raymond Fowler's *UFOs—Interplanetary Visitors* (1974). It is casually presented as a possibility among a range of intentions that aliens might possess. The idea of friendly contact is raised, but it is muted by concerns over loss of national pride as allegiance is transferred to a superior force. In a chapter archly titled "The Impact—Disintegration or Survival?" the existence of unprovoked hostile acts is pondered as either unwarranted aggression or an amoral act comparable to the swatting of a fly. Fowler believed the American military complex had treated UFOs as a threat, but would be helpless if they proved to be enemies. The blackouts, abductions, attacks, and burns associated with UFOs help to demonstrate that super-intelligent aliens are becoming an intimate part of our environment to which we will have to adapt.

Ralph and Judy Blum's *Beyond Earth* (1974) asserts UFOs may be the "the biggest story ever," but they are not sure if they are extraterrestrial or "living holograms projected on the sky by the laser beams of man's unconscious mind." The tone is decidedly upbeat with suggestions that UFOs might represent "an almost unimaginable energy source for mankind." They also have a habit of unorthodox healing, a converse of all the ills alleged in the prior decade. The Blums quote Hynek's opinion that UFOnauts indulge in "seemingly pointless antics," and they include James Harder's response to a question about whether UFOs pose a threat: "If you pick up a mouse in a laboratory situation, it's very frightening for the mouse. But it doesn't mean you meant the mouse any harm."

Robert Emenegger's *UFOs: Past, Present, and Future* (1974) also took an upbeat view of UFOs. Contacts were friendly and he concurred with the Air Force that they posed no threat. Understanding UFOs could lead to the discovery of a new energy source and a new relationship to life throughout the universe. Fantastic revelations to questions that have puzzled philosophers throughout history were near, and he hoped a reputable organization like the American Institute of Aeronautics and Astronautics and the National Academy of Sciences would move forward to study the phenomenon. "The immediate future looks promising."

In a December 1974 editorial for *Flying Saucer Review*, Charles Bowen warned that people should endeavor to avoid physical contact, because UFOs have been shown to cause harm. There is perhaps a struggle for possession of our planet between good and evil forces, but UFOs may not be greatly concerned with the ultimate welfare of the human race. Noting how much the phenomenon trades in gibberish, Bowen laments "Hoaxing, we feared, was not the prerogative of earth men."

Hynek and Vallée's *The Edge of Reality* (1975) posits that "there appears to be no desire for involvement with the human race." While UFOs are documented as causing harm, it is observed that electrical outlets also cause harm without being innately hostile. The study of UFOs is regarded as an opportunity to move to a new reality. New departures in methodology will, however, be needed. The Center for UFO Studies (CUFOS) will be set up to serve those ends.

The same general sentiment appears in Vallée's *The Invisible College* (1975). UFOs are indifferent to the welfare of the individual and pose no threat to national defense. The primary impact of UFOs appears to be on human belief. Could it be someone is playing a fantastic trick on us?

The Lorenzens answer with a big yes. "Somebody is putting us on!" UFO encounters are in a sense a charade. They also, however, appear to involve coldly scientific experiments on some humans. They may be trying to stock some distant exotic zoo. There is a threat from UFOs after all, despite government assurances, but not from invasion. Fortunately this threat is avoidable, according to the Lorenzens. Stay away from lovers' lanes and isolated camping sites. They argue the time has come to "educate the aliens" with radio broadcasts inviting them to visit openly.

John Keel decides in *The Mothman Prophecies* (1975) that the battle cry of the phenomenon is "Make him look like a nut!" He muses after Fort, "If there is a universal mind, must it be sane?" The "worldwide spread of UFO belief and its accompanying disease" fills him with great consternation.

In *The Eighth Tower* (1975) the dangerous character of the UFO phenomenon is played up with talk of a high rate of death among contactees and UFO hobbyists. Keel adds, "Any force that can sear your eyeballs, paralyze your limbs, erase your memory, burn your skin, and turn you into a coughing, blubbering wreck can also maim and kill you.'' It is dispassionate and ruthless. We are puppets to the super-spectrum.

In bizarre contrast, Hans Holzer rejects ''monster'' theories of aliens bent on destroying us. They may regard themselves as potential saviors. Their attempts at crossbreeding suggest we are ''not totally unworthy.'' Brad Steiger believed UFOs would be a transformative symbol that will unite our entire species into one spiritual organism. They would be the spiritual midwife that brings about mankind's starbirth into the universe. Paris Flammonde, on the other hand, takes the view that man will never achieve inter-communication or a symbiotic relationship with extraterrestrials.

The Hynek UFO Report (1977) reflects the emerging consensus. UFO study could perhaps ''be the springboard to a revolution in man's view of himself and his place in the universe.'' Yet, they also appear to be ''playing games with us.'' D. Scott Rogo similarly felt UFOs demonstrate that our world plays host to a force that seeks to mystify us.

Bill Barry's account of the Travis Walton controversy evaluates the phenomenon as having never expressed hostility toward its alleged victims. Abductees are merely treated as guinea pigs.

As in his book in the fifties, Leonard Stringfield's *Situation Red—The UFO Siege* (1978) is a portrait of confusion. Looking at airplane accidents, disappearances, and persistent spying, he admits to being stumped by the pointless harassment. UFO activity resembles a military strike force, but the randomness and absence of widespread destruction falls short of open hostility. If they wanted to destroy our civilization, clearly they could. Their effects are sometimes deleterious and sometimes beneficial. The paradox may be sinister or profound, but the main point is that it remains unresolved.

Art Gatti's *UFO Encounters of the 4th Kind* (1978) focuses on sexual incursions and he feels they, at minimum, show aliens are questionably motivated. Maybe they are curi-ous. Maybe they are milking our emotions like cattle. Maybe they involve two forces; one benevolent, the other wicked. Maybe they are seeding Earth with warriors for a future Armageddon.

Brad Steiger's *Alien Meetings* (1978) comes across as a curious regression to the fears of the sixties. One chapter head warns ''UFO Encounters May Be Hazardous to Your Health!'' After a survey of the usual troubles, he offers motives like invasion, domination, territorial acquisition, and commercial exploitation, but manages to dismiss the ''War of the Worlds'' idea as ''paranoid mutterings.'' Perhaps this indicates some progress over his books of the sixties, given that he did pose the possibility seriously then. Whether they are on some spiritual mission or merely pursuing history lessons, aliens at least seem to be intensely interested in us.

Rogo and Clark's *Earth's Secret Inhabitants* (1979) sees the phenomenon as a source both of good things like raised IQs and healings, plus bad things like burns and radiation effects. It provides us with visions of things humans want to believe. ''In fact, up to a certain point it may be a good thing for us to believe in these things—providing, of course, that we don't become so superstitious in the process that we lose our grip on common sense. Maybe they are clues to some larger truth.'' Vallée's *Messengers of Deception* (1979) essentially shows that losing one's grip on common sense is the usual result of UFO belief. As such, he felt it could be a useful political tool and agent of social control. On the brighter side, UFO study might clarify exciting theoretical and practical opportunities to understand energy and information.

In 1979 Yurko Bondarchuk foresaw imminent contact with extraterrestrials (before the year 2000). ''It is inconceivable that their journeys to a peripheral planet are merely haphazard or mindless.'' They are surveying our self-destructive capabilities and our resource base. He expects contact to lead to the emergence of a ''new world order'' in which existing territorial and ideological conflicts will be gradually eliminated. Creation of a restructured world economic order eventually follows. A universal reevaluation of spiritual convictions could also be expected. Raymond Fowler similarly speculates UFOs represent a "much-needed bridge between science and religion." The events of *The Andreasson Affair* (1979) strike him as a stage-managed religious experience by interstellar missionaries. Betty Andreasson and others like her have been primed subconsciously with information that might burst into consciousness all over the planet.

FUN OR RUN

Rogo, in *UFO Abductions* (1980), confesses the whole UFO abduction syndrome appears to be "slightly ridiculous." There is too much misinformation that appears designed to makes abductees look like "total fools." His guess is that these experiences are an elaborate façade, a camouflage forcing the individual to confront a secret aspect of himself. Rogo's book includes Ann Druffel's article "Harrison Bailey and the Flying Saucer Disease" that chronicled the medical misadventures of a man who said he was told his internal organs were three times older than they should have been. Druffel diagnoses his problems as resulting from microwave radiation in an UFO encounter. Druffel doesn't know if Bailey was harmed accidentally or deliberately, but Bailey thinks it was unintentional. In *The Tujunga Canyon Contacts* (1980) she opts for a view of UFOs as looking after man's continuing evolution. They take a special interest in our procreative activities or they are interested in expanding our consciousness.

The Proceedings of the First International UFO Congress (1980) presents views typical of the seventies. Leo Sprinkle thinks contact messages are seemingly reliable because of their similarities to each other and thus offer information on the scientific and spiritual development of humankind. Berthold Schwarz thinks the messages are garbage. Frank Salisbury remarks that UFOs seem too irrational and perverse—they verge on the truly diaboli-

cal. Jim Lorenzen characterizes the phenomenon as an insult to human intelligence, but Stanton Friedman begs to disagree.

In their study of several abductees, Judith and Alan Gransberg reported there was not one where the extraterrestrials were cruel to humans. Indeed, one abductee thought they were angels. They conclude, in contrast to Vallée, the concept of extraterrestrials is doing man no harm and could potentially be helpful.

Raymond Fowler continues ruminating on the Andreasson affair in *Casebook of a UFO Investigator* (1981), but in a somewhat larger context. He thinks that super-intelligent beings have possibly been nurturing man along his evolutionary way. We are under intense attention, perhaps as potential candidates for the intergalactic community. They love mankind. In *The Andreasson Affair—Phase Two,* he reaffirms the religionist slant of phase one, and this includes the millennial expectation that the Second Coming of Jesus Christ will happen during the adult lives of Bob and Betty Luca.

UFO by Milt Machlin with Tim Beckley is an interesting minor work having some regressive concerns. An odd case of a UFO murder is recounted in which people were killed either because they knew too much or they were being experimented upon. It closes with a flying saucer health warning that is charming in its simple tone: "Do not approach UFOs. People get shocks or even end up in the hospital. You could also get hit by a ray gun."

The appearance of Budd Hopkins's *Missing Time* (1981) represents a significant albeit ambivalent return to the UFO menace mindset. Hopkins regards abductions as an epidemic, but because people are protected by an induced anmesia it may be almost entirely invisible. He writes: "I do not believe the UFO phenomenon is malign or evilly intentioned. I fear, instead, that it is merely indifferent, though I fervently hope to be proven wrong." He adds, "For all any of us knows the whole UFO phenomenon may be ultimately blissfully benign—there is firm evidence for this position—and so having been abducted may turn out to be a peculiar privilege." Even so, he is "thoroughly alarmed" and calls for the establishment of a UFO investigatory arm to the United Nations, so that everyone would recognize UFOs as a serious reality to the governments of the world. The contradiction between his alarm and the consensus of the prior decade he has trouble abandoning is unresolved.

Brad Steiger's *Star People* (1981) and *The Seed* (1983) is basically contactee literature for the eighties crowd. John Magor's *Aliens Above, Always* (1983) also has the paternalistic quality of contacteeism: they are watching us for our benefit. Cynthia Hind offers the speculation in passing that aliens are here to be entertained or to blow our minds a little in *African Encounters* (1982).

Larry Fawcett and Barry Greenwood in *Clear Intent* (1984) say the human race could be in danger, but the laconic counterpoint that we haven't been conquered yet seems a call for ennui rather than concern.

In Extraterrestrials Among Us (1986), George Andrews returns to the sixties mind-set and comes up with an extraordinary variation of the viral metaphor: "It is an odd fact that among the viruses there are some that look like UFOs, such as the virus T. Bacteriophage." Some UFOs may have the ability to operate in either the macro-dimension of outer space or the micro-dimension of viruses, switching back and forth. He frets that our survival as a species may be at stake. "Have we been transforming our planet into a cancer cell in the body of the galaxy instead of making it the garden of the universe?" Terry Hansen, in a 1981 article, offered a more appropriate somatic metaphor for the period. He suggested UFOs may be a sort of "liver medicine" to make us function normally as part of a cosmic organism.

Night Siege (1987) chronicles power blackouts, surges, interference, and pain associated with an UFO flap, but offers no generalizations of their significance.

Intruders (1987) shares the same quality of unresolved contradiction as the prior Hopkins book. Aliens are committing a species of rape, their activities related to an unthinkable systematic breeding experiment to enrich their stock, reduce our differences, and acquire the ability to feel human emotions. What they do is "cruel" and each case is "a personal tragedy." Yet he also avers: "In none of the cases I've investigated have I ever encountered the suggestion of deliberate harm or malevolence. They don't realize the disasters they are causing because of an ignorance of human psychology."

Richard Hall titled his 1988 book *Uninvited Guests*. It is one of the more flaccid titles in the literature and more connotative of pushy salesmen than an alien menace. Hall finds little evidence of overt hostility and suggests harm is accidental or a matter of self-defense. Encounters probably represent mutual learning experiences. There is a strong interest in us and he hopes this means we are beginning a new phase and maturity, and perhaps a new relationship to the universe.

Steiger, in *The UFO Abductors* (1988) decides there must be at least two types of aliens. One is "genuinely concerned about our welfare and our spiritual and physical evolution." The other is indifferent to our needs and is sinisterly programming people for an Armageddon, a mass invasion of Earth so imminent it would have already taken place had not an Interplanetary Council intervened. The Forces of Light and Darkness "are about to square off" and humankind could find itself an unwilling pawn in this ultimate battle.

When *Tujunga Canyon Contacts* was reissued in 1988, Ann Druffel modified her views in the light of new developments on the abduction scene. Aliens were now malevolent and traumatizing, wily and harmful. The good news was that humans have the ability to battle them off.

The eighties saw another significant development. Paul Bennewitz introduced the story of the Dulce Base: a secret facility in the southwest that was populated by aliens called Grays. They had a secret agreement with the government that allowed them to abduct humans in exchange for technological advances. Grays were devious and should never be trusted. "This particular group can only be dealt with no differently than one must deal with a mad dog. They have invaded our country, our air, and they are freely violating the personal and mental integrity of our people."

In late 1987 John Lear released a statement giving his support to the Dulce Base story. He indicates people are killed to serve as sources for biological materials and to protect secrets. Females are impregnated to secure cross-breed infants. "The EBEs claim to have created Christ," but Lear warns this is disinformation "to disrupt traditional values for undetermined reasons." They have "obviously hostile intentions." In a finale he asks:

Are the EBES, having done a hundred thousand or more abductions—possibly millions worldwide—built an untold number of secret underground bases getting ready to return to wherever they came from? Or from the obvious preparations are we to assume that they are getting ready for a big move? Or is the more probable situation that the invasion is essentially complete and it is all over except the screaming?

Any good invasion would be done before anyone realized it had happened. His advice: Next time you see a saucer—"Run like hell."

UFOlogists rejected the body of claims surrounding the Dulce Base for the most part, but they spread in the general culture, particularly by radio talk shows and the Internet. The spread of the word Grays to label bald bigheaded aliens was one side effect of this development, but it also formed a basis for further tales of malevolence in the nineties.

GRANDER OR GRANDEUR

Raymond Fowler's third book on the Andreasson case, *The Watchers* (1990) brings the viral metaphor back. He feels "Like a medical researcher who has inoculated himself in order to experience and treat a disease under study." To his horror, he finds the UFO phenomenon linked to the future extinction of mankind through sterility. He calls it inconceivable, but he also feels it is authentic.

Vallée returns to the UFO scene in 1990 with *Confrontations*. He tallies up twelve cases of fatal injuries attributable to UFOs, and announces the phenomenon is more dangerous and technologically complex than we thought. He feels "a renewed sense of urgency" about UFO study.

In a 1990 interview, Donald Ware expressed his belief that the Hybrid Program is intended to develop bodies to house our souls in future incarnations—a future species with a 35 percent larger brain, telepathy, and a capacity for unconditional love. This has some resonance to a revelation passed along by Strieber that the visitors say they recycle souls.

Terence McKenna, more a high-profile thinker than UFOlogist, notes that UFO contact is perhaps the most common motif that is found in recreational psilocybin experiences. They are real in some sense. They are "apocalyptic concrescences that haunt the historical continuum, igniting religions and various hysterias, and seeping ideas into highly tuned nervous systems." They "act as a kind of ideological catalyst." UFOs will wreck science, sweep it away. A UFO-related religion would embody an archetype of enormous power. The UFO represents a crisis between the individual and the Overmind. "It comes from this murky region, beyond the end of history, beyond the end of life. . . . It is both the apotheosis and the antithesis of the monkey's journey toward mind."

In *Revelations* (1991) Vallée debunks the Dulce Base stories and warns that belief in the imminent arrival of aliens is a powerful fantasy, poisonous as any of the great irrational upheavals of history. The 1997 Heaven's Gate tragedy might give this line a cachet of prescience. Vallée also speculates UFO entities *"could even be fractal beings. The Earth could be their home port."* (Emphasis in the original.) He calls upon Oscar Wilde's dictum that an aesthetic truth was such that its opposite is equally true: "Perhaps the truths about alien contact, like those of the metaphysical kind, are the truths of masks.''

David Jacobs, in *Secret Life* (1992), echoes Hopkins in his belief that aliens are neither malevolent nor benevolent and share the anthropological policy of noninterference to save us cultural shock, or perhaps prefer secrecy to avoid human efforts of resistance. They do not seem headed for conquest or colonization, at least as we know the term.

George Andrews collects much of the Dulce Base or EBE mythos into his 1993 work, *ExtraTerrestrial Friends and Foes.* Grays are ''other-dimensional predatory parasites'' and may lack souls. We ''must confront the all-or-nothing emergency situation that is now staring us in the face.'' They are ''paralyzing our evolutionary development.'' Insectoids are invading us to complete their own evolution. Negative material like this is common on the Web. Lear's talk of future invasion is elaborated upon, for example, by Cosmic Awareness in a 1993 reading that predicted a full-force invasion by reptoids in 1999.

Linda Howe's *Glimpses of Other Realities* volumes (1993, 1998) similarly builds upon this mythos and includes portrayals of aliens as *''neither benevolent nor neutral,''* with some considered a ''black group'' thriving on control, destruction, and chaos. Despite a lot of negative material, Howe ends with a curiously positive gloss: ''Ultimately, there is a common bond among all life-forms ebbing and flowing on different spirals of different frequencies supported by a singular force, an invisible matrix of energy from which everything emerges and to which everything returns.'' They are watching us, guarding our future as a species, ''and will not allow humans to destroy the earth.'' Our concept of them ''has shifted from fear to curiosity to maybe even 'one of the guys' in cozy, human social terms.''

Timothy Good concludes *Alien Contact* (1993) with his assessment that we are being visited by several different groups of extraterrestrials. Some are less than benign, but others are lending us a helping hand ''as we reach, falteringly, toward the stars.'' Advantages

hopefully will outweigh disadvantages, ''leading to a more complete and profound understanding of our place in the universal scheme.''

In 1994, John Mack concludes in his study of the phenomenon that ''Abductions seem to be concerned primarily with two related projects: changing human consciousness to prevent the destruction of earth's life, and the joining of two species for the creation of a new evolutionary form.'' It might be an educational mythic drama intended by a ''transcendent intelligence to move our being to a higher level.'' It ''is not evil.''

Similarly, Richard Boylan says his hopes for humanity took a ''decided upturn . . . with politically correct, large-minded neighbors like the ETs vowing to step in if necessary to make sure we don't blow up each other . . .'' ETs will soon land and ''The open presence of ETs on earth will mean that we will have the benefit of some of the wisest minds from some of the older and more enduring minds in the galaxy available to help us design a civilization that really works for all.''

Jenny Randles's *The Star Children* (1995) suggests alien experiences are part of a spiritual evolution. We are being turned into cosmic citizens, our consciousness is being raised. ''We are climbing a stairway to the stars with a dazzling light far ahead of us at the top . . . We will all get there in the end.'' Our joy may be short-lived, however, when we learn we have only reached the first floor of a very tall building. Still, there is symbolic beauty in the Hybrid Program where people are helping ''to build a new and better race.'' She was clearly not being pessimistic: ''Yes, something wonderful might well be happening.''

With *Watchers II* (1995), Raymond Fowler suggests a connection between near-death experiences (NDEs) and UFOs: ''I am convinced that there is no other explanation—barring alien deception—that UFOs and their entities come from behind death's Great Door.'' They come from a world of light unimpeded by physical laws. They care about our health. The Light Beings give a treatise on life and death that tells us "life is wonderfully fair." Evil will be wiped out at some distant time, but on this plane, it must exist. They are monitoring the life-essence of the forms dwelling on Earth as we develop in our paraphysical evolution.

Hopkins in *Witnessed* (1996) thinks it evident aliens unwittingly add to the world's health problems. The proposition that aliens are here to teach us environmental consciousness is firmly termed "a colossal failure." He sees more devoted ecologists among skeptics than abductees. All evidence points to the Hybrid Program as their central concern. Reprising earlier conclusions, "Despite the fears of many, nothing in my 20 years of research into this phenomenon suggests that the UFO occupants are inherently malevolent. I have seen absolutely no evidence that they are bent upon invasion and enslavement of the human race." But neither are they benign or saviors from eco-doom. Forget demonic conquest or angelic rescue. Their goals are their own. Their presence will in time become inescapable even to the most die-hard skeptic.

Looking at cases in Brazil, Bob Pratt remarks that while "some UFO beings may be kind and well-intentioned . . . others definitely are not . . . UFOs may or may not be significant to mankind in the long run, but until we find out, we should treat them with the greatest of caution."

Joe Lewels in *The God Hypothesis* (1997) sees UFOs as part of a transformation of reality. The aliens may be god-like by having evolved beyond our understanding, or were simply created at a higher level of God's natural hierarchy of intelligences. He knows religious fundamentalists will brand them demonic, but fear can be averted by "the calmer voices of those who are able to embrace the grander perspective," accept the paradoxes, and go beyond good and evil to realize they are but the same thing from God's perspective. "The ET presence can have a positive result." We must all love unconditionally and understand we are all one.

Colin Wilson argues in *Alien Dawn* (1998) that aliens have moved beyond the stage of human evolution where we merely mark time and know how consciousness can operate at full pressure. They are not malevolent or hostile, but like Neanderthals, an evolutionary dead-end stuck in a spiritual cul-de-sac. They are creating a new kind of human being and evidence exists in the form of hundreds of super-intelligent kids. The UFO phenomenon is making an increasing impact on the human mind by a Sheldrakean morphogenetic induction.

In 1998, Jacobs changes his mind and announces that abductions are indeed the threat some people had earlier thought they were. He chronicles the views of the Positives faction of abductionology, including Leo Sprinkle, Dr. Hunter Gray, Richard Boylan, John Mack, Joseph Nyman, and Leah Haley. Curiously, no word of Fowler. He echoes Hopkins's conclusion that the environmental messages of the Positives look useless, since abductees don't become activists. A change is coming with hybrids and insectoid aliens assuming control of the planet. Non-abductees are expendable and only a small breeding population will be maintained in case the Hybrid Program has unforeseen problems. "It may very well be too late" to do anything to stop this. "I have come to the conclusion," Jacobs says, "that human civilization may be in for a rapid, and perhaps disastrous change, not of our own design . . ." Human freedom is doomed. "The aliens have fooled us . . . I do not think we will have to wait very long."

Michael Hesemann exults that contact with a superior civilization could be the greatest chance for humanity, opening up new perspectives. Communication with them could give us a new perspective, a holistic view of creation and our role in the universe. "That would be the first step in the next phase of our evolution: the birth of 'homo cosmicus,' . . . this alone probably makes the UFO phenomenon the secret key to our entrance into the 21st century."

Steiger returns fully to the Positives camp

in 1999 with *UFO Odyssey*. The UFO phenomenon awakens one to an awareness that "there exists one central, unifying energy on this planet that has the potential to transform our entire species." Contactees maintain that the evolution of humanity successively brings him to a more ethereal, purely spiritual state, a perfection of the soul. UFOs are a mythological symbol, in some way more real than the Internet or industrial averages, helping us regain our lost paradise as spiritual beings.

Mack's *Passport to the Cosmos* (1999) broadens the conclusion of his earlier book. "The abduction phenomenon seems to me to be part of a shift of consciousness that is collapsing duality and enabling us to see that we are connected beyond the Earth at a cosmic level." One must posit "an ultimate or overarching creative principle or intelligence in the cosmos that is doing its work through this and other phenomena . . ." Abductees variously call this intelligence God, Source, Home, One, "God-Goddess-All that is." Grays and the like are "intermediaries between us and the Divine Source."

ASSESSMENT

Credit must be given where it is due. The Air Force got it right and told it straight. No material threat to national security existed. The invasion never took place. Mirarchi's Pearl Harbor, Riordan's knockout attack, Keyhoe's final operation, Wilkins's death ceiling blockade, Michel's Sword of Damocles, NICAP's danger to the fabric of society, the Lorenzens' mass drugging and toppling of civilization, Edwards's imminent Overt Contact, Fawcett's disaster beyond imagination, Steiger's full-scale annihilation, Hynek's Russian Breakthrough, Clark's swamp-lurking village-slayers, Palmer's ongoing titanic war, Fowler's cultural disintegration: all were concerns with more basis in fantasy than reality.

The sense of urgency, the sense that it may be too late, the sense that our existence depended on a properly conducted investigation was an irrational fear. The Air Force repeatedly tried to get across the message that UFOlogists were wrong, but they were in no mood to listen. It is dogma among UFOlogists that the Air Force was incompetent or worse, yet if that is accepted as a proper, measured evaluation, what word is proper to describe the body of thought presented by these UFOlogists? The Air Force did not perform flawlessly in the details, but they had the big picture in more than sufficient focus to understand it was a nuisance problem and not one of life-and-death significance.

The same cannot be said of UFOlogists. For them the big picture keeps changing. In the fifties UFOs were considerate and peace loving. In the sixties they were a source of danger and death. In the seventies they were perversely irrational and a source of hope. In the eighties they were traumatizing though they didn't realize it. In the nineties they are grand things involved in our spiritual evolution and linked with God. Are these changes a progressive march to truth? Doubtful. The sixties were clearly worse than the fifties. The nineties' drift into theological and metaphysical realms is worse than the seventies and pretty overtly anti-scientific. Are these changes in fashion? Possibly, though the word doesn't seem right since the conclusions are at times laced with fear and dread rather than enthusiasm.

Much of this resembles the way paranoia changes over time. The initial presumption of alien benevolence is a puzzle I have yet to fully understand. My sense is that aliens tended to be malevolent in science fiction. Perhaps it was a carryover from the writings of science popularizers and astronomers. The myth of the canal-builders of Mars implied a superior race that was also industrious and evolved beyond war. Specifically, Lowell said "international conflicts and wars are unknown" for the inhabitants had united against the common enemy of a dying world. I can't point to any more contemporary source of the idea. We can dismiss the idea it was somehow obliged by the roundness of saucers for the dominant theory that they were secret weapons by either us or the Russians, possibly developed from Nazi scientists, and implicitly had a malevolent, future war connotation.

Regardless, the interpretative drift toward malevolence is consonant with the darkening worldview of paranoids as they withdraw from social contact and turn inward. The hypochondriacal stage is entered as the ego collapses and the fear of death asserts itself in a variety of forms. End-of-world fears are a common feature of collapse and these are numerous among the early UFOlogists. Persecution fantasies arise and this feature has led some to call this phase the ''pursuit'' stage of paranoia. The sixties, of course, did have such themes in the spread of UFO chases, UFOs shadowing people, and the Men-in-Black stories, but they constitute a subset of a much wider range of fears more broadly recognizable as dealing with encroaching death.

To term the sixties a hypochondriacal era seems apt on several points. There is a universal call for some authority who will tell everyone that UFOs are real. The authorities decline. The idea appearing in both Lorenzen and Steiger that UFOs would put sleeping drugs in reservoirs is an obvious parallel to poisoning fantasies found in individual paranoia. The concerns over blackouts and vehicle interference might be analogous to the loss-of-life-energy notions that develop around the depression aspects of some cases of schizophrenia. Concerns over war and the toppling of civilization or endangerment of the social fabric seem familiar variants on projective world destruction fantasies. The talk of invasion is as well, having obvious parallels in prior invasion panics like the 1789 Great Fear rumor-panic in France, the 1913 Scareship mania, and the sizable literature ruminating on invasion and future war that spawned *The War of the Worlds*.

The viral metaphors indulged in by UFO writers are a delightful expression of the hypochondriacal style. Though some will dismiss them as a mere literary device, it is perhaps worth mentioning that they routinely appear in other genres of paranoia. Believers in the Jewish world conspiracy usually described their enemies as bacilli, syphilis, the plague, and viruses. They entertained poisoning fantasies such as the fear that mass inoculation programs were plots to inject Gentiles with syphilis.

Hypochondria is not a permanent condition. The ego attempts to reintegrate eventually through the building of psychological defenses against the masochistic attacks of the conscience. Ideas of reference form to disown the crazier aspects of one's fears. Retrospective falsifications arise to rewrite personal history. Conspiracy logic forms pseudo-communities to organize the chaos of social reality. Later, delusions of grandeur arise and overcompensate the injured ego. The final stage is cosmic identity—the individual is God, the universe, and interlinked with everything.

As we pass from the sixties to the seventies, the calls for investigation drop away, ''urgent'' slips from the language, invasion and mass drugging is replaced by more upbeat thoughts. The bizarre aspects of alien nightmares and horrors become more evident and efforts are made to discount them on some level—enter control systems. Ancient astronaut lore rewrites Darwin to make us descendants from Starfolk rather than merely apes, and rewrites the Bible to be a product of superscience rather than superstition. In the eighties we get Roswell, MJ-12, and some other conspiracy theories. The Dulce Base secret agreement manages to incorporate both conspiracy and new threats of invasion for the Internet generation. With the nineties, delusions of grandeur and cosmic identity come to the fore among the Positives. The Dulce Base crowd and other Regressives stir in the background to retrace the cycle.

It is human nature that people don't often go around proclaiming their mistakes and there is no point in feigning surprise when observing that it seems impossible to find any UFOlogist who has reflected on the remarkable misjudgments and the spectacle of error that took place in sixties UFOlogy. It would have been nice to even find someone who expressed relief that the invasion was called off. Look through the UFO histories of people like Paris Flammonde, David Jacobs, Jerome Clark, even Curtis Peebles and Steven Dick, and they are sanitized of any account of the wild fears that UFOlogy had about aliens and UFOs. It is an open question if UFOlogy learns from its mistakes given such silence, and it is one probably left unasked for the obvious answer will be emotionally incorrect.

—MARTIN S. KOTTMEYER

References

Adamski, George, and Desmond Leslie. *Flying Saucers Have Landed* (The British Book Centre/Werner Laurie, 1953).

Adamski, George. *Inside the Space Ships* (Abelard-Schuman, 1955).

Andrews, George C. *Extraterrestrials Among Us* (Llewellyn, 1986).

———. *Extra-Terrestrial Friends and Foes* (IllumiNet Press, 1993).

Angelucci, Orfeo M. *The Secret of the Saucers* (Amherst Press, 1955).

Arnold, Kenneth, and Ray Palmer. *The Coming of the Saucers* (privately published, 1952).

Barker, Gray. *They Knew Too Much About Flying Saucers* (University Books, 1956).

Barry, Bill. *Ultimate Encounter* (Pocket Books, 1978).

Bender, Albert K. *Space Review—Complete File* (Saucerian Books, 1962).

Binder, Otto. *Flying Saucers Are Watching Us* (Tower, 1968).

———. *What We Really Know About Flying Saucers* (Fawcett, 1967).

Bloecher, Ted. *Report on the UFO Wave of 1947* (privately published, 1967).

Blum, Ralph and Judy. *Beyond Earth: Man's Contact with UFOs* (Bantam Books, 1974).

Boylan, Richard J. *Close Extraterrestrial Encounters* (Wild Flower Press, 1994).

Cohn, Norman. *Warrant for Genocide* (Harper & Row, 1967).

Creighton, Gordon. "The Villa Santina Case" in *The Humanoids*, edited by Charles Bowen (Henry Regnery, 1969).

Crowe, Michael J. *The Extraterrestrial Life Debate, 1750-1900* (Dover, 1999).

Dickhoff, Robert E. *Homecoming of the Martians* (Health Research, 1958, 1964).

Druffel, Ann, and D. Scott Rogo. *The Tujunga Canyon Contacts* (Prentice-Hall, 1980).

Edwards, Frank. *Flying Saucers—Serious Business* (Lyle Stuart/Bantam Books, 1966).

———. *Flying Saucers—Here and Now!* (Lyle Stuart, 1967; Bantam Books, 1968).

Emenegger, Robert. *UFO's: Past Present and Future* (Ballantine Books, 1974).

Fawcett, George. "UFO Repetitions," *Flying Saucers* (February 1965).

———. "Flying Saucers: Explosive Situation for 1968," *Flying Saucers* (April 1968).

Fawcett, Lawrence, and Barry Greenwood. *Clear Intent* (Prentice-Hall, 1984). Reprinted as *The UFO Cover-Up* (Fireside, 1992).

Flammonde, Paris. *The Age of Flying Saucers* (Hawthorne, 1971).

———. *UFO Exist!* (Ballantine, 1976).

Fowler, Raymond E. *Casebook of a UFO Investigator* (Prentice-Hall, 1981).

———. *The Andreasson Affair* (Prentice-Hall, 1979; Bantam Books, 1980; Wild Flower Press, 1994).

———. *The Andreasson Affair—Phase Two* (Prentice-Hall, 1982; Wild Flower Press, 1994).

———. *The Watchers* (Bantam Books, 1990).

———. *The Watchers II* (Wild Flower Press, 1995).

———. *The Andreasson Legacy* (Marlowe, 1997).

———. *UFOs: Interplanetary Visitors* (Prentice-Hall, 1974).

Frosch, John. *The Psychotic Process* (International University Press, 1983).

Fuller, Curtis G., ed. *Proceedings of the First International UFO Congress* (Warner Books, 1980).

Fuller, John G. *The Interrupted Journey* (The Dial Press, 1966; Dell, 1967).

———. *Incident at Exeter* (G. P. Putnam's Sons, 1966; Berkley, 1974).

———. *Aliens in the Skies* (G. P. Putnam's Sons/Berkley, 1969).

Gaddis, Vincent H. *Mysterious Fires and Lights* (David McKay, 1967; Dell, 1968).

Gatti, Art. *UFO Encounters of the 4th Kind* (Zebra, 1978).

Gibbons, Gavin. *The Coming of the Space Ships* (The Citadel Press, 1958).

Gillmor, Daniel S., ed. *Scientific Study of Unidentified Flying Objects* (Bantam, 1969).

Girvan, Waveney. *Flying Saucers and Common Sense* (The Citadel Press, 1955).

Good, Timothy. *Above Top Secret* (Sidgwick and Jackson, 1987; Morrow/Quill, 1988).

———. *Alien Contact* (William Morrow, 1993).

———. *Alien Base* (Avon, 1998).

Gross, Loren. *UFOs: A History* (Arcturus Book Service, 1982).

Hall, Richard, ed. *The UFO Evidence* (NICAP, 1964).

———. *Uninvited Guests* (Aurora, 1988).

Heard, Gerald. *Is Another World Watching?* (Harper, 1951).

Hesemann, Michael. *UFOs: The Secret History* (Marlowe, 1998).

Hind, Cynthia. *African Encounters* (Gemini, 1982).

Hopkins, Budd. *Intruders* (Random House, 1987; Ballantine, 1988).

———. *Missing Time* (Richard Marek, 1981; Ballantine, 1988).

———. *Witnessed* (Pocket Books, 1996).

Howe, Linda. *Glimpses of Other Realities: Volume 1: Facts and Eyewitnesses* (1993, 1998).

Hynek, J. Allen. *The UFO Experience: A Scientific Inquiry* (Henry Regnery, 1972).

Hynek, J. Allen, and Jacques Vallée. *The Edge of Reality* (Henry Regnery, 1975).

Jacobs, David M. *Secret Life* (Simon & Schuster, 1992).

———. *The Threat* (Simon & Schuster, 1998).

Jessup, Morris K. *The Case for the UFO* (The Citadel Press, 1955; Vero edition/Saucerian, 1973).

Jung, C. G. *Flying Saucers: A Modern Myth of Things Seen in the Skies* (Routledge & Kegan Paul/Harcourt, Brace & Co. 1959; Signet/NAL, 1969; Princeton University Press, 1978).

Keel, John A. *UFOs: Operation Trojan Horse* (G. P. Putnam's Sons, 1970). Also published as *Why UFOs* (Manor Books, 1976).

———. *The Mothman Prophecies* (Saturday Review Press/E. P. Dutton, 1975; Signet/NAL, 1976).

———. *The Eighth Tower* (Saturday Review Press/E. P. Dutton, 1975).

———. *Our Haunted Planet* (Fawcett, 1971).

Keyhoe, Donald E. *Aliens From Space* (Doubleday, 1973).

———. *Flying Saucers From Outer Space* (Henry Holt, 1953).

———. *Flying Saucers—Top Secret* (G.P. Putnam's Sons, 1960).

———. *The Flying Saucer Conspiracy* (Henry Holt, 1955).

———. *The Flying Saucers Are Real* (Fawcett, 1950).

Kottmeyer, Martin S. "What's Up Doc?" *Magonia* (October 1992).

———. "Swinging Through the Sixties," *Magonia* (March 1993).

———. "Shams and Shepherds," *Magonia* (June 1993).

Lewels, J. *The God Hypothesis* (Wild Flower Press, 1997).

Loftin, Robert. *Identified Flying Saucers* (McKay, 1968).

Lore, Gordon. *Strange Effects from UFOs* (NICAP, 1969).

Lorenzen, Coral and Jim. *Abducted! Confrontations with Beings from Outer Space* (Berkley, 1977).

———. *Encounters with UFO Occupants* (Berkley, 1976).

———. *Flying Saucer Occupants* (Signet/NAL, 1967).

———. *UFOs Over the Americas* (Signet/NAL, 1968).

———. *UFOs: The Whole Story* (Signet/NAL, 1969).

Lorenzen, Coral E. *Flying Saucers: The Startling Evidence of the Invasion from Outer Space* (Signet/NAL, 1962, 1966).

Machlin, Milt. *UFO* (Quick Fox, 1981).

Mack, John E. *Abducted* (Charles Scribner's Sons, 1994).

———. *Passport to the Cosmos* (Crown, 1999).

Magor, John. *Aliens Above, Always* (Hancock House, 1983).

Melges, Frederick T., and Arthur Freeman. "Persecutory Delusions: A Cybernetic Model," *American Psychiatry* (October 1975).

Michel, Aimé. *The Truth About Flying Saucers* (S. G. Phillips, 1956; Pyramid Books, 1967).

———. *Flying Saucers and the Straight Line Mystery* (Criterion, 1958).

Miller, Max B. *Flying Saucers: Fact or Fiction?* (Trend Books, 1958).

Moseley, James W. "The Solution to the Flying Saucer Mystery," *Saucer News* (June-July 1956).

Official Guide to UFOs, The. Editors of Science & Mechanics (Davis Publications/Ace Books, 1968).

Peebles, Curtis. *Watch the Skies: A Chronicle of the Flying Saucer Myth* (Smithsonian Institution Press, 1994; Berkley Books, 1995).

Randles, Jenny. *Star Children* (Sterling, 1995).

Reeve, Helen and Bryant. *Flying Saucer Pilgrimage* (Amherst Press, 1957).

Rogo, D. Scott. *The Haunted Universe* (Signet/NAL, 1977).

Rogo, D. Scott, ed. *Alien Abductions* (Signet/NAL, 1980).

Rogo, D. Scott, and Jerome Clark. *Earth's Secret Inhabitants* (Tempo, 1979).

Rogo, D. Scott, and Ann Druffel. *The Tujunga Canyon Contacts* (Prentice-Hall, 1980; Signet/NAL, 1989).

Ruppelt, Edward J. *The Report on Unidentified Flying Objects* (Doubleday/Ace Books, 1956).

Scully, Frank. *Behind the Flying Saucers* (Henry Holt, 1950).

Steiger, Brad, and Joan Writenour. *Flying Saucers Are Hostile* (Award Books, 1967).

———. *Flying Saucer Invasion Target Earth* (Award/Tandem, 1969).

Steiger, Brad. *The Seed* (Berkley, 1983).

———. *Strangers From the Skies* (Award Books, 1966).

———. *The UFO Abductors* (Berkley Books, 1988).

———. *Alien Meetings* (Grosset & Dunlap/Ace Books, 1978).

———. *The Flying Saucer Menace* (Award Books, 1967).

———. *Gods of Aquarius: UFOs and the Transformation of Man* (Harcourt Brace Jovanovich, 1976).

Steiger, Brad, and Sherry Hansen. *UFO Odyssey* (Ballantine Books, 1999).

———. *The Rainbow Conspiracy* (Kensington Books, 1994).

Steiger, Brad and Francie. *The Star People* (Berkley Books, 1981).

Story, Ronald D., ed. *The Encyclopedia of UFOs* (Doubleday/New English Library, 1980).

Stringfield, Leonard H. *Inside Saucer Post—3-0 Blue* (Moeller, 1957).

———. *Situation Red: The UFO Siege* (Doubleday, 1977).

Trench, Brinsley Le Poer. *The Flying Saucer Story* (Ace, 1966).

Vallée, Jacques. *Anatomy of a Phenomenon* (Henry Regnery, 1965; Ace Books, 1966).

———. *Challenge to Science* (Henry Regnery/Ace Books, 1966).

———. *Passport to Magonia* (Henry Regnery, 1969; Neville Spearman, 1970).

———. *Messengers of Deception* (And/Or Press, 1979; Bantam Books, 1980).

———. *The Invisible College* (E. P. Dutton, 1975).

———. *Dimensions* (Contemporary Books, 1988).

———. *Revelations* (Ballantine Books, 1991).

———. *Confrontations* (Ballantine Books, 1990).

———. *Forbidden Science* (Marlowe, 1996).

Ware, Donald, in *UFOs and the Alien Presence*, edited by Michael Lindemann (Wild Flower Press, 1998).

Wilkins, Harold T. *Flying Saucers on the Attack* (Ace, 1967).

———. *Flying Saucers Uncensored* (The Citadel Press, 1955).

Wilson, Colin. *Alien Dawn* (Fromm International, 1998).

Timmerman, John P.   (b. 1923). As a Lima, Ohio, businessman, Timmerman became associated with astronomer J. Allen Hynek in 1979 and provided major funding for the operation of the Center for UFO Studies (CUFOS) for many years. Timmerman graduated from Cornell University in 1950, at which time he became interested in investigating UFO sighting reports.

In 1980 Timmerman became Chairman and Treasurer of the Center and created the traveling UFO Photo Exhibit Research Project, which began appearing in shopping centers, universities, and at conferences throughout the United States and Canada. In May 1980 he created the *CUFOS Associate Newsletter* and served as its editor and publisher until it was discontinued in July 1985.

When CUFOS moved from a public office located in Evanston in 1981, Timmerman assumed much of the business operation responsibility for Dr. Hynek and opened a public access office with paid staff in Lima, Ohio, where he produced the *International UFO Reporter* edited by Dr. Hynek from January 1982 until the Lima office was combined with a new facility near Chicago, which was opened when Dr. and Mrs. Hynek moved from Evanston, Illinois, to Scottsdale, Arizona, in 1985.

In 1981, Timmerman successfully negotiated the transfer of the NICAP files from their location in Gaithersburg, Maryland, to Chicago where they are now combined with the case files in the offices of the J. Allen Hynek Center for UFO Studies.

In December of 1985 Timmerman retired as Chairman of CUFOS. He continues to serve on the Board of Directors of the J. Allen

John Timmerman

Hynek Center for UFO Studies as Public Relations Vice President, Treasurer, and Manager of the photo exhibit project.

Address:　P.O. Box 1621
　　　　　Lima, OH 45802
　　　　　U.S.A.

POSITION STATEMENT: The UFO Phenomenon is still far more complex than originally thought to be by most researchers. The proper study of the subject will require consideration of the complex nature of human mental processes as well as a better understanding of the physical nature of our planet and of the universe using our best scientists and technologies. Anecdotal information will remain our major public source for study until a way is found to share with the many varied cultural groups in today's world without serious social disruption the realities now held secretly by agencies of many governments of the world regarding the UFO Phenomenon.

　　　　　　　　　　—JOHN TIMMERMAN

Top Secret/Majic (Marlowe, 1996). Stanton Friedman tries to make a case that the Majestic-12 documents are authentic and reveal a secret government cabal controlling public knowledge about UFO crashes and the retrieval of alien bodies. He expands upon his earlier contentions that "the wreckage of at least two very advanced flying saucers in New Mexico in 1947" resulted in a back-engineering program which developed the transistor and other technological breakthroughs.

　　　　　　　　　　—RANDALL FITZGERALD

transformation required to join the Galactic Society　As we enter the new millennium, the pace of human activity is increasing rapidly. This also seems to be true for the non-human intelligence in this part of the galaxy, whether we call them aliens, visitors, watchers, angels, or archangels. We are in the process of joining a Galactic Society, both individually and collectively. Not everyone will do it in this lifetime; however, I sense that 700-800 million of us have at least started that process. Some of these people are called New Agers. In The RA Material they are called 4th-density beings. (Elkins and Rueckert, 1982)

In *Paradigm Wars: Worldviews for a New Age* (1996), Dr. Mark Woodhouse calls them the rising culture. My observation of a rapidly increasing spiritual awareness, of environmental activism from the grass roots to the highest levels of government, and of the prophecy in *The Urantia Book* suggests that these 4th-density beings will become the dominant culture in this century. The Old Agers are on the way out. The meek will inherit the Earth.

In 1952 my world was mainly my family and friends and the woods, streets, and schools of Arlington, Virginia. Then I saw seven UFOs and became a truthseeker. Now my world has been transformed. We are not all at the same level of acceptance of what is happening on this planet. Some of my ideas may seem very strange. However, *please keep a large mental hold basket to store those ideas that don't make sense to you.* You may reject them later if you choose. I am not tying to convince anyone of anything, but just sharing with other truthseekers what I have come to accept as real after forty-eight years of study.

UFOs represent, in part, the angelic force associated with the Second Coming operation. Ascended masters are real. Pleiadians are real. Zeta Reticulans are real. Arcturians, Aethiens, Andromies, and Essasanies are real. And I hope you do not feel slighted if I left out your favorite aliens. There are others out there.

Crop circles are real, and some are faked. Underground and undersea bases are real. The 1952 MJ-12 briefing and the 1954 Special Operations Manual 1-01 are real. The covert release of the MJ-12 manual, entitled "Extraterrestrial Entities and Technology, Recovery and Disposal," I believe, is a result of the 1993 Rockefeller White House initiative. I also believe that pressure from members of the not-so-secret world government caused a covert release of the alien autopsy film.

Because of the "prime directive" of the local galactic council, most of the information associated with the film is disinformation to protect the worldviews of those who are not ready for the alien presence. One pragmatic reason for the prime directive is to separate the necessary fact of human/alien hybrids from the awake consciousness of the Old Agers. I also believe that both spiritual inspiration and alien liaison are real.

SPIRITUAL ASPECTS OF TRANSFORMATION

Intelligent life is abundant throughout the universe. God is abundant throughout the universe. He is in you and me, in Zetas and Pleiadians, and in angels and archangels. Everything evolves. Galaxies, planets, our physical bodies, and spirit all evolve. God evolves. In considering human evolution I think it is important to recognize that we have at least four bodies: our physical body and three energy bodies. These energy bodies are the mental body, the emotional body, and the spiritual body. As we join the Galactic Society and gain greater access to the consciousness of "heaven," I think we are upgrading our physi-

cal and mental bodies. This seems to be a joint human-alien program. The universe is so complex it is beyond our ability to fully comprehend. However, with considerable effort and assistance from our guides, we can greatly expand our awareness of it.

Levels of Evolution: We have been taught about levels of evolution from several sources. I will outline two that I find useful. Seven "densities of reality" are taught in the RA material. The 1st density includes non-living matter: water, minerals, rock. Second in the hierarchy of evolutionary existence are plants and animals that are not self-aware. Third are humans and cetaceans, which include dolphins and whales. At this level, veils separate the conscious from the unconscious mind to expedite evolutionary polarization of consciousness through free-will. The soul's mission through multiple incarnations is to choose either service to others or service to self.

Souls that become sufficiently polarized are ready to graduate to the next level, where the mission then becomes to develop unconditional love. RA said it only takes about 50 percent positive polarization toward service to others to graduate. This planet is being transformed into a 4th-density positive planet, and those souls not sufficiently polarized will have an opportunity to incarnate on another 3rd-density planet. After a soul has learned to express unconditional love, it then becomes ready for the 5th-density experience of developing true wisdom. Many 5th-density souls may combine to become a galactic teacher, a 6th-density being that some call an archangel. RA, a galactic teacher, who was once worshipped here as the Egyptian Sun God, said he went through his 3rd-density experience on the planet Venus, 2.6 billion years ago. He said that halfway through the 6th density those of positive and negative polarization become one, and graduate to the 7th density as part of God's plan.

My second description of the levels of evolution comes from Deepak Chopra's July 20, 1996, lecture at the Institute of Noetic Science's (IONS) conference in Boca Raton, Florida. He described the "shades of awareness" detailed in ancient Vedic teachings. He described the first shade of awareness as deep sleep, and the second as a dream state. The third is the awake state that I hope most people reading this are experiencing. He said if you "woke up" from this state you would think it is not real. Chopra describes the 4th as transcendental awareness. One characteristic is that you acquire non-local awareness. It seems to me that the rising culture on this planet is acquiring non-local awareness through telepathy, through remote viewing, and through out-of-body experiences. At this level, Chopra said, "You can get a glimpse of the soul." The 5th shade he describes as cosmic awareness, where one can have simultaneous local and non-local awareness. (I think Pleiadians can do that.) The 6th level he describes as divine or God awareness. Here a being can cognate, or cause to be born, objects in both local and non-local awareness. (Perhaps Sai Baba is one of these.) At this level, intentionality assumes awesome power. The 7th level is described as Unity. He says, "The spirit within merges with the spirit without, and the universe is experienced as one's body." These seven "shades of awareness" seem to be parallel descriptions of the seven "densities" or levels in the evolution of the soul as described by RA in 1982.

Assistance from a Galactic Council: We have been told through various sources that Ashtar has been given responsibility by a local galactic council to coordinate the activities of the various beings helping us with our transformation. Ashtar says that Sananda or Jesus, is his spiritual adviser. This is primarily a transformation of consciousness, so Jesus is directing that process. Perhaps he decides when we are ready for more Marian apparitions or more phantom hitchhikers.

Marian apparitions, sometimes associated with UFOs, are increasing around the world, and I have found that the phantom hitchhiker phenomenon is also widespread. Evidence indicates that on November 22, 1993, eight differ-

ent cars traveling on I-10 east of Tallahassee, Florida, encountered a phantom hitchhiker. Most drivers felt compelled to stop and pick up a strange-looking man along a lonely stretch of the highway. He looked a lot like Jesus, and once in the car he said, "Gabriel is about to blow his horn." Then he just vanished. On one occasion two children were in the backseat, and the man just appeared in the front seat next to their mother. The children were quite disturbed, and the man said, "It's time for Gabriel to blow his horn." He then vanished. Seven such events happened that day just west of a speed trap, and each driver sped up and was stopped. Each of the seven related their story to the state trooper, and the eighth felt compelled to report the event by phone. Within a three-day period I received reports of these events from three independent sources in Niceville, Panama City, and Yalaha, Florida. I wonder if they were each inspired to tell me so that these events would become public knowledge.

I mentioned these events at a couple of UFO conferences and learned that a series of similar events took place on the Washington, D.C., Beltway, near Los Angeles, and in Illinois. Foreign investigators said the phantom hitchhiker gave the same message in Great Britain, Germany, and Italy. Gabriel blowing his horn is mentioned in the Bible in relation to the end times. I think someone is trying to tell us something, and if it is not Jesus, I think it must be one of his angels.

In July 1996 the late Willis Harmon, then president of IONS, was speaking on the Pathfinder Project. This project is defining the path from here to there, where there is a sustainable society, a new world order, or heaven on Earth. A question from the audience was, "How can we get from here to there when there are so many selfish people on Earth?" After Harmon, my answer was, "We can't do it without celestial assistance." I think we are getting that assistance. We are being guided. But, beyond that, I think that whoever decides which souls reincarnate here will send the highly selfish souls somewhere else. Perhaps only those souls oriented primarily toward service to others will reincarnate here, and their mission will be to develop unconditional love of others. Encouraging evidence of this celestial intervention can be found in the recent book, *The Millennium Children* (1997) by Caryl Dennis.

PHYSICAL ASPECTS OF TRANSFORMATION

Three of the physical aspects of our transforming to a 4th-density society are an increasing number of photos and videos of alien vehicles, advanced technology that is kept away from 3rd-density society until all national leaders choose peace, and a human/Zeta hybridization program. Some people might add to this list the crop circles and amazing pictograms that have increased in magnitude and meaning in recent years.

Photographs: Because photographs can be faked, photographic evidence of the alien presence is usually a non-threatening way to raise the awareness of those who are ready, without destroying the worldview of those who are not. Albums of good UFO photos fill several shelves in the archives of Wendelle Stevens in Tucson, Arizona. When Jaime Maussan, a top TV journalist and UFO researcher in Mexico, requested that people send him UFO videos, he received over 5,000 of them. Some showed groups of up to 50 objects. As the transformation progresses our alien visitors become bolder in their careful indoctrination program. They have now made an appearance at each of the last eight independence day celebrations in Mexico.

Carlos Dias and his lovely wife Margarita are an intelligent and spiritually oriented young couple who have willingly cooperated with Pleiadians. Carlos was contacted in 1979 by human-like beings, and he received guidance for many years before being allowed to take close photos and videos of Pleiadian vehicles. One video shows him in a field inviting contact as the vehicle pops into view above him, wakes the roosters and dogs, and then pops out. After one missing-time experience in the mountains a man got out of his car and said, "If you want to know what you went through today, I will wait for you tomorrow at noon . . ." at a certain location in Mexico City. When they met, the man was teaching schoolchildren to respect all living things. The man told Carlos we humans should open our minds and hearts. Carlos was offered further education about the transformation while in his community and while on their vehicles.

Another interesting set of pictures are the Almintaka photos taken on September 27, 1989, in Tennessee. The object appeared to be twice the size of the full Moon and was photographed with the best film Kodak makes, using a 2000mm lens with special filters. Graham E. Bethune of Toms River, New Jersey, a retired Navy fighter pilot, is the chief investigator and a longtime friend of the anonymous photographer. The man was apparently inspired to put the camera and film in the trunk of his car, and when driving near Nashville the object flew over. He stopped, and his wife said he appeared to be in a trance as he got the camera and took a whole roll of film. The photos show the object demonstrating a great variety of lighting effects, including a blue beam coming from a protrusion. Some type of smoke or water vapor condensation was used to delineate some of the light beams.

Photo opportunities of strange vehicles in Gulf Breeze, Florida, have been newsworthy for more than a decade. Phase one started on November 11, 1987, and included forty-one excellent photos of three types of vehicles taken by Ed and Frances Walters during eighteen sessions over five and a half months.

These were well documented in their first book *The Gulf Breeze Sightings* (1990). I have seen seventy-five photos of the vertical-sided vehicles taken by various people in that area. Ed and Frances later published *UFO Abductions in Gulf Breeze* (1994) to relate information about six abductions and other strange events that we investigators advised they leave out of the first book. Phase two of the Gulf Breeze sightings included an eighteen-month period when anomalous objects, usually over a mile away, were recorded by the Gulf Breeze Research Team 175 times. During this period they were documented by every news reporter and seen by most of the visitors that came from around the world. Phase three involved continuing daylight photo and video opportunities by Ed Walters. Three additional types of vehicles and a number of Ed's interesting encounters are now documented in *UFOs Are Real! Here is the Proof* (1997), co-authored with Dr. Bruce Maccabee.

One of these vehicles was photographed as an F-15 made a close identification pass. It was 29 feet in diameter and 19 feet high. It had similar domes top and bottom and was rimmed by eight egg-shaped protrusions. A later photo of this type of vehicle was made as a column of water rose up from the sound to contact the vehicle. A hamburger-shaped object was photographed three times. The last time, after it came closer, Ed said he just pointed the camera and something else clicked the shutter. He said that during this event a strange thumping noise was coming from the window, and an anomalous black dot appears there in the picture.

Ed even wrote about his opportunity to video his own abduction, but after he viewed it on TV it was apparently erased by some alien technology as he watched. A third type of object is an apparently unmanned disk 8 feet in diameter that hovered over the beach behind Ed's house in November 1995. Unfortunately this photo was inadvertently left out of the book by the editor. In November 1996 he took a closer photo of this type of object after it appeared 25 feet away in his backyard, about 3 feet above the ground. The shadow is plainly evident in both photos.

My conclusion after studying the Gulf Breeze UFOs for nearly ten years is that the vertical-sided, Type-I vehicles come in two sizes: one about 12 feet in diameter that is too small to take on humans, and one about twice that diameter that is designed to carry humans. These have the capability to energize the surrounding air so that it produces orange photons. I think they do this because the orange-ball

UFOs are less frightening than structured vehicles.

In the summer of 1994 Bland Pugh photographed, from Ed Walters's front yard, an unseen disk immediately above a frequently seen red light during a moonlit night. He used Ektar 1000 film. This disk had the same shape as the 8-foot-diameter disk Ed photographed in November 1995 and November 1996. If it is the same, the red light was 2 feet in diameter. Investigators of other red-light UFOs in Gulf Breeze determined that the lights were about 2 feet in diameter by using triangulation. I think some of the many red-light type UFOs are produced by unmanned vehicles, while others may be the reddish veil of plasma that hangs below Gulf Breeze Type-II vehicles shown in *The Gulf Breeze Sightings*. I have seen evidence to suggest that these Type-II vehicles belong to Ashtar's observers.

4th-Density Technology Programs: For several decades UFO investigators have heard stories about secret underground bases and humans and aliens working together. One story has President Eisenhower getting demonstrations of alien technology in April 1954 and asking them to please minimize their effect on our society. William F. Hamilton III has written several books about underground bases, and Dr. Richard Sauder speaks about the machines, mostly built by companies associated with Hughes Tool and Die, Inc., used to construct the bases and connecting tunnels. Magnetic levitation vehicles are postulated for rapid underground transport, and strange air vents, many on AT&T facilities, suggest the base and tunnel system is widespread. Tunnel evacuation is probably necessary for the high speeds reported to investigators.

Bill Uhouse claims to have worked for twenty-five years in two underground facilities, one near Area 51 and one near Dulce, New Mexico, that he was told are no longer under U.S. jurisdiction. World territories perhaps? Uhouse was told there were six such bases in, or beneath, the United States. He was working on a flying saucer simulator in the 1970s.

Uhouse said their team had an alien consultant. On the 1988 NBC special, "UFO Coverup Live," a shadowy figure called "Falcon" showed diagrams of alien physiology and said aliens have operational control of parts of Nevada. Amazing devices, some perhaps made by Lockheed-Martin, are test-flown in Nevada at night and photographed by many people. Bob Lazar claims to have worked on a vehicle designed for small aliens.

One young technician told me he has seen evidence that transporter technology, à la *Star Trek*, is used to move people from Area 51 to Pine Gap, Australia. I wonder how much of this is U.S. technology and how much is world technology being kept out of the 3rd-density society by a world-level organization operating under a galactic prime directive.

Retired Army intelligence officer, Philip J. Corso, recently wrote *The Day After Roswell* (1997) with William J. Birnes. They indicate that secrets from confiscated UFOs led to laser technology, fiber optics, night-vision capability, and the microchip.

Others have provided interesting evidence suggesting an electrogravitic propulsion system for the B-2. In 1996 Al Gore, a dual-hatted member of government, announced the contract award to Lockheed-Martin for the next generation space shuttle. This is a delta-shaped single-stage vehicle with "linear aerospike engines" that carries a large payload into space and lands like a plane. These engines burn hydrogen and oxygen through a linear aerospike nozzle. When I got my Mechanical Engineering degree I was taught there was not enough energy in that chemical reaction, even with zero waste, to accomplish that mission without reducing the effects of gravity. Perhaps electrogravitic propulsion, *Star Trek*-type transporters, and most zero-point energy devices are being reserved for use by 4th-density society until all national leaders choose peace.

Members of world government, which include many dual-hatted members of national governments, are working hard to cause all national leaders to choose peace. Meanwhile, some new technology is being released for lim-

ited use. I have been told that the Patterson Power Cell is a cold-fusion heat source that can now be leased for $5,000 per year. It is not likely to be used for war. Electrogravitic propulsion systems seem to be used only where they can remain highly controlled by unselfish people. And I wonder if the reason nations don't spend more money on the ability to go to Mars is because some humans already have the ability to go, either on their own vehicles or perhaps on vehicles of their alien friends.

Human-alien hybridization: Budd Hopkins introduced many of us to evidence of human-alien hybridization through the experiences of "Kathy Davis" and others in the 1987 book, *Intruders.* While she raised two of her children, she apparently carried two for over three months that were raised by aliens, and she was told there were seven more developed from her eggs. Kathy later met on alien vehicles the two she had carried for three months. She thought they were beautiful, but she agrees that because of their larger heads and eyes most of us would not accept them in 3rd-density society. During at least four of Ed Walters's eight abductions, he apparently provided emotional training for a total of thirty-five hybrid children two feet tall.

My friend "Pam" is raising two children born of Immaculate Conception. Both have been able to see people's auras since birth, and they recall many onboard experiences with aliens and many backyard experiences with hybrids, all without fear. One even said she could see through the ceiling while waking up, like Superwoman. Her mother was standing over her bed watching her expressions change as this happened. In 1996 Pam said she often felt a presence nearby. Later, when she was taken on board by aliens and presented with a baby to hold, she felt the same presence. I wonder if the spirit of this child was not checking out mom while the new body was growing in an artificial womb.

I think we, as a species, are being genetically enhanced. The result may be called *Homo noeticus*: humans with increased consciousness or ways of knowing. At the 1993 Human Potential Foundation Conference in Washington, D.C., "When Cosmic Cultures Meet," a recently retired legal counsel to the National Research Council and legal consultant to NASA called the next species *Homo alterios spatialis* in his talk on "Extraterrestrial Progeny of Humankind and a Declaration of Interdependence."

George S. Robinson's paper in *The Proceedings* was given the lead position, but the title was changed to "Homo Alterios Spatialis: A Transgenic Odyssey." My interpretation of one of his sentences is truly profound. He said, "In short, Earth-kind may well be the common progenitor when cosmic cultures meet." Perhaps more of us will soon meet our space-kind sons and daughters, brothers and sisters, and perhaps some missing twins.

Three of the 1996 movies I saw were *Phenomenon*, *Powder*, and *Independence Day*. The first two seemed to address the public reaction to people who are different, as does the TV series *Alien Nation*. They show that many people in our society are not yet ready to accept 4th-density capabilities. I think we all need to give serious thought to these messages, because it is happening among us. *Independence Day* seemed to be designed primarily to attract a big audience, but one underlying message was that to survive we must give more thought to being a citizen of the world rather than of a nation.

We are being given greater awareness, greater knowledge of all, that is, *greater knowledge of God*. We are being given greater telepathic ability to the point that I think it will become a normal means of communication as we join the Galactic Society.

POLITICAL TRANSFORMATION

If God wanted to get something done, like transform Earth to a 4th-density planet, how would he do it? He does it through individual human beings: through Zetas and Pleiadians, and through our guides—angels and archan-gels. God also works through those who have the resources to bring about world change. The primary resources are money and influence. Many of these people are part of the not-so-secret world government.

God's helpers from various levels of "reality" have assisted and influenced human evolution since its beginnings. (Newbrough, 1882) They influenced the ancient mystery religions of Babylon, Egypt, India, Persia, and Greece with various forms of pantheism. These wise spirits from "above" have throughout many centuries influenced our thought and action through Kabbalism, Gnosticism, the Knights Templars, the Rosicrucians, Freemasonry/Illuminati, and more recent spiritually oriented groups like the Theosophical Society, all culminating in what many call the New Age movement.

The rate of interaction may have increased since World War II to keep our technological development from getting too far ahead of our spiritual development. I have seen various signs that one primary purpose of Freemasonry is to build a widespread mind-set that will make a world government possible. A democratically elected world government seems to be a prerequisite to the people of Earth joining the Galactic Society.

The not-so-secret world government: Though not an expert on world government, I have focused my attention on it since January 1994. We have been living with a world government for seventy-nine years. I found an important book that seems to have greatly influenced the not-so-secret world government in 1972: *The Limits of Growth: A Report for the Club of Rome's Project on the Predicament of Mankind.* (Meadows et al., 1972)

I view the Club of Rome (COR) as a think-tank for the not-so-secret world government, much as the expertise of the Rand Corporation is used to provide guidance for the U.S. Air Force on complicated issues. The COR used the world's best system modelers and the big computer at MIT to model growth in the world system from 1900 to 2100. All relevant data collected from 1900 to 1970 was used, and the computer was asked what happens if we keep doing what we have been doing? Parameters plotted included birth and death rates, natural resources, capital, population, food per capita, industrial output per capita, and pollution. The curves showed many peaks in the first half of the next century, and by 2050 the death rate was nearly vertical. Population growth is finally halted by death due to decreased food and medical services. If many stabilizing policies were implemented in 1975, including an average of two children per family, the charts were less scary, and a stabilized society was nearly reached by 2050. However, if these policies were delayed until the year 2000, the decline continued through the end of this century without stabilization.

There is a 13-page commentary at the end of *The Limits of Growth* by The Executive Committee of the Club of Rome: Alexander King, Saburo Okita, Aurelio Peccei, Eduard Pestel, Hugo Thiemann, and Carroll Wilson. The commentary is concluded with the following paragraphs:

"The concept of a society in a steady state of economic and ecological equilibrium may appear easy to grasp, although the reality is so distant from our experience as to require a Copernican revolution of the mind. Translating the idea into deed, though, is a task filled with overwhelming difficulties and complexities. We can talk seriously about where to start only when the message of *The Limits of Growth,* and its sense of extreme urgency, are accepted by a large body of scientific, political, and popular opinion in many countries. The transition in any case is likely to be painful, and it will make extreme demands on human ingenuity and determination. As we have mentioned, only the conviction that there is no other avenue to survival can liberate the moral, intellectual, and creative forces required to initiate this unprecedented human undertaking.

"But we wish to underscore the challenge rather than the difficulty of mapping out the road to a stable state society. We believe that an unexpectedly large number of men and women of all ages and conditions will readily respond to the challenge and will be eager to discuss not *if* but *how* we can create this new future.

"The Club of Rome plans to support such activity in many ways. The substantive research begun at MIT on world dynamics will be continued both at MIT and through studies conducted in Europe, Latin America, the Soviet Union, and Japan. And, since intellectual enlightenment is without effect if it is not also political, The Club of Rome also will encourage the creation of a world forum where statesmen, policy-makers, and scientists can discuss the dangers and hopes for the future global system without the constraints of formal intergovernmental negotiation.

"The last thought we wish to offer is that man must explore himself—his goals and values—as much as the world he seeks to change. The dedication to both tasks must be unending. The crux of the matter is not only whether the human species will survive, but even more whether it can survive without falling into a worthless state of existence."

These words must have had a profound effect on the three branches of the world government: the Council on Foreign Relations, the Royal Institute of International Affairs, and the Institute of Pacific Relations founded in 1921. I suspect that *The Limits of Growth* influenced the formation of a unifying organization, the Trilateral Commission, in 1973.

Conclusions

There is much evidence that aliens and angels are working with humans to transform this planet. In 1959 Pope John XXIII, political head of the Roman Catholic Church, wrote in his diary that he had visits by both Jesus and Mary. Now there are Marian apparitions, often associated with UFOs, in many parts of the world. During one of these Giorgio Bongiovanni was stigmatized, and he was told to tell the world about the transformation. I was told by a retired CIA agent that in 1985 Gorbachev had a visit by two Ascended Masters. That visit is still changing the world.

I have recently heard evidence that suggests the public is being deceived about the A-10 that mysteriously went to Colorado on April 2, 1997. It was apparently briefly captured by aliens as a way to get the attention of authorities. Captain Buttons is reported to have been removed from the plane to openly join the Galactic Society. U.S. proliferation of sophisticated weapons of war may have been an issue there. Perhaps the people in our Space Command headquarters know. Human-alien liaison is real, and I think many of us are now ready to know what's going on. Greater knowledge of joint human-alien efforts to transform this planet should not cause too much stress for those who don't care much about the broader issues facing humanity, but it can give much-needed hope to the unknowing participants.

—DONALD M. WARE

References

Elkins, Don, and Carla Rueckert. *The RA Material* (L/L Research, 1982).

Dennis, Caryl, with Parker Whitman. *The Millennium Children* (Rainbows Unlimited, 1997).

"The Fellowship." *The Urantia Book: A Revelation for Humanity* (Uversa Press, 1996).

Human Potential Foundation. *When Cosmic Cultures Meet, The Proceedings* (1997).

Meadows, Donella and Dennis, et al. *The Limits to Growth* (Signet/NAL, 1972).

Newbrough, John Ballou. *Ohaspe: A New Bible* (Kosmon Press, 1944).

Walters, Ed. *The Gulf Breeze Sightings* (Avon, 1990).

Walters, Ed and Frances. *UFO Abductions in Gulf Breeze* (Avon, 1994).

Walters, Ed and Bruce Maccabee. *UFOs are Real! Here Is the Proof* (1997).

Woodhouse, Mark B. *Paradigm Wars: Guidelines for a New Age* (Frog, 1996).

Tremonton (Utah) movie On July 2, 1952, Navy Warrant Officer Delbert C. Newhouse was driving toward a new duty station with his wife and two children. Just after eleven in the morning, his wife noticed a group of bright objects that she couldn't easily identify. Newhouse, a trained Navy photographer, stopped the car to retrieve his 16mm camera from the trunk.

By the time he got his camera out, the objects had moved away from the car. Newhouse said later that when one object broke from the formation, he tracked it so that analysts would have something to work with. He let it fly across the field of view. He did that two or three times. When he turned back, the whole formation was gone.

The details of the story vary, depending on the source. Air Force files, based on the information supplied by others, show that Newhouse and his wife saw the objects at close range. By the time he got the car stopped and the camera out of the trunk, the objects had moved to a longer range. In an interview conducted by UFO investigators in 1976, Newhouse confirmed he had seen the objects at close range. He said they were large, disk-shaped, and brightly lighted. Major Dewey Fournet, once a member of the Pentagon's UFO office, said Newhouse had said the same thing to him.

After filming the objects, Newhouse stored his camera, got back into the car and drove on to his new duty station. Once there, he had the film processed and sent a copy to the Air Force suggesting they might find it interesting.

The Air Force investigation lasted for months, including analysis of the film. They tried everything to identify the objects but failed. When coupled to the report and the reliability of the photographer, the Air Force was stuck. They had no explanation. When the Air Force finished, the Navy asked for it. They made a frame-by-frame analysis that took more than a thousand man-hours. They studied the motion of the objects, their relation to one another in the formation, the lighting of the objects, and every other piece of data they could find on the film. In the end, like their Air Force counterparts, they were left with no explanation.

But, unlike their Air Force counterparts, the Navy experts were not restricted in their praise of the film. Their report said that the objects were internally lighted spheres that were not reflecting sunlight. They also estimated the speed at 3,780 miles per hour, if the spheres were five miles away. At twice the distance, they would have been moving twice as fast. At half the distance, half the speed. If the objects were just under a mile distant, they were traveling at 472 miles an hour.

When the Robertson Panel reviewed the film, Dr. Luis Alverez, a physicist and winner of the Nobel prize, said that they might be birds (specifically, seagulls which are known to be in the area). Fournet said, "Dr. Alverez suggested that as a possible solution to that Tremonton movie."

In the years that followed, the Tremonton movie's suggested explanation became a solid explanation. Donald H. Menzel and L. G. Boyd, in their book, *The World of Flying Saucers,* wrote of the Tremonton film: "The pictures are of such poor quality and show so little that even the most enthusiastic home-movie fan today would hesitate to show them to his friends. Only a stimulated imagination could suggest that the moving objects are anything but very badly photographed birds." (Menzel and Boyd, 1963)

The Condon Committee investigator on the case, Dr. William K. Hartmann, reexamined the film. After reviewing the evidence, Hartmann concluded: "These observations give strong evidence that the Tremonton films do show birds, as hypothesized above, and I now regard the objects as so identified." (Gillmor, 1969)

So a possible answer, suggested by the Robertson Panel, became the final explanation for the Newhouse film. However, in the analysis that appeared after the Robertson Panel, one fact was left out. Newhouse saw the objects at close range. Fournet said, ". . . when you look at what Newhouse said when he was interviewed after that . . . when you put all that together, the seagull hypothesis becomes flimsier and flimsier." As with most others, this case stands or falls with the credibility of the witnesses.

—KEVIN D. RANDLE

References

Gillmor, Daniel S., and Edward U. Condon, eds. *Scientific Study of Unidentified Flying Objects* (E. P. Dutton/Bantam Books, 1969).

Menzel, Donald, and Lyle G. Boyd. *The World of Flying Saucers* (Doubleday, 1963).

Randle, Kevin D. "Tremonton (Utah) movie" in Story, Ronald D., ed. *The Encyclopedia of UFOs* (Doubleday/New English Library, 1980).

———. *Conspiracy of Silence* (Avon Books, 1997).

———. *Scientific UFOlogy* (Avon Books, 1999).

Ruppelt, Edward J. *The Report on Unidentified Flying Objects* (Doubleday, 1956).

Truth About Flying Saucers, The (S.G. Phillips, 1956). French mathematician Aimé Michel examines the observed characteristics of UFOs and various theories about their pro-

Photo courtesy of Ground Saucer Watch (GSW)

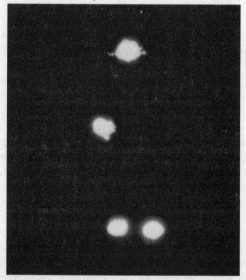

Computer enhancement of the Tremonton, Utah, UFOs

pulsion systems. He searches for patterns in UFO sightings and finds a tendency in European records for reports to be clustered during periods when Mars is aligned to the Sun and in areas where military bases were located.

—RANDALL FITZGERALD

Truth About The UFO Crash At Roswell, The (Avon Books, 1994). Kevin Randle and Donald Schmitt claim to have three hundred witnesses attesting to a military recovery of an extraterrestrial spacecraft and alien bodies near Roswell in 1947. This book was written, they say, to ''correct errors'' and add data collected since the 1991 publication of their first book on the subject, *UFO Crash at Roswell*. Several chapters of this book debunk the credibility of MJ-12 documents dealing with Roswell and challenge the veracity of Stanton Friedman's principal source for his book claiming a second spacecraft also crashed to the west of Roswell.

—RANDALL FITZGERALD

Tujunga Canyon Contacts, The (Prentice-Hall, 1980). Ann Druffel and D. Scott Rogo investigate in this book a contagion of alien abductions which spread over a period of decades between five Los Angeles women who were involved with each other as friends and lovers. The authors speculate that since all of the women were interested in metaphysical subjects, or displayed psychic talents, and all were lesbians, the ''UFO entities'' may have been intrigued about their reproductive habits and the effect on human evolution.

—RANDALL FITZGERALD

Tujunga Canyon (California) contacts In 1975, a group of five young women came to the attention of the NICAP (National Investigations Committee on Aerial Phenomena) investigative subcommittee in Los Angeles. All had lived or were still living in the area of the Tujunga Canyons, which wind up into the San Gabriel Mountains in Southern California. The first case documented was that of Sara Shaw and Jan Whitley, who had been awakened one

night in 1953 by a bright light outside their isolated cabin. An unexplained two-hour lapse of time occurred, after which the two young women fled down the mountain. The episode remained a mystery for twenty years, but when ''missing time'' experiences began to receive publicity, Sara Shaw sought our advice. After months of investigation, the two witnesses were hypnotically regressed separately by a clinical hypnotist, Bill McCall, M.D.

Sara recalled several thin humanoids in black garments coming through the closed window of their bedroom. They transported the two women onto a Saturn-shaped UFO hovering over a nearby stream. Jan was taken away, protesting violently, but Sara cooperated with the creatures as they examined her with an x-ray-type device. Afterwards, they held a ''conference'' with her, telling her about a ''cancer cure.'' Afterwards, the two women were ushered from the ''craft'' down a beam of light.

Later, Jan was repeatedly harassed by invisible ''presences'' in houses where she lived alone. The presences invariably urged her to ''come with them'' but Jan struggled mentally each time with them until they vanished.

At the last encounter they became visible as disembodied heads surrounding her bed. She resisted verbally, insisting they leave her alone. They never returned.

Unlike Sara, Jan was unable to recover visual memories of her 1953 encounter, but under hypnosis she experienced a certainty that the creatures were essentially invisible to her. She recalled being terrorized, a ''crunching pain'' in her head and a feeling that ''the atmospheric pressure had changed.'' Although she was convinced that the intruders were essentially invisible to her, she conceded other witnesses might see them in a visible form.

A separate encounter involved Jan and a third Tujunga witness, Emily Cronin. (All five witnesses preferred to be given pseudonyms to protect their identity.) In 1956, the two young women were driving home late at night along a mountain road but pulled over because of heavy truck traffic. Sleeping in a wayside rest stop, they were suddenly awakened by a bright light. Both felt completely paralyzed. For a few minutes Emily struggled against the paralysis and eventually was able to move one finger, breaking her entire paralysis. Jan also abruptly came out of her paralyzed state. She had been unable to resist by herself, but apparently Emily broke the paralyzed state for both. The two sped down the mountain, not speaking a word until they came to a cafe where they shared their impressions of what had happened. They remembered terror, paralysis, and the unexplained light but could not recover more details. When regressed by Dr. McCall, Emily remembered two entities clad in black emerging from a brightly lit landed "craft" nearby. The creatures circled their car, apparently curious about Emily's small son who was sleeping on the back seat. The entities were tall with elongated, thin heads. She had the impression that the creatures had "made a mistake" because a third entity in the craft was urging the others to return to the "UFO." The "craft" departed about the time Emily broke though her paralysis.

Later, Emily repeatedly perceived whitish entities which urged her to come with them but succeeded in breaking the altered state each time with a mental struggle. Subsequently, her roommate, Toni Fox, was able to help her by becoming aware she was "struggling" and gently waking her. Toni never saw the entities or experienced any paralysis.

In 1975, two other young women contacted Emily late one night in 1975, frightened and puzzled. Lori Briggs and Jo Maine, living in a nearby town, had experienced a terrorizing event involving paralysis and vague perception of small white-skinned entities. They were as rational and honest as the other three women and were eventually hypnotically regressed. Lori remembered being abducted by several thin, small creatures into a room with strange machines. She was examined by an X-ray type of equipment.

When the creatures suggested she come with them to an unexplained destination, Lori used a metaphysical technique, "internal sound," which she instinctively employed for meditation, protection, and relaxation. The creatures seemed surprised at her resistance and quickly transported her back to her own apartment, Jo at her side. Jo retrieved memories only of lying on a platform and of seeing "lights" and a dim "dome-shape." Throughout the ensuing years, after she moved to Tujunga, Lori at times became aware that the creatures were trying to recontact her. She would hear a loud, piercing noise the creatures made during the first encounter. When she promptly used her "own sound" against theirs, the entities left each time.

Seven separate types of events were experienced by the five Tujunga women, three of which had two witnesses. In 1980 these events became the subject of a book by this author and parapsychologist D. Scott Rogo. This was *The Tujunga Canyon Contacts* published by Prentice-Hall in 1980 with an updated paperback in 1989.

The book was the first to describe multiple-witness abductions and the possibility of "defense techniques" to fend off abduction scenarios, leading to this author's subsequent research presented in the 1998 publication of *How to Defend Yourself Against Alien Abduction*.

Since the Tujunga witnesses were of differing ages and were not in close contact during the 22-year period of the abduction events, it was hypothesized that Jan, who shared three of the experiences, might be somehow a "source of contagion" which made the other witnesses subject to abduction experiences. This "source of contagion" hypothesis was later interpreted by other researchers as being generational in nature, since many abductees have grandparents, parents, and children who have abduction experiences.

Scott Rogo and I wrote separate chapters on their interpretations of the events. Rogo hypothesized that the UFO phenomenon is essentially quasi-physical and is the product of a "supermind" that controls human consciousness and produces temporary energy forms that mold themselves into various shapes based on the predispositions of the viewer—in essence, a type of "mental projection."

I hypothesized that, while ordinary UFO phenomena seem physical and possibly extraterrestrial, so-called alien abductors are an order of creation which share the Earth with us in a hidden form and are essentially posing as UFO occupants in order to frighten and overcome human beings. Orders of intelligent creation, such as the Al-Jinn described in the Muslim Koran, Sidhe or Faery-folk described in academic writings by W. B. Yeats and others, and Incubi researched by prominent theologians such as Lodovico Sinistrari of Italy, have many characteristics in common with our modern-day alien UFO abductor: (1) materializing and de-materializing; (2) shape-shifting in size and form; (3) passing through solid matter; (4) sexually harassing nature; and (5) deceptive, or traumatizing by nature.

The California town of Tujunga and its treasured, wild canyons has long been regarded as a "window area" for strange events, both paranormal and UFOlogical.

—ANN DRUFFEL

12th Planet, The (Stein & Day, 1976). Zecharia Sitchin translates Sumerian, Babylonian, and Assyrian texts, along with the original Hebrew version of the Old Testament, to piece together a theory that visitors from an undiscovered 12th planet in our solar system inspired creation of the Sumerian civilization and Biblical stories of miracles and divine intervention. These visitors, called the Nefilim, came to Earth in search of minerals, mostly gold, and used genetic engineering to create humankind from *Homo erectus*. Some of the Nefilim opposed this experiment and caused the great flood to purify the planet of their creation.

—RANDALL FITZGERALD

2001: A Space Odyssey (Produced and directed by Stanley Kubrick for MGM, 1968).

This Academy Award-winning motion picture pushed the boundaries of the popular imagination to new limits.

The movie was based on a short story by Arthur C. Clarke entitled "The Sentinel," which first appeared in 1950. In it, an extraterrestrial artifact was discovered on the moon by Earth astronauts. What made the discovery such a powerful case of "future shock" was not just its otherworldly origin, but its age: *four million years*. This meant that long before human development was under way, other beings of a very high order of intelligence had been winging their way across the cosmos. The rest of the story concerns the odyssey of the spacecraft *Discovery*, as its lone surviving astronaut encounters an unknown intelligence that turns out to be our lord and savior.

Although not a religious film *per se,* it was in effect a space-age Genesis—a creation story featuring mankind as the product of a cosmic experiment being carried out, not by the traditional Judeo-Christian God, but by extraterrestrial intelligences who, because of attributes acquired during their own long evolution, might themselves be defined as gods.

In other words, *2001* contained the essential elements of the ancient astronaut theory prior to the fame of Erich von Däniken.

Moreover, the artifact in the story was more than a stone monument, indicating the possible existence of otherworldly visitors. The black monolith was both an alarm and a teaching device, which had been deliberately buried on the moon four million years before. Once excavated and exposed to light, it would serve as a signal to the beings who put it there. Thus, the "sentinel" would beam the message that man had reached a new step in his evolution—the capability of leaving the Earth and venturing into the cosmos.

In the novel version of *2001,* Arthur Clarke tells of the monolith's crystalline counterpart, used as a teaching machine for the man-apes back on Earth. It was in effect a highly complicated computer that thoroughly probed and mapped the brains and bodies of the early hominids, studied their reactions, evaluated their potential, and gave them "human" intelligence. Kubrick told *Playboy* magazine in 1968: "I will say that the God concept is at the heart of *2001*—but not any traditional, anthropomorphic image of God. I don't believe in any of Earth's monotheistic religions, but I do believe that one can construct an intriguing *scientific* definition of God." And so he did.

But Clarke and Kubrick gave their "gods" a much higher level of technology than von Däniken gave his. First of all, they were not of human form. Indeed, having freed themselves from matter, they existed as pure energy. Even the Earth people of *2001* that evolved from ape-men were far more advanced than von Däniken's ancient astronauts. They

had talking and thinking computers, an enormous space station, full-scale colonization of the moon, and artificially induced hibernation for long space journeys. No evidence of this kind of technology has ever been found as testimony to the presence of ancient astronauts. If and when it is, we will then have the kind of indications that can be taken seriously.

—RONALD D. STORY

References

Clarke, Arthur C. *2001: A Space Odyssey* (New American Library, 1968).

Interview with Stanley Kubrick in *Playboy* magazine (September 1968).

U

UFO Abductions: A Dangerous Game
(Prometheus Books, 1988). Philip Klass writes that movies and books have inspired an epidemic of alien abduction hoaxes, delusions, and fantasies. The use of hypnotic regression to extract memories of alien abduction is dangerous and deceptive because hypnotized subjects can willfully and convincingly lie, or hypnotic subjects can be pressured to produce pseudomemories which can wreak psychological harm.
—RANDALL FITZGERALD

UFO and the Bible (The Citadel Press, 1956). Astronomer Morris K. Jessup believes that many miracles recounted in the Bible provide evidence of alien visitors sent here as "sheep dogs" to tend the human flock. This was the first book-length attempt to reconcile the miraculous events in the Bible with the modern UFO phenomenon and with science. Jessup gives numerous striking examples to support his view that the UFO is the missing link, or common denominator, uniting the "miracles" of the Bible with the universal concepts sought by modern science.
—RANDALL FITZGERALD

"UFO" defined One of the major confusions besetting UFO research is that of basic definition. Unfortunately, the term "UFO" (which was coined by Captain Edward J. Ruppelt, a former chief of the U.S. Air Force's Project Blue Book) has been muddied, because it is both a technical term (i.e., given a specific meaning by various specialists) and a common-language term that has, in ordinary, everyday usage, taken on certain connotations, such as: UFO = extraterrestrial spaceship. The acronym has become so common, in fact, that it was defined in *Webster's New Twentieth Century Dictionary*, as follows: "any of the unidentified objects frequently reported, especially since 1947, to have been seen flying at varying heights and speeds and variously regarded as light phenomena, hallucinations, secret military missiles, spacecraft from another planet, et cetera." It has since been shortened in the 1997 tenth edition of *Merriam-Webster's Collegiate Dictionary* as simply: "unidentified flying object; *esp*: FLYING SAUCER."

The dictionary definition is usually intended as a close approximation of how a word or term is actually used in common practice, i.e., as a word comes to have a "meaning" in ordinary use. No single person can "assign" an ordinary use to a word; all must go along with the "meanings" of ordinary language that have evolved culturally.

This phenomenon was made strikingly clear to me by an experience with my son. He was five years old at the time (in 1979). I had just compiled the first *Encyclopedia of UFOs* (published by Doubleday and NEL in 1980) and wondered—without having any prior discussions on the matter—what a typical five-year-old child would have in his mind regarding the subject of UFOs. I asked my son, Brian: "What is a UFO?" He answered without hesitation, "a flying saucer." Just like the new *Merriam-Webster's Collegiate Dictionary*, Brian thought "flying saucer" answered the question. So, I rephrased the question this way: "What is *inside* a flying saucer?" To which he replied, matter-of-factly: "People from other planets." Nothing could better illustrate to me that "UFO" had become a living symbol in our culture for the vehicle that carries "humanoids from another planet."

Technical definitions are another matter.

Individuals do assign specific meanings to terms for a specific purpose. "UFO" has many such technical definitions, which vary from one "expert" to another. The Aerial Phenomena Research Organization defines a UFO as "any airborne object which cannot be identified by the witness." The astronomer Carl Sagan says something similar, in that "A UFO is a moving aerial or celestial phenomenon, detected visually or by radar, but whose nature is not immediately understood." A more precise definition is that offered by astronomer J. Allen Hynek: "We can define the UFO simply as the reported perception of an object or light seen in the sky or upon the land, the appearance, trajectory, and general dynamic and luminescent behavior of which do not suggest a logical, conventional explanation and which is not only mystifying to the original percipients but remains unidentified after close scrutiny of an available evidence by persons who are technically capable of making a commonsense identification, if one is possible."

There are, of course, instances in which the "UFO" is not "flying" and is not seemingly an "object." In fact, one possibility often suggested is that UFOs may be "psychic projections" (i.e., something like a hologram), which would not be definable as "objects" in the ordinary sense. Although a perfect definition is probably impossible (since, after all, the subjects of our study are "unidentified"), it may be advisable to limit the field of UFOlogy to those cases of sightings and encounters that do not seem (after a thorough and proper study by qualified persons) to be explainable in terms of any known phenomenon of nature or man-made device.

—RONALD D. STORY

UFO Enigma, The (Doubleday, 1977). Harvard astrophysicist Donald Menzel and psychiatrist Ernest Taves heatedly argue in this book that UFOs, ancient astronaut theories, parapsychology, and other pseudo-sciences are irrational aberrations which must be eradicated. Miracles described in the Bible have meteorological explanations. UFO sightings are all the result of liars, hoaxers, and misidentifications of natural phenomena. The authors admit their perspective is founded on a belief that we have never been visited, and we will never be visited by aliens from another star system.

—RANDALL FITZGERALD

UFO Exist! (G.P. Putnam's Sons, 1976). Paris Flammonde tries to make a case that powerful secret cabals "of enormous influence and incalculable economic strength" control human affairs and have conspired to keep the UFO secret from humanity. He believes UFOs could represent the private air force of a nongovernmental cabal, or these craft could be a monstrous creation of human intellect, some sort of energies or entities, over which control has been lost. "The enigmas may be a more developed stage of life, of which Man is a low form. The possibility of contact in such a circumstance seems improbable in the extreme."

—RANDALL FITZGERALD

UFO Incident, The   This made-for-TV movie, starring James Earl Jones and Estelle Parsons, was first aired on October 20, 1975, on NBC. It was a two-hour, prime-time special presentation of the alleged UFO-abduction experience of Betty and Barney Hill.

The Universal/NBC production was based on the book, *The Interrupted Journey* (1966) by John Fuller, that chronicled this most famous of all UFO-abductions, which allegedly occurred in 1961. The movie was repeated many times and is believed to have triggered a number of other UFO-abduction reports—as well as the popular image of the classic "Gray" alien. The large almond-shaped, wraparound eyes, no ears, small nose and mouth, and bald, oversized cranium—all of these features would later form the standard icon for the alien image.

Philip Klass, Martin Kottmeyer, and others have pointed out just how critical the timing of this media event happened to be in UFO-abduction history. Within weeks after the show,

Now It's a TV Movie . . .

ABOARD A FLYING SAUCER!

This Fall You Can See Couple's Incredible Story Of How They Were Kidnapped by a UFO

GROUP OF HUMANOIDS leads the captured couple aboard the saucer-shaped spaceship

Some believe this TV alien was the prototype for thousands of imaginary abductions by the "Grays" that were to follow.

UFO abductions were occurring in epidemic proportions and have continued that way ever since.

Among the famous cases to closely follow the first airing of the show were: Travis Walton (November 5, 1975), Charles Moody (claimed abduction was on August 13, 1975, but went public only *after* the show aired in November), and the Liberty, Kentucky, abduction (January 6, 1976). These cases, and most of the succeeding ones, followed the standard format that millions of viewers saw in *The UFO Incident*:

- captured and taken aboard a "flying saucer"
- undressed and placed on a table
- examined with special instruments, usually with special attention paid to the reproductive organs
- tour of the ship
- briefing or special message
- return to the original spot where the abduction occurred

- "missing time," or temporary loss of memory regarding the details of the event, which are usually recalled later through the use of time-regression hypnosis

These elements of UFO abduction accounts did not originate with *The UFO Incident,* but for the first time ever, they were dramatized and shown to millions of TV viewers—in repeated showings—of a very well-made, realistic movie that was presented as a true story.

—RONALD D. STORY

UFO Missionaries Extraordinary (Pocket Books, 1976). Hayden Hewes and Brad Steiger explore the origins of the Heaven's Gate cult two decades before most of the group committed mass suicide. From their start as UFO contactees recruiting followers on the West Coast, leaders Bo and Peep, two former Houston church choir members, expressed a desire for an ascension "to the next level" from planet Earth. Their philosophy of salvation by UFOs and the devotion of their followers remained largely unshaken even after their first apocalyptic prediction of mass deliverance aboard UFOs failed to come true in 1975.

—RANDALL FITZGERALD

UFO Retrievals (Blandford, 1995). British researcher Jenny Randles examines the chronology and evidence for thirty-two UFO crashes worldwide during the 20th century. She finds at most six accounts which may qualify as potential candidates for authentic spacecraft. But "the majority of evidence is peppered with misperception, mistaken identity and a pinch of fabrication."

—RANDALL FITZGERALD

UFO Verdict, The (Prometheus Books, 1986). Robert Sheaffer concludes in this book that UFOs do not exist because they spring entirely from the imaginations of the observers. UFO photos are all hoaxes, for example, because "all supposed UFO photographs produced to date have been taken by a single photographer, using a single camera.''

—RANDALL FITZGERALD

UFO's—A Scientific Debate (Cornell University Press, 1972) edited by Carl Sagan & Thornton Page. This book summarizes the proceedings of the American Association for the Advancement of Science special symposium held in December 1969. Fifteen American scientists challenge each other and the evidence of whether extraterrestrial visitation is physically real.

—RANDALL FITZGERALD

UFO's: Nazi Secret Weapon? (Samisdat, 1975). In this Canandian published tract, Mattern Friedrich claims that Adolf Hitler and a group of Nazi scientists escaped to Antarctica in flying saucers and account for the subsequent spate of worldwide UFO reports. Extraterrestrial visitors from another galaxy may have given the Nazis a helping hand in designing these craft because the Germans spoke a univeral technological language.

—RANDALL FITZGERALD

UFOlogy (Celestial Arts, 1973). James M. McCampbell, a nuclear power technician, theorizes that UFOs and their propulsion systems are electromagnetic energy phenomena. He cites numerous cases where the reported effects of UFOs—such as their interference with auto electrical systems and television and radio transmissions—resemble electromagnetic energy effects, especially those produced by microwaves.

—RANDALL FITZGERALD

UFOlogy Originally defined by Morris K. Jessup (in 1955) as follows: ''UFOlogy (You-fol-o-gy) has been coined in *The UFO Annual* to cover the field of investigation of what the Air Force has called Unidentified Flying Objects. Thus we have the science and study of the Unidentified Flying Object.''

Jessup coined the term in 1955, which appeared in his book *The UFO Annual*, when it

was published in 1956—the same year the term ''ufology'' also appeared, without any definition or explanation, in Britain's *Flying Saucer Review* (January-February 1956 issue); so, it appears that credit must be shared between these two sources.

The term first found its way into *The World Book Dictionary* in 1969. UFOlogy (or ufology) is presently defined in *Merriam-Webster's Collegiate Dictionary* simply as ''the study of unidentified flying objects.'' *(This entry was prepared from research conducted by Richard W. Heiden for the Aerial Phenomena Research Organization in 1983.)*

—ETEP STAFF

References

Flying Saucer Review (Jan.-Feb. 1956)

Heiden, Richard W. ''The Word 'UFOlogy','' *The A.P.R.O. Bulletin* (Vol. 31, No. 10, 1983).

Jessup, Morris K. *The UFO Annual* (The Citadel Press, 1956).

Merriam-Webster's Collegiate Dictionary, Tenth Edition (Merriam-Webster, 1993; 1997).

UFOnauts, The (Fawcett, 1976). Ghost hunter Hans Holzer thinks space visitors are abducting humans for breeding experiments because they find something about us appealing. He says these alien abductors resemble us, with the same sexual appetites, and do not ''consider us totally unworthy'' or they would not seek us out for breeding.

—RANDALL FITZGERALD

UFOs Explained (Random House, 1974). In his second book about the UFO phenomenon Philip Klass drops his theory that plasmas can account for sightings to argue that other logical scientific explanations can be found for any seemingly unexplained occurrence. He dissects a few dozen sightings to show how misidentifications of natural phenomena explain some, while others are simply hoaxes promulgated by publicity seekers and the greedy.

—RANDALL FITZGERALD

UFOs—Identified (Random House, 1968). Aviation magazine writer Philip Klass began his career as a UFO debunker with this book in which he attempted to offer an unusual natural explanation for a series of UFO sightings in New Hampshire recounted in John G. Fuller's book, *Incident at Exeter*. UFOs may be produced by a family of plasmas which include ball lightning and other freak atmospheric phenomena, Klass concluded, abandoning his previously held belief UFOs were just the result of hoaxes or misidentifications of conventional aircraft. When his plasma theory attracted considerable skepticism and ridicule from atmospheric scientists, Klass discarded the idea and fell back upon a strategy of trying to prove UFOs were mostly hoaxes and misperceptions of natural and human objects.

—RANDALL FITZGERALD

UFOs—Operation Trojan Horse (G.P. Putnam's Sons, 1970). John A. Keel writes that entities that are cosmic tricksters have deceived humans into thinking UFOs are extraterrestrial in origin. He warns that dabbling in the UFO subject can cause paranoia and schizophrenia, and recommends that parents forbid their children from becoming involved.

—RANDALL FITZGERALD

UFOs Over the Americas (Signet/NAL, 1968) by Jim and Coral Lorenzen. This book carries a quote on the cover by Carl Jung: "I hope you will continue your courageous fight for the truth." The Lorenzens think the truth may be that UFOs are projected images to deceive us and that the CIA has infiltrated civilian UFO groups to manipulate them, perhaps even their own group, The Aerial Phenomena Research Organization (APRO). They suggest that UFOs might be projected images of what contactees want to see, or what UFO occupants want them to see. Even though our technical equipment, our own minds, and the UFOs themselves may be deceiving us, it is the CIA that remains the chief agent of deception.

—RANDALL FITZGERALD

UFOs: What on Earth Is Happening? (Harvest House, 1975). John Weldon and Zola Levitt make an evangelical Christian case that demons pilot UFOs and they are preparing humanity for a satanic dictatorship under the Antichrist. These demons are manipulating the magnetic field of our planet "to affect the perceptions of those who see or contact them."

—RANDALL FITZGERALD

Ultimate Encounter (Pocket Books, 1978). Bill Barry recounts the story of Travis Walton, an Arizona woodcutter zapped by a UFO in front of six co-workers, who subsequently disappeared for five days and resurfaced claiming to have been abducted by aliens. His story was made into a movie and continues to generate controversy.

—RANDALL FITZGERALD

UMMO affair UMMO is, without any doubt, the longest-running hoax in UFOlogy. It drove wedges between believers and nonbelievers— between those who had received the "Good News" purveyed by the Space Brothers and those who took a more skeptical approach. The scientific jargon which characterized the UMMO reports led many to consider it the real thing.

The Ummites—tall, blond visitors from the planet UMMO, located some 14 light-years away from Earth—would have been perfectly at home in the company of Adamski's Venusians or the tall Nordics which have become part and parcel of modern UFOlogical taxonomy. Often endowed with names like DEI 98, ASOO 3, and IAUDU 3, they purportedly represented a civilization which had overcome planetary disharmony and mastered the secret of spaceflight (but apparently not the use of lowercase letters), trekking throughout neighboring solar systems in their OAWOLEA UEWA OEM, which humans referred to as "flying saucers."

These putative space travelers were in possession of a science completely undreamed of by human thinkers: their numerical system operated on a base of 12 rather than 10; they had discovered that the link between body and soul was a chain of 84 atoms of krypton lodged in the hypothalamus; their physicists had rejected our concept of Euclidean geometry and discovered that the universe was formed of an unsuspected number of dimensions and that matter, energy, and mass were in fact the result of three independent axes known collectively as IBOZOO UU. It was precisely this control of IBOZOO UU which enabled them to leave their homeworld and reach our solar system in some seven or eight months of travel time. Ummite cosmologists spoke of a "multiverse," the WAAM-WAAM, and were fascinated by magnetohydrodynamics, which they employed to power the small remote spheres (UULEWA) employed by their agents on Earth.

All information concerning their society, organization, and beliefs was gleaned from endless, erudite "reports" aimed at familiarizing humans with their culture, and acquainting humans with their perspective on our affairs, such as war, inequality, etc. These reports were allegedly transmitted by means of dictation to a human typist (who was strictly ordered never to attempt contact with the addressees), and then sent to scientists, philosophers, and broad-minded individuals who, in the Ummites' opinion, would be able to understand them and put them to good use.

A 1968 article appearing in Spain's conservative *ABC* newspaper openly discussed the existence of an "extraterrestrial colony" operating within that country at the time. The source of this information was a Catholic priest, Father Eduardo López, whose secondhand knowledge of the UMMO affair had been misconstrued by an eager journalist who wished to create the impression that the priest was actually in contact with the supposed aliens.

None of this quenched the public's appetite for UMMO, its progressive society, and its marvelous machinery. In 1971, the First UMMO Conference, organized by Rafael Farriols, was held outside Madrid. The public was treated to recorded readings of the various UMMO documents, along with a variety of slides.

Two years later, the Second UMMO Conference, held in Barcelona, featured a symposium of readings on humanity's place in the universe, daily life on UMMO, and other topics of interest. Farriols's and Antonio Ribera's book *UMMO: un caso perfecto* (*UMMO: A Perfect Case*) would appear shortly later.

Jacques Vallée pursued the phenomenon to Argentina, where a medical establishment dispensing miraculous cures had become UMMO's most tangible manifestation to date. In his book *Messengers of Deception*, Vallée had intimated the possibility of an espionage link with UMMO as part of the Cold War. In 1970, a British company known as UMO Plant Hire Ltd. was exposed as a front for KGB activities. One year later, over a hundred Soviet officials were expelled from the U.K. under suspicion of espionage, and UMO closed down.

The distinguished UFOlogist hinted at the strong possibility that UMMO was in fact some sort of covert exercise by one of the world's intelligence agencies, possibly aimed at the creation of a cult which would later be put to other uses. He was not alone in his observation: it had already been suggested by certain Spanish investigators that life on UMMO—an antiseptic society obsessed with personal cleanliness, heavily dependent on gadgetry for every detail of their existence, flitting about in aircars straight out of *The Jetsons*—reflected the ideal futuristic society from an American cultural perspective, thus hinting at the possible motive behind the entire affair.

—Scott Corrales

Unidentified, The (Warner Books, 1975). Jerome Clark and Loren Coleman theorize that the UFO phenomenon is a planetary poltergeist generating apparitions from humankind's repressed unconscious. Relying upon the work of Carl Jung, the authors write that the "otherworld" realm of the collective unconscious produces UFO manifestations and the Men in Black, who symbolically represent archetypal depictions of the Devil. (Clark, a former editor of *Fate* magazine, has since disavowed many of the ideas in this book.)

—RANDALL FITZGERALD

Uninvited Visitors (Cowles, 1967). Biologist Ivan T. Sanderson believes UFOs are a form of life sent here to keep watch over the cosmic nursery called Earth. These life-forms were manufactured by higher intelligence to duplicate a variety of Earth species and may live in outer space, visiting this planet periodically to feed on natural and human-produced electricity.

—RANDALL FITZGERALD

University of Colorado UFO Project In a March 1966 report to the U.S. Air Force Scientific Advisory Board, an *ad hoc* Committee to Review Project Blue Book, chaired by Dr. Brian O'Brien, recommended that the Air Force contract with several leading universities to conduct comprehensive investigations into UFO reports. A panel was then created to implement the recommendations, and confidential inquiries were sent to some well-known institutions. Harvard University, the Massachusetts Institute of Technology (MIT), the University of North Carolina, and the University of California reportedly declined the Air Force offer.

After further efforts, a contract was signed with the University of Colorado on October 6, 1966, for a fifteen-month, $313,000 study (later increased to twenty-four months and $525,000). The project officially began on November 1, 1966, under the direction of Dr. Edward U. Condon of the Department of Physics and Astrophysics, and terminated on October 31, 1968.

Air Force officials were quick to point out that Condon was both a distinguished physicist, having made significant wartime contributions to the development of the atomic bomb and radar, and a staunch individualist, not likely to be successfully pressured by the Air Force into explaining UFOs away. Condon had been a victim of the McCarthy era persecutions, had clashed with Representative Richard Nixon, and had had his security clearance revoked twice, in 1953 and 1954.

Condon's commitment to the project was only half time, so much of the organizing and direction was left to Robert J. Low, assistant dean of the Graduate School, who was appointed as full-time project coordinator. Low was later to become the focus of controversy and dissent within the project. Dr. Franklin E. Roach, of the Department of Astrogeophysics, contributed 100 percent of his time as a principal investigator, and Dr. Stuart W. Cook, head of the Department of Psychology, served as the second principal investigator, with the understanding that his department's responsibilities would be met by other faculty members; Dr. David R. Saunders, a psychometrician, agreed to allocate 100 percent of his time as a coprincipal investigator, Dr. William A. Scott, a social psychologist, contributed 20 percent, and Dr. Michael W. Wertheimer, an experimental psychologist, also contributed 20 percent. Scott withdrew from the project after a few months, however.

The project also retained the consulting services of a number of other specialists, both at the university and elsewhere, in the areas of physics, nuclear physics, solar physics, meteorology, physical chemistry, electrical engineering, psychology, and psychiatry. Various research approaches were followed: on-site field investigations were conducted and radar cases were analyzed, as were some UFO sightings by U.S. astronauts. Dr. William K. Hartmann, an astrogeophysicist at the University of Arizona, was contracted to conduct the photographic analyses. A historical review and an attitude survey were commissioned, as were various essays on perceptual and psychological problems, optics, radar, sonic booms, plasmas, and balloons, much of which had little direct bearing on the UFO question. Stanford Research Institute (SRI), for example, agreed to prepare the written reviews on optical mirages and radar anomalies (reportedly for about $50,000), provided their staff did not have to examine any UFO reports. These reviews appeared as chapters in the final report.

Most UFO researchers and organizations offered to assist the project, and consultations were held with many of them, including the head of Project Blue Book, Major Hector Quintanilla, Jr.; its consultant, Northwestern University astronomer Dr. J. Allen Hynek; Dr. James E. McDonald, an atmospheric physicist at the University of Arizona, who had actively been advocating an in-depth UFO study; and Dr. Jacques Vallée, a French computer specialist, as well as with officials and members of the two national UFO groups, the Aerial Phenomena Research Organization (APRO) and the National Investigations Committee on Aerial Phenomena (NICAP). There was a feeling among many UFO proponents that the Colorado project would make or break the future study of UFOs, and that it was important to cooperate with, advise, and even influence the project as much as possible.

The project, however, got off to a precarious start. First, the project staff had not previously been involved in UFO matters. Although this helped to ensure a new and impartial analysis of the data, it also meant that valuable time was expended in attempts to determine what the problem actually was, and how to go about studying it. The UFO subject, the Colorado investigators found, has many complex facets, and by the time they felt they were beginning to understand them, it was time to start writing up the final report.

Second, few of the older "classic" UFO incidents were reinvestigated because of the difficulty in doing so after several (sometimes many) years. Rather, it was felt that resources would be better expended in the investigation of cases reported during the course of the study (only twenty of the fifty-nine case reports in the final report predated the project). Consequently, a number of older unexplained cases, which still have not been satisfactorily explained, such as Exeter, New Hampshire; Ravenna, Ohio (Portage County); and Levelland, Texas, were not addressed by the project. However, during the course of the study, a few classic UFO reports were reinvestigated, such as McMinnville, Oregon (Trent); Great Falls, Montana; Lakenheath-Bentwaters, England; and some new ones, later to become classics,

were tackled for the first time, such as the Michalak (Falcon Lake, Canada) incident, and the Schirmer (Ashland, Nebraska) incident. Although tentative or speculative solutions were proposed for many of these in the final report, publicly released in January of 1969, it has been estimated that between a third and half of the total case reports remained unexplained.

Another problem that surfaced early in the project was the approach taken by the director. Dr. Condon, who had a keen sense of humor, very much enjoyed the UFO subject, but more for its entertainment value than for the data it generated. He paid close personal attention to the claims of contactees, but did not personally participate in any of the field investigations. In short, he felt that "flying saucers" were merely a nagging social/psychological problem which the Air Force rightfully wanted buried once and for all, and he practically admitted as much in a speech in January of 1967, before the project had barely begun, hinting also that the final report would be negative. These kinds of comments raised many doubts among the individuals and organizations cooperating with the project (NICAP eventually broke off relations) and led to conflict within the project.

The situation deteriorated further when, in July of 1967, coprincipal investigator Saunders and research associate Dr. Norman Levine, an electrical engineer, found a memorandum written by coordinator Low before the contract had been awarded. In the memo, addressed to the university's higher administration, Low had outlined some of his ideas about the conduct of the project and the possible perceptions of it by others. He stated that ". . . the trick would be, I think, to describe the project so that, to the public, it would appear a totally objective study, but to the scientific community would present the image of a group of nonbelievers trying their best to be objective, but having an almost zero expectation of finding a saucer."

Low's unfortunate terminology, particularly the word "trick," incensed the two investigators, already bothered by Condon's derogatory public remarks, and they sent a copy of the memo to NICAP. James McDonald eventually received a copy, and he referred to it in a January 31, 1968, letter to Low, who then reported the matter to Condon. Two days later, on February 8, 1969, Condon fired Saunders and Levine from the project for "incompetence." Soon afterward, the project's administrative assistant, Mary Louise Armstrong, resigned, claiming low morale due to Low's participation in the project.

Public release of the memo and the firings created nationwide publicity. *Look* magazine featured it, and several scentific journals and some Congressmen began questioning the credibility of the Colorado study. Some UFO organizations even became convinced that the project was a fraud and that Condon and Low had conspired with the Air Force to produce a "whitewash." Others simply thought that Low, at best, had acted irresponsibly in writing such a memo and in leaving it in the project's open files. It should be recognized that the word "trick" has common usage when referring to a possible solution to a problem, be it technical or political, and does not necessarily imply deceit. It can appear deceitful, however, if taken out of context. Condon stated, furthermore, that he had been unaware of the memo's existence and that it had not influenced his direction of the study.

The final months of the project, after the departure of Saunders and Levine, were quiet ones. Under Condon's direction, the final report began taking shape. Low's participation practically ended in May 1968, and Condon made no more derogatory public statements. Saunders, meanwhile, published his own book, *UFOs? Yes! Where the Condon Committee Went Wrong*, assisted by Boulder journalist Roger Harkins. The book represented a sort of "minority report" and gave an embarrassing "inside story" of the Colorado project from its planning in September of 1966 until his departure in February of 1968.

In November of 1968, the Condon team completed The Final Report of the Scientific Study of Unidentified Flying Objects and it was then reviewed by a special panel set up by the National Academy of Sciences. On January 8,

1968, NAS submitted its review to the U.S. Air Force. The review fully endorsed the Colorado report's scope, methodology, and conclusions. The so-called Condon Report was released publicly the following day and was published commercially soon afterward. (See SCIENTIFIC STUDY OF UNIDENTIFIED FLYING OBJECTS.)

The report left many UFO incidents unexplained, but the conclusions, written by Condon, were, as predicted by many observers, that UFO phenomena were not worthy of further scientific study. Condon also stated that the Earth could not be visited by extraterrestrial intelligence for another 10,000 years, although nobody has determined how this figure was arrived at. These conclusions were highly publicized by the press, which generally ignored the case studies in the report, some of which tended to contradict Condon's conclusions. It has remained unclear to what extent the other project members agreed with his conclusions.

The University of Colorado UFO Project had a lasting impact on the study of UFOs in general and on the scientific community in particular, which generally accepted Condon's conclusions without question. It led to the closing of Project Blue Book in December of 1969. It remains today as the most comprehensive federally supported UFO probe, and attempts by private UFO organizations, some scientists, members of Congress, and even the White House to initiate a new federal inquiry have not met with success.

—ETEP STAFF

Uri (Doubleday, 1974). American physician Andrija Puharich tells the story of his friend, Israeli spoon-bender Uri Geller, who claims to have been given his psychic powers as a three-year-old child by alien visitors to help prepare humans for alien contact. These visitors from the future—who resemble "certain exotic types of Japanese" and supposedly materialize their spacecraft at will—first visited the Earth 20,000 years ago, landing in Israel. They have made Israel a protected country and the Jews a protected race.

—RANDALL FITZGERALD

V

Valensole (France) encounter On the morning of July 1, 1965, near Valensole, France, farmer Maurice Masse reportedly saw an egg-shaped "craft" resting in his lavender field. The "saucer" stood on six legs and had a door, through which Masse could see two seats, back to back. Standing by the object were two small humanoids, who seemed startled by Masse's presence and instantly immobilized him. The object then vanished, and the farmer's temporary paralysis soon faded away.

It was about 5:45 A.M., and Maurice Masse was finishing a cigarette before commencing work in his field (named l'Olivol). He was standing near a hillock of pebbles and rakings by the end of a small vineyard alongside the field. Suddenly, he heard a whistling noise and glanced around the side of the hillock expecting to see a helicopter; instead, he saw a "machine," shaped like a rugby football, the size of a Dauphine car, standing on six legs connected by a central pivot. There were also, he said, "two boys of about eight years" near the object, bending down by a lavender plant.

Incensed, Masse approached stealthily through the vineyard and saw that the creatures were not boys at all; he broke cover and advanced toward them. When he was within fifteen feet (five meters), one turned and pointed a pencil-like device at him. Masse was stopped in his tracks, unable to move.

According to Masse's testimony, the creatures were less than four feet tall, and were clad in close-fitting gray-green clothes, without any covering on their heads. They had "pumpkin-like" heads, high fleshy cheeks, large eyes which slanted away, mouths without lips, and very pointed chins. They made "grumbling" noises from their middles.

Masse will not disclose what else happened during the encounter, saying merely that they returned to their "machine." He said he could see them looking at him from inside, while the legs whirled and retracted. With a thump from the central pivot, the machine took off to float silently away. At twenty meters, it just disappeared, although traces of its passage in the direction of Manosque were reportedly found on lavender plants for four hundred meters.

When he recovered mobility, so the story goes, a confused and frightened M. Masse rushed back to Valensole. There, the proprietor of the Café des Sports saw him and, alarmed by his appearance, questioned him. Masse blurted out part of his story; the proprietor could not contain himself, and the news quickly broke.

—AIMÉ MICHEL & CHARLES BOWEN

Vallée, F. Jacques (b. 1939). French computer scientist, world-renowned UFO investigator—and real-life model for "Lacombe" in the film *Close Encounters of the Third Kind*. Dr. Jacques Vallée, a former principal investigator on Department of Defense computer networking projects, was born in France, where he was trained in astrophysics. He moved to the United States in 1962 and received his Ph.D. in computer science in 1967 from Northwestern University, where he was a close associate of the late Dr. J. Allen Hynek.

The author of numerous articles and three books about high technology, Dr. Vallée first became interested in UFOs when he witnessed the destruction of tracking tapes of unknown objects at a major observatory. His research into the phenomenon has taken him to many places in the United States and to many coun-

Jacques Vallée

tries around the world, including France, Scotland, Australia, Brazil, and Russia.

Vallée has published dozens of scientific articles in British, French, and American professional journals, and twelve books in English on UFOs: *Anatomy of a Phenomenon* (1965); *Challenge to Science: The UFO Enigma* (with his wife, Janine Vallée, 1966), *Passport to Magonia* (1969), *The Edge of Reality* (with J. Allen Hynek, 1975), *The Invisible College* (1975), *Messengers of Deception* (1979), *Dimensions* (1988), *UFO Chronicles of the Soviet Union* (1989), *Confrontations* (1990), *Revelations* (1991), *Forbidden Science* (1992), and *Fastwalker* (1996), a novel.

Address: 1550 California St. #6L
San Francisco, CA 94109
U.S.A.

POSITION STATEMENT: I propose the hypothesis that there is a control system for human consciousness. I have not been able to determine whether it is natural or spontaneous; whether it is explainable in terms of genetics, of social psychology, or of ordinary phenomena—or if it is artificial in nature and under the power of some superhuman will. It may be entirely determined by laws that we have not yet discovered. . . .

I am suggesting that what takes place through close encounters with UFOs is control of human beliefs, control of the relationship between our consciousness and physical reality, that this control has been in force throughout history and that it is of secondary importance that it should now assume the form of sightings of space visitors.

It could represent the Visitor Phenomenon of Whitley Strieber or some form of "supernature," possibly along the lines of the Gaia hypothesis.

Alternately, in a Jungian interpretation of the same theme, the human collective unconscious could be projecting ahead of itself the imagery which is necessary for our own long-term survival beyond the unprecedented crises of the twenty-first century.

When the object we call UFO is visible to us in the reality of everyday life, I think it constitutes both a physical entity with mass, inertia, volume, etc., which we can measure, and a window toward another mode of reality for at least some of the percipients. Is this why witnesses can give us at the same time a consistent narrative and a description of contact with forms of life that fit no acceptable framework? These forms of life may be similar to projections; they may be real, yet a product of our dreams. Like our dreams, we can look into their hidden meaning, or we can ignore them. But like our dreams, they may also shape what we think of as our lives in ways that we do not yet understand.

—JACQUES VALLÉE

(Position statement was adapted from an interview in the February 1978 issue of *Fate* magazine and from Vallée's books *The Invisible College* and *Revelations*.)

Valentich (Bass Strait, Australia) UFO encounter On the evening of October 21, 1978, Mr. Frederick Valentich, a twenty-year-old civilian pilot, disappeared while on a solo fight between Moorabbin airport, Victoria, Australia—across Bass Strait—and King Island, in a single-engine Cessna 182 aircraft.

At about 7:06 P.M., Valentich radioed Melbourne Air Flight Service with a report that "a large aircraft" with "four bright lights" passed close to his plane, then apparently hovered over him, at which time Valentich began experiencing engine trouble followed by a radio "blackout."

A taped transcript of the conversation between Valentich and Melbourne Air Flight Service controller Steve Robey contains the following dialogue between pilot and ground:

7:06 P.M.: Pilot to ground: "Is there any known traffic in my area below 5,000 feet?"

Flight Service Unit: "Negative—No known traffic."

Pilot: "Seems to be a large aircraft below 5,000 feet."

Ground: "What type of aircraft?"

Pilot: "I cannot confirm. It has four bright lights that appear to be landing lights . . . aircraft has just passed over me about 1,000 feet above."

Ground: "Is large aircraft confirmed?"

Pilot: "Affirmative; at the speed it is traveling are there any RAAF (Royal Australian Air Force) aircraft in vicinity?"

Ground: "Negative."

Ground: "What is your altitude?"

Pilot: "4,500 feet."

Ground: "Confirm you cannot identify aircraft?"

Pilot: "Affirmative."

Then, three minutes after his original transmission, Valentich reported again:

"Aircraft . . . It's not an aircraft. It's" (break in transmission)

Ground: "Can you describe aircraft?"

Pilot: "It's flying past. It has a long shape. Cannot identify more than that . . . coming for me right now. It seems to be stationary. I'm orbiting and the thing is orbiting on top of me. It has a green light and sort of metallic light on the outside."

Valentich then told ground control the object had vanished.

Ground: "Confirm it has vanished?"

Pilot: "Affirmative. Do you know what sort of aircraft I've got? Is it military?"

Ground: "No military traffic in the area."

7:12 P.M.: Pilot: "Engine is rough idling and coughing."

Ground: "What are your intentions?"

Pilot: "Proceeding King Island. Unknown aircraft now hovering on top of me."

Ground: "Acknowledge."

The pilot's final transmission was: "Delta Sierra Juliet [Valentich's call sign] Melbourne . . ." followed by seventeen seconds of a loud metallic sound. Thus began the mystery, which has yet to be satisfactorily explained. An extensive search in Bass Strait failed to turn up any trace of the pilot or his plane.

A number of suggestions have been made in an attempt to explain the patently bizarre circumstances of Valentich's disappearance. Suicide, hoax, disorientation, UFO abduction, and a host of other theories have been put forward—none of which has ended the mystery. But Valentich's enigmatic conversation with Melbourne Flight Service demands that we at least consider the evidence for some sort of UFO connection.

Perhaps predictably, many people reported seeing UFOs on the same day and during the night of Valentich's disappearance. While many of these sightings might have been generated by some sort of hysterical contagion mechanism, some of the reports remain difficult to explain. Some fifteen distinct sightings have survived the gauntlet of civilian research group investigations. They all occurred between midday and 9 P.M. on October 21. Six of these occurred in Victoria, one on King Island; and the rest in New South Wales, Tasmania, and South Australia. These reports seem to confirm that something quite odd was happening on that day.

While the precedent for UFO activity on the same day as Valentich's disappearance is remarkable in itself, the situation becomes even more extraordinary, when one considers the UFO precedent for the areas that figure in the Valentich mystery—namely Cape Otway (his last land call), Bass Strait (the apparent location of his disappearance), and King Wand (his apparent destination).

During a two-month period, centered around January 1978, vacationers, fishermen, schoolteachers, local police, and lighthouse keepers in the Cape Otway area, saw UFOs.

Even earlier, during July 1977, local residents and the lighthouse keeper at Cape Otway saw an inexplicable brilliant light source that hovered out to sea for half an hour. Estimates of its brilliance were made, which suggested that the airborne power would have been of the order of five kilowatts (for a pencil-beam source) and fifteen megawatts (for an omni-directional source).

As we move out over Bass Strait, more curious mysteries are evident. A number of planes have disappeared or gone down there without a trace. A few years ago, a Tiger Moth with two people on board vanished, apparently only within a few miles of Cape Otway. In 1969, a pilot and his Fuji aircraft apparently went down in the sea, again only a few miles from the Cape.

During February 1944, a Beaufort bomber crew gained a most unusual companion out over the Strait, at an altitude of 4,500 feet. At about 2:20 A.M., a "dark shadow" appeared with what looked like a flickering light and flame belching from its aft end. The "unknown" stayed with the plane at a distance of some 100 to 150 feet, for eighteen to twenty minutes, during which time all radio and direction-finding instruments failed to function. It finally accelerated away from the plane at approximately three times the speed of the bomber—some 700 mph.

In October 1935, the Tasmanian airliner, the "Loina," crashed "unseen" into Bass Strait, while en route to Flinders Island. Some wreckage was found, but no bodies were recovered.

One year earlier, during the morning of October 19, 1934, the new Tasmanian mail-plane, "Miss Hobart," with twelve passengers on board, disappeared without a trace, apparently within a few miles of Wilson's Promontory. Two surveyors in the area heard the plane pass over; however, they were baffled when the engine sound suddenly ceased. A large, motionless white "flare" was seen from a surface vessel near Cape Liptrap. The ship went to investigate and saw another light, this time pink in color. To put a final seal on the whole mystery, the "Miss Hobart" had not even been carrying flares!

Back in July 1920, a schooner went missing in Bass Strait. An extensive air-sea search, by contemporary standards, was initiated. Rather than solve the mystery, the search served only to compound it. Crews and captains on two ships reported seeing "large flares," which they thought must have been from the missing schooner. Captain J. Stut and Sergeant A. G. Daizell flew toward the area where the flares were observed. They and their plane, along with the schooner, were never seen again.

The *Melbourne Argus* newspaper of the day even tells us of many people reportedly seeing "cigar shaped" objects flying over the Strait, as far back as 1896.

King Island's 425 square miles played host to a "mini-flap" of unidentified nocturnal aerial lights for at least three months prior to the disappearance of Frederick Valentich. Oval-shaped lights followed cars and mystified local residents. Strange lights or flares appeared off the north shore of New Year Island.

One of the most spectacular sightings of a UFO in the area, occurred at a wild and uninhabited part of the King Island coast, near Whistler Point, just before dawn, on April 10, 1976. "A beam of light" emanating from a "cross-shaped object" approached a duckshooter's car, in a direct line. The light display, eventually receded directly along its line of approach, ending a silent inspection, when it disappeared over the distant skyline.

Conflicting evidence, and the reluctance of certain officials to release their information, has effectively short-circuited any legitimate conclusions. The evidence presented here in summary form indicates that if some other explanation for the disappearance of Valentich and the Cessna aircraft is not forthcoming, then the possibility of some sort of UFO connection must be considered. As is stands now, the disappearance of the pilot and his plane remains a mystery.

—WILLIAM C. CHALKER

Van Tassel, George (1910-1978). Van Tassel was a major UFO contactee, theoretician, and entrepreneur. He was operator of the Giant Rock Airport in California's Mojave desert, where he hosted the fabled Giant Rock Space Conventions, at which important contactees and their followers gathered annually, between 1954 and 1970. Furthermore, Van Tassel was founder and leading light of the Ministry of Universal Wisdom, incorporated in 1958, and the related College of Universal Wisdom. These nearly one-man organizations, which among other activities built a large structure for research known as the "Integratron," were concerned with the advancement of "science and scientific philosophy," partly on the basis of principles believed communicated by UFOs.

From 1927 until 1947 Van Tassel was employed in a variety of positions by such major aviation concerns as Douglas, Hughes, and Lockheed. In 1947 he moved to Giant Rock to manage the airport.

In 1951, he became absorbed in the UFO contactee movement, beginning with his own contact. In that year, he reportedly went into a trance at the base of the huge rock, for which Giant Rock is named, and was taken up to meet the "Council of Seven Lights," a body of discarnate Earthlings inhabiting a spaceship circling our planet. Then on August 24, 1952, according to his book *I Rode a Flying Saucer,*

he was sleeping in the desert with his wife when he was awakened by an alien named Solgonda, whose ship was hovering nearby. His wife continued sleeping, but Van Tassel went aboard with the extraordinary visitors. This dramatic encounter led directly to the first Space Convention the following spring.

(Photo by Gabriel Green)

George Van Tassel

Later writings of Van Tassel expounded complex theories, derived from OSCs (Outer Space Contacts), that the human race is partly nonterrestrial in origin, and that cosmic reality can be reduced to "resonances." He built the four-story-high nonmetallic "Integratron" containing an electrostatic armature 55 feet in diameter, driven by air turbines and jets. The huge apparatus was never wholly completed, but was designed for the purpose of "research into the unseen truths of life" and particularly to develop technologies to rejuvenate the elderly and prevent aging.

The colorful "Sage of Giant Rock" was a popular media personality. He appeared as guest on over 400 radio and television shows during his life and gave nearly 300 lectures in the United States and Canada. Besides *I Rode a Flying Saucer,* his books include: *Into This World and Out Again, The Council of Seven Lights, Religion and Science Merged,* and *When Stars Look Down.*

George Van Tassel was married and had three daughters. The hospitality of Giant Rock was legendary among UFO buffs who made the trek to the remote desert airport to meet the "Grand Old Man" of the contactee world. His extensive friend-ships, lectures, mailings, and above all the Giant Rock Space Convention made him a pivotal figure to that world—one whose presence did much to give it coherence and vitality. He was an American individualist of strong character in the classic mold of the weathered pioneer, the aviator of the "barnstorming" era, and the tinkering backyard inventor, to which was added the newer mystiques of space and other worlds. With him, a UFO epoch also passed.

—ROBERT S. ELLWOOD, JR.

Varginha (Brazil) encounters of 1996 On January 20, 1996, at 0100 hrs., a farmer outside the prosperous Brazilian city of Varginha was startled to observe a strange vehicle about the size of a small bus hovering some sixteen feet above the ground. The silent, darkened craft appeared to have sustained damage to its fuselage and spewed smoke as it moved away slowly toward Varginha.

At 0830 hrs., the Varginha Fire Department received an anonymous phone call regarding the presence of a "bizarre creature" in the Jardim Andere neighborhood. Suspecting a prank, the firemen nonetheless responded to the call and were surprised to find a group of adults and children already hot in pursuit of the "creature," which was hiding in a gully within a small wooded area. The firemen managed to capture the creature by means of a net, and dragged it out. The civilian onlookers would later inform investigators that the being offered no resistance to its captors, and was placed in a wooden box which was driven away by a truck belonging to the Brazilian army.

Apparently there was more than one non-human creature on the loose, and a mop-up operation had been ordered by the military. Residents of Jardim Andere claimed to have seen platoons in combat gear scouring the area, punctuating their actions with occasional bursts of automatic fire. Two more beings, unceremoniously dumped into bags, were allegedly taken away by the military.

At 1530 hrs. that same day, the Da Silva sisters, Valquiria and Liliana (ages 14 and 16 respectively) and their friend Katia Xavier, 22, were returning home from work and decided to cut across a field along a street not far from where the Varginha firemen had captured the first creature. As the threesome crossed the field, they suddenly noticed a "man" with bulging blood-red eyes, greasy brown skin, and a bald head with noticeable veins and strange osseous protuberances. The strange mannikin was huddling in fear next to a brick wall, its hands between its legs. Astonishment soon gave way to fear, and the young women broke into a mad dash to reach the safety of their homes.

Exactly twenty-four hours after the presumably crippled UFO hovered over a farm on Varginha's outskirts, the Brazilian military was in possession of at least three extraterrestrial biological entities (EBEs). At 0130 hrs., under cover of darkness, Army trucks moved their prized catch to Humanitas Hospital, apparently until the fate of the alien creatures had been determined. UFOlogists on the scene believe the creatures were subjected to a battery of medical tests, and that at least one of them died at the hospital.

On January 22, 1996, the alien bodies were transferred to the refrigerated lab section of the University of Campiñas, where a number of distinguished pathologists would have had access to them. By all accounts, there was a considerable military presence on the campus.

The military's cover-up unraveled when an Army officer was interviewed on Brazilian television, discussing his role in the operations involving the transfer of the putative aliens to the hospital, where the initial tests were conducted.

But the Varginha story continued long after the initial events: On the evening of April 21, 1996, Teresa Clepf had gone out to dinner at a restaurant located within the confines of the Varginha Zoo. Mrs. Clepf had stepped out onto the restaurant's covered porch to smoke a cigarette when she noticed a figure moving in the darkness, lighting its way with blood-red eyes. She then returned into the restaurant to collect her thoughts before going out again: the creature was still there, staring back at her.

According to UFOlogist Claudeir Covo, a number of zoo animals died shortly after the creature was reported. Veterinarians at the Varginha Zoo diagnosed the strange deaths as "caustic intoxication," and discouraged any speculation that the animals may have been infected by an alien disease borne by the creature.

—SCOTT CORRALES

Villas Boas abduction Many researchers and writers agree that if UFOlogy could be summed up by a single case, it would be the one involving the experiences of Brazilian farmer Antonio Villas Boas.

Villas Boas, twenty-three years old at the time of the ordeal, was a farmer by profession. He lived on a *fazenda* on the outskirts of São Francisco de Sales, Minas Gerais, where it was customary to work day and night shifts during the planting season, he himself being responsible for nocturnal planting.

On October 5, 1957, Villas Boas went to bed at 11:00 P.M. following a party at the farmhouse. He and his younger brother Joáo were witnesses to a strange nocturnal light which lit up the entire room.

Ten days later—on the night of October 15—Antonio Villas Boas would have his historic experience. While driving his tractor, he noticed a shining star that increased in brightness, as if descending to earth. The light turned into a very shiny oval object headed straight for him. He tried to escape by speeding up the tractor, but the object had already landed some 10 to 15 meters ahead: It resembled a large, elongated egg with three spurs in front.

Seized by terror, Antonio jumped off the tractor in hopes of eluding his pursuers, but the furrowed terrain made a speedy getaway impossible. He was then seized by a small figure wearing a "strange outfit" and a helmet. The farmer managed to knock it to the ground, but three more similarly dressed figures overpowered him and bore him off to the waiting craft.

Villas Boas struggled and hurled insults at his helmeted captors even as the humanoids dragged him into the craft, where he was stripped naked and subjected to several indignities. His captors drew a blood sample from his chin using a chalice-like device, and after slathering him with a strange liquid over his entire body, he was taken to a room—unfurnished but for a couch—where he was left alone for some twenty minutes, by his account. At this point, a mixture of fear, nausea and coldness, coupled with the stench of a strange gas that was pumped into the room, led him to vomit in one of the corners.

"After a long time," Villas Boas said, "a noise at the door startled me. I turned in that direction and was shocked to see that it was now open and a woman was entering the room, walking toward me. She was approaching slowly, perhaps amused at the astonishment that must have been visible on my face. My jaw had dropped and with good reason. This woman was completely naked, as was I, and barefoot. She was also pretty, although different from the women I'd known. Her hair was an almost whitish shade of blonde, as if peroxided, straight and not very abundant, neck-length and with the ends curled inward. Her eyes were blue and large, more narrow than round and slanted outward—like the pencil-painted eyes of those girls who fancy themselves Arabian princesses and make their eyes look slanted; that's what they were like. Only it was a completely natural effect, since there was no paint at all involved."

The strange liquid which had been spread over his body, apparently some sort of aphrodisiac, began to work as Antonio felt less tense as the small woman began to caress him, ultimately seducing him. "It sounds incredible," he confessed to Fontes and Martins during the interview, "given the situation I was in. I believe that the liquid they rubbed on me was the cause of it. All I know is that I felt an uncontrollable sexual excitement, which had never happened to me before. I forgot about everything and held the woman, returning her caresses with my own. We ended up on the couch, where we had sexual relations for the first time. It was a normal act and she responded like any woman. Then came a period of more caressing followed by more sexual relations. In the end, she was tired and breathing quickly. I was still excited, but she now refused and tried to get away. When I noticed that, I cooled down too. That was what they wanted from me, a good stallion to improve their stock."

The door opened once more and two of the "crewmen" appeared, summoning the woman away. Before leaving, she turned to the farmer and pointed at her belly, then pointing at him, and finally at the heavens. Curiously, Villas Boas took this to mean that "she would return to take me to where it was she came."

After having served as breeding stock, Antonio was unceremoniously led off the vehicle, which took off immediately. Returning to his tractor, Villas Boas learned that the time was now five-thirty in the morning. Estimating that it had been around 1:15 A.M. when he was abducted, his entire experience had lasted some four hours and fifteen minutes.

After his traumatic experience, Villas Boas withdrew from public life to pursue his studies, earning a law degree and becoming a practicing attorney in the city of Formosa, Goias, while running a small business on the side. He died in late 1992 in the city of Uberaba, in Brazil's Triángulo Minero.

In June 1993, the late Dr. Walter K. Buhler, president of Brazil's SBDEDV organization, revealed that between 1962-63 his organization had received an anonymous letter from the U.S., inviting Villas Boas to visit this country in order to examine a recovered flying

Artist's rendering of a scene inside the space ship, as described by Villas Boas (Drawing by Gloria Alderson)

saucer in the possession of the American military. Villas Boas's son advised Buhler that his father had indeed visited the United States to inspect the object, but had kept silent about the visit for the rest of his life.

—SCOTT CORRALES

Von Däniken, Erich (b. 1935). Born in Zofingen, Switzerland, Erich von Däniken was educated at the College of Saint-Michel, in Fribourg, where even as a student he occupied his time with the study of ancient holy writings. While managing director of a Swiss five-star hotel, he wrote his first book, *Chariots of the Gods?* (1968), which quickly became an international bestseller.

Von Däniken has since written twenty-five more books; his most recent being *Odyssey of the Gods: The Alien History of Ancient Greece* (2000). He is internationally known as the leading popular spokesman for the ancient astronaut theory. In fact, with sales approaching

Erich von Däniken

58 million copies (translated into 28 different languages), he must be considered one of the most successful authors of all time.

In the United States, von Däniken won instant fame as a result of the television special *In Search of Ancient Astronauts* in 1970. In 1993, the German television station SAT-1 ran a twenty-five-part TV series with von Däniken entitled *Aug den Spuren der All-Mächtigen* ("Pathways of the Gods"). Since then, von Däniken has done other film work with both American and German TV companies, which is ongoing.

Address: Chalet Aelpli
            CH-3803 Beatenberg
            Switzerland

E-mail: evd@aas-fg.org
Web site: www.Daniken.com

POSITION STATEMENT: Unfortunately, I have never had the chance to see a UFO with my own eyes. Among UFO believers you find a great number of hysteric, credulous, intimidated, hoping, and good honest people. Real scientists are rather scarce among them.

Some reports on UFOs which I have followed up personally have made me startled. Take this Pascagoula case. I have had a lengthy discussion at the time with Charlie Hickson. Today I am of the opinion that there does in fact exist something which we call "unidentified flying objects." I am convinced that from time to time strange things are happening around us for which at the moment we have no reasonable explanation. But don't ask me what UFOs are. I simply don't know. Extraterrestrial visitors? Extraterrestrial technical probes? Objects of another dimension? Physical phenomena which will only be explained by the future? Again, I do not know. Considering that the UFO problem has taken grip of such a huge number of people, I feel that it should be investigated scientifically. Regardless of whether there are, in fact, UFOs or not. Perhaps the answer is to be found in psychology or somewhere in the human brain.

My critics have said that the ancient astronaut theory is dangerous, because its followers can no longer see the actual problems in our life and instead would hope for some sort of "salvation from space." This is real nonsense!

Religious people, regardless what faith they belong to, hope for "salvation from above." The greater part of the UFO followers do exactly the same. The Ancient Astronaut movement, however, sees the problem from the opposite side.

The extraterrestrials were here thousands of years ago. They have left behind rules and regulations but also a promise to return in the remote future (time dilation). Considering that the "Gods" of ancient times did not always treat mankind gently and quite often became angry and punished brutally, a "hope from above" is not realistic. Rather the contrary! Mankind should be prepared technically and also morally for the return of the "Gods."

—ERICH VON DÄNIKEN

W

walk-in This term describes a process of inter-dimensional, inter-planetary soul exchange, as well as the individuals who experience it. In this process, a soul from an older ET or angelic civilization (or a more evolved Earth soul) enters the voluntarily surrendered body and personality-system of a human being, to better serve humanity and Earth. Interestingly, some Walk-ins don't consider themselves ET souls and have little interest in such matters. In my view, however, *most* so-called Walk-ins are actually Wanderers, as I believe that genuine Walk-ins are far more rare than people imagine.

—SCOTT MANDELKER

Walton abduction *This case was the subject of a* National Enquirer *headline and cover story, three books, numerous magazine accounts, and a major motion picture. It made a tidy sum of money for its claimant, Travis Walton, and is considered a "classic" by the UFO community. The case was supported by the Aerial Phenomena Research Organization (APRO), but considered a probable hoax by the National Investigations Committee on Aerial Phenomena (NICAP). Thanks to the leading skeptical UFO investigator, Philip Klass, the probable truth about the incident was uncovered and reported by NICAP as follows:*

A summary of the incident as it was presented by the news media is included for your information.

On the evening of Nov. 5, 1975, at approximately 6:15 P.M. MST, a crew of seven young woodcutters, headed by Michael Rogers, was returning home. Rogers (age 28) was under contract to the U.S. Forest Service to thin out 1,277 acres of National Forest land near Turkey Springs. According to the story later told by Rogers, and other members of his crew (ages 17-25), they saw a UFO hovering nearby. They claim that Travis Walton jumped out of the moving car and walked/ran under the UFO, that he was "zapped" by an intense glowing beam from the UFO and that the rest of the crew panicked and drove off, leaving their friend behind. A short time later, they claim they returned to the spot to seek Travis but that he had disappeared—seemingly carried off by the UFO. It was not until more than two hours later that Rogers and his crew decided to report the incident to Under-Sheriff L. C. Ellison in nearby Heber, Arizona.

While Travis was missing, Rogers and the other five young men took a polygraph test, on Nov. 10, administered by C. E. Gilson of the Arizona Department of Public Safety of Phoenix. Five of the young men "passed" the examination but the results for one (Allen M. Dalis) were "inconclusive," according to Gilson. The reported test results have been widely interpreted endorsing the authenticity of the alleged UFO abduction.

Shortly after midnight on Nov. 11, Travis telephoned his sister, Mrs. Grant Neff, of Taylor, Arizona (near Snowflake), from a phone booth in Heber, about 30 miles away. Mr. Neff and Travis's older brother Duane, who had come to Snowflake from his home in Phoenix shortly after the alleged UFO incident, both drove to Heber to pick up Travis. They reported finding him crumpled on the floor of the phone booth, and in a very "confused" mental state. A short time after returning Travis to his mother's home in Snowflake, Duane decided to drive Travis to Phoenix, reportedly to obtain medical assistance. Later that same day he was examined by two physicians at the request of APRO.

On Feb. 7, 1976, almost three months after Travis's return, he and Duane took polygraph tests administered by George J. Pfeifer, then employed by Tom Ezell & Associates of Phoenix. According to published reports, both men passed the exam which involved many questions dealing with Travis's claim of having been abducted by a UFO. The widely publicized results of these tests seemed to confirm that such an incident actually occurred.

In evaluating the authenticity of such a case, UFO researchers must concentrate on the validity of available data. After reading the reports published by other organizations and national newspapers, one would think that the Walton case was a very strong one for the following reasons:

It was reported that:
1. Walton passed the polygraph examination.
2. There were six other witnesses. Five of the six passed the polygraph examination.
3. Walton is of high character.
4. Walton and his family had very little prior interest in UFOs. Therefore, it would be unlikely that he would concoct a story relating to UFOs.
5. None of the other six witnesses had any motivation to participate in a hoax.

For the information of NICAP members, these points are discussed in detail. They give even stronger indication that NICAP's original conclusion is the correct one, i.e., the case is a hoax.

Walton's Polygraph Examination

Mr. Philip Klass revealed to NICAP that a lie detector test had been administered to Travis Walton THREE MONTHS EARLIER, ON NOVEMBER 15, 1975. WALTON FAILED THE POLYGRAPH EXAMINATION AT THAT TIME.

This first test was given in the Sheraton Hotel in Scottsdale, Arizona, on the afternoon of November 15. The arrangements for the examination were made by Mr. James Lorenzen, APRO's director, and the test was paid for by the *National Enquirer.* The examination was administered by Mr. John J. McCarthy, director of the Arizona Polygraph Laboratory in Phoenix. Mr. McCarthy's credentials are excellent. He was trained at the Army's polygraph school at Fort Gordon. Mr. McCarthy is a member of the American Polygraph Association and has been licensed by the State of Illinois since 1964. At present, Arizona does not require that polygraph examiners be licensed to practice in the state.

The examiner reported his findings as instructed to the *National Enquirer* and Dr. James Harder, APRO's director of research, immediately upon the completion of the test taken by Walton. Dr. Harder reported that information to APRO's James Lorenzen.

McCarthy was further instructed to send a written report to the *National Enquirer.* The *Enquirer* instructed McCarthy not to reveal that he had tested Walton. An excerpt from the report which was sent is, "Attempting to perpetrate a UFO hoax, and that he has not been on any spacecraft." The report further stated that Travis Walton had tried unsuccessfully to distort his respiration pattern in an attempt to deceive the examiner. However, he was unsuccessful.

APRO published a full account of the Travis Walton case in their November 1975 newsletter which included the events that had transpired during the week following Travis's return through November 16. No mention of the November 15 lie detector test was included.

Mr. Klass has hard physical evidence in his possession, which has been checked by NICAP, that Mr. McCarthy did test Travis Walton on November 15, 1975, and that Walton failed the test. The evidence includes such documents as:

1. The polygraph examination statement of consent dated Nov. 15, 1975, and signed by Travis Walton.
2. McCarthy's written report to the *National Enquirer* dated Nov. 16, 1975, which includes his conclusion that the UFO account was a hoax.
3. The voucher receipt from the *National Enquirer* payable to McCarthy's Arizona Polygraph Laboratory dated Jan. 14, 1976, for "Travis Walton UFO Incident."
4. Agreement to conduct test and supply report to *National Enquirer.* This statement is dated Feb. 1, 1976, rather than Nov. 15, 1975. This is clearly a typographical error.

Three months after Travis Walton failed the first polygraph exam, he took another one administered by George J. Pfeifer, an examiner with only two years' experience, who was employed by Tom Ezell & Associates of Phoenix. The results of this test were widely publicized because he seemingly passed the test with flying colors. Mr. Klass discovered that Travis Walton dictated the questions that he wanted to be asked. Mr. Pfeifer complied with Walton's request. To check the validity of the method of testing, the president of Tom Ezell & Associates, Mr. Tom Ezell, was contacted. He stated that it is perfectly proper for the sponsor of a test (APRO) to indicate the area which should be explored. However Mr. Ezell in later correspondence with Mr. Klass stated, "Because of the dictation of questions to be asked, this test should be invalidated." He further stated that after examining the Travis Walton charts, "The reactions on the charts, to my way of interpretation, would not be readable. You would not be able to say if he [Travis Walton] is telling the truth or if he's lying."

CORROBORATING WITNESSES' POLYGRAPH EXAMINATIONS

As reported in the January 1976 issue of the *UFO Investigator*, the polygraph exam given to the other alleged witnesses was designed to determine whether or not Walton might be the victim of foul play instigated by his associates. Three of the four relevant questions asked during the test dealt entirely with this issue. The test was given by C. E. Gilson, an examiner with five years' experience. His statement to Mr. Klass was, "That was our sole purpose . . . to determine whether or not there had been a crime committed." The single question about the UFO was added at the request of Sheriff Gillespie. Gilson stressed, "That one question does not make it a valid test as far as verifying the UFO incident."

WALTON'S CHARACTER

In the evaluation of witness testimony, the credibility of the witness must also be evaluated.

On May 5, 1971, Travis Walton and Charles Rogers pleaded guilty to first degree burglary and forgery charges. (Charles Rogers is a younger brother of Michael Rogers, who was also involved in the UFO incident.) This information was revealed by Travis Walton himself during a preliminary discussion with the polygraph examiner, Mr. McCarthy, and confirmed by state authorities.

The young men agreed to make restitution of the funds and were placed on a two-year probation. Arizona law provides that if probation is fulfilled satisfactorily the party may later return and ask the Court to expunge the record. Both of the boys retracted their original pleas after the completion of the probation period.

At the time of the report there is no indication that Walton was continuing his youthful misbehavior.

PRIOR INTEREST IN UFOS

Interest in UFOs does not prohibit the interested party from having a valid sighting. However, in a large majority of hoax reports, prior interest is usually present. It has been reported elsewhere that Walton had little or no prior interest in the field. Dr. Howard Kandell, one of the two physicians who examined Walton at APRO's request was asked if the Waltons had indicated any prior interest in UFOs. Kandell replied: "They admitted to that freely, that he (Travis) was a 'UFO Freak' so to speak. . . ." He had made remarks that if he ever saw one, he'd like to go aboard.

Dr. Jean Rosenbaum, a psychiatrist who examined Walton was asked whether he had mentioned any prior interest in UFOs. He replied, "Everybody in the family claimed that they had seen them (UFOs) . . . Travis has been preoccupied with this almost all of his life : . . then he made the comment to his mother just prior to this incident that if he was ever abducted by a UFO, she was not to worry because he'd be all right." Duane Walton has stated that he and Travis had often discussed the possibility of getting a ride on a UFO.

MOTIVATION OF THE SIX WITNESSES

It has been stated that there was no motivation, other than possible friendship for the other six witnesses to corroborate Walton's story if it were not true. Investigation has revealed a strong financial possible motive for Mike Rogers and the other five crew members to perpetrate a hoax.

Mike Rogers had submitted a bid in the spring of 1974 to the U.S. Forest Service for a timber thinning operation of 1,277 acres of land in a National Forest, located in the Apache-Sitgreaves area. His bid was accepted and was 27 percent under the mid-figure submitted by the other companies. By the following summer (1975) it became clear to Rogers that he had grossly underestimated the magnitude of the job and could not complete it on time. He applied for an extension which was granted but he was penalized $1.00 per acre for all work performed after expiration of the original contract date. The new work completion date was November 10, 1975. As the new deadline approached, it became clear that once again, they could not possibly complete the work by that time and he would have to ask for another extension that would result in another pay cut. More serious, the Forest Service was withholding 10 percent of the payments until the job was done. With winter at hand, Rogers could not finish until the next spring to collect these funds. The alleged UFO incident gave Rogers a legal basis terminating his money-losing contract on the ground that his crew would not return to the work site out of fear, allowing Rogers to collect the withheld funds and pay his crew.

SUMMARY

The reaction of the Travis Walton family when informed that he had been "zapped" away on a UFO provides a valuable measure of whether they had prior knowledge of a planned hoax. If they believed that the incident actually took place, they would realize that they might never see Travis again. Troopers from the Navajo County Sheriff's Department assembled late on the night of November 5th, and returned to the alleged site to search for Travis. It was not until several hours after midnight on Nov. 6th that the group proceeded to inform Travis's mother that her son could not be found.

One member of the troopers informed Mr. Klass that when he explained the horrible fate of her son, she simply replied, "I'm not surprised."

Mrs. Kellet suggested to the law enforcement officials that the search be abandoned, saying, "I just don't think there's any use of looking any further . . . I don't think he's on this earth." Travis' brother, Duane, stated that he would stay on the site and wait because they always return their victims to the same spot.

At no time during the entire episode did the family or crew members show or express any concern for his well-being. Mr. Klass stated that, "One possible explanation for the reaction of Rogers and the members of his family is that they knew the incident was a hoax and that Travis was safe in a terrestrial hideout, rather than aboard an extraterrestrial spacecraft that might be taking him to a distant world from which he might never return."

On November 8, while Travis was "still

missing,'' Duane said he was not at all concerned for his brother's safety. Duane said he regretted that "I haven't been able to experience the same thing."

In any scientific investigation, all data must be considered. Any organization or corporation reporting on investigations has the responsibility to disclose all facts to its readers . . . not just the information which supports a preconceived position.

When the strengths and weaknesses of the Walton Case are evaluated, the indications are that a hoax has been perpetrated.

—NICAP

References

The APRO Bulletin (November 1975).
The APRO Bulletin (December 1975).
The APRO Bulletin (February 1976).
The APRO Bulletin (March 1976).
The APRO Bulletin (July 1976).
The APRO Bulletin (August 1976).
Barry, Bill. *Ultimate Encounter* (Pocket Books, 1978).
Klass, Philip J. *UFOs: The Public Deceived* (Prometheus Books, 1983).
———. *UFO Abductions: A Dangerous Game* (Prometheus Books, 1988).
UFO Investigator (June 1976).
Walton, Travis. *The Walton Experience* (Berkley, 1978).
———. *Fire in the Sky* (Marlowe & Co., 1996).

wanderer   This poetic term, used by George Hunt Williamson and other UFO contactees in the 1950s, describes a process of inter-dimensional, inter-planetary soul transfer. In this process, a higher-dimensional ET soul incarnates in the normal way (e.g., as a baby), and agrees to forget their own memory of ET identity and purpose, to aid the evolution of humanity and the planet. This process of cosmic soul-wandering has occurred since the beginning of human experience on Earth and is common throughout the Universe, and expresses the basic Law of Service in which elder souls freely go to serve worlds in need. The Law of Service is said to be the primary

motivation for the majority of UFO visitation occurring on Earth today.

—SCOTT MANDELKER

War of the Worlds, The   A classic science fiction novel, *The War of the Worlds* by H. G. Wells, is about an invasion from Mars. It first appeared in serial form in *Cosmopolitan* magazine during the summer of 1897. The first edition of the book was published by William Heinemann of London in 1898, and of course has been reprinted many times.

Alvin Correa's classic illustration of a Martian emerging from its spacecraft-cylinder in H. G. Wells's *The War of the Worlds*.

The concept of an invasion from space as a purgative horror owes much to this early literary effort, which has had considerable impact on later fiction writing, to say nothing of its obvious influence on speculations about the possible motives behind UFO activity.

The talented Orson Welles produced a realistic radio dramatization of the story in October 1938, causing a panic in the Eastern United

States. The stampede triggered by the broadcast is often referred to by students of the UFO problem as an example of potential havoc that could be generated by the sudden release of startling UFO information, or by a mass landing of alien craft.

The novel inspired an American movie in 1953 which won an Academy Award for special effects. The UFO flap in France in 1954, which was notable for many "little men" reports, may have been encouraged by the George Pal production, which at that time was enjoying a successful run in French theaters.

The Wellsian "UFOs are hostile" theory has been best developed by UFO authors Brad Steiger, Harold T. Wilkins, Coral E. Lorenzen, and Donald E. Keyhoe. The problem of an unprepared public is a theme that pervades many UFO books and articles, especially by Keyhoe, who served for many years as director of the National Investigations Committee on Aerial Phenomena (NICAP), thus providing a stimulus to the policy of that organization.

—LOREN E. GROSS

POSTSCRIPT: The original magazine serialization and resulting novel by H. G. Wells introduced the idea of aliens having big heads and degenerated bodies due to the future evolution of a body shaped by civilization. It was taken up with enthusiasm by science fiction (SF) writers in the pulp era and came forward into our time via comics and SF film culture.

Wells mentions the influence of the astronomer Schiaparelli explicitly in his 1898 novel and no doubt was influenced by Percival Lowell as well. Lowell had introduced the idea of Mars as a dying planet inhabited by technologically advanced beings.

Wells also described the Martian space vehicles as "huge cylinders," a description suggestive of later flying saucers and cigar-shaped UFOs. How he visualized the beings is captured in the words of the protagonist of Wells's novel: "A big grayish rounded bulk, the size perhaps of a bear, was rising slowly and painfully out of the cylinder. As it bulged up and caught the light, it glistened like wet leather.

Two large dark-colored eyes were regarding me steadfastly." A few pages later, Wells again emphasizes the eyes: "Those who have never seen a living Martian can scarcely imagine the strange horror of its appearance . . . above all, the extraordinary intensity of the immense eyes. . . ." One could forget for a moment he is reading Wells and could easily imagine hearing the voice of Barney Hill.

Here we have the gray color, large dark-colored eyes, and leathery skin as described in later years by many people who claimed to be abducted by UFO-aliens. By the time the George Pal movie was released in 1954, we have a modified version of spindly bodies with large heads, large eyes, and even hands with sucker-tipped fingers, as described in later abduction accounts.

—MARTIN S. KOTTMEYER
& RONALD D. STORY

Ware, Donald M. (b. 1935). Donald Ware has studied UFOs since he saw seven UFOs (which he believes were alien vehicles) over Washington, D.C., on July 26, 1952.

He received a B.S. in Mechanical Engineering from Duke University in 1957 and an M.S. in Nuclear Engineering from the Air Force Institute of Technology in 1970. After serving his country as a fighter pilot, staff scientist, test manager, and teacher, he retired from the Air Force in 1983.

Ware has studied birds around the world, and has had three articles published in scientific journals. He served as State Director and Eastern Regional Director for MUFON, and he is a Director of the International UFO Congress. Ware says that his search for truth has led to physical, mental, and spiritual interactions with the larger reality represented by the alien presence.

Address: 662 Fairway Ave.
            Ft. Walton Beach, FL 32547
            U.S.A.

POSITION STATEMENT: Some UFOs are vehicles controlled by a more advanced intelligence. They originally came from Zeta Reticuli, the Pleiades, Tau Ceti, Sirius, Arcturus, Andromeda, and perhaps other places. Some UFOs are vehicles made in secret facilities on this planet by humans, with assistance from one or more alien species. I suspect that some of the vehicles made here have the capability of reaching the Moon or Mars, using advanced propulsion systems that are restricted from use by the general society until all national leaders choose peace. At least one system reduces the effect of gravity.

We are joining the Galactic Society, one person at a time, as our consciousness evolves toward service-to-others through free-will choices. Then our souls enter our bodies for a new purpose: to develop unconditional love of others. We are getting new genetically engineered bodies: *Homo sapiens alterios* that may be among us and *Homo alterios spacialis* that must be separated from the general society until the lesser evolved souls are ready to accept them.

Perhaps a billion people are ready for open contact, many of whom are now contacted in their secret night life. Others who have not yet accepted humans of different races or religions would have serious ego problems. The main criteria for determining rules of engagement seems to involve our state of spiritual evolu-

tion, and only God knows when we are all ready for open contact.

Don Ware's position statement is continued below in an essay (published here for the first time in book form) that captures the essence of a viewpoint that is widely held in UFOlogy today.

Is My World Different Than Yours?

Each of us lives in a world defined by our experiences; by our actions and reactions; by who we meet, what we read, and what we watch on TV, film, and the stage. We each have the ability to change our world by our thoughts and our actions. Many people apparently do not realize this is true. Their reactions to the world are based on fear, and they don't experience the love they deserve.

My world is a world in the midst of a transformation. My world is a world full of beauty that can be seen, heard, touched, smelled, tasted, and felt emotionally. I have not felt the emotions of fear or anger since I learned to perceive the universe from the perspective of my soul, rather than as Donald Ware. My physical body only has five senses, so where did that sixth sense of emotion come from? I think it came from my emotional body, an energy body that occupies the same general space as my physical body. I also think I have a mental body and a spiritual body. All three of my energy bodies are part of the soul that will continue to exist after my physical body ceases to function.

My mental body contains the knowledge of all of my past experience, whether in this life or a previous one. I think my brain can be likened to a computer. The mental body then becomes the software. The brain is a processor for both new information and information stored in my mental body. The storage process is probably based on holographic principles as described in Michael Talbot's 1991 book, *The Holographic Universe.* In our waking state of consciousness we don't usually have the access

Donald Ware

codes for past life experience. This information is normally trapped behind the veils between our conscious, subconscious, and unconscious mind. However, if we choose to do so, we can find methods to pierce those veils. When we pierce the veil to our unconscious mind we gain access to a modem that can connect us to universal consciousness.

My spiritual body is part of the great spirit that pervades all that is. Some people call that great spirit God. Some define it as Love and Light. This pervasive spirit has become part of my world. It is in each of us whether our choices are mostly unselfish or selfish. Some form of this spirit is in the animals and the trees and even in the planet. I have been taught to believe this spirit is eternal.

Everything in the universe evolves, whether it be a galaxy, a solar system, a planet, or a person. When we do harm to any part of the universe we adversely affect the evolution of the universe. When we pollute the water, kill the animals, cut the trees, and fill our lungs with smoke we do harm to God.

The present transformation of the planet is a major step in the evolution of the solar system. The reason that the spirit is in our physical bodies on this planet is changing. Throughout recorded history we have been here to make choices. These choices tend to polarize the soul, our energy bodies, toward service to others or service to self. I have been taught that on this planet many souls are now sufficiently polarized through free-will choices to be ready to graduate to the next level in their evolution. They are ready to get on with the task of developing unconditional love. This planet is evolving to become a place where people develop unconditional love of others. Billions of spiritual beings, our guides, are here to assist. This transformation marks the end of the human experience as we have known it, and it marks the beginning of a more loving and peaceful experience.

Not only is our planet being transformed, but our physical bodies are being genetically altered. Evidence from my UFO research indicates that some of our souls will reincarnate into a body that has a larger brain and greater telepathic ability. Descriptions from several of my friends who have met their hybrid offspring on alien vehicles include a head with larger eyes and perhaps a 2000-cc brain. My friends who have learned to communicate telepathically say the new bodies have greater telepathic ability. We are soon to join a Galactic Society, and telepathy is the normal means of communication among the many intelligent species that interact with each other.

UFO researchers who specialize in people's onboard experiences say that the number of such experiencers is in the millions, perhaps 10 million just in the U.S.A. Most seem to have multiple hybrid offspring. We are told that these hybrid physical bodies, compatible with expanded consciousness, house the souls of both their human and their Zeta Reticulan relatives. They also seem to be compatible with this biosphere as evidenced by many children's circles, where hybrid children play in backyards with human children. I wonder when they will be allowed to live on the surface of this planet with adults in their awake state of consciousness.

I have high hopes for our future, although I do recognize that the great changes I see occurring involve great stress. These rapid changes also provide great opportunity for meaningful choices and great opportunity to express unconditional love. I see both human and ET influence to encourage all national leaders to choose peace. This is a prerequisite for establishing a demilitarized world. I see courageous national and world leaders working to safely eliminate nuclear weapons and other weapons of mass destruction. I see people with great influence working to help us overcome the destructive habits to which our society has become addicted. I see new thought entering the churches, holistic medicine entering the mainstream, and a more efficient and healthy diet being chosen by many.

More people are recognizing that a growth-driven economy with ever-increasing material wealth is not a sustainable path to happiness. In order to avoid a worldwide environmental crisis we should stop taking all we can get from mother nature and leaving the excess profit to our children. We should adopt the sustainable mode of living of the indigenous peoples who take only what they need from mother nature and leave the rest.

As we acquire the consciousness necessary to join the galactic society, we need representatives elected by all mankind. I think we need world leaders who can help us realize we are all members of one planet. With this broader perspective we can devote more energy to the evolution of our souls, and we can avoid the strife and inefficiency that accompany extreme nationalism and materialism.

—DONALD M. WARE

Washington National radar-visual sightings This extraordinary series of events occurred in the vicinity of Washington, D.C., on July 19-20, July 23, July 26-27, July 28, and July 29, 1952. In the midst of a summer heat wave (tied in later with an attempt to explain the Washington sightings and radar returns as being caused by temperature inversions), radar controllers, ground observers, and pilots and crews of both civilian airliners and military jet fighters experienced a "mini-invasion" of UFOs, which created headlines around the world.

The ten-day episode began shortly after midnight on July 19-20, as the Civil Aeronautics Agency's Air Route Traffic Control (ARTCC) radar operators at Washington National Airport picked up seven unknown targets on their screens (the first at 11:40 P.M., July 19), which appeared to be in the vicinity of Andrews Air Force Base in Maryland, fifteen miles south-southwest of Washington National. The targets appeared to be traveling between 100 and 130 miles per hour, although their motion was described as "completely radical compared to those of ordinary aircraft." They would hover in one position at times and also dart up and down. When two of the "objects" suddenly streaked off the

screen, air traffic controller Edward Nugent requested his supervisor, senior controller Harry G. Barnes, to look at the scope. After one look, Barnes in turn called over two more experienced controllers, Jim Copeland and Jim Ritchey, who verified the observations. Technicians were also called in to check the equipment for possible malfunction which was determined not to be the case, and Barnes then contacted the airport control tower, confirming that the targets were present on their scopes as well. Andrews radar operators also picked up strange blips on their scopes, which correlated with those being tracked by Washington National.

The first visual confirmation came at 3:15 A.M. (July 20) from Capitol Airlines flight #807, southbound from Washington National. The pilot, "Casey" Pierman (a seventeen-year veteran with the airline), sighted seven objects, where radar showed them to be, which he could not identify. The objects, which were observed for twelve minutes, were described by Captain Pierman as bright lights. "They were like falling stars without tails," he said, and two of them traveled at tremendous speed.

At times, some of the targets sending back radar returns were invisible to planes in the area, but a second confirmation came from Capitol-National Airlines flight #610, inbound from Herndon, Virginia, reporting a light, which followed the plane to within four miles of the runway. Ruppelt reports that: ". . . ARTCC called for Air Force interceptors to come in and look around. But they didn't show, and finally ARTCC called again—then again. Finally, just about daylight, an F-94 arrived, but by that time the targets were gone. The F-94 crew searched the area for a few minutes but they couldn't find anything unusual so they returned to their base."

On July 26, at about 10:30 P.M., strange blips were again picked up on radar, and again tracked simultaneously by ARTCC radar, the Washington National control tower, and the radar station at Andrews AFB. There were four to twelve targets, moving between 100 and 120 miles per hour, spread out in an arc around Washington, D.C., from Herndon, Virginia, to

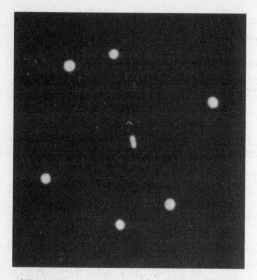

Allegedly a once classified USAF photo showing six UFOs over Washington, D.C., on July 20, 1952. The oblong luminosity (center) is supposed to be the exhaust trail of a jet fighter sent to intercept the objects.

Andrews AFB in Maryland. United Airlines flight #640 confirmed one colorful light visually and personnel at Andrews reported "three strange lights streaking across the sky." After a two-hour delay, two jet interceptors from New Castle Air Force Base, Delaware, arrived in the area and began a search for the objects. As before, most of the targets were invisible except on radar, but one pilot did pursue for two minutes four bright lights, which he could not overtake even at full throttle. After about twenty minutes, the jets ran low on fuel and returned to base.

On July 29, Major General John A. Samford, Air Force Director of Intelligence, held a major news conference at the Pentagon. He stated: "There has been no pattern that reveals anything remotely like purpose or remotely like consistency that we can in any way associate with any menace to the United States." And that "the radar and visual sightings . . . were due to mirage effects created by a double temperature inversion."

However, all four operators at the CAA Radar Traffic Control Center at Washington's National Airport, who tracked the UFOs on those harrowing nights in July 1952, consistently maintained that they had good, solid returns from something—not mirage effects with which they were all familiar and could easily recognize—that had never appeared before or since.

Captain Ruppelt later remarked that: "On each night that there was a sighting there was a temperature inversion but it was never strong enough to affect the radar the way inversions normally do. Hardly a night passed in June, July, and August in 1952 that there wasn't an inversion in Washington, yet the slow-moving, 'solid' radar targets appeared on only a few nights.

"So the Washington National Airport Sightings are still unknowns."

—Ronald D. Story

References

Hall, Richard H., ed. *The UFO Evidence* (NICAP, 1964).
NICAP, "Washington National radar/visual sightings" in Story, Ronald D., ed. *The Encyclopedia of UFOs* (Doubleday/New English Library, 1980).
Ruppelt, Edward J. *The Report on Unidentified Flying Objects* (Doubleday, 1956).
Story, Ronald D. *UFOs and the Limits of Science* (William Morrow/New English Library, 1981).
The New York Times (July 22, 1952).
UFO Investigator (NICAP, July 1972).

Watch the Skies! (Smithsonian Institution Press, 1994). Curtis Peebles provides a historical review of the flying saucer myths which evolved since 1947 and have spawned conspiracy theories and dangerous, cultish fanaticism. He demonstrates how the myth of a Roswell saucer crash emerged and how an Air Force sergeant created a fictitious MJ-12 government group complete with faked secret documents to ingratiate himself with a pretty female UFO researcher.

—Randall Fitzgerald

Watchers, The (Bantam, 1990). Longtime UFO investigator Raymond Fowler relates in this book how he uncovered his own memories of lifelong abductions by aliens and odd phenomena afflicting his family stretching back three generations. A scoop mark he finds on his lower leg, similar to one described by abductee Betty Andreasson, leaves Fowler convinced "the scar is the result of a biopsy taken as part of the aliens' ongoing genetic research within families of human beings."

—RANDALL FITZGERALD

waves (or flaps), UFO Periods of time when reports of UFOs amass at well above average rates are variously termed "waves" or "flaps." Both terms possess connotative prejudgments. Waves suggest a natural semirhythmic phenomenon or the arrival of masses of people, as in the waves of an invasion or waves of immigration. Captain Edward Ruppelt of Project Blue Book defined flaps as "a condition or situation, or state of being of a group characterized by an advanced degree of confusion that has not yet reached panic proportions" and is thus diagnosing a psychology problem, a crazy time. (Ruppelt, 1956) The presence of two terms to denote these times of accelerated UFO reporting behavior reflect the absence of consensus in UFOlogy's attempts to understand what is behind the simple arithmetical truth that UFO numbers change rather than remain constant over time.

It is not immediately obvious why the UFO phenomenon should not be a more or less constant occurrence over time whether one regards them as real or illusory. If they were alien transports connected with a survey of the planet or a study of mankind, the natural expectation would be that their presence should be methodical and unceasing. If they were accidents of circumstance or cognitive error, one would expect their occurrences to be fairly stable across time in a manner similar to the way traffic accidents remain numerically stable from year to year without showing periods of several-fold increases.

THE FIRST THEORY

The earliest forms of the Reconnaissance Theory of flying saucers only had to account for the 1947 wave of sightings. Given the extraordinary development of the atomic bomb a couple years earlier, it was somewhat natural to wonder if the equally new phenomenon of flying saucers was somehow connected. The idea was taken seriously in government intelligence circles; at least seriously enough to set up a UFO reporting net in the region of the Eniwetok bomb test. It failed to turn up anything. (Gross, 1986) Donald Keyhoe was a prominent spokesman for this theory and expanded on it with attempts to offer additional evidence in support of it. He observes there had been "a steadily increasing survey after our atomic bomb explosions in New Mexico, Japan, Bikini, and Eniwetok," and a second burst of activity after explosions in Soviet Russia. Attention was focused on the U.S. since it was "the present leader in atomic weapons." (Keyhoe, 1950)

These observations however do not bear scrutiny. The June-July 1947 wave did not coincide with any bomb test. The first Soviet A-bomb was exploded on August 29, 1949, and was revealed to the world three weeks later. Yet UFO numbers are seen declining consistently from July to October 1949 and the only thing resembling a surge does not take place until March 1950. The concentration of UFOs in the U.S. was true for 1947, but 1954 UFO reports were concentrated in France and still later waves were focused in Spain and Latin America; places that have never been in the forefront of nuclear developments. In February 1951 Keyhoe predicted there would be an upswing in UFO activity in the spring of 1951 due to scheduled atomic bomb tests near Las Vegas, Nevada. UFO historian Loren Gross has already pointed out the period happened to be the quietest on record. (Gross, 1983) The belief that the first waves of UFOs involved the monitoring of atomic bomb developments persists to the present day; as one can see in Raymond Fowler's book *The Watchers* (1990).

But it rests on no reasoned argument and can point to no successes, either in prediction or interpreting any of the waves since 1947.

THE MARTIAN HYPOTHESIS

Around 1952 a new interpretation of waves arose based on the recognition that waves seemed to peak around the time that Mars came closest to the Earth. Researchers in that era favored Mars as the likeliest abode of life, and it made some sense that travelers might time their arrivals to conserve fuel. Numerous predictions were offered. In January 1952, Lonzo Dove predicted the arrival of a saucer armada on April 15-16 of that year. Dove claimed success with a photograph of a huge circular cloud 30 miles across that he took on April 16th. (Dove, 1953)

The UFO numbers in the Blue Book files, however, tell a different story. There were only three UFO reports for the 15th, four for the 16th, and six on the 17th. Though this is trivially better than the numbers in March, it is pretty small for an armada and not very impressive placed against July's numbers, which ran in the dozens daily. Edgar Jarrold of the Australian Flying Saucer Bureau predicted 1954 and 1956 would be exceptionally heavy and 1953 and 1955 would be fairly light. He called it right for the light periods, but 1954 was exceptionally heavy only in France, and 1956 saw nothing of consequence. (Jarrold, 1953)

Aimé Michel first thought the Martian hypothesis was confirmed when a prediction he made for a wave in the late summer of 1954 came true. In his second effort he predicted a wave for eastern Europe or the Middle East in October or November 1956. When this was "double refuted," he endorsed the verdict of the Civilian Saucer Intelligence that the Mars correlation failed. (Michel, 1958) Harry Lord of the Tynesdale UFO Society issued a forecast in 1963 utilizing the Mars theory. He predicted flaps for late '62-early '63 (No), early '65 (No), late '67 (Yes), late '69 (No way!), and a large peak in late '72 (No). (Lord, 1963)

Jacques Vallée further discredited the theory by pointing out that pre-1947 waves did not conform to the Mars cycle. The space probes to Mars pitched additional dirt on the grave when showed it to be quite lifeless. Richard Hall offered a variant that proposed that flaps correlated with Venus, but it was DOA.

MATHEMATICAL MODELS

A number of attempts to predict UFO waves eschew any theoretical justification and simply base themselves on patterns in the data that suggest cyclicity. Keyhoe tried this in his historic article for *True*. Noting peaks of saucer activity in July 1947 and July 1948, he predicted it would peak again in July 1950. Activity peaked in March that year. (Girard, 1989) In December 1971 NICAP reported on the discovery of a five-year cycle and predicted there would be a flap in 1972. That year had 152 reports compared to 137 in 1971 and they proclaimed success in bold headlines proclaiming "1972 Upholds Five-Year UFO Cycle." By November 1973, however, NICAP was reminded what a true flap is all about: "First Flap in Six Years Resurrects UFOs as National Controversy."

Jenny Randles spoke of a 21-month cycle in the Pennine area of Great Britain and confidently predicted May/June 1984 would prove to be rather interesting. By her own later account, 1984 saw only 23 UFO cases and the best clustering happened around April 15 and 25. She found these cases rather interesting, while admitting they may be associated with military exercises. Writing in 1986 she acclaims her prediction came true: "I don't know how." (Randles, 1983, 1986)

The most famous cycle theory was a 61-month pattern offered by David Saunders. He claims it led him to predict in advance a 1972 wave in South Africa. (Saunders, 1976) Allan Hendry characterized the South African reports as a minor flurry and not a wave and also questioned the propriety of using Bloecher's 1947 data in Saunders's since it was a special delimited study. When removed from consideration, the remaining data show the baseline collection of 1947 reports in Blue Book's files had only a small swell of numbers inconsonant with a major flap. (Hendry, 1976) There have been a number of efforts to rehabilitate Saunders's work, but the absence of waves in January 1983 and February 1988 spelled an end to its believability. (Partain, 1985) With such failures, hope has faded for a simple mathematical model of mass UFO appearances.

BEHAVIORIST NOTIONS

Jacques Vallée looked at the pattern of UFO flaps and theorized it was a schedule of reinforcement like that used by behaviorists to instill irreversible behavior. The pattern of periodicity and unpredictability would help us learn new concepts. This control system allegedly also explains the absence of contact and why the phenomenon misleads us. That would preclude genuine learning. (Vallée, 1975)

This theory is amazingly perverse at even the simplest level. Within behaviorist theory, to be reinforcing, a stimulus must be of a positive, rewarding character. (Ruch and Zimbardo, 1971) It must induce pleasure instead of pain. The overwhelming majority of UFO cases involve fear. (Vallée, 1977; Swiatek-Hudej, 1981; Moravec, 1987) UFO flaps are usually times of anxiety, confusion, and near-hysteria. During the 1973 wave, mothers kept their children from going to school for fear they might be kidnapped. Clearly, learning in any form is unlikely in such an emotional atmosphere.

The suggestion, usually made in passing, that flaps are a way of desensitizing humanity to their presence, of getting us used to them perhaps in preparation for The Landing, at least gets the emotional valences of UFO experiences right. (Hall, 1988) The manner of presentation, however, is wrong. Desensitization is best accomplished by gradual increases in the intensity of the aversive stimuli. (Skinner, 1974) Appearing in sudden waves and withdrawing for long intervals only favors anxiety and acute fright. (Smelser, 1963)

TOURIST THEORY

A more promising line of speculation in the extraterrestrial mode exists in DeLillo and Marx's Tourist Theory of UFOs. They offer as a model the whims of Earthly tourism. This year we go Europe; next year the fares to South America look inviting. Maybe a few will brave Africa for a safari in between. Unsystematic but curious gatherings might follow news of Earth-Zoo personnel capturing an unusual specimen of wild humanity. Concerted campaigns by this or that agency competing for business might also yield an occasional bustle of traffic. (Marx and DeLillo, 1979) This is quite ingenious and would seem to be virtually untestable and immune to argument with respect to the numbers. There are, however, broader considerations that work against the theory. The most interesting things in a foreign culture tend to be located in urban settings: their museums, architecture, shops, churches, and shrines. UFO experiences tend to be in rural settings and the aliens don't debark for tour busses. Souvenir hunting is rarely seen. There's only one or two cases of an alien with a camera.

Gillespie and Prytz (1984) offer a cruder variation in their thoughts about UFO waves. "Flaps stick out like sore thumbs, and can be explained readily by External Intelligence for similar reasons that the Sydney Cricket Ground receives a 'flap' of Sydney-siders on Rugby Grand Final Day—it is a unique place for a certain people at a unique time!" So why were UFOs drawn to Earth and the United States in June/July 1947, July/August 1952, November 1957, August 1965, March/April 1966, and so forth? What made these times uniquely interesting for the aliens? Gillespie and Prytz don't seem ready to say. Instead they complain that those who advocate the idea that UFO phenomena are internally generated haven't explained why these are unique times either "probably because it is in the 'too hard' basket."

Difficulty is not disproof. The necessity of a psychological and sociological approach is mandated by the fact that nine out of ten UFO reports involve misinterpreted stimuli. This percentage does not alter significantly during flaps or periods of calm. (Ballester-Olmos, 1987) UFOs never outnumber IFO reports in any period. Take away all the unsolved cases, and the IFOs still display the large changes present in the total report population. If extra-terrestrial craft are causing flaps, you still need an explanation for why one true report spawns nine false ones. Copycat behavior would be the first possibility, yet IFO cases do not generally seem to be in the proximity of unsolved cases during major flaps. This is particularly troubling in the 1965 wave that seemed to lack national coverage of a major case off which a rash of copycats could work.

SILLY SEASONS

Sociological explanations of UFO flaps can be divided into two general categories, which for convenience can be termed "silly season theories" and "crisis theories." Silly season theories build on the premise that news media are a sufficient cause of flaps. The spread of news causes the spread of copycat behavior. The example of the Forkenbrook experiment forms the model of these theories. This hoax for a sociology class demonstrated how a false report could generate so much excitement in a locale that it spawned reports in several neighboring communities, including one from a man who said he had seen the UFO for some two weeks and knew it was going to land. (Klass, 1974)

There is no denying this model has application in certain local flaps. The Socorro case of April 24, 1964, spawned misidentifications of things like aircraft, birds, and a fire in a dump in nearby locales. Yet the Socorro case allegedly got national attention. Why didn't it spawn a nationwide wave of reports? Why didn't the Mantell crash spawn a nationwide flap? Why didn't the Val Johnson case or the Travis Walton (Snowflake, Arizona) case spawn nationwide reactions? These questions are relevant since some silly season theorists put great weight on the assumed effects of sin-

gle cases that get wide coverage. The Air Force cited the Levelland Whatnik as the primary cause of the November 1957 wave. (Strentz, 1982) This is plausible if one regards the slowly elevating numbers of mid and late October as not a true beginning of the flap, but a more or less irrelevant flurry that would have been disregarded if the post-Levelland spike had not appeared.

Herbert Hackett indicates the week of the 1947 flap was "a slow week from an editor's viewpoint" and he felt the newspapers milked the story by continually repeating the Kenneth Arnold flying saucer story with different experts consulted for their opinions. Hackett (1948) regarded Air Force denials as a paradoxical reinforcement of the concept. He gives a tally of the amount of space given to the story in the *Los Angeles Times* each day, presumably to offer some measure of the amount of reinforcement they gave. It is curious to note that if one juxtaposes Hackett's tally to a tally of UFO report numbers from the Los Angeles area the effect of media is not compelling. One half of the reports occur before the story ever reaches Page One, and by July 10th there are no UFOs reported, even though it was still on the front page the day before. (Gross, 1976) This finding parallels remarks by John Keel (1969/89) and Richard Hall (1988) that media coverage often seems to lag behind the increase in UFO numbers rather than precede it.

The reason for this can be discovered in Herbert Strentz's analysis of UFO journalism. Strentz posits that creating a flap is a "lowering of barriers" that newsmen set up before they will put a UFO report in their paper. Strentz is not clear what creates that drop in standards. But data in questionnaires he gathered provide a rather clear answer. The major reason given for reporting UFOs is an increase in the number of UFO reports! Coverage is obviously going to lag events and not initiate them if this is true. (Strentz, 1982)

The relevance of slow news days to lowering barriers is hard to sustain upon critical reflection. Kenneth Arnold's report of a new craft traveling at 1,200 miles per hour was a sensation for its time and would have merited coverage in any period regardless of its doubtful character and lack of corroboration. Flaps have happened in conjunction with major news events like the Sputnik furor in 1957. Philip Klass (1974) has suggested the 1973 wave was, in part, a reaction to a late-summer doldrums following the sordid disclosures of the Watergate affair. The UFO reports were printed to lighten things up for a nation weary of the big news that was dominating the front page. What is troublesome in this characterization of the period is that the 1973 flap reached its peak simultaneously with the Saturday Night Massacre which unleashed a flood of negative sentiment, described by others as a fevered rage that swept the nation. (Lukas, 1976)

Klass devotes a chapter of *UFOs Explained* (1974) to an extended tracing of the effects of media on UFO numbers. His reconstruction is impressive and seductive, but suffers from many difficulties when subjected to close scrutiny. A modest surge of reports in 1950 is tied to the publication of Donald Keyhoe's book *The Flying Saucers Are Real*, but nothing is said of the article in *True* magazine that spawned it. This was one of the most widely discussed articles of its time. Prominent newsmen like Walter Winchell and Frank Edwards did items on it. The Associated Press carried quotes from it. (Gross, 1983) A look at the daily UFO numbers for late December 1949 and January 1950 are astonishing for their total lack of a reaction.

Klass observes that UFO reports skyrocketed the same month that *Life* featured a major story titled "Have We Visitors from Outer Space?" More articles in *Look* and *Life* were published in June 1952 and yielded a tenfold increase for that month. Years earlier, Blue Book investigators looked at the daily tallies, however, and were not convinced there was a relationship. A brief increase was noted after the April 4 release of *Life*, but numbers seemed basically the same before as after. (Jacobs, 1975) The tally dropped to zero on the 8th and the bulk of the reports pop up two weeks after the article. The June 17, 1952, *Look* article was a debunking piece by Donald Menzel who wrote off the phenomenon as a bunch of mirages. Shouldn't this have decreased numbers?

Klass skips lightly over the 1957 wave and ignores the July/August 1965 wave entirely because the media did not show much interest in UFOs until the swamp gas flap of 1966. This flap is not tackled either, but it set in motion Congressional action and led to six books being published in 1966 and ten books in 1967. *The Invaders* TV series also appears in January 1967. This increased media attention is held to account for a high total of 937 UFO reports in 1967. What is left unsaid is that this represents a decrease from the 1966 total of 1,060 reports. Peak media coverage once again lags behind peak UFO numbers.

Hans van Kampen offers a subtle variant of the silly season theory in a 1978 article that relates the story of people seeing a panda that the media said had wandered out of a zoo. Unbeknownst to everyone, the panda was found dead just as the story went out. Van Kampen felt this flap of panda sightings indicated that human curiosity and sympathetic sharing of feelings was involved. (van Kampen, 1979) Do such factors underlie UFO flaps?

Curiosity about UFOs fortunately has a way of being measured. For a period in 1965 and 1966 there exists a tally of letters to the Pentagon by people making inquiries about UFOs. Often they are youngsters writing public school essays. (Lear, 1966) Overlap this tally of queries on a chart of UFO numbers and one quickly sees they do not match to a significant degree. Interestingly the queries do peak the same month that *Life*, *Time*, *Newsweek*, and *U.S. News and World Report* did stories on the swamp gas debacle, but UFO numbers were already falling. The factor of sympathetic feelings is potentially correct, but not as easy to test or verify. Given the failure of so many seemingly commonsense notions about UFOs, however, it is perhaps best to suspend judgement about that factor.

Menzel (1963) has suggested the 1952

wave was nurtured in part by the movie *The Day the Earth Stood Still* playing in theaters all spring. He points out that the spaceship in the movie reappeared in many reports during the wave. The movie's initial release actually took place in September 1951. UFO numbers from August to November run 18-16-24-16, which minimally proves any reaction was neither immediate nor sharply forceful. It is unsurprising in this context that a prediction that Steven Spielberg's *Close Encounters of the Third Kind* would spawn a major flap failed. (Klass, 1977; Hendry, n.d.) A chart of monthly report totals perversely shows a lull throughout the period it was generating major box-office figures. When it leaves the theaters, the numbers start upward in a manner that begs the suggestion the movie somehow suppressed UFO reporting. (Hendry, 1981) It is relevant to add that none of the major UFO flaps coincide with the release of major films of the alien invasion genre. This may not forbid the possibility that lesser effects on UFO numbers exist. A look at UFO numbers before and after the release of twenty popular alien invasion films turns up minor increases for fourteen of them. Even if the effect is real, we can still doubt whether this is due to enhanced interest in or attention to aliens, or if the malevolence of movie aliens adds a darker tone to the UFO mythos and increases numbers by increasing fear. (Lucaniao, 1988)

We can also add that Paul Ferrughelli did a correlation study of prime time television events and the frequency of UFO reports in a 36-month period from 1987 to 1989 involving 683 sightings reports. The correlation coefficient calculated from the data was +.086, which was effectively indistinguishable from no causal relationship whatsoever. (Ferrughelli, 1991)

There is another problem with the silly season theory. J. Allen Hynek raised it in a memoir of the swamp gas debacle. Why was there so much excitement and hysteria over the incredibly trivial Dexter sightings? The media circus makes no sense from the perspective of newsworthiness. Strentz's news judgment barriers had tumbled in a collective mania of the period. They were clamoring for an authoritative statement from the Air Force on what amounted to some faint lights and a glow in a swamp. They posed no danger. There were no aliens seen. It was less dramatic than dozens of cases seen over the years. Why should this be? Hynek had not a clue and pleaded for sociologists to take a crack at the problem. (Hynek, 1976)

It would be an exaggeration to regard silly season theories as refuted by all the above considerations. It may be that a more detailed study or some novel perspective might yield more convincing results. According to the Condon report, however, there have been other attempts to correlate UFO maxima with waves of press publicity without compelling evidence of a real association. It is hard to escape the sense that there is some missing factor or factors.

REACTIONS TO SCIENCE

The problem that presents itself is figuring out which of the myriad changing aspects of the human environment it is that UFO numbers are responding to. Is it political climates (liberal vs. conservative, individualism vs. collectivism, democratic vs. totalitarian)? Is it war and peace? Is it economic climates? Is it changing styles in the exercise of power? Is it changes in collective perceptions of powerlessness? Is it a response to fluctuating religious-secularist fashions of living? Is it a response to different educational fashions? Are there changes in skepticism and gullibility, cynicism and trust? Are people more sky-oriented and filled with wanderlust in some times more than others?

One interesting stab in the dark was John A. Rimmer's guess that for every scientific advance there is an equal and opposite mystical reaction. The ghost rockets of 1946 and the saucers of 1947 would thus be a reaction to the introduction of nuclear weapons in 1945. The 1957 Levelland wave would be the obvious reaction to the introduction of space travel represented by the Sputniks the same month. Did the other flaps follow major scientific advances? Was there a reaction associated with the moon landing? (Rimmer, 1969) The depressing answers are no and no, despite the poetry of the idea.

CRISIS THEORIES

One of the venerable mainstays of sociological thought is the concept of crisis as an agent of social change. There is a sizeable literature devoted to crisis cults and how stressful events prompt new interpretations of religious doctrines, visions, and myths. (LaBarre, 1972) Among the axioms of crisis theory is the proposition that crises create wishes for supernatural solutions. (Stark and Bainbridge, 1987) UFOs can be regarded as supernatural in the official sense that they are forces outside of nature that suspend, alter, and ignore physical forces. Are UFOs a magical reaction to crises? Otto Billig has offered the most extended argument that they are. His application of crisis theory to the data of the UFO phenomenon is probably as close to textbook as can be expected and one cannot deny there are facets to his thesis that work. In the specific realm of UFO flaps, however, difficulties are clearly evident. In his usage, the concept of crisis embodies such a wide range of events one is left wondering why we do not see a steady stream of reports instead of the widely separated peaks of activity that are actually present. This is vividly exemplified by Billig's annotations on a chart of Air Force-compiled monthly UFO tallies. Periods of crisis cover roughly 67 percent of the time interval from 1947 to 1969 by his own illustration. Yet only eight percent of this interval shows numbers that could be reasonably termed flaps. (Billig, 1982) Even if we regard crisis not as a primary causal agent, but as a necessary catalytic factor, there is no way to discount the plausibility that these flaps overlap the 67 percent regions of crisis simply by chance.

Lloyd de Mause's psychohistorical investigations of the fantasy-life of American politics provide a more useful definition of crisis. Utilizing a protocol called fantasy analysis on a mass of historical documents and news stories, de Mause charted a regular sequential change of the perception of the strength and impotence of American leadership. For our purposes we will only look at one of the recurring stages that is specifically perceived as a phase of crisis and collapse. It is identified by a proliferation of emotional metaphors involving fantasies of death and dying. Unnamed poisonous enemies multiply as the group displaces rage outwards. Apocalyptic and millennial overtones are generally present. De Mause's group fantasy definition allows a restriction and demarcation between crises that are merely annoyances and crises that are felt with intense emotion. It has the added virtue of having been constructed independent of any interest in UFOs. There would be no question of crises being selected in a manner to skew acceptance of the crisis theory. (De Mause, 1982)

Six group fantasy crises occurred between 1952 and 1977, the period that de Mause limited himself to. They comprise only 18 percent of this 25-year interval. If all five major national flaps fell into these well-defined bands of crisis, we would have impressive statistical proof of a true relationship. Regrettably, only one wave, 1957, occurs during these crises and this is no better than chance.

It might be that political crisis is the wrong form of crisis to be looking at. Charles Fair offers a variant restriction of crisis theory that suggests UFO graphs are gauges of collective anxiety corresponding to alignments of power during the Cold War. Thus flaps happen at the times of Dulles' "brinkmanship," the opening phases of the space race, and the entanglement in Vietnam. (Fair, 1974) There is one killer problem that stares any potential convert of such crisis theories in the face. The Cuban missile crisis of 1962 was the single most terrifying event in the 20th century. Fear of nuclear annihilation was palpable and imminent. If ever an impetus for salvationist fantasy and magical escape existed, it had to be then. We should have seen the biggest UFO flap imaginable. This not only failed to happen, but UFO numbers actually dropped during the crisis.

Billig tries to excuse this incongruity in his application by trying to draw a distinction between crises that focus on specific situations and those that pose a vague threat, which leaves the individual without adequate defenses. The distinction sounds phony since every individual without a fallout shelter had no defense against a nuclear exchange. The wish for aliens to come down and rescue us naturally seems a logical supernatural solution obliged by the axioms of crisis theory. Peter Rogerson (1981) alternately proposed the crisis was over so fast that there was not enough time for a salvationist fantasy to develop. The 1957 wave, however, showed a tenfold increase in the matter of three days. And, to repeat, the numbers actually went down during the crisis. Surely some kind of increase should have been registered. Such excuses just don't wash to anyone who lived through this collective staredown with death.

Crisis theory probably does not work here because the salvationist impulse does not form the core of the dominant rumor complex about UFOs. While the impulse is certainly present in the contactee complex of people like George Adamski and George Hunt Williamson, this is distinct from the beliefs of people like Donald Keyhoe and Coral Lorenzen who saw UFOs as spycraft and potential invaders. (Rogerson, 1978/79) It is also distinct from those who felt saucers were secret weapons: the true dominant belief of the fifties and sixties in the general public. Most cases speak not of escaping Earth and all its sorrows (the John Lennon UFO is a well-known but nearly unique exception to the rule), but express fears of many varieties from being spied upon, being captured, being chased, being contaminated, and being run into.

MASS HYSTERIA

The suggestion that flaps are a form of collective hysteria seems initially more promising as a way to account for the fears seen in UFO experiences. Mark Rhine in the Condon report and Robert Hall point to certain episodes of mass hysteria or hysterical contagion like the June bug epidemic, the Seattle windshield pitting epidemic, and the Mad Gasser of Mattoon, wondering if they may serve as explanatory models for what is going on with the UFO phenomenon. Neither takes the idea very far and Hall pointed out several difficulties in comparing these phenomena, probably the most notable being the fleeting character of these model epidemics. (Sagan and Taves, 1974) Michael Swords suggests these models are more properly labeled as anxiety attacks and adds the point that the people involved do not display psychotic symptoms: ". . . they do not add unreal experiences to their beliefs." He firmly denies hysteria or mass psychogenic illness makes any contribution to the great mass of UFO reports and his detailed argument is strongly recommended as a thorough demolition of this line of inquiry. It further warns us that the etiology of flaps will not be analogous to neuroses, but to psychoses. (Swords, 1984)

Allan Hendry's study of 1,158 IFO reports demonstrates conclusively there are important emotional forces connected to the UFO mythos that compromises the objectivity of percipients of UFOs. Commonplace stimuli like stars, balloons, and the like are imaginatively reconstructed with unreal traits like domes and the saucer shape. Witnesses are totally sincere and most are eminently articulate even when offering greatly distorted observations. IFO witnesses are found in skilled trade jobs and with both general and specialized education. Competency and the ability to reason critically are not the issues. Emotions and expectations are subverting the perception process. (Hendry, 1979)

PARANOIA THEORY

Many facets of the UFO mythos are identifiably forms of paranoid ideation. The core belief that aliens are making a reconnaissance of our planet, that, to borrow a title from the sixties, *Flying Saucers Are Watching Us*, is a collective variant on the common paranoid delusion of observation, the erroneous impression that one is being watched by persecuting others. Allied to this is a large complex of suspicions.

The government knows more than it is telling. It is purposefully misleading the public. It secretly gathers up all important evidence like photos and crashed saucers. The saucers may be secret weapons of America, Russia, and even Nazi scientists. Concerns about invasion, poisoning, irradiation, mind-tampering, doppelgangers, night-doctors, and sexnappings are seen. Myriad fantasies of world destruction have been ubiquitous among both UFOlogists and experiencers.

Norman Cameron guesses the incidence of paranoid reactions in the general population to be quite high. Transient paranoid misinterpretations may happen to virtually anyone in the right set of circumstances. (Cameron, 1959) In certain individuals paranoid ideation becomes fixed and chronic. Even in these instances, there is no loss of mental competency in most other aspects of their lives. Indeed they may often perform at superior levels. (Rosen, Fox, and Gregory, 1972) Paranoia is essentially an intellectual disorder which is strikingly, meticulously logical after the basic emotional axioms are laid in. (Fried and Agassi, 1976) The point is that Hendry's facts about IFO reports are consistent with either transient or chronic paranoia. This allows one to speculate on the origins of the waves of misinterpretation generated by the UFO mythos, for there is no mystery about the origins of paranoiac reactions.

Kenneth Mark Colby has critically reviewed the formulations offered by several researchers for the origin of paranoia and convincingly concluded that only shame and humiliation adequately explained the range of known precipitants of paranoia. Injuries to the ego in such forms as personal slights, job failures, false arrests, accidents, deformities, and sexual defeat exemplify the varied events seen at the beginning of paranoid psychoses. (Colby, n.d.) Underscoring the primacy of personal pride over personal danger is the fact that paranoia is more often associated with people experiencing thwarted ambitions than with people holding few expectations in a hazardous environment. (Meissner, 1978) If flaps are being governed by the dynamics of paranoia, we should be asking if they are being generated by episodes of collective shame.

APPLICATION

In the case of the major UFO flaps in America, such a question yields good answers. The 1947 wave was obviously triggered by the phrase "flying saucer" entering the language and the presumption that they represented a superweapon closely analogous to the atomic bomb developed in supersecrecy by the Manhattan Project a couple years earlier. This fed into a hysterical anti-communism that was spawned earlier in 1947, specifically March 12th. On that date Truman addressed a joint session of Congress and spoke in sweeping, apocalyptic terms of communism as an insidious world menace. Those who loved freedom would have to struggle with it at all times and on all fronts. Truman quickly set up a federal loyalty review program. One aim of this speech was to garner military aid to support a Greek regime in the throes of a civil war by scaring the hell out of the American people. The aid was granted, but it succeeded too well in scaring people. Norman Thomas was making a trip through California that spring and was amazed at how quickly "hysterical anti-communism swept the state." Historians David Caute and Athan Theoharis confirm this pervasive fear of communism quickly gripped the nation. A poll in 1947 showed 66 percent of Americans believed the Soviet Union was "aggressive" compared to 38 percent in 1945. (Boyer, 1994) One of the earliest moves by the government in investigating the flying saucer problem included background checks of those who claimed to have seen saucers to determine if they had communist ties. They didn't. The erosion of basic trust by loyalty tests of Americans could be a key factor in the escalation of paranoia in this period.

The 1952 wave begins with the rising furor of an upcoming steel strike planned by laborers in the steel industry. In that era, steel was a major force in the American economy and an integral part of American national identity. The strike deeply divided the nation because the nation was then fighting a war in Korea and such an action was perceived as a traitorous threat to the strength of the nation. President Truman seized the steel industry to keep the mills running. In due course, however, the courts declared the seizure unconstitutional and the strike began in earnest.

UFO numbers responded to developments in the steel strike in a convincing manner. Numbers grew up to the time of the seizure and then fell for a time. After the courts ruled and the strike proceeded, UFO numbers began upwards and skyrocket to record proportions, culminating in the frenzy of the Washington National sightings. Three days after the first Washington National sighting the strike was settled. Within a week, the numbers begin to collapse, assisted by an announcement that the D.C. cases were caused by a temperature inversion.

Sputnik

Sputnik was indisputably the central trauma of the fifties generation and a profound blow to American self-esteem. The U.S. prided itself on being the most technologically advanced nation on Earth. Yankee ingenuity was a term of self-endearment. Sputnik called all this into question. The Russians were the first to orbit a satellite around the Earth and we were not. This event gnawed away at the American psyche such that millions were funneled into the space program over the following decade in a race to put a man on the moon before the Russians and restore self-confidence in our superiority.

A look at the UFO numbers are puzzling at first glance because the peak happens after the launch of Sputnik II, a month after Sputnik I. Shouldn't the Levelland flap follow the initial Sputnik more closely? A memoir of the period by NASA clarifies the paradox. The alarm did not materialize immediately. Planetariums and ham radio operators became more active after the first announcement, but *Newsweek* correspondents first found "massive indifference" and a vague feeling that we had entered a new era. After a week, this bewilderment melted away before a mounting and almost universal furor. Between October 9th and 15th a lot of blaming was going on in Washington, D.C., and calls went up for improving education. Successful rocket tests between October 17th and October 23rd offered hope we were catching up, but then on November 3rd Russia announced the launch of a second even more spectacular Sputnik with a dog on board named Laika. (Green and Lomask, 1970) Add into this emotional brew news of a UFO incident in which an UFO caused automobiles to fail and the numbers exploded tenfold.

Numbers dropped off from the 6th onwards probably because of the whimsical Trasco case, wherein aliens tried to kidnap a guy's dog, an obvious spin on Laika. The Schmidt contact may also have been a factor, for authorities quickly proclaimed the man an ex-con. Numbers remain elevated in the ensuing weeks. There is a temporary sharp decline accompanying the explosion of a Vanguard rocket on December 6th and some see that as a point against paranoia theory. Yet while this was clearly a humiliation for workers on the Vanguard project and they were treated as if they had committed treason, people in general seemed disappointed and depressed. Paranoia is in part a defense against depression and does not manifest itself in the depths of mourning. (Meissner, 1978) It is more usually associated with frenzy and manic thought. The flap resumed briefly in the days that followed, but by late December it was essentially over. The launch of Explorer I on January 31, 1958, was a relief, but UFO numbers were already so low by that date that no further decline was immediately apparent since there were only one to three reports per day. Even so, the total for February was 41, down from January's 61, and potentially indicative of restored pride.

SIXTIES

The UFO wave of July-August 1965 coincides with two major events that introduced the nation to two extended nightmares: the Vietnam debacle and the race riots. The first U.S. ground combat operation began on June 28, 1965. While the U.S. had been involved in Vietnam with aerial bombing before this date, the ground combat denoted a new level of development. Unfortunately it quickly turned out that the troops were engaged in a "futile assault." On July 4th, Hanoi repulsed overtures for peace. On July 20th U.S. Secretary of Defense Robert McNamara reported the situation in Vietnam was deteriorating. On July 28th a troop build-up was announced and draft calls issued. UFO numbers were virtually flat from January to June, but with July, gradual but erratic increases are unmistakable. A small two-day decline around July 15th coincides with news of Mariner 4 reaching Mars—a brief moment of technological triumph.

The flap reaches a peak on August 4th as the reality of the draft sinks in, then drops down quickly for a week when the second blow hits. On August 11th: the Watts riot. From the 11th to the 16th the Watts suburbs go up in flames when racial tensions erupted. UFO numbers seem to go up in response for a secondary peak on the 11th and 12th of August. Beginning on August 18-19 and in mid-September successful Vietnam operations at Chulai, Da Nang, and Ankhe are accompanied by declines of UFO numbers and the flap gradually fizzled out.

The swamp gas flap is significantly smaller than the other flaps we are considering here, but we can answer Hynek's question posed earlier. Five days before Dexter-Hillsdale, on March 15, 1966, a new Watts riot came into the headlines. UFO numbers that had been running flat for weeks amid stories of truces, peace bids, and talk of the Great Society, began to surge in response. Then on March

23rd, two days before Hynek's press conference, came the first anti-American demonstrations in Hue and DaNang. The flap peaked on March 30th and presumably declined for lack of further race riots or anti-American demonstrations. News of Saigon riots and further anti-U.S. outbursts on April 4th was followed the next day by a secondary peak. An anti-U.S. riot in Hue on May 26th and the flaming suicide of a religious figure on May 29th were also accompanied by brief, lesser increases.

Over the months that followed, UFO numbers tended to remain at elevated levels, but visibly fluctuated in response to developments in Vietnam. During a period of record casualties in March 1967, UFOs were clearly swarming about. During the Christmas truce and peace proposals of late December 1966, the UFOs vanished. A curious proof of the importance of Vietnam War news in modulating UFO numbers came in June 1967. Between June 5th and 10th, Vietnam was completely knocked off the front page by an Arab-Israeli war. For four days straight Blue Book did not receive a single report! This interesting fact, we can add, calls into question Thomas Bearden's linking the 1973 flap with mid-East war tensions. (Bearden, 1980)

OTHER RESOLUTIONS

Blue Book went out of business at the end of the 1960s and with it ended any conveniently accessible daily tally of UFO numbers. This precluded detailed comparison of the 1973 wave with the events of the Watergate crisis. But we can point out that David Jacobs called mid-October the peak period of the flap and this roughly corresponds with Vice President Agnew's resignation on October 10th followed ten days later by the Saturday Night Massacre. (Jacobs, 1975) It unleashed a flood of negative public sentiment and calls for impeachment. This was against a leader who less than a year before had been reelected in a landslide of popular support. (Lukas, 1976)

The ups and downs of national pride also seem to correlate with lesser swings of UFO numbers. News of poverty in Appalachia, charges that Reds had infiltrated the State Department, and some of the desegregation conflicts seem to relate to increases in UFO activity. Conversely when we landed on the moon, when the Reds were retreating during the Korean war, and when Ike went on his "Peace Tour," UFO reports vanished.

The drop of UFOs during the Cuban missile crisis, so troubling to crisis theory, is readily understood when one remembers the salient issue is not fear and anxiety, but pride. It was the Soviets who backed down from that face-off, not America. A drop-off in UFO numbers following the Kennedy assassination, another if lesser conundrum to crisis theory, is fully explicable with the observation on how mourning and melancholy decreases paranoid ideation. (Meissner, 1978)

PROBLEMS AND CONFUSIONS

It must be said that efforts to extend the theory forward to events after 1973 have been disappointingly ambiguous. National pride was clearly present with such events as the November 1989 fall of the Berlin Wall, the successful 1989 invasion of Panama, and the victorious Persian Gulf War of February 1992. Each of these events can be linked to periods of zero activity in data collected by the National Sighting Research Center. Stretches of zero activity, however, are so common in this data set that one could fairly dismiss the correlation as due to chance.

The televangelism sex scandals of the 1980s seemed a rather blatant episode of collective shame and should have prompted paranoiac reactions among the faithful. In fact, there is unequivocal evidence that they did in the form of satanic rumor panics. One swept North and South Carolina on March 14, 1987, five days before Jim Bakker finally resigned, and another swept the region of the Alexandria and Baton Rouge ministries of Jimmy Swaggert on April 1, 1988, the week before he was defrocked for sins he confessed to the prior February. (Victor, 1990) Inspection of daily UFO tallies does not show a parallel increase of UFO activity either nationally or in the region of the ministries. One might be tempted to shrug this off by saying UFOs would be too secular a way to express paranoia in a religious population, but it gets worse.

The Watts riots of the 1960s seem clearly linked to a spike in UFO activity, but when riots struck Miami in mid-January 1989 and in Los Angeles after the Rodney King verdict near the end of April 1992, no spike in UFO activity was visible. Post hoc, one can say that only riots in Watts seem linked to UFO spikes and that other race riots in the sixties generated no response. Perhaps it was special in some way, but why that should be is not immediately apparent.

The most puzzling development occurred during the Monica Lewinsky scandal. The emotional highpoint seemed to occur in the wake of the confession of wrongdoing by the President in the summer of 1998. Angry discussions of the shame it had brought to the country prompted me to check the National UFO Reporting Center's database for activity. The site's home page remarked "September has been an incredibly active month for UFO reports, including mass sightings of blue-green fireballs across the United States." The next month a message was posted reading, "A UFO wave sweeping the country characterized by mass sightings of spheres and fireballs continued throughout October." In November, the description is upgraded even further: "Our report database (updated Nov 21) continues to document an incredible UFO wave sweeping the country." This description was retained through January 1999. Seemingly this was proof positive of the paranoia theory, but then the number of reports continued increasing well after tempers calmed down. Numbers slowly mount to a peak in the fall of 1999 and then fall from December through the start of the new Millennium. (NUFORC, August 2000) Critics wonder if this was really a flap or if there was some form of collection artifact of Internet growth—a new link from a popular site bringing in more people or some such development that just coincidentally started in at the time of the scandal. The situation is thoroughly confusing.

Another issue that draws comment is the absence of Blue Book era sized flaps since 1973. Was there some factor that suppressed the creation of flaps other than pride? This seems plausible in terms of changing perceptions about the nature of the saucer menace. Where the fifties was dominated by concerns saucers were secret weapons and the sixties by fears of invasion, the seventies ushered an era of speculations that UFOs were a charade and perhaps harmless. The movie *Close Encounters of the Third Kind* in particular advanced a vision of aliens as children of light and awe which was a polar opposite to the paranoid fantasies that dominated the prior decades. Such changes would act to reduce fears about what unexplained lights portend and subvert the superego—think parental oversight—aspects of earlier UFOlogy. Obsessions with Roswell and abduction in later years decreased interest in interpreting aerial puzzles in favor of talk about conspiracies and dream interpretation.

While this might seem to render the theory immune to further test until such time as we see a return to enthusiastic belief in reconnaissance and invasion, further work can yet be done in the area of foreign flaps. Was France's Great Martian Panic of 1954 connected to the fall of Dien Bien Phu and the pullout of troops from the Indochina war? What caused the Latin American Wave of 1965? What of the British Scareships of 1912-13?

Criticisms of paranoia theory have been few and generally obtuse. It has been called unfalsifiable, but a pattern of high UFO activity congruent with events of pride such as the Persian Gulf War, the tearing down of the Berlin Wall, the moon landing, the Red retreat of the Korean War, etc., would quickly sink the theory in the eyes of any theorist. A pair of people wondered about the absence of Bullard's 1988 paper on flaps in the discussion. Simply, Bullard did not advance any theory. His paper boils down to the proposition, "Silly season theory is wrong, ergo UFOs are real."

But IFOs are real, too, and he offers no explanation why either changed in frequency when they did. Jerome Clark singles out the explanation of the 1952 wave as "incredible," using the phrase "a hysterical reaction to a steel strike" to describe his understanding of the theory. In fact, mass hysteria was rejected as an explanation of flaps generally in the first presentation of the theory. There are no details on why he feels it doesn't bear consideration. Philip Klass has termed the theory "simplistic" and can show anyone that silly season theory has been common among the skeptical.

That the theory is simplistic is true enough and it is by design. The possibility of multifactor approaches giving better insight has not been denied, but focused argument on a single factor has advantages over tangled commentaries invoking the interaction of multiple elements. At this stage, some standard elements may not be relevant and it seems best to test the limits of applying this new element before bringing back in excuses for the confusion we have seen in this subject.

—MARTIN S. KOTTMEYER

References

Ballester-Olmos, Vicente Juan. *Characteristics of Close Encounters in Spain* (Fund for UFO Research, 1987).

Bearden, Thomas. *The Excalibur Briefing* (Strawberry Hill, 1980).

Billig, Otto. *Flying Saucers: Magic in the Skies: A Psychohistory* (Schenkman, 1982).

Boyer, Paul. *By the Bomb's Early Light* (University of North Carolina, 1994).

Bullard, Thomas E. "Waves," *International UFO Reporter* (November/December 1988).

Cameron, Norman. "Paranoid Conditions and Paranoia," in Arieti, Silvano, ed., *American Handbook of Psychiatry, Volume One* (Basic Books, 1959).

Clark, Jerome. "UFO Update," *UFO Report* (August 1978).

Clark, Jerome. "The Anomalist #3 Reviewed," *MUFON UFO Journal* (February 1996).

Colby, Kenneth Mark. "Appraisal of Four Psychological Theories of Paranoid Phenomena," *Journal of Abnormal Psychology* (n.d.).

Dove, Lonzo. "The Mars Explosions and the Flying Saucers," *Space Review* (July 1953).

Fair, Charles. *The New Nonsense* (Simon & Schuster, 1974).

Ferrughelli, Paul. *National Sighting Yearbook 1990* (National Sighting Research Center, 1991).

Fowler, Raymond. *The Watchers* (Bantam, 1990).

Fried, Yehuda, and Joseph Agassi. *Paranoia: A Study in Diagnosis* (D. Reidel, 1976).

Gillespie, F.C., and John Prytz. "An Inductive Proof of External Intelligence UFO Theories," *UPIAR Research in Progress* (1984).

Girard, Robert. *An Early UFO Sourcebook* (Arcturus Book Service, 1989).

Green, Constance McLaughlin, and Milton Lomask. *Vanguard: A History* (NASA, 1970).

Gross, Loren E. "The UFO Wave of 1947: California: June 25-July 16" in Dornbos, Nancy, ed. *Proceedings of the 1976 CUFOS Conference* (CUFOS, 1976).

———. *UFOs: A History: 1949* (Arcturus Book Service, 1983).

———. *UFOs: A History: September-October 1952* (privately published, 1986).

Hackett, Herbert. "The Flying Saucer: A Manufactured Concept," *Sociology and Social Research* (May-June 1948).

Hall, Richard. "Venus as a UFO Source," *UFO Investigator* (n.d.).

———. *Uninvited Guests* (Aurora, 1988).

Hall, Robert L. "Sociological Perspectives on UFO Reports" in Sagan, Carl, and Thornton Page, eds. *UFOs: A Scientific Debate* (W.W. Norton, 1974).

Hendry, Allan. "The Great UFO Flap that Flopped . . . So Far," *International UFO Reporter* (1978).

———. *The UFO Handbook* (Doubleday, 1979).

———. Letter to Philip Klass, February 11, 1981.

Hynek, J. Allen. "Swamp Gas Plus Ten and Counting" in *1976 MUFON Symposium Proceedings* (MUFON, 1977).

Jacobs, David. *The UFO Controversy in America* (Signet/NAL, 1975).

Jarrold, Edgar R. "Spotlight on Australia," *Space Review* (July 1953).

Keel, John. "The Flap Phenomenon in the United States," NY Fortean Society reprint from *Flying Saucer Review* Special Issue #2, June 1969 (1989).

Keyhoe, Donald. *The Flying Saucers are Real* (Fawcett, 1950).

Klass, Philip J. *UFOs Explained* (Vintage, 1974).

———. "An Argument Against UFOs." *Current* (October 1977).

La Barre, Weston. *The Ghost Dance: The Origins of Religion* (Delta, 1972).

Lord, Harry. "Search for Patterns," *Flying Saucers* (January 1963).

Lucaniao, Thomas. *Them or Us: Archetypal Interpretations of Fifties Alien Invasion Films* (Indiana University Press, 1988).

Lukas, J. Anthony. *Nightmare: The Underside of the Nixon Years* (Viking, 1976).

Marx, R.H., and R. DeLillo. "The Tourist Theory," *Flying Saucer Review* (July 1979).

Meissner, W.W. *The Paranoid Process* (Jason Aronson, 1978).

Menzel, Donald, and Boyd, Lyle G. *The World of Flying Saucers* (Doubleday, 1963).

Michel, Aimé. *Flying Saucers and the Straight-Line Mystery* (Criterion, 1958).

Moravec, Mark. "UFOs as Psychological and Parapsychological Phenomena" in Evans, Hilary, and Dennis Stacy, eds. *UFOs: 1947-1987 The 40-Year Search for an Explanation* (Fortean Tomes, 1987).

Partain, Keith. "A Preliminary Study of the Relationship between So-Called UFO Waves, Natural Constants and Planetary Cycles," *Pursuit* (1985).

Randles, Jenny. *The Pennine UFO Mystery* (Granada, 1983).

———. "Anatomy of a UFO Wave," *International UFO Reporter* (March/April 1986).

Rimmer, John A. "The UFO as an Anti-Scientific Symbol," *Merseyside UFO Bulletin* (July/August 1969).

Rogerson, Peter. "Towards a Revisionist History of UFOlogy," *MUFOB* new series (Winter 1978/79).

———. "Why Have All the UFOs Gone?" *Magonia* (1981).

Rosen, Ephraim, Ronald E. Fox, and Jan Gregory. *Abnormal Psychology* (W.R. Saunders, 1972).

Ruch, Floyd L., and Philip G. Zimbardo. *Psychology and Life* (Scott, Foresman, 1971).

Ruppelt, Edward J. *The Report on Unidentified Flying Objects* (Doubleday, 1956).

Saunders, D.R. "A Spatio-Temporal Invariant for Major UFO Waves" in Dornbos, Nancy, *Proceedings of the 1976 CUFOS Conference* (CUFOS, 1976).

Skinner, B. F. *About Behaviourism* (Vintage, 1976).

Smelser, Neil J. *Theory of Collective Behavior* (Free Press, 1963).

Stark, Rodney, and William Sims Bainbridge. *A Theory of Religion* (Peter Lang, 1987).

Strentz, Herbert J. *A Survey of Press Coverage of*

Unidentifiied Flying Objects (Arcturus Book Service, 1982).

Swiatek-Hudej, Paul and Cassandra. "Perceptual Implications of a UFO Sighting" in *Proceedings of the Sixth Annual UFO Conference, Adelaide, South Australia, 1981* (CUFOS, 1981).

Swords, Michael D. "Mass Hysteria & Multiple-Witness Sightings," *MUFON UFO Journal* (September 1984).

Vallée, Jacques. *Anatomy of a Phenomenon* (Ace, 1966).

———. *The Invisible College* (E.P. Dutton, 1975).

Vallée, Jacques and Janine. *Challenge to Science* (Ballantine, 1977).

Van Kampen, Hans. "The Case of the Lost Panda," *Skepical Inquirer* (Fall 1979).

Victor, Jeffrey S. "The Spread of Satanic Cult Rumors," *Skeptical Inquirer* (Spring 1990).

Webb, Walter N.   (b. 1934). Perhaps best known as the original investigator of the Barney and Betty Hill case, Webb has been associated with UFO research since his own sighting in 1951.

After graduating from Ohio's Mount Union College in 1956 (B.S. degree in biology), Webb's interest in astronomy developed into a career. First he served under the late J. Allen Hynek at the Smithsonian Astrophysical Observatory's Optical Satellite Tracking pro-

Walter Webb

gram (1957-58). Duties included tracking the world's first artificial satellites from Hawaii. Then he spent 32 years at Boston's Charles Hayden Planetarium, Museum of Science, as senior lecturer, assistant director, and operations manager. He is now retired.

Webb has served four national UFO organizations, three of them as an astronomy consultant. For six months in 1995, the UFO Research Coalition (represented by the three major U.S. UFO organizations) hired Webb as its full-time investigator. Currently he writes "The Night Sky" column in the *MUFON UFO Journal* and is the author of *Encounter at Buff Ledge: A UFO Case History*. His honors include the 1996 Isabel L. Davis Memorial Award of the Fund for UFO Research and an appointment by the J. Allen Hynek Center for UFO Studies as its first Senior Research Associate. Both awards recognized Webb's many years of work in the UFO field.

POSITION STATEMENT: My personal investigations into the UFO matter cover almost half a century. During this time I have been lucky enough to experience my own anomalous sighting. That event alone convinced me that the phenomenon was something real and unknown. Add to this my interviews with several hundred witnesses, many of them claiming close encounters with highly structured and maneuverable objects. Some of these sources even testified to confrontations with humanoid entities associated with landed craft.

My professional science background and firsthand knowledge of known sky phenomena lead me to believe that beyond the huge category of misperceived objects and phenomena, there exists a small subset of manifestations which are totally unique and yet indicative of intelligent activity. I continue to believe only one hypothesis truly can explain the available data. I feel that very strong circumstantial evidence exists supporting an extraterrestrial origin for some of these reported sightings and encounters.

It seems obvious that open contact with

extraterrestrials would have a profound effect on the human race and on our fundamental institutions—in some ways unforeseen. This awareness may well explain, at least in part, our visitors' enigmatic behavior. I also believe, however, Earth's citizens deserve a truthful and complete disclosure of any and all facts that governments may be privy to regarding UFOs. Only through an informed populace can we and our scientists meet the challenge facing us. In the meantime the following courses of action need to be taken:

1. Science professionals must be encouraged to explore the UFO problem without fear of ridicule, and UFO witnesses should be encouraged to come forth with their experiences, again without fearing derision.

2. UFO researchers need to document their investigations much more thoroughly and in a scientific manner.

3. We must continue to seek out physical evidence.

4. Sleep paralysis imagery, a little known phenomenon, is creating false entity reports, especially in bedroom encounter claims. Both UFO investigators and mental health professionals must learn to recognize this phenomenon's potential role in UFO encounter and abduction cases.

—WALTER N. WEBB

Web sites, UFO/ET-related For all the latest information on UFO and SETI-related subjects, check the following sites on the World Wide Web:

Above Top Secret
www.abovetopsecret.com

Aliens and the Scalpel
www.alienscalpel.com

The Anomalist
www.anomalist.com

Archaeology, Astronautics and
SETI Research Association
www.aas-ra.org

Argonaut-Greywolf
William & Lori McDonald
www.alienufoart.com

Art Bell
www.artbell.com

Beyond Roswell
www.beyondroswell.com

The British UFO Research Association
www.bufora.org.uk

Center for the Study of
Extraterrestrial Intelligence
www.cseti.com

Citizens Against UFO Secrecy
www.caus.org

Committee for the
Scientific Investigation
of Claims of the Paranormal
www.csicop.org

The Computer UFO Network
www.cufon.org

Mark Davenport
www.greenleafpublications.com

Deb's UFO Research Information
Clearinghouse
www.debshome.com

Earth Files
www.earthfiles.com

The Extraterrestrial Encyclopedia Project
www.RonaldStory.com

Filer's Research Institute
www.filersfiles.com

Fund for UFO Research
www.fufor.org

Stanton Friedman
www.v-j-enterprises.com/sfpage

Malcolm Hathorn
www.uforeality.com

J. Allen Hynek
Center for UFO Studies
www.cufos.com

David Icke
www.davidicke.com

Inexplicata
www.inexplicata.com

International Space
Sciences Organization
www.isso.org

Kennedy Space Center
Visitor Complex
www.kennedysnacecenter.com

Kal Korff
www.kalkorff.com

Ronald Story
www.RonaldStory.com

Mothership
www.ufomind.com

Mutual UFO Network
www.mufon.com

NASA Headquarters
www.hg.nasa.gov

NASA Home Page
www.nasa.gov

National UFO Reporting Center
www.ufocenter.com

PEER
www.peer-mack.org

Phenomenon
www.stateoftheart.nl/phenomenon

Planetary Society
www.planetaa.org

Project 1947
www.Project1947.com

Jeff Rense
www.sightings.com

Saucer Smear
www.martiansgohome.com

Dan Sherman
www.aboveblack.com

Zecharia Sitchin
www.sitchin.com

SETI Institute
www.seti.org

Whitley Strieber
www.whitleysworld.com

UFO Roundup
www.ufoinfo.com

UFO Magazine
www.ufomag.com

UFO Magazine
www.ufomag.co.uk

The Ultimate UFO Resource
www.ufocin.com

Univeral Vision
www.universal-vision.com

Katharina Wilson
www.alienjigsaw.com

Wellington-Kaikoura (New Zealand) radar/ visual sightings On New Year's Day, 1979, the news quickly spread around the world that UFOs sighted over New Zealand's Canterbury coast were being taken seriously by the Royal New Zealand Air Force to the extent that Skyhawk fighter-bombers had been placed on standby alert. Not since the famed Washington National sightings of 1952 had such a furor arose within the news media over the subject of UFOs, and for good reason.

Never before had there been a case of simultaneous radar-visual-photographic observations. The New Zealand sightings of December 21 and 31, 1978, involved several airborne observers, which included the pilots and crewmembers of three separate aircraft-radar operators, both in the air and on the ground, and on December 31, a professional TV cameraman shot several thousand frames of 16mm color movie film of unidentified lights. The brightest object to be captured on film was described by the camerman, David Crockett, as having "a transparent sphere on top with brightly lit saucer-shaped bottom." Other "objects" were variously described as saucer- or egg-shaped with rotating bands of red light going around the white or yellowish-white globules of light. Up to four lights were reportedly seen at one time during the high point of UFO activity. (However, lights were seen in many different places, so it is difficult to determine exactly how many UFOs might have been present.)

Here are the essentials of the story from the beginning:

The first sightings occurred around 12:30 A.M., December 21-22, 1978, as an Argosy cargo plane owned by Safe-Air Ltd., departed Blenheim en route (along the eastern coast of New Zealand's South Island) to Christchurch. Captain John B. Randle reported "a number of white lights," near the mouth of the Clarence River "similar to landing lights," in the sky. Five objects were confirmed by the powerful Wellington Air Traffic Control (WATC) radar and were considered unexplained.

Around 3:30 A.M., a second Safe-Air Ar-

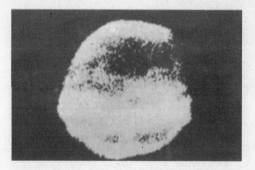

One of the famous New Zealand UFOs, as photographed by an Australian TV crew from a plane

gosy, flying approximately the same course as the first, also encountered UFOs. WATC received five strong returns, which Captain Vern L. A. Powell and his copilot, Ian B. Perry, were asked to identify. Wellington said there was a large return on the port side of the plane at nine o'clock at a distance of forty kilometers. The two pilots looked out and there it was. Somewhat later, Powell blurted out over the radio: "Something is coming towards us at a tremendous speed on our radar. It has traveled some twenty-four kilometers [fifteen miles] in five seconds. Now it has abruptly veered off [an estimated speed of 10,800 miles per hour]. It was moving so fast it was leaving a tail behind it on the radar screen," Powell said. Air traffic controller Eric McNae at Wellington reported that one object paced the Argosy freighter for twelve miles along the Kaikoura coast before disappearing off their screens.

On December 26, after a flurry of news reports in the New Zealand papers, Australian television Channel 0 in Melbourne decided to do a feature story on Vern Powell's experience. Reporter Quentin Fogarty, vacationing in New Zealand at the time, was contacted for the assignment. Fogarty soon arranged for a camera crew (which turned out to be David Crockett and his wife, Ngaire) to accompany him on a similar trip to reconstruct for the television audience what had happened on the same flight path ten days before.

The plane, an Argosy four-engine turbo-prop freighter, as before, left Blenheim at 9:30 P.M. on December 30th for an uneventful trip to Wellington, where it would be loaded with newspapers for the trip south to Christchurch. Upon arrival at Wellington, Fogarty interviewed the controllers at WATC. Then, at 11:46 P.M., the Argosy, piloted by Captain William Startup and First Officer Robert Guard, departed Wellington, with Fogarty, the Crocketts, and a full load of newspapers on board.

At ten minutes past midnight, as the plane had just passed Cape Campbell below (twenty-five miles south of Wellington over Cook Strait), Startup and Guard observed some unusual lights in the direction of a town called Kaikoura. Meanwhile, Fogarty and the Crocketts were in the loading bay working on a "stand-up" to use in their story on the previous UFO sightings. Fogarty had just recorded this statement: "We are now approaching the Clarence River where the highest concentration of UFOs was sighted on the morning of December 21. We're at an altitude of 14,000 feet and we're on exactly the same route taken by Captain Powell when he encountered those mysterious objects. It's a beautiful clear night outside and naturally we'll be looking out for anything unusual." Just then, pilot Bill Startup yelled: "Get up here quick!"

"There were bright globules of light pulsating and expanding and lighting up the fore-shore and town of Kaikoura," Fogarty said. A radio call to WATC confirmed that Wellington also saw radar targets located in the direction of Kaikoura, about thirteen miles from the plane. The encounter had begun.

Over the next fifty minutes or so, until the aircraft landed at Christchurch, those on board were treated to a spectacular, and at times frightening, UFO display. Some of the activity was also captured on film, but because of the objects' apparent ability to appear and disappear at will, filming was very difficult.

There were times when Wellington radar confirmed an unidentified target on the tail of the aircraft. Reporter Fogarty, who did a taped

commentary throughout the flight, perhaps best summed up the feelings of everyone on board, when he said: "Let's hope they're friendly." Just before the aircraft landed, Captain Startup invited the television crew back on the return leg.

December 31, 2:15 A.M.: The Argosy took off for Blenheim. It was only a couple of minutes out of Christchurch when a bright object was observed outside the starboard window.

The object was also picked up on the aircraft radar. At first it was within the twenty-mile range. Later it came as close as ten miles. This time the object didn't disappear or fade, and David had a lot more success with his filming. He described it as having a brightly lit base with a sort of transparent dome. Fogarty, who was continuing his taped commentary, said at the time that it sounded suspiciously like a "flying saucer."

About thirty-seven nautical miles out of Christchurch, with the object still outside the window, Captain Startup decided to turn toward it. He put the aircraft into a 90-degree turn. The object kept its relative distance from the plane until Startup decided to get back on course. As he turned, the object maintained its location at the right of the aircraft, then approached the aircraft and passed beneath the right-hand side and disappeared. During the turn, the captain saw another bright object appear, at first higher than the aircraft and in front. This object then passed to the left and beneath. From this point until landing at Blenheim, those on board occasionally saw bright, pulsating lights. Some "objects" were also picked up by ground radar.

About 10:05 P.M., Fogarty, with the film firmly clutched in his hand, took off from Christchurch for Melbourne. News of the morning's incredible events was already making headlines around the world. He arrived back in Melbourne as the New Year was dawning. Then began the major task of getting the story together for distribution around the world.

A week after the sightings, the film was on its way to the United States for scientific analysis. Channel 0 chose NICAP for the task. The investigation was conducted on behalf of NICAP by Dr. Bruce Maccabee, a Navy physicist. He spent ten days in New Zealand and a week in Australia interviewing the witnesses and analyzing the film. He subsequently presented his findings to several groups of scientists in the U.S. Not one of the scientists was able to explain the radar-visual-photographic sightings in conventional terms.

Mr. Jack Acuff, former director of NICAP, said that his organization had never previously endorsed a UFO film as being genuine but added that the evidence in this case pointed to some new phenomenon that was probably related to other UFO reports.

Dr. Maccabee has been a member of NICAP for twelve years. He is also on the Scientific Board of the Center for UFO Studies, and in that capacity he presented the evidence to Dr. J. Allen Hynek. Hynek stated his opinion that the New Zealand evidence clearly suggests some phenomenon that cannot be explained in ordinary terms. He criticized those in responsible scientific positions who had publicly stated that the New Zealand film showed Venus, Jupiter, meteors, etc., without even bothering to talk to the witnesses or to find out at what times and in which directions the various portions of the film were shot.

Some of the other scientists joining Dr. Maccabee and Dr. Hynek in the opinion that the film shows something unusual are Dr. Peter Sturrock, a plasma physicist; Dr. Richard Haines, an optical physiologist; Dr. Gilbert Levin, a biophysicist; and Neil Davis, an electronics specialist. Other scientists, most notably several government and industry radar specialists, requested that their names not be used because of their sensitive positions.

—RONALD D. STORY

References

Maccabee, Bruce. "Wellington/Kaikoura radar/visual sightings" in Story, Ronald D., ed. *The Encyclopedia of UFOs* (Doubleday/New English Library, 1980).

Story, Ronald D. *UFOs and the Limits of Science* (William Morrow/New English Library, 1981).

We Are Not Alone (McGraw-Hill, 1964).
New York Times science reporter Walter Sullivan writes the first book providing an overview of attempts by astronomers to intercept extraterrestrial radio signals. He also provides summaries of interviews he conducted with astronomers Frank Drake and Carl Sagan who urged that we reexamine ancient myths, such as those produced by Sumeria and the Hebrews, for clues about ancient astronaut landings which may have influenced the growth of human civilization.

—RANDALL FITZGERALD

We Are Not The First (G.P. Putnam, 1971).
Australian author Andrew Tomas finds numerous examples of unexplained knowledge from antiquity which indicate that galactic visitors established contact with humans to inspire the creation of civilization. Among the examples he cites: the Mayans had a more precise calendar than we do today; the Dogon tribe of Mali have known for centuries that Sirius has a companion star even though it is invisible to the naked eye; Stonehenge is an astronomical computer built four thousand years ago; and the Catholic Church lists 200 saints who levitated, perhaps utilizing alien secrets of anti-gravity.

—RANDALL FITZGERALD

We Met the Space People (Saucerian Books, 1959).
Helen and Betty Mitchell, two sisters in St. Louis, describe their alleged contacts with visitors from Mars and Venus, who appear indistinguishable from male humans, and who warn the sisters to speak out against nuclear weapons. Otherwise, humans will face the same fate as "their ancestors from Atlantis," according to these Venusians.

—RANDALL FITZGERALD

When Time Began (Avon Books, 1993).
Zecharia Sitchin, in book five of his Earth Chronicles series on the ancient astronaut theme, theorizes that Stonehenge was built or

inspired by alien visitors as a solar clock to chart the passage of Celestial Time. Among other enigmas, he wonders why seven was chosen as the number of days to represent a slice of a year known as a week. He answers his own question by concluding that the extra-terrestrial visitors we call God first passed the six outer planets of our solar system before reaching Earth, the seventh planet, and thus the number seven has held sacred symbolism for humans ever since.

—RANDALL FITZGERALD

Whispers from Space (Macmillan, 1973). Scottish astronomer John Macvey became, in this book, one of the first scientists to admit publicly to having had his own UFO sighting, prompting him to urge an open mind about UFOs and ancient astronaut theories. He suspects that alien contact with our species may have occurred but evidence of it remains far beyond our comprehension or ability to detect.

—RANDALL FITZGERALD

window areas Particular geographical locations where UFO sightings and other odd happenings frequently occur. Examples are: Sedona, Arizona; Gulf Breeze, Florida; and Hudson Valley, New York. These and other window areas are described in the book *UFO USA* (Hyperion, 1999) compiled by SPACEAGE: The Society for the Preservation of Alien Contact Evidence and Geographic Exploration.

—RONALD D. STORY

Witnessed   (Pocket Books, 1996). Budd Hopkins details in this book what he describes as the most important alien abduction case "in recorded history." Manhattan housewife Linda Napolitano was floated into a hovering UFO at night from her twelfth-floor apartment window, witnessed by Perez de Cuellar, Secretary General of the United Nations, and two of his American bodyguards.

—RANDALL FITZGERALD

X

X-Files, The (Twentieth Century Fox Film Corp./Fox-TV; Producer: Chris Carter). This popular TV series, which premiered in 1993, has a pronounced symbiotic relationship with modern UFO-ET mythology. So much so that virtually every element of UFO lore has been incorporated into these weekly sci-fi mystery dramas.

Heavily laden with conspiracies and cover-ups—covert liaisons between the U.S. Government and aliens, UFO-abduction tie-ins, genetically engineered deviants, and virtually every aspect of paranormal phenomena that can be imagined—the show basically follows the exploits of two young FBI agents, Fox Mulder and Dana Scully, as they investigate all of it in pursuit of the "truth."

Their credo is summed up by two catch-phrases: "The truth is out there" and "trust no one"—which taps into the paranoid suspicions of many. However, the greater appeal probably has to do with the series' visual artistry, interesting and attractive lead characters, and the bizarre nature of the horrors endured. And, of course, almost everyone enjoys a good mystery, which *The X-Files* usually provides.

The show has been called "provocative," "intriguing," "spooky," "incredible," "eerie," "creepy," "intelligent," "paranoid," and "preposterous"—all of which is true.

—RONALD D. STORY

Y

Yorba Linda (California) photo At twilight on January 24, 1967, fourteen-year-old "Tom X" (name withheld by request) was reportedly startled by a dark, hat-shaped object hovering outside a second-story window of his home in Yorba Linda, California. He rushed quickly to an adjacent room and returned within seconds with his inexpensive Mark XII fixed-focus camera. Tom said that the object had moved farther away from the windowpane, but that he was still able to snap one black-and-white picture before running downstairs, shouting for his family to come and view the bizarre visitor.

Tom X's family lived in a small, relatively isolated town on the edge of rapidly growing Orange County. He regularly used a mail-order film company to process his photos, but they had lost a roll of film shortly before this incident. So instead of trusting his UFO picture to the mails, he had a fourteen-year-old friend develop it for him.

Tom's friend tried his best, but the negative and photo emerged scratched and dulled. In addition, it was light-struck and/or fogged. Later, professional cleaning restored it to reasonable clarity, but nothing could be done about several long scratches which had been produced by the camera's faulty winding mechanism.

When the sighting and photo came to this writer's attention in June 1967, it was subjected to analysis by six photographic experts during the next four years. Equipment used included sophisticated aerospace photogrammetric systems. The consensus of the experts was that the hat-shaped image denoted a solid, three-dimensional, free-flying object. It seemed to be either stationary or moving at slow speed.

Tom X had reported four thin appendages hanging down from the bottom rim, but by the time he snapped the photo, the object had apparently withdrawn or otherwise folded up one of them, one expert theorized. Double exposure, cutouts, hand-thrown, or string-suspended models were ruled out. The object's true size was judged to be about twenty inches in diameter along its horizontal axis and about two feet in height, and was about one hundred feet from the camera.

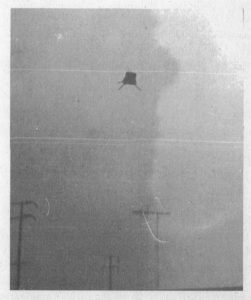

The dark, hat-shaped object photographed by "Tom X" on January 24, 1967. (Lines across the photo are scratches from camera's faulty winding mechanism.)

Tom's character and reliability were checked. He was determined to be an honest, intelligent individual, who was well thought of by his friends and school authorities. His family verified the fact that he was in a highly excitable state after viewing and photographing the object. However, they could not corroborate the sighting itself, because the object had disappeared by the time other family members hurried back upstairs with him.

The entire X family, which included Tom, his parents, and sister, had witnessed a large silvery object with lighted windows on January 4, 1967, just twenty days before the hat-shaped object was photographed. Prior to that time, none of the family had any interest in UFOs, and even considered the subject unreal and uninteresting. Following the January 24th occurrence, a considerable number of other more-distant UFOs were sighted by members of the X family and other residents of Yorba Linda and surrounding communities.

Tom X had the impression that the January 24th object was "gigantic," but this might have been due either to his excited state, an optical illusion, or the fact that the object when first seen was actually very close to the window. Investigation revealed that when first seen, it subtended an angle of about sixteen degrees and about one degree when the photo was taken.

Tom's visual impression was that the bottom rim was continuous and slanted like a top hat; however, the photo showed the rim was actually composed of egg-shaped bulges, from which the legs apparently protruded.

Another sighting of a similar object was reported from Wapello, Iowa, by another fourteen-year-old boy, Douglas Eutsler, on March 22, 1967, about two months after Tom's sighting. Douglas reported the sighting to the Air Force, and his sketch appeared in a December 1967 U.S. magazine. The two witnesses did not know each other.

Douglas reported that the bottom part of the object was rotating. This might be a possible clue why Tom X saw the rim as a continuous slope, rather than as egg-shaped protrusions as revealed in the photo. Eutsler reported the object as large, also, but there was no objective way to measure the Wapello object's true size. Perhaps the phenomenon of

size constancy, in which the brain zooms in like a telephoto lens, could be applied to both cases.

The initial decision by NICAP (the National Investigations Committee on Aerial Phenomena) was that the photo was a hoax (a cutout or small model at the window, photographed with a close-up lens). The object was further studied by means of comparison photos, and the NICAP conclusion was proved to be in error.

Densitometer readings by a major California aerospace firm yielded the fact that the object had photographed much darker than it should have, if its true color was black, as reported by Tom X. This situation was clarified when further analysis by a Southern California geodetic survey firm revealed that the object's color was probably red, which would photograph darker than black. It was subsequently learned that Tom X's color perception was faulty. He saw deep red (or maroon) metal and/or light as black sometimes. Therefore, the possibility that the object was metal and/or glowing red must be considered.

As in most of the best UFO photos, the investigation of the Yorba Linda picture is ongoing. The witness/photographer "Tom X" has generously granted permission for researchers to use it without restrictions, and it is no longer copyrighted. It has become accepted by prominent researchers in the UFO field and is now a part of the official UFO packet distributed to the media by the Fund for UFO Research. In 1999, a computer-enhancement expert studied the Yorba Linda photo and confirmed its three-dimensionality. He also found a faint highlight on the body of the craft, indicating probable reflection of sunlight off the rounded surface, consistent with the position of the sun at the time of sighting.

The object in the Yorba Linda photo does not conform to any classic UFO category. However, small, apparently unoccupied UFOs have been reported often. Because of the care taken by photogrammetric analysts, however, it is a potentially important piece of evidence.

It is certainly among the closest UFO photographs taken to date.

—ANN DRUFFEL

Yungay (Peru) photos   These photos were reportedly taken in 1967 by Augusto Arranda while he was trekking in the mountains near Yungay, located at about 10,000 feet in the Huaylas Valley of north-central Peru. Arranda had borrowed a camera from Cesar Ore, an acquaintance, who operated a tourist office in Yungay. The photos were given to the Aerial Phenomena Research Organization (APRO) for analysis.

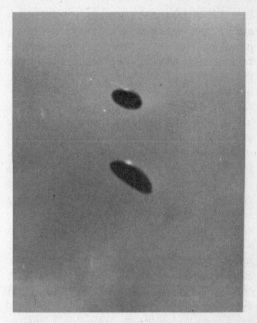

Yungay photo #2

Yungay photo #1

One of the photos came to APRO's attention, in 1968, through an indirect means. After some investigation, the photo was traced back to the Kodak Peruana S.A. processing laboratory, where an employee, in violation of company rules, had retained copies of the photos at the time they were being commercially developed. Kodak officials confiscated the photos from their employee before the writer could locate him and refused to produce them (they were obtained in 1969 through Eastman Kodak's International Markets Division in Roch-

ester, New York). No Kodak records were available to trace the photos to their original source.

The location of a full set of the photos, in Yungay, was made known to APRO by an official in the Peruvian Ministry of the Navy. A trip was made to Yungay, where the three missing photos (being retained by Kodak Peruana S.A.) were found and obtained from Mr. Ore. Arranda, the photographer, had mailed copies to Mr. Ore after the former returned to Lima, the capital. Arranda had presumably sent the negatives to Kodak for processing, explaining the two independent sources brought to APRO's attention.

In spite of intensive investigation, Mr. Arranda was not located by APRO, although conclusive evidence of his existence was obtained. Consequently, the details concerning the observation and the photography are not known; neither are the original negatives available for analysis. Although original prints exist in the United States, and several scientists have examined them, they have not been subjected to a comprehensive analysis. Their authenticity has thus been occasionally questioned. However, nothing emerged during APRO's investigation to indicate a hoax. No publicity or commercialization was ever attempted by the photographer or by Ore. On the contrary, it took much effort to trace the photographs.

In May 1970, a strong earthquake struck central Peru, resulting in the death of over 70,000 persons. During the earthquake, a glacier was dislodged from Mount Huascaran, one of the tallest peaks in the Andes mountain range, causing a large avalanche of ice, rocks, and mud to descend on Yungay at a speed of about 200 miles per hour. The entire town and almost its entire population of 20,000 persons were buried instantly. The earthquake has been called ''the most catastrophic natural disaster in the history of the Western Hemisphere and ranks high among the world's greatest natural disasters'' (see Reps, William F., and Simiu, Emil, ''Case Study: Engineering Geology and Siting Problems Related to the Peru Earthquake of May 31, 1970,'' in *Design, Siting and Construction of Low-Cost Housing and Community Buildings to Better Withstand Earthquake and Windstorms*. National Bureau of Standards Building Science Series 48, U. S. Department of Commerce).

The original camera and one original print which remained with Mr. Ore were lost in the avalanche. It is not known if Mr. Ore survived, and further in-country investigation was not undertaken.

—ETEP STAFF

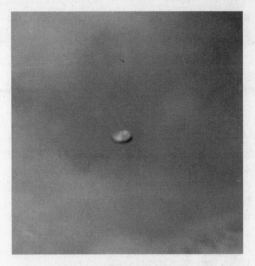

Yungay photo #3

Yungay photo #4

Z

Zeidman, Jennie R. (b. 1932). Jennie Zeidman has been involved in UFOlogy since 1953, when, as a senior at Ohio State University (where she earned her B.A. degree in English), she was a student of Dr. J. Allen Hynek, and later his secretary and research assistant in the early days of Project Blue Book. She is now retired and divides her time between Columbus, Ohio, and Mt. Crested Butte, Colorado.

Jennie Zeidman

E-mail: zeidman@crestedbutte.net

POSITION STATEMENT: I am by nature a skeptic. When I first became associated with Dr. Hynek and UFOlogy in 1953, I was convinced that all reported events could be explained in terms of already understood and identified phenomena: The only requirements were better investigations and better analysis. My position remained thus until about 1966. No single incident changed my mind; rather the sheer weight of the evidence, building case by case, and my personal involvement in interviewing dozens of witnesses, in the United States and abroad. My awareness of the history and philosophy of science and my accessibility to the reliable data contributed to my growing uneasiness. During the period of 1966-70, I gradually backed away from a "there's nothing to it" stance, opening my eyes to the astounding similarity of global reports and the undeniable credibility of many of the witnesses. With the advent of more sophisticated investigatory techniques, I have seen the data strengthened and their validity sustained.

I now believe unequivocally that "there is something" to UFO phenomena. What, I cannot say. I have never proposed a theory of extraterrestrial intelligence to explain the reported events, yet certainly that theory cannot be ruled out. Whatever their meaning, their origin, their *motives,* UFO phenomena have, I believe, demonstrated their validity as a challenge to both physical and behavioral scientists. The subject is eminently worthy of serious research.

—JENNIE ZEIDMAN

Zwischbergen (Switzerland) photo On the afternoon of July 26, 1975, three Dutch hikers (B., his brother H., and their friend M.), were about to take on the last kilometers of a two-day mountain trip in the Swiss Alps, when at approximately 3 P.M. they allegedly encountered a circular object hovering in the air in front of them. The "UFO" seemed to be made of "some sort of metal, not unlike aluminum." It had a dull gray color and its shape resembled that of an inverted soup plate, "at least 15 meters in diameter."

The object appeared to be suspended over the small village of Zwischbergen, at a distance of 100 to 500 meters. B. succeeded in

Zwischbergen photo, taken in Switzerland on July 26, 1975: a stereotype image of a "flying saucer"-type UFO from the seventies.

findings were published in 1994 in a book called *Unidentified Aerial Object Photographed near Zwischbergen, Switzerland, on July 26, 1975.*

A closer view

taking a color slide of the phenomenon. Immediately after the photo was taken, the object started to move and glided behind the trees where it disappeared from view.

Back in the Netherlands, B., H., and M. showed the slide to a fellow member of a local parochial choir, whom they knew was a co-worker of the country's largest (now defunct) UFO group NOBOVO. In the years that followed, the case received worldwide publicity. It is usually referred to as "the Saas Fee photo," because of the proximity of this well-known ski resort to the location of the alleged sighting.

The late Dr. J. Allen Hynek once referred to the "Saas Fee photo" as one of the best UFO photos ever, and UFO photoanalyst William H. Spaulding, after conducting a computerized image evaluation in 1977, concluded that "the object size is 25-30 feet in diameter" and "was 'removing' some of the fog/haze layer as it moved toward the camera."

Eight years after details of the case had been published, additional "eye-witness testimony" surfaced. A group of Belgian tourists reportedly photographed "something odd in the sky" on that same day, at the same time. This second photo was taken from the village of Eison, only 49 km west of the location where the three Dutchmen had taken their picture.

These exceptional circumstances prompted CAELESTIA, a Belgian research and publication project for atmospheric anomalies, to undertake a follow-up investigation. Their

Study of the original slide by photo experts confirmed that the photo showed a three-dimensional object. With the image itself being explicit enough, only two possible interpretations remained: either the object is a meters-wide craft of unknown origin, or a small model. Although the investigation did not make it possible to decide either way, several circumstantial elements were uncovered that seem to point in the direction of a hoax. To wit:

- The analysis conducted by Spaulding proved seriously flawed and was found to be conducted, not on the original slide, but on a third- or fourth-generation print.
- It turned out that the slides preceding and succeeding the unidentified object photo were missing from B.'s slide collection (creating a suspicion that they were removed from the collection because they showed less succesful attempts to create a UFO shot).
- The rim of the object appears to be "dented" (possibly as a result of ungentle landings from previous attempts to get the object in the air in front of the camera.
- The dark coloration of the bottom side of the object indicates that the image was not affected by aerial perspective, suggesting

that the object was small and close to the camera.

- Attempts to imitate the photo with the help of an aluminum camping-plate yielded similar "flying saucer" pictures (video images of the sighting location confirmed that it is quite easy to launch and recuperate Frisbee-type objects at the site).
- Witness M., who emigrated to New Zealand in 1983, confirmed the sighting only after he contacted the other two witnesses.
- There existed a suitable climate for concocting a practical joke of this nature: (a) similar bogus "flying saucer" pictures were common in the press those days; (b) only hours before the UFO shot was taken, the witnesses had created and photographed a funny face using a rock and dressing it up with a pair of glasses and a sun-cap; and (c) a few days before the trip to Zwischbergen, the group had already sighted a strange, light-reflecting object in the sky—"probably a weather balloon"—which they had jokingly referred to as a "UFO."

- In spite of the large number of potential witnesses (popular ski resorts in the valleys adjacent to the Zwischbergen valley, an air show at a nearby airfield and a major traffic congestion 20 km north northwest of the sighting location), no corroborative eye-witness testimonies were found that confirm the presence of an unconventionally shaped, meters-wide airborne vehicle over the Zwischbergen valley on the day the photo was taken.

Furthermore, the second photo taken at Eison that same day proved irrelevant after study. Most likely it depicts a bird and was taken, not at the same time, but approximately one hour after B.'s UFO shot.

—WIM VAN UTRECHT

ACKNOWLEDGMENTS

The following acknowledgments and credits are considered an extension of the copyright page:

ABDUCTED: CONFRONTATIONS WITH BEINGS FROM OUTER SPACE and all other mini-book-review entries by Randall Fitzgerald were revised and adapted by the author from his book *Cosmic Test Tube: Extraterrestrial Contact, Theories & Evidence.* Copyright © 1998. Reprinted by permission of Randall Fitzgerald, the author, and Donald Altman, publisher, Moon Lake Media, Los Angeles, CA (www.moonlakebooks.com).

ABDUCTION TRANSCRIPTION PROJECT. Copyright © 2001 by Dan R. Wright. POSTSCRIPT copyright © 1999, 2001 by Philip J. Klass. Adapted and reprinted by permission from *The Skeptics UFO Newsletter (SUN).*

ABDUCTIONS and all other glossary-style entries by Scott Mandelker were revised and adapted by the author from his book *Universal Vision: Soul Evolution and the Cosmic Plan.* Copyright © 2000. Reprinted by permission of Scott Mandelker, the author, and Universal Vision, publisher, San Francisco, CA (www.universal-vision.com).

ADAMSKI, GEORGE. Copyright © 1980, 2001 by Ronald D. Story. Revised and adapted from *The Encyclopedia of UFOs* (Doubleday/New English Library, 1980).

AETHERIUS SOCIETY. Copyright © 1980, 2001 by Ronald D. Story. Revised and adapted from *The Encyclopedia of UFOs* (Doubleday/New English Library, 1980).

AIRSHIP WAVE OF 1896. Copyright © Loren E. Gross 1980, 2001. Revised and adapted from Story, Ronald D., ed., *The Encyclopedia of UFOs* (Doubleday/New English Library, 1980).

AIRSHIP WAVE OF 1897. Copyright © Lucius Farish 1980, 2001. Revised and adapted from Story, Ronald D., ed., *The Encyclopedia of UFOs* (Doubleday/New English Library, 1980).

ALIEN AUTOPSY FILM. Copyright © Joe Nickell 1995, 2001. Reprinted from the *Skeptical Inquirer* (November 1995) by permission of the author.

ALIEN GALLERY (text and illustrations). Copyright © 2001 by David W. Chace.

ALIEN ICONOGRAPHY. Copyright © Joe Nickell 1997, 2001. Reprinted from the *Skeptical Inquirer* (September/October 1997) by permission of the author.

ALIEN MOTIVES. Copyright © 2001 by Stanton T. Friedman.

ALIEN ROOTS. Copyright © 1979, 2001 by Alvin H. Lawson. Revised and adapted from "Alien Roots: Six Entity Types and Some Possible Earthly Ancestors" by Alvin H. Lawson. First published in the *1979 MUFON UFO Symposium Proceedings* (Mutual UFO Network, 1979). Illustrations have either been redrawn or are in public domain. Reprinted by permission of the author and MUFON.

ALIEN TYPES. Copyright © 2001 by Patrick Huyghe.

ALLAGASH ABDUCTIONS. Copyright © 2001 by Raymond E. Fowler.

ALLENDE LETTERS. Copyright © by Kevin D. Randle 1980, 2001. Revised and adapted from Story, Ronald D., ed., *The Encyclopedia of UFOs* (Doubleday/New English Library, 1980).

AMERICA WEST AIRLINES SIGHTING. Copyright © 2001 by Robert Swiatek.

ANCIENT ASTRONAUT THEORY. Copyright © 1980, 2001 by Ronald D. Story. Revised and adapted from *The Encyclopedia of UFOs* (Doubleday/New English Library, 1980).

ANCIENT UFOs. Copyright © 1980, 2001 by Ronald D. Story. Revised and adapted from *The Encyclopedia of UFOs* (Doubleday/New English Library, 1980).

ANDREASSON ABDUCTIONS. Copyright © 2001 by Raymond E. Fowler and Betty Andreasson Luca.

ANGELS AND UFOs. Copyright © 1980, 2001 by Barry H. Downing. Revised and adapted from Story, Ronald D., ed., *The Encyclopedia of UFOs* (Doubleday/New English Library, 1980).

ANGELUCCI, ORFEO. Copyright © Robert S. Ellwood 1980, 2001. Revised and adapted from Story, Ronald D., ed., *The Encyclopedia of UFOs* (Doubleday/New English Library, 1980).

ANIMAL MUTILATIONS and all other entries by CORAL & JIM LORENZEN and those credited to APRO are reprinted by prior arrangement with the Lorenzens, APRO, and by permission of Lawrence E. Lorenzen, executor of the Lorenzen estate. Copyright to all entries reprinted from *The Encyclopedia of UFOs* (Doubleday/New English Library, 1980) are held in trust by Ronald D. Story.

ANTHROPIC PRINCIPLE. Copyright © 2001 by Ronald D. Story.

APOCALYPTIC THOUGHT. Copyright © 1991, 2001 by Martin S. Kottmeyer. Revised and adapted from *UFO Brigantia* (January 1991). Original title: "Dying Worlds, Dying Selves." Reprinted by permission of the author.

ARCHETYPES. Copyright © 2001 by Gregory L. Little.

AREA 51. Copyright © 2001 by Arlan K. Andrews.

ARNOLD SIGHTING. Copyright © 1980, 2001 by Ronald D. Story. Revised and adapted from *The Encyclopedia of UFOs* (Doubleday/New English Library, 1980)

ASTRONAUTS, UFO SIGHTINGS BY. Copyright © 1978, 1980, 2001 by James E. Oberg. Revised and adapted from Story, Ronald D., ed., *The Encyclopedia of UFOs* (Doubleday/New English Library, 1980). Published separately in *The Skeptical Inquirer,* fall 1978.

ATOMIC BOMB AND UFOs. Copyright © 2001 by Daniel Cohen.

AVELEY (ENGLAND) ABDUCTION. Copyright © 1980, 2001 by Jenny Randles. Revised and adapted from Story, Ronald D., ed., *The Encyclopedia of UFOs* (Doubleday/New English Library, 1980).

B-57 BOMBER PHOTO. Copyright © 1980, 2001 by Ronald D. Story. Revised and adapted from *The Encyclopedia of UFOs* (Doubleday/New English Library, 1980).

BELGIAN UFO WAVE OF 1989-90. Copyright © 2001 by Wim Van Utrecht.

BENDER MYSTERY. Copyright © 1980, 2001 by Jerome Clark. Revised and adapted from Story, Ronald D., ed., *The Encyclopedia of UFOs* (Doubleday/New English Library, 1980).

BERMUDA TRIANGLE–UFO LINK. Copyright © 1980, 2001 by Ronald D. Story. Revised and adapted from *The Encyclopedia of UFOs* (Doubleday/New English Library, 1980).

BETHURUM, TRUMAN. Copyright © 1980, 2001 by David M. Jacobs. Revised and adapted from Story, Ronald D., ed., *The Encyclopedia of UFOs* (Doubleday/New English Library, 1980).

BIBLICAL MIRACLES AS SUPER-TECHNOLOGY. Copyright © 2001 by Barry H. Downing.

BIBLICAL UFOs. Copyright © 1980, 2001 by Barry H. Downing. Revised and adapted from Story, Ronald D., ed., *The Encyclopedia of UFOs* (Doubleday/New English Library, 1980).

BIRTH MEMORIES HYPOTHESIS. Copyright © 2001 by Alvin H. Lawson.

BOUNDARY DEFICIT HYPOTHESIS. Copyright © 1989, 1994, 2001 by Martin S. Kottmeyer. Revised and adapted from *Magonia* (March 1989) and from the *Bulletin of Anomalous Experience* (August 1994). Original titles: "Abduction: The Boundary-Deficit Hypothesis" and "Testing the Boundaries" respectively. Reprinted by permission of the author.

BUFF LEDGE (VERMONT) ABDUCTION. Copyright © 2001 by Walter N. Webb.

CASH-LANDRUM UFO ENCOUNTER. Copyright © 2001 by John Schuessler.

CATEGORIES OF UFO REPORTS. Copyright © 1980, 2001 by J. Allen Hynek and Ronald D. Story. Revised and adapted from *The Encyclopedia of UFOs* (Doubleday/New English Library, 1980).

CHUPACABRAS. Copyright © 2001 by Scott Corrales.

CLOSE ENCOUNTERS OF THE THIRD KIND. Copyright © 2001 by Martin S. Kottmeyer and Ronald D. Story.

COMMUNION FOUNDATION. Copyright © 2001 by Whitley Strieber.

CONTACTEES. Copyright © 1980, 2001 by Ronald D. Story. Revised and adapted from *The Encyclopedia of UFOs* (Doubleday/New English Library, 1980).

COSMIC CONSCIOUSNESS. Copyright © 2001 by R. Leo Sprinkle.

COSMONAUTS, UFO SIGHTINGS BY. Copyright © 2001 by Michael Hesemann.

COYNE (MANSFIELD, OHIO) HELICOPTER CASE. Copyright © 1980, 2001 by Jennie Zeidman. Revised and adapted from Story, Ronald D., ed., *The Encyclopedia of UFOs* (Doubleday/New English Library, 1980).

DAWSON ENCOUNTER. Copyright © 2001 by Billy J. Rachels.

DAY THE EARTH STOOD STILL, THE. Copyright © 2001 by Martin S. Kottmeyer and Ronald D. Story.

DELPHOS (KANSAS) LANDING TRACE. Copyright © 1981, 2001 by Ronald D. Story. Revised and adapted from *UFOs and the Limits of Science* (William Morrow, 1981).

DEMONIC THEORY OF UFOs. Copyright © 1980, 2001 by Barry H. Downing. Revised and adapted from Story, Ronald D., ed., *The Encyclopedia of UFOs* (Doubleday/New English Library, 1980).

DRAKE EQUATION. Copyright © 1998, 2001 by the SETI Institute.

"EARTH CHRONICLES." Copyright © 2001 by Zecharia Sitchin.

ELK ABDUCTION. Copyright © 2001 by Peter B. Davenport.

ELOHIM. Copyright © 2001 by Ronald D. Story.

EXETER (NEW HAMPSHIRE) SIGHTINGS. Copyright © 2001 by Peter B. Davenport and Peter Geremia.

EXTRATERRESTRIAL HYPOTHESIS. Copyright © 1980, 2001 by J. Richard Greenwell. Revised and adapted from Story, Ronald D., ed., *The Encyclopedia of UFOs* (Doubleday/New English Library, 1980).

EXTRATERRESTRIAL LIFE, HISTORY OF. Copyright © 2001 by Steven Dick.

EZEKIEL'S WHEEL. Copyright © 1980, 2001 by Walter N. Webb. Revised and adapted from Story, Ronald D., ed., *The Encyclopedia of UFOs* (Doubleday/New English Library, 1980).

"FACE" ON MARS. Copyright © 2001 by Gary Posner.

FAIRY LORE AND UFO ENCOUNTERS. Copyright © 2001 by Thomas Eddie Bullard.

FATIMA (PORTUGAL), MIRACLE AT. Copyright © 1980, 2001 by Ann Druffel. Revised and adapted from *The Encyclopedia of UFOs* (Doubleday/New English Library, 1980).

FAWCETT'S "REPETITIONS." Copyright © 1991, 2001 by George D. Fawcett. Originally published by the *International UFO Library* magazine (1991). Reprinted by permission of the author.

FLATWOODS (WEST VIRGINIA) MONSTER. Copyright © Joe Nickell 2000, 2001. Reprinted from the *Skeptical Inquirer* (November/December 2000) by permission of the author.

"FLYING SAUCER." Copyright © 1980, 2001 by Loren E. Gross. Revised and adapted from Story, Ronald D., ed., *The Encyclopedia of UFOs* (Doubleday/New English Library, 1980).

FORT, CHARLES. Copyright © 1980, 2001 by Loren E. Gross. Revised and adapted from Story, Ronald D., ed., *The Encyclopedia of UFOs* (Doubleday/New English Library, 1980).

FRY, DANIEL W. Copyright © 1980, 2001 by Ronald D., Story. Revised and adapted from

Story, Ronald D., ed., *The Encyclopedia of UFOs* (Doubleday/New English Library, 1980).

GALICIA UFO WAVE OF 1995. Copyright © 2001 by Scott Corrales.

GARDEN GROVE (CALIFORNIA) ABDUCTION HOAX. Copyright © 2001 by Alvin H. Lawson.

GEOMAGNETIC EXPLANATIONS OF UFOS. Copyright © 2001 by Gregory L. Little.

GEOMAGNETIC INTELLIGENT ENERGY THEORY OF UFOS. Copyright © 2001 by Gregory L. Little.

GHOST ROCKETS OF 1946. Copyright © 1980, 2001 by Loren E. Gross. Revised and adapted from Story, Ronald D., ed., *The Encyclopedia of UFOs* (Doubleday/New English Library, 1980).

GILL SIGHTING. Copyright © 1980, 2001 by Richard Hall. Revised and adapted from Story, Ronald D., ed., *The Encyclopedia of UFOs* (Doubleday/New English Library, 1980).

GRAYS. Copyright © 1994, 1998, 2001 by Martin S. Kottmeyer. Revised and adapted from the *MUFON UFO Journal* (November 1994) and *Magonia* (February 1998). Original titles: "Why Are the Grays Gray?" and "Varicose Brains: Entering a Gray Area" respectively. Reprinted by permission of the author.

GREAT FALLS (MONTANA) MOVIE. Copyright © 2001 by Kevin D. Randle and Ronald D. Story.

GULF BREEZE (FLORIDA) INCIDENTS. Copyright © 2001 by Bruce Maccabee.

HILL ABDUCTION. Copyright © 2001 by Walter N. Webb.

HUDSON VALLEY (NEW YORK) UFO SIGHTINGS. Copyright © 2001 by Philip J. Imbrogno.

HYPNOSIS, USE OF, IN UFO INVESTIGATIONS. Copyright © 2001 by R. Leo Sprinkle. POSTSCRIPT copyright © 2001 by Robert A. Baker.

IATROGENESIS. Copyright © 2001 by Robert A. Baker.

IMAGINARY ABDUCTEE STUDY. Copyright © 2001 by Alvin H. Lawson.

IMPLANTS, ALIEN. Copyright © 2001 by Roger K. Leir.

INSECTOIDS. Copyright © 1997, 2001 by Martin S. Kottmeyer. Revised and adapted from *UFO Magazine* (July/August 1997). Original title: "Bugs Baroque."

INTERSTELLAR TRAVEL. Copyright © 2001 by Stanton T. Friedman.

INVADERS FROM MARS. Copyright © 2001 by Martin S. Kottmeyer and Ronald D. Story.

INVASION OF THE BODY SNATCHERS. Copyright © 2001 by Martin S. Kottmeyer and Ronald D. Story.

JESSUP, MORRIS K. Copyright © 1980, 2001 by James E. Oberg. Revised and adapted from Story, Ronald D., ed., *The Encyclopedia of UFOs* (Doubleday/New English Library, 1980).

JESUS AS AN EXTRATERRESTRIAL. Copyright © 2001 by Ronald D. Story.

JORDAN-KAUBLE, DEBRA. Copyright © 2001 by Debra Jordan Kauble.

JUNG, CARL GUSTAV. Copyright © 1980, 2001 by Ronald D. Story. Revised and adapted from *The Encyclopedia of UFOs* (Doubleday/New English Library, 1980).

KECKSBERG (PENNSYLVANIA) INCIDENT. Copyright © 2001 by Stan Gordon.

KELLY CAHILL ABDUCTION. Copyright © 2001 by William C. Chalker.

KELLY-HOPKINSVILLE (KENTUCKY) GOBLINS. Copyright © 1976 by Coral & Jim Lorenzen. Adapted from *Encounters with UFO Occupants* (Berkley, 1976). Reprinted by permission of Lawrence E. Lorenzen and prior arrangement with APRO.

KENTUCKY ABDUCTION. Copyright © 1976, 1980, 2001 by Coral & Jim Lorenzen and R. Leo Sprinkle. Revised and adapted from Story, Ronald D., ed., *The Encyclopedia of UFOs* (Doubleday/New English Library, 1980).

KINROSS (MICHIGAN) JET CHASE. Copyright © 1980, 2001 by Richard Hall. Revised and adapted from Story, Ronald D., ed., *The Encyclopedia of UFOs* (Doubleday/New English Library, 1980).

KLASS, PHILIP J. Biography copyright © 2001 by Gary Posner and Philip J. Klass.

KLASS'S UFOLOGICAL PRINCIPLES. Copyright © 1974, 2001 by Philip J. Klass.

LAKENHEATH-BENTWATERS RADAR-VISUAL

UFOs. Copyright © 1981, 2001 Ronald D. Story. Revised and adapted from *UFOs and the Limits of Science* (William Morrow, 1981).

LEVELLAND (TEXAS) LANDINGS. Copyright © 1981, 2001 Ronald D. Story. Revised and adapted from *UFOs and the Limits of Science* (William Morrow, 1981).

LUBBOCK (TEXAS) LIGHTS. Copyright © 1980, 2001 by Kevin D. Randle. Revised and adapted from Story, Ronald D., ed., *The Encyclopedia of UFOs* (Doubleday/New English Library, 1980).

MACK'S ABDUCTEES. Copyright © 1995, 2001 by Joe Nickell. Reprinted from the *Skeptical Inquirer* (November 1995) by permission of the author.

MAJESTIC 12 (MJ-12) DOCUMENTS. Copyright © 2001 by Joe Nickell.

MAN-MADE UFOs. Copyright © 2001 by Tim Matthews.

MARS AND MARTIANS. Copyright © 2001 by Thomas Eddie Bullard.

MARS ROCK. Copyright © 2001 by Ronald D. Story.

McDONALD, JAMES E. Copyright © 1980, 2001 by J. Richard Greenwell. Revised and adapted from Story, Ronald D., ed., *The Encyclopedia of UFOs* (Doubleday/New English Library, 1980).

McMINNVILLE (OREGON) PHOTOS. Copyright © 1980, 2001 by Bruce Maccabee. Revised and adapted from Story, Ronald D., ed., *The Encyclopedia of UFOs* (Doubleday/New English Library, 1980).

MEIER CONTACTS. Copyright © 2001 by Michael Horn.

MENGER, HOWARD. Copyright © 1980, 2001 by Ronald D. Story. Revised and adapted from Story, Ronald D., ed., *The Encyclopedia of UFOs* (Doubleday/New English Library, 1980).

METÁN (ARGENTINA) UFO CRASH-RETRIEVAL. Copyright © 2001 by Scott Corrales.

METAPHYSICAL ASPECTS OF UFOs AND ETs. Copyright © 2001 by Scott Mandelker.

MEXICAN UFO WAVE OF THE 1990S. Copyright © 2001 by Scott Corrales.

MICHALAK ENCOUNTER. Copyright © 1981, 2001 by Ronald D. Story. Revised and adapted from *UFOs and the Limits of Science* (William Morrow, 1981).

MIND CONTROL BY ALIENS. Copyright © 1994, 2001 by Martin S. Kottmeyer. Revised and adapted from *Magonia* (June 1994 and September 1994). Original titles: "Alienating Fancies" Parts One and Two. Reprinted by permission of the author.

"MISSING TIME" Copyright © 2001 by Robert A. Baker and Ronald D. Story.

MOTHMAN. Copyright © 1980, 2001 by Gray Barker. Revised and adapted from Story, Ronald D., ed., *The Encyclopedia of UFOs* (Doubleday/New English Library, 1980).

NAZCA "SPACEPORT." Copyright © 2001 by James W. Moseley, Joe Nickell, and Ronald Story.

OCCULT CONNECTION WITH UFOs AND ET ENCOUNTERS. Copyright © 2001 by Paris Flammonde.

OPERATION MAINBRACE SIGHTINGS. Copyright © 1980, 2001 by Richard Hall. Revised and adapted from Story, Ronald D., ed., *The Encyclopedia of UFOs* (Doubleday/New English Library, 1980).

PALENQUE "ASTRONAUT." Copyright © 1976, 2001 by Ronald D. Story. Revised and adapted from *The Space-Gods Revealed* (Harper & Row, 1976).

PALMER, RAYMOND A. Copyright © 1980, 2001 by Daniel Cohen. Revised and adapted from Story, Ronald D., ed., *The Encyclopedia of UFOs* (Doubleday/New English Library, 1980).

PARALLEL TIME LINE. Copyright © 2001 by Martin S. Kottmeyer and Ronald D. Story.

PARANOIA AND UFOs. Copyright © 1989, 1992, 2001 by Martin S. Kottmeyer. Revised and adapted from "UFOlogy Considered as an Evolving System of Paranoia" in Stillings, Dennis, ed., *Cyberbiological Studies of the Imaginal Component in the UFO Contact Experience* (Archaeus Project, 1989) and *UFO Magazine* (May/June 1992). Reprinted by permission of the author and Dennis Stillings of the Archaeus Project.

PASCAGOULA (MISSISSIPPI) ABDUCTION. Copyright © 1980, 2001 by Kevin D. Randle.

SLEEP PARALYSIS. Copyright © 2001 by Kevin D. Randle.

SOCORRO (NEW MEXICO) LANDING. Copyright © 1981, 2001 by Ronald D. Story. Revised and adapted from *UFOs and the Limits of Science* (William Morrow, 1981).

STAR PEOPLE, THE. Copyright © 2001 by Brad Steiger.

STORY'S UFO "OBSERVATIONS." Copyright © 2001 by Ronald D. Story.

TEHRAN (IRAN) JET CHASE. Copyright © 1981, 2001 by Ronald D. Story. Revised and adapted from *UFOs and the Limits of Science* (William Morrow, 1981).

THREAT, UFO-ET. Copyright © 1992, 1993, 2001 by Martin S. Kottmeyer. Revised and adapted from *Magonia*. Original titles: "What's Up, Doc?" (October 1992), "Swinging Thru the Sixties" (March 1993), and "Sham and Shepherds: The Seventies and So Forth" (June 1993). Reprinted by permission of the author.

TRANSFORMATION REQUIRED TO JOIN THE GALACTIC SOCIETY. Copyright © 2001 by Donald M. Ware.

TREMONTON (UTAH) MOVIE. Copyright © 1980, 2001 by Kevin D. Randle. Revised and adapted from Story, Ronald D., ed., *The Encyclopedia of UFOs* (Doubleday/New English Library, 1980).

TUJUNGA CANYON (CALIFORNIA) CONTACTS. Copyright © 2001 by Ann Druffel.

2001: A SPACE ODYSSEY. Copyright © 1976, 2001 by Ronald D. Story. Revised and adapted from *The Space-Gods Revealed* (Harper & Row, 1976).

"UFO" DEFINED. Copyright © 2001 by Ronald D. Story.

"UFO INCIDENT, THE." Copyright © 2001 by Ronald D. Story.

UFOLOGY. Copyright © 2001 by Ronald D. Story.

UMMO AFFAIR. Copyright © 2001 by Scott Corrales.

VALENSOLE (FRANCE) ENCOUNTER. Copyright © 1980, 2001 by Charles Bowen and Aimé Michel. Revised and adapted from Story, Ronald D., ed., *The Encyclopedia of UFOs* (Doubleday/New English Library, 1980).

VALENTICH (BASS STRAIT, AUSTRALIA) UFO ENCOUNTER. Copyright © 1980, 2001 by William C. Chalker. Revised and adapted from Story, Ronald D., ed., *The Encyclopedia of UFOs* (Doubleday/New English Library, 1980).

VAN TASSEL, GEORGE. Copyright © 1980, 2001 by Robert S. Ellwood, Jr. Revised and adapted from Story, Ronald D., ed., *The Encyclopedia of UFOs* (Doubleday/New English Library, 1980).

VARGINHA (BRAZIL) ENCOUNTERS OF 1996. Copyright © 2001 by Scott Corrales.

VILLAS BOAS ABDUCTION. Copyright © 2001 by Scott Corrales.

WAR OF THE WORLDS, THE. Copyright © 2001 by Martin S. Kottmeyer and Ronald D. Story.

WASHINGTON NATIONAL RADAR-VISUAL SIGHTINGS. Copyright © 1981, 2001 by Ronald D. Story. Revised and adapted from *UFOs and the Limits of Science* (William Morrow, 1981).

WAVES (OR FLAPS), UFO. Copyright © 1995, 1996, 2001 by Martin S. Kottmeyer. Revised and adapted from *The Anomalist*. Original title: "UFO Flaps: An Analysis" (Winter 1995/96). Reprinted by permission of the author and Patrick Huyghe of *The Anomalist*.

WELLINGTON-KAIKOURA (NEW ZEALAND) RADAR-VISUAL SIGHTINGS. Copyright © 1981, 2001 by Ronald D. Story. Revised and adapted from *UFOs and the Limits of Science* (William Morrow, 1981).

X-FILES, THE. Copyright © 2001 by Ronald D. Story.

YORBA LINDA (CALIFORNIA) PHOTO. Copyright © 1980, 2001 by Ann Druffel. Revised and adapted from Story, Ronald D., ed., *The Encyclopedia of UFOs* (Doubleday/New English Library, 1980).

ZWISCHENBERGEN (SWITZERLAND) PHOTO. Copyright © 2001 by Wim Van Utrecht.

Unless otherwise noted, all material in this book is copyrighted (© 2001) by the author whose name appears at the end of the individual entry. Compilation copyright is held by Ronald D. Story. www.RonaldStory.com